S0-AIN-065

White Sox

J O U R N A L

Year by Year & Day by Day with
the Chicago White Sox Since 1901

White Sox
JOURNAL

JOHN SNYDER

Copyright © 2009 by John Snyder

All rights reserved. No portion of this book may be reproduced in any fashion, print, facsimile, or electronic, or by any method yet to be developed, without express permission of the copyright holder.

For further information, contact the publisher at:

 Clerisy Press
1700 Madison Road
Cincinnati, OH 45206
www.clerisypress.com

Library of Congress Cataloging-in-Publication Data:

Snyder, John, 1951–
    White Sox journal : year by year & day by day with the Chicago White Sox since 1901 / John Snyder.
    p. cm.
    ISBN-13: 978-1-57860-341-1
    ISBN-10: 1-57860-341-2
    1. Chicago White Sox (Baseball team)—History. I. Title.

GV875.C58S685 2009
796.357'640977311--dc22

2008049754

Edited by Jack Heffron
Cover designed by Stephen Sullivan
Interior designed by Mary Barnes Clark
Distributed by Publishers Group West

Front cover photo © Tannen Maury/epa/Corbis
Interior photos and back cover photos appear courtesy of Dennis Goldstein.
    Baseball cards appear courtesy of the Topps Company Inc.

R0421246958

About the Author

John Snyder has a master's degree in history from the University of Cincinnati and a passion for baseball. He has authored more than fifteen books on baseball, soccer, hockey, tennis, football, basketball, and travel and lives in Cincinnati.

Acknowledgments

This book is part of a series that takes a look at Major League Baseball teams. The first was *Redleg Journal: Year by Year and Day by Day with the Cincinnati Reds Since 1866*, the winner of the 2001 Baseball Research Award issued by *The Sporting News* and SABR. That work was followed by *Cubs Journal: Year by Year and Day by Day with the Chicago Cubs Since 1876*, *Red Sox Journal: Year by Year and Day by Day with the Boston Red Sox Since 1901*, *Indians Journal: Year by Year and Day by Day with the Cleveland Indians Since 1901*, *Cardinals Journal: Year by Year and Day by Day with the St. Louis Cardinals since 1882* and *Dodgers Journal: Year by Year and Day by Day with the Dodgers Since 1884*. Each of these books is filled with little-known items that have never been published in book form.

Greg Rhodes was my co-author on *Redleg Journal*, in addition to publishing the book under his company's name Road West Publishing. While Greg did not actively participate in the books about the Cubs, Red Sox, Cardinals, or Indians, he deserves considerable credit for the success of these books because they benefited from many of the creative concepts he initiated in *Redleg Journal*.

The idea for turning *Redleg Journal* into a series of books goes to Richard Hunt, president and publisher of Emmis Books and its successor company Clerisy Press, and editorial director Jeff Heffron.

I would also like to thank the staff at the Public Library of Cincinnati and Hamilton County. The vast majority of the research for this book came from contemporary newspapers and magazines. The library staff was extremely helpful with patience and understanding while retrieving the materials for me, not only for this book but for all of my other endeavors as well. Dick Miller deserves thanks for providing me with material from his personal collection of baseball books. Dick was a lifelong friend of my father, who passed away in 1999, and installed in me a love of both history and baseball.

And finally, although they should be first, thanks to my wife, Judy, and sons Derek and Kevin, whose encouragement and support helped me through another book.

Contents

PART ONE: CHICAGO WHITE SOX DAY BY DAY

PART TWO: CHICAGO WHITE SOX BY THE NUMBERS

The Birth of the White Sox

The creation of the Chicago White Sox and the American League as major league entities are due to the vision, energy and perseverance of Charlie Comiskey and former Cincinnati sportswriter Ban Johnson. The American League had its genesis in November 1893, when a new minor league called the Western League was formed with clubs in Grand Rapids, Sioux City (Iowa), Minneapolis, Milwaukee, Kansas City, Toledo, Indianapolis and Detroit. With the backing of Cincinnati Reds owner John Brush, who had an interest in the Indianapolis franchise, Johnson was asked to head the Western League as president, treasurer and secretary.

From 1892 through 1900, the National League was baseball's only major league. It had prior competition from the American Association, which existed from 1882 through 1891, the Union Association in 1884, and from the Players League, which lasted only the 1890 season. From 1892 through 1899, the National League was a 12-team circuit with clubs in Baltimore, Boston, Brooklyn, Chicago, Cincinnati, Cleveland, Louisville, New York, Philadelphia, Pittsburgh, St. Louis and Washington. The Chicago club was the present day Cubs (known as the Colts during the 1890s) and had been a charter member of the National League since it was established in 1876.

Like many monopolies, the NL had grown arrogant during the 1890s. Tight controls were placed on the players, including a maximum salary of $2,400. Competitive balance was nonexistent. In 1899, the Cleveland Spiders compiled a record of 20–134 and finished 84 games behind the first-place Brooklyn Dodgers. Meanwhile, Johnson's Western League had grown stronger each year as the top circuit in the minor leagues. Comiskey became involved in the Western League in 1894 as the owner of the Sioux City franchise, which he quickly moved to St. Paul.

Comiskey was only 35 when he took over the St. Paul franchise, but he was one of the most respected individuals in the game. He made his major league debut in 1882 as a first baseman in the American Association with the St. Louis Browns (the present-day Cardinals franchise) and was named manager of the club a year later. Aggressive, demanding and innovative, he led St. Louis to four consecutive American Association pennants beginning in 1885. Comiskey left the Browns following the 1891 season and assumed a position as manager of the Reds. It was in Cincinnati that Comiskey and Johnson met and formed a fast friendship. The two ambitious men had plans to jettison some of the smaller cities in the Western League, move them to larger cities in the East and turn the circuit into a second major league.

The National League reduced its roster from 12 to eight on March 8, 1900 by dropping clubs in Baltimore, Cleveland, Louisville and Washington. This gave Johnson the opening he needed. Within days after the NL contracted to eight teams, Johnson changed the name of his organization to the American League. Teams in the smaller towns of Grand Rapids, St. Paul and Toledo were replaced by new ones in Chicago, Cleveland and Buffalo. Many players were without jobs because of the reduction of four clubs in the National League and cast their lot with the American League.

The new Chicago franchise in the American League was headed by Comiskey. It was a natural fit, because he grew up in the Windy City, the son of a well-known alderman. In an agreement with Cubs owner James Hart, the AL club could not build its ballpark north of 35th Street. Comiskey built a new home for his ball club at the site of a former cricket field on 39th Street between Princeton and Wentworth. The location was four miles from The Loop in what was then a remote part of Chicago. The new club was not permitted to use Chicago in its official name, but Hart said nothing about nicknames. Comiskey borrowed the historic moniker White Stockings, used by Chicago's first professional team in 1870 and by the National League club from 1876 through the late 1880s. (The nickname was shortened to White Sox by 1904).

Hart was convinced that Comiskey's White Stockings would receive little patronage and would go bankrupt in trying to compete with the well-established Cubs. Previously, Chicago had teams in the Union Association (1884) and the Players League (1890), but each lost money and lasted only a year. The task of Comiskey and Johnson to place a second team in Chicago was daunting. Comiskey knew the hazards full well since he was the manager of the 1890 Players League club in Chicago. The White Stockings were successful in their first season, however, by turning a profit and winning the American League pennant. Comiskey served as field manager in addition to his duties as owner and guided the club to a record of 82–53.

Shortly after the end of the 1900 season, Johnson announced his plans for his American League to become a second major league to compete with the NL. The franchises in Minneapolis, Kansas City and Indianapolis were eliminated in favor of those in the larger eastern cities of Baltimore, Philadelphia and Washington. Johnson wrote a letter in late-October 1900 to National League president Nick Young seeking peace and an arrangement in which each league would respect the contracts of the other, which would prevent player raids and player salaries from escalating. The NL immediately rejected the plan. The league owners had vanquished all previous opposition and had no doubt that the American League would soon follow into oblivion.

Johnson retaliated by announcing that his new American League would attempt to sign the top players in baseball away from the NL. They certainly found a receptive audience. Players were not only saddled with a maximum salary of $2,400 but had to pay for their uniforms and other basic amenities.

With the opening of the 1901 season fast approaching, Comiskey had to work quickly. He gained instant credibility by signing Clark Griffith, one of the best pitchers in baseball, away from the Cubs on March 1. Griffith was not only acquired to head the pitching staff, but to serve as player-manager as well. Griffith also persuaded Cubs regulars Sam Mertes and Nixey Callahan to join the White Stockings along with Fielder Jones of the Dodgers and Billy Sullivan of the Braves. Our story begins with the start of the 1901 season.

THE STATE OF THE WHITE SOX

After winning the American League pennant in 1900 when the circuit was designated a minor league, the White Sox also captured the AL's first pennant as a major league entity in 1901. The Sox finished first again in 1906. There was no World Series in 1901. In 1906, the White Sox won the world championship by stunning the crosstown Cubs in the Fall Classic. Other AL pennant winners were the Athletics (1902, 1904 and 1905), Red Sox (1903) and Tigers (1907, 1908 and 1909). Overall, the White Sox had the best record of any AL franchise from 1901 through 1909 with 744 wins and 575 losses, just nosing out the Athletics, who were 734–568. The White Sox had a winning percentage of .5641 compared to the Athletics' percentage of .5637.

THE BEST TEAM

The best team was the 1906 outfit, which ended the season in first place in the American League with a record of 93–58. Nicknamed the Hitless Wonders, the club won the pennant despite the worst batting average (.230) and slugging percentage (.288) and the fewest home runs (seven) in the league. The White Sox then went on to win the World Series in a tremendous upset over the crosstown Cubs, a club which won a major league-record 116 games in 1906.

THE WORST TEAM

The 1903 club was the only one that lost more often than it won, finishing in seventh place with a record of 60–77.

THE BEST MOMENT

The best moment lasted six days, from October 9 through October 14, 1906, when the White Sox and the Cubs met in the first, and to date only, all-Chicago World Series.

THE WORST MOMENT

In a winner-take-all showdown for the 1908 American League pennant on the last day of the season, the White Sox lost to the Tigers 7–0. Had the White Sox won that afternoon, Chicago would have witnessed its second White Sox-Cubs World Series.

THE ALL-DECADE TEAM • YEARS WITH WS

Billy Sullivan, c	1901–12, 1914
Jiggs Donahue, 1b	1904–09
Frank Isbell, 2b	1901–09
Lee Tannehill, 3b	1903–12
George Davis, ss	1902, 1904–09
Patsy Dougherty, lf	1906–11
Fielder Jones, cf	1901–08
Danny Green, rf	1902–05
Ed Walsh, p	1904–16
Doc White, p	1903–13
Frank Smith, p	1904–10
Nixey Callahan, p	1901–05, 1911–13

Walsh and Davis are in the Hall of Fame. According to Bill James' Win Shares system, Jones ranked as the 12th-best player in the majors during the 1900s. White was 22nd. Isbell was arguably both the best first baseman and second baseman in White Sox togs during the 1900s. He is listed here as a second baseman, although he played 618 games as first and 347 at second with the Sox. Other outstanding White Sox players during the decade were pitchers Roy Patterson (1901–05, 1911–13), Nick Altrock (1903–09) and Frank Owen (1903–09), right fielder Ed Hahn (1906–10) and catcher Ed McFarland (1902–07).

THE DECADE LEADERS

Batting Avg:	Danny Green	.284
On-Base Pct:	Danny Green	.366
Slugging Pct:	Danny Green	.370
Home Runs:	Frank Isbell	13
RBIs:	Frank Isbell	447
Runs:	Fielder Jones	693
Stolen Bases:	Frank Isbell	250
Wins:	Doc White	124
Strikeouts:	Ed Walsh	901
ERA:	Ed Walsh	1.68
Saves:	Ed Walsh	14

THE HOME FIELD

The White Sox established themselves as Chicago's South Side team upon the founding of the franchise in 1900 by building a ballpark on West 39th Street between Princeton and Wentworth. The facility had no official name but is designated in most histories as South Side Park. The field opened as an athletic venue around the time of the 1893 World's Fair for a professional cricket team known as the Chicago Wanderers. By 1900, the year that Charles Comiskey brought his St. Paul Saints to Chicago, the cricket field had long been abandoned, and the lot was overgrown with weeds and strewn with debris. It was located in the Irish neighborhood of Bridgeport, which included some small industrial plants, St. George Church, Kidwell Greenhouse and several saloons. The ballpark was easily accessible from the Wentworth Avenue streetcar. South Side Park was built entirely of wood with a whitewashed exterior. It was purely functional, with no architectural embellishments whatsoever. The distance to the left field wall was 355 feet, and it was 450 feet to deep center and 400 feet to right. The spacious dimensions were typical of the period, in which batters were expected to use a combination of power and speed to hit home runs. Balls hit over the fence were rare and most circuit blasts were inside the park. In 1901, the seating capacity numbered fewer than 5,000. In 1902, 1,000 bleacher seats were added in the outfield. Over the years, seating was boosted to 15,000. When the demand for seats exceeded the supply, which was often during the 1900s, the overflow crowd stood in foul territory and along the deep outfield walls. On October 2, 1904, 30,084 fans were shoehorned into the ballpark. South Side Park served the White Sox until June 1910, when the first Comiskey Park was built four blocks to the north.

THE GAME YOU WISH YOU HAD SEEN

On October 14, 1906, the White Sox won their first world championship by defeating the heavily favored Cubs in Game Six of the World Series. It is the only time in franchise history that the Sox clinched a World Series in Chicago. The final victories in the Fall Classics in 1917 and 2006 occurred on the road.

THE WAY THE GAME WAS PLAYED

In this decade of pitching and defense, the AL set all-time lows in ERA and batting average. In 1908, the AL batting average was .239 and the league earned run average was 2.39. In part, this was the result of a 1903 rule change that counted foul balls as strikes. The merits of the foul-strike rule were hotly debated for years afterward. Offense started a gradual decline that was not reversed until the introduction of the cork center ball in 1910.

THE MANAGEMENT

Charlie Comiskey founded the White Sox in 1900 and continued as owner of the club until his death in 1931. Field managers were Clark Griffith (1901–02), Nixey Callahan (1903–04), Fielder Jones (1904–08) and Bill Sullivan (1909).

THE BEST PLAYER MOVE

The best player move was the drafting of Ed Walsh from Newark of the Eastern League during the 1903–04 off-season. The best deal with another big-league club was the purchase of Nick Altrock from the Red Sox in April 1903.

THE WORST PLAYER MOVE

The worst move sent Gavvy Cravath, Nick Altrock and Jiggs Donahue to the Senators for Bill Burns on May 16, 1909.

1901

Season in a Sentence

With an infusion of talent from the crosstown Cubs, the Clark Griffith-led White Sox capture the American League pennant.

Finish • Won • Lost • Pct • GB

First   83   53   .610   +4.0

Manager

Clark Griffith

Stats

Stats	WS	AL	Rank
Batting Avg:	.276	.277	5
On-Base Pct:	.350	.333	2
Slugging Pct:	.370	.371	4
Home Runs:	32		4
Stolen Bases:	280		1
ERA:	2.98	3.66	1
Fielding Avg:	.941	.938	5
Runs Scored:	818		1
Runs Allowed:	631		2

Starting Lineup

Billy Sullivan, c
Frank Isbell, 1b
Sam Mertes, 2b
Fred Hartman, 3b
Frank Shugart, ss
Herm McFarland, lf
Dummy Hoy, cf
Fielder Jones, rf
Joe Sugden, c
Jimmy Burke, ss

Pitchers

Clark Griffith, sp
Roy Patterson, sp
Nixey Callahan, sp
John Katoll, sp
Erwin Harvey, sp-rp

Attendance

354,350 (first in AL)

Club Leaders

Batting Avg:	Fielder Jones	.311
On-Base Pct:	Fielder Jones	.412
Slugging Pct:	Dummy Hoy	.400
Home Runs:	Sam Mertes	5
RBIs:	Sam Mertes	98
Runs:	Fielder Jones	120
Stolen Bases:	Frank Isbell	52
Wins:	Clark Griffith	24
Strikeouts:	Roy Patterson	127
ERA:	Nixey Callahan	2.42
Saves:	Clark Griffith	1
	Erwin Harvey	1

MARCH 1	The White Sox sign Clark Griffith after he jumps his contract with the Cubs.

As player-manager, Griffith conducted the White Sox's first spring training as a major league club. It was held in the resort town of Excelsior Springs, Missouri. During the early years of the 20th century, people came from around the world to experience the healing and therapeutic powers of the springs.

MARCH 14	The White Sox sign Fielder Jones after he jumps his contract with the Brooklyn Dodgers.
MARCH 21	The White Sox sign Billy Sullivan after he jumps his contract with the Boston Braves.
MARCH 27	The White Sox sign Sam Mertes after he jumps his contract with the Cubs.
APRIL 1	The White Sox sign Nixey Callahan after he jumps his contract with the Cubs.
APRIL 24	The White Sox play their first game as a major league club and defeat the Cleveland Indians 8–3 before 6,000 at South Side Park. The ballpark was decorated for the occasion, and the contest was preceded by a music concert and the hoisting of the 1900 American League pennant. The Sox pulled ahead early, scoring twice in the first inning and five in the second. The White Sox lineup in the opener was Dummy Hoy,

center field; Fielder Jones, right field; Sam Mertes, left field; Frank Shugart, shortstop; Frank Isbell, first base; Fred Hartman, third base; Dave Brain, second base; Billy Sullivan, catcher; and Roy Patterson, pitcher. Brain played only five games in a White Sox uniform. He was released despite hitting .350 in 20 at-bats. A native of Hereford, England, Brain was later a starting infielder in the National League for five seasons.

The April 24 meeting between the White Sox and Indians is recognized as the first in the history of the American League. The first batter in AL history was Cleveland outfielder Ollie Pickering, who flied out on Patterson's second pitch. Three other contests were scheduled that day, but each was rained out.

APRIL 28   A crowd of 16,000 overwhelms the tiny grandstand at South Side Park for a Sunday game between the White Sox and Indians. The overflow crowd from the stands was placed around the outfield, severely impeding play. By a pre-game agreement, any ball hit into the multitude in the outfield was a ground-rule single. The Sox collected 23 singles to win 13–1.

APRIL 29   Frank Shugart hits the first homer in White Sox history, but the Sox lose 3–2 to the Detroit Tigers at South Side Park.

APRIL 30   John Skopec hits the first home run by a pitcher in White Sox history during a 4–2 win over the Tigers at South Side Park.

The homer was the only one by Skopec during his major league career, which spanned two seasons, 15 games and 43 at-bats.

MAY 1   Herm McFarland and Dummy Hoy both hit grand slams during a 19–9 rout of the Tigers at South Side Park. The slam by McFarland, struck during an eight-run second inning off Joe Yeager, was the first in American League history. All 19 runs were scored in the first five innings and were aided by 12 Detroit errors, an AL record.

No White Sox player hit another grand slam until Jesse Tannehill in 1910. The club didn't have two slams in a game until Robin Ventura hit a pair of them in 1995. McFarland had a close call during spring training in Excelsior Springs, Missouri, in 1902 when manager Clark Griffith took his players on a 10-mile run. Griffith, McFarland and two others were halfway over a train trestle that traversed a ravine when they heard a train approaching. With no time to reach either end of the trestle, Griffith ordered his men to grab a railroad tie and dangle over the edge. After the train rumbled past, teammates ran to pull them up.

MAY 2   The White Sox lose a forfeit to the Tigers at South Side Park. The Sox ended the eighth inning with a 5–2 lead. As the Tigers' half of the ninth started, rain and darkness threatened to end play. During the downpour, Detroit scored six times to move ahead 8–5. Knowing that the score would revert back to the eighth inning unless the ninth was completed, Clark Griffith ordered his players to stall as long as possible between pitches and make no attempt to retire a Tigers batter or runner. The patience of umpire Tom Connolly was tested, however, and he declared the game a forfeit in favor of the Tigers. After he signaled the end of the game, fans stormed the field heading straight for Connolly. Charlie Comiskey pushed his way through the mob trying to mollify his fans while police hustled Connolly from the ballpark.

Connolly was the only umpire on the field, a common practice during the early 1900s.

MAY 3   The White Sox score seven runs in the third inning and defeat the Brewers 11–3 in Milwaukee.

MAY 5   The White Sox suffer a 21–7 defeat at the hands of the Brewers in Milwaukee. Roy Patterson pitched the complete game and allowed 25 hits. He faced 57 batters, the most ever by a pitcher in a nine-inning American League game.

MAY 9   The White Sox win 4–2 over the Indians in Cleveland despite being held hitless by Earl Moore over the first nine innings. In the fourth inning, the White Sox put runners on second and third on an error, a walk and a sacrifice. In an attempt to pick Fielder Jones off third base, Moore threw the ball past the bag and both runners scored. The contest went into extra innings with the score 2–2 and Chicago still looking for its first hit. In a drizzling rain, Sam Mertes broke the spell with a single leading off the tenth. Mertes moved to third on another single by Fred Hartman. Frank Shugart hit a slow roller to shortstop Danny Shay, who threw to the plate. Mertes slid under the tag for the go-ahead run. Later, Hartman scored on another infield out and the Sox held on for the win. John Katoll pitched the complete game for the Sox.

Fielder Jones was a key player on the pennant-winning team of 1901, batting .311.

There have been 12 games in major league history in which a pitcher held the opposition hitless for nine innings, then gave up a hit in extra innings. Mertes collected the first hit in two of the 12 games. The other was in 1904, when he was a member of the Giants. In that contest, Mertes ended the no-hit bid of Long Tom Hughes of the Cubs. Sam was nicknamed Sandow after a famous strongman of the period. Mertes batted .277 for the Sox in 1901.

MAY 16   The White Sox wallop the Brewers 14–1 at South Side Park. Three runs scored in the first inning in unusual fashion. The Sox loaded the bases on a close call on a play at first base. The entire Milwaukee club encircled umpire Tom Connolly to protest the decision, but no one called time. During the argument, all three Chicago runners scored.

MAY 19	The White Sox pummel the Brewers 14–3 at South Side Park.
MAY 23	The White Sox score seven runs in the third inning and survive a four-run Athletics rally in the ninth to win 11–9 at South Side Park. During the final inning, Clark Griffith put himself into the game as a reliever, replacing Erwin Harvey with the score 11–7, the bases loaded and no one out. Griffith walked Nap Lajoie intentionally to force in a run, then recorded three ground outs for the win.
MAY 25	Frank Shugart makes four errors at shortstop, three of them in the third inning, during a 6–5 triumph over the Athletics at South Side Park.
MAY 26	Clark Griffith pitches the first shutout in White Sox history, defeating the Orioles 5–0 at South Side Park.
MAY 30	The White Sox play two games in one day for the first time and win twice against the Red Sox at South Side Park. The double-header was a split admission affair, with one contest in the morning and the other in the afternoon. The White Sox won the opener 8–3 and the second tilt 5–3.

In the White Sox's first season as a major league entry, the South Siders outdueled the Cubs, then located on Chicago's West Side in a ballpark bounded by Taylor, Wood, Polk and Lincoln. The Sox won the AL pennant and drew an attendance of 354,350. Shorn of some of their best players in the player raids by the Sox, the Cubs finished sixth, attracted 205,071 fans and were called the "Remnants" by local sportswriters.

JUNE 7	The White Sox hammer the Senators 15–4 in Washington.
JUNE 10	The White Sox win a thrilling 10-inning, 13–10 decision over the Senators in Washington. The Sox led 10–1 before the Senators scored a run in the eighth and staged an incredible eight-run rally in the ninth to deadlock the game 10–10. Chicago won the contest on a three-run homer by Fred Hartman in the tenth. It was the first extra-inning homer in White Sox history.

In his lone season with the White Sox, Hartman batted .309.

JUNE 13	The White Sox annihilate the Orioles 12–0 in Baltimore. Roy Patterson not only pitched a shutout but also contributed a three-run homer off future Hall of Famer Joe McGinnity.
JUNE 24	The White Sox win a remarkable 14-inning decision over the Athletics in Philadelphia by a score of 7–5. Nixey Callahan allowed four runs in the first before hurling 12 consecutive scoreless innings. The Sox tied the score 4–4 with two runs in the sixth, one in the seventh and one in the ninth. Chicago surged ahead with three runs in the top of the 14th before withstanding a one-run Philadelphia rally in the bottom half.
JUNE 28	Roy Patterson collects four hits in five at-bats and pitches ten innings to lead the White Sox to a 7–6 win over the Indians at South Side Park.
JULY 3	The White Sox win their tenth game in a row with a 4–3 decision over the Indians in 11 innings in Cleveland.

JULY 9   The White Sox outlast the Brewers 17–9 at South Side Park.

JULY 12   The White Sox score seven runs in the fifth inning and defeat the Brewers 14–1 at South Side Park. In his first game with the Sox in Chicago, Jimmy Burke collected four hits, including a double, in five at-bats.

The Brewers moved to St. Louis in 1902 and were renamed the Browns.

JULY 18   The White Sox take over first place with a 9–1 victory over the Orioles at South Side Park.

The Sox remained in first place for the rest of the season, finishing the year four games ahead of the Red Sox. There were some tense moments when Boston pulled within one-half game of the White Sox on August 27, but Chicago pulled away in early September. Oddly, the White Sox lost all ten games to the Red Sox in Boston during the 1901 season and were 8–12 against the New Englanders overall.

JULY 24   The White Sox collect 20 hits and score seven runs in the fifth inning while thrashing the Senators 17–3 at South Side Park.

JULY 31   Clark Griffith pitches the White Sox to a 2–0 win over the Tigers at South Side Park.

AUGUST 1   Nixey Callahan pitches a one-hitter to defeat the Tigers 4–0 at South Side Park. The lone Detroit hit was a single by opposing pitcher Joe Yeager.

AUGUST 2   The White Sox pitching staff records its third consecutive complete-game shutout when Roy Patterson throws a two-hitter to defeat the Tigers 7–0 at South Side Park. The only Detroit hits were singles by Kid Elberfield and Sport McAllister.

AUGUST 8   Fielder Jones collects five hits in five at-bats during an 18–8 win over the Tigers in Detroit.

Fielder was Jones's given name when he was born in Shinglehouse, Pennsylvania, in 1871, which proved to be prophetic when he became one of the best defensive center fielders in the game. The unusual name derived from a great uncle who was a Civil War general. Jones studied engineering at Alfred University, but due to the economic depression of the 1890s, he couldn't find a job in the field and turned to baseball. Fielder was offered a land deed by his mother worth $1,000 if he gave up the sport for a business career, but he declined. Jones batted .311 in 1901. He is best known as the manager of the 1906 White Sox club, which won the American League pennant and was known as the "Hitless Wonders."

AUGUST 10   Frank Isbell fails in the clutch, leaving an American League-record 11 runners stranded during an 11–7 loss to the Indians in Cleveland.

Isbell led the AL in stolen bases with 52 in 1901. Nicknamed "Bald Eagle," Isbell was sensitive about his lack of hair and rarely removed his cap on the field. He was upset when team photos were taken with all of the players bareheaded. Isbell played for the Sox for nine seasons (1901–09) and played all nine positions.

AUGUST 12   The White Sox obliterate the Indians 17–2 in Cleveland.

AUGUST 13   A day after scoring 17 runs, the White Sox go from the ridiculous to the sublime by collecting one hit in the first game of a double-header and 22 in the second while facing the Indians in Cleveland. In the opener, the Sox were the victims of a one-hitter and a 4–0 loss at the hands of Earl Moore, who pitched another gem against the club earlier in the year (see May 9, 1901). It was also the first time in White Sox history that the club was shut out. In the second tilt, the Sox routed the Indians 14–1.

AUGUST 21   Shortstop Frank Shugart and pitcher John Katoll disgrace themselves during an 8–0 loss to the Senators in Washington. In the fourth inning, Katoll became exasperated over the calls of umpire John Haskell, fired a ball at the arbiter's shins and was thrown out of the contest. Pandemonium followed as the whole Chicago team surrounded the arbiter. During the ensuing argument, Shugart dealt a heavy blow to Haskell's face. Haskell tore off his mask and flailed away at Shugart's head. Katoll also tried to assault the ump, but his right hook failed to connect. The crowd overflowed onto the field and one spectator punched Shugart. Police stormed the field and staved off a riot.

Shugart and Katoll were arrested by Washington police for the attack of Haskell and were suspended for two weeks by American League President Ban Johnson. As a result of Shugart's violent actions in the August 21 contest, he was blacklisted by Johnson at the end of the 1901 season and never played another big-league game.

AUGUST 24   Making his first, and only, major league appearance, White Sox starting pitcher Frank Dupee pitches to only three batters at the beginning of a 10–4 loss to the Orioles in Baltimore. Dupee walked all three batters he faced and was relieved by Roy Patterson.

AUGUST 31   The White Sox sweep the Orioles 12–2 and 5–2 in a double-header at South Side Park.

SEPTEMBER 8   Dummy Hoy hits a two-run walk-off double in the ninth inning to beat the Red Sox 4–3 at South Side Park.

William (Dummy) Hoy played center field for the White Sox in 1901 at the age of 39 in the 13th season of a 14-year career. He scored 112 runs during the season, batted .294, and led the AL in walks with 86. Hoy had a long career despite being deaf and possessing a slight, five-foot-six build. An average hitter, he stayed in the majors largely because of his speed and defensive attributes. Hoy is called a "deaf-mute" in most baseball histories, but that is not entirely true. He learned to speak a few phrases to help him in his profession, such as "you are rotten," which was directed at umpires who displeased him. Many other authors have also written that Hoy's deafness was the reason that umpires adopted hand signals to go along with the vocal calls of "out," "safe," and "strike." This is not true. Umpires did not begin using hand signals until 1905, three years after Hoy's career ended. In 1961, at the age of 99, Hoy threw out the ceremonial first pitch before Game Three of the World Series in Cincinnati.

SEPTEMBER 9   The White Sox complete a four-game sweep of the Red Sox with a double-header sweep at Comiskey Park by scores of 4–3 and 6–4. The wins gave Chicago a seven-game lead in the AL pennant race.

SEPTEMBER 15   In the final home games of the 1901 season, the White Sox sweep the Brewers 5–4 and 9–4 before a crowd of 18,000 at South Side Park. Because of the overflow of fans surrounding the outfield, any ball hit into the crowd was a ground-rule triple. As a result, the White Sox set major league records for most triples in an inning (five in the eighth inning of the second game) and a double-header (nine), and an American League mark for most triples in a game (six).

SEPTEMBER 18   Roy Patterson records his 20th win of the season with a 10–3 decision over the Orioles in Baltimore. The Sox scored eight times in the sixth inning.

Patterson had a record of 20–16 and an ERA of 3.37 in 1901.

SEPTEMBER 19   The White Sox game against the Orioles in Baltimore is postponed by the funeral of President William McKinley. He was shot by Leon Czolgosz at a reception in Buffalo on September 6 and died on September 14. Theodore Roosevelt became the new president.

SEPTEMBER 20   Clark Griffith records his 24th win of the season with an 8–3 decision over the Athletics in Philadelphia.

Griffith had a record of 24–7 and an earned run average of 2.67 in 1901.

SEPTEMBER 23   The White Sox lose 5–2 to the Athletics in Philadelphia, but they clinch the American League pennant when the Red Sox lose twice to the Tigers in Boston.

There was no postseason series for the White Sox despite winning the AL crown. The American and National Leagues were at "war," raiding each other's rosters for playing talent, which made a meeting between the champions of the two circuits impossible. The first World Series between AL and NL champions took place in 1903.

OCTOBER 24   The White Sox sign Danny Green after he jumps his contract with the Cubs.

What is a White Sox?

The White Sox were known as the White Stockings when the club was founded in 1900. The nickname was originally attached to Chicago's first professional team, created in 1870. Civic leaders raised $20,000 to organize a strong team, believing it would boost the city's image. This was accomplished when the White Stockings, named because of the color of their hosiery, knocked off the Cincinnati Red Stockings - baseball's first professional team - twice in two meetings in October 1870. The Cincinnati club arrived in the Windy City with an incredible record of 113–2–1. The wins were cause for a city-wide celebration in Chicago.

The White Stockings became part of the National Association - baseball's first professional league - in 1871. The club disbanded for two years after the disastrous fire that destroyed much of Chicago on October 8, 1871, but the team returned in 1874. The National Association ceased to exist after the 1875 season, and the National League was formed in its place, beginning play in 1876. The White Stockings were a part of the NL. The franchise is today known as the Chicago Cubs.

The club changed the color of its stockings from white to black in 1888 and the White Stockings nickname passed out of use. The club went through a variety of nicknames before Cubs was coined in 1902.

When Charlie Comiskey brought his franchise from St. Paul to Chicago in 1900 he revived the White Stockings nickname, but soon newspapers began calling the club White Socks and White Sox. The change was gradual as the term White Stockings was utilized less and less often, and White Sox more frequently, and took place over a period of five or six years. By 1906, the nickname White Stockings had passed almost entirely out of use. In 1911, White Sox received official club sanction when the word "Sox" appeared on the uniforms for the first time.

The reason for the change from White Stockings to White Sox isn't clear, but there are two probable explanations. First, Sox fit more easily into headlines than Stockings. Secondly, between 1870 and the start of the 20th century, the name "stockings" took on a more feminine meaning. In 1870, stockings described footwear worn by both men and women. During the late 19th century, the meaning had changed. Women wore stockings. Men wore socks.

1902   Sox

Season in a Sentence

The White Sox lead the AL for 77 days and hold a 5½-game lead in mid-July before fading to fourth.

Finish • Won • Lost • Pct • GB

Fourth   74   60   .552   8.0

Manager

Clark Griffith

Stats

Stats	WS	AL	Rank
Batting Avg:	.268	.275	6
On-Base Pct:	.332	.331	5
Slugging Pct:	.335	.369	7
Home Runs:	14		8
Stolen Bases:	265		1
ERA:	3.41	3.57	5
Fielding Avg:	.955	.949	1
Runs Scored:	675		5
Runs Allowed:	602		2

Starting Lineup

Billy Sullivan, c
Frank Isbell, 1b
Tom Daly, 2b
Sammy Strang, 3b
George Davis, ss
Sam Mertes, lf
Fielder Jones, cf
Danny Green, rf
Ed McFarland, c

Pitchers

Roy Patterson, sp
Nixey Callahan, sp
Clark Griffith, sp
Wiley Piatt, sp
Ned Garvin, sp

Attendance

337,898 (third in AL)

Club Leaders

Batting Avg:	Fielder Jones	.321
On-Base Pct:	Fielder Jones	.390
Slugging Pct:	George Davis	.402
Home Runs:	Frank Isbell	4
RBIs:	George Davis	93
Runs:	Sammy Strang	108
Stolen Bases:	Sam Mertes	46
Wins:	Roy Patterson	19
Strikeouts:	Wiley Piatt	96
ERA:	Ned Garvin	2.21
Saves:	None	

APRIL 23   In the season opener, the White Sox defeat the Tigers 12–2 at South Side Park. Nixey Callahan was the winning pitcher, and also collected three hits, one of them a double. Frank Isbell had four hits, including three doubles, in five at-bats. A chilling wind from Lake Michigan held the crowd to 6,500. The stands were decked with red, white and blue bunting and a military band played throughout the contest. Before the first pitch, both teams marched to the flag pole where the American flag and the 1901 American League pennant were unfurled.

APRIL 27   Sammy Strang draws five walks in five plate appearances during a 9–0 victory over the Indians at South Side Park.

Strang hit .295 for the White Sox in 1902, his only season with the club. He was one of the five regulars who jumped from the National League to the White Sox during the 1901–02 off-season. Strang came from the Giants, along with George Davis. Tom Daly moved to Chicago from the Dodgers, Ed McFarland from the Phillies and Danny Green from the Cubs. The NL counter attacked, and two starters on the 1901 White Sox left the club. Dummy Hoy went to the Reds and Fred Hartman joined the Cardinals. During the last week of the 1902 season, Strang also returned to the NL by signing a contract to the Cubs, then went back to the Giants in 1903 in a trade.

MAY 9   The White Sox score six runs in the ninth inning to beat the Indians 12–8 in Cleveland.

The White Sox wore distinctive dark blue road uniforms with "Chicago" written across the front in white from 1902 through 1916. The dark blue uniforms had one-season revivals in both 1926 and 1930.

MAY 14   The White Sox smack the Browns 12–2 at South Side Park.

There were only seven home runs, five by the White Sox, struck at South Side Park in 1902. The Sox hit nine homers in road games, while the pitching staff surrendered 28.

MAY 16   White Sox pitcher Wiley Piatt pitches a one-hitter to defeat the St. Louis Browns 2–1 at South Side Park. The only hit off Piatt was a double by Dick Padden.

MAY 18   The White Sox and Browns play 17 innings to a 2–2 tie at South Side Park. The game was called on account of darkness. Nixey Callahan of the Sox and Red Donahue of the Browns both pitched complete games. Callahan also chipped in with five hits, all singles, in eight at-bats. Neither pitcher allowed a run after the sixth inning.

MAY 19   Clark Griffith pitches the White Sox to a 1–0 win over the Tigers in Detroit.

MAY 23   The White Sox edge the Red Sox 4–3 in 10 innings in Boston. The contest was 1–1 after 10 innings. Sam Mertes clubbed a three-run homer in the top of the 10th inning before Chicago survived a two-run Boston rally in the bottom half.

The homer was the only one that Mertes hit in 1902. The White Sox's top hitter during the year was Fielder Jones, who hit .321.

JUNE 9	Roy Patterson wins his own game with a walk-off single in the ninth inning to defeat the Senators 2–1 at South Side Park.

Patterson had a 19–14 record and a 3.06 ERA.

JUNE 13	The White Sox record their eighth victory in a row with a 9–0 decision over the Red Sox at South Side Park.
JULY 25	The White Sox capture the first game of a double-header with a 15–4 thrashing of the Orioles in Baltimore. The Sox lost the nightcap 5–4.
JULY 30	The start of White Sox's 1–0 loss to the Indians in Cleveland is delayed for more than an hour because of a train wreck. The previous day, the White Sox played in Washington and the Indians in Baltimore. An accident on the Baltimore & Ohio line delayed the two clubs until the accident could be cleared from the tracks.
AUGUST 9	The White Sox score two runs in the ninth inning to defeat the Red Sox 8–7 at South Side Park. Danny Green tripled in the tying run and scored on a walk-off sacrifice fly by George Davis. The White Sox held a 6–1 advantage at the end of the seventh inning, but Boston plated five runs in the eighth and one in the ninth to pull ahead 7–6.

Davis played in the majors from 1890 through 1909 and was one of the outstanding shortstops of his era. His long overdue election to the Hall of Fame occurred in 1998. He was with the White Sox in 1902 and again from 1904 through the end of his career. The one-year gap was due to the war between the American and National Leagues from 1901 through 1903. Davis jumped from the New York Giants to the White Sox in 1902 at a salary reported to be $4,000, which made him one of the highest, if not the highest, paid players in the game. However, Davis didn't enjoy his first season in Chicago, in which he hit .299, and jumped back to the Giants. The 1903 peace agreement between the two leagues (see January 10, 1903) returned Davis to Chicago, but he refused to comply with the edict. Comiskey secured an injunction barring Davis from playing with the Giants after the shortstop appeared in four games with the New York club. Comiskey won the court battle, and Davis returned to the White Sox in 1904. He was a key member of the 1906 White Sox world championship team.

AUGUST 13	The White Sox are knocked out of first place with a 9–0 loss to the Red Sox in Boston.

The White Sox spent 77 days in first place in 1902. The peak point of the season occurred on July 16 when the Sox had a record of 42–25 and a 5½-game lead. A six-game losing streak started the following day and sent the club into a tailspin. By the end of the season, the White Sox were 74–60 and in fourth place, eight games out of first.

AUGUST 22	Trailing the Senators 6–0 after seven innings in Washington, the White Sox score six times in the eighth inning and three in the ninth to win 9–6.
AUGUST 25	The White Sox are hammered 21–6 by the Orioles in Baltimore.

AUGUST 26   The day after Baltimore scores 21 runs off White Sox pitching, Ned Garvin shuts out the Orioles 10–0 in Baltimore.

Four days later, Garvin was arrested in Chicago for shooting Lawrence Flanigan, the proprietor of a bar, in the shoulder. Garvin was released by the White Sox, and since Flanigan's wound wasn't serious, Garvin escaped with a fine for assault. He died in 1908 at the age of 32 from tuberculosis.

SEPTEMBER 20   Nixey Callahan pitches a no-hitter to defeat the Tigers 3–0 in the first game of a double-header at South Side Park. Callahan walked two and struck out two. All three runs scored in the first inning when George Davis tripled in two runs and scored on an error.

Before the games, there was a parade of some 200 of the top amateur players in Chicago through the downtown streets and on to the White Sox ballpark. The grand marshall was future Hall of Famer Cap Anson, who starred for the Cubs from 1876 through 1897. The procession reached South Side Park in the seventh inning, and the game was stopped as the players marched around the field. Charles Comiskey was presented with a fishing outfit and his wife with a bunch of roses.

SEPTEMBER 21   Clark Griffith wins his own game in the ninth inning to defeat the Tigers 5–4 in the first game of a double-header at South Side Park. Griffith tripled in the tying run, then he scored on an error when Detroit second baseman Kid Gleason threw the ball past third base trying to retire the White Sox pitcher-manager. The Sox also won the second tilt 2–0.

Griffith didn't return to the White Sox in 1903. During the summer of 1902, American League President Ban Johnson decided to establish an American League club in New York to begin play in 1903. The Baltimore Orioles were the club that would be moved to Gotham to establish the franchise that was eventually named the Yankees. Johnson approached Griffith about heading the New York club as manager. Griffith chafed under the direction of autocratic and tight-fisted Charlie Comiskey and was happy to comply. Griffith managed the New York club from 1903 through 1908, the Cincinnati Reds from 1909 through 1911, and the Senators from 1912 through 1920. When Griffith moved to Washington he also became part-owner of the club. He bought out many of his partners in 1920 to obtain a controlling interest in the Senators, which he held until his death in 1955.

SEPTEMBER 28   On the last day of the season, the White Sox and the Browns play a farcical double-header in St. Louis. The Browns won the opener 10–9 and the White Sox the second 10–4. In the nightcap, many players on both teams played out of position. Frank Isbell was the starting pitcher. Sam Mertes began the game as a catcher and finished as a pitcher. It was his only big-league game as a pitcher and allowed him to play all nine positions during his 10 seasons in the majors. (Mertes played at least one game at every position but center field with the White Sox in 1902.) Nixey Callahan appeared in the season finale as the shortstop and Clark Griffith was in left field.

1903

Sox

Season in a Sentence

The White Sox are in first place on May 31, but they wilt over the summer and finish with a losing record under new manager Nixey Callahan.

Finish • Won • Lost • Pct • GB

Seventh 60 77 .438 30.5

Manager

Nixey Callahan

Stats

	WS	AL	Rank
Batting Avg:	.247	.255	6
On-Base Pct:	.301	.303	6
Slugging Pct:	.314	.344	7
Home Runs:	14		6
Stolen Bases:	180		1
ERA:	3.02	2.96	6
Fielding Avg:	.949	.953	7
Runs Scored:	516		6
Runs Allowed:	613		7

Starting Lineup

Jack Slattery, c
Frank Isbell, 1b
George Magoon, 2b
Nixey Callahan, 3b
Lee Tannehill, ss
Ducky Holmes, lf
Fielder Jones, cf
Danny Green, rf
Bill Hallman, lf
Ed McFarland, c
Tom Daly, 2b

Pitchers

Doc White, sp
Patsy Flaherty, sp
Roy Patterson, sp
Frank Owen, sp
Davey Dunkle, sp-rp
Nick Altrock, sp-rp

Attendance

286,183 (fifth in AL)

Club Leaders

Batting Avg:	Danny Green	.309
On-Base Pct:	Danny Green	.375
Slugging Pct:	Danny Green	.425
Home Runs:	Danny Green	6
RBIs:	Danny Green	62
Runs:	Danny Green	75
Stolen Bases:	Danny Green	29
Wins:	Doc White	17
Strikeouts:	Doc White	114
ERA:	Doc White	2.13
Saves:	Four tied with	1

JANUARY 10   The National and American Leagues reach a peace accord at a meeting in Cincinnati, ending the costly war and contract jumping that had driven salaries skyward. The two leagues agreed to refrain from raiding one another's rosters and set up a three-man governing body consisting of the presidents of the two organizations and Cincinnati Reds President Garry Herrmann.

MARCH 16   The White Sox name Nixey Callahan as manager to replace Clark Griffith.

Callahan was two days shy of his 29th birthday when he was hired as the player-manager of the Sox. He was an unlikely choice to run the club because as a player he had always been a hard drinker and undisciplined in addition to suffering from weight problems. Nothing went right in 1903, as the White Sox had a record of 60–77. After a 23–18 start to the 1904 season, Callahan resigned as manager, although he continued with the Sox as a player through the end of the 1905 season.

APRIL 22   The White Sox win the season opener 14–4 over the Browns in St. Louis. Frank Isbell, Fielder Jones and Ed McFarland each collected three hits. Two of Isbell's hits were doubles. In his first game with the White Sox, Patsy Flaherty was the winning pitcher.

Flaherty had a record of 11–25 in 1903 and still holds the White Sox record for most losses in a season. The Sox released him in May 1904, after he lost two of three decisions. The Pirates immediately picked him up, and Flaherty was 19–9 over the remainder of the season. He finished his career in 1911 with a mark of 67–84.

MAY 1   In the home opener, the White Sox defeat the Tigers 5–1. Cold and high winds kept the crowd at South Side Park to 3,800.

MAY 2   The White Sox score eight runs in the fourth inning and wallop the Indians 16–6 at South Side Park.

MAY 6   The White Sox commit an American League-record 12 errors, but they pull out a 10–9 win over the Tigers at South Side Park. Down 6–0, the Sox scored two runs in the fourth inning and five in the fifth to take a 7–6 lead. After falling behind again 9–7, the White Sox plated three tallies in the ninth for the win. Shortstop Lee Tannehill made four of the errors. First baseman Frank Isbell and pitcher Patsy Flaherty each committed three errors.

MAY 8   Nixey Callahan collects five hits, including a triple and a double, in six at-bats, but is ineffective as a pitcher in an 11-inning, 13–12 loss to the Browns at South Side Park. He pitched the complete game, allowing two runs in the ninth to tie the score 9–9 and four in the 11th. The Sox scored three runs in the bottom half in a futile rally.

It was games like this that brought Callahan to the decision to give up pitching and to move to third base and the outfield. After pitching in three games in 1903, he never returned to the mound, although he was still playing in the majors as late as 1913. As a pitcher, Callahan had a record of 93–73, and he was 32–24 with the Sox. As a hitter, Nixey had a batting average of .292 in 1904 and a lifetime mark of .273.

MAY 27   Patsy Flaherty pitches the White Sox to a 1–0 win over the Indians in Cleveland.

The White Sox peaked in 1903 on May 29 with a record of 19–12 and a 2½-game lead in the American League pennant race. The Sox were knocked from their first-place perch two days later, however, and lost 50 of their last 80 games, beginning with a July 4 double-header defeat.

JUNE 9   The White Sox trade Tom Daly and Cozy Dolan to the Reds for George Magoon.

JUNE 16   The White Sox play in New York for the first time and win 6–3 over the Yankees.

JUNE 21   The White Sox hammer the Athletics 11–1 in Philadelphia.

JUNE 25   Darkness ends an 18-inning marathon between the White Sox and Yankees at South Side Park with the score knotted 6–6. New York scored two runs in the ninth to send the contest into extra innings. Relievers Roy Patterson of the White Sox and Jess Tannehill of the Yankees each pitched shutout ball over the last nine innings.

JUNE 30   Red Sox pitcher Nick Altrock gives up eight White Sox runs in the first inning of a 10–3 Chicago victory at South Side Park.

Despite the performance, the White Sox acquired Altrock seven days later (see July 7, 1903).

JULY 7   Danny Green and umpire Jack Sheridan fight during a 10-inning, 3–2 victory over the Yankees in New York. In the seventh inning, Green was called out at first base and objected strongly to Sheridan's decision. Green was ejected but continued his verbal assault on the arbiter from the dugout. Sheridan walked toward Green and struck the White Sox outfielder with his mask, inflicting a nasty cut. Green retaliated by belting the ump. Sheridan was arrested by park police for disorderly conduct and hauled off to the station house. Since he was the only umpire assigned to the game, Pasty Flaherty of the Sox and Monty Beville of the Yankees were called upon to officiate the remainder of the contest. Sheridan was bailed out of jail by Yankees President Joseph Gordon. The case was closed when Green refused to press charges.

On the same day, the White Sox purchased Nick Altrock from the Red Sox. Altrock proved to be an excellent acquisition. He won 19 or more games in 1904, 1905 and 1906, posting a 62–39 record over those three seasons. Altrock is best-known, however, for his comedic talents. After his playing days were over, Altrock was a coach with the Senators for four decades and kept fans in stitches with his clowning in the coaching lines. He also teamed with Al Schacht, another former big-league pitcher, to form a pantomime act. The two appeared on the field before several World Series games during the 1920s and 1930s.

JULY 30   The White Sox rout the Indians 10–0 at South Side Park.

AUGUST 19   Despite a fluke homer by Frank Isbell, the White Sox lose 4–3 to the Red Sox at South Side Park. In the seventh inning with two runners on base, Isbell hit a ball into right field that rolled under the bleachers.

AUGUST 21   White Sox left fielder Ducky Holmes ties a major league record for most assists by an outfielder with four, although the White Sox lose 11–3 to the Red Sox at South Side Park.

SEPTEMBER 6   Doc White pitches a 10-inning, one-hitter to defeat the Indians 1–0 at South Side Park. The lone Cleveland hit was a double by Bill Bradley. The Sox collected only three hits off Indians hurler Marty Glendon. The 10th-inning run scored on two errors and a passed ball.

Guy (Doc) White jumped his contract with the Phillies to join the White Sox just before the American and National Leagues reach a peace accord that prevented such practices (see January 10, 1903), and just after he received a degree in dental surgery from Georgetown University. White was also an accomplished violinist and balladeer who wrote song lyrics in his spare time. After his playing career ended, White toured the country as an evangelist. His diverse talents included a repertoire of pitches that led to a lifetime record of 189–156 over a career that lasted from 1901 through 1913. He is best known for pitching five consecutive shutouts in September 1904 (see September 30, 1904). White was 159–123 in 11 seasons in Chicago. He ranks sixth all-time among White Sox hurlers in wins and is second in shutouts (43), fourth in complete games (206), fifth in games started (301), fifth in ERA (2.30) and sixth in innings (2,498⅓).

SEPTEMBER 18   Shortstop Lee Tannehill commits four errors during a 7–1 loss to the Yankees in the first game of a double-header in New York. The Sox also lost the second tilt 6–3.

Danny Green was the White Sox's top hitter in 1903 with a .309 average. Doc White topped the pitchers with a 17–16 record and a 2.13 earned run average.

OCTOBER 1   The Cubs and the White Sox play each other for the first time in a postseason "City Series." The Cubs were the home team and won the first game 11–0 at West Side Grounds. The original schedule called for 15 games, with one played each day through October 15.

After 10 days of the City Series, the Cubs had six victories, the White Sox three, and one contest was postponed by rain. The Sox won four of the next five, three of them on 2–0 shutouts by Doc White, Frank Owen and Nick Altrock.

OCTOBER 15   The White Sox defeat the Cubs 2–0 at South Side Park, ending the first City Series. Each team won seven games, but no more were played to determine the championship. The White Sox wanted to play a deciding fifteenth game, but Cubs management refused. The players' contracts expired on October 15, and Cubs President James Hart didn't want to pay his players for another day of work.

The City Series

A largely forgotten aspect of the histories of the White Sox and the Cubs is the Chicago City Series, which was played nearly every fall from 1903 through 1942. The Series was held just after the close of the regular season at the same time as the World Series and was a highly anticipated event in Chicago. Weekend games usually drew capacity crowds, and those played on weekday afternoons drew well above the regular season figures, even though they were held in the city's fickle October weather. Attendance remained high even in seasons in which both clubs finished with losing records. There were cases in which managers on both clubs either saved their jobs by winning the City Series or wound up unemployed by losing to their crosstown rivals.

The first City Series was played in 1903. The White Sox were founded in 1900, and in 1901 they began raiding National League rosters for players, taking several Cubs. Naturally, there was a great deal of animosity between the established National League and the upstart American League. It was soothed in part by a peace accord in January 1903 in which each league agreed to respect the player contracts of the other. At the end of the 1903 season, the Boston Red Sox and the Pittsburgh Pirates met in baseball's first World Series. At the same time, the White Sox and the Cubs agreed to play 15 games against each other from October 1 through October 15. Bragging rights were at stake, but in the end nothing was settled in that initial City Series, as each team won seven games with another contest postponed by rain and never played.

From 1903 through 1942, the Cubs and the White Sox met in the post-season 26 times, with the White Sox winning 19 times, the Cubs six, and the one draw in 1903. Beginning in 1905, the City Series was played under the same rules that governed the World Series. In 1906, the White Sox and the Cubs won their league championships and played each other in the World Series. Although fan interest was still high, the last City Series was played in 1942. Cubs management, led by P. K. Wrigley and Charlie Grimm, hadn't beaten the White Sox since 1930, were embarrassed by the one-sided nature of the affair and declined to play any more of them. Wrigley called winning the City Series a "booby prize" unworthy of the effort.

Following are the results of the series:

1903	White Sox 7 games, Cubs 7 games.
1904	No series played.
1905	Cubs 4 games, White Sox 1 game.
1906	White Sox 4 games, Cubs 2 games in the World Series.
1907	No series held (Cubs in the World Series).
1908	No series held (Cubs in the World Series).
1909	Cubs 4 games, White Sox 1 game.
1910	No series played (Cubs in the World Series).
1911	White Sox 4 games, Cubs 0 games.
1912	White Sox 4 games, Cubs 3 games, 2 ties.
1913	White Sox 4 games, Cubs 2 games.
1914	White Sox 4 games, Cubs 3 games.
1915	White Sox 4 games, Cubs 1 game.
1916	White Sox 4 games, Cubs 0 games.
1917	No series played (White Sox in the World Series).
1918	No series played (Cubs in the World Series).
1919	No series played (White Sox in the World Series).
1920	No series played (White Sox roster devastated by the suspensions of eight players in the Black Sox scandal, which broke in September 1920).
1921	White Sox 5 games, Cubs 0 games.
1922	Cubs 4 games, White Sox 3 games.
1923	White Sox 4 games, Cubs 2 games.
1924	White Sox 4 games, Cubs 2 games.
1925	Cubs 4 games, White Sox 1 game.
1926	White Sox 4 games, Cubs 3 games.
1927	No series played (Cubs declined to participate).
1928	Cubs 4 games, White Sox 3 games.
1929	No series played (Cubs in World Series).
1930	Cubs 4 games, White Sox 2 games.
1931	White Sox 4 games, Cubs 3 games.
1932	No series played (Cubs in World Series).
1933	White Sox 4 games, Cubs 0 games.
1934	No series played (Cubs declined to participate).
1935	No series played (Cubs in World Series).
1936	White Sox 4 games, Cubs 0 games.
1937	White Sox 4 games, Cubs 3 games.
1938	No series played (Cubs in World Series).
1939	White Sox 4 games, Cubs 3 games.
1940	White Sox 4 games, Cubs 3 games.
1941	White Sox 4 games, Cubs 0 games.
1942	White Sox 4 games, Cubs 2 games.

1904

Sox

Season in a Sentence

After a change in managers in June and a six-day stay in first place in August, the White Sox fade to third in September despite five consecutive shutouts by Doc White.

Finish • Won • Lost • Pct • GB

Third   89   65   .578   6.0

Managers

Nixey Callahan (23–18) and Fielder Jones (66–47)

Stats

Stats	WS	AL	Rank
Batting Avg:	.242	.244	5
On-Base Pct:	.300	.295	4
Slugging Pct:	.316	.321	5
Home Runs:	14		5
Stolen Bases:	216		1
ERA:	2.30	2.60	3
Fielding Avg:	.964	.959	1
Runs Scored:	600		3
Runs Allowed:	482		2 (tie)

Starting Lineup

Billy Sullivan, c
Jiggs Donahue, 1b
Gus Dundon, 2b
Lee Tannehill, 3b
George Davis, ss
Nixey Callahan, lf
Fielder Jones, cf
Danny Green, rf
Frank Isbell, 1b-2b
Ducky Holmes, lf
Ed McFarland, c

Pitchers

Frank Owen, sp
Nick Altrock, sp
Doc White, sp
Frank Smith, sp
Roy Patterson, sp
Ed Walsh, rp-sp

Attendance

557,123 (second in AL)

Club Leaders

Batting Avg:	Danny Green	.265
On-Base Pct:	Danny Green	.352
Slugging Pct:	George Davis	.359
Home Runs:	Fielder Jones	3
RBIs:	George Davis	69
Runs:	Danny Green	83
Stolen Bases:	George Davis	32
Wins:	Frank Owen	21
Strikeouts:	Doc White	115
ERA:	Doc White	1.78
Saves:	Frank Owen	1
	Ed Walsh	1

APRIL 14   Four months after Orville and Wilbur Wright's first successful flight, and four months following the terrible Iroquois Theater fire in downtown Chicago that killed 578 people, the White Sox lose the season opener 6–1 to the Indians at South Side Park.

The White Sox opened the 1904 season with a Jones in center field, but it was Charlie Jones, not Fielder. Fielder Jones had signed his 1903 contract without a reserve clause and during the following off-season signed with the New York Giants. He reported to the Giants for spring training in 1904, but the National Commission ruled that Jones belonged to the White Sox. "I am practically a slave," Jones said. "The baseball slave accepts the restrictions placed upon him by the great magnates, and smiles." Jones missed the first six White Sox games before joining the club. Six weeks later, he was the manager of the Sox (see June 5, 1904).

APRIL 18   Patsy Flaherty pitches a two-hitter to defeat the Tigers 9–2 at South Side Park. The only Detroit hits were a double by Charlie Carr and a single by Ed Gremminger.

APRIL 24   Trailing 4–0, the White Sox score a run in the eighth inning and four in the ninth to stun the Indians 5–4 at South Side Park. With a runner on third and two out in the ninth, Ducky Holmes was hit by a pitch and Fielder Jones walked. Player-manager Nixey Callahan tied the score with a three-run double and crossed the plate with the winning tally on Danny Green's double.

Green led the White Sox in batting average (.265), on base percentage (.352) and runs (83) in 1904.

MAY 1   The White Sox wallop the Browns 13–0 in St. Louis.

MAY 12   Future Hall of Fame pitcher Ed Walsh makes his major league debut as a reliever during a 9–3 loss to the Athletics in Philadelphia.

MAY 19   In his first big-league start, Ed Walsh pitches a two-hitter to defeat the Senators 5–0 on a rainy afternoon in Washington. The only hits off Walsh were singles by Jake Stahl and Joe Cassidy.

Walsh made his big-league debut two days before his 23rd birthday, and by the time his career ended in 1917 he had a lifetime record of 195–126. Walsh's ERA of 1.81 is the best all-time among major league pitchers with at least 1,500 innings pitched. With the exception of four games in his last season, Walsh spent his entire career with the Sox. He was one of 13 children born to an impoverished family of Pennsylvania coal miners, and for Walsh baseball provided an escape from the grueling, life-shortening work. He was drafted by the White Sox from Newark in the Eastern League in 1903. Walsh was taught to throw a spitball by Elmer Stricklett, a teammate at Newark and with the White Sox. Stricklett is credited by some historians as the individual who invented the pitch. It took a few years for Walsh to master the spitball, which remained a legal pitch in baseball until 1920. He didn't move into the White Sox starting rotation until late in the 1905 season, but he soon established himself as one of the best pitchers of the era. Full of confidence, Walsh was described by one sportswriter as "the only man I ever saw who could strut while standing still." From 1906 through 1912, Walsh won 168 games, including an astonishing figure of 40 in 1908. On the White Sox all-time lists, he ranks first in earned run average (1.80), first in shutouts (57), second in strikeouts (1,732), third in wins (195), third in complete games (249), third in innings pitched (2,947⅓), fourth in winning percentage (.609) and fourth in games started (312).

JUNE 1   Frank Owen not only pitches a two-hit shutout to defeat the Senators 1–0 at South Side Park, but he drives in the game's lone run with a fifth-inning single. The only Washington hits were singles by Barry McCormick and Charles Moran.

Owen had a spectacular three-year run with the White Sox from 1904 through 1906, posting a cumulative record of 64–41. In 1904, he was 21–15 with an ERA of 1.94. A physician, Owen set up a medical practice in Ypsilanti, Michigan, during the off-season and continued it after his playing days ended.

JUNE 5   The White Sox collect 21 hits and hammer the Athletics 14–2 at South Side Park. In his first game as manager, Fielder Jones picked up four hits, including a double, in four at-bats and scored five runs.

Jones replaced Nixey Callahan earlier in the day. Callahan resigned with the club holding a record of 23–18, preferring a role as a player only. Jones was in his ninth season as a major league player and 30 years old when appointed as manager. He proved to be the perfect choice as an antidote to Callahan, a lax disciplinarian. Quiet but possessing a fiery temper, Jones was a stern disciplinarian who had no tolerance for overweight or lazy players. He was also an innovator who was seldom afraid to try out a new strategy. Jones is credited with devising the "motion" infield to thwart hit-and-run plays and sacrifice bunts. He led the White Sox until 1908, a period that included the 1906 world championship. Jones's clubs in Chicago were 427–293, a winning percentage of .593.

Though never a good hitter, Billy Sullivan provided excellent defense behind the plate for the Sox throughout the team's first decade.

JUNE 21   Charles Comiskey honors good friend Garry Herrmann at South Side Park before a 2–1 win over the Indians. Herrmann was president of the Cincinnati Reds as well as the head of the National Commission, which was then baseball's governing body. He was honored to signify the peace between the National and American Leagues. Herrmann was in Chicago for the Republican National Convention. Herrmann and his party arrived at the ballpark in six decorated horse-drawn wagons, which had carried them from their hotel downtown, and circled the field prior to the game to great applause.

JUNE 27   The White Sox collect 24 hits and demolish the Tigers 18–6 in Detroit. Jiggs Donahue scored five runs.

A weak hitter but one of the best-fielding first basemen of the 1900s, Donahue played for the White Sox from 1904 through 1909. He died of syphilis at the age of 34 in 1913.

JULY 1   Nick Altrock pitches a two-hitter to defeat the Browns 5–0 at South Side Park. The only St. Louis hits were singles by Jesse Burkett and Charlie Hemphill. Center fielder Fielder Jones pulled off an unassisted double play during the game by catching a shallow fly ball and stepping on second before the runner could return.

| JULY 7 | Frank Owen pitches the White Sox to a 1–0 win over the Browns in St. Louis. |
| JULY 9 | Nick Altrock pitches the White Sox to a 1–0 win over the Browns in St. Louis. |

Altrock was 19–14 with a 2.96 earned run average in 1904.

JULY 11	The White Sox rout the Indians 11–1 in a game in Cleveland called after eight innings to allow both teams to catch a train.
JULY 18	The White Sox easily defeat the Senators 11–1 in Washington.
JULY 29	Frank Owen wins his own game with a 10th-inning homer that provides the winning run in a 4–3 decision over the Red Sox in Boston.

The homer was the second of two that Owen hit during his eight-year career in which he accumulated 483 at-bats. As a team, the White Sox hit just 14 homers in 1904, all of them on the road. It was next to impossible to hit a home run at South Side Park. There were only two homers struck there during the season, both by visiting players.

AUGUST 2	Frank Owen pitches a two-hitter to defeat the Senators 5–1 at South Side Park. Owen also stole home in the third inning. The only Washington hits were singles by Jake Stahl and opposing pitcher Beany Jacobson.
AUGUST 3	The White Sox score two runs in the ninth inning and one in the 10th to beat the Senators 3–2 at South Side Park.
AUGUST 6	Nick Altrock sets a major league record (since tied) for most total chances accepted by a pitcher in a game with 13 during an 8–1 win over the Athletics at South Side Park. Altrock had 10 assists and three putouts.

In 1904, Altrock set an American league record (since tied) for most putouts in a season by a pitcher with 49.

| AUGUST 11 | Doc White pitches the White Sox to a 1–0 win over the Yankees in New York. George Davis drove in the winning run with a single in the sixth inning. |

Davis led the White Sox in hits (142), triples (15), RBIs (69) and stolen bases (32) in 1904.

| AUGUST 17 | Jesse Tannehill of the Red Sox pitches a no-hitter to defeat the White Sox 6–0 at South Side Park. The final out was recorded on a bouncer off the bat of Fielder Jones to second baseman Hobe Ferris. Jesse's brother Lee contributed to the no-hitter by going 0-for-3 as the White Sox third baseman. |
| AUGUST 22 | The White Sox drop from first place to third after losing 4–3 to the Yankees in New York. The Sox not only dropped past the Yanks but Boston as well. |

Chicago spent six days in August on top of the AL standings. The club never led after August 22, but the White Sox were in contention for the pennant until the final week.

SEPTEMBER 8   After being held scoreless in the first 17 innings of a double-header in Cleveland, the White Sox score three runs in the ninth inning of the second tilt to defeat the Indians 3–2. The Sox lost the opener 6–0.

SEPTEMBER 10   The White Sox lose a double-header 5–4 and 11–6 to the Indians in Cleveland. The defeats placed Chicago in fourth place, 7½ games out of first with 26 contests left on the schedule.

SEPTEMBER 12   Doc White pitches the White Sox to a 1–0 win over the Indians in Cleveland.

The shutout was the first of five in a row pitched by White in September 1904. The five consecutive shutouts pitched by White is still the American League record. It was the major league mark until Don Drysdale of the Dodgers hurled six in a row in 1968. White lived just long enough to see his record broken. He died in 1969 at the age of 90.

SEPTEMBER 16   Doc White pitches his second shutout in a row with a one-hitter to defeat the Browns 1–0 in St. Louis. The only hit off White was a triple by Tim Jones.

White pitched seven shutouts in 1904, all of them between August 11 and September 30. During the season, he had a 16–12 record and a 1.78 ERA.

SEPTEMBER 18   Roy Patterson pitches the White Sox to a 1–0 win over the Tigers at South Side Park.

SEPTEMBER 19   Doc White pitches his third consecutive shutout, beating the Tigers 3–0 at South Side Park.

In eight consecutive starts from September 5 through October 2, White pitched six shutouts and allowed only four runs in 72 innings.

SEPTEMBER 25   Doc White pitches his fourth consecutive shutout, downing the Athletics 3–0 at South Side Park.

While pitching five shutouts in a row, White allowed just 17 hits in 45 innings.

SEPTEMBER 30   Doc White pitches his fifth straight shutout and runs his streak of consecutive scoreless innings to 45 with a 4–0 triumph over the Yankees at South Side Park.

The win put the White Sox two games behind the Yankees in the AL pennant race. Chicago was in third place with Boston in second three percentage points behind New York. There were 10 games left to play.

OCTOBER 2   A crowd of 30,084 jams into South Side Park for a double-header against the Yankees in a showdown for the pennant. Doc White started the first game on just one day of rest and aiming for his sixth consecutive shutout. His streak ended when he allowed a run in the first inning, but White shut down the Yanks the rest of the way and won 2–1. Fielder Jones sent White to the mound again to start the second contest. The White Sox led 2–0 after three innings. At that point, White had allowed only one run over his last 57 innings, but he succumbed to the strain of pitching so many innings in such a short span of time, and the Sox lost 6–3 before the game ended after seven innings on account of darkness.

At the end of the twin bill, the White Sox were 3½ games behind with seven left to play. The Sox were swept in a three-game series against the Red Sox at South Side Park from October 3 through October 5, ending any hopes for a pennant on the South Side of Chicago. The Red Sox nosed out the Yankees for the 1904 AL flag.

OCTOBER 9   On the last day of the season, the White Sox sweep the Browns 6–2 and 1–0 at South Side Park. Frank Smith pitched the second-game shutout.

1905   Sox

Season in a Sentence

The White Sox fall just short of first place in a grueling pennant race despite a pitching staff that compiles an earned run average of 1.99.

Finish • Won • Lost • Pct • GB

Second   92   60   .605   2.0

Manager

Fielder Jones

Stats

Stats	WS	AL	Rank
Batting Avg:	.237	.241	5
On-Base Pct:	.305	.299	4
Slugging Pct:	.304	.314	6
Home Runs:	11		8
Stolen Bases:	194		2
ERA:	1.99	2.65	1
Fielding Avg:	.968	.957	1
Runs Scored:	612		2
Runs allowed:	451		1

Starting Lineup

Billy Sullivan, c
Jiggs Donahue, 1b
Gus Dundon, 2b
Lee Tannehill, 3b
George Davis, ss
Nixey Callahan, lf
Fielder Jones, cf
Danny Green, rf
Frank Isbell, 2b-rf
Ducky Holmes, lf
Ed McFarland, c

Pitchers

Nick Altrock, sp
Frank Owen, sp
Doc White, sp
Frank Smith, sp
Ed Walsh, sp
Roy Patterson, sp

Attendance

687,419 (first in AL)

Club Leaders

Batting Avg:	Jiggs Donahue	.287
On-Base Pct:	George Davis	.353
Slugging Pct:	Jiggs Donahue	.349
Home Runs:	Three tied with	2
RBIs:	Jiggs Donahue	76
Runs:	Fielder Jones	91
Stolen Bases:	Jiggs Donahue	32
Wins:	Nick Altrock	23
Strikeouts:	Frank Smith	171
ERA:	Doc White	1.76
Saves:	None	

APRIL 14   On a cold afternoon following a morning snowstorm, the White Sox open the season with a 2–1 loss to the Browns before 8,654 at South Side Park. The Sox collected only two hits off Harry Howell, both singles by Danny Green. Frank Smith pitched for Chicago.

Smith was 19–13 with a 2.13 ERA in 1905. He was part of a staff of pitchers that compiled a team record earned run average of 1.99. The White Sox used only six pitchers all season in Smith, Nick Altrock, Frank Owen, Doc White, Ed Walsh and Roy Patterson. Smith, Altrock, Owen and White formed the starting rotation, logging 80 wins and 1,201⅔ innings between them.

Altrock led the group with a 23–12 record and a 1.88 ERA. Owen was 21–13, had a 2.10 earned run average, completed 32 of his 38 starts, and hurled 334 innings. Doc White won 17, lost 13, and his 1.76 ERA led the White Sox. Smith contributed 19 wins, including a no-hitter and a pair of one-hitters, and struck out 171 batters.

APRIL 16   With light snow falling periodically, the White Sox defeat the Browns 5–0 at South Side Park.

The White Sox led the American League in attendance four consecutive seasons from 1905 through 1908.

APRIL 17   An 11-inning complete game shutout by Doc White beats the Browns 1–0 at South Side Park. Danny Green's single drove in the winning run.

APRIL 29   The White Sox score eight runs in the third inning to take an 11–0 lead and move on to defeat the Tigers 15–5 at South Side Park.

MAY 13   Frank Smith allows no runs and four hits in an 11-inning complete game, but he fails to receive a victory for his efforts because the contest against the Yankees at South Side Park ends in a 0–0 tie. The game was called on account of darkness. Bill Hogg pitched the shutout for New York.

MAY 21   Frank Smith pitches a one-hitter to beat the Senators 2–1 at South Side Park. Jake Stahl's single in the first inning was the only Washington hit.

MAY 26   Nick Altrock pitches the White Sox to a 1–0 win over the Red Sox at South Side Park.

JUNE 3   Ducky Holmes is ejected from a 5–4 loss to the Indians at South Side Park for cursing umpire Silk O'Loughlin. After the game was over, Holmes stood outside the park when O'Loughlin happened to be leaving. A youngster hurled a bottle at the umpire, barely missing his head. O'Laughlin believed that it was Holmes who threw the bottle and reported the incident to AL president Ban Johnson.

Holmes was suspended for two games by Johnson. The Sox had only four outfielders on the roster, and Danny Green was sidelined with an injury. For the two games that Holmes missed, the Sox used pitchers in the outfield as fill-ins. Charlie Comiskey thought the suspension was unwarranted. Comiskey and Johnson had long been close friends and their partnership helped lead to the creation of the American League. The two even shared an office in downtown Chicago. But Johnson ruled the AL like a dictator and his decisions often ran counter to Comiskey's best interests. Their differences, years in the making, came to the surface with the suspension of Holmes and led to a rift that never healed. Comiskey vacated the office he shared with Johnson at the Fisher Building on May 1, 1906, and moved to the Marquette Building a few blocks away. For more than two decades, until the death of both men in 1931, the two battled almost constantly and it nearly led to the break-up of the American League on more than one occasion.

JUNE 9	The White Sox slip past the Athletics 3–2 in 14 innings in Philadelphia. Doc White pitched the complete game and struck out 13 batters. The winning run scored on a double by George Davis off Rube Waddell.
JUNE 13	Pitcher Frank Owen steals home in the eighth inning of a 7–0 win over the Senators in Washington.
JUNE 14	George Davis steals four bases and collects four hits in four at-bats during a 5–3 win over the Senators in Washington.
	Davis hit .278 in 1905, second on the club to Jiggs Donahue's .287. Fielder Jones batted just .245 but scored 91 runs.
JULY 1	Frank Owen performs the unusual feat of pitching two complete-game victories in one day against the Browns in St. Louis. Owen allowed only two runs and seven hits in 18 innings in winning 3–2 and 2–0.
JULY 2	Doc White pitches the White Sox to a 1–0 win over the Tigers at South Side Park.
AUGUST 1	Jiggs Donahue is involved in altercations with the umpires both during and after a 5–4 loss in 10 innings to the Athletics in Philadelphia. Donahue wasn't around at the finish because he had been ejected by Tom Connor. Police were needed to escort Donahue off the field. Donahue headed for the umpires' dressing room after the game but was stopped by Jack McCarthy, Connor's partner. McCarthy dropped his mask and fought Donahue until police broke them apart.
	The defeat dropped the White Sox out of first place. The Sox failed to regain the top spot in 1905, but they battled for the pennant until the final week.
AUGUST 22	Nick Altrock allows only one run and six hits in 13 innings to beat the Athletics 2–1 in the second game of a double-header at South Side Park. Philadelphia won the opener 4–0.
	The White Sox played five double-headers in six days at South Side Park starting on August 22. Chicago split twin bills against the A's on the 22nd and 23rd. After the postponement of a game against Philadelphia on the 24th, the Sox swept Boston in three straight double-headers on the 25th, 26th and 27th.
AUGUST 30	Frank Owen allows one run and seven hits in a 15-inning complete game, but he receives little hitting support from his teammates and the score is 1–1 when the contest ends because of darkness.
AUGUST 31	Frank Smith just misses a perfect game with a 2–0 win over the Senators at South Side Park. The only Washington base runner was Jake Stahl, who singled with two out in the eighth inning. It was Smith's second one-hitter of 1905, and Stahl had the lone hit in both of them (see May 21, 1905).
SEPTEMBER 2	Second baseman Gus Dundon suffers a peculiar injury before a 6–3 win, called after five innings by rain, over the Indians in Cleveland. Dundon was hit in the mouth by a bat that slipped from the hands of Lee Tannehill. Seven teeth were knocked out and Dundon was unconscious when an ambulance took him to the hospital.

SEPTEMBER 6   The White Sox win both ends of a double-header against the Tigers in Detroit by shutout, the second a no-hitter by Frank Smith. In the opener, Doc White allowed four hits in a 2–0 win. Smith won the second tilt 15–0. It is the largest margin of victory in a no-hitter in the major leagues since 1890. The Sox put the game out of reach early with eight runs in the first inning. Smith walked three and struck out eight. The final out was recorded on a strikeout of Bobby Lowe. Nixey Callahan, who pitched a no-hitter for the White Sox in 1902, played left field behind Smith.

SEPTEMBER 8   The White Sox wallop the Indians 12–2 at South Side Park.

SEPTEMBER 16   The White Sox score eight runs in the first inning and three in the season and cruise to a 12–2 victory over the Browns at South Side Park. Nixey Callahan swiped four bases.

                Due to a scheduling quirk, the White Sox had to fight for the AL pennant by playing their final 24 games on the road.

SEPTEMBER 20   Trailing 4–1, the White Sox score eight runs in the eighth inning and move on to beat the Indians 9–6 in Cleveland.

SEPTEMBER 26   Ed Walsh wins both ends of a double-header against the Red Sox in Boston. Doc White started the first game but left with an injury after throwing to only one batter. Walsh relieved, but according to the rules of the day he was not permitted any warm-up pitches. Unable to get loose, Walsh gave up five runs before the first inning ended, but he shut down Boston the rest of the way and the White Sox won 10–5. Walsh started game two and pitched an eight-inning complete game, called by darkness, winning by the score of 2–1.

SEPTEMBER 27   Bill Dinneen of the Red Sox no-hits the White Sox in the first game of a double-header in Boston, but Chicago rebounds to win the nightcap in convincing fashion. Dinneen won 2–0, recording the final out on a pop-up by George Davis to third baseman Bob Unglaub. With Cy Young starting the second fray for Boston, the White Sox exploded for nine runs in the first inning and five in the second, winning 15–1 in a contest shortened to six innings by darkness. Dinneen later became a longtime AL umpire and officiated no-hitters thrown by White Sox pitchers Ed Scott in 1914 and Bill Dietrich in 1937.

                At the end of the day, the White Sox were in second place, only three percentage points behind the Athletics, with a three-game series slated between the Sox and A's in Philadelphia from September 28 through September 30.

SEPTEMBER 28   The Athletics win the first game of the pennant showdown series 4–3 in Philadelphia. The winning run was scored by A's left fielder Topsy Hartsel on a single into short left field by Harry Davis. The flare by Davis hit Hartsel's glove, which was left on the field. (Major leaguers left their gloves on the field while their team was at-bat until 1954.) In the ninth inning, the Sox had the bases loaded with two out, but Billy Sullivan hit a tapper back to pitcher Eddie Plank for the final out.

SEPTEMBER 29   The White Sox are routed by the Athletics 11–1 in Philadelphia.

SEPTEMBER 30   The White Sox salvage the third game of the series with a 4–3 win over the Athletics
                in Philadelphia. A two-run single by Danny Green in the seventh inning broke a 2–2
                tie. It was Frank Owen's 21st win of the year.

                *The win placed the Sox one game behind the A's with six games left to play.
                Chicago had a golden opportunity to make up ground with two series against
                the Senators and Browns, the two worst teams in the league, to close the season.
                However, the White Sox won three, lost two and tied one at Washington and
                St. Louis, allowing the Athletics to clinch the crown. At the time, there was
                no rule requiring teams to make up postponements or tie games should they
                occur in the last series between the two clubs in a particular city, even if they
                had a bearing on the pennant race. The Athletics had six unplayed contests and
                finished the season with a 92–56 record. The White Sox matched Philadelphia's
                92 wins, but they were 92–60 and failed make up two games. One of them was
                an August 24 game against the Athletics in Chicago that was postponed by rain.
                The A's lost the World Series five games to one to the New York Giants.*

OCTOBER 7   On the final day of the season, Nick Altrock wins his 23rd game of 1905 with a
                2–1 decision over the Browns in the first game of a double-header in St. Louis.
                The second contest resulted in a 7–7 tie called after nine innings by darkness.

OCTOBER 11   In the opener of the Chicago City Series against the Cubs, the White Sox lose 5–4
                at South Side Park.

                The Cubs won the best-of-seven series, four games to one.

1906

Season in a Sentence

With a team dubbed the "Hitless Wonders," the White Sox overcome a nine-game deficit by winning 19 contests in a row in August to capture a thrilling American League pennant race, then stun the heavily-favored Cubs in an all-Chicago World Series.

Finish • Won • Lost • Pct • GB

First   93   58   .616   +3.0

Manager

Fielder Jones

World Series

The White Sox defeated the Chicago Cubs four games to two.

Stats

Stats	WS	AL	Rank
Batting Avg:	.230	.249	8
On-Base Pct:	.302	.303	5
Slugging Pct:	.286	.318	8
Home Runs:	7		8
Stolen Bases:	214		3
ERA:	2.13	2.69	2
Fielding Avg:	.963	.957	2
Runs Scored:	570		3
Runs Allowed:	460		1

Starting Lineup

Billy Sullivan, c
Jiggs Donahue, 1b
Frank Isbell, 2b
Lee Tannehill, 3b
George Davis, ss
Ed Hahn, lf-rf
Fielder Jones, cf
Bill O'Neill, rf
Patsy Dougherty, lf
George Rohe, 3b

Pitchers

Frank Owen, sp
Nick Altrock, sp
Ed Walsh, sp
Doc White, sp
Roy Patterson, sp
Frank Smith, sp-rp

Attendance

585,302 (first in AL)

Club Leaders

Batting Avg:	Frank Isbell	.279
On-Base Pct:	Fielder Jones	.346
Slugging Pct:	George Davis	.355
Home Runs:	Fielder Jones	2
	Billy Sullivan	2
RBIs:	George Davis	80
Runs:	Ed Hahn	80
Stolen Bases:	Frank Isbell	37
Wins:	Frank Owen	22
Strikeouts:	Ed Walsh	171
ERA:	Doc White	1.52
Saves:	Frank Owen	2

APRIL 17   The White Sox open the season with a "frank" 5–3 win over the Tigers in Detroit. Frank Owen was the winning pitcher and Frank Isbell collected three hits.

Isbell led the 1906 Sox in batting average (.279) and stolen bases (37).

APRIL 20   Two days after the great San Francisco earthquake and fire, the White Sox open the home portion of the schedule and defeat the Tigers 6–1 before 14,100 at South Side Park.

MAY 2   One-half of the gate receipts from the Tigers-White Sox game in Detroit go to the San Francisco relief fund to aid victims of the April 18 earthquake and fire. The Tigers won 5–3.

MAY 6   Ed Walsh pitches a one-hitter to defeat the Indians 6–0 at South Side Park.

Walsh led the AL in shutouts in 1906 with 10. Overall, he was 17–13, had an ERA of 1.88 and struck out 171 batters.

MAY 9   The White Sox purchase Ed Hahn from the Yankees.

Hahn was picked up to bolster the outfield. The White Sox lost both starting corner outfielders and the club's top outfield reserve during the 1905–06 off-season. Danny Green was only 29 years old, but he had trouble with his throwing arm. Charlie Comiskey let him manage half the club during split-squad spring training in 1906. Green had his players roller skating, believing it was better than jogging, but his training ideas displeased Comiskey. After Green's spring squad lost most of its games, Comiskey sent him to the minors. Green was still playing in the minor leagues when he died of complications from a beaning in 1914. Nixey Callahan left the club after a falling out with Comiskey over Nixey's excessive drinking and weight problems. Callahan quit the White Sox to take over the Logan Squares, a famous Chicago semipro club. His 1906 team defeated both the White Sox and the Cubs in post-World Series exhibitions. Callahan returned to the White Sox in 1911. Ducky Holmes, a divisive force in the clubhouse, was released.

MAY 17   Roy Patterson pitches a two-hitter to beat the Senators 6–2 in Washington. The only hits off Patterson were by Smith and Jones. Opposing pitcher Charley Smith homered and Charlie Jones singled.

MAY 18   Player-manager Fielder Jones ties a White Sox record for most extra-base hits in a game with four by collecting two doubles, a triple and a homer in five at-bats during a 10–6 win over the Senators in Washington. The Sox led 6–0, allowed the Senators to tie the contest with six tallies in the seventh, then broke the deadlock with four in the ninth.

MAY 25   Entering the game with a 20-game losing streak, the Red Sox end their misery with a 3–0 victory over the White Sox in Boston.

JUNE 5   Doc White pitches a one-hitter to beat the Athletics 7–1 at South Side Park. The only Philadelphia hit was a double by Bris Lord in the seventh inning.

White's ERA of 1.52 led the American League in 1906. His won-lost record was 18–6.

JUNE 10 The White Sox collect only one hit off Yankee pitcher Al Orth, but they win 1–0 at South Side Park. A third-inning single by Fielder Jones, combined with two errors, led to the lone run of the game. Frank Owen pitched the shutout.

The White Sox entered the game with a record of 19–23. The Sox were in sixth place, 8½ games out of first. It seemed as though a pennant was out of the question in 1906, but the Sox went 74–35 the rest of the way.

JUNE 18 The White Sox outlast the Red Sox 4–3 in 15 innings at South Side Park.

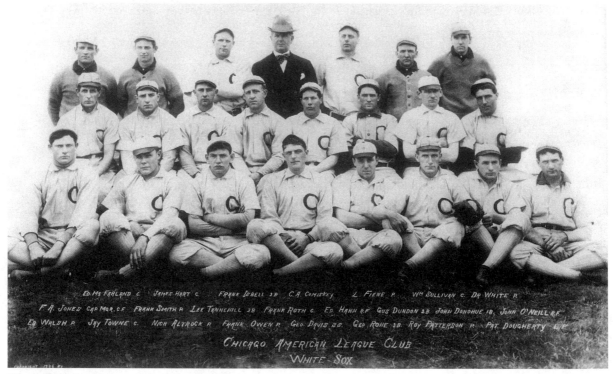

The 1906 World Champion Chicago White Sox

JUNE 30   The White Sox sweep the Indians 6–4 and 12–11 in a double-header in Cleveland. The first game went 12 innings. In the second, the Sox trailed 10–6 before scoring six runs in the eighth and surviving a Cleveland rally in the ninth.

JULY 3   The White Sox sweep the Browns 5–3 and 3–0 in a double-header at South Side Park. Doc White pitched a one-hitter in the second encounter. He was robbed of a no-hitter by a single from Jack O'Connor.

                 Jiggs Donahue helped win both games by collecting hits while ducking away from pitches. In the opener, Browns pitcher Ed Smith threw a fastball that headed straight for Donahue's head. As he whirled away, the ball hit Jiggs's bat and shot into right field, scoring a runner from second. In the second tilt, Donahue dove out of the way of an inside pitch from Beany Jacobson. Again, the ball hit the bat for a line-drive RBI single.

JULY 4   Ed Hahn's single leading off the ninth inning robs Barney Pelty of the Browns of a no-hitter in the second game of a double-header at South Side Park. Pelty retired the next three hitters for a one-hit, 3–0 win. Chicago won the opener of the holiday twin bill 5–1.

JULY 5   Fielder Jones threatens umpire Billy Evans with a bat after being ejected from a 4–3 win over the Indians in Cleveland.

JULY 6   The White Sox purchase Patsy Dougherty from the Yankees.

Dougherty was available because he got into a fistfight with Yankee manager Clark Griffith. Dougherty was the second ex-Yankee claimed by the Sox to reinforce the outfield in 1906, following Ed Hahn, who was purchased on May 9. Considering that the White Sox edged the Yankees in the 1906 pennant race by three games, the purchase of Hahn and Dougherty might well have been the difference. Dougherty proved to be an excellent acquisition. He was a starter for the Sox until 1910 and led the AL in stolen bases in 1908.

JULY 7   The White Sox score seven runs in the seventh inning and hammer the Red Sox 12–0 in Boston.

JULY 25   The White Sox lose a double-header to the Athletics in Philadelphia by scores of 5–1 and 4–2.

The losses dropped the White Sox to 46–42 on the season. The club was in fourth place, nine games out of first. The Sox overcame the deficit by winning 47 of their last 63 games.

AUGUST 2   Doc White shuts out the Red Sox 3–0 at South Side Park.

The victory started the White Sox's club-record 19-game winning streak. It occurred over a period of 20 games through August 23, marred only by a 0–0 tie against the Yankees on August 13 between victories number 11 and 12.

AUGUST 3   Ed Walsh pitches a one-hitter to beat the Red Sox 4–0 at South Side Park. The only Boston hit was a single by Jack Hayden.

AUGUST 4   Roy Patterson pitches the White Sox to a 1–0 win over the Red Sox at South Side Park. It was Chicago's third consecutive shutout, each of them over Boston. The lone run of the game scored in the ninth inning on a triple by Jiggs Donahue and a walk-off single by Patsy Dougherty.

The White Sox set a major league record for most shutouts in a season with 32 in 1906. The Cubs matched the figure in both 1907 and 1909, but it has never been exceeded. The 32 shutouts in 1906 were recorded by Ed Walsh (ten), Frank Owen (seven), Doc White (seven), Nick Altrock (four), Roy Patterson (three) and Frank Smith (one).

AUGUST 8   Roy Patterson pitches a 1–0 shutout in his second consecutive start, defeating the Athletics at South Side Park. And, as in the August 4 game, Patterson won on a walk-off hit in the ninth inning by Patsy Dougherty, whose triple followed a walk to George Davis. Dougherty's three-bagger was only the White Sox's second hit off Eddie Plank.

The 19-game winning streak was due in part to the work of University of Chicago athletic director Hiram "Doc" Connibear, an expert in physical conditioning. He was hired by Charlie Comiskey and put the White Sox through rigorous exercise regimens that helped restore the club in the second half. Connibear departed in mid-September to accept a coaching job at the University of Washington.

AUGUST 11   George Moriarty of the Yankees fights a Chicago fan during an 8–1 White Sox win at South Side Park. Moriarty was subdued by police before he could do any physical damage to the heckler. It was the Sox's tenth win in a row.

Moriarty was an American League umpire from 1917 through 1940.

AUGUST 12   The White Sox leap from third place to first in one day with a 3–0 victory over the Yankees at South Side Park. It was the Sox's 11th win in a row.

Chicago was involved in a four-team race with the Yankees, Athletics and Indians. The Athletics and Indians dropped out of contention in early September, leaving the White Sox to battle the Yanks for the AL crown during the final weeks.

AUGUST 13   The White Sox and the Yankees play to a 0–0 tie, called after nine innings to allow the New York club to catch a train.

AUGUST 18   The White Sox win their 15th game in a row with a 10–0 pummeling of the Yankees in New York. The Sox broke open a tight game with nine runs in the ninth inning.

AUGUST 23   The White Sox win their 19th game in a row by beating the Senators 4–1 in Washington. The victory gave the White Sox a 5½-game lead in the pennant race.

AUGUST 25   The White Sox's 19-game winning streak comes to an end with 5–4 and 4–3 losses to the seventh-place Senators in a double-header in Washington. In the opener, the Sox seemed poised to win their 20th game in a row, but the Senators scored three times in the ninth inning off Ed Walsh.

Walsh had seven victories during the 19-game winning streak. Doc White won five, Frank Owen three, Roy Patterson three and Nick Altrock one. The staff was almost unhittable. There were nine shutouts, counting the 0–0 tie against the Yankees on August 13. The Sox allowed only one run in five other games during the streak and outscored the opposition by a count of 100–24. The 19-game winning streak by the 1906 White Sox is still tied for the second-longest in American League history and the fourth-longest in the majors since 1900. The only three longer ones were compiled by the New York Giants, who won 26 in succession in 1916, the Cubs with 21 in a row in 1935, and most recently by the 20 consecutive victories strung together by the Oakland Athletics in 2002. The Yankees matched the 1906 White Sox with 19 wins in a row in 1953.

AUGUST 27   In a game called after six innings by rain, Ed Walsh allows only one hit and beats the Athletics 1–0 in Philadelphia.

SEPTEMBER 4   The idle White Sox are knocked out of first place when the Yankees sweep the Red Sox 7–0 and 1–0 in a double-header in Boston.

The Yankees used a 15-game winning streak to overcome the White Sox.

SEPTEMBER 5   Doc White pitches a two-hitter to defeat the Tigers 2–0 in Detroit. The only hits off White were singles by Ty Cobb and Bill Coughlin.

SEPTEMBER 6   The White Sox score eight runs in the first inning and wallop the Tigers 13–5 in Detroit.

SEPTEMBER 11   Umpire Billy Evans leaves South Side Park under police protection after unfavorable calls against the home team lead to a 7–3 loss to the Browns in St. Louis. The defeat left the Sox two games behind the Yankees in the AL pennant race.

SEPTEMBER 12   The White Sox score nine runs in the second inning and rout the Browns 13–5 at South Side Park.

SEPTEMBER 13   The White Sox and Browns play to a 10-inning, 0–0 tie at South Side Park. The game was called on account of darkness. Frank Owen pitched the shutout for Chicago.

SEPTEMBER 15   The White Sox regain first place with a 6–4 win over the Browns in St. Louis.

SEPTEMBER 17   Ed Walsh strikes out 12 batters in a 12-inning complete-game, 5–4 win over the Athletics at South Side Park.

SEPTEMBER 21   The White Sox fall back out of first place by losing a double header 6–3 and 4–1 to the Yankees at South Side Park.

                 The White Sox staged an Old-Timers Day at South Side Park as 147 former major leaguers responded to invitations and attended the games. Among them was future Hall of Famer Cap Anson.

SEPTEMBER 22   The White Sox tie the Yankees for first place with a 7–1 win over the New York club in a pennant showdown at South Side Park.

SEPTEMBER 23   The Yankees take sole possession of first place with a 1–0 win before 25,000 at South Side Park. The Yanks scored their run in the first inning off Ed Walsh. Bill Hogg hurled the shutout.

SEPTEMBER 25   The White Sox move back on top of the American League standings with a 3–2 win over the Red Sox at South Side Park while the Yankees lose 6–5 to the Tigers in Detroit.

OCTOBER 1   The White Sox take a 2½-game lead with a 1–0 win over the Browns in 13 innings in St. Louis. Nick Altrock pitched the complete game for his 20th victory of the season, allowing only six hits. Lee Tannehill drove in the winning run with a single.

                 Altrock was 20–13 with a 2.06 ERA in 1906.

OCTOBER 2   Frank Owen records his 22nd win of the season with a 4–0 decision over the Browns in St. Louis.

                 Owen was 22–13 with a 2.33 earned run average in 1906.

OCTOBER 3   The White Sox are rained out, but they clinch the American League pennant when the Yankees split a double-header against the Athletics in Philadelphia.

OCTOBER 5   The White Sox score seven runs in the sixth inning to beat the Indians 9–3 at South Side Park.

The White Sox met the Cubs in the only all-Chicago World Series ever played. Managed by Frank Chance, the 1906 Cubs were one of the greatest teams in history. The club finished 116–36. Its .763 winning percentage is the best in the modern (post-1900) era. With the Cubs winning 23 more regular-season games than the White Sox, the series appeared to be a mismatch and the National Leaguers were heavy favorites, with a betting margin of 3–1. In addition, the Cubs played their best ball over the final two months of the season, winning 55 of their last 63 games. Even the staunchest White Sox fans didn't believe their club stood a chance, but privately Chance worried about overconfidence. The White Sox were also crippled at the start of the World Series by the loss of shortstop George Davis. Davis was the White Sox's best overall player, hitting .277 and leading the club in RBIs with 80. To replace Davis, Lee Tannehill moved from third base to shortstop and reserve George Rohe took over at third. Rohe turned out to be the hero of the series, one of the many unheralded players who have starred in the Fall Classic. When Davis returned for Game Four, Tannehill was benched and Rohe remained in the lineup. The playing sites during the series alternated, with the odd-numbered games played at the Cubs' home of West Side Grounds and the even-numbered contests at South Side Park. The city was at a virtual standstill for the six days in which the two clubs battled for the world title. Two teenage fans, desperate for money so they could buy tickets from scalpers, held up a grocery store. City alderman Charles Martin, a White Sox fan, was arrested after brawling with a drunken Cubs supporter.

OCTOBER 9   With snow flurries blowing throughout the game at West Side Grounds, Nick Altrock bests Cubs pitcher Three Finger Brown 2–1 in a Game One matchup of four-hitters. The Sox scored first in the fifth inning when George Rohe tripled and scored on an error. The White Sox took a 2–0 lead in the sixth on an RBI single by Frank Isbell. The Cubs scored in their half of the sixth, but the White Sox held on for the win.

With the advent of radio and television still in the future, the Chicago Tribune *secured two downtown arenas where fans could "watch" the games on electric scoreboards. One was the Auditorium, seating 4,000. The other was the First Regiment Armory, with a capacity of 5,000. A 20-foot baseball diamond was erected on each stage. Balls and strikes were indicated by light bulbs. The batter's names were illuminated. Bulbs at first, second and third indicated the base runners. An announcer, using a megaphone, called the play as it came over the telegraph wire.*

OCTOBER 10   With freezing winds pounding the 12,595 present at South Side Park, the Cubs even the series by winning Game Two 7–0 on a one-hitter by Ed Reulbach. The only White Sox hit was a single by Jiggs Donahue in the seventh inning.

In the bottom of the first, play was halted when Fielder Jones was presented with a complete set of silver contained in a chest of polished wood.

OCTOBER 11   With the autumn cold continuing, the White Sox win Game Three 3–0 at West Side Grounds behind the pitching of Ed Walsh and the clutch hitting of George Rohe. With the score 0–0, Lee Tannehill led off the sixth inning with a single. Ed Walsh walked, and Ed Hahn was hit by a pitch to load the bases with none out. Hahn was hit in the face with the pitch, and play stopped as Hahn was taken from the field and rushed to a hospital. The next two batters were retired and it appeared the opportunity would be wasted, but Rohe hit a bases-clearing triple to score the only three runs of the game. Walsh allowed only two hits and struck out 12. The only Cubs hits were in the first inning when Solly Hofman singled and Wildfire Schulte doubled.

White Sox catcher Billy Sullivan was hitless in 21 at-bats with nine strikeouts in the 1906 World Series, the only time during his career that he played in the postseason. The only individual with more career at-bats in the World Series without a hit is Athletics pitcher George Earnshaw, who was 0–for–22 with 11 strikeouts in 1929, 1930 and 1931.

OCTOBER 12   The Cubs even the series at two games apiece, winning 1–0 in another pitchers' duel before 18,385 at South Side Park. Nick Altrock allowed only a run and seven hits, but White Sox batters were stymied by Three Finger Brown, who hurled a two-hitter. The lone run of the contest scored in the seventh inning on a two-out single by Johnny Evers.

The 1906 World Series was the first in which umpires raised their right hand to signal a strike. The innovation was introduced in the minors in 1905 and is credited to Chief Zimmer, who umpired in the Southern League. Previously, umpires used only voice calls to signal balls and strikes, but most fans couldn't hear them and were left in the dark as to whether a pitch was a ball or a strike. The new method of raising a right hand for a strike and making no signal for a ball was immediately popular with fans and players alike, and was universal in baseball by 1907.

OCTOBER 13   The two Chicago clubs break their bats out of cold storage as the White Sox move within one win of a world championship with an 8–6 victory over the Cubs at West Side Grounds. The Sox won despite committing six errors. It was the fifth consecutive game in which the visiting team was the victor. The Saturday afternoon crowd of 23,257 spilled over into the deep part of the outfield. Balls hit into the crowd were doubles. There were eleven two-baggers struck by the two clubs, four of them from Frank Isbell, which is still a World Series record. The Sox scored in the top of the first on Isbell's first double, but the Cubs came back with three in their half off Ed Walsh. The White Sox evened the count at 3–3 in the third when Isbell and George Davis hit back-to-back doubles, and after Davis moved to third he swiped home on a double steal with Patsy Dougherty. The Sox broke the game open with four runs in the fourth and never relinquished the lead. Doc White pitched three shutout innings to earn a save. George Rohe continued his hot hitting with three hits, including a double.

OCTOBER 14   The White Sox claim the world championship with an easy 8–3 win over the White Sox before 19,249 at South Side Park. The gates were closed 90 minutes before the 2:30 p.m. start because of the crush of fans desiring tickets. A crowd of thousands, unable to gain entrance, remained in the streets outside and received reports of the game from those who shouted out the play-by-play from the upper rows of the grandstand. Cubs manager Frank Chance gambled by pitching Three Finger Brown, making his third start in six days, but Brown's weary arm wasn't up to the task. The White Sox scored three runs in the first and four in the second. Doc White pitched the complete game The hitting stars were Ed Hahn (four hits), Frank Isbell (three hits), George Davis (three RBIs) and Jiggs Donahue (three RBIs).

The White Sox's reputation as "Hitless Wonders" continued in the World Series as the club hit just .198. The leading hitter was George Rohe. During the regular season, Rohe batted .258 with just six extra base hits in 225 at-bats. In the World Series, Rohe batted .333 with seven hits, including two triples and a double, in 21 at-bats. Baseball didn't grant Most Valuable Player awards in the World Series until 1955, but if the honor existed in 1906 it certainly would have gone to Rohe. After the Series, Charlie Comiskey proclaimed, "Whatever George Rohe may do from now on, he's signed on for life with me!" Rohe was the Sox's regular third baseman in 1907, but he hit only .213 and was released at the end of the season and never played in the majors again.

The Cubs rebounded from the World Series upset to the White Sox by winning the Fall Classic in both 1907 and 1908. The White Sox didn't return to post-season play until 1917.

The Hitless Wonders

The 1906 White Sox won the world championship with an aggregation that has become forever known as the "Hitless Wonders." No one knows who coined the phrase, but it was in use by the end of the 1905 season and is certainly apropos. The 1906 club finished last in the eight-team American League in batting average with a mark of .230, seven percentage points below the next-worst team. The slugging percentage of just .286 was 18 points worse than any other AL team. The White Sox also finished last in hits (1,133) and home runs (seven) but were third in runs scored (570). The resourceful offense was built around speed and taking advantage of every opportunity. The 1906 White Sox led the league in walks (453), hit batsmen (51) and sacrifices (227) and was third in stolen bases (214).

The manager of the White Sox in 1906 was Fielder Jones. He led the club from June 1904 through the end of the 1908 seasons. The Sox were contenders all five seasons that Jones was at the helm, and it's possible that no manager ever generated more offense with less.

The following is a chart of the White Sox's rankings in various offensive categories during Jones's tenure.

	1904	1905	1906	1907	1908
Runs Scored:	3	2	3	3	5
Batting Avg:	5	5	8	7	8
On-Base Pct:	4	4	5	5	2
Slugging Pct:	5	6	8	8	8
Extra-Base Hits:	5	4	8	8	8
Home Runs:	5	8	8	8	8
Stolen Bases:	1	2	3	4	2
Walks:	1	2	1	1	1
Sacrifices:	1	1	1	2	1

Jones retired at the end of the 1908 season. After he left, the White Sox were still hitless, but no longer were wonders, and slipped out of contention with an aging club. The 1910 White Sox hit all-time lows for offensive futility with a batting average of .211, an on-base percentage of .275 and a slugging percentage of .261. The team batting average was the worst of any big league club since 1900 and the slugging percentage was an all-time low. There were also American League records for fewest hits (1,058) and fewest doubles (115) in a season. No one on the club with 175 or more at-bats hit higher than .250. Among the regulars, Patsy Dougherty's .248 "led" the team. The Sox pitching staff in 1910 had a team ERA of 2.03, but the excellent pitching couldn't overcome an abysmal offense and the team had a record of 68–85.

1907

Sox

Season in a Sentence

With no roster changes to the central cast, the defending world champion "Hitless Wonders" hold first place for 102 days but continue to be offensively challenged and end the season in third.

Finish • Won • Lost • Pct • GB

Third 87 64 .576 5.5

Manager

Fielder Jones

Stats

Stats	WS	AL	Rank
Batting Avg:	.238	.247	7
On-Base Pct:	.302	.302	5
Slugging Pct:	.283	.309	8
Home Runs:	5		8
Stolen Bases:	175		5
ERA:	2.22	2.54	1
Fielding Avg:	.966	.957	1
Runs Scored:	588		3
Runs Allowed:	474		1

Starting Lineup

Billy Sullivan, c
Jiggs Donahue, 1b
Frank Isbell, 2b
George Rohe, 3b-2b
George Davis, ss
Patsy Dougherty, lf
Fielder Jones, cf
Ed Hahn, rf
Lee Quillen, 3b

Pitchers

Ed Walsh, sp
Doc White, sp
Frank Smith, sp
Nick Altrock, sp
Roy Patterson, sp

Attendance

666,307 (first in AL)

Club Leaders

Batting Avg:	Patsy Dougherty	.270
On-Base Pct:	Ed Hahn	.359
Slugging Pct:	Patsy Dougherty	.315
Home Runs:	George Rohe	2
RBIs:	Jiggs Donahue	68
Runs:	Ed Hahn	87
Stolen Bases:	Patsy Dougherty	33
Wins:	Doc White	27
Strikeouts:	Ed Walsh	206
ERA:	Ed Walsh	1.60
Saves:	Ed Walsh	4

MARCH 5 The White Sox leave Chicago for a spring training jaunt to Mexico City.

One of Charlie Comiskey's dreams was to internationalize baseball, and the trip to Mexico was part of the plan. The Sox were the first major league club to train in a foreign country. The team steamed out of the Windy City on the Sunset Limited to New Orleans, where they changed to a train bound for south of the border. The train was pulled by two brightly decorated engines. The trip took five days, and just two hours after arrival, the Sox played an intra-squad game before a crowd of curious Mexicans. The team remained in Mexico for two weeks before completing training in Eagle Pass, Texas, a Rio Grande town located on the Mexican border. Comiskey had a discontented club on his hands. Most players didn't want to train in Mexico, and those who did were unhappy about their contracts. Each player received $1,874.01 for winning the 1906 World Series, in part because Comiskey was so pleased with the results that he threw an extra $15,000 into the pot. The players were shocked when they received their contracts during the following off-season, however. Comiskey considered the additional World Series share as an advance on their 1907 salaries and not as a bonus for winning the 1906 world championship.

APRIL 11   The White Sox lost the season opener 1–0 to the Browns in St. Louis. Nick Altrock took the hard luck defeat. Harry Howell pitched for the Browns and allowed only five hits, three of them to Fielder Jones. Howell also beat the White Sox on Opening Day in 1905 by a 2–1 score with a two-hitter.

APRIL 17   George Davis is ejected from a 4–1 win over the Tigers in Detroit for throwing a ball at umpire Jack Stafford.

APRIL 18   In the home opener, Nick Altrock hurls a shutout to defeat the Browns 2–0 on a frigid day at South Side Park.

APRIL 19   The White Sox edge the Browns 1–0 at South Side Park. The lone run of the contest scored on a steal of home by Fielder Jones in a double-steal attempt with Jiggs Donahue, who swiped second. With his spitball working to near perfection, Ed Walsh pitched the shutout and tied the major league record for most assists by a pitcher in a nine-inning game with 11.

            Before the game, the White Sox raised the 1906 American League pennant. The hoisting of the world championship banner was scheduled for four weeks later, but it didn't go as planned (see May 14, 1907).

MAY 4   During the fourth inning of a 2–1 win over the Tigers in Detroit, the White Sox pull off an unusual triple play in which three outs were recorded on tag plays on the bases. It was also the first triple play in White Sox history. The Tiger base runners were Claude Rossman on third and Germany Schaefer on second. Butch Schmidt hit a grounder to shortstop George Davis. Rossman was tagged out in a rundown between third and home. Schmidt was out trying to reach second, and Schaefer was gunned down attempting to score to complete the triple play. Schaefer barreled hard into Ed Walsh, and the pitcher was hurt badly enough that he had to leave the game and miss his next start.

            The White Sox held onto first place continually from May 2 through August 6.

MAY 14   The White Sox attempt to raise the 1906 world championship

Though overshadowed by the great Ed Walsh during the club's early years, Doc White annually posted a very low ERA, and in 1907 he won a career-high 27 games.

pennant before a game against the Senators at South Side Park, but the flag pole breaks and the game is postponed by rain.

The day started with a parade that started downtown and ended at South Side Park, where a standing room-only crowd of 15,000 assembled on a Tuesday afternoon. City employees, many of whom boarded carriages and waved to crowd that lined the streets during the length of the procession, were given the day off to participate. Also in the parade were numerous bands, players from both teams, and AL President Ban Johnson. The pennant was presented to Charlie Comiskey by the mayor of Chicago. Unfortunately, as the pennant was being hoisted to a position below the American flag and the 1906 American League pennant, the flag pole snapped in two and the flags came crashing to earth. The two teams began the game, but during the first inning, a heavy shower moved in, stopping play and resulting in a postponement.

MAY 26   Ed Walsh pitches a five-inning no-hitter in a game against the Yankees at South Side Park shortened by rain. The White Sox won a controversial 8–1 decision. It began to rain in the fourth inning with the Sox ahead 4–1. New York manager Clark Griffith removed pitcher Al Orth and took over the mound duties himself. Hoping to have the contest washed out before it could be declared an official game, Griffith took as much time as possible between pitches and loaded the bases on walks before yielding a single to Walsh. The Sox, on the other hand, wanted the game to go as quickly as possible. Billy Sullivan sauntered slowly from third base toward home plate and the Yankees made no attempt to tag him out. Umpire Jack Sheridan threatened a forfeit for the next team that failed to play the game on the level, and the shenanigans ceased.

JUNE 1   Doc White pitches the White Sox to a 1–0 victory over the Tigers at South Side Park. Jiggs Donahue ended the game with a sacrifice fly with two out in the ninth.

Donahue led the White Sox in 1907 in RBIs (68) and hits (158).

JUNE 12   The White Sox score seven runs in the seventh inning and outclass the Senators 13–1 in Washington.

JUNE 23   Jiggs Donahue is hitless in six at-bats and leaves an American League-record 11 runners on base during a 12-inning, 7–5 loss to the Indians at South Side Park.

JUNE 26   Doc White pitches a shutout to defeat the Browns 1–0 in St. Louis.

JULY 15   The White Sox administer a 15–0 shellacking on the Yankees at South Side Park.

JULY 16   Frank Isbell drives in all three White Sox runs for a 13-inning, 3–2 victory over the Yankees at South Side Park. Isbell entered the game in the ninth as a pinch-hitter for George Rohe and delivered a game-tying single. Isbell remained in the contest at second base. The Sox trailed 2–1 in the bottom of the 13th when Isbell came to bat with the bases loaded and singled in two runs for the win. Ed Walsh pitched the complete game and set a record, since tied, for most assists in an extra inning game with 12. With his three putouts, Walsh set another record for most total chances in a game with 15.

The win marked the peak of the 1907 season. The White Sox were 51–26 and had a five-game lead in the AL race. A month-long slump soon followed, however, and the Sox were knocked out of first on August 6. After regaining the top spot in a three-way race with the Tigers and Athletics, the Sox were in first for the final time on August 25. Nonetheless, Chicago still had a shot at the American League pennant up to the final week of the season.

AUGUST 1   The White Sox purchase Charlie Hickman from the Indians.

AUGUST 12   Ed Walsh ties his own record for most assists in a nine-inning game with 11, but he loses 5–3 to the Red Sox at South Side Park.

                  Walsh was 24–18 in 1907. He led the American League in earned run average (1.60), games pitched (56), games started (46), complete games (37), innings pitched (422⅓) and saves (four) and was second in strikeouts (206).

AUGUST 19   The White Sox score seven runs in the second inning to take an 11–0 lead and move on to punish the Senators 16–2 at South Side Park. The game was called by umpire Billy Evans after eight innings by threatening storm clouds. Ten minutes later, rain came down in torrents.

AUGUST 21   Frank Smith pitches the White Sox to a 1–0 win over the Athletics at South Side Park. The lone run of the contest crossed the plate in the ninth inning on a sacrifice fly by Jiggs Donahue off Chief Bender.

AUGUST 25   The White Sox score three runs in the ninth inning to take a 3–2 victory from the Yankees in the first game of a double-header at South Side Park. All three runs scored with two out.

AUGUST 27   Frank Isbell is badly cut on the hand by Patsy Dougherty during practice at South Side Park during an off day. The accident occurred during sliding drills. Isbell missed a month of action, hampering the Sox's drive for the pennant.

SEPTEMBER 11   Doc White pitches a shutout to beat the Browns 2–0 in the first game of a double-header in St. Louis. But he issues a walk, ending a streak of 65⅓ consecutive innings without a walk, dating back to August 15. The Sox completed the sweep with a 5–4 triumph in the nightcap.

SEPTEMBER 20   The White Sox sweep the Senators 2–1 and 13–6 in Washington. In the opener, Frank Smith picked up his 22nd win of the season. The Sox collected 21 hits in the second tilt. George Davis was 5-for-5 with three singles and two doubles.

                  Smith was 22–11 with an ERA of 2.47.

SEPTEMBER 24   In the first game of a pennant showdown series against the Athletics in Philadelphia, the White Sox win 8–3. It was Ed Walsh's 24th win of the season.

                  The victory put the third-place Sox one-half game out of first with 12 contests left on the schedule. The A's and Tigers were tied for the top spot in the AL. With the Cubs having already clinched the NL crown, a second consecutive all-Chicago World Series was possible.

SEPTEMBER 25   With a chance to move ahead of the Athletics in the standings, the White Sox lose in Philadelphia. Eddie Plank pitched a two-hitter for the A's.

SEPTEMBER 26   The White Sox's pennant aspirations take another hit with a 3–1 loss to the Athletics in Philadelphia. Ed Walsh, pitching on one day of rest, was the losing pitcher. Jimmy Dygert pitched a two-hitter for the A's.

OCTOBER 1   The White Sox are eliminated from pennant contention with a 3–1 loss to the Yankees in New York.

The Tigers went to the World Series and suffered four losses and a tie in five games against the Cubs.

OCTOBER 6   A month before Oklahoma becomes the 46th state, Doc White earns his 27th win of the season with a 4–2 victory over the Indians at South Side Park. Frank Isbell came in to pitch to the final batter, with White moving to second base.

White was 27–13 with an ERA of 2.26 in 1907.

1908   Sox

Season in a Sentence

In one of the greatest pitching feats of all time, Ed Walsh wins 40 games, but the White Sox fall just short of a pennant by losing the final game of the season in a nail-biting three-team race with the Tigers and the Indians.

Finish • Won • Lost • Pct • GB

Finish	Won	Lost	Pct	GB
Third	88	64	.579	1.5

Manager

Fielder Jones

Stats

Stats	WS	AL	Rank
Batting Avg:	.224	.239	7
On-Base Pct:	.298	.294	2
Slugging Pct:	.271	.304	8
Home Runs:	3		8
Stolen Bases:	209		2
ERA:	2.22	2.39	3
Fielding Avg:	.966	.958	1
Runs Scored:	537		5
Runs Allowed:	470		2

Starting Lineup

Billy Sullivan, c
Frank Isbell, 1b
George Davis, 2b
Lee Tannehill, 3b
Freddy Parent, ss
Patsy Dougherty, lf
Fielder Jones, cf
Ed Hahn, rf
John Anderson, rf
Jiggs Donahue, 1b
Jake Atz, 2b

Pitchers

Ed Walsh, sp
Doc White, sp
Frank Smith, sp
Frank Owen, sp
Nick Altrock, sp

Attendance

636,096 (first in AL)

Club Leaders

Batting Avg:	Patsy Dougherty	.278
On-Base Pct:	Patsy Dougherty	.367
Slugging Pct:	Patsy Dougherty	.326
Home Runs:	Three tied with	1
RBIs:	Fielder Jones	50
Runs:	Fielder Jones	92
Stolen Bases:	Patsy Dougherty	47
Wins:	Ed Walsh	40
Strikeouts:	Ed Walsh	269
ERA:	Ed Walsh	1.42
Saves:	Frank Smith Moxie Manuel	1 1

MARCH 23   On a spring training trip, the White Sox are marooned for more than a day when a 20-car freight train ahead of them skids into a ditch near Bay Minette, Alabama. The passengers bought out the few nearby stores and had to forage for food until the tracks were cleared.

APRIL 14   The White Sox open the 1908 season by hammering the Tigers 15–8 at South Side Park. The Sox had a 13–0 lead at the end of the fifth inning. Patsy Dougherty was the top Chicago batter, collecting three hits.

Dougherty was also the White Sox's top hitter over the course of the season. He led the club in batting average (.278), on-base percentage (.367), slugging percentage (.326) and stolen bases (41). That he could lead the club with a slugging percentage of only .326 highlights the uniqueness of both the 1908 season and the White Sox during the dead-ball era. The league-wide batting average during the year was .239 and the slugging percentage was .304. The White Sox had a team batting average of .224 and a slugging percentage of only .271. The club hit only three home runs all season, the fewest of any major league club since 1900. Fielder Jones, Frank Isbell and Ed Walsh accounted for the only three homers struck by the Sox player all year. In a game on July 4, Walsh hit the only home run at South Side Park by the home team. The pitching staff surrendered 11 homers, four of them at home.

APRIL 19   The White Sox collect only two hits off Browns pitcher Bill Graham but win 3–0 at South Side Park. Ed Walsh pitched the shutout.

Walsh had one of the most remarkable seasons of any pitcher in history in 1908. He won 40 games, posting a record of 40–15. No other AL pitcher that season won more than 24 contests. Walsh not only led the league in wins, but in winning percentage (.727), games pitched (66), games started (42), shutouts (11), saves (six), innings pitched (464) and strikeouts (269). His earned run average of 1.42 ranked third. Between his 42 complete games and 15 games finished as a reliever, Walsh was on the mound at the end of 57 of the White Sox's 156 games in 1908. His 40 wins and 42 complete games are both the most of any major league hurler from 1904 to the present. Walsh's 464 innings are the most of any pitcher since 1893, the year that the 60-foot, six-inch pitching distance to home plate was established. The 66 games were the most of any pitcher between 1892 and 1943. The figures for wins, games started, complete games, shutouts, innings pitched and strikeouts are all White Sox single-season records to this day. Walsh's 464 innings in 1908 came a year after he pitched 422⅓ innings. He struggled in 1909 with a 15–11 record and pitched 230⅓ innings, less than half of his 1908 total, although his ERA was still a sparkling 1.41 and he led the AL in shutouts with eight. The limited activity was due to a holdout that kept him out of action until May 9 and strained ligaments in his arm. Walsh recovered to lead the AL in earned run average in 1910 and won 27 games in both 1911 and 1912.

MAY 19   Doc White pitches a one-hitter to defeat the Senators 2–0 in Washington. The only hit off White was a single by Bob Ganley.

MAY 31   Ed Walsh pitches the White Sox to a 1–0 win over the Tigers in the first game of a double-header at South Side Park. Detroit won the second tilt 2–1.

JUNE 7	Nick Altrock hits a double leading off the 10th inning and scores the winning run in a 2–1 win over the Senators at South Side Park. The run was driven in by John Anderson. Altrock also tied a major league record for most assists by a pitcher in an extra-inning game with 12.

Anderson played for the White Sox in the last year of a 14-year career. He was born in Sarpsborg, Norway.

JUNE 9	The White Sox trounce the Athletics 10–0 at South Side Park.

JUNE 15	In the fifth inning, Patsy Dougherty triples and steals home to defeat the Yankees 2–1 at South Side Park. It was the White Sox's 12th win in a row.

JUNE 16	The White Sox win their 13th consecutive game by defeating the Yankees 3–2 at South Side Park.

The 13-game winning streak helped the White Sox overcome a sluggish start in which they posted an 18–20 record through June 3. At the end of the streak, the Sox were 31–20 and had a 2½-game lead over the second-place Indians.

JUNE 17	Alice Roosevelt Longworth, the daughter of President Theodore Roosevelt, watches the White Sox end their 13-game winning streak by losing 5–2 to the Yankees at South Side Park. Alice attended the game with her husband Nicholas Longworth, an Ohio Congressman. They were in Chicago to attend the Republican National Convention.

JUNE 20	In a battle of future Hall of Fame pitchers, Ed Walsh beats Cy Young and the Red Sox 1–0 at South Side Park.

For a period of six years, Walsh was not only the White Sox's number one starter but the first choice as a reliever as well. He led the Sox in innings pitched in 1907, 1908, 1910, 1911 and 1912. Walsh topped the club in saves six straight seasons from 1907 through 1912. He was the club leader in both games started and games relieved in 1907, 1908 and 1911.

JUNE 25	The White Sox are knocked out of first place with a 3–2 loss to the Indians in Cleveland.

The Sox didn't regain the top perch in the American League in 1908, but they were not eliminated from the pennant race until the final day of the season.

JULY 7	The White Sox take two from the Senators in a double-header in Washington. In the opener, the Sox won 1–0 behind the pitching of Doc White. The nightcap went 13 innings. Chicago scored twice in the ninth inning to send the contest into extra innings, then plated three runs in the 13th to win 7–4.

JULY 10	The White Sox and Senators play 16 innings to a 2–2 tie in Washington. Neither team scored after the fifth inning. Nick Altrock pitched all 16 innings for the Sox.

JULY 11	After traveling to Philadelphia, the White Sox play 16 innings for the second day in a row, defeating the Athletics 5–4. Ed Walsh pitched the entire game. The winning run

scored on a double by Fielder Jones, an error that moved him to third and a sacrifice fly by Patsy Dougherty. Third baseman Lee Tannehill ended the game with an unassisted double play by snaring a hot liner and stepping on third before the runner could return. The original schedule called for a double-header, but the umpires determined that it was too dark to start the second tilt.

Jones led the White Sox in runs (92), hits (134) and walks (86) in 1908.

JULY 25   The White Sox score seven runs in the seventh inning and win 12–2 over the Athletics at South Side Park.

AUGUST 2   Frank Smith pitches a 10-inning, two-hitter to defeat the Senators 2–1 at South Side Park. The winning run scored on Ed Hahn's double and Patsy Dougherty's single. The only Washington hits were singles by Buck Freeman and Clyde Milan.

Smith was a perpetual malcontent who often threatened to jump the club. Both Charlie Comiskey and Fielder Jones disliked Smith's boozing, careless personal habits and indifference to conditioning. During one drunken episode, Smith challenged heavyweight boxing champion James Jeffries to a fight. Smith made good on his threat to bolt and left the club for two weeks in July 1908 before returning after a reconciliation with Sox management. Smith's nickname was "Piano Mover," his off-season occupation in Pittsburgh.

AUGUST 15   The White Sox wrest a 15-inning, 5–3 decision over the Senators in Washington. Ed Walsh pitched a complete game for the win.

AUGUST 21   Trailing 5–0, the White Sox score seven runs in the fourth inning as a springboard to an 8–7 win over the Red Sox in Boston.

Walsh pitched the final 3⅓ innings in relief and was credited with a victory. At the time, it was up to the discretion of the official scorer to assign the winning pitcher. Under today's scoring rules, the win would have gone to the starting pitcher and Walsh would have received a save. This happened three other times during the season. If present-day rules were applied, Walsh would have 36 wins and 10 saves in 1908 instead of 40 wins and six saves. Nonetheless, the 36 wins would easily be the single-season White Sox record. The second-best total is 29 by Ed Cicotte in 1919.

AUGUST 29   The White Sox sweep the Yankees 1–0 and 6–2 in New York. Doc White pitched the shutout in the opener.

SEPTEMBER 1   After being shut out for six innings, the White Sox erupt for four runs in the seventh inning and nine more in the eighth to defeat the Browns 13–3 in St. Louis.

SEPTEMBER 9   The White Sox blow a 6–0 lead and lose 7–6 in 12 innings to the Tigers in Detroit. The loss dropped the Sox three games behind the first-place Tigers in the American League pennant race.

SEPTEMBER 10   Fielder Jones collects five hits in five at-bats, but the White Sox allow runs in the ninth and 10th innings to lose 6–5 to the Tigers in Detroit.

SEPTEMBER 11   The White Sox defeat the Tigers 4–2 in 11 innings in Detroit. Patsy Dougherty drove in the go-ahead run with a triple and scored on a single by Frank Isbell.

SEPTEMBER 12   The White Sox win 2–1 in 10 innings against the Tigers in Detroit. It was the fourth consecutive extra-inning game between the two clubs, establishing a major league record. Each team won two of the four. Frank Smith pitched a complete game and started the game-winning rally with a single. He moved to third base on Freddy Parent's double and scored on Billy Sullivan's sacrifice fly.

SEPTEMBER 13   The White Sox win 1–0 over the Indians in the second game of a double-header at South Side Park. Ed Walsh pitched the shutout. Cleveland won the first game 3–2.

SEPTEMBER 18   Ed Walsh pitches the White Sox to a 1–0 win over Walter Johnson and the Senators at South Side Park. The run scored in the seventh inning when John Anderson doubled, moved to third on a fielder's choice, and scored on a sacrifice fly by Freddy Parent. Johnson allowed only three hits.

One of the most dominant pitchers in an era dominated by pitchers, Ed Walsh won an eye-popping 40 games in 1908.

SEPTEMBER 20   Frank Smith pitches his second career no-hitter to defeat the Athletics 1–0 at South Side Park. He walked one and struck out two. Opposing pitcher Eddie Plank surrendered only four hits. Smith pitched the gem with a partially disabled pitching hand. The little finger of his right hand was stiff and sore from the blow he received during his previous start when he tried to stop a line drive through the middle. Smith recorded the last two outs of the ninth inning himself by fielding grounders from Simon Nicholls and Rube Oldring. The score was still 0–0, however. In the bottom of the ninth, Frank Isbell reached first base on a grounder fielded by first baseman Danny Murphy because Plank failed to cover the bag. Isbell moved to second on a passed ball and to third on a wild pitch. Plank intentionally walked George Davis and intended to do the same to Freddy Parent. On the third pitch, Parent reached out and got a piece of the ball sending a slow roller to second baseman Scotty Barr. The throw to the plate was too late to retire Isbell, and the Sox had a victory.

At the end of the day, the White Sox were in third place, 1½ games behind the first place Tigers. The Indians were in second, one-half game out.

SEPTEMBER 26   With the help of 13 walks from New York pitchers, the White Sox beat the Yankees 12–0 at South Side Park.

SEPTEMBER 27   Ed Walsh pitches the White Sox to a 3–0 victory over the Red Sox in a drizzly rain at South Side Park.

At the end of the day, the Tigers were in first place, one percentage point ahead of the Indians. The Sox were third, just one-half game behind. There were nine days left in the season.

SEPTEMBER 28   Vice presidential candidate James Sherman takes a break from campaigning to watch the White Sox and Red Sox play to a 10-inning, 2–2 tie at South Side Park. The contest was called by darkness.

Sherman was the running mate of Republican Party nominee William Howard Taft. The ticket of Taft and Sherman won the November election.

SEPTEMBER 29   Pitching on one day of rest, Ed Walsh hurls two nine-inning complete-game victories to defeat the Red Sox 5–1 and 2–0 in a double-header at South Side Park. Walsh allowed only seven hits and struck out 15, 10 of them in the opener, while performing the iron-man feat.

OCTOBER 2   Ed Walsh strikes out 15 batters and hurls a four-hitter, but loses 1–0 to the Indians in Cleveland when Addie Joss pitches a perfect game. The contest is regarded by many as the greatest pitching duel in major league history. To add to the suspense, it came near the end of a heated pennant race. Cleveland scored the game's lone run in the third inning. Joe Birmingham singled and took a large lead off first in an attempt of a delayed steal. Walsh threw to first baseman Frank Isbell, and Birmingham took off for second. Isbell's throw struck Birmingham in the shoulder, and as the ball caromed into the outfield, the Cleveland runner reached third. Birmingham scored on a wild pitch as Walsh and catcher Ossee Schreckengost crossed signals. In the ninth, Fielder Jones sent three pinch-hitters to the plate to face Joss. Doc White grounded out to second baseman Nap Lajoie and Jiggs Donahue struck out. One out from a perfect game, Joss induced John Anderson to ground to third baseman Bill Bradley, whose low throw to first baseman George Stovall was scooped up just in time to beat the runner.

At the end of the day, the White Sox were in third place 2½ games behind the first-place Tigers. The Indians were in second, one-half game out. Each club had four games left to play. The White Sox and Tigers closed the season with three games against each other in Chicago from October 4 through October 6. The Sox needed to win all three games to take the pennant.

OCTOBER 3   Pitching in relief, Ed Walsh preserves a 3–2 win over the Indians in Cleveland by striking out Nap Lajoie with the bases loaded and two out in the ninth inning.

OCTOBER 4   The White Sox stay in the pennant race with a 3–1 victory over the Tigers at South Side Park. In true "Hitless Wonder" fashion, the Sox won the game despite collecting only one hit off Detroit hurler Ed Killian. Doc White pitched a complete game for the White Sox. All three Chicago runs crossed the plate in the first without the benefit of a hit. A walk to Ed Hahn was followed by an error, a sacrifice, another error, a stolen base, a sacrifice fly by George Davis, a walk, and a double steal in which Patsy Dougherty swiped home. The only hit against Killian was a single by Freddy Parent in the second.

Play was stopped when Fielder Jones stepped to the plate in the first inning. He was presented with a large silver loving cup. During the game, spectators cheered when the Cubs' 5–2 victory over the Pirates at West Side Grounds was posted on the scoreboard. There were visions of another all-Chicago World Series as the Cubs were also involved in a tight three-way pennant race with the Pirates and Giants.

OCTOBER 5   Ed Walsh records his 40th win of the season with a 6–1 victory over the Tigers at South Side Park.

The Indians were eliminated from the race by splitting a double-header against the Browns. The winner of the October 6 contest between the White Sox and Tigers would claim the AL title.

OCTOBER 6   The White Sox lose a chance to win the American League pennant by losing 7–0 to the Tigers before 30,000 on a Tuesday afternoon at South Side Park. Fielder Jones made a controversial choice of starting pitcher in Doc White that has been debated for nearly a century. The Sox played 16 games from September 17 through October 5 and used only three starters during that span, alternating Ed Walsh, White and Frank Smith. Walsh was his best hurler by far, but he pitched nine innings the previous day and 38$\frac{2}{3}$ innings in a seven-day span from September 29 through October 5. White pitched nine innings on October 4. Smith started on October 3 but failed to finish the game. It was the third consecutive start in which Smith had to be relieved in a season in which Sox starters combined for 107 complete games. Jones went with White in the season finale. White wasn't up to the task, however, retiring only one batter and allowing four runs in the first inning. Walsh and Smith both pitched well in relief, but it was too late. Wild Bill Donovan hurled the shutout for Detroit, allowing only two hits while striking out 10.

The Tigers went to the World Series and lost to the Cubs in five games.

1909

Season in a Sentence

Fielder Jones decides not to return as manager, and without his leadership an aging team slips out of pennant contention to fourth place.

Finish • Won • Lost • Pct • GB

Fourth   78   74   .513   20.0

Manager

Billy Sullivan

Stats

Stats	WS	AL	Rank
Batting Avg:	.221	.244	8
On-Base Pct:	.291	.303	5
Slugging Pct:	.275	.309	8
Home Runs:	4		8
Stolen Bases:	211		3
ERA:	2.05	2.47	2
Fielding Avg:	.964	.957	1
Runs Scored:	492		6
Runs Allowed:	463		2

Starting Lineup

Billy Sullivan, c
Frank Isbell, 1b
Jake Atz, 2b
Billy Purtell, 3b
Lee Tannehill, ss-3b
Patsy Dougherty, lf
Freddy Parent, cf-ss
Ed Hahn, rf
Dave Altizer, rf-1b
Frank Owens, c
Willis Cole, cf

Pitchers

Frank Smith, sp
Ed Walsh, sp
Jim Scott, sp
Doc White, sp
Bill Burns, sp
Rube Suter, rp-sp

Attendance

478,400 (fifth in AL)

Club Leaders

Batting Avg:	Patsy Dougherty	.285
On-Base Pct:	Patsy Dougherty	.359
Slugging Pct:	Patsy Dougherty	.391
Home Runs:	Four tied with	1
RBIs:	Patsy Dougherty	55
Runs:	Patsy Dougherty	71
Stolen Bases:	Patsy Dougherty	36
Wins:	Frank Smith	25
Strikeouts:	Frank Smith	177
ERA:	Ed Walsh	1.41
Saves:	Ed Walsh	2

JANUARY 19   Charlie Comiskey buys a 600-acre parcel of land for $100,000 with the idea of building a new ballpark, which became known as Comiskey Park and opened about a year-and-a-half later (see July 1, 1910).

The lot was on the Wentworth Avenue streetcar line and was bounded by 35th Street, Wentworth, 34th and Shields. It was part of the Canal Trustees Subdivision, owned by Roxanna A. Bowen, the granddaughter of John Wentworth, Chicago's colorful and outlandish mayor during the Civil War era who fired the entire police force one night in a moment of pique. The site of Comiskey's proposed new park was located four blocks north of South Side Park. A previous ballpark, also named South Side Park, was built on almost exactly the same spot. It was used by Chicago's Players League club, on which Comiskey was player-manager, in 1890, and by the Cubs from 1891 through 1893. After the Cubs moved to West Side Grounds in 1894, the grandstand was razed and the property evolved into a community dumping ground. It was also used as a truck farm, where individuals rented small plots to grow vegetables before selling them from horse-drawn wagons. Wild alfalfa grew in what was to become center field.

APRIL 12   The White Sox name Billy Sullivan as manager, replacing Fielder Jones.

Jones announced at the end of the 1908 season that he was retiring from baseball to tend to business interests, which included vast timberlands near Portland, Oregon. Jones had threatened to retire in previous years, only to return when Charlie Comiskey reluctantly increased Fielder's salary. This time Jones was adamant and refused all of Comiskey's offers. Comiskey named Sullivan to direct spring training, still holding out hope that Jones would come back to Chicago. Just two days before Opening Day, Sullivan was named permanent manager. Sullivan had been one of the White Sox's catchers since 1901. He had a career batting average of just .212 in 16 big-league seasons, the second lowest of any player with at least 3,000 at-bats. He was a tremendous defensive catcher, however, in an era in which teams routinely stole 200 bases in a season and pitching ruled the game. Sullivan helped revolutionize the position. Before he reached the majors, catchers stood up to 20 feet behind the batter in order to guard against injury. Sullivan is believed to be the first to crouch right behind the batter. He also patented a chest protector in 1909 which injected compressed air into a wind bag in order to absorb the impact of foul tips. Previously, chest protectors were simple flat pieces of leather. The White Sox were pennant contenders in each of Jones's five years as manager, but under Sullivan they started slowly in 1909 and were out of the race by Memorial Day. Sullivan was fired at the end of the season and replaced by Hugh Duffy (see October 19, 1909), but not before Comiskey tried one more time to coax Jones out of retirement. Sullivan remained with the club as a catcher for three more seasons, however, long enough to see Duffy replaced as White Sox manager during the 1911–12 off-season. Fielder Jones returned to baseball in 1914 as manager of the St. Louis club in the Players League. After that organization folded at the end of the 1915 campaign, Jones managed the St. Louis Browns from 1916 through 1918.

APRIL 14   The White Sox open the season with a 2–0 defeat against the Tigers in Detroit. George Mullin hurled a one-hit shutout. Gavvy Cravath's single was the only Chicago base hit. Sox starting pitcher Frank Smith allowed only four hits, but he lost on two unearned runs following an error by shortstop Freddy Parent.

APRIL 22   The White Sox lose the home opener 3–1 to the Tigers at South Side Park.

APRIL 25   In his first major league start, White Sox pitcher Jim Scott pitches a shutout, defeating the Browns 1–0 at South Side Park. Scott allowed only three hits. The lone run of the game scored in the ninth inning on a single by Freddy Parent, a stolen base, a sacrifice and an error.

Scott pitched nine seasons in the majors, all of them with the White Sox, and had a career record of 107–114. He won 20 games in 1913, pitched a no-hitter in 1914, and hurled 24 victories in 1915. Scott was born in Deadwood, South Dakota, and grew up in the Death Valley town of Imperial, California. After his playing career ended, Scott served as a captain in the Army in France during World War I, married a sister of teammate Buck Weaver, worked as a minor league umpire, formed a religious cult in Los Angeles and was employed as an electrician in one of Hollywood's movie studios.

APRIL 26   The White Sox win 1–0 against the Browns at South Side Park for the second day in a row. Frank Smith pitched the shutout, surrendering only two hits on singles to

Jimmy Williams and opposing pitcher Jack Powell. The lone run of the game scored in the first inning when Ed Hahn singled and toured the bases on an error, a sacrifice and an infield out.

Smith's shutout on April 26 was his third complete game in a span of just five days in which he allowed only two runs. He was pressed into the role of staff ace when Ed Walsh held out for a higher salary and didn't pitch until May 9. During the 1909 season, Smith was 25–17 with an ERA of 1.80. He led the American League in games (51), games started (41), complete games (37), innings pitched (365) and strikeouts (177). The workload ruined a pitcher who was only 29 years old. Smith was never the same after the 1909 season. He was dealt to the Red Sox in August 1910 with a record of 4–9.

APRIL 27   The White Sox defeat the Browns 1–0 at South Side Park for the third day in a row. Doc White hurled the shutout. The lone run of the contest scored on a walk-off single by Billy Sullivan off Rube Waddell.

MAY 1   The game between the White Sox and Indians in Cleveland is postponed by snow.

MAY 2   Amid snow flurries, the White Sox lose 6–5 to the Tigers at South Side Park.

MAY 10   The White Sox edge the Senators 1–0 in an 11-inning contest at South Side Park. Both Doc White and Walter Johnson pitched complete games. White also started the game-winning rally with a two-out single and scored on singles by Ed Hahn and Mike Welday.

MAY 13   The White Sox and the Senators play to a 17-inning, 1–1 tie at South Side Park. The contest was called by darkness. Doc White pitched a complete game for the White Sox and surrendered only one hit over the last 10 innings.

Platooning and pinch-hitting to exploit lefty-righty matchups were relatively new concepts in 1909. In the 17th inning, the Sox had runners on second and third with one out. Billy Sullivan took himself out of the game, and sent Mike Welday, a left-handed batter, to face right-hander Tom Hughes. When Washington manager Joe Cantillion saw this move, he brought in southpaw hurler Dolly Gray. Hughes went to right field. Sullivan countered by taking out Welday and substituting Frank Owens, a right-handed hitter. When Cantillion tried to replace Gray with Hughes, the umpires informed him of a new rule which stated that a reliever had to pitch to at least one batter. After some heated debate between Cantillion and the umps, Gray walked Owens to load the bases. Hughes came back to the mound, and retired the White Sox without a run being scored.

MAY 16   The White Sox lose 1–0 in 13 innings to the Athletics at South Side Park. Over the first 12 innings, Ed Walsh allowed no runs and four hits before allowing doubles to Harry Davis and Pinch Thomas in the 13th. Jack Coombs pitched the complete game for the A's.

On the same day, the White Sox traded Gavvy Cravath, Nick Altrock and Jiggs Donahue to the Senators for Bill Burns. This deal proved to be one of the worst in White Sox history. After the Senators also gave up on Cravath, he resurfaced with the Phillies in 1912 and became one of the best hitting stars of the decade.

Cravath led the NL in home runs six times, twice in RBIs, on-base percentage and slugging percentage, and once each in runs, hits and walks. Burns had a record of only 7–13 with the White Sox when he was traded to the Reds early in the 1910 season. He had the pitching abilities of a 20-game winner, but he seemed to have no ambition and frustrated Sox management with a heavy gambling problem in which he bet heavily on craps, cards, horse races and prize fights. Burns was known to doze on the bench during games. Later, he was involved in the gambling cartel that sought to fix the 1919 World Series between the White Sox and the Reds. Burns was one of the liaisons between the gamblers and the White Sox players that were a part of the fix.

MAY 17   For the second day in a row, the White Sox lose 1–0 in extra innings to the Athletics at South Side Park, this time in 12 innings. Jim Scott pitched a complete game, allowing only five hits. The winning run scored on a single by Home Run Baker and a triple by Eddie Collins.

The White Sox were held without a run for 38 consecutive innings from May 16 through May 19.

JUNE 2   The White Sox play at Shibe Park in Philadelphia for the first time and lose 5–4 to the Athletics. Ed Walsh left the club to attend the funeral of his younger brother David, who died from injuries sustained in a coal mining accident in Plains, Pennsylvania.

Shibe Park was baseball's first double-decked ballpark constructed of concrete and steel. The Athletics played there until 1954, when the club moved to Kansas City. Renamed Connie Mack Stadium in 1953, it was the home of the Phillies from 1939 through 1970.

JUNE 11   Ed Walsh pitches the White Sox to a 1–0 win over the Yankees in New York.

JUNE 20   Ed Walsh pitches a one-hitter to defeat the Indians 4–0 in the first game of a double-header in Cleveland. The only hit off Walsh was a single by Terry Turner. Cleveland won the second tilt 5–0.

JULY 2   The White Sox steal 11 bases and bury the Browns 15–3 at South Side Park. The Sox stole home three times to tie a major league record. Billy Purtell led the stolen bases parade with three. Patsy Dougherty swiped two and Dave Altizer, Jake Atz, Freddy Parent, Ed Hahn, Ed Walsh and Barney Reilly had one each. It was Reilly's first major league game. Chicago scored five runs in the first inning, three of them on a bases-loaded single by catcher Fred Payne.

Altizer served in the Army in the Philippines during the Spanish-American War and in China during the Boxer Rebellion. He was known for shouting "No, no, no" whenever he was tagged out. While playing for the Senators in 1908, Altizer invented a postcard with a photo of William Jennings Bryan which, when held up to the light, also showed a photo of the White House.

JULY 18   Frank Smith pitches a one-hitter to defeat the Senators 1–0 at South Side Park. The only Washington hit was a single by Bob Unglaub.

JULY 23   Jim Scott shuts out the Athletics 3–0 at South Side Park, but is unhappy with the calls of umpire Bull Perrine. Scott tried to attack Perrine under the grandstand after the game, but he was held back by teammates.

JULY 25   The White Sox record their eighth win in a row with a 3–0 decision over the Athletics at South Side Park.

               The win gave the White Sox a 42–45 record. The club overcame a slow start to win 44 of their last 73 games, but it wasn't enough to rise above fourth place.

JULY 31   The White Sox win both ends of a double-header against the Senators in Washington with shutouts. In the opener, Bill Burns had a no-hitter in progress when Otis Clymer singled with two out in the ninth. Burns had to settle for a one-hit, 1–0 victory. Frank Smith won the second contest 4–0.

AUGUST 3   Jim Scott pitches a two-hitter but loses 2–1 to the Athletics in the first game of a double-header in Philadelphia. The A's also won the nightcap 10–4. In the eighth inning, Philadelphia second baseman Eddie Collins objected to a call by Umpire Tim Hurst, and Hurst spit tobacco juice in Collins's face. At the end of the game, several hundred fans rushed at the umpire, but policemen and A's players went to his assistance and Hurst made his escape. The American League fired him because of the incident.

AUGUST 5   Pitching on one day of rest, Jim Scott hurls a two-hitter in his second consecutive start, beating the Athletics 1–0 in the second game of a double-header in Philadelphia. Playing center field, Doc White tripled in the fourth inning and scored on Lee Tannehill's single for the lone run of the game. White was injured in the sixth inning sliding into third base and was carried from the field. Philadelphia won the opener 3–0.

AUGUST 28   Senators pitcher Dolly Gray sets major league records for most walks in an inning (eight) and most consecutive walks (seven) during a 6–4 loss to the White Sox in Washington. To add to the bizarre nature of the contest, the Sox collected only one hit during the entire game, a single by Patsy Dougherty in the second. All six runs came in the inning during which Gray became unhinged. The second time that Dougherty hit in the second inning, he went to the plate without a bat and drew a walk. The White Sox also won the second game 2–1.

               Dougherty led White Sox hitters in 1909 with a .285 batting average and 38 stolen bases.

AUGUST 29   Ed Walsh pitches a two-hitter and wins 1–0 over the Senators at South Side Park. The only Washington hits were singles by Germany Schaefer and Jack Lelivett.

SEPTEMBER 5   Frank Smith strikes out 12 batters but loses 6–1 to the Indians at South Side Park.

SEPTEMBER 12   Frank Smith pitches the White Sox to a 1–0 win over the Indians at South Side Park. It was Smith's 25th win of the season. Billy Purtell drove in the lone run of the game with a single in the second inning.

SEPTEMBER 25   The White Sox collect only two hits off Senators pitcher Bob Groom, but win 2–1 in the first game of a double-header in Washington. Doc White was the winning pitcher. The Sox also won the second contest 2–0 as Bill Burns outpitched Walter Johnson.

OCTOBER 8   The Cubs win the first game of the Chicago City Series, defeating the White Sox 4–0 at West Side Grounds.

OCTOBER 15   Cubs pitcher Three Finger Brown closes out the City Series with a one-hitter and a 1–0 win over the White Sox at West Side Grounds. The only Sox hit was a single by Freddy Parent in the fifth inning. The Cubs won the series, four games to one. The five games drew a total of 74,512 fans.

OCTOBER 19   The White Sox hire 43-year-old Hugh Duffy as manager, replacing Billy Sullivan.

During the 1909 season, Duffy was the manager and owner of the Providence club in the Eastern League. He had previously managed the Milwaukee Brewers (1901) and Philadelphia Phillies (1904–06) at the big league level, but only one of those four clubs had a winning record. Duffy was one of the greatest players in baseball during the 1890s, batting .440 for Boston in the National League in 1894, which is still the all-time record for the highest average in a season and helped him earn a berth in the Hall of Fame. Comiskey and Duffy played together on Chicago's team in the Players League in 1890. Duffy wasn't able to revive an aging White Sox team, however, and lasted only two seasons, in which the club posted a record of 145–159.

THE STATE OF THE WHITE SOX

The White Sox were in a rebuilding mode at the start of the 1910s and spent the first half of the decade struggling to find a winning combination. By 1915, the Sox had a contender and won the AL pennant in both 1917 and 1919. The 1917 club won the World Series over the Giants. It would be the last world baseball championship in the city of Chicago until the Sox won again in 2006. The White Sox were one of only three clubs to win pennants during the 1910s. The other two were the Athletics (1910, 1911, 1913 and 1914) and Red Sox (1912, 1915, 1916 and 1918). Overall, the White Sox were 798–692 during the decade, a winning percentage of .536 that was second-best behind the .579 posted by the Red Sox.

THE BEST TEAM

The 1917 White Sox, under Pants Rowland, were 100–54, won the AL pennant race by nine games and defeated the New York Giants in the World Series.

THE WORST TEAM

The 1910 Sox were 68–85 and finished sixth with Hugh Duffy as manager.

THE BEST MOMENT

The White Sox won the 1917 World Series with a sixth-game victory by a 4–2 score over the Giants, helped by a strange play in which New York third baseman Heinie Zimmerman chased Eddie Collins across the plate in attempt to tag Collins.

THE WORST MOMENT

One of the worst moments in baseball history occurred during the 1919 World Series, when the White Sox lost to the Reds after several players met with gamblers in an attempt to fix the series.

THE ALL-DECADE TEAM • YEARS WITH WS

Ray Schalk, c	1912–28
Jack Fournier, 1b	1912–17
Eddie Collins, 2b	1915–26
Harry Lord, 3b	1910–14
Buck Weaver, ss	1912–20
Joe Jackson, lf	1915–20
Happy Felsch, cf	1915–20
Shano Collins, rf	1910–20
Ed Walsh, p	1904–16
Ed Cicotte, p	1912–20
Jim Scott, p	1909–17
Joe Benz, p	1911–19

Other outstanding White Sox players during the 1910s were pitchers Red Faber (1914–33), Reb Russell (1913–19), Lefty Williams (1916–20), center fielder Ping Bodie (1911–14) and right fielder Nemo Leibold (1915–20). Eddie Collins, Walsh, Schalk and Faber are all in the Hall of Fame. Jackson would likely be in the Hall of Fame if he wasn't permanently barred from baseball for his role in fixing the 1919 World Series. Cicotte and Weaver were building Hall of Fame resumes when they, too, were implicated in the scandal.

THE DECADE LEADERS

Batting Avg:	Joe Jackson	.326
On-Base Pct:	Eddie Collins	.410
Slugging Pct:	Joe Jackson	.470
Home Runs:	Ping Bodie	20
RBIs:	Shano Collins	478
Runs:	Buck Weaver	521
Stolen Bases:	Eddie Collins	194
Wins:	Eddie Cicotte	135
Strikeouts:	Eddie Cicotte	874
ERA:	Ed Walsh	1.96
Saves:	Ed Walsh	20

THE HOME FIELD

The period from 1909 and 1914 was a significant one in the history of stadium construction as wooden ballparks were being replaced by double-decked facilities constructed of concrete and steel. Among them were such classic baseball venues as Shibe Park (1909), Forbes Field (1909), Crosley Field (1912), Tiger Stadium (1912), Fenway Park (1912), the Polo Grounds (1912), Ebbets Field (1913) and Wrigley Field (1914). The White Sox were a part of this trend, replacing wooden South Side Park during the 1910 season with Comiskey Park, built four blocks to the north of the club's previous home and constructed of concrete and steel. Comiskey Park opened on July 1, 1910, and served the Sox until 1990.

THE GAME YOU WISHED YOU HAD SEEN

On October 13, 1917, the White Sox set up their Game Six win in the World Series with a fifth-game victory over the Giants by overcoming a 5–2 deficit with three runs in the seventh inning and three in the eighth to win 8–5.

THE WAY THE GAME WAS PLAYED

Pitching and defense continued to dominate baseball. Offense spiked in the early years of the decade after the AL adopted the cork-centered ball in 1910, but by the mid-teens, the league batting average was back around .250. Home runs were at a premium. There were more than twice as many triples as home runs and speedy outfielders were a necessity to cover playing fields that were much larger than those common today. AL pitchers completed 56 percent of their starts, but this was a significant drop from the 79 percent of the previous decade. During the 1910s, the strategic use of relief pitching, pinch-hitters and platooning became an important aspect of the game for the first time.

THE MANAGEMENT

Charles Comiskey was in his second decade as owner of the White Sox. Harry Grabiner came on board in 1915 as vice president with the duties of a present-day general manager. Field managers were Hugh Duffy (1910–11), Nixey Callahan (1912–14), Pants Rowland (1915–18) and Kid Gleason (1919–23).

THE BEST PLAYER MOVE

The best move was the purchase of Eddie Collins from the Athletics for $50,000 in December 1914. Comiskey also used his cash to buy Eddie Cicotte from the Red Sox in 1912 and to acquire Joe Jackson in a trade with the Indians in 1915. In addition, Ray Schalk and Buck Weaver were bought from minor league clubs.

THE WORST PLAYER MOVE

The White Sox sent Edd Roush back to the minors following a nine-game trial in 1913. He left the organization to join the Federal League a year later and went on to a Hall of Fame career as an outfielder.

1910

Season in a Sentence

The White Sox open Comiskey Park, but the disintegration of the Hitless Wonders continues and the club compiles a batting average of only .211 while landing in sixth place.

Finish • Won • Lost • Pct • GB

Sixth   68   85   .444   35.5

Manager

Hugh Duffy

Stats

Stats	WS	AL	Rank
Batting Avg:	.211	.243	8
On-Base Pct:	.275	.308	8
Slugging Pct:	.261	.313	8
Home Runs:	7		8
Stolen Bases:	183		7
ERA:	2.03		2
Fielding Avg:	.954	.956	7
Runs Scored:	457		7
Runs Allowed:	479		2

Starting Lineup

Fred Payne, c
Chick Gandil, 1b
Rollie Zeider, 2b-ss
Billy Purtell, 3b
Lena Blackburne, ss
Patsy Dougherty, lf
Freddy Parent, cf
Shano Collins, rf-lf
Paul Meloan, rf
Lee Tannehill, ss-1b
Charlie French, 2b-rf
Harry Lord, 3b
Bruno Block, c

Pitchers

Ed Walsh, sp
Doc White, sp
Jim Scott, sp-rp
Fred Olmstead, sp-rp
Irv Young, sp-rp
Frank Lange, sp-rp
Frank Smith, sp

Attendance

552,084 (third in AL)

Club Leaders

Batting Avg:	Patsy Dougherty	.248
On-Base Pct:	Patsy Dougherty	.318
Slugging Pct:	Patsy Dougherty	.300
Home Runs:	Chick Gandil	2
RBIs:	Patsy Dougherty	43
Runs:	Rollie Zeider	57
Stolen Bases:	Rollie Zeider	49
Wins:	Ed Walsh	18
Strikeouts:	Ed Walsh	2.58
ERA:	Ed Walsh	1.27
Saves:	Ed Walsh	5

MARCH 12   At the White Sox training camp in San Francisco, Billy Sullivan steps on a rusty nail. He ignored the advice of his teammates to consult a physician, but instead relied on the word of a quack pharmacist who prescribed a near-lethal dose of turpentine to cure the malady. Sullivan developed blood poisoning and almost lost a leg before seeking competent medical attention. He didn't play in a regular season game until early July.

MARCH 17   On St. Patrick's Day, official groundbreaking ceremonies take place at Comiskey Park. Architect Zachary Taylor Davis laid in place a "lucky" Irish green brick, and a piece of sod brought from Ireland was planted. The ballpark opened on July 1, 1910.

APRIL 14   In the greatest Opening Day pitching performance in White Sox history, Frank Smith hurls a one-hitter to defeat the Browns 3–0 at South Side Park. The only St. Louis hit was a single by Ray Demmitt.

APRIL 20   Indians pitcher Addie Joss pitches a no-hitter against the White Sox for a 1–0 win at South Side Park. It was the second time that Joss pitched a no-hitter against the Sox (see October 2, 1908). The final out was recorded on a grounder by Rollie Zeider to third baseman Bill Bradley.

APRIL 23   The White Sox game against the Browns in St. Louis is postponed by snow. The April 24 contest was also called off because of the wintry weather.

APRIL 30   Doc White pitches a two-hitter to defeat the Tigers 1–0 at South Side Park. The only Detroit hits were singles by Ty Cobb and Oscar Stanage.

MAY 1   The White Sox eke out a 5–4 win in 15 innings against the Tigers at South Side Park. Ed Walsh pitched a complete game and struck out 15. Detroit scored twice in the ninth to take a 4–3 lead, but the Sox tied it up in their half on an RBI single by Billy Purtell. In the 15th, Lee Tannehill doubled, went to third on a sacrifice and scored on a wild pitch.

Ed Walsh had an earned run average of 1.27 in 1910, but he seldom had any hitting support and finished with a won-lost record of 18–20. He had the rare achievement of leading the league in both ERA and defeats. He also completed 33 of his 36 starts, seven of them with shutouts, recorded two wins and five saves in nine relief appearances, and struck out 258 batters in 369²/₃ innings.

MAY 7   The White Sox barely escape from Bennett Field in Detroit following a 5–3 win over the Tigers. Once the game ended, Chicago players were pelted with cushions and other missiles before they could reach the safety of the clubhouse.

MAY 23   The White Sox defeat the Red Sox 4–3 in 15 innings in Boston. Ed Walsh not only pitched a complete game, but he drove in the winning run with a single that scored Lee Tannehill.

MAY 24   The White Sox score one run in the eighth inning and three in the ninth to tie the score 5–5 against the Yankees in New York, but the contest ends in a 5–5 deadlock when it is called because of darkness at the end of the 12th inning.

JUNE 3   The White Sox collect only one hit off Jack Warhop of the Yankees but win 3–1 at South Side Park behind the pitching, hitting, and base running of Ed Walsh. Walsh collected the only Chicago hit with a two-run single in the sixth inning. He reached third on a two-base error and scored the third run on an infield out.

JUNE 6   Ed Walsh pitches a one-hitter to beat the Red Sox 1–0 at South Side Park. Duffy Lewis picked up the lone Boston hit with a single.

JUNE 11   The White Sox purchase George Browne from the Senators.

JUNE 15   The White Sox win 4–3 in a 14-inning marathon against the Athletics at South Side Park. Ed Walsh pitched a complete game and delivered a walk-off single to win the game. Sox second baseman Rollie Zeider committed four errors during the contest.

Zeider was nicknamed "Bunions" because he once contracted blood poisoning after a spiking from Ty Cobb sliced open a bunion. Zeider played for the White Sox (1910–13), the Chicago Whales of the Federal League (1914–15) and the Cubs (1916–18). The only other individual to play for all three 20th-century Chicago clubs was Dutch Zwilling, who is also last among all major leaguers alphabetically. Zwilling appeared in 27 games with the Sox in 1910, the Whales in 1914 and 1915 and the Cubs in 1916.

JUNE 20   Fred Olmstead pitches the White Sox to a 1–0 victory over the Indians in Cleveland.

JUNE 21   White Sox pitcher Irv Young, whose nickname was "Young Cy Young" when he
               debuted with the Braves in 1905, starts both ends of a double-header against the
               Indians in Cleveland. In the opener, Young squared off against the original Cy
               Young, who was gunning for his 498th career win. Irv Young didn't last long, being
               removed from the game in the first after allowing two runs. Jim Scott relieved for the
               Sox and didn't allow a run until the 12th, which resulted in a 3–2 loss. Irv was nearly
               invincible in the nightcap, pitching a 10-inning shutout for a 3–0 Chicago win.

JUNE 27   The White Sox play at South Side Park for the last time, losing 7–2 to the Indians.

               *South Side Park remained in use for Negro League baseball until 1940 as the
               home field of the Chicago American Giants. After the grandstand was torn down
               the city of Chicago developed the site for low-income housing.*

JULY 1   The White Sox open Comiskey Park with a 2–0 loss to the Browns before a crowd of
               24,000. Barney Pelty pitched the shutout while Ed Walsh took the loss. Attendance
               was estimated at between 28,000 and 32,000. The elaborate pre-game celebration
               included a downtown parade, four military bands and speeches by a score of local
               dignitaries, including Chicago Mayor Fred Busse.

               *The new ballpark was located four blocks north of South Side Park on a plot
               bounded by 35th, Wentworth, 34th and Shields. The new facility was designed
               by architect Zachary Taylor Davis, who also drew up the plans for Wrigley Field
               (then known as Weeghman Park) four years later. Comiskey Park was one of the
               first double-decked, concrete and steel baseball parks, a trend that started with
               the opening of Shibe Park in Philadelphia a year earlier. Comiskey Park was
               built in the same Beaux Arts style as the Philadelphia ballpark, with a pressed
               brick exterior that was common to the ballparks of the period. The letter "C"
               was set in bas-relief along the exterior walls. The arches at the back of the lower
               grandstand formed another distinct feature. (The masonry walls of present-
               day U.S. Cellular Field, which opened in 1991, loosely echo those arches.) The
               atmosphere that set the first Comiskey Park apart from other ballparks came
               from the stockyards, which were located nearby and sent unwanted odors
               wafting over the neighborhood. If the stench from the stockyards could be
               detected it meant that the wind was blowing toward the fences and that it would
               likely be a good day for the hitters. In 1910, the double-decked portion
               of Comiskey Park extended only about 30 feet beyond first base and third base
               and was the only concrete and steel portion of the park. Separate wooden
               single-decked pavilions were located along the deeper portions down the first-
               and third-base lines from the ends of the double-decked stands to the foul poles.
               Wooden bleachers were constructed behind the outfield walls in left and right.
               The original dimensions were 363 feet down the foul lines and 420 feet to dead
               center, where a massive wooden scoreboard loomed over the field. The foul
               lines were old water hoses that were flattened and painted white. Total cost was
               pegged at about $700,000, including the cost of the land, all of the cash raised
               privately by Charles Comiskey. The ball park would last 80 years, although it
               never developed the cult status of many of the ballparks of the period. From the
               outside, Comiskey Park looked more like a factory than a work of architecture.
               It was as never as picturesque as Wrigley Field, as charming as Fenway Park*

or as historic as Yankee Stadium. With a symmetrical field, it didn't possess the eccentric dimensions of places like the Polo Grounds or the angles of Ebbets Field. Nonetheless, generations of largely blue-collar White Sox fans from the South Side of Chicago could imagine the club playing nowhere else but utilitarian Comiskey Park and viewed places like Wrigley Field as pretentious and full of pompous yuppies.

JULY 2   The White Sox win for the first time at Comiskey Park with a 3–2 decision over the Browns.

JULY 20   The White Sox lose their 11th game with a row, dropping a 2–0 decision to the Athletics in Philadelphia.

JULY 31   Lee Tannehill hits a grand slam off Wild Bill Donovan in the fourth inning of a 6–5 loss to the Tigers at Comiskey Park. It was not only the first grand slam at the new ballpark, but the first homer of any kind. The drive by Tannehill skipped through the wickets of a small fence connecting the left-field pavilion to the grandstand about 30 feet past third base. Under the rules of the day, it was a home run. There were several other unusual aspects to Tannehill's homer. It was his first home run since 1903 and the last of three homers that he struck in a major league career that spanned ten seasons and 3,778 at-bats from 1903 through 1912. It was also the first grand slam by a White Sox player since Herm McFarland and Dummy Hoy both hit bases-loaded homers in the same game on May 1, 1901.

AUGUST 4   The White Sox and the Athletics battle to a 0–0 tie in a contest at Comiskey Park that is called after 16 innings by darkness. Ed Walsh and Jack Coombs both pitched complete games in the spectacular mound duel. Walsh allowed only six hits while striking out 10. Coombs was even better, hurling a three-hitter and fanning 18.

AUGUST 7   Just two days after pitching a 16-inning shutout, Ed Walsh tosses a two-hitter to defeat the Senators 4–0 at Comiskey Park. Wid Conroy collected both Washington hits with a pair of singles.

AUGUST 9   The White Sox trade Frank Smith and Billy Purtell to the Red Sox for Harry Lord and Amby McConnell.

The White Sox pulled off a great deal in the short term as they gave up two players near the end of their careers for Lord, who was Chicago's starting third baseman for four seasons.

AUGUST 11   Ed Walsh strikes out 15 batters while defeating the Red Sox 1–0 at Comiskey Park. It was Walsh's third consecutive shutout. The lone run of the contest scored in the second inning on a triple by Patsy Dougherty and a single from Billy Purtell.

Including a relief stint of 1$\frac{2}{3}$ innings on August 9, Walsh pitched 35$\frac{2}{3}$ innings during an eight-day span from August 4 through August 11 and allowed no runs and just 11 hits while striking out 39 batters.

AUGUST 14   Ed Walsh's streak of consecutive scoreless innings ends at 40$\frac{2}{3}$ during a double-header against the Yankees before a crowd of 32,498 at Comiskey Park. Walsh saved the opener by pitching the eighth and ninth innings in relief of Frank Lange for a 4–1 victory. Walsh started the second game and hurled three shutout innings before his scoreless streak ended in a hurry when the Yankees scored five runs in the fourth to win 5–1.

AUGUST 15   Ed Scott pitches a two-hitter for a 3–2 win over the Yankees at Comiskey Park. Scott also figured in all three Chicago runs. In the fifth inning, he hit a sacrifice fly. Trailing 2–1 in the seventh, Scott singled in a run and scored on Amby McConnell's triple. The only New York hits were singles by Birdie Cree and Jimmy Austin.

AUGUST 23   Ed Walsh and Walter Johnson both strike out 10 batters in a game between the White Sox and Senators in Washington. The Sox won 1–0 on back-to-back triples by Paul Meloan and Patsy Dougherty in the sixth inning.

AUGUST 24   Billy Sullivan catches three balls out of 11 dropped 555 feet from the top of the Washington Monument.

The feat had been performed previously by Pop Shriver of the Cubs in 1894 and Gabby Street of the Senators in 1908. Sullivan had obtained a permit from Washington city officials to perform the stunt, but he didn't announce the time to avoid the formation of a large crowd. Ed Walsh and Doc White dropped the regulation American League baseballs from one of the windows near the top of the monument. Sullivan made no attempt to catch the first drop, wishing to see how it would fall. Using the same mitt that he used to catch Walsh and White fastballs during games, Sullivan missed the first seven balls but caught the eighth and snared two more on the 10th and 11th tries.

AUGUST 27   A night game is staged at Comiskey Park before a curious crowd of 3,500. The opponents were Nixey Callahan's Logan Squares and a team from the neighborhood of Rogers Park, two of Chicago's top amateur clubs. The Logan Squares won 3–0.

Charles Comiskey was one of the investors in the Night Baseball Development Company, formed in 1908. Comiskey, George Cahill and Cincinnati Reds President Garry Herrmann put up $50,000 to explore the possibility of staging baseball games at night. Cahill, along with his two brothers, owned a floodlight manufacturing firm in Holyoke, Massachusetts. The first test run took place at Cincinnati's Palace of the Fans, the Reds' home field, with an exhibition game between two Elks Club teams on June 18, 1909. For the game in Chicago on August 27, 1910, 10 lamps were installed by Cahill either on top of the grandstand or on the top of towers around the outfield facing downward. Ten others were placed like floodlights around the edge of the field facing skyward. Reviews of the first night game at Comiskey were generally favorable, but Comiskey, Herrmann and other big league owners did not deem the light sufficient for major league play. The first regular night game between two major league clubs didn't take place until May 24, 1935. It was played at Crosley Field in Cincinnati. The first regular season night game at Comiskey Park took place exactly four years later on May 24, 1939.

SEPTEMBER 8   Fred Olmstead pitches a one-hitter to defeat the Browns 1–0 in the first game of a double-header at Sportsman's Park. The only St. Louis hit was a single by Jack Truesdale on the first pitch of the first inning. The Browns won the second contest 6–4.

SEPTEMBER 9   Ed Walsh pitches a two-hitter to beat the Browns 8–1 in the first game of a
                   double-header at Sportsman's Park. The only St. Louis hits were singles by
                   Danny Hoffman and opposing pitcher Farmer Ray.

SEPTEMBER 13   Ed Walsh strikes out 13 batters but loses 1–0 to the Browns at Comiskey Park.

SEPTEMBER 18   Ed Walsh pitches a shutout to defeat the Red Sox 6–0 at Comiskey Park. The White
                   Sox pulled off a triple play in the second inning. With Boston runners on first and
                   second moving with the pitch, Billy Purtell lined to second baseman Freddy Parent,
                   who threw to shortstop Rollie Zeider. A relay from Zeider to first baseman Chick
                   Gandil completed the triple play.

                   *The next day, Gandil was sold to Montreal in the Eastern League. He returned
                   to the majors with the Senators in 1912. Gandil played for the Sox again from
                   1917 through 1919 and was a key instigator in the scandal to fix the 1919
                   World Series.*

SEPTEMBER 19   Fred Olmstead pitches the White Sox to a 1–0 win over the Red Sox at Comiskey
                   Park.

SEPTEMBER 20   Ed Walsh strikes out 13 batters to beat the Yankees 3–0 at Comiskey Park. It was
                   the third straight shutout by White Sox pitchers. Walsh also drove in two runs with
                   a single in the eighth inning. The only New York hits were singles by Harry Wolter
                   and Frank LaPorte.

SEPTEMBER 24   The White Sox winning streak reaches 10 games with a double-header sweep of the
                   Athletics by scores of 8–4 and 3–2 at Comiskey Park. The second game went 11
                   innings.

                   *The Sox won 18 of their last 23 games in 1910, but the fast finish couldn't
                   prevent a 68–85 record, creating the worst winning percentage by the club
                   between 1903 and 1924.*

SEPTEMBER 27   Jim Scott and Senators pitcher Dolly Gray both pitch two-hitters in the first game of
                   a double-header at Comiskey Park. The White Sox won 2–0. Kid Elberfield collected
                   both Washington hits with singles. The Sox lost the nightcap 3–2.

1911

Season in a Sentence

With an infusion of new talent, the White Sox post a winning record.

Finish • Won • Lost • Pct • GB

Fourth   77   74   .510   24.0

Manager

Hugh Duffy

Stats

Stats	WS	AL	Rank
Batting Avg:	.269	.273	6
On-Base Pct:	.326	.338	7
Slugging Pct:	.350	.358	6
Home Runs:	20		5 (tie)
Stolen Bases:	201		6
ERA:	2.97		2
Fielding Avg:	.961	.953	2
Runs Scored:	719		3
Runs Allowed:	624		2

Starting Lineup

Billy Sullivan, c
Shano Collins, 1b
Amby McConnell, 2b
Harry Lord, 3b
Lee Tannehill, ss
Nixey Callahan, lf
Ping Bodie, cf
Matty McIntyre, rf
Rollie Zeider, 1b-ss
Patsy Dougherty, lf

Pitchers

Ed Walsh, sp-rp
Jim Scott, sp
Doc White, sp
Frank Lange, sp
Fred Olmstead, rp-sp
Irv Young, rp-sp
Jesse Baker, rp-sp

Attendance

583,208 (second in AL)

Club Leaders

Batting Avg:	Matty McIntyre	.323
On-Base Pct:	Matty McIntyre	.397
Slugging Pct:	Harry Lord	.433
Home Runs:	Ping Bodie	4
	Shano Collins	4
RBIs:	Ping Bodie	97
Runs:	Harry Lord	103
Stolen Bases:	Nixey Callahan	45
Wins:	Ed Walsh	27
Strikeouts:	Ed Walsh	255
ERA:	Ed Walsh	2.22
Saves:	Ed Walsh	4

APRIL 12	The scheduled season opener against the Tigers in Detroit is rained out.
APRIL 13	The White Sox get the 1911 season under way with a 4–2 loss to the Tigers in Detroit.
APRIL 20	In the first game of the season at Comiskey Park, the White Sox lose 6–3 to the Tigers. Chicago Mayor Carter Harrison threw out the ceremonial first pitch.
APRIL 27	The White Sox wallop the Browns 14–4 at Comiskey Park.
MAY 11	The White Sox put aside their image as "hitless wonders" and bury the Senators 20–6 at Comiskey Park. The score was 7–6 when the Sox plated seven runs in the seventh, then poured it on with six more in the eighth. A shell-shocked Bob Groom pitched a complete game for Washington.
MAY 18	The White Sox outlast the Red Sox 12–8 at Comiskey Park. Chicago broke a 7–7 tie with two runs in the sixth.
MAY 28	The White Sox score four runs in the ninth inning to send the game against the Indians at Comiskey Park into extra innings, but it winds up in a 5–5 tie when a torrential rain stops play at the end of the 10th. During the ninth-inning rally, Ping Bodie tripled with the bases loaded and scored on a single by Shano Collins.

Ping Bodie's given name was Francesco Stephano Pezzullo. A native of San Francisco, he was among the first Italian-Americans to play in the majors. Naturally funny and garrulous, Bodie played for the White Sox from 1911 through 1914. Chicago Tribune *columnist Ring Lardner blended elements of Bodie into the brash ballplayer of Lardner's "You Know Me, Al" stories, which amused and delighted readers of the sports page during the period.*

MAY 30   Irv Young pitches a two-hitter to beat the Browns 2–0 in the second game of a double-header at Comiskey Park. The only hits off Young were singles by Frank LaPorte and Ed Hallinan. St. Louis won the first game 4–1.

JUNE 2   The White Sox score seven runs in the fourth inning and forge ahead to beat the Red Sox 13–8 in Boston.

JUNE 5   Hugh Duffy sends three consecutive pinch-hitters to the plate in the ninth inning, and all three strike out against Smoky Joe Wood, closing out a 5–4 loss to the Red Sox in Boston. The three pinch-hitters were Patsy Dougherty, Fred Payne and Bruno Block.

JUNE 8   During a 7–3 win against the Yankees in New York, White Sox shortstop Roy Corhan is hit on the head by a pitch from Russ Ford. Yankee manager Hal Chase allows Ping Bodie as a courtesy runner, even though Bodie is already in the lineup. Corhan was unable to continue and was replaced at shortstop by Lee Tannehill.

JUNE 10   After breaking a scoreless tie with nine runs in the second inning, the White Sox defeat the Senators 18–7 in Washington.

JUNE 18   Leading 13–1 after 4½ innings, the White Sox blow the huge lead and lose 16–15 to the Tigers in Detroit. The Sox collected seven runs in the first inning, and after the Tigers scored a single run in the second, Chicago added three in the fourth and three in the fifth. The Tigers started the incredible comeback with four runs in the fifth and three in the sixth. After the Sox scored twice in the seventh to take a 15–8 advantage, Detroit added five in the eighth and three in the ninth. Ty Cobb scored the winning run when Sam Crawford hit a drive over the head of center fielder Ping Bodie. The Sox pitchers in the debacle were Doc White, Fred Olmstead and Ed Walsh. The loss was pinned on Walsh for allowing the three ninth-inning tallies.

              The 12-run deficit overcome by the Tigers is the largest ever overcome in a major league game. It has been matched twice, by the Athletics against the Indians in 1925 and the Indians against the Mariners in 2001.

JUNE 20   The White Sox sweep the Browns 6–3 and 13–6 in St. Louis.

JULY 4   Ed Walsh snaps Ty Cobb's 40-game hit streak during a 7–1 win over the Tigers in the first game of a double-header in Detroit. The Tigers also won the nightcap 11–10 in 11 innings.

JULY 11   In the first game of a double-header, Doc White pitches a three-hitter against the Red Sox at Comiskey Park with Clyde Engle collecting all three hits. The White Sox won 4–0 with all four runs scoring in the eighth. Boston won the second contest 6–4.

JULY 16   The White Sox shock the Senators with four runs in the ninth to win 6–5 at Comiskey Park.

JULY 22   Several hundred soldiers from Fort Sheridan attend the game at Comiskey Park, won 5–4 by the White Sox over the Athletics. The soldiers paraded around the field before the game and stood at attention while the "Star Spangled Banner" was played. The Stars and Stripes were then raised while the crowd waved hats and handkerchiefs.

                 At the time, the "Star Spangled Banner" was played prior to sporting events only on special occasions. It did not became the National Anthem until 1933 and was not performed before games on a regular basis until the United States became involved militarily in World War II in December 1941.

JULY 28   The White Sox win 7–5 over the Yankees in 14 innings in New York. Harry Lord tripled in one 14th-inning run and scored on a sacrifice fly by Nixey Callahan. The Sox held a 5–1 lead before the Yankees scored one run in the eighth and three in the ninth.

                 Lord hit .321 and scored 103 runs in 1911.

JULY 29   Trailing 5–2, the White Sox score one run in the eighth inning, two in the ninth and three in the tenth to pull ahead 8–5, then withstand a two-run Yankee rally in the bottom of the 10th to win 8–7 in the second game of a double-header in New York. The Sox also won the first game 10–2.

JULY 30   The White Sox hammer the Yankees 13–0 in New York.

AUGUST 4   Unusual plays highlight an 11-inning, 1–0 win over the Senators in Washington as Doc White outduels Walter Johnson. First, White Sox shortstop Lee Tannehill tied a major league record with two unassisted double plays. Then in the ninth, Washington's Germany Schaefer tried to steal first base. He was a base runner on second with teammate Clyde Milan on third when Schaefer took off for first in an attempt to draw a throw that would allow Milan to score. Sox manager Hugh Duffy raced onto the field to protest the peculiar tactic, and during the argument with umpire Doc Parker, Schaefer tried to make it back to second. Catcher Fred Payne pegged a throw to second baseman Amby McConnell, and Schaefer was caught in a rundown between first and second. During the rundown, Milan broke for the plate and was out on a bullet from first baseman Shano Collins to Payne. Washington won the second game 3–2.

                 John Francis (Shano) Collins played for the White Sox from 1910 through 1920, alternating between first base and the outfield.

AUGUST 7   Jim Scott pitches a shutout through 12 innings and takes a 1–0 lead into the bottom of the 13th, only to allow a run that frame and another in the 14th to lose 2–1 to the Athletics in the first game of a double-header in Philadelphia. The Sox also lost the nightcap in extra innings, dropping a 3–2 decision in 10 innings.

AUGUST 14   Ed Walsh pitches a one-hitter to defeat the Tigers 2–0 at Comiskey Park. The only Detroit hit was a single by Oscar Stanage.

AUGUST 18   Catcher Fred Payne has to leave a 7–5 win over the Athletics at Comiskey Park
               under unusual circumstances. Payne was hit in the mouth by a ball thrown to him
               by the ball boy. Payne was taking off his mask and didn't see the ball headed in his
               direction. He was out for the rest of the year with the resulting injuries and never
               played another big-league game.

AUGUST 20   The White Sox trounce the Senators 11–0 at Comiskey Park.

AUGUST 25   The increased use of relief pitching, pinch-hitting and tactical substitutions is
               apparent during a 6–5 White Sox win over the Yankees at Comiskey Park. Hugh
               Duffy used five pitchers, starting with Joe Benz and following with Jim Scott, Jesse
               Baker, Irv Young and Doc White. Frank Lange and Ed Walsh, two other pitchers,
               were used as pinch-hitters and both delivered hits.

AUGUST 27   Ed Walsh pitches a no-hitter and beats the Red Sox 5–0 at Comiskey Park. Walsh
               walked one and struck out eight. The only Boston base runner was Clyde Engle,
               who walked in the fourth inning. In the ninth, Steve Yerkes made the first out on a
               bouncer back to Walsh. Pinch-hitter Les Nunamaker struck out. Joe Riggert made
               the final out on a ground ball to second baseman Amby McConnell.

               *Walsh led the league in games pitched (56), innings pitched (368²/₃) and
               strikeouts (255) in 1911. He had a 27–18 record, a 2.22 ERA and completed
               33 of his 37 starts.*

SEPTEMBER 1   Inserted into the game as a pinch-hitter, Felix Chouinard of the White Sox helps kill
               a ninth-inning rally by being tagged out on a "hidden ball trick" at second base by
               Indians shortstop Ivy Olson. The White Sox lost 2–1 at Comiskey Park.

SEPTEMBER 8   Matty McIntyre collects five hits, including a triple and a double, in five at-bats
               leading the White Sox to 9–3 win over the Tigers in Detroit.

               *In his first season with the White Sox following a trade with the Tigers, McIntyre
               hit .323 and scored 102 runs in 1911. He played only one more season in the big
               leagues, however, dropping to an average of .167 in 49 games in 1912.*

SEPTEMBER 11   The White Sox score four runs in the ninth inning to stun the Browns 7–6 in the
               first game of a double-header in St. Louis. The Sox completed the sweep with a 2–0
               triumph in the nightcap.

SEPTEMBER 22   The White Sox win two games with shutouts in a double-header against the Senators
               in Washington. Jim Scott won the opener 5–0. Frank Lange (eight innings) and
               Ed Walsh (one inning) combined to take game two 1–0.

OCTOBER 4   Ed Walsh wins his 27th game of the season with a 14–6 decision over the Browns in
               the first game of a double-header at Comiskey Park. St. Louis won the second tilt,
               called after eight innings by darkness, 2–1.

OCTOBER 8   On the last day of the season Rollie Zeider ties a club record by scoring five runs
               during a 10–4 win over the Indians at Comiskey Park.

OCTOBER 13   In the first game of the City Series, the White Sox score three runs in the ninth inning to beat the Cubs 4–3 at Comiskey Park. Cubs center fielder Solly Hofman misjudged a fly ball, opening the way for the three-run rally. Reserve catcher Ralph Kreitz drove in the winning run with a single.

Kreitz played in only seven regular season games during his career and failed to collect a single RBI.

OCTOBER 15   A crowd of 36,308, the largest ever to see a baseball game in Chicago up to that time, watches the White Sox beat the Cubs 4–2 at Comiskey Park in game three of the Chicago City Series.

The White Sox swept the Cubs four games to none in the 1911 City Series. The four games drew 99,359.

OCTOBER 22   The White Sox and Cubs play a benefit game for St. Ann's Hospital. The White Sox won 6–2, although the teams exchanged pitchers before the contest. Ed Walsh pitched for the Cubs, while Cubs hurler Lew Richie took the mound for the Sox. Before the game, Walsh was presented with a $4,000 Lincoln.

OCTOBER 23   The White Sox hire Nixey Callahan as manager, replacing Hugh Duffy.

Duffy was let go because Comiskey wanted a manager who resided in Chicago year-round, and Duffy preferred to spend his off-seasons at his residence in Boston. Callahan had previously managed the White Sox in 1903 and 1904. His second tour with the club lasted three seasons. Duffy managed the Red Sox in 1921 and 1922 and later served the Boston organization as director of its tryout camp and baseball school and as a general goodwill ambassador. Until 1953, when he was 86 years old, Duffy traveled south with the Red Sox every spring, putting on a uniform every day.

1912

Season in a Sentence

The White Sox win 23 of their first 29 games and spend 49 days in first place before sinking to fourth.

Finish • Won • Lost • Pct • GB

Fourth   78   76   .506   28.0

Manager

Nixey Callahan

Stats

Stats	WS	AL	Rank
Batting Avg:	.255	.265	7
On-Base Pct:	.317	.333	7
Slugging Pct:	.329	.348	7
Home Runs:	17		7
Stolen Bases:	205		5
ERA:	3.06	3.34	3
Fielding Avg:	.956	.952	3
Runs Scored:	639		6
Runs Allowed:	648		3

Starting Lineup

Walt Kuhn, c
Rollie Zeider, 1b-3b
Morrie Rath, 2b
Harry Lord, 3b
Buck Weaver, ss
Nixey Callahan, lf
Ping Bodie, cf-rf
Shano Collins, rf-1b
Wally Mattick, cf

Pitchers

Ed Walsh, sp-rp
Joe Benz, sp
Frank Lange, sp-rp
Doc White, sp-rp
Eddie Cicotte, sp-rp
Rube Peters, rp-sp

Attendance

602,241 (first in AL)

Club Leaders

Batting Avg:	Ping Bodie	.294
On-Base Pct:	Morrie Rath	.380
Slugging Pct:	Ping Bodie	.407
Home Runs:	Harry Lord	5
	Ping Bodie	5
RBIs:	Shano Collins	81
Runs:	Morrie Rath	104
Stolen Bases:	Rollie Zeider	47
Wins:	Ed Walsh	27
Strikeouts:	Ed Walsh	254
ERA:	Ed Walsh	2.15
Saves:	Ed Walsh	10

APRIL 11   Two months after New Mexico and Arizona become the 47th and 48th states, the White Sox beat the Browns 6–2 before 30,000 at Comiskey Park in the season opener. Ed Walsh pitched a complete-game shutout.

APRIL 20   Six days after the sinking of the Titanic, the White Sox and the Browns play 15 innings to a 0–0 tie at Sportsman's Park. The contest was called on account of darkness. Jim Scott pitched a complete game, allowing just six hits. George Baumgardner went the distance for St. Louis.

APRIL 27   The White Sox play at Navin Field in Detroit for the first time and win 2–0 behind the pitching of Ed Walsh.

Known first as Navin Field, then as Briggs Stadium and Tiger Stadium, the ballpark served the Tigers from 1912 through 1999.

MAY 7   The White Sox beat the Senators 1–0 in a game at Washington shortened to five innings by rain. Harry Lord accounted for the lone run of the game with a homer in the fourth inning off Bob Groom. Frank Lange hurled the shutout.

MAY 8   The White Sox purchase Jack Fournier from the Red Sox.

Fournier hit over .300 with power in both 1914 and 1915 as a starting first baseman, but he frustrated the club with his inconsistent hitting and fielding deficiencies. He was released in 1917, but the club should have shown a little more patience. Fournier was one of the top first sackers in the National League during the first half of the 1920s with the Cardinals and the Dodgers.

MAY 11   The White Sox score seven runs in the ninth inning to stun the Athletics 9–5 in Philadelphia.

MAY 17   The White Sox play at Fenway Park for the first time and score four runs in the ninth inning to defeat the Red Sox 5–2. All four runs scored with two out. The rally started on a single by Ed Walsh.

Arriving in 1912 as a young, light-hitting shortstop, Buck Weaver became, by the late teens, one of the best fielding third baseman in the game as well as a productive hitter.

Nixey Callahan put Walsh under an unbearable workload in 1912. Walsh made 41 starts, completing 32, and made 21 relief appearances. His 62 games pitched as well as his 393 innings led the AL. Walsh had a record of 27–17 with 10 saves, an earned run average of 2.15, and 254 strikeouts. From 1907 through 1912, he pitched 2,247²/₃ innings, an average of 375 per year, and the strain proved to be too much. Walsh wasn't nearly the same pitcher after 1912. He never pitched as many as 100 innings in a season again, and won only 13 more big-league games.

MAY 18   The White Sox record on the 1912 season is 23–6 after a 3–1 win over the Red Sox in Boston.

The 23–6 mark gave the Sox a 5½-game lead and Nixey Callahan looked like a genius in his second go-around as manager of the club. But on the way to losing 70 of their next 120 games, Chicago dropped out of first on June 9. The Sox needed to win their last five games to finish above the .500 mark at 78–76 and ended up in fourth, 28 games behind the pennant-winning Red Sox.

MAY 21   The White Sox lose a bizarre 9–8 decision to the Yankees in New York when the Yankees score three runs in the ninth inning. With runners on second and third and the score 8–8 with two out, Frank Lange attempted to issue an intentional walk to Roy Hartzell. On the fourth ball, Sox catcher Walt Kuhn stepped out of the box too early and umpire Bill Evans called a balk, bringing the winning run across the plate.

MAY 25   The White Sox edge the Tigers 5–4 in a 17-inning marathon at Comiskey Park. Harry Lord opened the final inning with a double and scored on Ping Bodie's single. Neither team scored from the eighth through the 16th. Frank Lange pitched 10 scoreless innings of relief for the Sox.

JUNE 21   Rollie Zeider steals five bases during an 8–1 win over the Browns at Comiskey Park.

JUNE 28   The White Sox score four runs in the ninth inning to tie the score 9–9, only to lose 10–9 to the Tigers in Detroit. In the 10th inning, Joe Benz walked Ty Cobb with the bases loaded to force in the winning run.

JUNE 30   The White Sox pummel the Tigers 12–0 in the first game of a double-header in Detroit. The Sox kept up the slugging in the second contest, but they lost 11–9. It was called at the end of the sixth inning to allow the White Sox to catch a train.

JULY 10   The White Sox purchase Eddie Cicotte from the Red Sox.

Cicotte came to the White Sox at the age of 28 with a lifetime record of 53–47 and a reputation as a surly troublemaker. He was available because he couldn't get along with Red Sox manager Jake Stahl. Cicotte's name will always live in infamy as one of the eight players barred for life because of his participation in fixing the 1919 World Series, but for nine seasons he compiled one of the best pitching records in club history. He ranks seventh all-time among White Sox pitchers in wins (156), third in ERA (2.24), fifth in winning percentage (.605), fifth in complete games (183), fifth in shutouts (28), seventh in innings pitched (2,321²/₃), eighth in games started (258). Cicotte won 29 games in 1919 and 28 in 1917, both seasons in which the White Sox reached the World Series. He was a source of controversy long before his role in throwing the World Series. Cicotte was accused by opponents of illegally doctoring the ball with a sticky substance and throwing a pitch called a "shine ball."

JULY 17   Ed Walsh pitches a two-hitter to beat the Red Sox 1–0 in the first game of a double-header at Fenway Park. The only Boston hits were singles by Larry Gardner and Duffy Lewis. The Red Sox won the nightcap 7–3.

JULY 25   The actions of Nixey Callahan nearly result in a forfeit before the White Sox pull out a 10-inning, 6–4 win over the Yankees in New York. Callahan was ejected in the top of the10th for protesting a call by umpire Jack Sheridan. Instead of retiring to the clubhouse, as required by the rules, Callahan jumped into the grandstand and hid behind a railing. Sheridan discovered the ruse and was on the verge of forfeiting the game when Callahan ran off the field. Nixey was suspended for three days by AL President Ban Johnson because of the incident.

AUGUST 11   At the age of 20, Ray Schalk makes his major league debut with a single in three at-bats during a 9–6 loss to the Athletics in the first game of a double-header in Philadelphia. The White Sox also lost the second game 2–1.

Schalk was obtained from Milwaukee of the American Association for $18,000. He was a catcher for the White Sox from 1912 through 1928 and also managed the club in 1927 and 1928. Schalk appeared in 1,757 games for the Sox, 1,722 of them behind the plate. In 1925 he passed Deacon McGuire as the all-time leader in games as a catcher and held the mark until 1939 when passed by Gabby Hartnett. Schalk caught four no-hitters, which remains the major league record. At five-foot-nine and 165 pounds, he was small for his position. Ray's career batting average was .253 and he hit only 11 homers in 5,306 at-bats. Yet, Schalk was elected to the Hall of Fame on the basis of his defensive prowess, endurance, leadership, intelligence and mental toughness.

AUGUST 13   President William Howard Taft attends a contest between the White Sox and the Senators in Washington. The White Sox win 5–3.

SEPTEMBER 19   Ed Walsh pitches a three-hitter to defeat the Athletics 3–0 at Comiskey Park. Walsh held the A's hitless until the eighth inning.

Second baseman Morrie Rath had an unusual set of statistics in 1912, his first season with the White Sox. Playing in 157 games, Rath scored 104 runs and drove in only 19 runs, a direct result of his leadoff position in the batting order, an ability to get on base and a lack of power. Only 13 of his 161 hits went for extra bases, and Rath drew 95 walks. He hit .272 in 1912, but slumped to .200 in 1913 and was released. Rath spent five full seasons in the minors before returning to the big leagues as the starting second baseman with the 1919 Reds, a club which met the White Sox in the World Series.

OCTOBER 4   Ed Walsh records his 27th win of the season with a 7–2 decision over the Tigers at Comiskey Park.

OCTOBER 9   The 1912 Chicago City Series begins at Comiskey Park with a 0–0 tie, called after nine innings by darkness. Ed Walsh held the Cubs to one hit.

Game two, played at West Side Grounds on October 11, also resulted in a tie after the contest was called on account of darkness at the end of 12 innings with the score 3–3. After four days of the City Series, neither team had a victory with two rainouts and two ties.

OCTOBER 13   A crowd of 30,393 at West Side Park watches the Cubs defeat the White Sox 4–2 to take a two games to none lead in the City Series.

The crowd became so unmanageable in the early part of the game that it was impossible for a large detail of police to keep them from crowding onto the infield. A dozen or more park attaches and ushers went to the assistance of the police, and when this failed to push the crowd back, the Cubs players, each armed with a bat, went to the rescue. The fans were intimidated by the show of force and were shoved far enough into the outfield to allow play to continue.

OCTOBER 14   The Cubs take a three games to none lead in the City Series with an 8–1 win over the White Sox at Comiskey Park.

After five games, the White Sox had three losses and two ties in the City Series.

OCTOBER 15   The White Sox finally win a game in the 1912 City Series with a run in the 11th to beat the Cubs 5–4 at West Side Grounds.

OCTOBER 17   The White Sox even the City Series at three wins apiece by scoring four runs in the ninth to defeat the Cubs 8–5 at West Side Grounds. Wally Mattick figured in all four of the ninth-inning runs by scoring on an infield out after smacking a bases-loaded triple.

OCTOBER 18   Three weeks before the election of Woodrow Wilson as President, the White Sox win their fourth game in a row to take the City Series with a 16–0 trouncing of the Cubs at Comiskey Park. The Sox scored all of their runs in the first five innings, eight of them in the third. Ed Walsh pitched the shutout. After the game, several thousand fans rushed the field and led Walsh around the diamond after draping a large American flag around his shoulders.

Incredibly, the White Sox mounted a comeback to win four games in a row to win the championship of Chicago despite the fact that they didn't win a single contest in the best-of-seven series until the sixth game.

1913

Sox

Season in a Sentence

The White Sox score the fewest runs in the American League and allow the fewest in finishing just above the .500 mark.

Finish • Won • Lost • Pct • GB

Fifth   78   74   .513   17.5

Manager

Nixey Callahan

Stats

Stats	WS	AL	Rank
Batting Avg:	.236	.256	8
On-Base Pct:	.299	.325	8
Slugging Pct:	.311	.336	7
Home Runs:	24		2 (tie)
Stolen Bases:	156		8
ERA:	2.33		1
Fielding Avg:	.960	.959	4
Runs Scored:	488		8
Runs Allowed:	498		1

Starting Lineup

Ray Schalk, c
Hal Chase, 1b
Morrie Rath, 2b
Harry Lord, 3b
Buck Weaver, ss
Ping Bodie, lf-cf
Wally Mattick, cf
Shano Collins, rf
Joe Berger, 2b
Larry Chappell, lf
Jack Fournier, 1b-rf

Pitchers

Reb Russell, sp
Jim Scott, sp
Eddie Cicotte, sp
Joe Benz, sp-rp
Ed Walsh, sp
Doc White, rp-sp

Attendance

644,501 (first in AL)

Club Leaders

Batting Avg:	Buck Weaver	.272
On-Base Pct:	Harry Lord	.327
Slugging Pct:	Ping Bodie	.397
Home Runs:	Ping Bodie	8
RBIs:	Buck Weaver	52
Runs:	Harry Lord	62
Stolen Bases:	Harry Lord	24
Wins:	Reb Russell	22
Strikeouts:	Reb Russell	158
ERA:	Eddie Cicotte	1.58
Saves:	Reb Russell	4

FEBRUARY 1   The White Sox and the New York Giants sign an agreement to stage a world tour at the close of the 1913 season (see October 18, 1913).

APRIL 10   The scheduled season opener between the White Sox and Indians in Cleveland is rained out.

APRIL 11   The White Sox get the regular season under way with a 3–1 loss to the Indians on a chilly and windy day in Cleveland.

APRIL 12   The White Sox trounce the Indians 13–3 in a game in Cleveland halted after seven innings to allow the Sox to catch a train bound for St. Louis.

APRIL 17   In the home opener before a crowd of about 28,000 at Comiskey Park, the White Sox defeat the Indians 2–1 behind the three-hit pitching of Jim Scott.

Scott had an unusual season in 1913 by winning 20 games but losing 21. He had a 1.90 earned run average in 312⅓ innings.

APRIL 23   Outfielder Davy Jones walks four times in four plate appearances during a 2–1 victory over the Tigers at Comiskey Park.

Jones played only 12 games with the White Sox near the end of a 14-year career.

APRIL 26   Rookie pitcher Reb Russell pitches a two-hitter to defeat the Browns 1–0 at Comiskey Park. The only St. Louis hits were singles in the fifth inning by Bobby Wallace and opposing pitcher Dwight Stone. The lone run of the game scored on a walk-off single by Shano Collins.

In his first season in the majors, Ewell (Reb) Russell was 22–16 with a 1.91 ERA in 316²/₃. He led the AL in games pitched with 52 by making 36 starts and 16 relief appearances. Probably due to the heavy workload, Russell was only 7–12 in 1914. He gave the White Sox a couple more good seasons, including a 15–5 mark for the 1917 world champions, but made his final pitching appearance in 1919. After a few seasons back in the minors, Russell played as an outfielder for the Pirates in 1922 and 1923. He had a career won-lost record of 80–59 and a .268 batting average with 22 homers in 976 at-bats.

MAY 17   On an eventful day with 36,000 in attendance at Comiskey Park, the White Sox honor Frank Chance, and part of the stands collapse, before a 6–4 win over the Yankees.

Chance was the manager of the Yankees following a career with the Cubs that lasted from 1898 through 1912. He was also manager of the Cubs from 1904 until he was unceremoniously fired at the end of the 1912 season. Chance became a Chicago institution by guiding the Cubs into the World Series four times. "Frank Chance Day" began with a two-mile-long downtown parade that began in Grant Park and featured 700 automobiles. At the ballpark, Chicago Mayor Carter Harrison presented Chance with a floral horseshoe. There was also a display of fireworks, along with troupes of acrobats, contortionists and tumblers, trained dogs and monkeys, vocalists and brass bands. Chance played an inning at first base before giving way to Hal Chase. The day was not without serious problems, however. Part of the temporary stands built for the occasion collapsed, injuring three. One of the gate tenders severed a finger. He was in the act of pushing back the steel gate when the crowd surged against it and caught his hand between the hinge and the gate.

MAY 21   The White Sox score six runs in the ninth inning before the rally falls short, resulting in a 10–9 loss to the Red Sox at Comiskey Park. The game ended on a bases-loaded grounder by Babe Borton.

The White Sox started the season with a 20–12 record before drifting out of the pennant race.

JUNE 1   The White Sox trade Rollie Zeider and Babe Borton to the Yankees for Hal Chase.

When he arrived in Chicago, Chase had played in the majors for nine seasons, all with the Yankees, and was considered by contemporaries as the best first baseman in baseball. His statistics, however, fail to back this claim either offensively or defensively. At the time of the trade, an article in The Sporting News *said of Chase, "That he can play first as it never was and perhaps never will is a well known truth. That he will is a different matter." The problem wasn't laziness. Chase often threw games in collusion with gamblers in exchange for cash. A complex personality, he was also a moody and disruptive force in the clubhouse. Despite the problems, he had an odd appeal to both baseball management and the fans. Chase was even the manager of the Yankees in 1910 and 1911, and he played 15 years in the majors because of his unquestioned talent. His ability to mask the fact that he was throwing games probably led to this dichotomy. Chase had the innate ability to look like he was hustling at the same time he was trying to lose the game on purpose with tactics like diving after balls just a second too late to make a play. The crowd would cheer Chase for his effort, and the miscue would allow him to collect on his bet. How much Charles Comiskey knew of Chase's gambling proclivities in 1913 isn't known, but the Sox owner was willing to take a flyer on the controversial first baseman to rejuvenate an anemic offense. "He is a grand player, although during the last few seasons he has not played his best owing to his desire to get away from*

Though only 20 years old in his first full season in 1913, catcher Ray Shalk quickly established himself as a team leader, a position he maintained until 1928.

New York, where he has played since 1905," said Comiskey. "A change is what he needs to bring out his best." Chase batted .280 while playing in 158 games for the Sox before jumping to the Federal League in June 1914.

JUNE 11   Reb Russell pitches the White Sox to a 1–0 win over the Yankees in New York. The run scored in the fourth inning on a triple by Ping Bodie and a single by Wally Mattick.

JUNE 22   Jim Scott strikes out 15 batters, including the first six to face him in the first and second inning, but he loses 2–0 to the Browns in the first game of a double-header at Comiskey Park. The Sox won the second tilt by the same 2–0 score behind the pitching of Ed Walsh.

JULY 14   Reb Russell pitches a one-hitter to beat the Red Sox 8–0 at Comiskey Park. The only Boston hit was a single by Harry Hooper in the third inning.

JULY 22   The White Sox score three runs in the ninth inning to defeat the Senators 6–5 at Comiskey Park. The final two runs crossed the plate on a single by Morrie Rath.

JULY 23   Hal Chase makes four errors at first base, three of them in the sixth inning, during a 7–1 loss to the Senators at Comiskey Park.

AUGUST 9   Reb Russell pitches a shutout to edge the Athletics 1–0 in Philadelphia. The lone run of the game scored on a single by rookie outfielder Larry Chappell.

Chappell was an expensive mistake. He was purchased from Milwaukee in the American Association in July for $20,000 and two players. Chappell's ballyhooed debut was delayed a few days because he went to McCloskey, Illinois, without club permission to visit his mother. He played in only 109 big league games and hit just .226 with no homers. Chappell became part of the U.S. Army Medical Corps during World War I and treated soldiers in San Francisco during the great influenza epidemic of 1918, which caused an estimated 400,000 to 500,000 deaths in the United States and 20 million worldwide. Chappell became one of the victims of the epidemic, dying on November 6, 1918, at the age of 28.

AUGUST 20   Jim Scott pitches the White Sox to a 1–0 triumph over the Red Sox at Comiskey Park. Joe Berger drove in the winning run with a sacrifice fly in the sixth inning. Larry Chappell tied a major league record when he was caught stealing three times.

Edd Roush made his major league debut in the game, going hitless in three at-bats. After a nine-game tryout in which he was 1-for-10, Roush was optioned to the Sox farm club in Lincoln, Nebraska. Instead of reporting to Lincoln, Roush jumped to the Federal League. Charles Comiskey was normally an excellent judge of talent, but he had two huge lapses in judgment during the 1913 season. One was buying Larry Chappell (see August 9, 1913). The other was letting Roush out of the White Sox organization. After the Federal League collapsed, Roush joined the Giants and from there was traded to the Reds. With Cincinnati, he won two NL batting titles and finished his big league career in 1931 with a .323 batting average. Roush played against the White Sox in the 1919 World Series and was elected to the Hall of Fame in 1962.

SEPTEMBER 9   Ping Bodie drives in both runs of a 2–0 win over the Athletics in Philadelphia. Bodie homered in the second inning and singled in a run in the fourth, both off Chief Bender.

SEPTEMBER 27   Jim Scott strikes out 14 batters during a 6–2 win over the Browns at Comiskey Park. It was Scott's 20th win of the season.

SEPTEMBER 28   Eddie Cicotte pitches the White Sox to a 1–0 victory over the Indians at Comiskey Park.

                   Cicotte was 18–11 in 1913 with an ERA of 1.58.

OCTOBER 4   Reb Russell collects his 22nd win of the season with a 1–0 decision over the Tigers in the second game of a double-header in Detroit. The contest was called after six innings by darkness. The Tigers won the opener 7–5.

OCTOBER 8   The White Sox win the first game of the Chicago City Series 4–2 over the Cubs at West Side Grounds. The Cubs won games two and three, but the Sox rallied to take game four to even the series.

OCTOBER 12   The White Sox take a three-games-to-two lead in the City Series with an 11-inning, 2–0 win over the Cubs at West Side Grounds. Joe Benz pitched a complete-game shutout. Shano drove in the winning run with a single, and after reaching third on Jack Fournier's base hit, Collins drove him in.

OCTOBER 13   The White Sox win the City Series with a 6–2 win over the Cubs at Comiskey Park.

OCTOBER 18   The world tour of games between the White Sox and Giants begins in Cincinnati. The Giants won 11–2 before a crowd of 5,000.

                   The two clubs made their way west across North America, playing games scheduled for cities in Illinois (Springfield and Peoria), Iowa (Ottumwa and Sioux City), Kansas (Blue Rapids), Missouri (St. Joseph, Kansas City and Joplin), Oklahoma (Tulsa and Muskogee), Texas (Bonham, Dallas, Beaumont, Houston, Marlin, Abilene and El Paso), Arizona (Douglas and Bisbee), California (Los Angeles, San Diego, Oxnard Sacramento, Oakland and San Francisco), Oregon (Medford and Portland) and Washington (Seattle and Tacoma).

NOVEMBER 19   The White Sox and Giants board the R.M.S. Empress of Japan at Victoria, British Columbia, and set sail for Japan.

DECEMBER 6   The White Sox beat the Giants 9–4 at Keio University in Tokyo.

DECEMBER 14   The Giants defeat the White Sox 7–4 in Hong Kong.

DECEMBER 17   The White Sox beat the Giants 2–1 at Manila in the Philippines.

The World Tour

It was one of Charles Comiskey's dreams to make baseball a worldwide sport. To set his plan in motion, the White Sox and the New York Giants, led by John McGraw, played all around the globe between the 1913 and 1914 seasons. It was the second such venture. From October 1888 through March 1889, the Chicago Cubs (then known as the White Stockings) played a team of All-Stars from clubs in the National League and American Association in places such as Hawaii, New Zealand, Australia, Ceylon, India, Egypt, Italy, France and England.

The White Sox-Giants tour followed a similar path, with games taking place on every inhabited continent except South America. It started on October 18, 1913, in Cincinnati. From that date, the tourists were scheduled to play every day while traveling through cities in Illinois, Iowa, Missouri, Kansas, Oklahoma, Texas, Arizona, California, Oregon and Washington. The two clubs left the United States on November 19, crossing into Canada to sail across the Pacific Ocean for Japan from Victoria, British Columbia. By then, the Giants, and White Sox's rosters were fortified by players from other clubs due to the travel schedule and because a few players on each team refused to participate. Other AL players who joined the White Sox for the tour included Tris Speaker from the Red Sox, Sam Crawford from the Tigers and Germany Schaefer of the Senators.

The first games on foreign soil were played in Tokyo, where enthusiastic crowds greeted the players, particularly Jim Thorpe of the Giants, who enjoyed international acclaim for winning both the decathlon and the pentathlon at the 1912 Olympics. Giants manager John McGraw was also one of the most famous men in baseball and led the Giants to NL pennants in 1911, 1912 and 1913. Baseball was thriving in Japan and had been for several years, particularly as a college sport. Keio University's team had made a tour of the United States two years previously.

The tour went west from Japan to China, where a game was played at Hong Kong. Next stop was Manila for two games, then a long hop to Australia, where the cities of Brisbane, Sydney and Melbourne were visited. From Australia, the clubs went to Ceylon. Then came Cairo, Egypt, where the White Sox and Giants appeared before royalty for the first time as Abbas Hilmi II, Khedive of Egypt, watched a game with his 43 wives. The next day, the tourists visited the Pyramids.

From Egypt, the group went to Rome and had an audience with Pope St. Pius X. In France, a contest was played in Nice, but rained canceled four games in Paris. On February 26, 1914, the White Sox beat the Giants 5–4 in 11 innings at the Chelsea Football Grounds before a crowd of 30,000 that included King George V. Tom Daly won the game with a home run. The teams left Liverpool aboard the *Luisitania* on February 28 and reached American soil in New York to a raucous welcome on March 7, 110 days after that first game in Cincinnati.

The world tour was conducted just in time. By August 1914, Europe was embroiled in a World War, with England and France pitted against Germany. The *Luisitania*, which brought the White Sox and Giants across the Atlantic, was sunk by a German submarine on May 7, 1915, costing over 1,200 their lives, including 128 Americans. The United States became involved militarily on the side of England and France in April 1917. The war ended in November 1918 with a German defeat.

1914

Season in a Sentence

Exhausted from their off-season world tour, the White Sox limp to sixth place.

Finish • Won • Lost • Pct • GB

Sixth (tie) 70   84   .455 30.5

Manager

Nixey Callahan

Stats

Stats	WS	AL	Rank
Batting Avg:	.239	.248	8
On-Base Pct:	.302	.319	8
Slugging Pct:	.311	.323	8
Home Runs:	19		3
Stolen Bases:	167		7 (tie)
ERA:	2.48	2.73	2
Fielding Avg:	.955	.959	6
Runs Scored:	487		8
Runs Allowed:	560		5

Starting Lineup

Ray Schalk, c
Jack Fournier, 1b
Lena Blackburne, 2b
Jim Breton, 3b
Buck Weaver, ss
Ray Demmitt, lf
Ping Bodie, cf
Shano Collins, rf-cf
Hal Chase, 1b
Scotty Alcock, 3b
Joe Berger, ss-2b

Pitchers

Joe Benz, sp
Jim Scott, sp
Eddie Cicotte, sp-rp
Reb Russell, sp-rp
Red Faber, rp-sp
Mellie Wolfgang, rp-sp

Attendance

469,290 (second in AL)

Club Leaders

Batting Avg:	Jack Fournier	.311
On-Base Pct:	Jack Fournier	.368
Slugging Pct:	Jack Fournier	.443
Home Runs:	Jack Fournier	6
RBIs:	Shano Collins	65
Runs:	Buck Weaver	64
Stolen Bases:	Shano Collins	30
Wins:	Joe Benz	14
	Jim Scott	14
Strikeouts:	Joe Benz	142
ERA:	Eddie Cicotte	2.04
Saves:	Red Faber	4

JANUARY 1   The Giants down the White Sox 2–1 in Brisbane, Australia.

The two clubs also played two games each in Sydney and Melbourne on the Australian continent.

JANUARY 23   The White Sox beat the Giants 4–1 in Colombo, Ceylon.

FEBRUARY 1   The White Sox and Giants play to a 3–3 tie at Cairo, Egypt in a contest called after 10 innings by darkness.

FEBRUARY 2   The world tourists visit the Pyramids. Photographs were taken of White Sox and Giants players in front of the Great Sphinx and a mock game was filmed by motion picture cameras with the Pyramids as a backdrop. Later that afternoon, the Giants defeated the White Sox 6–3 in Cairo.

FEBRUARY 11   The White Sox and Giants meet Pope St. Pius X at the Vatican.

There were three games scheduled in Rome from February 11 through February 13, but each was rained out.

FEBRUARY 15   Wearing their baseball uniforms, the White Sox and Giants mingle with the crowds during Mardi Gras at Nice, France.

                There were four games scheduled for Paris from February 18 through February 21, but each was rained out.

FEBRUARY 26   The White Sox and Giants play before King George V at the Chelsea Football Grounds in London with the Sox winning 5–4 in 11 innings on a homer by Tom Daly.

                At the time, Daly had played in only one big-league game. He was born a British subject in St. John's, New Brunswick, Canada. Daly played 244 major league games over eight seasons with the White Sox, Indians and Cubs, and he never hit a single regular-season homer as a major leaguer.

FEBRUARY 28   The White Sox and Giants board the *Luisitania* at Liverpool, England, for a return to the United States.

MARCH 7   The White Sox and Giants arrive back in the States when the *Luisitania* docks in New York.

APRIL 14   The White Sox open the season with a 5–2 victory over the Indians at Comiskey Park. Trailing 2–0, the Sox scored three runs in the seventh inning and two in the eighth. Jim Scott was the winning pitcher.

                There were three major league clubs in Chicago in 1914 and 1915. The new franchise in the Windy City was a part of the Federal League, which declared itself a major circuit during the 1913–14 off-season and began raiding the rosters of the American and National Leagues. The Chicago entry was owned by popular and wealthy restaurateur Charles Weeghman and was nicknamed the Whales. The franchise gained immediate credibility by signing former Cubs star Joe Tinker as player-manager and by building a new ballpark at the corner of Clark and Addison called Weeghman Park. At first, Charles Comiskey managed to sign all of his key players despite the offers of higher salaries, but he lost Harry Lord and Hal Chase to the Federals during the 1914 season. The Federal League folded after the 1915 season. Weeghman bought the Cubs in December 1915 and moved the club from West Side Grounds into Weeghman Park. William Wrigley, Jr. bought out Weeghman a few years later, and renamed the park Wrigley Field.

APRIL 16   Joe Benz pitches the White Sox to a 1–0 win over the Indians at Comiskey Park. Shano Collins drove in the lone run of the contest with a double in the seventh inning.

APRIL 17   The White Sox run their season record to 4–0 with a 6–5 victory over the Indians at Comiskey Park. The game ended on an inside-the-park homer by Shano Collins. Red Faber made his major league debut and allowed three runs and four hits in 4⅓ innings as the starting pitcher.

APRIL 18   The White Sox are 5–0 in 1914 after defeating the Browns 5–3 at Comiskey Park.

                The fast start wasn't indicative of the way the season would progress. By early June, the club's record dipped to 18–23. The Sox rebounded and were just

2½ games behind the first-place Athletics in early July, then collapsed again, ending the year in a tie for sixth place.

APRIL 23   The Federal League Chicago Whales play their first regular-season game at Weeghman Park (present-day Wrigley Field). Chicago defeated Kansas City 9–1.

APRIL 30   The White Sox lose a strange 5–4 decision to the Tigers in Detroit. The only Chicago hit during the contest was a double by Ray Demmitt leading off the first inning. In the ninth, the Sox scored three runs by drawing six walks from three Tiger pitchers.

MAY 10   Ed Cicotte beats the Tigers 1–0 at Comiskey Park. Shano Collins drove in the lone run with a single in the seventh inning.

MAY 13   Lena Blackburne steals four bases during a 9–2 win over the Senators in Washington.

             On the same day, starting third baseman Harry Lord unexpectedly left the club and went to his home in Maine. He said that he was tired of baseball. With the exception of 97 games as player-manager with Buffalo in the Federal League in 1915, Lord never appeared in another big league game.

MAY 14   Jim Scott holds the Senators hitless through nine innings in Washington, but he loses 1–0 when he allows two hits in the 10th. In the last of the 10th, Chick Gandil led off with a single to center and scored on a double by Howard Shanks. Scott walked two and struck out two. Doc Ayers pitched a complete game for Washington and surrendered only three hits.

MAY 19   Eddie Cicotte pitches a one-hitter to defeat the Athletics 3–0 at Shibe Park. The only Philadelphia hit was a single by Stuffy McInnis with one out in the eighth inning.

MAY 25   Jim Scott shuts out the Yankees for a 1–0 win in New York. In the seventh inning, Buck Weaver doubled, took third on an infield out, and scored on a sacrifice fly by Shano Collins.

MAY 31   Joe Benz pitches a no-hitter, defeating the Indians 6–1 at Comiskey Park. He walked two and struck out three. The Cleveland run scored in the fourth inning on two errors and an infield out. In the ninth, Benz walked Ray Wood with one out. The game ended on a double play struck by Rivington Bisland that went from shortstop Buck Weaver to second baseman Joe Berger to first baseman Hal Chase.

JUNE 4   Jim Scott faces the minimum 27 batters in pitching a one-hitter and a 2–0 victory over the Indians at Comiskey Park. The only base runners were Joe Jackson on a second-inning single and Nemo Leibold on a walk. Both were erased on stolen base attempts.

JUNE 6   Joe Benz pitches a two-hitter in a contest against the Yankees at Comiskey Park that ends in a 1–1 tie.

JUNE 8   Reb Russell of the White Sox and Ray Fisher of the Yankees match two-hitters in a 1–0 Chicago win at Comiskey Park. The first hit of the game for either team was a bunt single by New York's Doc Cook in the seventh inning that Russell was slow in fielding. Jack Truesdale collected the second hit off Russell in the ninth.

Both Chicago base hits produced the lone run of the contest. In the eighth, Ping Bodie tripled and Ray Schalk singled Bodie home.

JUNE 10   Joe Benz is two outs from his second no-hitter in less than two weeks before settling for a one-hitter and a 2–0 defeat of the Senators at Comiskey Park. With one out in the ninth inning, Eddie Ainsmith hit a slow grounder toward shortstop Buck Weaver. Third baseman Scotty Alcock cut in front of Weaver, bobbled the ball momentarily and couldn't make the throw to first. The official scorer ruled the play a hit in a controversial decision.

In three consecutive starts from May 31 through June 10, Benz allowed two runs and three hits in 26 innings. Despite the streak, he had a record of 15–19 in 1914.

JUNE 17   Red Faber pitches a one-hitter and defeats the Athletics 5–0 at Comiskey Park. Faber was three outs from a no-hitter when Jack Lapp collected an infield single on a grounder to Lena Blackburne at second base. Blackburne would have probably thrown Lapp out if he had charged the ball, but Blackburne backed up a few steps, allowing Lapp to reach safely.

Russell Aubrey (Lena) Blackburne made an unusual contribution to baseball. He discovered and marketed the special mud from the Delaware River that is used by umpires to rub the gloss off of new baseballs.

JUNE 21   Hal Chase leaves the White Sox to join the Buffalo club in the Federal League.

JULY 3   Five days after Archduke Ferdinand of Austria is assassinated, an event which precipitates the start of World War I in August, Red Faber pitches 13 innings, allowing five hits in beating the Browns 3–2 at Comiskey Park. Joe Berger's single drove in the winning run.

Urban (Red) Faber pitched his entire big-league career with the White Sox. Although 25 when he made his big-league debut, Faber lasted 20 seasons in the majors from 1914 through 1933 and posted a 254–213 record. He is second in career wins with the Sox, ranking behind only Ted Lyons, who won 260 times with the club. Faber ranks first in games pitched (669), second in games started (483), second in complete games (274), second in innings pitched (4,087^{2}/$_{3}$), third in strikeouts (1,471) and fourth in shutouts (30). He was purchased by the White Sox from Des Moines in the Western League for $3,500. Faber was invited on the 1913–14 world tour, but he was lent to the Giants when John McGraw's club was short of pitching. Faber was at his peak from 1920 through 1922 when he had a record of 69–45 and led the AL in ERA in 1921 and 1922. He was elected to the Hall of Fame in 1964.

JULY 5   With the White Sox trailing the Indians 3–1 in the seventh inning at Comiskey Park, Ray Demmitt hits a grand slam off Rip Hagerman. The Sox added an insurance run in the eighth and won 6–3.

JULY 28   Joe Benz pitches a 13-inning shutout, allowing six runs to beat the Yankees 1–0 at Comiskey Park. New York's Jack Warhop surrendered just four hits, two of them in the 13th, while pitching a complete game. Ray Demmitt led off the 13th with a bunt single. He went to third on a bunt by Shano Collins that Warhop threw past first base. Jack Fournier drove in the winning run with a single.

AUGUST 11   The White Sox defeat the Indians in a double-header at Comiskey Park with a pair of 2–0 victories. Mellie Wolfgang won the opener and Eddie Cicotte took the nightcap.

AUGUST 29   Two weeks after the opening of the Panama Canal, Mellie Wolfgang ties a major league record for most assists in a nine-inning game by a pitcher with 11 during a 2–1 win over the Senators in Washington.

AUGUST 31   Jack Fournier hits two inside-the-park homers off Walter Johnson during a 10-inning, 4–3 victory at Griffith Stadium. Fournier broke a 2–2 tie with a homer in the eighth. After Washington knotted the score again in the ninth, Fournier struck a game-winning home run in the tenth.

SEPTEMBER 1   The White Sox win a 15-inning marathon 5–4 over the Senators in Washington. Jim Scott pitched a complete game after allowing three runs in the ninth inning to tie the score 4–4. Shano Collins drove in the winning run with a single.

SEPTEMBER 18   The White Sox score all seven of their runs in the fifth inning of a 7–5 victory over the Yankees at Comiskey Park.

OCTOBER 7   In the first game of the Chicago City Series, the Cubs defeat the White Sox 4–2 at Comiskey Park.

The Sox lost three of the first four games of the series before winning the final three.

OCTOBER 15   The White Sox take the City Series four games to three over the Cubs with a 3–2 victory at Comiskey Park.

DECEMBER 8   The White Sox purchase Eddie Collins from the Athletics for $50,000.

Charles Comiskey purchased one of the greatest second basemen in major league history in Eddie Collins. At the time he arrived in Chicago, Collins had played in 1,013 major league games over nine seasons, carried a career batting average of .338 and had just won the Chalmers Award as the American League's most valuable player of 1914. He was also a major base-stealing threat and led the AL in runs in 1912, 1913 and 1914. Collins was a member of four AL pennant winners in Philadelphia, three of which went on to win the World Series. Despite being a success in the standings, the Athletics struggled financially. Attendance dropped dramatically in 1914 as Philly fans took the success for granted. Meanwhile, the Federal League was offering huge contracts to AL and NL stars and club owner and manager Connie Mack couldn't compete financially. He decided to sell his star players who hadn't already jumped to the Federals to other AL clubs. The White Sox had problems for years finding a competent second baseman and Comiskey put up the cash to buy Collins's contract. It was a great move. Collins played for the Sox from 1915 through 1926, managing the club during those last two seasons. Among White Sox players, Collins ranks first in stolen bases (368), second in batting average (.331), second in on-base percentage (.426), third in triples (102), fourth in runs (1,065), fourth in hits

(2,007), fifth in RBIs (804), fifth in doubles (266), fifth in at-bats (6,085) and sixth in games (1,670). He ended his career with 1,821 runs, 3,315 hits, 745 stolen bases and a .333 batting average. The only player to exceed those figures in all four categories is Ty Cobb, which goes a long way toward explaining why Collins has never received the recognition he deserves from baseball historians. Collins played at the same time in the same league as Cobb. Eddie never won a batting title, but he finished second to Cobb in 1909, 1914 and 1915.

DECEMBER 17 The White Sox hire 35-year-old Clarence (Pants) Rowland as manager, replacing Nixey Callahan.

The announcement by Charles Comiskey to hire Rowland was a complete surprise. Rowland had never played or managed in the major leagues prior to his appointment as manager of the Sox. As a result of his lack of big-league experience, Rowland never received the respect he deserved, even after taking a team that finished sixth in 1914 to third in 1915, second in 1916 and a world championship in 1917. Rowland was fired after a sixth-place finish in 1918. Callahan later managed the Pirates in 1916 and 1917.

1915   Sox

Season in a Sentence

With the addition of Eddie Collins and Joe Jackson, the White Sox win 93 games and leap to third place under new manager Pants Rowland.

Finish • Won • Lost • Pct • GB

Third   93   61   .604   9.5

Manager

Pants Rowland

Stats

	WS	AL	Rank
Batting Avg:	.258	.248	3
On-Base Pct:	.345	.325	2
Slugging Pct:	.348	.326	2
Home Runs:	25		2
Stolen Bases:	233		2
ERA:	2.43	2.93	3
Fielding Avg:	.965	.959	2
Runs Scored:	717		2
Runs Allowed:	509		3

Starting Lineup

Ray Schalk, c
Shano Collins, 1b-rf
Eddie Collins, 2b
Lena Blackburne, 3b
Buck Weaver, ss
Jack Fournier, lf-1b
Happy Felsch, cf
Eddie Murphy, rf
Braggo Roth, 3b-lf
Joe Jackson, cf-lf
Bunny Brief, 1b

Pitchers

Red Faber, sp-rp
Jim Scott, rp
Joe Benz, sp
Eddie Cicotte, sp-rp
Reb Russell, sp-rp

Attendance

539,461 (second in AL)

Club Leaders

Batting Avg:	Eddie Collins	.332
On-Base Pct:	Eddie Collins	.460
Slugging Pct:	Jack Fournier	.491
Home Runs:	Jack Fournier	5
RBIs:	Shano Collins	85
Runs:	Eddie Collins	118
Stolen Bases:	Eddie Collins	46
Wins:	Red Faber	24
	Jim Scott	24
Strikeouts:	Red Faber	182
ERA:	Jim Scott	2.03
Saves:	Eddie Cicotte	3

APRIL 14   The White Sox celebrate Opening Day by defeating the Browns 7–6 in 13 innings at Sportsman's Park. With the score 4–4 in the 13th, Bunny Brief and Ray Schalk both singled and scored on Jack Fournier's triple. Fournier crossed the plate on an infield out. The Sox survived a two-run St. Louis rally in the bottom of the inning. Hi Jasper was the winning pitcher despite allowing three runs in four innings. Eddie Collins was two-for-five in his debut with the White Sox.

It was also the White Sox's debut for Brief, who homered earlier in the game. It was the first ever Opening Day home run for a Sox batter. He was born Anthony John Grzeszkowski before settling on a briefer name at the start of his baseball career. Brief's brief stay with the White Sox lasted 48 games. During a long minor league career, Brief hit 340 home runs.

APRIL 15   The White Sox score seven runs in the first inning during a 16–0 pasting of the Browns in St. Louis. Red Faber pitched the shutout and collected four hits, including a double, in five at-bats.

APRIL 23   In the home opener at Comiskey Park, the White Sox win 4–3 over the Browns.

Harry Grabiner was named team secretary and vice president of the White Sox in 1915, taking a role analogous to a modern day general manager. He was first employed by Charles Comiskey in 1905. Harry was 14 years old and was given a job sweeping out the grandstand and selling scorecards. Comiskey recognized his hard work, and 10 years later, still only in his mid-20s, Grabiner was granted the responsibility of supervising the team's financial affairs and negotiating contracts. By the 1920s, with Comiskey advancing in years and heart-broken over the news that eight of his players conspired to fix the 1919 World Series, Grabiner practically ran the club. That role increased after Comiskey died in 1931 and his son and wife owned the White Sox. Grabiner continued as vice-president until 1945.

APRIL 26   The White Sox pummel the Indians 12–1 at Comiskey Park.

MAY 5   During the second inning of a 1–0 loss to the Indians in Cleveland, all four White Sox batters reach base on a walk, two singles and an error, but none scored. The four batters were Jack Fournier, Shano Collins, Buck Weaver and Bunny Brief. Two were thrown out at third base and one at home.

MAY 12   Five days after the sinking of the luxury liner *Luisitania,* resulting in the death of over 1,200, including 128 Americans, Red Faber uses only 67 pitches in beating the Senators 4–1 at Comiskey Park. Faber faced 32 batters, allowed three hits, walked one, and struck out four.

Faber was 24–14 in 1915 with an ERA of 2.55 in 299²/₃ innings. He led the AL in games pitched with 50, making 32 starts and 18 relief appearances.

MAY 17   Jim Scott pitches a one-hitter in beating the Athletics 6–2 at Comiskey Park. The only Philadelphia hit was an infield single by Nap Lajoie. Shortstop Buck Weaver knocked the ball down but couldn't make the play at first. The victory started a nine-game winning streak.

Scott had a 24–11 record in 1915 and a 2.03 ERA. He pitched seven shutouts.

MAY 21   The White Sox edge the Red Sox 3–2 in a 17-inning marathon at Comiskey Park. In the 17th, Buck Weaver doubled, Finners Quinlan was hit by a pitch and Ray Schalk beat out a bunt to load the bases. Tom Daly batted for Red Faber and delivered a game-winning single. Faber pitched all 17 innings and didn't allow a run after the seventh.

Weaver hit .268 and scored 83 runs in 1915.

MAY 31   Reb Russell starts both games of a double-header against the Tigers at Comiskey Park. In the opener, Russell lasted only 1²/₃ innings and had a no decision in a 4–3 loss. In the second tilt, Russell pitched a complete game for a 3–1 decision.

JUNE 4   Jim Scott hurls the White Sox to a 2–0 victory over the Red Sox in Boston. In the first inning, Tris Speaker was struck in the head by a Scott pitch. By courtesy of Chicago manager Pants Rowland, Bill Rodgers ran for Speaker, and Speaker was allowed to resume his place in center field.

JUNE 9   Eddie Cicotte pitches a two-hitter, leading the White Sox to a 13–0 thrashing of the Yankees at the Polo Grounds in New York. The only hits off Cicotte were singles by Doc Cook and Luke Boone.

JUNE 11   The White Sox lead 8–1 in the fifth inning but blow the advantage and lose 10–9 to the Yankees in New York. Holding what appeared to be a safe lead, Pants Rowland took center fielder Happy Felsch and catcher Ray Schalk out of the game for a rest only to have the Yanks mount a comeback. The game had a lively finish when Braggo Roth tripled with one out, but was doubled at the plate on a throw from center fielder Hugh High after catching Tom Daly's fly ball. The Chicago players were incensed at umpire Silk O'Loughlin's decision on the play, gathered around the arbiter and jeered him all the way to the dressing room.

Roth hit seven home runs in 1915, which was good enough to lead the American League in the category during the dead ball era. He hit three of them with the White Sox and four as an Indian after an August 20 trade.

JUNE 17   In his first game in Philadelphia since being sold by the Athletics to the White Sox, Eddie Collins collects two doubles and a single in three at-bats and steals two bases in a 3–0 Chicago victory.

In his first season with the White Sox, Collins hit .332, scored 118 runs, stole 46 bases and walked a league-leading 119 times. Collins was runner-up to Ty Cobb in the AL batting race. Jack Fournier was the third-leading batter with an average of .322.

JUNE 18   Happy Felsch hits a grand slam off Joe Bush in the fourth inning of an 11–4 win over the Athletics in Philadelphia. On the negative side, the Sox tied a major league record when six players were caught stealing. The club had five successful stolen base attempts.

One of 12 children born to a poor German immigrant, Oscar (Happy) Felsch was a 20-year-old rookie when he won the White Sox starting center field job in 1915. Growing up in Milwaukee, Felsch quit school in the sixth grade to take a $10-a-week factory job. He remained a regular with the Sox until September 1920 when he was one of the eight players accused of fixing the 1919 World Series and was given a lifetime suspension.

JUNE 24   On the day the steamer *Eastland* explodes and capsizes in the Chicago River, killing 811 people, the White Sox outlast the Indians 5–4 in 19 innings in Cleveland. The Indians scored two runs in the eighth to take a 4–3 lead, but the Sox deadlocked the contest in the ninth. There was no more scoring until the 19th, when Buck Weaver singled and Eddie Collins doubled with two out. Red Faber pitched 11 innings of relief and allowed no runs and three hits.

JUNE 28   In the third inning, Happy Felsch hits a bases-loaded triple, then scores on a Buck Weaver single to account for all of the Chicago runs in a 4–2 victory over the Browns at Comiskey Park.

The peak of the 1915 season occurred on July 1 when the Sox were 46–21 and held a six-game lead over the second-place Tigers in the AL pennant race.

JULY 6   The White Sox wallop the Browns 12–2 in St. Louis.

JULY 7   The White Sox purchase Nemo Leibold from the Indians.

Harry (Nemo) Leibold played for the White Sox from 1915 through 1920, a period in which he was the starting outfielder on two World Series teams. Only five-foot-seven, he was nicknamed for the comic strip character Little Nemo.

JULY 12   Courtesy may be a fine virtue, but it costs the White Sox a victory in a game against the Senators at Comiskey Park. In the third inning, Washington first baseman Chick Gandil wrenched his ankle swinging at a ball, and Pants Rowland permitted Rip Williams to finish Gandil's turn at-bat and allowed Chick to remain in the game. Gandil proceeded to drive in the go-ahead run in the fifth inning, leading to a 5–3 Senators win over the Sox.

JULY 14   Dilatory tactics in an attempt to have the game called on account of rain cost the Athletics a victory against the White Sox at Comiskey Park. The contest started five minutes early to try and beat the rain. The Sox were leading by two runs in the fourth inning when the roar of thunder inspired the A's to delay the contest until the legal number of innings could be played. Philadelphia pitcher Joe Bush didn't put the ball anywhere near the plate, but the Sox swung at the errant tosses in order to speed play. Red Faber was hit by a pitch and circled the bases without any attempt by the A's to retire him. Faber was credited with steals of second, third and home. After being threatened by the umpires with forfeit, the Athletics began to play on the level. The threatening clouds cleared in time to allow nine innings to be played, and the Sox went on to win 6–4.

JULY 15   The White Sox purchase Eddie Murphy from the Athletics.

JULY 18   The White Sox are knocked out of first place with a 6–2 loss to the Red Sox at
               Comiskey Park.

               *The White Sox spent 59 days in first place in May, June and July. Chicago was
               out of the pennant race by the end of August.*

JULY 28   Jim Scott not only pitches a shutout, but he drives in the lone run of a 1–0 victory
               over the Red Sox in Boston with a single in the third inning.

AUGUST 20   The White Sox send Braggo Roth, Larry Chappell, Ed Klepfer and $31,500 to the
               Indians for Joe Jackson.

               *The major league career of Joe Jackson ended with a lifetime suspension for
               his role in fixing the 1919 World Series, but regardless of the tragic outcome,
               this was one of the best trades in White Sox history. Jackson was available
               because of the financial problems of Cleveland owner Charles Somers. The deal
               cost Charles Comiskey $31,500 and three journeyman players. At the time he
               arrived in Chicago, Jackson was 26 years old and had a career batting average
               of .371 in 2,544 at-bats. In six seasons with the Sox, Jackson batted .339, the
               best of any player in club history with at least 2,000 plate appearances. Jackson
               also ranks third in on-base percentage (.407) and fourth in slugging percentage
               (.498).*

AUGUST 21   The White Sox win 1–0 in 11 innings against the Yankees in the first game of a
               double-header at Comiskey Park. Jim Scott pitched a complete game. The winning
               run scored when Eddie Murphy walked, reached third on a single by Shano Collins,
               and scored on a squeeze bunt by Eddie Collins. It was also the first game played
               by Joe Jackson as a member of the White Sox. He was 1-for-3. New York won the
               second contest 3–2.

AUGUST 23   The White Sox sweep the Yankees in a double-header at Comiskey Park, taking the
               first game 5–0 and the second 4–3 in 11 innings.

AUGUST 24   The White Sox score two runs in the bottom of the 13th inning to edge the Senators
               6–5 at Comiskey Park. After the Sox loaded the bases with two out, Eddie Murphy
               walked and Eddie Collins singled to drive in the tying and winning runs.

AUGUST 25   The White Sox played their third consecutive extra-inning game, losing 7–4 to the
               Senators in 14 innings at Comiskey Park.

AUGUST 26   The White Sox play their fourth straight extra-inning contest, losing 2–1 to the
               Senators in 13 innings at Comiskey Park. The game was scoreless through 11 innings
               in a duel between Walter Johnson and Reb Russell. Both teams scored in the 12th.
               In the 13th, Johnson hit a long foul to left field with a runner on third and one out.
               Chicago left fielder Nemo Leibold should have let the ball drop foul, but he caught it
               instead, allowing the runner to cross the plate with the winning run.

               *The White Sox played eight games and 89 innings in six days from August 21
               through August 26.*

AUGUST 29   The White Sox play the shortest game in club history, polishing off the Athletics 5–0 in 68 minutes at Comiskey Park. Jim Scott was the Chicago pitcher. He faced 30 batters, allowed three hits, walked one, and struck out six.

SEPTEMBER 3   A rule book would have come in handy during a 6–5 loss to the Indians in the second game of a double-header at Comiskey Park. In the Cleveland half of the fourth inning, two men had scored and Elmer Smith was the runner on first with one out. Jay Kirke swung at a wild pitch for the third strike, Smith took second and Kirke took first. Under the rules, Kirke should have been called out because first base was already occupied, but the umpires failed to notice. Two more wild pitches and an error enabled Smith and Kirke to score. The White Sox filed a protest, and American League President Ban Johnson ordered that the entire contest be replayed.

SEPTEMBER 6   Eddie Murphy collects seven hits in 10 at-bats during a 7–1 and 8–0 sweep of the Indians at Comiskey Park.

SEPTEMBER 8   The White Sox overcome an 8–0 deficit to defeat the Tigers 10–9 at Comiskey Park. Detroit scored four runs in the first inning and four more in the second before the Sox tied the contest with a run in the second, two in the fourth and five in the seventh. After the Tigers regained the lead with a tally in the eighth, the White Sox won it with two in the ninth.

SEPTEMBER 11   Red Faber pitches a one-hitter to beat the Red Sox 3–1 at Fenway Park. The lone Boston hit was a single by Tris Speaker.

Manager Pants Rowland seems delighted to have the great Eddie Collins join the Sox in 1915.

SEPTEMBER 29   The White Sox rout the Indians 13–6 in Cleveland.

OCTOBER 3   On the final day of the season, the White Sox record their 11th win in a row with a 6–2 decision over the Browns at Comiskey Park.

OCTOBER 6   The White Sox rally from a 4–0 deficit to defeat the Cubs 9–5 in game one of the 1915 Chicago City Series. The contest attracted 19,513 to Comiskey Park on a Wednesday afternoon.

OCTOBER 9   Shano Collins hits an inside-the-park grand slam off Jimmy Lavender in the third inning of a 5–0 win over the Cubs in game four of the City Series, played at White Sox Grounds.

OCTOBER 10   The White Sox conclude the City Series with an 11–3 win over the Cubs before 32,666 at Comiskey Park. The Sox won the series four games to one.

1916   Sox

Season in a Sentence

After falling below the .500 mark in late June, the White Sox put on a late surge and nearly capture the American League pennant.

Finish • Won • Lost • Pct • GB

Second   89   65   .578   2.0

Manager

Pants Rowland

Stats

Stats	WS	AL	Rank
Batting Avg:	.251	.248	2
On-Base Pct:	.319	.321	5
Slugging Pct:	.339	.324	2
Home Runs:	17		3 (tie)
Stolen Bases:	197		2
ERA:	2.36	2.82	1
Fielding Avg:	.968	.965	2
Runs Scored:	601		3
Runs Allowed:	497		2

Starting Lineup

Ray Schalk, c
Jack Fournier, 1b
Eddie Collins, 2b
Buck Weaver, 3b-ss
Zeb Terry, ss
Joe Jackson, lf
Happy Felsch, cf
Shano Collins, rf
Jack Ness, 1b
Fred McMullin, 3b

Pitchers

Red Faber, sp-rp
Lefty Williams, sp
Joe Benz, sp-rp
Jim Scott, sp-rp
Mellie Wolfgang, sp-rp
Reb Russell, rp-sp
Eddie Cicotte, rp-sp
Dave Danforth, rp

Attendance

679,923 (first in AL)

Club Leaders

Batting Avg:	Joe Jackson	.341
On-Base Pct:	Eddie Collins	.405
Slugging Pct:	Joe Jackson	.495
Home Runs:	Happy Felsch	7
RBIs:	Joe Jackson	78
Runs:	Joe Jackson	91
Stolen Bases:	Eddie Collins	40
Wins:	Reb Russell	18
Strikeouts:	Lefty Williams	138
ERA:	Eddie Cicotte	1.78
Saves:	Eddie Cicotte	5

APRIL 12   The White Sox lose the season opener 4–0 to the Tigers before a crowd of about 30,000 at Comiskey Park. Harry Coveleski pitched the three-hit shutout for Detroit.

It was a costly defeat for Sox owner Charles Comiskey. The fresh green paint on many of the seats was not yet dry, and Comiskey had to pay cleaning bills for thousands of fans.

APRIL 15   The White Sox score seven runs in the first inning and defeat the Tigers 9–4 at Comiskey Park.

APRIL 16   Ray Shook starts and completes one of the shortest careers in big league history during a 6–5 loss to the Browns at Comiskey Park. In his lone appearance in the majors, Shook was in the game only as a pinch-runner for Jack Lapp in the seventh inning.

MAY 2   The White Sox score three runs in the ninth inning to defeat the Browns 5–4 in St. Louis. Zeb Terry delivered a two-out, two-run, walk-off, pinch-hit double to account for the tying and winning runs. Five Sox pitchers (Red Faber, Eddie Cicotte, Dave Danforth, Mellie Wolfgang and Lefty Williams) combined on a three-hitter.

Despite weighing only 128 pounds, Terry played seven seasons in the majors with the White Sox, Braves, Pirates and Cubs.

MAY 5   The Indians score three runs in the sixth inning to beat the White Sox 3–2 at Comiskey Park. Jack Graney led off the sixth carrying a bat that was flat on one side. Catcher Ray Schalk pointed out the rules infraction to the home plate umpire, and Graney went back to the bench for a new bat. He then singled to spark the game-winning rally.

MAY 20   The White Sox lambaste the Athletics 11–0 in Philadelphia.

MAY 28   The White Sox win a double-header against the Indians at Comiskey Park with a pair of 2–0 decisions. Jim Scott and Red Faber hurled the shutouts.

Faber was 17–9 with a 2.02 ERA in 1916.

JUNE 1   Joe Jackson collects three hits, including a triple, in three at-bats during a 6–3 win over the Tigers in Detroit. The perfect day extended his streak of hits in consecutive at-bats to nine over three games, all off Tigers pitching. Among the nine hits by the hot-hitting Jackson were four doubles and two triples.

Jackson led the AL in triples (21) and total bases (293) in 1916, in addition to batting .341 with 202 hits and 40 doubles. The triples total is also a Sox record for a single season.

JUNE 21   The White Sox lose 11–1 and 2–1 in a double-header against the Browns in St. Louis.

The defeats dropped the White Sox's record to 26–28 amid rumors that the firing of manager Pants Rowland was imminent. The club was in sixth place and five games out of first. Despite the slow start, the Sox leaped into contention and were in first place by August 3.

June 22   Reb Russell pitches a two-hitter to defeat the Browns 2–0 at Sportsman's Park.
           The only St. Louis hits were a double by Jimmy Austin and a single by Doc Lavan.

           Russell had an 18–11 record and a 2.42 earned run average in 1916.

July 2   The White Sox outlast the Tigers 1–0 in 12 innings at Comiskey Park. Reb Russell
           pitched a four-hit, complete game shutout.

           *In the third inning, Ty Cobb was called out on strikes. Cobb heaved his bat
           into the stands after directing a few choice remarks at umpire Dick Nallin.
           Fortunately, the bat struck no one because fans had recently vacated the area
           after a light rain started falling.*

July 4   In the second game of a double-header against the Browns at Comiskey Park, the
           White Sox score two runs in the ninth inning and one in the 13th to win 7–6. The
           winning run scored on a single by Buck Weaver, a stolen base and a single by Eddie
           Collins. St. Louis won the first game.

           Collins hit .308 in 1916. He had 17 triples, but only 14 doubles.

July 10   The White Sox win a double-header against the Red Sox in Boston with a pair of
           shutouts. Lefty Williams won the opener 4–0 and Red Faber the nightcap 3–0.

           *Claude (Lefty) Williams was 26 when he reached the majors in 1916. He
           emerged as a star during the 1919 pennant drive with a record of 23–11, then
           lost three games in the World Series. Williams was 22–14 late in the 1920 season
           when it was revealed that he was one of the eight White Sox who conspired to
           throw the Series.*

July 15   The White Sox sweep the Athletics 4–1 and 1–0 in Philadelphia. Joe Benz pitched the
           second-game shutout. Buck Weaver drove in the lone run with a triple in the third
           inning.

July 23   The White Sox collect 20 hits and edge the Tigers 12–9 in Detroit. First baseman
           Jack Ness collected five of the hits, including two doubles and a triple, in six at-bats.
           The two clubs arrived an hour late after a long train trip from the East, then battled
           nearly three hours in the broiling sun. The game ended in turmoil. With two on and
           two out in the bottom of the ninth, Donie Bush hit a high foul that Sox catcher Ray
           Schalk caught, then dropped when he crashed into the stands. Umpire Dick Nallin
           ruled that Schalk held the ball long enough for the putout, incurring the wrath of the
           Tigers and their fans. Nallin had to leave with a police escort after a few spectators
           tossed bottles in his direction.

July 25   The White Sox defeat the Yankees 13–8 at Comiskey Park. Eddie Cicotte was the
           starting pitcher but lasted only 1⅓ innings.

July 26   A day after failing to complete the second inning in a start the previous day, Eddie
           Cicotte pitches a one-hitter to beat the Yankees 2–0 at Comiskey Park. The only
           New York hit was a single by Wally Pipp in the fifth inning.

           Cicotte was 15–7 with a 1.78 ERA in 1916.

JULY 30   Joe Jackson hits a grand slam off Marsh Williams in the sixth inning of a 7–0 win in the second game of a double-header against the Athletics at Comiskey Park. The Sox also won the opener 10–1.

Fritz Von Kolnitz, who played 24 games as an infielder with the White Sox in 1916, retired at the end of the season to set up a legal practice in Charleston, South Carolina. During World War I, he enlisted in the Army and reached the rank of major, the highest rank achieved by any major leaguer. Later, Von Kolnitz amassed considerable wealth in the Charleston real estate market and wrote several books on South Carolina history.

AUGUST 3   The idle White Sox take first place when the Red Sox lose to the Browns in St. Louis.

AUGUST 4   The White Sox win their ninth game in a row with a 3–2 decision over the Senators in the first game of a double-header at Comiskey Park. Washington broke the streak with an 8–3 win in the nightcap.

AUGUST 9   The Red Sox nose the White Sox out of first place with a 3–1 victory in 12 innings at Comiskey Park.

The White Sox failed to regain the top spot in the American League in 1916 but were in the pennant race until the final week of the season.

SEPTEMBER 3   Red Faber shuts out the Browns for a 1–0 win in St. Louis. Ray Schalk drove in the lone run of the game with a double in the ninth inning.

SEPTEMBER 15   The White Sox beat the Senators 3–2 at Comiskey Park.

With the win, the White Sox had a record of 80–60 and were in third place, one-half game behind the first-place Red Sox. The Tigers were second, two percentage points back of Boston. The Sox had a three-game series against the Red Sox from September 16 through September 18.

SEPTEMBER 16   The White Sox win the first game of a pennant-showdown series against the Red Sox at Comiskey Park by a 6–4 score. The Tigers also won to take over first place. Chicago was second, one-half game out. The Red Sox fell from first to third.

SEPTEMBER 17   The Red Sox shove the White Sox back into third place with a 6–3 win before a crowd estimated at 40,000 at Comiskey Park.

SEPTEMBER 18   The White Sox lose again 4–2 to the Red Sox at Comiskey Park.

The White Sox closed the series 1½ games out of first. The club was unable to get any closer and finished the season two games behind the Red Sox. The Tigers, who lost three games in a row to Boston from September 19 through 21, ended the year in third, four games out.

SEPTEMBER 19   The White Sox score three runs in the ninth inning to defeat the Athletics 5–4 at Comiskey Park. Four consecutive pinch-hitters (Eddie Murphy, Jack Fournier, Ray Schalk and Happy Felsch) produced two singles, a sacrifice and a walk to load the bases. Shano Collins hit a sacrifice fly, and Eddie Collins drove in two runs with a double. The Sox tied a major league record for most runs scored by pinch-hitters in an inning with three.

SEPTEMBER 22   Eddie Collins runs his consecutive hitting streak to 20 games with a 6–3 victory over the Yankees at Comiskey Park.

SEPTEMBER 30   Happy Felsch pops an inside-the-park, game-winning grand slam in the 12th inning off Indians pitcher Pop Boy Smith for the winning runs in a 7–3 Chicago triumph in the second game of a double-header in Cleveland. The White Sox also won the opener 7–2.

Felsch hit .300 for the White Sox in 1916.

In his first full season with the club, Shoeless Joe Jackson led the White Sox in many offensive categories, as he would through the 1920 season, when he was banned from baseball.

OCTOBER 4   The White Sox win 8–2 against the Cubs in game one of the Chicago City Series. The Sox went on to sweep the series, four games to none. It was the sixth consecutive year that the White Sox won the City Series. The Cubs and the White Sox didn't meet in the post-season again until 1921, because the White Sox went to the World Series in 1917 and 1919, and the Cubs appeared in the Fall Classic in 1918. The 1920 City Series was canceled because eight White Sox players were suspended just prior to the end of the regular season for throwing the 1919 World Series.

1917

Season in a Sentence

In a season that begins less than a week after the United States enters World War I, the White Sox streak to a pennant with a club record 100 victories, then defeat the Giants in the World Series.

Finish • Won • Lost • Pct • GB

First   100   54   .649   +9.0

Manager

Pants Rowland

World Series

The White Sox defeated the Giants four games to two.

Stats

Stats	WS	AL	Rank
Batting Avg:	.253	.248	3
On-Base Pct:	.329	.318	1
Slugging Pct:	.326	.320	2
Home Runs:	18		3
Stolen Bases:	219		1
ERA:	2.16	2.66	1
Fielding Avg:	.967	.964	2
Runs Scored:	656		1
Runs Allowed:	464		2

Starting Lineup

Ray Schalk, c
Chick Gandil, 1b
Eddie Collins, 2b
Buck Weaver, 3b
Swede Risberg, ss
Joe Jackson, lf
Happy Felsch, cf
Nemo Leibold, rf
Shano Collins, rf
Fred McMullin, 3b

Pitchers

Eddie Cicotte, sp
Lefty Williams, sp-rp
Red Faber, sp-rp
Reb Russell, sp-rp
Jim Scott, sp
Joe Benz, sp-rp
Dave Danforth, rp

Attendance

684,521 (first in AL)

Club Leaders

Batting Avg:	Happy Felsch	.308
On-Base Pct:	Eddie Collins	.389
Slugging Pct:	Joe Jackson	.429
Home Runs:	Happy Felsch	6
RBIs:	Happy Felsch	102
Runs:	Joe Jackson	91
	Eddie Collins	91
Stolen Bases:	Eddie Collins	53
Wins:	Eddie Cicotte	28
Strikeouts:	Eddie Cicotte	150
ERA:	Eddie Cicotte	1.53
Saves:	Dave Danforth	9

MARCH 1   The White Sox purchase Chick Gandil from the Indians.

The White Sox entered the 1917 season believing they only needed a first baseman and a shortstop to win the AL pennant. To meet that end, the club bought Gandil from Cleveland and Swede Risberg from the Pacific Coast League. Gandil and Risberg were both regulars on the 1917 and 1919 pennant-winning clubs in Chicago, but both were also involved in the fix of the 1919 World Series and were suspended for life in 1920.

APRIL 12   The scheduled season opener against the Browns in St. Louis is rained out.

APRIL 13   The White Sox get the 1917 season under way with a 4–3 loss to the Browns in St. Louis.

The opener was played amid patriotic fervor, as the United States declared war on Germany on April 6, beginning the country's military involvement in World War I.

APRIL 14   In his first appearance of the 1917 season, Eddie Cicotte pitches a no-hitter and defeats the Browns 11–0 in St. Louis. The Sox put the game away with seven runs in the second inning to take an 8–0 lead. All three ninth-inning outs were recorded on pop-ups by Ward Miller to catcher Ray Schalk, George Sisler to first baseman Chick Gandil and Del Pratt to shortstop Swede Risberg. Cicotte walked three and struck out five.

The no-hitter was the beginning of a brilliant season for Cicotte in which he posted a record of 28–12. He not only led the AL in wins, but in earned run average (1.53) and innings pitched (346⅓) as well. Cicotte also pitched seven shutouts and 29 complete games in 35 starts, and made 14 relief appearances. The tremendous year was unexpected because Cicotte turned 33 in August 1917, his previous high in victories in a season was 18 in 1913 and his career record was 119–100. After his record dipped to 12–19 in 1918, Cicotte was 29–7 in 1919 and 21–10 in 1920 before drawing a lifetime ban for his participation in the 1919 World Series fix.

APRIL 16   Red Faber pitches a two-hitter to defeat the Tigers 4–0 in Detroit. The only hits off Faber were a double by Ty Cobb and a single by Donie Bush.

APRIL 19   In the home opener, the White Sox lose 6–2 to the Browns at Comiskey Park. Prior to the game, players on both clubs put on an exhibition military drill with the Sox wearing regulation Army uniforms.

Charles Comiskey donated a portion of the gate receipts collected at Comiskey Park in 1917 to the Red Cross. A total of $17,113 was raised.

APRIL 24   The White Sox collect only two hits off Indians pitcher Stan Coveleski but win 1–0 at Comiskey Park behind the pitching of Jim Scott. The run scored in the ninth inning on a triple by Swede Risberg and a sacrifice fly by Eddie Collins.

Collins hit .289 and scored 91 runs in 1917.

APRIL 28   The White Sox outlast the Tigers 2–1 in 14 innings at Comiskey Park.

MAY 5   Ernie Koob of the Browns defeats the White Sox 1–0 with a no-hitter in St. Louis. The losing pitcher was Eddie Cicotte, who no-hit the Browns three weeks earlier on April 14. The run scored in the sixth inning and was unearned, courtesy of an error by shortstop Swede Risberg. Koob's no-hitter wasn't without controversy. With one out in the first inning, Buck Weaver hit a grounder that was booted by second baseman Ernie Johnson. Official scorer J. B. Sheridan was late getting to the park that day and missed the play. Many of the other writers at the game, both from Chicago and St. Louis, thought it was a hit and Sheridan entered it as such in the scorebook. Following the game, Sheridan consulted the umpires and players concerning the Weaver hit, and most told him that the play should have been scored an error. Sheridan reversed his decision, and Koob had his no-hitter.

MAY 6

The White Sox are the victims of a no-hitter in St. Louis for the second day in a row, this time by Bob Groom of the Browns in the second day of a double-header. In the opener, the Sox won 4–3. Groom pitched the eighth and ninth inning in relief and didn't allow a hit. Groom started the second game and hurled nine more hitless innings for a 3–0 St. Louis win. The game ended on a grounder by Nemo Leibold to first baseman George Sisler. The losing pitcher was Joe Benz, who tossed a no-hitter for the Sox in 1914.

The White Sox season record at the end of the twinbill was 11–10.

MAY 13

Eddie Cicotte pitches a two-hitter to defeat the Yankees 1–0 at Comiskey Park. Happy Felsch drove in the lone run of the game with a single on the fourth inning. The only New York hits were singles by Frank Baker and Roger Peckinpaugh.

Felsch batted .308 and drove in 102 runs in 1917.

MAY 15

Buck Weaver collects five hits, including a double, in five at-bats leading the White Sox to an 11–0 win over the Yankees at Comiskey Park.

Weaver had a .284 batting average in 1917.

MAY 19

The White Sox record their eighth win in a row with an 8–2 decision over the Red Sox at Comiskey Park.

MAY 23

Members of the White Sox register for the military draft at the Chicago city clerk's office. According to a proclamation issued by President Woodrow Wilson on May 18, all men in the U.S. between the ages of 21 and 30 were required to register on June 5. The Sox players eligible for the draft registered two weeks early because the club was on the road on June 5.

MAY 24

Reb Russell pitches a 12-inning shutout to defeat the Senators 1–0 at Comiskey Park. The winning run scored on a wild pitch by George Dumont, who also hurled a complete game.

JUNE 5

On a day in which more than 10 million men register for the military draft, the White Sox defeat the Athletics 6–3 in Philadelphia. In honor of the day, the two teams drilled and raised the American flag, and the Chicago players sang the "Star Spangled Banner."

JUNE 15

Lefty Williams pitches a four-hitter to beat the Red Sox 8–0 at Fenway Park. Williams held Boston without a hit until the eighth inning.

Williams started the season winning his first nine decisions. He finished the year at 17–8.

JUNE 16

The White Sox down the Red Sox 7–2 during an event-filled afternoon at Fenway Park. When it began raining in the fifth inning with Chicago leading 2–0, the game was interrupted by a crowd that swarmed from the bleachers to the playing field hoping to have the contest delayed long enough so that the rain would prevent it from being completed before the regulation five innings. The game was stopped by rain for 30 minutes before being resumed, and all nine innings were played.

After the contest, it was revealed that those who ran on to the field were gamblers who had bet heavily on the Red Sox to win. At the time, gamblers took bets in the open at nearly every major league ballpark, including Comiskey Park, with little interference from the police or the ball clubs.

JUNE 23   The White Sox edge the Indians 2–1 in 15 innings at Comiskey Park. Due to the use of pinch-hitters and pinch-runners, Pants Rowland ran out of position players and had to use pitcher Reb Russell during the last four innings in left field. Playing the outfield for the first time in his career, Russell contributed two sensational catches.

JUNE 24   Dave Danforth shuts out the Indians for a 1–0 win in Cleveland. Shano Collins drove in the lone run of the game with a single in the eighth inning.

Danforth often used his large hands to loosen the covers on baseballs to sharpen the break on his curveball. The shutout on June 24, 1917, was the first of only two he recorded during his 10-year big league career. The other one came with the Browns in 1924. Danforth was used mainly as a reliever in 1917 and led the AL in games pitched (50) and saves (nine).

JULY 13   The Yankees score the winning run in the 11th inning of a 6–5 win over the White Sox at Comiskey Park in an unusual manner. With Roger Peckinpaugh the runner on second, Wally Pipp singled to center. Happy Felsch threw home as Peckinpaugh headed for the plate. As Peckinpaugh slid, he was tagged by Schalk, but the Sox catcher dropped the ball as soon as he made contact with the runner. Schalk, while sitting on Peckinpaugh a foot from home plate, recovered the ball and tagged him again. Umpire Billy Evans ruled Peckinpaugh was safe because of interference by Schalk.

JULY 17   Eddie Cicotte pitches a one-hitter for a 5–0 win over the Senators in the first game of a double-header at Comiskey Park. The only Washington hit was a single by Ray Morgan in the second inning. The White Sox also won the second tilt 3–2 in 11 innings.

Cicotte's 28 wins in 1917 is the third-highest in White Sox history. His 29 victories in 1919 ranks second. The all-time record is Ed Walsh's 40 wins in 1908.

JULY 31   The Red Sox knock the White Sox out of first place with a 5–2 win at Fenway Park. Boston's Harry Hooper hit a fluke three-run homer in the first inning that glanced off the glove of Chicago right fielder Shano Collins and into the bleachers.

AUGUST 10   Walter Johnson pitches a one-hitter against the White Sox for a 4–0 Washington win at Griffith Stadium.

AUGUST 11   The White Sox are the victims of a one-hitter for the second game in a row, losing 3–2 to the Senators in Washington. Three Senators pitchers (George Dumont, Jim Shaw and Doc Ayers) combined on the one-hitter.

AUGUST 18   The White Sox regain first place with a 5–4 victory over the Athletics at Comiskey Park.

The Sox remained in first for the rest of the season.

AUGUST 19   The White Sox wallop the Athletics 14–6 at Comiskey Park. During the game, $550 was collected to buy baseball equipment for servicemen serving in France. The fund was started by Senators owner Clark Griffith and collections were taken at every major league ballpark during the 1917 and 1918 seasons.

AUGUST 21   Chick Gandil fights Doc Gainer of the Red Sox during a 2–0 Chicago win at Comiskey Park. Gandil claimed that Gainer tried to spike him during the fourth inning. After the game, the two met in the White Sox dugout and swapped punches until they were separated.

                The White Sox were Gandil's third team in three years, playing as a regular first baseman with the Senators in 1915 and the Indians in 1916. He was passed from club to club because he was a disruptive force in the clubhouse, helping to divide each club into rival cliques that would have little to do with each other off the field.

AUGUST 23   Military drills by White Sox and Senators players precede a 6–0 Chicago win at Comiskey Park. Among those in the crowd were some 6,000 soldiers and sailors.

                Before the season, AL President Ban Johnson ordered all eight teams in the organization to practice military drills. A prize of $500 was to be awarded to the best-drilled team, with Army Colonel Raymond Sheldon acting as judge. The White Sox and Senators performed before Sheldon before the August 23 game outfitted in khaki uniforms and toting Springfield rifles. The Browns won the league-wide competition, with the White Sox finishing fourth.

AUGUST 27   Eddie Cicotte records his 20th win of the season with a 3–0 decision over the Yankees at Comiskey Park.

AUGUST 29   The White Sox sweep the Browns 6–0 and 11–1 at Comiskey Park.

AUGUST 31   The White Sox win their ninth game in a row with an 8–2 decision over the Browns at Comiskey Park.

SEPTEMBER 2   A wild finish leads to a 10-inning 6–5 win over the Tigers in the first game of a double-header at Comiskey Park. Detroit scored four runs in the ninth inning to take a 5–3 lead, but the White Sox scored two in their half and one in the tenth for the win. The winning run scored when Eddie Collins singled, stole second and third, and scored on a sacrifice fly by Joe Jackson. The Sox also won the second game 7–2.

                Jackson hit .301 and scored 91 runs in 1917.

SEPTEMBER 3   The White Sox sweep the Tigers 7–5 and 14–8 in a double-header at Comiskey Park. The wins gave the Sox a 6½-game lead over the Red Sox in the AL pennant race.

                Two weeks later, while staying at the Ansonia Hotel in New York, the White Sox collected $45 from each player, allegedly as a gift for beating the Red Sox. Years afterward, Chick Gandil, Swede Risberg and Happy Felsch claimed that the White Sox collected the money to give to the Tigers for "laying down" *during the double headers of September 2 and 3. The charges of crookedness were not proven one way or the other (see December 30, 1926).*

SEPTEMBER 4   The White Sox score eight runs in the eighth inning and defeat the Browns 13–6 in St. Louis. Happy Felsch collected two doubles in the inning.

SEPTEMBER 8   Joe Jackson doubles in a run in the third inning, then scores on Chick Gandil's single for both runs in a 2–0 victory over the Indians at Comiskey Park. More than 8,000 soldiers and sailors were present and each was presented with baseball uniforms with the names "America" and "U.S.A" on the shirts as gifts of Charles Comiskey and the Woodland Bards, a White Sox rooting organization.

Pitcher Jim Scott left the White Sox in September to travel to San Francisco for an officers' training camp. By the time the war was over, Scott reached the rank of captain.

SEPTEMBER 9   The White Sox win a game against the Indians at Comiskey Park by forfeit as a result of some juvenile behavior. After Cleveland outfielder Jack Graney was called out for interfering with White Sox third baseman Fred McMullin during the top of the 10th inning with the score 3–3, the Indians argued for 10 minutes. When they finally took the field, the Cleveland players threw their gloves in the air and a couple of them rolled on the field. After Indians hurler Fritz Coumbe struck out Chicago's Dave Danforth, Indians catcher Steve O'Neill pegged the ball into left field. At that point, umpire Brick Owens had enough and declared the forfeit.

SEPTEMBER 21   The White Sox clinch the 1917 American League pennant with a 2–1 win in 10 innings over the Red Sox in Boston. Red Faber retired the first 18 batters to face him before Harry Hooper tripled leading off the seventh. In the 10th, Ray Schalk doubled and Shano Collins singled to score the winning run. The pennant was the first for the Sox since the "Hitless Wonders" won the world championship in 1906.

SEPTEMBER 25   The White Sox steal 10 bases during a 7–5 win over the Senators in Washington. Nemo Leibold, Fred McMullin and Eddie Collins each swiped two bases, while Shano Collins, Byrd Lynn, Buck Weaver and Chick Gandil stole one each.

SEPTEMBER 29   The White Sox win their 100th game of the 1917 season with a 3–1 decision over the Yankees in the second game of a double-header at the Polo Grounds. It was also Eddie Cicotte's 28th win of the season. New York won the first game 12–8.

The 1917 club is also the only one in White Sox history to reach the 100-win mark. The Sox played the New York Giants in the World Series. Managed by John McGraw, the 1917 Giants were 98–56 and won the NL pennant by 10 games. Comiskey Park was enlarged to a capacity of 32,000 with the construction of an additional bleacher section in center field and more boxes behind home plate.

OCTOBER 6   The White Sox open the World Series with a 2–1 win over the Giants before 32,000 at Comiskey Park behind the seven-hit pitching of Eddie Cicotte. The first run scored in the third inning when Fred McMullin doubled home Shano Collins. Happy Felsch gave the Sox a 2–0 lead with a homer into the left-field bleachers in the fourth.

During the game, Red Cross volunteers roamed the stands asking for contributions. A military band played patriotic tunes. Two thousand doughboys marched into the park, then made their way single file to the grandstand.
The White Sox also looked the part in this wartime World Series as Charles Comiskey commissioned specially-designed uniforms. The "SOX" logo on the left breast, which was solid blue during the regular season, was changed for the post-season as the blue was trimmed in red and contained white stars inside the letter "S." A red and blue stripe was added to the white socks.

OCTOBER 7

The White Sox win Game Two with a 7–2 decision over the Giants before 32,000 at Comiskey Park. New York scored first with two runs in the top of the second inning, but the Sox tied it up in their half, then broke the contest open with five tallies in the fourth. Chicago collected 14 hits, all singles, including three by both Joe Jackson and Buck Weaver. Red Faber was the winning pitcher, tossing a complete game. He also provided some comic relief. With two out in the fifth inning, Faber was a base runner on second base with Buck Weaver at third. Faber tried to steal third, quickly forgetting that Weaver already occupied the bag. Faber was tagged out after a beautiful headfirst slide in which he collided with Weaver's feet as he arrived.

Starting shortstop Swede Risberg was knocked out of the lineup during the World Series because he was bothered by a boil. Buck Weaver moved from third base to short and Fred McMullin started all six games of the Series at third.

OCTOBER 9

The scheduled third game of the 1917 World Series is postponed by rain.

OCTOBER 10

The Giants take Game Three 2–0 over the White Sox at the Polo Grounds in New York. Rube Benton pitched the shutout, allowing five hits. The two Giants runs scored in the fourth inning off Eddie Cicotte.

OCTOBER 11

The Giants even the World Series with another shutout, defeating the White Sox 5–0 in New York behind the pitching of Ferdie Schupp. Benny Kauff smashed two homers off Red Faber, pinning him with the loss.

OCTOBER 13

The White Sox move within one game of the world championship with an 8–5 come-from-behind win over the Giants before 27,323 fans at Comiskey Park. A walk and a base hit chased Sox starter Reb Russell from the mound in the first inning before he could retire a batter, and manager Pants Rowland brought in Eddie Cicotte to put out the fire. The Giants came out of the first with two runs and ran their lead to 5–2 after 6½ innings. The Sox scored three times in their half of the seventh to knot the contest at 5–5, then scored three more in the eighth for the win. The comeback was led by Eddie Collins, Joe Jackson and Happy Felsch, the 3–4–5 hitters in the lineup, who combined for nine hits in 14 at-bats. Credit for the victory went to Red Faber, who retired all six batters he faced in two innings of relief. The game was marred by nine errors, six of them by the White Sox.

OCTOBER 15

The White Sox take the world championship with a 4–2 win over the Giants in New York. The Sox struck first with three runs in the fourth. Leadoff batter Eddie Collins reached second when third baseman Heinie Zimmerman fielded his easy grounder and heaved the ball past first baseman Walter Holke. Then Joe Jackson hit a routine fly ball to right field, which Dave Robertson dropped, putting Collins on first and Jackson on first. Felsch hit a Rube Benton pitch back to the mound, and Collins was caught in a rundown between home and third, creating one of the strangest and most controversial plays in World Series history. Benton threw to Zimmerman, who in turn relayed to catcher Bill Rariden. Rariden chased Collins back within 15 feet of third and threw the ball back to Zimmerman. Zimmerman tried to tag Collins and missed, and Collins headed back in the direction of home plate. Zimmerman chased Collins instead of throwing the ball back to Rariden, who had to leap out of the base line to avoid being called for interference. Zimmerman was unable to place the tag on Collins, who raced across the plate for the first run of the game with the Giants third baseman a couple of steps behind in hot pursuit. Unnerved by the lack of support, Benton gave up a two-run single to Chick Gandil. Taking the mound only two days after earning a victory in a two-inning relief appearance, Faber pitched a complete game for his third win of the Series against one loss. He was the winner in games two, five and six, and the loser in game four. Faber pitched 16 more years in the majors but never appeared in another Fall Classic. He missed the 1919 Series with a sore arm.

The run scored by Collins in the fourth inning was debated in the sports pages of the country for the next several weeks over whether Zimmerman or Rariden was responsible for the gaffe. Many writers who witnessed the play blamed Rariden, rather than Zimmerman, for running Collins back too close to third base, which made a return throw from the third baseman difficult. Others cited Benton and Holke for failing to cover home plate. Zimmerman was later expelled from organized baseball in 1919 for trying to induce his teammates to throw a September game.

OCTOBER 16   The White Sox and the Giants play an exhibition game at Camp Mills in Mineola, New York, before 6,000 soldiers who were about to be shipped off to war in France. The Sox won 6–4.

Red Faber warms up before a game in the 1917 World Series. Faber spent his entire 20-year, Hall-of-Fame career with the White Sox.

1918

Season in a Sentence

The defending world champion White Sox free fall into sixth place in a season that ends on Labor Day at the request of the federal government because of World War I.

Finish • Won • Lost • Pct • GB

Sixth   57   67   .460   17.0

Manager

Pants Rowland

Stats

Stats	WS	AL	Rank
Batting Avg:	.256	.254	5
On-Base Pct:	.322	.323	5
Slugging Pct:	.321	.322	4
Home Runs:	8		6
Stolen Bases:	116		5
ERA:	2.73	2.77	4
Fielding Avg:	.967	.964	3
Runs Scored:	457		6
Runs Allowed:	446		3

Starting Lineup

Ray Schalk, c
Chick Gandil, 1b
Eddie Collins, 2b
Fred McMullin, 3b
Buck Weaver, ss
Nemo Leibold, lf
Eddie Murphy, rf
Shano Collins, cf-rf
Swede Risberg, ss-3b
Happy Felsch, cf
Wilbur Good, cf

Pitchers

Eddie Cicotte, sp
Fred Shellenback, sp
Joe Benz, sp-rp
Reb Russell, sp
Lefty Williams, sp
Red Faber, sp
Dave Danforth, rp-sp

Attendance

195,091 (fifth in AL)

Club Leaders

Batting Avg:	Buck Weaver	.300
On-Base Pct:	Eddie Collins	.407
Slugging Pct:	Shano Collins	.392
Home Runs:	Eddie Collins	2
RBIs:	Shano Collins	56
Runs:	Nemo Leibold	57
Stolen Bases:	Eddie Collins	22
Wins:	Eddie Cicotte	12
Strikeouts:	Eddie Cicotte	104
ERA:	Joe Benz	2.51
Saves:	Three tied with	2

APRIL 16   The White Sox open the season with a 6–1 loss to the Browns before 18,000 at Comiskey Park. A parade of soldiers from Fort Sheridan and sailors from the Great Lakes Naval Training Station preceded the game.

With a labor shortage due to the war, Charles Comiskey purchased a flock of sheep in 1918 to help keep the grass at Comiskey Park neat and trim. He was following the lead of President Woodrow Wilson, who put sheep to pasture on the White House lawn.

APRIL 30   The White Sox pummel the Indians 13–3 in Cleveland.

MAY 3   Eddie Collins misses a contest against the Tigers in Detroit with an injured knee, ending a streak of 479 consecutive games played dating back to 1914. Without Collins in the lineup, the White Sox collected 25 hits and walloped the Tigers 19–3. Buck Weaver picked up five hits in seven at-bats. Collins was out of action until May 13.

Collins hit .276 in 1918 before volunteering for service in the Marines on August 15. He was one of many White Sox to join the service before the end of the season. The others included Jim Scott (who enlisted in 1917), Red Faber, Swede Risberg, Ted Jourdan, Pat Hardgrove, Joe Jenkins and Tom McGuire. Joe Jackson, Lefty Williams, Byrd Lynn and Happy Felsch avoided military service by working in a war-related industry, actions that created considerable controversy (see May 13, 1918 and July 1, 1918).

MAY 13   Joe Jackson announces he has accepted a position as a ship painter for the Harlan & Hollingsworth Shipbuilding Company in Wilmington, Delaware. Jackson had recently received word from the draft board in his hometown of Greenville, South Carolina that he was placed in 1-A status. Jackson sought an exemption from active service, claiming that he was employed in a war-related industry. In June, Lefty Williams and Byrd Lynn also avoided military service by working as ship painters at the same Delaware concern. The trio received extra pay to play baseball for the factory team. Charles Comiskey was outraged by the actions of Jackson, Williams and Lynn, believing that it amounted to draft-dodging. "I don't consider them to be fit to play on my ball club," complained Comiskey. "I would gladly lose my whole team if the players wished to do their duty for the country, as hundreds of thousands of other young men are doing." The Sox owner swore that Jackson, Williams and Lynn would never play again for the White Sox, but once the war ended in November, all was apparently forgiven. The three were employed by the Chicago club again in 1919.

MAY 14   Red Faber retires the first 20 batters to face him before settling for a three-hitter and a 3–0 win over the Athletics at Shibe Park. The first Philadelphia hit was a single by Tilly Walker.

MAY 15   The White Sox lose an 18-inning marathon 1–0 to the Senators in Washington. All 18 players in the starting lineups of the two squads were still in the game at the end, including pitchers Lefty Williams and Walter Johnson. Williams set a White Sox record (since tied) by striking out five times in six at-bats. On the mound, he allowed eight hits, all singles. In the Washington 18th, Eddie Ainsmith and Johnson singled before Williams threw a wild pitch that allowed Ainsmith to score. The game was completed in two hours and 47 minutes.

MAY 22   Eddie Cicotte pitches a 14-inning complete game but loses 1–0 to the Yankees in New York. Cicotte allowed only four hits through the first 13 innings, but in the 14th he surrendered three singles to lose. Hank Thormahlen pitched a complete game for the Yankees.

After posting a 28–12 record in 1917, Cicotte lost his first seven decisions in 1918 and finished the season with a 12–19 mark.

JUNE 1   The White Sox hit into a game-ending triple play against the Yankees in New York. The Sox went into the ninth inning trailing 6–3, but they scored twice and loaded the bases with none out. Chick Gandil hit a liner that appeared to be headed for left field, but Yankee third baseman Frank Baker made a spectacular catch, threw to second baseman Del Pratt to beat Happy Felsch, and Pratt fired to first sacker Wally Pipp before Buck Weaver could return to the bag.

JUNE 2   Happy Felsch hits a grand slam off Slim Love in the fifth inning of a 6–2 win over the Yankees in New York.

The White Sox were 22–17 on June 7 and in third place, 2½ games behind.

JUNE 11   The 1917 American League pennant is raised before a 4–1 win over the Red Sox at Comiskey Park. Red Faber pitched his last game before enlisting in the Navy.

JUNE 20   The gate receipts from a 10-inning, 5–4 win over the Indians at Comiskey Park go toward a fund to build a recreation pavilion for servicemen on the lakefront in Chicago. Special features were staged before the game, including an auction. A baseball autographed by President Woodrow Wilson was sold for $5,650. A ball bearing the signature of Mrs. Wilson garnered $1,450. One signed by evangelist Billy Sunday, who played for the Cubs during the 1880s, netted $50.

JUNE 22   The 1917 world championship pennant is raised before a 4–3 loss to the Indians at Comiskey Park. Red Faber, attired in his Navy uniform, assisted in the flag-raising.

JUNE 26   Frank Shellenback pitches a two-hitter for a 3–0 win over the Tigers in Detroit. The only hits off Shellenback were singles by Donie Bush and Harry Heilmann.

JULY 1   Happy Felsch leaves the White Sox to work in a munitions plant in Milwaukee and play for the factory team. The plant made poison gas for use in chemical warfare.

JULY 29   Joe Benz pitches a 13-inning, complete-game shutout to defeat the Senators 1–0 at Comiskey Park. The Sox collected only two hits over the first 11 innings off Harry Harper, who was removed for a pinch-hitter. The winning run scored on a double by Ray Schalk and a single from Wilbur Good off reliever Walter Johnson.

AUGUST 1   The National Commission, baseball's governing body, announces that the 1918 season will end on September 2 in order to comply with a draft order issued by the federal government requiring that all men of draft age to either enter the military or find a war-related job. The World Series participants were given an extension until September 15. The Cubs won the NL crown and lost to the Red Sox in the Fall Classic. The Cubs played their home games in the series at Comiskey Park because the White Sox's ballpark had a greater seating capacity than Weeghman Park.

AUGUST 6   The White Sox outlast the Yankees 5–4 in 15 innings at Comiskey Park. Shano Collins drove in the winning tally with a sacrifice fly.

           Collins tied a major league record with three bases-loaded triples in 1918. He also holds the major league record for most bases-loaded triples in a career with eight, all of which were struck while he played for the White Sox.

SEPTEMBER 2   On the final day of the war-shortened season, Buck Weaver collects eight hits in 10 at-bats in a double-header against the Tigers in Detroit, although the White Sox lose both games 11–5 and 7–3. Weaver had six singles and two doubles. Five of the hits occurred in the opener.

           The batting outburst gave Weaver a final season average of exactly .300.

NOVEMBER 11   An armistice is signed with Germany ending World War I.

When the 1918 season came to a close, it appeared that there would be no baseball in 1919 because the end of the war was nowhere in sight. But a series of victories by the Allies, led by the United States, Great Britain and France, hastened a conclusion of the war by November 1918. Owners hastily made plans for the 1919 season, but due to the late start in preparing for the campaign and the anticipation of a poor year at the gate, baseball executives shortened the season to 140 games. It was a decision that officials came to regret, as attendance reached record levels in 1919.

DECEMBER 31   Kid Gleason replaces Pants Rowland as manager of the White Sox.

Rowland was canned following the disappointing sixth-place finish in 1918. He never managed another big league club, but he had a long career in baseball serving in such posts as an American League umpire (1923–27), president of the Pacific Coast League (1944–53) and vice president of the Cubs (from 1956 until his death at the age of 89 in 1969). Gleason's playing career started as a pitcher with the Phillies in 1888. After his arm went dead, he became a second baseman and remained in the big leagues until 1908. Gleason was a coach with the White Sox from 1912 through 1914, and again in 1917 and 1918. He was 53 when appointed as manager of the Sox. Gleason won an American League pennant in his first season as manager, but he had the misfortune of guiding a club that threw the World Series in collusion with gamblers. He managed the White Sox until the end of the 1923 season.

1919

Season in a Sentence

With World War I over and a new manager in Kid Gleason, the White Sox win the club's second AL pennant in three years before losing the most controversial World Series in history.

Finish • Won • Lost • Pct • GB

First   88   52   .629   +3.5

World Series

The White Sox lost five games to three to the Cincinnati Reds.

Manager

Kid Gleason

Stats

	WS	AL	Rank
Batting Avg:	.287	.268	1
On-Base Pct:	.351	.333	2
Slugging Pct:	.380	.359	3
Home Runs:	25		5
Stolen Bases:	150		1
ERA:	3.04	.322	4
Fielding Avg:	.969	.965	2
Runs Scored:	667		1
Runs Allowed:	534		2

Starting Lineup

Ray Schalk, c
Chick Gandil, 1b
Eddie Collins, 2b
Buck Weaver, 3b
Swede Risberg, ss
Joe Jackson, lf
Happy Felsch, cf
Nemo Leibold, rf
Shano Collins, rf
Fred McMullin, 3b

Pitchers

Eddie Cicotte, sp
Lefty Williams, sp
Red Faber, sp
Grover Lowdermilk, sp-rp
Dickie Kerr, rp-sp

Attendance

627,186 (second in AL)

Club Leaders

Batting Avg:	Joe Jackson	.351
On-Base Pct:	Joe Jackson	.422
Slugging Pct:	Joe Jackson	.506
Home Runs:	Joe Jackson	7
	Happy Felsch	7
RBIs:	Joe Jackson	96
Runs:	Buck Weaver	89
Stolen Bases:	Eddie Collins	33
Wins:	Eddie Cicotte	29
Strikeouts:	Lefty Williams	125
ERA:	Eddie Cicotte	1.82
Saves:	Three tied with	1

APRIL 23   In the season opener, the White Sox collect 21 hits and thrash the Browns 13–4 in St. Louis. Eddie Collins had a home run among his three hits. Buck Weaver collected four hits, including a triple. Joe Jackson and Swede Risberg picked up three hits each. Lefty Williams was the winning pitcher.

MAY 2   In the first game of the year at Comiskey Park, the White Sox lose 11–4 to the Browns. Before the game, the U.S. flag was raised by a contingent of Marines, assisted by Eddie Collins, who enlisted in the Marines in August 1918 and was discharged shortly after World War I ended.

Collins hit .319 in 1919.

MAY 14   Eddie Cicotte pitches the White Sox to a 1–0 win over the Red Sox at Comiskey Park.

MAY 18   Eddie Cicotte pitches his second consecutive 1–0 victory, defeating the Athletics at Comiskey Park.

MAY 22   Lefty Williams downs the Yankees 1–0 at Comiskey Park. The run scored in the first inning on a double by Buck Weaver and a single from Joe Jackson.

              Williams was 23–11 with a 2.64 ERA in 1919.

MAY 23   Eddie Cicotte pitches his third consecutive shutout, beating the Yankees 5–0 at Comiskey Park.

              Cicotte had a record of 29–7 in 1919. He led the AL in victories, winning percentage (.806), innings pitched (306²/₃) and complete games (30 in 35 starts). Cicotte pitched five shutouts and had an ERA of 1.82.

MAY 31   A fight between Chick Gandil and Tris Speaker highlights a 5–2 win over the Indians at Comiskey Park. At the end of the eighth inning, Gandil claimed that Speaker had tried to spike him when he slid into first base. The two players fought for three minutes and several healthy wallops were exchanged before they could be separated.

              The White Sox ended the month of May with a 24–7 record and a five-game lead in the AL race. The Sox dropped out of first in mid-June, but they took over the top spot for keeps on July 10.

JUNE 5   Eddie Collins breaks a 1–1 tie with an inside-the-park grand slam off Ernie Shore in the eighth inning of a 5–1 victory over the Yankees in New York.

JUNE 14   The White Sox score three runs in the 14th inning to beat the Athletics 6–3 in Philadelphia.

JUNE 23   Happy Felsch sets an American League record (since tied) for most total chances by a center fielder in a game. Felsch had 11 putouts and one assist during a 3–2 loss to the Indians at Comiskey Park.

              Beginning in June, Charles Comiskey began a crackdown on gamblers who openly took bets in the Comiskey Park stands. Chicago police made several arrests. Beer sales also ceased at Comiskey Park at the end of June 1919 as Prohibition took effect in the state of Illinois. Prohibition became a national law in January 1920 with the passage of the 18th amendment to the Constitution. Alcohol sales didn't make a return to major league ballparks until 1933 when Prohibition was lifted.

JUNE 30   The White Sox beat the Indians 5–2 during a stormy afternoon in Cleveland. Kid Gleason was ejected from the field in the first inning for protesting a decision. Later, the Cleveland team delayed the contest for 10 minutes, insisting that Eddie Cicotte had made a balk. The Sox won despite the fact that four runners were thrown out at the plate.

JULY 3   The White Sox score 10 runs in the fourth inning and pummel the Indians 17–1 in Cleveland. Chick Gandil drove in five runs during the big rally.

JULY 9   Red Faber wins both games of a double-header against the Athletics at Comiskey Park. Faber entered the first game as a reliever in the eighth inning with the score 5–5. The Sox scored three in the eighth, the last two on Faber's single, then survived a two-run Philadelphia rally in the ninth to win 8–7. Faber pitched a complete game in the nightcap to win 6–2.

JULY 13   The White Sox win a 14–9 slugging match over the Red Sox at Comiskey Park. Buck Weaver contributed a bases-loaded single.

                Weaver batted .296 and scored 89 runs in 1919.

JULY 20   A ninth-inning walk-off homer by Joe Jackson into the right field bleachers at Comiskey Park beats the Yankees 2–1.

                Jackson hit .351 and drove in 96 runs in 1919.

JULY 21   Dickie Kerr wins both games of a double-header in relief against the Yankees at Comiskey Park. He pitched one-third of an inning in the opener, won by the White Sox 7–6. Kerr hurled two innings in the second tilt, a 5–4 Chicago victory in 10 innings.

JULY 24   Eddie Cicotte pitches a 10-inning shutout to defeat the Browns 1–0 at Comiskey Park. Happy Felsch hit a bases-loaded single to drive in the winning run.

JULY 27   Race riots erupt in Chicago after an African-American youngster drifts into the white section of the segregated 29th Street Beach. The youngster drowned after whites threw rocks at him. A week of unrest resulted in the deaths of 40 people.

AUGUST 2   After being held hitless for the first six innings by Herb Pennock, the White Sox erupt for a run in the seventh inning, eight tallies in the eighth and a run in the ninth to win 10–1 in the second game of a double-header against the Red Sox at Fenway Park. Boston won the first game 5–3.

AUGUST 10   Eddie Cicotte pitches a 12-inning shutout to defeat the Senators 1–0 in Washington. In the 12th, Buck Weaver reached on an infield single, advanced to second on an infield out and scored on an error.

AUGUST 14   Happy Felsch ties the major league record for most assists by an outfielder in a game with four, although the White Sox lose 15–6 to the Red Sox at Comiskey Park.

AUGUST 19   Down 7–2, the White Sox score four runs in the seventh inning and two in the eighth to win 8–7 over the Athletics at Comiskey Park.

AUGUST 22   In his first game with the White Sox, Bill James shuts out the Senators 3–0 at Comiskey Park.

                James was a 32-year-old veteran with a 61–68 lifetime record in his eighth season in the majors when acquired from the Red Sox to help an ailing Chicago pitching staff down the pennant stretch. He pitched five games for the White Sox and was 3–2 with two shutouts.

AUGUST 24   The White Sox record their 10th win in a row with a 4–1 decision over the Yankees at Comiskey Park.

AUGUST 26   Eddie Collins homers over the right-field fence in the 10th inning to beat the Browns 4–3 in St. Louis.

SEPTEMBER 5   Eddie Cicotte wins his 28th game of the season, defeating the Indians 9–1 at Comiskey Park.

Cicotte didn't pitch again for two weeks due to a lame shoulder. He had been overworked for years, pitching 346²/₃ innings in 1917, 266 in 1918 in a season that ended four weeks early on September 2, and had logged 288¹/₃ innings on the mound in 1919 following his September 5 start. The ache in his shoulder may have influenced Cicotte's decision to help throw the 1919 World Series. He was 35 years old and feared that his career might be over. The money he received from gamblers would provide a "nest egg" on which to retire.

SEPTEMBER 6   Buck Weaver steals second, third and home in the sixth inning of an 11–2 loss to the Indians at Comiskey Park.

SEPTEMBER 11   National Commission Chairman Garry Herrmann announces that the 1919 World Series will be a best-of-nine affair following a vote of the 16 club owners.

Every World Series from 1905 through 1918 was a best-of-seven. The extension in 1919 was due in part to the owners reducing the length of the regular season from 154 games to 140 in anticipation of a drop in attendance following the end of World War I. Instead, attendance boomed in record numbers. In order to recoup some of the money lost from shortening the regular season, major league owners decided on a longer World Series. The 154-game schedule was brought back in 1920. The World Series had a best-of-nine format again in 1920 and 1921 before returning to the traditional best-of-seven.

SEPTEMBER 12   Making his first major league start, Sox pitcher Roy Wilkinson pitches a shutout to defeat the Athletics 7–0 in Philadelphia.

Wilkinson made 36 more big league starts and never pitched another shutout. In 1921, he was moved into the starting rotation following the suspensions of Eddie Cicotte and Lefty Williams and posted a record of 4–20. Wilkinson ended his big-league career a year later with 12 wins and 31 losses.

SEPTEMBER 15   The White Sox survive a six-run, ninth-inning rally by the Athletics to win 11–10 in Philadelphia.

SEPTEMBER 16   The Cincinnati Reds clinch the National League pennant. It was the first pennant for the franchise since 1882, when it was a part of the American Association. Managed by Pat Moran, the Reds had an impressive 96–44 record in 1919 and were a club that has been vastly underrated by historians. The winning percentage of .686 was the best of any NL club between 1912 and 1942 and the best of any major league team from 1912 through 1927. Despite winning more than two-thirds of their games, the Reds were decided underdogs in the World Series against the White Sox, however. The club was a surprise winner in 1919. Cincinnati was a last-place team as recently as 1916, had not finished above third place since 1887 and hadn't ended a season within 10 games of first since 1884. The 1919 Reds were largely a group of average players who had career years at the same time, which led to their underdog status. The only future Hall of Famer on the roster was Edd Roush, and the only other stars at their peaks were Heinie Groh and Jake Daubert. Also, the American League had won eight of the nine World Series from 1910 through 1918.

SEPTEMBER 18   The World Series fix is born in a room in Boston's Hotel Buckminster when Chick Gandil tells bookmaker Sport Sullivan that he believes that enough White Sox players would participate in losing on purpose to throw the Series to the Reds. Gandil asked Sullivan for $80,000.

SEPTEMBER 19   Making his first start in three weeks, Eddie Cicotte earns win number 29 in 1919 with a 3–2 win over the Red Sox in Boston.

On the same day, Chick Gandil solicited teammates for his World Series fix, including Cicotte, who asked for $10,000 up front. Gandil recruited Swede Risberg was overheard by reserve infielder Fred McMullin, who demanded that he be included. Lefty Williams was at first not interested, but he agreed to join the conspiracy when he learned it will go forward without him.

SEPTEMBER 20   Gandil and fellow plotters Eddie Cicotte, Happy Felsch, Joe Jackson, Fred McMullin, Swede Risberg, Buck Weaver and Lefty Williams, meet at the Hotel Ansonia in New York and decide to see if bookmaker Sport Sullivan delivers the cash. The amounts originally offered by the gamblers were more than most of the players made during the entire 1919 season. The eight players involved are forever known as the "Black Sox" for their participation in throwing the Series. Weaver, though he sat in on meetings, decided not to participate in the fix and accepted no money. But because he had prior knowledge of the conspiracy and did not divulge the information, Weaver was banned from organized baseball for life along with the seven others.

SEPTEMBER 21   Eddie Cicotte meets with Bill Burns, a gambler and a former major league pitcher who played for the White Sox in 1909 and 1910. Cicotte agreed to involve Burns in the fix, along with Burns associate Billy Maharg.

SEPTEMBER 23   Bill Burns and Billy Maharg offer to meet with gambler Arnold Rothstein and former world featherweight champion Abe Attell at Jamaica Race Track. Rothstein turned down their proposal. A day later, Rothstein reconsidered and said he would provide $100,000 for the fix as long as his name wasn't used.

SEPTEMBER 24   The White Sox score two runs in the ninth inning to clinch the American League pennant with a 6–5 victory over the Browns at Comiskey Park. Eddie Cicotte was the starting pitcher in search of his 30th victory of the season, but he was removed from the contest for a pinch-hitter in the seventh inning with the White Sox trailing 5–2. Dickie Kerr pitched the final two innings and started the rally in the ninth with a single. Kerr went to third on Nemo Leibold's single and scored on Buck Weaver's sacrifice fly. Leibold raced from first to third on a fly ball by Eddie Collins to deep center field. Joe Jackson's walk-off hit drove in the winning run.

It has often been written that Charles Comiskey kept Eddie Cicotte out of the starting rotation in both 1917 and 1919 because there was a clause in the pitcher's contract that awarded him with a bonus if he won 30 games. There is absolutely no evidence that Comiskey kept Cicotte on the bench in either 1917, when Cicotte won 28 games, or in 1919. Cicotte started the September 24 game with 29 wins to his credit. Two years earlier, Cicotte didn't miss a start and needed a late rush just to win 28 games. He had nine victories from August 27 through the end of the regular season.

SEPTEMBER 26   Sport Sullivan discusses the World Series fix with Arnold Rothstein, who sends Nat Evans, one of his partners, to talk to the Chicago players.

SEPTEMBER 28   In the final game of the season, the White Sox lose 10–9 to the Tigers at Comiskey Park. Eddie Cicotte started the game as a final tune-up before the post-season. He allowed a run in two innings and was taken out of the game to rest for his start in Game One of the World Series, which was three days away.

On the same day, Sport Sullivan and Nat Evans met with Chick Gandil amid growing suspicion between the players and the gamblers. The gamblers worried that the players wouldn't go through with the fix. The players feared the gamblers would fail to come through with the money promised. Lefty Williams wanted out. Joe Jackson demanded $20,000.

SEPTEMBER 29   Arnold Rothstein decides to finance the World Series fix. The plan called for Nat Evans to deliver $40,000 to Sport Sullivan for distribution to the eight White Sox involved in the conspiracy. An additional $40,000 was to be put in the safe at the Hotel Congress in Chicago for the players if the fix was successful. Sullivan siphoned off $29,000 and bet on the Reds. He gave Chick Gandil only $10,000 of the $40,000 promised. Unwilling to take a lesser amount, Eddie Cicotte demanded the entire $10,000 in order to carry on with the fix. He found the ten grand under his pillow and sewed into the lining of his jacket. Rothstein bet $90,000 with oilman Harry Sinclair. Rothstein's bets totaled $270,000 and drove the odds from 3–1 on the White Sox to 8–5 on the Reds within a few days, thereby reducing the winnings of others who had bet on the Reds to win the Series. In Cincinnati, the players, minus Joe Jackson, met in Eddie Cicotte's room with Bill Burns and Rothstein associate Abe Attell. The players were told they would receive $20,000 after each loss. Meanwhile, rumors of the fix begin to circulate and some newspapermen were suspicious, but most dismissed the allegations as idle gossip. It was believed in baseball circles that a World Series couldn't be fixed because it would require too many players and too much money in contests held in a ballpark before thousands in an event that was front-page news in almost every newspaper in the country.

OCTOBER 1   The White Sox lose the opening game of the World Series 9–1 in Cincinnati. Eddie Cicotte hit Reds leadoff batter Morrie Rath with a pitch in the first inning, a signal to gamblers that the fix was on. Arnold Rothstein responded by betting an additional $100,000 on Cincinnati. Rath later scored on a sacrifice fly by Heinie Groh. The Sox tied the score with an unearned run in the second but fell behind after a five-run Cincinnati fourth. All five runs scored with two out when Cicotte surrendered hits to five consecutive batters, including a two-run triple to opposing pitcher Dutch Ruether.

The players were shortchanged by the gambling syndicate again, as Abe Attell did not deliver the $20,000 as promised to Bill Burns and Billy Maharg. The latter told the White Sox in on the fix that the money was tied up in bets.

J. G. Taylor Spink, publisher of The Sporting News, informed AL President Ban Johnson of the rumors that the White Sox were throwing the Series. At 11 p.m., Charles Comiskey and Kid Gleason discussed the possibility that the Series was fixed. Gleason told Comiskey that he believed his players were just overconfident. After midnight, Comiskey talked to NL President John Heydler, who agreed with Gleason's assessment that the White Sox simply took the Reds too lightly. Then, at 3:00 a.m., Comiskey expressed his concerns to Johnson. The two held a simmering hatred for each other after bitterly feuding for over 10 years. Johnson responded that Comiskey's suspicions were "the yelp of a beaten cur."

OCTOBER 2   The Reds win game two 4–2 in Cincinnati. Lefty Williams, one of the best control pitchers in the American League, was uncharacteristically wild. In the fourth inning, the Reds struck for three runs when Williams walked Morrie Rath and Heinie Groh and allowed a single to Edd Roush and a triple to Larry Kopf. Slim Sallee, who pitched for the Giants club that lost to the White Sox in the 1917 Fall Classic, was the winning pitcher. A bizarre incident occurred in the seventh inning when a stuffed dummy was dropped out of a low-flying airplane and landed between second and third base. This was apparently a practical joke. No players were injured, nor was anyone arrested.

Before the game, Chick Gandil told Abe Attell, Bill Burns and Billy Maharg that he wanted $20,000. Attell insisted there was no money until after the game, but he left a Texas oil lease as security. When the contest was over, Gandil was beaten up by Kid Gleason, and Ray Schalk attacked Lefty Williams. During the first two games, both Eddie Cicotte and Williams repeatedly crossed up Schalk by failing to throw the pitches he signaled. On the train from Chicago to Cincinnati, Chicago columnist Ring Lardner sang a parody of a popular song of the day titled "I'm Forever Blowing Bubbles" within earshot of the White Sox players. In Lardner's version, the signature line was "I'm forever blowing ball games."

OCTOBER 3   The White Sox win game three 3–0 before 29,126 at Comiskey Park as Dickie Kerr tosses a three-hit shutout. The White Sox scored two runs in the second inning on Chick Gandil's single.

Before the game, Gandil told Bill Burns that the fix was still on and that the Sox would lose. Burns and Billy Maharg bet all of their money on the Reds, and lost every cent.

OCTOBER 4   The Reds take a three-games-to-one lead in the World Series with a 2–0 win before 34,363 at Comiskey Park behind the three-hit pitching of Jimmy Ring. Both Cincinnati runs scored in the fifth inning with the aid of two errors by Eddie Cicotte. The first miscue occurred when the Chicago pitcher threw wildly to first after fielding a grounder by Pat Duncan. The second Cicotte error happened when he dropped a throw at second base in an attempt to retire Larry Kopf, who was trying to stretch a single into a double.

Sport Sullivan panicked when another gambler wanted to bet on the White Sox. Chick Gandil told Sullivan that the fix was off. Sullivan then offered $20,000 prior to Game Four and another $40,000 before Game Five if the White Sox agreed to keep losing on purpose. Gandil took the $20,000 and distributed $5,000 each to Happy Felsch, Joe Jackson, Swede Risberg and Lefty Williams to ensure their continued cooperation in the fix.

OCTOBER 6   After a rainout of the October 5 game, the Reds take a four-games-to-one lead in the best-of-nine World Series with a 5–0 win before 34,379 at Comiskey Park as Hod Eller pitches a three-hit shutout. Eller struck out nine batters, including six in succession in the second and third innings. The Reds bunched four runs in the sixth inning off Lefty Williams, two of them coming on an Edd Roush triple that was misplayed by Happy Felsch in center field.

The White Sox who were in on the fix did not receive the promised $20,000 when Sport Sullivan failed to show up for a meeting. The "Black Sox," outraged at being double-crossed, decided to try and win the Series. It would take four consecutive victories to accomplish the feat.

OCTOBER 7   The White Sox prolong the Series with a 5–4 win in 10 innings in Game Six, played in Cincinnati. The Reds jumped out to an early 4–0 lead with two runs in the third inning and another pair in the fourth, prompting Cincinnati fans to prepare for a championship celebration. The Sox postponed those plans with a run in the fifth, ending a 26-inning scoreless streak, and three in the sixth in a rally started by a double from Buck Weaver.

The ace of the White Sox staff, Ed Cicotte had an outstanding season in 1919, though his actions during the World Series cost him his career.

The winning run in the 10th scored on another Weaver double and singles by Joe Jackson and Chick Gandil.

OCTOBER 8   The White Sox keep their world championship hopes afloat with a 4–1 win at Cincinnati behind the seven-hit pitching of Eddie Cicotte. Shano Collins contributed a double, two singles and two runs scored.

OCTOBER 9   The Reds take the world championship with a 10–5 win over the White Sox before 32,930 at Comiskey Park. The game was decided in the first inning when the Reds connected for four runs off Lefty Williams, who lost his third game of the series. By the eighth inning, the score was 10–1. It was Lefty's third loss of the Series.

The gamblers who had bet heavily on the Reds told Williams the night before that unless he lost the game convincingly in the first inning, he and his wife would be physically harmed. Lefty wasted no time, grooving pitches. He retired only one of the five batters to face him and surrendered two singles and two doubles. Sport Sullivan and Nat Evans retrieved $40,000 from the Congress

Hotel safe. In Chick Gandil's room they distributed $15,000 to Swede Risberg, $5,000 to Fred McMullin and the rest to Gandil.

OCTOBER 10   Charles Comiskey offers a reward of $20,000 for information about the fix of the World Series. He kept the monetary inducement open throughout the off-season, although he later reduced the amount to $10,000.

The details of the "Black Sox" plan to throw the World Series was not made public until September 1920. It is fruitless to speculate as to which team would have won if the World Series had been played on the level. The depth of the fix is still unknown. The games were thrown mainly on pitching and defense. Eddie Cicotte and Lefty Williams, both excellent control pitchers, had sudden lapses of wildness throughout the Series. The "Black Sox" who were in on the fix made few glaring errors. The defensive omissions were mostly on throws that were just a little off line, relays that were held a second too long, fly balls that were missed by a step and by slowing down slightly on the base paths.

DECEMBER 19   Charles Comiskey reports on the investigation involving the possibility of a fix of the 1919 World Series. "I am very happy to state," said the Sox owner, "that we have discovered nothing to indicate any member of my team double-crossed me or the public last fall. We have been investigating all these rumors and I have had men working 24 hours a day running down clues that promised to produce facts. Nothing came of them. Do not get the impression that we are through investigating. I am still working on the case and will go to the limit to get any evidence to bear out the truth of these accusations. If I land the goods on any of my ballplayers I will see that there is no place in organized ball for them. There will be no whitewashing or compromising with crooks as long as I am in the American League. But as yet, not one bit of reliable information has been turned up to prove there was anything wrong." Comiskey also conferred with Maclay Hoyne, State's Attorney for Cook County, about bringing criminal proceedings against the White Sox suspected of throwing the Series. Hoyne expressed the opinion that it would be extremely difficult to prove the case. Only Gandil and Cicotte had shown any signs of coming into any extraordinary sum of money. Gandil had purchased a new automobile, diamonds and other marks of affluence. Cicotte had lifted the mortgage on his farm. Of the eight players eventually implicated in the fix, seven returned to play for the White Sox in 1920, and most of them received a large increase in salary. The only one who didn't come back to the Sox was Gandil, who decided to retire on the money he received from gamblers. Meanwhile, the fix was debated on the sports pages throughout the winter. The first publication to break the story just days after the Series ended was *Collier's Eye,* a weekly based in Chicago. Windy City sportswriter Hugh Fullerton accused the players of crookedness in a series of articles beginning in December 1919, but few took him seriously. Francis C. Richter, editor of the prestigious Reach Baseball Guide, weighed in on the World Series scandal in the 1920 edition of the publication. "Any man who knows anything at all about base ball and base ball players," wrote Richter, "knows absolutely that both the game and its exemplars are absolutely honest so far as its public presentation is concerned, and any man who insinuates that the 1919 World Series was not honorably played by every participant therein not only does not know what he is talking about, but is a menace to the game quite as much as the gamblers would be if they had the ghost of a chance to get in their nefarious work."

Don't Blame Charles Comiskey for the 1919 World Series Scandal

Charles Comiskey's reputation as a miser whose penurious ways led to eight of the players conspiring to lose the 1919 World Series in collusion with gamblers is fixed in cement. In the excellent 1990 book *The Ballplayers: Baseball's Ultimate Biographical Reference,* it is written that "Comiskey's own greed is considered to have been the real motivation for the 'Black Sox' selling out to gamblers in 1919. When it was revealed that the players threw the Series for $10,000 because Comiskey had underpaid them for years, his reputation was tarnished." *Baseball: The Biographical Encyclopedia*, published in 2000, says that Comiskey was "a tightwad owner whose ill treatment of his personnel helped bring on the Black Sox scandal of 1919." In the 2002 work, *The New Biographical History of Baseball,* the passage under Comiskey discloses that "his 1919 pennant winners were woefully underpaid, some of them getting only half of what comparable players on other teams received; this made them ripe for the plucking by the gambling fraternity." Richard C. Lindberg in *The White Sox Encyclopedia* summed up the verdict on the White Sox founder when he wrote: "Baseball historians who study the national pastime have long considered Charles Comiskey a tightfighted misanthrope whose shabby treatment of his eight underpaid players on the 1919 squad was the catalyst of the Black Sox scandal." The four books cited above were written by some of baseball's best historians and were invaluable resources in the writing of this book. However, the accepted historical record of Comiskey's role in the Black Sox scandal is inaccurate.

The primary research for *White Sox Journal* was done by carefully looking at contemporary newspapers and publications such as *The Sporting News*. One of the goals of this book was to see if Comiskey was considered to be a "tightfisted misanthrope." In fact, Comiskey was portrayed as one of baseball's more generous owners before the Black Sox scandal broke in 1920. The shift toward labeling him as a tightwad began in 1921 when the eight players involved in the World Series were defending themselves against the charges. They were acquitted, but nonetheless were suspended for life from participating in Organized Baseball

by commissioner Kenesaw Landis. Later, several of the players returned to the courtroom to seek back pay from Comiskey because of the suspensions.

During these trials, the eight "Black Sox" related tales of Comiskey's ill-treatment, both on the stand and to the assembled press. The trials were covered extensively in the newspapers, especially in Chicago. The players' stories of Comiskey's tight-fisted practices were generally believed, leading to a change in the public perception of the White Sox owner. Were the players truthful in their portrayal of Comiskey? Or, has Comiskey been "convicted" by baseball historians of being a "tightwad" based on exaggerated, false or even perjurious testimony given by the "Black Sox?" The historical record suggests that the latter is true.

The years leading up to the 1919 World Series were a particularly acrimonious period in owner-player relations. The existence of the Federal League in 1914 and 1915 escalated salaries because players had the option of joining a third league outside the structure of Organized Baseball. When the Federal League folded in 1916, owners naturally tried to cut salaries back to their pre-1914 levels, leading to difficulties in signing players to contracts. In 1918, the country was at war and owners, forecasting a drop in attendance, again tried to cut costs by reducing salaries. By the time the 1919 season started, World War I was over, but owners didn't believe the public would return to the ballparks and scaled back the schedule from 154 games to 140. Players' salaries were decreased as well.

Despite this, Charles Comiskey had little trouble signing his players to contracts during this period. Had Comiskey truly paid his players "half of what comparable players on other teams received," the White Sox would have been hit much harder than other teams with players defecting to the Federal League. In fact, the Sox came out of the Federal League "war" with a much stronger roster because of Comiskey's willingness to spend money. With the exception of Harry Lord and Hal Chase, none of his 1914 or 1915 players left for the Federals. In addition, Comiskey exploited the financial difficulties of fellow owners to acquire

Eddie Collins from the Athletics and Joe Jackson from the Indians. Collins and Jackson were two of the greatest stars of the period, and to keep them out of the clutches of the Federal League, Comiskey signed the pair to three-year contracts. At the time, multiyear deals were almost unheard of.

In addition, spring training holdouts were common throughout baseball during the 1914–1919 period. The problem should hit the White Sox harder than most clubs because of the up and down nature of the club's position in the standings. The Sox won the World Series in 1917, and many world championship teams have trouble signing players because they are anxious to "cash in" on their good season with a significant salary increase. The 1918 squad limped home in sixth place. Such a drop usually prompts another difficult cycle in inking players to contracts because owners tend to take a hard line following a disappointing season. Yet, Comiskey had few problems getting his players into camp. In 1918, players were signed well in advance of spring camp. In 1919, Buck Weaver was the last member of the team to put his signature on a contract. He signed the deal in Chicago's LaSalle station as the club was boarding a train for camp in Mineral Wells, Texas. Comiskey did have well-publicized salary squabbles with Fielder Jones in 1909 and Dickie Kerr in 1921, but these were widely-spaced aberrations.

Unlike many owners before and after the era in which he owned the White Sox, Comiskey did not trade players to cut payroll costs. He founded the franchise in 1901 and owned it until his death in 1932. The only regular during this period who was traded to another club was Willie Kamm in 1931, when Comiskey was ill and was no longer running the club on a day-to-day basis. In addition, Comiskey freely spent money in order to put a winning team on the field, both before and after 1919. In many ways, he was the George Steinbrenner of the first three decades of the 20th century.

Rumors swirled throughout the 1919 World Series that the games were fixed and that many of the players conspired with gamblers to lose on purpose. The day after the Series ended, Comiskey offered a $20,000 reward for any information about the fix. Two months later, he admitted that no information had been found linking any of his players to dumping the games, but he said that he would remain vigilant in his pursuit of any wrongdoing. Well into the 1920 season, Comiskey continued to make bold statements that he would get rid of any of the offending players if solid evidence could be found that they threw games.

Many historians have viewed Comiskey's statements as a mere smoke screen and allege that the Sox owner had no intention of allowing incriminating information about the 1919 World Series scandal to become public, and in fact conspired to keep it hidden. There was, in fact, little that Comiskey could do under the circumstances. Those with concrete knowledge of the fix were the gamblers, many connected with organized crime, and the players themselves. No one was willing to talk. Even 40 years later, when Eliot Asinof wrote his book *Eight Men Out* about the scandal, he confronted a "wall of silence." Asinof interviewed the surviving members of the 1919 White Sox and found that no one was willing to go on record concerning what they knew about the fix. Asinof found just as many doors closed by the innocent players as the culprits for fear of physical reprisals from organized crime, even though four decades had passed. "I was told by more than one ballplayer," Asinof noted, "that it was safer to keep one's mouth shut about this whole affair."

Comiskey also found that baseball's hierarchy was unwilling to cooperate. The office of the commissioner was not created until 1921, when Kenesaw Landis was given the position. From 1903 through 1920, baseball was run by a three-man commission consisting of Reds President Garry Herrmann, National League President John Heydler and American League President Ban Johnson. Comiskey couldn't turn to any one of the three for help. Herrmann's Cincinnati club had defeated the White Sox in the 1919 World Series and didn't want his championship tarnished. Heydler, due to league pride, didn't want a National League club to be robbed of an undisputed title. It was the first time since 1914 that the NL won the Fall Classic. Heydler publicly expressed the notion that he believed the Series was won on the level. Comiskey and Johnson were bitter enemies and had been for about 15 years. Johnson offered no help in Comiskey's investigation.

Comiskey had no choice but to bring seven of the eight players suspected of fixing the World Series back to the White Sox in 1920. The only one who didn't return was Chick Gandil, who retired. Releasing the other seven players wasn't a viable option. They would have become free agents, and there is little doubt that they would have been snapped up by another club, likely at an increase in salary. Had they not been signed by another big-league team, both the White Sox and baseball would have been subject to legal action for wrongful termination and "blacklisting."

In addition, the public didn't seem to care about the scandal, as major league baseball set attendance records in 1920. The 16 clubs attracted 9,120,875 fans that season, breaking the previous mark of 7,234,114 set in 1909. The White Sox drew 833,492, shattering the former high of 687,419 established in 1905.

The fix finally became public in September 1920, when a grand jury began investigating the allegations surrounding the 1919 World Series. On September 28, many admitted on the witness stand that they took money from gamblers to throw the Series. The revelation came at a particularly bad time for the White Sox, who were in the final week of a heated pennant race and had a shot at returning to the World Series again. After hearing the admissions of guilt, Comiskey didn't wait for an indictment or a conviction to take action. He immediately suspended the seven players who were involved in the fix and were still on the roster. "Until there is a finality to this investigation, it is due to the public that I take this action even though it costs Chicago the pennant," Comiskey said. Six days later, Comiskey paid the rest of the players on the 1919 squad $1,500, the difference between the winner's and loser's share of the World Series purse. Comiskey stated that he didn't believe that those who played in the Series honestly should "suffer from the perfidy of others."

The eight "Black Sox" were indicted on October 22, 1920, for "attempting to defraud the public," as there was no law on the books that made fixing baseball games illegal. The trial took place in July and August of 1921. On August 2, a jury found the players innocent of all charges.

By this time, Kenesaw Landis had taken over as commissioner. The following day, Landis suspended the eight players from Organized Baseball for life in spite of the not-guilty verdict. While Landis has long been given credit for the banishments, it was actually Comiskey who had suspended the players. When Landis took his action, the "Black Sox" hadn't played in a big-league game for over 10 months, thanks to Comiskey's bold action of September 28, 1920.

Comiskey had his faults, but he was far from the worst owner of his era, and in fact, was better than most. Over the years, his negative traits have been magnified and his words and actions have too often been turned against him by historians, while his positive qualities have largely been ignored. Charles Comiskey should be absolved of any responsibility in the 1919 World Series scandal. The blame rests solely on the individuals who purposely lost the Series for their own personal financial gain.

THE STATE OF THE WHITE SOX

The decade began under a cloud as eight White Sox players were suspected of throwing the 1919 World Series. Seven of the eight played for the club in 1920, and it appeared that the Sox might return to the postseason when the seven were suspended by Charles Comiskey after a grand jury indicted the "Black Sox" for conspiracy to fix the 1919 Fall Classic. A year later, they were banned for life by baseball commissioner Kenesaw Landis. The White Sox spent the rest of the 1920s, and the 1930s and 1940s as well, trying to recover from the scandal. Overall, the Sox were 731–804 during the '20s, a winning percentage of .476 that ranked seventh in the league, ahead of only the Red Sox. AL pennant winners were the Indians (1920), Yankees (1921, 1922, 1923, 1926, 1927 and 1928), Senators (1924 and 1925) and Athletics (1929).

THE BEST TEAM

The 1920 White Sox were 96–58 and finished in second place, two games behind the Indians. It would be 1936 before another White Sox club ended a season higher than fifth, and 1964 before another Comiskey Park team won more than 96 games.

THE WORST TEAM

The worst team was the last one. The 1929 edition was 59–93 and finished seventh.

THE BEST MOMENT

Journeyman pitcher Charlie Robertson hurled the only perfect game in White Sox history on April 30, 1922, against the Tigers in Detroit.

THE WORST MOMENT

The worst moment in the history of the franchise occurred on August 3, 1921, when Kenesaw Landis issued a lifetime suspension from organized baseball to the eight White Sox players implicated in the fix of the 1919 Series.

THE ALL-DECADE TEAM • YEARS WITH WS

Ray Schalk, c	1912–28
Earl Sheely, 1b	1921–27
Eddie Collins, 2b	1915–26
Willie Kamm, 3b	1922–31
Bill Cissell, ss	1928–32
Bibb Falk, lf	1920–28
Johnny Mostil, cf	1918, 1921–29
Harry Hooper, rf	1921–25
Red Faber, p	1914–33
Ted Lyons, p	1923–42, 1946
Tommy Thomas, p	1926–32
Ted Blankenship, p	1922–30

Despite an overall lack of team success, the White Sox had their share of future Hall of Famers during the 1920s. The list included Collins, Lyons, Faber, Hooper and Schalk. Collins, Faber and Schalk were also on the 1910s All-Decade Team. Other outstanding White Sox players during the 1920s included outfielders Alex Metzler (1927–30) and Bill Barrett (1923–29). Finding a capable shortstop was a decade-long problem for the White Sox during the 1920s.

THE DECADE LEADERS

Batting Avg:	Eddie Collins	.348
On-Base Pct:	Eddie Collins	.435
Slugging Pct:	Eddie Collins	.447
Home Runs:	Bibb Falk	50
RBIs:	Bibb Falk	627
Runs:	Eddie Collins	631
Stolen Bases:	Johnny Mostil	175
Wins:	Red Faber	149
Strikeouts:	Red Faber	804
ERA:	Tommy Thomas	3.24
Saves:	Sarge Connally	25

THE HOME FIELD

At the start of the decade, Comiskey Park was 10 years old and had a second deck only between first and third bases. During the winter of 1926–27, the ballpark was double-decked around its entire expanse with the exception of an elevated bleacher section in direct center field. The detached outfield pavilions were connected to the baseline grandstand seats for the first time. Manually operated scoreboards were built into the outfield walls. The $600,000 remodeling boosted capacity to 52,000.

THE GAME YOU WISH YOU HAD SEEN

Offensive outbursts were rare at pitcher-friendly Comiskey Park, but September 9, 1921, was the exception to the rule as the White Sox outslugged the Tigers 20–15.

THE WAY THE GAME WAS PLAYED

Rule changes in 1920 and the emergence of Babe Ruth as a star transformed baseball from a low-scoring defensive affair to a high-scoring offensive carnival. AL teams went from averaging 3.5 runs per game in 1917 to 5.1 per game in 1921 and 5.4 per game in 1930. As a result, team ERAs jumped by nearly two runs. Pitchers completed fewer than half their starts in the AL in 1923, the first time that had happened, as relief pitching continued to gain importance.

THE MANAGEMENT

Charles Comiskey, who owned the White Sox from the franchise's inception until his death in 1931, had to rebuild the club in the wake of the suspension of the seven "Black Sox" who remained with the team in 1920. Harry Grabiner was team secretary and vice-president, serving a role similar to a modern day general manager. Field managers during the 1920s were Kid Gleason (1919–23), Johnny Evers (1924), Eddie Collins (1925–26), Ray Schalk (1927–28) and Lena Blackburne (1928–29). In addition, Frank Chance was hired as manager in October 1923, but resigned due to health reasons in February 1924. Ed Walsh and Collins were interim managers in 1924 while Evers was absent following an appendectomy.

THE BEST PLAYER MOVE

Charles Comiskey tried to revive the White Sox during the 1920s by spending a small fortune on minor league players and amateurs. In most cases, Comiskey overpaid for the amount of talent he received. He definitely struck gold in 1923, however, by signing pitcher Ted Lyons off the campus of Baylor University.

THE WORST PLAYER MOVE

There were no disastrous trades during the 1920s, but on the other hand, there were also no deals that had a lasting positive impact on the franchise.

1920

Season in a Sentence

The White Sox are in contention for their second consecutive American League pennant when eight players are indicted for attempting the fix the 1919 World Series.

Finish • Won • Lost • Pct • GB

Second   96   58   .623   2.0

Manager

Kid Gleason

Stats

Stats	WS	AL	Rank
Batting Avg:	.295	.284	3
On-Base Pct:	.357	.347	3
Slugging Pct:	.402	.387	4
Home Runs:	37		4
Stolen Bases:	109		3
ERA:	3.59	3.79	3
Fielding Avg:	.968	.966	4
Runs Scored:	794		4
Runs Allowed:	665		3

Starting Lineup

Ray Schalk, c
Shano Collins, 1b
Eddie Collins, 2b
Buck Weaver, 3b
Swede Risberg, ss
Joe Jackson, lf
Happy Felsch, cf
Nemo Leibold, rf
Amos Strunk, rf
Ted Jourdan, 1b

Pitchers

Red Faber, sp
Lefty Williams, sp
Eddie Cicotte, sp
Dickie Kerr, sp-rp
Roy Wilkinson, rp-sp

Attendance

833,492 (third in AL)

Club Leaders

Batting Avg:	Joe Jackson	.382
On-Base Pct:	Joe Jackson	.444
Slugging Pct:	Joe Jackson	.589
Home Runs:	Happy Felsch	14
RBIs:	Joe Jackson	121
Runs:	Eddie Collins	117
Stolen Bases:	Eddie Collins	19
	Buck Weaver	19
Wins:	Red Faber	23
Strikeouts:	Lefty Williams	128
ERA:	Red Faber	2.99
Saves:	Dickie Kerr	5

FEBRUARY 9   Baseball's rules committee adopts new regulations that usher in the era of the lively ball. The changes were spurred in part by the owners' recognition of the positive impact of Babe Ruth upon the game. Ruth clubbed a then-record 29 home runs for the Red Sox in 1919 and helped the American League set an all-time attendance record. Baseball's rules committee adopted a more-lively ball, agreed to keep a fresh ball in play at all times and banned pitchers from using foreign substances to deface a ball. These included paraffin, resin, powder, emery boards, files and saliva.

APRIL 14   The White Sox begin the 1920 season with an 11-inning, 3–2 win over the Tigers at Comiskey Park. Lefty Williams pitched a complete game. Buck Weaver had four hits, including a double, in five at-bats. Eddie Collins collected two doubles and a single.

Lefty Williams was one of four pitchers to win 20 or more games for the White Sox in 1920. The only other club in major league history with four 20-game winners was the 1971 Baltimore Orioles. The stellar rotation with the Sox in 1920 included Williams, Red Faber, Eddie Cicotte and Dickie Kerr. Faber was

23–13 with an ERA of 2.99, 28 complete games and 319 innings. Williams had a record of 22–14, 128 strikeouts, and an earned run average of 3.91. Cicotte's mark was 21–10 with 28 complete games, 303⅓ innings and an ERA of 3.26. The pitching hero of the 1919 World Series, Kerr started the 1920 season in the bullpen before moving into the rotation in May. He was 21–9, had a 3.37 ERA, and led the AL in saves with five.

APRIL 20   The game between the White Sox and Browns at Comiskey Park is halted in the third inning when a fog from Lake Michigan blows in and obscures the field. The fog failed to lift, and the contest was postponed.

The rumors that eight players had conspired to throw the 1919 World Series didn't affect attendance at Comiskey Park in 1920. The club drew a then-record 833,492, shattering the old mark of 687,419 set in 1905. The 1920 attendance standard remained the record until the Sox drew 983,403 in 1946.

APRIL 25   The White Sox run their record on the 1920 season to 6–0 with a 10-inning, 2–1 victory over the Tigers in Detroit.

APRIL 29   Lefty Williams pitches a two-hitter to defeat the Indians 6–1 in Cleveland. The only hits off Williams were singles by Tris Speaker and Larry Gardner.

MAY 20   The White Sox erupt for eight runs in the 16th inning to defeat the Senators 13–5 in Washington. The Sox scored twice in the top of the 15th to take a 5–3 lead, but the Senators rallied to tie the game again in their half. The White Sox put the game away, scoring the eight runs on two triples, a double, two singles and four errors. Red Faber pitched all 16 innings for Chicago.

MAY 21   The White Sox win in extra innings for the second day in a row, scoring three times in the 10th inning and defeating the Senators 11–9 in Washington.

MAY 22   The White Sox score seven runs in the third inning and beat the Senators 10–6 in Washington.

MAY 29   The White Sox score five times in the ninth inning to stun the Indians 8–7 in the first game of a double-header in Cleveland. The last three Chicago runs scored on bases-loaded walks. The Indians won the second tilt 6–1.

JUNE 19   With the White Sox trailing 5–4 in the 10th inning, Happy Felsch hits a two-run, walk-off triple to defeat the Yankees 6–5 at Comiskey Park.

JUNE 26   The White Sox score seven runs in the fourth inning and beat the Indians 12–7 at Comiskey Park.

JUNE 28   The White Sox win a 13–5 slugging match against the Tigers in Detroit.

JUNE 30   The White Sox wallop the Tigers 14–0 in Detroit.

JULY 1   The White Sox split a double-header against the Browns on an eventful day at Comiskey Park, winning the opener 3–2 in 11 innings and losing the nightcap 4–1. The 1919 American League pennant was unfurled before the game and Ray Schalk was presented with a chest of silver for his loyal service to the club. In the opener, Nemo Leibold hit his first career homer. Leibold made his major league debut in 1913 and the homer occurred in his 2,527th at-bat.

JULY 4   The White Sox supply the fireworks in the first game of an Independence Day double-header at Comiskey Park by overcoming a 5–0 deficit with six runs in the eighth inning to defeat the Indians 6–5. The Sox collected eight hits in the tremendous rally off future Hall of Famer Stan Coveleski. The big blow was a bases-loaded triple by Eddie Murphy. Shano Collins broke the 5–5 tie with a single. Chicago completed the sweep with a 5–3 win in the nightcap.

Murphy was a key figure off the bench for the White Sox in 1919 and 1920. As a pinch-hitter those two seasons, he had 21 hits in 54 at-bats for an average of .389, and hit .373 overall in 152 at-bats.

JULY 6   Happy Felsch hits a walk-off home run in the 11th inning to defeat the Indians 5–4 at Comiskey Park. Eddie Murphy tied the score 4–4 with a pinch-single in the 10th.

During the 1920 season, Felsch and Joe Jackson became the first White Sox players to reach double-digits in home runs. Felsch had 14 homers, 115 RBIs, 40 doubles, 15 triples, and a .338 batting average. Jackson hit .382 with 12 home runs, 121 RBIs, 105 runs, 218 hits, 42 doubles and 20 triples. Other batting leaders in 1920 were Buck Weaver, who hit .331 and had 102 runs and 208 hits, and Eddie Collins, with a .372 average, 117 runs and 224 hits. The hit totals of Collins, Jackson and Weaver still rank as the three highest single-season figures in White Sox history. Rip Radcliff is fourth with 207 in 1936.

JULY 8   In an odd 8–5 win over the Athletics in Philadelphia, both teams score five runs in the ninth inning.

Ray Schalk caught 151 of the White Sox's 154 games in 1920.

JULY 12   Shano Collins hits a home run in the ninth inning off Scott Perry to account for the only run in a 1–0 victory over the Athletics in Philadelphia. Dickie Kerr pitched the shutout.

JULY 16   With the White Sox trailing 5–4 in the ninth inning of the second game of a double-header in Washington, Joe Jackson hits an inside-the-park grand slam off Senators hurler Eric Erickson for an 8–5 victory. The Sox also won the opener 4–1.

JULY 20   The White Sox score four runs in the ninth inning to beat the Yankees 7–5 in the first game of a double-header at the Polo Grounds. All four runs scored after two were out. New York took the second game 6–3.

JULY 23   Down 5–0 in the fifth inning, the White Sox rally to win 8–7 in Boston. The Sox scored four runs in the eighth inning, the last two on a pinch-single by Eddie Murphy.

On the same day, the White Sox purchased Amos Strunk from the Athletics.

AUGUST 5   The White Sox fall into third place, five games back of the first-place Indians after a 4–2 loss to the Red Sox at Comiskey Park.

Following a resurgence, the Sox moved back into first place 16 days later.

AUGUST 20   The White Sox sweep the Athletics in a double-header in Philadelphia, with the second resulting in a forfeit. The Sox won the opener 7–4. With two out in the bottom of the ninth and Chicago leading 5–2 in the second tilt, the crowd swarmed on to the field. When the multitude refused to leave, umpire Ollie Chill declared the forfeit. The first game was halted in the fifth inning for a moment of silence for Indians shortstop Ray Chapman, who was buried that day. Chapman died three days earlier from the effects of being hit in the head from a pitch thrown by Carl Mays of the Yankees.

AUGUST 21   The White Sox take over control of first place with a 5–2 win over the Senators in Washington.

AUGUST 26   On the day that women are granted the right to vote with the passage of the 19th amendment, the White Sox take a 3½-game lead in the American League pennant race with a 16–4 victory over the Yankees in New York.

AUGUST 31   Cubs president Bill Veeck, Sr. receives a telegram informing him of heavy betting on that day's game between the Cubs and Phillies in Chicago. The message warned him of rumors that the game was fixed. The Cubs replaced starting pitcher Claude Hendrix with Grover Alexander, but the Cubs lost anyway 3–0.

The game would have major implications on the future of the White Sox. Cook County District Attorney MacClay Hoyne and a grand jury looked into the events surrounding the Cubs-Phillies game of August 31, which led to the investigation of the 1919 World Series fix (see September 7, 1920).

SEPTEMBER 1   The White Sox are knocked out of first place with a 6–2 loss to the Red Sox in Boston.

The loss was the fifth in a row, including two to the Yankees and three to the Red Sox. Many White Sox players were convinced that the players involved in the 1919 World Series fix also threw the five games against the Yankees and Red Sox in collusion with gamblers, who had bet on the Yankees or Indians to win the American League pennant. Eddie Collins voiced his suspicions to Charles Comiskey on September 2. Comiskey listened patiently and said he would look into it, but like the World Series the previous autumn, he had nothing but unverifiable rumors to act upon.

SEPTEMBER 6   In his major league debut, White Sox pitcher Shovel Hodge holds the Tigers hitless for the first 7⅓ innings before settling for a 10-inning two-hitter and a 5–4 win in the second game of a double-header at Comiskey Park. Detroit scored four runs in the eighth inning with the help of singles by Sammy Hale and Donie Bush and four Hodge walks. The Sox also won the opener 6–2.

Clarence (Shovel) Hodge had a 14–15 record and a 5.17 ERA during a three-year big league career.

SEPTEMBER 7   A Cook County grand jury convenes to investigate gambling in baseball. In
               addition to investigating the August 31 Phillies-Cubs game, presiding judge Charles
               McDonald recommends that the panel look into the rumors that the 1919 World
               Series was fixed (see September 21, 1920).

SEPTEMBER 11   Shano Collins is given a check for $2,500 from his Chicago admirers before a 9–7
               loss to the Red Sox at Comiskey Park.

SEPTEMBER 13   Trailing 5–4, the White Sox score seven runs in the sixth inning to spark a 15–6 win
               over the Senators at Comiskey Park. Happy Felsch hit a grand slam in the big inning.
               Eddie Collins extended his hitting streak to 22 games.

SEPTEMBER 17   The White Sox tie an American League record with six triples during a 7–4 win over
               the Yankees at Comiskey Park. The Sox collected three consecutive triples from
               Eddie Collins, Joe Jackson and Happy Felsch off Hank Thormahlen with two out in
               the first inning. Later, Felsch and Jackson tripled again, and Swede Risberg added
               another three-bagger.

SEPTEMBER 18   The White Sox take a 14–2 lead in the fifth inning, collect 21 hits, and defeat the
               Yankees 15–9 before a crowd of 43,000 at Comiskey Park. The seating capacity
               of the ballpark in 1920 was about 32,000. The excess crowd was placed 10 deep
               around the field. Any ball hit into the crowd was a ground-rule double.

SEPTEMBER 20   The White Sox thrash the Athletics 13–6 at Comiskey Park. It was Red Faber's 23rd
               win of the season.

SEPTEMBER 21   Assistant Illinois State Attorney Hartley Replogle announces he will suppoena
               players, owners, managers and gamblers to testify before the grand jury. Charles
               Comiskey was among the first to testify. He told the grand jury: "If any of my
               players are not honest, I'll fire them no matter who they are, and if I can't get honest
               players to fill their places, I'll close the gates of the park that I have spent a lifetime
               to build and in which, in the declining years of my life, I take the greatest measure of
               pride and pleasure."

SEPTEMBER 25   The White Sox pull within one game of first place with a 5–1 win over the Indians
               in Cleveland. Lefty Williams won his 22nd game of 1920 in what would prove to be
               the last game of his career. After hitting a home run, Joe Jackson twice made obscene
               gestures towards the fans while circling the bases. He was booed lustily by the crowd
               at Dunn Field, which included thousands of ex-soldiers attending an American
               Legion convention in Cleveland. Many fans chanted "shipyard" repeatedly in
               Jackson's direction, a reference to his controversial decision not to join the military
               during World War I (see May 13, 1918).

SEPTEMBER 26   It what would prove to be the last game of his career, Eddie Cicotte earns his 21st
               win of 1920 with an 8–1 decision over the Tigers at Comiskey Park.

SEPTEMBER 27   Dickie Kerr wins his 20th game of the season and keeps the White Sox one-half game
               behind the Indians in the AL pennant race with a 2–0 win over the Tigers
               at Comiskey Park.

SEPTEMBER 28   Eddie Cicotte admits to the grand jury he accepted $10,000 to throw the first game of the 1919 World Series, which the Reds won 9–1. Joe Jackson also testified for nearly two hours, said that he received $5,000 of the $20,000 he was promised and implicated Chick Gandil and Swede Risberg in the scandal. Lefty Williams and Happy Felsch also took their turns before the board of inquiry and confessed their involvement. Charles Comiskey was not in court to hear the confessions of Cicotte, Jackson, Williams and Felsch on the witness stand. Instead, he remained in his office and issued suspensions for the eight players involved in the fix, seven of whom were still with the club. The eight were Cicotte, Jackson, Gandil, Risberg, Lefty Williams, Buck Weaver, Happy Felsch and Fred McMullin. The move cost the White Sox the services of two starting pitchers and their starting left fielder, center fielder, third baseman and shortstop. In his letter to his players, Comiskey remarked: "Until there is a finality to this investigation, it is due to the public that I take this action even though it costs Chicago the pennant." (See October 22, 1920.)

OCTOBER 1   In the first game since the suspension of the eight members of the "Black Sox," the White Sox lose 8–6 to the Browns in St. Louis to fall two games behind the Indians with two games to play.

OCTOBER 2   The White Sox win 10–7 over the Browns in St. Louis behind Dickie Kerr's 21st win, but the Indians clinch the AL pennant with a 10–1 victory over the Tigers in Detroit.

OCTOBER 4   Charles Comiskey gives each of the players on the 1919 White Sox who did not participate in the fix a check for $1,500. The amount was the difference between the winner's share and the loser's share. Comiskey stated that he didn't believe that those who played in the Series honestly should suffer from the perfidy of others.

OCTOBER 22   Two weeks before the election of Warren Harding as president, eight members of the 1919 White Sox are indicted for throwing the World Series. Also indicted were New York gamblers Arnold Rothstein and Abe Attell. The case went to trial on July 19, 1921.

1921

Season in a Sentence

With a roster decimated by the suspensions of the players involved in the fix of the World Series, the White Sox sink to seventh place.

Finish • Won • Lost • Pct • GB

Seventh 62 92 .403 36.5

Manager

Kid Gleason

Stats

	WS	AL	Rank
Batting Avg:	.283	.292	5
On-Base Pct:	.343	.357	5
Slugging Pct:	.379	.408	7
Home Runs:	35		7
Stolen Bases:	93		3
ERA:	4.94	4.28	8
Fielding Avg:	.969	.965	2
Runs Scored:	683		6
Runs Allowed:	858		7

Starting Lineup

Ray Schalk, c
Earl Sheely, 1b
Eddie Collins, 2b
Joe Mulligan, 3b
Ernie Johnson, ss
Bibb Falk, lf
Amos Strunk, cf-rf
Harry Hooper, rf
Johnny Mostil, cf
Harvey McClelland, 2b-ss-rf

Pitchers

Red Faber, sp
Dickie Kerr, sp
Roy Wilkinson, sp-rp
Dominic Mulrenen, sp
Shovel Hodge, rp-sp
Doug McWeeny, rp-sp

Attendance

543,650 (fourth in AL)

Club Leaders

Batting Avg:	Eddie Collins	.337
On-Base Pct:	Eddie Collins	.412
Slugging Pct:	Harry Hooper	.470
Home Runs:	Earl Sheely	11
RBIs:	Earl Sheely	95
Runs:	Ernie Johnson	93
Stolen Bases:	Ernie Johnson	22
Wins:	Red Faber	25
Strikeouts:	Red Faber	124
ERA:	Red Faber	2.48
Saves:	Roy Wilkinson	3

JANUARY 21   Kenesaw Landis takes over officially as baseball's first commissioner.

MARCH 4   The White Sox trade Shano Collins and Nemo Leibold to the Red Sox for Harry Hooper.

Hooper was acquired for some star quality in the outfield after Joe Jackson and Happy Felsch were suspended for trying to fix the 1919 World Series. Hooper was 33 years old, had been a starter in the Boston outfield since 1909 and played on world championship clubs in 1912, 1915, 1916 and 1918. He hit .302 overall in five seasons with the White Sox and was elected to the Hall of Fame in 1971.

APRIL 13   The scheduled season opener against the Tigers in Detroit is postponed by rain.

APRIL 14   The White Sox open the 1921 season with a 6–5 loss to the Tigers in Detroit in a contest played in a constant drizzle. The Sox led 5–1 before Detroit scored four runs in the seventh inning and one in the ninth.

APRIL 21	In the home opener, the White Sox win 8–3 against the Tigers before 25,000 at Comiskey Park. The game was stopped by rain in the top of the eighth inning.
APRIL 29	Red Faber pitches a two-hitter to defeat the Indians 1–0 at Comiskey Park. The only Cleveland hits were singles by Charlie Jamieson and Jack Graney. The lone run of the contest scored in the fourth inning on a double by Earl Sheely and a single by Amos Strunk.

Sheely was the White Sox's starting first baseman for six seasons and hit .305 with the club, which ranks 10th all-time among Sox players with at least 2,000 plate appearances.

MAY 5	Red Faber pitches another two-hitter against the Indians, winning 4–0 in Cleveland. The only hits off Faber were a double by Tris Speaker in the seventh inning and a single by Charlie Jamieson in the ninth.
MAY 18	The White Sox trounce the Yankees 12–2 at Comiskey Park.

Despite a 62–92 record, the White Sox were 13–9 against the pennant-winning Yankees in 1921.

MAY 22	Bibb Falk hits a grand slam off Harry Courtney in the fifth inning of a 6–2 win over the Senators at Comiskey Park.

A rookie in 1921, Falk replaced Joe Jackson in left field. Falk was a regular at the position for eight seasons. He played in 1,067 games and hit .315 as a member of the Sox. His batting average ranks sixth-best among players with at least 2,000 plate appearances with the club. Before becoming a professional baseball player, Falk was a star tackle on the University of Texas football team. In 1939, he returned to Texas as the school's baseball coach. Falk won 20 consecutive Southwest Conference championships and national titles in 1949 and 1950.

JUNE 27	The trial of eight White Sox players and 10 gamblers accused of fixing the 1919 World Series begins in Chicago. The presiding judge was Hugo Friend.
JULY 2	Trailing 6–2, the White Sox score nine runs in the eighth inning and beat the Browns 11–8 in the first game of a double-header at Sportsman's Park. St. Louis won the second encounter 9–4.
JULY 3	Judge Hugo Friend turns down a defense motion to dismiss the indictments in the "Black Sox" trial and jury selection begins.
JULY 9	The White Sox gain a thrilling 10–9 victory in 16 innings against the Yankees at Comiskey Park. Down 8–0, the Sox scored three runs in the seventh. The Yanks added a run in the top of the eighth to take a 9–3 lead before Chicago rallied with two tallies in their half and four in the ninth to send the game into extra innings. Earl Sheely delivered hits that drove in the tying run in the ninth and the winning run in the 16th. Bibb Falk had five hits, including a triple, in five at-bats.

JULY 11   The "Black Sox" meet some of their former teammates in the courtroom. Dickie Kerr, Eddie Collins, Red Faber, Ray Schalk, Harvey McClellan and Roy Wilkinson and manager Kid Gleason were called as witnesses in the trial. The indicted eight "Black Sox" were in good spirits and their ex-teammates slapped them on the back and offered encouraging words. Even Gleason chatted amiably with them.

JULY 17   Red Faber pitches a 10-inning shutout to beat the Red Sox 1–0 at Comiskey Park.

JULY 21   Bibb Falk hits a walk-off homer into the right-field bleachers in the 14th inning to defeat the Athletics 2–1 at Comiskey Park. Red Faber pitched all 14 innings to earn his 20th win of the season.

The win gave Faber a 20–6 record to account for half of his club's wins. At the time, the White Sox had won 40 and lost 49. Faber seemed headed for 30 wins, but after a late-season slump he finished at 25–15. He led the league in ERA (2.48 in 330²/₃ innings) and complete games (32 in 39 starts). Number-two starter Dickie Kerr was 19–17, but his ERA of 4.72 was well above the league average and nearly double the figure posted by Faber. The pitchers on the White Sox staff other than Faber and Kerr won only 18 games and lost 60. Before the start of the 1922 season, Faber was given a three-year contract with a substantial raise by Charles Comiskey. Kerr also wanted the security of a three-year deal, with a modest raise of $500 a year, but Comiskey refused to grant the request. Kerr declined to sign a contract. Although a holdout, he was not allowed to play for any other team according to the rules of organized baseball. Kerr hooked up with an independent semi-pro team in Paris, Texas, that played against the club that employed a couple of Black Sox players who were under suspension for their role in fixing the 1919 World Series. As a result, Kerr was suspended by baseball commissioner Kenesaw Landis in April 1922. With the exception of 12 games with the White Sox in 1925, Kerr never played in the majors again. Later, he worked for several years as a minor league manager and was responsible for switching future Cardinals star Stan Musial from a pitcher into an outfielder in 1941. Musial's first child was named Dickie in honor of Kerr. In 1959, Musial bought Kerr a house in Houston.

JULY 23   The grand jury confessions and immunity waivers of Eddie Cicotte, Joe Jackson and Lefty Williams are missing from the files of the Illinois state attorney. The players repudiated their confessions. Jackson, who was illiterate, said that he didn't know what he was signing.

Exactly what happened to the confessions, signed in September 1920, is a source of controversy. AL President Ban Johnson charged that Arnold Rothstein paid $10,000 to get rid of the files. According to writers Donald Dewey and Nicholas Acocella, Rothstein arranged for Alfred Austrian, Charles Comiskey's attorney, to steal the documents from the state's attorney's office. Eliot Asinof, author of Eight Men Out, *attributed the action to defense attorney William Fallon. In a 1924 suit by Jackson for $18,000 in back pay, the confessions resurfaced in the possession of George B. Hudnall, another of Comiskey's attorneys.*

JULY 28   The White Sox have to play the Senators in Washington without Dickie Kerr, Eddie Collins, Red Faber, Ray Schalk, Harvey McClellan and Roy Wilkinson. The six were called to Chicago to testify in the Black Sox trial. The Sox appealed to the

Senators to postpone the game, but Washington owner Clark Griffith refused to do so. The Sox lost 8–5. The players made a 1,500-mile round trip from Washington to Chicago and were on the stand for only a few minutes.

JULY 29   The state makes its final argument in the "Black Sox" case and demands five-year sentences plus $2,000 fines for each of the eight players. The defense argued that the players' contracts didn't require that they try and win games.

AUGUST 2   Judge Hugo Friend instructs the Black Sox jury that in order to reach a guilty verdict there must be proof that the games were thrown plus an intention to defraud the public. After only two hours of deliberation, the eight Black Sox were acquitted on charges of fixing the 1919 World Series. The jurors lifted the players onto their shoulders and marched them around the courtroom. The jurors then retired to an Italian restaurant with the players they just acquitted. Chick Gandil said, "I guess that will learn Ban Johnson he can't frame an honest bunch of ballplayers."

AUGUST 3   Despite their acquittal, the eight White Sox players are given lifetime suspensions from organized baseball by commissioner Kenesaw Landis. "The doors are closed to them for good." Landis said. "The most scandalous chapter in the game's history is closed."

AUGUST 7   The White Sox's uniforms fail to arrive from Boston in time for a game against the Yankees in New York. The Sox played in the gray road uniforms of the Yankees and lost 2–0 in a contest called by rain after five innings.

AUGUST 18   In his first game with the White Sox, John Russell pitches 13 innings, only to lose a 1–0 heartbreaker to the Senators at Comiskey Park. The run scored on a double and three walks. Eric Erickson pitched a complete game for Washington and allowed only three hits.

Russell's only prior major league experience consisted of six games, one start, and an 0–1 record with the Dodgers in 1917 and 1918. He appeared in 15 games for the White Sox over two seasons and finished his career with a 2–7 record, no shutouts and a 5.40 ERA.

AUGUST 25   The White Sox outslug the Athletics 13–6 at Comiskey Park.

Life After a Lifetime Ban

The eight White Sox suspended by Charles Comiskey in September 1920 and banned for life from baseball in August 1921 by Commissioner Kenesaw Landis for fixing the 1919 World Series did not go quietly. The eight went to their graves trying to clear their names.

Chick Gandil

Chick Gandil was the only one of the eight "Black Sox" to leave the White Sox voluntarily. Bowing to the wishes of his wife, Chick refused to sign a 1920 contract with the White Sox. He played for an independent team in Idaho that paid him a salary commensurate with the $4,000 he earned from Charles Comiskey in 1919. As the ringleader in the Series fix, some sources claim Gandil pocketed $35,000 from gamblers. Following his banishment by Kenesaw Landis, Gandil played semipro baseball on the West Coast and in Arizona. After his playing days ended, he became a plumber in the San Francisco Bay area during the late 1930s and retired in 1952.

Even in his final days, Gandil defiantly continued to deny his guilt in the World Series scandal. Famed criminal attorney Melvin Belli was approached about representing Gandil in a suit against baseball to clear his name, but it never moved past the discussion stage. Gandil died in 1970 at the age of 82 in Calistoga, California.

Swede Risberg

Swede Risberg was considered to be Chick Gandil's "second lieutenant" in the plan to fix of the World Series. Like Gandil, Risberg spent the remainder of his life vehemently professing his innocence by denying any complicity in the conspiracy. Swede sued Charles Comiskey for back pay and won a pittance in 1925 in a jury trial.

For several years, Risberg played on semipro and independent teams outside the reach of organized baseball. On one, in Sioux Falls, South Dakota, Risberg was kicked off the team for trying to foment a revolt among his teammates against management.

Risberg's life savings were wiped out during the Great Depression. He later operated a tavern in the northern California town of Red Bluff. Risberg died in 1975 on his 91st birthday.

Joe Jackson

Angry and resentful toward Charles Comiskey, Joe Jackson sued the White Sox owner for slander and breach of contract in April 1924. Jackson's attorney demanded $119,000 in punitive damages. But Comiskey's attorneys produced Joe's confession, which had been missing and presumed stolen since 1920 (see July 23, 1921). No one could explain how these documents surfaced after all that time. Because of the confession, Jackson's case against Comiskey collapsed.

Using an assumed name, Jackson played sandlot games with "outlaw" teams outside the governance of organized baseball through 1933. He was 45 when he finally hung up his spikes. Later, Jackson owned a dry cleaning business and a liquor store with his wife Kate in Greenville, South Carolina.

Jackson was scheduled to appear on Ed Sullivan's "Toast of the Town" live television program in December 1951 to tell his side of the Black Sox scandal, but Jackson died of a heart attack 10 days before airing.

Many groups and individuals have petitioned baseball to have Jackson admitted to the Hall of Fame based on his .356 lifetime batting average, the third-highest of all-time behind only Ty Cobb and Rogers Hornsby. Thus far, those efforts have proved to be futile.

Happy Felsch

Like Swede Risberg and Joe Jackson, Happy Felsch sued Charles Comiskey for back pay. In 1925, a jury awarded Felsch $661 plus interest, which brought the sum to $1,166. Claiming he "never had anything to do with the conspiracy," Felsch raised six children in Milwaukee as a crane operator and as a tavern and grocery store proprietor. He died in 1964 at 72.

Fred McMullin

The least known of the Black Sox conspirators, Fred McMullin was only a reserve infielder in 1919.

He received $5,000 as "hush money" because he overheard a locker-room conversation between Chick Gandil and Swede Risberg concerning the fix. Ironically, McMullin went into law enforcement following the ban. He worked in the Los Angeles office of the U.S. Marshal. McMullin died in 1952 at the age of 61.

Lefty Williams

Lefty Williams refused to talk about the 1919 World Series for publication for the remainder of his life. He pitched for independent clubs until about 1927 before settling in Chicago, where he operated a pool room. Later, Williams moved to California to run a plant nursery business in Laguna Beach. He died in 1959 at the age of 66.

Eddie Cicotte

Cicotte was one of the few Black Soxers who admitted his guilt. After his ban, he took an assumed name to protect his family and worked in a Ford plant in Detroit for many years until retiring in 1944. In his declining years, Cicotte tended to a strawberry patch on his property and patiently answered letters sent to him by baseball fans around the country. "I don't know of anyone who ever went through life without making a mistake," admitted Cicotte. "Everybody who has ever lived has committed sins of his own."

Late in life, Eddie Cicotte was interviewed by baseball writer Joe Falls of the *Detroit Free Press*. When asked about the burden of guilt he shouldered, Cicotte replied, "I admit I did wrong, but I've paid for it. I've tried to make up for it by living as clean a life as I could. Nobody can hurt me anymore." Cicotte died in 1969 at the age of 84 in Detroit.

Buck Weaver

Buck Weaver played to the level of his abilities during the 1919 World Series and accepted no money from gamblers, but he was banned because he knew about the fix but failed to alert baseball authorities. He spent the rest of his life trying to clear his name. Weaver exhausted his life savings on legal appeals. He wrote letters to commissioners Kenesaw Landis, Happy Chandler and Ford Frick to be allowed back into Organized Baseball, but to no avail. "It hasn't been easy earning a living since I was thrown out of baseball in 1920," Weaver said years later, "but I've been able to live with my conscience." Weaver was working as a clerk at the $50 window at Chicago's three racetracks up to the moment of his death of a heart attack at the age of 65 in 1956.

SEPTEMBER 3   The White Sox go on a batting rampage and beat the Browns 12–1 at Comiskey Park.

SEPTEMBER 4   Down 8–4, the White Sox score seven runs in the seventh inning and defeat the Browns 11–10 at Comiskey Park.

SEPTEMBER 9   The White Sox outlast the Tigers 20–15 in a slugfest at Comiskey Park. In addition to the 35 runs, there were 42 hits in the contest, 22 of them by Chicago. Earl Sheely was the batting star with five hits, including a homer and a triple, in five at-bats. He also scored five runs. The Sox led 9–2 after two innings, but Detroit pulled ahead 11–9 in the top of the fourth. The White Sox tied it with two tallies in their half. In the fifth, Detroit scored again before the Sox countered with five in the bottom half to take a 16–12 advantage. By the end of the seventh the score was 20–15.

The leading hitters on the White Sox in 1921 were Eddie Collins (.337) and Harry Hooper (.327).

SEPTEMBER 24   The White Sox lose their 11th game in a row, dropping a 7–4 decision to the Athletics in the first game of a double-header in Philadelphia. The Sox broke out of the slump in a big way, winning the nightcap 16–1.

SEPTEMBER 30   Ray Schalk ties a major league record with three assists in the eighth inning of a 3–2 loss to the Indians at Comiskey Park by picking three runners off first base. The three Cleveland runners were Charlie Jamieson, Joe Wood and Elmer Smith.

OCTOBER 5   The Chicago City Series begins with a 2–0 White Sox win over the Cubs before 16,000 at Comiskey Park. Dickie Kerr pitched the shutout. In the first City Series played since 1916, the Sox won all five games of the best-of-nine series.

OCTOBER 8   In game three of the City Series, the White Sox score three runs in the ninth inning and one in the 10th to defeat the Cubs 4–3 at Comiskey Park. With the Cubs leading 3–1, runners on second and third and two out in the ninth inning, Earl Sheely flied to right fielder Max Flack, who dropped the ball allowing the two runners to cross the plate and tie the score. Amos Strunk drove in the winning run with a single.

OCTOBER 10   The White Sox complete a sweep of the Cubs with a 9–5 victory at Wrigley Field.

1922   Sox

Season in a Sentence

Despite the loss of Dickie Kerr in a contract dispute, the White Sox improve by 15 games over the 1921 record and reach the .500 mark.

Finish • Won • Lost • Pct • GB

Fifth   77   77   .500   17.0

Manager

Kid Gleason

Stats

Stats	WS	AL	Rank
Batting Avg:	.278	.285	5
On-Base Pct:	.343	.348	5
Slugging Pct:	.373	.398	6
Home Runs:	45		5 (tie)
Stolen Bases:	109		2
ERA:	3.94	4.03	4
Fielding Avg:	.975	.969	1
Runs Scored:	691		6
Runs Allowed:	691		3

Starting Lineup

Ray Schalk, c
Earl Sheely, 1b
Eddie Collins, 2b
Joe Mulligan, 3b
Ernie Johnson, ss
Bibb Falk, lf
Johnny Mostil, cf
Harry Hooper, rf
Amos Strunk, cf
Harvey McClellan, 3b

Pitchers

Red Faber, sp
Charlie Robertson, sp
Dixie Leverett, sp
Ted Blankenship, sp-rp
Henry Courtney, sp-rp
Shovel Hodge, rp

Attendance

602,860 (fourth in AL)

Club Leaders

Batting Avg:	Eddie Collins	.324
On-Base Pct:	Eddie Collins	.401
Slugging Pct:	Johnny Mostil	.472
Home Runs:	Bibb Falk	12
RBIs:	Earl Sheely	80
	Harry Hooper	80
Runs:	Harry Hooper	111
Stolen Bases:	Ernie Johnson	21
Wins:	Red Faber	21
Strikeouts:	Red Faber	148
ERA:	Red Faber	2.80
Saves:	Red Faber	2
	Dixie Leverett	2

APRIL 12   The White Sox open the season with a 3–2 loss to the Browns at Comiskey Park. Both starting pitchers were named Urban, as Urban Shocker defeated Urban (Red) Faber.

APRIL 21   At St. Louis, the White Sox score two runs in the ninth inning to tie the game 4–4, then score six in the top of the 10th before the Browns score a meaningless tally in the bottom half to make the final 10–5.

                  Faber was 21–17 in 1922 and lead the league in ERA for the second year in a row with a mark of 2.81. He also topped the circuit in innings pitched (352) and complete games (31 in 38 starts).

APRIL 23   Ken Williams of the Browns hits three homers off White Sox pitching to lead his club to a 10–7 win in St. Louis.

                  Williams was the first American Leaguer to hit three homers in a game and the first major league batter to do so since 1897.

APRIL 30   Charlie Robertson pitches the only perfect game in White Sox history, defeating the Tigers 2–0 in Detroit. Tigers star outfielder-manager Ty Cobb accused Robertson, who struck out six, of doctoring the ball. The White Sox scored both of their runs thanks to an Earl Sheely single. Left fielder Johnny Mostil preserved the perfect game with a running catch in the second inning. It was the only time all season that Mostil, normally a center fielder, played in left.

The Unlikeliest Perfect Game in Baseball History

There have been 17 starting pitchers in major league history who are credited with pitching a perfect game by retiring all 27 batters they have faced, including the one thrown by Don Larsen in the 1956 World Series. There were two others in which a pitcher retired the first 27 batters to face him before allowing one or more base runners in extra innings. None of the perfect games was more unlikely than the one that Charlie Robertson of the White Sox pitched on April 30, 1922 against the Tigers in Detroit.

Robertson finished his career with only 49 wins, the fewest number of victories by a perfect-game pitcher. He had a 49-80 career record for a .380 winning percentage. The only other perfect game pitchers to end a career with a losing record are Len Barker, who was 74–76, and Don Larsen with a record of 81–91. Barker had his perfect game with the Indians in 1981, and Larsen's came in the 1956 World Series for the Yankees against the Dodgers.

Robertson had the highest earned run average (4.44) of any pitcher with a perfect game and the fewest shutouts (six). Robertson's perfect game was only his second career victory and fourth big-league start, making him by far the least experienced hurler to ever accomplish the feat. In addition, no perfect game pitcher ever faced a tougher lineup. The 1922 Tigers finished the season with a composite batting average of .306. It is not only the highest batting average of any team to have been set down in a perfect game, but the highest of any club that has been the victim of any type of no-hitter. Robertson's gem was also the only perfecto pitched in the majors between 1908 and 1956 and the only one during the regular season from 1908 through 1964.

Robertson's perfect game was played on a sunny Sunday afternoon at Navin Field in Detroit. There was a crowd of 25,000, which overflowed the stands. Ropes were set up in the outfield, and much of the crowd stood behind the ropes.

Any ball hit into the crowd was a ground-rule double.

The 27 Outs

First inning- Robertson struck out Lu Blue. George Cutshaw popped out to second baseman Eddie Collins. Ty Cobb grounded out to third baseman Harvey McClellan.

Second inning- In the top of the inning, the White Sox scored twice to take a 2–0 lead. Earl Sheely drove in both runs with a single. In the Tigers' half, Bobby Veach hit a fly ball to deep left. Johnny Mostil, playing left field for the first time in his career and the only time in 1922, caught the ball after a long run against the ropes that held back the overflow crowd. An accommodating Detroit crowd moved out of the way to give Mostil room to make the catch. Harry Heilmann and Bob Jones flied out to Harry Hooper in right field.

Third inning- Topper Rigney popped out to Collins. Clyde Manion fouled out to catcher Ray Schalk. Opposing pitcher Herm Pillette grounded out to shortstop Eddie Mulligan.

Fourth inning- Blue struck out. Cutshaw popped out to Collins. Cobb flied out to Mostil.

Fifth inning- Veach flied out to Hooper on a 3–2 pitch. Cobb, who was also the manager of the Tigers, riled at umpire Dick Nallin claiming that Robertson was putting an illegal substance on the ball. The game was stopped as Nallin searched Robertson. The umpire was satisfied that nothing was amiss, and play resumed. Heilmann tapped the ball back to Robertson, who threw to first. Cobb then asked Nallin to check the glove of first baseman Earl Sheely. The mitt was clean. Jones popped out to McClelland.

Sixth inning- Rigney popped out to Collins. Manion flied to Hooper in right. Pillette struck out.

Seventh inning- Blue grounded out to Collins. Cutshaw grounded to McClellan. Cobb struck out and continued to holler at Nallin. Every time that a ball was thrown out of play, Cobb would grab it looking for signs that Robertson was using an illegal pitch.

Eighth inning- Veach struck out. Heilmann popped out to Sheely. Jones grounded out to Collins.

Ninth inning- Cobb brandished balls he claimed had oil on them and brought the evidence to Nallin. The umpire said he saw nothing, Cobb went back to the dugout flinging bats and profanity. Danny Clark went to the plate as a pinch-hitter for Rigney. Clark struck out on three pitches. Manion popped out to Collins, placing Robertson one out from a perfect game. Johnny Bassler pinch-hit for Pillette. After taking a ball and a strike, Bassler went back to the bench for a different bat. The partisan Detroit crowd booed Bassler. On the next pitch, Bassler lifted a fly ball to left. After a long jaunt, Mostil caught the ball near the foul line.

Cobb sent the baseballs he claimed had oil on them to AL President Ban Johnson, but no action was taken.

Robertson was traded by the White Sox to the Browns in 1926. His career ended in 1928. Robertson went back to Texas to work as a pecan broker. For the next 34 years, he was the last pitcher to throw a perfect game. On October 9, 1956, Larsen set down 27 Brooklyn Dodgers in order in Game Five of the World Series.

Five days later, on October 14, Robertson appeared on the television program *What's My Line?* He signed the blackboard as "C. C. Robertson" of Fort Worth, Texas. After six questions, panelist Bennett Cerf correctly identified the mystery guest as Charlie Robertson of perfect-game fame. Robertson died in 1984 at the age of 88.

MAY 17   Red Faber pitches a complete game and strikes out 13 batters, but loses 3–1 when the Athletics score two runs in the 13th on a walk-off homer by Tilly Walker. Fred Heimach pitched a complete game for the A's and failed to strike out a batter.

MAY 22   President Warren Harding and his wife Florence attend a 4–3 White Sox win over the Senators in Washington.

MAY 26   Bibb Falk singles with one out in the eighth inning to break up Urban Shocker's bid for a perfect game during a meeting with the Browns at Comiskey Park. Ray Schalk doubled to tie the game, and the Sox scored an unearned run in the 10th to win 2–1.

JUNE 9   At Comiskey Park, the Yankees use a courtesy runner with permission from White Sox manager Kid Gleason during a 10–6 Chicago victory. On a two-out single in the sixth inning, Wally Schang was injured when he slid into first base and was replaced by pinch-runner Al DeVormer. After the third out, Schang returned to his catching position. When Schang reached base again in the eighth inning, DeVormer ran for him again, this time staying in the game to catch.

JUNE 11   White Sox pitcher Dixie Leverett pitches a 13-inning complete game and hits a walk-off double to beat the Red Sox 7–6 at Comiskey Park.

JUNE 13   Charlie Robertson pitches a two-hitter and defeats the Red Sox 5–0 at Comiskey Park. Robertson held Boston hitless until Frank O'Rourke singled leading off the eighth. Mike Menosky added another single in the ninth.

JUNE 16   A two-run, two-out, walk-off single by Ernie Johnson in the ninth inning beats the Athletics 9–8 at Comiskey Park. Earlier, the Sox blew leads of 2–0 and 6–5.

JUNE 22   An inside-the-park, walk-off homer by Harry Hooper in the 10th inning defeats the Indians 6–5 at Comiskey Park.

JUNE 27   Ray Schalk hits for the cycle in four at-bats during a 9–5 win over the Tigers in Detroit.

              Schalk hit only 11 home runs in 5,306 career at-bats.

JULY 1   Bibb Falk hits a grand slam off Hooks Dauss in the first inning of a 7–3 win over the Tigers at Comiskey Park. The victory was Chicago's eighth in a row and gave the club a record of 35–30.

JULY 3   Still popular with Philadelphia fans where he began his career, Eddie Collins is presented with a lawn mower and a traveling bag when he steps to the plate for the first time in the second game of a double-header at Shibe Park. He collected four hits, including a triple, in seven at-bats as the White Sox beat the Athletics 4–1, then lost 3–2.

              Collins hit .324 for the White Sox in 1922.

JULY 19   Dixie Leverett pitches a complete game shutout and is 4-for-4 at the plate with two doubles and two singles, leading the way to an 8–0 win over the Red Sox in Boston.

AUGUST 1   The White Sox fail to win a game at Comiskey Park because of the dilatory tactics of the Yankees. The Sox led 5–1 in the bottom of the fourth when rain threatened. The Yankees responded by doing everything possible to prevent the contest from becoming an official game. Shortstop Everett Scott refused to field a weakly hit ball hit by Red Faber and the White Sox pitcher reached third base before any effort was made to put him out. Outfielders threw the ball around to each other on hits instead of returning it to the infield, and the Yanks used three pitchers, each change causing a delay. The rain arrived in torrents, turning the field into a quagmire. A corps of men with sawdust, gasoline and brooms tried to get the diamond into condition but failed, and the game was called before the required five innings were completed.

AUGUST 15   The White Sox collect 25 hits and defeat the Red Sox 19–11 in Boston. Chicago scored seven runs in the ninth to break open a close game. The 25 hits were 21 singles, three doubles and a triple. The Red Sox had 15 singles. The combined total of 36 one-base hits tied a modern major league record.

AUGUST 23   Elmer Pence has one of the shortest careers in big-league history when he subs in right field for Harry Hooper at the end of an 11–3 loss to the Senators in Washington in what proves to be Pence's only game in the majors. Pence had one putout defensively and no plate appearances.

AUGUST 29   Earl Sheely hits a two-run homer in the 10th inning to defeat the Tigers 5–3 in Detroit.

               Sheely hit .317 with six home runs in 1922.

AUGUST 31   The White Sox collect 21 hits and smash the Tigers 10–1 in Detroit. Ernie Johnson had five singles in five at-bats.

SEPTEMBER 5   The White Sox score seven runs in the eighth inning to cap a 15–5 win over the Tigers in the second game of a double-header at Comiskey Park. Detroit won the opener 9–8.

SEPTEMBER 7   White Sox catcher Yam Yaryan hits a walk-off homer in the 10th inning to defeat the Indians 9–8 at Comiskey Park. Yaryan entered the game in the top of the 10th when Ray Schalk injured his finger.

               The homer was the second of two that Clarence (Yam) Yaryan hit in 173 major league at-bats.

SEPTEMBER 20   The White Sox sweep the Athletics 1–0 and 3–2 in a double-header at Comiskey Park with the second contest lasting 10 innings. Red Faber pitched the shutout in the opener for his 21st win of the season.

OCTOBER 1   A National Football League game is played at Comiskey Park for the first time, with the Chicago Cardinals defeating the Milwaukee Badgers 3–0 before 3,500.

               Comiskey Park was the Cardinals' home field from 1922 through 1925; 1929 and 1930; 1939 through 1943; and 1945 through 1958. The Cardinals used Normal Park at Racine and 61st Street from 1926 through 1928, Wrigley Field from 1931 through 1938, and Soldier Field in 1959. The club disbanded in 1944 because of World War II. The Cardinals moved to St. Louis in 1960 and to Phoenix in 1988.

OCTOBER 3   The Chicago City Series opens with a 6–3 White Sox win over the Cubs before 17,434 at Wrigley Field.

OCTOBER 14   The White Sox even the City Series at three game apiece with a 1–0 win over the Cubs at Comiskey Park. Red Faber pitched the shutout. Ray Schalk drove in the winning run with a bases-loaded squeeze play in the ninth inning.

OCTOBER 15   The Cubs win the City Series four games to three with a 2–0 win over the White Sox
              at Wrigley Field. Grover Alexander pitched the shutout. It was the first time that the
              Sox lost the City Series since 1909.

1923   Sox

Season in a Sentence

The White Sox tumble back into seventh place, bringing about an end to Kid Gleason's reign as manager.

Finish • Won • Lost • Pct • GB

Seventh   69   85   .448   30.0

Manager

Kid Gleason

Stats

Stats	WS	AL	Rank
Batting Avg:	.279	.282	5
On-Base Pct:	.350	.351	4
Slugging Pct:	.373	.388	6
Home Runs:	42		5
Stolen Bases:	191		1
ERA:	4.05	3.98	5
Fielding Avg:	.971	.968	2
Runs Scored:	692		5
Runs Allowed:	741		3 (tie)

Starting Lineup

Ray Schalk, c
Earl Sheely, 1b
Eddie Collins, 2b
Willie Kamm, 3b
Harvey McClellan, ss
Bibb Falk, lf
Johnny Mostil, cf
Harry Hooper, rf
Roy Elsh, lf
Bill Barrett, lf

Pitchers

Charlie Robertson, sp
Red Faber, sp
Mike Cvengros, sp
Dixie Leverett, sp
Ted Blankenship, sp-rp
Sloppy Thurston, rp

Attendance

573,778 (third in AL)

Club Leaders

Batting Avg:	Eddie Collins	.360
On-Base Pct:	Eddie Collins	.455
Slugging Pct:	Eddie Collins	.453
Home Runs:	Harry Hooper	10
RBIs:	Willie Kamm	87
Runs:	Johnny Mostil	91
Stolen Bases:	Eddie Collins	49
Wins:	Red Faber	14
Strikeouts:	Red Faber	91
	Charlie Robertson	91
ERA:	Red Faber	3.41
Saves:	Sloppy Thurston	4

APRIL 18   The White Sox open the season with a 6–5 loss to the Indians in Cleveland. The Sox
            scored four runs in the eighth for a 5–4 lead, but Cleveland struck back with two in
            the ninth off Frank Mack for the win.

            *The White Sox lost all four games of the opening series against the Indians.
            The Sox had a 2–9 record in April.*

APRIL 22   A unknown perpetrator throws a bomb at Comiskey Park.

            *Thomas Healey, a former Chicago police officer who was moonlighting as
            a night watchman at Comiskey Park, was situated in the stadium offices just
            above the main entrance at 35th Street and Shields Avenue when he was thrown
            out of his chair by the detonation of a pipe bomb. The bomb burst while still in
            the air and windows of the office were blown out by the concussion. A portable
            hot dog stand at street level was demolished, but there was no significant
            damage to the ballpark and no one was injured. The blast could be heard a mile
            away at the Stanton Avenue Police Station and officers rushed to the scene.*

Detectives searched for clues, but no suspects were ever identified. Some blamed gamblers for the dastardly deed. There had been a crackdown to bring about a halt to bookmaking in the grandstand. A large sign had been placed on the front of the bleachers at Comiskey park which read: "No Betting." Others blamed trade unionists. Comiskey Park had recently been painted by nonunion workers.

APRIL 26   The White Sox lose the home opener 3–0 to the Indians at Comiskey Park. Pants Rowland, who managed the White Sox from 1915 through 1918, was one of the umpires. Before the game, Rowland was presented with a basket of flowers.

The starting third baseman for the White Sox in 1923 was rookie Willie Kamm, who was purchased from the San Francisco Seals of the Pacific Coast League for $100,000. Up to that time, the only player who moved from one club to another in a six-figure financial transaction was Babe Ruth, who was bought by the Yankees from the Red Sox in 1920. With only 29 homers in 1,693 major league games, Kamm was never confused with Ruth, but he forged a long career as the best defensive third baseman of his generation. He played for the White Sox from 1923 through 1931 and compiled a .279 batting average with the club. Kamm's 243 doubles are the eighth-best in club history. Defensively, he led AL third basemen eight times in fielding average, eight times in total chances per games, seven in putouts, four in assists and three in double plays.

MAY 3   Leo Taylor has one of the shortest careers in big league history when he appears as a pinch-runner during a 6–3 loss to the Browns at Comiskey Park in what proves to be his only game in the majors.

MAY 12   The White Sox purchase Sloppy Thurston from the Browns.

MAY 16   The White Sox score seven runs in the fourth inning and defeat the Senators 14–8 at Comiskey Park.

Eddie Collins was once again the top hitter on the White Sox with a .360 batting average in 1923.

MAY 31   The White Sox sell Ernie Johnson to the Yankees.

JUNE 5   The White Sox play at Yankee Stadium for the first time, and lose 7–6 in 10 innings. The Sox scored two runs in the ninth inning and two more in the 10th to take a 6–4 lead, only to have three Yankees cross the plate in the bottom of the 10th.

JUNE 6   Playing in his 11th big league season, Red Faber hits his first career homer during a 4–1 win over the Yankees in New York. The drive, which bounced into the left-field stands, broke a 1–1 tie in the seventh inning.

Faber hit three career homers in 1,269 career at-bats over 20 seasons. The other two were struck in 1928 and 1929.

JUNE 17   The White Sox collect only four hits in 11 innings, but they win 5–3 against the Senators at Griffith Stadium. Washington pitcher Skipper Friday, making his major league debut, walked 14 batters.

JUNE 18   A two-run rally in the ninth inning beats the Athletics 6–5 in Philadelphia. With two out, Sloppy Thurston singled, Harry Hooper tripled, and Harvey McClelland doubled. The game ended when left fielder Roy Elsh threw out a runner at the plate.

JUNE 24   Trailing 8–3, the White Sox erupt for six runs in the ninth inning to shock the Tigers 9–8 in Detroit.

JUNE 30   Harry Hooper homers on the first pitch of the game from Guy Morton of the Indians, sparking the White Sox to a 3–1 win in the first game of a double-header in Cleveland. The Sox completed the sweep with a 5–4 victory in the nightcap.

JULY 2   Ted Lyons makes his major league debut, pitching one inning of perfect relief during a 7–2 loss to the Browns in St. Louis.

Lyons was a fixture in Chicago for more than two decades, pitching for the White Sox from 1923 through 1942, and again in 1946, with the intervening three spent with the Marines during World War II. Lyons also managed the White Sox from 1946 through 1948. A native of Lake Charles, Louisiana, he was signed off the campus of Baylor University and went to directly to the White Sox without playing in the minor leagues. Lyons compiled a 260–230 lifetime record, good enough for election into the Hall of Fame in 1955. He would have certainly exceeded the 300-win mark if he had pitched on contending teams. During Ted's 21-season career, the White Sox had only six winning seasons. Lyons holds the all-time White Sox career records for wins, games started (484), complete games (356), and innings pitched (4,161). He is second in games pitched (594), fifth in strikeouts (1,073) and sixth in shutouts (27).

JULY 6   The White Sox purchase Leon Cadore from the Dodgers.

JULY 18   The White Sox score seven runs in the second inning and win 11–3 over the Red Sox in the second game of a double-header at Comiskey Park. Boston won the first game 6–3.

AUGUST 3   The White Sox game against the Red Sox in Boston is postponed to observe a national day of mourning following the August 2 death of President Warren Harding, who died during a trip to San Francisco. The White Sox game against the Senators in Washington on August 10 was also postponed for Harding's funeral. Calvin Coolidge succeeded Harding as president.

AUGUST 9   The White Sox suffer a humiliating 21–5 loss to the Athletics in Philadelphia.

AUGUST 22 Pitching in relief, Sloppy Thurston strikes out three batters on nine pitches in the 12th inning, but gives up a run in the 13th to lose 3–2 to the Athletics at Comiskey Park. The strikeout victims were Beauty McGowan, Chick Galloway and Sammy Hale. Thurston is the only pitcher in White Sox history to fan three batters in an inning on the minimum nine pitches.

AUGUST 25 In his first major league start, White Sox pitcher Claral Gillenwater pitches a four-hit shutout, beating the Red Sox 4–0 at Comiskey Park.

The performance was not just Gillenwater's only career shutout, but his only win and lone complete game as well. His career lasted five games, three of which were starts. He had a 1–1 record and a 5.48 earned run average in 21⅓ innings.

SEPTEMBER 1   The White Sox defeat the Indians 14–6 in a game at Comiskey Park called in the bottom of the eighth inning by rain.

SEPTEMBER 24   Charlie Robertson pitches the White Sox to a 1–0 win over the Senators in Washington. Earl Sheely drove in the lone run of the game with a single in the sixth inning.

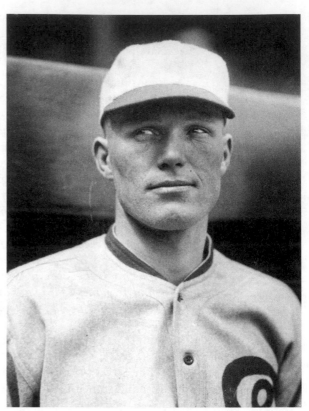

OCTOBER 6   Ted Lyons picks up the first two wins of his career, both in relief against the Indians in Cleveland. Lyons tossed 4⅔ innings in the opener and three in the nightcap as the Sox swept by scores of 6–3 and 7–6.

OCTOBER 10   The Cubs defeat the White Sox 5–4 at Wrigley Field in the first game of the City Series.

OCTOBER 14   Game four of the City Series draws a paid crowd of 41,825 to Comiskey Park, the largest ever to see a baseball game in Chicago up to that time. The White Sox won 5–3 to even the series at two games apiece. Earl Sheely ended the contest with a two-run homer in the ninth inning.

One of the league's best hitters in the mid-1920s, Bib Falk posted better than a .300 average from 1923 through 1927.

OCTOBER 16   The White Sox win the City Series four games to two with a 10-inning, 4–3 win over the Cubs at Comiskey Park. The Sox scored two runs in the ninth to tie the contest. The pair of ninth-inning runs were driven in on a two-run single by Harry Hooper. The winning tally scored following an error by Cubs second baseman George Grantham.

Moments after winning the City Series, Kid Gleason resigned as manager. In his first season in Chicago, Gleason led the Sox to the 1919 American League pennant, but the club was shattered by the Black Sox scandal. He valiantly tried to rebuild the club, but by the end of the 1923 season Gleason was suffering from chronic depression and was unable to eat. He later served as a coach with the Athletics from 1926 until his death in January 1933.

OCTOBER 26   The White Sox hire 46-year-old Frank Chance as manager.

A future Hall of Famer, Chance was already a hero in Chicago for his role in leading the Cubs to their greatest period of glory. He joined the Cubs in 1898 as a catcher and switched to first base in 1902. Chance became manager in 1905. A year later, the Cubs compiled a record of 116–36 for a winning percentage of .763 that is still the best in modern major league history. The Cubs lost to the White Sox in the 1906 World Series, but recovered by winning the world championship in 1907 and 1908 and by reaching the Fall Classic again in 1910. Chance was let go by the Cubs at the end of the 1912 season after a dispute with owner Charles Murphy. Chance's record as Cubs manager was 768–389 (.664). He was hired by two other clubs, but had little success. The Yankees were 117–168 under Chance in 1913 and 1914 and, after a spell out of baseball, he returned to manage the Red Sox to a 61–93 mark in 1923. Frank never managed a regular season game for the White Sox, however (see February 16, 1924).

DECEMBER 11   The White Sox hire former Cubs star Johnny Evers as a coach.

Evers played second base for the Cubs alongside Frank Chance in the World Series in 1906, 1907, 1908 and 1910. After a stint as player-manager of the Cubs in 1913, Evers played in another Fall Classic for the Boston Braves in 1914. By the start of the 1924 season, Evers was manager of the White Sox (see February 16, 1924).

1924

Sox

Season in a Sentence

The White Sox lose two managers to illness and suffer through a club-record 13-game losing streak in August on the way to the first last-place finish in franchise history.

Finish • Won • Lost • Pct • GB

Eighth   66   87   .431   28.5

Managers

Frank Chance (0–0), Johnny Evers (10–11), Ed Walsh (1–2), Eddie Collins (14–12) and Evers (41–61)

Stats

Stats	WS	AL	Rank
Batting Avg:	.288	.290	6
On-Base Pct:	.365	.358	3
Slugging Pct:	.382	.396	7
Home Runs:	41		4 (tie)
Stolen Bases:	137		1
ERA:	4.74	4.23	8
Fielding Avg:	.963	.969	8
Runs Scored:	793		3
Runs Allowed:	858		8

Starting Lineup

Buck Crouse, c
Earl Sheely, 1b
Eddie Collins, 2b
Willie Kamm, 3b
Bill Barrett, ss
Bibb Falk, lf
Johnny Mostil, cf
Harry Hooper, rf
Maurice Archdeacon, cf
Ray Schalk, c

Pitchers

Sloppy Thurston, sp
Ted Lyons, sp-rp
Red Faber, rp
Charlie Robertson, sp-rp
Mike Cvengros, sp
Dixie Leverett, sp
Sarge Connally, rp
Ted Blankenship, rp-sp

Attendance

606,658 (third in AL)

Club Leaders

Batting Avg:	Eddie Collins	.349
On-Base Pct:	Eddie Collins	.441
Slugging Pct:	Bibb Falk	.487
Home Runs:	Harry Hooper	10
RBIs:	Earl Sheely	103
Runs:	Eddie Collins	108
Stolen Bases:	Eddie Collins	42
Wins:	Sloppy Thurston	20
Strikeouts:	Sarge Connally	55
ERA:	Sloppy Thurston	3.80
Saves:	Sarge Connally	6

FEBRUARY 16   Frank Chance resigns as manager of the White Sox due to ill health.

Chance contracted a cold in December that developed into bronchial pneumonia and asthma. Prior to the illness, he had chronic sinus troubles dating back to his playing days, when he was beaned several times. When Chance resigned just prior to the start of spring training in 1924, Comiskey said that he would keep the job open and appointed Johnny Evers as acting manager. After resting for a few weeks at his home in Los Angeles, Chance went to the mountains for two weeks to live in the open and try to clear his lungs. He felt well enough to leave California for Chicago and resume his duties as manager on April 7, but on the long train trip he contracted a severe cold. A physician recommended that Chance spend two months in a hot, dry climate. Chance went to Palm Springs, California, where his condition continued to worsen. Johnny Evers, who had been acting manager, was given the job on a permanent basis on April 19. Chance died on September 14, 1924, of complications from influenza, just five days after his 47th birthday.

MARCH 3   The White Sox arrive for their spring training headquarters in Winter Haven, Florida, and find they have no place to stay. The club was promised that a newly built hotel would be finished in time to accommodate the players and staff, but it wasn't close to completion. The players had to stay at boarding houses and private homes scattered all over town.

The 1924 season was the first time that the White Sox trained in Florida. From 1901 through 1923, the Sox held training camp in various towns in Missouri, Alabama, Texas, Louisiana and California in addition to the trip to Mexico City in 1907. Following their experience in Winter Haven, the Sox didn't train in Florida again until 1954.

APRIL 15   The White Sox lose the season opener 7–3 to the Browns before 28,000 at Comiskey Park.

Despite the last-place finish, the White Sox were third in the American League in attendance in 1924 with a figure of 606,658.

APRIL 30   The White Sox sell Amos Strunk to the Athletics.

MAY 1   Bill Barrett steals home twice and second base once during a 13–7 win over the Indians in Cleveland. The steals of home occurred in the first and ninth innings.

MAY 14   Johnny Evers leaves the club in Boston because of stomach problems.

At first, Evers was diagnosed with ptomaine poisoning and was sent to his home in Troy, New York. There, it was determined that he had appendicitis and underwent surgery. He was away from the club for a month. Pitching coach Ed Walsh filled in as acting manager for only three games when Eddie Collins was appointed to the post. Collins guided the Sox to a 14–12 record before Evers returned.

MAY 28   After being shut out 5–0 in the first game of a double-header against the Indians in Cleveland, the White Sox erupt for a 13–6 win in the nightcap.

MAY 31   The White Sox pummel the Browns 12–2 in St. Louis.

JUNE 10   Bibb Falk hits a walk-off home run in the 13th inning to beat the Red Sox 3–2 at Comiskey Park.

Falk had a career year in 1924, batting .352.

JUNE 16   The White Sox win an exciting 9–8 decision over the Senators at Comiskey Park. Harry Hooper hit a grand slam off Walter Johnson in the seventh inning for a 5–3 Chicago lead. Washington scored five times in the top of the eighth for an 8–5 advantage, but the Sox countered with four in their half for the win.

The White Sox games were heard on the radio for the first time in 1924. WMAQ carried the home contests of both the Sox and the Cubs. The announcer was 23-year-old Hal Totten.

JUNE 21   The White Sox split an event-filled double-header against the Browns in St. Louis, winning 8–5 and losing 7–6. Trouble came in the sixth inning of the second game when umpire Ducky Holmes banished Browns manager George Sisler for protesting balls and strikes calls. About a half-dozen bottles were fired at Holmes, some of which narrowly missed the arbiter. Policemen in plain clothes rushed onto the field. At the same time, a crowd of fans broke down the gate in right field and swarmed the field, further delaying the contest.

JUNE 28   The White Sox lose 13–12 to the Browns in 14 innings at Comiskey Park. The Sox scored three runs in the eighth inning and one in the ninth to tie the contest 12–12, only to wind up losing. St. Louis pulled off a triple play in the second inning. With Ray French, Bill Barrett and Buck Crouse on base, Sloppy Thurston grounded to shortstop Wally Gerber, who threw to second to force Crouse. Second baseman Marty McManus threw to first in time to retire Thurston. Barrett tried to score on the play, and was thrown out on a toss from first baseman George Sisler to catcher Hank Severeid.

JUNE 30   Johnny Mostil scores five runs during a 14–4 win over the Tigers at Comiskey Park. Mostil reached base on a double, a single and three walks.

JULY 11   Bibb Falk hits a grand slam off Joe Bush of the Yankees in the third inning, but the White Sox lose 12–9 in New York.

JULY 12   The White Sox wallop the Red Sox 17–8 in Boston.

JULY 17   The White Sox smother the Athletics 13–5 in Philadelphia. Most of the scoring was done late in the contest. The Sox trailed 4–1 before scoring five runs in the seventh inning, three in the eighth and four in the ninth.

               The White Sox were 43–42 on July 19, then went 23–45 the rest of the way.

JULY 22   Sloppy Thurston wins his 10th game in a row with a 4–0 decision over the Senators in the first game of a double-header in Washington. The Sox lost the second tilt 4–1.

JULY 26   Maurice Archdeacon collects five hits in six at-bats, but the White Sox lose 5–4 to the Yankees at Comiskey Park when Babe Ruth hits a homer in the 14th inning.

               A center fielder, Archdeacon hit .333 in 127 major league games, but a lack of power (no home runs and only 18 extra base hits in 384 at-bats) and size (five-foot-eight and 153 pounds) along with too many injuries prevented him from becoming a long-term success.

JULY 27   The White Sox score four runs in the ninth inning to stun the Yankees 7–6 at Comiskey Park. The winning run crossed the plate on a bases-loaded walk by Milt Gaston to Ray Schalk.

JULY 30   The White Sox win a thrilling 7–6 decision over the Red Sox at Comiskey Park. Down 5–1, the White Sox scored three runs in the eighth inning. After Boston scored in the top of the ninth, the White Sox rallied for three in their half for the victory. Willie Kamm collected five hits, including a double, in five at-bats.

AUGUST 26   The White Sox suffer their 13th consecutive defeat, dropping a 4–3 decision to the Athletics in 12 innings in Philadelphia. The 13 losses in a row is still the club record.

AUGUST 27   Harry Hooper hits a grand slam in the fourth inning of a 12–9 win over the Athletics in the first game of a double-header in Philadelphia. The win broke the White Sox's 13-game losing streak.

SEPTEMBER 10   On the day that Chicago teenagers Nathan Leopold and Richard Loeb receive life sentences for the "thrill murder" of 14-year-old Bobby Franks, the White Sox outlast the Tigers 12–8 in Detroit. The Sox broke a 5–5 tie with four runs in the sixth inning.

SEPTEMBER 13   The White Sox are hammered 16–1 by the Yankees at Comiskey Park.

SEPTEMBER 14   Sloppy Thurston records his 20th win of the season with a 5–2 decision over the Yankees at Comiskey Park.

At the start of the 1924 season, Hollis (Sloppy) Thurston was a 24-year-old pitcher with a lifetime record of 7–8. He was 20–14 in 1924, had a 3.80 ERA and led the league in complete games with 28 in 36 starts. Thurston fanned only 37 batters in 291 innings, however, which may explain his lack of later success. He was 10–14 in 1925 and never won more than 13 games in a season after 1924.

SEPTEMBER 18   Eddie Collins collects five hits, including a double, in five at-bats leading the White Sox to a 7–3 win over the Red Sox at Comiskey Park. The game was stopped at 4:30 p.m. for a moment of silence in the memory of Frank Chance, who was buried that day in Los Angeles. Chance died four days earlier.

Collins hit .349 and scored 108 runs in 1924.

SEPTEMBER 28   Harry Hooper collects two triples and two doubles during a 10–10 tie against the Tigers at Comiskey Park. The game was called at the end of the 10th inning by darkness.

SEPTEMBER 29   The White Sox close the season with a 16–5 trouncing of the Tigers at Comiskey Park.

OCTOBER 1   The Chicago City Series begins with the White Sox losing 10–7 to the Cubs at Wrigley Field.

OCTOBER 4   At Comiskey Park, the White Sox hammer the Cubs 13–0 in game four of the City Series.

OCTOBER 6   The White Sox win the City Series four games to two with a 5–3 decision over the Cubs at Comiskey Park.

The City Series didn't end play for the White Sox in 1924. The club traveled through Canada on the way to a European trip that included visits to England, Ireland, France, Germany and Italy in a series of games against the New York Giants. Managed by John McGraw, the trip was a smaller version of the around-the-world sojourn that took place between the 1913 and 1914 seasons.

OCTOBER 12   In the first game of the post-season tour, the White Sox lose to the Giants 13–5 in Montreal.

OCTOBER 15   Following a 6–2 loss to the Giants in Quebec City, Quebec, the White Sox and their New York counterparts board the ocean liner *Montroyal* for a trip across the Atlantic.

OCTOBER 23   The White Sox defeat the Giants 16–11 in Liverpool at the Everton Football Grounds.

OCTOBER 24   The White Sox lose 3–2 at the Stamford Bridge Football Grounds in London before a crowd that included the Duke and Duchess of York.

NOVEMBER 6   The White Sox lose 8–5 to the Giants in London before a crowd that includes King George V, Queen Mary, and the Prince of Wales. Before the game, the King came out onto the diamond and the players lined up to be formally presented to him. King George also saw the White Sox and Giants play in London on February 26, 1914.

NOVEMBER 20   Ten days after the murder of bootlegger Dion O'Bannon in his Chicago flower shop, players from both the White Sox and Giants are presented to Pope Pius XI at the Vatican.

              The players left Europe for a return trip to the United States on November 24. The trip was a financial failure.

DECEMBER 11   Eddie Collins is appointed manager of the White Sox, replacing Johnny Evers.

              A member of the team since 1915, Collins had been interim manager for 26 games in May and June 1924 while Evers was recuperating from an appendectomy. Evers never managed another big-league club. In his dual role as manager and starting second baseman, Collins guided the Sox to winning records in both 1925 and 1926 before being unceremoniously fired by Charles Comiskey.

1925

Season in a Sentence

In his first year as manager, Eddie Collins brings the South Side of Chicago its first winning season since the Black Sox were indicted in 1920.

Finish • Won • Lost • Pct • GB

Fifth	79	75	.513	18.5

Manager

Eddie Collins

Stats

Stats	WS	AL	Rank
Batting Avg:	.284	.292	7
On-Base Pct:	.369	.360	3
Slugging Pct:	.385	.407	7
Home Runs:	38		8
Stolen Bases:	131		2
ERA:	4.29	4.40	3
Fielding Avg:	.968	.967	4
Runs Scored:	811		5
Runs Allowed:	770		3

Starting Lineup

Ray Schalk, c
Earl Sheely, 1b
Eddie Collins, 3b
Willie Kamm, 3b
Ike Davis, ss
Bibb Falk, lf
Johnny Mostil, cf
Harry Hooper, rf
Bill Barrett, 2b-rf

Pitchers

Ted Lyons, sp
Ted Blankenship, sp-rp
Red Faber, sp
Sloppy Thurston, sp-rp
Charlie Robertson, sp
Mike Cvengros, sp-rp
Sarge Connally, rp

Attendance

831,231 (second in AL)

Club Leaders

Batting Avg:	Eddie Collins	.346
On-Base Pct:	Eddie Collins	.461
Slugging Pct:	Earl Sheely	.442
	Eddie Collins	.442
Home Runs:	Willie Kamm	6
	Harry Hooper	6
RBIs:	Earl Sheely	111
Runs:	Johnny Mostil	135
Wins:	Ted Lyons	21
Strikeouts:	Ted Blankenship	81
ERA:	Ted Blankenship	3.16
Saves:	Sarge Connally	8

APRIL 14	The White Sox lose the season opener 4–3 to the Tigers in Detroit. Earl Sheely clubbed a home run for the Sox.
APRIL 18	The White Sox smash the Browns 14–5 in St. Louis. The Sox took a 3–2 lead with two runs in the sixth inning, then piled on with six in the seventh and four in the eighth.
APRIL 20	The White Sox outlast the Browns 11–10 in St. Louis.
APRIL 22	In the home opener, the White Sox down the Tigers 3–1 before 30,000 at Comiskey Park.
APRIL 23	Charlie Robertson pitches the White Sox to a 1–0 victory over the Tigers at Comiskey Park. The lone run of the contest scored in the ninth inning on three Detroit errors.
APRIL 26	The White Sox lose a forfeit to the Indians at Comiskey Park. The game was attended by 44,000, the largest ever to attend a game at the facility up to that time, with the overflow standing on the field. In the eighth inning, the fans started a cushion fight with the grandstand patrons throwing cushions at the overthrow crowd, which returned the fusillade. With two out in the bottom of the ninth and

Sporting colorful striped uniforms, White Sox players gather before a game. From left to right: Eddie Collins, Ray Schalk, Dickie Kerr, Red Faber and Harry Hooper.

the Sox losing 7–2, many of the fans stormed the field. The umpires and police were helpless to clear the diamond. With continued play an impossibility, the umpires declared a forfeit.

APRIL 27   Trailing 4–3, the White Sox erupt for nine runs in the eighth inning and beat the Indians 12–4 at Comiskey Park.

MAY 10   Johnny Mostil hits a two-run, walk-off homer in the 12th inning to beat the Senators 10–8 at Comiskey Park before a crowd of over 40,000. Washington scored seven runs in the sixth inning to take an 8–4 lead before Chicago countered with two tallies in the seventh and two more in the eighth.

            Mostil led the American League in runs (135), walks (89) and stolen bases (42) in 1925. Player-manager Eddie Collins batted .346 and collected his 3,000th career hit in early June.

MAY 11   During a publicity stunt, Ray Schalk catches a ball dropped 460 feet from the Tribune Tower in downtown Chicago. Schalk stood on Michigan Avenue wearing a suit and tie, dress shoes and a wide-brimmed fedora. A crowd estimated at 10,000 witnessed the event.

MAY 14   The White Sox edge the Yankees 1–0 at Comiskey Park in a pitching duel between future Hall of Famers Ted Lyons and Herb Pennock.

MAY 18   The White Sox win 6–5 in 14 innings against the Athletics at Comiskey Park. Sloppy Thurston pitched a complete game. Earl Sheely tied the score 5–5 with a two-run homer in the ninth inning. Ray Schalk drove in the winning run with a single.

MAY 28   Willie Kamm hits a grand slam in the eighth inning off Earl Whitehill of the Tigers to give the White Sox a 4–2 lead, but the Sox wind up losing 7–5 in 10 innings at Comiskey Park.

JUNE 2   The White Sox wipe out a 10-run Tiger lead but lose 16–15 in Detroit. The Tigers led 15–5 at the end of the sixth inning, but the Sox rallied with seven runs in the seventh inning and three runs in the ninth to tie the contest 15–15. Detroit won on a walk-off homer by Ty Cobb in the bottom of the ninth off Ted Blankenship.

JUNE 12   The White Sox slaughter the Athletics 15–1 in Philadelphia.

JUNE 30   The White Sox score five runs in the 12th inning to defeat the Browns 6–1 in St. Louis.

JULY 4   The White Sox overwhelm the Indians 14–5 in the first game of a double-header in Cleveland. The Sox lost the second tilt 5–4.

JULY 5   Down 3–1, the White Sox score four runs in the top of the ninth inning, then withstand an Indians rally in the bottom half to win 5–4.

JULY 21   Ray Schalk appears in his 1,575th game as a catcher, breaking the record for most career games at the position, passing Deacon McGuire, who played from 1884 through 1912. The White Sox lost 6–3 to the Red Sox in the first game of a double-header at Comiskey Park. Schalk also played in the second contest, an 8–3 Chicago victory.

            Schalk finished his career with 1,727 games as a catcher. He held the record until Gabby Hartnett passed Schalk in 1938.

JULY 23   Sarge Connally allows only one hit in 7²/³ innings of scoreless relief during the White Sox 8–3 win over the Tigers in Detroit.

            George (Sarge) Connally picked up his nickname from his rank in the Army during World War I.

JULY 28   Four days after John Scopes is convicted and fined $100 for teaching evolution in the Scopes Monkey Trial in Dayton, Tennessee, rookie center fielder Spencer Harris hits a grand slam off Curly Ogden of the Senators during a six-run ninth inning that caps a 10–5 win in the first game of a double-header in Washington. The Sox completed a sweep with a 6–2 win in the second tilt, called after eight innings by darkness.

The homer was the first of Harris's career. He hit three home runs in 377 career at-bats over three seasons.

JULY 30   The White Sox trounce the Senators 11–1 in Washington.

AUGUST 1   The White Sox win 5–3 in 15 innings against the Athletics in Philadelphia. In the 15th, Ray Schalk doubled in the first run and scored on a single by Ted Lyons and a sacrifice fly from Ike Davis. Lyons pitched the first 14$\frac{1}{3}$ innings before he was relieved by Sarge Connally, who recorded the final two outs with two men on base.

AUGUST 4   Dickie Kerr is reinstated by Commissioner Kenesaw Landis. Kerr had been suspended since 1922 (see July 21, 1921). He pitched only 12 more games, two of them starts, and compiled an 0–1 record and a 5.15 ERA in 36$\frac{2}{3}$ innings.

AUGUST 6   The White Sox romp to a 10–0 win over the Red Sox in Boston.

AUGUST 9   Sloppy Thurston pitches a complete game and drives in the winning run in the 12th inning with a single that defeats the Yankees 4–3 in New York.

AUGUST 11   The White Sox score seven runs in the seventh inning of a 15–2 win over the Yankees in New York. Harry Hooper collected five hits, including a triple, in five at-bats.

AUGUST 24   Ted Blankenship wins his 10th consecutive game with a 3–1 decision over the Athletics at Comiskey Park.

Blankenship had a record of 17–8 in 1925.

AUGUST 26   Red Faber pitches the White Sox to a 1–0 victory over the Yankees at Comiskey Park. The winning run scored in the second inning on a double by Harry Hooper and a single from Willie Kamm.

SEPTEMBER 19   Ted Lyons comes within one out of a no-hitter before defeating the Senators 17–0 in the second game of a double-header at Griffith Stadium. The lone Washington base hit was a single by Bobby Veach with two out in the ninth inning. The Sox scored seven runs in the second inning and eight in the fifth. The Senators won the opener 3–2.

SEPTEMBER 26   Ted Lyons records his 20th win of 1925 with a 6–0 decision over the Red Sox in the second game of a double-header at Fenway Park. Lyons was helped by Bibb Falk, who took a spill in left field and caught a fly ball while lying on his back. Boston won the opener 6–5.

Lyons was 21–11 in 1925. He led the league in wins and shutouts (five) and posted a 3.26 ERA.

OCTOBER 7   The Chicago City Series starts with the White Sox and Cubs playing to a 2–2, 19-inning tie at Comiskey Park. The game ended because of darkness. Ted Blankenship and Grover Alexander both pitched complete games. Alexander gave up 20 hits to the Sox. Blankenship yielded 11 hits. Neither team scored after the fifth inning.

The Cubs won four of the next five games to take the city championship.

NOVEMBER 6   White Sox shortstop Harvey McClellan dies at the age of 30 in Cynthiana, Kentucky, following surgery for liver cancer. During the off-season, McClellan was a buyer for the Liggett and Myers Tobacco Company.

1926   Sox

Season in a Sentence

The White Sox continue to improve, winning 81 games, but it's not enough for Charles Comiskey, who fires Eddie Collins as manager at the end of the season.

Finish • Won • Lost • Pct • GB

Fifth   81   72   .529   9.5

Manager

Eddie Collins

Stats

Stats	WS	AL	Rank
Batting Avg:	.289	.281	3
On-Base Pct:	.361	.351	4
Slugging Pct:	.390	.392	5
Home Runs:	32		6 (tie)
Stolen Bases:	123		1
ERA:	3.74		3
Fielding Avg:	.973	.969	1
Runs Scored:	730		5
Runs Allowed:	655		3

Starting Lineup

Ray Schalk, c
Earl Sheely, 1b
Eddie Collins, 2b
Willie Kamm, 3b
Bill Hunnefield, ss
Bibb Falk, lf
Johnny Mostil, cf
Bill Barrett, rf
Spencer Harris, rf
Ray Morehart, 2b

Pitchers

Ted Lyons, sp
Tommy Thomas, sp
Red Faber, sp
Ted Blankenship, sp
Jim Joe Edwards, sp-rp
Sloppy Thurston, rp-sp
Sarge Connally, rp

Attendance

710,339 (fourth in AL)

Club Leaders

Batting Avg:	Bibb Falk	.345
On-Base Pct:	Eddie Collins	.441
Slugging Pct:	Bibb Falk	.477
Home Runs:	Bibb Falk	8
RBIs:	Bibb Falk	108
Runs:	Johnny Mostil	120
Stolen Bases:	Johnny Mostil	35
Wins:	Ted Lyons	18
Strikeouts:	Tommy Thomas	127
ERA:	Ted Lyons	3.01
Saves:	Sloppy Thurston	3
	Sarge Connally	3

APRIL 13   In the season opener, the White Sox play before an overflow crowd of 37,000 at Comiskey Park and win 5–1 over the Tigers behind the pitching of Ted Lyons. At one juncture, the large throng crowded almost to the infield, bringing a brief halt to the game. Eddie Collins helped police convince the surging mass to retreat far enough back to permit play to continue.

The White Sox started the season with a 14–7 record, but slipped to 63–66 by the end of August. The club was 18–6 in September.

APRIL 15   The White Sox score eight runs in the first inning and wallop the Browns 11–4 at Comiskey Park.

MAY 19   Trailing 4–2, the White Sox score seven times in the fourth inning and hold on to defeat the Red Sox 9–7 in Boston.

MAY 20   Earl Sheely collects three doubles during a 13–4 victory over the Red Sox in Boston.

MAY 21   In the first four at-bats, Earl Sheely picks up a homer and three doubles during an
               8–7 loss to the Red Sox at Fenway Park.

               *Combined with his three doubles the previous day, Sheely set an American
               League record and tied a major league mark for most extra-base hits in
               consecutive games. The only other players with seven extra-base hits in
               consecutive games are Ed Delahanty with the Phillies in 1896, Red Schoendienst
               (Cardinals, 1948), Joe Adcock (Braves, 1954) and Jim Edmonds (Cardinals,
               2003).*

MAY 23   Ted Lyons pitches the White Sox to a 1–0 win over the Indians in Cleveland. The
               lone run of the game scored on a ninth-inning single by Eddie Collins.

               At the age of 39, Collins hit .344 in 106 games in 1926.

JUNE 2   The White Sox score four runs in the ninth inning with five singles to defeat the
               Browns 6–5 in St. Louis.

JUNE 8   The White Sox defeat the Athletics 1–0 at Comiskey Park in a battle between future
               Hall of Fame pitcher Red Faber and Lefty Grove. The winning run scored in the
               ninth inning on a bases-loaded squeeze bunt by Ray Schalk that brought Bibb Falk
               home from third base.

               Falk hit .345 and drove in 108 runs in 1926.

JUNE 13   Tommy Thomas pitches a two-hitter to defeat the Senators 2–0 at Comiskey Park.
               The only Washington hits were singles by Roger Peckinpaugh and Jim Tobin.

               *Thomas had a record of 83–92 with the White Sox from 1926 through 1932,
               but he was an above-average pitcher on below-average clubs. His best season
               was 1927, when he was 19–16 with a 2.98 ERA and his 307²/₃ innings pitched
               led the league. In 1929, Thomas topped the AL in complete games with 24 in
               31 starts.*

JUNE 19   Cardinal Patrick O'Donnell, Primate of Ireland, witnesses a 6–5 loss to the Yankees
               at Comiskey Park. O'Donnell watched the game from a box decorated with the
               Eucharist colors and the American flag. He also threw out the ceremonial first pitch.
               Several players, including Babe Ruth, kissed the Cardinal's ring. Eddie Collins was
               also honored and received a truckload of gifts.

JUNE 20   An overflow crowd of 44,000 at Comiskey Park watches the White Sox lose 4–3 to
               the Yankees.

               *The problem of squeezing 44,000 people into a ballpark with 32,000 seats
               was solved by the start of the 1927 season when Charles Comiskey expanded
               capacity to 52,000 by adding double-decks down the foul lines and behind the
               outfield walls.*

JULY 6   The White Sox sell Everett Scott to the Reds.

JULY 10   The White Sox lose 17–14 to the Athletics at Shibe Park. The game was scoreless until the A's scored six times in the fourth. The Sox bounced back and moved ahead 14–11 before Philadelphia delivered another six-run salvo in the eighth.

JULY 20   The White Sox pummel the Red Sox 13–2 in Boston. All 13 runs were scored in the first four innings.

AUGUST 4   Bill Barrett hits an inside-the-park grand slam in the seventh inning, breaking a 3–3 tie and leading to a 7–3 victory over the Red Sox at Comiskey Park. The blow was struck against Fred Heimach.

AUGUST 7   White Sox pitches Jim Joe Edwards pitches a shutout to defeat the Athletics 1–0 in the second game of a double-header at Comiskey Park. Edwards was hit on the kneecap by a line drive from opposing pitcher Eddie Rommel in the eighth inning but refused to leave the game. Philadelphia won the opener 3–2.

AUGUST 11   The White Sox explode for five runs in the 13th inning to defeat the Indians 7–2 in Cleveland.

AUGUST 15   The White Sox and Tigers play to a 0–0 tie at Comiskey Park. The game ended after five innings when a heavy rain swept through the Windy City.

AUGUST 16   After the two clubs travel to Detroit for a one-game series, the White Sox and Tigers play to a 0–0 tie for the second day in a row. The contest on August 16 ended after 10 innings to allow both clubs to catch trains bound for the East Coast. Ted Lyons and Tigers pitcher Sam Gibson both pitched three-hit, complete-game shutouts.

AUGUST 21   Ted Lyons pitches a no-hitter to beat the Red Sox 6–0 in Boston. Lyons struck out two and walked one. Another batter reached on an error. The final batter was Topper Rigney, who grounded to first baseman Earl Sheely with Lyons covering the bag for the putout.

Lyons pitched 41 consecutive scoreless innings from August 9 through August 26. He finished the season with an 18–16 record and a 3.01 ERA.

Ted Lyons spent his entire 21-year, Hall-of-Fame career with the White Sox. In this photo, taken in 1926, he warms up before a game.

AUGUST 22   The White Sox and Athletics defy the law and play on a Sunday in Philadelphia. It was the first professional baseball game ever played on a Sunday in the state of Pennsylvania. The A's obtained a court injunction that prevented police interference. The game was an outgrowth of an exposition in Philadelphia during the summer of 1926 honoring the 150th anniversary of the signing of the Declaration of Independence. The exposition was open on Sunday and charged admission. A's owner and manager Connie Mack believed that if the exposition could charge admission on Sunday, so could his ball club. The Athletics won the game 3–2. There would be no more Sunday games in Philadelphia until 1934, however.

AUGUST 31   White Sox second baseman Ray Morehart, playing in place of the injured Eddie Collins, ties a major league record with nine hits in a double-header against the Tigers in Detroit. In the opener, Morehart collected five hits, two of them doubles, in six at-bats. The Sox had 23 hits in all and mauled the Tigers 19–2, with 15 of the runs coming in the final three innings, including eight in the eighth. In the second tilt, a 7–6 Detroit victory, Morehart was 4-for-4 with four singles and two walks.

There have been only nine players, six of them since 1900, who have collected nine hits in a double-header. Morehart is the only Sox player to accomplish the feat. During a three-year, 177-game big league career with the White Sox and the Yankees, he hit .269.

SEPTEMBER 1   A ball hit by Johnny Mostil travels only a few feet but scores three runs during an 11–7 win over the Tigers in Detroit. With the bases loaded in the eighth inning, Mostil chopped a ball in front of the plate. Tiger catcher Larry Woodall fielded it, and his throw toward first base hit Mostil in the back and caromed into right field, scoring all three runners.

Mostil hit .328, scored 120 runs and led the American League in stolen bases with 35 in 1926.

SEPTEMBER 10   Catcher Harry McCurdy sets a White Sox record (since tied) with hits in 10 consecutive at-bats during a 5–4, 10-inning loss to the Browns at Comiskey Park. McCurdy came into the contest with eight straight hits, achieved over four games from September 6 through September 9. During the September 10 contest, he singled twice before being retired in his third plate appearance.

McCurdy had eight singles and two doubles during his streak. He played for the White Sox from 1926 through 1928 and hit .288 in 451 at-bats. McCurdy had a 10-year major league career, mostly as a back-up catcher, and batted .282 with four clubs.

SEPTEMBER 22   The White Sox score two runs in the ninth inning to defeat the Yankees 2–1 at Comiskey Park. Bill Hunnefield hit a two-out, two-strike, RBI double to tie the score, then scored on a single from Bill Barrett.

SEPTEMBER 25   A walk-off homer by Bill Barrett off Walter Johnson beats the Senators 2–1 in the first game of a double-header at Comiskey Park. Washington won the second contest 3–2.

SEPTEMBER 29   In the first game of the Chicago City Series, the Cubs defeat the White Sox 6–0 at Wrigley Field.

OCTOBER 3   Ted Blankenship pitches the White Sox to a 4–0 win over the Cubs at Comiskey Park in game four of the City Series, which evens the series at two games apiece.

OCTOBER 7   The White Sox win the seventh and final game of the City Series with a 3–0 victory over the Cubs at Wrigley Field. Ted Blankenship pitched his second shutout of the series.

NOVEMBER 11   Ray Schalk replaces Eddie Collins as manager.

Collins was appointed as the White Sox manager on a permanent basis at the 1924 season. He took a club that had finished in last place that year to a 79–75 record in 1925. The club continued to improve in 1926, finishing 81–72. That wasn't good enough for Charles Comiskey, however. Comiskey had poured a small fortune into the purchase of minor league and amateur stars and expected better results. He was 67 years old and in failing health in 1926, and he wanted to bring Sox fans another pennant before he died. Despite his 12 years of loyal service to the club as a player and manager, Collins was dismissed without so much as a phone call. He learned about it from newspapermen. Collins never managed another club on the field. Eddie played and coached with the Philadelphia Athletics, where he began his career, from 1927 through 1932. After Tom Yawkey bought the Red Sox in February 1933, Collins went to Boston to serve as the club's general manager until he retired in 1947. Schalk had been a player for the White Sox since 1912. His record as manager of the club was 102–125 before resigning in July 1928. Comiskey not only never saw a another pennant for his ball club, he never saw another winning season after 1926. Beginning in 1927, the Sox had nine consecutive losing campaigns, the longest stretch in franchise history. Comiskey passed away on October 26, 1931.

DECEMBER 30   The *Chicago Tribune* breaks a story that the Tigers had thrown a four-game series to the White Sox in 1917 to help Chicago win the pennant (see September 3, 1917). Commissioner Kenesaw Landis announced he would hold hearings investigating the matter (see January 5, 1927).

1927

Season in a Sentence

Charles Comiskey renovates Comiskey Park but is unable to rejuvenate a White Sox team that loses 11 more games than the previous season under new manager Ray Schalk.

Finish • Won • Lost • Pct • GB

Fifth   70   83   .458   39.5

Manager

Ray Schalk

Stats

Stats	WS	AL	Rank
Batting Avg:	.278	.285	6
On-Base Pct:	.344	.351	5
Slugging Pct:	.378	.399	7
Home Runs:	36		5
Stolen Bases:	89		6
ERA:	3.51	4.14	2
Fielding Avg:	.971	.967	1
Runs Scored:	662		7
Runs Allowed:	708		2

Starting Lineup

Harry McCurdy, c
Bud Clancy, 1b
Aaron Ward, 2b
Willie Kamm, 3b
Bill Hunnefield, ss
Bibb Falk, lf
Alex Metzler, cf
Bill Barrett, rf
Buck Crouse, c
Roger Peckinpaugh, ss

Pitchers

Ted Lyons, sp
Tommy Thomas, sp
Ted Blankenship, sp
Red Faber, sp
Sarge Connally, rp-sp

Attendance

614,423 (third in AL)

Club Leaders

Batting Avg:	Bibb Falk	.327
On-Base Pct:	Alex Metzler	.396
Slugging Pct:	Bibb Falk	.465
Home Runs:	Bibb Falk	9
RBIs:	Bibb Falk	83
	Bill Barrett	83
Runs:	Alex Metzler	87
Stolen Bases:	Bill Barrett	20
Wins:	Ted Lyons	22
Strikeouts:	Tommy Thomas	107
ERA:	Ted Lyons	2.84
Saves:	Sarge Connally	5

JANUARY 5   Commissioner Kenesaw Landis begins a three-day hearing on the charges that four games between the White Sox and Tigers on September 2 and 3, 1917, had been thrown to the White Sox. Former Sox player Swede Risberg, one of the eight "Black Sox" suspended for fixing the 1919 World Series, contended that some Chicago players contributed $45 each to reward Detroit players for "laying down" during the four games in questions. Risberg fingered Sox manager Pants Rowland as the mastermind behind the plan and said that Ray Schalk and Eddie Collins were among the ringleaders. Many White Sox players admitted giving money to the Tigers, but they said that it was a reward for beating the Red Sox, Chicago's chief rival during the 1917 pennant chase, three times in a series later in September. Such gifts were a common practice at the time. Landis interviewed 29 players on the two clubs, but no witnesses confirmed any part of the story that the games were fixed. A week after the hearing opened, Landis cleared all those accused, citing a lack of evidence. Landis instituted a new rule which stated that anyone who gave a gift to an opposing player for any reason would receive a one-year suspension.

JANUARY 13   The White Sox trade Johnny Grabowski and Ray Morehart to the Yankees for Aaron Ward.

Ward was the starting second baseman on Yankees World Series teams in 1921, 1922 and 1923, but by the time he arrived in Chicago was past his prime. He lasted only one season with the Sox.

JANUARY 15   The White Sox trade Sloppy Thurston and Leo Mangum to the Senators for Roger Peckinpaugh.

Like Aaron Ward, who was obtained two days earlier, Peckinpaugh was a middle infielder with world championship rings. He was the starting shortstop in the Fall Classic for the Yankees in 1921 and the Senators in 1924 and 1925. Like Ward, Peckinpaugh was well into the downside of his career when he put on a White Sox uniform. The 1927 campaign was his last in the majors. Fortunately, the White Sox gave up little of substance to acquire Ward and Peckinpaugh.

MARCH 8   Johnny Mostil attempts suicide during spring training in Shreveport, Louisiana.

Mostil slashed his arms, wrists, throat and left side with 13 cuts while alone in his bathroom in the Hotel Youree, where the White Sox were quartered. Pat Prunty, a friend of Mostil, left the player about 4 o'clock in the afternoon, and upon returning about 6:30 found the door locked. Prunty obtained a pass key and found Mostil on the bathroom floor. The player was rushed to a hospital. The most serious wounds consisted of two deep gashes in the left side of the neck just below the ear. Mostil hovered near death for several days, then slowly began to discover his strength and the will to live. He never gave a reason for committing suicide, other than he had been "feeling badly." An agonizing nerve disease diagnosed as neuritis that caused him many sleepless nights was the official explanation issued by the White Sox's front office. There was also speculation that he was carrying on an affair with the wife of teammate Red Faber. Mostil returned to the playing field in September 1927, but he played in just 13 games that season. In 1928, he regained his starting position in center field, but a broken ankle in 1929 ended his career. Johnny rejoined the White Sox in 1949 as a scout and held the position until retiring in 1968 at the age of 72.

APRIL 12   The White Sox open the season with a 3–2 loss to the Indians in Cleveland. The Sox left 14 runners on base.

APRIL 13   After being to one-hit by Indians pitcher Dutch Levsen through the first seven innings, the White Sox score a run in the eighth inning and six in the ninth to win 7–2 in Cleveland.

APRIL 17   The White Sox put together a nine-run rally in the ninth inning to beat the Browns 12–5 in St. Louis.

APRIL 20   In the first game at expanded Comiskey Park, the White Sox lose 5–4 to the Indians. The White Sox Rooter's Association staged a massive downtown parade and presented Manager Ray Schalk with a floral horseshoe, symbolizing good luck.

During the 1926–27 off-season, the seating capacity of Comiskey Park was increased from 32,000 to 52,000 by double-decking the entire ballpark with the exception of a small section of unroofed bleachers in center field.

The addition cost $600,000 and was supervised by architect Zachary Taylor Davis, who designed both the original Comiskey Park structure, opened in 1910, and Wrigley Field.

APRIL 26   Following a 9–3 win over the Tigers at Comiskey Park, three Detective Bureau squads connected with the Chicago police force – 21 men in all – rush into the park at breakneck speed in response to a riot call. It proved to be a false alarm. There was no riot, just a group of celebrating White Sox fans.

MAY 7   U.S. Vice President Charles Dawes attends a game against the Yankees at Comiskey Park and watches the White Sox lose 8–0. Dawes was a resident of Evanston, Illinois, and served under Calvin Coolidge. Lou Gehrig hit a grand slam in the ninth inning into the right-field stands to account for the first homer at the remodeled ballpark.

MAY 17   White Sox starting pitcher Joe Brown retires no one in what proves to be his only big-league appearance. Brown faced three batters and allowed two hits and a walk. The White Sox lost 6–3 to the Red Sox in Boston.

MAY 18   Now a player with the Athletics, Eddie Collins makes his first appearance in Chicago since being fired as manager of the White Sox. He was given a wrist watch and a diamond stick pin in pre-game ceremonies, but the contest was called during the first inning by rain.

MAY 25   Four days after Charles Lindbergh lands in Paris at the end of his historic solo flight across the Atlantic, the White Sox sweep the Browns 14–8 and 1–0 in St. Louis. Ted Lyons pitched the game-two shutout.

In the best season of his 21-year career, Lyons had a record of 22–14 and a 2.84 earned run average in 1927. He led the AL in wins, complete games (30 in 34 starts) and innings pitched (307²/₃). Tommy Thomas just missed the 20-win circle with a mark of 19–16. The rest of the staff combined had 29 wins and 53 losses.

MAY 30   The White Sox hammer the Browns 10–0 in the second game of a double-header at Sportsman's Park. St. Louis won the opener 11–3.

JUNE 6   The White Sox rout the Red Sox 10–2 in Boston.

The win gave the White Sox a record of 31–17 and put the club only one game back of the first-place Yankees, but hopes for a pennant soon went up in smoke. The Sox were 39–66 over the remainder of the year and ended up 39¹/₂ games behind the Yanks. The 1927 White Sox are one of only four clubs in major league history to fall 14 games under .500 (a position they held in September) after being 14 games above .500. The others are the 1890 Philadelphia Athletics of the American Association, the 1978 Oakland Athletics, and the 2005 Baltimore Orioles.

JUNE 8   Tony Lazzeri hits three homers for the Yankees during an 11-inning, 12–11 White Sox loss in New York. Lazzeri's third homer capped a five-run Yankee ninth inning that tied the score 11–11. During the 11th-inning rally, Lazzeri was walked intentionally.

JUNE 28   The White Sox score three runs in the ninth inning to win 8–7 over the Indians at Comiskey Park with the help of 41-year-old coach Lena Blackburne, who was playing in his first major league game in eight years. With the score 7–6, one out and the tying run on second, Blackburne put himself into the game as a pinch-hitter. He was serving as acting manager following the second-inning ejection of Ray Schalk by the umpire Brick Owens. Blackburne delivered a single to tie the game. Earl Sheely singled and Willie Kamm hit a sacrifice fly to score Blackburne with the winning run.

The plate appearance was Blackburne's first in the majors since 1919. He previously played for the White Sox from 1910 through 1915 and returned to the club as a coach in 1927. Following his dramatic pinch-hit on June 28, 1927, Blackburne never stepped to the plate in the majors again. His only future appearance in a big-league contest came two years later as a pitcher for one-third of an inning when he managed the Sox (see June 5, 1929).

JULY 2   Bibb Falk hits a home run in the 10th inning to defeat the Browns 6–5 in St. Louis.

JULY 3   The White Sox explode for eight runs in the seventh inning to take an 11–2 lead, then hold on for an 11–10 victory over the Browns at Sportsman's Park. St. Louis attempted a comeback with four runs in the eighth inning and four more in the ninth.

JULY 11   The White Sox win 7–6 over the Red Sox at Comiskey Park on two errors during a stolen base attempt. In the ninth inning, Bill Barrett took off for second, and Boston catcher Fred Hofmann threw the ball past the base. Barrett went to third on the overthrow and scored when center fielder Ira Flagstead fumbled the ball. The White Sox tied a major-league record with eight sacrifices in the game. Bibb Falk and Aaron Ward each had two sacrifices, with Roger Peckinpaugh, Bill Barrett, Willie Kamm and Harry McCurdy accounting for one each.

JULY 12   Sarge Connally collects four hits in four at-bats, and while generally ineffective on the mound, he pitches a complete game to defeat the Athletics 8–6 at Comiskey Park.

JULY 13   On Eddie Collins Day at Comiskey Park, the former White Sox star and manager is given an automobile prior to a 7–5 Athletics victory.

JULY 15   White Sox first baseman Bud Clancy hits an inside-the-park grand slam off Rube Walberg in the first inning of an 11–10 loss to the Athletics in the second game of a double-header at Comiskey Park. Philadelphia also won the opener 3–1.

AUGUST 16   Babe Ruth becomes the first player to hit a home run over the new double-decked stands at Comiskey, a feat that architect Zachary Taylor Davis declared was impossible. The ball landed in an adjacent soccer field after traveling 474 feet. Ruth's blast was struck off Tommy Thomas during an 8–1 Yankees win.

SEPTEMBER 6   Bill Barrett's grand slam in the seventh inning breaks a 4–4 tie and sparks the White Sox to a 9–6 win over the Tigers in Detroit. Barrett was the first batter to face George Smith, who relieved Haskell Billings.

SEPTEMBER 22   The White Sox extend their losing streak to 12 games, dropping a 10-inning 2–1 decision to the Red Sox in Boston. The White Sox broke their losing streak the next day, with a 2–1 win over the Red Sox at Fenway Park.

1928

Season in a sentence

The disappointment of 1927 leads to a youth movement in 1928 and a mid-season change in managers from Ray Schalk to Lena Blackburne.

Finish • Won • Lost • Pct • GB

Fifth   72   82   .468   29.0

Managers

Ray Schalk (32–42) and Lena Blackburne (40–40)

Stats

Stats	WS	AL	Rank
Batting Avg:	.270	.281	7
On-Base Pct:	.334	.344	7
Slugging Pct:	.358	.397	8
Home Runs:	24		8
Stolen Bases:	139		1
ERA:	3.98	4.04	4
Fielding Avg:	.970	.969	4
Runs Scored:	656		7
Runs Allowed:	725		4

Starting Lineup

Buck Crouse, c
Bud Clancy, 1b
Bill Hunnefield, 2b
Willie Kamm, 3b
Bill Cissell, ss
Bibb Falk, lf
Johnny Mostil, cf
Alex Metzler, rf-lf-cf
Carl Reynolds, rf
Buck Redfern, 2b-ss
Bill Barrett, rf-2b
Moe Berg, c

Pitchers

Tommy Thomas, sp
Ted Lyons, sp-rp
Red Faber, sp
Grady Atkins, sp
Ted Blankenship, sp
Ed Walsh Jr., sp
George Cox, rp

Attendance

494,152 (third in AL)

Club Leaders

Batting Avg:	Willie Kamm	.308
On-Base Pct:	Alex Metzler	.410
Slugging Pct:	Alex Metzler	.422
Home Runs:	Alex Metzler	3
	Bill Barrett	3
RBIs:	Willie Kamm	84
Runs:	Alex Metzler	71
Stolen Bases:	Johnny Mostil	23
Wins:	Tommy Thomas	17
Strikeouts:	Tommy Thomas	129
ERA:	Tommy Thomas	3.08
Saves:	Ted Lyons	6

March 4   The White Sox sell Aaron Ward to the Indians.

APRIL 11   The White Sox open the season with an 8–3 loss to the Indians at Comiskey Park. In his first major league game, shortstop Bill Cissell collected three hits but made two errors. Ray Schalk was out of action with an injury. It was the first time that he was not in the Opening Day lineup since 1912.

> *Cissell was another of Charles Comiskey's high-priced acquisitions. He was purchased from Portland in the Pacific Coast League for $123,000, then a record for a minor league player. Cissell never panned out, however. He craved alcohol, and with Prohibition the law of the land, Cissell spent many a night prowling the streets looking for speakeasies. He often reported to the ballpark hung over or in no condition to play before being traded to the Indians in 1932. When Cissell died of a heart attack in March 1949 at the age of 45, he was destitute, suffering from malnutrition and living in a Chicago rooming house. A serious nerve condition had cost him both of his legs. The funeral was paid for by the Comiskey family after it was determined that the Cissell family lacked the financial resources for a decent burial.*

APRIL 20   The Indians hammer the Indians 11–1 in Cleveland.

MAY 23   Johnny Mostil is the star of a 4–3 win over the Indians at Comiskey Park. In center field, he tied an American League record for most chances accepted by an outfielder in a game with 12, accumulating 11 putouts and an assist. In the eighth inning, he broke a 3–3 tie by scoring from second base on a wild pitch.

MAY 26   Red Faber pitches the White Sox to a 1–0 victory over the Tigers at Comiskey Park.

JUNE 20   Harry McCurdy hits a grand slam off Dutch Levsen in the fourth inning of a 6–4 win over the Indians in the first game of a double-header in Cleveland. The Sox won despite being outhit 15–6. Cleveland won the second tilt 4–3.

JUNE 21   The White Sox defeat the Indians 4–3 in the second game of a twin bill in Cleveland. The Indians won the first contest by the same 4–3 score.

JULY 4   Tommy Thomas pitches a shutout to edge the Browns 1–0 in the second game of a double-header at Comiskey Park. St. Louis won the opener 11–8.

          After the games, Ray Schalk resigned as manager of the White Sox and was replaced by Lena Blackburne. The club had a record of 32–42 at the time of the switch. The resignation as manager also ended Schalk's playing career with the Sox. He had a brief five-game trial with the Giants in 1929, then retired from professional baseball. For a number of years, Schalk ran a bowling alley on Chicago's South Side. Under Blackburne, the Sox were 40–40 over the remainder of the 1928 season, but were 59–93 in 1929 leading to his dismissal.

JULY 6   The White Sox score seven runs in the fifth inning against the Senators at Griffith Stadium to take an 8–4 lead, then hang on to win 9–8 after Washington scores four runs in the ninth inning.

JULY 8   The White Sox pound out 20 hits and win 13–7 over the Senators in Washington.

JULY 14   The White Sox sweep the Red Sox 11–4 and 11–8 in Boston. The opener was the first career win for Ed Walsh Jr., son of the former star pitcher Ed Walsh. Bill Cissell drove in nine runs during the day, with five RBIs in the first game and four in the second. He had a homer, double and three singles in eight at-bats.

          A graduate of Notre Dame, Ed Walsh Jr. had a record of 11–24 and an earned run average of 5.57 in four seasons with the White Sox. He was only 32 when he died of rheumatic fever in 1937 at his parent's home in Meriden, Connecticut.

JULY 22   Red Faber changes his hitting approach before delivering a game-winning hit that beats the Yankees 6–4 in New York. With the score 4–4 and two Chicago runners on base in the eighth, the switch-hitting Faber went against the odds and hit right-handed against right-hander Wilcy Moore. After swinging and missing at two Moore pitches, Faber went to the left side of the plate and hit a single to score both runners.

JULY 25   The White Sox lose 16–0 and 8–7 to the Athletics at Comiskey Park. The Sox led the nightcap 7–4 before the A's score four times in the ninth inning.

AUGUST 6 The White Sox edge the Yankees 5–4 in 15 innings at Comiskey Park. Willie Kamm drove in the winning run with a two-out triple.

During the game, a fan behind the Yankee dugout shined a mirror in the eyes of Babe Ruth. Police were called to confiscate the mirror and expel the fan from the park.

AUGUST 20   In his major league debut, White Sox first baseman Art Shires collects four hits, including a triple, in five at-bats during a 6–4 win over the Red Sox in Boston.

Shires's contract was bought from the Waco club in the Texas League. He refused to report to the White Sox for several days because he demanded a portion of the purchase price. That should have given the Sox a heads up on the problems that lay ahead. A native of Italy, Texas, Shires was rarely out of trouble before was he traded to the Senators in June 1930. An after-hours reveler who stepped out on the town almost every night attired in a derby hat, spats and a walking cane, Shires loved to boast about his baseball abilities. Players began calling him "The Great" Shires, and Art loved the nickname. Appointed team captain during spring training in 1929, Shires used his duties to foment a rebellion against manager Lena Blackburne. Stripped of his captaincy before Opening Day, Shires was suspended three times during the season. His first suspension came after going on a bender one night in the team's spring training hotel in Dallas, Texas. The second occurred after he fought Blackburne in the clubhouse (see May 15, 1929). Blackburne moved Shires into his room on the road to try to curb the player's late-night carousing, but in September, Shires tore up his hotel room in Philadelphia and got in another fistic battle with his manager (see September 15, 1929). Squandering his money on Prohibition-era booze and nightclubs, Shires was broke at the end of the season. He approached fight promoter Nessie Blumenthal for a loan. Blumenthal agreed with the proviso that Shires put his pugilistic prowess on display before an audience at Chicago's White City Amusement Park. A series of amateur bouts pitting Shires against all comers was hastily arranged. The biggest bout came in December against Chicago Bears lineman George Trafton. Shires lost, but he agreed to fight Cubs outfielder Hack Wilson, another player who was often in monetary distress because of his love of a good time. Commissioner Kenesaw Landis threaten to suspend both Shires and Wilson if they stepped into the ring, and the bout was called off. In 1948, Shires was implicated in the murder of W. W. Erwin, a former minor league umpire he had beaten to a pulp in a Dallas street brawl. Art was exonerated after a coroner determined that Erwin had died of natural causes, and not by the beating administered by Shires.

SEPTEMBER 9   Scoreless through nine innings, the White Sox score two runs in the eighth inning and eight times in the ninth to defeat the Indians 10–1 in Cleveland.

SEPTEMBER 30   On the last day of the season, Sox pitcher Bob Weiland pitches a shutout in his first major league game, beating the Athletics 1–0 at Comiskey Park. Willie Kamm drove in the lone run of the contest with a single in the seventh inning.

A native of Chicago, Weiland didn't pitch another shutout in the majors until 1937 with the St. Louis Cardinals. He was 5–15 with a 5.39 ERA in four seasons with the White Sox, and 20–57 during his career when he suddenly became a steady starter with the Cards. Weiland won 15 games in 1937 and 16 in 1938. His career ended in 1940 with a 62–94 record.

OCTOBER 3   In the opening game of the Chicago City Series, the Cubs defeat the White Sox 3–0 before 25,885 at Comiskey Park.

OCTOBER 5   After losing the first two games of the City Series, the White Sox outlast the Cubs 13–11 at Wrigley Field. The Sox took a 13–10 lead with a five-run seventh inning.

OCTOBER 9   A month before Herbert Hoover defeats Al Smith in the presidential election, the Cubs win the seventh and deciding game of the City Series 13–2 at Comiskey Park. The seven games drew 184,951 fans.

The White Sox Catch a Spy

Moe Berg played for the White Sox as a catcher from 1926 through 1930, near the start of a 15-year career. He might have been the most intelligent man ever to play professional baseball. Berg read and spoke twelve languages, including Sanskrit, and held degrees from Princeton University, Columbia Law School and the Sorbonne. He enthralled newsmen with discourses on a wide variety of topics, including ancient Greek history and astronomy. Berg appeared on the popular radio program *Information Please*, correctly answering questions on Roman mythology, French impressionism, spatial geometry and the infield fly rule.

With the exception of 1929, when he played 107 games for Chicago, Berg was never more than a reserve. He hit .243 with just six homers in 1,813 career at-bats, but stayed in the majors because of his intelligence and defensive abilities behind the plate. Berg was reportedly the subject of Mike Gonzalez's legendary scouting report: "Good field, no hit." White Sox pitcher Ted Lyons once quipped, "Berg can speak in twelve languages, but can't hit in any of them."

Berg was traded by the White Sox to the Indians in April 1931 and from there moved on to play with the Senators and Red Sox. Sometime during this period, he began working as a spy for the United States government. At the end of the 1934 season, Berg was added at the last minute to a team of All-Stars, headed by Babe Ruth, on a goodwill trip to Japan. Organizers cited Berg's fluent Japanese as the reason for including him on the roster of stars. However, instead of playing, Berg spent much of his time taking photographs. By order of the State Department, Berg was to photograph key Japanese military installations and other potential targets from the roof of a Tokyo hospital. In April 1942, Major General Jimmy Doolittle used these photos in making the first American air attack on Japan during World War II.

Once the war started, Berg quit his job as a coach with the Red Sox and joined the Office of Strategic Services (OSS), the forerunner of the CIA. His primary objective was to determine Germany's nuclear potential. Berg undertook several missions behind enemy lines to keep track of German scientists. To add to the danger, Berg was Jewish. Some of these missions were rumored to have involved assassinations. His gift for languages served him well, and he also returned home safely.

1929   Sox

Season in a Sentence

Lena Blackburne has to battle first baseman Art Shires as well as the opposition, and the White Sox manager loses 93 games and his job.

Finish • Won • Lost • Pct • GB

Seventh   59   93   .388   46.0

Manager

Lena Blackburne

Stats

Stats	WS	AL	Rank
Batting Avg:	.268	.284	7
On-Base Pct:	.325	.349	7
Slugging Pct:	.363	.407	8
Home Runs:	37		7
Stolen Bases:	109		1
ERA:	4.41	4.25	6
Fielding Avg:	.969	.969	4
Runs Scored:	627		7
Runs Allowed:	792		6

Starting Lineup

Moe Berg, c
Art Shires, 1b
John Kerr, 2b
Willie Kamm, 3b
Bill Cissell, ss
Alex Metzler, lf
Dutch Hoffman, cf
Carl Reynolds, rf
Bud Clancy, 1b
Johnny Watwood, cf

Pitchers

Tommy Thomas, sp
Ted Lyons, sp
Red Faber, sp
Ed Walsh Jr., sp
Hal McKain, rp
Grady Atkins, rp-sp

Attendance

426,795 (fifth in AL)

Club Leaders

Batting Avg:	Carl Reynolds	.317
On-Base Pct:	Alex Metzler	.367
Slugging Pct:	Carl Reynolds	.474
Home Runs:	Carl Reynolds	11
RBIs:	Carl Reynolds	67
Runs:	Bill Cissell	83
Stolen Bases:	Bill Cissell	26
Wins:	Tommy Thomas	14
	Ted Lyons	14
Strikeouts:	Ted Lyons	68
ERA:	Tommy Thomas	3.19
Saves:	Ted Lyons	2

FEBRUARY 28   Two weeks after seven of Al Capone's rivals are machine-gunned to death in a North Side garage in the St. Valentine's Day massacre, the White Sox trade Bibb Falk to the Indians for Chick Autry.

APRIL 16   The White Sox open the season with a 3–1 loss to the Browns in St. Louis.

APRIL 22   The White Sox mop up on the Indians 10–0 in Cleveland.

APRIL 25   In the home opener, the White Sox lose 3–2 to the Browns before 9,000 on a cold and windy day at Comiskey Park. Bud Clancy hit a home run.

APRIL 29   The White Sox clobber the Indians 13–4 at Comiskey Park.

APRIL 30   A hidden-ball trick creates the third out of a White Sox triple play during an 8–4 win over the Indians at Comiskey Park. With Cleveland's Charlie Jamieson on second and Johnny Hodapp on third, Carl Lind grounded out to shortstop Bill Cissell. Both runners tried to advance. Hodapp was retired on a throw from first baseman Bud Clancy to catcher Buck Crouse. Jamieson barely reached third safely on a throw from Clancy to third baseman Willie Kamm. Instead of returning the ball to the pitcher, Kamm kept it and tagged Jamieson when he took a lead off the bag.

MAY 4   Lou Gehrig becomes the first player to hit three home runs in a game at Comiskey Park during an 11–9 Yankees win over the White Sox. Babe Ruth, Gehrig and Bob Meusel hit consecutive home runs in the seventh inning. It was also the first time that three players in a row hit home runs at Comiskey.

MAY 12   A two-out, two-run, walk-off double by Willie Kamm in the ninth inning beats the Senators 4–3 at Comiskey Park. It was Kamm's fourth hit and third double of the afternoon.

MAY 15   Art Shires fights White Sox manager Lena Blackburne during batting practice before a game against the Red Sox at Comiskey Park.

Third sacker Willie Kamm was a consistently productive hitter for the team during the 1920s, a key part of the team that replaced the legendary Black Sox.

Shires took his swings during batting practice wearing a red felt hat. Blackburne told him to remove it, and Shires refused. The argument culminated in a clubhouse fight in which Blackburne, who was 42 years old, five-foot-eleven and weighed 160 pounds, knocked out the 21-year-old Shires, who was two inches taller and 35 pounds heavier than the Sox manager. Shires was suspended by the club for three weeks.

MAY 19   In the fourth inning of a 10–3 win over the Tigers in Detroit, Johnny Mostil breaks his leg tripping over home plate on the uncontested front end of a double steal. Mostil never played another major league game.

MAY 23   The White Sox trade Bill Barrett to the Red Sox for Doug Taitt.

MAY 24   Ted Lyons pitches a 21-inning complete game against the Tigers at Comiskey Park, only to lose 6–5. Lyons allowed 24 hits, but he kept them scattered well enough to pitch 13 consecutive scoreless innings from the eighth through the 20th. George Uhle hurled the first 20 innings for Detroit and started the 21st with a single. Uhle was lifted by player-manager Bucky Harris, who inserted himself into the game as a pinch-runner and crossed the plate on a single by Roy Johnson and a sacrifice fly from Charlie Gehringer. The 21 innings were completed in three hours and 31 minutes.

MAY 26   Red Faber pitches a one-hitter for a 2–0 win over the Tigers at Comiskey Park. The only Detroit hit was a single by Charlie Gehringer in the fourth inning.

MAY 27

The White Sox win a thrilling 14-inning, 6–5 decision over the Tigers in the second game of a double-header at Comiskey Park. Bill Cissell homered in the ninth inning to tie the score 3–3. Detroit scored in both the 12th and 13th innings, but the Sox rallied each time to knot the contest. The winning run crossed the plate on a walk-off single by relief pitcher Tommy Thomas. Chicago also won the opener 7–4 with Thomas earning a save.

JUNE 5

Manager Lena Blackburne pitches during the White Sox's 17–2 loss to the Red Sox in Boston. Nine of Boston's 24 hits came consecutively with two out in the eight-run eighth inning. Chicago rookie pitcher Dan Dugan allowed the first eight hits. The ninth was surrendered to Jack Rothrock by Blackburne, who was so disgusted with the performance that he took the mound himself. Blackburne faced only one batter because Rothrock was out trying to stretch a single into a double. It was the last of 548 games that Blackburne played during his big-league career, and his only game as a pitcher.

JULY 2

The White Sox lose both games of a double-header in extra innings against the Indians in Cleveland. The Sox lost the opener 4–3 in 10 innings and the nightcap 5–4 in 11.

JULY 3

The White Sox and Indians play their third extra-inning contest in two days, with the Sox winning 6–3 in 10 innings in Cleveland.

JULY 21

The White Sox clobber the Red Sox 10–0 at Comiskey Park.

AUGUST 18

Ted Lyons wins his own game with a walk-off single in the ninth inning off Herb Pennock to beat the Yankees 3–2 at Comiskey Park.

AUGUST 20

Before a game against the Yankees at Comiskey Park, Red Faber is showered with gifts and presented with a check for $2,700. On the mound, Faber pitched eight innings but lost 5–4.

SEPTEMBER 11

The White Sox lose an odd 7–4 decision to the Athletics in Philadelphia in which all 11 runs scored in the first inning. Stranger still, the starting pitchers were future Hall of Famers Ted Lyons and Lefty Grove.

SEPTEMBER 14

Art Shires fights Lena Blackburne again, this time in a Philadelphia hotel room.

> *Shires tore apart his hotel room in a drunken frenzy. Blackburne's attempts to pacify Shires ended in a wild free-for-all involving traveling secretary Lou Barbour, who came to Blackburne's rescue. Barbour's thumb was nearly bitten off during the melee, although he wasn't sure whether it was Shires or Blackburne who bit him. Hotel detectives arrived a few minutes later and arrested Shires. The troubled first baseman was suspended for the remainder of the season (see December 9, 1929).*

SEPTEMBER 28

All American League games are postponed out of respect for Yankee manager Miller Huggins, who was buried that day in Cincinnati. Huggins died three days earlier from blood poisoning.

SEPTEMBER 30   With fan apathy at a new low, Donie Bush replaces Lena Blackburne as manager, effective at the end of the season.

Blackburne never managed another big-league club, but he had a profitable business bottling and selling mud from the Delaware River, along the borders of Pennsylvania and New Jersey, to the American and National Leagues. The mud was used by umpires to remove the gloss from new baseballs prior to game time. Bush was 40 years old. He was a star shortstop in the American League, mainly with the Tigers, from 1908 through 1923. Bush managed the Pirates to the National League pennant in 1927, his first season with the club, but couldn't get along with his players and was fired in August 1929. He took the White Sox job just hours before the Yankees called to offer him a position as manager. Bush was tempted to take the offer from the prestigious Yankees, but AL President Ernest Barnard would not let Bush break his contract with the talentless Sox. Bush managed the Chicago club for two seasons to a lackluster record of 118–189.

OCTOBER 2   A crowd of only 200 at Comiskey Park watches the White Sox beat the Tigers 3–1.

OCTOBER 4   The White Sox score eight runs in the eighth inning of a 14–6 walloping of the Tigers. Only 350 attended the game at Comiskey Park.

DECEMBER 9   Six weeks after the historic stock market crash, which starts the country on the road to the Great Depression, Art Shires begins his professional boxing career by knocking out "Dangerous Dan" Daly in only 21 seconds before a capacity crowd of 5,000 at Chicago's White City arena. According to the AP story, "Shires and his opponent fought like a couple of amateurs showing no boxing skill, no preliminary training or other tricks of the trade." The crowd included White Sox traveling secretary Lou Barbour, who nearly had his thumb bitten off in a row with Shires (see September 14, 1929).

DECEMBER 15   Art Shires is decisively defeated by Chicago Bears lineman George Trafton before a packed house of 5,000 at the White City arena. Thousands more were turned away. The 218-pound Trafton outweighed Shires by 40 pounds. Bloodied and beaten, Shires refused to go down. By the end of the fifth round, both fighters were so exhausted that they could barely raise their arms.

Shires had another bout scheduled with Cubs outfielder Hack Wilson, but Wilson backed out of the fight on December 18. Undeterred, Shires challenged Gene Tunney and Jack Dempsey to matches. Commissioner Kenesaw Landis put an end to Shires's boxing career on January 18, 1930, by threatening him with a suspension from baseball if he ever stepped into the ring again.

THE STATE OF THE WHITE SOX

The 1930s was the worst decade in White Sox history. With the country mired in the Great Depression, the club posted an overall record of 678–841, a winning percentage of .446 that was the seventh-best among the eight clubs in the American League, ahead of only the St. Louis Browns. In 1935, the Sox had a losing record for the ninth season in a row and finished in the lower half of the AL standings for the 15th year in succession. The only clubs on the South Side of Chicago with winning records during the '30s were at the end of the decade (1936, 1937 and 1939). The White Sox began their first serious forays into creating a farm system, but it produced next to nothing in the way of talent. Throughout the '30s, the White Sox fielded teams that were either the oldest or among the oldest in the majors. American League pennant winners were the Athletics (1930, 1931), Yankees (1932, 1936, 1937, 1938 and 1939), Senators (1933) and Tigers (1934 and 1935).

THE BEST TEAM

The 1937 White Sox had a record of 86–68 and finished in third place, 19 games out of first. The modest .558 winning percentage was the best of any Sox club between 1920 and 1953.

THE WORST TEAM

In terms of winning percentage, the 1932 White Sox were the worst in club history, posting a record of 49–102 (.325). The team finished 56½ games behind the pennant-winning Yankees but did manage to avoid last place, because the Red Sox fielded a club that was 43–111.

THE BEST MOMENT

At Yankee Stadium on July 2, 1930, Carl Reynolds hits homers in the first, second and third innings, two of them inside-the-park homers, and later added two singles. In all, he had eight RBIs in a 15–2 win.

THE WORST MOMENT

The career of a promising young pitcher was ruined in November 1938 when Monty Stratton had to have one of his legs amputated following a hunting accident.

THE ALL-DECADE TEAM • YEARS WITH WS

Luke Sewell, c	1935–38
Zeke Bonura, 1b	1934–37
Jackie Hayes, 2b	1932–40
Jimmie Dykes, 3b	1933–39
Luke Appling, ss	1930–43, 1945–50
Al Simmons, lf	1933–35
Mike Kreevich, cf	1935–41
Carl Reynolds, rf	1927–31
Ted Lyons, p	1923–42, 1946
Thornton Lee, p	1937–47
John Whitehead, p	1935–39
Vern Kennedy, p	1934–37

Appling, Simmons and Lyons all are in the Hall of Fame. Lyons was also on the 1920s All-Decade Team. Other outstanding players on the White Sox during the 1930s were left fielder Rip Radcliff (1934–39) and center fielder Mule Haas (1933–37).

THE DECADE LEADERS

Batting Avg:	Zeke Bonura	.317
On-Base Pct:	Luke Appling	.399
Slugging Pct:	Zeke Bonura	.518
Home Runs:	Zeke Bonura	79
RBIs:	Luke Appling	615
Runs:	Luke Appling	695
Stolen Bases:	Luke Appling	86
Wins:	Ted Lyons	117
Strikeouts:	Ted Lyons	536
ERA:	Monty Stratton	3.71
Saves:	Clint Brown	43

THE HOME FIELD

There were three significant changes to Comiskey Park during the 1930s. The infield was moved 14 feet closer to the outfield walls in 1934, the first public address system was installed in 1935 and light towers were added in 1939. The first regular-season major league night game was played at Comiskey Park on August 18, 1939.

THE GAME YOU WISH YOU HAD SEEN

Comiskey Park was the site of the first All-Star Game on July 6, 1933. There were 17 future Hall of Famers in the contest. The American League won 4–2.

THE WAY THE GAME WAS PLAYED

The offensive explosion that changed baseball during the 1920s continued throughout the 1930s. Batting averages in the AL floated around .280, with a peak of .289 in 1936, when the teams in the circuit averaged 5.7 runs per game. In 1930 there were more home runs than stolen bases in the American League for the first time.

THE MANAGEMENT

Charles Comiskey, who founded the franchise in 1900, died on October 26, 1931. The mantle was passed to his son, Louis. Never in robust health, Louis died on July 19, 1939, at the age of 54. Grace Comiskey, Charles's widow, became head of the club following the death of her son. Harry Grabiner, who had been employed by the White Sox since 1905, served as general manager throughout the 1930s. Field managers were Donie Bush (1930–31), Lew Fonseca (1932–34) and Jimmie Dykes (1934–46).

THE BEST PLAYER MOVE

The best move was the purchase of Luke Appling from the Atlanta Crackers of the Southern Association in 1930. The best trade brought Thornton Lee from the Indians for Jack Salveson on December 8, 1936.

THE WORST PLAYER MOVE

The worst trade of the decade sent Bump Hadley and Bruce Campbell to the Browns for Red Kress in April 1932.

1930

Sox

Season in a Sentence

Following a massive roster turnover, new manager Donie Bush proves to be no more successful than predecessor Lena Blackburne, as the White Sox finish in seventh place for the second year in a row.

Finish • Won • Lost • Pct • GB

Seventh   62   92   .405   40.0

Manager

Donie Bush

Stats

Stats	WS	AL	Rank
Batting Avg:	.276	.288	6
On-Base Pct:	.328	.351	7
Slugging Pct:	.391	.421	6
Home Runs:	63		6
Stolen Bases:	74		5
ERA:	4.71	4.65	5
Fielding Avg:	.962	.968	8
Runs Scored:	729		7
Runs Allowed:	884		5

Starting Lineup

Bernie Tate, c
Johnny Watwood, 1b-cf
Bill Cissell, 2b
Willie Kamm, 3b
Greg Mulleavy, ss
Smead Jolley, lf-rf
Red Barnes, cf
Carl Reynolds, rf-cf-lf
John Kerr, 2b
Bud Clancy, 1b

Pitchers

Ted Lyons, sp
Pat Caraway, sp-rp
Red Faber, sp
Tommy Thomas, sp
Garland Braxton, sp-rp
Dutch Henry, rp-sp
Ed Walsh, Jr., rp
Hal McKain, rp

Attendance

406,123 (seventh in AL)

Club Leaders

Batting Avg:	Carl Reynolds	.359
On-Base Pct:	Carl Reynolds	.388
Slugging Pct:	Carl Reynolds	.584
Home Runs:	Carl Reynolds	22
RBIs:	Smead Jolley	114
Runs:	Carl Reynolds	103
Stolen Bases:	Carl Reynolds	16
	Bill Cissell	16
Wins:	Ted Lyons	22
Strikeouts:	Pat Caraway	83
ERA:	Ted Lyons	3.78
Saves:	Hal McKain	5

APRIL 15   The White Sox season opener, scheduled for Comiskey Park against the Indians, is postponed by rain. The April 16th contest was also rained out.

Rain and cold postponed seven of the White Sox's first 10 games in 1930.

APRIL 17   The White Sox finally get the 1930 season under way and win 8–7 over the Indians in 10 innings before 25,000 at Comiskey Park. Cleveland led 4–0 before the Sox took the lead with six runs in the sixth, but the Indians rallied and sent the contest into extra innings. The winning run scored on a double by Alex Metzler.

Dutch Henry was the winning pitcher. He won only once more in 1930, however, and finished the season with a horrendous record of 2–17.

APRIL 27   First baseman Bud Clancy fails to record a putout or an assist during a 2–1 win over the Browns in St. Louis. Clancy is one of only four first baseman in major league history to play a game of nine innings or more without a fielding chance. Tommy Thomas ($6^1/_3$ innings) and Hal McKain ($2^2/_3$ innings) struck out eight batters. Two Browns were retired on force outs at second base and one was thrown out on a stolen base attempt. The other 16 outs were the result of fly balls.

The White Sox began wearing uniform numbers for the first time in 1930. The Yankees became the first team to permanently affix numbers to their uniforms in 1929. By 1932, all major leaguers sported identifying numerals on the backs of their jerseys.

MAY 24   Trailing 6–1, the White Sox score six runs in the seventh inning and hold off the Tigers to win 7–6 in Detroit.

The most celebrated rookie on the White Sox in 1930 was outfielder Smead Jolley, who was purchased from San Francisco in the Pacific Coast League for $50,000. He batted .313 and hit 16 homers with 114 RBIs in 1930, but Jolley was slow afoot and possessed a glove of iron. Because of his fielding deficiencies and a broken ankle, Jolley's playing time was reduced to 110 at-bats in 1931 and he was traded to the Red Sox in April 1932. Jolley's big-league career lasted only four seasons.

JUNE 4   A walk-off homer by John Kerr in the 10th inning beats the Yankees 8–7 at Comiskey Park.

JUNE 10   After the Athletics score two runs in the top of the 10th inning, the White Sox counter with two in their half and win 7–6 with a tally in the 11th at Comiskey Park. Bud Clancy drove in the winning run with a single off Lefty Grove.

JUNE 16   The White Sox trade Art Shires to the Senators for Bennie Tate and Garland Braxton.

The White Sox finally had enough of Shires and his eccentric behavior. Due his rampant ego, abhorrent behavior and gift for publicity, Shires was one of the most well-known players in baseball during a brief stay in the majors, even though it lasted only 291 games. He played his last big-league game in 1932 when he was only 25.

JULY 2   Carl Reynolds hits homers during his first three at-bats of a 15–2 win over the Yankees in the second game of a double-header at Yankee Stadium. In both the first and second innings, Reynolds hit inside-the-park homers to left field off Red Ruffing. In the third, Reynolds hit an opposite-field homer into the right-field bleachers facing Ken Holloway. Babe Ruth tore the nail completely off the ring finger of his left hand when he caught it in the fence vainly trying to catch Reynolds's drive. Reynolds later added two singles and drove in a total of eight runs in six at-bats. In the opening act of the twin bill, he was hitless in four at-bats as the Sox lost 5–1.

Reynolds was the first White Sox player to hit three home runs in a game. Nonetheless, the Associated Press story of the game featured Ruth's injury and speculation of how it would affect the Babe's home runs swing, rather than on Reynolds's batting feats. In 1930, Reynolds hit .359 with 22 home runs, 18 triples, 103 runs and 104 RBIs. He was the first Sox player to hit at least 20 homers in a season, breaking the previous mark of 14 set by Happy Felsch in 1920. Reynolds never came close to reaching those figures again, however. Considered to be injury-prone, temperamental and quarrelsome, he was traded to the Senators following the 1931 season.

JULY 15   Making his first major league start, White Sox third baseman Blondy Ryan hits a home run, but the Sox lose 9–5 to the Yankees at Comiskey Park.

Ryan didn't hit another home run in the majors until 1933, when he played for the Giants. He batted only .207 in 87 at-bats with the Sox.

JULY 18   The White Sox purchase Fats Fothergill from the Tigers.

Charitably listed at 230 pounds on a five-foot-10 body, Bob (Fats) Fothergill played three seasons in the White Sox outfield during a career that began in 1922 and lasted 12 years.

JULY 20   The White Sox sweep the Red Sox 16–4 and 5–4 in a double-header at Comiskey Park. Chicago collected 21 hits in the opener.

JULY 21   The White Sox sell Alex Metzler to the Browns.

JULY 31   The White Sox sweep the Browns 10–2 and 1–0 during a double-header at Comiskey Park. Ted Lyons pitched the second-game shutout.

AUGUST 27   The White Sox down the Indians 14–5 and 5–4 during a double-header in Cleveland. Ted Lyons recorded his 20th win of the season in the second tilt.

On a club that had a record of 62–92, Lyons was 22–15 in 1930 and had an ERA of 3.78. He led the AL in innings pitched ($297^1/3$) and complete games (29 in 36 starts).

AUGUST 29   White Sox pitcher Pat Caraway pitches a spectacular 13-inning shutout, allowing only three hits, to defeat the Indians 3–0 in Cleveland. Caraway also drove in the first run of the game with a double in the 13th.

Caraway had a bizarre, accordion-like wind-up, nearly doubling over his six-foot-four-inch frame before delivering.

SEPTEMBER 10   Luke Appling makes his major league debut. Playing shortstop and batting sixth, Appling had a single in four at-bats during a 6–2 loss to the Red Sox at Comiskey Park.

The September 10, 1930, contest was the beginning of a career with the White Sox that lasted until 1950. Appling would establish himself as one of the greatest players in franchise history. He was a sophomore at Oglethorpe in 1930 when he signed a professional contract with Atlanta of the Southern Association. The Sox paid Atlanta $20,000 for Appling's contract. After a few rough seasons, he blossomed into stardom in 1933 when he batted .322, the first of nine consecutive seasons in which he batted .300 or better. His peak season was in 1936 when he hit .388 and won the first of two career batting titles. Appling was a hypochondriac, constantly complaining of some ailment, which earned him the nickname "Old Aches and Pains." Yet he had only one major injury, a broken leg in 1938, and batted .301 in 142 games at the age of 42 in 1949. Appling holds career club records in games played (2,422), at-bats (8,857), runs (1,319), hits (2,749), doubles (440), RBIs (1,116) and walks (1,302). He is also third in *triples (102), fourth in on-base percentage (.399) and eighth in batting average (.310). Appling also played 2,218 career games at shortstop, ranking fifth all-time behind Luis Aparicio, Ozzie Smith, Cal Ripken and Larry Bowa. Appling held the all-time record for games played by a shortstop from 1949, when he passed Rabbit Maranville, until 1970. Appling was elected to the Hall of Fame in 1964. Unfortunately, a World Series ring is not among his trophies. Appling played during one of the worst stretches in White Sox history. He was a member of only five teams with a winning record, none of which finished higher than third place or closer than eight games from first place.*

SEPTEMBER 21   The White Sox bash the Yankees 15–7 at Comiskey Park.

OCTOBER 1   In the first game of the City Series, the White Sox defeat the Cubs 5–1 at Comiskey Park.

The Cubs rebounded from the game one defeat and won the series, four games to two.

1931   Sox

Season in a Sentence

Irascible manager Donie Bush makes enemies out of nearly everyone on the club, as the White Sox crash land into last place.

Finish • Won • Lost • Pct • GB

Eighth   56   97   .366   51.5

Manager

Donie Bush

Stats

Stats	WS	AL	Rank
Batting Avg:	.260	.278	8
On-Base Pct:	.323	.344	7
Slugging Pct:	.343	.396	8
Home Runs:	27		8
Stolen Bases:	94		3
ERA:	5.04	4.38	8
Fielding Avg:	.961	.968	8
Runs Scored:	704		6
Runs Allowed:	939		8

Starting Lineup

Bennie Tate, c
Lu Blue, 1b
John Kerr, 2b
Billy Sullivan, Jr., 3b
Bill Cissell, ss
Lew Fonseca, lf
Johnny Watwood, cf
Carl Reynolds, rf
Fats Fothergill, lf-rf
Luke Appling, ss
Frank Grube, c
Irv Jeffries, 3b
Mel Simons, cf

Pitchers

Vic Frasier, sp-rp
Tommy Thomas, sp
Pat Caraway, sp-rp
Ted Lyons, sp-rp
Red Faber, rp-sp
Jim Moore, rp
Hal McKain, rp

Attendance

403,550 (sixth in AL)

Club Leaders

Batting Avg:	Lu Blue	.304
On-Base Pct:	Lu Blue	.430
Slugging Pct:	Carl Reynolds	.442
Home Runs:	Carl Reynolds	6
RBIs:	Carl Reynolds	77
Runs:	Lu Blue	119
Stolen Bases:	Bill Cissell	18
Wins:	Vic Frasier	13
Strikeouts:	Vic Frasier	87
ERA:	Red Faber	3.82
Saves:	Vic Frasier	4

MARCH 21   Two after Congress adopts "The Star-Spangled Banner" as the National Anthem, the White Sox and New York Giants play a night game before 2,500 fans in an exhibition game in Houston, Texas. It was the first time that two major league clubs played each other at night. The Sox scored five runs in the 10th inning to win 11–6.

The first regular season night game in the majors occurred in 1935 between the Reds and Phillies in Cincinnati. The White Sox began playing at night during the regular season in 1939.

APRIL 3   The White Sox purchase Lu Blue from the Browns.

Blue was 34 years old when he was purchased by the White Sox. He gave the club one good season, batting .304 with 119 runs scored and 127 walks in 1931.

APRIL 14   The White Sox open the season with a 5–4 loss to the Indians in Cleveland. The Indians took the lead with two runs in the eighth inning.

APRIL 22   In the home opener, the White Sox lambaste the Indians 10–2. Temperatures in the low 40s kept the crowd at Comiskey Park to 5,000.

APRIL 26   Rookie pitcher Vic Frasier walks 10 in 7$\frac{1}{3}$ innings during an 8–4 loss to the Tigers at Comiskey Park.

APRIL 30   Down 9–4, the White Sox score three runs in the fourth inning, two in the seventh and one in the 11th to defeat the Browns 10–9 at Comiskey Park. Bill Cissell drove in the winning run.

MAY 1   The White Sox score seven runs in the sixth inning of an 8–2 win over the Browns at Comiskey Park.

MAY 9   A run-filled ninth inning caps a 13–9 loss to the Yankees at Comiskey Park. New York scored six runs in the top of the inning to take a 13–2 lead before the Sox countered with seven in their half.

MAY 15   The White Sox commit eight errors during a 12–8 loss to the Red Sox at Comiskey Park.

MAY 17   The White Sox trade Willie Kamm to the Indians for Lew Fonseca.

Kamm had been the White Sox's regular third baseman since 1923, but things began to turn sour when Donie Bush was appointed manager. Bush accused Kamm of loafing and indifference, and Willie was benched for several stretches during the 1930 season. After leaving Chicago, Kamm was the Indians' regular third baseman for four years. Fonseca won the American League batting title as recently as 1929 with a .369 average, but he was seldom healthy during his 12-year career, which began in 1922. He played in at least 100 games only four times. Among his injuries were broken shoulders (four times), a fractured wrist, a chipped bone in his ankle, a dislocated hip, a concussion, a broken nose and a severed artery in his leg. While playing for Cincinnati, Fonseca once missed several games after slicing open his abdomen with his belt buckle. With the White Sox, he was a regular for only one season. At the end of the 1931 season, Fonseca succeeded Bush as manager (see October 12, 1931).

MAY 18   Down 8–3, the White Sox stun the Red Sox with six runs in the ninth inning to win 9–8 at Comiskey Park. Lu Blue drove in the first three runs with a bases-loaded triple. After the next two hitters were retired, Smead Jolley and Ike Eichrodt singled and pinch-hitter Mel Simons smacked a two-run double for the victory.

MAY 27   Pat Caraway collects four hits, including a double, in four at-bats and pitches a complete game to defeat the Tigers 10–1 in the second game of a double-header at Comiskey Park. The Sox also won the opener 5–4.

JUNE 5   Lew Fonseca hits a homer in the 11th inning, which sparks the White Sox to a 7–5 win over the Athletics in Philadelphia. It was one of only two home runs that Fonseca hit in 561 at-bats with the Sox over three seasons.

JULY 7   The White Sox defeat the Browns 10–8 in 12 innings in St. Louis in the longest extra-inning game in major league history without a strikeout. Sox pitchers were Tommy Thomas ($7^1/_3$ innings), Red Faber ($3^2/_3$ innings) and Hal McKain (one inning). Browns hurlers were Lefty Stewart (nine innings) and Chad Kimsey (three innings).

JULY 9   Vic Frasier walks nine batters and allows six hits but pitches a shutout to defeat the Indians 3–0 at Comiskey Park. Cleveland loaded the bases three times without scoring and left 14 men on base during the afternoon.

JULY 22   Johnny Watwood collects five hits, including a triple and a double, in five at-bats during a 9–3 win in the second game of a double-header against the Red Sox in Boston. Watwood also had a double and a single in four at-bats in the opener, a 3–2 Chicago defeat.

JULY 23   Pat Caraway is shelled for 11 runs in $4^2/_3$ innings during a 13–4 loss to the Red Sox in Boston. Caraway begged manager Donie Bush to take him out of the game, but Bush berated the pitcher in the dugout in full view of the fans at Fenway Park and sent Caraway back to the mound.

                Bush completely destroyed the confidence of Caraway, who was 10–24 with a 6.22 earned run average in 1931. Caraway's next start was even worse (see July 26, 1931).

JULY 26   After winning the first game of a double-header 5–4 over the Yankees in New York, the White Sox are pummeled in the second tilt 22–5. Starting pitcher Pat Caraway allowed eight walks, seven hits and 13 runs in two innings.

                Before the twin bill, Bill Cissell raced Dusty Cooke and Ben Chapman in a 100-yard dash. Cissell finished third with Chapman breaking the tape at 10.4 seconds. Famed tap-dancer Bill "Bojangles" Robinson competed in the same race. Robinson was given a 25-yard start and raced backwards, finishing behind Chapman, but ahead of Cooke and Cissell.

JULY 28   The White Sox turn a hopeless cause into a 14–12 victory over the Yankees in New York. The Sox trailed 12–3 before shocking the Yanks with 11 runs in the eighth inning off three future Hall of Fame pitchers. With one out and no one on base, Carl Reynolds doubled off Herb Pennock. Lew Fonseca followed with a single, and Fats Fothergill drove a pitch into the left field stands. John Kerr singled and Red Ruffing replaced Pennock. Ruffing yielded singles to Bill Cissell and Frank Grube, a double to Smead Jolley and a triple to Lu Blue. The triple bounced off the chest of second baseman Tony Lazzeri and rolled across the foul line. Lefty Gomez replaced Ruffing and retired Irv Jeffries for the second out. Then came Reynolds's second double of the inning, and a single by Lew Fonseca, tying the score 12–12. Fothergill followed by poking a fly ball to right field. Babe Ruth tried for a shoestring catch but missed, and Fothergill wound up with a triple to score the go-ahead run. In addition to the home run and triple, Fothergill collected two doubles earlier in the contest.

AUGUST 7   At the age of 42, Red Faber pitches a complete-game shutout to defeat the Browns 2–0 at Comiskey Park.

AUGUST 12   The White Sox overwhelm the Senators 11–1 at Comiskey Park.

AUGUST 22   Jimmie Foxx of the Athletics drives a ball out of Comiskey Park during a 7–1 Philadelphia win. The ball landed on the left field roof and bounced out.

AUGUST 30   The White Sox commit eight errors, and four pitchers combine to walk 12 batters, but the club survives to defeat the Tigers 10–8 in 12 innings in Detroit.

SEPTEMBER 9   The Cubs defeat the White Sox 3–0 in a charity exhibition game to benefit the unemployed before 34,865 at Comiskey Park. A total of $44,489 was turned over to the Illinois State Unemployment Fund. Al Capone sat in the front row with his bodyguard.

SEPTEMBER 12   During an odd double-header against the Yankees in New York, the White Sox win 8–5 in 13 innings and tie 13–13 in 10 innings. In the opener, the Yankees scored three times in the ninth inning to tie the score 3–3. In the 13th, the Sox plated five runs and the Yankees two. In the second game, Chicago had leads of 6–1, 10–8 and 13–10, but on each occasion, the Yanks came back to take the lead or tie the contest. Both clubs scored three runs in the ninth. The game was called on account of darkness.

SEPTEMBER 20   Pitching in relief in each contest, Pat Caraway is the losing pitcher in both ends of a double-header against the Senators in Washington, as the White Sox drop 4–3 and 6–4 decisions.

SEPTEMBER 30   In the first game of the Chicago City Series, the White Sox defeat the Cubs 9–0 at Wrigley Field. Red Faber pitched the shutout. Smead Jolley smacked a grand slam off Charlie Root during a seven-run sixth.

                The City Series appeared to be a mismatch. The White Sox finished the regular season in last place, while the Cubs were third in the NL.

OCTOBER 3   Boasting that he could beat the White Sox with eight bloomer girls from an old-ladies home, Cubs pitcher Pat Malone loses 4–3 to the Sox at Comiskey Park in game four of the City Series. Malone was pelted by a barrage of lemons from angry fans during the contest.

OCTOBER 4   The White Sox take a three-games-to-two lead in the City Series with a 13–6 victory over the Cubs before 41,523 at Comiskey Park.

OCTOBER 6   The White Sox win the City Series with a 7–2 triumph at Wrigley Field in the seventh and deciding game.

OCTOBER 9   Donie Bush resigns as manager of the White Sox. "I don't mind losing ball games if there is a prospect of better days ahead," said Bush, "but I feel that whatever reputation I possess as a manager would be jeopardized by remaining another year." Bush managed only one more big-league club, guiding the 1933 Cincinnati Reds to a last-place finish. He remained active in baseball until his death at the age of 86, however. Bush managed in the minors for 10 years, scouted for the Red Sox and White Sox, and owned the Indianapolis club in the American Association. The ballpark in Indianapolis, Bush's hometown, was named in his honor. Bush Stadium was the set locale for the baseball scenes in John Sayles's 1988 film *Eight Men Out*, based on the Black Sox scandal.

OCTOBER 12   Lew Fonseca is named manager of the White Sox.

The White Sox sank to new depths under Fonseca, sporting a 49–102 record in 1932 and 120–196 overall before he was fired in May 1934. His greatest contribution to baseball came after his playing days ended when he became major league director of motion picture production. Fonseca produced some 53 baseball movies, including the official World Series film from its inception in 1943 through 1965. He served as narrator in many of them. In the 1970s, Fonseca served as a roving hitting instructor in the Reds organization and tutored many members of the Big Red Machine, including Pete Rose, Johnny Bench and George Foster.

OCTOBER 26   Nine days after Al Capone is imprisoned for tax evasion, Charles Comiskey dies at the age of 72.

Comiskey had been in ill health for years. He passed away at his hunting lodge in Eagle River, Wisconsin. Comiskey left a sizable estate valued at $1,529,707. Control of the club passed to his son, Lou. Born in 1885, Lou was a robust and athletic young man groomed to take over the family business when he was stricken with a malignant case of scarlet fever when he was only 27. Lou never shook off the after-effects of the disease. For years, he carried a portable oxygen mask around with him and his weight ballooned to 300 pounds. Despite his physical limitations, Lou laid out an ambitious plan to revive the White Sox. He created the farm system and made bold moves such as the purchase of Athletics stars Al Simmons, Jimmie Dykes and Mule Haas (see September 28, 1932). Lou wasn't able to turn the White Sox into pennant contenders, but the franchise moved from AL doormats to respectability by the late 1930s. His health deteriorated, however, and Lou Comiskey died in 1939 at the age of 54.

DECEMBER 2   The White Sox trade Bob Weiland to the Senators for Milt Gaston.

DECEMBER 4   The White Sox trade Carl Reynolds and John Kerr to the Senators for Jackie Hayes, Bump Hadley and Sad Sam Jones.

Known as "Sad Sam" because of his downcast demeanor, Jones had a record of 193–171 and was a veteran of four World Series and 18 big-league seasons when he arrived in Chicago. He was 38–46 in four seasons with the White Sox before hanging up his spikes at the age of 43.

1932   Sox

Season in a Sentence

In the first season following the death of founder Charles Comiskey and with the country mired in the Great Depression, the White Sox field the worst team in the history of the franchise.

Finish • Won • Lost • Pct • GB

Seventh   49   102   .325   56.5

Manager

Lew Fonseca

Stats

Stats	WS	AL	Rank
Batting Avg:	.267	.277	7
On-Base Pct:	.327	.346	7
Slugging Pct:	.360	.404	7
Home Runs:	36		8
Stolen Bases:	89		2
ERA:	4.82	4.48	6
Fielding Avg:	.957	.969	8
Runs Scored:	687		7
Runs Allowed:	897		6

Starting Lineup

Frank Grube, c
Lu Blue, 1b
Jackie Hayes, 2b
Carey Selph, 3b
Luke Appling, ss
Fats Fothergill, lf-rf
Liz Funk, cf
Red Kress, rf-ss
Bob Seeds, rf-cf-lf
Billy Sullivan Jr., 3b
Charlie Berry, c
Johnny Hodapp, lf

Pitchers

Ted Lyons, sp
Sad Sam Jones, sp
Milt Gaston, sp
Vic Frasier, sp
Red Faber, rp
Paul Gregory, rp

Attendance

233,198 (sixth in AL)

Club Leaders

Batting Avg:	Bob Seeds	.290
On-Base Pct:	Red Kress	.346
Slugging Pct:	Red Kress	.435
Home Runs:	Red Kress	9
RBIs:	Luke Appling	63
Runs:	Red Kress	83
Stolen Bases:	Lu Blue	17
	Liz Funk	17
Wins:	Ted Lyons	10
	Sad Sam Jones	10
Strikeouts:	Sad Sam Jones	64
ERA:	Ted Lyons	3.28
Saves:	Red Faber	6

APRIL 12   Six weeks after the kidnapping of the Lindbergh baby, the White Sox win 9–2 in an Opening Day victory over the Browns at Comiskey Park. In his first game with the Sox, Sad Sam Jones pitched a complete game. Third baseman Carey Selph also made his debut with the Pale Hose and blasted out three doubles. Lu Blue contributed two doubles and a single.

The White Sox won four of their first five games, then dropped 20 of their next 25.

APRIL 24   The White Sox trade Bill Cissell and Jim Moore to the Indians for Johnny Hodapp and Bob Seeds.

Lew Fonseca was given permission by Lou Comiskey to make his own trades, and Fonseca turned over almost the entire roster with no positive effect.

APRIL 27   The White Sox trade Bump Hadley and Bruce Campbell to the Browns for Red Kress.

This turned out to be one of the worst trades in club history. Kress looked like a coming star when he hit .311 with 16 homers and 114 RBIs as a 24-year-old with the Browns in 1931. He never came close to repeating those numbers in Chicago and was traded to the Senators in 1934. In the process, the White Sox lost two quality players. Hadley was an above-average pitcher on some terrible Browns teams and was a member of four consecutive World Series clubs with the Yankees from 1936 through 1939. Campbell was a starting outfielder with the Browns, Indians and Tigers into the early 1940s.

APRIL 29   The White Sox trade Bennie Tate, Smead Jolley and Cliff Watwood to the Red Sox for Charlie Berry and Jack Rothrock.

Berry played only two seasons with the White Sox and Rothrock only one. They weren't worth the loss of three players. Berry was an All-American end at Lafayette University and later played pro football. In 1925, he led the National Football League in scoring while playing for the Pottsville Maroons. After his playing career ended, Berry was an umpire in the American League from 1942 through 1962 and served as an NFL official from 1941 until 1961. In 1958, he was an umpire in the World Series and an official in the NFL championship game.

MAY 17   Milt Gaston sets a major league fielding record for pitchers (since tied) by taking part in four double plays during a 7–3 win over the Red Sox in Boston.

In 1932, the White Sox discarded the navy blue road uniforms that the club had worn off and on since 1902 in favor of the standard gray. The home uniforms had a new look as well. The primary design featured a new arrangement of the S-O-X letters, intertwined diagonally with a baseball (inside the "O") and an orange bat worked into the layout. The letters were deep red outlined in navy blue. The uniform was used for four seasons. An alternate home uniform was also showcased in 1932 with two interlocking horse shoes constituting the "S," a baseball representing the "O" and criss-crossed bats forming an "X."

MAY 22   The White Sox win twice with ninth inning rallies during a double-header against the Tigers at Comiskey Park. In the opener, Johnny Hodapp hit a walk-off homer for a 3–2 triumph. In the second tilt, Chicago trailed 7–1 before erupting for two runs in the eighth inning and five in the ninth. All five of the ninth inning runs scored after two were out. The contest ended on a bases-loaded triple by Lu Blue.

MAY 23   Milt Gaston pitches a two-hitter to defeat the Indians 4–0 at Comiskey Park. The only Cleveland hits were singles by Joe Vosmik and Bill Cissell.

MAY 30   The White Sox fight 47-year-old umpire George Moriarty following a 12–6 and 12–11 double-header loss to the Indians in Cleveland. The Indians scored four runs in the ninth inning to win the nightcap. Umpiring at home plate, Moriarty called a 2–2 pitch to Earl Averill from Pat Caraway a ball with the Sox leading 11–9 and two on base. Averill then lined the next pitch for a triple that tied the game and later scored the winning run. During a confrontation between Moriarty and the players in the runway leading from the field to the dressing room, Moriarty offered to fight the White Sox one by one. Milt Gaston stepped forward and said, "You might as well start with me," and the arbiter decked the Sox pitcher with two punches.

Lew Fonseca, catcher Charlie Berry and Frank Grube ganged up on Moriarty, kicking and punching him before he was rescued by the Cleveland players. Fonseca charged that Moriarty "deliberately brought on the fight by sneering at the Chicago players all day," and that the umpire issued the first challenge to fight. Moriarty, who once beat Ty Cobb to a pulp when they were teammates with the Tigers, had to be hospitalized for a broken hand (from hitting Gaston), bruises and spike wounds.

Gaston was fined $500 and suspended for 10 days by AL President Will Harridge. Fonseca was fined $500, Berry $250 and Grube $100. Moriarty was "severely reprimanded for his neglect of duty on the ball field."

JUNE 4
Player-manager Lew Fonseca inserts himself into the lineup in the ninth inning as a pinch-hitter and delivers a two-out, two-strike, walk-off single to beat the Browns 6–5 at Comiskey Park.

JUNE 8
The White Sox win a thrilling 3–2 decision over the Senators at Comiskey Park. The Sox were shut out for eight innings, then loaded the bases in the ninth before Charlie Berry clubbed a two-out, bases-loaded triple for the win.

JUNE 11
The White Sox sell Tommy Thomas to the Senators.

JUNE 13
Down 6–0, the White Sox score two runs in the sixth inning and five in the seventh to beat the Red Sox 7–6 at Comiskey Park.

JUNE 20
The Athletics let loose on five White Sox pitchers, collecting 26 hits to win 18–11 in a slugfest at Comiskey Park. Doc Cramer had six hits in six at-bats for the A's.

JULY 2
The White Sox swamp the Browns 15–5 in St. Louis.

JULY 7
The White Sox collect 20 hits to defeat the Athletics 13–3 in the first game of a double-header in Philadelphia. The A's won the second contest 9–3.

JULY 23
After the Indians score a run in the top of the 12th inning, the White Sox rally to win 6–5 with two tallies in their half on four consecutive singles by Charlie English (playing in his first major league game), Frank Grube, Billy Sullivan Jr. and Bob Seeds.

Sullivan was the son of Billy Sullivan Sr., who played for the White Sox from 1901 through 1914. The younger Sullivan was a member of the Sox from 1931 until 1933.

AUGUST 19
The White Sox extend their losing streak to 10 games with 4–3 and 3–1 losses in a double-header against the Senators in Washington.

AUGUST 20
The White Sox break their 10-game losing streak with a 6–4 win over the Athletics in the first game of a double-header in Philadelphia but blow a commanding lead in the second contest. The Sox held an 8–4 advantage before allowing 10 runs in the eighth inning for a 14–8 loss.

SEPTEMBER 3
The White Sox score six runs in the first inning and defeat the Browns 13–8 in St. Louis. Making his first big-league start, Sox pitcher Charlie Biggs had a six-run lead before he took the mound. But he allowed a homer to Debs Garms, the first

batter he faced. Nonetheless, Biggs lasted until the seventh inning and received credit for the victory. It proved to be his only win in the majors. Biggs pitched only six games during his brief career and had a 1–1 record and a 6.93 ERA.

SEPTEMBER 4 Billy Sullivan Jr. collects five hits, including a home run, in five at-bats during a 5–1 win over the Browns in the second game of a double-header at Sportsman's Park. St. Louis won the opener 7–5.

The homer was the only one that Sullivan hit in 1932. He didn't strike another one in the majors until 1935, when he played for the Reds.

SEPTEMBER 11 The starting battery in the second game of a double-header against the Senators at Comiskey Park is pitcher Ed Walsh Jr. and catcher Billy Sullivan Jr., the sons of White Sox stars of the dead ball era. Despite the bloodlines of Walsh and Sullivan, the Senators won 9–4. Washington also won the opener 2–1.

Ed Walsh Jr. and Billy Sullivan Jr. both matriculated at Notre Dame. Early in the 1932 season, Sullivan played for the Sox only on weekends while attending classes in South Bend.

SEPTEMBER 19 The White Sox lose their 100th game of 1932, dropping a 9–6 decision to the Athletics at Comiskey Park.

With the combination of the Depression and a terrible team, the White Sox drew only 233,198 fans in 1932. With the exception of the war-shortened 1918 campaign, it is the lowest attendance figure in franchise history.

SEPTEMBER 21 Red Kress collects seven hits, five of them for extra bases, in nine at-bats during an 11–3 and 3–1 double-header sweep of the Tigers in Detroit. Kress swatted a homer, four doubles and two singles.

SEPTEMBER 23 The White Sox play at massive Municipal Stadium in Cleveland for the first time and lose 13–6 in Cleveland. Lew Fonseca pitched the sixth inning and retired the side in order. It was the only pitching appearance of his 12-year career.

SEPTEMBER 28 The White Sox purchase Al Simmons, Jimmie Dykes and Mule Haas from the Athletics for $150,000.

With the country near the nadir of the Great Depression, and following a season in which the White Sox were 49–102 and drew only 233,198 fans, Lou Comiskey served notice that he was going to take a new direction in order to improve the health of the franchise. Comiskey revealed that the team had spent upwards of a million dollars during the previous 12 seasons buying largely unproductive minor league players. All that would change, he vowed. In the future, the money would go toward proven players and a revamped farm system. Simmons, Dykes and Haas were all key components on Athletics clubs that won the AL championship in 1929, 1930 and 1931. A's owner and manager Connie Mack let them go because he could no longer afford to pay their salaries in a Depression-era economy. Although the three failed to help the White Sox move into pennant contention, the club did advance from laughingstocks to respectability by the end of the 1930s. A future Hall of Famer, Simmons was one of the top players in baseball when acquired by the Sox. In nine years with the Athletics, he had a .351 batting average and had averaged 128 RBIs and 104 runs per season. While he didn't reach those standards with the Sox, Simmons hit .337 and drove in 223 runs during his first two seasons in Chicago and made the All-Star team in all three seasons with the club. Haas stuck around in the Sox outfield for six seasons. Dykes had by far the longest stay with the club. A third baseman by trade, he was named manager in May 1934 and held the job until 1946. The tenure is the longest of any Sox skipper.

DECEMBER 15   Six weeks after Franklin Roosevelt defeats Herbert Hoover in the presidential election, the White Sox trade Johnny Hodapp, Fats Fothergill, Bob Seeds and Greg Mulleavy to the Red Sox for Ed Durham and Hal Rhyne.

1933   Sox

Season in a Sentence

With nowhere to go but up after a 49–102 record in 1932, the White Sox win 67 games with a revamped lineup and host baseball's first All-Star game.

Finish • Won • Lost • Pct • GB

Sixth   67   83   .447   31.0

Manager

Lew Fonseca

Stats | WS • AL • Rank

Stats	WS	AL	Rank
Batting Avg:	.272	.273	4
On-Base Pct:	.342	.342	4
Slugging Pct:	.360	.390	7
Home Runs:	43		8
Stolen Bases:	43		6
ERA:	4.45	4.28	6
Fielding Avg:	.970	.972	6
Runs Scored:	683		6
Runs Allowed:	814		6

Starting Lineup

Charlie Berry, c
Red Kress, 1b
Jackie Hayes, 2b
Jimmie Dykes, 3b
Luke Appling, ss
Al Simmons, lf
Mule Haas, cf
Evar Swanson, rf
Frank Grube, c

Pitchers

Ted Lyons, sp
Sad Sam Jones, sp
Ed Durham, sp
Milt Gaston, sp
Paul Gregory, sp
Jake Miller, sp-rp
Joe Heving, rp
Red Faber, rp
Chad Kimsey, rp
Whit Wyatt, rp

Attendance

397,789 (third in AL)

Club Leaders

Batting Avg:	Al Simmons	.331
On-Base Pct:	Evar Swanson	.411
Slugging Pct:	Al Simmons	.481
Home Runs:	Al Simmons	14
RBIs:	Al Simmons	119
Runs:	Evar Swanson	102
Stolen Bases:	Evar Swanson	19
Wins:	Three tied with	10
Strikeouts:	Ted Lyons	74
ERA:	Sad Sam Jones	3.36
Saves:	Joe Heving	6

APRIL 12   The White Sox open the season with a 4–2 victory over the Browns in St. Louis. Al Simmons hit a fourth-inning home run in his first game with the Sox. Ex-Brown Red Kress drove in the other three runs.

The White Sox held spring training in Pasadena, California, for the first time in 1933. The Sox trained in Pasadena from 1933 through 1952 with the exception of three seasons during World War II (1943–45), when the club was headquartered in Indiana due to wartime travel restrictions.

APRIL 13   The White Sox pound out 20 hits and score four runs in the 11th inning to beat the Browns 11–7 at Sportsman's Park. St. Louis outfielder Sammy West collected six hits in six at-bats.

APRIL 18   The White Sox hammer the Tigers 12–0 in Detroit.

APRIL 19   In the home opener, the White Sox defeat the Browns 3–0 before 10,000 at Comiskey Park. Ted Lyons pitched the shutout.

With the end of Prohibition, beer was sold at Comiskey Park for the first time since 1919.

APRIL 20   Al Simmons pulls off an unassisted double play in the ninth inning of a 5–4 win over the Browns at Comiskey Park. Playing left field, Simmons raced in for Rick Ferrell's short liner and continued on to second base to retire Oscar Melillo, who had already rounded third base.

In his first season with the Sox, Simmons hit .331 with 14 homers, 119 RBIs and 200 hits. However, a great deal of tension existed between Simmons and Lew Fonseca, who ripped his star for failing to hustle. Simmons's batting average was above .380 in late-June, and a second half slump coincided with the club's slide into the second division.

APRIL 23   Ted Lyons pitches a two-hitter and collects three hits, including a home run, in three at-bats for a 4–1 win over the Indians at Comiskey Park. The only Cleveland hits were by Sarge Connally, an ex-teammate of Lyons, and Mike Powers.

The White Sox started the season with an 8–3 record. On June 7, the club was 26–20 and in second place, six games out of first, but the Sox were 41–63 the rest of the way.

APRIL 25   The White Sox-Tigers game at Comiskey Park is postponed by snow.

MAY 11   Lou Comiskey orders his players to forget about making catches of baseballs from the 628-foot-high sky ride tower at the Chicago World's Fair. Under an agreement made with World's Fair officials, Al Simmons, Jimmie Dykes and Red Kress consented to try for a world's record by attempting to catch balls dropped from a higher point than previously tried. Ted Lyons was to throw three balls to each player from the tower. A mathematician said that a baseball thrown from 628 feet would be traveling 146.88 miles an hour and would strike with an impact of 60.7 foot pounds. Fearing injury to his star players, Comiskey put a stop to the stunt.

Called a "Century of Progress," the fair lasted two years and extended over 341 acres on two man-made islands off Lake Michigan. In 1933, the fair attracted 22 million visitors.

MAY 14   The White Sox purchase Earl Webb from the Tigers.

MAY 18   The first major league All-Star Game is announced for July 6 in Chicago for either Comiskey Park or Wrigley Field. A few days later, Comiskey was chosen because of its greater seating capacity. It was played as part of the Chicago World's Fair celebration and was sponsored by the *Chicago Tribune*. A fan vote was held to pick the starting lineups. The proceeds were to benefit the Association of Professional Baseball Players of America, which was formed in 1925 to care for old and disabled players and umpires.

MAY 21   White Sox pitcher Jake Miller pitches a two-hitter to defeat the Senators 6–0 at Griffith Stadium. The only Washington hits were singles by Heinie Manush in the first inning and Goose Goslin in the seventh.

MAY 27   The White Sox lead 11–3 heading into the bottom of the eighth, but allow 12 runs in the inning to lose 15–11 to the Yankees in New York. The Yanks collected eight hits and four walks off Ted Lyons, Jake Miller and Ed Durham. The last four runs scored on a grand slam by Bill Dickey.

JUNE 3   The White Sox score seven runs in the second inning and win 11–6 over the Tigers in Detroit.

          On the same day, the White Sox traded Vic Frasier to the Tigers for Whit Wyatt. Wyatt was 25 years old when acquired by the White Sox and seemed to possess all the tools necessary to be a top-of-the-line pitcher. He was 8–17 with a 5.90 ERA in four seasons with the Sox, however. A classic late-bloomer, Wyatt found his form later with the Dodgers and had a record of 78–39 with Brooklyn from 1939 through 1943, a period in which he was named to four All-Star teams and pitched in the World Series.

JUNE 4   The White Sox swamp the Browns 13–6 and 10–2 during a double-header in St. Louis.

JUNE 5   The White Sox continue their heavy hitting by gathering 23 hits during a 14–7 victory over the Browns in St. Louis. All nine players in the starting lineup had at least two hits.

JUNE 9   The White Sox pick up an exhilarating 14-inning, 10–9 win over the Tigers at Comiskey Park. The Sox trailed 7–1 in the fifth inning and were still behind 9–4 when a five-run uprising in the bottom of the ninth tied the score. Luke Appling hit the first pitch of the 14th for a walk-off homer.

          With Jimmie Dykes providing a steadying influence, Appling had a breakout year in 1933, with a .322 batting average, six homers and 197 hits.

JUNE 13   Just 10 days after being acquired by the White Sox, Whit Wyatt loses a no-hitter with two out in the ninth inning on a single by Ted Gullic of the Browns. Wyatt had to settle for a 6–1 win at Comiskey Park. St. Louis scored a run in the third inning on two walks, a sacrifice and an infield out.

JUNE 18   Before 53,398 at Comiskey Park, the White Sox score three runs in the ninth inning and one in the 10th to defeat the Yankees 5–4 in the second game of a double-header. The Yanks won the opener 6–4.

JULY 6   The first All-Star Game is played, with the American League winning 4–2 before 47,595. Babe Ruth, then 38 years old and near the end of his career, hit the first home run in the Mid-Summer Classic with a clout in the third inning. Later, Frankie Frisch homered for the NL. Al Simmons and Jimmie Dykes were in the starting lineup and played the entire game. Simmons was 1-for-4 and Dykes had two hits in three at-bats. The managers were Connie Mack for the AL and John McGraw for the NL. The American League players wore the home uniforms of their clubs, while the opposition donned specially made gray uniforms with "National League" written across the front.

There were 17 future Hall of Famers who made an appearance in the contest, including Earl Averill, Joe Cronin, Rick Ferrell, Frankie Frisch, Lou Gehrig, Charlie Gehringer, Lefty Gomez, Lefty Grove, Chick Hafey, Gabby Hartnett, Carl Hubbell, Chuck Klein, Babe Ruth, Al Simmons, Bill Terry, Pie Traynor and Paul Waner. Future Cooperstown enshrinees Bill Dickey, Jimmie Foxx and Tony Lazzeri were on the rosters of the two clubs but didn't play.

The First All-Star Game

The American League began play as a major league in 1901, and two years later the first World Series between the champions of the AL and NL was held in 1903. It took until 1933, however, before the first All-Star Game was played.

The tradition was conceived by Arch Ward, the sports editor of the *Chicago Tribune*. Ward saw the game as a way to promote the city and Chicago's Century of Progress Exposition, commonly known as the World's Fair. Ward began to petition for the game in his columns and secured approval for the game from AL President Will Harridge and Bill Veeck Sr., president of the Chicago Cubs. Each lobbied for the All-Star Game among owners in their respective leagues. Many of the magnates disliked the idea, however, and when they finally agreed to it they firmly stipulated it would be a one-time event. Final approval wasn't granted until May 18.

Plans were made to play the game at Comiskey Park on July 6. The proceeds would go to the Association of Professional Baseball Players of America, which was formed in 1925 to care for old and disabled players and umpires. The starting lineups, with the exception of the pitchers, were chosen by a vote of the fans, with ballots printed in 55 newspapers around the country. Ten more players were selected by the managers of the two leagues. The two rosters of 18 players each included 20 future Hall of Famers.

A total of 47,595 paid a $1.10 admission fee to see the novel concept in action. The managers were Connie Mack of the Philadelphia Athletics, who had managed his club since its inception in 1901, and NL skipper John McGraw. He had managed the New York Giants from 1902 until his retirement in 1932.

The American League scored the first run of the game in the second inning. After two walks, Yankees pitcher Lefty Gomez, a .113 hitter that season, lined a single to center. Babe Ruth, then 38 and near the end of his career, put his stamp on the classic game by smacking a two-run homer just inside the right-field foul line in the third off Cardinals hurler Wild Bill Hallahan. Frankie Frisch homered for the Nationals in the sixth to make the score 3–2 before the AL added a tally in the bottom half of the inning. There was no more scoring in the 4–2 American League victory.

The game immediately caught the public's imagination. Major league owners quickly made the All-Star Game an annual event and clamored to bring the game to their towns. It has been played every season with the exception of 1945, when wartime travel restrictions canceled the contest.

Ward wasn't done creating All-Star Games. In 1934 he conjured up the idea of pitting college football's All-Stars against the champions of the NFL. Played at Soldier Field, the contest was held annually during the preseason until 1976.

JULY 8 — Luke Appling collects seven hits, including four doubles, in 10 at-bats during a double-header in Philadelphia. The White Sox lost the opener 10–4 and won the second 11–6.

JULY 30 — Mule Haas and Al Simmons star in a sweep of the Browns at Comiskey Park. The White Sox won the opener 8–7 in 10 innings, and the nightcap 15–2. Haas had eight hits, including two doubles, in 12 at-bats. Al Simmons collected seven hits on a triple, two doubles and four singles, in an even dozen at-bats.

> *Simmons's given name was Aloys Szymanski. He was born in Milwaukee, the son of Polish immigrants. When he entered baseball, he changed his surname to Simmons, which he had seen on a billboard advertising a hardware company.*

AUGUST 2 — The White Sox beat the Tigers twice with ninth-inning rallies during a double-header in Detroit. In the first game, Charlie Berry homered in the ninth inning for a 2–1 win. In the second tilt, Evar Swanson doubled in Berry to break a 3–3 tie and lift the Sox to a 4–3 victory.

> *Swanson played three seasons in the NFL (1925–27) as an end with the Chicago Cardinals before turning exclusively to baseball. He played with the White Sox from 1932 through 1934, a period in which he was considered one of the fastest players in the majors.*

AUGUST 11 — A double by Luke Appling, a triple from Jimmie Dykes and Hal Rhyne's single in the seventh inning accounts for the only two runs of a 2–0 win over the Tigers at Comiskey Park. Rhyne entered the game as a substitute at second base as a replacement after Jackie Hayes was injured.

AUGUST 19 — Down 7–0, the White Sox score a run in the fifth inning, one in the sixth, five in the eighth and one in the 12th to win 8–7 over the Yankees at Comiskey Park. A bases-loaded triple by Evar Swanson climaxed the eighth-inning rally. The winning run scored on a double by Charlie Berry and a single by Hal Rhyne.

AUGUST 21 — The White Sox and Yankees play 18 innings at Comiskey Park to a 3–3 tie. The contest was called on account of darkness. Following eight shutout innings, both clubs scored once in the ninth inning and twice in the 11th. The Sox tied the score 3–3 on Evar Swanson's two-run single. All 22 hits in the contest, 11 by each club, were singles. Milt Gaston (11 innings) and Red Faber (seven innings) pitched for Chicago.

AUGUST 23 — The White Sox sweep the Red Sox 3–1 and 12–1 at Comiskey Park. Red Kress belted a grand slam during a seven-run fourth inning in the second game of the twinbill.

SEPTEMBER 7 — Sad Sam Jones pitches the White Sox to a 1–0 victory over the Senators at Griffith Stadium. The Sox were held to one hit through eight innings by Washington pitcher Monty Weaver. In the ninth, the lone run of the contest scored on a single by Al Simmons, a walk to Luke Appling and a one-base hit from Red Kress.

SEPTEMBER 10 — The first Negro League East-West All-Star Game is played at Comiskey Park. The West won 11–7.

The Negro League All-Star Game was played at Comiskey Park every season from 1933 through 1953.

SEPTEMBER 13   Two pitchers over the age of 40 start for the White Sox during a double-header against the Athletics in Philadelphia, with 41-year-old Sad Sam Jones taking the mound in game one and 45-year-old Red Faber in the second tilt. Jones pitched a complete-game 3–2 victory. Faber went six innings and took a 4–2 loss.

OCTOBER 4   In the first game of the City Series, the White Sox defeat the Cubs 3–2 at Wrigley Field.

The White Sox went on to sweep the series four games to none. Sox pitchers held the Cubs to three runs, with Sad Sam Jones, Red Faber, Ted Lyons and Joe Heving hurling complete games. Faber and Lyons pitched shutouts. Faber's shutout, a 2–0 victory in game two, was thrown a month after his 45th birthday and was his last appearance in a White Sox uniform. He retired at the close of the season after 22 years with the Sox. Al Simmons drove in both runs. Stung by the loss, the Cubs refused to play in the City Series in 1934. There was also no postseason matchup between the two Chicago clubs in 1935 because the Cubs played in the World Series. The City Series resumed in 1936.

NOVEMBER 1   The White Sox announce an alteration of Comiskey Park. In order to increase the number of home runs, home plate was brought 14 feet closer to the outfield walls. The change reduced the foul lines from 352 feet to 348, and center field from 436 feet to 422. Al Simmons demanded the modification, charging the deep outfield fences hampered his power. Simmons clouted only 14 homers in 1933, his fewest since his rookie year of 1924. Comiskey Park was not entirely to blame, however, as Simmons had seven homers at home and seven on the road. The new dimensions did have the desired effect of increasing home runs, but they failed to help the home club. In 1933, there were 62 home runs hit at Comiskey, 42 of them by the opposition. There were 129 struck at the ballpark in 1934, with opposing players continuing to reap the most benefit with 82 homers, compared with 47 by the Sox. Simmons was sold to the Tigers in December 1935, and home plate was moved back 14 feet to its previous location in 1936.

DECEMBER 12   Five days before the Bears win their first NFL championship be defeating the New York Giants 23–21 in the championship game, the White Sox send Charlie Berry and $20,000 to the Athletics for George Earnshaw and Johnny Pasek.

Earnshaw was 86–41 with the A's from 1929 though 1932 but was past his prime by the time he put on a White Sox uniform. In two seasons with the Sox, he was 15–13 with an ERA of 4.85.

1934

Season in a Sentence

The reign of Jimmie Dykes as manager begins during a disastrous season in which the White Sox tumble into last place while fielding one of the oldest teams in the league.

Finish • Won • Lost • Pct • GB

Eighth   53   99   .346   47.0

Managers

Lew Fonseca (4–11) and Jimmie Dykes (49–88)

Stats

Stats	WS	AL	Rank
Batting Avg:	.263	.279	8
On-Base Pct:	.336	.351	7
Slugging Pct:	.363	.399	8
Home Runs:	71		5
Stolen Bases:	36		8
ERA:	5.41	4.50	8
Fielding Avg:	.966	.970	8
Runs Scored:	704		7
Runs Allowed:	946		8

Starting Lineup

Hal Madjeski, c
Zeke Bonura, 1b
Jackie Hayes, 2b
Jimmie Dykes, 3b
Luke Appling, ss
Al Simmons, lf
Mule Haas, cf
Evar Swanson, rf
Bob Boken, 2b
Jocko Conlan, cf
Marty Hopkins, 3b
Merv Shea, c
Frenchy Uhalt, rf-cf

Pitchers

George Earnshaw, sp
Ted Lyons, sp
Sad Sam Jones, sp
Milt Gaston, sp
Les Tietje, sp-rp
Phil Gallivan, rp
Joe Heving, rp

Attendance

236,559 (seventh in AL)

Club Leaders

Batting Avg:	Al Simmons	.344
On-Base Pct:	Al Simmons	.403
Slugging Pct:	Zeke Bonura	.545
Home Runs:	Zeke Bonura	27
RBIs:	Zeke Bonura	110
Runs:	Al Simmons	102
Stolen Bases:	Evar Swanson	10
Wins:	George Earnshaw	14
Strikeouts:	George Earnshaw	97
ERA:	George Earnshaw	4.52
Saves:	Joe Heving	4

APRIL 17   The White Sox open the season with an 8–3 loss to the Tigers before 16,000 at Comiskey Park.

APRIL 18   In his second major league game, Zeke Bonura clubs two home runs, although the White Sox lose 6–5 to the Tigers at Comiskey Park.

APRIL 19   The White Sox score two runs in the ninth inning to defeat the Tigers 9–8 at Comiskey Park. Zeke Bonura doubled in the tying run and scored on a single by Luke Appling.

Henry "Zeke" Bonura made an immediate impression by hitting 10 home runs in his first 25 big-league games. During his rookie year, he batted .302 with 27 home runs and 110 RBIs. The 27 home runs set a club record that was not broken until 1950. In four seasons with the Sox, Bonura thrilled White Sox fans with his long-distance clouts, but he frustrated them with his lack of defense at first base. He caught the balls he got to, leading the AL in fielding three times, but his range was limited and he pursued batted balls with a decided lack of enthusiasm. Bonura often got where the ball had just been a second too late and made a great flourish with his gloved hand waving in the direction of the drive as it whizzed by him into right field. Chicago Tribune writer Ed Burns coined it "The Mussolini Salute." He further aggravated the front office with outspoken comments, reporting late for spring training on an annual basis in salary disputes and was rumored to be romantically involved with Lou Comiskey's daughter Dorothy.

APRIL 30   The White Sox outlast the Indians 20–10 at Comiskey Park. The Sox scored nine runs in the fourth inning to take a 14–1 lead, and scored all 20 runs in the first six innings.

The White Sox went the entire 1934 season without using a single left-handed pitcher.

MAY 8   Zeke Bonura hits a grand slam off Earl Whitehill in the third inning to give the White Sox a 4–1 lead, but the Senators rally to win 7–6 in Washington.

After the game, Lou Comiskey announced a change in managers with Jimmie Dykes replacing Lew Fonseca. Dykes was 37 years old and was the White Sox's starting third baseman. He had been in the majors since 1918, the first of 15 seasons with the Athletics. Dykes came to the Sox along with Al Simmons and Mule Haas at the end of the 1932 season (see September 28, 1932). Dykes was the Sox regular at third through the 1936 season and remained as manager until May 1946. During that period, the Sox had a record of 894–923 and never finished higher than third place or closer than eight games from first place. Still, he was given considerable credit for his abilities as manager. The Sox in that period simply didn't have the talent to contend, and with a minuscule and ineffective

Jimmie Dykes guided the Sox through the Depression and war years, never winning a pennant but usually mustering a competitive team.

scouting staff, the farm system produced almost nothing in the way of top-of-the-line talent. Dykes was particularly adept at perusing the waiver wire and turning discards from other organizations into useful players.

MAY 9   The White Sox trade Red Kress to the Senators for Bob Boken.

MAY 11   Zeke Bonura hits into three double plays during a 7–6 loss to the Yankees in 14 innings in New York.

MAY 13   Bucky Walters and Eddie Morgan of the Red Sox both hit grand slams during a 14–2 trouncing of the White Sox in Boston. Walters hit his slam in the first inning off Milt Gaston. Morgan went deep with the bases loaded in the third against Joe Heving.

MAY 18   Jimmie Foxx of the Athletics becomes the first player to hit a home run into the center-field bleachers at Comiskey Park since that section was built in 1927. The bleachers were 426 feet from home plate in 1934, and the ball landed in the seventh row above a 15-foot high fence. The White Sox won the game 5–4.

MAY 19   The White Sox defeat the Athletics 14–10 at Comiskey Park.

MAY 21   At Comiskey Park, Jimmie Dykes hits a grand slam in the eighth inning that ties the Red Sox 10–10, but the White Sox lose 13–10 in 10 innings.

MAY 23   The White Sox score seven runs in the eighth inning of a 14–2 win over the Yankees at Comiskey Park.

MAY 30   Hal Trosky of the Indians hits three home runs during a 5–4 White Sox loss in the second game of a double-header in Cleveland. The Sox won the opener 8–7 in 12 innings.

MAY 31   The White Sox score eight runs in the third inning of a 12–5 victory over the Indians in Cleveland.

JUNE 16   Bob Boken hits a grand slam off Bob Kline in the eighth inning of a 9–7 win over the Athletics in the first game of a double-header in Philadelphia. In the second tilt, Bob Johnson of the A's collected six hits, including two homers, in six at-bats during a 7–6 Philadelphia win in 11 innings.

JUNE 27   Al Simmons hits a grand slam off Lefty Gomez in the third inning, but the White Sox lose 8–7 in 11 innings in New York.

          Simmons hit .344 with 18 homers and 104 RBIs in 1934. Luke Appling batted .303.

JUNE 29   The White Sox lose an odd 11-inning, 5–2 decision to the Indians at Comiskey Park. All seven runs scored in the final inning. Les Tietje of the White Sox and Mel Harder of Cleveland each pitched 10 shutout innings before tiring. Neither pitcher retired a batter in the 11th before being lifted for relievers.

JUNE 30   Catcher Ed Madjeski hits a walk-off homer in the ninth inning that beats the Indians 2–1 at Comiskey Park. The victory broke an eight-game losing streak.

JULY 1   The White Sox score eight runs in the second inning of a 12–5 win in the first game of a double-header against the Indians at Comiskey Park. Cleveland won the second tilt 4–3 in 11 innings.

JULY 10   In the All-Star Game, played at the Polo Grounds in New York, Al Simmons collects two doubles and a single in five at-bats, drives in a run, and scores three. His infield single in the fifth inning scored the run which tied the contest 4–4. The American League won 9–7.

JULY 24   Two days after John Dillinger is killed by FBI agents outside the Biograph Theater in Chicago, the White Sox defeat the Senators 4–1 in the sweltering heat at Comiskey Park. The official high temperature in the Windy City that day was 104 degrees.

JULY 26   Pitching on his 42nd birthday and 18th wedding anniversary, Sad Sam Jones hurls a complete game shutout to defeat the Senators 9–0 at Comiskey Park.

JULY 29   The White Sox lose 16–15 to the Tigers in the first game of a double-header at Comiskey Park. The Sox scored seven runs in the seventh inning to take a 13–11 lead, but couldn't hold the advantage. Detroit relief pitcher Schoolboy Rowe provided the winning margin by hitting a two-run homer in the ninth inning off Sox pitcher Joe Heving. Chicago won the second contest 6–4.

AUGUST 1   A two-run homer by Zeke Bonura in the 10th inning beats the Browns 4–2 in the second game of a double-header in St. Louis. The White Sox also won the first game 10–6.

AUGUST 11   Jocko Conlan is presented with an auto and several hundred dollars in cash as well as a floral horseshoe before a 9–8 loss to the Browns at Comiskey Park.

               Conlan was a 33-year-old outfielder picked up by the White Sox in July 1934. He was a longtime minor leaguer, but despairing of ever reaching the majors, he retired from organized baseball. At the time he was signed by the White Sox, Conlan was working as a Chicago playground instructor who played semi-pro ball on the weekends. He played two years in the majors with a .263 batting average and no home runs in 365 at-bats before embarking on a long career as an umpire (see July 28, 1935).

AUGUST 22   Red Sox pitcher Wes Ferrell hits two late-inning homers off Les Tietje to defeat the White Sox 3–2 in Boston. The first one, struck in the eighth inning, tied the score at 2–2, and the second in the 10th sailed over the center field wall to win the game.

SEPTEMBER 6   The White Sox blow a chance at victory with some inventive base running that results in a 5–3 loss to the Yankees at Comiskey Park. In the ninth inning, the Sox base runners were Jimmie Dykes on second and Marty Hopkins on first with none out. Charlie Uhlir was sent to bat for Ed Madjeski with instructions to bunt. Dykes was caught off second on a throw by Yankee catcher Arndt Jorgens. Uhlir missed an attempt to bunt and struck out. As Uhlir fanned, Hopkins tried to steal second and was thrown out, Jorgens to shortstop Frankie Crosetti, to end the game.

SEPTEMBER 9   Third baseman Marty Hopkins hits a grand slam off Al Thomas in the eighth inning of an 11–3 win over the Senators in the first game of a double-header at Comiskey Park. Washington won the second contest 2–1 in 10 innings.

SEPTEMBER 11   Jimmie Dykes inserts himself into the game as a pinch-hitter and delivers a walk-off single in the 11th inning to beat the Senators 3–2 at Comiskey Park.

SEPTEMBER 14   Milt Gaston pitches the White Sox to a 1–0 victory over the Red Sox at Comiskey Park. The winning run scored in the first inning on a bases-loaded walk by Wes Ferrell to Jackie Hayes.

SEPTEMBER 16   The White Sox sweep the Red Sox 2–1 and 12–10 during a double-header at Comiskey Park. In the opener, George Earnshaw pitched a two-hitter. Both hits were singles by opposing pitcher Johnny Welch. In the nightcap, the White Sox scored seven runs in the fourth inning to take a 10–5 lead, but allowed Boston to tie. A two-run eighth broke the deadlock.

SEPTEMBER 26   The White Sox losing streak reaches 10 games with 12–10 and 10–3 defeats at the hands of the Tigers in a double-header in Detroit. The second game was called after eight innings by darkness.

SEPTEMBER 27   The White Sox break their 10-game losing streak with an 11–0 win over the Tigers in Detroit.

SEPTEMBER 30   On the last day of the season, Al Simmons collects five hits, including two doubles, in five at-bats during a 9–5 win over the Indians in the first game of a double-header in Cleveland. The Sox lost the second game, called after five innings by darkness, 5–3.

1935   Sox

Season in a Sentence

With an infusion of new players, the White Sox are early season surprises (51–35 record on July 31) before winding up with a losing season (74–78) that is a vast improvement over the previous season (53–99).

Finish • Won • Lost • Pct • GB

Fifth   74   78   .487   19.5

Manager

Jimmie Dykes

Stats

Stats	WS	AL	Rank
Batting Avg:	.275	.280	7
On-Base Pct:	.348	.351	5
Slugging Pct:	.382	.402	8
Home Runs:	74		5
Stolen Bases:	46		6
ERA:	4.38	4.46	5
Fielding Avg:	.976	.972	2
Runs Scored:	738		5
Runs Allowed:	750		5

Starting Lineup

Luke Sewell, c
Zeke Bonura, 1b
Jackie Hayes, 2b
Jimmie Dykes, 3b
Luke Appling, ss
Rip Radcliff, lf
Al Simmons, cf
Mule Haas, rf
George Washington, rf
Tony Piet, 2b
Marty Hopkins, 3b

Pitchers

Ted Lyons, sp
John Whitehead, sp
Vern Kennedy, sp
Les Tietje, sp
Sad Sam Jones, sp
Ray Phelps, sp-rp
Carl Fischer, rp-sp

Attendance

470,281 (fourth in AL)

Club Leaders

Batting Avg:	Luke Appling	.307
On-Base Pct:	Luke Appling	.437
Slugging Pct:	Zeke Bonura	.485
Home Runs:	Zeke Bonura	21
RBIs:	Zeke Bonura	92
Runs:	Zeke Bonura	107
Stolen Bases:	Luke Appling	12
Wins:	Ted Lyons	15
Strikeouts:	John Whitehead	72
ERA:	Ted Lyons	3.02
Saves:	Whit Wyatt	5

JANUARY 22   The White Sox purchase Luke Sewell from the Browns.

APRIL 16   The scheduled season opener against the Tigers in Detroit is postponed by cold weather.

APRIL 17   The White Sox open the season with a 7–6 win over the Tigers in Detroit. Luke Sewell drove in three runs in his White Sox debut, and Zeke Bonura contributed two doubles and a single.

APRIL 23   In the home opener, the White Sox defeat the Tigers 7–2 at Comiskey Park.

APRIL 26   The White Sox hit five home runs during an 11–1 win over the Browns at Comiskey Park. The homers were struck by Rip Radcliff, Jackie Hayes, Al Simmons, Zeke Bonura and Luke Appling.

                  Appling hit .307 and drew 122 walks in 1935 for an on-base percentage of .437.

APRIL 27   The White Sox score eight runs in the fifth inning of a 16–4 win over the Browns at Comiskey Park.

MAY 8   The White Sox defeat the Yankees 7–4 at Comiskey Park.

                  The victory gave the Sox a 13–4 record and a 1½-game lead in the AL pennant race.

MAY 11   Rookie pitcher John Whitehead pitches a two-hitter to defeat the Red Sox 13–3 at Comiskey Park. Babe Dahlgren collected both Boston hits and drove in all three runs with a double in the third inning and a homer in the fifth.

MAY 16   The White Sox sell George Earnshaw to the Dodgers.

MAY 18   The White Sox score three runs in the ninth inning to defeat the Red Sox 3–2 in Boston. The rally consisted of a double by Jackie Hayes, a single by Al Simmons, Zeke Bonura's double and a single from Jimmie Dykes.

MAY 19   The White Sox win 6–5 over the Red Sox in Boston to take a 2½-game lead in the AL pennant race with a record of 17–7.

MAY 26   Jimmie Dykes hits a two-run homer in the 10th inning to lift the Athletics 5–3 in Philadelphia. It was his second homer of the game.

MAY 30   John Whitehead runs his career won-lost record to 8–0 with an 8–4 victory over the Indians in the first game of a double-header at Comiskey Park. Cleveland won the second tilt 4–0.

                  The second-game loss dropped the White Sox out of first place. The Sox never regained the top spot during the 1935 season, but they closed July with a 51–37 record and a position in third place, just 3½ games out of first. The White Sox were 23–41 in August, September and October, however. With the fast start and overall improvement, attendance almost doubled from 236,559 in 1934 to 470,281 in 1935.

JUNE 4   The White Sox purchase Tony Piet from the Reds.

                *Piet played only three seasons with the White Sox but was a fixture on the
                South Side of Chicago for years as a prominent auto dealer. He owned Tony
                Piet Motors from 1938 until his death in 1981. Piet's given name was Anthony
                Pietruszka, but he shortened it upon entering professional baseball.*

JUNE 5   After starting his first season in the majors with eight consecutive wins, John
                Whitehead loses for the first time, dropping a 2–0 decision to the Browns in St. Louis.

                *After his 8–0 beginning, Whitehead lost six in a row and finished the season with
                a 13–13 record. He was 46–47 with the White Sox over five seasons.*

JUNE 11   Al Simmons hits a grand slam off Bobby Burke in the seventh inning, tying the score
                8–8, but the White Sox lose 9–8 to the Senators in the first game of a double-header
                at Comiskey Park. The Sox won the second tilt 9–3 as Simmons hit another homer.

JUNE 13   Concentrating their fire on one big inning, the White Sox score nine times in the fifth
                after two are out and beat the Senators 10–6 at Comiskey Park.

JUNE 14   Al Simmons hits a grand slam in the eighth inning to tie the score 11–11, but the
                White Sox lose 16–11 in 11 innings to the Senators at Comiskey Park. It was the
                second time in four days that Simmons hit a game-tying grand slam during a White
                Sox defeat.

JUNE 16   A double-header against the Yankees at Comiskey Park is postponed with more
                than 50,000 in attendance. Game one started but was halted in the fourth inning by
                torrential rain with the Yanks leading 8–0. After a wait of an hour and 40 minutes,
                the twin bill was called off.

JULY 8   Al Simmons collects a double and a single in four at-bats during the American
                League's 4–1 victory in the All-Star Game, played at Municipal Stadium in Cleveland.

JULY 12   The White Sox score in seven of nine innings and defeat the Red Sox 13–2 in Boston.

JULY 20   Carl Fischer pitches a one-hitter to defeat the Senators 1–0 in the first game of a
                double-header at Griffith Stadium. Fischer was three outs from a no-hitter when
                Ossie Bluege led off the ninth inning with a single. Washington won the second
                contest 9–2.

                *The shutout was the only one that Fischer pitched in a White Sox uniform.
                Overall, he was 5–5 with a 6–19 ERA in his only season with the club.*

JULY 28   The White Sox score 10 runs in the second inning and win the first game of a double-
                header 14–6 over the Browns at Sportsman's Park. St. Louis won the second tilt 4–3.

                *Umpire Red Ormsby was overcome by the heat and could not continue in the
                second game. Only two umpires were assigned to the twin bill, which left Harry
                Geisel without a partner. In Ormsby's place, Jocko Conlan of the White Sox and
                Ollie Bejma served as base umps. Conlan was already a licensed boxing referee.*

The next season, he began umpiring in the minors. From 1941 through 1964, Conlan was an umpire in the National League, a period in which he officiated six World Series and six All-Star Games. Jocko was elected to the Hall of Fame in 1974, only the fourth umpire so honored.

AUGUST 7   Outfielder George Washington breaks a 0–0 tie with a two-run single in the top of the 10th inning, and the White Sox survive an Indian rally in the bottom of the inning to win 2–1 in the second game of a double-header in Cleveland. The Sox lost the opener 5–2.

AUGUST 16   Vern Kennedy pitches a 14-inning complete game to defeat the Red Sox 4–3 at Comiskey Park. A single by Tony Piet drove in the winning run.

AUGUST 17   Luke Appling collects five hits, including a double, in five at-bats during a 3–2 loss to the Athletics in the first game of a double-header at Comiskey Park. The second contest, called after five innings by darkness, was won by the Sox 8–2.

AUGUST 20   The White Sox sweep the Athletics 13–4 and 11–4 at Comiskey Park. Jocko Conlan was taken off the bench to replace slumping George Washington, and collected seven hits, including two doubles, in eight at-bats. Conlan also drove in six runs and contributed a sacrifice and a walk.

AUGUST 26   The White Sox take a thrilling 15-inning, 9–8 decision from the Yankees in the first game of a double-header at Comiskey Park, with the winning run coming on a steal of home by Zeke Bonura. The Yankees scored twice in the ninth to tie the score 5–5 and both teams plated two in the 13th. After the Yankees took an 8–7 advantage in the top of the 15th, the Sox countered with two in their half. Bonura stole home with two outs on Jimmy DeShong's deliberate wind-up. The Yanks won the second tilt, called after seven innings by darkness, 7 5.

AUGUST 27   The White Sox and Yankees combine to leave 30 men on base, tying a major league record for a nine-inning game, during a 13–10 New York win in the first game of a double-header at Comiskey Park. Each club stranded 15. The Sox won the second tilt 4–3.

AUGUST 31   Rookie Vern Kennedy pitches a no-hitter to defeat the Indians 6–0 at Comiskey Park. He struck out five batters and walked four. Kennedy also hit a bases-loaded triple in the sixth inning. In the ninth, pinch-hitter Kit Carson fanned for the first out. Left fielder Al Simmons recorded out number two with a spectacular diving catch of Milt Galatzer's hard smash. Earl Averill walked, extending the drama, before Joe Vosmik struck out on a 3–2 pitch to end the game.

Kennedy was an all-around athlete at Central Missouri State Teachers College before entering professional baseball and won the decathlon at the Penn relays. As a 26-year-old rookie in 1935, he had an 11–11 record with an ERA of 3.91. Kennedy posted an earned run average of 4.62 and walked 147 batters in 274^{1}/$_{3}$ innings in 1936, but with the help of some generous offensive support, posted a record of 21–9. Kennedy was traded by the White Sox to the Tigers after the 1937 season and never came close to the 20-win circle again. He finished his career in 1945 with a record of 104–132.

SEPTEMBER 16   Luke Appling collects five hits, including a double, in five at-bats during a 9–1 win over the Senators in Washington.

SEPTEMBER 17   The White Sox score two runs in the 14th inning to win 3–1 over the Senators in Washington. A double by Jimmie Dykes broke the 1–1 tie.

SEPTEMBER 29   On the last day of the season, the White Sox defeat the American League champion Tigers 3–2 and 14–2 during a double-header at Comiskey Park. The second game lasted only 5½ innings before it was called to allow the Tigers to catch a train back to Detroit for the start of the World Series against the Cubs. The Sox scored eight runs in the second inning and six in the third.

DECEMBER 10   The White Sox sell Al Simmons to the Tigers for $75,000.

The Sox soured on Simmons after he batted just .267 in 1935 and had several heated clashes with Jimmie Dykes. The club jumped at the chance to sell the 33-year-old outfielder when the Tigers came calling. Simmons had three years left as a productive starter in the majors.

1936   Sox

Season in a Sentence

With a record of 81–70 and a third-place finish, the White Sox enjoy their best season since 1920 as Jimmie Dykes begins to mold a competitive ball club.

Finish • Won • Lost • Pct • GB

Third   81   70   .536   20.0

Manager

Jimmie Dykes

Stats

Stats	WS	AL	Rank
Batting Avg:	.292	.289	5
On-Base Pct:	.373	.353	4
Slugging Pct:	.397	.421	7
Home Runs:	60		8
Stolen Bases:	66		4 (tie)
ERA:	5.06	5.04	6
Fielding Avg:	.973	.971	3
Runs Scored:	920		4
Runs Allowed:	873		6

Starting Lineup

Luke Sewell, c
Zeke Bonura, 1b
Jackie Hayes, 2b
Jimmie Dykes, 3b
Luke Appling, ss
Rip Radcliff, lf
Mike Kreevich, cf-rf
Mule Haas, rf
Tony Piet, 2b-3b
Larry Rosenthal, cf

Pitchers

Vern Kennedy, sp
John Whitehead, sp
Sugar Cain, sp
Ted Lyons, sp
Monty Stratton, sp
Bill Dietrich, sp
Clint Brown, rp
Italo Chelini, rp-sp

Attendance

500,391 (fourth in AL)

Club Leaders

Batting Avg:	Luke Appling	.388
On-Base Pct:	Luke Appling	.473
Slugging Pct:	Luke Appling	.508
Home Runs:	Zeke Bonura	12
RBIs:	Zeke Bonura	138
Runs:	Zeke Bonura	120
	Rip Radcliff	120
Stolen Bases:	Tony Piet	15
Wins:	Vern Kennedy	21
Strikeouts:	Vern Kennedy	99
ERA:	Vern Kennedy	4.63
Saves:	Clint Brown	5

APRIL 11   The White Sox purchase Clint Brown from the Indians.

Brown had been a capable starting pitcher for the Indians from 1930 through 1933, but after two off-seasons seemed to be washed-up when he arrived in Chicago. Jimmie Dykes turned Brown into one of baseball's first successful closers by utilizing him exclusively in relief at the end of games to preserve a victory. Using a tantalizing curveball and a deceptive sidearm delivery, Brown saved 18 games in 1937, had seven relief wins and set a record for games finished with 48 in 53 relief appearances. He missed almost the entire 1938 season with elbow trouble. In 1939, Brown saved 18 again and won 11. He appeared in 61 games to become the first pitcher ever to record at least 60 relief appearances in a season and broke his own record for games finished with 56, a mark that stood until 1950. Unlike today's closers, however, Brown often pitched multiple innings. He totaled 100 innings in 1937 and 118$^{1}/_{3}$ in 1939.

APRIL 14   In the season opener, the White Sox trail 6–2 before scoring two runs in the sixth inning and three in the eighth to defeat the Browns 7–6 before 12,000 at Comiskey Park. Tony Piet hit a home run during the contest.

The White Sox and the Cubs were on five radio stations in 1936. Due to an agreement between the two Chicago clubs, only home games were broadcast. Bob Elson was the play-by-play man for WGN, Russ Hodges for WIND, Pat Flanagan on WBBM, Hal Totten on WCFL and John Harrington on WJJD. All five announcers covered both the Sox and the Cubs. Elson did the play-by-play for White Sox games from 1931 through 1970 on five different stations (WGN, WIND, WJJM, WCFL and WMAQ). In addition, stations in such places as Rock Island, Illinois; Lincoln, Nebraska; Davenport, Iowa; and Des Moines, Iowa did telegraphic recreations of White Sox and Cubs games during the 1936 season. In Des Moines, the games of both Chicago clubs were broadcast on station WHO by Ronald (Dutch) Reagan, who would leave the Midwest for a career as a movie actor in 1937. In 1936, The Sporting News conducted a reader poll to determine the most popular radio play-by-play broadcaster in the country. Despite the fact that he broadcast no games live and emanated from the relatively small town of Des Moines, Reagan finished ninth in the poll. He fared much better in future elections, winning two terms each as governor of California and president of the United States.

MAY 4   The White Sox purchase Dixie Walker from the Yankees.

Walker was given a regular spot in the outfield in 1937 and responded with a .302 batting average, 105 runs and a league-leading 15 triples. The acquisition of Walker would have been one of the greatest transactions in club history if the White Sox had hung on to him for another decade (see December 2, 1937).

MAY 5   The White Sox trade Les Tietje to the Browns for Sugar Cain.

MAY 11   With a barrage of 22 hits, the White Sox win 19–6 over the Browns in a game played in a steady drizzle in St. Louis. The Sox scored seven runs in the fourth inning and seven more in the ninth. Only a week after being purchased from the Yankees, Dixie Walker collected five hits, including two doubles, in six at-bats.

MAY 14   The White Sox score eight runs in the first inning and lead 10–1 at the end of the third, but they barely hang on for a 13–12 win over the Senators at Comiskey Park. The Sox needed a run in the ninth to break a 12–12 tie.

MAY 21   The White Sox win a 14-inning marathon by a 3–2 score over the Athletics at Comiskey Park. The Sox loaded the bases on walks in the 14th before Luke Appling stroked a two-out single. All 18 players in the starting lineups of the two clubs finished the game, including pitchers John Whitehead of Chicago and Harry Kelley of Philadelphia.

              Appling won the 1936 batting title by hitting .388. He also had 111 runs, 204 hits, six homers and 128 RBIs.

MAY 28   The White Sox score four runs in the ninth inning to defeat the Tigers 6–5 in Detroit. Jackie Hayes started the inning with a home run. Tony Piet hit a two-run single to tie the score and Mule Haas singled to drive in the winner.

JUNE 2   Rip Radcliff drives in seven runs with two homers and a single during an 11–9 win over the Yankees in New York. The Yanks scored seven runs in the first inning to take a 7–0 lead before the Sox came back. Two runs in the eighth broke the 9–9 tie.

              Radcliff was 28 before he reached the majors in 1934 in part because of his limited defensive abilities. He played six seasons for the White Sox and compiled a .310 batting average, ninth-best of all-time among hitters with at least 2,000 plate appearances with the club. In 1936, Radcliff had his best year with 207 hits and a .335 average.

JUNE 7   Mike Kreevich hits a grand slam off Wes Ferrell in the sixth inning, breaking a 5–5 tie in a 12–5 win over the Red Sox in Boston.

              As a boy in Mount Olive, Illinois, Kreevich accidentally shot off a finger on his left hand in a hunting mishap. Despite the handicap and several years working in the coal mines in Mount Olive, Kreevich fought his way to the majors, although he was 28 before playing his first full season in the big leagues.

JUNE 13   The White Sox bombard the Senators 15–2 in Washington.

JUNE 16   Jimmie Foxx hits a tape-measure homer over the left-field roof at Comiskey Park during a 4–2 win over the Red Sox. The other Boston run scored on another long Foxx homer that landed in the stands in left-center, just to the left-field side of the bleachers.

JUNE 19   John Whitehead pitches the White Sox to a 1–0 win over the Red Sox at Comiskey Park. The lone run scored in the fifth inning on a double by Jimmie Dykes and a single from Frank Grube.

JUNE 23   The White Sox break a 3–3 tie with nine runs in the sixth inning and defeat the Yankees 13–4 at Comiskey Park.

JUNE 24   The Yankees score 10 runs in the fifth inning of an 18–11 victory over the White Sox at Comiskey Park. Joe DiMaggio hit two home runs in the big inning.

JULY 1   The Tigers torch the White Sox with 25 hits and win 21–6 at Comiskey Park.

              The White Sox were 31–37 on July 2, and it looked as though the club was headed
              for its 10th losing season in a row before posting a 50–33 record the rest of way.

JULY 7   Luke Appling drives in two runs with a single in the seventh inning during the All-
              Star Game at Braves Field in Boston, won by the National League 4–3. Rip Radcliff
              contributed a dramatic catch in the third inning on a liner by Joe Medwick.

JULY 17   The White Sox take a 14–1
              lead after four innings and
              defeat the Senators 16–5 in
              Washington.

JULY 18   Rip Radcliff collects
              six hits, including two
              doubles, in seven at-bats
              during a 21–14 victory
              over the Athletics in the
              second game of a double-
              header in Philadelphia. The
              Sox scored seven runs in
              the fifth inning to take a
              12–6 lead and were never
              headed. The score was
              14–8 at the end of the
              sixth and 17–8 at the end
              of the eighth. In the ninth,
              Chicago scored four times
              and Philadelphia countered
              with six. The White Sox
              also won the opener 7–4.

JULY 19   The White Sox extend their
              winning streak to eight
              games with an 11–5 and
              8–2 sweep of the Athletics
              in Philadelphia.

One of the greatest players in White Sox history, Luke Appling
hit .388 in 1936, leading the league. He was the runner-up for
the MVP award that year, just one of his many great seasons.

JULY 20   The White Sox purchase Bill Dietrich from the Senators.

              Although never more than an end-of-the-rotation starter and long reliever,
              Dietrich was a favorite of Jimmie Dykes and pitched 11 seasons for the White
              Sox. Wearing thick glasses, Dietrich had an 80–91 record for the White Sox,
              pitched a no-hitter in 1937 and lost two-hitters in the ninth inning during a
              five-week span in 1941.

JULY 25   The White Sox lose 5–3 to the Yankees at Comiskey Park highlighted by a dispute
              with the umpires. In the sixth inning, umpire Bill Johnston ejected manager Jimmie
              Dykes, catcher Luke Sewell and coach Merv Shea for arguing balls and strikes calls.

As a result, the crowd of 15,000 booed the umpiring crew so loudly that a cordon of police escorted the arbiters from the field at the end of the game.

JULY 26   During a riotous double-header against the Yankees at Comiskey Park, the umpires are the targets of hundreds of missiles thrown by fans. The Sox lost both games 12–3 and 11–8 in 11 innings. Umpire Bill Summers made a call against the Sox in the eighth inning of game two, leading to a bombardment of bottles, beer cans, seat cushions, oranges and lemons. Time was called as Jimmie Dykes appealed to the fans to desist, but the ploy failed. Summers was injured just as Zeke Bonura was rounding second base with the game-tying homer in the ninth. A bottle hurled by an unidentified fan in the upper grandstand back of third base, where Summers was stationed, hit him in the groin and he collapsed. After he received first aid, Summers was able to walk to the clubhouse, but he did not return to the diamond. Commissioner Kenesaw Landis, who was in a first-row box, authorized an announcement over the public address system offering a $5,000 reward for information leading to the arrest and conviction of the assailant.

JULY 27   The Athletics collect 25 hits and win 15–8 over the White Sox at Comiskey Park.

JULY 28   The White Sox score seven runs in the fifth inning to take a 15–2 lead and win 19–6 over the Athletics at Comiskey Park. In his first start with the White Sox, Bill Dietrich pitched a complete game and collected four hits in six at-bats.

JULY 30   Vern Kennedy records his 10th win in a row with a 7–4 decision over the Athletics at Comiskey Park.

AUGUST 1   In his second start with the White Sox, Bill Dietrich pitches a two-hitter to defeat the Red Sox 3–0 at Comiskey Park. The only Boston hits were a single by Doc Cramer in the fourth inning and a double by Joe Cronin in the fifth.

AUGUST 2   The White Sox sweep the Red Sox 9–1 and 12–11. The second game went 12 innings as Chicago overcame a nine-run deficit. Boston took a 10–1 lead with six runs in the fifth inning and led 11–3 at the end of the sixth. The White Sox rallied with a run in the seventh inning, five in the eighth, two in the ninth and one in the 12th.

AUGUST 18   The White Sox edge the Indians 11–10 in 10 innings at Comiskey Park. The winning run scored on a triple by Rip Radcliff and a single by Luke Appling.

AUGUST 31   Luke Appling runs his hitting streak to 27 games during a 5–1 loss to the Yankees in New York.

SEPTEMBER 6   The White Sox sweep the Indians 15–1 and 6–3 in a double-header at Comiskey Park. In the opener, Rip Radcliff collected four hits, including a double, in six at-bats and drove in five runs.

SEPTEMBER 11   The White Sox collect 26 hits during a 17–2 pounding of the Athletics at Comiskey Park. Mike Kreevich, Luke Appling and Zeke Bonura each collected five hits and Rip Radcliff picked up four hits. In the process, the White Sox tied American League records for most players with five or more hits in a game, and most players with four or more hits in a game. Kreevich had a triple, two doubles and a single, and Radcliff added two doubles and two singles. Appling and Bonura both had five singles.

Despite his ineffectiveness, Hod Lisenbee pitched a complete game for the A's. His 26 hits allowed tied a modern major league record for a nine-inning game.

SEPTEMBER 14   Vern Kennedy records his 21st win of the season with an 11–3 decision over the Senators in the second game of a double-header at Comiskey Park. The White Sox also won the first game 5–4 in 10 innings.

OCTOBER 2   In game one of the Chicago City Series, the White Sox defeat the Cubs 5–1 at Wrigley Field.

OCTOBER 3   In game two of the City Series, the White Sox score eight runs in the sixth inning and defeat the Cubs 11–3 at Comiskey Park.

OCTOBER 5   The White Sox complete the four-game sweep of the Cubs in the City Series with an 8–2 win over the Cubs at Comiskey Park. Zeke Bonura had a 5-for-5 day.

DECEMBER 10   Five weeks after Franklin Roosevelt defeats Alf Landon in the presidential election, the White Sox trade Jack Salveson to the Indians for Thornton Lee.

When acquired by the White Sox, Lee was a 30-year-old pitcher with a 12–17 lifetime record. With the Sox, he lasted 11 seasons and compiled a record of 104–104. Lee was much better than a .500 pitcher, however, as he pitched on some dismal teams. From 1937 through 1941 he was 74–57 before being hobbled by injuries. Salveson won only five big-league games after the trade, all on teams during World War II depleted by the military draft and enlistments.

DECEMBER 31   The White Sox and the Cubs jointly announce that they will be charging radio stations for the rights to broadcast games from Comiskey Park and Wrigley Field in 1937. Previously, stations were permitted to broadcast games free of charge. WGN and WBBM paid both the Sox and the Cubs $7,500, while WIND, WCFL and WJJD each paid the two clubs $3,000.

1937

Season in a Sentence

The White Sox remain in pennant contention into early August and win 86 games, the most compiled by the franchise in a single season between 1920 and 1953.

Finish • Won • Lost • Pct • GB

Third   86   68   .558   16.0

Manager

Jimmie Dykes

Stats

Stats	WS	AL	Rank
Batting Avg:	.280	.281	4
On-Base Pct:	.350	.355	6
Slugging Pct:	.400	.415	5
Home Runs:	67		7
Stolen Bases:	70		5
ERA:	4.17	4.62	2
Fielding Avg:	.971	.972	6
Runs Scored:	780		5
Runs Allowed:	730		2

Starting Lineup

Luke Sewell, c
Zeke Bonura, 1b
Jackie Hayes, 2b
Tony Piet, 3b
Luke Appling, ss
Rip Radcliff, lf
Mike Kreevich, cf
Dixie Walker, rf

Pitchers

Vern Kennedy, sp
Monty Stratton, sp
Thornton Lee, sp
Ted Lyons, sp
John Whitehead, sp
Bill Dietrich, sp-rp
Clint Brown, rp
Johnny Rigney, rp

Attendance

589,235 (third in AL)

Club Leaders

Batting Avg:	Zeke Bonura	.345
On-Base Pct:	Zeke Bonura	.412
Slugging Pct:	Zeke Bonura	.573
Home Runs:	Zeke Bonura	19
RBIs:	Zeke Bonura	100
Runs:	Dixie Walker	105
	Rip Radcliff	105
Stolen Bases:	Luke Appling	18
Wins:	Monty Stratton	15
Strikeouts:	Vern Kennedy	114
ERA:	Monty Stratton	2.40
Saves:	Clint Brown	18

APRIL 20   The White Sox scheduled season opener against the Browns in St. Louis is postponed by rain.

APRIL 21   The White Sox open the season with a 15–10 loss to the Browns in St. Louis. Zeke Bonura was 4-for-5. Dixie Walker collected a triple, double and single and drove in four runs.

APRIL 23   In the home opener, the White Sox lose 10–2 to the Tigers at Comiskey Park. Luke Sewell hit a home run in a losing cause.

> *The Sox started the season with a 3–9 record, then won 22 of the next 30. A 10-game winning streak catapulted the Sox into a first-place tie on June 8 with a record of 25–17. The club relinquished the lead the next day but remained in contention for nearly two months. On August 1, Chicago was 57–36 and five games out of first place, but they lost seven games in a row to the Yankees and Red Sox beginning on August 3 to end any hopes for a pennant in Chicago.*

APRIL 29   The White Sox hammer the Browns 12–0 at Comiskey Park.

MAY 12   Six days after the German dirigible *Hindenburg* erupts in flames at Lakehurst, New Jersey, killing 56 people, the White Sox trounce the Senators 13–5 at Comiskey Park.

MAY 23   The White Sox come from behind to defeat the Red Sox 6–4 in 10 innings at Fenway Park. Trailing 3–1, Chicago scored twice in the ninth inning and three times in the 10th before Boston tallied one in their half of the 10th.

MAY 26   Trailing 5–1, the White Sox score one run in the seventh inning, one in the eighth and three in the ninth to win 6–5 over the Senators in Washington. Dixie Walker tied the score 5–5 with a two-run triple, then crossed the plate on Zeke Bonura's double.

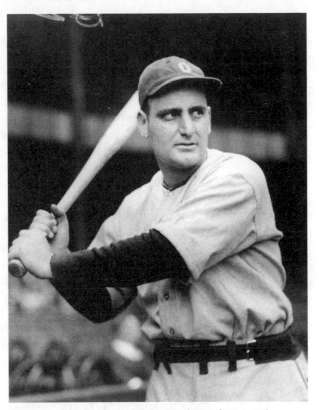

          Bonura hit .345 with 19 homers and 100 runs batted in during the 1937 season.

JUNE 1   Bill Dietrich pitches a no-hitter, defeating the Senators 8–0 at Comiskey Park. He walked two and struck out five. The two walks were issued in the sixth inning after Dietrich started the game by retiring 15 batters in a row. In the ninth inning, Jim Bottomley led off in a pinch-hit role and flied out to Mike Kreevich in center field. Harry Davis made the 26th out of the game by grounding out to

Zeke Bonura was a very productive hitter for several years in the late 1930s. In 1937 he batted .345 and knocked in 100 runs.

second baseman Jackie Hayes. Sammy West struck out to end the contest.

          There were only two no-hitters pitched in the majors between September 21, 1934 and June 11, 1938, and White Sox pitchers accounted for both of them. The other was by Vern Kennedy on August 31, 1935.

JUNE 7   The White Sox score seven runs in the fifth inning and defeat the Athletics 12–6 at Comiskey Park. It was Chicago's ninth win in a row.

JUNE 8   The White Sox extend their winning streak to 10 games with a 5–4 win over the Yankees at Comiskey Park.

JUNE 11   In pre-game ceremonies at Comiskey Park, Zeke Bonura is presented with an automobile as Chicago's "most popular player," then collects four hits, including two doubles and a homer, and five RBIs during a 14–8 victory over the Senators.

JUNE 13   The White Sox score eight runs in the eighth inning of a 9–4 win over the Senators in the first game of a double-header at Comiskey Park. Washington won the second tilt 3–2.

JUNE 19   The White Sox score four runs in the ninth inning off Red Ruffing to defeat the Yankees 5–2 in New York. Rip Radcliff's double sent across the first run. Mike Kreevich broke the 3–3 tie with a three-run homer.

JUNE 22   The heavyweight boxing championship of the world takes places before 65,000 at Comiskey Park with Joe Louis taking the crown from James J. Braddock with an eighth-round knockout.

> *The ring was set up at second base and about 15,000 seats were placed all over the field to accommodate the large crowd, causing large divots and bare spots in the grass from the foot traffic and from the temporary seats sinking into the ground. American League fielders had trouble fielding balls for the rest of the year because of the uneven surface. According to Ed Burns of the* Chicago Tribune, *the fight "ripped up the field more than a troupe of Kansas grasshoppers could have done."*

JUNE 26   The White Sox score three runs in the ninth inning to beat the Senators 6–5 in Washington.

JUNE 29   Monty Stratton pitches a three-hitter to beat the Tigers 3–2 at Comiskey Park. Stratton retired the first 18 batters to face him before Pete Fox singled leading off the seventh.

JULY 1   The White Sox garner 20 hits during a 15–8 thrashing of the Tigers at Comiskey Park. In his first start of the season, Jimmy Dykes reached base in all five plate appearances with a double, three singles and a walk.

JULY 3   Rip Radcliff collects five hits, including a triple and a double, during a 10–5 win over the Browns in St. Louis.

JULY 10   Clint Brown pitches four shutout innings and drives in the winning run with a walk-off single in the 11th inning for a 5–4 triumph over the Browns at Comiskey Park.

JULY 18   On the day that Amelia Earhart disappears over the Pacific, the White Sox sweep the Red Sox 6–5 and 1–0 at Comiskey Park. The first contest went 10 innings. Monty Stratton pitched the second game shutout.

JULY 29   The White Sox win 2–0 over the Senators in Washington behind the pitching of Thornton Lee. The two runs scored in the fifth inning on a double by Luke Appling and singles by Tony Piet and Lee.

> *Appling hit .317 and collected 42 doubles in 1937.*

AUGUST 1   Dixie Walker homers in the 11th inning to beat the Athletics 4–3 in the first game of a double-header in Philadelphia. The White Sox completed a sweep with a 3–2 victory in game two.

AUGUST 8   The White Sox break a seven-losing streak and end Boston's 12-game winning skein with a 13–0 pounding of the Red Sox in the second game of a double-header at Fenway Park. Zeke Bonura hit a grand slam. The contest was called after six innings because of the Massachusetts sports law that stipulated that Sunday games end precisely at 6:30 p.m. The Red Sox won the opener 7–6.

AUGUST 14   Jimmie Dykes puts himself into the game as a pinch-hitter with the score tied 4–4 in the 10th inning and delivers a two-run single for a 6–4 win over the Tigers in the second game of a double-header in Detroit. The Tigers won the opener 11–8.

AUGUST 18   Rip Radcliff runs his hitting streak to 20 games during a 6–0 win over the Tigers at Comiskey Park.

AUGUST 29   The Athletics score 12 runs in the first inning off Monty Stratton and Johnny Rigney and beat the White Sox 16–0 in the first game of a double-header at Comiskey Park. The Sox rebounded from the debacle to take the second tilt 5–3.

> A native of the Chicago suburb of Oak Park, Rigney was a key figure with the White Sox for more than two decades. He pitched for the club from 1937 through 1942 and again in 1946 and 1947, with the intervening three years spent in the service during World War II. Rigney was 63–64 with the club. During the 1939 season, in which he was 15–8, Rigney won 11 games in a row. Two years later, on October 8, 1941, he married Dorothy Comiskey, the eldest daughter of Grace and Louis Comiskey. After his playing career ended, Rigney moved into the front office as director of the farm system, a job he held for eight years, and was a vice president from 1955 until Bill Veeck bought the club in 1959. In those roles, Rigney greatly improved the scouting operation and deserves much of the credit for the success that the Sox enjoyed during the 1950s and 1960s.

SEPTEMBER 2   The White Sox use four solo homers to defeat the Red Sox 4–2 in the first game of a double-header at Comiskey Park. Boze Berger and Mike Kreevich, the first and second hitters in the lineup, led off the first inning with home runs off Johnny Marcum. In the third, Berger and Dixie Walker homered. Chicago completed the sweep with a 10–8 victory in the second tilt.

SEPTEMBER 4   Mike Kreevich hits four consecutive doubles during a 9–1 win over the Tigers in Detroit.

SEPTEMBER 23   John Whitehead pitches the White Sox to a 1–0 win over the Athletics in Philadelphia.

OCTOBER 3   On the last day of the regular season, the White Sox sweep the Browns 2–0 and 7–3 in St. Louis. The first game went 11 innings, with Thornton Lee hurling a complete-game shutout. The runs scored on a triple by Rip Radcliff, an intentional walk to Luke Appling and a two-run double from Zeke Bonura. The second contest was called after five innings by darkness.

OCTOBER 6   The Cubs win the first game of the Chicago City Series, defeating the White Sox 7–3 at Wrigley Field.

OCTOBER 9   The White Sox even the City Series at two games apiece with a 14–2 thrashing of the Cubs at Comiskey Park.

OCTOBER 13   The White Sox take the seventh and deciding game of the City Series by a 6–1 score at Wrigley Field.

DECEMBER 2   The White Sox trade Dixie Walker, Vern Kennedy and Tony Piet to the Tigers for Gee Walker, Mike Tresh and Marv Owen.

The White Sox had concerns about Dixie Walker's health. Shortly after being acquired by the White Sox in 1936, he had suffered a severe shoulder injury, then tore cartilage in his knee. The Tigers had the same concerns and passed him onto the Dodgers in 1939, where he became an instant hero in Brooklyn. After being dealt by the Sox, Dixie was a four-time All-Star, played in two World Series and won a batting title. Tresh was a starting catcher for nine seasons with the Sox, Gee Walker was a regular outfielder for two years and Owen was the starter at third base for a season, but the three combined still weren't worth the loss of Dixie Walker.

1938   Sox

Season in a Sentence

After a third-place finish in 1937, the White Sox drop to sixth as injuries and miserable spring weather ruin the season.

Finish • Won • Lost • Pct • GB

Sixth   67   83   .439   32.0

Manager

Jimmie Dykes

Stats

Stats	WS	AL	Rank
Batting Avg:	.277	.281	5
On-Base Pct:	.343	.358	8
Slugging Pct:	.383	.415	8
Home Runs:	67		8
Stolen Bases:	56		6
ERA:	4.36	4.79	2
Fielding Avg:	.967	.971	7
Runs Scored:	709		8
Runs Allowed:	752		3

Starting Lineup

Luke Sewell, c
Joe Kuhel, 1b
Jackie Hayes, 2b
Marv Owen, 3b
Boze Berger, ss-2b
Rip Radcliff, lf
Mike Kreevich, cf
Gee Walker, rf-lf
Hank Steinbacher, rf
Luke Appling, ss
Tony Rensa, c

Pitchers

Thornton Lee, sp
Monty Stratton, sp
John Whitehead, sp
Ted Lyons, sp
Jack Knott, sp
Johnny Rigney, rp-sp

Attendance

338,278 (seventh in AL)

Club Leaders

Batting Avg:	Hank Steinbacher	.331
On-Base Pct:	Hank Steinbacher	.393
Slugging Pct:	Gee Walker	.493
Home Runs:	Gee Walker	16
RBIs:	Gee Walker	87
Runs:	Marv Owen	84
Stolen Bases:	Mike Kreevich	13
Wins:	Monty Stratton	15
Strikeouts:	Monty Stratton	82
ERA:	Thornton Lee	3.49
Saves:	Three tied with	2

MARCH 18   The White Sox trade Zeke Bonura to the Senators for Joe Kuhel.

The White Sox patience with the temperamental Bonura ran out during the spring of 1938 when he was a holdout, although the deal was not a hit with White Sox fans because of Zeke's popularity. In contrast to Bonura, who was flamboyant and inept with the glove, Kuhel was quiet, hard-working and the best defensive first baseman in baseball. Despite the initial animosity of Sox fans,

Kuhel eventually won them over. He served as the club's starting first baseman until 1943. Bonura flopped in Washington and by 1941 was out of the majors.

APRIL 19

The White Sox open the season with a 4–3 win over the Tigers before 18,000 at Comiskey Park. The Sox broke a 1–1 tie with three runs in the fourth inning and held on for the win.

The 1938 season was a disaster from the start. Heavy flooding at the club's spring training base in Pasadena made it virtually impossible to conduct workouts. Injuries and bad weather were a problem all year. In late March, Luke Appling fractured an ankle and would miss three months. Monty Stratton battled arm miseries and Clint Brown missed most of the season following an operation to remove bone chips from his elbow. Only one player appeared in more than 130 games and just one pitcher made more than 25 starts. The lousy weather encountered in California followed the White Sox after Opening Day. During the first five weeks of the regular season, 11 games were postponed. Six more contests were lost in June. The bad weather also wiped out many lucrative weekend games at Comiskey Park, and combined with a losing team, attendance plummeted from 589,245 in 1937 to 338,278 in 1938. To make up the postponements, the Sox had to play 38 games in August, including 13 double-headers. During one brutal stretch from August 21 through 28, the White Sox played 15 games in eight days in four different cities (Cleveland, New York, Boston and Philadelphia). The ultimate blow came after the season ended when Stratton had to have his right leg amputated following a hunting accident (see November 28, 1938).

MAY 5

Boze Berger hits the first pitch of the game for a home run and later adds three singles during a 10–4 win over the Athletics in Philadelphia.

Berger volunteered for service in the Army during World War II. He rose to the rank of major and made the military his career after the war was over.

MAY 13

The White Sox score three runs in the ninth inning to defeat the Indians 7–6 in Cleveland.

Radio play-by-play of White Sox and Cubs home games was available on four stations in 1939. On WJJD, former Sox manager Lew Fonseca and ex-Cubs manager Charlie Grimm were teamed.

A 28-year-old rookie in 1936, Mike Kreevich was a consistent hitter for the White Sox through 1940, earning a spot on the All-Star team in 1938.

Fonseca and Grimm shared the same booth for two seasons and entertained Chicago baseball fans with a hilarious comedy routine during games.

MAY 21   A home run by Yankee pitcher Spud Chandler off Thornton Lee in the eighth inning is the only run of a 1–0 New York win over the White Sox at Comiskey Park.

MAY 22   Ted Lyons records his 200th career victory with a 9–2 decision over the Senators at Comiskey Park.

MAY 27   Hank Greenberg hits a home run into the distant center-field bleachers at Comiskey Park during a 5–2 Detroit win over the White Sox. In 1938, the bleacher wall was 15 feet high and 440 feet from home plate. Greenberg was the first to reach the bleachers at that distance. Jimmie Foxx hit a homer into the bleachers in 1934, when the distance from the plate was 426 feet (see May 18, 1934).

JUNE 4   The White Sox lose their 10th game in a row, dropping a 9–4 decision to the Athletics in Philadelphia.

JUNE 8   Down 10–6, the White Sox score a run in the eighth inning, three in the ninth and one in the 13th to defeat the Yankees 11–10 in the first game of a double-header in New York. Gee Walker drove in the last four Chicago runs with a three-run homer in the ninth and a single in the 13th.

JUNE 10   Pitcher Monty Stratton hits a grand slam during the second inning of a 15–2 trouncing of the Red Sox in Boston. The White Sox collected 20 hits and scored in seven of the nine innings.

JUNE 22   Right fielder Hank Steinbacher collects six hits in six at-bats during a 16–3 win over the Senators at Comiskey Park. Steinbacher singled off Wes Ferrell in the first and second innings, hit a single in the fourth and a double in the fifth against Monty Weaver, and singled twice facing Chief Hogsett during the seventh and eighth. The Sox scored in each of the first seven innings.

              Steinbacher played three seasons in the majors (1937–39), all with the White Sox, and posted a career batting average of .292 with 170 hits in 203 games. He is one of three Sox players with six hits in six at-bats in one game. The others are Floyd Robinson in 1962 and Lance Johnson in 1995. Rip Radcliff also had six hits in seven-at-bats during a contest in 1936.

JUNE 30   The White Sox hammer the Browns 11–1 in St. Louis. Pitching against a club that traded him to the White Sox 19 days earlier, Jack Knott retired 21 of the first 22 batters to face him.

JULY 17   The White Sox score seven runs in the fifth inning of a 12–1 triumph over the Senators in Washington.

JULY 24   Thornton Lee pitches a two-hitter, but loses 2–0 to the Yankees in the first game of a double-header in New York. The two runs scored in the second inning on two errors, one of them by Lee, and a double by Bill Dickey. The White Sox won the second tilt 5–2.

JULY 29 | Yankee outfielder Jake Powell inflames racial passions in the Windy City by making remarks during a radio interview that are derogatory to African-Americans. The comments were made prior to a 4–3 White Sox loss to New York at Comiskey Park. During the interview, Powell took delight in telling listeners how he discriminated against African-Americans in his role as a policeman in Maryland during the off-season and said that he would like to "hit every colored person in Chicago over the head with a club."

On July 30, Powell was suspended for 10 days by Kenesaw Landis for comments that the commissioner described as "unethical" and "disparaging." Extra police were on hand to protect the Yankees players during the remainder of the series at Comiskey Park. Powell moved away from his club's hotel in Chicago. At the age of 40 in 1948, Powell committed suicide in a Washington, D.C., police station while being questioned on a bad-check charge.

JULY 30 | Gee Walker and Yankees second baseman Joe Gordon fight at the end of a 9–6 White Sox loss at Comiskey Park. Walker was retired on a force play at second base for the final out of the game and tangled with Gordon after an exchange of heated words. The two exchanged punches until separated by umpire Steve Basil.

AUGUST 4 | Rip Radcliff collects eight consecutive hits during a double-header against the Athletics at Comiskey Park. In the opener, won by the White Sox 8–7, Radcliff was 5-for-5 on four singles and a double. During Chicago's 7–3 triumph in the nightcap, Radcliff had three singles in his first three at-bats before being retired twice. Counting two hits in his last two at-bats of a 13–5 loss to A's in Chicago on August 3, Radcliff had 10 consecutive hits on eight singles and a double. The 10 hits tied a club record set by Harry McCurdy in 1926.

AUGUST 5 | The White Sox go from one extreme to another, winning 14–5 and losing 12–5 during a double-header against the Senators at Comiskey Park.

AUGUST 11 | Concentrating all of their firepower in two innings, the White Sox score seven runs in the third inning and six in the eighth to defeat the Tigers 13–1 at Comiskey Park.

AUGUST 27 | The White Sox go from one extreme to the other, losing a double-header 19–6 and 1–0 to the Red Sox in Boston.

SEPTEMBER 17 | Playing first base to give Joe Kuhel a rest in the second game of a double-header against the Athletics at Comiskey, Merv Connors clubs three home runs in consecutive plate appearances, pacing the White Sox to a 7–4 victory. All three home runs were struck off Jim Reninger, who was making his major league debut, in the second, fourth and sixth innings. Connors also doubled and drove in five runs. He had been called up from Shreveport in the Texas League only two weeks earlier. Connors didn't play in the first game, an 8–4 Chicago win.

Connors played only two seasons in the majors (1937–38), both with the White Sox, and hit just eight homers while batting .279 in 52 games and 165 at-bats.

SEPTEMBER 28 | The White Sox outlast the Indians 14–11 in Cleveland. Five runs in the fifth inning broke a 5–5 tie.

NOVEMBER 28   A month after Orson Welles fools many Americans into believing that Martians are invading New Jersey during his Mercury Theater radio program on Halloween Eve, Monty Stratton undergoes an operation to have his right leg amputated at the knee following a hunting mishap the previous day. Stratton accidentally shot himself in the leg while hunting rabbits near his farm in Texas. The surgery was necessary to halt the spread of gangrene and save Stratton's life.

Monty Stratton's Story

At the close of the 1938 season, Monty Stratton looked as though he might be headed for stardom, if not Cooperstown. He was 26 years old and had a record of 30–14 over the previous two seasons.

On November 27, he went hunting in the woods alone near his Greenville, Texas, home when he spotted a rabbit hopping through the brush. Monty fired his .32-caliber pistol at the animal, but as he holstered the weapon a bullet discharged and went into his thigh and downward severing the femoral artery of his right leg behind the knee. Stratton crawled toward his home a half-mile away, where he was found by one of his brothers. When doctors examined the wound, they arrived at the conclusion that the leg would have to be amputated because of poor blood circulation.

With his playing career over, Stratton became a coach with the White Sox during the 1939, 1940 and 1941 seasons. Fitted with an artificial leg, he occasionally pitched batting practice. In 1942, he became a manager for a club in Lubbock, Texas, in the White Sox farm system, but the job lasted only a year. Returning to his 52-acre ranch in Greenville, Stratton began heaving baseballs at a painted target on the side of his barn. By 1944, the former Sox pitcher figured he had overcome his handicap enough to pitch for a pick-up team in Greenville. Two years later, Stratton pitched in organized baseball again for the Sherman club in the East Texas League and posted an 18–8 record.

About this time, a Hollywood scriptwriter named Douglas Morrow approached Stratton about doing a screenplay of his life. Morrow figured that Stratton's story would be an inspiration to World War II veterans who lost their limbs in combat. Released in 1949 with the title *The Stratton Story*, Jimmy Stewart was cast as Stratton with June Allyson as Ethel. Morrow's treatment won the Academy Award for best original screenplay.

DECEMBER 19   The White Sox sell Luke Sewell to the Dodgers.

DECEMBER 21   The White Sox trade Boze Berger to the Red Sox for Eric McNair.

1939

Season in a Sentence

The White Sox right the ship and post a winning record during a season in which Lou Comiskey dies and night baseball is introduced in Chicago.

Finish • Won • Lost • Pct • GB

Fourth   85   69   .552   22.5

Manager

Jimmie Dykes

Stats	WS	AL	Rank
Batting Avg:	.275	.279	6
On-Base Pct:	.349	.352	5
Slugging Pct:	.379	.407	8
Home Runs:	64		7
Stolen Bases:	113		1
ERA:	4.31	4.62	4
Fielding Avg:	.972	.969	2
Runs Scored:	755		5
Runs Allowed:	737		3

Starting Lineup

Mike Tresh, c
Joe Kuhel, 1b
Ollie Bejma, 2b
Eric McNair, 3b
Luke Appling, ss
Gee Walker, lf
Mike Kreevich, cf
Rip Radcliff, rf
Larry Rosenthal, rf
Jackie Hayes, 2b
Marv Owen, 3b

Pitchers

Thornton Lee, sp
Johnny Rigney, sp
Ted Lyons, sp
Jack Knott, sp
Eddie Smith, sp
Bill Dietrich, sp
Clint Brown, rp
Johnny Marcum, rp-sp

Attendance

594,104 (third in AL)

Club Leaders

Batting Avg:	Eric McNair	.324
On-Base Pct:	Luke Appling	.430
Slugging Pct:	Joe Kuhel	.460
Home Runs:	Joe Kuhel	15
RBIs:	Gee Walker	111
Runs:	Joe Kuhel	107
Stolen Bases:	Mike Kreevich	23
Wins:	Thornton Lee	15
	Johnny Rigney	15
Strikeouts:	Johnny Rigney	112
ERA:	Ted Lyons	2.76
Saves:	Clint Brown	18

APRIL 18   The White Sox lose 6–1 to the Tigers at Detroit on Opening Day. Jimmie Dykes was ejected in the seventh inning for objecting to the umpiring decisions.

APRIL 22   The White Sox open the home schedule with a 5–1 loss to the Browns before 10,000 at Comiskey Park.

The White Sox had seven consecutive preseason exhibition games at Comiskey Park rained out as well as the April 21 regular season opener before finally playing a home game in 1939.

APRIL 23   Marv Owen collects four doubles during a 17–4 win over the Browns at Comiskey Park. Owen was helped by the ineffectiveness of the St. Louis outfielders. Left fielder Beau Bell and center fielder Mel Almada both got their gloves on Owen drives, but couldn't hang on to them. Another fly ball was badly misjudged by right fielder Myril Hoag.

APRIL 24   White Sox batters draw 15 walks from Cleveland pitchers Johnny Humphries and Tom Drake during a 9–3 win in Cleveland.

APRIL 27   The White Sox purchase Eddie Smith from the Athletics.

Smith was 25 and had a 9–28 record when acquired from the A's. He pitched for the White Sox until 1947 with seasons ranging from a 14–9 mark in 1940 to 7–20 in 1942. A victim of pitching largely for bad teams, Smith was 73–113 over a career from 1936 though 1947 despite posting a 3.82 ERA that was below the league average for that period.

MAY 1   The White Sox and Cubs play a benefit game for former Sox pitcher Monty Stratton, who lost his right leg in a hunting accident the previous November (see November 28, 1938). The White Sox won 4–1 before 25,594, raising $28,000, all of which went to Stratton. Everybody paid to enter the park, including reporters, umpires and players. Stratton also received the take from the concessions. Before the game, he was presented with an automobile from former teammate Tony Piet, who owned a dealership on the South Side of Chicago. Stratton also walked to the mound on his artificial leg to throw out the ceremonial first pitch.

MAY 6   The White Sox win 14–12 over the Senators at Comiskey Park. Trailing 8–2, the Sox scored eight times in the fourth inning to take a 10–8 advantage, only to allow Washington to retake the lead 11–10. Three runs in the sixth inning put Chicago on top 13–11.

MAY 24   The White Sox play a regular season game at night for the first time in club history and win 4–1 over the Athletics at Shibe Park in Philadelphia.

The Cincinnati Reds were the first big-league club to play night games in 1935. They were followed by the Dodgers in 1938, the Athletics, Phillies, Indians and White Sox in 1939, the Giants, Browns, Pirates and Cardinals in 1940, the Senators in 1941, the Braves and Yankees in 1946, the Red Sox in 1947 and Tigers in 1948. The last holdout among the 16 pre-expansion teams to play home games at night were the Cubs, who first played at night at Wrigley Field in 1988 (see August 18, 1939).

MAY 28   Members of the White Sox and Indians nearly come to blows during a 6–0 Chicago loss in Cleveland. Jimmie Dykes and Indians pitcher Johnny Allen threatened to punch each other during a heated exchange in the third inning, and Gee Walker charged Allen after being hit on the head with a pitched ball in the sixth. Players of both teams stepped in before any blows were struck, however.

JUNE 2   The White Sox trade John Whitehead to the Browns for Johnny Marcum.

JUNE 4   The White Sox score eight runs in the first inning and defeat the Athletics 14–9 in the first game of a double-header at Comiskey Park. Philadelphia won the second tilt 11–6.

JUNE 5   The White Sox wallop the Athletics 12–1 at Comiskey Park.

JUNE 24   The White Sox score seven runs in the second inning to spark a 14–6 win over the Red Sox in Boston.

JULY 1   The White Sox and Tigers spilt a double-header in Detroit, with the Tigers taking the opener 6–5 and the Sox taking the nightcap 4–3. The sixth inning of the second game was enlivened when Hank Greenberg charged that Joe Kuhel deliberately spiked him while sliding into first base, and the Tiger slugger swung one punch at Kuhel. Both teams rushed to the scene and prevented a fight. Umpire Ed Rommel banished Greenberg from the game. Police removed several fans from the park following a deluge of bottles flung toward the Chicago dugout.

JULY 2   Trouble surfaces again in Detroit during an 8–1 White Sox loss to the Tigers. Before the game, Jimmie Dykes received a telegram from AL president Will Harridge that advised the Sox manager that he blamed the Chicago players in part for the row that occurred the previous day between Hank Greenberg and Joe Kuhel. Dykes sent all of his players who were not actually in the game to the center-field bullpen. All went well until the fourth inning, when umpire Ed Rommel called a third strike on Sox third baseman Eric McNair, who tossed his bat high in the air. Rommel chased McNair, and when Dykes and Ted Lyons got into the argument, they too were ejected.

JULY 3   Eric McNair collects five hits in five at-bats during an 8–3 win over the Browns in St. Louis.

JULY 5   Eddie Smith pitches a two-hitter to defeat the Indians 2–1 at Comiskey Park. Smith went into the game with an 0–9 career record against Cleveland. The only two Indians hits were singles by Rollie Hemsley and Moose Solters.

JULY 8   Down 5–2, the White Sox score seven runs in the seventh inning and beat the Tigers 10–5 at Comiskey Park.

JULY 13   The White Sox lead 8–0 after four innings but wind up losing 12–10 to the Athletics at Comiskey Park.

JULY 18   Club owner Lou Comiskey dies from congestive heart failure at his summer home in Eagle River, Wisconsin. Comiskey was 56 years old.

                Under the terms of the will, Comiskey bequeathed half of the club to his wife, Grace, who he married in 1913, with the other half to be divided equally among his children, 13-year-old son Charles II, 18-year-old daughter Grace and 22-year-old daughter Dorothy. Comiskey further stipulated that it was his wish that no shares of stock be sold prior to the time that Charles II reached the age of 35, which would be in 1961. The First National Bank of Chicago was named trustee for the estate, valued at $2,250,000. It was Lou Comiskey's heartfelt desire that his only son, nicknamed Chuck, would someday assume command of the franchise that had been in the family since 1900. The language of the will was vague, however, as to who would run the franchise until Chuck became of legal age. The problem would eventually split the Comiskey family into rival factions (see February 29, 1940).

AUGUST 18   The White Sox play their first night game at Comiskey Park and win 1–0 in 11 innings over the Indians before 46,000. Through the first 10 innings, Bob Feller allowed only one hit, a single by Jackie Hayes in the third inning. Feller started the 11th by walking Eddie Smith, who pitched a complete-game shutout for the Sox. Hayes tried twice to bunt Smith to second but was unsuccessful, and then hit a double, putting the pitcher on third. Mike Kreevich drove in the winning run with a single.

> *Rules in both leagues limited clubs to playing only seven night games at home in 1939. The White Sox did not play a majority of their home schedule at night until 1966.*

AUGUST 20   After the Indians take a 5–4 lead in the top of the 10th inning, the White Sox rally for a pair of tallies in their half to win 6–5 at Comiskey Park. The two runs scored on a bases-loaded pinch-single by Eric McNair.

> *Twelve days later, Germany invaded Poland, triggering a declaration of war from England and France and the beginning of World War II. The conflict would embroil the United States militarily on December 7, 1941, with the attack by the Japanese on Pearl Harbor.*

SEPTEMBER 2   Johnny Rigney pitches a two-hitter to defeat the Tigers 2–0 at Comiskey Park. It was Rigney's 10th victory in a row. The only Detroit hits were a single by Pete Fox in the seventh inning and a double by Rudy York in the ninth.

SEPTEMBER 6   Johnny Rigney extends his streak of consecutive wins to 11 with a 7–2 decision over the Browns in St. Louis.

> *Rigney had a record of 15–8 and a 3.70 ERA in 1939.*

SEPTEMBER 10   Trailing 9–6, the White Sox score three runs in the seventh inning and two in the eighth to win 11–9 over the Tigers in the second game of a double-header in Detroit. The Sox lost the opener 5–1, a contest that ended Johnny Rigney's 11-game losing streak.

SEPTEMBER 24   The White Sox sweep the Browns 11–9 and 4–3 at Comiskey Park. The second game was called after 4½ innings by darkness.

SEPTEMBER 27   The first day-night double-header in major league history takes place at Comiskey Park. The Indians won both games 5–2 and 7–5.

OCTOBER 4   The Chicago City Series starts with a 10–9 Cubs win over the White Sox before 42,767 in a night game at Comiskey Park. The Cubs scored three times in the ninth for the win.

OCTOBER 7   Hank Leiber's three-run, walk-off homer in the ninth inning gives the Cubs a 5–3 win over the White Sox at Wrigley Field and a three-games-to-one lead in the City Series.

OCTOBER 8   Trailing 5–0 in game five of the City Series and facing elimination, the White Sox rally with two runs in the sixth inning, three in the eighth and three in the 10th for an 8–5 win over the Cubs at Wrigley Field. In the 10th, Norm Schleuter smacked a two-run double and scored on an error. He entered the game as a catcher in the eighth inning.

OCTOBER 9   The White Sox even the series with a 6–1 win over the Cubs at Comiskey Park.

OCTOBER 10   At Comiskey Park, the White Sox win the City Series with a 7–1 victory over the Cubs in the seventh and deciding game.

Over the last 23 innings of the series, the White Sox outscored the Cubs 21–2. The seven games drew 128,818 fans.

DECEMBER 8   On a busy day, the White Sox trade Rip Radcliff to the Browns for Moose Solters, swap Gee Walker to the Senators for Taffy Wright and Pete Appleton, and sell Marv Owen to the Red Sox.

Wright was an outstanding pickup for the White Sox at little cost. He played for the club from 1940 through 1942 and again from 1946 through 1948, with the intervening three seasons spent in the military during World War II. Wright hit .312 for the Sox, which ranks sixth among players with at least 2,000 career plate appearances with the club.

THE STATE OF THE WHITE SOX

The White Sox were 82–72 in 1940 and finished in fourth place, just eight games out of first. It was the Sox's fourth winning season in five years and the closest that the club had come to reaching the World Series since the suspension of the Black Sox in 1920. The Sox gradually declined over the remainder of the 1940s, however, and had losing records in each season from 1944 through 1950. Overall, the club had a record of 707–820 during the decade, a winning percentage of .463 that was the fifth-best in the American League. AL pennant-winners were the Tigers (1940 and 1945), Yankees (1941, 1942, 1943, 1947 and 1949), Browns (1944), Red Sox (1946) and Indians (1948).

THE BEST TEAM

Both the 1940 and 1943 teams were 82–72 and finished in fourth place. The 1940 team finished eight games behind while the 1943 outfit was 16 games from first place.

THE WORST TEAM

The 1948 White Sox thudded into last place with a record of 51–101. The winning percentage of .336 is the worst of any Sox club between 1932 and the present day.

THE BEST MOMENT

Pat Seerey clubbed four home runs in a game against the Athletics in Philadelphia on July 18, 1948.

THE WORST MOMENT

Baseball commissioner Happy Chandler suspended the White Sox from the American League during the 1947–48 off-season when general manager Leslie O'Connor challenged Chandler by breaking an arcane rule over the signing of an amateur pitcher.

THE ALL-DECADE TEAM • YEARS WITH WS

Mike Tresh, c	1938–48
Joe Kuhel, 1b	1928–43, 1946–47
Cass Michaels, 2b	1943–50, 1954
Ralph Hodgin, 3b	1943–44, 1946–48
Luke Appling, ss	1930–43, 1945–50
Guy Curtright, lf	1943–46
Thurman Tucker, cf	1942–44, 1946–47
Taffy Wright, rf	1940–42, 1946–48
Thornton Lee, p	1937–47
Joe Haynes, p	1941–48
Ed Lopat, p	1944–47
Eddie Smith, p	1939–43, 1946–47

Wally Moses (1942–46) was the second-best outfielder to play for the White Sox during the 1940s, but he was a right fielder and ranks behind Wright. Curtwright was essentially a wartime fill-in and reflects the White Sox's problems in left field during the 1940s. No one on the club played 100 games in left in back-to-back years between Gee Walker (1938–39) and Minnie Minoso (1952–58). Other top players with the Sox during the 1940s were pitchers Johnny Humphries (1941–45), Orval Grove (1940–49) and Ted Lyons (1923–42, 1946) and second baseman Don Kolloway (1940–43, 1946–49).

THE DECADE LEADERS

Batting Avg:	Taffy Wright	.312
On-Base Pct:	Luke Appling	.402
Slugging Pct:	Taffy Wright	.415
Home Runs:	Joe Kuhel	52
RBIs:	Luke Appling	488
Runs:	Luke Appling	613
Stolen Bases:	Wally Moses	106
Wins:	Thornton Lee	64
Strikeouts:	Thornton Lee	474
ERA:	Thornton Lee	3.10
Saves:	Gordon Maltzberger	33

THE HOME FIELD

There were no significant additions or alterations made during the 1940s to Comiskey Park, which was in its fourth decade of use.

THE GAME YOU WISH YOU HAD SEEN

It was Ted Lyons Day at Comiskey Park on September 15, 1940. Lyons pitched a three-hitter against the Red Sox in the first game of a double-header and Joe Kuhel hit a walk-off homer in the 10th inning of the nightcap. The wins put the White Sox four games out of first, the closest the club came to the top of the American League during the month of September between 1920 and 1955.

THE WAY THE GAME WAS PLAYED

There were two significant developments during the 1940s. The first was World War II, which involved the United States from 1941 through 1945 and depleted major league rosters, as many players donned military uniforms and saw combat. The second was integration, with the arrival of Jackie Robinson in 1947. The White Sox integrated in 1951 by adding Minnie Minoso to the roster. League stats and averages in 1949 looked very similar to those of 1940, although offense dipped during the war years and there was a surge of home runs at the end of the decade.

THE MANAGEMENT

The Comiskey family owned the White Sox, as they had since 1900, but direction at the top was somewhat of a muddle. Lou Comiskey, son of founder Charles Comiskey, died in 1939. He left the club to his wife, Grace, and three children. It was Lou's dying wish that his son Chuck eventually run the club, but Chuck was only 14 years old in 1940. Grace was club president during the decade, with Chuck taking his increasing role in running the club. Although they often spent their money unwisely, Charles and Lou Comiskey had always been willing to allocate funds to build a winner. Grace, on the other hand, was frugal and the club atrophied during the 1940s, fielding rosters largely of retreads, castoffs and reclamation projects. She drove away general manager Harry Grabiner, who had been employed by the organization since 1905. Grabiner resigned in 1945. He was replaced Leslie O'Connor, who was general manager from 1945 through 1948, and the club continued to decline under O'Connor's

leadership. Frank Lane, who ran the front office from 1948 until 1955, revived the franchise by making brilliant trades and by rebuilding the farm system. Field managers were Jimme Dykes (1934–46), Ted Lyons (1946–48) and Jack Onslow (1949–50).

THE BEST PLAYER MOVE

The best player moves during the 1940s had no effect on White Sox fortunes during that decade, but they set the tone for the success the franchise enjoyed during the 1950s and early 1960s. Billy Pierce came from the Tigers in November 1948 for Aaron Robinson and $10,000. Nellie Fox was acquired from the Athletics in exchange for Joe Tipton in October 1949. They were both engineered by Frank Lane within a year after he became general manager of the Sox and are arguably the two greatest trades in club history.

THE WORST PLAYER MOVE

The White Sox made a horrible deal by trading Ed Lopat to the Yankees in February 1948 for Aaron Robinson, Bill Wight and Fred Bradley, although Robinson was used nine months later as trade bait to bring Billy Pierce to Chicago.

1940s

1940   Sox

Season in a Sentence

In last place in late May, the White Sox roar into pennant contention in September, only to finish in fourth place, eight games behind the Tigers.

Finish • Won • Lost • Pct • GB

Fourth 82 72 .532 8.0
(tie)

Manager

Jimmie Dykes

Stats   WS • AL • Rank

	WS	AL	Rank
Batting Avg:	.278	.271	3
On-Base Pct:	.340	.342	4
Slugging Pct:	.387	.401	6
Home Runs:	73		7
Stolen Bases:	52		6
ERA:	3.74	4.38	2
Fielding Avg:	.969	.970	5
Runs Scored:	735		5
Runs Allowed:	672		3

Starting Lineup

Mike Tresh, c
Joe Kuhel, 1b
Skeeter Webb, 2b
Bob Kennedy, 3b
Luke Appling, ss
Moose Solters, lf
Mike Kreevich, cf
Taffy Wright, rf
Larry Rosenthal, lf
Eric McNair, 2b

Pitchers

Johnny Rigney, sp
Eddie Smith, sp
Thornton Lee, sp
Ted Lyons, sp
Jack Knott, sp
Bill Dietrich, sp

Attendance

660.366 (fifth in AL)

Club Leaders

Batting Avg:	Luke Appling	.348
On-Base Pct:	Luke Appling	.420
Slugging Pct:	Joe Kuhel	.488
Home Runs:	Joe Kuhel	27
RBIs:	Joe Kuhel	94
Runs:	Joe Kuhel	111
Stolen Bases:	Mike Kreevich	15
Wins:	Johnny Rigney	14
	Eddie Smith	14
Strikeouts:	Johnny Rigney	141
ERA:	Johnny Rigney	3.11
Saves:	Clint Brown	10

FEBRUARY 29 Probate judge John F. O'Connell clears the way for Grace Comiskey, the widow of Louis Comiskey, to retain the White Sox. She had been engaged in a legal battle with the First National Bank of Chicago over the estate of her late husband, who died on July 18, 1939.

The bank had been a partner in White Sox affairs since 1900 and continued on as executor of Louis's will. In January 1940, bank trustee John Gleason made known his intention to solicit outside bids after revealing that the ball club had lost $675,029 during the previous 11 years. Operating the White Sox, he argued, was a "hazardous enterprise." To counteract the move, Grace Comiskey went to court, claiming that the trustee's sole function was to preserve the estate, not dissolve it. She won the case and was formally elected team president on March 4, 1941, the third Comiskey in the position. Grace did little to improve the ball club under her leadership, however. Older players were kept on the roster until their trading value dwindled to almost nothing. Almost no money was put into the farm system, especially during World War II, when signing young ball players was a risky business because of their susceptibility to the military draft and the risk of serious injury and death in combat. Once the war ended in 1945, the Sox were far behind other clubs, as Mrs. Comiskey's conservative fiscal policies and lack of vision doomed the club to a succession of losing clubs.

APRIL 6   Second baseman Jackie Hayes is hospitalized with an eye infection.

Hayes had complained of vision problems throughout spring training in 1940, his 14th season in the big leagues. He thought a speck of coal dust might have lodged in his eye, causing inflammation. Team doctors advised Hayes that it was probably just a minor infection that would most likely clear up in a few days. When the problem failed to improve, physicians determined that it was a cataract. By July, he had completely lost his vision in one eye but gamely insisted on playing. He appeared in 18 games late in the season and hit .195 in 41 at-bats. To protect against injury because of his difficulty following the flight of the ball, the White Sox demanded that Hayes wear a batting helmet. He was the first Sox player in history to use the protective device (batting helmets didn't become commonplace until the late 1950s). By 1942, Hayes was completely blind in both eyes, a condition that remained until his death in 1983.

APRIL 16   In the opening game of the season, the White Sox are the victims of a no-hitter by Bob Feller and a 1–0 Indians win before 14,000 on a bitterly cold day at Comiskey Park in which the temperature was 47 degrees. Eddie Smith was the hard-luck losing pitcher. With two out in the ninth inning, Luke Appling fouled off four straight pitches before drawing a walk. Taffy Wright hit a sharp grounder to the right side, but second baseman Ray Mack darted to his left, knocked the ball down and made a throw to first baseman Hal Trosky that beat Wright by an eyelash.

In the second inning, Cleveland center field Roy Weatherly got his glove on a drive by Wright that was ruled an error. At the time, official scoring decisions were not made available to the crowd at Comiskey Park, nor were the total number of hits by each club posted on the scoreboard. Fans were in the dark as to whether or not Feller had a no-hitter in progress until an announcement was made over the public address system in the sixth inning.

APRIL 22   White Sox pitcher Vallie Eaves walks 12 batters in $7^2/_3$ innings during a 6–5 loss to the Tigers at Comiskey Park.

APRIL 26   The White Sox score seven runs in the seventh inning of an 11–1 trouncing of the Indians in Cleveland.

MAY 11   The White Sox defeat the Tigers 1–0 in Detroit in a contest in which opposing pitchers Jack Knott and Tommy Bridges both hurled two-hitters. The Sox collected their hits in the third inning. Mike Tresh singled, moved to second on an error and crossed the plate on a single from Bob Kennedy. The only Detroit hits were singles by Bruce Campbell in the sixth inning and Dick Bartell in the ninth.

Kennedy was a native of Chicago and a 19 years old when he made his big league debut in 1939. The night before he signed his first professional contract in 1937, Kennedy worked as a popcorn vendor at Comiskey Park during the Louis-Braddock fight. He played for the White Sox from 1939 through 1942, 1946 through 1948 and 1955 through 1957. Kennedy served with the Marines for three years during World War II and another year during the Korean War. He was later manager of the Cubs from 1963 through 1965 and general manager from 1977 until 1981.

MAY 20
The White Sox win at Comiskey Park for the first time in 1940 with a 5–4 decision over the Senators. The Sox lost their first nine games at home.

The White Sox had a 9–16 record and were in last place entering the May 20 game.

MAY 21
Joe Kuhel collects five hits, including two doubles and a homer, in five at-bats during a 9–8 win over the Senators at Comiskey Park.

MAY 23
Trailing 4–3, the White Sox explode for 10 runs in the eighth inning and win 13–4 over the Athletics at Comiskey Park.

JUNE 3
Skeeter Webb collects five hits, including a double and a homer, in six at-bats during a 7–4 win over the Red Sox in Boston.

A solid hitter during his six years with the White Sox, Joe Kuhel slammed 27 homers in 1940, a career high.

JUNE 11
Two weeks after the surrender of Holland and Belgium to Germany, and five days following the evacuation of 350,000 British troops at Dunkirk, a two-run, pinch-hit homer by Moose Solters in the ninth inning defeats the Athletics 5–4 in Philadelphia.

JUNE 19
The White Sox win 1–0 over the Yankees at Comiskey Park. Thornton Lee pitched the shutout. Luke Appling drove in the lone run of the game with a single in the eighth inning.

JUNE 20
The White Sox defeat the Yankees 1–0 at Comiskey Park, this time in 11 innings. Johnny Rigney pitched a complete game. Bob Kennedy drove in the winning run with a walk-off double.

Due to a protest made by the Yankees, AL President Will Harridge ordered on July 1 that the entire game be replayed, cruelly wiping out the White Sox victory. In the second inning, Bill Dickey of the Yanks hit a foul fly to left fielder Moose Solters, whose cap fell as he caught the ball. Trying to catch his cap, Solters dropped the ball. Umpire John Quinn ruled that Solters dropped it in the act of throwing, but Harridge stated that "this decision is not borne out by the three other officials, who claim no throw was attempted. Quinn's decision was plainly a violation of the playing rule and the major leagues' interpretation." The game was replayed on September 18. On that date, the Sox played a double-header against the Yankees, winning the first 6–3 and losing the second, called after eight innings by darkness, 9–8 in a contest that ended in controversy (see September 18, 1940).

JULY 2   Ten days after France surrenders to Germany, the White Sox and Tigers combine to score in 14 different turns at bat during a 10–9 Chicago defeat in Detroit. The Sox scored in every inning but the first and eighth. The Tigers scored in every inning except the second. They did not bat in the ninth. There were five two-run innings and nine one-run innings during the game.

At the conclusion of the game, the White Sox had a record of 28–36 and were in sixth place, 11¹/₂ games out of first. The club was 50–28 over the next 2¹/₂ months (see September 15, 1940).

JULY 3   The White Sox score seven runs in the ninth to take a 12–3 lead, then withstand a four-run Tiger uprising in the bottom half of the inning to win 12–7 in Detroit.

JULY 9   Luke Appling collects a double and a single in three at-bats in the All-Star Game at Sportsman's Park in St. Louis. The American League garnered only one other base hit, however, in a 4–0 loss.

JULY 13   The White Sox blank the Red Sox in both ends of a double-header in Boston, winning 5–0 and 7–0. Ted Lyons won the opener. In the second tilt, Jack Knott pitched a two-hitter. The only Boston hits were singles by Tom Carey and Jimmie Foxx.

Beginning in 1939, Lyons pitched only on Sundays. It was an enormously successful strategy, both at the box office and in helping Lyons to extend his career. At the age of 39, he was 12–8 in 1940, led the AL in shutouts with four, posted an ERA of 3.24 and completed 17 of his 22 starts.

JULY 17   Third baseman Eric McNair makes four errors during a 5–2 loss to the Senators at Washington.

JULY 20   The White Sox defeat the Athletics 19–7 in Philadelphia. The Sox scored all of their runs in three different innings, with eight in the first, seven in the fifth and four in the ninth.

JULY 24   The White Sox score six runs in the first inning and bang out 20 hits during a 12–10 win over the Red Sox at Comiskey Park on a day in which the temperature in Chicago reaches 102 degrees.

On July 21, Ted Williams created controversy by telling a Cleveland writer that he would rather be a fireman than a baseball player. During the series between the White Sox and Red Sox at Comiskey Park from July 23 through 25, Jimmie Dykes tormented Williams by supplying his club with bells, sirens and fire hats.

JULY 27   Moose Solters homers in the 12th inning to defeat the Yankees 6–5 at Comiskey Park. Solters was hitless in his first five at-bats. The White Sox scored a run in the first inning thanks to two errors on one play by Joe DiMaggio in the first inning. With two out, Joe Kuhel lifted a fly ball to DiMaggio, who dropped it as he started to run off the field. DiMaggio picked up the ball and fired it to third base, but no one was at the bag because his teammates had headed for the dugout believing the third out was made. Kuhel circled the bases on the play to tie the score 1–1.

Kuhel had a career year in 1940. He hit .280 with 27 homers, 94 RBIs and 111 runs scored. The 27 homers tied a club record set by Zeke Bonura in 1934. It remained the Sox record until Gus Zernial clubbed 29 home runs in 1950.

JULY 28   Charlie Keller collects three homers for the Yankees during a 10–9 win over the Yankees in the first game of a double-header at Comiskey Park. The Sox won the second game 8–4.

AUGUST 2   Thornton Lee pitches a two-hitter to defeat the Senators 10–2 at Comiskey Park. The only Washington hits were a single by Buddy Myer in the first inning and a homer from Jimmy Bloodworth in the ninth.

AUGUST 6   Thornton Lee pitches a two-hitter in his second consecutive start, beating the Indians 5–1 in the first game of a double-header in Cleveland. The only hits off Lee were singles by Lou Boudreau and Roy Weatherly. The Sox lost the nightcap 3–2.

AUGUST 16   The White Sox score nine runs in the eighth inning and defeat the Tigers 13–4 in Detroit.

AUGUST 18   Ted Lyons collects four hits in five at-bats and pitches a complete game to defeat the Tigers 7–5 in Detroit. The Sox scored three runs in the ninth inning for the win.

AUGUST 25   In the first of a double-header before 70,740 at Yankee Stadium, Ted Lyons outduels Red Ruffing for a 1–0 White Sox win. The lone run of the contest scored on a double by Taffy Wright in the ninth inning. The Yankees won the second tilt 3–1.

SEPTEMBER 2   Johnny Rigney pitches a two-hitter to defeat the Tigers 4–0 in the second game of a double-header at Comiskey Park. The only Detroit hits were a single by Barney McCosky and a double from Charlie Gehringer. The Sox also won the opener 2–1.

The White Sox entered the day with a record of 63–61 in fourth place, 11½ games behind.

SEPTEMBER 3   The White Sox score seven runs in the first inning and defeat the Tigers 10–2 at Comiskey Park.

The White Sox were 13–9 against the pennant-winning Tigers in 1940.

SEPTEMBER 12   The White Sox sweep the Athletics 1–0 and 4–3 during a double-header at Comiskey Park. In the opener, Bill Dietrich pitched the shutout. The second tilt ended on a two-run, pinch-hit homer in the ninth inning by Ken Silvestri.

SEPTEMBER 15   On Ted Lyons Day at Comiskey Park, the White Sox extend their winning streak to eight games with a 5–1 and 4–2 sweep of the Red Sox. Before the games, Lyons received cash and gifts worth $4,500, then pitched a three-hitter in the opener. The second contest went 10 innings and ended on a two-run homer by Joe Kuhel.

The wins gave the White Sox a record of 78–64 and placed the club just four games out of first place. The Sox lost eight of the remaining 12 contests left on the schedule, however.

SEPTEMBER 18   After winning the first game of a double-header 6–3 against the Yankees at Comiskey Park, the White Sox drop the second 9–8 when umpire Harry Geisel creates a firestorm by calling the contest because of darkness after eight innings. Chicago nursed an 8–7 lead into the eighth inning before the Yankees pushed across two runs to take a one-run advantage. After the Sox failed to score in their half, Geisel motioned to the dugouts signaling his intention to call the game because of darkness. Jimmie Dykes was livid and screamed hysterically at Geisel. Almanacs were produced to demonstrate to Geisel that sunset would occur at 6:54 p.m., 47 minutes after the umpire ended the contest, but he remained firm in his decision.

Lights had been installed at Comiskey Park the previous season, but an American League rule prevented them from being turned on to finish day games. The rule was in place until 1951.

SEPTEMBER 22   The White Sox drub the Browns 10–0 in St. Louis.

SEPTEMBER 29   On the final day of the season, the White Sox lose 2–1 to the Browns at Comiskey Park. Luke Appling collected two hits in four at-bats but fell just shy of winning the batting title.

Appling batted .348 in 1940, finishing second to Joe DiMaggio, who hit .352.

OCTOBER 1   The White Sox open the Chicago City Series with a 5–3 win over the Cubs at Wrigley Field. The Sox went on to win the series, four games to two.

DECEMBER 18   Six weeks after Franklin Roosevelt defeats Wendell Willkie in the Presidential election and 10 days after the Bears annihilate the Washington Redskins 73–0 in the NFL championship game, the White Sox sell Eric McNair to the Tigers.

1941

Season in a Sentence

The White Sox finish last in almost every major offensive category, post the lowest earned run average in the American League, hold first place on June 1 and end up with a .500 record.

Finish • Won • Lost • Pct • GB

Third   77   77   .500   24.0

Manager

Jimmie Dykes

Stats

Stats	WS	AL	Rank
Batting Avg:	.255	.266	8
On-Base Pct:	.322	.341	8
Slugging Pct:	.343	.389	8
Home Runs:	47		8
Stolen Bases:	91		1
ERA:	3.52	4.18	1
Fielding Avg:	.971	.972	5
Runs Scored:	638		8
Runs Allowed:	649		2

Starting Lineup

Mike Tresh, c
Hal Trosky, 1b
Billy Knickerbocker, 2b
Dario Lodigiani, 3b
Luke Appling, ss
Myril Hoag, lf
Mike Kreevich, cf
Taffy Wright, rf
Don Kolloway, 2b
Bob Kennedy, 3b
Moose Solters, lf
Ben Chapman, cf-lf

Pitchers

Thornton Lee, sp
Eddie Smith, sp
Johnny Rigney, sp
Ted Lyons, sp
Bill Dietrich, sp
Buck Ross, sp-rp

Attendance

677,077 (fifth in AL)

Club Leaders

Batting Avg:	Taffy Wright	.322
On-Base Pct:	Taffy Wright	.399
	Luke Appling	.399
Slugging Pct:	Taffy Wright	.468
Home Runs:	Joe Kuhel	12
RBIs:	Taffy Wright	97
Runs:	Luke Appling	93
Stolen Bases:	Joe Kuhel	20
Wins:	Thornton Lee	22
Strikeouts:	Thornton Lee	130
ERA:	Thornton Lee	2.37
Saves:	Four tied with	1

JANUARY 4   The White Sox purchase Joe Haynes from the Senators.

At the time he was purchased by the White Sox, Haynes was 23 years old with a 9–18 record and a history of arm problems. He gave the White Sox eight effective seasons as a reliever and a spot starter. Haynes led the AL in games pitched in 1942 and in earned run average in 1947.

FEBRUARY 7   The White Sox trade Clint Brown to the Indians for Johnny Humphries.

APRIL 15   The White Sox win the season opener 4–3 over the Indians in Cleveland. Bill Dietrich was the winning pitcher. Bob Feller, who no-hit the Sox on Opening Day in 1940, took the defeat. Third baseman Dario Lodigiani, in his first game for Chicago, collected three hits.

Lodigiani played second base at Lowell Junior High School in San Francisco, where his double play partner was Joe DiMaggio, who then played shortstop.

APRIL 18   In the home opener, 40-year-old Ted Lyons is the winning pitcher in a 6–3 decision over the Browns before 6,406 at Comiskey Park.

APRIL 22   Bill Dietrich is two outs from a no-hitter before being forced to settle for a two-hit, 6–3 victory over the Tigers in Detroit. With one out in the ninth inning, Luke Appling put a runner on base with an error, Hank Greenberg singled and Rudy York homered.

MAY 10   Lord Halifax, the British ambassador to the United States, attends a 4–3 White Sox win over the Tigers at Comiskey Park.

MAY 15   The White Sox humiliate the Yankees 13–1 in New York. Eddie Smith pitched a complete game for the Sox. He allowed a single in four at-bats to Joe DiMaggio. At the moment, it appeared like an insignificant hit during a one-sided loss, but the single started DiMaggio on his record-breaking 56-game hitting streak.

MAY 20   Taffy Wright drives in a run for the 13th game in a row to set an American League record (since tied) during a 5–2 win over the Senators in Washington.

Wright drove in 22 runs during his 13-game streak from May 4 through May 20. He drove in 88 runs and batted .337 in 147 games in 1940. Wright's record was tied by Mike Sweeney of the Royals in 1999. The major league mark for RBIs in consecutive games is 17 by Ray Grimes of the Cubs in 1922.

MAY 24   Eddie Smith throws a wild pitch with two out in the ninth inning while facing opposing pitcher Johnny Gorsica, scoring Rudy York from third base for the only run of a 1–0 loss to the Tigers in Detroit.

MAY 27   Luke Appling hits his first home run since August 1937 during a 5–2 loss to the Browns at Comiskey Park.

The home run was the only one that Appling hit in 1941. He batted .314 that season.

MAY 29   Bill Dietrich pitches a one-hitter to defeat the Browns 4–0 at Comiskey Park. The only St. Louis hit was a single by Chet Laabs in the fourth inning.

On the same day, the White Sox signed Ben Chapman as a free agent following his release by the Senators.

JUNE 1   The White Sox split a double-header against the Senators at Comiskey Park, but they take first place when the Indians lose twice to the Yankees. The Sox lost the first game 3–2 and won the second 4–3 in 11 innings.

The White Sox had a record of 26–17 at the conclusion of play on June 1. The club bottomed out in late July at 47–52, then won 18 of the next 21 games to take second place. Chicago lost 22 of their final 34 games to finish at .500 and in third place. Only two of the eight clubs in the American League (the Yankees and Red Sox) had winning records in 1941.

JUNE 22   On the day that Germany invades the Soviet Union, the White Sox score seven runs in the third inning to take a 10–0 lead and lambaste the Athletics 14–0 in the first game of a double-header at Shibe Park. Chicago bats went silent in the second tilt, as Philadelphia won 3–0.

JUNE 25   Johnny Rigney pitches a 13-inning complete-game shutout, allowing six hits to defeat the Senators 3–0 in Washington. The Sox collected only three hits against Sid Hudson through the first 12 innings. In the 13th, Mike Kreevich singled and Joe Kuhel doubled Kreevich to third. Taffy Wright was intentionally walked and Luke Appling drew another base on balls to force in the first run of the game. The second scored on a triple steal, with Kuhel swiping home.

JUNE 26   Eddie Smith pitches a 16-inning complete game but loses 3–2 to the Senators in Washington. The winning run scored on a bases-loaded single by Jimmy Bloodworth.

JUNE 28   Don Kolloway hits two homers and steals four bases during a 6–4 win over the Indians in Cleveland. He came into the game with a .163 batting average, and the home runs were the first two of Kolloway's major league career. He homered in the fifth and eighth innings. In the ninth, Kolloway reached base on a force out, then stole second, third and home.

> *A native of the south-Chicago suburb of Blue Island, Kolloway played for the Sox from 1940 through 1943 and again from 1946 through 1949. During the two-year gap, Kolloway served in the Army during World War II. In 1942, he led the AL in doubles with 40.*

JUNE 29   The White Sox score eight runs in the sixth inning and defeat the Indians 9–3 in Cleveland. All eight runs scored after the first two batters were retired, as 10 consecutive Sox hitters reached base. Dario Lodigiani, Luke Appling, Taffy Wright and Moose Solters all singled. Ben Chapman walked and Mike Tresh singled. Ted Lyons, Don Kolloway and Joe Kuhel walked on 12 straight balls thrown by Cleveland hurlers Mel Harder and Harry Eisenstat. Lodigiani hit a single before Appling ended the inning by flying out.

JULY 6   Jimmie Dykes is suspended indefinitely by AL president Will Harridge for arguing too vociferously with the umpires during a 5–3 loss against the Indians at Comiskey Park the previous day.

> *Dykes was banished in the ninth inning of the July 5 game after a prolonged protest in which he maintained that players in the Cleveland bullpen had interfered with right fielder Taffy Wright's opportunity to catch a long foul ball. The suspension was levied in large part because of Dykes's long-standing problems with the AL umpiring crew. In a strongly worded message informing the Sox manager of his suspension, Harridge wrote that Dykes's "tactics in delaying our games, attempting to bulldoze and browbeat the umpires while filing protests, which have no basis in fact or justification in the rules, have become very offensive, not only to the spectators in other cities throughout the circuit, but to our entire organization." The suspension was lifted a week later.*

JULY 18   The White Sox prevent Lefty Grove from winning his 300th career game by defeating the Red Sox 4–3 in 10 innings at Comiskey Park.

JULY 23   In Boston, Jimmie Dykes tries a shift against Ted Williams, deploying the shortstop to the right side of second, moving the third baseman into the vacant hole at short, and swinging the entire outfield around to the right so that the left fielder stood just to the left of center. Williams foiled the strategy by poking a double into left field.

The White Sox won 10–4. Dykes didn't try the shift again, nor did any other AL manager until Lou Boudreau of the Indians used it in 1946.

JULY 29   Eddie Smith pitches a shutout and fights Al Simmons during a 1–0 victory over the Athletics in Philadelphia. Luke Appling's triple in the fourth inning drove in the lone run of the game. Simmons, who pinch-hit in the ninth, lined out to center field to end the game. He and Smith came to blows on the first-base line as both were returning to their respective dugouts. Jimmy Dykes rushed into the fray and pulled the combatants apart. Simmons, who had been coaching at third base until called upon as a pinch-hitter, spent the better part of the afternoon taunting Smith and was warned by the umpires to cease.

AUGUST 2   Moose Solters is struck on the head during fielding practice prior to a 3–1 win over the Senators in Washington.

After examination by physicians, the injury wasn't immediately considered to be serious, but by the end of the month Solters began suffer from debilitating headaches. Further tests revealed a fractured skull. Solters's eyesight slowly deteriorated, and he eventually became totally blind.

AUGUST 7   The White Sox trounce the Browns 11–1 in St. Louis.

AUGUST 8   Taffy Wright drives in six runs on two homers and a double during a 16–2 win over the Browns in St. Louis. The White Sox outscored the Browns 27–3 in consecutive games.

AUGUST 9   Taffy Wright homers off Bob Feller in the 10th to break a 5–5 tie against the Indians in Cleveland. The White Sox added an insurance run later in the inning for a 7–5 victory.

AUGUST 11 A fight marks a 14–9 White Sox win over the Browns during the first game of a double-header at Comiskey Park. The Sox broke an 8–8 tie with six runs in the eighth inning. Fisticuffs flared after Joe Kuhel was struck on the shoulder by one of Eldon Auker's pitches in the seventh. The two exchanged remarks as Kuhel walked to first base and Auker charged over as Kuhel neared the bag. Kuhel met Auker with a swing to the face, the first of a dozen blows that were exchanged before Sox coach Mule Haas and pitcher Eddie Smith pulled Auker to one side. Meantime, Alan Strange of the Browns rushed from the dugout and joined in the altercation. Strange was wrestled to the ground by Jimmie Dykes. Kuhel, Auker and Strange were each ejected. St. Louis won the second tilt 10–3.

AUGUST 14 Johnny Humphries defeats the Tigers 3–0 at Comiskey Park.

AUGUST 16 Johnny Rigney pitches the White Sox to a 1–0 win over the Indians in Cleveland. Taffy Wright drove in the winning run with a single in the first inning.

AUGUST 19 The White Sox sweep a double-header against the Athletics at Comiskey Park with a pair of shutouts. Thornton Lee won the opener 4–0, and Johnny Humphries took the nightcap 1–0.

AUGUST 20   The White Sox record their third consecutive shutout over the Athletics at Comiskey Park as Johnny Rigney wins a 9–0 decision. It was Rigney's second consecutive three-hit shutout. The victory also extended Chicago's winning streak to nine games.

During the fall of 1941, Rigney married Dorothy Comiskey, the daughter of club owner Grace Comiskey. Rigney was one of two White Sox players to marry the offspring of a major league club executive during the 1941–42 off-season. Joe Haynes wedded Thelma Griffith, the adopted daughter of Senators owner Clark Griffith. They met while Haynes played for the Washington club.

AUGUST 23   Johnny Humphries pitches his third consecutive shutout, defeating the Red Sox 3–0 at Comiskey Park.

Humphries was in his fourth season in the majors and first with the White Sox in 1941. He was used mainly as a reliever until being placed in the starting rotation in August. The three consecutive shutouts came in his second, third and fourth starts of the season and were the first three shutouts of his career. Humphries pitched 35 straight scoreless innings from July 19 through August 30. He was 4–2 in 1941, with all four wins coming on shutouts.

SEPTEMBER 20   Thornton Lee wins his 20th game of 1941 with a 4–3 decision over the Tigers at Comiskey Park. The White Sox trailed 3–0 before scoring two runs in the eighth

Thorton Lee pitched 11 years for the Sox, enjoying a career year in 1941, leading the league in ERA and posting 22 victories.

inning and twice more in the ninth. The tying and winning runs scored on a bases-loaded walk-off single by Don Kolloway.

A 23-year-old outfielder named Stan Goletz made his big-league debut with the White Sox in 1941 and collected three hits in five at-bats, all as a pinch-hitter. He went into the military service before the start of the 1942 season and never returned to the majors, finishing his brief career with a batting average of .600.

SEPTEMBER 24   Thornton Lee pitches a two-hitter to defeat the Indians 2–1 at Comiskey Park. The only Cleveland hits were a homer by Ken Keltner in the fourth inning and a double from Gee Walker in the seventh.

Lee had a career year in 1941, a season in which he turned 35 years old in September. He had a record of 22–11, pitched 300¹/₃ innings and led the league in earned run average (2.37) and complete games (30 in 34 starts). The heavy workload damaged his arm, however. In 1942, Lee didn't appear in a regular season game until July and finished the season pitching only 76 innings with a 2–6 record. Although his career lasted through 1948, Lee was never nearly as effective as he was in 1941.

SEPTEMBER 27   The White Sox score eight runs in the fourth inning and beat the Tigers 10–6 in Detroit.

OCTOBER 4   In the first game of the Chicago City Series, the White Sox score four runs in the ninth inning to defeat the Cubs 4–1 at Wrigley Field.

OCTOBER 7   The White Sox complete a four-game sweep of the Cubs in the City Series with a 3–1 win at Comiskey Park.

DECEMBER 7   The Japanese attack Pearl Harbor in Honolulu with an early morning air raid. A day later, the United States declared war on Japan, signaling the involvement of the U.S. militarily in World War II. On December 11, the U.S. declared war on Germany (see January 15, 1942).

DECEMBER 9   The White Sox trade Mike Kreevich and Jack Hallett to the Athletics for Wally Moses.

Moses was a .319 career hitter when acquired by the White Sox and had never hit below .300 in his seven seasons in the majors. He was 31 years old, however, and was in the decline phase of his career. Moses served as the White Sox starting right fielder for four seasons during the war, batting .272. He led the AL in triples in 1943 and doubles in 1945. He also stole 56 bases in 1943 to set a White Sox franchise record that wasn't surpassed until Rudy Law swiped 77 in 1983.

1942

Season in a Sentence

The White Sox lose 18 of their first 22 games and finish the season in the sixth place.

Finish • Won • Lost • Pct • GB

Finish	Won	Lost	Pct	GB
Sixth	66	82	.446	34.0

Manager

Jimmie Dykes

Stats

Stats	WS	AL	Rank
Batting Avg:	.246	.257	8
On-Base Pct:	.316	.329	6
Slugging Pct:	.318	.357	8
Home Runs:	25		8
Stolen Bases:	114		1
ERA:	3.58	3.66	4
Fielding Avg:	.970	.971	5
Runs Scored:	538		8
Runs Allowed:	609		4

Starting Lineup

Mike Tresh, c
Joe Kuhel, 1b
Don Kolloway, 2b
Bob Kennedy, 3b
Luke Appling, ss
Taffy Wright, lf
Myril Hoag, cf-lf
Wally Moses, rf
Tom Turner, c
Dario Lodigiani, 3b
Sammy West, cf

Pitchers

Johnny Humphries, sp
Ted Lyons, sp
Eddie Smith, sp
Bill Dietrich, sp
Buck Ross, sp-rp
Jake Wade, sp-rp
Thornton Lee, sp
Joe Haynes, rp

Attendance

425,734 (fifth in AL)

Club Leaders

Batting Avg:	Don Kolloway	.273
On-Base Pct:	Wally Moses	.353
Slugging Pct:	Wally Moses	.369
Home Runs:	Wally Moses	7
RBIs:	Don Kolloway	60
Runs:	Luke Appling	78
Stolen Bases:	Joe Kuhel	22
Wins:	Ted Lyons	14
Strikeouts:	Eddie Smith	78
ERA:	Ted Lyons	2.10
Saves:	Joe Haynes	6

JANUARY 15   Three weeks after the Bears win the NFL championship by defeating the Washington Redskins 14–6, President Franklin Roosevelt gives baseball commissioner Kenesaw Landis the go-ahead to play ball despite the nation's involvement in World War II. In his statement, Roosevelt said that he believed the continuation of the sport would be beneficial to the country's morale.

The military draft and enlistments began to have an impact on the White Sox during the 1942 season. At the start of spring training, outfield prospects Dave Short and Stan Goletz were in the service. Before the end of the season, the Sox lost starting pitcher Johnny Rigney and third baseman Bob Kennedy to the Navy. Others who donned military uniforms before the close of the 1942 baseball campaign were catcher George Dickey, outfielder Van Helm and first baseman Jake Jones.

MARCH 18   Two African-American players work out for the White Sox during spring training in Pasadena, California. One was future Hall of Famer Jackie Robinson, who was a native of Pasadena and broke Major League Baseball's color barrier with the Dodgers in 1947. The other was Nate Moreland. "He's worth $50,000 of anybody's money," Jimmie Dykes said of Robinson, but no attempt was made to sign Robinson by club management.

APRIL 3   The White Sox sell Billy Knickerbocker to the Athletics.

APRIL 14   In the season opener, the White Sox drop a 3–0 decision to the Browns before 9,879 at Comiskey Park. Bob Muncrief pitched a three-hit shutout for St. Louis. Johnny Rigney was the losing pitcher.

The game was played five days after the fall of Bataan, one of the many shocking military defeats suffered at the hands of Japan early in 1942. Four days after the opener, Major General James Doolittle staged a daring air raid on Tokyo.

APRIL 17   The White Sox edge the Indians 1–0 in Cleveland's home opener. Ted Lyons pitched the shutout. The lone run of the game scored on a double by Myril Hoag and a single from Dario Lodigiani.

APRIL 26   After Jimmie Dykes makes a series of changes to the lineup just prior to game time, the White Sox bat out of turn during the first two innings before discovering the gaffe during a 3–2 loss to the Indians at Comiskey Park. Rookie Harry Sketchley failed to bat in his turn in the second inning, but without penalty because the Sox called the mix-up to the attention of umpire Steve Basil. Batting in the correct order, Chicago scored twice in the third to take a 2–0 lead, but Cleveland rallied to win with three tallies in the eighth.

During the duration of World War II, balls hit into the stands at Comiskey Park were returned by the fans and donated to the recreation departments of the Armed Forces.

MAY 9   Despite being held hitless over the last eight innings of a game against the Browns in St. Louis, the White Sox win 2–1 with both runs and all three hits recorded in the first inning.

MAY 17   Johnny Rigney makes his last appearance before leaving for the Navy and defeats the Senators 4–3 in the second game of a double-header at Comiskey Park. The Sox also won the opener 7–1.

Rigney spent better than three years in the service. He didn't pitch in the majors again until 1946, although he would appear in one more game at Comiskey Park (see July 2, 1942).

MAY 29   Trailing 8–3, the White Sox score four runs in the eighth inning and five in the ninth to win 12–8 over the Browns in St. Louis. Don Kolloway drove in six runs on a double and two singles.

MAY 30   The White Sox score seven runs in the ninth inning to break a 5–5 tie and defeat the Tigers 12–5 in the second game of a double-header in Detroit. The Sox lost the opener 9–8.

MAY 31   The White Sox score five runs in the 10th inning to defeat the Tigers 9–4 in Detroit.

JUNE 7   The day after America's victory over Japan in the Battle of Midway, the Red Sox defeat the White Sox with two 3–2 decisions during a double-header at Fenway Park. The second game ended just after the ejection of Jimmie Dykes. A Massachusetts law stipulated that games on Sunday must end precisely at 6:30 p.m. With that time fast approaching and the score 2–2 in the eighth inning, Jimmie Dykes tried to prolong the game as long as possible. If the eighth didn't end before 6:30, the entire inning would be wiped out and the game would have gone into the books as a seven-inning 2–2 tie. With the crowd in an uproar, Dykes changed pitchers three times and was prevented from making a fourth only because the umpires threatened a forfeit. The Red Sox drove in the winning run seconds before the clocks in Boston struck 6:30.

Dykes was fined $250 by AL President Will Harridge for the stalling tactics.

JUNE 9   Eddie Smith pitches a two-hitter but loses 2–0 to the Athletics in Philadelphia.

The June 9 defeat dropped Smith's record to 0–10. He was 3–19 in August before winning four of his last five decisions to finish at 7–20. Despite the won-lost record, Smith was the White Sox's lone representative on the 1942 American League All-Star team.

JUNE 19   The Red Sox defeat the White Sox 1–0 at Comiskey Park on a freak inside-the-park homer by Dom DiMaggio. In the fifth inning, DiMaggio hit a ball into right field that rolled under the bench in the Boston bullpen. By the time Chicago right fielder Wally Moses retrieved the ball, DiMaggio had circled the bases.

The 1942 season was one of the few that the entire team nickname appeared on the uniforms. At home, "White Sox" was written in script in red outlined in blue. The design lasted only one season, however.

JUNE 21   Ted Lyons records his 250th career victory with a 6–5 decision over the Red Sox in the first game of a double-header at Comiskey Park. Boston won the second tilt 7–0.

Pitching exclusively on Sundays, Lyons started 20 games in 1942 and completed every one of them. He was 14–6 and his 2.10 ERA led the American League. After the season ended, he enlisted in the Marines and missed three seasons. Lyons pitched only five games in 1946 before retiring as an active player.

JUNE 24   Tom Turner hits a grand slam off Early Wynn in the eighth inning of a 6–0 win over the Senators at Comiskey Park. It was also Turner's first major league home run.

JUNE 28   The White Sox sweep the Yankees 6–2 and 13–1 at Comiskey Park.

JULY 2   All of the gate receipts from a White Sox-Indians game at Comiskey Park go to the Army-Navy Relief Fund. A total of 29,062 fans paid their way into the game, earning the fund $33,352. The Indians won the game 7–5. The contest was preceded by a game between a team from the Great Lakes Naval Training Station and another from Chanute Field, two military bases located in Illinois. Great Lakes, managed by Mickey Cochrane, won 7–1. Johnny Rigney pitched six innings for Great Lakes and allowed no runs and one hit in six innings.

JULY 5   The White Sox trounce the Browns 14–2 in the first game of a double-header at Comiskey Park, only to be walloped 13–2 by St. Louis in the second encounter.

JULY 26   Sixteen-year-old heir-to-the-throne Chuck Comiskey gets thrown out of a game during a double-header against the Athletics. The Sox won the opener 2–1 and lost the nightcap 3–2 in 10 innings. The row started in the first game when Don Kolloway swung at a pitch that resulted in a tap in front of the plate. Umpire John Quinn ruled that the Sox second baseman had run into the ball in fair territory. Jimmie Dykes roared out of the dugout, closely followed by Comiskey, who was sitting on the bench in uniform. Both were ejected. A few days later, AL President Will Harridge barred Comiskey from sitting in the dugout in the future. For the second year in a row, Harridge also reprimanded Dykes for conduct unbecoming a big-league manager. This time a written apology was demanded from the Sox manager.

JULY 29   The White Sox play a twi-night double-header at Comiskey Park for the first time, winning 6–5 in 11 innings and 7–5 in the regulation nine against the Yankees.

AUGUST 3   The White Sox play at Camp Grant (Illinois) against soldiers on the base team and win 9–2.

AUGUST 5   Don Kolloway steals home in the sixth inning for the only run of a 1–0 win over the Tigers at Comiskey Park. The Tigers disputed the call by umpire Bill Summers. Detroit catcher Eddie Parsons, who claimed he tagged Kolloway, was put out of the game as a result of his noisy protest. Thornton Lee pitched the shutout in a duel with Hal Newhouser.

AUGUST 9   The White Sox extend their winning streak to eight games with a 11–1 and 3–2 sweep of the Indians at Comiskey Park.

               Between games, Bob Kennedy was sworn into the Naval Air Corps by Lieutenant Commander Russell Cook. Kennedy won the second game with a walk-off single. He served in the Navy until the end of the war, returning to the White Sox in 1946. Kennedy also served in Korea with the Marine Air Corps during the 1952 season while playing for the Indians. He is one of only two players to have his major league career interrupted by service in both World War II and the Korean War. The other one was Ted Williams.

AUGUST 10   The White Sox run their winning streak to nine games with a 3–1 decision over the Indians at Comiskey Park.

SEPTEMBER 11   Eddie Smith pitches the White Sox to a 1–0 win over the Yankees at Comiskey Park. Don Kolloway drove in George Dickey in the eighth inning for the lone run of the game.

               Dickey was the brother of Bill Dickey, a Hall of Fame catcher with the Yankees. George was the White Sox backup catcher in 1941 and 1942, and after three years in the service during World War II, he returned to the Sox for the 1946 and 1947 seasons.

SEPTEMBER 30   In the Chicago City Series, the White Sox defeat the Cubs 3–0 at Wrigley Field. Ted Lyons pitched the shutout three days after enlisting in the Marines. (He was a captain in the Marine Corps when discharged in 1945.) The Sox went on to win the series, four games to two. The six games drew 45,818.

               This was the last time that the Chicago City Series was played. The Cubs and the White Sox played each other 26 times in the post-season between 1903 and 1942, including the 1906 World Series. The White Sox won 19 of the series and the Cubs six, with another ending in a tie.

1943

Sox

Season in a Sentence

The White Sox lose stars such as Ted Lyons, Johnny Rigney, Taffy Wright and Bob Kennedy to the military, but they improve in the standings and win 82 games.

Finish • Won • Lost • Pct • GB

Fourth   82   72   .532   16.0

Manager

Jimmie Dykes

Stats

Stats	WS	AL	Rank
Batting Avg:	.247	.249	5
On-Base Pct:	.322	.322	5
Slugging Pct:	.320	.341	7
Home Runs:	33		7
Stolen Bases:	173		1
ERA:	3.20	3.30	5
Fielding Avg:	.973	.973	6
Runs Scored:	573		6
Runs Allowed:	594		4

Starting Lineup

Mike Tresh, c
Joe Kuhel, 1b
Don Kolloway, 2b
Ralph Hodgin, 3b-rf-lf
Luke Appling, ss
Guy Curtright, lf
Thurman Tucker, cf
Wally Moses, rf
Skeeter Webb, 2b
Jimmy Grant, 3b
Tom Turner, c
Dick Culler, 3b-2b

Pitchers

Orval Grove, sp
Bill Dietrich, sp
Johnny Humphries, sp
Eddie Smith, sp
Buck Ross, sp
Thornton Lee, sp
Gordon Maltzberger, rp
Joe Haynes, rp

Attendance

508,962 (fourth in AL)

Club Leaders

Batting Avg:	Luke Appling	.328
On-Base Pct:	Luke Appling	.419
Slugging Pct:	Luke Appling	.407
Home Runs:	Joe Kuhel	5
RBIs:	Luke Appling	80
Runs:	Wally Moses	82
Stolen Bases:	Wally Moses	56
Wins:	Orval Grove	15
Strikeouts:	Orval Grove	76
ERA:	Orval Grove	2.75
Saves:	Gordon Maltzberger	14

MARCH 18   Two months after Franklin Roosevelt and Winston Churchill meet in Casablanca, Morocco, to formulate strategy for the war in Europe, the White Sox open their spring training camp in French Lick, Indiana.

During World War II, major league teams had to train north of the Ohio River and east of the Mississippi to save on travel expenses. The White Sox shared the French Lick facility with the Cubs. A diamond was laid out between the practice fairway and the parallel 18th fairway of the golf course adjoining the elegant French Lick Hotel, headquarters for both clubs. When the field was flooded or the weather was too cold, Jimmie Dykes moved the club indoors. Calisthenics were conducted in the ballroom of the hotel to the jumping rhythms of big-band music. The Sox trained at French Lick in 1943, 1944 and 1945, and returned to Pasadena, California, after the war ended.

APRIL 21   The White Sox lose the opener 3–0 to the Browns in St. Louis. Al Hollingsworth pitched the shutout.

Due to a shortage of available materials due to the war, an inferior batch of baseballs manufactured with different specifications was used at the start of the 1943 season. After a series of low-scoring games throughout both major leagues, a more resilient ball was rushed into use.

APRIL 27   In the home opener, the White Sox lose 4–2 to the Indians before 4,177 at Comiskey Park.

Several White Sox players entered military service between the 1942 and 1943 seasons, including Myril Hoag, Dario Lodigiani, Ted Lyons, Len Perme, Dave Philley, Roy Schalk, Ed Weiland, Leo Wells, Sammy West and Taffy Wright. During the 1943 campaign, Frank Kalin joined the service.

MAY 7   Johnny Humphries pitches a 10-inning shutout and scores the winning run for a 1–0 win over the Tigers at Comiskey Park. In the 10th, Humphries walked and score on a double by Luke Appling. A "crowd" of only 513 attended the contest.

MAY 14   Two days after Germany surrenders in the North African campaign, Buck Ross pitches a one-hitter and faces only 28 batters in defeating the Yankees 3–0 at Comiskey Park. Ross narrowly missed a no-hitter. In the second inning, Nick Etten hit a bouncer up the middle. Ross knocked it down and threw to first baseman Joe Kuhel, but Etten beat the throw by inches.

During his 10-year major league career with the Athletics and White Sox, Ross was 56–95 with a 4.94 ERA.

MAY 21   Johnny Humphries pitches the White Sox to a 1–0 victory over the Senators at Comiskey Park. Thurman Tucker drove in the lone run with a single in the fifth inning.

One of the fastest players of the era, Tucker played five seasons with the White Sox during the 1940s. He bore a striking resemblance to nightclub comic and actor Joe E. Brown. Fans began calling the outfielder Joe E. Tucker.

JUNE 20   The White Sox score seven runs in the fourth inning of a 10–6 win over the Indians in the second game of a double-header at Comiskey Park. Cleveland won the opener 7–2.

JUNE 30   A crowd of 29,495 pays to see the White Sox win 7–1 over the Senators at Comiskey Park. All of the receipts, a figure which reached $32,624, were turned over to war charities. Orval Grove was the winning pitcher. Earlier in the day he was rejected by doctors for service in the Army because of bad knees. In a preliminary game, a combined team of White Sox and Senators played the team from the Great Lakes Naval Training Station and won 4–0.

JULY 1   Guy Curtright runs his hitting streak to 26 games during a 2–0 win over the Senators at Comiskey Park.

Curtright was one of many players who received a shot at the majors during World War II because the rosters were depleted by players joining the military. He spent nine seasons in the minors before making his major league debut with the White Sox in 1943 at the age of 30. During the off-season, he worked as a high school mathematics teacher in Missouri. He earned a master's degree in education at the University of Missouri during the off-season while a minor leaguer. Curtright hit .291 in 138 games in 1943, his only season as a regular. His 26-game hitting streak is still the fourth-longest in White Sox history.

Another "elderly" rookie with the White Sox in 1943 was 30-year-old relief pitcher Gordon Maltzberger. He was 7–4 with an ERA of 2.46 and a league-leading 14 saves. Maltzberger was the 13th of 14 children born to a Texas farm couple. He wore glasses because of a 1934 automobile accident that required two stitches to repair one of his eyeballs. Later, Maltzberger was a minor league manager in the White Sox system. He was a leading contender as the next White Sox manager in 1971 before Chuck Tanner was given the job.

JULY 7   Wally Moses steals home with two out and the bases loaded in the 14th inning to defeat the Red Sox 3–2 at Comiskey Park.

JULY 8   Orval Grove comes with one out of a no-hitter before settling for a one-hit, 1–0 victory over the Yankees at Comiskey Park. The lone New York hit was a bloop double by Joe Gordon that landed inches inside the third-base line with two out in the ninth inning.

JULY 12   Jimmie Dykes winds up in "jail" during a 6–5 win in an exhibition game played at the Camp Grant Army base. Dykes had been shouting insults at umpire Art Passarella, a former American League arbiter who was serving as a private in the camp. Passarella had enough of Dykes and called the military police, who slapped the White Sox manager in a cell for a half-hour.

JULY 21   Orval Grove runs his record to 9–0 with an 8–6 win over the Red Sox in the second game of a double-header at Fenway Park. Boston won the opener 3–2.

              Grove entered the season with a 4–6 career record and a 5.45 ERA. He was 15–9 and posted an earned run average of 2.75 in 1943. He pitched 10 big league seasons, all with the Sox, and was 63–73.

JULY 23   White Sox catcher Vince Castino hits a grand slam off Dick Newsome in the fourth inning of a 5–1 win over the Red Sox in the second game of a double-header at Fenway Park. Boston won the opener 8–7 in 10 innings.

              The homer was the first of Castino's career. He hit only two home runs in 215 career at-bats over three seasons.

JULY 28   The White Sox pound out 21 hits and defeat the Senators 12–7 in Washington.

AUGUST 12   The White Sox score two runs in the ninth inning and one in the 14th to defeat the Red Sox 7–6 in the second game of a double-header at Comiskey Park. Luke Appling tripled and Skeeter Webb singled to account for the winning run. Boston took the opener 10–6.

AUGUST 13   Luke Appling collects hits 2,000th career hit during a 3–2 win over the Red Sox at Comiskey Park. The milestone hit was an RBI single off Tex Hughson in the first inning.

AUGUST 14   Luke Appling's double in the third inning drives in both runs of a 2–0 win over the Red Sox at Comiskey Park. Thornton Lee pitched the shutout.

              Appling collected 192 hits and led the AL in batting average (.328) and on-base percentage (.415) in 1943. Appling is the only White Sox player ever to win a batting title, accomplishing the feat twice. The other time was in 1936 when he batted .388.

AUGUST 18   The White Sox defeat the Senators 3–2 in 14 innings in the first game of a double-header at Comiskey Park. Guy Curtright drove in the winning run with a single. Washington won the second tilt 4–2. The Senators recorded 10 double plays during the afternoon, a major league record for one club during a double-header.

AUGUST 19   Sox third baseman Cass Kwietniewski makes his major league debut at the age of 17 years, 168 days during a 3–1 win over the Senators at Comiskey Park.

Kwietniewski jumped straight from American Legion ball in Detroit to the White Sox. He played only two games in 1943 and 27 in 1944 before becoming a regular at shortstop in 1945 while Luke Appling was in the service. Also in 1945, Kwietniewski changed his name to Cass Michaels. He moved to second base in 1946 when Appling returned. Michaels played for the Sox until 1950, and after brief stints with three other AL clubs, again in 1954. He was an All-Star in 1949.

AUGUST 23   Tony Cuccinello smacks a walk-off homer in the ninth inning to beat the Athletics 3–2 in the second game of a double-header at Comiskey Park. The Sox also won the opener 5–2.

AUGUST 24   The Athletics lose their 20th game in a row by dropping a 6–5 decision to the White Sox in the first game of a double-header at Comiskey Park. The Sox scored two runs in the ninth for the win. The A's broke their long losing streak by defeating Chicago 8–1 in the second tilt.

SEPTEMBER 22   Three weeks after the beginning of the Allied invasion of the Italian mainland, Ralph Hodgin hits a two-run double in the ninth inning to defeat the Athletics 2–1 in the second game of a double-header in Philadelphia. The Sox also won the opener 6–0.

SEPTEMBER 24   The White Sox and Athletics battle 16 innings to a 3–3 tie in a contest in Philadelphia called on account of darkness.

SEPTEMBER 26   In the fourth inning, the White Sox break a scoreless tie with a 13-run assault on the Senators' pitching staff to win 15–3 in the first game of a double-header at Griffith Stadium. The nine players in the lineup who contributed to the big inning were Wally Moses, Thurman Tucker, Guy Curtright, Luke Appling, Dick Culler, Ralph Hodgin, Joe Kuhel, Skeeter Webb and pitcher Eddie Smith. The Sox pounded out 10 hits in the inning off hapless pitchers Early Wynn, Jim Mertz and Bill Lefebvre. Smith contributed the only home run he struck in 531 major league at-bats over a 10-year career. The highlight of the surprising display of offensive prowess was a triple-steal executed perfectly by Tucker, Curtright and Appling. Washington won the second contest 5–2.

NOVEMBER 6   The White Sox purchase Hal Trosky from the Indians.

Trosky was a huge star at first base for the Indians before suffering from migraine headaches. From 1934, when he was a 21-year-old rookie, through 1940, Trosky hit .314 and averaged 101 runs, 29 homers and 122 RBIs per season. When acquired by the Sox, he hadn't played a major league game in over two years. Trosky appeared in 135 games for Chicago in 1944, batted .241, and hit 10 of the club's 23 homers that season. He sat out the 1945 campaign, then came back for 88 more games in 1946 before retiring for good.

NOVEMBER 24   The White Sox sell Joe Kuhel to the Senators.

1944   Sox

Season in a Sentence

The loss of Luke Appling and Don Kolloway to the military is too much to overcome, and the White Sox sink into seventh place.

Finish • Won • Lost • Pct • GB

Seventh   71   83   .451   18.0

Manager

Jimmie Dykes

Stats

Stats	WS	AL	Rank
Batting Avg:	.247	.260	7
On-Base Pct:	.307	.325	8
Slugging Pct:	.320	.353	8
Home Runs:	23		8
Stolen Bases:	66		3
ERA:	3.58	3.43	6
Fielding Avg:	.970	.971	6
Runs Scored:	543		7
Runs Allowed:	662		5

Starting Lineup

Mike Tresh, c
Hal Trosky, 1b
Roy Schalk, 2b
Ralph Hodgin, 3b
Skeeter Webb, ss
Eddie Carnett, lf
Thurman Tucker, cf
Wally Moses, rf
Guy Curtwright, lf-rf
Grey Clarke, 3b
Johnny Dickshot, lf

Pitchers

Bill Dietrich, sp
Orval Grove, sp
Ed Lopat, sp
Johnny Humphries, sp-rp
Thornton Lee, sp
Gordon Maltzberger, rp
Joe Haynes, rp
Buck Ross, rp

Attendance

563,539 (third on AL)

Club Leaders

Batting Avg:	Ralph Hodgin	.295
On-Base Pct:	Thurman Tucker	.388
Slugging Pct:	Wally Moses	.379
Home Runs:	Hal Trosky	10
RBIs:	Hal Trosky	70
Runs:	Wally Moses	82
Stolen Bases:	Wally Moses	21
Wins:	Bill Dietrich	16
Strikeouts:	Orval Grove	105
ERA:	Ed Lopat	3.28
Saves:	Gordon Maltzberger	12

APRIL 18   The scheduled season opener against the Indians at Comiskey Park is rained out.

APRIL 19   The White Sox get the 1944 season under way and win 3–1 over the Indians before 5,706 at Comiskey Park. Orval Grove was the winning pitcher.

The White Sox were hit hard by the military draft between the 1943 and 1944 seasons with the loss of Luke Appling, Don Kolloway and Eddie Smith. Teams during World War II had to search high and low for replacements. The Sox's starting second baseman in 1944 and 1945 was Roy Schalk. A classic wartime performer, Schalk played three games with the Yankees in 1932 then spent 12 years in the minors before making it back to the majors at the age of 35. Outfielder Johnny Dickshot appeared in 130 games in the majors from 1936 through 1939, then after four years in the minors, he played for the Sox during the final two years of the war. In 1945, Dickshot played in 130 games for Chicago and hit .302 at the age of 35, but wasn't invited back for 1946 when the veterans returned home from the armed forces.

APRIL 28 — Thornton Lee pitches 11 shutout innings before allowing two runs in the 12th inning to lose 2–0 to the Tigers in Detroit. Hal Newhouser hurled a complete game for the Tigers.

MAY 6 — The White Sox erupt for four runs in the ninth inning to defeat the Tigers 4–2 in Detroit. Roy Schalk's two-run single provided the winning margin.

MAY 11 — Hal Trosky steals home in the 16th inning to break a 2–2 tie against the Athletics in Philadelphia. The White Sox added an insurance run for a 4–2 victory.

MAY 14 — The White Sox score four runs in the ninth inning to defeat the Senators 6–4 in the second game of a double-header in Washington. Thurman Tucker broke the 4–4 tie with a two-run single. The Sox lose the opener 4–0.

JUNE 6 — All major league games are postponed in observance of the D-Day landing in France. President Franklin Roosevelt urged Americans to spend the day in prayer at home or in church.

JUNE 11 — The White Sox run their winning streak to eight games with a 4–2 decision over the Tigers in the first game of a double-header at Comiskey Park. The steal ended with a 1–0 loss in the nightcap.

JUNE 18 — Wally Moses stars as the White Sox sweep the Indians in Cleveland with two late-inning rallies. In the opener, Moses hit a homer in the 10th for a 3–2 Chicago win. In the second tilt, the Sox scored two in the ninth for a 7–6 triumph. Moses tripled in the tying run and scored on Roy Schalk's single.

JUNE 22 — The White Sox score seven runs in the eighth inning and defeat the Browns 10–3 in St. Louis.

JUNE 25 — The White Sox sweep the Indians 11–0 and 4–3 at Comiskey Park. The second game ended in controversy in the top of the eighth inning. Cleveland had a runner on base and one out when it began to rain. Though the downpour soon ceased, the game was called because the field was unplayable. Indians manager Lou Boudreau accused the White Sox grounds crew of moving slowly to cover the diamond with the tarpaulin.

JULY 1 — Trailing 3–0, the White Sox score three times in the ninth inning for a 3–2 victory over the Yankees in New York. The Sox were helped by four New York errors. Eddie Carnett broke the tie with a single. Going into the ninth, the White Sox had been held scoreless for 21 consecutive scoreless innings.

AUGUST 17 — Bill Dietrich pitches the White Sox to a 1–0 win over the Senators in Washington. Hal Trosky drove in the lone run with a sacrifice fly in the ninth inning.

The White Sox had a 50–50 record in mid-August before going 21–33 the rest of the way.

AUGUST 27   Johnny Humphries allows a walk-off homer in the ninth inning to Roy Cullenbine of the Indians, resulting in a 1–0 loss to the Indians in Cleveland. The Sox also lost the opener 4–3.

SEPTEMBER 1   Seven days after Allied troops liberate Paris, Joe Haynes pitches a 12-inning complete game and drives in the deciding run of a 5–4 win over the Indians at Comiskey Park. Haynes ended the contest with a single with two out and the bases loaded.

SEPTEMBER 10   Orval Grove hits a walk-off triple to beat the Browns 3–2 in the second game of a double-header at Comiskey Park. St. Louis won the opener 6–2.

SEPTEMBER 15   The White Sox lose a first-inning run during a 5–1 loss to the Browns in St. Louis due to a batting order mix-up. The problem occurred because coach Mule Haas turned in the wrong lineup card. Eddie Carnett batted out of turn and singled in Wally Moses. Carnett was declared out, and the run was nullified.

OCTOBER 1   The White Sox and Red Sox play a double-header in just two hours and 48 minutes on the final day of the regular season. Boston won the opener 3–1 in an hour and 38 minutes. Chicago took the second contest 4–1 in 1:10.

1945   Sox

Season in a Sentence

In the last year of World War II, the White Sox hold first place for 37 days before limping to a sixth-place finish.

Finish • Won • Lost • Pct • GB

Sixth   71   78   .477   15.0

Manager

Jimmie Dykes

Stats

Stats	WS	AL	Rank
Batting Avg:	.262	.255	1
On-Base Pct:	.326	.325	5
Slugging Pct:	.337	.346	7
Home Runs:	22		8
Stolen Bases:	78		2
ERA:	3.69	3.36	7
Fielding Avg:	.970	.973	8
Runs Scored:	596		6
Runs Allowed:	633		6

Starting Lineup

Mike Tresh, c
Kerby Farrell, 1b
Roy Schalk, 2b
Tony Cuccinello, 3b
Cass Michaels, ss
Johnny Dickshot, lf
Oris Hockett, cf
Wally Moses, rf
Guy Curtright, cf-lf
Bill Nagel, 1b
Floyd Baker, 3b

Pitchers

Thornton Lee, sp
Orval Grove, sp
Ed Lopat, sp
Johnny Humphries, sp
Bill Dietrich, sp
Joe Haynes, sp
Earl Caldwell, rp-sp
Frank Papish, rp

Attendance

657,981 (third in AL)

Club Leaders

Batting Avg:	Tony Cuccinello	.308
On-Base Pct:	Tony Cuccinello	.379
Slugging Pct:	Wally Moses	.420
Home Runs:	Johnny Dickshot	4
	Guy Curtright	4
RBIs:	Roy Schalk	65
Runs:	Wally Moses	79
Stolen Bases:	Johnny Dickshot	18
Wins:	Thornton Lee	15
Strikeouts:	Thornton Lee	108
ERA:	Thornton Lee	2.44
Saves:	Earl Caldwell	4
	Frank Papish	4

APRIL 17   Five days after Franklin Roosevelt dies of a cerebral hemorrhage and is succeeded
              by Harry Truman as president, the White Sox win 5–2 over the Indians in Cleveland
              on Opening Day. Thornton Lee was the winning pitcher. Cleveland player-manager
              Lou Boudreau was the victim of a hidden-ball play. When Boudreau stepped off third
              base, he was tagged by Tony Cuccinello, who took a throw from the outfield and
              kept the ball instead of returning it to the pitcher.

APRIL 19   The White Sox trounce the Indians 14–6 in Cleveland.

APRIL 20   In the home opener, the White Sox defeat the Browns 3–2 in 10 innings before 3,649
              at Comiskey Park. Eddie Lopat was the winning pitcher and hit a home run. The
              winning run scored on Roy Schalk's double.

              *The war in Europe was winding to a close, but the end of the conflict with
              Japan was nowhere in sight. The country was well into its fourth year of war,
              and everyone in the Comiskey Park stands could claim a loved one, friend or
              neighbor who had been or currently was involved in fighting somewhere in the
              world. While the 1945 opener was taking place, U.S. forces were involved in
              a deadly struggle to capture Okinawa. Between the 1944 and 1945 seasons,
              pitchers Gordon Maltzberger and Don Hanski, catcher Ed Fernandes, infielder
              Bill Metzig and outfielders Thurman Tucker and Ralph Hodgin entered the
              service, leaving the Sox to scramble for replacements. The starting shortstop in
              1945 was 19-year-old Cass Michaels. The other eight players who appeared in
              90 or more games that season were all past 30. Pitcher Clay Touchstone was
              42 years old and made six relief appearances. It was the first time that he had
              played in the majors in 16 years. Touchstone's previous big-league experience
              was six games with the Boston Braves in 1928 and 1929. Earl Caldwell, a
              39-year-old pitcher who hadn't played in the majors since 1937, was another
              reclamation project on the Opening Day roster. Unlike most of the others
              picked up off the scrap heap, however, Caldwell gave the Sox one good postwar
              season. As a closer, Caldwell was 13–4 with eight saves and a 2.08 ERA in
              1946.*

APRIL 22   The White Sox run their season record to 5–0 with a sweep of the Browns at
              Comiskey Park by scores of 4–3 in 10 innings and 5–3.

MAY 1   Six days before Germany's surrender closes the European phase of World War II,
              Joe Haynes pitches a one-hitter and just misses a perfect game in defeating the Tigers
              5–0 in Detroit. The only Tiger base runner was ex-White Sox infielder Skeeter Webb,
              who hit a bouncing single leading off the third inning. Haynes retired the first six and
              last 21 batters to face him.

MAY 25   The White Sox are knocked out of first place with a 5–4 loss to the Yankees in
              New York.

              *The Sox went into the game with a 15–9 record. The club was in first place for
              37 of the first 42 days of the 1945 season. Chicago failed to regain the top spot
              in the American League for the rest of the season, but it remained within striking
              distance of first until late summer. In August, the White Sox were 58–51 and in
              third place, 4$^1/_2$ games out of first. Jimmie Dykes's crew lost 27 of their final
              40 games, however.*

MAY 27 | The White Sox collect only three hits off Red Sox pitching during a double-header at Comiskey Park. In the opener, Boo Ferriss pitched a one-hitter for a 7–0 win. The only Chicago hit was a single by Tony Cuccinello in the second inning. In the nightcap, Emmett O'Neill hurled a two-hitter for a 2–1 victory.

JUNE 1 | The White Sox outlast the Senators 11–9 in an 11-inning seesaw battle at Griffith Stadium. The Sox had a 6–3 lead in the eighth, but Washington scored four in the last half of the inning to take a 7–6 advantage. Chicago plated three tallies in the ninth to move ahead 9–7, but the Senators countered with two in their half to force extra innings. The two runs by the Sox in the 11th came home on bases-loaded walks.

JUNE 12 | Thornton Lee strikes out 13 batters and defeats the Indians 1–0 at Comiskey Park. Bill Nagel drove in the winning run with a bases-loaded single in the ninth inning.

Lee was 15–12 with a 2.44 ERA in a comeback year in 1945. He was 22–11 in 1941, then posted a record of 10–25 during three injury-plagued seasons from 1942 through 1944.

JUNE 17 | Joe Haynes suffers a compound fracture of his ankle sliding into third base during a 7–5 win over the Tigers in the second game of a double-header at Comiskey Park. The Sox also won the opener 6–1.

"It is the worst athletic injury I have ever seen," exclaimed Dr. John Claridge of Mercy Hospital in Chicago. Haynes was out for the rest of the 1945 season, but returned in 1946.

JUNE 20 | The day before Japan surrenders Okinawa to U.S. forces, a four-run eighth inning climaxed by a near-riot highlights a 4–1 win over the Browns in St. Louis. The excitement began after the runs had scored and two were out. Browns manager Luke Sewell waved pitcher Tex Shirley into the game to replace George Caster. Instead of handing the ball to Shirley, Caster fired it into the White Sox dugout in response to the heckling he received from Sox batting practice pitcher Karl Scheel, a 23-year-old ex-Marine. The Browns leaped off the bench intent on inflicting bodily harm to Scheel. The White Sox ran forward to meet the advance, and during the ensuing melee, Scheel was beaten to a pulp. A squad of St. Louis police was necessary to quell the disturbance.

JULY 2 | A week after the signing of the United Nations charter, the White Sox hammer the Yankees 11–0 in the first game of a double-header at Comiskey Park. New York won the second tilt 6–2.

JULY 7 | The White Sox sweep the Athletics 1–0 and 12–4 at Comiskey Park. Bill Dietrich pitched the shutout. Wally Moses stole home in the first inning for the lone run of the game.

Moses hit .295 with 35 doubles and a league-leading 15 triples in 1945.

JULY 9 | The White Sox defeat the Cubs 5–4 in 10 innings in an exhibition game before 47,144 at Comiskey Park. The entire proceeds, in excess of $50,000, were donated to the War Relief Fund and the Red Cross.

JULY 23   Bill Dietrich pitches an 11-inning complete game shutout to defeat the Yankees 1–0 in New York. Oris Hockett drove in the lone run with a single in the 11th.

AUGUST 5   The White Sox sweep the Tigers 12–8 and 3–2 at Comiskey Park. The Sox trailed 6–2 in the opener, then scored 10 unanswered runs with four in the sixth inning, four in the seventh and two in the eighth.

AUGUST 6   On the day that the atom bomb is dropped on Hiroshima, Oris Hockett steals four bases during a 7–0 win over the Tigers in the second game of a double-header against the Tigers at Comiskey Park. Detroit won the opener 6–2.

                 On the same day, a bullet was fired into Hockett's hotel room door. His room at the Broadview Hotel in Chicago was not entered, as the bullet jammed the lock. Hockett was not in the room at the time. The hotel clerk said that moments earlier, a man came to the front desk looking for the White Sox outfielder.

AUGUST 15   The day after Japan's surrender ends World War II, the White Sox sweep the Red Sox 5–1 and 11–0 at Comiskey Park.

AUGUST 18   The White Sox score eight runs in the seventh inning to polish off the Red Sox 16–1 at Comiskey Park.

AUGUST 22   Trailing 5–2, the White Sox score three runs in the ninth inning and one in the 11th to defeat the Yankees 6–5 in 11 innings at Comiskey Park. Mike Tresh contributed doubles during both late-inning rallies. He scored on a single by Kerby Farrell.

SEPTEMBER 5   The White Sox sweep the Athletics 15–6 and 6–5 during a double-header against the Athletics at Comiskey Park. The second contest went 14 innings. Floyd Baker broke a 4–4 tie with a two-run single in the top of the 14th before the A's came back with a tally in their half.

SEPTEMBER 11   The White Sox score two runs in the ninth inning to defeat the Senators 2–1 in Washington. The winning run scored on a squeeze bunt by Guy Curtright, which scored Johnny Dickshot from third base.

                 Mike Tresh caught all 150 White Sox games in 1945. The club used only two catchers all season. Vince Castino played in 25 games behind the plate.

SEPTEMBER 26   Harry Grabiner resigns as general manager of the White Sox, ending 40 years of service with the club.

                 Grabiner had been employed by the White Sox since 1905. He started as a 14-year-old, sweeping out the grandstand and selling scorecards. Grabiner worked his way up the ladder and was appointed by Charles Comiskey as team secretary and vice president in 1915, holding duties analogous to those of the modern-day general manager. He continued to work under Louis Comiskey after the death of his father Charles in 1931, and for Grace Comiskey following the passing of her husband Louis in 1939. By the terms of Louis's will, Grabiner was guaranteed 10 years of employment with the White Sox if he chose to remain with the organization. Grabiner and Grace Comiskey had never gotten along, however, and Grace made it impossible for Harry to continue.

The breaking point came when Bill Veeck tried to purchase the White Sox in 1945. Mrs. Comiskey mistrusted Grabiner's motives, believing that he was too friendly with Veeck and was conspiring against her. After Veeck bought the Indians in June 1946, Grabiner joined him in Cleveland. Unfortunately, Grabiner was soon stricken with cancer and died in 1948.

SEPTEMBER 30   Rain costs Tony Cuccinello a chance at the batting title. September 30 was the last day of the regular season, and the Sox's double-header against the Indians at Comiskey Park was postponed by a downpour. Cuccinello went into the day holding down first place in the batting race by a percentage point over Snuffy Stirnweiss of the Yankees. Cuccinello was batting .308. The rainout denied the Sox third baseman a chance for the title because Stirnweiss collected three hits that day to beat Cuccinello .30854 to .30846. The difference of .00008 made it the closest batting race of all-time.

Even though he was second in the AL in batting average, Cuccinello never played another big-league game, ending his 15-year big league career. Nearly 38 years old when the 1945 season came to a close, he was released after the season was over along with many other aging wartime players, including outfielders Johnny Dickshot and Oris Hockett, each of whom finished in the top 10 in batting average. Dickshot hit .302, third-best in the AL, and Hockett batted .293 to finish 10th. Starting second baseman Roy Schalk and first baseman Kerby Farrell were also released before the start of the 1946 season. In all, five of the eight players who appeared in at least 100 games for the Sox in the final wartime season didn't play a single big-league game after 1945. Cuccinello would return to the Sox as a coach from 1957 through 1966 and again in 1969 under Al Lopez.

OCTOBER 3   Leslie O'Connor is named general manager of the White Sox, replacing Harry Grabiner.

A former Chicago attorney, O'Connor was the trusted secretary and treasurer in the commissioner's office from 1921 through 1945. He was hired by Kenesaw Landis, who was impressed by O'Connor's trying of a case while Landis was a federal judge. After Landis's death in November 1944, O'Connor served as interim commissioner until Happy Chandler was appointed to the post in April 1945. Grace Comiskey hired O'Connor because of his wealth of baseball experience. He was a more-than-competent as an administrator, but he lacked a background in making trades and building a farm system, qualities that the Sox sorely needed as the franchise stagnated during World War II. Hampered by Grace Comiskey's unwillingness to spend the money necessary to build a contending club, the franchise went from bad to worse under O'Connor, who resigned following a 51–101 season in 1948.

1946

Season in a Sentence

The war veterans return, Jimmie Dykes departs, Ted Lyons replaces Dykes as manager, and the White Sox post a losing record for the third year in a row.

Finish • Won • Lost • Pct • GB

Fifth   74   80   .481   30.0

Managers

Jimmy Dykes (10–20) and Ted Lyons (64–60)

Stats

Stats	WS	AL	Rank
Batting Avg:	.257	.256	4
On-Base Pct:	.323	.328	5
Slugging Pct:	.333	.364	8
Home Runs:	37		8
Stolen Bases:	78		1
ERA:	3.10	3.50	1
Fielding Avg:	.972	.973	6
Runs Scored:	562		6
Runs Allowed:	595		4

Starting Lineup

Mike Tresh, c
Hal Trosky, 1b
Don Kolloway, 2b
Dario Lodigiani, 3b
Luke Appling, ss
Bob Kennedy, lf
Thurman Tucker, cf
Taffy Wright, rf
Cass Michaels, 2b
Ralph Hodgin, lf
Whitey Platt, lf-cf-rf
Joe Kuhel, 1b
Frankie Hayes, c
Wally Moses, rf-cf

Pitchers

Ed Lopat, sp
Orval Grove, sp
Joe Haynes, sp
Eddie Smith, sp
Johnny Rigney, sp
Earl Caldwell, rp
Frank Papish, rp-sp

Attendance

983,403 (sixth in AL)

Club Leaders

Batting Avg:	Luke Appling	.309
On-Base Pct:	Luke Appling	.384
Slugging Pct:	Luke Appling	.378
Home Runs:	Taffy Wright	7
RBIs:	Luke Appling	55
Runs:	Thurman Tucker	62
Stolen Bases:	Don Kolloway	14
Wins:	Ed Lopat	13
Strikeouts:	Ed Lopat	89
ERA:	Ed Lopat	2.73
Saves:	Earl Caldwell	8

FEBRUARY 20   The White Sox open spring training camp in Pasadena, California, the first held in peacetime in five years.

The 1946 major league training camps were unique as returning war veterans competed with wartime fill-ins for spots on the roster. The White Sox spring training roster included 32 players who had spent all or most of the 1945 season in the military. Many of them, such as Luke Appling, Taffy Wright, Ralph Hodgin, Thurman Tucker, Bob Kennedy, Don Kolloway, Dario Lodigiani, Johnny Rigney and Eddie Smith reclaimed their positions. Of the 27 players who played for the White Sox in 1945, only 13 returned in 1946.

APRIL 16   The White Sox lose the season opener 1–0 to the Indians before 20,106 at Comiskey Park. Bob Feller pitched a three-hit shutout. Bill Dietrich was the hard-luck loser.

Coach Mule Haas was the acting manager for the first 12 games of the 1946 season while Jimmie Dykes recovered from a gallstone attack.

APRIL 28   Ted Lyons records the last of his 260 career wins with a 4–3 decision over the Browns in the first game of a double-header at Comiskey Park. In the nightcap, St. Louis scored nine unearned runs in the first inning and won 11–8.

MAY 6   Thornton Lee pitches a complete game and drives in both Chicago runs with a
              second-inning single to defeat the Yankees 2–1 in New York.

MAY 8   Johnny Pesky of the Red Sox ties a major league record by scoring six runs during
              a 14–10 Boston win over the White Sox at Fenway Park.

MAY 19   Ted Lyons makes his last major league appearance, losing 4–3 when the Senators
              score two runs in the ninth inning in the first game of a double-header at Comiskey
              Park. Washington won the second contest 7–1.

              *Lyons completed each of his last 28 career starts. He finished his last three
              starting assignments in 1941, all 20 in 1942, and after three years in the Marines,
              all five in 1946.*

MAY 24   Jimmie Dykes resigns as manager and is replaced by Ted Lyons.

              *Dykes had been the White Sox manager since 1934. He resigned after
              demanding a contract extension through the 1947 season, which was refused
              by Grace Comiskey. The club had a 10–20 record at the time of Dykes's
              resignation. Lyons had been with the White Sox as a pitcher since 1923. He took
              himself off the roster as an active player at the time he was appointed manager.
              The Sox bottomed out at 38–58 on July 30 in 1946 before winning 36 of their
              last 58 games. The club appeared to be on the upswing after the strong finish,
              but it was 70–84 in 1947 and 51–101 in 1948 before Lyons was fired. He never
              managed another big-league club. Dykes, on the other hand, would go on to
              manage the Athletics (1951–53), Orioles (1954), Reds (1958), Tigers (1959–60)
              and Indians (1960–61).*

MAY 27   The White Sox collect 20 hits and defeat the Browns 9–2 in St. Louis.

JUNE 11   Eddie Smith pitches the White Sox to a 1–0 win over the Athletics in Philadelphia.
              Whitey Platt drove in the lone run of the game with a single in the seventh inning.
              The Sox pulled off a triple play in the first inning. With Elmer Valo on second
              base and Barney McCosky on first, Irv Hall lined a pitch to second baseman
              Don Kolloway, who tossed to shortstop Luke Appling to double Valo. Appling
              fired the ball to first baseman Hal Trosky before McCosky could return to complete
              the triple play.

              Appling hit .309 in 1946.

JUNE 13   The White Sox purchase Joe Kuhel from the Senators.

JULY 7   Ed Lopat pitches a two-hitter to defeat the Indians 2–0 in the second game of a
              double-header at Municipal Stadium. The only hits off Lopat were singles by
              George Case and Gene Woodling. Cleveland won the opener 3–2.

JULY 15   The White Sox purchase Frankie Hayes from the Indians.

JULY 19   Fourteen White Sox players are ejected during a 9–2 loss to the Red Sox in Boston.
              The group was banished for heckling an umpire after he issued a warning following
              a "dust off" pitch to Ted Williams by Joe Haynes in the third inning. As a result of

the pitch, umpire Red Jones cautioned Haynes. The chorus of yammering from the Chicago bench led Jones to eject four players. When the jeering continued, 10 others were chased in the next inning. The only three individuals on the Chicago bench when the Red Sox were at bat were manager Ted Lyons, coach Mule Haas and the trainer.

JULY 21   The White Sox score eight runs in the second inning of a 9–3 win in the second game of a double-header at Yankee Stadium. New York won the opener 3–2.

JULY 23   The White Sox sell Wally Moses to the Red Sox.

JULY 29   Relief pitcher Earl Caldwell hits a walk-off single in the 12th inning to defeat the Yankees 4–3 at Comiskey Park.

JULY 31   The White Sox score three runs in the ninth inning to defeat the Athletics 3–2 at Comiskey Park. Luke Appling drove in the winning run with a walk-off triple.

AUGUST 3   Taffy Wright's home run in the fourth inning off Ray Scarborough is the only run of a 1–0 victory over the Senators in Washington. Orval Grove didn't allow a hit until the seventh inning and finished with a three-hitter.

AUGUST 4   The White Sox sweep the Senators 3–1 and 1–0 at Comiskey Park. Frank Papish pitched the second game shutout. The lone run scored when Early Wynn walked Sox first baseman Frank Whitman with the bases full.

           The bases-loaded walk accounted for the only run batted in of Whitman's career and was one of just two bases on balls he drew in the majors. It also happened in his only career game as a first baseman. Whitman played in 20 big-league contests and had one hit, a single, in 22 at-bats for a batting average of .045. In another oddity, Whitman scored seven runs because he was often used as a pinch-runner. His nickname was "Hooker."

AUGUST 6   The White Sox score nine runs in the fifth inning of an 11–1 win over the Indians at Comiskey Park.

AUGUST 8   Reliever Earl Caldwell collects his second extra-inning walk-off single in a span of 10 days with a 10th-inning base hit to defeat the Indians 7–6 in the second game of a double-header at Comiskey Park. Cleveland won the opener on a one-hitter by Bob Feller.

           Despite a terrible start and a losing record, it was a great year at the box office for the White Sox. The club drew 983,403 to break the previous record of 833,492 set in 1920. The Sox were sixth in the American League and 11th in the majors in attendance in 1946, however. The boost was part of a nationwide trend as fans flocked to the ballparks in the first year following World War II. The 16 big league clubs drew 18,534,444 fans in 1946, shattering the previous high of 10,951,502 established in 1945.

AUGUST 22 The White Sox score three runs in the ninth inning and one in the 11th to defeat the Red Sox 4–3 in Boston. Batting as a pinch-hitter, Ed Lopat drove in the tying run with a single. Don Kolloway's RBI-single accounted for the game-winner.

SEPTEMBER 3   The White Sox score two runs in the 16th inning to win 4–3 over the Tigers at Comiskey Park. After Detroit scored in the top of the 16th, the Sox plated two in their half on doubles by Ralph Hodgin, Whitey Platt and Taffy Wright.

SEPTEMBER 14   Ed Lopat allows only one run and five hits during an 11-inning complete game, but he loses 1–0 to the Athletics at Comiskey Park.

SEPTEMBER 21   The White Sox sweep the Browns 11–10 and 9–1 during a double-header at Sportsman's Park. In the opener, the Sox trailed 6–1 at the end of the sixth inning before mounting a comeback with three runs in the seventh inning, five in the eighth and two in the ninth to take an 11–7 lead and survive a three-run St. Louis rally in the last of the ninth.

DECEMBER 6   The White Sox sign Red Ruffing as a free agent following his release by the Yankees.

Ruffing had 270 wins during a Hall of Fame career when he arrived in Chicago as a 42-year-old pitcher. With the Sox, Ruffing had a 3–5 record and a 6.11 ERA before calling it a career.

1947   Sox

Season in a Sentence

Fielding a roster mostly of players that were well past their prime, the White Sox lose 84 games.

Finish • Won • Lost • Pct • GB

Finish	Won	Lost	Pct	GB
Sixth	70	84	.455	27.0

Manager

Ted Lyons

Stats

Stats	WS	AL	Rank
Batting Avg:	.256	.256	5
On-Base Pct:	.321	.333	6
Slugging Pct:	.342	.364	7
Home Runs:	53		7
Stolen Bases:	91		1
ERA:	3.64	3.71	5
Fielding Avg:	.975	.977	7
Runs Scored:	553		7
Runs Allowed:	661		5

Starting Lineup

Mike Tresh, c
Rudy York, 1b
Don Kolloway, 2b
Floyd Baker, 3b
Luke Appling, ss
Taffy Wright, lf-rf
Dave Philley, cf
Bob Kennedy, rf
Cass Michaels, 2b-3b
Thurman Tucker, cf
George Dickey, c
Jack Wallaesa, ss-lf
Ralph Hodgin, lf
Jake Jones, 1b

Pitchers

Ed Lopat, sp
Joe Haynes, sp
Frank Papish, sp-rp
Orval Grove, sp
Bob Gillespie, sp-rp
Thornton Lee, sp-rp
Earl Caldwell, rp
Earl Harrist, rp

Attendance

876,948 (sixth in AL)

Club Leaders

Batting Avg:	Luke Appling	.306
On-Base Pct:	Luke Appling	.386
Slugging Pct:	Luke Appling	.412
Home Runs:	Rudy York	15
RBIs:	Rudy York	64
Runs:	Luke Appling	67
Stolen Bases:	Dave Philley	21
Wins:	Ed Lopat	16
Strikeouts:	Ed Lopat	109
ERA:	Ed Lopat	2.81
Saves:	Earl Caldwell	8

APRIL 15   The White Sox win the season opener 2–0 over the Indians on a day in Cleveland in which the temperatures are near freezing. Ed Lopat pitched the shutout to win a duel with Bob Feller. Don Kolloway contributed three hits.

Lopat had a 16–13 record and a 2.81 ERA in 1947.

APRIL 18   In the White Sox second game of 1947, Johnny Rigney records the club's second shutout with a 1–0 win over the Browns. It was also the first game of the year at Comiskey Park and attracted a crowd of 8,718. The lone run crossed the plate in the first inning on a single by Dave Philley.

APRIL 23   Ed Lopat allows five home runs during a 7–4 loss to the Tigers in Detroit. Lopat surrendered home runs in the third inning to Roy Cullenbine and Eddie Lake and three consecutive homers in the eighth to Cullenbine, Dick Wakefield and Hoot Evers.

MAY 4   The White Sox sweep the Athletics 8–7 and 1–0 in a double-header at Comiskey Park. In the opener, the Sox trailed 6–2 before scoring six times in the eighth inning. The big inning was highlighted by a pinch-hit grand slam from Jack Wallaesa. Orval Grove pitched the game-two shutout. The lone run scored in the first inning on a single by Bob Kennedy.

The sweep gave the White Sox a 10–5 record and a hold on first place. Five days later, the Sox dropped out of first place and were out of the pennant race by the end of May.

JUNE 8   The White Sox lose 1–0 in an 18-inning marathon to the Senators in the first game of a double-header at Comiskey Park. Frank Papish pitched the first 13 innings for the Sox and allowed only five hits. Earl Harrist surrendered just one hit in his first four innings of relief. At that point, Chicago hurlers had put together 33 consecutive scoreless innings over three games against the Senators. But in the 18th, Al Evans tripled and Sherry Robertson hit a sacrifice fly off Harrist for the lone run of the game. The Sox collected only six hits off Walt Masterson (16 innings) and Early Wynn (two innings). Chicago won the second tilt 8–2.

It was Luke Appling Day at Comiskey Park. He was given a new car, a watch with a gold wristband and a check for $1,700. Appling was 40 years old in 1947, but he hit .306 in 139 games and played in the All-Star Game.

JUNE 9   Down 8–2, the White Sox rally to defeat the Yankees 9–8 at Comiskey Park with two runs in the fourth inning, two in the sixth, two in the eighth and one in the 10th. The score was tied in the eighth on a two-out, two-run homer on a 3–0 pitch by Luke Appling. Jake Jones drove in the game-winning run with a single in the 10th.

JUNE 14   In a trade of starting first baseman, the White Sox swap Jake Jones to the Red Sox for Rudy York.

JUNE 15   In his first two games with the Red Sox, Jake Jones hits homers in both ends of a double-header and drives in seven runs against the White Sox a day after the Chicago club trades him. In the nightcap, he thrilled the Fenway Park crowd by clubbing a walk-off grand slam off Orval Grove to give Boston an 8–4 win.

JUNE 22   The White Sox defeat the Athletics 1–0 in 10 innings in the first game of a double-header at Shibe Park. Bob Gillespie (nine innings) and Earl Caldwell (one inning) combined on the shutout. The lone run scored on two singles and an error. Philadelphia won the second contest 3–0.

Gillespie never pitched a complete-game shutout in the majors. He finished his four seasons in the big leagues with a 5–13 record and a 5.07 ERA.

JUNE 23   The White Sox score seven runs in the ninth inning to break a 3–3 tie, then withstand a three-run Senators rally in the bottom half to win 10–6 in Washington.

JULY 5   Larry Doby makes his major league debut for the Indians against the White Sox at Comiskey Park. Doby struck out as a pinch-hitter for Bryan Stephens in the seventh inning facing Earl Harrist. The Sox won the game 6–5.

Doby was the first African-American player in American League history and the second in the majors following Jackie Robinson, who debuted with the Dodgers on April 15, 1947. The White Sox integrated their roster in 1951 with the arrival of Minnie Minoso. Doby played for the White Sox in 1956, 1957 and 1959 and served as manager in 1978.

AUGUST 2   The White Sox wallop the Senators 13–1 in Washington.

AUGUST 7   The White Sox score two runs in the ninth inning and two more in the 10th to defeat the Tigers 4–2 in Detroit. The Sox tied the score on a single by Red Ruffing, who was in the game as a pinch-hitter. Rudy York broke the deadlock with a two-run homer in the 10th.

AUGUST 17 Taffy Wright homers in the eighth inning off Fred Hutchinson for the only run in a 1–0 victory over the Tigers at Comiskey Park. Ed Lopat pitched the shutout.

AUGUST 23 Rudy York sets his hotel room on fire for the second time in 1947 to set the unofficial major league record for "most hotel fires started in a season."

On April 26 while playing for the Red Sox, York fell asleep while smoking in bed. He was dragged to safety by the hotel night engineer, who found smoke billowing from beneath the door of York's second-floor room. Unable to arouse York by knocking, the night engineer entered the room with a passkey. The whole room was blazing. As a result of Rudy's negligence, 450 guests at the Miles Standish Hotel were forced to evacuate. York suffered only slight burns and smoke inhalation. After a June trade to the White Sox, York took up residence at the Stevens Hotel in Chicago. He left his 15th-floor room at the hotel on August 23 with a lit cigarette on a window sill. The drapes and window sash were destroyed before the fire was extinguished. Ironically, one of York's post-playing career jobs was as a fire prevention officer with the Georgia State Forestry Commission.

AUGUST 28 Joe Haynes pitches a 12-inning complete game and drives in the winning run in a 4–2 win over the Indians in Cleveland. Haynes broke the 2–2 deadlock with an RBI-single.

SEPTEMBER 10   Dave Philley is hurt by a nail during a 3–1 loss to the Senators in Washington. Philley cut a deep gash in the little toe of his left foot after making a sensational one-handed catch. He went hurtling headlong over a low temporary fence being constructed in the outfield for extra bleacher seats to be used for the upcoming Washington Redskins football games and cut the toe on a rusty nail. Philley was rushed immediately to the hospital for a tetanus shot and was out of the lineup for a week.

SEPTEMBER 15   At Fenway Park, the White Sox and Red Sox combine for 12 double plays to tie an American League record for a double-header. Boston pulled off seven of the double plays, including five in the second game. The White Sox won the opener 6–3 and the Red Sox took the nightcap 7–5.

SEPTEMBER 16   Jack Wallaesa hits a grand slam in the ninth inning to cap an 8–3 win over the Red Sox in the second game of a double-header at Fenway Park. Boston won the opener 5–0.

Wallaesa hit eight homers in 253 at-bats over two seasons for the White Sox, but his batting average was only .194.

SEPTEMBER 23   A crowd of only 942 attends a 4–1 loss to the Tigers at Comiskey Park.

OCTOBER 29   Commissioner Happy Chandler suspends the White Sox for failure to pay a fine over the signing of a high school pitcher.

Sox general manager Leslie O'Connor defied a major league edict by signing prep pitching sensation George Zoeterman. He attended Chicago's Christian High School. The rule barred professional teams from negotiating for the services of an athlete playing while still in high school. O'Connor paid Zoeterman a $2,000 bonus and dared Chandler to act. O'Connor had a different interpretation of the rule, and believing he had the law on his side, stood his ground and refused to withdraw the original contract offer. Chandler responded by fining the White Sox $500 and suspending the club from the American League until the impasse was resolved to his satisfaction. The suspension prevented the Sox from asking waivers on players, claiming players on waivers, signing contracts or participating in any transactions or activities with other clubs. O'Connor threatened to take Chandler to civil court and counted on the support of the Comiskey family, but on November 4, Chuck Comiskey quietly paid the fine. Zoeterman was declared a free agent and upon completion of high school, signed a contract with the Cubs. But he never reached the major leagues.

DECEMBER 28   The NFL championship game is played at Comiskey Park, with the Chicago Cardinals defeating the Philadelphia Eagles 28–21 on a frozen field that requires players from both clubs to wear basketball shoes.

1948

Season in a Sentence

After years of penny-pinching policies by Grace Comiskey and the direction of incompetent general manager Leslie O'Connor, the White Sox lose 101 games.

Finish • Won • Lost • Pct • GB

Eighth   51   101   .336   44.5

Manager

Ted Lyons

Stats

Stats	WS	AL	Rank
Batting Avg:	.251	.266	7
On-Base Pct:	.329	.349	7
Slugging Pct:	.331	.382	7
Home Runs:	55		7
Stolen Bases:	46		4
ERA:	4.89	4.29	7
Fielding Avg:	.973	.977	7
Runs Scored:	559		8
Runs Allowed:	814		7

Starting Lineup

Aaron Robinson, c
Tony Lupien, 1b
Don Kolloway, 2b
Cass Michaels, 3b-2b
Luke Appling, ss-3b
Pat Seerey, lf
Dave Philley, cf
Taffy Wright, rf
Floyd Baker, 3b
Ralph Hodgin, lf-rf
Ralph Weigel, c

Pitchers

Bill Wight, sp
Joe Haynes, sp
Al Gettel, sp
Marino Pieretti, sp
Randy Gumbert, sp
Howie Judson, rp
Glen Moulder, rp
Frank Papish, rp-sp
Orval Grove, rp-sp

Attendance

777,844 (seventh in AL)

Club Leaders

Batting Avg:	Luke Appling	.314
On-Base Pct:	Luke Appling	.423
Slugging Pct:	Dave Philley	.387
Home Runs:	Pat Seerey	18
RBIs:	Pat Seerey	64
Runs:	Tony Lupien	69
Stolen Bases:	Tony Lupien	11
Wins:	Bill Wight	9
	Joe Haynes	9
Strikeouts:	Bill Wight	68
ERA:	Joe Haynes	3.97
Saves:	Howie Judson	8

JANUARY 27   The White Sox trade Thurman Tucker to the Indians for Ralph Weigel.

FEBRUARY 24   The White Sox trade Ed Lopat to the Yankees for Aaron Robinson, Bill Wight and Fred Bradley.

> *In an appallingly bad trade, Leslie O'Connor traded his staff ace and received next to nothing in return. Lopat had a record of 109–51 from 1948 through 1954 with the Yanks and pitched on five consecutive world championship clubs. Wight packed his family and drove from his home in Delano, California, to the Yankees spring camp in St. Petersburg, Florida, only to be told he was traded. He had to immediately drive back to California, where the White Sox trained in Pasadena. In his first season with the White Sox, Wight had a record of 9–20, a 4.80 ERA, 135 walks and only 68 strikeouts. Robinson lasted only a year in Chicago as the starting catcher, but he was used as trade bait after the season was over for a pitcher who was every bit the equal of Lopat (see November 10, 1948).*

APRIL 16   In the first game telecast on WGN-TV, the White Sox defeat the Cubs 4–1 in an exhibition game at Wrigley Field. Jack Brickhouse was at the microphone. He was teamed with Harry Creighton from 1948 through 1954.

WGN-TV began its long association with Chicago baseball by telecasting all of the home games of both the White Sox and the Cubs in 1948. Brickhouse and Creighton covered both teams.

APRIL 20   The White Sox open the season with a 5–2 loss to the Tigers before 14,801 at Comiskey Park. Mike Tresh hit a homer, his first since May 19, 1940.

Tresh hit only two home runs in 3,189 career at-bats.

MAY 8   Two weeks after the start of the Berlin airlift, the White Sox are the victims of a triple play and lose 16–1 to the Athletics in Philadelphia.

The White Sox lost 19 of their first 23 games in 1948.

JUNE 2   The White Sox trade Bob Kennedy to the Indians for Pat Seerey and Al Gettel.

Nicknamed "Fat Pat" because of his 200 pounds on a five-foot-10-inch body, Seerey could hit the ball a long way, but not often enough to satisfy his employers. He played for the Indians from 1943 through 1948, and the White Sox in 1948 and 1949. Seerey hit 86 home runs in 1,815 major league at-bats despite playing in poor hitter's parks. He clubbed 54 of those 86 homers on the road. On the negative side, he led the AL in strikeouts in each of the four seasons he appeared in at least 100 games and had a lifetime batting average of .224. With the Sox in 1948, Seerey fanned 94 times in 340 at-bats. The batter ranking second on the club in strikeouts that season was Cass Michaels with 42. Seerey did give fans one thrill, however, walloping four homers in a single game (see July 18, 1948).

JUNE 6   The White Sox sweep the Senators 10–4 and 11–4 in Washington.

JUNE 15   The White Sox score seven runs in the third inning to take an 8–4 lead, but are forced to play 11 innings before defeating the Yankees 9–8 at Comiskey Park. Relief pitcher Earl Caldwell drove in the winning run with a single.

Luke Appling was 41 years old in 1948, but he was the White Sox's top player, batting .314 in 139 games.

JULY 4   The White Sox rout the Tigers 12–1 in the second game of a double-header at Comiskey Park. Detroit won the opener 6–3.

JULY 18   Pat Seerey ties a major league record by clubbing four home runs during an 11-inning, 12–11 victory over the Athletics in the first game of a double-header in Philadelphia. After striking out in the second inning, Seerey led off in the fourth with the Sox trailing 6–1. On the first pitch from Carl Scheib, Seerey hit a home run that completely cleared the roof of the double-decked stands in left field at Shibe Park. Facing Scheib again in the fifth with two out and one on base, Seerey homered onto the roof. With Bob Savage on the mound in the sixth, Seerey hit a three-run homer onto the roof on a 2–2 pitch. It was his third consecutive home run in three consecutive innings. Chicago took an 11–7 lead in the top of the seventh, during which Seerey fouled out to the catcher, but the A's tied the contest with four tallies in their half. He walked in the ninth and the score remained 11–11 heading into the

11th inning. Batting with two out, Seerey hit Lou Brissie's first pitch into the upper deck of the left field stands for his fourth home run of the game and the winning run. Philadelphia won the second game 6–1. It was called after five innings by the Sunday curfew in observance of a Pennsylvania law that stipulated that games on the Christian Sabbath must end at 6 p.m.

Through the 2006 season, there have been 15 players who struck four homers in a game. Seerey is the only member of the White Sox to accomplish the feat. Of the 15 players with four-homer games, only two hit fewer than 100 career homers. Seerey hit 86. Bobby Lowe, who belted four homers for the Boston Braves on May 30, 1894, accounted for 71 lifetime home runs.

JULY 22   Pitcher Al Gettel is forced to play second base during a 5–3 loss to the Red Sox in the second game of a double-header at Fenway Park. In the fifth inning, Cass Michaels was ejected for objecting to an umpire's call, and Ted Lyons had no available infielders because of injuries to reserves Don Kolloway and Jack Wallaesa. Boston also won the first game 3–0.

JULY 24   Pat Seerey strikes out seven times in a double-header against the Yankees in New York. The White Sox lost the first game 6–2 and won the second 8–4 in 10 innings.

JULY 27   Pat Seerey hits a two-out, two-run, walk-off homer in the ninth inning to defeat the Senators 2–1 at Comiskey Park.

JULY 28   The White Sox purchase Randy Gumpert from the Yankees.

AUGUST 13   Satchel Paige pitches for the Indians in front of a sellout crowd of 51,013 at Comiskey Park and shuts out the White Sox 5–0.

AUGUST 21   The White Sox score three runs in the ninth inning to defeat the Indians 3–2 in Cleveland. Facing Bob Lemon, Pat Seerey walked, then Eddie Robinson and Dave Philley swatted back-to-back homers for the win. The Cleveland pitching staff came into the game with four straight shutouts and had a streak of 47 consecutive scoreless innings before the Sox's ninth-inning rally.

SEPTEMBER 15   The White Sox score 10 runs in the seventh inning and trounce the Red Sox 17–10 at Comiskey Park. Taffy Wright drove in five runs in the big inning with a grand slam and a fielder's choice. He had a total of six runs batted in during the contest, including an earlier single.

SEPTEMBER 29   The White Sox lose their 100th game of the season, dropping a 5–2 decision to the Indians in Cleveland.

OCTOBER 2   The White Sox trade Frank Papish to the Indians for Bob Kuzava and Ernie Groth.

The 1948 World Series between the Boston Braves and the Cleveland Indians was the first one shown on Chicago television. Only the games from Cleveland were telecast in Chicago, however, because it was not yet possible to transmit images from Boston to the Midwest. The first World Series telecast was in 1947 between the Yankees and Dodgers, but it was seen only on stations in New York, Washington, Philadelphia and Schenectady, New York.

OCTOBER 3   Jack Onslow replaces Ted Lyons as manager of the White Sox.

Lyons was a coach with the Tigers from 1949 through 1953 and with the Dodgers in 1954 before returning to the White Sox as a scout in 1955, a position he held until retiring in 1966. Onslow was 60 years old when appointed as the Sox manager and had spent the previous two seasons as a manager in the organization's farm system. He had spent a lifetime in baseball as a catcher, coach, minor league manager and scout. Onslow's big-league experience consisted of 45 games as a player during the 1910s and seven seasons as a coach with five different clubs in the 1920s and 1930s. A rigid and unyielding disciplinarian, he proved to be the wrong man to guide the youth movement on which the White Sox embarked upon after the disastrous 1948 season. He was fired in May 1950 with a 71–113 record as manager.

OCTOBER 4   At the age of 22, Chuck Comiskey is appointed vice president of the White Sox. He had been working for the club without a title in various capacities since his ather, Louis, died in 1939.

OCTOBER 9   Frank Lane is hired as general manager, replacing Leslie O'Connor.

Frank Lane, was the general manager from 1948 through 1955, and under his guidance and leadership, the franchise moved from perpetual losers to pennant contenders. During his seven seasons with the club, he made 241 deals involving 353 players. Among his acquisitions were Billy Pierce, Nellie Fox, Minnie Minoso, Sherm Lollar and Chico Carrasquel. Lane got into baseball management at a rather advanced age. He was a football and basketball official and ran a semipro league in Cincinnati when he was hired at the age of 37 by Larry MacPhail in 1933 as the Reds' business manager. Later, Lane served as an assistant to Warren Giles, MacPhail's successor as Cincinnati general manager. After Lane served a hitch in the Navy during World War II and MacPhail purchased the Yankees, Lane went to work for his former boss again running the Kansas City club in the Yankees' farm system. In 1947 and 1948, he was president of the American Association. Lane was 52 when hired by the White Sox and was warned not to take the job. The club was 51–101 in 1948, with a majority of the roster past the age of 30 and little in the way of talented prospects at either the big-league level or in the farm system. The club didn't improve overnight. The 1950 season was the seventh in a row in which the White Sox posted a losing record. The 1951 campaign, however, marked a turning point. After hiring Paul Richards as manager, the Sox won 81 games, the first of 17 straight winning seasons. Lane was impulsive and had an explosive temper, however, and often argued with upper management over team policies. In addition, the White Sox could never seem to get past the Yankees or Indians in the standings. After the 1955 season, the fourth of five consecutive third-place finishes, the Comiskey family fired Lane, but his legacy survived for a few more years. Many of the players Lane acquired in trades were key contributors to the 1959 American League pennant-winning team.

NOVEMBER 10   The White Sox send Aaron Robinson to the Tigers for Billy Pierce and $10,000.

In his first major trade, Frank Lane pulled off one of the greatest deals in White Sox history. For a 33-year-old catcher, the Sox received a 21-year-old pitcher who was named to seven All-Star teams while with the club. Over his big-league career, Pierce had a record of 211–169 with a 3.27 ERA, better numbers than many in the Hall of Fame, including contemporary Jim Bunning. Pierce, a quiet class act who was never flashy, has never received serious consideration for induction into Cooperstown in spite of his credentials. As a member of the White Sox, Pierce was 186–152. He ranks fourth among Sox pitchers in career wins, first in strikeouts (1,796), third in games started (390), third in shutouts (35), fourth in games (456), fourth in innings pitched (2,931) and fifth in complete games (183).

NOVEMBER 15   Two weeks after Harry Truman defeats Thomas Dewey in the presidential election, the White Sox sell Taffy Wright to the Athletics.

NOVEMBER 22   The White Sox trade Joe Haynes to the Indians for Joe Tipton.

Tipton hit only .204 in 67 games with the White Sox, then was traded a year later even up for Nellie Fox.

1949   Sox

Season in a Sentence

Frank Lane begins a long overdue youth movement and the White Sox take a small step toward respectability.

Finish • Won • Lost • Pct • GB

Sixth   63   91   .409   34.0

Manager

Jack Onslow

Stats

	WS	AL	Rank
Batting Avg:	.257	.263	6
On-Base Pct:	.347	.353	5
Slugging Pct:	.347	.379	8
Home Runs:	43		8
Stolen Bases:	62		1
ERA:	4.30	4.20	6
Fielding Avg:	.977	.977	4
Runs Scored:	648		7
Runs Allowed:	737		6

Starting Lineup

Don Wheeler, c
Chuck Kress, 1b
Cass Michaels, 2b
Floyd Baker, 3b
Luke Appling, ss
Steve Souchock, lf
Catfish Metkovich, cf
Dave Philley, rf
Herb Adams, cf
Gus Zernial, lf
Joe Tipton, c
Eddie Malone, c

Pitchers

Bill Wight, sp
Randy Gumpert, sp
Bob Kuzava, sp-rp
Billy Pierce, sp
Mickey Haefner, sp
Max Surkont, rp
Marino Pieretti, rp
Howie Judson, rp-sp

Attendance

937,151 (fifth in AL)

Club Leaders

Batting Avg:	Cass Michaels	.308
On-Base Pct:	Luke Appling	.439
Slugging Pct:	Cass Michaels	.421
Home Runs:	Steve Souchock	7
RBIs:	Cass Michaels	83
Runs:	Dave Philley	84
Stolen Bases:	Dave Philley	13
Wins:	Bill Wight	15
Strikeouts:	Billy Pierce	95
ERA:	Bill Wight	3.31
Saves:	Max Surkont	4
	Marino Pieretti	4

JANUARY 12   The White Sox sell Mike Tresh to the Indians.

APRIL 19   In the season opener, the White Sox lose 5–1 to the Tigers in Detroit.

APRIL 22   In the home opener, the White Sox defeat the Browns 5–2 before a crowd of 9,568. Gus Zernial hit a home run in his first game with the Sox at Comiskey Park.

              The White Sox started well and had a 17–15 record on May 22, but the season soured quickly with a 46–76 mark the rest of the way. Nonetheless, the 63 victories was an improvement of 12 over the 51–101 won-lost ledger of 1948.

MAY 1   The White Sox sweep the Browns 7–6 and 14–11 at Sportsman's Park. The Sox had to stave off ninth-inning rallies in both games. The Browns put together a pair of ninth-inning rallies with three in the ninth of the opener and eight in the nightcap that nearly wiped out a 14–3 Chicago lead. After the second game, manager Jack Onslow and catcher Joe Tipton nearly came to blows after Onslow accused Tipton of failing to cover up his signals to the pitcher.

MAY 3   The Senators outhomer the home team 7–2 at Comiskey Park and defeat the White Sox 14–12 in 10 innings. Clyde Vollmer hit two home runs for Washington with Mark Christman, Eddie Robinson, Bud Stewart, Al Evans and Gil Coan adding the others. Gus Zernial and Joe Tipton homered for Chicago.

              Before the 1949 season, the White Sox moved in the home run distances at Comiskey Park by building a chicken-wire fence 20 feet inside the outfield wall. The foul lines were reduced from 352 to 332 feet, the power alleys from 382 to 362 and center field from 440 to 420. The fence was built to take advantage of the power of Gus Zernial, a rookie outfielder who clubbed 40 homers for the Hollywood Stars of the Pacific Coast League in 1948. After nine homers were struck in the May 3 game, the fence was ripped down and the previous dimensions restored. In the first eight games of 1949, there were 23 homers hit at Comiskey, 11 of them between the new fence and the old barrier. The Sox hit only 43 home runs as a team in 1949, far fewer than any other team in the major leagues. The Senators were the next worst with 81. The White Sox leader in home runs in 1949 was Steve Souchock with seven. Zernial missed two months with a broken collarbone and hit only five out of the ballpark in 73 games.

MAY 7   The White Sox trade Don Kolloway to the Tigers for Vern Rapp.

MAY 11   The White Sox score in all eight turns at bat and defeat the Red Sox 12–8 at Comiskey Park. Chicago tallied once in the first and second innings, twice in the third, once in the fourth, twice in the fifth, once in the sixth and seventh, and three times in the eighth.

              On the same day, the White Sox purchased Clyde Shoun from the Braves.

MAY 14   The White Sox nose out the Indians 11–10 at Comiskey Park. The Sox wiped out an 8–4 deficit with five runs in the fifth inning.

              The White Sox sported new uniforms in 1949, displaying the interlocking "S," "O," and "X" in Old English script for the first time, with the letters arranged in a downward slope. The primary color was changed from blue with some red trim, to black.

MAY 15

Before a crowd of 53,325 assembled for a double-header at Comiskey Park, the White Sox beat the Indians twice by shutouts, 10–0 and 2–0. Bill Wight hurled the shutout in the opener. Al Gettel provided the second-game whitewash. It was Gettel's only shutout as a member of the Sox. Both runs in the nightcap scored on the first major league home run by Gordon Goldsberry, a sixth-inning shot off Mike Garcia.

Chuck Comiskey and Frank Lane celebrated the double-shutout by digging up home plate and mailing it to Indians owner Bill Veeck with a note reading: "We thought you might like to know what this looks like." Going along with the gag, Veeck went one better and had the plate installed at Municipal Stadium in Cleveland with ceremonies before an Indians game on May 27.

JUNE 3

The White Sox install the first members in the club's Hall of Fame. The original White Sox Hall of Famers were Luke Appling, Eddie Collins, Charles Comiskey, Jimmy Dykes, Red Faber, Harry Hooper, Joe Kuhel, Ted Lyons, Johnny Mostil, Ray Schalk, Al Simmons, Billy Sullivan, Ed Walsh and Doc White. Large murals of the players were placed within the Comiskey Park foyer near the front entrance.

Appling was 42 years old in 1949, but he hit .301 in 142 games.

JULY 19

Rookie outfielder Herb Adams severely burns his hands while cooking eggs for breakfast. It was his third injury of the season. Earlier, Adams went on the shelf with a broken finger, then hurt his shoulder crashing into a fence while attempting a catch. Adams was born in Hollywood, California. His mother had bit parts as an actress in several silent films. Herb's aunt was Anne Shirley, who had featured roles in many movies during the 1930s and 1940s and earned an Academy Award nomination for *Stella Dallas.*

Howie Judson set a White Sox club record for consecutive losses in a season with 14 in 1949. After winning his first decision, he ended the season 1–14 with a 4.58 earned run average.

JULY 21

The White Sox purchase Mickey Haefner from the Senators.

JULY 22

The White Sox erupt for eight runs in the first inning and pummel the Athletics 12–0 at Comiskey Park.

JULY 26

The Red Sox score 10 runs in the eighth inning and maul the White Sox 11–2 in Boston.

AUGUST 15

Bill Wight shuts out the Browns 8–0 in St. Louis.

AUGUST 16

Bob Kuzava pitches a shutout to defeat the Browns 4–0 in St. Louis.

The shutout was the only one for Kuzava as a member of the White Sox.

AUGUST 17

Mickey Haefner accounts for the third consecutive White Sox shutout, defeating the Tigers 1–0 at Comiskey Park. The shutout was the only one Haefner pitched as a member of the White Sox. Outfielder Johnny Ostrowski, a Chicago native in his Comiskey Park debut, drove in the winning run with a single in the seventh inning.

The Sox participated in six consecutive shutouts, including losses on August 14, 18 and 19.

AUGUST 28   The White Sox blow a 7–2 lead by allowing six runs in the ninth inning for an 8–7 loss to the Yankees in the first game of a double-header at Comiskey Park. The Sox also lost the nightcap in a contest called after eight innings by darkness.

AUGUST 30   Bill Wight pitches a 10-inning shutout but loses 1–0 to the Senators at Comiskey Park.

In pre-game ceremonies, Jackie Hayes was honored and given $8,000 in cash and gifts. Hayes played for the Sox from 1932 until 1940, when deteriorating eyesight ended his career (see April 6, 1940). He had been blind since 1942.

SEPTEMBER 20   Bob Kuzava allows only three hits in eight innings, but he walks 10 and loses 2–1 to the Yankees in New York.

SEPTEMBER 21   After falling behind 8–1, the White Sox score three runs in the sixth inning, three in the eighth and three in the ninth and defeat the Yankees 10–9 in New York. Gus Zernial's pinch-hit homer accounted for all three ninth-inning runs.

One of the September call-ups was second baseman Jim Baumer, who was 18 years old and signed a contract calling for a $50,000 bonus out of high school. He had the unusual distinction of playing in the majors during the 1940s and 1960s, but not in the 1950s. In 1949, he collected four hits in 10 at-bats with the Sox, but he spent the next 12 years in the minors. In 1961, Baumer was the Reds' Opening Day second baseman, but he was traded to the Tigers after only 10 games and a .125 batting average. Detroit sent him back to the minors and he never played in another big league game, although Baumer served as general manager of the Milwaukee Brewers from 1971 through 1977.

SEPTEMBER 29   Six days after President Harry Truman announces that the Soviet Union has developed and tested an atomic bomb, a meager crowd of 801 at Comiskey Park watches the White Sox lose 8–3 to the Indians.

SEPTEMBER 30   The White Sox purchase Chico Carrasquel from the Dodgers.

Carrasquel played in three All-Star Games with the White Sox as the club's starting shortstop from 1950 through 1955, bridging the gap between Luke Appling and Luis Aparicio.

OCTOBER 2   On the last day of the season, nine St. Louis pitchers hurl one inning each during a 4–3 White Sox win in the first game of a double-header at Sportsman's Park. The Browns won the second contest, called after five innings by darkness, 5–3.

OCTOBER 19   The White Sox trade Joe Tipton to the Athletics for Nellie Fox.

Frank Lane and the White Sox pulled off what is arguably the greatest player-for-player deal in club history. For a 26-year-old reserve catcher who hit .204 for the Sox in 1948, the club acquired a future Hall of Famer who played 14 seasons in Chicago. The acquisition of Fox didn't create any newspaper headlines at the time it was announced, however. He was two months shy of his 22nd birthday, stood only five-foot-nine, weighed just 150 pounds and had a career batting average of .247 with no homers in 263 at-bats. The White Sox already had an All-Star at second base in Cass Michaels, who was only 23 in 1949 and hit 308 with 83 RBIs. Fox took over the position in May 1950, however, after Michaels was traded to Washington. Nellie made the first of his 12 All-Star teams in 1951. Despite his slight stature, he once played in 798 consecutive games. He appeared in 2,295 games at second base during his big-league career, the fifth-best of all-time. Fox ranks second in double plays by a second baseman, trailing only Bill Mazeroski. Almost impossible to strike out, Foxx fanned just 216 times in 9,232 at-bats. In 1958, he went 98 straight games without striking out. He never struck out as many as 20 times in a season. Among White Sox players all-time, Fox ranks second in games (2,115), tied for first in triples (104), second in at-bats (8,486), second in hits (2,470), third in runs (1,187), third in doubles (335), third in total bases (3,118), fifth in walks (658) and eighth in runs batted in (740).

DECEMBER 14   The White Sox trade Eddie Klieman to the Athletics for Hank Majeski.

THE STATE OF THE WHITE SOX

At the beginning of the decade, the White Sox were one of baseball's worst franchises. From 1921 through 1950, the Sox had only seven winning seasons and never finished a season higher than third place or closer than eight games from the top of the AL standings. A turnaround began in 1951, the first of 17 consecutive winning seasons that included an American League pennant in 1959. Overall, the Sox were 847–693 during the 1950s, a winning percentage of .550 that was the third-best in the league behind the Yankees and Indians and the best of any decade in White Sox history. The Yankees won eight of the 10 American League titles during the '50s, missing only in 1954 and 1959. Cleveland won the 1954 pennant under Al Lopez, who was also the manager of the 1959 White Sox.

THE BEST TEAM

The 1959 White Sox captured the only AL pennant won by the franchise between 1919 and 2005. The 1959 club was 94–60 before losing the World Series to the Dodgers in six games.

THE WORST TEAM

The 1950 White Sox were 60–94 and landed in sixth place.

THE BEST MOMENT

The White Sox ended 40 years of frustration by clinching the pennant on September 22, 1959. Mayor Richard Daley ordered that the city's air raid sirens be turned on, setting off a panic.

THE WORST MOMENT

Chuck Comiskey resigned as vice president in 1952 when his mother, Grace, the club president, reneged on her promise to grant him a modest raise. The petty squabbles among members of the Comiskey family created headlines throughout the 1950s.

THE ALL-DECADE TEAM • YEARS WITH WS

Sherm Lollar, c	1952–63
Eddie Robinson, 1b	1950–52
Nellie Fox, 2b	1950–62
Bubba Phillips, 3b	1956–59
Chico Carrasquel, ss	1950–55
Minnie Minoso, lf	1951–57, 1960–61, 1964, 1976, 1980
Jim Landis, cf	1957–64
Jim Rivera, rf	1952–61
Billy Pierce, p	1949–61
Dick Donovan, p	1955–60
Early Wynn, p	1958–62
Gerry Staley, p	1956–61

Fox is the only member of the 1950s All-Decade Team in the Hall of Fame, but Pierce, Minoso and Lollar also deserve admission. The inclusion of Phillips highlights the White Sox's problems in finding a consistently adequate third baseman, a situation that existed for 30 years. No one on the White Sox played 100 or more games at third in consecutive seasons between Willie Kamm (1923–30) and Pete Ward (1963–65). Other outstanding players of the 1950s included shortstop Luis Aparlcio (1956–62, 1968–70) and pitchers Jack Harshman (1954–57) and Virgil Trucks (1953–55).

THE DECADE LEADERS

Batting Avg:	Minnie Minoso	.307
On-Base Pct:	Minnie Minoso	.405
Slugging Pct:	Minnie Minoso	.475
Home Runs:	Minnie Minoso	100
RBIs:	Minnie Minoso	616
Runs:	Nellie Fox	902
Stolen Bases:	Minnie Minoso	145
Wins:	Billy Pierce	155
Strikeouts:	Billy Pierce	1,487
ERA:	Billy Pierce	3.06
Saves:	Harry Dorish	36

THE HOME FIELD

The bullpens at Comiskey Park were moved to center field in 1950, shortening the distance from home plate in dead center from 440 feet to 410. A large scoreboard was built in 1951 in back of the center-field bleachers, replacing the boards on the outfield walls. The brick exterior of the ballpark was whitewashed in 1959.

THE GAME YOU WISHED YOU HAD SEEN

Bob Keegan pitched a no-hitter at Comiskey Park against the Senators on August 20, 1957.

THE WAY THE GAME WAS PLAYED

The increase in the number of home runs continued during the 1950s, with AL teams averaging 120 homers per season, compared with 85 during the 1930s. Playing in a large ballpark, however, the White Sox relied more on speed. The Sox hit fewer home runs than the American League team average every season from 1917 through 1971. On the other hand, the Sox led the league in stolen bases for 11 consecutive seasons beginning in 1951, and the club was dubbed the "Go-Go Sox." The number of complete games in the AL continued to decline, from an average of 63 per team in 1950 to 46 in 1959. Relievers were making more appearances, and the relief specialist emerged, including such White Sox hurlers as Harry Dorish, Turk Lown and Gerry Staley. The increased use of relievers to close out victories led to a new statistic called the "save," although it wasn't officially recognized until 1969. Games were also taking longer to play. The average length of a game rose from two hours and 23 minutes in 1950 to two hours and 38 minutes in 1959. In addition, the first franchise shifts in 50 years took place. In the NL, the Boston Braves moved to Milwaukee in 1953. In the AL, the St. Louis Browns moved to Baltimore in 1954, where the club was renamed the Orioles and the Athletics transferred from Philadelphia to Kansas City a year later. In 1958, major league baseball was played west of the Rocky Mountains for the first time when the Dodgers and Giants moved from New York to California. The integration of baseball accelerated during the 1950s. In 1950, there were only nine African-American or dark-skinned Latin players in the major leagues. By 1959, that number increased to 67. The White Sox were among the teams that integrated during the 1950s (see July 28, 1950 and April 30, 1951).

THE MANAGEMENT

Charles Comiskey founded the franchise in 1900, but by the 1950s his descendants quarreled constantly. Grace Comiskey, who was Charles's daughter-in-law, was club president from 1941 until her death in 1956. There was no individual with the title of president from 1956 until 1959. Following Grace's passing, her son Chuck and son-in-law John Rigney were co-heads of the franchise as vice presidents. The reign of the Comiskeys ended in 1959 when Bill Veeck bought the club and left no doubt as to who was in charge. General managers were Frank Lane (1948–55), the dual heads of Chuck Comiskey and John Rigney (1955–59) and Hank Greenberg (1959–61). Field managers were Jack Onslow (1949–50), Red Corriden (1950), Paul Richards (1951–54), Marty Marion (1954–56) and Al Lopez (1957–65).

THE BEST PLAYER MOVE

In November 1951, the White Sox picked up Sherm Lollar from the Browns along with Al Widmar and Tom Upton for Jim Rivera, Joe DeMaestri, Gordon Goldsberry and Gus Niarhos.

THE WORST PLAYER MOVE

The Sox damaged their future in December 1959 by trading prospects Norm Cash and Johnny Romano, along with Bubba Phillips, to Cleveland for Minnie Minoso, Dick Brown, Don Ferrarese and Jake Striker.

1950s

1950   Sox

Season in a Sentence

The rebuilding project hits a bump in the road as the White Sox post 94 defeats, the club's seventh consecutive losing season.

Finish • Won • Lost • Pct • GB

| Sixth | 60 | 94 | .390 | 38.0 |

Managers

Jack Onslow (8–22) and Red Corriden (52–72)

Stats

Stats	WS	AL	Rank
Batting Avg:	.260	.271	6
On-Base Pct:	.333	.356	8
Slugging Pct:	.364	.402	7
Home Runs:	93		7
Stolen Bases:	19		8
ERA:	4.66	4.58	4
Fielding Avg:	.977	.976	5
Runs Scored:	625		8
Runs Allowed:	749		4

Starting Lineup

Phil Masi, c
Eddie Robinson, 1b
Nellie Fox, 2b
Hank Majeski, 3b
Chico Carrasquel, ss
Gus Zernial, lf
Dave Philley, cf-rf
Marv Rickert, rf
Floyd Baker, 3b

Pitchers

Billy Pierce, sp
Bill Wight, sp
Bob Cain, sp-rp
Ray Scarborough, rp
Ken Holcombe, sp-rp
Howie Judson, rp
Luis Aloma, rp
Randy Gumpert, rp-sp

Attendance

781,330 (fifth in AL)

Club Leaders

Batting Avg:	Eddie Robinson	.311
On-Base Pct:	Eddie Robinson	.402
Slugging Pct:	Eddie Robinson	.486
Home Runs:	Gus Zernial	29
RBIs:	Gus Zernial	93
Runs:	Gus Zernial	75
Stolen Bases:	Dave Philley	6
Wins:	Billy Pierce	12
Strikeouts:	Billy Pierce	118
ERA:	Bill Wight	3.58
Saves:	Luis Aloma	4

FEBRUARY 2   The White Sox purchase Phil Masi from the Pirates.

APRIL 18   The White Sox open the season with a 5–3 loss to the Browns before 9,987 at Comiskey Park. Cass Michaels hit a home run. Nellie Fox made his White Sox debut as a pinch-runner for Dave Philley in the ninth inning.

The bullpens were moved in 1950 from the foul lines to a spot in center field, which reduced the home run distance in that direction from 440 feet to 410.

APRIL 30   Bill Wight pitches a two-hitter to defeat the Tigers 5–0 in the first game of a doubleheader at Comiskey Park. The only Detroit hits were doubles by Johnny Lipon and Dick Kryhoski. The second game was called on account of darkness at the end of the ninth inning, resulting in a 7–7 tie. A late rally prevented an almost certain defeat. The Sox trailed 7–0 before scoring four runs in the seventh inning and three in the ninth.

MAY 4   In his first major league start, Bob Cain pitches a shutout to defeat the Yankees 15–0 in New York. The White Sox erupted for 23 hits in the contest.

The shutout was the only one that Cain pitched as a member of the White Sox. He was 10–14 with the club before being traded to the Tigers in 1951. He finished his career in 1953 with a 37–44 record, a 4.50 ERA and three shutouts.

MAY 22   The White Sox roar back with three runs in the 10th inning to beat the Red Sox 10–9 at Comiskey Park. Chicago led 7–5 before Boston scored two runs in the ninth inning and two in the 10th. During the bottom half, Hank Majeski tied the score 9–9 with a two-run double, then scored on a pinch-single by Eddie Malone.

MAY 26   The White Sox fire 61-year-old Jack Onslow as manager and replace him with 62-year-old coach Red Corriden.

The Sox were 8–22 when the switch was made. Onslow's abilities as manager had been the subject of heated debate among the White Sox hierarchy for the better part of a year. Frank Lane and Chuck Comiskey wanted to get rid of Onslow. Grace Comiskey and her two daughters wanted to keep Onslow. Finally, Chuck Comiskey threatened to resign his post as the club's vice president if Onslow wasn't ousted. Despite his rather advanced age, Corriden had never before managed a big league team. He was hired merely to finish out the 1950 season until a more suitable alternative could be found (see October 10, 1950). The Sox had a record of 52–72 with Corriden as manager.

MAY 28   Gus Zernial hits a two-run homer in the third inning off Early Wynn to account for the only runs in a 2–0 win over the Indians in the first game of a double-header at Comiskey Park. Bill Wight pitched the shutout. Cleveland won the second contest 7–0.

MAY 29   Trailing 8–6, the White Sox score four runs in the eighth inning and two in the ninth to defeat the Browns 12–8 in St. Louis. Howie Judson was the winning pitcher in relief, ending a 15-game losing streak spread over two seasons. He lost his last 14 decisions in 1949 and his first one in 1950.

MAY 30   The White Sox sweep the Browns 14–2 and 12–9 at Sportsman's Park. The two wins gave Chicago 38 runs in three consecutive games. The Sox pounded out 38 hits during the twin bill, 21 of them in the opener. Gus Zernial drove in eight runs, including six in the first game, on two homers and three singles. In his final two games with the White Sox, Cass Michaels collected six hits, among them a homer and a triple.

MAY 31   The White Sox trade Cass Michaels, Bob Kuzava and Johnny Ostrowski to the Senators for Eddie Robinson, Ray Scarborough and Al Kozar.

Robinson gave the White Sox some much needed power in the middle of the lineup. He hit 20 or more home runs in each of his three seasons with the club before a trade to the Athletics in January 1953. Robinson smacked 20 homers in 1950, 29 in 1951 and 22 in 1952. No one hit 20 or more home runs in three straight seasons again until Bill Melton collected 23 in 1969, 33 in 1970 and 33 more in 1971. Michaels's career mysteriously went downhill after an All-Star season in 1949 at the age of 23. In 1950, he held out for a $3,000 raise, then reported to spring training 15 pounds overweight. By 1954, Michaels's big league career was over. The trade with Washington opened the way for Nellie Fox to take over as the White Sox's starting second baseman, a job he would hold until 1962.

JUNE 15   Billy Pierce pitches a one-hitter to defeat the Yankees 5–0 at Comiskey Park. The only New York hit was a single by Billy Johnson in the fifth inning. Pierce pitched his gem despite dismal weather conditions. The contest was delayed by rain in the second, fourth and fifth innings. The three interruptions totaled 93 minutes.

JUNE 16   Ray Scarborough walks 10 batters and allows five hits but defeats the Senators 7–1 at Comiskey Park. Scarborough was traded by Washington to Chicago on May 31. All seven White Sox runs scored in the third inning.

JUNE 19   Marv Rickert hits a ninth-inning, RBI-single to tie the Senators 3–3 at Comiskey Park, then swats an 11th inning walk-off homer for a 4–3 White Sox victory.

JULY 8   Down 5–0, the White Sox score two runs in the sixth inning and five in the seventh to win 7–5 over the Browns in the first game of a double-header at Sportsman's Park. St. Louis won the second contest 11–5.

The game was played two weeks after North Korean military forces attacked South Korea. The United States quickly entered the conflict on the side of South Korea. By the time the Korean War ended in 1953, military call-ups affected the White Sox roster. Outfield prospect Bill Wilson missed the 1951 and 1952 seasons while serving in the armed forces. In 1952, Sammy Esposito, Herb Adams and Joe Kirrene were also in the service. Esposito and Kirrene were on active duty into the 1953 campaign.

JULY 11   The National League wins the All-Star Game 4–3 in 14 innings before a crowd of 46,127 at Comiskey Park. It was the first All-Star Game to be nationally televised. Red Schoendienst accounted for the winning run with a homer off Ted Gray of the Tigers. Ralph Kiner tied the score 3–3 with a home run in the ninth. Ted Williams broke his elbow crashing into the left-field wall chasing a Kiner drive in the first inning. Williams remained in the contest until the seventh, when the pain became too great to continue. He even put the AL ahead 3–2 with an RBI-single in the fifth.

Future Hall of Famers on the rosters of the two clubs included Yogi Berra, Roy Campanella, Joe DiMaggio, Larry Doby, Bobby Doerr, Bob Feller, George Kell, Ralph Kiner, Bob Lemon, Stan Musial, Pee Wee Reese, Phil Rizzuto, Robin Roberts, Jackie Robinson, Red Schoendienst, Duke Snider, Enos Slaughter Warren Spahn and Ted Williams.

JULY 14   The Red Sox score 11 runs in the third inning of a 13–1 win over the White Sox in Boston.

JULY 28   The White Sox sign their first African-American players when Sam Hairston and Bob Boyd ink contracts. Both were sent to the minors. Hairston's big-league career lasted only four games in 1951, although his son Jerry played for the White Sox from 1973 through 1977 and from 1981 through 1989. Jerry's son, Jerry Jr., reached the majors in 1998 and was still active in 2006. Boyd also reached the White Sox's roster in 1951 and lasted nine seasons in the majors. The first black player to appear in a major league game for the White Sox was Minnie Minoso on May 1, 1951.

AUGUST 3   Randy Gumpert pitches the White Sox to a 1–0 win over the Athletics at Comiskey
               Park. The lone run scored on an RBI-triple by Eddie Robinson when right fielder
               Elmer Valo tried to make a shoe string catch on a sinking liner and missed.

AUGUST 5   Chico Carrasquel runs his hitting streak to 24 games during a 12–7 loss to the
               Red Sox at Comiskey Park.

               *There were only seven players born in Latin America playing in the major
               leagues in 1950. The seven were Carrasquel from Venezuela, Luis Olmo from
               Puerto Rico and Mike Guerra, Sandy Consuegra, Roberto Ortiz, Luis Aloma
               and Connie Marrero from Cuba. Five of the seven played for two clubs. In
               addition to Carrasquel, Luis Aloma was a member of the White Sox and served
               as an interpreter for Carrasquel, who spoke little English. Marrero, Consuegra
               and Ortiz played for the Washington Senators.*

AUGUST 8   After spotting the Indians a 5–0 lead, the White Sox bounce back with four runs in the
               sixth inning, two in the seventh and three in the eighth to win 9–6 at Comiskey Park.

               On the same day, the White Sox sold Mickey Haefner to the Braves.

SEPTEMBER 10   Randy Gumpert pitches a 12-inning complete game, but he loses 1–0 in a duel with
               Hal Newhouser and the Tigers in the first game of a double-header at Comiskey
               Park. The White Sox won the second fray 5–4.

SEPTEMBER 30   Eddie Robinson hits a grand slam off Cuddles Marshall in the eighth inning of an
               8–2 win over the Browns. Only 839 fans attended the game at Comiskey Park on a
               Saturday afternoon.

OCTOBER 1   On the final day of the season, Gus Zernial hits four homers and drives in eight
               runs during a double-header against the Browns at Comiskey Park. In the opener,
               Gus homered in the fifth inning off Ned Garver in a 4–3 Chicago win. Zernial hit
               three home runs in the nightcap, which the Sox lost 10–6. He went deep off Stubby
               Overmire in the second and third innings and Jack Bruner in the eighth. The home
               runs allowed Zernial to break the club record for homers in a season with 29.
               The previous mark was 27, set by Zeke Bonura in 1934 and Joe Kuhel in 1940.
               The second tilt was also the 2,422nd and final game of Luke Appling's career. He
               collected a single in four at-bats. The starting pitcher for the Sox was 19-year-old
               Gus Keriazakos, who made his major league debut after signing for a bonus of
               $67,000 out of high school in Montclair, New Jersey, where he was a classmate of
               future astronaut Buzz Aldrin. Keriazakos never came close to reaching such heights
               in baseball. In his big-league debut, he lasted only 2⅓ innings, allowing five runs,
               seven hits and five walks. Keriazakos never played another game for the White Sox.

               *After hitting .301 in 142 games in 1949 at the age of 42, Appling lost his starting
               shortstop job to Chico Carrasquel. In 1950, Appling batted .234 in 50 games.
               White Sox fans clamored for Luke to be named manager for the 1951 season,
               but management had other ideas. He remained in the organization for a few
               more years as a minor league manager.*

OCTOBER 10   The White Sox hire 42-year-old Paul Richards as manager.

Richards was a catcher during his playing career, which ended in 1946 with the Tigers. He was hired by the White Sox after a run of success as a manager in the minor leagues. An excellent teacher and motivator and a stickler for fundamentals, Richards was considered to be one of the smartest men in baseball and an excellent handler of pitchers. He was a quiet but commanding presence in the dugout and wasn't afraid to use unorthodox strategy. Under Richards, the long-dormant White Sox suddenly awoke from a 30-year slumber. After finishing 60–94 in 1950, the Sox were in first place in July in 1951 and ended up with an 81–73 record. The club had winning seasons in each of Richards's four seasons as manager, the first time that the Sox were above .500 for that length of time since doing it six years in a row from 1904 through 1909. Difficulties with general manager Frank Lane, however, led Richards to leave the White Sox for the Orioles just prior to the end of the 1954 campaign.

DECEMBER 10   The White Sox trade Bill Wight and Ray Scarborough to the Red Sox for Joe Dobson, Al Zarilla and Dick Littlefield.

1951   Sox

Season in Sentence

Sparked by a rejuvenated, speed-based offense under new manager Paul Richards, the White Sox stage a 14-game winning streak in May and hold first place in July before fading to fourth.

Finish • Won • Lost • Pct • GB

Fourth   81   73   .526   17.0

Manager

Paul Richards

Stats

Stats	WS	AL	Rank
Batting Avg:	.270	.262	1
On-Base Pct:	.349	.342	4
Slugging Pct:	.385	.381	5
Home Runs:	86		6 (tie)
Stolen Bases:	99		1
ERA:	3.50	4.12	2
Fielding Avg:	.975	.975	4
Runs Scored:	714		4
Runs Allowed:	644		3

Starting Lineup

Phil Masi, c
Eddie Robinson, 1b
Nellie Fox, 2b
Bob Dillinger, 3b
Chico Carrasquel, ss
Minnie Minoso, lf-3b-rf
Jim Busby, cf
Al Zarilla, rf
Bud Stewart, lf
Don Lenhardt, lf
Ray Coleman, cf-lf
Gus Niarhos, c

Pitchers

Billy Pierce, sp
Saul Rogovin, sp
Ken Holcombe, sp
Joe Dobson, sp
Lou Kretlow, sp-rp
Howie Judson, sp-rp
Randy Gumpert, rp-sp
Harry Dorish, rp

Attendance

1,328,234 (third in AL)

Club Leaders

Batting Avg:	Minnie Minoso	.324
On-Base Pct:	Minnie Minoso	.419
Slugging Pct:	Minnie Minoso	.498
Home Runs:	Eddie Robinson	29
RBIs:	Eddie Robinson	117
Runs:	Minnie Minoso	109
Stolen Bases:	Minnie Minoso	31
Wins:	Billy Pierce	15
Strikeouts:	Billy Pierce	113
ERA:	Saul Rogovin	2.48
Saves:	Joe Dobson	3
	Luis Aloma	3

MARCH 11   During spring training, Marilyn Monroe poses for photographs with White Sox players Gus Zernial, Hank Majeski and Joe Dobson.

At the time, Monroe was a largely unknown actress who had yet to play a featured role in a movie and was described in the stories surrounding the photo opportunity as a "starlet." Within two years, however, she became one of the biggest stars in show business. Marilyn was photographed with the White Sox while acting as hostess for the annual Kiwanis Club Crippled Children's Fund baseball game in Los Angeles. The Hollywood Stars of the Pacific Coast played a team of major league All-Stars from the four clubs that trained in Southern California, which were the White Sox (Pasadena), Cubs (Los Angeles), Browns (Burbank) and Pirates (San Bernardino).

APRIL 17   On Opening Day, the White Sox hammer the Browns 17–3 in St. Louis. The Sox collected 19 hits and drew 14 walks. Seven runs scored in the eighth inning. Al Zarilla homered, doubled and singled, scored three runs and drove in four in his White Sox debut. Gus Zernial also had four RBIs. Jim Busby collected three hits and drove in three runs. Floyd Baker scored three runs. Billy Pierce pitched a complete game.

APRIL 19   After scoring 17 runs in the opener, the White Sox win the second game of the season 13–5 over the Browns in St. Louis. Al Zarilla homered, giving him two home runs in two games with the White Sox.

APRIL 20   In the home opener, the White Sox win 5–0 over the Tigers before 8,731 at Comiskey Park. After three games, the White Sox were 3–0, outscoring the opposition 35–8. Randy Gumpert held Detroit hitless until the eighth inning, when Charlie Keller slammed a single. Gumpert finished with a three-hit complete game. He also drove in two runs. AL president Will Harridge commemorated the 50th anniversary of the founding of the American League by throwing out the ceremonial first pitch with a gold baseball.

A huge scoreboard was erected at Comiskey Park above the center field bleachers in 1951. It was topped by a large sign for Chesterfield cigarettes and a Longines clock. The previous scoreboards were located on the outfield walls in left and right fields. The White Sox also sported new home uniforms. Navy blue pinstripes were added and the "Sox" logo on the front was made larger and was outlined in red. The caps had "Sox" on the front instead of the letter "C."

APRIL 25   Eddie Robinson becomes the first White Sox player to homer onto the roof at Comiskey Park. The blast came during an 8–6 win over the Browns in the first game of a double-header. St. Louis won the second contest 7–4. Robinson hit 29 homers, drove in 117 runs and batted .282 in 1951.

There were two games on April 25 because the April 26 contest was moved up a day as a result of a visit to Chicago from General Douglas MacArthur. A parade was held in his honor and was attended by an estimated two million people. MacArthur was the head of United States forces in Korea, but he was removed from his command by President Harry Truman on April 11 in a move that was unpopular with the majority of the American public.

APRIL 30   In a three-team trade, the White Sox trade Gus Zernial and Dave Philley to the Athletics and receive Paul Lehner from the A's and Minnie Minoso from the Indians. A native of Cuba, Minoso became the first player of African descent to play for the White Sox. In 1949, while a member of the Indians, Minoso became the first dark-skinned Latin player in major league history. Colorful and gregarious, Orestes (Minnie) Minoso became an immediate fan favorite with his infectious enthusiasm for the game. He was as productive as he was exciting. Minoso hit over .300 eight times, scored over 100 runs in four seasons, drove in over 100 runs in four years and led the AL in stolen bases (three times), triples (three times) and hits, doubles and slugging percentage once each. He was able to accomplish these feats in spite of the fact that he didn't become a big-league regular until he was 28 years old. Among White Sox players, Minoso ranks 10th in games played (1,379), ninth in at-bats (5,011), fourth in extra-base hits (474), fourth in runs batted in (808), fifth in on-base percentage (.397), fifth in runs (893), fifth in walks (658), sixth in total bases (2,346), sixth in doubles (260), sixth in triples (79), eighth in hits (1,523) and 10th in slugging percentage (.468). Although the trade to acquire Minoso is one of the best in club history, it wasn't without cost. Zernial led the AL in home runs and RBIs in 1951 and drove in over 100 runs three times with the A's.

MAY 1   In his first at-bat with the White Sox, Minnie Minoso thrills the Comiskey Park crowd by hitting a home run into the center-field bleachers. It was also his first big-league homer. Minoso batted third in the lineup and played third base during the 8–3 win over the Yankees. In addition, Mickey Mantle hit his first home run in the majors, a sixth-inning bomb off Randy Gumpert.

In 138 games with the Sox in 1951, Minoso hit .324 with 14 triples, 10 homers, 74 RBIs, 109 runs scored and a league-leading 31 stolen bases. In 1950, the entire White Sox team

It was a sign of positive changes for the Sox when young Minnie Minoso arrived in 1951 in a trade from Cleveland. He went back to Cleveland in 1958 and then returned to Chicago in 1960 for two more productive years.

stole only 19 bases, the worst figure in the majors. In a remarkable turnaround, the Sox led the big leagues in stolen bases in 1951 with 99. Fleet-footed Jim Busby (26 stolen bases) and Chico Carrasquel (14 bases) also contributed to the stolen base mark, which became a trend for several more years. Frank Lane and Paul Richards realized that speed and defense were necessary to win at spacious Comiskey Park. The White Sox led the AL in steals 11 consecutive seasons from 1951 through 1961. The Sox also increased their run production from a major league worst 625 runs in 1950 to 714 in 1951, which ranked fourth in the AL and seventh in the majors.

MAY 11   Joe Dobson pitches a one-hitter and defeats the Indians 12–1 at Comiskey Park. The only Cleveland hit was a double by Bobby Avila in the eighth inning.

Dobson was the youngest of 14 children born to a Texas farming family. At the age of nine, he lost his left thumb and forefinger playing with a dynamite cap.

MAY 15   Nellie Fox hits a two-run homer in the 11th inning to defeat the Red Sox 9–7 in Boston. It was Nellie's first major league home run and was struck in his 804th career at-bat. Paul Richards used unorthodox strategy earlier in the contest. Ted Williams was the first Boston batter in the ninth. Richards brought left-hander Billy Pierce into the game to relieve Harry Dorish and face Williams, but in order to keep Dorish in the game, Richards moved the pitcher to third base. Williams popped up, and Dorish went back to the mound. The victory was the first of a 14-game winning streak.

On the same day, the White Sox traded Bob Cain to the Tigers for Saul Rogovin. When acquired by the White Sox, Rogovin was 27 years old and had a 3–3 lifetime record and a 5.56 ERA but had played for Paul Richards in the minors. After Richards made a few corrections in Rogovin's delivery, he was a pleasant surprise, posting an 11–7 record and a 2.45 ERA with the Sox in 1951. Rogovin was 14–9 in 1952 before a sore arm in 1953 reduced his effectiveness.

MAY 16   The White Sox purchase Bob Dillinger from the Pirates.

MAY 18   Bud Stewart hits a grand slam off Spec Shea in the eighth inning to break a 3–3 tie during a 7–4 win over the Yankees in New York. Stewart entered the game in the second inning as a replacement for Jim Busby, who injured his thumb.

MAY 28   The White Sox take first place with their 12th win in a row, a 4–2 defeat of the Browns at Comiskey Park. Saul Rogovin pitched a two-hitter. The only St. Louis hits were singles by Bobby Young and Don Lenhardt in the seventh inning.

MAY 29   The White Sox trade Hank Majeski to the Athletics for Kermit Wahl.

MAY 30   The White Sox win their 14th game in a row, the second-longest win streak in club history, with a 5–2 and 8–1 sweep of the Browns at Comiskey Park. The White Sox outscored the opposition 89–48 in the 14 games.

After a 6–7 start, the White Sox won 20 of their next 22 games for a 26–9 record. After seven consecutive losing seasons, the enthusiasm of White Sox fans was revived. The team was called the "Go-Go Sox" and bumper stickers with the slogan began appearing all over Chicagoland. Attendance increased from 781,330 to 1,328,234. It was the first time that the club drew over one million. The giant leap from a 51–101 record in 1948 to 81–73 in 1951 was made with little help from the farm system. The only regular on the 1951 club who was developed in the club's minor league chain was Jim Busby. The rest were acquired from other clubs during a remarkable turnover of the roster. Of the 27 players who played in at least 15 games for the White Sox in 1948, only Randy Gumpert remained in 1951.

JUNE 2   The 14-game winning streak is snapped with a 5–1 loss to the Athletics at Comiskey Park.

JUNE 11   A two-ton safe at Comiskey Park that contained $75,000 in receipts from concession sales is stolen. The safe was recovered two weeks later, but of course it was found empty. Police said the strongbox was opened with an acetylene torch.

JUNE 14   The White Sox sweep the Senators 8–7 and 14–5 in Washington. It was the Sox's 14th and 15th consecutive wins on the road.

             At the end of the day, the White Sox had a record of 36–14 and a 4½-game lead in the AL pennant race. The team had won 30 of their last 37 games. The Sox held first place until July 12, but quickly dropped out of the race soon after.

JUNE 15   A brawl highlights an 11-inning, 4–3 loss to the Athletics in the first game of a double-header in Philadelphia that ends the White Sox's 15-game road winning streak. In the 11th inning, Elmer Valo of the A's tried to score from first base on Gus Zernial's double. The throw beat Valo to the plate, but catcher Gus Niarhos dropped the ball when Valo slammed into the Sox catcher. Pitcher Saul Rogovin, backing up the play, swung at Valo and players from both teams rushed to the scene. Order was restored after a few blows were struck. Valo required three stitches to close a gash over his eye, suffered when he fell on Niarhos's mask. Niarhos had a slight cut on his forehead and severe contusions. Philadelphia also won the second tilt 12–5.

JUNE 17   The White Sox sweep the Athletics 4–0 and 9–1 in a double-header in Philadelphia. In the only start of his major league career, Luis Aloma pitched a shutout in the opener.

             Aloma was a reliever who was pressed into a starting role because the White Sox played three double-headers in four days. He never started another game. In four big-league seasons, all with the White Sox from 1950 through 1953, Aloma relieved in 115 games. He had an 18–3 lifetime record, 15 saves, and a 3.44 ERA. From 1950 through 1952, Aloma won 13 straight decisions. He won his last four games in 1950, all six in 1951, and his first three in 1952.

JULY 1   A walk-off homer by Minnie Minoso in the 11th inning beats the Browns 2–1 in the first game of a double-header at Comiskey Park. St. Louis won the second contest 3–1.

JULY 3   A vicious fight erupts in the Comiskey Park stands during a 4–1 win over the Indians. A group of fans in the area overlooking the bullpen had been heckling White Sox pitcher Marv Rothblat. Other fans took exception and a fight ensued involving clubs and knives. Several people were hospitalized.

JULY 12   The White Sox are knocked out of first place with a twi-night double-header loss to the Red Sox by scores of 3–2 and 5–4 before a crowd of 52,593 at Comiskey Park. The second contest was a 17-inning marathon, Saul Rogovin pitched all 17 innings, allowing 10 hits. A two-base error by the Sox pitcher led to the 17th-inning run. The contest ended at 1 a.m.

JULY 13   A day after competing in a 26-inning double-header, the White Sox and Red Sox play a 19-inning game, with the White Sox winning 5–4 with a spectacular rally. The score was 2–2 after five innings before the two clubs combined for 13 consecutive scoreless innings. The Red Sox seemed to have the game in hand when they scored twice in the top of the 19th, but the White Sox came back with three in their half for the victory. Floyd Baker, Bobby Dillinger and Nellie Fox singled to load the bases. Pinch-hitter Bud Stewart singled in two to tie the score. Al Zarilla beat out a bunt to load the bases again. Don Lenhardt's sacrifice fly ended the contest at 1:17 a.m.

           Fox became a star in 1951, batting .313 with 12 triples among his 189 hits.

JULY 26   Clyde Vollmer hits three homers for the Red Sox during a 13–10 White Sox loss in Boston.

JULY 27   Stalling tactics by the Yankees cost the White Sox a victory in New York. After the White Sox scored three runs in the top of the ninth for a 4–3 lead, rain washed out the rest of the contest, reverting the score back to the end of the eighth and a 3–1 Yankees win. With storm clouds looming, the Yanks tried to delay play as long as possible to prevent the ninth from being completed. Third baseman Gil McDougald was ejected for lingering on the mound too long to talk to the pitcher. Yank manager Casey Stengel then engaged in a prolonged argument over McDougald's ouster. Stengel used four different pitchers during the inning and was preparing to call in a fifth from the bullpen when the rain struck. The umpires called the contest after a 62-minute wait.

AUGUST 2   Jim Busby homers in the 10th inning to defeat the Athletics 4–3 in Philadelphia. Busby went into the game in the eighth inning as a defensive replacement for Bud Stewart.

AUGUST 21 The White Sox overwhelm the Athletics 13–5 at Comiskey Park.

AUGUST 26 Bert Haas hits a pinch-hit home run during an 8–6 loss to the Yankees at Comiskey Park. The Sox released Haas the following day, and he never played in another big-league game.

           The White Sox outdrew the Cubs 1,328,234 to 894,415 in 1951. It was the first time the that Sox attracted more fans than their North Side rivals since 1944. The Sox outdrew the Cubs every season from 1951 through 1967 with the exception of 1958.

SEPTEMBER 19 Gus Niarhos hits his only major league home run during a 5–3 loss to the Yankees in New York.

           Niarhos appeared in 315 games and had 691 at-bats over a nine-year career with four clubs. He played for the White Sox in 1950 and 1951.

SEPTEMBER 28   Bud Stewart homers in the 10th inning off Satchel Paige to defeat the Browns 4–3 in St. Louis.

NOVEMBER 13   The White Sox trade Randy Gumpert and Don Lenhardt to the Red Sox for Chuck Stobbs and Mel Hoderlein.

NOVEMBER 27   The White Sox trade Jim Rivera, Joe DeMaestri, Gus Niarhos, Dick Littlefield and Gordon Goldsberry to the Browns for Sherm Lollar, Al Widmar and Tom Upton.

Frank Lane resuscitated a franchise that had been on life support when he took over in 1948 with five brilliant deals in 48 months through 1952. The transactions brought Billy Pierce, Nellie Fox, Minnie Minoso, Chico Carrasquel and Sherm Lollar to Chicago. One of the most underrated players of his era, Lollar was a seven-time All-Star during his career, six of them during his 12 seasons with the White Sox.

1952   Sox

Season in a Sentence

The White Sox prove that the sudden leap forward in 1951 wasn't a fluke, but they finish 81–73 for the second year in a row.

Finish • Won • Lost • Pct • GB

Third   81   73   .525   14.0

Manager

Paul Richards

Stats

Stats	WS	AL	Rank
Batting Avg:	.252	.253	5
On-Base Pct:	.327	.330	5
Slugging Pct:	.348	.365	7
Home Runs:	80		7
Stolen Bases:	61		1
ERA:	3.25		2
Fielding Avg:	.980	.977	1
Runs Scored:	610		5
Runs Allowed:	568		2

Starting Lineup

Sherm Lollar, c
Eddie Robinson, 1b
Nellie Fox, 2b
Hector Rodriguez, 3b
Chico Carrasquel, ss
Bud Stewart, lf
Minnie Minoso, cf-lf
Sam Mele, rf
Jim Rivera, cf
Ray Coleman, cf-lf-rf
Willy Miranda, ss

Pitchers

Billy Pierce, sp
Saul Rogovin, sp
Joe Dobson, sp
Marv Grissom, sp
Lou Kretlow, sp-rp
Bill Kennedy, rp
Harry Dorish, rp
Chuck Stobbs, rp-sp

Attendance

1,231,675 (third in AL)

Club Leaders

Batting Avg:	Eddie Robinson	.296
	Nellie Fox	.296
On-Base Pct:	Eddie Robinson	.382
Slugging Pct:	Eddie Robinson	.466
Home Runs:	Eddie Robinson	22
RBIs:	Eddie Robinson	104
Runs:	Minnie Minoso	96
Stolen Bases:	Minnie Minoso	22
Wins:	Billy Pierce	15
Strikeouts:	Billy Pierce	144
ERA:	Joe Dobson	2.51
Saves:	Harry Dorish	11

JANUARY 13   Minnie Minoso steals the show at the 12th annual Diamond Dinner of the Chicago baseball writers in the Palmer House Grand Ballroom. Minoso was on hand to accept *The Sporting News* Rookie of the Year award. After receiving the plaque from J. G. Taylor Spink, the publisher of the weekly publication, Minoso rattled off a 90-second speech in Spanish, then concluded with one sentence in English saying, "Anyhow, Mr Spink, I thank you."

JANUARY 18   Chuck Comiskey resigns as vice president of the White Sox when his mother reneges on a promise to give him a modest raise from his salary of $10,000. Chuck took a position as vice president in charge of sports coverage for the Liberty Broadcasting Network, a chain of radio stations, but the operation folded in May. Chuck returned to the White Sox on June 10, but the rift with his mother was irreconcilable. Grace never completely forgave her son for displaying the family's dirty laundry in public. Chuck had a burning desire to run the club on his own the way his grandfather and father had done, but his mother and sister Dorothy consistently thwarted those ambitions until the Comiskey family lost control of the club in 1959.

APRIL 15   The White Sox lose the opener before 25,037 at Comiskey Park. It was the largest Opening Day crowd since 1926. Billy Pierce was the losing pitcher. Sherm Lollar homered in his White Sox debut.

APRIL 27   The White Sox win a thrilling 14-inning, 7–6 decision over the Browns in the first game of a double-header at Comiskey Park. The Sox trailed 6–4 when Eddie Robinson hit a disputed two-run homer in the ninth. St. Louis right fielder Jim Delsing contended that he could have caught the ball, but a fan reached out and grabbed it. Minnie Minoso's single drove in the winning run. The second contest was suspended at the end of the fifth inning with the Sox leading 3–1. The suspension occurred because of an American League rule that stipulated that lights could not be turned on to complete games on Sundays. The game was concluded on July 3, with Chicago winning 6–3.

APRIL 30   Eddie Robinson hits a homer in the 11th inning to defeat the Senators 4–3 in Washington. The White Sox also won the opener 7–3.

Robinson hit .296 with 22 homers and 104 RBIs in 1952.

MAY 1   Joe Dobson pitches a two-hitter to defeat the Athletics 3–0 at Shibe Park. Joe Dobson had a no-hitter in progress until George Kell beat out an infield roller with one out in the eighth inning. Dave Philley collected the other Philadelphia hit with a single in the ninth.

Dobson allowed only one earned run in the first 34²/₃ innings of 1952. He finished the season with a 14–10 record and a 2.51 ERA.

MAY 2   Seven White Sox pitchers combine for 16 walks during a 13–12 loss to the Athletics in Philadelphia.

MAY 3   The White Sox trade Jim Busby and Mel Hoderlein to the Senators for Sam Mele.

MAY 9   The White Sox win a 16-inning marathon 8–5 against the Tigers in Detroit. Both teams scored in the 14th inning. In the 16th, Minnie Minoso hit a two-run triple, then scored on Eddie Robinson's single.

Minoso led the AL in stolen bases with 22 in 1952 in addition to hitting .281 with 13 homers.

MAY 25   The White Sox win twice with shutouts in a double-header against the Tigers at Comiskey Park. Joe Dobson pitched the opener, a 2–0 victory. Marv Grissom won game two 1–0. The lone run scored in the first inning on Al Zarilla's triple and a wild pitch.

JUNE 10   The White Sox erupt for 12 runs in the fourth inning and defeat the Athletics 15–4 in Philadelphia. Sam Mele tied an American League record and set a White Sox record with six runs batted in during the inning. Mele belted a three-run homer off Harry Byrd, followed by a bases-loaded triple off Ed Wright.

JUNE 12   Nellie Fox ties an American League record for most total chances in a game by a second baseman, with 17 during a 10–4 win over the Athletics in Philadelphia. Fox had 10 putouts and seven assists.

              Fox hit .296 and led the AL in hits with 192 in 1952.

JUNE 15   Gracie Lou Comiskey, the youngest daughter of White Sox president Grace Comiskey, dies of a heart attack at the age of 31. The June 18 game between the White Sox and Athletics at Comiskey Park was postponed for Gracie Lou's funeral. According to her will, her 948 shares in the White Sox went to her mother. This gave Grace a majority of the stock, with 4,062 out of a total of 7,500.

              On the same day, the White Sox trade Al Zarilla and Willie Miranda to the Browns for Tom Wright and Leo Thomas. The Sox purchased Miranda from the Browns on waivers 13 days later, then traded him back to St. Louis on October 16. In 1959, Miranda escaped Cuba by hiding in the cockpit of a Miami-bound PanAm plane. He returned two decades later to help family members leave the country during the Mariel boat lift.

JUNE 17   The White Sox sweep the Athletics 13–1 and 2–1 at Comiskey Park. In the opener, Minnie Minoso collected a homer, a triple and a double. The second contest went 10 innings.

JUNE 20   The White Sox stun the Yankees 8–5 in 11 innings at Comiskey Park. The Sox trailed 5–1 entering the bottom of the ninth. A two-run single by Minnie Minoso capped a four-run rally that sent the game into extra innings. The contest ended on a three-run homer by Sam Mele.

JUNE 27   Bud Stewart goes on the injured list when he tears the nail off one of his toes after it became stuck in a folding bed. Stewart missed three days of action.

JULY 6   Minnie Minoso homers in the 13th inning to beat the Indians 3–2 in Cleveland.

JULY 8   In the All-Star Game at Shibe Park in Philadelphia, Minnie Minoso doubles in the fourth inning and scores on Eddie Robinson's single, but the American League loses 3–2. The game ended after five innings because of rain.

JULY 10   Billy Pierce pitches a two-hitter to beat the Senators 2–0 in the first game of a double-header at Griffith Stadium. The only Washington hits were singles by Eddie Yost and Mickey Vernon. The Sox completed the sweep with a 4–2 win in the nightcap. With the two wins, the Sox were 46–34 and in second place, just 2½ games behind the Yankees. Chicago spiraled out of the race by the end of July, however.

Pierce was 15–12 with a 2.57 earned run average in 1952.

JULY 13   Nellie Fox collects five hits, including three doubles, in five at-bats during a 7–4 win in the second game of a double-header in Philadelphia. Fox also had two hits in the opener, but the A's won 6–0.

JULY 24   Lou Kretlow pitches a two-hitter to defeat the Red Sox 3–0 in the first game of a double-header against the Red Sox at Comiskey Park. The only Boston hits were a double by Sammy White and a single by Faye Throneberry.

JULY 28   The White Sox trade Ray Coleman and J. W. Porter to the Browns for Jim Rivera and Darrell Johnson.

Nickname "Jungle Jim," Rivera played for the White Sox as an outfielder from 1952 through 1961. He didn't reach the majors until he was 28 years old because of a stretch of nearly four years in the Atlanta Federal Penitentiary after being court-martialed on a charge of attempted rape while serving in the Army. The complainant was the daughter of Rivera's commanding officer. Despite another serious brush with the law (November 12, 1952), Rivera caught the imagination and adoration of Sox fans with his enthusiasm, hustle, charity work and colorful and humorous observations.

JULY 30   Lou Kretlow pitches his second consecutive two-hit shutout, beating the Yankees 7–0 at Comiskey Park. The only New York hits were a double by Phil Rizzuto in the third inning and a single by Joe Collins in the sixth.

The back-to-back gems pitched by Kretlow in July 1952 weren't indicative of his career. They accounted for half of his four victories in 1952, and he pitched only three shutouts during his entire career. The other one was recorded with the Sox in 1951. Kretlow finished his 10-year career in 1956 with a record of 27–47 and an ERA of 4.87.

AUGUST 8   The White Sox score four runs in the ninth inning to defeat the Tigers 4–3 in the first game of a double-header at Comiskey Park. Hector Rodriguez tied the score 3–3 with a two-run single before Nellie Fox's walk-off single scored the winning run. The Sox completed the sweep with a 2–1 win in the nightcap.

AUGUST 14   Hitless in his previous 20 at-bats, Nellie Fox connects for a two-run triple in the 10th inning to beat the Tigers 2–0 in Detroit. Marv Grissom (nine innings) and Luis Aloma (one inning) combined on the shutout.

AUGUST 30   The White Sox score seven runs in the third inning of an 11–6 win over the Indians at Comiskey Park.

SEPTEMBER 1   The White Sox trade Howie Judson to the Reds for Hank Edwards.

SEPTEMBER 2   Rocky Krsnich hits a two-run walk-off triple in the ninth inning to defeat the Tigers
                   6–5 in the first game of a double-header at Comiskey Park. He entered the game at
                   third base in the eighth inning after Hector Rodriguez was lifted for a pinch-hitter.
                   The Sox completed the sweep in the second tilt with a 7–4 victory.

SEPTEMBER 3   The White Sox defeat the Browns 1–0 at Comiskey Park despite collecting only two
                   hits off Dick Littlefield. The lone run scored on a homer by Sam Mele in the seventh
                   inning. Saul Rogovin pitched the shutout.

SEPTEMBER 9   Sam Mele hits a walk-off homer in the ninth inning to defeat the Senators 3–2 in the
                   second game of a double-header at Comiskey Park. The Sox also won the opener 3–2
                   in 12 innings.

SEPTEMBER 13   Marv Grissom strikes out 13 batters in eight innings, but the White Sox lose 6–5 to
                   the Yankees at Comiskey Park.

SEPTEMBER 14   The White Sox outlast the Red Sox 4–3 in a 17-inning marathon at Comiskey Park.
                   Saul Rogovin pitched the first 15 innings, striking out 14. Luis Aloma hurled the final
                   two frames. Rocky Krsnich drove in the winning run with a single.

OCTOBER 16   The White Sox trade Hank Edwards and Willie Miranda to the Browns for Tommy
                   Byrne and Joe DeMaestri.

NOVEMBER 12   Eight days after Dwight Eisenhower defeats Illinois Governor Adlai Stevenson in the
                   presidential election, Jim Rivera is placed on probation by Major League Baseball
                   Commissioner Ford Frick for one year.

                   *Rivera was arrested in September on charges of rape. The accusation was
                   brought by the 22-year-old wife of a soldier. Rivera previously spent almost
                   four years in prison on an attempted rape charge (see July 28, 1952). He was
                   exonerated two weeks later by a Chicago grand jury. Frick placed Rivera on
                   indefinite probation because "of a certain type of moral delinquency." The Sox
                   were not allowed to trade him or sell him to another club for a year.*

DECEMBER 10   The White Sox trade Chuck Stobbs to the Senators for Mike Fornieles.

1953

Sox

Season in a Sentence

The White Sox win 89 games, the most by the franchise since 1920, but finish 11½ games behind the dominant Yankees.

Finish • Won • Lost • Pct • GB

Third   89   65   .578   11.5

Manager

Paul Richards

Stats

Stats	WS	AL	Rank
Batting Avg:	.258	.262	6
On-Base Pct:	.341	.337	4
Slugging Pct:	.364	.383	7
Home Runs:	74		7
Stolen Bases:	73		1
ERA:	3.41	3.99	2
Fielding Avg:	.980	.978	1
Runs Scored:	716		3
Runs Allowed:	592		2

Starting Lineup

Sherm Lollar, c
Ferris Fain, 1b
Nellie Fox, 2b
Bob Elliott, 3b
Chico Carrasquel, ss
Minnie Minoso, lf
Jim Rivera, cf'
Sam Mele, rf
Bob Boyd, 1b-lf
Red Wilson, c

Pitchers

Billy Pierce, sp
Virgil Trucks, sp
Saul Rogovin, sp
Joe Dobson, sp-rp
Bob Keegan, sp-rp
Harry Dorish, sp
Mike Fornieles, rp-sp
Sandy Consuegra, rp-sp

Attendance

1,191,353 (second in AL)

Club Leaders

Batting Avg:	Minnie Minoso	.313
On-Base Pct:	Minnie Minoso	.410
Slugging Pct:	Minnie Minoso	.466
Home Runs:	Minnie Minoso	15
RBIs:	Minnie Minoso	104
Runs:	Minnie Minoso	104
Stolen Bases:	Minnie Minoso	25
Wins:	Billy Pierce	18
Strikeouts:	Billy Pierce	186
ERA:	Billy Pierce	2.72
Saves:	Harry Dorish	18

JANUARY 27   The White Sox trade Eddie Robinson, Joe DeMaestri and Ed McPhee to the Athletics for Ferris Fain and Bob Wilson.

Robinson led the White Sox in home runs and RBIs in both 1951 and 1952, and although Fain lacked Robinson's power, he topped the AL in batting average those same two seasons. Fain was a flop in Chicago, however. After hitting .344 in 1951 and .327 in 1952, his average plummeted to .256 in 1953. In addition, he was a disciplinary problem all year. In August, Fain was involved in a drunken brawl in a Maryland night club (see August 2, 1953). Robinson's numbers also dropped after the trade, though not as dramatically as Fain's.

FEBRUARY 9   The White Sox trade Marv Grissom, Hal Brown and Bill Kennedy to the Red Sox for Vern Stephens.

The Sox gave up two good pitchers for an over-the-hill third baseman. When he arrived in Chicago, Stephens had a .288 career batting average, 231 homers and 1,090 RBIs, but he was 32 and was no longer capable of playing every day. Stephens was sold to the Browns in July 1953. Grissom had an odd career. He was 34 years old and had only a 2–6 lifetime record with a 5.74 when the White Sox took a chance on him in 1952. Grissom was 12–10 as a starter that season. The Red Sox passed him on to the Giants, where he became one of the top relief pitchers in the National League during the second half of the 1950s. Brown was never a star, but was a capable spot starter and long reliever and lasted in the majors until 1964.

APRIL 14   On Opening Day, the White Sox are stopped by a one-hitter pitched by Bob Lemon, losing 6–0 to the Indians in Cleveland. Minnie Minoso provided the only hit with a single in the first inning with two out.

Don Wells joined Bob Elson in the White Sox radio booth in 1953. Wells teamed with Elson until 1960.

APRIL 16   In the Sox's second game of the season, Billy Pierce hurls a one-hitter to defeat the Browns 1–0 in the home opener before 11,354 at Comiskey Park. Harry Brecheen pitched a two-hitter for St. Louis. The only hit off Pierce was a double by Bobby Young in the seventh inning. The Chicago run scored in the seventh on a walk, a sacrifice and an error.

APRIL 17   Only 972 fans are in attendance at Comiskey Park to watch the White Sox lose 6–4 to the Browns with the thermometer reading 36 degrees.

APRIL 18   The White Sox win an odd 7–6 decision over the Indians at Comiskey Park. Seven pitchers on the two teams combined for 26 walks and two hit batsmen, but they allowed only seven hits.

MAY 2   The White Sox score four runs in the ninth inning to defeat the Yankees 8–7 at Comiskey Park. Ferris Fain's three-run homer tied the contest 7–7. Two walks and an error produced the winning tally.

Fain's father was a jockey who rode Duval to a second-place finish in the 1912 Kentucky Derby.

MAY 12   The White Sox score two runs in the 10th inning to defeat the Red Sox 9–7 in Boston. Ellis Kinder was the losing pitcher. He had won 18 consecutive decisions over the Sox dating back to 1948. Chico Carrasquel hit a grand slam off Mel Parnell in the second inning.

On the same day, the White Sox purchased Sandy Consuegra from the Senators. He proved to be an excellent acquisition. In four seasons with the Sox, Consuegra was 30–15 with a 2.85 ERA as a spot starter and reliever. In 1954, his record was 16–3.

MAY 16   A hunch by Paul Richards pays off in a 5–3 win over the Yankees in New York. The White Sox trailed 3–0 entering in the ninth, scored a run, then loaded the bases with two outs. Vern Stephens was due to bat against right-handed pitcher Ewell Blackwell. Stephens, a right-handed batter, had 10 career grand slams, but Richards lifted him for pitcher Tommy Byrne, who swung from the left side. A former Yankee, Byrne stunned the Yankee Stadium crowd by hitting a home run on a 2–2 pitch into the right-field stands, clearing the bases.

Byrne batted .235 with 14 homers in 601 career at-bats. He also hit a grand slam with the Browns in 1951.

JUNE 11   The White Sox sell Tommy Byrne to the Senators.

                 *Despite his grand slam on May 16, the White Sox were unimpressed with
                 Byrne's pitching after he posted a 10.13 ERA in 16 innings with the club. The
                 Senators sent him to the minors late in the 1953 campaign, where he remained
                 until the Yankees re-acquired Byrne in 1954. He had previously played for the
                 club in 1943 and from 1946 through 1951. In 1955, Byrne was 16–5 in New
                 York, and pitched in the World Series in 1955, 1956 and 1957.*

JUNE 13   Sherm Lollar hits a grand slam off Mickey McDermott in the sixth inning of a 5–2
                 victory over the Red Sox at Comiskey Park.

                 *On the same day, the White Sox send Lou Kretlow, Darrell Johnson and
                 $95,000 to the Browns for Virgil Trucks and Bob Elliott. Trucks was a
                 34-year-old veteran when he arrived in the White Sox locker room. He gave
                 the pitching staff a huge lift, winning his first eight decisions with the White Sox
                 and posting a 15–6 record and a 2.86 record over the remainder of the 1953
                 season. Counting his 5–4 mark with the Browns, Trucks was 20–10 in 1953,
                 the lone 20-win season of his 17-year career. He had a record of 47–26 in three
                 seasons with the Sox.*

JUNE 14   The White Sox win twice with shutouts during a double-header against the Red Sox
                 at Comiskey Park. Billy Pierce pitched a two-hitter in the opener for a 6–0 win.
                 He had a no-hitter in progress until Del Wilber doubled in the eighth. Jimmy Piersall
                 singled in the ninth to account for the other Boston hit. Sandy Consuegra won the
                 second tilt 1–0. The lone run scored in second inning on a single by Jim Rivera, a
                 stolen base, and a single from Chico Carrasquel.

JUNE 16   In his White Sox debut, Bob Elliott hits a bases-loaded single in the 11th inning to
                 break a 3–3 tie against the Senators in Washington. Ferris Fain followed with
                 a three-run triple for a 7–3 win.

JUNE 19   The White Sox sign a contract to train in Tampa, Florida, beginning with the 1954
                 season.

                 *The White Sox trained in Pasadena, California, from 1933 through 1952, with
                 the exception of three seasons during World War II (1943–45), when the club
                 headquartered in French Lick, Indiana. After a one-year stopover in El Centro,
                 California, in 1953, the Sox conducted spring drills in Tampa from 1954
                 through 1959. The White Sox's home games and workouts during training camp
                 were held at Al Lopez Field, which was built by the city of Tampa for the Sox.
                 A Tampa native, Lopez was the manager of the Indians when the Sox moved
                 there in 1954. He was the skipper of the White Sox from 1957 through 1965,
                 and again in 1968 and 1969, managing games at a diamond named in his honor
                 during his first three seasons at the helm of the Sox.*

JUNE 25   Paul Richards uses a major league-record five first basemen, including Billy Pierce,
                 during a 4–2 win over the Yankees in New York. The other four to play at first were
                 Ferris Fain, Sherm Lollar, Freddie Marsh and Sam Mele. Fain was the starter at the
                 position, but he was banished by the umpires for arguing in the third inning. He was

replaced by Lollar, who played at first base for the first time in his career. (He didn't play there again until 1959). Lollar moved to his normal position as a catcher in the eighth and was succeeded at first by Marsh. Pierce was the starting pitcher, but opening the ninth, Richards moved Pierce to first base and brought Harry Dorish in to pitch to Hank Bauer. Casey Stengel pinch-hit Don Bollweg for Bauer. Bollweg beat out a bunt, and Richards was thumbed by the umps for protesting the decision. Dorish pitched to one more batter, and Pierce returned to the mound, recording the final two outs with Mele at first.

Lollar batted .287 with eight home runs in 1953.

JUNE 27   The White Sox score three runs in the ninth inning to win 6–5 over the Red Sox in Boston. Jim Rivera homered to put Chicago within a run. A walk and a single followed before Minnie Minoso dropped a windblown two-run double into the outfield with two outs for the winning tallies.

In 1953, Minoso batted .313, clubbed 15 homers, drove in 104 runs, scored 104 and led the AL in steals with 25.

JUNE 28   The White Sox overwhelm the Red Sox 13–4 in Boston.

JULY 1   A seven-run outburst in the sixth inning leads to a 13–4 victory over the Browns at Comiskey Park.

JULY 4   The White Sox celebrate the holiday with a 13–0 and 4–2 sweep of the Browns in St. Louis.

JULY 8   The White Sox score eight runs in the third inning and thrash the Tigers 14–4 at Comiskey Park. Sam Mele hit a grand slam of Dick Weik.

JULY 10   The White Sox erupt for 10 runs in the seventh inning and down the Indians 16–5 in the second game of a double-header at Comiskey Park. The 16-run outburst came after the Sox were shut out over 10 innings in the opener. Billy Pierce was seven outs from a no-hitter and carried a shutout into extra innings, only to lose. The first Cleveland hit was a single by George Strickland with two out in the seventh. The Indians scored three times in the 10th for a 3–0 win.

JULY 12   The White Sox sweep the Indians 14–2 and 3–1 in a double-header at Comiskey Park.

JULY 14   Two White Sox players shine in the All-Star Game, although the National League wins 5–1 at Crosley Field in Cincinnati. Billy Pierce was the AL starting pitcher and threw three shutout innings. Minnie Minoso collected a double and a single and drove in the only American League run.

JULY 18   The White Sox stretch their winning streak to eight games with a 10–6 win over the Senators at Comiskey Park. Ferris Fain collected five hits in five at-bats.

JULY 19   The Yankees cool off the White Sox with a 6–2 and 3–0 sweep before a packed house of 54,215 at Comiskey Park. Sam Mele extended his hitting streak to 22 games in the opener but was held hitless in the nightcap.

Chicago entered the day with a 56–32 record and were four games back of the Yankees. The Sox had cut nine games off the Yankees' lead in five weeks. On June 14, the margin between the Yanks and the White Sox was 13 games.

JULY 20   The White Sox sell Vern Stephens to the Browns.

JULY 22   The White Sox edge the Red Sox 1–0 at Comiskey Park. Virgil Trucks pitched the shutout. The lone run scored in the fifth inning on a triple by Chico Carrasquel and a sacrifice fly by Nellie Fox.

JULY 24   Billy Pierce strikes out 12 batters during a 12-inning complete game but loses 4–2 to the Athletics at Comiskey Park.

JULY 29   Two days after the signing of the armistice ending the Korean War, the White Sox score eight runs in the ninth inning against the Red Sox at Fenway Park to take an 8–1 lead. Boston scored two in their half of the ninth for an 8–3 final. The White Sox had been held scoreless for 25 consecutive innings before the ninth-inning explosion.

JULY 30   The White Sox whip the Red Sox 17–1 in Boston.

AUGUST 2   Following a 1–0 loss against the Senators in Washington, Nellie Fox is injured in a freak accident in the Griffith Stadium locker room. Fox reached for a toothbrush when a row of four lockers tipped over on him. He was pinned for several minutes. Nellie's legs above the ankles took the brunt of the crash, causing a cut on the left one.

Fox sat on the bench the next two games nursing his injuries. They were the only two contests he missed all year. Exactly how the lockers tipped over remained in dispute, but a few players accused Ferris Fain of shoving them from the other side in anger over his dwindling batting average. Later that evening, Fain because involved in a fight in a night club at the Romano Inn in Colmar Park, Maryland, one of Washington's suburbs. He broke a finger during the altercation, which put him out of action for four weeks. Fain said he was dancing with the girlfriend of a friend of his when a man named James Judge asked to cut in. According to Fain's account, he first knocked down the man, and in turn was punched between the eyes. Several blows were exchanged before the fracas was broken up. Three days later, Judge sued Fain for $50,000 in damages, claiming assault and battery and the loss of six teeth.

AUGUST 3   The White Sox win 1–0 over the Senators in Washington. Billy Pierce hurled the shutout. Sherm Lollar drove in the lone run of the game with a sacrifice fly in the ninth inning.

AUGUST 5   A two-run homer by Sam Mele in the 14th inning beats the Athletics 9–7 in Philadelphia. Billy Pierce pitched $6^2/_3$ innings of shutout relief.

AUGUST 8   The White Sox lose twice to the Yankees 1–0 and 3–0 in New York. In the second game, Bob Boyd broke up the no-hit bid of former White Sox hurler Bob Kuzava by clouting a double with one out in the ninth inning.

The White Sox entered the four-game series against the Yankees with a 66–41 record and were four games out of first. The Sox lost three of four and never threatened the Yanks again over the remainder of the 1953 season.

Catcher Sherm Lollar and pitcher Billy Pierce formed a potent battery for 10 years, beginning in 1952 when Lollar arrived in Chicago.

AUGUST 9   Billy Pierce pitches his second consecutive shutout, beating the Yankees 5–0 in New York.

AUGUST 12   Sherm Lollar is ejected during a 7–4 loss to the Indians in Cleveland for bumping into umpire Joe Paparella, who called Bobby Avila safe at home plate. Lollar was suspended for six days for AL president Will Harridge.

AUGUST 14   Billy Pierce pitches his third consecutive shutout, defeating the Tigers 7–0 in Detroit.

                Over four starts and two relief appearances, Pierce pitched 39 consecutive scoreless innings. Pierce led the AL in strikeouts (186 in 271⅓ innings) and lowest opponent's batting average (.218) in 1953. Overall, he was 18–12 with a 2.72 ERA and seven shutouts.

AUGUST 18   Virgil Trucks strikes out 12 batters during a 3–2 win over the Browns in the first game of a double-header in St. Louis. The White Sox completed the sweep with a 2–1 victory in the second contest.

AUGUST 25   The White Sox purchase Connie Ryan from the Phillies.

AUGUST 28   Jimmy Piersall of the Red Sox touches off a near riot in the third inning of a 4–3
               Boston win over the White Sox at Comiskey Park. In the third inning, Piersall upset
               Chico Carrasquel with a slide to break up a double play. Carrasquel rose from
               the tangle as if ready to throw a punch at Piersall, and as players from both clubs
               swarmed onto the field, Gus Niarhos of the Red Sox started swinging and was
               ejected from the game.

AUGUST 29   A triple play by the White Sox ends a 5–1 win over the Red Sox at Comiskey Park.
               Starting pitcher Connie Johnson was removed in the ninth inning after allowing a
               single to Floyd Baker and a walk to Al Zarilla. Virgil Trucks came into the game in
               relief and recorded three outs while facing only one batter. Trucks induced
               Karl Olson to hit a line drive to Ferris Fain, who stepped on first base and threw
               to Chico Carrasquel for a force of Baker at second.

AUGUST 30   Billy Pierce pitches the White Sox to a 1–0 win over the Yankees in the second game
               of a double-header at Comiskey Park. The run scored in the sixth inning on a triple
               by Ferris Fain and an infield out by Connie Ryan. New York won the opener 10–6.

SEPTEMBER 14   The White Sox score eight runs in the sixth inning and defeat the Red Sox 10–6 in
               Boston.

SEPTEMBER 27   In St. Louis, the White Sox win 2–1 in 12 innings in the final game of the St. Louis
               Browns franchise. It is the duty of the home team to supply the balls, and with
               the Browns' coffers almost empty, the stock of new baseballs became completely
               exhausted by the ninth inning. As a result, scuffed balls used earlier in the contest
               were put into use. "Knocking the cover off the ball" became a literal phrase instead
               of a figurative one as they were coming apart at the seams by game's end. The ball
               caught by White Sox outfielder Bill Wilson to end the contest had a large cut down
               the middle.

               *The Browns formally moved to Baltimore two days later and were renamed
               the Orioles. The White Sox were also the opponent for the first game played in
               Baltimore by the new Orioles team (see April 15, 1954). It was the first time
               that an American League franchise moved from one city to another since the
               1902–03 off-season when a previous Baltimore club moved to New York, where
               they were eventually named the Yankees.*

DECEMBER 8   The White Sox purchase Cass Michaels from the Athletics.

DECEMBER 10   The White Sox trade Saul Rogovin, Connie Ryan and Rocky Krsnich to the Reds
               for Willard Marshall.

1954

Season in a Sentence

The White Sox reach first place in June, remain in pennant contention into August and win 94 games, the most by the club since 1917, but finish 17 games behind the Indians.

Finish • Won • Lost • Pct • GB

Third   94   60   .610   17.0

Managers

Paul Richards (91–54) and Marty Marion (3–6)

Stats

Stats	WS • AL • Rank		
Batting Avg:	.267	.257	2
On-Base Pct:	.350	.334	2
Slugging Pct:	.379	.373	4
Home Runs:	94		4 (tie)
Stolen Bases:	98		1
ERA:	3.05	3.72	2
Fielding Avg:	.982	.977	1
Runs Scored:	711		3
Runs Allowed:	521		2

Starting Lineup

Sherm Lollar, c
Ferris Fain, 1b
Nellie Fox, 2b
Cass Michaels, 3b
Chico Carrasquel, ss
Minnie Minoso, lf
Johnny Groth, cf
Jim Rivera, rf
George Kell, 1b-3b
Matt Batts, c
Phil Cavarretta, 1b

Pitchers

Virgil Trucks, sp
Bob Keegan, sp
Jack Harshman, sp
Billy Pierce, sp
Don Johnson, rp-sp
Sandy Consuegra, rp-sp
Harry Dorish, rp

Attendance

1,231,629 (third in AL)

Club Leaders

Batting Avg:	Minnie Minoso	.320
On-Base Pct:	Minnie Minoso	.411
Slugging Pct:	Minnie Minoso	.535
Hone Runs:	Minnie Minoso	19
RBIs:	Minnie Minoso	116
Runs:	Minnie Minoso	119
Stolen Bases:	Minnie Minoso	18
	Jim Rivera	18
Wins:	Virgil Trucks	19
Strikeouts:	Virgil Trucks	152
ERA:	Sandy Consuegra	2.69
Saves:	Don Johnson	7

FEBRUARY 5   The White Sox trade Neil Berry and Sam Mele to the Orioles for Johnny Groth and Johnny Lipon.

APRIL 13   The White Sox lose the season opener 8–2 to the Indians before 31,026 at Comiskey Park.

The White Sox installed television sets in the concession stands at Comiskey Park in 1954 so that fans who left their seats would not miss any of the action on the field.

APRIL 15   The White Sox participate in the first major league game played in Baltimore since 1902. The Sox defeated the Orioles 3–1 before a crowd of 46,354. The first batter in the history of Memorial Stadium was Chico Carrasquel, who faced Bob Turley

Memorial Stadium was the home of the Orioles from 1954 through 1991.

APRIL 18   The White Sox trade Johnny Lipon to the Reds for Grady Hatton.

APRIL 24   The White Sox pummel the Orioles 14–4 at Comiskey Park.

APRIL 30   Bob Keegan pitches the White Sox to a 5–0 win over the Red Sox in Boston.

MAY 1   Virgil Trucks pitches a one-hitter to down the Red Sox 3–0 at Fenway Park. The only Boston hit was a single by Billy Goodman with two out in the sixth inning.

MAY 2   The White Sox post their third straight shutout when Don Johnson two-hits the Athletics for a 4–0 win in the first game of a double-header in Philadelphia. The only hits off Johnson were a single by Eddie Joost in the fourth inning and a double by opposing pitcher Morrie Martin in the sixth. The A's won the second contest 2–1.

MAY 3   The brilliant pitching by the White Sox staff continues as Sandy Consuegra hurls a two-hitter to defeat the Athletics 14–3 in Philadelphia. Consuegra retired the first 19 batters to face him before Spook Jacobs doubled in the seventh to break his 0-for-22 slump. Jacobs also accounted for the second hit by beating out a bunt in the ninth, when the A's scored three runs with the help of two errors, a walk and a sacrifice fly. The Sox scored eight runs in the third inning to build a 9–0 lead.

MAY 4   Minnie Minoso hits a grand slam off Mickey McDermott in the second inning of an 8–6 win over the Senators in Washington.

Minoso had the best season of his career in 1954. He led the league in triples (18) and slugging percentage (.535), in addition to batting .320 with 19 homers, 116 RBIs and 119 runs scored.

MAY 9   Billy Pierce strikes out 12 batters in 10 shutout innings against the Tigers in the second game of a double-header at Comiskey Park, but the contest ends in a 0–0 tie. It was called on account of darkness at the end of the 10th because of an American League rule stipulating that lights couldn't be turned on to finish games played on Sundays. Detroit won the opener 3–2 in 11 innings.

MAY 10   Don Johnson pitches his second two-hitter in a span of 11 days, defeating the Red Sox 1–0 at Comiskey Park. Boston pitcher Tom Brewer allowed just three hits. The lone run scored in the first inning when Brewer walked four of the first six batters to face him. The only hits against Johnson were singles by Charlie Maxwell in the first inning and Sammy White in the second.

MAY 16   Minnie Minoso drives in six runs on a homer, a triple and a single during a 10–5 win in the first game of a double-header against the Senators at Comiskey Park.

MAY 22   Five days after the Supreme Court rules in the case of *Brown vs. the Board of Education of Topeka* that segregation of public schools is illegal, Minnie Minoso smacks a three-run homer in the ninth inning to defeat the Tigers 5–3 in Detroit.

MAY 23   The White Sox send Grady Hatton and $100,000 to the Red Sox for George Kell.

A future Hall of Famer, Kell played in eight All-Star Games during his career, but none of them were with the White Sox. He was supposed to solve the Sox's long-standing problems at third base. Kell played well when healthy, batting .303 in 742 at-bats with Chicago before a May 1956 trade to the Orioles, but he was often sidelined with a bad back.

MAY 24

The White Sox sign Phil Cavarretta.

Cavarretta played for the Cubs from 1934 through 1953 and managed the club from 1951 through 1953. He made his major league debut as an 18 year old. Cavarretta was fired as Cubs manager during spring training in 1954. He was of some help to the White Sox in 1954, batting .316 in 71 games and 158 at-bats.

Slick-fielding shortstop Chico Carrasquel started three All-Star games in the early 1950s and provided great defense for the Sox.

MAY 28

The White Sox rout the Orioles 11–6 and 14–8 during a double-header in Baltimore. Cass Michaels hit a grand slam in the sixth inning of the first game off Jay Heard.

MAY 29

The White Sox extend their winning streak to eight games with an 11–4 victory over the Orioles in Baltimore.

JUNE 8

The White Sox take first place with a 9–3 win over the Athletics in Philadelphia.

The Sox held first place for four days.

JUNE 16

Ferris Fain hits an inside-the-park grand slam off Sonny Dixon to cap a seven-run seventh inning and an 11–6 win over the Athletics at Comiskey Park. Fain hit a low line drive to center field, where Bill Wilson missed a running catch, allowing the ball to roll to the wall.

JULY 1

A gambling ring is broken up during the Boys' Benefit exhibition game against the Cubs, won 7–6 by the North Side rivals at Comiskey Park. The annual charity game was designed to purchase equipment for youth baseball in the city. Several gamblers were rounded up and arrested by plainclothes detectives of the Chicago police department.

JULY 4

Mike Garcia (1⅓ innings), Ray Narleski (5⅔ innings) and Early Wynn (two innings) combine on a one-hitter to beat the White Sox 2–1 in Cleveland. The Indians were one out away from a three-pitcher no-hitter when Minnie Minoso singled with two out in the ninth.

JULY 6

Virgil Trucks pitches a one-hitter in a 4–0 win over the Tigers in Detroit. The only hit off Trucks was a single by Harvey Kuenn in the third inning.

Trucks was 19–12 with a league-leading five shutouts and an ERA of 2.79 in 1954. He failed to win three September starts in an attempt to record his 20th victory of the season.

JULY 11   The White Sox sweep the Indians 3–0 and 8–2 at Comiskey Park. Billy Pierce pitched a two-hitter in the opener. The only Cleveland hits were singles by Al Rosen in the first inning and George Strickland in the ninth.

At the All-Star break, the White Sox were 54–32 and in third place, four games behind the first-place Indians.

JULY 13   Nellie Fox and Minnie Minoso contribute to an 11–9 win by the American League in the All-Star Game at Municipal Stadium in Cleveland. Fox broke a 9–9 tie with a two-run single in the eighth inning. Minoso singled twice in four at-bats and scored a run. Unfortunately, White Sox pitchers were far from successful. Sandy Consuegra allowed five runs and five hits in one-third of an inning. Bob Keegan surrendered two runs and three hits in two-thirds of an inning. The earned run average of Chicago pitchers in the 1954 All-Star Game was 63.00.

Fox led the AL in hits in 1954 with 201 in addition to scoring 111 runs and batting .391.

JULY 21   The White Sox clobber the Yankees 15–2 in New York.

JULY 25   Jack Harshman strikes out a club record 16 batters during a 5–2 win over the Red Sox in the first game of a double-header in Boston. Chicago also won game two 4–2.

Despite all of the Hall of Fame pitchers who have worn a White Sox uniform, Harshman's 16-strikeout performance still stands alone as the club record for a single game. Harshman opened the 1950 season as the New York Giants' starting first baseman. He was converted into a pitcher in the minors in 1951 and appeared in two contests as a hurler with the Giants in 1952. Harshman was purchased by the White Sox in September 1953. Relying on a slip pitch taught to him by Paul Richards, Harshman was 48–34 with an ERA of 3.33 in four seasons with the Sox. He hit six home runs in 1956, the all-time White Sox record for home runs by a pitcher in a season.

AUGUST 1   The White Sox sweep the Athletics 6–5 and 12–1 in Philadelphia.

AUGUST 4   Phil Cavarretta hits a grand slam off Russ Kemmerer in the first inning for a 4–0 lead, but the White Sox need 10 innings to defeat the Red Sox 6–5 at Comiskey Park. Matt Batts drove in the winning run with a single.

AUGUST 7   Controversial Wisconsin Senator Joseph McCarthy attends a 4–3 loss to the Washington Senators at Comiskey Park. McCarthy's arrival was greeted by a mixture of cheers and jeers. He sat in the box of general manager Frank Lane and was surrounded by a bodyguard of Chicago policemen. In December 1954, McCarthy was censured by his fellow U.S. senators by a 67–22 vote for abusing his investigative powers during his attempts to root out suspected communists employed by the federal government.

AUGUST 8   The White Sox record their eighth win in a row with a 10–5 decision over the
                Senators at Comiskey Park.

                *The Sox closed the day with a 70–39 record and were five games behind the
                Indians. The Chicago club could draw no closer, however.*

AUGUST 11   Virgil Trucks pitches the White Sox to a 1–0 win over the Orioles at Comiskey Park.
                George Kell drove in the lone run with a single.

AUGUST 13   Jack Harshman pitches a 16-inning complete game shutout to defeat the Tigers 1–0
                at Comiskey Park. Harshman allowed nine hits, walked seven and struck out 12.
                Al Aber also pitched a complete game for Detroit. The winning run scored on an
                RBI-triple by Minnie Minoso. The Tigers protested the play, claiming that an usher
                stationed along the right-field line to retrieve foul balls interfered with Al Kaline's
                attempt to field Minoso's drive.

                Harshman pitched 32 consecutive scoreless innings over four starts in August.

AUGUST 27   The White Sox score eight runs in the third inning and overwhelm the Athletics
                11–0 at Philadelphia. It was a costly victory, however, as Cass Michaels suffered a
                fractured skull as a result of being hit by a pitch from Marion Fricano. The injury
                impaired Michaels's vision and he never played in another major league game.

AUGUST 28   The White Sox play the Athletics in Philadelphia for the last time and win 5–2.

                The Athletics moved to Kansas City at the end of the 1954 season.

AUGUST 31   Hurricane Carol postpones the game between the White Sox and Red Sox in Boston.

SEPTEMBER 7   The White Sox purchase Dick Donovan from the Tigers.

                *At the time, Donovan was 26 years old, had pitched 62⅓ major league innings
                and had an 0–4 record with a 7.22 ERA. He hardly looked like a prospect,
                but Donovan proved to be a tremendous addition. In six seasons in Chicago,
                Donovan posted a record of 73–50.*

SEPTEMBER 11   The White Sox score two runs in the ninth inning and one in the 10th to defeat the
                Yankees 6–5 at Comiskey Park. In the ninth, Minnie Minoso doubled in a run and
                scored on a single by Nellie Fox. Chico Carrasquel's single drove in the winning run.

SEPTEMBER 14   Paul Richards resigns as manager of the White Sox, and is replaced by 36-year-old
                Marty Marion.

                *Although he failed to win a pennant in Chicago, Richards dramatically improved
                the White Sox. Taking over a club that had won only 60 games in 1950, the
                Sox had 81 wins in both 1951 and 1952, 89 victories in 1953 and were 91–56
                in 1954 when Richards submitted his resignation. Despite his success, Richards
                had problems with the front office. Richards and general manager Frank
                Lane were both strong-willed individuals, and Richards grew weary of Lane's
                temperamental outbursts and meddling. In addition, the Comiskey family was
                split over the direction of the club and dragged their feet over salary negotiations*

with regard to an extension of Richards's contract. He felt it was time to leave when he received an opportunity to join the Orioles in the dual role of general manager and field manager. Richards ran the Orioles until 1961, again building a dysfunctional franchise into a winner, but fell shy of a pennant. Later, he was the first general manager of the Houston Astros, an expansion franchise that began play in 1962, and after that became vice president in charge of baseball operations with the Atlanta Braves. Richards came out of retirement to manage the White Sox again in 1976. Marion was one of the best shortstops in baseball during the 1940s and won the NL MVP Award in 1944. His entire playing career was spent with the Cardinals, and he managed the club in 1951. He was fired after just one season on the job in spite of an 81–73 record. Marion next managed the moribund St. Louis Browns for Bill Veeck from June 1952 through the end of the 1953 season. He was a coach for the White Sox under Richards when promoted to manager. Under Marion, the White Sox were 91–63 in 1955 and 85–69 in 1956, but he was often under fire from both the management of the club and the fans. The 1956 season was the fifth in a row that the Sox finished in third place behind the Yankees and Indians, and the frustration was mounting. Marion resigned at the end of that season and was replaced by Al Lopez.

SEPTEMBER 25   The White Sox wallop the Orioles 11–0 in Baltimore.

The White Sox were 94–60 in 1954, the most wins by the franchise in any season since 1917, but they finished a distant third, 17 games behind the Indians, who went 111–43.

DECEMBER 6   The White Sox trade Ferris Fain, Leo Christante and Jack Phillips to the Tigers for Walt Dropo, Ted Gray and Bob Nieman. On the same day, the Sox also dealt Don Ferrarese, Don Johnson, Matt Batts and Freddie Marsh to the Orioles for Clint Courtney, Jim Brideweser and Bob Chakales.

Dropo and Nieman both cracked the starting lineup in 1955 following a deal in which the White Sox gave up little of consequence. Nieman started fast with five homers in his first nine games with the Sox in 1955, but he finished the season with only 11. Fain played only one more year in the majors. In 1985, he was arrested at his Georgetown, California, farm for marijuana possession. Authorities confiscated 25 pounds of plants and Fain was sentenced to four months' house arrest. Two years later, Fain was arrested again and charged with possessing more than 400 marijuana plants.

1955   Sox

Season in a Sentence

The White Sox close the month of August in first place, but a 12–12 record in September results in another third-place finish.

Finish • Won • Lost • Pct • GB

Third   91   63   .591   5.0

Manager

Marty Marion

Stats

	WS	AL	Rank
Batting Avg:	.268	.258	1
On-Base Pct:	.347	.339	4
Slugging Pct:	.388	.381	5
Home Runs:	116		
Stolen Bases:	69		1
ERA:	3.37	3.96	2
Fielding Avg:	.981	.977	2
Runs Scored:	725		4
Runs Allowed:	557		1

Starting Lineup

Sherm Lollar, c
Walt Dropo, 1b
Nellie Fox, 2b
George Kell, 3b
Chico Carrasquel, ss
Minnie Minoso, lf
Jim Busby, cf
Jim Rivera, rf
Bob Nieman, lf-rf
Bob Kennedy, 3b

Pitchers

Billy Pierce, sp
Dick Donovan, sp
Virgil Trucks, sp
Jack Harshman, sp
Connie Johnson, sp
Sandy Consuegra, rp
Mike Fornieles, rp-sp
Harry Byrd, rp-sp

Attendance

1,175,684 (sixth in AL)

Club Leaders

Batting Avg:	George Kell	.312
On-Base Pct:	George Kell	.389
Slugging Pct:	Walt Dropo	.448
Home Runs:	Walt Dropo	19
RBIs:	George Kell	81
Runs:	Nellie Fox	100
Stolen Bases:	Jim Rivera	25
Wins:	Billy Pierce	15
	Dick Donovan	15
Strikeouts:	Billy Pierce	157
ERA:	Billy Pierce	1.97
Saves:	Sandy Consuegra	7

APRIL 12   Seven days after Richard Daley is elected mayor of Chicago, the White Sox open the season with a 5–1 loss to the Indians in Cleveland.

Vince Lloyd joined the television broadcasting team of both the White Sox and Cubs in 1955, taking a seat alongside Jack Brickhouse. Lloyd was at the TV mike for both Chicago clubs until 1967 and for the Cubs until 1986.

APRIL 14   In the home opener, the White Sox defeat the Kansas City Athletics 7–1 before 14,067 at Comiskey Park. The game was the Sox's first against the Athletics since their move from Philadelphia to Kansas City. Sandy Consuegra threw just 74 pitches in throwing a complete game in which he surrendered just three hits.

APRIL 16   Walt Dropo hits a grand slam off Ray Narleski in the fifth inning of a 9–4 win over the Indians at Comiskey Park.

A multitalented star at the University of Connecticut, Dropo was chosen by the Providence Steamrollers in the first round of the 1947 NBA draft and in the ninth round of the NFL draft by the Chicago Bears in 1948.

APRIL 21   George Kell hits a grand slam off Ned Garver in the third inning of a 9–1 win over the Tigers in Detroit.

At the conclusion of the game, the White Sox made a trip by airplane for the first time in club history, traveling from Detroit to Kansas City. The first team to travel by air was the Cincinnati Reds in 1934, but airplane journeys by big-league teams did not become commonplace until the late 1950s.

APRIL 22   The White Sox play the Athletics in Kansas City for the first time and win 5–3 at Municipal Stadium.

Municipal Stadium was the home of the Athletics from 1955 through 1967 and the Royals from 1969 through 1972.

APRIL 23   The White Sox tie a modern major league record for most runs in a game during a 29–6 thrashing of the Athletics in Kansas City. Chicago scored four runs in the first inning, seven in the second, three in the third, two in the fourth, six in the sixth, three in the seventh and four in the eighth. The Sox also established club records for most hits (29), most total bases (55) and most home runs (seven) in a game. Bob Nieman and Sherm Lollar each hit two of the homers, with Minnie Minoso, Walt Dropo and Jack Harshman each adding one. The long drives were aided by a 30 mile-per-hour wind. Lollar tied a major league mark by picking up two hits in an inning twice in one game, a feat accomplished by just four players in history. Lollar homered and singled in the second inning and singled twice in the sixth. He had a total of five hits in six at-bats. Chico Carrasquel also collected five hits in six at-bats. Nieman drove in seven runs. Carrasquel and Minoso scored five runs. The six Athletics pitchers to undergo the pummeling were Bobby Shantz, Lee Wheat, Bob Trice, Moe Burtschy, Bob Spicer and Ozzie Van Brabant.

Other than the White Sox on April 23, 1955, the only other club during the 20th century to score as many as 29 runs in a game was the Boston Red Sox on June 8, 1950, with a 29–4 win over the St. Louis Browns in Boston. Dropo was the starting first baseman on both clubs that scored 29 runs in a contest. Harry Dorish witnessed the 1950 game from the bench as a member of the Browns and pitched two innings of shutout relief for the White Sox in the 1955 contest. The 1950 Red Sox and 1955 White Sox shared the modern major league record and the American League record for most runs in a game until the Texas Rangers defeated the Orioles 30–3 in Baltimore on August 22, 2007.

APRIL 24   The day after scoring 29 runs, the White Sox are shut out by the Athletics and lose 5–0 in Kansas City. Alex Kellner pitched a five-hitter for the A's.

APRIL 26   The White Sox are shut out for the second game in a row following their 29-run explosion on April 23, losing 5–0 to the Yankees at Comiskey Park. Bob Turley pitched a one-hitter for New York.

APRIL 27   After being shut out two games in a row, the White Sox's bats awaken again with a 13–4 win over the Yankees at Comiskey Park. The Sox scored five runs in the first inning off Whitey Ford and Johnny Sain.

Over a four-game span, the White Sox's run totals were 29, 0, 0 and 13.

MAY 6   Virgil Trucks pitches a two-hitter to defeat the Tigers 1–0 at Comiskey Park. The only Detroit hits were singles by Al Kaline in the sixth inning and Bill Tuttle in the seventh.

MAY 8

The White Sox sweep the Tigers 5–4 and 1–0 during a double-header at Comiskey Park. The first game went 11 innings. A two-run, pinch-hit homer by Ron Jackson in the ninth inning tied the score. A single by Nellie Fox drove in the winning run. Dick Donovan pitched the game-two shutout. The lone run scored in the eighth inning on a triple by Nellie Fox and a single from Minnie Minoso.

Fox hit .311, scored 100 runs and collected 198 hits in 1955.

MAY 28

Batting out of the lead-off spot, Johnny Groth collects four extra-base hits on two homers and two doubles, leading the White Sox to a 16–4 win over the Tigers in Detroit.

MAY 30

The White Sox purchase Bob Kennedy from the Orioles.

JUNE 5

Jim Rivera hits a grand slam off Tommy Byrne in the first inning of a 5–3 win over the Yankees in the first game of a double-header at Comiskey Park. New York won the second tilt 3–2 in 10 innings.

JUNE 6

The White Sox trade Harry Dorish to the Orioles for Les Moss.

JUNE 7

The White Sox trade Clint Courtney, Johnny Groth and Bob Chakales to the Senators for Jim Busby.

JUNE 11

The White Sox clobber the Senators 10–0 at Comiskey Park.

JUNE 12

The White Sox win two from the Senators 1–0 and 8–4 during a double-header at Comiskey Park. Billy Pierce pitched the shutout. The Sox scored seven runs in the third inning of game two.

Pierce had a record of 15–10, pitched 205²/₃ innings and had a league-leading earned run average of 1.97. He lost four 1–0 decisions. The ERA was the lowest of any White Sox pitcher (minimum of 150 innings) between 1919 and 1964.

JUNE 14

The White Sox edge the Orioles 1–0 in Baltimore. Jack Harshman (8⅓ innings) and Sandy Consuegra (two-thirds of an inning) combined on the shutout. Sherm Lollar drove in the lone run with a bases-loaded walk issued by Saul Rogovin in the eighth inning.

Lollar hit .261 in 16 homers in 1955.

JULY 2

Jack Harshman strikes out 10 batters, pitches a three-hitter and clouts a homer in the seventh inning off Herb Score, breaking a 1–1 tie in a 2–1 victory over the Indians in Cleveland.

JULY 7

Walt Dropo hits a grand slam off Babe Birrer in the sixth inning of a 12–1 win over the Tigers in Detroit.

JULY 9

Connie Johnson strikes out 12 batters during a 6–0 win over the Indians at Comiskey Park.

Johnson pitched in the Negro Leagues for the Kansas City Monarchs for many years. Because of the color barrier, he didn't make his major league debut until 1953 when he was 30-years-old.

JULY 12   Billy Pierce is the starting pitcher for the American League in the All-Star Game, played at County Stadium in Milwaukee. Pierce pitched three shutout innings, allowing one hit and striking out three. Chico Carrasquel collected two singles in three at-bats. Despite the contributions from the White Sox, the AL lost 6–5 in 12 innings.

JULY 14   The White Sox sweep the Senators 13–4 and 5–2 in a double-header at Comiskey Park. The Sox scored seven runs in the fourth inning of the opener.

JULY 15   Pinch-hitter Bob Kennedy hits a two-run, walk-off triple in the ninth inning to beat the Senators 5–4 at Comiskey Park.

JULY 16   After the Orioles score two runs in the top of the ninth inning to break a 1–1 tie, the White Sox counter with three runs in their half to win 4–3 at Comiskey Park. Gil Coan, purchased from the Baltimore club earlier in the day, singled in a run with the bases loaded to make the score 3–2. Ray Moore hit Sherm Lollar with a pitch and walked Dick Donovan, at the plate as a pinch-hitter, to force in the winning run.

JULY 26   The White Sox purchase Bobby Adams from the Reds.

JULY 31   Jack Harshman pitches an 11-inning, two-hit complete game to defeat the Senators 3–1 in the first game of a double-header in Washington. The 11th-inning runs scored when George Kell was hit by a pitch from Pedro Ramos with the bases loaded, followed by a walk to Jim Rivera. The Sox also won the opener 6–5.

            On the same day, pitcher Dick Donovan underwent an emergency appendectomy. At the time, he was 13–4 with an ERA of 2.64. Donovan tried to pitch three weeks later, but he wasn't ready. Over the remainder of the 1955 season he was 2–5 with an earned run average of 5.36.

AUGUST 6   Nellie Fox is benched for a rest by manager Marty Marion during an 8–1 loss to the Orioles on a 98-degree day in Baltimore, ending his playing streak of 273 consecutive games. Marion also benched Jim Busby, who came into the game with a playing streak of 297 games.

            The August 6 game was the only one that Fox missed in 1955. He played in the next contest two days later, the first of a White Sox-record 798 consecutive games (see September 3, 1960). The 798-game streak is the longest ever by a second baseman. If he had played on August 6, 1955, Fox would have appeared in 1,072 straight games, a mark that has been exceeded by only six players in big-league history. From 1951 through 1962, Fox played in 1,848 of the White Sox 1,872 games, a figure of 98.7 percent and an average of only two games missed per year over a 12-year period.

AUGUST 9   Billy Pierce pitches a two-hitter for a 4–1 win over the Athletics in Kansas City. The only hits off Pierce were by Red Wilson, who singled in the second inning and homered with two out in the ninth.

AUGUST 11	The White Sox overwhelm the Athletics 14–1 in Kansas City.
AUGUST 13	Bob Kennedy hits a grand slam off Frank Lary in the third inning to give the White Sox a 5–2 lead, but the Tigers rally to win 9–8 after scoring two runs in the ninth.
AUGUST 24	The White Sox smash 20 hits to defeat the Orioles 14–1 in the first game of a double-header at Comiskey Park. Baltimore won the second tilt 2–1.
AUGUST 27	The White Sox trounce the Senators 11–1 at Comiskey Park.
AUGUST 30	The White Sox defeat the Red Sox 7–5 at Comiskey Park to move into first place. The Sox were five percentage points ahead of the Indians and Yankees, who were tied for second.

Despite the victory that put the Sox on top of the American League, general manager Frank Lane railed at the umpires. The Sox had been on umpire Larry Napp all day following an incident in which Red Sox outfielder Jimmy Piersall threw a handful of dirt at him. Piersall remained in the game. Lane was once a top football referee in the Big Ten and couldn't stand officiating blunders. When Sherm Lollar got the thumb for waving a towel at Napp, Lane rushed toward the private box of AL President Will Harridge and launched a profane tirade over what Lane believed was incompetent umpiring. Joining Harridge in the box that day was Cal Hubbard, the American League supervisor of umpires. The next day, commissioner Ford Frick ordered Lane to apologize to Harridge and to pay a $500 fine for "conduct unbecoming a baseball official and for using violent and profane language." Lane obliged, but Chuck Comiskey publicly berated Lane, stating that his gutter language was "absolutely inexcusable." The two had been privately bickering for years, but with their differences out in the open, any hopes for a reconciliation were ended. Comiskey thought that Lane was making too many deals and was trading players just to make trades. Chuck thought that the constant roster turnover made players jittery and hurt their performance because they didn't know when they were going to be shipped out of town. A generation gap also contributed to the acrimony between Lane and Comiskey. Lane was 59 years old and had been in baseball for 20 years and wasn't the type to back down from anyone. He didn't think he should be taking orders from Chuck, who was 29. Lane felt that it was impossible to continue with the club (see September 23, 1955).

| SEPTEMBER 4 | The White Sox drop out of first place with a double-header loss to the Indians in Cleveland, both by scores of 5–3. |

The Sox were in first place in September for the first time since 1920, but they lost a chance for a pennant in 1955 by losing 12 of their last 23 games.

| SEPTEMBER 10 | The White Sox take a come-from-behind 9–8 win over the Yankees in New York. Down 7–3, the Sox score two runs in the seventh inning and three in the ninth for an 8–7 advantage. The last two runs scored on a single by Walt Dropo. The Yankees forced extra innings with a tally in their half of the inning. In the 10th, Minnie Minoso walked and scored on a sacrifice, passed ball and an error. |

The Sox closed the day two games behind the first-place Indians and one-half game back of the second-place Yankees, but they could draw no closer to either club.

SEPTEMBER 23   Frank Lane's resignation is accepted by the White Sox board of directors.

Lane resigned despite having a contract that lasted through the 1960 season. He and Chuck Comiskey had been sparring for years, and Lane's vulgar outburst at what he believed was inadequate umpiring (see August 30, 1955) upset young Comiskey's sense of propriety, greasing Lane's departure. Chuck's mother, Grace, and his sister, Dorothy, wanted Lane to remain with the White Sox and tried to convince him to stay. But as Lane explained to reporters, "one of the owners has held me up to public ridicule, and I feel the only solution is for me to leave." Grace in turn maliciously scolded her son in reaction to Lane's departure. "Charles just talks too much," snapped Mrs. Comiskey. "He's my son and when he was nine years old I could tell him to shut up, but after all he's 29 now." Two weeks later, Lane took a job as general manager of the Cardinals, a job he held for two years before leaving after a series of disagreements with owner August Busch Jr. Lane then went to the Indians, where he stayed for three seasons and committed the unpardonable sin of trading fan favorite Rocky Colavito. In Chicago, St. Louis and Cleveland, Lane took a losing club and built it into a pennant contender. But he couldn't seem to leave well enough alone and continued making trades that prevented his teams from reaching a pennant. In 1961, he became Charlie Finley's first general manager after Finley purchased the Kansas City Athletics, but Lane lasted only a few months as the two mercurial personalities failed to mesh. Lane later worked in the front offices of the Orioles and Brewers.

SEPTEMBER 25   On the last day of the season, Billy Pierce strikes out 12 batters during a 5–0 win over the Athletics at Comiskey Park.

OCTOBER 18   The White Sox trade Bobby Adams to the Orioles for Cal Abrams.

OCTOBER 25   The White Sox trade Chico Carrasquel and Jim Busby to the Indians for Larry Doby.

The White Sox sent Carrasquel to Cleveland because Luis Aparicio was ready to take over as the starting shortstop. Doby was a future Hall of Fame outfielder near the end of his career, but he gave the White Sox two fine seasons.

NOVEMBER 16   The White Sox board of directors eliminate the job of general manager and appoint Chuck Comiskey and Johnny Rigney to jointly run the day-to-day operation of the club. Rigney was the husband of Chuck's sister Dorothy. Comiskey and Rigney ran the club until Bill Veeck purchased the White Sox in March 1959. The alliance between Comiskey and Rigney was uneasy from the start and grew bitter in 1957, when Chuck sued his sister for control of the majority of the shares (see December 10, 1956).

NOVEMBER 30   The White Sox trade Virgil Trucks to the Tigers for Bubba Phillips.

1956   Sox

Season in a Sentence

An 11-game losing streak in July ends any hope for a pennant and the White Sox finish in third place for the fifth straight season, leading to the resignation of Marty Marion and the hiring of Al Lopez.

Finish • Won • Lost • Pct • GB

Third   85   69   .552   12.0

Manager

Marty Marion

Stats

Stats	WS	AL	Rank
Batting Avg:	.267	.260	4
On-Base Pct:	.352	.344	3
Slugging Pct:	.397	.394	4
Home Runs:	128		5
Stolen Bases:	70		1
ERA:	3.73		3
Fielding Avg:	.979	.975	1
Runs Scored:	776		4
Runs Allowed:	634		3

Starting Lineup

Sherm Lollar, c
Walt Dropo, 1b
Nellie Fox, 2b
Fred Hatfield, 3b
Luis Aparicio, ss
Minnie Minoso, lf
Larry Doby, cf
Jim Rivera, rf
Dave Philley, 1b-rf
Sammy Esposito, 3b

Pitchers

Billy Pierce, sp
Jack Harshman, sp
Dick Donovan, sp
Jim Wilson, sp
Bob Keegan, sp
Gerry Staley, rp-sp

Attendance

1,000,090 (fifth in AL)

Club Leaders

Batting Avg:	Minnie Minoso	.316
On-Base Pct:	Minnie Minoso	.425
Slugging Pct:	Minnie Minoso	.525
Home Runs:	Larry Doby	24
RBIs:	Larry Doby	102
Runs:	Nellie Fox	109
Stolen Bases:	Luis Aparicio	21
Wins:	Billy Pierce	20
Strikeouts:	Billy Pierce	192
ERA:	Jack Harshman	3.10
Saves:	Dixie Howell	4

APRIL 16   The White Sox sell Howie Pollet to the Pirates.

APRIL 17   The White Sox win 2–1 over the Indians on Opening Day before 16,773 at Comiskey Park. Billy Pierce pitched a five-hitter. Sherm Lollar contributed two doubles and a single in three at-bats. The winning run scored in the seventh inning on a bases-loaded walk by Bob Lemon to Jim Busby. Luis Aparicio made his major league debut and collected a single in three at-bats.

Aparicio hit .266 with a league-leading 21 stolen bases and won the Rookie of the Year Award. He played in the majors from 1956 through 1973, and with the White Sox from 1956 through 1962 and again from 1968 through 1970. During his first seven seasons he teamed with Nellie Fox as one of the best double-play combinations in big-league history. Luis played in 2,581 games at shortstop, which set the major league record until Omar Vizquel passed him in 2008. Aparicio led the American League in stolen bases nine consecutive seasons, from his rookie campaign through 1964, and totaled 506 steals in the career. For eight straight years beginning in 1959, he topped AL shortstops in fielding percentage, in addition to leading in assists seven times, putouts four, total chances per game three and double plays once. These stats helped him to earn seven Gold Gloves and to make the All-Star teams in eight different seasons. Luis also collected 2,677 career hits. Among White Sox players, he is eighth in games (1,511), second in stolen bases (318), seventh in at-bats (5,856), sixth in runs (791) and seventh in hits (1,576). Aparicio became the first Venezuelan elected to the Hall of Fame in 1984.

APRIL 19   The White Sox win 1–0 at Comiskey Park as Jack Harshman and Indians pitcher Herb Score both hurl two-hitters. The lone run scored without a hit in the seventh inning when Minnie Minoso walked, moved up two bases on a wild pitch and scored on a sacrifice fly from Larry Doby. The two hits for both teams were back-to-back. Bobby Avila and Al Smith singled in the fourth inning for Cleveland, and Walt Dropo and Luis Aparicio collected singles for Chicago in the eighth to break up Score's no-hit bid.

In his first season with the White Sox, Doby hit .268 with 24 homers and 102 RBIs.

APRIL 21   The Athletics explode for 13 runs in the second inning and defeat the White Sox 15–1 in Kansas City. Each of the 13 runs scored with two outs off Sandy Consuegra, Bill Fischer and Harry Byrd. A total of 13 consecutive batters reached base on nine singles, two walks, a triple and a double during the onslaught. The Sox collected only one hit off A's hurler Art Ditmar.

MAY 14   The White Sox sell Sandy Consuegra to the Orioles.

MAY 21   The White Sox trade George Kell, Bob Nieman, Mike Fornieles and Connie Johnson to the Orioles for Jim Wilson and Dave Philley.

MAY 27   The White Sox win 5–4 in 15 innings against the Indians in the first game at Comiskey Park. Jim Wilson, in his first appearance with the White Sox, pitched two scoreless innings of relief and singled in the winning run in the 15th. The Sox tied the score 4–4 with a run in the ninth. The rally was almost cut short by fan interference. With two away, Minnie Minoso walked and Sherm Lollar doubled to apparently score Minoso, who crossed the plate on the play. However, a fan reached out of his box seat and touched the ball. As a result, umpires ordered Minoso back to third. Fox followed with a single to score Minoso and send the contest into extra innings. Cleveland won the second encounter 4–2.

Wilson's career almost ended as a rookie with the Red Sox in 1945 when his skull was fractured by a line drive from Hank Greenberg. He recovered to last in the big leagues until 1958. He spent three seasons with the White Sox and fashioned a 15–8 record in 1957.

MAY 28   The White Sox purchase Gerry Staley from the Yankees.

The Yankees didn't make many personnel mistakes during the 1950s, but letting Staley go to the White Sox was one of them. A lumberjack in the Pacific Northwest before entering pro ball, Staley certainly looked washed up when he arrived in Chicago as a 35-year-old pitcher. The Sox converted him from a starter to a reliever, and Staley had a run as one of the top closers in baseball.

From 1957 through 1960, Staley pitched 422 innings in 228 games and posted an earned run average of 2.42 along with a 30–19 record and 39 saves. He led the AL in game pitched during the 1959 pennant-winning year and made the All-Star team in 1960 just prior to his 40th birthday.

JUNE 2   The White Sox wallop the Orioles 12–0 and 9–2 during a double-header in Baltimore. Dick Donovan pitched the opening-game shutout and collected two singles and a double. In the fourth inning of the first game, Nellie Fox was hit by a pitch twice in one plate appearance. Fox was first struck in the seat of the pants by a curve from Oriole lefty Johnny Schmitz. In the judgment of umpire Hank Soar, however, Fox wasn't entitled to first base because he made no effort to evade the pitch. Two pitches later, Fox was plunked again, however, and Soar ruled the play a hit by pitch.

JUNE 4   The White Sox wallop the Orioles 13–4 in Baltimore.

JUNE 9   During an 8–0 win against the Red Sox in Boston, the White Sox try a "man in motion" play. With Ted Williams at bat, Marty Marion shifted three of his infielders to the right side, with Fred Hatfield guarding the third base line. As the pitch was delivered, Hatfield raced over to cover the shortstop position, but umpire Ed Runge ruled the maneuver illegal as a distraction to the hitter.

JUNE 14   In a game at Yankee Stadium played in 95-degree heat, tempers are short during a 5–1 White Sox loss. In the sixth inning, Dave Philley precipitated a vociferous outbreak when he argued a second strike called by umpire Charlie Berry and the Sox outfielder planted himself squarely on top of the plate with his back to pitcher Bob Grim. Berry ordered Grim to pitch, Philley got back into the batter's box, and when Berry called a strike on the next offering that looked high and wide, pandemonium broke loose. Marty Marion stormed out of the dugout and both he and Philley were ejected. On his way back to the bench, Philley tossed his bat 30 feet into the air.

The Sox were already seething at Grim because he beaned Minnie Minoso the previous season. Another altercation between Philley and Grim would occur nine days later (see June 23, 1956).

JUNE 17   The White Sox collect 20 hits and blast the Senators 20–2 in the first game of a double-header at Comiskey Park. The Sox scored in seven of eight turns at bat. Washington won the second tilt 10–4.

JUNE 20   The White Sox outlast the Orioles 12–8 at Comiskey Park. The Sox broke a 5–5 tie with three runs in the fifth inning.

JUNE 21   Both teams collect only one hit during a 1–0 White Sox win over the Orioles at Comiskey Park. The sensational pitching performances were accomplished with Jack Harshman on the mound for the Sox and Connie Johnson (seven innings) and George Zuverink (one inning) for Baltimore. The lone run and Chicago hit occurred in the first inning. Jim Rivera led off the inning with a walk, stole second, and scored on a double by Nellie Fox. Gus Triandos ended Harshman's no-hit bid with a double in the seventh.

Fox hit .296 with 108 runs and 192 hits in 1956.

JUNE 22   Sammy Esposito stars during a 12-inning, 5–4 win over the Yankees at Comiskey Park. The Yanks scored two runs in the 11th for a 4–2 lead. Esposito tied the contest with a two-run double in the bottom of the inning, then drove in the winning tally with a single in the 12th. Dick Donovan held New York hitless for the first 7⅓ innings.

A native of Chicago who attended Fenger High School, Esposito played for the Sox in 1952 and again from 1955 through 1963 as an infielder. Although he lasted 10 seasons in the majors, Esposito never played more than 100 games in a season and hit just .207 in 792 career at-bats.

JUNE 23   In a game marked by a fistfight between Dave Philley and Yankees pitcher Bob Grim, the White Sox win 2–0 at Comiskey Park. The brawl occurred in the sixth inning after Philley had been struck by the Yankee hurler. The Chicago outfielder raced to the mound, where he skirmished briefly with Grim before the combatants were pried apart by teammates.

JUNE 24   The White Sox sweep the Yankees 14–2 and 6–3 during a double-header at Comiskey Park. Larry Doby hit a three-run homer in the first inning of each game.

The wins completed a four-game sweep over the Yankees that put the White Sox one game out of first place with a record of 36–22. The Sox drew no closer to the Yankees in 1956, however. An 11-game losing streak in July ended any chance for a pennant.

JUNE 26   The White Sox extend their winning streak with a 4–1 decision over the Red Sox at Comiskey Park.

JUNE 28   The White Sox clobber the Indians 13–2 in the second game of a double-header in Cleveland. The Sox lost the opener 5–2.

JULY 6   The White Sox trounce the Tigers 14–0 at Comiskey Park.

JULY 7   Dick Donovan allows consecutive homers to Harvey Kuenn, Earl Torgeson and Charley Maxwell in the fifth inning of a 12–8 loss to the Tigers at Comiskey Park.

JULY 10   Billy Pierce starts for the American League in the All-Star Game at Griffith Stadium in Washington and allows a run in three innings while striking out five. Nellie Fox collected two singles in four at-bats, but the National League won 7–3.

JULY 11   The White Sox purchase Ellis Kinder from the Cardinals.

JULY 14   Mel Parnell of the Red Sox pitches a no-hitter to defeat the White Sox 4–0 in Boston. The game ended when Walt Dropo tapped the ball to the right of the mound, where Parnell fielded it and raced all the way to first base for the unassisted out.

JULY 18   The White Sox lose their 11th game in a row, a 4–3 decision to the Orioles in Baltimore.

JULY 19   The White Sox break their 11-game losing streak with a 3–2 win over the Orioles in Baltimore.

JULY 29   Larry Doby drives in eight runs during a double-header against the Red Sox at
             Comiskey Park, leading to 11–2 and 6–3 White Sox wins. Doby collected five RBIs in
             the opener on two homers, and three during the nightcap with a double and a single.

AUGUST 3   The White Sox explode for 11 runs in the first inning and defeat the Orioles 13–2 at
             Comiskey Park. The runs scored on a home run, two doubles, four singles and four
             walks.

AUGUST 4   The White Sox club four home runs during a 15–4 thrashing of the Orioles at
             Comiskey Park. Jim Rivera connected for two of the homers, with Les Moss,
             Larry Doby, Walt Dropo and Jack Harshman each adding one.

AUGUST 8   Sherm Lollar smacks a walk-off homer in the 14th inning to defeat the Indians 7–6 at
             Comiskey Park.

Luis Aparicio led the American League in stolen bases for the first of nine consecutive times in
1956, on his way to the Rookie of the Year Award.

AUGUST 14   The White Sox trample the Athletics 12–1 in Kansas City.

AUGUST 15   Dick Donovan pitches a two-hitter for a 10–0 win over the Athletics in Kansas City.
             The only hits off Donovan were singles by opposing pitcher Wally Burnette in the
             sixth inning and from Al Pilarcik in the eighth.

AUGUST 23   Nellie Fox collects seven consecutive hits during an 8–3 and 6–4 sweep of the
             Yankees in New York. Fox was 5-for-5 in the opener, with four singles and a triple.
             He had singles in the first two of his five plate appearances in game two.

AUGUST 31   Dick Donovan pitches a 10-inning shutout and drives in the winning run with a
             single off Early Wynn to beat the Indians 1–0 in the second game of a double-header
             at Comiskey Park. Cleveland won the opener 3–2.

SEPTEMBER 13   Billy Pierce earns his 20th win of the season with a 4–3 decision over the Red Sox at Comiskey Park.

> *Pierce's ERA jumped from 1.97 in 1955 to 3.32 in 1956, but with better hitting support, his record improved from 15–10 to 20–9. His 21 complete games in 1956 led the American League.*

SEPTEMBER 22   The White Sox collect 20 hits and maul the Athletics 17–3 at Comiskey Park.

SEPTEMBER 24   The White Sox take an 11–0 lead in the fourth inning and hang on for a 14–11 win over the Tigers in Detroit. The Sox collected 22 hits in the contest.

SEPTEMBER 30   Jim Derrington becomes the youngest player in White Sox history by starting the final game of the season, a 7–6 loss to the Athletics in Kansas City. Derrington's age was 16 years, 305 days. He allowed six runs and nine hits in six innings. Derrington also singled to become the youngest player in American League history to collect a hit.

> *Derrington was on the team because of the rule passed in 1955 stipulating that any amateur player who signed a contract with a bonus of at least $4,000 would have to remain on the major league roster for two years. The rule was rescinded in 1958. Derrington was signed by the White Sox to a contract calling for $78,000 when he graduated from high school in South Gate, California. He is the last 16-year-old to play in the major leagues. Derrington's last game in the majors was as a 17-year-old. He played in 20 games in 1957, five as a starter, and finished his brief career with an 0–2 record and a 5.23 ERA in 43 innings. Derrington went back to the minors in 1958 but hurt his arm. After a conversion to first base failed, he was out of professional baseball by the time he was 22.*

OCTOBER 2   Fire destroys the press box, radio booths and adjoining sections of the upper deck of Comiskey Park. The Chicago Cardinals football team was working out at the time of the blaze, which shot 40 feet above the roof and was visible in the Loop. Chuck Comiskey promptly announced that the press box would be replaced by an air-conditioned one with shatterproof glass.

OCTOBER 24   Marty Marion resigns as manager.

> *The White Sox had high hopes for a pennant in both 1955 and 1956, but the club finished in third place both seasons, earning Marion the ire of both the fans and the Comiskey family. With rumors swirling that the Sox were courting Al Lopez as manager, Marion resigned with a year left on his contract. Although only 37 when he left Chicago, Marion never managed another big-league club.*

OCTOBER 29   A week before Dwight Eisenhower wins a second term as president by defeating Adlai Stevenson, the White Sox name Al Lopez as manager.

> *The son of Spanish immigrants who settled in Tampa, Florida, Lopez was a catcher in the majors leagues from 1928 through 1947. He appeared in 1,918 games behind the plate, a record that stood until Bob Boone passed him in 1987. A big-league manager for 15 full seasons and parts of two others, Lopez wasn't inclined to resort to shrieking tirades at players and managers. Instead, he brought a calm and rational approach to leading a club. He was the manager of*

the Indians from 1951 through 1956, winning the pennant in 1954 and finishing second to the Yankees the other five seasons. In 1954, Cleveland won 111 games and posted a winning percentage of .721 that is still the American League record and the best of any big-league club since 1909. Yet the Indians lost the World Series in a shocking four-game sweep at the hands of the New York Giants. Lopez resigned as Cleveland manager at the end of the 1956 season because of disagreements with general manager Hank Greenberg. With the White Sox, Lopez finished second to the Yankees in 1957 and 1958, then was the manager of the 1959 club that won the AL pennant, the only one that flew over Chicago between 1919 and 2005. The Sox lost the 1959 World Series to the Dodgers in six games, before dropping to third in 1960, fourth in 1961 and fifth in 1962. After landing in second place the next three seasons, twice to the hated Yankees, Lopez resigned at the end of the 1965 campaign, although he returned to the Sox briefly in 1968 and 1969 on an interim basis.

DECEMBER 10   Club president Grace Comiskey dies of a heart attack at the age of 63.

The passing of Grace Comiskey threw the future of the franchise into disarray and led to the family losing control of the franchise 27 months later. Grace had been president of the club since 1941, following the death of her husband Louis in 1939. Prior to her death, Grace and her eldest daughter, Dorothy, had presented a united front to the media and attempted to make Chuck Comiskey appear ridiculous, believing he was too young and too rash to run the club on his own, as his grandfather and father had done. Chuck had just turned 31 when his mother died. In her will, Grace showed her favoritism toward her daughter by awarding Dorothy 3,975 shares of the club (54 percent), while Chuck received 3,475 (46 percent). The decision to bequeath more stock to Dorothy was a painful rebuke to her only son. Although she owned a majority of the stock, Dorothy shunned publicity and had little interest in running the club. She married John Rigney, a former White Sox pitcher, in 1941. After his playing days ended, Rigney joined the front office and rose through the ranks. In 1956, Chuck Comiskey and John Rigney were both vice presidents and served as co-general managers. In November 1957, Chuck initiated a legal proceeding in order to force his sister to distribute the 2,582 shares of remaining stock held in trust by their mother's estate. The family feud reached the boiling point late in 1958. In an attempt to gain control of the team, Dorothy sought to have the White Sox's board of directors increased from four to five. Had Dorothy been able to elect three directors, as she desired, she theoretically could have demoted or ousted her brother. The messy court battle continued, as Chuck went to court to and succeeded in blocking the move and the board of directors remained at four. The four were Dorothy and Chuck and their attorneys. Chuck's attorney was his father-in-law, which added to the family drama. With his legal bills mounting, Chuck tried to purchase Dorothy's stock and submitted several bids. Dorothy rejected Chuck's best offer and instead accepted Bill Veeck's proposition in 1959 (see March 10, 1959), ending the Comiskey family's 59-year ownership of the White Sox. It wasn't the end of the Comiskey family litigation, however. Chuck sued Dorothy, claiming that she illegally sold the club to Veeck. The Illinois Appellate Court ruled against Chuck in January 1960. In another matter, Dorothy and Grace had a joint checking account prior to Grace's death. Chuck took Dorothy to court seeking to have that checking account made part of the estate. Following another trial, that decision also went against Chuck.

1957   Sox

Season in a Sentence

Under new manager Al Lopez, the White Sox hold a six-game lead in the pennant race in June before ending the year in second, the club's highest finish since 1920.

Finish • Won • Lost • Pct • GB

Second   90   64   .584   8.0

Manager

Al Lopez

Stats

Stats	WS	AL	Rank
Batting Avg:	.260	.255	3
On-Base Pct:	.347	.329	1
Slugging Pct:	.375	.382	6
Home Runs:	106		7
Stolen Bases:	109		1
ERA:	3.35	3.79	2
Fielding Avg:	.982	.979	1
Runs Scored:	707		3
Runs Allowed:	566		2

Starting Lineup

Sherm Lollar, c
Earl Torgeson, 1b
Nellie Fox, 2b
Bubba Phillips, 3b
Luis Aparicio, ss
Minnie Minoso, lf
Larry Doby, cf
Jim Rivera, rf
Jim Landis, rf-cf
Walt Dropo, 1b
Sammy Esposito, 3b

Pitchers

Billy Pierce, sp
Dick Donovan, sp
Jim Wilson, sp
Bob Keegan, sp
Jack Harshman, sp
Gerry Staley, rp
Bill Fischer, sp-rp

Attendance

1,135,668 (fourth in AL)

Club Leaders

Batting Avg:	Nellie Fox	.317
On-Base Pct:	Minnie Minoso	.408
Slugging Pct:	Minnie Minoso	.464
Home Runs:	Minnie Minoso	14
	Jim Rivera	14
RBIs:	Minnie Minoso	103
Runs:	Nellie Fox	110
Stolen Bases:	Luis Aparicio	28
Wins:	Billy Pierce	20
Strikeouts:	Billy Pierce	171
ERA:	Dick Donovan	2.77
Saves:	Gerry Staley	7
	Paul LaPalme	7

APRIL 16   The White Sox open the season with an 11-inning, 3–2 win over the Indians in Cleveland. Billy Pierce pitched a complete game. The winning run scored in the 11th off Herb Score on two walks and a double by Larry Doby.

Vince Lloyd replaced Harry Creighton in the television booth, joining Jack Brickhouse. As had been the case since 1948, and would continue until 1968, the White Sox and the Cubs shared TV broadcast teams. Only the daytime home games of both clubs were telecast.

APRIL 18   In the home opener, the White Sox defeat the Athletics 6–2 before 10,814 at Comiskey Park. Jack Harshman pitched a complete game and hit a home run. Sherm Lollar and Minnie Minoso also homered.

Minoso hit .310 with 12 homers, 103 RBIs, 96 runs scored and a league-leading 36 doubles in 1957.

APRIL 20   Down 6–0, the White Sox score three runs in the third inning, three in the fourth, three in the sixth and two in the seventh to defeat the Athletics 11–7 at Comiskey Park.

The White Sox led the majors in stolen bases in 1957 with 109. The Giants were second in the category with 64 steals.

APRIL 21   On Easter Sunday, Jim Wilson is two outs from a no-hitter before settling for a three-hit, 10-inning, 1–0 win over the Athletics at Comiskey Park. The no-hit bid was spoiled when Hector Lopez singled with one out in the ninth. The winning run scored when Sherm Lollar, pinch-hitting for Wilson, hit a sacrifice fly.

MAY 2   Walt Dropo hits a pinch-hit grand slam off Chuck Stobbs in the sixth inning of a 6–1 win over the Senators at Comiskey Park.

> *The Sox had a record of 11–2 on May 3.*

MAY 9   Ted Williams hits three homers off Bob Keegan to drive in all four runs of a 4–1 Red Sox win over the White Sox at Comiskey Park.

MAY 16   Bubba Phillips collects five hits, including a home run and a triple, in five at-bats during an 8–3 win over the Senators in Washington.

> *Phillips was an outfielder who was converted into a third baseman to solve the White Sox's decades-long problem of filling the position. He played 246 games at third for Chicago over four seasons before the club looked for another solution.*

MAY 18   White Sox pitcher Paul LaPalme costs his team a victory against the Orioles in Baltimore by throwing a pitch a half-minute too early. The contest was originally scheduled for the afternoon, but was switched to nighttime to avoid conflict with the Preakness. The game started at 7 p.m., and it was agreed beforehand to end play precisely at 10:20 p.m., regardless of the score, in order to allow the Sox to catch a train midnight for Boston. Heading into the bottom of the ninth the White Sox led 4–3 with about 30 seconds remaining before the 10:20 p.m. deadline. League rules did not call for a suspended game, so the Sox could have won the game by stalling, or by issuing an intentional walk. La Palme threw a pitch over the plate, however, and Dick Williams hit it for a home run. Time was called by the umpires immediately after the home run.

MAY 20   The White Sox sell Bob Kennedy to the Dodgers.

MAY 22   The White Sox extend their winning streak to nine games with an 8–4 decision over the Yankees in New York. The victory gave the Sox a 20–7 record and a three-game lead in the pennant race.

MAY 25   Dick Donovan pitches a one-hitter to defeat the Indians 1–0 in Cleveland. The only hit off Donovan was a single by Eddie Robinson in the second inning.

> *With a 16–6 record, Donovan topped the American League in winning percentage in 1957. He also led in complete games with 16 and compiled a 2.77 earned run average.*

MAY 26   The White Sox edge the Indians 1–0 in 10 innings in the first game of a double-header in Cleveland. Billy Pierce and Indians hurler Bud Daley both pitched complete games. In the 10th, Luis Aparicio singled, went to third on a two-base error by Daley on an attempted pick-off throw and scored on an infield out. Cleveland won game two 4–3.

MAY 31   Walt Dropo hits a grand slam off Frank Lary in the eighth inning of a 6–0 win over the Tigers at Comiskey Park.

JUNE 4   Billy Pierce pitches a 10-inning two-hitter to win 1–0 over the Red Sox at Comiskey Park. Nellie Fox drove in the winning run with a single. The only Boston hits were singles by Billy Klaus in the third inning and Norm Zauchin in the seventh.

             Fox had the best offensive year of his career in 1957. He batted .317 with six home runs, 110 runs scored and a league-leading 196 hits.

JUNE 8   Billy Pierce shuts out the Orioles 2–0 at Comiskey Park.

             The win gave the White Sox a 32–13 record and a six-game lead in the American League pennant race. It was the Sox's largest advantage at any point in a season since 1919.

JUNE 12   During a 7–6 win over the Yankees at Comiskey Park, New York hurler Al Cicotte nearly skulls Minnie Minoso with a fastball. On the next pitch, Minoso swung and missed but let go of the bat, which sailed past Cicotte's head.

JUNE 13   The hostilities between the White Sox and Yankees continue as a brawl that lasts nearly half an hour highlights a 4–3 Chicago loss at Comiskey Park. The fight erupted in the Sox half of the first inning while Larry Doby was at bat and two men were on base. New York pitcher Art Ditmar threw a high and inside pitch and Doby hit the dirt. The ball got away from catcher Elston Howard and Ditmar ran in to cover the plate. Doby and Ditmar immediately exchanged words and began swinging. Billy Martin blindsided Doby with a punch. A contingent of New York police was needed to help quell the melee. When order was restored, Doby and Walt Dropo were thrown out along with Yankee players Enos Slaughter and Martin. Slaughter left the field with his uniform shirt torn to shreds. Ditmar was allowed to remain in the game despite vigorous protests from the White Sox and emerged as the winning pitcher.

JUNE 14   The White Sox trade Dave Philley to the Tigers for Earl Torgeson.

             Torgeson was acquired to fill a need at first base. Jim Rivera was the Opening Day starter at first and played 31 games at the position. It was a project doomed to fail, as Rivera had never before played in the infield and his speed was wasted at first.

JUNE 16   Dixie Howell hits two home runs and pitches 3²/₃ innings of scoreless relief during an 8–6 win over the Senators in the second game of a double-header at Comiskey Park. The Sox trailed 6–0 before scoring three runs in the fifth inning, one in the sixth and four in the eighth. Howell homered in the fifth and sixth. The White Sox also won the opener 4–2.

JUNE 30   The White Sox score four runs in the ninth inning to defeat the Senators 7–6 in the first game of a double-header at Griffith Stadium. A two-out triple by Larry Doby broke the 6–6 tie. Washington won the second tilt 11–9 in 10 innings on a walk-off homer by Roy Sievers.

The game-two loss dropped the White Sox out of a first-place tie with the Yankees. The Sox failed to regain the top spot in the league for the remainder of the year but were within sight of first place until the last week of August.

JULY 5   The White Sox rout the Indians 14–4 at Comiskey Park.

JULY 8   The White Sox sweep the Indians 9–8 and 7–2 at Comiskey Park. The opener was a thrilling come-from-behind victory that lasted 13 innings. Down 6–0, the Sox scored one run in the second inning, four in the fourth and three in the seventh for an 8–6 lead, but Cleveland tied the score 8–8 with two tallies in the ninth. In the 13th, Jim Rivera hit a triple and scored on Luis Aparicio's single.

JULY 9   Minnie Minoso is one of the heroes of the All-Star Game, won 6–5 by the American League at Busch Stadium in St. Louis. He entered the game in the eighth inning and doubled during a three-run ninth that staked the AL to a 6–2 lead. The game seemed to be in the bag with Billy Pierce on the mound, but Pierce gave up three runs. With one out, Gus Bell tried to advance two bases on a single, but Minoso threw out Bell at third base. Gil Hodges was the next hitter and lined to left field, where Minoso made a running catch to end the game.

JULY 20   Dick Donovan pitches a one-hitter to defeat the Red Sox 4–0 at Comiskey Park. The only Boston hit was a single by Ted Williams.

JULY 26   Jim Wilson (8⅓ innings) and Billy Pierce (two-thirds of an inning) combine on a two-hitter to defeat the Orioles 1–0 in the second game of a double-header at Memorial Stadium. Pierce struck out the only two batters he faced after Wilson walked two. The only Baltimore hits were a double by Al Pilarcik in the first inning and a single by Joe Ginsberg in the second. The Orioles won the first game 5–2.

           Pierce was 20–12 with a 3.26 ERA in 1957. He tied for the league lead in wins and complete games (16).

JULY 28   Jim Landis strikes out five times in five at-bats, but the White Sox win 4–3 over the Orioles in Baltimore.

JULY 30   President Dwight Eisenhower attends a 7–1 White Sox win over the Senators in Washington.

AUGUST 1   Larry Doby hits a grand slam off Chuck Stobbs in the fourth inning for a 4–0 lead, but the White Sox lose 5–4 to the Senators in Washington.

AUGUST 7   Jim Wilson pitches a two-hitter to defeat the Athletics 7–0 at Comiskey Park. The only Kansas City hits were a double by Billy Hunter in the first inning and a single by Irv Noren in the fourth.

AUGUST 9   Nellie Fox drives in the tying runs twice and scores the winner during an 11-inning, 5–4 win over the Yankees at Comiskey Park. Fox deadlocked the contest at 3–3 with an RBI-single in the ninth. After New York tallied in the top of the 11th, Fox tied the game again in the White Sox's half with another single and crossed the plate on Larry Doby's double.

AUGUST 17   Minnie Minoso hits a grand slam off Harry Byrd to give the White Sox a 4–0 lead before a batter is retired, but the Tigers rally to win 9–8 in 10 innings in Detroit.

AUGUST 20   Bob Keegan pitches a no-hitter on the 49th birthday of Al Lopez, beating the Senators 6–0 in the second game of a double-header at Comiskey Park. He walked two and struck out one. In the ninth inning, Jim Lemon grounded to Luis Aparicio at shortstop for the first out, followed by a strikeout of Julio Becquer. The final out was recorded on a pop up by Eddie Yost to first baseman Walt Dropo. Washington won the opener 5–4.

Keegan was 37 years old when he threw his no-hitter, the first by a White Sox pitcher since 1937. He won only two more big league games after the gem, one on a three-hitter in his next start (see August 25, 1957) and another on a two-hitter (see September 15, 1957).

AUGUST 21   The White Sox score seven runs in the third inning and defeat the Senators 12–6 at Comiskey Park.

AUGUST 25   In his first start since his no-hitter, Bob Keegan allows only three hits during a 6–2 win over the Orioles in the first game of a double-header at Comiskey Park. He retired the first 10 batters to face him, extending his hitless streak to 12⅓ innings, before Bob Boyd tripled. The White Sox also took game two 7–0.

The White Sox were 75–48 and 3½ games behind the Yankees on August 26, then they lost three games in a row to the Yankees at Comiskey Park from August 27 through August 29 to all but destroy any of the club's pennant hopes. The Sox closed the gap to 4½ games on September 7 but could get no closer.

SEPTEMBER 6   Dixie Howell not only pitches two innings of scoreless relief, but he also smacks a walk-off home run to defeat the Athletics 4–3 at Comiskey Park. It was his third homer of the season. He hit two in a game 10 weeks earlier (see June 16, 1957).

Howell was a prisoner of war in Germany during World War II. During his big-league career, he hit five home runs and compiled a .243 batting average in 74 at-bats. Howell suffered a fatal heart attack on March 18, 1960, at the age of 40 while in spring training with the Indianapolis club of the American Association.

SEPTEMBER 7   Luis Aparicio hits the first two of his three 1957 home runs during the same game, an 8–3 win over the Athletics at Comiskey Park. The first was an inside-the-park homer leading off the first inning. Aparicio hoisted a pop fly to right field, where Lou Skizas attempted to make a catch, but when he lunged for the ball, he lost his balance and went skidding into foul territory. As the ball bounced toward the right-field corner, Skizas lay sprawled on the warning track for several moments, apparently stunned. By the time Skizas regained his feet, retrieved the ball and fired it toward the infield, Aparicio had raced across the plate.

The September 7, 1957, game was the only one of Aparicio's 18-year career in which he hit two or more homers in a game.

SEPTEMBER 15   Bob Keegan (seven innings) and Barry Latman (two innings) combine on a two-hitter to defeat the Senators 3–1 in Washington. Jim Lemon collected both hits with a single in the fifth inning and a homer in the seventh.

SEPTEMBER 19   The White Sox score four runs in the 13th inning to defeat the Senators 7–3 in Washington. During the rally, Nellie Fox and Minnie Minoso hit home runs on consecutive pitches from Pedro Ramos.

SEPTEMBER 21   Down 6–1, the White Sox score one run in the sixth inning, three in the seventh and two in the eighth to defeat the Indians 7–6 in Cleveland.

During his 14 seasons with the White Sox, Nellie Fox played with a ferocity few players could match. Though not the most gifted athlete, his never-ending desire to win made him one of the most respected players in the game.

SEPTEMBER 22   Two days before President Eisenhower sends federal troops to Little Rock, Arkansas, to integrate Central High School and two weeks before the Soviet Union launches the earth satellite Sputnik, Billy Pierce collects his 20th win of the season with a 9–5 decision over the Indians in Cleveland.

DECEMBER 3   The White Sox trade Larry Doby, Jack Harshman, Jim Marshall and Russ Herman to the Orioles for Tito Francona, Billy Goodman and Ray Moore.

DECEMBER 4   The White Sox trade Minnie Minoso and Fred Hatfield to the Indians for Early Wynn and Al Smith.

The White Sox needed to make a bold move to surge past the Yankees in the American League standings and risked trading Minoso, the most popular player on the team among Sox fans, for Wynn, a pitcher who many believed was too old to be of much help. The controversial deal helped the White Sox win the 1959 AL pennant, however, as Wynn became the ace of the pitching staff. Mickey Mantle once said that Wynn was "so mean he'd knock you down in the dugout." Early had pitched under Al Lopez for six years in Cleveland. When acquired by the Sox, Wynn was 38 years old and had a lifetime record of 249–203. He recorded the fourth 20-win season of his career in 1956, when he was 20–9 with a career-low 2.72 ERA. But in 1957, Wynn had a record of 14–17 and his earned run average soared to 4.31. He was 14–16 for Chicago in 1958, but he had one more 20-win season left in him, with a 22–10 mark in 1959. Overall, Wynn won 64 and lost 55 in five seasons in Chicago. Minoso returned to the White Sox in another trade with the Indians in December 1959.

1958   Sox

Season in a Sentence

The White Sox finish second again but are never a factor in the pennant race after stumbling out of the gate and thudding into last place in mid-June.

Finish • Won • Lost • Pct • GB

Second   82   72   .532   10.0

Manager

Al Lopez

Stats

Stats	WS	AL	Rank
Batting Avg:	.257	.254	3
On-Base Pct:	.329	.325	3
Slugging Pct:	.367	.383	6
Home Runs:	101		8
Stolen Bases:	101		1
ERA:	3.61		4
Fielding Avg:	.981	.979	2
Runs Scored:	634		6
Runs Allowed:	615		4

Starting Lineup

Sherm Lollar, c
Earl Torgeson, 1b
Nellie Fox, 2b
Billy Goodman, 3b
Luis Aparicio, ss
Al Smith, lf-rf
Jim Landis, cf
Jim Rivera, rf-lf
Bubba Phillips, 3b-lf-cf
Ray Boone, 1b
Earl Battey, c
Don Mueller, rf
Ron Jackson, 1b

Pitchers

Billy Pierce, sp
Dick Donovan, sp
Early Wynn, sp
Jim Wilson, sp
Ray Moore, sp
Gerry Staley, rp

Attendance

797,451 (sixth in AL)

Club Leaders

Batting Avg:	Nellie Fox	.300
On-Base Pct:	Sherm Lollar	.367
Slugging Pct:	Sherm Lollar	.454
Home Runs:	Sherm Lollar	20
RBIs:	Sherm Lollar	84
Runs:	Nellie Fox	82
Stolen Bases:	Luis Aparicio	29
Wins:	Billy Pierce	17
Strikeouts:	Early Wynn	179
ERA:	Billy Pierce	2.68
Saves:	Gerry Staley	8
	Turk Lown	8

MARCH 21   The White Sox purchase Don Mueller from the Giants.

APRIL 15   The White Sox open the season with a 4–3 loss to the Tigers before 28,319 at Comiskey Park. The Sox led 3–1 before Detroit rallied with runs in the fifth, sixth and eighth innings off Billy Pierce.

APRIL 25   The White Sox score three runs in the ninth inning and one in the 12th to defeat the Athletics 6–5 at Comiskey Park. Jim Rivera's two-run single tied the score. In the 12th, Rivera singled, reached second on a sacrifice and crossed the plate on a hit by Luis Aparicio.

MAY 9   Early Wynn pitches a two-hitter against his former Indians teammates for a 5–0 win in Cleveland. The only Cleveland hits were a single by Russ Nixon and a double by Rocky Colavito. White Sox outfielder Ted Beard hit his first major league homer since 1951 and the last of the six he struck during his career.

MAY 22   A crowd of only 632 attends a 5–1 win over the Orioles on a windy, 46-degree day at Comiskey Park.

MAY 23   Early Wynn pitches the White Sox to a 1–0 win over the Orioles at Comiskey Park. The lone run scored in the third inning when Wynn and Luis Aparicio singled and Nellie Fox struck a sacrifice fly.

JUNE 8   Billy Goodman collects five hits, including a double, in six at-bats, but the White Sox lose 6–5 in 10 innings against the Red Sox in the first game of a double-header at Fenway Park. Boston also won the second tilt 4–1.

JUNE 13   The White Sox and the Orioles play to a 5–5 tie against the Orioles in at Memorial Stadium. The game was called on account of a curfew in the city of Baltimore that stipulated that no inning could start after 11:59 p.m. The Sox trailed 4–0 heading into the ninth and scored five times, but the Orioles countered with one tally in their half.

              The White Sox were 22–30 on June 13 and in last place in the American League standings. The Sox were 60–42 the rest of the way and rose to second place by August 11. But they never got close to the Yankees, who ran away with the pennant.

JUNE 15   The White Sox sweep the Orioles twice with shutouts during a double-header at Memorial Stadium. In the opener, Jim Wilson pitched a two-hitter for a 3–0 win. The only Baltimore hits were singles by Brooks Robinson in the second inning and Gus Triandos in the fifth. Both were retired on the base paths. Robinson was nailed on a pick-off attempt and Triandos on a double play. Wilson faced the minimum 27 batters. Dick Donovan won game two 4–0.

              On the same day, the White Sox traded Tito Francona and Bill Fischer to the Tigers for Ray Boone and Bob Shaw. Boone was the head of a Major League Baseball's first three-generation family. His son Bob played in the majors from 1972 through 1990, and two of Bob's sons also reached the big leagues. Bret played from 1992 through 2005, and Aaron debuted in 1997 and was still active in 2007. Joining the White Sox in the 11th season of a 13-year career, Ray Boone was one of the many veteran retreads unsuccessfully tried out at first base by the White Sox during the 1950s. The Sox would have been much better keeping Francona. He hit .363 in 1959 and was a regular for the Indians at both first base and in the outfield for five seasons before playing another half-dozen seasons with several clubs as a valued reserve. After leaving the Sox, Francona played in 1,442 big league games. The White Sox received one good season from Shaw. He was 18–6 with a 2.69 earned run average during the pennant-winning season of 1959, but he regressed to a 13–13 mark and a league-average ERA in 1960. Shaw was dealt to the Athletics in 1961.

JUNE 17   The White Sox record their third consecutive shutout as Billy Pierce pitches a complete game for a 4–0 victory over the Red Sox at Comiskey Park.

JUNE 19   Early Wynn hurls a two-hitter to defeat the Red Sox 4–0 at Comiskey Park. It was the White Sox's fourth shutout in five games. The only Boston hits were singles by Frank Malzone in the second inning and opposing pitcher Frank Sullivan in the fifth.

JUNE 21   Billy Pierce throws a two-hitter to win 1–0 over the Orioles at Comiskey Park. The only Baltimore hits were singles by Dick Williams in the fourth inning and Al Pilarcik in the ninth.

JUNE 23   Sherm Lollar hits a two-run homer off Whitey Ford in the first inning for the only runs in a 2–0 win over the Yankees at Comiskey Park. Ray Moore pitched the shutout. It was Chicago's sixth shutout during a span of nine games, a feat accomplished by five different pitchers. The other four were Jim Wilson, Dick Donovan, Early Wynn and Billy Pierce.

           On the same day, the White Sox trade Turk Lown to the Reds for Walt Dropo. Lown didn't look like much of an acquisition. He was 34 years old and had a 30–46 lifetime record along with a 4.61 ERA. But Lown gave the White Sox five solid seasons out of the bullpen. He was tremendous during the 1959 pennant-winning season, posting a 9–2 record, a league-leading 15 saves and an earned run average of 2.89.

JUNE 24   The White Sox telecast a night game for the first time since 1949 and lose 6–2 to the Yankees at Comiskey Park.

JUNE 27   Billy Pierce retires the first 26 batters to face him before settling for a one-hit, 3–0 win over the Senators at Comiskey Park. He started the ninth by retiring Ken Aspromonte and Steve Korcheck. He was one batter from a perfect game when Ed Fitz Gerald, batting for Russ Kemmerer, lined an opposite-field double into right field that landed fair by a foot. Pierce next faced Albie Pearson and struck him out to end the game.

           The game was Pierce's third consecutive shutout, a stretch in which he allowed only eight hits in 27 innings. He had a scoreless streak of 33 consecutive innings over four starts. Over the course of the 1958 season, Pierce was 17–11 with a 2.68 earned run average and a league-leading 19 complete games.

JUNE 29   Billy Goodman collects five hits, including a triple, in six at-bats during an 11-inning, 12–11 win over the Senators in the second game of a double-header at Comiskey Park. The Sox collected 21 hits in all. Chicago led 7–1 in the fourth inning, fell behind 10–7 in the sixth, took an 11–10 advantage in the eighth, then allowed Washington to tie the score in the ninth. Jim Rivera drove in the winning run with a double. The Senators won the opener 12–0.

JULY 8   Nellie Fox collects two singles in four at-bats during the American League's 4–3 win in the All-Star Game, played at Memorial Stadium in Baltimore.

JULY 12   The White Sox sweep the Red Sox 7–4 and 13–5 in Boston. Sherm Lollar hit a grand slam off Riverboat Smith in the first inning of the opener.

              Lollar had the best offensive season of his career in 1958 with 22 homers, 84 RBIs and a .273 batting average.

JULY 18   Al Smith hits a grand slam off John Romonosky in the fifth inning of a 9–2 win over the Senators in Washington.

JULY 30   The White Sox score eight runs in the third inning for an 8–2 win, then hang on to defeat the Senators 11–9 at Comiskey Park.

AUGUST 9   Sherm Lollar drives in six runs on a grand slam and two singles during a 9–3 win over the Tigers in Detroit. Lollar bashed the homer off Herb Moford in the fifth inning.

AUGUST 16   The White Sox outlast the Indians 7–6 in 14 innings at Comiskey Park. The winning run scored on two walks and an error.

AUGUST 22   Nellie Fox strikes out during an 8–5 loss to the Yankees in New York. It ended Nellie's streak of 98 consecutive games without striking out, a major league record.

AUGUST 31   Early Wynn pitches a two-hitter for a 3–0 win over the Tigers at Comiskey Park. The only Detroit hits were singles by Johnny Groth in the third inning and Harvey Kuenn in the ninth.

SEPTEMBER 3   The White Sox collect only two hits but win 1–0 over the Tigers in Detroit. The lone run scored in the seventh inning on a single by Billy Goodman and a double from Sherm Lollar off Frank Lary. Dick Donovan pitched the shutout.

              Donovan was 15–14 with a 3.01 ERA in 1958.

SEPTEMBER 14 The White Sox hit five home runs during a 6–5 win over the Tigers in the second game of a double-header at Comiskey Park. Earl Torgeson struck two of them, with Johnny Callison, Bubba Phillips and Sherm Lollar each adding one. The homers by Callison and Phillips were of the inside-the-park variety. It was Callison's first homer in the majors. He was 19 years old and made his big league debut five days earlier. Torgeson's second homer broke a 5–5 tie in the eighth inning. The Sox also won the opener 7–1.

SEPTEMBER 25 A crowd of only 799 watches the White Sox lose 7–1 to the Tigers at Comiskey Park.

              Attendance dropped from 1,135,668 in 1957 to 797,451 in 1958.

SEPTEMBER 26   Barry Latman pitches the White Sox to a 1–0 win over the Athletics at Comiskey
                Park. The lone run scored in the sixth on a sacrifice fly by Johnny Callison.

                *Latman looked like a coming star in 1958. He was 20 years old and compiled a
                3–0 record and a 0.76 earned run average in 13 games and 47²/₃ innings. Latman
                never developed, however. He was traded to the Indians in April 1960 and
                finished his career in 1967 with a 59–68 record.*

SEPTEMBER 28   In his first major league at-bat, Chuck Lindstrom hits an RBI-triple off the left field
                wall during an 11–4 win over the Athletics at Comiskey Park on the final day of the
                1958 season. He later drew a walk. Lindstrom entered the game as a substitute at
                catcher for Johnny Romano, who was playing in only his fourth big league contest.

                *A native of Chicago, Lindstrom was 22 years old and the son of Hall of Famer
                Fred Lindstrom. Chuck's triple in his debut proved to be the only official at-bat
                of his only big league game. In fact, it was his only game above the Class A level
                in the minors. Sent to the Sox farm club in Charleston, South Carolina, in 1959,
                Chuck hit .219 and retired from baseball as a player. He finished his "career" in
                the majors with a batting average of 1.000 and a slugging percentage of 3.000.*

In Search of a Third Baseman

The White Sox had a slick-fielding, solid-hitting third baseman from 1923 through 1931 named Willie Kamm, who played in 1,159 games at the position for the club. After Kamm was traded to the Indians in May 1931, the Sox spent more than 30 seasons finding another individual to play 100 or more games in consecutive seasons at third.

Year	Leader in Games Played at 3B	Games Played at 3B
1930	Willie Kamm	105
1931	Billy Sullivan, Jr.	83
1932	Carey Selph	71
1933	Jimmie Dykes	151
1934	Jimmie Dykes	74
1935	Jimmie Dykes	98
1936	Jimmie Dykes	125
1937	Tony Piet	86
1938	Marv Owen	140
1939	Eric McNair	103
1940	Bob Kennedy	154
1941	Dario Lodigiani	86
1942	Bob Kennedy	96
1943	Ralph Hodgin	56
1944	Ralph Hodgin	82
1945	Tony Cuccinello	112
1946	Dario Lodigiani	44
1947	Floyd Baker	101
1948	Luke Appling	64
1949	Floyd Baker	122
1950	Hank Majeski	112
1951	Bob Dillinger	70
1952	Hector Rodriguez	113
1953	Bob Elliott	58
1954	Cass Michaels	91
1955	George Kell	105
1956	Fred Hatfield	100
1957	Bubba Phillips	97
1958	Billy Goodman	111
1959	Bubba Phillips	100
1960	Gene Freese	122
1961	Al Smith	80
1962	Al Smith	105
1963	Pete Ward	154
1964	Pete Ward	138

1959

Season in a Sentence

With a club that leads the majors in earned run average and stolen bases, and hits fewer home runs than any other club in the big leagues, the White Sox win the AL pennant for the first time since 1919.

Finish • Won • Lost • Pct • GB

First   94   60   .610   +5.0

Manager

Al Lopez

World Series

The White Sox lost four games to two to the Los Angeles Dodgers

Stats

Stats	WS	AL	Rank
Batting Avg:	.250	.253	6
On-Base Pct:	.330	.326	3
Slugging Pct:	.364	.384	7
Home Runs:	97		8
Stolen Bases:	113		1
ERA:	3.29		1
Fielding Avg:	.979	.977	1
Runs Scored:	669		6
Runs Allowed:	588		1

Starting Lineup

Sherm Lollar, c
Earl Torgeson, 1b
Nellie Fox, 2b
Bubba Phillips, 3b
Luis Aparicio, ss
Al Smith, lf-rf
Jim Landis, cf
Jim McAnany, rf
Billy Goodman, 3b
Jim Rivera, rf-lf

Pitchers

Early Wynn, sp
Bob Shaw, sp-rp
Billy Pierce, sp
Dick Donovan, sp
Barry Latman, sp-rp
Gerry Staley, rp
Turk Lown, rp
Ray Moore, rp

Attendance

1,423,144 (third in AL)

Club Leaders

Batting Avg:	Nellie Fox	.306
On-Base Pct:	Nellie Fox	.380
Slugging Pct:	Sherm Lollar	.451
Home Runs:	Sherm Lollar	22
RBIs:	Sherm Lollar	84
Runs:	Luis Aparicio	98
Stolen Bases:	Luis Aparicio	56
Wins:	Early Wynn	22
Strikeouts:	Early Wynn	179
ERA:	Bob Shaw	2.69
Saves:	Turk Lown	15

MARCH 10   Two months after Alaska is admitted as the 49th state, Bill Veeck completes the purchase of a majority of the White Sox's stock for $2.7 million. The deal ended 59 years of Comiskey family control of the club. Veeck had arranged for a 90-day option to purchase the majority stock in the club from Dorothy Comiskey Rigney in December 1959. During the 90-day period, Dorothy tried to back out of the deal and sell the club to Chicago insurance executive Charlie Finley, but Veeck thwarted the deal with Finley. Veeck headed a syndicate called the CBC Corporation in which he owned 30 percent of the stock, Hank Greenberg 40 percent and John Allyn, Sr. 24 percent, with the remainder split among small investors. Veeck became club president. Greenberg was named general manager. A former major league first baseman during the 1930 and 1940s, mainly with the Tigers, Greenberg was elected to the Hall of Fame in 1956 based on a .313 batting average and 331 home runs in 1,394 games. Greenberg worked under Veeck with the Indians as farm director and was later the general manager in Cleveland from 1950 through 1957. Allyn died in

1960, and his stock was divided between his sons Arthur Jr. and John. Both would be majority owners of the Sox during the 1960s and 1970s.

Veeck's lifelong dream of owning a team in his hometown became a reality when he completed the purchase of the majority stock of the White Sox from Dorothy Comiskey Rigney. The transaction climaxed a feud between Dorothy and her brother Chuck, the club's vice president and owner of the other 46 percent (see December 10, 1956). Chuck Comiskey remained in the organization as vice president, but he had little authority and wasn't consulted on major personnel issues. He was instrumental in building one of the best farm systems in baseball, only to see Veeck trade the White Sox's top prospects for veterans. Chuck was unhappy over his secondary role. Comiskey believed running a club once owned by his father and grandfather was his birthright. He resigned his post as vice president in June 1960, although he retained his 46 percent share until December 1961. Veeck's father, William Sr., was president of the Cubs from 1918 until his death in 1932. The younger Veeck was employed by Cubs owner P. K. Wrigley in a variety of capacities, including the 1937–38 supervision of the renovation of Wrigley Field that included the building of the present-day scoreboard and the planting of the ivy on the outfield walls. At the age of 27, Veeck bought the Milwaukee Brewers of the American Association in 1941 and turned a franchise on the brink of bankruptcy into one of the most profitable in the minor leagues by displaying a genius for promotional gimmicks that would bring people into the ballpark. While owning the Brewers, Veeck served in the Marines during World War II and suffered an injury from the recoil of an artillery piece that cost him his right leg. Once out of the service, Veeck purchased the Indians in 1946, a losing club with a spotty attendance record. By 1948, the Indians won the world championship and drew a then-major league record 2,620,627 fans. He sold the club in 1949, looking for new horizons. Veeck bought the St. Louis Browns in 1951, in yet another attempt to remake a moribund franchise. The Browns proved to too much of a challenge, however, and Veeck sold the franchise to a group that moved the club to Baltimore and renamed it the Orioles. In Chicago, Veeck won an American League title in 1959, the first for the team in 40 years, and used a winning club and his promotional bag of tricks to set franchise attendance records in both 1959 and 1960. Plagued by ill health, Veeck sold the Sox in June 1961.

APRIL 6   The White Sox announce the move of their spring training base from Tampa to Sarasota. The White Sox had trained in Tampa since 1954 but had trouble drawing crowds. The Reds also trained in Tampa, and the Sox believed that the city couldn't support two teams. The White Sox remained in Sarasota until 1997.

APRIL 10   In the season opener, the White Sox defeat the Tigers 9–7 in 14 innings on a 37-degree day in Detroit. The two 14th-inning runs scored on a home run by Nellie Fox, who had failed to connect for a homer in 623 at-bats in 1958. Fox also collected a double and three singles in seven trips to the plate. Jim Landis hit a two-run homer in the fifth.

              Fox had an MVP season in 1959. He batted .306 with 191 hits, including 34 doubles, six triples and two home runs.

APRIL 11   Early Wynn records his 250th career victory with a 5–3 decision over the Tigers in Detroit. Luis Aparicio broke a 3–3 tie with a home run in the seventh inning.

Aparicio was the runner-up to Nellie Fox in the MVP balloting in 1959. Luis hit just .257, but he won the Gold Glove, scored 98 runs and led the majors in stolen bases with 56. The 56 steals tied a White Sox record set by Wally Moses in 1943 and stood until Rudy Law swiped 77 in 1983. Early Wynn was third in the Most Valuable Player voting. He had a record of 22–10 and compiled an ERA of 3.16 in a league-leading 255²/₃ innings.

APRIL 14   In the home opener, the White Sox defeat the Athletics 2–0 before 19,303 at Comiskey Park. Billy Pierce pitched the shutout. The victory ran the club's record to 4–0 on the 1959 season.

Bill Veeck threw out the ceremonial first pitch, with Chuck Comiskey serving as the "catcher" in an attempt to show that harmony existed between the two.

Early Wynn played a crucial role in the drive for the pennant in 1959. One of the most intimidating pitchers of the 1950s, Wynn won 22 games and the Cy Young Award that season.

Nellie Fox and Luis Aparicio were presented with a huge loaf of bread that was 20 feet in length, weighed 200 pounds and was wheeled in on a truck. Early Wynn was presented with 500 silver dollars that were rolled out on a wheelbarrow. Veeck also provided a round of free drinks for everyone in the house during the seventh-inning stretch.

APRIL 22

In a remarkable rally, the White Sox score 11 runs on just one hit in the seventh inning of a 20–6 win over the Athletics in Kansas City. With Tom Gorman on the mound for the A's at the start of the seventh and the Sox leading 8–6. Ray Boone led off and reached on an error by shortstop Joe DeMaestri. Al Smith sacrificed Boone to second and was safe when catcher Hal Smith fumbled the ball. Johnny Callison singled to score Boone for the first run and only hit of the inning. Right fielder Roger Maris couldn't get a hold of Callison's drive, allowing Smith to score and Callison to move to third. Luis Aparicio walked and stole second. Bob Shaw walked to load the bases and Mark Freeman replaced Gorman as the Kansas City hurler. Earl Torgeson and Nellie Fox both walked, forcing in two runs. Jim Landis bounced back to Freeman, who threw home to force Shaw. Sherm Lollar walked and Freeman was relieved by George Brunet. Boone and Smith walked in succession for two more runs. Callison was hit by a pitch to score another. After Aparicio walked for run number nine, Shaw struck out. Bubba Phillips hit for Torgeson and drew a walk, as did Nellie Fox for the 11th run of the inning. With the bases still loaded, Jim Landis grounded out to end the inning. The A's walked 10, hit a batter, and made three errors.

APRIL 25

Trailing 5–3, the White Sox continue to find ways of manufacturing runs by scoring five times in the ninth inning on just one hit and beat the Indians 8–6 in Cleveland. The lone hit was a three-run homer by Earl Torgeson following two errors and two walks.

MAY 1

In one of the greatest one-man shows in White Sox history, Early Wynn not only pitches a one-hitter, but he accounts for the lone run of a 1–0 win over the Red Sox at Comiskey Park with a home run in the eighth inning off Tom Brewer. Wynn also struck out 14 batters and walked seven. The only Boston hit was a single by Pete Runnels with one out in the first inning.

On the same day, the White Sox traded Don Rudolph and Lou Skizas to the Reds for Del Ennis. Rudolph pitched 16 games for the White Sox from 1957 through 1959 and left with one of the most unusual legacies in club history. He was married to an exotic dancer named Patti Waggin and managed her career. The two met in 1954 in Colorado Springs, where Don was a minor leaguer in the White Sox organization. She was working her way through college as a stripper who was billed as the "Coed with the Educated Torso." Rudolph was killed in an industrial accident in 1968 at the age of 37.

MAY 2

The White Sox trade Ray Boone to the Athletics for Harry Simpson.

MAY 12

Al Smith breaks a 2–2 tie with a two-run homer in the top of the 12th inning, lifting the White Sox to a 4–3 win over the Red Sox in Boston.

MAY 13

The White Sox purchase Larry Doby from the Tigers.

MAY 14

The White Sox trounce the Red Sox 14–6 in Boston.

MAY 16   The White Sox run their winning streak to eight games with an 11-inning, 4–3 decision over the Yankees in New York. Del Ennis drove in the game-winner with a single.

                The White Sox won the 1959 AL pennant despite scoring 669 runs, the sixth-best figure in an eight-team league. The Sox were first in the majors in stolen bases (113) and topped the American League in triples (46). On the other end of the spectrum, the club hit the fewest home runs in the big leagues (97). The only two players to reach double figures in homers were Sherm Lollar (22) and Al Smith (17). The only player with more than 160 plate appearances with a slugging percentage over .400 was Lollar. Nellie Fox was the only Sox player with a batting average above .280. The White Sox topped the majors in earned run average (3.29) and the AL in fielding average (.979). Much of the success can be attributed to the use of the pitching staff by Al Lopez. The Sox manager led the league in relief pitchers called upon over the course of the season (242) and in saves (36).

MAY 23   The Athletics pummel the White Sox 16–0 in Kansas City.

MAY 26   In another stunt by Bill Veeck, "Martians" try to "kidnap" Luis Aparicio and Nellie Fox prior to a 3–0 loss to the Indians at Comiskey Park.

                Prior to the game, a helicopter landed at second base and four midgets dressed in space costumes dashed onto the field. En route to the dugout, one of the "invaders" grabbed the public address microphone and said "We have come to Earth to carry away the only two men we consider worth joining us Nellie Fox and Luis Aparicio. However, since they are doing such a fine job here, we've decided to let them stay." One of the midgets was three-foot-seven-inch Eddie Gaedel, who batted in a game for the Browns in 1951 in another Veeck stunt.

JUNE 2   Gnats cause an 18-minute stoppage of play during the first inning of a 3–2 win over the Orioles at Comiskey Park. A swarm of the pesky insects zeroed in on Baltimore pitcher Hoyt Wilhelm. Umpire Bill Simmers signaled for some help. First, a couple of grounds crew workers came out and waved towels. That didn't help. Next, the White Sox batboy ran out with DDT bottles and the air was sprayed around the mound. Wilhelm tried pitching again, but the gnats were still there. This was followed by a couple of workmen with garden-type flitguns. Then torches were lit. Finally, the Sox summoned the crew that was ready to touch off the fireworks display scheduled for after the game. Three men set off a smoke bomb on the mound, routing the gnats.

JUNE 4   A walk-off homer in the 17th inning by Earl Torgeson beats the Orioles 6–5 at Comiskey Park. Both teams scored in the 13th.

JUNE 11   Billy Pierce pitches a one-hitter to defeat the Senators 3–1 at Griffith Stadium. The lone Washington hit was a double by Ron Samford in the third inning.

JUNE 14   Early Wynn collects four hits, including two doubles, in five at-bats during a 9–6 win over the Orioles in Baltimore. The Sox also won the second tilt 3–2 in 10 innings.

JUNE 20   The White Sox tumble from second place to fifth in the standings with 8–2 and 9–0 losses to the Red Sox in Boston.

The defeats stretched Chicago's losing streak to six games. The club was 33–30, but only a game-and-a-half out of first place in the close AL pennant race. From June 21 through the end of the season, the Sox were 61–30.

JUNE 27   Harry Simpson hits a grand slam off Bob Turley in the eighth inning of a 5–4 win over the Yankees at Comiskey Park.

One of Bill Veeck's favorite gags was to give away unusual prizes. On this day, he observed International Specialty Food and Confection Week in Chicago with gifts to fans that included 500 tins of eels in seaweed, fried caterpillars, french-fried ants, fried grasshoppers, 500 jars of whale meat, barbecued snake meat, iguana meat, smoked octopus and smoked sparrows on skewers. Waiters from the famous Pump Room served some of the delicacies in the aisles of the ball park.

JULY 2   Al Smith swats a grand slam off Don Mossi in the ninth inning, but the White Sox lose 9–7 to the Tigers in Detroit.

JULY 3   Al Smith homers in the 10th inning to defeat the Tigers 6–5 in Detroit.

JULY 4   Jim Landis collects five hits, including a double, in five at-bats during a 7–4 win over the Athletics in the first game of a double-header in Kansas City. The A's won the second tilt 8–3.

One of the best defensive outfielders of his era, Landis won four Gold Gloves while playing for the White Sox from 1957 through 1964.

JULY 7   At Forbes Field in Pittsburgh, Nellie Fox hits two singles in five at-bats, but the American League loses 5–4 in the first of two All-Star Games played in 1959.

There were two All-Star Games played each season from 1959 through 1962.

JULY 12   Jim McAnany hits a bases-loaded triple in each game of a 5–3 and 9–7 double-header sweep of the Athletics at Comiskey Park.

JULY 17   Early Wynn and Yankees hurler Ralph Terry both pitch two-hitters during a 2–0 White Sox win in New York. An infield hit by Terry in the sixth inning was the only hit by either team until the ninth. Jim McAnany spoiled Terry's no-hit bid with a single to open the ninth. Early Wynn bunted, and Terry threw too late to second to retire McAnany. Luis Aparicio advanced both runners with a sacrifice, Nellie Fox was intentionally walked to load the bases. After Yankee catcher Yogi Berra failed to catch a foul tip on a two-strike delivery, Jim Landis struck a two-run single. Norm Siebern collected the second Yankee hit leading off the ninth.

JULY 24   A walk-off homer by Al Smith beats the Orioles 2–1 at Comiskey Park.

JULY 25   The White Sox beat the Orioles 3–2 at Comiskey Park. Harry Simpson drove in the winning run with a pinch-single. Turk Lown pitched six innings of shutout relief for the win.

JULY 26   Early Wynn pitches his second consecutive two-hitter to defeat the Orioles 4–1 in the first game of a double-header at Comiskey Park. The only Baltimore hits were a double by Albie Pearson in the fourth inning and a single from Gene Woodling in the ninth.

JULY 28 | The White Sox move into first place with a 4–3 win over the Yankees at Comiskey Park.

The Sox remained in first for the rest of the season.

AUGUST 1 | Held to one hit through eight innings, the White Sox score two runs in the ninth inning to defeat the Senators 2–1 at Comiskey Park. Jim Landis drove in both runs with a double.

AUGUST 3 | In the second All-Star Game of 1959, Nellie Fox collects two singles in four at-bats to help the American League to a 5–3 win at Memorial Coliseum in Los Angeles.

AUGUST 6 | The White Sox and Orioles battle 18 innings to a 1–1 tie at Memorial Stadium. The game was called by a curfew law in Baltimore that stated that no inning could start after 11:59 p.m. Billy Pierce pitched 16 innings for the Sox. There was no scoring by either club after the eighth.

AUGUST 21 | On the day that Hawaii is admitted as the 50th state in the Union, the White Sox celebrate Nellie Fox Night at Comiskey Park prior to a 5–4 win over the Senators. Fox was showered with a wide range of gifts, including cigars, a shotgun, a TV set, two automobiles and a sailboat.

AUGUST 22 | Barry Latman pitches the White Sox to a 1–0 win over the Senators at Comiskey Park. The lone run scored in the second inning. Sherm Lollar walked, stole second and scored on a single by Bubba Phillips.

Lollar hit 22 homers, drove in 84 runs and batted .265 in 1959.

AUGUST 25 | The White Sox score two runs in the ninth inning and one in the 10th to defeat the Red Sox 5–4 at Comiskey Park. Billy Goodman drove in the winning run with a double.

On the same day, the White Sox traded Harry Simpson and Bob Sagers to the Pirates for Ted Kluszewski. Wearing sleeveless jerseys to show off his bulging biceps, Kluszewski hit 171 home runs for the Reds from 1953 through 1956, but a back injury sapped his tremendous power. By the time he arrived in Chicago, he was near the end of his career, but he played a starring role for the White Sox in the 1959 World Series and remained with the club through the end of the 1960 season, batting .294 with seven home runs in 282 at-bats.

AUGUST 26 | All individuals named Smith are admitted free of charge to a 7–6 loss to the Red Sox on a night at Comiskey Park honoring Sox outfielder Al Smith. All the Smiths had to do to get into the park was to show some identification. They were then given buttons reading, "I'm a Smith. We're all for Al Smith." All the guests sat in the left-field seats behind Al Smith. For his part, Smith dropped a fly ball that led to the Boston victory.

The White Sox entered a four-game, pennant-showdown series against the Indians on August 28 with a lead of 1½ games over Cleveland.

AUGUST 28 | The White Sox defeat the Indians 7–3 before a crowd of 70,398 in Cleveland.

AUGUST 29 | The White Sox extend their lead in the pennant race to 3½ games with a 2–0 victory over the Indians in Cleveland. Dick Donovan pitched the shutout.

AUGUST 30   The White Sox complete a four-game sweep of the Indians with 6–3 and 9–4 wins before 68,586 at Cleveland.

The sweep gave the White Sox a lead of ½ games. The Indians cut the gap to two games on September 20 but could get no closer. During the 1959 season, the White Sox were 15–7 against Cleveland.

SEPTEMBER 2   The White Sox score 11 runs in the fifth inning off Paul Foytack and Tom Morgan to account for all of the runs of an 11–4 win over the Tigers in the second game of a double-header at Comiskey Park. Al Smith homered to lead off the big inning, but the next two hitters were retired. From there, Luis Aparicio and Nellie Fox singled and Jim Landis walked to load the bases. Then, in quick succession, the Sox ripped off singles by Ted Kluszewski, Sherm Lollar, Billy Goodman, Smith, Jim McAnany and Joe Stanka. Aparicio was hit by a pitch before Fox finished off the 11-run rally with a bases-loaded triple. The Sox also won the opener 7–2.

Stanka was also the winning pitcher in his debut in the majors. He pitched only one more big-league game. Stanka later won 100 games while pitching in Japan.

SEPTEMBER 7   The White Sox win two from the Athletics by scores of 2–1 and 13–7 during a double-header at Comiskey Park.

SEPTEMBER 11   The White Sox are shut out for 25 innings in a 3–0 and 1–0 double-header loss to the Orioles at Memorial Stadium. The second game was a playoff of the 18-inning tie played on August 6 and went 16 innings. The winning run scored on a two-out single by Brooks Robinson. Barry Latman (9⅓ innings) and Gerry Staley (6⅓ innings) pitched for Chicago. Jerry Walker, a 20-year-old rookie, pitched all 16 innings for Baltimore. Jack Fisher, another 20-year-old, hurled the game-one shutout.

During the 1959 season, the White Sox and Orioles played an 18-inning game, two 17-inning contests and a 16-inning tilt.

SEPTEMBER 12   Early Wynn records his 20th win of the season with a 6–1 decision over the Orioles in Baltimore.

SEPTEMBER 18   Sherm Lollar homers in the fifth inning off Jim Bunning to account for the lone run of a 1–0 win over the Tigers at Comiskey Park. Bob Shaw pitched the shutout.

The White Sox drew a then-record 1,423,144 fans, breaking the previous mark of 1,328,234 set in 1951.

SEPTEMBER 22   The White Sox clinch the pennant with a 4–2 win over the Indians before 54,293 in Cleveland. Early Wynn was the winning pitcher with Bob Shaw and Gerry Staley combining for 3⅓ innings of scoreless relief. Al Smith and Jim Rivera provided the key blows with back-to-back homers in the sixth. There was tension in the ninth when Cleveland loaded the bases with one out. Staley came into the game to replace Shaw and induced Vic Power to hit a grounder to Luis Aparicio, who raced to second base for the force and threw to Ted Kluszewski for the pennant-clinching out.

Mayor Richard Daley, a diehard White Sox fan, decided to celebrate the first pennant by the franchise in 40 years by ordering Fire Commissioner

Robert Quinn to activate the city air-raid sirens at 10:30 p.m. The sirens wailed for five minutes. The situation set off a panic, as many believed the Russians had launched their ICBMs at Chicago. Thousands scurried to their basements and backyard bomb shelters. Television and radio shows were interrupted to tell Chicagoans that there was no air raid. An independent poll later determined that 33 percent of all Chicagoans believed the city was under attack.

SEPTEMBER 25   A boneheaded move by Norm Cash leads to a 6–5 loss to the Tigers in Detroit. The Tigers scored three times in the ninth inning. With the bases loaded and the score 5–5, Lou Berberet grounded to second baseman Billy Goodman, whose peg to the plate retired Harvey Kuenn. Catcher Johnny Romano threw to Cash at first base, where umpire John Rice ruled Berberet safe on a close play. While Cash argued the decision, Al Kaline streaked home and beat Cash's belated throw to the plate.

SEPTEMBER 26   Johnny Callison hits a grand slam off Ray Narleski in the eighth inning of a 10–5 win over the Tigers in Detroit.

SEPTEMBER 27   Bubba Phillips makes two outs at third base during a triple play as the White Sox win 6–4 over the Tigers in Detroit. With runners on first and third, Gail Harris bounced to pitcher Bob Shaw near the mound. Shaw flipped the ball to Phillips, who tagged Tom Morgan between third and home. Harris had rounded first and headed for second. Phillips then raced across the diamond with the ball in his hand to tag out Harris near first. While that was going on, Harvey Kuenn, who started the play at first, tried to score. Kuenn was out on a throw from Phillips to catcher Johnny Romano to shortstop Luis Aparicio, who applied the tag near third base.

SEPTEMBER 29   The Los Angeles Dodgers clinch the National League pennant.

The Dodgers and the Milwaukee Braves ended the regular season with identical 86–68 records. A best-of-three playoff was set up to decide the National League champion, and the Dodgers won two games to none. The club was managed by Walter Alston. It was the Dodgers' second season in Los Angeles after finishing seventh in 1958. While in Brooklyn, the Dodgers won six pennants from 1947 through 1956.

OCTOBER 1   The White Sox show a surprising display of power in defeating the Dodgers 11–0 before 48,013 at Comiskey Park in Game One of the 1959 World Series. The Sox scored two runs in the first inning, exploded for seven in the third, then added two in the fourth. Ted Kluszewski hit two home runs and a single in four at-bats and drove in five runs. Jim Landis collected three singles and scored three times. Early Wynn (seven innings) and Gerry Staley (two innings) combined on the shutout.

During the 1959 World Series, the White Sox truly became the White Sox as the solid navy blue hose with white and red stripes worn during the regular season was replaced by white socks with red and blue stripes.

OCTOBER 2   The Dodgers even the Series with a 4–3 win in the second game of the 1959 World Series, played before 47,368 at Comiskey Park. The White Sox opened up a two-run lead in the first inning. Bob Shaw shut out Los Angeles for the first four innings, but he allowed a run in the fifth inning and three in the seventh. Charlie Neal hit two home runs for the Dodgers and Chuck Essegian added a pinch-homer. A Chicago rally in the eighth inning fell short when Sherm Lollar was thrown out at the plate for the first out while trying for the tying run. Had Lollar been held at third by coach Tony Cuccinello, the Sox would have had runners on second and third with none out. As it was, the Sox had a runner on third and one out, but Billy Goodman struck out and Jim Rivera fouled out. Larry Sherry, a rookie called up from the minors in midseason, pitched three innings of relief for the Dodgers, earning the save.

White Sox left fielder Al Smith was involved in a bizarre incident in the fifth inning, when Neal homered into the lower stands. A fan scrambling for the ball knocked a beer cup off the top of the wall. Smith had backed up to the wall in an attempt to catch Neal's drive and was looking straight up when the sudsy contents came tumbling down and splashed him in the face. Smith played 12 years in the majors and appeared in two All-Star Games, but he is best-remembered for the incident. When he died in 2002, the first sentence of Smith's obituary in The New York Times *read: "Al Smith, the Chicago White Sox outfielder who became the subject in one of baseball's most famous photographs when a fan accidentally spilled a cup of beer on him as Smith watched a home run sail over his head in the 1959 World Series, died Thursday at a hospital in Hammond, Ind." Accompanying the obit was the photo of Smith being doused with the cup and the stream of beer caught in midair. The image was captured by* Chicago Tribune *photographer Ray Gora using a new model camera developed by the government to film rockets blasting into space. The infamous fan who knocked over the cup was Melvin Piehl, an executive with a motor oil company.*

OCTOBER 4   The Dodgers take a lead in the Series with a 3–1 win over the White Sox in Los Angeles. The Dodgers broke a scoreless tie with two runs in the seventh inning off Dick Donovan. Don Drysdale was the winning pitcher with two innings of relief help from Larry Sherry.

Game Three was the first in World Series history played west of St. Louis. The contests in Los Angeles were played at Memorial Coliseum, which was the home of the Dodgers from 1958 through 1961. The crowds during the three games in L.A. totaled 92,394, 92,650 and 92,706. They were the three largest crowds in major league history. Built for football and track, the massive Coliseum had little to recommend it for baseball, outside of the large seating capacity. The left-field line was only 251 feet long, topped by a 40-foot high screen. Because of the large crowds at the massive single-decked facility, players on both teams had extreme difficulties tracking the ball on throws, line drives, and low fly balls against the backdrop of fans, wearing mostly white or light-colored outfits.

OCTOBER 5   The Dodgers move within one game of the world championship by taking a three-games-to-one lead in the Series with a 5–4 decision over the White Sox in Los Angeles. The Dodgers jumped ahead 4–0 with four runs in the third inning off Early Wynn, but the Sox countered with four in the seventh, the last three on a home run by Sherm Lollar. Gil Hodges broke the 4–4 tie with a homer off Gerry Staley in the eighth. Larry Sherry was the winning pitcher, with two innings of scoreless relief.

OCTOBER 6   The White Sox stay alive with a 1–0 win over the Dodgers in Los Angeles. The Sox scored the lone run of the game off Sandy Koufax in the fourth inning on singles by Nellie Fox and Jim Landis and a Sherm Lollar double-play ball. A great running catch by Jim Rivera on Charlie Neal snuffed out a seventh-inning Dodgers rally.

In what proved to be an amazingly prophetic move, Rivera entered the game as a defensive replacement for Jim McAnany just before Neal stepped to the plate with runners on first and second and two out. Bob Shaw pitched 7⅓ innings and was the winning pitcher. Dick Donovan notched a save by retiring all five batters to face him. Chicago pitchers stranded 11 runners.

OCTOBER 8   The Dodgers close out the Series in Game Six with a 9–3 win over the White Sox before 47,653 at Comiskey Park. Al Lopez gambled by starting 39-year-old Early Wynn on two days' rest, and Wynn allowed five runs in 3⅓ innings. Dick Donovan surrendered three runs in relief without retiring a batter and Los Angeles led 8–0 in the fourth inning. The three Sox runs crossed the plate on a homer by Ted Kluszewski in the bottom of the fourth. The final run scored in the ninth on Chuck Essegian's second pinch-homer of the Series. Larry Sherry hurled 5⅔ innings of relief.

Manager Al Lopez shares a word with owner Bill Veeck during the pennant race of 1959.

During the 1959 World Series, Sherry picked up two wins and two saves and allowed only one run in 12⅔ innings. Kluszewski was the Chicago hero with three homers, 10 RBIs and nine hits in 23 at-bats for a .391 batting average.

NOVEMBER 3   The White Sox trade Ron Jackson to the Red Sox for Frank Baumann.

A former high school pitching sensation in St. Louis, Baumann gave the White Sox one good season. His 2.67 ERA in 185⅓ innings in 1960 lead the American League. Baumann's won-lost record was 13–6, but arm trouble prevented any further success.

DECEMBER 6   The White Sox trade Norm Cash, Johnny Romano and Bubba Phillips to the Indians for Minnie Minoso, Dick Brown, Don Ferrarese and Jake Striker.

The White Sox won the 1959 pennant with an aging team. Early Wynn was 39, Gerry Staley 38, Jim Rivera 36, Turk Lown and Earl Torgeson 35, Ted Kluszewski and Sherm Lollar 34 and Billy Pierce 32. Nellie Fox, Bubba Phillips, Al Smith and Dick Donovan were all 31. The cadre of tremendous young talent on both the World Series roster and in the farm system was the envy of baseball, however. Players in the White Sox organization at the end of the 1959 season who were 25 years old or younger included Luis Aparicio, Earl Battey, Johnny Callison, Norm Cash, Joe Horlen, Barry Latman, Jim Landis, J. C. Martin, Ken McBride, Don Mincher Gary Peters, Claude Raymond and Floyd Robinson. Despite the rosy future, Bill Veeck decided to make a run at his second consecutive pennant by trading some of those unproven prospects for proven veteran talent. The December 6, 1959, trade with Cleveland was the first of three such trades during the 1959–60 off-season (see December 9, 1959, and April 4, 1960). White Sox fans were ecstatic over the return of Minoso, who filled the team's need for a corner outfielder. White Sox outfielders in 1959 combined to hit only .243 with 33 homers in 1,727 at-bats. Minoso had two solid seasons during his return engagement in Chicago. In 1960, he hit .311 with 20 homers, 105 RBIs and a league-leading 184 hits. The deal inflicted considerable long-term damage to the franchise, though. Cash was traded by the Indians to the Tigers in April 1960. He played in Detroit until 1974 and hit 377 career homers, won the batting title in 1961 and made four All-Star teams. A power-hitting catcher who topped the 20-home run, 80-RBI mark twice in his career, Romano was an All-Star in both 1961 and 1962 for Cleveland.

DECEMBER 9   The White Sox trade Johnny Callison to the Phillies for Gene Freese.

Freese filled the White Sox's need for a third baseman for one season before being traded to the Reds in December 1960. Like the trade completed three days earlier, this transaction had long-range negative consequences on the future of the White Sox. Callison lasted in the majors until 1973 as an outfielder. He made the NL All-Star three times with the Phillies.

THE STATE OF THE WHITE SOX

The White Sox entered the decade as defending American League champions after winning the pennant in 1959. The 1959 club was also the ninth in a row in which the White Sox posted a winning record. The streak was extended to 17 by 1967 as the Sox finished above .500 in each of the first eight seasons of the decade. In addition, from 1961 through 1967, the White Sox had a better record (630–504) than any other team in the American League, but there were no more pennants flying over Chicago. Overall, the Sox were 852–760 during the 1960s, for a .529 winning percentage that was the fifth-best figure in the American League. AL pennant winners were the Yankees (1960, 1961, 1962, 1963 and 1964), Twins (1965), Orioles (1966 and 1969), Red Sox (1967) and Tigers (1968).

THE BEST TEAM

The 1964 White Sox were 98–64 and finished a close pennant race just one game behind the Yankees.

THE WORST TEAM

After nearly winning the pennant in 1967, the 1968 White Sox lost their first 10 games and ended the year with a record of 67–95. The club tied for eighth place in a 10-team league.

THE BEST MOMENT

Take your pick. Was it in 1964 when the White Sox were in first place as late as September 16? Or in 1967, when the Sox were in first during the first week of September?

THE WORST MOMENT

Take your pick. Was it in 1964 when the White Sox finished one game behind the Yankees in the three-team pennant race in which the Orioles were also involved? Or was it in 1967, when with a chance to win the American League pennant in a tight four-team race with the Red Sox, Twins and Tigers, the White Sox lost their final five games to finish in fourth place, three games out of first?

THE ALL-DECADE TEAM • YEARS WITH WS

Johnny Romano, c	1958–59, 1965–66
Tommy McCraw, 1b	1963–70
Don Buford, 2b	1963–67
Pete Ward, 3b	1963–69
Luis Aparicio, ss	1956–62, 1968–70
Al Smith, lf	1958–62
Jim Landis, cf	1957–64
Floyd Robinson, rf	1960–66
Joe Horlen, p	1961–71
Gary Peters, p	1959–69
Tommy John, p	1965–71
Hoyt Wilhelm, p	1963–68

Aparicio and Wilhelm are in the Hall of Fame. John also deserves a spot in Cooperstown. Other outstanding players on the White Sox during the 1960s included pitchers Juan Pizarro (1961–66) and Eddie Fisher (1962–66, 1972–73), shortstop Ron Hansen (1963–69), second baseman Nellie Fox (1950–62), center fielder Ken Berry (1962–70), first baseman Roy Sievers (1960–61) and catcher Sherm Lollar (1952–63).

THE DECADE LEADERS

Batting Avg:	Al Smith	.295
On-Base Pct:	Floyd Robinson	.370
Slugging Pct:	Al Smith	.473
Home Runs:	Pete Ward	97
RBIs:	Pete Ward	407
Runs:	Floyd Robinson	433
Stolen Bases:	Luis Aparicio	176
Wins:	Joe Horlen	99
Strikeouts:	Gary Peters	1,098
ERA:	Hoyt Wilhelm	1.92
Saves:	Hoyt Wilhelm	98

THE HOME FIELD

Comiskey Park reached its 50th birthday in 1960, the year that Bill Veeck unveiled baseball's first exploding scoreboard, which boomed fireworks whenever a White Sox batter hit a home run. The Sox drew 1,644,460 fans that season, which was not only a franchise record, but a Chicago mark, exceeding the figure of 1,485,166 attracted by the Cubs in 1929. Attendance slipped under the one million mark in 1966, however, and would remain there for six seasons. Racial tensions in Chicago contributed to the decline, as the perception that Comiskey Park was located in a high-crime area kept many suburban fans away from the ballpark. In 1968 and 1969, the Sox played nine "home" games at County Stadium in Milwaukee in preparation for a possible move of the franchise 90 miles to the north, which fortunately never took place.

THE GAME YOU WISHED YOU HAD SEEN

In the heat of the 1967 pennant race, Joe Horlen pitched a no-hitter on September 10 against the Tigers at Comiskey Park.

THE WAY THE GAME WAS PLAYED

Baseball was played in new cities and ballparks during the 1960s, with franchise shifts and expansion from 16 teams to 24. American League baseball was played for the first time in Minnesota, Southern California, Oakland and Seattle. The expansion of the strike zone in 1963 brought a decline in offense in the 1960s until the owners lowered the mound for the 1969 season. The league ERA dipped to 2.98 in 1968, the only time it has been below 3.00 since 1918.

THE MANAGEMENT

Bill Veeck purchased a majority of the stock in the club in March 1959, then sold it in June 1961 to Arthur Allyn Sr. Arthur sold the Sox to his brother John in September 1969. General managers were Hank Greenberg (1959–61) and Ed Short (1961–70). Field managers were Al Lopez (1957–65), Eddie Stanky (1966–68), Les Moss (1968), Lopez again (1968–69) and Don Gutteridge (1969–70).

THE BEST PLAYER MOVE

The best trade sent Juan Pizarro to the Pirates for Wilbur Wood in October 1966. A close second was the Sox's part of a three-team deal in which the White Sox sent Jim Landis, Fred Talbot and Mike Hershberger to the Athletics and Cam Carreon to the Indians in exchange for Tommy John, Tommie Agee and Johnny Romano from Cleveland.

THE WORST PLAYER MOVE

The worst transaction was the placing of Denny McLain on waivers in April 1963, allowing him to be picked up by the Tigers. The worst trade sent Earl Battey and Don Mincher to the Senators along with $150,000 for Roy Sievers.

1960s

1960   Sox

Season in a Sentence

The White Sox improve their offense by scoring 72 more runs than the 1959 pennant-winners and hold first place in mid-August, but they fade to third by the end of the season.

Finish • Won • Lost • Pct • GB

Third   87   67   .565   10.0

Manager

Al Lopez

Stats

Stats	WS	AL	Rank
Batting Avg:	.270	.255	1
On-Base Pct:	.348	.331	1
Slugging Pct:	.396	.388	2
Home Runs:	112		7
Stolen Bases:	122		1
ERA:	3.60	3.87	3
Fielding Avg:	.982	.978	1
Runs Scored:	741		2
Runs Allowed:	617		2

Starting Lineup

Sherm Lollar, c
Roy Sievers, 1b
Nellie Fox, 2b
Gene Freese, 3b
Luis Aparicio, ss
Minnie Minoso, lf
Jim Landis, cf
Al Smith, rf
Ted Kluszewski, 1b

Pitchers

Early Wynn, sp
Billy Pierce, sp
Bob Shaw, sp
Herb Score, sp
Frank Baumann, rp-sp
Gerry Staley, rp
Turk Lown, rp
Russ Kemmerer, rp

Attendance

1,644,460 (first in AL)

Club Leaders

Batting Avg:	Al Smith	.315
On-Base Pct:	Roy Sievers	.396
Slugging Pct:	Roy Sievers	.534
Home Runs:	Roy Sievers	28
RBIs:	Minnie Minoso	105
Runs:	Minnie Minoso	89
	Jim Landis	89
Stolen Bases:	Luis Aparicio	51
Wins:	Billy Pierce	14
Strikeouts:	Early Wynn	158
ERA:	Frank Baumann	2.67
Saves:	Gerry Staley	10

MARCH 13   The White Sox become the first team in American professional sports history to place the names of the players on the backs of their uniforms. The names first appeared during a 2–0 loss to the Reds in Tampa.

APRIL 4   The White Sox send Earl Battey, Don Mincher and $150,000 to the Senators for Roy Sievers.

The team of Bill Veeck and Hank Greenberg made three trades during the 1959–60 off-season in which the club swapped prospects for a veteran who filled an immediate need. Like the first two (see December 6, 1959, and December 9, 1959), the deal of April 4, 1960, hurt the club severely in the long term. Sievers was acquired to fill a chronic need for a first baseman. He was 33 years old and a three-time All-Star who hit 42 homers in 1957 and 39 more in 1958. Sievers gave the White Sox two good seasons. He batted .295 with 28 homers and 93 RBIs in 1960 and posted nearly identical numbers in 1961. Although Sievers helped in the short term, the long-term effects of the transaction were disastrous. The loss of Battey hurt the club for years. He was the starting catcher for the Senators and Twins for seven seasons, made four All-Star teams, won three Gold Gloves, and played in the World Series in 1965. Mincher had a fine career as a first baseman that lasted until 1972 and included two All-Star Game appearances. The attempt at wringing another pennant out of an aging team after the fairy tale season of 1959 failed. Had the Sox held on to Battey, Mincher, Norm Cash, Johnny Callison and Johnny Romano, they would certainly have won the pennant in 1964 and 1965, and possibly 1963 and 1967 as well.

APRIL 18   The White Sox trade Barry Latman to the Indians for Herb Score.

Score had a record of 16–10 for the Indians as a rookie in 1955 and topped that with a 20–9 mark in 1956. In both seasons, he led the AL in strikeouts and finished in the top five in earned run average. He appeared to be off to another stellar season in 1957 when on May 7 he was struck in the face with a line drive off the bat of Yankees infielder Gil McDougald. Score suffered eye damage and a broken nose and didn't pitch again that season. He struggled with a combined record of 11–15 with Cleveland in 1958 and 1959. Al Lopez managed Score during the pitcher's first two seasons in the majors and hoped to revive his career. Score was only 26 when he arrived in Chicago, but he posted a 6–12 won-lost ledger with the White Sox.

APRIL 19   In his first game with the White Sox since 1957, Minnie Minoso collects two homers and drives in six runs during a 10–9 win over the Athletics before an Opening Day crowd of 41,661 at Comiskey Park. Minoso struck a grand slam off Johnny Kucks in the fourth inning for a 9–2 lead. Kansas City battled back, however, tying the contest 9–9. Batting in the ninth, Minoso clobbered a walk-off homer for the victory. Luis Aparicio also played a key role with three hits and three runs.

In addition to putting names on the backs of the uniforms (see March 13, 1960), Bill Veeck inaugurated another innovation in 1960 with an exploding scoreboard at Comiskey Park. It was the first of its kind. Whenever a White Sox player hit a home run, fireworks and aerial bombs were shot from 10 towers atop the board. Pinwheels on the facing of the towers swirled and sound effects were played over the public address system that included a cacophony of shrieks, crashes, whistles, roars, howls, train wrecks, fire engine sirens, foghorns, machine gun fire, a cavalry charge bugle, diving planes, the William Tell overture, a chorus whistling "Dixie" and a circus calliope. Strobe lights at the base of the board flashed simultaneously. The routine lasted about 30 seconds. Opposing players hated the idea and traditionalists were appalled, but it was a huge hit with most of the fans. Although Veeck sold the club a year later, his scoreboard design remained virtually intact until the ballpark was torn down after the 1990 season and was incorporated into the scoreboard at the new Comiskey Park. Veeck also added a picnic area in left field in 1960 with an opening in the wall to allow fans to watch the game from a field-level vantage point behind the left fielder.

APRIL 26   Al Smith collects five hits in five at-bats during an 8–0 win over the Athletics in Kansas City. Smith led off the first inning with a homer and later added a double and three singles.

APRIL 28   Al Smith runs his streak of hits in consecutive at-bats to eight with three singles in his first three plate appearances of a 3–1 win over the Indians at Comiskey Park.

Smith hit .315 with 12 homers in 1960.

MAY 8   The White Sox explode for five runs in the 10th inning to defeat the Yankees 8–3 in New York. Jim Landis climaxed the outburst with a three-run homer.

MAY 10   The White Sox surrender two grand slams during a 9–7 loss to the Red Sox at Fenway Park. Vic Wertz delivered a bases-loaded wallop off Early Wynn in the first inning. Rip Repulski cleared the bases with an eighth-inning wallop facing Turk Lown, who had just entered the game as a reliever to face Repulski.

MAY 30   Indians outfielder Jimmy Piersall puts on a show during a double-header before 54,731 at Comiskey Park in which Cleveland won 9–4 and 4–1. After being ejected from the opener for arguing a call, Piersall threw bats, balls, helmets, towels and everything else that wasn't nailed down out of the Cleveland dugout. While stalking to the clubhouse via a runway next to the Sox bench, Piersall heaved a sand bucket onto the field. It took 10 minutes for the batboys to put everything back into their proper place. In the second game, Piersall stood motionless while a Minnie Minoso drive sailed over his head for a double. The scoreboard operator through it was a home run and set off the fireworks. After catching the final out of the game, Piersall immediately turned and threw a ball toward the scoreboard, breaking a couple of light bulbs. Bill Veeck wasn't amused by Piersall throwing at his new toy. "I like Jim very much," said the White Sox owner. "But if he throws at my scoreboard again, we'll use our rocket launchers on him and we'll put him into orbit."

JUNE 5   The White Sox win two from the Athletics during a double-header at Comiskey Park, both by 2–0 scores. Russ Kemmerer and Frank Baumann hurled the shutouts. It was the second of only two shutouts thrown by Kemmerer during his nine-year big league career. The first one came in his first big-league start with the Red Sox in 1954.

             The White Sox drew 1,644,460 fans in 1960 to set an all-time Chicago record, breaking the previous mark set by the 1929 Cubs, who attracted 1,485,166. It remained the White Sox's standard until 1977. The Sox also outdrew the Cubs by more than a 2–1 margin in 1960, the only season in history that has happened. The attendance figure at Wrigley Field in 1960 was 809,770.

JUNE 10   The White Sox trounce the Red Sox 13–3 in Boston.

JUNE 11   The White Sox purchase Bob Rush from the Braves.

JUNE 17   The Yankees poke fun at the exploding scoreboard at Comiskey Park during a 4–2 win over the White Sox. After Clete Boyer homered in the second inning, Casey Stengel and his coaches and players lit sparklers and waved them while marching back and forth in the dugout.

             White Sox home games were telecast in color for the first time in 1960.

JUNE 21   Jim Landis hits a walk-off homer in the ninth inning to defeat the Orioles 4–3 at Comiskey Park.

JUNE 23   Early Wynn pitches a two-hitter to defeat the Orioles 3–1 at Comiskey Park. The only Boston hits were singles by Marv Breeding leading off the first inning and Clint Courtney in the eighth.

JUNE 26   The White Sox crush the Red Sox 21–7 with a 22-hit attack in the second game of a double-header at Comiskey Park. Chicago scored 11 runs in the fourth inning to take an 18–1 lead. The White Sox also won the opener 4–3.

The White Sox won all 11 games in 1960 from the Red Sox at Comiskey Park.

JULY 2   The White Sox score seven runs in the fourth inning for an 8–4 lead, then hold on to win 8–7 from the Red Sox in Boston.

JULY 3   Roy Sievers hits a home run in the 11th inning to defeat the Orioles 2–1 in Baltimore.

JULY 11   At Municipal Stadium in Kansas City, Al Lopez manages the American League to a 5–3 loss in the first of two All-Star Games played in 1960. Nellie Fox drove in a run with a single.

JULY 13   At Yankee Stadium, Al Lopez manages the American League to a 6–0 loss in the second of two All-Star Games played in 1960. Sherm Lollar collected a double in two at-bats. Early Wynn retired all six batters to face him, striking out two.

JULY 18   Roy Sievers runs his hitting streak to 21 games during a 9–1 win over the Red Sox at Comiskey Park.

JULY 24   Nellie Fox collects the 2,000th hit of his career with a first-inning single off Jim Coates during a 6–3 win over the Yankees in the first game of a double-header in New York. It was the White Sox's eighth win in a row. The Sox lost game two 8–2.

JULY 26   The White Sox pick up 21 hits during a 16–3 thrashing of the Red Sox in Boston. Gene Freese collected five hits, including a homer and two doubles, in six at-bats.

Freese hit .273 with 17 homers in 1960.

JULY 28   Gene Freese winds up in a Washington, D.C., jail after having words with a police officer.

The Sox played a game against the Red Sox in Boston earlier in the day, losing 4–2, and arrived in Washington late in the afternoon for a game the following day against the Senators. Freese and Aparicio decided to take in a night game between the Senators and Tigers at Griffith Stadium. According to Freese, he was talking to Pete Whisenant and Pedro Ramos of the Senators next to the Washington dugout. Along came a police officer, who advised Freese that he couldn't stand there. The Sox third baseman thought the officer was an usher, made an unwise choice of words and was arrested. After being taken to police headquarters in a paddy wagon, Freese was fined $10 for disorderly conduct.

AUGUST 7   The White Sox win both ends of a double-header with ninth inning, walk-off hits against the Senators at Comiskey Park. In the opener, Gene Freese hit a two-run homer in the ninth inning for a 9–7 Sox victory. In the nightcap, Minnie Minoso's single drove in the winning run for a 3–2 Chicago triumph. Relief pitcher Gerry Staley was the winning pitcher in both games. He pitched 3 1/3 innings of the first game and two-thirds of an inning in the second tilt.

AUGUST 14   The White Sox move into a tie for first place with the Orioles by sweeping the Athletics 9–3 and 7–2 at Comiskey Park.

AUGUST 15   The White Sox drop back out of first place with a 4–1 loss to the Tigers at Comiskey Park.

AUGUST 19   The White Sox clobber the Athletics 10–0 in Kansas City.

AUGUST 20   Herb Score pitches a two-hitter to defeat the Athletics 3–0 in Kansas City. The only hits off Score were singles by opposing pitcher Don Larsen in the sixth inning and Norm Siebern in the seventh.

AUGUST 23   Starting pitcher Billy Pierce is relieved before throwing a pitch prior to a game against the Yankees in New York. After Pierce threw a few preliminary pitches from the mound, he complained of a pulled muscle. When Lopez notified umpire Charlie Berry of the injury, the arbiter allowed the Sox to start Early Wynn in Pierce's place. Wynn proceeded to pitch a complete game for a 5–1 victory.

AUGUST 28   The White Sox suffer a tough loss to the Orioles in Baltimore in a key game in the 1960 pennant race. The Sox came into the game trailing the first place Yankees by 2$\frac{1}{2}$ games. In the eighth inning with the White Sox trailing 3–1 with two runners on base, Al Lopez called on Ted Kluszewski to pinch-hit for Minnie Minoso. On the second pitch from Milt Pappas, Kluszewski lined a pitch into the right-field seats for what appeared to be a 4–3 Chicago lead. Third-base umpire Ed Hurley claimed he had called time, however, just before Pappas delivered the ball to the plate. Hurley said he called a halt to play because White Sox substitutes Floyd Robinson and Earl Torgeson were warming up their arms outside of the bullpen. A violent argument followed and Nellie Fox was ejected for using abusive language. Sent back to the plate, Kluszewski flied out and the Sox lost 3–1. Bill Veeck filed a formal protest, but it was denied by AL President Joe Cronin.

AUGUST 30   The White Sox outlast the Senators 11–10 in a 10-inning thriller in Washington. At the end of the seventh inning, the Senators led 1–0. In the eighth, however, the offenses of both clubs suddenly broke loose. In that inning, Chicago scored two runs and Washington returned fire with four tallies. In the ninth, the Sox took a 7–5 lead with five runs in the top half, only to have the Senators tied it up in their half. The scoring spree continued in the 10th, as the Sox scored four runs and survived a three-run rally by the opposition for the victory.

SEPTEMBER 4   The playing streak of Nellie Fox comes to an end at 798 consecutive games, dating back to 1955 (see August 6, 1955). Fox was sidelined by a virus and missed both games of a double-header against the Tigers at Comiskey Park. Billy Goodman started in Fox's place as the Sox lost 6–4, then won 5–4.

SEPTEMBER 7   Sammy Esposito is confronted by an enraged fan during a 6–4 loss to the Yankees at Comiskey Park. Playing second base for the ailing Nellie Fox, Esposito made a key error that led to the New York victory. With the Sox leading 4–1 in the eighth inning, Esposito booted what appeared to be a tailor-made double-play grounder that would have ended the inning. Instead, the Yanks erupted for four runs before the inning could be completed. A 41-year-old fan named Willie Harris jumped the box-seat railing and went after Esposito. Harris berated the Sox infielder and threw a punch. Esposito ducked and threw one of his own, but missed. Harris was arrested and fined $25 for disorderly conduct.

SEPTEMBER 10   A walk-off homer by Jim Landis off Hoyt Wilhelm in the 11th inning beats the Orioles 3–2 at Comiskey Park.

SEPTEMBER 13   Nellie Fox homers in the 11th inning to defeat the Senators 6–5 at Comiskey Park. It was one of only two homers that Fox hit all year.

The White Sox finished the day with an 81–59 record and a position in third place, two games from the top. The Yankees were in first place and the Orioles in second, one game back. The Sox lost eight of their last 14 games, however, while the Yankees finished the season with a 15-game winning streak.

SEPTEMBER 21   Minnie Minoso smashes a home run onto the left-field roof just inside the foul line during a 7–2 win over the Athletics at Comiskey Park.

SEPTEMBER 23   In only his second major league at-bat, Stan Johnson collects his first home run as a result of Minnie Minoso's ejection during a 7–0 win over the Indians in Cleveland. Minoso stepped to the plate in the ninth inning after Ted Kluszewski belted a home run. Frank Funk threw a high, inside pitch that made Minoso hit the dirt. Minnie stood up, flipped his bat in the direction of Funk and was tossed by umpire Bill Stewart. The incident proved to be a break for Johnson, a rookie outfielder recently called up from the minors. Johnson was sent in to complete Minoso's at-bat and hit a home run over the right-field fence in his second plate appearance in the majors.

The home run proved to be Johnson's only hit as a major leaguer. He accumulated only seven more at-bats and finished his career with a .111 batting average.

OCTOBER 26   The American League announces plans to expand to 10 teams for the 1961 season with the addition of two new franchises. The Washington Senators moved to Minnesota, where they were renamed the Twins. A new expansion team was created in Washington, also named the Senators. Another expansion outfit was installed in Los Angeles and named the Angels.

DECEMBER 14   Six weeks after John Kennedy wins the presidential election over Richard Nixon, the White Sox lose Ken McBride, Earl Averill, Ted Kluszewski and Jim McAnany to the Angels and Dick Donovan, Jim Hicks and Ed Hobaugh to the Senators in the expansion draft.

Donovan looked finished when he posted a 5.38 ERA in 78²/₃ innings in 1960. He led the AL in earned run average in 1961 with Washington, however, and won 20 games for the Indians in 1962. McBride gave the Angels three good seasons before fading.

DECEMBER 15   The White Sox trade Gene Freese to the Reds for Juan Pizarro and Cal McLish.

The White Sox pulled off a terrific deal in acquiring Pizarro to bolster the pitching staff. During his six seasons with the White Sox, he was 75–47 to post the second-highest winning percentage (.615) in club history.

Only Lefty Williams (.648) was better. McLish's given name was Calvin Coolidge Julius Caesar Tuskahoma McLish. He pitched one season for the White Sox before being dealt to the Phillies. Freese hit 26 homers for the Reds in 1961 and played in the World Series that fall, but a broken ankle suffered during spring training in 1962 ended his days as an effective player.

1961 — Sox

Season in a Sentence

Bill Veeck sells the club and the White Sox crash-land into last place in June before winning 19 of 20 later in the month on the way to a fourth-place finish.

Finish • Won • Lost • Pct • GB

Fourth 86 76 .531 23.0

Manager

Al Lopez

Stats

Stats	WS	AL	Rank
Batting Avg:	.265	.256	3
On-Base Pct:	.338	.332	2
Slugging Pct:	.395	.395	6
Home Runs:	138		7
Stolen Bases:	100		1
ERA:	4.06	4.02	4
Fielding Avg:	.980	.976	3
Runs Scored:	765		3
Runs Allowed:	726		4

Starting Lineup

Sherm Lollar, c
Roy Sievers, 1b
Nellie Fox, 2b
Al Smith, 3b-rf
Luis Aparicio, ss
Minnie Minoso, lf
Jim Landis, cf
Floyd Robinson, rf
J. C. Martin, 1b-3b
Cam Carreon, c

Pitchers

Juan Pizarro, sp-rp
Billy Pierce, sp
Cal McLish, sp
Ray Herbert, sp
Early Wynn, sp
Frank Baumann, rp-sp
Turk Lown, rp
Russ Kemmerer, rp

Attendance

1,146,019 (fourth in AL)

Club Leaders

Batting Avg:	Floyd Robinson	.310
On-Base Pct:	Floyd Robinson	.389
Slugging Pct:	Roy Sievers	.537
Home Runs:	Al Smith	28
RBIs:	Al Smith	93
Runs:	Minnie Minoso	91
Stolen Bases:	Luis Aparicio	53
Wins:	Juan Pizarro	14
Strikeouts:	Juan Pizarro	188
ERA:	Juan Pizarro	3.05
Saves:	Turk Lown	11

APRIL 10 With President John F. Kennedy in attendance, the White Sox open the season against the Senators in Washington and win 4–3. The Sox trailed 3–1 before rallying for the victory. Roy Sievers homered in the third inning and broke the 3–3 tie with a sacrifice fly in the eighth. Early Wynn started the game, but lasted only two innings. Russ Kemmerer and Frank Baumann combined for seven innings of shutout relief. The game was the first in the history of the expansion Washington Senators (see October 26, 1960). The club moved to Texas and was renamed the Rangers after the 1971 season.

Jim Rivera received an autograph from Kennedy on a baseball, but he wasn't happy after looking at the inscription. "The guy's got bad handwriting," muttered Rivera. "How can I even prove the president signed this? It could be anybody's signature. And he went to Harvard."

APRIL 18   The day after the launching of the unsuccessful Bay of Pigs invasion of Cuba, and two days after the Blackhawks win the Stanley Cup, the scheduled home opener against the Senators at Comiskey Park is postponed by a heavy, wet snow that covered the playing field.

APRIL 19   The White Sox get the home opener under way, but lose 7–2 to the Senators before 16,637 at Comiskey Park.

The first ball was tossed out by John F. Kennedy, a fan from suburban Oaklawn whose name was plucked out of the phone book. "We couldn't get the president, so we came up with the next best thing," chuckled Bill Veeck. "Our Mr. Kennedy is a politician, too, you know, even though he did lose." Oaklawn's Mr. Kennedy ran for trustee of the village in an election held the previous day. Another gimmick Veeck sprang on the crowd was the hiring of eight midgets to work as vendors in the box-seat sections. "The fans are always complaining about not being able to see because the vendors get in the way." said Veeck. "so we hired the midgets." One of the midgets was Eddie Gaedel (see May 26, 1959). Gaedel died two months later at the age of 36 of a heart attack after he had been the victim of a brutal mugging in Chicago.

APRIL 30   The White Sox play a regular-season game in Minnesota for the first time and defeat the Twins 5–3 in 11 innings.

Ralph Kiner joined Bob Elson in the White Sox radio booth in 1961. He went to the Mets in 1962 and was still on the broadcasting scene in New York into the 21st century.

MAY 7   Two days after Alan Shepard becomes the first American in space, Roy Sievers drives in six runs on a two-run homer in the fourth inning and a grand slam in the sixth, both off Frank Lary. The six runs batted in accounted for all of the Chicago runs in an 8–6 loss in the first game of a double-header at Comiskey Park. The Sox also lost the second game 5–3.

To celebrate National Raisin Week, Bill Veeck gave away a ton of raisins to a "lucky" fan. The ton amounted to a total of 5 million raisins.

MAY 9   Herb Score pitches a two-hitter to defeat the Indians 4–2 at Comiskey Park. The only Cleveland hits were a triple by Jimmy Piersall in the sixth inning and a single by Johnny Temple in the eighth. In an oddity, the Indians tied a major league record for the fewest official at-bats in a nine-inning game with 23. A total of 34 Cleveland batters went to the plate. Six walked, three collected sacrifice bunts and two hit sacrifice flies.

MAY 10   The White Sox purchase Wes Covington from the Braves.

MAY 15   The Twins play in Chicago for the first time and defeat the White Sox 5–0 at Comiskey Park.

MAY 18   The White Sox play a regular season in California for the first time and win 6–4 over the Angels. The game was played at Wrigley Field in Los Angeles, which served as the Angels' home for one year.

Wrigley Field was used by L.A.'s Pacific Coast League club, also named the Angels, from 1925 through 1957. The ballpark was built by the Wrigley family, which owned the Chicago Cubs from 1919 through 1981. The Los Angeles version of Wrigley Field can still be seen on the 1959 TV series Home Run Derby, *which is available on DVD, and as a backdrop for many Hollywood movies. It was torn down in 1965. The Angels franchise has been known as the Los Angeles Angels (1961–65), the California Angels (1965–96), the Anaheim Angels (1997–2004) and the Los Angeles Angels of Anaheim (since 2005).*

MAY 21   Jim Landis breaks a 4–4 tie with a two-run homer in the 10th inning, and the White Sox defeat the Red Sox 6–5 in the first game of a double-header at Fenway Park. Boston won the second contest 4–1.

MAY 23   Billy Pierce strikes out 12 batters in six innings, but the White Sox lose 3–1 to the Orioles in Baltimore.

MAY 28   Wes Covington hits a grand slam off Bob Turley in the third inning of a 14–9 victory over the Yankees in the first game of a double-header in New York. The Sox lost the nightcap 5–3.

JUNE 3   Roy Sievers hits the first pitch of the 13th inning off Art Ditmar to lift the White Sox to a 6–5 win over the Yankees at Comiskey Park. Ditmar had just entered the game as a reliever.

          Sievers hit .295 with 27 homers and 92 RBIs in 1961.

JUNE 9   The White Sox lose an excruciating double-header to the Senators in Washington 1–0 in 10 innings and 10–9. The Senators scored four runs in the ninth inning of the second contest.

          The White Sox were in last place on June 11 with a record of 19–33. The club won 19 of 20 from the second game of a double-header on June 11 though June 28 but it wasn't enough to vault the Sox into pennant contention.

JUNE 10   The White Sox trade Bob Shaw, Gerry Staley, Wes Covington and Stan Johnson to the Athletics for Ray Herbert, Don Larsen, Andy Carey and Al Pilarcik.

          Herbert came to the White Sox as a 31-year-old pitcher with a 49–62 lifetime record. He had one great season in Chicago, with a 20–9 record and a 3.27 ERA in 1962. Larsen was acquired by the Sox less than five years after pitching a perfect game in the 1956 World Series while with the Yankees. He was a reliever while in Chicago, and posted a 7–2 record and a 4.12 ERA before being traded to the Giants in November.

JUNE 11   Bill Veeck sells shares of White Sox stock to Arthur Allyn Jr. Hank Greenberg also sold his shares to Allyn and resigned as general manager two months later.

          A serious illness kept Veeck away from the ball club during the early part of the 1961 season, although the exact nature of the malady wasn't revealed. Veeck decided to sell his majority share. He and Hank Greenberg spurned an offer from Chicago attorney (and future mayoral candidate) Bernard Epson and *entertainer Danny Thomas, who were acting in concert with Chuck Comiskey, who desired to regain control of the ball club. Veeck and Greenberg instead sold their shares to Allyn, thwarting the move by Comiskey (see December 15, 1961). The price was pegged at $3.25 million. After taxes, Veeck netted a profit of about $370,000 for the 27 months he owned the club. Veeck would return to the White Sox, buying the club again in 1975. Allyn was a Chicagoan who managed the LaSalle Street securities and investments firm he and his brother John had inherited in 1960. Known as Artnell, the diversified corporation included subsidiaries such as Eastman Oil; Kickaway Garments of Chicago; National Seating Company of Mansfield, Ohio; Artnell Exploration of Southwest Africa; the Transcontinental Bus System (Trailways); and some Georgia chicken farms. Arthur Allyn Sr. had owned 24 percent of the stock in the corporation that Veeck put together to buy the majority stock of the White Sox in 1959. He also backed Veeck when he owned the Cleveland Indians (1946–49) and St. Louis Browns (1951–53). Arthur Sr.'s shares of White Sox stock were split evenly between Arthur Jr. and John upon their father's death. Arthur Jr. knew little about baseball and left the operation of the club to general manager Ed Short (see August 26, 1961). Art Allyn was an avid butterfly collector, amateur pilot, pianist and a former chemist. He had some progressive ideas about baseball, such as revenue sharing, that would have limited many of the problems the sport experienced in future years. But Art was a relative newcomer to baseball, and that along with an abrasive nature with those who disagreed with him kept his notions from becoming a reality. Arthur ran the Sox until 1969, when he sold the club to his brother John.*

JUNE 13   The Angels play in Chicago for the first time and lose 2–1 and 10–2 in a double-header against the White Sox at Comiskey Park. Al Smith hit a grand slam off Ron Kline in the fifth inning of game two.

JUNE 14   The White Sox sweep the Angels in a double-header for the second day in a row, winning 4–1 and 9–4. The Sox scored seven runs in the first inning of the second game.

JUNE 18   The White Sox get three runs in the ninth inning from unlikely power sources to defeat the Twins 4–3 in the first game of a double-header at Comiskey Park. Billy Goodman hit a two-run, pinch-hit homer to tie the score 3–3. Then Nellie Fox smacked a walk-off home run.

The home run by Goodman was his first since 1959 and the last of 19 that he struck in 5,644 major league at-bats. Fox hit only two home runs in 1961.

JUNE 21   Roy Sievers drives in nine runs during a double-header against the Indians at Comiskey Park. The White Sox won 15–3 and 11–1. Sievers entered the first game in the fourth inning as a pinch-hitter, but still found time to drive in seven runs. He whacked a grand slam in his pinch-hit appearance off Johnny Antonelli as the Sox scored eight times in the inning. Sievers added a three-run homer in the sixth. In the second tilt, Sievers hit another homer among his three hits, drove in two more runs, and scored four. Al Smith tied an American League record for most times hit by a pitch during a double-header. He was struck by Antonelli in the first game, and Barry Latman and Frank Funk in the second.

JUNE 24   The White Sox score seven runs in the second inning and win 12–6 over the Senators at Comiskey Park. It was Chicago's eighth win in a row.

JUNE 28   The White Sox extend their winning streak to 12 with a 6–5 and 11–1 sweep of the Tigers in Detroit. The two victories also gave the Sox 19 wins in the last 20 games.

JULY 4   White Sox pitcher Warren Hacker pitches to only one batter and gives up a walk-off grand slam to Julio Becquer for a 6–4 loss to the Twins in Minnesota.

JULY 9   The White Sox score five runs in the ninth inning to defeat the Indians 7–5 in the first game of a double-header in Cleveland. Batting as a pinch-hitter with the Sox trailing 5–3, Sherm Lollar delivered a grand slam off Frank Funk for the winning runs. Chicago also won the second game 9–8 despite three home runs from Indians outfielder Willie Kirkland off Cal McLish.

JULY 14   Battery mates Sherm Lollar and Frank Baumann hit back-to-back home runs in the fifth inning, but they account for the only two runs in a 6–2 loss to the Yankees at Comiskey Park.

JULY 16   The White Sox score three runs in the ninth inning, the last two on a walk-off single by Minnie Minoso, to defeat the Red Sox 4–3 at Comiskey Park.

AUGUST 11 Luis Aparicio's homer off Jim Archer in the third inning accounts for the only run of a 1–0 win over the Athletics at Comiskey Park. Billy Pierce pitched the shutout.

AUGUST 25 Juan Pizarro strikes out 13 batters during a 3–2 win over the Indians at Comiskey Park.

AUGUST 26 Al Smith drives in six runs with two homers and a single during a 10–5 win over the White Sox at Comiskey Park.

> On the same day, Hank Greenberg resigned as general manager and was replaced by Ed Short. A lifelong Chicagoan, Short was hired by the White Sox in 1950 as public relations director and later served as traveling secretary. Prior to joining the Sox organization, he was the sports director at radio station WJJD. Short joined the club at a time when it needed a general manager who was not afraid to make bold decisions. The White Sox had an aging roster, and many of the top players in the farm system had been traded away by Bill Veeck and Greenberg. "We cannot afford to let this club grow old and fall apart completely," Short said. The 1961 White Sox possessed the oldest roster in either league. Regulars included Early Wynn (age 41), Minnie Minoso (38), Turk Lown (37), Sherm Lollar (36), Warren Hacker (36), Cal McLish (35), Billy Pierce (34), Roy Sievers (34), Nellie Fox (33), Al Smith (33) and Ray Herbert (31). Short traded away fan favorites like Luis Aparicio, Fox, Pierce, Minoso, Smith and Jim Landis, but his deals brought the club Tommy John, Pete Ward, Hoyt Wilhelm, Wilbur Wood, Tommie Agee, Eddie Fisher, Ron Hansen and Johnny Romano. In two years, Short pulled off the nearly impossible feat of transforming the oldest roster in baseball into one of the youngest while vastly improving the team. The Sox finished in second place in 1963, 1964 and 1965 and came close to winning the pennant in 1967. The team suddenly collapsed in 1968, however, and Short was fired in 1970.

SEPTEMBER 3   A two-run pinch-double by Billy Goodman in the ninth inning beats the Senators 5–4 in the first game of a double-header in Washington. The Sox completed the sweep with a 4–1 win in the second contest.

SEPTEMBER 8   Minnie Minoso hits a two-run homer in the 10th inning to defeat the Angels 5–3 in Los Angeles.

Al Smith put up the best power numbers of his career in 1961, forging a .506 slugging percentage.

The major story in baseball during the 1961 season was Roger Maris's pursuit of Babe Ruth's single-season home run record. Maris hit 61 homers, surpassing Ruth's total of 60 in 1927. The White Sox contributed mightily to Maris's record, surrendering 13 of his 61 home runs from 10 different pitchers. Chicago hurlers giving up homers to Maris in 1961 were Cal McLish (two), Russ Kemmerer (two), Billy Pierce (two), Bob Shaw (one), Early Wynn (one), Ray Herbert (one), Frank Baumann (one), Don Larsen (one), Warren Hacker (one) and Juan Pizarro (one).

SEPTEMBER 17   Al Smith hits a grand slam off Johnny James in the fourth inning of an 8–1 win over the Angels in the first game of a double-header at Comiskey Park. The Sox also won the second tilt 4–3 in 10 innings.

                Smith hit .278 with 28 homers and 93 RBIs in 1961.

SEPTEMBER 22   Floyd Robinson hits a grand slam off Milt Pappas in the ninth inning, but it comes too late to forestall an 8–6 loss to the Orioles at Comiskey Park.

                An outfielder, Robinson showed considerable promise early in his career. At the end of the 1964 season, he was 28 years old and had a lifetime batting average of .301 in 2,130 at-bats. Thereafter, he batted only .254 in 414 games before his sojourn in the majors ended in 1968. Robinson played in 880 contests for the White Sox from 1960 though 1966.

SEPTEMBER 29   Juan Pizarro strikes out 13 batters in nine innings but receives a no-decision as the White Sox lose 3–2 to the Orioles in 10 innings in Baltimore.

NOVEMBER 9   The White Sox purchase the 117-room Sarasota Terrace Hotel adjacent to Payne
                Field where the club conducted spring training. The price was $500,000.
                The purchase was made because no hotel in Sarasota would house the club's
                African-American players because of the city's strict policies of segregation.
                Previously, the club's black players were quartered a mile away at a hotel that
                catered only to African-Americans. Black players on the White Sox's 40-man spring
                training roster in 1962 were Juan Pizarro, Floyd Robinson and Al Smith.

NOVEMBER 27   The White Sox trade Minnie Minoso to the Cardinals for Joe Cunningham.

                *Minoso was finished as an everyday player. Cunningham was nearly done, but
                he had enough left to hit .295 with eight home runs for the White Sox in 1962.*

NOVEMBER 28   The White Sox trade Roy Sievers to the Phillies for John Buzhardt and Charley
                Smith.

NOVEMBER 30   The White Sox trade Billy Pierce and Don Larsen to the Giants for Eddie Fisher,
                Dom Zanni and Bobby Tiefenauer.

                *Pierce has one solid year left, posting a 16–6 record with the Giants in 1962 and
                pitching in the World Series that fall. Using a baffling knuckleball taught to him
                by Hoyt Wilhelm, Fisher gave the White Sox several excellent seasons out of the
                bullpen. He was 34–26 with 44 saves and a 3.02 ERA for Chicago from 1962
                through 1966.*

DECEMBER 15   The White Sox trade Cal McLish and Frank Barnes to the Phillies for Bob Sadowski,
                Taylor Phillips and Lou Vassie.

                *On the same day, Chuck Comiskey sold his 46 percent share of the White Sox
                to an 11-man group for an amount believed to be $3.3 million. The group was
                headed by William Bartholomay, a 33-year-old insurance executive. The sale
                ended the involvement of the Comiskey family in the affairs of the White Sox.
                Chuck's grandfather Charles founded the club in 1900. Chuck still harbored
                hopes that Bartholomay's group would eventually buy out Arthur Allyn, who
                bought a 54 percent majority of the stock in the club six months earlier (see
                June 11, 1961). In this way, Comiskey could then re-purchase his stock plus the
                54 percent. That plan was soon thwarted. Deprived of their stock dividends and
                unable to influence club policy, Bartholomay and his friends sold the 46 percent
                to Allyn on May 5, 1962. This made Allyn the sole owner. Bartholomay and his
                cohorts then bought the Milwaukee Braves in November 1962 and moved the
                franchise to Atlanta at the end of the 1965 season.*

1962

Season in a Sentence

The White Sox allow fewer runs than any other team in the American League, but they also hit the fewest home runs, leading to a lackluster fifth-place finish.

Finish • Won • Lost • Pct • GB

Fifth   85   77   .525   11.0

Manager

Al Lopez

Stats

Stats	WS	AL	Rank
Batting Avg:	.257	.255	5
On-Base Pct:	.336	.328	3
Slugging Pct:	.372	.394	10
Home Runs:	92		10
Stolen Bases:	76		2 (tie)
ERA:	3.73	3.97	4
Fielding Avg:	.982	.978	1
Runs Scored:	707		7
Runs Allowed:	658		1

Starting Lineup

Cam Carreon, c
Joe Cunningham, 1b
Nellie Fox, 2b
Al Smith, 3b
Luis Aparicio, ss
Floyd Robinson, lf-rf
Jim Landis, cf
Mike Hershberger, rf-cf
Sherm Lollar, c
Charlie Maxwell, lf

Pitchers

Ray Herbert, sp
Juan Pizarro, sp
John Buzhardt, sp
Early Wynn, sp
Joe Horlen, sp
Eddie Fisher, rp
Dom Zanni, rp
Turk Lown, rp
Frank Baumann, rp

Attendance

1,131,562 (fifth in AL)

Club Leaders

Batting Avg:	Floyd Robinson	.312
On-Base Pct:	Joe Cunningham	.410
Slugging Pct:	Floyd Robinson	.475
Home Runs:	Al Smith	16
RBIs:	Floyd Robinson	109
Runs:	Joe Cunningham	91
Stolen Bases:	Luis Aparicio	31
Wins:	Ray Herbert	20
Strikeouts:	Juan Pizarro	173
ERA:	Ray Herbert	3.27
Saves:	Turk Lown	6

MARCH 24   The White Sox trade Andy Carey to the Dodgers for Ramon Conde and Jim Koranda.

MARCH 31   The White Sox sign University of Detroit pitcher Dave DeBusschere for $100,000.

DeBusschere was one of the most interesting athletes in White Sox history. Standing six-foot-six, he was not only a dominating pitcher in college, but an All-American basketball player who was drafted in the first round by the Detroit Pistons. While playing for the White Sox in 1962 and 1963, DeBusschere had a 3–4 record and a 2.90 ERA in 102$^1/_3$ innings, mostly as a reliever. He played for the Pistons in between those two seasons in the majors, then decided to concentrate solely on basketball. In November 1964, at the age of 24, the Pistons made him the youngest coach in NBA history. DeBusschere was later a forward on two New York Knicks championship teams, and served as commissioner of the American Basketball Association. He was elected to the NBA Hall of Fame in 1982.

APRIL 10   Before a shivering crowd of 18,124 at Comiskey Park, the White Sox claim a 2–1 Opening Day victory over the Angels. Sherm Lollar drove in the winning run with a single, one of his four hits on the day. He also tied a major league record for most foul balls caught in a game with six. Juan Pizarro pitched a complete game. The Sox left 16 men on base.

Nat King Cole sang the National Anthem.

APRIL 13   Mike Hershberger collects five hits, including a double, in six at-bats during a 12–5 win over the Athletics in Kansas City.

The cramped dressing rooms at Comiskey Park, which were part of the original 1910 design of the ballpark, were replaced in 1962 with much roomier quarters.

APRIL 17   Floyd Robinson drives in seven runs by whacking a homer, two doubles and a single during an 8–0 win over the Twins in Minnesota.

Milo Hamilton joined Bob Elson in the White Sox radio booth in 1962.

APRIL 19   The White Sox score nine runs in the first inning to spark a 10–3 win over the Twins in Minnesota. Jim Landis hit a grand slam off Jim Kaat during the opening salvo, then added a solo homer in the seventh.

MAY 3   Jim Landis accounts for the only run of a 1–0 win over the Yankees at Comiskey Park with a homer in the fourth inning off Whitey Ford. John Buzhardt pitched the shutout.

MAY 4   The Red Sox score 12 runs in the fifth inning and defeat the White Sox 13–6 in Boston.

MAY 6   Turk Lown checks a three-run Red Sox rally in the ninth inning by fanning all three batters he faces, preserving a 4–3 White Sox win in Boston.

MAY 9   The White Sox play at D. C. Stadium in Washington for the first time and lose 9–3 and win 7–6 in a double-header against the Senators.

D. C. Stadium was renamed Robert F. Kennedy Stadium in 1968. It was the home of the Senators from 1962 until the franchise moved to Texas after the 1971 season and was renamed the Rangers. In 2005, the facility was re-introduced to baseball with the arrival of the Nationals and served the club through the 2007 season.

MAY 11   The White Sox play at Dodger Stadium, also known as Chavez Ravine, for the first time and lose 4–2 to the Angels.

The Angels shared Dodger Stadium with the Dodgers from 1962 through 1965 before moving to Anaheim.

MAY 13   The White Sox score seven runs in the eighth inning and win 15–6 over the Angels in Los Angeles.

JUNE 2   The White Sox score seven runs in the fifth inning and win 10–2 in the first game of a double-header against the Orioles at Memorial Stadium. Baltimore won the second contest 11–4.

JUNE 7   Al Smith collects five hits in five at-bats during an 8–4 win over the Angels in Los Angeles.

JUNE 15   A two-run walk-off triple by Floyd Robinson in the ninth inning defeats the Angels 7–6 at Comiskey Park.

              Robinson hit .312 with 11 homers, 109 RBIs and a league-leading 45 doubles in 1962. The doubles mark set a White Sox record that stood until Frank Thomas collected 46 in 1992.

JUNE 23   Luis Aparicio collects five hits in five at-bats during a 6–1 win over the Athletics at Comiskey Park.

              The White Sox had an oddly constructed lineup in 1962. The club was last in the majors in home runs (92), but it was second in the AL in both doubles (250) and triples (56). The Sox tied for second in the league in stolen bases with 76. It was the first time since 1950 that the White Sox failed to lead the circuit in steals.

JUNE 25   The White Sox trade Bob Farley to the Tigers for Charlie Maxwell.

JULY 1   Cam Carreon hits a bases-loaded, walk-off triple in the ninth inning to defeat the Indians 5–4 in the first game of a double-header at Comiskey Park. It was his only triple of the season in 313 at-bats. In the second tilt, the White Sox set a major league record (since tied) for most sacrifice flies in an inning with three in the fifth during a 7–6 win over the Indians.

              Three sacrifice flies in an inning would seem to be a statistical impossibility but is conceivable under the scoring rules. According to the rule a sacrifice fly can be credited when "before two are out, the batter hits a fly ball which is dropped and the runner scores, if, in the scorer's judgment, the runner could have scored after the catch had the fly been caught." There were two such plays in the fifth inning of game two on balls caught, then dropped, by Cleveland right fielder Gene Green.

JULY 10   At D. C. Stadium in Washington, Luis Aparicio plays the entire game for the American League at shortstop in the All-Star Game and hits a triple, but the NL wins 3–1.

JULY 12   Juan Pizarro pitches a two-hitter and defeats the Tigers 3–2 at Comiskey Park. Two doubles by Steve Boros in the second and fourth innings accounted for the pair of Detroit hits.

JULY 14   With the White Sox and the Cubs playing in Chicago at the same time, WGN-TV carries both games. The station switched back and forth between the two contests, with Vince Lloyd doing the play-by-play at Comiskey Park and Jack Brickhouse at Wrigley Field. The Sox downed the Tigers 4–2, while the Cubs beat the Reds 6–3.

JULY 21   Juan Pizarro hurls a two-hitter and strikes out 12 for a 5–0 win over the Red Sox at Fenway Park. The only Boston hits were a double by opposing pitcher Gene Conley in the third inning and a single from Carl Yastrzemski in the fourth.

JULY 22   Floyd Robinson collects six singles in six at-bats during a 7–3 win over the Red Sox in Boston. Robinson connected off five different pitchers. Bill Monbouquette gave up two of the six hits, and Mike Fornieles, Hal Kolstad, Galen Cisco and Dick Radatz surrendered one each.

Rookie sensation Floyd Robinson helped launch the era of the Go-Go Sox, bringing a new level of speed to the team.

AUGUST 1   Bill Monbouquette of the Red Sox pitches a no-hitter against the White Sox, winning 1–0 at Comiskey Park. The lone Chicago base runner was Al Smith, who walked on a 3–2 pitch with two out in the second inning. The final out was recorded on a strikeout of Luis Aparicio. Early Wynn was the hard-luck loser. Wynn was attempting to win the 298th game of his career.

AUGUST 4   Al Smith is hit by a Bill Stafford pitch with the bases loaded in the ninth inning to score the winning run of a 2–1 victory over the Yankees at Comiskey Park.

AUGUST 5   A crowd of 44,444 at Comiskey Park watches the White Sox win 3–2 in 13 innings over the Yankees. A single by Mike Hershberger drove in Juan Pizarro with the winning run.

AUGUST 7   Ray Herbert pitches a three-hitter to beat the Orioles 4–0 at Comiskey Park. Herbert retired the first 17 batters to face him and had a no-hitter until Russ Snyder singled in the seventh inning.

Herbert put together a streak of 31 consecutive scoreless innings over four starts in August 1962.

AUGUST 11   The White Sox erupt for seven runs in the fourth inning and win 11–2 over the Athletics in Kansas City. Joe Cunningham had a triple and a double in the inning.

AUGUST 12   Jim Landis homers off Bill Fischer in the eighth inning to account for the lone run of a 1–0 win over the Athletics in Kansas City. It was the second time in 1962 that Landis won a 1–0 game with a home run. Ray Herbert (7⅔ innings) and Juan Pizarro (1⅓ innings) combined on the shutout.

AUGUST 15   Shut out through eight innings, the White Sox suddenly explode for 10 runs in the ninth to defeat the Indians 10–2 in the first game of a double-header in Cleveland. The Sox lost game two 3–2.

AUGUST 16   The White Sox plate seven runs in the first inning and win 11–6 over the Indians in Cleveland.

AUGUST 19   Charlie Maxwell drives in six runs, four of them on a grand slam, during an 11–5 win over the Tigers in the first game of a double-header at Comiskey Park. The bases-loaded poke came at the expense of Sam Jones in the sixth inning. Chicago lost the second tilt 8–3.

Maxwell had his big day on a Sunday, which was typical of his career. Maxwell struck 40 of his 148 career homers on Sundays.

AUGUST 31   Joe Cunningham collects five hits in five at-bats during a 5–2 loss to the Tigers in Detroit.

SEPTEMBER 8   Early Wynn wins the 299th game of his career in pitching a complete game for a 6–3 decision over the Senators in Washington. It was Wynn's fifth start since winning game number 298.

SEPTEMBER 18   Trying for his 300th career victory, Early Wynn allows eight runs in five innings and the White Sox lose 10–5 to the Red Sox at Comiskey Park.

After he won number 299 on September 8, the White Sox kept Wynn out of the rotation during a road trip to Minnesota and Washington so that he could try for his 300th victory before the home fans in Chicago in the hopes of drawing a large crowd. Club owner Arthur Allyn and general manager Ed Short were severely criticized by the Windy City media for the marketing ploy, especially after the attendance for the September 18 contest was only 14,498.

SEPTEMBER 19   Mike Hershberger hits a walk-off homer in the 10th inning to defeat the Red Sox 3–2 at Comiskey Park. Hershberger entered the game in the eighth inning as a pinch-runner and remained in the contest as a right fielder.

SEPTEMBER 21   The White Sox score six runs in the ninth inning without a batter being retired to stun the Yankees 7–6 at Comiskey Park. Nine batters in a row reached base. Nellie Fox and Cam Carreon singled, and Bob Roselli hit a pinch-hit double for the first run. Luis Aparicio drew a walk, Joe Cunningham smacked a three-run double to make the score 6–5, before Floyd Robinson walked. Al Smith failed twice to lay down a bunt to move the runners over, then doubled to tie the contest. Jim Landis was walked intentionally to load the bases, and Deacon Jones, pinch-hitting for Mike Hershberger, singled in the winning run.

SEPTEMBER 23   In his second attempt at winning his 300th career game, Early Wynn allows only one run through the first nine runs, then surrenders four in the 10th to lose 5–1 to the Yankees at Comiskey Park.

SEPTEMBER 28   Early Wynn tries for win number 300 again and loses 7–3 to the Yankees in New York.

Wynn had a 7–15 record and a 4.48 ERA in 1962. He finished the season with a 299–242 lifetime record and was 42 years old. Wynn was released by the White Sox in November, but was invited back to spring training in 1963 as a non-roster player. He failed to make the club, however. Early was unemployed for two months when the Indians, needing something to boost attendance, signed him in attempt to have him win number 300 in a Cleveland uniform. In a previous stint with the Indians (1949–57), Wynn won 163 games. He earned his 300th win on July 13, 1963. It proved to be his last big-league victory.

SEPTEMBER 30   On the last day of the season, Ray Herbert wins his 20th game of 1962 with an 8–4 decision over the Yankees in New York.

1963   Sox

Season in a Sentence

With an infusion of young talent, the White Sox reach first place in mid-June and win 94 games to finish second to the Yankees.

Finish • Won • Lost • Pct • GB

Second   94   68   .580   10.5

Manager

Al Lopez

Stats

Stats	WS	AL	Rank
Batting Avg:	.250	.247	5
On-Base Pct:	.325	.315	3
Slugging Pct:	.365	.380	7
Home Runs:	114		8
Stolen Bases:	64		4
ERA:	2.97		1
Fielding Avg:	.979	.978	5
Runs Scored:	683		4
Runs Allowed:	544		1

Starting Lineup

J. C. Martin, c
Tom McCraw, 1b
Nellie Fox, 2b
Pete Ward, 3b
Ron Hansen, ss
Dave Nicholson, lf
Mike Hershberger, cf-rf
Floyd Robinson, rf
Jim Landis, cf
Cam Carreon, c
Al Weis, 2b-ss
Joe Cunningham, 1b

Pitchers

Gary Peters, sp
Juan Pizarro, sp
Ray Herbert, sp
Joe Horlen, sp-rp
John Buzhardt, sp
Hoyt Wilhelm, rp
Jim Brosnan, rp
Eddie Fisher, rp-sp
Dave DeBusschere, rp-sp

Attendance

1,158,848 (third in AL)

Club Leaders

Batting Avg:	Pete Ward	.295
On-Base Pct:	Floyd Robinson	.361
Slugging Pct:	Pete Ward	.482
Home Runs:	Pete Ward	22
	Dave Nicholson	22
RBIs:	Pete Ward	84
Runs:	Pete Ward	80
Stolen Bases:	Tom McCraw	15
	Al Weis	15
Wins:	Gary Peters	19
Strikeouts:	Gary Peters	189
ERA:	Gary Peters	2.33
Saves:	Hoyt Wilhelm	21

JANUARY 14   Three months after America's nerves are frazzled by the Cuban missile crisis, the White Sox trade Luis Aparicio and Al Smith to the Orioles for Hoyt Wilhelm, Pete Ward, Ron Hansen and Dave Nicholson.

The trade was a huge gamble as the White Sox tried to bring more youth to their roster by trading two proven veterans for three question marks and a 39-year-old pitcher. Sox fans were angry over the deal at the time it was announced, particularly over the loss of Aparicio, but it proved to be one of the best transactions in club history. Aparicio had slumped to a career low batting average of .241 in 1962 and was at odds with Al Lopez. Smith had a solid season, batting .292 with 16 homers, but he was 34 years old and didn't want to play third base. He never again accumulated as many as 400 at-bats in a season after leaving Chicago. Hansen, who at six-foot-three was unusually tall for shortstops of the era, was acquired to replace Aparicio. After winning the Rookie of the Year award in 1960, he batted just .173 in 71 games in 1962, during which his Marine reserve unit was called up during the Cold War tensions of the period. While Aparicio had a far superior career to Hansen, over the five seasons following the trade with Baltimore, Hansen was the better player. Unfortunately, a back injury in 1966 started a decline. A native of Montreal, Ward was the son of former National Hockey League star Jimmy Ward. Pete gave the club a quality third baseman for the first time since Willie Kamm was traded in 1931. During his first season with the Sox, Ward batted .295 with 22 homers and 84 RBIs and was the runner-up to teammate Gary Peters in the Rookie of the Year balloting. Like Hansen, injuries curtailed a promising career. Ward suffered a neck injury during a car accident in 1965 on the way to a Blackhawks game (April 25, 1965) and his career took a serious turn for the worse. Nicholson could hit the ball as far as anyone in baseball history when he connected, but unfortunately, it wasn't very often. In three seasons with the White Sox he hit .213 with 37 homers in 828 at-bats. During his seven-year stay in the majors, Nicholson fanned once per 2.48 at-bats, the highest rate in big league history. Although he was 39 at the time he joined the White Sox, Wilhelm proved to be the best of the four players obtained from the Orioles. Using a knuckleball, Wilhelm pitched six seasons as a reliever with the Sox and posted a 41–33 record, 98 saves and a dazzling 1.91 ERA in 675²/₃ innings.

APRIL 8   The White Sox sell Denny McLain to the Tigers.

The White Sox had two young right-handers on the roster in McLain and Bruce Howard, both of whom were given large bonuses. Under the existing rules, the Sox were allowed to protect only one of them. General manager Ed Short had to subject one of the them to waivers, and to help the club make the final decision, Howard and McLain were pitted against each other in a spring training intrasquad game. Howard won 2–1, and McLain was placed on the waiver wire. The Tigers put in the claim on McLain, who was a native of Chicago. Letting McLain out of the organization proved to be a monumental mistake for the Sox. Howard never developed any consistency and had a 26–31 career record. McLain, on the other hand, won 20 games in 1966, 31 in 1968 and 24 more in 1969. He is the only pitcher since 1934 with a season of 30 wins or more. At the end of the 1969 season, McLain was only 25 and had a 114–57 lifetime record. But he was suspended by commissioner Bowie Kuhn for the first half of the 1970 season due to links with gamblers and was never the same afterward.

APRIL 9   In the season opener, the White Sox win 7–5 over the Tigers on a 42-degree day in Detroit. With the Sox trailing 5–4 in the seventh inning, Pete Ward drilled a three-run homer. It was Ward's first game with the White Sox and his first major league home run. Also making his White Sox debut, Hoyt Wilhelm pitched two shutout innings, striking out three. Ray Herbert was the starting pitcher, but he put Chicago in a 4–0 hole in the second inning.

APRIL 13   The White Sox waste brilliant pitching and lose 1–0 in 15 innings to the Angels in Los Angeles. Juan Pizarro started and pitched nine shutout innings, allowing only two hits. Hoyt Willhem pitched three scoreless innings and Gary Peters added two more before allowing a run in the 15th. Ed Kirkpatrick, a 19-year-old outfielder, drove in the winning run with a single.

Pizarro was 16–8 with a 2.39 ERA in 1963.

APRIL 16   In the home opener, the White Sox lose 7–4 to the Athletics before 24,760. Playing for the first time in a Sox uniform at Comiskey Park, Ron Hansen hit a home run.

APRIL 20   Dave Nicholson hits a grand slam off Frank Sullivan in the sixth inning of a 10–7 win over the Twins at Comiskey Park.

MAY 1   Ray Herbert shuts out the Orioles 7–0 in the first game of a double-header at Comiskey Park. The Sox also won the second game 6–4.

MAY 4   Al Lopez is ejected for arguing about the lights during an 8–1 win over the Senators at Comiskey Park. The sky darkened in the fourth inning, and umpire Bill Valentine ordered that the lights be turned on while Dave Nicholson was at-bat. Lopez complained that the sudden switch from semi-darkness to bright illumination was unfair to the batter and could result in injuries. The discussion became heated, and Lopez was tossed by umpire Bill McKinley. Nicholson hit the next pitch for a home run.

MAY 5   Ray Herbert pitches his second consecutive shutout, defeating the Senators 8–0 in the first game of a double-header at Comiskey Park. The Sox lost the second tilt 8–7 when Washington scored five runs in the ninth inning.

On the same day, the White Sox trade Dom Zanni to the Reds for Jim Brosnan, who was not only a pitcher, but a best-selling author. In 1960, Brosnan published The Long Season, *a diary account of the 1959 season, which he spent with the Cardinals and Reds. He followed with a similar book about the 1961 campaign called* The Pennant Race. *The books were among the first that presented an inside look at Major League Baseball from a player's point of view. The Reds tried to censor any further writing ventures, and when he refused he was traded to the White Sox. Brosnan posted a 2.84 ERA in 73 innings for the White Sox, but the club also tried to prohibit him from writing during the baseball season. Like he had in Cincinnati, Brosnan refused to go along with the edict and the club released him. No one else offered him a contract, and he retired.*

MAY 8   After being held hitless for six innings by Ed Rakow, the White Sox pour across eight runs in the seventh inning and whip the Athletics 8–3 in Kansas City.

MAY 9   Ray Herbert pitches a two-hitter to defeat the Yankees 2–0 in New York. Ron Hansen drove in both runs with a double in the second inning. It was Herbert's third consecutive shutout. The only Yankee hits were singles by Clete Boyer in the third inning and Joe Pepitone in the fifth.

MAY 10   Juan Pizarro is the whole show in a 2–0 win over the Angels at Comiskey Park. He not only pitched a complete game and threw a three-hit shutout, but he also drove in both runs with a homer and a single.

MAY 12   The White Sox overwhelm the Angels 14–2 in the first game of a double-header at Comiskey Park, but they lose the second tilt 7–6 in 13 innings.

MAY 14   Ray Herbert pitches his fourth consecutive shutout, beating the Tigers 3–0 at Comiskey Park. Jim Landis drove in all three runs with a homer and a single.

          Herbert pitched 38 consecutive scoreless innings from May 1 through May 19.

MAY 16   Jim Brosnan faces only one batter and gives up a walk-off homer to Max Alvis in the ninth inning for a 5–4 loss to the Indians in Cleveland.

JUNE 2   After losing the opener of a double-header 11–9 to the Red Sox at Comiskey Park, the White Sox bounce back to win the nightcap 10–0.

JUNE 3   Joe Cunningham breaks his collarbone in a freak accident during a 4–0 win over the Angels in Los Angeles. Running to first base, Cunningham tripped over the foot of Angels first baseman Charlie Dees.

JUNE 12   Dave Nicholson ties a major league record by striking out seven times during eight plate appearances in a double-header against the Angels at Comiskey Park. The White Sox won 3–1 and lost 5–0.

JUNE 14   Charlie Maxwell hits a walk-off homer in the ninth inning to defeat the Athletics 3–2 at Comiskey Park.

JUNE 19   Nellie Fox collects five hits in six at-bats and Tommy McCraw blasts two homers and drives in five runs during a 12–4 triumph over the Twins in Minnesota.

JUNE 20   The White Sox are knocked out of first place with a 9–4 loss to the Twins in Minnesota.

          The Sox failed to regain the top spot in 1963 and fell out of serious contention by the Fourth of July. The club finished in second place, but 10$\frac{1}{2}$ games behind the Yankees.

JUNE 21   The White Sox spoil Early Wynn's attempt at winning his 300th career game by defeating the Indians 2–0 at Municipal Stadium. Ron Hansen accounted for both Chicago runs with a two-run homer in the ninth inning.

JUNE 28   Early Wynn tries for win number 300 again, and has a no-decision in a 4–3 Indians win over the White Sox at Comiskey Park. Wynn allowed three runs in six innings.

          On the same day, the White Sox purchase Jim Lemon from the Phillies.

JULY 14   A two-out, two-run single by Nellie Fox in the ninth inning beats the Orioles 3–2 in the second game of a double-header at Comiskey Park. Baltimore won the opener 6–3.

JULY 15   Gary Peters pitches a one-hitter and strikes out 13 batters to beat the Orioles 4–0 at Comiskey Park. The only Baltimore hit was a single by opposing pitcher Robin Roberts in the third inning.

Peters pitched briefly for the White Sox in 1959, 1960, 1961 and 1962. He made 12 relief appearances and posted an ERA of 3.00 and an 0–1 record in 21 innings. Peters was considered to be somewhat of an oddball during his progress through the Sox farm system. Obsessed with aerodynamics, he whittled boomerangs in his spare time. Although 1963 was his fifth season in the majors, he was still considered a rookie because of his limited number of innings. Peters turned 26 just after Opening Day and made the roster only because he was out of options. The White Sox were about to place Peters on waivers when he made an emergency start on May 6 when Juan Pizarro was sidelined with the flu. Peters defeated the Athletics 5–1 and hit a home run. He

Runner-up to teammate Gary Peters for the Rookie of the Year Award, third baseman Pete Ward led the Sox in nearly every offensive category in 1963.

proved to be the surprise sensation of the season. Peters won the Rookie of the Year Award with a 19–8 record, a league-leading 2.33 ERA and 189 strikeouts in 243 innings. He won 20 games in 1964, but never reached that figure again. Overall, he was 91–78 with the White Sox before being traded to the Red Sox following the 1969 season. Peters ranks fifth all-time in strikeouts among White Sox pitchers with 1,098.

JULY 28   Nellie Fox collects his 2,500th career hit during a 4–1 win over the Orioles in Baltimore.

JULY 29   Joe Horlen loses a no-hitter and the game in the ninth inning of a 2–1 loss to the Senators in Washington. Horlen had a no-hitter in progress until Chuck Hinton singled with one out in the ninth. Horlen retired Bobo Osborne on a ground out, but gave up a homer to Don Lock to lose the contest.

Horlen was able to complete a no-hitter on September 10, 1967. He pitched for the White Sox from 1961 through 1971 and posted a 113–113 record. Among White Sox pitchers, Horlen ranks eighth all-time in wins, seventh in games started (284) and eighth innings pitched (1,918).

AUGUST 11   Dave Nicholson hits a walk-off homer in the 11th inning to defeat the Tigers 3–2 in the second game of a double-header at Comiskey Park. Detroit won the opener 7–2.

AUGUST 14   The White Sox lose a tough 1–0 decision to the Indians in 11 innings at Comiskey Park. Willie Kirkland accounted for the lone run of the game with a homer off Ray Herbert. Dick Donovan pitched the shutout for Cleveland.

AUGUST 17   Pete Ward drives in both runs of a 2–0 victory over the Yankees at Comiskey Park with a sacrifice fly in the first inning and a single in the fifth. Gary Peters pitched the shutout.

AUGUST 29   The day after Martin Luther King Jr.'s "I Have a Dream" speech in Washington, Gary Peters extends his winning streak to 11 games with a 7–2 decision over the Indians in Cleveland.

AUGUST 31   Back-to-back homers by Jim Landis and Floyd Robinson in the ninth inning defeats the Twins 2–0 in Minnesota. Joe Horlen (seven innings) and Hoyt Wilhelm (two innings) combined on the shutout.

SEPTEMBER 6   Dave Nicholson hits a grand slam in the second inning off Jim Kaat, but the White Sox lose 9–8 to the Twins at Comiskey Park.

SEPTEMBER 18   Gary Peters notches his 19th win of the season with a 4–3 decision over the Red Sox in the second game of a double-header at Comiskey Park. Chicago also won the opener 8–3.

               Peters lost his final two starts of 1963 in an attempt for win number 20.

SEPTEMBER 20   Eddie Fisher (seven innings) and Hoyt Wilhelm (two innings) combine on a two-hitter to defeat the Tigers 2–0 in Detroit. The only hits by the Tigers were singles by Don Wert in the second inning and Willie Horton in the fifth.

SEPTEMBER 24   Ray Herbert pitches a two-hitter to defeat the Orioles 15–0 at Memorial Stadium. The only Baltimore hits were singles by Bob Saverine in the third inning and Luis Aparicio in the sixth. The Sox scored eight runs in the fifth inning, highlighted by two doubles from Floyd Robinson.

DECEMBER 10   Three weeks following the assassination of President John F. Kennedy, the White Sox trade Nellie Fox to Houston for Jim Golden, Danny Murphy and cash.

               With the retirement of Sherm Lollar and the departure of Fox, Jim Landis was the only player from the 1959 pennant-winners still with the club. Fox was nearly 36 when dealt to Houston and fetched little on the trade market. He was a regular for one season with the Astros, and in 1965 he tutored the development of another undersized second baseman in future Hall of Famer Joe Morgan. Nellie died of cancer in 1975 at the age of 51. In 1985, he received 295 votes in the Hall of Fame balloting conducted by the baseball writers, just two short of the number necessary for election. By 1990, he was eligible for consideration for induction again by the Veterans Committee and was considered to be a lock to be quickly elected because of the near-miss in the writers's vote. But mysteriously, Fox wasn't selected until 1997. Many accuse Al Lopez, who was a member of the committee, with using his influence to keep Fox out of the Hall of Fame.

1964

Season in a Sentence

During a thrilling three-team pennant race, the White Sox lose 11 games in a row to the Yankees and finish in second place, one game behind the Yanks and one game ahead of the Orioles.

Finish • Won • Lost • Pct • GB

Second   98   64   .605   1.0

Manager

Al Lopez

Stats

Stats	WS	AL	Rank
Batting Avg:	.247	.247	7
On-Base Pct:	.323	.317	3
Slugging Pct:	.353	.382	8
Home Runs:	106		9
Stolen Bases:	75		3
ERA:	2.72		1
Fielding Avg:	.981	.980	5
Runs Scored:	642		7
Runs Allowed:	501		1

Starting Lineup

J. C. Martin, c
Tom McCraw, 1b
Don Buford, 2b
Pete Ward, 3b
Ron Hansen, ss
Dave Nicholson, lf
Mike Hershberger, cf-rf
Floyd Robinson, rf-lf
Al Weis, 2b
Jim Landis, cf
Bill Skowron, 1b
Jerry McNertney, c

Pitchers

Gary Peters, sp
Juan Pizarro, sp
Joe Horlen, sp
John Buzhardt, sp
Ray Herbert, sp
Hoyt Wilhelm, rp
Eddie Fisher, rp

Attendance

1,250,053 (second in AL)

Club Leaders

Batting Avg:	Floyd Robinson	.301
On-Base Pct:	Floyd Robinson	.388
Slugging Pct:	Pete Ward	.473
Home Runs:	Pete Ward	23
RBIs:	Pete Ward	94
Runs:	Ron Hansen	85
Stolen Bases:	Al Weis	22
Wins:	Gary Peters	20
Strikeouts:	Gary Peters	205
ERA:	Joe Horlen	1.88
Saves:	Hoyt Wilhelm	27

JANUARY 6   The White Sox unveil new road uniforms to be worn during the 1964 season. Instead of the traditional gray, the jerseys were powder blue. General manager Ed Short said that the suits would "add some color" to the club and would look better on television. The home uniforms were a little less colorful than in the past, however, as red was eliminated as a trim color. The "SOX" insignia on the front was changed from black to navy blue, as were the caps.

MARCH 18   The White Sox purchase Don Mossi from the Tigers.

APRIL 8   The White Sox sign 41-year-old Minnie Minoso as a free agent.

Minoso played in only 30 games in 1964, mostly as a pinch-hitter, before drawing his release in July.

APRIL 14   In the midst of Beatlemania, with the Fab Four holding the top five spots on the Billboard singles chart, the White Sox open the 1964 season with a 5–3 loss to the Orioles before 20,766 at Comiskey Park. A two-run homer by Boog Powell off Hoyt Wilhelm in the eighth inning broke a 3–3 tie.

Jim Landis was the Opening Day center fielder, but was benched two days later in favor of Mike Hershberger. Landis was at the center of a controversy over media interviews. On April 16, Ed Short told the players that they would not be receiving any remuneration for radio and television interviews. The players voted not to participate unless they received $25 for radio interviews and $50 for TV. Landis was the most vocal of the players and, after an argument with Short, demanded a trade. Al Lopez said that he wasn't going to play an individual who didn't want to be with the team, and as a result, Landis seldom appeared in the lineup for the next two months. Things hit rock bottom on June 10 when Jim Landis Night was held to honor his service to a club he played with for eight seasons. Instead of putting Landis in the lineup, Lopez gave Minnie Minoso a rare start. The Sox manager was hung in effigy in the players' parking lot. During the 1964 season, Landis hit only .208 with just one home run in 298 at-bats. In January 1965, he was dealt to the Athletics. During his last four seasons in the majors, Landis played for six different teams.

MAY 6   Dave Nicholson hits three home runs during a 6–4 and 11–4 sweep of the Athletics in a double-header at Comiskey Park. He hit two homers in the first game and one in the second.

Nicholson may or may not have hit a home run roughly 573 feet off Moe Drabowsky in the fifth inning of the opener. Nicholson's blast soared high above the upper-deck roof. The only question was whether or not the ball bounced onto the roof before exiting the park and landing in neighboring Armour Park, where a father and son were tossing a baseball to each other. If the drive didn't hit the roof, as the White Sox brass insisted, the ball traveled about 573 feet. Several of the fans in the upper level claimed they heard the ball hit the roof with an unmistakable thud. Sox general manager Ed Short said that an electrician working on the roof claimed the ball cleared it completely, and that the ball contained no scuff marks. If it had struck the roof, it would have shown signs of tar. Nicholson appeared to have finally turned his tremendous skills into production early in 1964. On June 5, he was hitting .294 with seven homers and 23 RBIs in 136 at-bats. Over the remainder of the season, however, he batted .127 in 156 at-bats and followed that with a .153 average in 85 at-bats in 1965. After one frustrating game, Nicholson used his tremendous strength to twist the shower knobs so tightly that no one on the team could take a shower. A plumber had to be called to loosen the knobs with a wrench. The Sox finally gave up on Nicholson, and dealt him to the Astros in December 1965.

MAY 22   Juan Pizarro strikes out 13 batters during a 3–1 win over the Senators at Comiskey Park.

Pizarro was 19–9 with an ERA of 2.56 in 1964.

MAY 23   The White Sox score nine runs in the second inning and beat the Senators 14–2 at Comiskey Park. Pete Ward hit a grand slam off Tom Cheney.

MAY 29   Pete Ward hits a grand slam off Dave Wickersham in the sixth inning for all of the White Sox runs in a 4–1 win over the Tigers in Detroit.

Ward hit 23 homers with 94 RBIs and a .282 batting average in 1964. Other batting leaders were Floyd Robinson (.301 average and 11 home runs) and Ron Hansen (.261 average and 20 homers).

JUNE 10   The White Sox edge the Orioles 2–1 at Comiskey Park with the help of clutch relief pitching from Eddie Fisher, who entered the game replacing Gary Peters with one out in the ninth inning and runners on first and third. With just one pitch, Eddie Fisher induced Dick Brown to ground into a double play.

The White Sox closed the game with a 31–14 record and a 2¹/₂-game lead. The Sox traveled to New York on June 12 for a five-game, three-day series and lost all five games to drop out of first place.

JUNE 15   In their first game after losing five straight to the Yankees, the White Sox score seven runs in the first inning and beat the Orioles 9–1 in Baltimore.

JUNE 18   The White Sox move back into first place with a 2–0 win over the Orioles in Baltimore.

The White Sox next played the Yankees at Comiskey Park for a four-game series.

JUNE 20   Gary Peters pitches shutout ball through 10 innings, then allows a run in the 11th to lose 1–0 to the Yankees at Comiskey Park. Whitey Ford pitched a complete game for New York.

JUNE 21   The White Sox score only one run in 26 innings during a double-header against the Yankees at Comiskey Park. The Sox lost the opener 2–0 and the second tilt 2–1 in 17 innings.

JUNE 22   The Yankees complete the four-game sweep at Comiskey Park with a 6–5 win over the White Sox.

The White Sox lost their first 11 games against the Yankees in 1964, including nine in a row during an 11-day period from June 12 through June 22. An inability to beat the contenders kept the Sox from reaching the World Series in 1964. The club was 6–12 against the Yanks and 8–10 versus the Orioles. Against the bottom three clubs (the Athletics, Senators and Red Sox), Chicago won 42 and lost 12.

JUNE 26   Mike Hershberger breaks up a no-hitter by Gerry Arrigo with a single leading off the ninth inning for the only White Sox hit in the first game of a double-header against the Twins in Minnesota. The Sox lost 2–0, then won the nightcap 9–4.

JUNE 30   Jerry McNertney hits a grand slam off Sonny Siebert in the fifth inning of a 12–3 win over the Indians in Cleveland.

JULY 4   Two days after the passage of the Civil Rights Act, prohibiting racial discrimination in employment and places of public accommodation, Gary Peters shuts out the Indians 4–0 at Comiskey Park.

JULY 5   The White Sox extend their streak of consecutive shutouts to three with a double-header sweep over the Indians at Comiskey Park. Juan Pizarro was the winning pitcher in the opener with a 2–0 decision. Joe Horlen won game two 5–0.

JULY 7

At Shea Stadium in New York, Al Lopez manages the American League to a 7–4 loss in the All-Star Game. The NL scored four runs in the ninth inning, the last three on a walk-off homer by Johnny Callison.

JULY 10

Joe Horlen pitches a two-hitter to defeat the Angels 6–1 in the second game of a double-header in Los Angeles. The only hits off Horlen were a double by Lenny Green in the third inning and a single by Felix Torres in the fifth. The White Sox also won the first game 7–4.

JULY 12

Pete Ward hits his third grand slam of the season by connecting off Orlando Pena during the White Sox seven-run eighth inning, which caps an 11–4 win over the Athletics in the second game of a double-header in Kansas City. The Sox also won the opener 3–1.

JULY 13

The White Sox trade Joe Cunningham and Frank Kreutzer to the Senators for Bill Skowron and Carl Bouldin.

JULY 19

Going to bat as a pinch-hitter with the White Sox trailing 2–1 in the 13th inning, Gary Peters smacks a two-run homer for a 3–2 win over the Athletics in the first game of a double-header at Comiskey Park. Peters failed at two bunt attempts before swinging away. The Sox also won the second game 4–3.

Peters had a 20–8 record and a 2.50 ERA in 274 innings in 1964. As a batter, he struck four homers in 120 at-bats. During his career, Peters hit 19 career home runs. As a member of the White Sox, Peters batted .212 with 15 homers in 599 at-bats.

JULY 25

The White Sox pick up a thrilling 13-inning, 6–5 win over the Twins at Comiskey Park. Ron Hansen's home run in the ninth tied the score 3–3. In the 12th inning, both teams scored, with the Sox tying the contest 4–4 with a single from Bill Skowron. Minnesota plated another run in the 13th. The Sox rallied with two tallies in the half, both crossing the plate on Mike Hershberger's bases-loaded single.

JULY 26

A walk-off single by reliever Eddie Fisher in the 12th beats the Twins 6–5 in the first game of a double-header at Comiskey Park. The Sox also won the second contest 3–0.

JULY 31

Juan Pizarro strikes out 14 batters during a 6–0 win over the Senators in Washington.

AUGUST 14

The White Sox score six runs in the first inning and three in the second to rout the Red Sox 11–1 in Boston.

AUGUST 17

In the first game of a four-game series against the Yankees at Comiskey Park, the White Sox win 2–1.

AUGUST 18

The White Sox score three runs in the eighth inning and one in the 10th to defeat the Yankees 4–3 at Comiskey Park. Floyd Robinson's homer tied the score. Mike Hershberger's walk-off single drove in the winning run.

AUGUST 19   The White Sox win their third in a row over the Yankees with a 4–2 decision at
                 Comiskey Park.

AUGUST 20   The White Sox complete a four-game sweep of the Yankees at Comiskey Park.
                 John Buzhardt pitched the shutout.

                 *At the conclusion of play on August 20, the White Sox were in first place, three
                 percentage points ahead of the Orioles. The Yankees were in third, four games
                 behind.*

AUGUST 25   Juan Pizarro pitches the White Sox to a 1–0 win over the Twins at Comiskey Park.
                 The winning run scored in the ninth inning on singles by Jim Landis, Floyd Robinson
                 and Ron Hansen.

SEPTEMBER 4   Trailing the Indians 5–4 in the bottom of the 10th at Comiskey Park, Pete Ward and
                 Bill Skowron hit back-to-back homers for a 6–5 victory.

SEPTEMBER 6   Gary Peters retires the first 19 batters to face him, but he loses 2–0 to the Indians in
                 the first game of a double-header at Comiskey Park on two runs in the ninth inning.
                 The White Sox bounced back to win the nightcap 3–2 in 13 innings.

SEPTEMBER 10   Ron Hansen homers on a 3–0 pitch in the 10th inning for a 2–1 win over the Twins
                 in Minnesota.

SEPTEMBER 12   The White Sox purchase Smoky Burgess from the Pirates.

                 *A rotund five-foot-eight and weighing in at 187 pounds, Burgess was a 37-year-
                 old catcher when acquired by the White Sox. He was no longer capable of
                 catching, except on an emergency basis, but he was proficient as a pinch-hitter.
                 Burgess became a fan favorite, and those at Comiskey Park looked forward to
                 seeing Smoky step to the plate with the game on the line. From 1964 through
                 1966, he had 149 at-bats for the White Sox and hit .295 with three homers and
                 40 RBIs. Burgess's 21 pinch-hits in 1966 is still the club record for a season.*

SEPTEMBER 15   A veteran and a rookie, each making their first appearance with the White Sox, come
                 through with keys hits in a 3–2 win over the Tigers in Detroit. Smoky Burgess hit a
                 pinch-hit homer in the eighth to tie the score 2–2. Making his major league debut,
                 Marv Staehle hit a pinch-single in the 10th to drive in the winning run.

                 *Staehle was born in the Chicago suburb of Oak Park. He played seven seasons
                 with the White Sox and batted .160 with only one extra-base hit in 81 at-bats.*

SEPTEMBER 16   The White Sox win 4–1 over the Tigers in Detroit.

                 *At the end of the day, the White Sox were tied for first place with the Orioles
                 with a record of 88–61. The Yankees were in third place, just one-half game and
                 one percentage point back of the co-leaders.*

SEPTEMBER 19   The White Sox pennant hopes receive a jolt with a 10-inning, 1–0 loss to the
                 Senators in Washington. Joe Horlen allowed only two hits through the first nine

innings before surrendering two hits in the 10th to lose the game. Bennie Daniels pitched the complete game for the Senators.

The loss left the White Sox in third place, two games from the top with 11 contests to play.

SEPTEMBER 22   The White Sox suffer another excruciating 1–0 loss to the Angels in Los Angeles. Al Lopez gambled by starting Bruce Howard, who was making his first major league start, in place of the slumping Juan Pizarro. Fred Newman pitched the shutout for the Angels.

The defeat left the Sox 3½ games behind the Yankees with nine games to play. The Orioles were second one game back.

OCTOBER 2   Five days after the release of the Warren Commission Report, which declared that Lee Harvey Oswald acted alone in the assassination of John F. Kennedy, the White Sox sweep the Athletics 3–2 and 5–4 at Comiskey Park.

With two days left in the season, the White Sox were two games behind the Yankees and still possessed a slim chance to win the pennant.

OCTOBER 3   Joe Horlen pitches a two-hitter to defeat the Athletics 7–0 at Comiskey Park. Dave Duncan collected both Kansas City hits with singles in the third and ninth innings.

The Yankees won the same day to clinch the pennant. The White Sox won their last nine games in 1964 but couldn't catch the Yanks, who won 15 of 17 from September 12 through September 30.

OCTOBER 4   On the last day of the season, Bruce Howard pitches a two-hitter to beat the Athletics 6–0 at Comiskey Park. The only Kansas City hits were singles by Bert Campaneris in the first inning and Larry Stahl in the seventh.

OCTOBER 15   The White Sox trade Rudy May to the Phillies for Bill Heath and Joel Gibson.

May was 20 years old when he was traded for two other minor league prospects who never panned out. He had a long productive career with four different clubs that lasted until 1983 and included 152 victories. May won 18 games for the Orioles in 1978 and led the AL in ERA in 1980 with the Yankees.

DECEMBER 1   A month after Lyndon Johnson defeats Barry Goldwater in the presidential election, the White Sox trade Ray Herbert to the Phillies for Danny Cater. On the same day, the Sox traded Frank Baumann to the Cubs for Jimmie Schaffer.

1965

Season in a Sentence

The White Sox look like sure pennant winners after winning 23 of their first 31 games to take a 4½-game lead, but Al Lopez finishes in his accustomed position of second place and resigns as manager in November.

Finish • Won • Lost • Pct • GB

Second   95   67   .586   7.0

Manager

Al Lopez

Stats

Stats	WS	AL	Rank
Batting Avg:	.246	.242	4
On-Base Pct:	.317	.314	3
Slugging Pct:	.364	.369	6
Home Runs:	125		7 (tie)
Stolen Bases:	50		7
ERA:	2.99		2
Fielding Avg:	.980	.978	4
Runs Scored:	647		5
Runs Allowed:	555		1

Starting Lineup

Johnny Romano, c
Bill Skowron, 1b
Don Buford, 2b
Pete Ward, 3b
Ron Hansen, ss
Danny Cater, lf
Ken Berry, cf
Floyd Robinson, rf
Tommy McCraw, 1b-lf-cf
J. C. Martin, c

Pitchers

Joe Horlen, sp
Tommy John, sp-rp
John Buzhardt, sp
Gary Peters, sp
Bruce Howard, sp
Juan Pizarro, sp
Eddie Fisher, rp
Hoyt Wilhelm, rp
Bob Locker, rp

Attendance

1,130,519 (third in AL)

Club Leaders

Club Leaders		
Batting Avg:	Don Buford	.283
On-Base Pct:	Don Buford	.358
Slugging Pct:	Bill Skowron	.424
Home Runs:	Bill Skowron	18
	Johnny Romano	18
RBIs:	Bill Skowron	78
Runs:	Don Buford	93
Stolen Bases:	Don Buford	17
Wins:	Tommy John	14
Strikeouts:	Tommy John	126
ERA:	Eddie Fisher	2.40
Saves:	Eddie Fisher	24

JANUARY 20   In a three-team deal, the White Sox trade Jim Landis, Mike Hershberger and Fred Talbot to the Athletics for Rocky Colavito, then ship Colavito and Cam Carreon to the Indians for Johnny Romano, Tommy John and Tommie Agee.

Most White Sox fans were outraged by the trade, believing that the club should have kept Colavito instead of passing him on to Cleveland. At the time of the deal, Romano was considered to be a player who would solve the White Sox's significant weakness at the catching position. John and Agee, however, were young players who had struggled in brief appearances in the big leagues. The trade turned out to be one of the best in White Sox history, however, as John and Agee developed into All-Stars. John had an 82–80 record with the White Sox, but his won-lost record was not reflective of his abilities. John posted an ERA below the league average in six of his seven seasons in Chicago and twice led the AL in shutouts. Fine efforts frequently went unrewarded because of the White Sox's pop-gun offense of the period. The 1967 season was an example. John posted a 2.47 ERA and threw six shutouts, but would up with a 10–13 record. Agee was the Rookie of the Year in 1966 and appeared in the All-Star

Game in each of his two full seasons with the White Sox. Romano gave the White Sox two solid seasons before being dealt to the Cardinals.

APRIL 13   Five weeks after the first combat troops arrive in Vietnam, the White Sox win the season opener 5–3 over the Orioles in Baltimore. Gary Peters was the winning pitcher.

APRIL 15   The White Sox lose the home opener 3–1 to the Senators before 18,283 at Comiskey Park. The score was 1–1 when Hoyt Wilhelm entered the game in the ninth inning, faced only two batters and gave up homers to Frank Howard and Willie Kirkland.

APRIL 17   Ken Berry drives in both runs during a 2–1 win over the Senators in 10 innings at Comiskey Park. Berry hit a sacrifice fly in the fourth inning and a walk-off single in the 10th.

APRIL 18   Danny Cater collects six hits in eight at-bats during a double-header against the Senators at Comiskey Park. The White Sox won the opener 5–1 and dropped the nightcap 4–1.

Cater collected nine hits in his first 14 at-bats with the Sox.

APRIL 21   A two-run homer by Bill Skowron in the 11th inning beats the Red Sox 3–1 in Boston.

APRIL 25   Pete Ward is injured in an auto accident on the way to a Chicago Blackhawks Stanley Cup playoff game.

Ward was in a car with Tommy John and two White Sox investors when the vehicle was rear-ended by another motorist. Ward didn't believe he was hurt and went to Chicago Stadium to watch the game. He woke up the next morning with a stiff neck, but he still didn't think that anything serious was amiss and kept on playing. Over the following months, however, the condition grew worse. Ward was only 25 on the day of the accident and was never again the same player. In 1963 and 1964 combined, he hit .289 with 45 home runs in 1,189 at-bats. From 1965 through the end of his career at the age of 31, Ward accumulated 1,900 at-bats and batted just .234 with 53 homers.

MAY 17   The White Sox extend their winning streak to eight games with a 13–2 rout of the Athletics in Kansas City.

MAY 18   The White Sox winning streak reaches nine games with a 5–4 decision over the Athletics in Kansas City.

The win gave the White Sox a 23–8 record and a 4 1/2-game lead over second-place Minnesota. The Sox were still in first place on June 28, but they soon sank out of the pennant race and were 53–45 on July 30. The Twins won the first AL pennant for the franchise since 1933, when the club was located in Washington.

MAY 31   Don Buford hits a homer in the 10th inning to defeat the Indians 4–3 in the first game of a double-header at Municipal Stadium. Cleveland won the second contest by the same 4–3 score.

Buford hit .283 with 10 homers in 1965. He was originally signed as an outfielder by the White Sox in 1960, but by the time he reached the majors in 1963, the club had converted him to third base and later to second after the trade of Nellie Fox.

JUNE 4   Danny Cater and Floyd Robinson each hit home runs in the 15th inning to break up a terrific pitcher's duel and lift the White Sox to a 2–0 win over the Yankees in New York. Joe Horlen (nine innings) and Eddie Fisher (six innings) combined on the shutout. Fisher allowed only one hit.

Fisher was outstanding in 1965, pitching 82 games in relief totaling 165$\frac{1}{3}$ innings. He had a 15–7 record, 24 saves and a 2.40 ERA. Fisher was also instrumental in keeping the bullpen loose with his humorous impersonation of Donald Duck. He was asked to perform it on the radio with Bob Elson and on TV with Jack Brickhouse. Fans often stopped Fisher on the street and asked him to speak as the famous cartoon character.

JUNE 6   The White Sox lose 6–1 and 12–0 to the Yankees in New York. Tom Tresh hit three home runs in the first game.

JUNE 8   In the first amateur free-agent draft in baseball history, the White Sox select catcher Ken Plesha from Notre Dame.

Plesha was a complete bust and never rose higher than Class A ball. The first draft yielded little. The only future major leaguers chosen were Fred Rath (fourth round), Ron Lolich (tenth), Paul Edmondson (21st) and Danny Lazar (31st). None had a big-league career lasting longer than three seasons.

JUNE 20   Pete Ward hits a walk-off homer on the first pitch of the 10th inning to defeat the Red Sox 4–3 at Comiskey Park.

JUNE 26   Shortstop Ron Hansen commits three errors, which contribute to a 14-inning, 2–0 loss to the Orioles at Comiskey Park, wasting excellent pitching from Gary Peters (9$\frac{2}{3}$ innings) and Eddie Fisher (4$\frac{1}{3}$ innings).

JUNE 27   Hoyt Wilhelm retires all 15 batters he faces in a double-header against the Orioles at Comiskey Park, as the White Sox sweep 6–2 and 4–0. Wilhelm pitched three innings in the opener and two in the nightcap.

JUNE 28   The White Sox score seven runs in the sixth inning and defeat the Twins 17–4 in Minnesota. The Sox trailed 3–0 in the fifth inning when Tommy McCraw blasted a grand slam off Dave Boswell.

JULY 4   A fifth-inning home run by Ken Berry off George Brunet beats the Angels 1–0 in Los Angeles. Tommy John (8$\frac{1}{3}$ innings) and Eddie Fisher ($\frac{2}{3}$ of an inning) combined on the shutout.

JULY 8   The White Sox trade Jimmie Schaffer to the Mets for Frank Lary.

JULY 13   At Metropolitan Stadium in Bloomington, Minnesota, Al Lopez manages the American League to a 6–5 loss in the All-Star Game.

Lopez managed five All-Star Games, and the American League lost all five. He led the AL squad in 1955, both games in 1960, and in 1964 and 1965.

JULY 14   The White Sox score three runs in the 12th inning, then hold off the Indians in the bottom half to win 12–10 in Cleveland. The Sox led 5–0 in the fifth inning, fell behind 8–6 in the seventh and scored three in the ninth to take a 9–8 advantage, only to have Cleveland send the contest into extra innings with a tally in their turn at bat.

JULY 24   Pete Ward collects five hits, including a double, in five at-bats, but the White Sox lose 7–4 to the Tigers in Detroit.

JULY 25   Trailing 4–1, the White Sox score eight runs in the sixth inning and defeat the Tigers 10–6 in the first game of a double-header in Detroit. Johnny Romano hit a grand slam off Juan Navarro. The Tigers won the second tilt 13–2.

JULY 29   Johnny Romano hits two homers and drives in five runs during a 9–4 win over the Indians in Cleveland.

Romano batted .242 and clubbed 18 homers in 1965. His 18 homers led the club. Bill Skowron also clubbed 18. Six others reached double-digits in home runs, including Floyd Robinson (14), Danny Cater (14), Ken Berry (12), Ron Hansen (11), Don Buford (10) and Pete Ward (10).

AUGUST 1   Joe Horlen pitches the White Sox to a 1–0 win over the Tigers in the first game of a double-header at Comiskey Park. Ron Hansen drove in the lone run with a sacrifice fly in the second inning. The Sox lost game two 2–1.

AUGUST 2   A two-run single by Pete Ward off Denny McLain in the first inning produces the only runs of a 2–0 win over the Tigers at Comiskey Park. Gary Peters ($7^1/_3$ innings) and Hoyt Wilhelm ($1^2/_3$ innings) combined on the shutout.

AUGUST 11   Juan Pizarro pitches a one-hitter for a 7–0 win over the Senators in the second game of a double-header at Comiskey Park. The only Washington hit was a single in the fifth inning by Woodie Held. The Sox lost the first game 5–2.

AUGUST 20   The Beatles perform at Comiskey Park during their second of three American tours. In 1964, the Fab Four played at the International Amphitheater.

AUGUST 22   The White Sox extend their winning streak to 10 games with an 8–3 and 2–1 sweep of the Athletics in Kansas City.

The streak caused a brief flurry of excitement in Chicago. The Sox had a 71–50 record and were $5^1/_2$ games behind the Twins.

AUGUST 23   Juan Pizarro strikes out 13 batters in 10 innings, but gets a no-decision as the White Sox lose 2–1 in 10 innings to the Orioles at Comiskey Park.

AUGUST 25   The White Sox purchase Gene Freese from the Pirates.

AUGUST 29   The White Sox sweep the Red Sox by identical 3–2 scores during a double-header at Comiskey Park. The first game went 14 innings. J. C. Martin drove in the winning run with a sacrifice fly.

SEPTEMBER 6   The White Sox sweep the Angels 2–1 in 10 innings and 4–3 during a double-header at Comiskey Park.

The Sox ended the day 4¹/₂ games behind Minnesota with 22 games left on the schedule. The Twins came to Chicago on September 8 and swept both games of a two-game series, virtually ending the Sox's chances for a pennant.

SEPTEMBER 28   Danny Cater hits a walk-off homer in the 11th inning to defeat the Tigers 4–3 in the first game of a double-header at Comiskey Park. Detroit won the second game by the same 4–3 score.

OCTOBER 2   Bruce Howard pitches a two-hitter to defeat the Athletics 12–0 at Comiskey Park. The only Kansas City hits were singles by Bert Campaneris in the sixth inning and Jose Tartabull in the seventh.

NOVEMBER 4   Al Lopez resigns as manager of the White Sox and accepts a position with the club as a vice president carrying out "special assignments."

Lopez was 57 years old when he stepped down and said he desired to spend more time with his family. He had managed 15 seasons in the majors, nine of them with the White Sox, and was also frustrated and worn down by an inability to take a club to a world championship. The Yankees won 14 pennants in 16 seasons from 1949 through 1964, and Al Lopez's teams were the only ones to break the streak. Lopez won the AL title with the Indians in 1954 and with the Sox in 1959. On both occasions, however, his clubs lost in the World Series, winning only two games while losing eight. During the Yankees' period of dominance from the late 1940s through the mid-1960s, Lopez finished second to the New York club nine times, falling short in 1951, 1952, 1953, 1955 and 1956 in Cleveland and 1957, 1958, 1963 and 1964 in Chicago. The 1965 season was particularly galling. The Yankees dynasty had finally collapsed and the team slipped all the way to sixth place. Yet, Lopez and the White Sox failed to take advantage and ended the year second to the Twins. It was Al's 10th second-place finish in 15 years.

DECEMBER 15   The White Sox hire 50-year-old Eddie Stanky as manager.

The Cubs create a stir on October 25, 1965, by luring Leo Durocher out of retirement to manage the club. The White Sox countered by hiring Eddie Stanky, one of Durocher's former players. Branch Rickey once said that Stanky "can't hit, he can't run, he can't throw. He can't do a thing except beat you." Stanky played in the majors for 11 seasons and was the starting second baseman in the World Series with the Dodgers in 1947, the Braves in 1948 and the Giants in 1951. He previously managed the Cardinals from 1952 through 1955. Stanky managed the White Sox until July 1968 and was almost always at the center of controversy as a result of his feisty and combative nature. He managed to alienate nearly every opposing player and manager, along with the Chicago-area sportswriters and most of the players on his own ball club.

1966

Season in a Sentence

Under new manager Eddie Stanky, the White Sox struggle to score runs and finish fourth with their worst winning percentage since 1950.

Finish • Won • Lost • Pct • GB

Fourth   83   79   .512   15.0

Manager

Eddie Stanky

Stats

Stats	WS	AL	Rank
Batting Avg:	.231	.240	10
On-Base Pct:	.299	.308	7
Slugging Pct:	.331	.369	10
Home Runs:	87		9
Stolen Bases:	153		1
ERA:	2.68		1
Fielding Avg:	.976	.978	9
Runs Scored:	574		7 (tie)
Runs Allowed:	517		1

Starting Lineup

Johnny Romano, c
Tom McCraw, 1b
Al Weis, 2b
Don Buford, 3b
Jerry Adair, ss-2b
Ken Berry, lf
Tommie Agee, cf
Floyd Robinson, rf
Bill Skowron, 1b
Pete Ward, lf
Lee Elia, ss
Wayne Causey, 2b
J. C. Martin, c

Pitchers

Tommy John, sp
Gary Peters, sp
Joe Horlen, sp
Bruce Howard, sp
John Buzhardt, sp
Jack Lamabe, sp-rp
Bob Locker, rp
Hoyt Wilhelm, rp
Dennis Higgins, rp
Juan Pizarro, rp

Attendance

990,016 (sixth in AL)

Club Leaders

Batting Avg:	Tommie Agee	.273
On-Base Pct:	Tommie Agee	.326
Slugging Pct:	Tommie Agee	.447
Home Runs:	Tommie Agee	22
RBIs:	Tommie Agee	86
Runs:	Tommie Agee	98
Stolen Bases:	Don Buford	51
Wins:	Tommy John	14
Strikeouts:	Tommy John	138
ERA:	Gary Peters	1.98

MARCH 5   The Major League Players Association hires Marvin Miller to be the new executive director of the organization. Miller formally took office on July 1. Under Miller's leadership, the association would take actions that led to a revolution in player-owner relations, including free agency beginning in 1976.

APRIL 11   The White Sox open the season with a 14-inning, 3–2 victory over the Angels at Comiskey Park before a crowd of 28,175 at Comiskey Park. Tommie Agee tied the score 2–2 with a two-run homer in the seventh. The winning run crossed the plate on a bases-loaded single by Tommy McCraw. Tommy John was the Chicago starting pitcher. Bob Locker, Eddie Fisher, Dennis Higgins and Juan Pizarro combined for eight innings of shutout relief.

Agee was 23 years old on Opening Day and won the AL Rookie of the Year Award in 1966, with a .273 batting average, 22 homers, 86 RBIs, 98 runs scored and 44 stolen bases.

APRIL 19   The White Sox play the Angels in Anaheim for the first time, and win 3–1 at Anaheim Stadium.

APRIL 29   The White Sox stop the Indians' 10-game, season-opening winning streak with a 4–1 victory in Cleveland.

The victory gave the White Sox a 10–3 record, but the club lost six of their next seven and hovered around the .500 mark for most of the season.

MAY 7   Tommy John pitches the White Sox to a 1–0 win over the Tigers at Comiskey Park. J. C. Martin drove in the lone run of the game with a single in the sixth inning.

The White Sox in 1966 were the first major league club to require their catchers to wear helmets behind the plate. The original protective head gear for the club's receivers were ordinary batting helmets with the peaks sawed off.

MAY 8   Gates Brown hits a two-run double off Bob Locker in the 11th inning as the Tigers beat the White Sox 3–1 at Comiskey Park.

After the game, Detroit sports writer Watson Spoelestra asked Eddie Stanky what pitch Locker threw to Brown. Stanky jumped into an explosive tirade directed at the writer when asked the innocuous question. The Sox manager performed a "strip tease" by ripping his jersey to shreds and threw his clothes one by one across the clubhouse, climaxing the display by slamming his spikes into a wall. The scene set the stage for a hostile relationship between Stanky and the media. He seemed to delight in delivering sarcastic answers to what he deemed to be "stupid" questions. As a result, Chicago writers criticized Stanky in print at every opportunity.

MAY 14   The White Sox clobber the Tigers 13–3 in Detroit.

The White Sox began the season by playing "God Bless America" prior to games at Comiskey Park instead of the National Anthem, inciting complaints from many fans. The club polled fans as to which music selection they would like to hear, and the "Star Spangled Banner" was the winner by a 5–1 margin. On May 20, the first home game following the poll, Mitch Miller of the popular television series "Sing Along With Mitch" led the Comiskey Park fans in the singing of the National Anthem.

MAY 27   The White Sox trade Danny Cater to the Athletics for Wayne Causey.

MAY 29   Tommy John shuts out the Yankees 2–0 in New York.

MAY 30   The White Sox run their streak of consecutive shutouts to three with a 1–0 and 11–0 sweep of the Red Sox at Comiskey Park. John Buzhardt whitewashed Boston in the opener. Bill Skowron drove in the lone run of the game with a single in the seventh inning. Jack Lamabe pitched a one-hitter in the nightcap. The only hit off Lamabe was a single by Joe Foy in the eighth inning.

JUNE 3   Jack Lamabe pitches his second consecutive shutout, beating the Senators 8–0 at Comiskey Park with a three-hitter.

The back-to-back shutouts, in which he allowed only four hits, were the first two of his career. He pitched only one more shutout as a major leaguer, that one coming as a Cardinal in 1967. Lamabe finished his career with a 33–41 record and a 4.24 ERA. On June 13, the pitching staff had an earned run average of 2.22, but the club had a record of only 26–28 because of an insufficient offense.

JUNE 5   The White Sox sweep the Senators 4–1 and 12–0 at Comiskey Park. Gary Peters pitched a two-hitter in the second tilt. The only Washington hits were singles by Ken McMullen in the seventh inning and Frank Howard in the ninth.

From May 29 through June 5, the White Sox played 10 games in eight days, with the pitchers hurling six shutouts and allowing a total of only nine runs.

JUNE 7   In the first round of the amateur draft, the White Sox select outfielder Carlos May from Parker High School in Birmingham, Alabama.

May was an American League All-Star in 1969 and 1972 and had a 10-year big-league career, nine of them with the White Sox. His older brother Lee played in the big leagues from 1965 through 1982. Other future major leaguers chosen by the Sox in 1966 were Jim Magnuson (third round), Ken Frailing (fifth round), Charles Brinkman (16th round) and Art Kusyner (37th round).

JUNE 12   The White Sox trade Eddie Fisher to the Orioles for Jerry Adair and Johnny Riddle.

JUNE 16   Tommy McCraw drives in all five Chicago runs during a 5–2 win over the Athletics in the second game of a double-header at Comiskey Park. McCraw struck a grand slam in the third inning and a run-scoring single in the sixth, both off Ralph Terry. The White Sox also won the first game 6–4.

JULY 1   John Buzhardt (eight innings) and Bob Locker (five innings) combine to allow only four hits during a 2–1 win over the Red Sox at Comiskey Park.

With a league-leading 1.98 ERA, Gary Peters deserved better than a 12–10 record in 1966. He was a stalwart of the Sox rotation throughout the 1960s.

JULY 30   Two weeks after the bodies of eight student nurses, murdered by Richard Speck, are found in Chicago, Gary Peters uses only 75 pitches to defeat the Yankees 6–0 at Comiskey Park. Peters faced 29 batters and pitched a three-hitter.

Peters led the AL in ERA in 1966 with a 1.98 mark, but a lack of batting support led to a 12–10 record.

AUGUST 12   The White Sox win their eighth game in a row with a 1–0 decision over the Angels at Comiskey Park. Tommy John pitched the shutout.

The star of the winning streak was Johnny Romano, who hit six homers in seven games from August 3 to August 11.

AUGUST 28   The White Sox win a pair of extra-inning games against the Twins in the first game of a double-header at Comiskey Park. The Sox won the opener 4–3 in 15 innings and the nightcap 7–6 in 11. In game one, Minnesota took a 3–1 lead in the 11th, but the Sox tied it on consecutive singles by Pete Ward, Wayne Causey, Smoky Burgess and Jerry Adair. With two out in the 15th, Tommie Agee struck a bases-loaded single to produce the winning run. The second tilt ended on a walk-off home run by Jerry Adair.

AUGUST 29   A two-run homer by Tommie Agee off Gary Bell in the sixth inning beats the Indians 2–0 at Comiskey Park. Tommy John pitched the shutout.

SEPTEMBER 9   The White Sox outlast the Senators 1–0 in 10 innings at Comiskey Park. Washington pitcher Pete Richert allowed only one hit through the first nine innings. In the 10th the Sox scored on a Tommie Agee double, a walk to Bill Skowron, a wild pick-off throw by Richert that advanced both runners and an error by third baseman Ken McMullen. Gary Peters (three innings), Joe Horlen (six innings) and Hoyt Wilhelm (one inning) combined on the shutout.

SEPTEMBER 10   The White Sox win 1–0 over the Senators at Comiskey Park for the second day in a row behind a two-hitter by Bruce Howard. The only Washington hits were singles by Dick Nen in the second inning and Paul Casanova in the eighth. The lone run scored in the sixth inning on a double by Ken Berry and a single by Tommie Agee.

SEPTEMBER 17   The White Sox end a 3–1 win over the Orioles at Memorial Stadium with a bizarre triple play. Dave Johnson opened the Baltimore ninth with a double, but he could only reach third base on a bloop double by Paul Blair. When Andy Etchebarren grounded out, Blair broke for third, only to find Johnson in possession of the bag. Blair retreated, was caught in a rundown and was tagged out as Johnson broke for the plate. On the throw home, where pitcher Tommy John was covering, Johnson was nailed for the third out.

SEPTEMBER 22   A crowd of 413, the smallest in Yankee Stadium history, watches the White Sox beat the Yankees 4–1.

A lack of attendance at Comiskey Park was also a problem in 1966. The White Sox drew 990,016 fans, the lowest total since 1958 and the second lowest since 1950. Eddie Stanky revived the "Go-Go" atmosphere that captivated fans during the 1950s, as the team stole 153 bases, which led the majors and was the most by the club since 1943. But the 1966 Sox were second-to-last in home runs with 87. Fans had become bored by the low-scoring affairs at Comiskey Park, especially in contrast to the frequent long-ball shootouts at Wrigley Field, a few miles to the north. The deep fences were the major factor in the low scores, but club management bears much of the responsibility. In order to help the pitching staff and inhibit enemy sluggers, the White Sox stored game balls for up to six months in the dank and damp underbelly of Comiskey Park. The practice began in 1965. By the time the balls were used, the storage boxes in which they were contained had become so mildewed that they fell apart when touched. To fool the umpires and opposing clubs, the White Sox placed the damp balls into new boxes. The club also watered down the area in front of the plate until it had the consistency of a swamp and let the infield grass grow high in order to slow down ground balls when White Sox sinkerball pitchers were on the mound. When a sinkerballer was pitching for the opposition, the dirt in front of the plate was mixed with clay and burned with gasoline. On orders from Eddie Stanky, the opposing team's bullpen mounds were lowered or raised from the standard height to upset the pitcher's rhythm.

SEPTEMBER 27   The White Sox edge the Red Sox 1–0 in the first game of a double-header at Comiskey Park. The lone run scored on a single by Ken Berry. Joe Horlen (eight innings) and Hoyt Wilhelm (one inning) combined on the shutout. Boston won the second tilt 2–1.

OCTOBER 12   The White Sox trade Juan Pizarro to the Pirates for Wilbur Wood.

After winning 19 games in 1964, Pizarro struggled for two years before being dealt to the Pirates in exchange for a 25-year-old pitcher who spent the entire 1966 season in the minors. Wood spent parts of five seasons with the Red Sox and Pirates from 1961 through 1975 and posted a 1–8 record and a 4.18 ERA. Using a knuckleball that put less strain on his arm than his hard-throwing mound contemporaries, Wood was the workhorse of the Sox staff for nearly a decade, first in the bullpen and then in the starting rotation. He led the AL in games pitched in 1968 (88 games), 1969 (76) and 1970 (77). Chuck Tanner converted Wood into a starter in 1971, and Wilbur pitched 334 innings that season, followed by 376^{2}/$_{3}$ in 1972, 359^{1}/$_{3}$ in 1973, 320 in 1974 and 291^{1}/$_{3}$ in 1975. Often pitching on two days' rest, Wood averaged 44.8 starts per year during those five seasons, peaking at 49 in 1972. He won 20 or more games four seasons in a row, with 24 in both 1972 and 1973. On the all-time White Sox lists, Wood ranks fifth in wins (163), third in games pitched (578), fourth in strikeouts (1,332), fifth in innings pitched (2,524^{1}/$_{3}$), sixth in games started (286), sixth in saves (57) and 10th in shutouts (24).

DECEMBER 14   The White Sox trade Johnny Romano to the Cardinals for Walt Williams and Don Dennis.

DECEMBER 15   The White Sox trade Floyd Robinson to the Reds for Jim O'Toole.

1967

Season in a Sentence

Despite a "sockless" offense that outscores only one team in the league, the White Sox lead a thrilling four-team pennant race for 92 days before losing their last five games to finish in fourth place.

Finish • Won • Lost • Pct • GB

Fourth   89   73   .549   3.0

Manager

Eddie Stanky

Stats

Stats	WS	AL	Rank
Batting Avg:	.225	.236	9
On-Base Pct:	.293	.305	9
Slugging Pct:	.320	.351	9
Home Runs:	89		9
Stolen Bases:	124		2
ERA:	2.45	3.23	1
Fielding Avg:	.979	.979	4
Runs Scored:	531		9
Runs Allowed:	491		1

Starting Lineup

J. C. Martin, c
Tom McCraw, 1b
Wayne Causey, 2b
Don Buford, 3b
Ron Hansen, ss
Pete Ward, lf
Tommie Agee, cf
Ken Berry, rf-lf-cf
Walt Williams, lf
Rocky Colavito, rf
Duane Josephson, c
Ken Boyer, 3b-1b

Pitchers

Joe Horlen, sp
Gary Peters, sp
Tommy John, sp
Bruce Howard, sp
Bob Locker, rp
Hoyt Wilhelm, rp
Don McMahon, rp
Bob Locker, rp
John Buzhardt, rp

Attendance

985,634 (sixth in attendance)

Club Leaders

Batting Avg:	Ken Berry	.241
	Don Buford	.241
On-Base Pct:	Pete Ward	.334
Slugging Pct:	Pete Ward	.392
Home Runs:	Pete Ward	18
RBIs:	Pete Ward	62
Runs:	Tommie Agee	73
Stolen Bases:	Don Buford	34
Wins:	Joe Horlen	19
Strikeouts:	Gary Peters	215
ERA:	Joe Horlen	2.06
Saves:	Bob Locker	20

APRIL 11   Three months after the Green Bay Packers defeat the Kansas City Chiefs in the first Super Bowl, the White Sox's scheduled season opener against the Red Sox in Boston is postponed by cold weather.

APRIL 12   The White Sox lost the opening game of the 1967 season 5–4 to the Red Sox in 40-degree weather in Boston. John Buzhardt was the starting pitcher for Chicago and put the White Sox in a 4–0 hole after three innings.

Red Rush joined Bob Elson in the White Sox radio booth in 1967.

APRIL 13   The White Sox erupt for five runs in the ninth inning to defeat the Red Sox 8–5 in Boston. A two-run double by Ron Hansen put Chicago into the lead.

APRIL 15   In the home opener, the White Sox lose 3–1 to the Senators before 18,388 at Comiskey Park.

Numbers appeared on the fronts of the White Sox jerseys for the first time in 1967. On the road uniforms, the name CHICAGO was featured in slanted script lettering with a wide underline flourish that also incorporated the White Sox nickname with small white lettering.

APRIL 16   The White Sox win a 16-inning marathon by a 4–3 score over the Senators in the second game of a double-header at Comiskey Park. The game ended on a bases-loaded walk to Jerry Adair. The Sox also won the opener 7–3.

APRIL 22   Joe Horlen pitches a two-hitter to defeat the Senators 1–0 in Washington. He held the opposition hitless until Cap Peterson singled with one out in the eighth inning. Paul Casanova singled in the ninth inning for the other Washington hit. The Sox also collected only two hits, one of them a second-inning home run by Tommie Agee off Phil Ortega.

Horlen had the best season of his career in 1967 with a 19–7 record. He led the AL in winning percentage (.731), earned run average (2.06), shutouts (six) and lowest opponents' on-base percentage (.253).

APRIL 28   A two-run walk-off single by Don Buford in the ninth inning beats the Indians 3–2 at Comiskey Park.

MAY 6   The White Sox trade Bill Skowron to the Angels for Cotton Nash.

Nash was a basketball star at the University of Kentucky and played in the NBA during the 1964–65 season with the Lakers and Warriors and in the ABA with the Kentucky Colonels in 1967–68. A six-foot-five-inch first baseman, he had three at-bats with the Sox and failed to collect a hit.

MAY 10   The White Sox wallop the Orioles 13–1 in Baltimore.

MAY 12   The White Sox collect only three hits, but defeat the Angels 1–0 at Comiskey Park. J. C. Martin drove in the lone run with a single in the fifth inning. Joe Horlen (8$\frac{1}{3}$ innings) and Bob Locker ($\frac{2}{3}$ of an inning) combined on the shutout.

MAY 13   Jim O'Toole pitches a 10-inning shutout while allowing only two hits to defeat the Angels 1–0 at Comiskey Park. Pete Ward led off the 10th with a double, moved to third on an error and scored on a sacrifice fly by Smoky Burgess. It was the White Sox's eighth win a row.

The shutout was O'Toole's first since 1964, his only one as a member of the White Sox and the last of 18 he threw as a major leaguer.

MAY 14   The White Sox extend their winning streak to 10 with a sweep of the Angels in a double-header at Comiskey Park by scores of 4–2 and 3–1. Gary Peters pitched a one-hitter in the second tilt and drove in two runs with a second-inning single that gave the Sox a 2–1 lead. Bill Skowron homered in the top of the second to account for the only California hit and run.

The wins gave the White Sox an 18–7 record and a 1$\frac{1}{2}$-game lead.

MAY 24   Tommy McCraw blasts three homers and drives in eight runs during a 14–1 win over the Twins in Minnesota. McCraw's first homer was struck off Dean Chance with a man on base in the fourth inning and gave the Sox a 2–1 lead. Chance was again the victim in the seventh when McCraw homered with two on base. The Sox scored seven times in the inning. McCraw closed his great offensive performance with a three-run blast in the ninth off Jim Kaat.

McCraw hit a career-high 11 home runs in 1967 and drove in 45 runs.

JUNE 3   The White Sox trade Jerry Adair to the Red Sox for Don McMahon and Bob Snow.

JUNE 4   With a bases-loaded single in the fourth inning, Ken Berry drives in both White Sox runs in a 2–0 victory over the Athletics in the first game of a double-header at Comiskey Park. Kansas City won the second contest 5–4.

JUNE 7   In the first round of the amateur draft, the White Sox select third baseman Don Haynes from Headland High School in East Point, Georgia.

Haynes never reached the majors, peaking at Class AAA. The 1967 draft was largely a wasted effort for the White Sox. The only future major leaguer drafted was sixth-rounder Dennis O'Toole, who played at DeLaSalle High School in Chicago. At the time he was drafted, his brother Jim was playing for the White Sox. Dennis reached the majors in 1969 at the age of 20, but he appeared in only 15 big-league games.

JUNE 8   Carl Yastrzemski collects six hits, including a homer and a double, in nine at-bats and makes three great catches in left field during a double-header against the White Sox at Comiskey Park. The White Sox won the first game 5–2 but lost the second 7–3.

Two days earlier, Eddie Stanky angered Yastrzemski and the Red Sox by saying that Yaz "was an All-Star, but only from the neck down."

JUNE 10   Gary Peters not only hurls a shutout, but collects a home run and a single during a 9–0 win over the Yankees in New York.

Peters had a 16–11 record and a 2.28 ERA in 260 innings in 1967.

JUNE 11   The White Sox move back into first place with a 2–1 and 3–2 sweep of the Yankees before 62,582 at Yankee Stadium.

The White Sox were in first place continually from June 11 through August 12. The club stayed on top despite an offense that ranked ninth in a 10-team league in runs (531), ninth in batting average (.225), ninth in slugging percentage (.220) and ninth in homers (89). No one with 200 or more at-bats hit higher than .241. Don Buford was the team leader in hits with 129 and no one accumulated 200 total bases. The pitching staff recorded a league-leading ERA of only 2.45, well ahead of the Twins, who ranked second at 3.14.

JUNE 12   A day after playing a double-header in New York, the White Sox travel to Washington and play a 22-inning marathon, only to lose 6–5 to the Senators on a night in which the game-time temperature was 90 degrees. The contest lasted six hours and 38 minutes. The Sox scored three times in the seventh inning to tie the score 4–4. Both teams plated runs in the 10th. From there, neither team crossed the plate until the bottom of the 22nd. John Buzhardt, who pitched eight innings of relief, allowed the winning run by loading the bases with one out, followed by a Paul Casanova single.

JUNE 15   Ken Berry runs his hitting streak to 20 games, but the White Sox lose 2–1 to the Red Sox in 11 innings in Boston.

> *On the same day, White Sox owner Arthur Allyn proposed a $50 million stadium-arena complex for the city of Chicago. The site Allyn suggested was in the downtown area, immediately south of the Loop, on the railroad air rights of the Dearborn station and its trackage area. It would encompass 50 acres. The gigantic complex, built on stilts, would include three separate venues. One would be designed for baseball seating 46,000, another for football and soccer, with a capacity of 60,000, and a third for basketball and hockey, which could handle 15,000. Target date for completion was 1972. Allyn continued to push for the athletic compound until he sold the White Sox in 1969, but his dream failed to materialize.*

JUNE 17   Joe Horlen runs his season record to 8–0 with a 1–0 win over the Yankees at Comiskey Park. Horlen pitched eight innings and Hoyt Wilhelm hurled the ninth. The lone run was driven in on a double by Walt Williams.

> *Going by the colorful nickname of "No Neck," Williams stood five-foot-six and weighed 190 pounds. With full-tilt hustle on the field and a fire hydrant-shaped physique, "No Neck" was a fan favorite during his six seasons with the White Sox from 1967 through 1972.*

JUNE 26   Ken Berry hits a two-run single in the ninth inning for a 5–4 win over the Orioles in Baltimore. He didn't start the game in his regular spot in left field because of an eye infection incurred during pre-game practice. Berry entered the contest in the eighth inning as a defensive replacement for Don Buford.

JUNE 28   Wayne Causey hits a three-run homer in the eighth inning to give the White Sox a 3–2 win over the Orioles in Baltimore. Causey was subbing at second base for Al Weis, who tore ligaments the previous day, which put him out of action for the rest of the season.

> *The win gave the White Sox a 42–26 record and a 5½-game lead in the American League pennant race.*

JULY 3   The White Sox lose a 13-inning, 1–0 decision to the Orioles at Comiskey Park.

JULY 4   Tommy John pitches a two-hitter to defeat the Orioles 4–0 at Comiskey Park. Luis Aparicio collected both Baltimore hits with a triple in the fourth inning and a single in the sixth.

JULY 7   Gary Peters (eight innings) and Hoyt Wilhelm (one inning) combine on a two-hitter to defeat the Twins 2–1 at Comiskey Park. The Minnesota tally scored on doubles by Cesar Tovar and Tony Oliva in the first inning. The two Chicago runs crossed the plate with one out in the ninth inning on an error by Twins shortstop Zoilo Versalles.

JULY 8   The White Sox edge the Twins 1–0 at Comiskey Park with a run in the ninth inning. Dick Kenworthy doubled, moved to third base on a sacrifice bunt and scored on a sacrifice fly by Wayne Causey. Tommy John pitched a three-hit shutout, with Tony Oliva collecting all three Minnesota hits.

JULY 11   At the All-Star Game at Anaheim Stadium in Anaheim, Gary Peters pitches three perfect innings (the sixth through the eighth) and fans four. Among his victims were Willie Mays and Roberto Clemente (both on strikeouts), Hank Aaron and Willie McCovey. The American League lost, however, 2–1 in 15 innings.

JULY 13   Gary Peters is the winning pitcher and scores the lone run in a 1–0 win over the Angels at Comiskey Park. In the sixth inning, he singled and scored on a double by Ken Berry. Peters pitched the first seven innings and Hoyt Wilhelm the final two.

JULY 22   The White Sox trade J. C. Martin to the Mets for Ken Boyer.

JULY 23   On the first day of rioting in Detroit that leaves 14 dead, the White Sox sweep the Athletics 8–4 and 1–0 in Kansas City. Gary Peters ($7^2/_3$ innings) and Hoyt Wilhelm ($1^1/_3$ innings) combined on the game-two shutout. The lone run of the game scored on a double by Jim King and a single from Ron Hansen in the second inning.

JULY 24   The White Sox play an exhibition game at County Stadium in Milwaukee and lose 2–1 to the Twins before a crowd of 51,144.

              Milwaukee became a major league baseball city in 1953 when the Braves moved there from Boston. The club set a National League attendance record in its first season in Wisconsin with a figure of 1,826,397, and drew over 2,000,000 each season from 1954 through 1957. Attendance soon declined, however, and the Braves moved to Atlanta following the 1965 season. The exhibition game was sponsored by 32-year-old Milwaukee businessman Bud Selig, who wanted to bring major league baseball back to Milwaukee. One of those intrigued was White Sox owner Arthur Allyn, who was having his own problems drawing fans into Comiskey Park (see October 30, 1967).

JULY 25   The White Sox win a thrilling double-header 3–1 and 6–5 over the Indians at Comiskey Park with a pair of walk-off homers. The opener was won in the ninth inning on a two-run shot from J. C. Martin. The second contest went 16 innings. Cleveland scored in the top of the 16th, but the Sox rallied in their half on a single by Ken Boyer and a homer by Ken Berry.

JULY 29   The White Sox trade Jim King and Marv Staehle to the Indians for Rocky Colavito.

              Colavito and Ken Boyer (see July 22, 1967) were acquired to add some veteran home run power to the lineup. Between them, the pair had been selected to 13 All-Star teams, but they were too far past their primes to be of much help to the Sox.

JULY 31   In his third game with the White Sox, Rocky Colavito hits a two-run homer in the 10th inning to beat his former Indians teammates 4–2 in Cleveland.

AUGUST 13   The Twins shove the White Sox out of first place with a 3–2 win over the Sox in Minnesota in a game highlighted by a controversial umpiring decision. In the ninth inning, Tommie Agee drilled a shot off the left-field wall. Agee tried for a triple on the play, but he was called out by umpire Bill Valentine. It appeared that Agee had the throw beaten, and Eddie Stanky and third base coach Grover Redsinger were both ejected during the ensuing argument.

Before the game, Eddie Stanky barred Vice President Hubert Humphrey from the Chicago clubhouse. "What do I want Humphrey for? Can he hit?" Stanky later asked.

AUGUST 15   The White Sox purchase Sandy Alomar Sr. from the Mets.

AUGUST 16   The White Sox wallop the Athletics 14–1 at Comiskey Park. Pete Ward contributed two homers and two singles.

AUGUST 21   The White Sox sell John Buzhardt to the Orioles.

AUGUST 25   Ken Berry drives in both White Sox runs during a 2–1 win over the Red Sox in the second game of a double-header at Comiskey Park. Berry homered in the fifth inning and hit a walk-off single in the ninth. Boston won the opener 7–1.

AUGUST 27   Gary Peters pitches an 11-inning complete game and beats the Red Sox 1–0 in the second game of a double-header at Comiskey Park. The lone run scored on a bases-loaded walk to Rocky Colavito from Darrell Brandon.

SEPTEMBER 6   The White Sox rally to beat the Angels 3–2 in 13 innings at Comiskey Park. The game was scoreless until California scored twice in the 11th. The Sox countered with two runs in their half and won in the 13th on a walk-off double by Ken Berry.

The day ended with the top four teams in the American League each exactly 17 games over .500. The White Sox and Twins were tied for first with a 78–61 record. The Tigers and Red Sox were one percentage point behind at 79–62.

SEPTEMBER 7   The idle White Sox drop from first place to third when the Twins and Red Sox both win.

SEPTEMBER 10   In the heat of 1967's thrilling four-team pennant race, Joe Horlen pitches a no-hitter to defeat the Tigers 6–0 in the first game of a double-header at

Joel Horlen's 19 victories paced the Sox in 1967 and helped keep the team in the pennant race. Horlen and teammate Gary Peters gave the Sox a formidable one-two pitching punch during the 1960s.

Comiskey Park. The White Sox entered the day in fourth place with a two-game losing streak and two games out of first. Horlen allowed only two batters to reach base. Bill Freehan was hit by a pitch in the third inning and Eddie Mathews reached on an error by first baseman Ken Boyer in the fifth. Detroit hit only two balls to the outfield, both on routine flies. Horlen struck out four batters and drove in a run with a single in the eighth inning. Jerry Lumpe led off the Tiger ninth inning and hit a sharp grounder up the middle. Second baseman Wayne Causey quickly moved to his right, backhanded the ball, whirled and threw Lumpe out at first on a close play that was argued by Detroit manager Mayo Smith. Bill Heath followed Lumpe and grounded out to third baseman Don Buford. Dick McAuliffe grounded out to shortstop Ron Hansen to seal Horlen's no-hitter. Horlen tossed his glove in the air as he leaped off the pitcher's mound. The Sox also won game two by a shutout with a 4–0 decision. Cisco Carlos (six innings), Hoyt Wilhelm (1$\frac{1}{3}$ innings) and Bob Locker (1$\frac{2}{3}$ innings) combined on the shutout.

SEPTEMBER 13   The White Sox outlast the Indians 1–0 in 17 innings at Comiskey Park. Gary Peters and Sonny Siebert were the starting pitchers, and each went 11 innings. Peters walked 10 men and hit a batter, but allowed only one hit, a triple by Joe Azcue in the third inning. Siebert surrendered just four Chicago hits. The 17th-inning rally started on a single by Ken Boyer, who was removed for pinch-runner Buddy Bradford. Bradford moved to second on a passed ball and, after Tommy McCraw was issued an intentional walk, Rocky Colavito singled. The three Sox relievers who completed the shutout after Peters left the contest were Bob Locker (two innings), Roger Nelson (three innings) and Don McMahon (one inning).

In 11 games from September 11 through September 24, the White Sox pitching staff allowed 17 runs in 109 innings.

SEPTEMBER 14   A walk-off grand slam by Don Buford off Orlando Pena in the 10th inning accounts for the only runs in a 4–0 win over the Athletics at Comiskey Park. It was the second game in a row that the White Sox won despite failing to score a run through the first nine innings. Cisco Carlos pitched the shutout.

The shutout was the only complete game of Carlos's career. He was nearly 27 when he made his major league debut on August 25, 1967. Carlos was a surprise sensation during the pennant race, with a 2–0 record and an ERA of 0.86 in 41$\frac{2}{3}$ innings. He was never consistently effective again, however, posting a 9–18 record and a 4.33 earned run average over the remainder of his career.

SEPTEMBER 15   In his first start since pitching a no-hitter, Joe Horlen allows only three hits in a 7–3 win over the Twins at Comiskey Park.

During his last 64 innings pitched in 1967, Horlen allowed only 33 hits and seven earned runs in 64 innings for an ERA of 0.99.

SEPTEMBER 16   The White Sox score four runs in the ninth inning to beat the Twins 5–4 at Comiskey Park. The rally consisted of four singles, two intentional walks and an error. The contest ended on a single by Pete Ward.

SEPTEMBER 17   The White Sox complete a three-game sweep of the Twins with a 4–0 win over the Twins at Comiskey Park. Gary Peters pitched the shutout.

At the conclusion of play on September 17, the White Sox were in second place one-half game back of the Tigers.

SEPTEMBER 26   The White Sox-Athletics clash in Kansas City is rained out.

At the conclusion of play on September 26, the Twins were in first place with a 91–68 record. The Red Sox were a game back at 90–69. The White Sox were 89–68, one game behind, with the Tigers at 89–69, 1¹/₂ games out. Chicago's next two games were against the A's, a club with a 60–96 record and 11 losses in their last 12 games heading into the series.

SEPTEMBER 27   The pennant hopes of the White Sox receive a stunning blow with a 5–2 and 4–0 double-header loss to the Athletics in Kansas City. The day has gone down in Sox lore as "Black Wednesday." Had the Sox won both games against the lowly A's, they would have taken sole possession of first place, as the Tigers were idle and the Red Sox and Twins both lost. Joe Horlen and Gary Peters, who ranked first and second in the American League in earned run average, were the starting pitchers. Horlen was gunning for his 20th win of the season. The games also marked the final two played by the Athletics in Kansas City. The A's moved to Oakland following the end of the season.

Following the debacle against the Athletics, the Sox played three games versus the Senators in Washington. The Senators were 73–85 and had lost 15 of their previous 24 games.

SEPTEMBER 29   The White Sox are eliminated from the pennant race with a 1–0 loss to the Senators at Comiskey Park. The lone run was unearned and scored in the first inning. Washington's Tim Cullen was safe at first base when first baseman Tommy McCraw dropped a throw from third baseman Ken Boyer. Hank Allen forced Cullen, but second baseman Don Buford threw wildly to first trying for the double play. Allen scored on a single by Fred Valentine. Tommy John was the hard-luck losing pitcher.

SEPTEMBER 30   The White Sox lose their third straight game by shutout, 4–0 to the Senators at Comiskey Park.

OCTOBER 1   The White Sox close the season with a five-game losing streak, dropping a 4–3 decision to the Senators at Comiskey Park. Joe Horlen lost his second chance at posting his 20th victory of the season. On the same day, the Red Sox defeated the Twins 5–3 in Boston to clinch the American League pennant.

OCTOBER 30   Arthur Allyn announces that the White Sox will play nine "home" games at County Stadium in Milwaukee in 1968.

The White Sox were at a crossroads at the end of the 1967 season, and Allyn made several moves that severely damaged the franchise for years. The Sox extended their streak of consecutive winning seasons to 17 in 1967, but the 1959 pennant was the only post-season appearance during that stretch. Attendance at Comiskey Park was an overriding issue. The Sox were in first place for 92 days and were involved in a thrilling pennant race until the final week, but drew only 985,634 fans at home, the sixth-best in the American League. Three years earlier, the White Sox attracted 1,230,053. Meanwhile, the Cubs in 1967 were in first place briefly in July and won 87 games, the most by the team since 1945. Wrigley Field was an exciting, happening place again and the Cubs drew 977,226, up from 635,891 in 1966. The overabundance of 1–0 and 2–1 games at cavernous Comiskey Park kept many fans away. Fans had become bored by low-scoring affairs, especially in contrast to the high-scoring games at Wrigley. In 1967, games at Wrigley averaged 8.4 runs per game, in comparison to just 5.7 per game at White Sox home games. There were fewer runs scored at Comiskey Park than any other American League ballpark in 1962, 1965, 1966, 1967 and 1968. Racial tensions and rioting that occurred across the country frightened many fans away from attending night games at Comiskey Park because of concerns about the safety of the surrounding neighborhood. The surprise announcement that the White Sox would play nine games in Milwaukee in 1968 further alienated Sox fans. The move was accompanied by rumors that the franchise would move to Wisconsin permanently. The White Sox also made a mistake by taking their telecasts off WGN-TV. Previously, WGN telecast both Chicago clubs and the two shared the same announcing team. No road games of either club were telecast at a time when the other club was playing at home. The White Sox moved to WFLD-TV in 1968, with Jack Drees and Dave Martin doing the play-by-play. The move hurt the Sox because WFLD was a UHF station at a time when many television sets couldn't pick up UHF channels. The signal from the station was so weak that many of those who could pick up the telecast had to attempt to watch the games through an almost impenetrable blanket of snow. Popular announcers Jack Brickhouse and Vince Lloyd, who had been handling the telecasts of both Chicago clubs, were now associated exclusively with the Cubs and helped reduce interest in the White Sox. Trades made by general manager Ed Short during the 1967–68 off-season also weakened the future of the White Sox. Promising players such as Don Buford and Tommie Agee were dealt for aging veterans Tommy Davis and Luis Aparicio in an attempt to push the Sox to the top of the league. The deals were a failure, as the White Sox slumped to a 67–95 record in 1968. By 1970, the Sox had a record of 56–106 and attracted only 495,355 fans while the Cubs drew 1,642,705. Only 10 years earlier, in 1960, the White Sox outdrew the Cubs 1,644,460 to 809,770.

NOVEMBER 29   The White Sox trade Don Buford, Bruce Howard and Roger Nelson to the Orioles for Luis Aparicio, Russ Snyder and John Matias.

Seventeen in a Row

The White Sox put together a streak of 17 consecutive winning seasons from 1951 through 1967, the third-longest in major league history.

Teams with 12 or more consecutive winning seasons

Team	Years	
New York Yankees	39	1926–64
Baltimore Orioles	18	1968–85
Chicago White Sox	17	1951–67
Boston Red Sox	16	1967–82
New York Yankees	16	1993–2008*
Pittsburgh Pirates	15	1899–1913
St. Louis Cardinals	15	1939–53
Atlanta Braves	15	1991–2005
Chicago Cubs	14	1926–39
Milwaukee/Atlanta Braves	14	1953–66
San Francisco Giants	14	1958–71
Chicago Cubs	13	1879–91
Brooklyn Dodgers	13	1945–57
Boston Braves	12	1888–99
Chicago Cubs	12	1903–14
New York Giants	12	1903–14

*Active at the end of the 2008 season

The White Sox were playing Buford out of position in the infield. Moved to left field by the Orioles, Don played in the World Series in 1969, 1970 and 1971. Aparicio was 33 when he was re-acquired by the Orioles, but he had three of the best offensive seasons of his career in his second engagement with the club.

DECEMBER 15   The White Sox trade Tommie Agee and Al Weis to the Mets for Tommy Davis, Jack Fisher, Billy Wynne and Dick Booker.

Following a trend established by the trade with the Orioles 16 days earlier, the White Sox traded established, rising young stars for veteran experience. Agee's numbers fell off in 1967 after his Rookie of the Year season of 1966. The Sox gave up on him too quickly. Agee and Weis were both key components on the Mets' 1969 World Series team. Davis won the NL batting title in 1962 and 1963, but was a huge disappointment in his only season with the White Sox, which came in the middle of an 18-year big league career.

1968   Sox

Season in a Sentence

The season begins with pennant aspirations, but those evaporate quickly with an 0–10 start, leading to the dismissal of Eddie Stanky and an eighth-place finish.

Finish • Won • Lost • Pct • GB

Eighth   67   95   .414   36.0
(tie)

Managers

Eddie Stanky (34–45), Les Moss (0–2), Al Lopez (6–5), Moss (12–22) and Lopez (15–21).

Stats

Stats	WS	AL	Rank
Batting Avg:	.228	.230	6
On-Base Pct:	.286	.300	10
Slugging Pct:	.311	.339	10
Home Runs:	71		10
Stolen Bases:	90		4 (tie)
ERA:	2.75	2.98	4
Fielding Avg:	.977	.978	7
Runs Scored:	463		10
Runs Allowed:	527		4

Starting Lineup

Duane Josephson, c
Tommy McCraw, 1b
Sandy Alomar, 2b
Pete Ward, 3b
Luis Aparicio, ss
Tommy Davis, lf
Ken Berry, cf
Buddy Bradford, lf-rf-cf
Jerry McNertney, c
Bill Voss, rf
Leon Wagner, rf
Tim Cullen, 2b

Pitchers

Joe Horlen, sp
Tommy John, sp
Jack Fisher, sp
Gary Peters, sp
Cisco Carlos, sp
Jerry Priddy, sp-rp
Wilbur Wood, rp
Hoyt Wilhelm, rp
Bob Locker, rp

Attendance

803.775 (ninth in AL)

Club Leaders

Batting Avg:	Tommy Davis	.268
On-Base Pct:	Pete Ward	.354
Slugging Pct:	Tommy McCraw	.375
Home Runs:	Pete Ward	15
RBIs:	Pete Ward	50
	Tommy Davis	50
Runs:	Luis Aparicio	55
Stolen Bases:	Sandy Alomar	21
Wins:	Joe Horlen	12
Strikeouts:	Tommy John	117
ERA:	Tommy John	1.98
Saves:	Wilbur Wood	16

FEBRUARY 9   The White Sox trade Lee Thomas to the Astros for Tom Murray and Levi Brown.

FEBRUARY 13   The White Sox trade Ron Hansen, Dennis Higgins and Steve Jones to the Senators for Tim Cullen, Buster Narum and Bob Priddy.

MARCH 26   The White Sox sell Rocky Colavito to the Dodgers.

APRIL 9   The season opener against the Indians at Comiskey Park is postponed to avoid conflict with the funeral of Dr. Martin Luther King Jr., who was murdered in Memphis on April 4.

APRIL 10   The White Sox lose 9–0 to the Indians in the season opener before a slim crowd of 7,756 at Comiskey Park. Sonny Siebert pitched a two-hit shutout.

APRIL 25   The White Sox record falls to 0–10 with a 3–2 loss to the Twins in Minnesota.

Counting the five losses in succession at the end of the 1967 season, the White Sox lost 15 regular season games in a row. During the season-opening 10-game losing streak in 1968, the Sox scored only 13 runs with a team batting average of .193 in 321 at-bats, along with an on-base percentage of .255 and an abysmal slugging percentage of .252. The offensive woes weren't soon corrected. The club scored 34 runs in their first 18 contests, and 124 in the first 52. The Sox finished the year with 463 runs scored, an average of 2.86 per game, which represented the lowest figure in club history. No one on the 1968 club scored more than 55 runs or drove in more than 50.

APRIL 26   The White Sox finally win after starting the season with 10 straight defeats, defeating the Twins 3–2 in Minnesota.

The White Sox fought their way back to a 15–17 record by May 19, but ended up with a 67–95 mark, the first losing season by the franchise since 1950. It was also the first time since 1950 that the Cubs had a better record than the Sox. The Cubs were 84–78 in 1968.

MAY 1   Tommy John strikes out 12 batters during a 4–1 win over the Senators in Washington.

MAY 3   Tommy McCraw ties a major league record for first basemen with three errors in one inning during a 3–2 loss to the Yankees at Comiskey Park. McCraw's miscues in the third inning contributed to the three New York runs. McCraw first bobbled a grounder from Gene Michaels. Three batters later, Roy White grounded to McCraw, who let the ball slip out of his hands in an attempt to throw to the plate. McCraw, without looking, then tossed to first base, but no one was covering the bag, giving him two errors on one play.

MAY 4   Cisco Carlos (eight innings) and Bob Locker (one inning) combine on a two-hitter for a 4–1 win over the Yankees at Comiskey Park. Carlos allowed only one hit, a single by Mickey Mantle with one out in the seventh inning. The other New York hit was a double by Steve Whitaker off Locker in the ninth.

MAY 5

Gary Peters hits a grand slam off Al Downing in the fourth inning of a 5–1 win over the Yankees in the first game of a double-header at Comiskey Park. New York won the second tilt 4–1.

MAY 7

Tommy McCraw hits a grand slam off Sammy Ellis in the third inning of a 6–4 win over the Angels in Anaheim.

MAY 9

The White Sox play the Athletics in Oakland for the first time and win 4–2.

On the same day, White Sox pitcher Bob Priddy was injured checking his car engine while driving several of his teammates in a borrowed car in Oakland. The car stalled, and Priddy opened the hood to see what was wrong. His fingers were nicked by the fan blades, requiring stitches.

MAY 11

The White Sox edge the Athletics 1–0 in Oakland. The lone run scored in the third inning on a double by Luis Aparicio. Joe Horlen (6²/₃ innings), Wilbur Wood (two innings) and Bob Locker (¹/₃ of an inning) combined on the shutout.

MAY 15

The White Sox play a home game in Milwaukee for the first time and lose 4–2 to the Angels before a crowd of 23,510 at County Stadium.

The Sox played nine home games in Milwaukee in 1968, drawing 265,452 fans, an average of 29,505 per game. The nine games were played at night, with four on Monday, one on Tuesday, one on Wednesday, two on Thursday and one on Friday. At Comiskey Park, the Sox drew 538,323 for a total of 803,865.

MAY 17

The White Sox win 1–0 in 10 innings against the Athletics at Comiskey Park. The lone run scored on a triple by Tommy McCraw, his second of the game, and a two-out, pinch-hit single by Duane Josephson. Joe Horlen pitched the shutout.

MAY 24

The White Sox play 13 innings, only to lose 1–0 to the Yankees in New York.

MAY 25

The White Sox lose 1–0 in extra innings to the Yankees in New York for the second game in a row, this time in 10 innings.

MAY 26

Gary Peters bats sixth in the White Sox starting lineup in game lost 5–1 by the White Sox to the Yankees in New York. Peters hit ahead of Duane Josephson, Luis Aparicio and Tim Cullen. The Sox also lost the second game 7–6.

MAY 28

In conjunction with expansion to 12 teams, the American League owners vote to split the circuit into two divisions along with a postseason playoff to determine the champion beginning with the 1969 season. The two new clubs were the Kansas City Royals and the Seattle Pilots. The White Sox were placed in the Western Division with the Twins, Athletics, Angels, Royals and Pilots. The Sox were not enamored with the situation, since it would mean playing 27 games a season on the West Coast.

MAY 31

A bases-loaded squeeze bunt in the 14th by Luis Aparicio scores Dick Kenworthy from third base for the winning run in a 2–1 decision over the Twins at Comiskey Park.

JUNE 1   The White Sox outlast the Twins 1–0 at Comiskey Park. On his 27th birthday, Minnesota pitcher Dean Chance hurled hitless ball for 8⅓ innings. Bill Voss beat out an infield roller for the first hit. Tommy McCraw followed with another infield hit. Dick Kenworthy looped a short fly ball into right field to score the winning run. Cisco Carlos (six innings), Bob Locker (two innings) and Wilbur Wood (one inning) combined on the shutout.

JUNE 6   In the first round of the amateur draft, the White Sox select shortstop Billy McKinney from Ohio University.

> *McKinney played in 341 big-league games and batted only .225. The White Sox chose eight future major leaguers in the June 1968 draft, but none reached stardom. In addition to McKinney, Hugh Yancy (second round), Lamar Johnson (third), Rich Moloney (14th) and Stan Perzanowski (16th) were picked in the regular phase. During the secondary phase, the club selected Bart Johnson, Ken Hottman and Daniel Neumeier.*

JUNE 9   The White Sox game against the Red Sox in Boston is postponed so as not to conflict with the funeral of Robert Kennedy, who was shot in Los Angeles on June 5 and died 25 hours later.

JUNE 11   Russ Snyder hits a grand slam off Bill Monbouquette in the third inning of a 9–5 win over the Yankees in New York.

> *Snyder stepped to the plate without a single RBI in 79 at-bats in 1968. He was traded two days later.*

JUNE 13   The White Sox trade Russ Snyder to the Indians for Leon Wagner.

> *Nicknamed "Daddy Wags," Wagner owned a clothing store with the slogan, "Get Your Rags at Daddy Wags." He hit 20 or more homers six consecutive seasons with the Angels and Indians from 1961 through 1966, but his power stroke was gone by the time he arrived in Chicago. Wagner hit just one home run in 162 at-bats with the Sox.*

JUNE 15   Ken Berry hits a grand slam off Joe Sparma in the fourth inning of a 7–4 win over the Tigers at Comiskey Park.

JUNE 30   Bill Voss hits a grand slam off Dennis Ribant in the third inning of a 12–0 triumph over the Tigers in Detroit. Tommy John pitched the shutout.

> *For much of the 1968 season, John was available to the White Sox only on weekends because he was serving with the Indiana Air National Guard.*

JULY 12   With the White Sox holding a 34–45 record, Al Lopez comes out of retirement to replace Eddie Stanky as manager of the White Sox.

> *Following the 1967 season, Stanky was given a four-year contract through 1971. But Stanky wasn't one to take losing well, and the 0–10 start of 1968 ate at him. Personal conflicts between Stanky and his players, which had been brewing for*

years, were magnified by the club's inability to win games. Petty fines were levied on players failing to advance runners, laying down a bunt and other various offenses which fueled the discontent. Angry and frustrated by the negative press surrounding the losing season, Stanky barred reporters from entering the clubhouse after games. The final straw came when he had his coaches dress in the same room as the players. It was perceived as spying on the manager's part. Despite owing money to Stanky for another 3½ seasons, Arthur Allyn and Ed Short decided to make a change. "I'm sorry if it's me," said Stanky. "But that's the way I am, and that's the way I do things. I'm not the sort to change my ways." Les Moss served as interim for one game until Al Lopez could arrive from his home in Tampa. Lopez, who had managed the club from 1957 through 1965, had been enjoying retirement, but was persuaded by Allyn and Short to help out the ball club. After just 11 games, Lopez was stricken with appendicitis and missed the next five weeks, with Moss again serving in an interim capacity. When Lopez returned, he restored calm and stability to the clubhouse, but couldn't return the Sox to their winning ways. He resigned for good 17 games into the 1969 season (see May 2, 1969).

JULY 17   The White Sox win 1–0 over the Orioles at Comiskey Park. The lone run came on a balk by Baltimore pitcher Tom Phoebus, which scored Tommy McCraw from third base. Joe Horlen (7⅓ innings), Wilbur Wood (one inning) and Hoyt Wilhelm (⅔ of an inning) combined on the shutout.

JULY 20   The White Sox trade Wayne Causey to the Angels for Woodie Held.

JULY 21   The White Sox trade Don McMahon to the Tigers for Dennis Ribant.

JULY 27   The White Sox edge the Angels 1–0 in Anaheim. The only run of the contest scored on a sacrifice fly by Sandy Alomar Sr. Bob Priddy (seven innings), Hoyt Wilhelm (one inning) and Wilbur Wood (one inning) combined on the shutout.

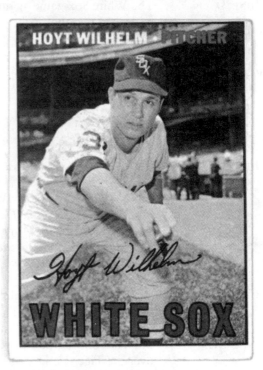

Already 40 years old in his first season with the White Sox, knuckle-balling reliever Hoyt Wilhelm gave the team six excellent years of service.

JULY 29   The White Sox explode for five runs in the 13th inning to defeat the Athletics 7–2 in Oakland.

JULY 31   Trailing 8–1, the White Sox score one run in the fifth inning, four in the sixth and six in the ninth to defeat the Twins 12–8 in Minnesota. The big blow was a three-run double by Tim Cullen that broke an 8–8 tie.

AUGUST 2   The White Sox trade Tim Cullen to the Senators for Ron Hansen.

Cullen and Hansen were traded for each other less than six months earlier (see February 13, 1968). Three days before the August 2 swap, Hansen pulled off an unassisted triple play for Washington against the Indians.

AUGUST 9   The White Sox defeat the Indians 1–0 at Comiskey Park. Tommy John (seven innings), Bob Locker (1²/₃ innings) and Hoyt Wilhelm (¹/₃ of an inning) combined on the shutout. John also scored the lone run of the game. In the fifth inning he singled, moved to second base on an error and scored on a double by Walt Williams.

AUGUST 20   Pete Ward hits a grand slam off Denny McLain in the sixth inning of a 10–2 win over the Tigers in the second game of a double-header in Detroit. The White Sox lost the opener 7–0, collecting only one hit off John Hiller.

AUGUST 22   A brawl that puts Tommy John out for the season is the feature of a 4–2 loss to the Tigers in Detroit.

With a 3–2 count on Tigers infielder Dick McAuliffe, John threw an inside pitch that was so high that catcher Jerry McNertney couldn't lay a glove on it. It was a walk for McAuliffe, but as he started for first he began yelling at the White Sox hurler. John shouted back and McAuliffe stormed the mound. John took a defensive stance, and McAuliffe bowled him over, ramming into John's left pitching shoulder with his knee. Tommy suffered a torn ligament of the shoulder and didn't pitch again for the rest of the season. AL President Joe Cronin fined McAuliffe $250 and suspended him for five days for his role in the altercation.

AUGUST 25   On the eve of the Democratic National Convention in Chicago, marred by violent confrontations between antiwar demonstrators and police, a riot with political overtones nearly erupts at Comiskey Park during a 10–2 loss to the Twins. A group of George Wallace supporters heaped a torrent of abuse toward Tommy Davis and other African-American players. Davis ignored the racial slurs, but several Eugene McCarthy people flashed their campaign buttons at them while chiding them for their narrow views. Angry words were exchanged, but park police thwarted the confrontation before it spiraled out of control.

AUGUST 28   White Sox rookie Jerry Nyman pitches a shutout in his first major league start, defeating the Yankees 3–0 at Comiskey Park. Nyman made one prior relief appearance, four days earlier, lasting two-thirds of an inning.

Nyman pitched only one more shutout during his three-year big league career. He finished in stay in the majors with a 6–7 record and a 4.57 ERA.

AUGUST 29   The White Sox defeat the Yankees 1–0 at Comiskey Park. The lone run scored on a single by Luis Aparicio in the seventh inning. Joe Horlen (8¹/₃ innings) and Wilbur Wood (²/₃ of an inning) combined on the shutout.

Aparicio batted .264 and led the Sox in hits (164), runs (55) and doubles (24) in 1968.

SEPTEMBER 4   Following 13 scoreless innings, the White Sox score three times in the 14th inning to defeat the Senators 3–0 in Washington. The first run crossed the plate on a bases-loaded squeeze bunt from third base to bring home Tommy Davis from third base. Luis Aparicio added a two-run single. Jack Fisher ($7^2/_3$ innings), Hoyt Wilhelm ($1^1/_3$ innings), Wilbur Wood ($1^1/_3$ innings), Bob Locker ($2^2/_3$ innings) and Dennis Ribant (one inning) combined on the shutout.

SEPTEMBER 6   Solo homers provide all three runs for an 11-inning, 3–2 win over the Orioles in Baltimore. Jerry McNertney homered in the fifth inning, Pete Ward in the sixth and Buddy Bradford in the 11th.

                 The White Sox set an American League record for most one-run games in a season in 1968 with 74. The club was 30–44 in the close encounters.

SEPTEMBER 28   Jack Fisher (seven innings) and Hoyt Wilhelm (two innings) combine on a two-hitter, but the White Sox lose 1–0 to the Angels in Anaheim.

OCTOBER 15   In the expansion draft, the White Sox lose Tommy Davis and Jerry McNertney to the Seattle Pilots and Buddy Booker, Alan Fitzmorris, Bill Haynes and Scott Northey to the Kansas City Royals.

DECEMBER 5   A month after Richard Nixon defeats Hubert Humphrey in the presidential election, the White Sox sell Leon Wagner to the Reds.

1969

Season in a Sentence

A second straight losing season brings about the lowest attendance figure in the major leagues, rumors that the club is headed for Milwaukee, a truckload of new players, the second retirement of Al Lopez and a change in ownership.

Finish • Won • Lost • Pct • GB

Fifth   68   94   .420   39.0

Managers

Al Lopez (8–9) and Don Gutteridge (60–85)

Stats

Stats	WS	AL	Rank
Batting Avg:	.247	.246	6
On-Base Pct:	.322	.324	6
Slugging Pct:	.357	.369	7
Home Runs:	112		9
Stolen Bases:	54		9 (tie)
ERA:	4.21	3.62	11
Fielding Avg:	.981	.978	2
Runs Scored:	625		8
Runs Allowed:	723		10

Starting Lineup

Ed Herrmann, c
Gail Hopkins, 1b
Bobby Knoop, 2b
Bill Melton, 3b
Luis Aparicio, ss
Carlos May, lf
Ken Berry, cf
Walt Williams, rf
Buddy Bradford, rf-cf
Tommy McCraw, 1b-rf-cf-lf
Pete Ward, 1b-3b
Don Pavletich, c
Ron Hansen, 2b-1b
Duane Josephson, c

Pitchers

Joe Horlen, sp
Gary Peters, sp
Tommy John, sp
Billy Wynne, sp
Paul Edmondson, sp
Wilbur Wood, rp
Dan Osinski, rp

Attendance

589,546 (12th in AL)

Club Leaders

Batting Avg:	Walt Williams	.304
On-Base Pct:	Bill Melton	.352
Slugging Pct:	Bill Melton	.433
Home Runs:	Bill Melton	23
RBIs:	Bill Melton	87
Runs:	Luis Aparicio	77
Stolen Bases:	Luis Aparicio	24
Wins:	Joe Horlen	13
Strikeouts:	Gary Peters	140
ERA:	Tommy John	3.25
Saves:	Wilbur Wood	15

APRIL 8   The White Sox open the 1969 season in Oakland and lose 6–2. Gary Peters hit a home run, but he allowed five runs in six innings.

Peters is the only pitcher in White Sox history to hit a home run on Opening Day.

APRIL 9   Carlos May drives in all three runs of a 3–0 win over the Athletics in Oakland. May hit the first two home runs of his major league career and contributed a single. Tommy John pitched the shutout.

The White Sox had new uniforms in 1969. The primary trim color was changed from navy blue to royal blue and pinstripes were removed from the home jerseys. The stirrup socks were white with blue stripes and blue sanitary hose. The pale blue road uniforms were shelved as the club went back to the traditional gray. The CHICAGO script design and the numbers on the back were white, outlined in blue. The road uniforms had to be sent back to the manufacturer in mid-April, however, because the numbers couldn't be read from the stands or by viewers on television, particularly those with black-and-white sets. A darker shade of blue was added for contrast.

APRIL 11   The White Sox play the first regular season major league game ever played in Seattle and lose 7–0 at Sicks Stadium.

The Pilots lasted only one season in Seattle. The franchise moved to Milwaukee in 1970 and the team was renamed the Brewers. Seattle received another big league franchise in 1977 when the Mariners began play.

APRIL 13   The White Sox smash five home runs and win 12–7 over the Pilots in Seattle. The homers were struck by Pete Ward, Bill Melton, Gail Hopkins, Woodie Held and Don Pavletich.

APRIL 16   In the home opener, the White Sox win 5–2 over the Royals before 11,163 at Comiskey Park. Carlos May hit two home runs and Buddy Bradford one. It was also the first time that the White Sox played the Royals.

Astroturf was placed in the infield at Comiskey Park in 1969. The outfield remained grass. The fences were also brought in 17 feet on the foul lines, from 352 feet to 335, and shortened from 375 to 370 in the power alleys and from 415 feet to 400 in center field. The change resulted in an additional 29 home runs, 15 of them by the White Sox. The inner fence was removed in 1971. A dugout cafe was also built for the fans in 1969. This area was served by the Soxettes, lovely young ladies who acted as hostesses.

APRIL 19   The Seattle Pilots play in Chicago for the first time and defeat the White Sox 5–1 at Comiskey Park.

APRIL 20   Bill Melton hits a walk-off homer in the 10th inning to defeat the Pilots 3–2 in the first game of a double-header at Comiskey Park. The Sox also won the second game 13–3.

Melton became the first White Sox batter to hit 30 or more homers in a season with 33 in 1970. A year later he hit 33 again to become the first White Sox batter to top the American League in home runs. Melton passed Minnie Minoso in 1974 to set the all-time White Sox record for home runs in a career. He hit 154 as a member of the Sox and still ranks seventh behind Frank Thomas, Harold Baines, Carlton Fisk, Paul Konerko, Magglio Ordonez and Robin Ventura. Melton may have clubbed many more homers were it not for a ruptured disc he suffered during the winter of 1971 after falling off the roof of his garage. Only 26 at the time, he never fully regained his power stroke. Problems with broadcaster Harry Caray also contributed to Melton's decline. Never a nimble fielder at third base, Melton became a target of Caray, who magnified every mistake. Melton was bothered by Caray's sarcastic barbs, and his play suffered as a consequence. The two nearly came to blows one night in Milwaukee's Marc Plaza Hotel.

APRIL 25   Buddy Bradford hits a home run over the left-field roof at Comiskey Park during a 6–5 win over the Twins.

APRIL 30   The White Sox play the Royals in Kansas City for the first time, and lose 3–2.

MAY 2   Al Lopez resigns as manager of the White Sox due to ill health.

Lopez suffered from stomach problems for years, and the stress of managing led to constant pain, a limited diet and many sleepless nights. He never managed again, living out his remaining days in peaceful retirement at his bayfront home in Tampa. Lopez passed away on October 30, 2006, at the age of 97, just four days after the Sox won their first world championship since 1917. Don Gutteridge succeeded Lopez as manager. Gutteridge was an infielder in the majors from 1936 through 1948 for four major league clubs, including the pennant-winning clubs with the Browns in 1944 and the Red Sox in 1946. He was a first-base coach with the White Sox from 1955 through 1966, then returned to the club in July 1968 when Lopez replaced Eddie Stanky as manager. Nearly 57 when he became a big-league skipper for the first time, Gutteridge proved to be ill-prepared for the job. Over two seasons, the Sox were 109–172 under his leadership.

MAY 6   Joe Horlen pitches the White Sox to a 1–0 win over the Orioles in Baltimore. The run scored on a walk to Sandy Alomar Sr., a stolen base and a single by Luis Aparicio.

Aparicio hit .280 in 1969.

MAY 14   The White Sox trade Sandy Alomar Sr. and Bob Priddy to the Angels for Bobby Knoop.

In a swap of starting second basemen, the White Sox would have been better served by keeping Alomar, who played in the majors until 1978. His son Sandy Jr. was a catcher for the White Sox from 2001 through 2004.

MAY 15   With a single off Earl Wilson, Luis Aparicio collects his 2,000th career hit during a 10-inning, 2–1 loss to the Tigers in Detroit.

MAY 16   The White Sox survive three homers by Mike Epstein to defeat the Senators 7–6 at Comiskey Park.

MAY 17   In his first starting assignment of the season, Jerry Nyman pitches a one-hitter to defeat the Senators 6–0 at Comiskey Park. Nyman also drove in three runs with a bases-loaded double. The only Washington hit was a single by Brant Alyea in the second inning.

MAY 24   Bill Melton hits a grand slam off Lee Stange in the third inning of a 9–3 win over the Red Sox at Comiskey Park.

MAY 25   Tommy John (seven innings) and Wilbur Wood (two innings) combine on a two-hitter against the Red Sox at Comiskey Park, but one is a fifth-inning homer by George Scott to beat the White Sox 1–0.

JUNE 2   Trailing 4–0, the White Sox score six runs in the eighth inning to defeat the Red Sox 6–4 in Boston. The rally was capped by a grand slam by Carlos May off Sparky Lyle.

May's birthday was May 17. With his name over his uniform number 17, he was the only player in history to wear his birthday on his uniform.

JUNE 5
In the first round of the amateur draft, the White Sox select third baseman Ted Nicholson from Oak Park High School in Laurel, Mississippi.

Nicholson was the third overall pick in the draft, but he proved to be a complete flop. He never advanced past Class A. The only future major leaguers chosen by the Sox in 1969 were Bruce Kimm (seventh round), Glenn Redmon (19th round) and Rich Hinton (third round of the secondary phase).

JUNE 8
The White Sox trade Bob Locker to the Seattle Pilots for Gary Bell.

JUNE 19
The White Sox come from behind three times to beat the Pilots 13–10 at Comiskey Park. Seattle scored four times in the first, but the Sox came back with five in their half. The Pilots plated two in the third, but Chicago rebounded for four in the bottom half to lead 9–6. The opposition took a 10–9 advantage with four in the seventh, and for the third time the Sox responded with a rally in the same inning, bringing four across the plate. Three scored without hitting the ball with the help of a couple of ex-White Sox players. With the contest deadlocked at 10–10 and the bases loaded, Seattle pitcher Bob Locker threw a wild pitch to bring the runner in from third base. The return throw from Jerry McNertney to Locker missed the pitcher and sailed into right field, and two more scored.

JUNE 20
In his major league debut, Paul Edmondson pitches a two-hitter to defeat the Angels 9–1 in the second game of a double-header in Anaheim. The only hits were singles by Rick Reichardt in the fourth inning and Jim Spencer in the fifth. California won the opener 2–1 in 12 innings.

Edmondson didn't win another big league game. He finished his rookie season with a 1–6 record and a 3.70 earned run average. On February 13, 1970, the day after his 27th birthday, Edmondson died in an auto accident near Santa Barbara, California.

JUNE 22
Billy Wynne pitches the White Sox to a 1–0 win over the Angels in Anaheim. The lone run scored on a double by Carlos May in the third inning.

The shutout was the only one of Wynne's career. He finished his five-year stay in the majors with an 8–11 record and a 4.33 earned run average.

JUNE 24
Bill Melton hits three homers in his first three plate appearances during a 7–6 win over the Pilots in the second game of a double-header in Seattle. All three were solo shots. Melton went deep on Fred Talbot in the second and fourth innings and John O'Donoghue in the sixth. After striking out in the seventh, Melton faced Jim Bouton in the ninth and belted a double that landed about seven feet short of the fence. The four extra-base hits in a game tied a White Sox record. Carlos May and Ed Herrmann also homered during the game. The Sox won the opener 6–4.

JULY 3
Bill Melton hits a walk-off homer in the 11th inning to beat the Twins 5–4 at Comiskey Park.

JULY 7
Gary Peters pitches a two-hitter to defeat the Athletics 2–0 at County Stadium in Milwaukee. The only Oakland hits were doubles by Danny Cater in the second

inning and Joe Rudi in the eighth. Luis Aparicio scored both runs following singles in the first and third innings.

JULY 18   With Tommy John pitching a complete game, the White Sox outfield fails to record a putout during a 6–1 win over the Royals in Kansas City.

JULY 27   Seven days after Neil Armstrong becomes the first man to walk on the moon, the White Sox are hammered by the Orioles 17–0 at Memorial Stadium. The Sox were outhit 20–2.

AUGUST 11   Carlos May loses part of his right thumb in an accident while training with the Marine Reserves at Camp Pendleton, California.

May seemed to be a shoo-in for the AL Rookie of the Year Award when the mishap occurred. He made the All-Star Game just two months after celebrating his 21st birthday and was batting .281 with 18 homers in 100 games. The injury happened while swabbing down a mortar tube during firing exercises. May thought the weapon was empty. The shell fired and the five-foot swabbing stick hit the thumb. After enduring several painful skin-graft operations, May came back to play in 150 games in 1970. He made the All-Star team again in 1972. Often criticized for lazy and indifferent outfield play, May peaked before he was 25, however, and was out of baseball by the time he was 30.

AUGUST 26   Nine days after the final day of the Woodstock Music Festival in Bethel, New York, the White Sox score two runs in the ninth inning and one in the 10th to defeat the Yankees 3–2 at Yankee Stadium. A two-run double by Bill Melton in the ninth inning tied the contest. Pete Ward's sacrifice fly drove in the winner.

AUGUST 30   Trailing 5–1, the White Sox score three in the seventh and two in the ninth to defeat the Indians 6–5 at Comiskey Park. Woodie Held's single drove in the winning run.

AUGUST 31   With a game-winning rally in their final at-bat for the second day in a row, the White Sox score three times in the ninth inning to beat the Indians 7–6 at Comiskey Park. Don Pavletich drove in the winning run with a single.

SEPTEMBER 2   Trailing 3–0, the White Sox score nine runs in the sixth inning and defeat the Orioles 10–3 at Comiskey Park.

SEPTEMBER 4   Tommy John (seven innings) and Danny Murphy (one inning) combine on a two-hitter, but the White Sox lose 1–0 to the Angels in Anaheim.

Murphy made his major league debut at the age of 17 as an outfielder with the Cubs in 1960. A native of Danvers, Massachusetts, Murphy was signed for a $125,000 contract. He was rushed far too soon, however, and had a .171 batting average in 123 at-bats over three seasons with the Cubs. He later became a pitcher and was 4–4 with the White Sox in 1969 and 1970.

SEPTEMBER 13   The Athletics explode for four runs in the 10th inning to defeat the White Sox 4–0 at Comiskey Park. Paul Edmondson pitched nine shutout innings, but Wilbur Wood allowed the four 10th-inning runs.

SEPTEMBER 14   The White Sox score seven runs in the second inning and win 12–8 over the Athletics in the first game of a double-header at Comiskey Park. The Sox also won the second tilt 9–8 on a walk-off homer in the ninth inning by Tommy McCraw.

The White Sox home attendance dropped to 589,546 in 1969, the club's lowest figure since 1944. The Sox attracted just 392,862 for 71 games at Comiskey Park and 196,684 in 11 contests at County Stadium in Milwaukee. The summer of 1969 belonged to the Cubs, who were in first place for most of the season prior to a September collapse. The White Sox received scant space in the newspaper in the midst of the hysteria at Wrigley Field, where the Cubs drew 1,674,993 fans.

SEPTEMBER 21   The White Sox score eight runs in the third inning of a 10–2 win over the Royals in Kansas City.

SEPTEMBER 24   Arthur Allyn sells his 50 percent share of the White Sox to his brother John, who was the owner of the other 50 percent of the franchise and thereby controlled 100 percent of the franchise.

Arthur was perturbed by the club's financial losses and a critical press, which was in the main hostile toward him. John Allyn said the split came when Arthur had a $13.7 million offer from a Milwaukee group headed by Bud Selig and wanted to sell. The price was more than double what the Allyns paid for the White Sox in 1961. John refused to approve such a sale and a complicated settlement followed in which Arthur, in effect, traded and sold his White Sox shares to his brother in exchange for other holdings in the huge financial complex owned by the family. At his first press conference, John assured White Sox fans that the club would remain in Chicago "for as long as I can envision." Arthur explained he would go into semi-retirement and devote much of his time to his butterfly collection, believed to be valued at $250,000. "I will become a full-time entomologist," he said. "I an mentally and physically tired." Previously, John Allyn had stayed completely in the background in the affairs of the White Sox, but upon purchasing control, he immediately began an ambitious program to rectify the sorry state of the franchise. The club dipped to a 56–106 record in 1970, but it improved to 87–67 in 1972, bringing about a boost in attendance from 495,335 in 1970 to 1,302,527 by 1973. Soon, the club's win totals and attendance figures began to lag again, however, and with rumors swirling that the White Sox were about to move to Seattle, John Allyn sold the club to a group headed by Bill Veeck in December 1975.

SEPTEMBER 25   Walt Williams hits a walk-off homer in the 10th inning to defeat the Royals 2–1 at Comiskey Park.

NOVEMBER 25   White Sox owner John Allyn announces that the White Sox will not play any home games in Milwaukee in 1970. Milwaukee received a major league franchise in March 1970 when the Seattle Pilots moved to the city and were renamed the Brewers.

DECEMBER 11   The White Sox trade Gary Peters and Don Pavletich to the Red Sox for Syd O'Brien and Gerry Janeski.

DECEMBER 18   The White Sox trade Pete Ward to the Yankees for Mickey Scott.

THE STATE OF THE WHITE SOX

The decade began with one of the worst seasons in franchise history as the White Sox lost 106 games. With a dramatic improvement under manager Chuck Tanner, the White Sox were 87–67 in 1972, but they slipped back to a 64–97 record in 1976. Then came the glorious summer of 1977, when the White Sox were in first place in August before finishing at 90–72. The decade ended with the club falling back into mediocrity, however. The 1972 and 1977 seasons proved to be the only ones during the decade in which the Sox posted a winning record. Overall, the White Sox posted a 752–853 mark for the decade, a winning percentage of .469 that ranked ninth in the American League. Pennant-winners included the Orioles (1970, 1971 and 1979), Athletics (1972, 1973 and 1974), Red Sox (1975) and Yankees (1976, 1977 and 1978). Western Division champions were the Twins (1970), Athletics (1971, 1972, 1973, 1974 and 1975), Royals (1976, 1977 and 1978) and Angels (1979).

THE BEST TEAM

T2he 1972 White Sox were 87–67 and finished just 5½ games behind the world champion Athletics.

THE WORST TEAM

The 1970 Sox lost more games than any club in franchise history, finishing with a record of 56–106.

THE BEST MOMENT

During the summer of 1977, the White Sox spent 61 days in first place and held the top position as late as August 19.

THE WORST MOMENT

The White Sox were forced to forfeit the second game of a double-header against the Tigers at Comiskey Park because of "Disco Demolition Night."

THE ALL-DECADE TEAM • YEARS WITH WS

Ed Herrmann, c	1967, 1969–74
Richie Allen, 1b	1972–74
Jorge Orta, 2b	1972–79
Bill Melton, 3b	1968–75
Bucky Dent, ss	1973–76
Carlos May, lf	1968–76
Chet Lemon, cf	1975–81
Pat Kelly, rf	1971–76
Lamar Johnson, dh	1974–81
Wilbur Wood, p	1967–78
Jim Kaat, p	1973–75
Goose Gossage, rp	1972–76
Terry Forster, rp	1971–76

Another top player was catcher Brian Downing (1973–77). Gossage, who was inducted in 2008, is the only Hall of Fame member on the 1970s All-Decade Team. But Allen and Kaat deserve Hall of Fame consideration, too.

THE DECADE LEADERS

Batting Avg:	Richie Allen	.307
On-Base Pct:	Richie Allen	.398
Slugging Pct:	Richie Allen	.589
Home Runs:	Bill Melton	129
RBIs:	Jorge Orta	456
Runs:	Jorge Orta	442
Stolen Bases:	Pat Kelly	119
Wins:	Wilbur Wood	136
Strikeouts:	Wilbur Wood	1,138
ERA:	Jim Kaat	3.10
Saves:	Terry Forster	75

THE HOME FIELD

In 1969, Arthur Allyn changed the official name of the club's home field from Comiskey Park to White Sox Park and installed Astroturf in the infield. Shortly after he bought the Sox in 1975, Veeck ripped up the artificial turf, returned to an all-grass field and changed the name of the facility back to Comiskey Park. Most people had been referring to the ballpark as Comiskey Park anyway, despite Allyn's 1969 edict. Attendance bottomed out at 495,355 in 1970, improved to 1,302,527 in 1973, fell again to 750,802 in 1975, then increased once more to 1,657,135 in 1977.

THE GAME YOU WISHED YOU HAD SEEN

On May 28, 1973, the White Sox and Indians completed a game that was suspended two nights earlier with the score 2–2 at the end of the 16th. The White Sox won the suspended game 6–3 on a three-run walk-off homer by Richie Allen in the 21st inning. Then they won the regularly scheduled meeting 4–0. Wilbur Wood was the winning pitcher in both games, with five innings of relief in the suspended game followed by a complete-game shutout.

THE WAY THE GAME WAS PLAYED

Speed and defense were more prominent during the 1970s than in any decade since the lively ball was introduced in 1920. Stolen bases per team in the American League rose from 72 in 1970 to 107 in 1979, while home runs per team declined from 146 in 1970 to 94 in 1976 before surging upward by the end of the decade. The designated hitter rule was introduced in the AL in 1973.

THE MANAGEMENT

John Allyn owned the White Sox from September 1969 until December 1975, when he sold the franchise to a group headed by Bill Veeck. Veeck previously owned the Sox from 1959 through 1961. He sold the club in January 1981 to Jerry Reinsdorf and Eddie Einhorn. Ed Short became general manager in August 1961 and served in that role until September 1970, when he was replaced by Roland Hemond, who ran the player development aspect of the club until 1985. There were eight different field managers in the '70s, including Don Gutteridge (1969–70), Bill Adair (1970), Chuck Tanner (1970–75), Paul Richards (1976), Bob Lemon (1977–78), Larry Doby (1978), Don Kessinger (1979) and Tony LaRussa (1979–86).

THE BEST PLAYER MOVE

The best player move was the selection of Harold Baines in the first round of the amateur draft in 1977.

THE WORST PLAYER MOVE

The worst deal by the White Sox sent Goose Gossage and Terry Forster to the Pirates in December 1976 for Richie Zisk and Silvio Martinez.

1970

Sox

Season in a Sentence

In a disastrous season, the White Sox lose a club-record 106 games and draw only 495,355 fans.

Finish • Won • Lost • Pct • GB

Sixth   56   106   .346   42.0

Managers

Don Gutteridge (49–87), Bill Adair (4–6) and Chuck Tanner (3–13)

Stats

Stats	WS	AL	Rank
Batting Avg:	.253	.250	4
On-Base Pct:	.317	.325	9
Slugging Pct:	.362	.379	9
Home Runs:	123		9
Stolen Bases:	53		9
ERA:	4.54	3.71	12
Fielding Avg:	.975	.978	11
Runs Scored:	633		8
Runs Allowed:	822		12

Starting Lineup

Ed Herrmann, c
Gail Hopkins, 1b
Bobby Knoop, 2b
Bill Melton, 3b-rf
Luis Aparicio, ss
Carlos May, lf
Ken Berry, cf
Walt Williams, rf
Syd O'Brien, 2b-3b
Tommy McCraw, 1b-lf-rf-cf
Duane Josephson, c

Pitchers

Tommy John, sp
Jerry Janeski, sp
Joe Horlen, sp
Bart Johnson, sp
Wilbur Wood, rp
Danny Murphy, rp
Jerry Crider, rp

Attendance

495,355 (12th in AL)

Club Leaders

Batting Avg:	Luis Aparicio	.313
On-Base Pct:	Luis Aparicio	.372
Slugging Pct:	Bill Melton	.488
Home Runs:	Bill Melton	33
RBIs:	Bill Melton	96
Runs:	Luis Aparicio	86
Stolen Bases:	Carlos May	12
	Tommy McCraw	12
Wins:	Tommy John	12
Strikeouts:	Tommy John	138
ERA:	Tommy John	3.27
Saves:	Wilbur Wood	21

FEBRUARY 13   White Sox pitcher Paul Edmondson dies in an auto accident near Santa Barbara, California. Edmondson was driving a vehicle that skidded on a rain-slicked highway, crashed into another car and burned. A female companion was also killed in the accident.

FEBRUARY 28   Ten days after the "Chicago Seven" are found not guilty of conspiring to start a riot during the 1968 Democratic National Convention, the White Sox sell Ron Hansen to the Yankees.

APRIL 4   A snowstorm in Chicago moves a two-game exhibition series between the White Sox and the Cubs to Tulsa, Oklahoma. The games were originally scheduled for April 4th and 5th, one at Comiskey Park and the other at Wrigley Field to conclude spring training. The April 4th contest in Tulsa was postponed, however, because of rain and temperatures in the 30s.

APRIL 7   Setting the stage for a miserable season, the White Sox lose 12–0 to the Twins on Opening Day before a crowd of 11,473 at Comiskey Park. Jim Perry pitched the Minnesota shutout and Brant Alyea slugged two homers and drove in seven runs. Sox starter Tommy John allowed six runs in 4^2/$_3$ innings.

Billy Pierce joined Jack Drees in the TV booth in 1970.

APRIL 10   The White Sox play the Milwaukee Brewers for the first time, and win 5–4 at Comiskey Park before a crowd of only 1,036.

APRIL 18   The White Sox play the Brewers in Milwaukee for the first time, and win 8–4.

APRIL 29   Orioles outfielder Paul Blair hits three home runs to lead his club to an 18–2 win over the White Sox at Comiskey Park.

The new organist at Comiskey Park in 1970 was 23-year-old Nancy Faust, who became a Chicago institution. She is arguably the first sports organist to include pop and rock themes while playing during games. Faust also played organ for the Bulls, Blackhawks, Sting and DePaul University. She performed full-time at White Sox contests until 2005. Beginning in 2006, she played only during day games. Her chief contributions were a rousing rendition of "Take Me Out To The Ballgame" during the seventh-inning stretch, inspiring Harry Caray to sing along (see April 9, 1976), and the playing of the song "Na, Na, Hey, Hey Kiss Him Goodbye." (see July 3, 1977).

MAY 1   Trailing 4–2, the White Sox score eight runs in the sixth inning and defeat the Tigers 13–6 at Comiskey Park.

MAY 5   The day after Ohio National Guardsmen shoot and kill four students at Kent State University, the White Sox win 2–1 over the Indians at Comiskey Park in a contest that features nine double plays. The Indians turned five of the twin-killings and the Sox four.

MAY 6   Carlos May scores both runs during a 2–1 win over the Indians at Comiskey Park. May tripled and scored on an error in the seventh inning, then smacked a walk-off homer in the ninth.

MAY 8   Playing third base, Bill Melton breaks his nose on a pop-up during a 6–1 loss to the Orioles in Baltimore. The ball glanced off the heel of Melton's glove and struck his nose, knocking him unconscious.

MAY 18   Ken Berry twice leaps above the center-field fence at Comiskey Park to take home runs away from both Alex Johnson and Bill Voss, but the White Sox lose 6–1 to the Angels.

MAY 20   The White Sox score three runs in the ninth inning to defeat the Angels 3–2 at Comiskey Park. The game was scoreless before California plated two in the top of the ninth. Chicago pinch-hitter Bob Christian hit a home run to tie the game 2–2. The Sox loaded the bases on a hit batsman, a single and a walk before Gail Hopkins ended the game with a sacrifice fly.

The home run by Christian was the only one he hit in 1970 and the last of four he struck during his major league career.

MAY 31   The White Sox win a 22–13 slugfest over the Red Sox at Fenway Park. The 35 runs scored in the contest was one shy of the American League record by the most by two teams in one game and the most of any game involving the White Sox. The White Sox scored six runs in the first inning, one in the third and three in the fourth to take an 11–7 lead before another seven-run explosion in the sixth. Four tallies in the eighth put Chicago ahead 22–10. Walt Williams scored five runs and collected five hits, including a double, in seven at-bats. Luis Aparicio was five-for-five on four singles and a triple. The White Sox picked up 24 hits in all, with 16 singles, six doubles, a triple and a homer. Floyd Weaver was the winning pitcher despite allowing six runs in five innings. It was his first major league win since 1965 and his only one as a member of the White Sox.

Aparicio batted .313 in 1970, his only season above .300 during his 18 years in the majors.

JUNE 4

Facing Dick Bosman, Walt Williams hits the first pitch of the game for a home run, sparking a 7–3 win over the Senators in Washington.

On the same day, the White Sox selected shortstop Lee Richard from Southern University in the first round of the amateur draft. Richard played in only 239 big league games and batted only .209 with two home runs. Nonetheless, it was one of the White Sox's best drafts. The Sox selected Terry Forster in the second round and Goose Gossage in the ninth round of the regular phase and Bucky Dent during the first round of the secondary phase. Other future major leaguers chosen in 1970 were Jerry Hairston Jr. (third round), Jim Geddes (sixth round) and Bruce Miller (20th round). The Sox also selected Archie Manning during the secondary phase as a shortstop prospect, but he declined to sign a contract. In the fall of 1970, Manning won All-American honors as a quarterback at the University of Mississippi. Then he was drafted by the New Orleans Saints as the second pick of the first round of the NFL draft in 1971.

JUNE 10

The Red Sox defeat the White Sox 7–6 in 14 innings at Comiskey Park with the help of a freak grand slam by Rico Petrocelli in the fourth inning. Petrocelli's drive bounced off the glove of right fielder Tommy McCraw and into the bullpen.

JUNE 12

Tommy John pitches a two-hitter to defeat the Senators 6–0 at Comiskey Park. The only Washington hits were singles by Wayne Comer in the fifth inning and Ed Brinkman in the ninth.

JUNE 15

The White Sox trade Buddy Bradford to the Indians for Bob Miller and Barry Moore.

JUNE 28

The White Sox outslug the Twins 11–10 in the second game of a double-header at Comiskey Park. Minnesota won the opener 9–1.

JULY 19

The White Sox celebrate Luis Aparicio Day before a double-header against the Orioles at Comiskey Park. Among his many gifts, Aparicio received a camper, a boat, an orange Opel sports car, a jeweled ring, fishing equipment, golf clubs, a tape recorder, a stereo and saving bonds. The White Sox lost 8–2 and won 7–3.

JULY 24

The White Sox score five runs in the ninth inning to defeat the Tigers 5–2 in the first game of a double-header in Detroit. The Sox collected six consecutive singles during the rally, by Duane Josephson, Bob Spence, Ken Berry, Bobby Knoop, Ed Herrmann and Syd O'Brien. Detroit won the second tilt 5–4. Bill Melton tied a major league record by striking out seven times during the twin bill.

AUGUST 2   Six days after three people are shot during a riot at a Sly and the Family Stone concert in Chicago, a two-out, two-run, walk-off homer by Bill Melton in the ninth inning beats the Indians 8–7 in the second game of a double-header at Comiskey Park. Cleveland won the first game 4–2.

AUGUST 5   Ed Herrmann hits a grand slam off Gene Brabender in the first inning of a 9–3 win over the Brewers at Comiskey Park.

In August, the "Big White Machine" was unveiled before Sox fans. The contraption was a 1929 Ford that Ed Herrmann, Bill Melton and Syd O'Brien helped restore. The car was installed with a V-8 engine and was driven around Comiskey Park after each victory.

AUGUST 19   Trailing 5–2, the White Sox erupt for 11 runs in the ninth inning to defeat the Red Sox 13–5 in Boston. The rally was accomplished with nine singles, a double, two walks, a sacrifice fly and an error. Luis Aparicio hit a pinch-double and later singled. Others who contributed to the 11 runs were Bill Melton (two singles), Ken Berry (two singles), Ossie Blanco (a single and a sacrifice fly), Wilbur Wood (single), Ed Herrmann (single), Bobby Knoop (single) and Carlos May (walk).

AUGUST 29   Trailing 7–1, the White Sox score eight runs in the sixth inning and four in the seventh and defeat the Red Sox 13–9 at Comiskey Park. Ed Herrmann started the sixth-inning rally with a lead-off single, then capped it with a grand slam off Chuck Hartenstein.

Herrmann batted .283 with 19 home runs in 1970.

AUGUST 30   For the second time in 1970, the White Sox and the Red Sox play a game at Fenway Park in which more than 30 runs are scored. The White Sox won the first one, on May 31 by a score of 22–13. This time Boston won 21–11 in the first game of a double-header. Boston also won the second game 4–1.

SEPTEMBER 1   The White Sox sell Bob Miller to the Cubs.

On the same day, the White Sox fired Ed Short as general manager. Short had been in the position since 1961. He took the Sox to the brink of the World Series in 1964, when the club finished a game out of first place. After the team just missed another pennant in 1967 it went into a slide that culminated with the 106-loss season of 1970 and an attendance figure that fell below 500,000, the lowest in the major leagues. The White Sox were outdrawn 1,642,705 to 495,355 by the Cubs.

SEPTEMBER 2   The White Sox fire Don Gutteridge as manager.

Gutteridge had a record of 109–172 as manager of the White Sox. He never managed another big-league team. Coach Bill Adair served as interim manager until Chuck Tanner arrived in Chicago on September 15 after his stint as manager of the Hawaii club in the Pacific Coast League came to a conclusion (see September 4, 1971).

SEPTEMBER 4   The White Sox hire Chuck Tanner as manager, Stu Holcomb as general manager and Roland Hemond as director of personnel.

The selections of the relatively unknown Tanner, Holcomb and Hemond came as somewhat of a surprise because most believed that John Allyn would hire "big names" to try to revive the franchise. "The entire White Sox operation has lost its public image," Allyn said. "We have to rebuild that image as well as the team. But we can't rebuild the image with the men we had in charge. The fans, the press and everyone else was down on them whether they admitted it or not." The hiring of Tanner and Hemond was the keys to restoring that image. Tanner was 41 years old and had been an outfielder in the majors with four different clubs from 1955 through 1962. After his playing days ended, he became a highly successful manager in the minors. In 1970 Tanner led Hawaii, a farm club in the Angels system, to a record of 98–48. Tanner was a player's manager who was in touch with the changing realities of the "swinging '70s." "When it comes to the mod styles," Tanner said, "that doesn't bother me. I'm just interested in their ability. I don't care how long the hair is if he can hit .300." With his infectious enthusiasm, Tanner elevated a club that was 56–106 to 87–67 in 1972 with the help of an MVP season from Richie Allen, and attendance nearly tripled. Expectations were high heading into 1973, but the Sox fell backward and were 77–85 that season. Tanner granted special privileges to the temperamental Allen, which led to dissension inside the clubhouse. Tanner also became engaged in a power struggle with Holcomb, with the treatment of Allen the central issue in the quarrel, and Holcomb resigned in June 1973. Allen walked out on the club in September 1974, and Tanner's bubbly optimism wasn't enough to turn things around. He was fired in 1975 following a 75–86 season and an alarming drop in attendance. Holcomb was 60 years old, had coached football at Purdue and worked as the athletic director at Northwestern. He was involved in the promotional and marketing aspects of the club, as well as negotiating player contacts. Hemond was 42 and also came from the Angels, where he served as farm director since the franchise's inception in 1961. Hemond was in charge of player trades and the farm system, and he became general manager in 1973 when Holcomb resigned his position and left the White Sox. Hemond remained the general manager of the White Sox until 1985. Another key addition was the hiring of Johnny Sain, who was considered one of the best pitching coaches in the game. It was Sain who suggested that Wilbur Wood be converted into a starting pitcher. Harry Caray was another White Sox hire during the fall of 1970 as the radio broadcaster. Caray replaced Bob Elson, who had

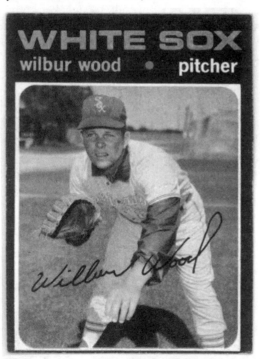

Few pitchers have achieved the level of success as both a starter and reliever that Wilbur Wood reached. After notching 21 saves in 1970, he moved to the rotation and won 20 games in four consecutive seasons.

announced White Sox games since 1931. Always controversial and never afraid to say what he believed, Caray handed the play-by-play during Cardinals games from 1945 through 1969 before he was dismissed amid rumors that he was having an affair with the daughter-in-law of club owner August Busch Jr. Caray spent one unhappy year with the Oakland Athletics in 1970 before jumping at the chance to return to the Midwest with the White Sox. Caray broadcast White Sox games for 11 years. Despite covering teams that lost more often than they won, Caray, through the sheer force of his personality, helped put fans in the seats at Comiskey Park by connecting with the South Side's blue-collar fans. Caray described himself as the fan's man in the booth. "I have always contended," Caray said when asked about the key to his success, "that if you put a microphone in front of anyone in the bleachers and told him to start talking about the game he was watching, he would sound very much the way I do." Caray loved Chicago's abundant nightlife, and his title as the "Mayor of Rush Street" originated during his years with the Sox.

SEPTEMBER 7   The White Sox set a record (since tied) for most players used during an 18-inning double-header with 41, but lose 7–4 and 7–5 to the Athletics at Comiskey Park. Interim manager Bill Adair put 18 players into the lineup in the first game and 23 in the second. Thirteen players appeared in both contests. Chicago also tied an American League record for most hits by pinch-hitters in a game with four during the second tilt. Duane Josephson, Gail Hopkins, Bob Spence and Ossie Blanco all singled.

SEPTEMBER 9   Alex Johnson of the Angels becomes the first player since 1938, and only the third overall, to smack a home run into the center-field bleachers at Comiskey Park. The only previous batters to accomplish the feat were Jimmie Foxx and Hank Greenberg. Johnson's blast was struck off Billy Wynne during a 3–1 White Sox win in the second game of a double-header. The contest was stopped after eight innings by rain. The Sox also won the opener 11–4.

On the same day, the White Sox purchased Stave Hamilton from the Yankees. He pitched only three games with the Sox before an off-season trade with the Giants but is noteworthy for once having played in the NBA. Standing six-foot-seven, he played for the Minneapolis Lakers from 1958 through 1960 before embarking on a baseball career. Hamilton played in the majors from 1961 through 1972.

SEPTEMBER 10   The White Sox purchase Lee Maye from the Senators.

SEPTEMBER 21   Bill Melton becomes the first batter in White Sox history to hit at least 30 homers in a season during an 8–4 win over the Royals in the first game of a double-header at Comiskey Park. Kansas City won game two 8–2. The "crowd" at Comiskey was only 672.

SEPTEMBER 23   Just 693 fans attend a 6–0 win over the Royals at Comiskey Park.

SEPTEMBER 25   Luis Aparicio sets a major league record for most games played at shortstop with 2,219 by appearing in both ends of a double-header against the Brewers at Comiskey Park. The White Sox won 5–1 and lost 3–2. The second-game loss was the 100th of the season by the Sox.

Aparicio broke the record previously held by Luke Appling, who played in 2,218 games at short, all with the White Sox. Aparicio finished his career with 2,581 games at the position and still holds the career record.

OCTOBER 1   The White Sox close the season with a 13-inning loss to the Angels in Anaheim. It was Chicago's 106th defeat of 1970.

OCTOBER 13   The White Sox trade Gail Hopkins and John Matias to the Royals for Pat Kelly and Don O'Riley.

Kelly proved to be a fine pickup. He played six seasons for the White Sox and made the All-Star team in 1973. Pat's older brother Leroy was a star running back for the Cleveland Browns.

NOVEMBER 30 The White Sox trade Ken Berry, Syd O'Brien and Billy Wynne to the Angels for Tom Bradley, Jay Johnstone and Tom Egan.

The White Sox made a great short-term deal with the Angels. The possessor of a degree in Latin from the University of Maryland, Bradley fanned over 200 batters and won 15 games in each of his two seasons with the Sox.

DECEMBER 1   The White Sox trade Luis Aparicio to the Red Sox for Mike Andrews and Luis Alvarado.

Aparicio hit .313 in 1970 but was 36 at the time of the trade, and the White Sox needed an infusion of youth to improve their lowly position in the standings. He played three seasons for the Red Sox before calling it a career. Neither Andrews nor Alvarado contributed much to the brief revival of the White Sox during the early 1970s.

1971

Season in a Sentence

A new attitude prevails with a revamped roster, new uniforms, Chuck Tanner as manager and Harry Caray in the broadcast booth and results in an improvement of 23 wins over the previous season.

Finish • Won • Lost • Pct • GB

Third   79   83   .488   22.5

Manager

Chuck Tanner

Stats

Stats	WS	AL	Rank
Batting Avg:	.250	.247	7
On-Base Pct:	.327	.320	4
Slugging Pct:	.373	.364	5
Home Runs:	138		5
Stolen Bases:	83		2
ERA:	3.12	3.46	4
Fielding Avg:	.975	.980	12
Runs Scored:	617		7
Runs Allowed:	597		5

Starting Lineup

Ed Herrmann, c
Carlos May, 1b
Mike Andrews, 2b
Bill Melton, 3b
Luis Alvarado, ss
Rick Reichardt, lf
Jay Johnstone, cf
Walt Williams, rf-lf
Rich McKinney, 2b
Lee Richard, ss
Tom Egan, c
Pat Kelly, rf
Rich Morales, ss
Mike Hershberger, cf

Pitchers

Wilbur Wood, sp
Tom Bradley, sp
Tommy John, sp
Joe Horlen, sp
Bart Johnson, rp
Steve Kealey, rp
Vicente Romo, rp
Terry Forster, rp

Attendance

833,891 (ninth in AL)

Club Leaders

Batting Avg:	Carlos May	.294
On-Base Pct:	Carlos May	.375
Slugging Pct:	Rick Reichardt	.429
Home Runs:	Bill Melton	33
RBIs:	Bill Melton	96
Runs:	Bill Melton	72
Stolen Bases:	Carlos May	16
Wins:	Wilbur Wood	22
Strikeouts:	Wilbur Wood	210
ERA:	Wilbur Wood	1.91
Saves:	Bart Johnson	14

JANUARY 8   The White Sox unveil dazzling new uniforms for the 1971 season.

The slanted "SOX" logo on the front of the home jerseys remained, as did the script "CHICAGO" on the road shirts with the underline that contained the team nickname. But in a dramatic departure from the past, blue was eliminated as a trim color and the uniforms were a vivid red, including the cap and sweatshirts. Even the shoes were red. The home jerseys contained pinstripes. The road uniforms were powder blue with the red lettering outlined in white. The names of the players were taken off the backs of the shirts. In their place were large block numbers. The red uniforms were in use through the 1975 season.

FEBRUARY 9   The White Sox trade Jerry Janeski to the Senators for Rick Reichardt.

Reichardt signed with the Angels for a then-record bonus of $200,000 after playing at the University of Wisconsin. He looked like he'd live up to expectations in 1966 when he hit .288 with 16 homers in 1966, but an illness forced the removal of a kidney and he was never again the same player.

Reichardt gave the White Sox one decent season as a regular outfielder before mounting injuries took their toll. Janeski won only one more big-league game following the trade.

MARCH 24   The White Sox trade Bobby Knoop to the Royals for Luis Alcaraz.

MARCH 29   The White Sox trade Tommy McCraw to the Senators for Ed Stroud.

MARCH 31   The White Sox trade Duane Josephson and Danny Murphy to the Red Sox for Vicente Romo and Tony Muser.

APRIL 7   The White Sox open the season with a double-header in Oakland and win twice 6–5 and 12–4. Bill Melton led the attack with a two-run homer in the opener and a grand slam in the nightcap in the sixth inning off Bob Locker. Mike Andrews and Jay Johnstone, two players acquired in deals the previous off-season, also homered in the second game, and both added a double and a single as well. Andrews scored three runs and drove in four. Johnstone scored four times.

                After the awful 1970 season, the White Sox were such an unattractive commodity that WMAQ-AM dropped the club from the station's lineup. The Sox couldn't find another Chicago station to take their games and were reduced to signing with suburban stations WEAW in Evanston and WTAQ in LaGrange. The Sox returned to WMAQ-AM in 1973 after a successful 1972 campaign.

APRIL 9   A crowd of 43,253 at Comiskey Park, the largest for a home opener up to that time, watches the White Sox win 3–2 over the Twins. Rich McKinney drove in the winning run with a two-out single in the ninth inning.

                The big Opening Day crowd came just one season after the White Sox drew only 495,355 fans, the lowest in the major leagues. With a revitalization of the franchise under owner John Allyn, manager Chuck Tanner and general manager Roland Hemond, the White Sox drew 833,891 fans in 1971 while improving the club's won-lost record from 56–106 to 79–83. The Sox were 51–41 from June 29 through the end of the season. With new pitching coach Johnny Sain at the controls, the staff ERA was lowered from 4.56 in 1970 to 3.12 in 1971. The Sox also had some home-run power. The team hit 138 homers, which ranked fifth in the league and was above the American League average of 124 per team. Amazingly, it was the first time since 1917 that the Sox hit more homers than the league average. That season, the club collected 18 home runs compared to the league average of 17.

MAY 2   Wilbur Wood records his first win as a starting pitcher since June 23, 1968, with a 3–1 decision over the Senators in Washington.

                Wood had made 239 appearances as a reliever from 1968 through 1970, leading the AL in games pitched all three seasons. When Joe Horlen went down with an injury during spring training, the Sox made the bold decision to convert Wood into a starting pitcher. The change of assignments couldn't have worked out better. With a knuckleball that placed less strain on his arm than hurlers with a more conventional array of pitches, Wood made 42 starts in 1971, completed 22 and pitched 334 innings while compiling a 22–13 record and an earned run average of only 1.91. During the 24-month period from June 1, 1971, through May 31, 1973, Wood had a record of 56–31.

MAY 6   The White Sox draw 511 fans into Comiskey Park, commit six errors and lose 10–1 to the Red Sox. The game had been re-scheduled hastily on an open date following the postponement of a game the previous evening and was played on a Thursday afternoon with the threat of rain and temperatures in the 40s.

MAY 9   Rick Reichardt collects seven hits in 10 at-bats during a double-header as the White Sox sweep the Senators 5–0 and 9–5 at Comiskey Park. His seven hits were five singles, a double and a homer. Reichardt had two hits in the opener and five during the second tilt.

MAY 22   The White Sox rout the Angels 13–0 in Anaheim.

MAY 31   The White Sox split an eventful double-header against the Orioles at Comiskey Park. The Sox won the opener 1–0 behind the pitching of Tommy John. Ed Herrmann drove in the lone run with a single in the sixth inning. In the second tilt, won 11–3 by Baltimore, Don Buford hit two home runs and fought both White Sox pitcher Bart Johnson and a fan. In the eighth inning, Johnson struck Buford with a pitch, the second time that the Orioles outfielder was plunked. Buford charged the mound dragging his bat behind him and landed a hard right to Johnson's chest. After Johnson was knocked down by the blow, he got up and delivered a punch to Buford's face. The benches of both teams emptied, but the umpires quickly restored order. Nobody was ejected, but Buford was asked to leave the premises after grappling with a fan in the ninth. The fan leaped onto the field and charged Buford while he was in the on-deck circle. Buford gave the intruder a bloody nose and split lip.

JUNE 8   With the first pick in the 1971 amateur draft, the White Sox select catcher Danny Goodwin from Central High School in Peoria, Illinois.

             The White Sox couldn't sign Goodwin, who opted to attend Southern University. Goodwin was once again the number-one pick in the draft in 1975 when he was selected by the California Angels, but he hit only .236 with 13 homers in 252 big-league games. The only future major leaguers drafted by the White Sox in 1971 were Samuel Ewing (first round of the secondary draft in January), Bill Sharp (second round of the June regular phase), Jeff Holly (17th round of the regular phase) and Pete Varney (first round of the secondary phase in June). None had a major league career longer than five years. A catcher, Varney was a hero in one of the most famous college football games of all-time. Trailing 29–13 with 42 seconds to play in 1968, Harvard scored two touchdowns and converted a pair of two-point conversions to tie Yale 29–29. Varney caught a pass in the end zone for the second two-point conversion after time expired.

JUNE 15   Bill Melton hits a grand slam off Mike Kilkenny in the sixth inning of a 6–1 win over the Tigers in Detroit.

JUNE 20   The White Sox trounce the Twins 18–8 in Minnesota. Trailing 4–0, the Sox erupted for nine runs in the sixth inning and six more in the seventh. Rick Reichardt hit a grand slam off Jim Strickland in the seventh.

JUNE 22   The White Sox score eight runs in the second inning and down the Royals 11–6 at Comiskey Park.

JUNE 23   The White Sox continue their hot hitting with a 12–3 victory over the Royals at Comiskey Park. The Sox scored 46 runs over a four-game span.

JULY 3   Tommy John pitches the White Sox to a 1–0 win over the Royals in Kansas City. Rich McKinney drove in the lone run with a triple in the eighth inning.

JULY 4   On Chuck Tanner's 42nd birthday, the White Sox win 1–0 over the Royals in Kansas City for the second day in a row. Wilbur Wood pitched the shutout. Carlos May drove in the lone run with a single in the fourth inning.

May hit .294 with seven homers in 1971.

JULY 7   With the help of speedster Lee Richard, the White Sox defeat the Athletics 2–1 at Comiskey Park. In the seventh inning, Richard broke a 1–1 tie by scoring from second base on Rich McKinney's sacrifice fly, a deep drive to center field.

A former first-round draft choice, Richard was possibly the fastest player in the game during the early 1970s, but he couldn't hit or field. Richard had a .209 career average in 492 at-bats and led the AL in errors by a shortstop in 1971 with 26 despite playing only 68 games at the position.

JULY 11   The White Sox trade 1–0 wins with the Brewers during a double-header at Comiskey Park. Milwaukee won the opener. Wilbur Wood hurled the Sox's shutout. The lone run scored on a home run by Ed Herrmann off Bill Parsons.

JULY 16   Bill Melton's two-run homer off Pete Broberg in the sixth inning accounted for the only runs in a 2–0 win over the Senators in Washington. Tommy John pitched the shutout.

The contest marked the final time that the White Sox played the Senators in Washington. The franchise moved to Texas after the conclusion of the 1971 season and was renamed the Rangers.

JULY 18   The White Sox lose a tough double-header 3–2 and 6–1 to the Yankees in New York. The Yanks scored three runs in the ninth to win the opener. In the second game, Mike Kekich pitched a one-hitter. The only Chicago hit was a home run by Mike Andrews in the fifth inning.

JULY 19   The White Sox explode for five runs in the 10th inning and defeat the Yankees 8–3 in the first game of a double-header in New York. Ed Herrmann capped the rally with a three-run homer. The Sox won the second game 3–1.

JULY 20   Carlos May collects five hits in five at-bats, but the Red Sox lose 5–4 in Boston.

JULY 25   White Sox catcher Tom Egan blasts a home run either onto or over the left-field roof at Comiskey Park during a 9–6 win over the Senators in the second game of a double-header. Witnesses disagreed as to whether or not the ball bounced on the roof or cleared it. The Sox also won the opener 5–1.

JULY 27   The White Sox score four runs in the 12th inning to defeat the Yankees 9–6 at Comiskey Park. The Yanks scored once in the top of the 12th on an error by Bill Melton at third base. In the bottom half, Pat Kelly drove in the tying run with a double, then Melton belted a three-run walk-off homer.

AUGUST 5   Wilbur Wood pitches the White Sox to a 1–0 win over the Angels in Anaheim. Tom Egan drove in the lone run with a single in the seventh inning.

AUGUST 6   Tom Bradley pitches a two-hitter and Mike Andrews hit a grand slam in the sixth inning off Blue Moon Odom to lead the White Sox to a 7–0 win over the Athletics in Oakland. The only hits off Bradley were a single by Sal Bando in the second inning and a triple by Bert Campaneris in the sixth.

AUGUST 8   Fisticuffs enliven a 9–7 win over the Athletics in the first game of a double-header in Oakland. Bert Campaneris accused Bart Johnson of throwing at him and charged the mound. Players poured onto the field from both sides and quite a few punches were thrown. Ed Herrmann kept his catcher's mask on and was in the thick of the melee. He was the only casualty, suffering a skinned nose. The Sox insisted that Angel Mangual of the A's struck Herrmann with a bat. Chicago also won game two 3–1.

AUGUST 17   White Sox infielder Steve Huntz hits two homers during a 6–5 win over the Tigers in the first game of a double-header in Detroit. The homers were the only two that Huntz struck in 1971, and were the last two of the 16 he collected during his big-league career. The Sox also won the second tilt 4–1.

AUGUST 26   Rain wipes out a White Sox rally in the ninth, resulting in an 8–7 loss to the Orioles at Memorial Stadium. The Sox fell behind 6–0 in the fourth inning, then battled back to tie the contest 7–7 before Baltimore plated a run in the eighth. In the ninth, Mike Andrews hit a pinch-homer, Bill Melton doubled and then scored on a single by Carlos May for a 9–8 lead. Before the inning could be completed, however, it began to rain heavily, preventing any further play. According to the rules then in effect, the score reverted back to the previous full inning of play, and the contest went into the books as an 8–7 Baltimore victory.

SEPTEMBER 1   The White Sox outlast the Twins for a 2–0 win in 11 innings at Minnesota. The runs were driven in on a single by Carlos May and a sacrifice fly from Walt Williams. Wilbur Wood (nine innings), Bart Johnson (one inning) and Vicente Romo (one inning) combined on the shutout.

               A power pitcher, Johnson reached the majors as a 19-year-old in 1969, but he had a career beset with arm injuries. In 1972, the Sox tried to convert him into an outfielder. Johnson was sent to Appleton in the Midwest League and played in 50 games, batting .329 with six homers and a .538 slugging percentage. He returned to pitching in the majors in 1973, but played in his last game in 1977 when he was only 27, finishing with a career record of 43–51.

SEPTEMBER 6   Steve Kealey hits the last White Sox home run by a pitcher prior to the passage of the designated hitter rule in 1973. It was struck during a 6–2 win over the Twins in the first game of a double-header at Comiskey Park. Minnesota won the second contest 10–2.

               The homer was the only one of Kealey's career in 26 at-bats.

SEPTEMBER 13   Rick Reichardt hits two homers and drives in five runs during a 6–3 win over the Royals in Kansas City.

SEPTEMBER 21   Bart Johnson strikes out 12 batters in eight innings and beats the Athletics 5–1 in Oakland. The White Sox also won the second game 6–2.

On the same day, the American League approved the move of the Washington Senators franchise to Dallas-Fort Worth, where the club was renamed the Texas Rangers. The vote to approve the transfer was 10–2, with White Sox owner John Allyn casting one of the two negative votes. For geographic balance, it was necessary to move the former Senators from the Eastern Division to the West. The White Sox and the Brewers where the two easternmost clubs in the Western Division and both campaigned to move to the East. Possibly because of Allyn's objection to the shift of the Washington club to Texas, the AL voted to place the Brewers in the East instead of the White Sox.

SEPTEMBER 29   Bill Melton accounts for both White Sox runs with a pair of homers during a 2–1 win over the Brewers at Comiskey Park. The first homer was struck off Jim Slaton in the first inning and reached the upper deck. The second was hit off Slaton in the third and landed in the deep regions of the lower deck in left field. The home runs lifted Melton into a three-way tie for the American League home run title with one game remaining. Melton, Norm Cash of the Tigers and Reggie Jackson of the Athletics each had 32 home runs. The Tigers and A's finished their seasons on September 29. The Sox had one game left to give Melton a shot at the home run title.

"Beltin' Bill" Melton belted 33 homers in 1971 to lead the American League. A power source at the hot corner, Melton hit over 20 home runs five times for the Sox.

SEPTEMBER 30   On the final day of the season, Bill Melton becomes the first player in White Sox history to win the American League home run title with a blast into the left-field stands off Bill Parsons during a 2–1 win over the Brewers at Comiskey Park. Chuck Tanner had put Melton in the lead-off spot in the lineup to give him the possibility of an extra at-bat. It was Melton's 33rd homer of the year, breaking a three-way tie for the lead with Norm Cash and Reggie Jackson. After the home run, Tanner took Melton out of the game and replaced him with Walt Williams, who played third base for the first time in his career.

In addition to his 33 homers, Melton hit .269 and drove in 86 runs in 1971.

DECEMBER 2   The White Sox trade Tommy John to the Dodgers for Richie Allen, then deal Rich McKinney to the Yankees for Stan Bahnsen.

The John-for-Allen trade was a long-term disaster for the White Sox, but in the short-term it might well have saved the Chicago White Sox franchise. Allen helped to reinvigorate a dying club by bringing a new level of excitement to the South Side and inducing people to come back to Comiskey Park after years in which the White Sox posted some of the lowest attendance figures in the American League. After leaving Chicago, John won 204 more big-league games, was named to four All-Star teams and played in four World Series. An enigmatic figure who was charming and gregarious one day and sullen and uncommunicative the next, Allen came to the club with considerable baggage. Rebellious and an iconoclast, he did things his own way and was almost always at odds with management and the center of controversy during his entire career. Allen won the National League Rookie of the Year Award with the Phillies in 1964 and had spent eight full seasons in the majors before playing for the White Sox. In 1969, his behavior led to a 28-day suspension by the Phils. Although there were concerns about his attitude and his deficiencies on defense, there was no question about his bat. At the end of the 1971 season, Allen had a lifetime batting average of .297 with 234 homers in 4,229 at-bats. He had not yet turned 30. But due in large part to his battles with management, Allen was traded to the Cardinals before the 1970 season. After one season in St. Louis, Allen was dealt to the Dodgers. The White Sox were his fourth team in four years. Manager Chuck Tanner had known the Allen family for decades. Both were from nearby towns in western Pennsylvania, and Tanner played high school basketball against Allen's older brother. The 1972 season didn't start well, though. Allen demanded a $135,000 contract from his new employers. The Sox agreed to Allen's request, but he failed to show up for spring training. The players called a strike on April 1, and finally Allen showed up in camp ready to play. Once the 1972 regular season began, a week late due to the strike, Allen was a man on a mission and silenced many of his critics. With easygoing Tanner as manager, Allen had what is arguably the greatest season in club history. He led the AL in home runs (37), runs batted in (113), walks (99), on-base percentage (.420) and slugging percentage (.603) and ranked second in total bases (305), third in batting average (.308) and fourth in runs (90). Allen was a divisive force in the clubhouse, however. To keep his slugging first baseman happy and content, Tanner had one set of rules for Allen and another for the rest of the team. The slugger was allowed to skip batting practice and to show up only a half-hour before game time, a courtesy that Tanner extended to no one else on the club. Richie was even on the cover of Sports Illustrated *with a lit cigarette hanging out of his mouth while juggling three baseballs in full uniform standing in the Comiskey Park dugout. Allen was off to a great start in 1973, but he broke his leg on June 28, ending his season. He had another great season in 1974 until September 14, when he walked out on the team. After tearing down much of what he built up, Allen was traded to the Braves during the 1974–75 off-season. Bahnsen was also a tremendous short-term acquisition. He won 21 games for the Sox in 1972 and 18 more in 1973. McKinney hit just .220 in 200 at-bats after the trade with the Yankees for Bahnsen.*

1972

Season in a Sentence

With Richie Allen leading the charge, the White Sox are in first place in late August before finishing second to the Athletics.

Finish • Won • Lost • Pct • GB

Second 87 67 .565 5.5

Manager

Chuck Tanner

Stats

Stats	WS	AL	Rank
Batting Avg:	.238	.239	6
On-Base Pct:	.311	.308	4
Slugging Pct:	.346	.343	6
Home Runs:	108		4
Stolen Bases:	100		2
ERA:	3.12	3.06	8
Fielding Avg:	.977	.979	9
Runs Scored:	566		4
Runs Allowed:	538		8

Starting Lineup

Ed Herrmann, c
Richie Allen, 1b
Mike Andrews, 2b
Ed Spiezio, 3b
Rich Morales, ss
Carlos May, lf
Jay Johnstone, cf
Pat Kelly, rf
Rick Reichardt, cf
Luis Alvarado, ss
Walt Williams, rf
Bill Melton, 3b

Pitchers

Wilbur Wood, sp
Stan Bahnsen, sp
Tom Bradley, sp
Dave Lemonds, sp-rp
Terry Forster, rp
Steve Kealey, rp
Goose Gossage, rp

Attendance

1,177,318 (third in AL)

Club Leaders

Batting Avg:	Richie Allen	.308
	Carlos May	.308
On-Base Pct:	Richie Allen	.420
Slugging Pct:	Richie Allen	.603
Home Runs:	Richie Allen	37
RBIs:	Richie Allen	113
Runs:	Richie Allen	90
Stolen Bases:	Pat Kelly	32
Wins:	Wilbur Wood	24
Strikeouts:	Tom Bradley	209
ERA:	Wilbur Wood	2.51
Saves:	Terry Forster	29

APRIL 6   The White Sox scheduled season opener against the Athletics at Comiskey Park is postponed by baseball's first players' strike. Chicago's first eight games were eliminated by the labor action, which began on April 1 and ended on April 13.

APRIL 15   With the strike settled, the White Sox open the 1972 season in Kansas City and lose 2–1 to the Royals in 11 innings. In his Chicago debut, Richie Allen hit a home run in the ninth inning for a 1–0 lead. With two out in the bottom of the ninth, Bob Oliver homered off Wilbur Wood to tie the score 1–1. Kansas City won the game with a run in the 11th off Bart Johnson.

APRIL 18   The White Sox romp over the Rangers 14–0 in the home opener before 20,943 at Comiskey Park. Carlos May drove in six runs on a homer, a double and two singles. Pat Kelly collected two triples and a double. Wilbur Wood pitched the three-hit shutout.

The White Sox were 55–23 at home in 1972 and just 32–44 on the road.

APRIL 22   Wilbur Wood pitches the White Sox to a 1–0 win over the Royals in the first game of a double-header in Kansas City. It was his second consecutive shutout. The Sox also won the second contest 3–2.

APRIL 25   Wilbur Wood pitches his third consecutive shutout, beating the Indians 6–0 on a
35-degree day at Comiskey Park.

*In his first four starts of 1972, Wood pitched 36 innings and allowed only one
run. The four starts came over a period of 11 days. Wood tied a White Sox
record for most games started by a pitcher in a season with 49. It was set by
Ed Walsh in 1908. Wood pitched on two days' rest 26 times in 1972. He
finished the year with a 24–17 record and a 2.51 ERA in 376²/₃ innings. Wood
was one of three White Sox pitchers with 40 or more starts in 1972. Stan
Bahnsen, in his first year with the club, was 21–16 with a 3.61 earned run
average in 252¹/₃ innings in 41 starts. Tom Bradley drew 40 starting assignments
and was 15–14 with a 2.98 ERA in 252 innings. The rest of the staff combined
to start only 24 games. The bullpen was anchored by a pair of 20-year-olds in
Terry Forster and Goose Gossage. Forster debuted with the Sox in 1971 at the
age of 19 after pitching only 10 minor league games. In 1972, he had a 6–5
record, a 2.25 ERA and 29 saves with 104 strikeouts in 100 innings. Gossage
won his first seven major league decisions, finishing the 1972 season with a 7–1
record, but he hadn't yet harnessed the skills that made him a Hall of Famer. He
had a 4.28 ERA with 44 walks and 57 strikeouts in 80 innings.*

Dick Allen hit 37 home runs in 1972 and won the MVP Award. His stay in
Chicago was brief, as it was with most teams who took a chance on Allen.

Both Forster and Gossage were converted into starters by the White Sox in 1976, then traded together to the Pirates (see December 10, 1976).

APRIL 26   A two-run, walk-off homer by Richie Allen in the ninth inning beats the Indians 7–5 at Comiskey Park.

MAY 20   Stan Bahnsen pitches a two-hitter to defeat the Angels 8–0 at Comiskey Park. Ken McMullen collected both California hits with singles in the second and eighth innings.

MAY 21   Carlos May hits a dramatic two-out, three-run homer in the ninth inning to beat the Angels 9–8 at Comiskey Park.

MAY 22   The White Sox play the Rangers in Texas for the first time and win 7–6 in 10 innings at Arlington Stadium.

JUNE 2   The White Sox purchase Phil Regan from the Cubs.

JUNE 3   The Yankees explode for eight runs in the 13th inning, all off Bart Johnson, and win 18–10 over the White Sox at Comiskey Park.

JUNE 4   Richie Allen thrills a Comiskey Park crowd of 51,904, the largest since 1954, by coming off the bench in the ninth inning as a pinch-hitter and delivering a three-run, walk-off homer for a 5–4 win in the second game of a double-header against the Yankees. The Sox also won the opener 6–1.

             Allen hit 27 of his 37 homers in 1972 at Comiskey Park.

JUNE 6   In the first round of the amateur draft, the White Sox select outfielder Mike Ordina from Rancho Cordova High School in Rancho Cordova, California.

             The 1972 draft was one of the worst in White Sox history. The only future major leaguers drafted and signed were George Enright (sixth round) and Nyls Nyman (16th round). Enright played in only two big league games, and Nyman appeared in just 106 over two seasons.

JUNE 11   The White Sox club five home runs during a 6–4 win over the Brewers in the first game of a double-header at Comiskey Park. Richie Allen hit two homers, with Ed Herrmann, Luis Alvarado and Mike Andrews each adding one.

JUNE 14   A two-run homer by Carlos May off Mel Stottlemyre in the eighth inning accounts for the only two runs in a 2–0 victory over the Yankees in New York. Wilbur Wood pitched the shutout. The decision was Wood's 10th win of the season, and occurred in Chicago's 49th game.

             May hit .308 with 12 home runs in 1972.

JUNE 21   Four days after the break-in of the Democratic Party National Committee headquarters at the Watergate complex in Washington, the White Sox score eight runs in the eighth inning to defeat the Brewers 9–3 in Milwaukee.

JUNE 25   The White Sox score seven runs in the fourth inning and defeat the Rangers 10–5 in Arlington. The big blow was a grand slam by Carlos May off Jim Panther.

JULY 18   The White Sox lose 4–3 in 12 innings to the Tigers in Detroit.

             The defeat gave the Sox a 45–40 record and a position 8½ games behind the first-place Athletics.

JULY 23   Chuck Tanner asks home plate umpire Mark Anthony three times to inspect Cleveland pitcher Gaylord Perry in a search for a foreign substance during a 2–1 win in the first game of a double-header at Comiskey Park. The inspections revealed nothing, but Perry seemed unnerved. Tanner asked for searches twice with Richie Allen at-bat in the seventh and ninth innings, and Allen followed with a home run in the seventh and a single in the ninth that led to the winning run. The Sox won game two 4–3.

JULY 24   Stan Bahnsen holds the Royals hitless for 7⅔ innings before giving up three singles in the eighth inning that produce two runs and lead to a 3–0 loss in the second game of a double-header at Comiskey Park. The first hit off Bahnsen was struck by opposing pitcher Roger Nelson. The Sox won the opener 7–3.

JULY 31   Richie Allen hits two inside-the-park homers during an 8–1 victory over the Twins at Comiskey Park. In the first inning with two men on base, Allen hit a drive that bounced over the head of center fielder Bobby Darwin, who slipped trying to field the ball. Batting again in the fifth, Allen hit another drive to center and circled the bases when Darwin missed an attempted shoestring catch. Both homers were struck off Bert Blyleven.

AUGUST 9   Wilbur Wood pitches and hits his way to a 1–0 win over the Angels in Anaheim. Wood not only threw a complete game, but he drove in the lone run with a single off Nolan Ryan with two out in the seventh inning.

AUGUST 10   The White Sox and Athletics play 17 innings in Oakland before the game is suspended by the American League's 1:00 a.m. curfew with the score 3–3. Both teams scored in the 14th. The contest was completed the following day.

AUGUST 11   The White Sox and Athletics finish their suspended game of August 10, with the A's winning 5–3 in 19 innings in Oakland. The contest ended on a two-run, walk-off homer by Joe Rudi off Stan Bahnsen. The White Sox won the regularly scheduled game 1–0. Dave Lemonds (6⅔ innings) and Cy Acosta (2⅓ innings) combined on a two-hitter. The only hits by the A's were singles by Sal Bando in the fifth inning and Dave Duncan in the seventh, both off Lemonds. Carlos May drove in the lone run with a single in the seventh.

AUGUST 12   Erasing an 8 ½-game deficit in just 25 days with 17 wins in 22 games, the White Sox take first place with an 11-inning, 3–1 win over the Athletics in Oakland. Wilbur Wood pitched a complete game and allowed only two hits, earning his 20th victory in Chicago's 107th game of the season. Brant Alyea collected both hits off Wood with singles in the seventh inning and a homer with two out in the bottom of the ninth that tied the score 1–1. The two runs in the 11th scored on a home run by Ed Spiezio, who hit only two out of the park in 277 at-bats in 1972.

Spiezio was the White Sox's starting third baseman during the second half of 1972 because Bill Melton was limited to 57 games during the season due to a herniated disc.

AUGUST 17   The White Sox trade Bruce Miller and Bruce Kimm to the Angels for Eddie Fisher.

AUGUST 20   After the Red Sox score three runs in the top of the ninth for a 7–5 lead, the White Sox bounce back with four in their half to win 9–7 in the first game of a double-header at Comiskey Park. Walt Williams drove in the first run with a single, then Pat Kelly belted a three-run walk-off homer. Boston won the second tilt 5–4.

AUGUST 23   Richie Allen becomes the first White Sox batter, and just the fourth overall, to homer into the center-field bleachers at Comiskey Park during a 5–2 win over the Yankees. The drive traveled approximately 460 feet and landed about 15 feet from Harry Caray, who was broadcasting from the bleachers. The ball was caught by Mark Liptak, a fan who was interviewed by Caray on the air. Those who had homered into the bleachers previously were Jimmie Foxx in 1934, Hank Greenberg in 1938 and Alex Johnson in 1970.

AUGUST 29   The White Sox are knocked out of first place with a 3–0 loss to the Red Sox in Boston.

SEPTEMBER 13   The White Sox play at Municipal Stadium in Kansas City for the last time and lose 6–4 to the Royals.

SEPTEMBER 15   The White Sox lose 1–0 to the Angels in Anaheim. The tough loss put the Sox four games behind the Athletics with 15 games left to play.

SEPTEMBER 16   A two-run homer by Richie Allen off Nolan Ryan in the fifth inning accounts for the only runs in a 2–0 win over the Angels in Anaheim. Stan Bahnsen (eight innings) and Terry Forster (one inning) combined on the shutout.

SEPTEMBER 19   Jorge Orta hits a home run in the 15th inning to defeat the Athletics 8–7 in Oakland. The A's scored twice in the ninth to tie the score 5–5. Both teams scored two runs in the 13th. Oakland manager Dick Williams used 30 players in the contest to set a major league record. The victory kept the White Sox's slim hopes of winning the pennant alive. The Sox were four games out with 12 left on the schedule.

SEPTEMBER 20   The White Sox lose 6–3 to the Athletics in Oakland, all but dashing hopes for a division pennant. The defeat left the Sox five games out with 11 to play.

SEPTEMBER 22   Stan Bahnsen earns his 20th win of the season with an 8–4 win over the Rangers at Comiskey Park.

OCTOBER 2   With the White Sox trailing 4–2, Buddy Bradford hits a pinch-hit grand slam off Dave LaRoche in the eighth inning to beat the Twins 6–4 in Minnesota.

OCTOBER 3   The White Sox score two runs in the ninth inning to beat the Twins 5–4 in Minnesota. Acting as a pinch-hitter, Terry Forster delivered a single to tie the score 4–4. The winning run scored on an error.

Forster collected 12 hits in his first 24 at-bats in the majors over the course of the 1971 and 1972 seasons, a batting average of an even .500. The designated hitter rule (see December 10, 1972) limited him to one at-bat over the next four seasons, but a trade to the Pirates in 1977 put a bat in his hands once more. Forster finished his career with a batting average of .397 on 31 hits in 78 at-bats.

OCTOBER 19   The White Sox trade Walt Williams to the Indians for Eddie Leon.

NOVEMBER 28   Three weeks after Richard Nixon defeats George McGovern in the presidential election, the White Sox trade Tom Bradley to the Giants for Ken Henderson and Steve Stone.

DECEMBER 10   The American League votes to adopt the designated hitter rule on a three-year experimental basis. Under the new rule, the designated hitter replaced the pitcher in the batting order unless otherwise noted before the game. The rule was adopted permanently by the AL in 1975, but to this day the NL has declined to go along with the change.

1973   Sox

Season in a Sentence

The White Sox draw more fans than in any season since 1960 and are in first place on June 29, but they limp to fifth and a losing season after Richie Allen breaks his leg.

Finish • Won • Lost • Pct • GB

Fifth   77   85   .475   17.0

Manager

Chuck Tanner

Stats

Stats	WS	AL	Rank
Batting Avg:	.256	.259	7
On-Base Pct:	.326	.331	7
Slugging Pct:	.372	.381	10
Home Runs:	111		10
Stolen Bases:	83		8
Fielding Avg:	.977	.977	7
ERA:	3.86	3.82	7
Runs Scored:	652		8
Runs Allowed:	705		8

Starting Lineup

Ed Herrmann, c
Tony Muser, 1b
Jorge Orta, 2b
Bill Melton, 3b
Eddie Leon, ss
Jerry Hairston, lf
Johnny Jeter, rf-cf-lf
Pat Kelly, rf
Carlos May, dh-lf
Ken Henderson, dh-cf
Dick Allen, 1b
Luis Alvarado, 2b
Bill Sharp, cf
Buddy Bradford, cf
Mike Andrews, dh

Pitchers

Wilbur Wood, sp
Stan Bahnsen, sp
Steve Stone, sp-rp
Eddie Fisher, sp-rp
Terry Forster, rp
Cy Acosta, rp

Attendance

1,302,527 (fourth in AL)

Club Leaders

Batting Avg:	Pat Kelly	.280
On-Base Pct:	Bill Melton	.363
Slugging Pct:	Bill Melton	.439
Home Runs:	Bill Melton	20
	Carlos May	20
RBIs:	Carlos May	96
Runs:	Bill Melton	83
Stolen Bases:	Pat Kelly	22
Wins:	Wilbur Wood	24
Strikeouts:	Wilbur Wood	199
ERA:	Wilbur Wood	3.46
Saves:	Cy Acosta	18

FEBRUARY 27   Richie Allen signs a contract for $750,000 over three years. The deal made Allen the
                highest-paid player in the history of the game up to that time. The previous record
                was held by Henry Aaron, who was paid $600,000 in a three-year deal. Allen earned
                $135,000 in 1971.

                *The deal for Allen helped to destroy team morale. Allen agreed to his record-
                breaking deal at a time when 13 other players were unsigned. In order to pay
                for Allen's hefty salary, the White Sox drew a hard line with many others on
                the roster. Two of the unsigned players, Jay Johnstone and Ed Spiezio, were
                released before the season opener. Three others, Stan Bahnsen, Rick Reichardt
                and Mike Andrews, refused to sign and had their contracts renewed by the club
                with significant pay cuts. Bahnsen signed a new pact in mid-June, but Reichardt
                and Andrews never agreed to terms and maintained a running squabble with the
                front office. Reichardt was released on June 28 and caught on with the Royals.
                Andrews was let go on July 10 and signed with the Athletics. The releases of the
                two players came as a surprise to the fans and the media because they came at a
                time when the Sox were in contention for the pennant, were beset with injuries
                and had several players out of action, including Allen (see June 28, 1973).
                Reichardt was hitting .275 in 46 games at the time of his departure. There were
                also indications, never confirmed, that club management agreed to carry Hank
                Allen, Richie's brother, on the roster all season at Richie's request. Hank, who
                had previously retired, got into only 28 games and had a .103 batting average in
                39 at-bats. Chuck Tanner continued to have a special set of rules governing his
                temperamental superstar and another set of demands for the rest of the team,
                further disrupting the peace and harmony on the team.*

APRIL 6   The scheduled season opener against the Rangers in Arlington is rained out.

APRIL 7   The White Sox open the season with a 3–1 win over the Rangers in Arlington.
                Richie Allen hit a home run and Carlos May contributed three singles. Wilbur Wood
                pitched a complete game. Mike Andrews was in the lineup as the White Sox's first
                designated hitter.

                *Comiskey Park organist Nancy Faust played a few bars from "Jesus Christ
                Superstar" when Allen stepped to the plate in 1973, but the practice was stopped
                because of complaints from many fans.*

APRIL 10   The White Sox scheduled home opener against the Athletics is postponed by cold
                weather.

APRIL 11   In the home opener, the White Sox lose 12–2 to the Athletics before 22,091 at
                Comiskey Park.

                *Harry Caray, who announced White Sox games on the radio only in 1971 and
                1972, was on radio and television both in 1973. On the radio he partnered with
                Gene Osborn and on TV with Bob Waller.*

APRIL 12   Ken Henderson hits a grand slam off Rollie Fingers in the eighth inning of a 6–3 win
                over the Athletics at Comiskey Park. It was Henderson's first homer as a member of
                the White Sox.

APRIL 20   The White Sox play at Royals Stadium in Kansas City for the first time and trounce the Royals 16–2.

APRIL 25   Wilbur Wood shuts out the Yankees 3–0 in New York.

APRIL 29   Wilbur Wood pitches his second consecutive shutout, defeating the Red Sox 5–0 in Boston.

MAY 2   Wilbur Wood pitches his third consecutive shutout, beating the Orioles 4–0 in Baltimore.

MAY 4   Stan Bahnsen (six innings) and Terry Forster (three innings) combine to shut out the Yankees 5–0 at Comiskey Park.

MAY 5   The White Sox defeat the Yankees 4–0 at Comiskey Park for their third shutout in a row. Eddie Fisher (5⅓ innings) and Terry Forster (3⅔ innings) combined on the victory. It was also the Sox's eighth win in a row.

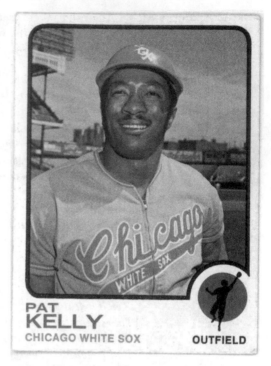

Pat Kelly added speed to the Chicago lineup, swiping 22 bases in 1973. No other teammate had more than eight.

MAY 6   The White Sox extend their winning streak to nine games with an 11–2 decision over the Yankees at Comiskey Park.

MAY 8   The White Sox win 1–0 over the Red Sox at Comiskey Park. The lone run scored on a triple by Pat Kelly and a single from Carlos May in the fourth. Eddie Fisher (6⅓ innings) and Terry Forster (2⅓ innings) combined on the shutout.

MAY 20   The White Sox play before a crowd of 55,555, the largest ever at Comiskey Park. The Sox split a double-header with the Twins, winning 9–3 and losing 3–0.

> *With the club in contention until the All-Star break, the White Sox drew 1,302,527 fans in 1973, the club's highest attendance figure since 1960.*

MAY 26   The White Sox and Indians battle 16 innings at Comiskey Park before the contest is suspended by the American League's 1:00 a.m. curfew with the score 2–2. The game was scheduled for completion the following day.

MAY 27   The completion of the May 26 game between the White Sox and Indians at Comiskey Park is postponed by rain.

MAY 28   At Comiskey Park, the White Sox and Indians complete their suspended game of May 26 with the White Sox winning 6–3 at Comiskey Park. The game resumed in the top of the 17th with the score 2–2. Wilbur Wood took the mound for the Sox and pitched the final five innings. He pitched four shutout innings before giving up an unearned run in the top of the 21st on an error by shortstop Eddie Leon. Wood became the winning pitcher, however, when the Sox rallied in the bottom half. Tony Muser doubled, moved to third on a sacrifice by Chuck Brinkman and scored on a single from Leon. After Pat Kelly singled, Richie Allen belted a three-run walk-off homer. Wood kept on pitching in the regularly scheduled game and pitched a complete game shutout for a 4–0 win. During the afternoon, he hurled 14 innings, gave up only an unearned run and added two victories to his total.

The two wins of May 28 gave the White Sox a record of 26–14. Wood had half of those victories, with a 13–3 record and a 1.70 ERA in 132 innings. He wasn't quite as effective over the remainder of the season, however, with 11 wins, 17 losses and a 4.49 earned run average. Wood finished the season with a 24–20 record and a 3.46 ERA. He became the first pitcher to win at least 20 and lose at least 20 in the same season since Walter Johnson, who was 25–20 with the Senators in 1916. Wood led the AL in wins, games started (48) and innings pitched (359⅓), but his decline over the last four months of the season contributed to the White Sox sinking in the standings. The Sox were 51–71 over the last 122 games.

MAY 31   Brian Downing is injured in his major league debut, a 10–2 win over the Tigers at Comiskey Park. With the game well in hand, he went into the game at third base in the eighth inning in place of Bill Melton. Chasing a foul pop, Downing tore up his knee sliding on the warning track and spent six weeks on the disabled list.

JUNE 5   In the first round of the amateur draft, the White Sox select catcher Steve Swisher from Ohio University.

Swisher was traded to the Cubs five months later and spent nine seasons in the majors. Other future major leaguers drafted and signed by the White Sox in 1974 were Jim Otten (second round), Ken Kravec (third round) and Mike Squires (18th round).

JUNE 17   The Brewers hit two grand slams during a 15–5 win over the White Sox at Comiskey Park. Darrell Porter cleared the bases with a homer off Stan Bahnsen in the second inning, and Joe Lahoud hit a slam off Goose Gossage in the third.

In keeping with the changing times, mustaches and beards began appearing on the faces of White Sox players in 1973 for the first time since the beginning of the 20th century. Among those sporting facial hair were Rick Reichardt, Rich Morales, Eddie Leon, Tony Muser, Luis Alvarado and Richie Allen.

JUNE 21   Stan Bahnsen allows 12 hits and walks one, but he pitches a complete-game shutout to defeat the Athletics 2–0 at Comiskey Park.

JUNE 24   Ed Herrmann drives in seven runs during an 11–1 win over the Athletics in the second game of a double-header in Oakland. Herrmann contributed a three-run homer, a two-run double and a two-run single. The A's won the opener 7–0.

JUNE 28   Richie Allen suffers a hairline fracture of his right leg during a 2–0 win over the Angels in Anaheim. Allen was injured in a collision with Mike Epstein while leaping for a high throw.

Allen batted only five more times in 1973. It was a devastating blow to the White Sox. In the 68 games he played, Allen hit 16 homers and drove in 41 runs, along with a .316 batting average and a .612 slugging percentage.

JULY 3   Tony Muser singles and draws a club-record five walks in six plate appearances during a 15–1 walloping of the Rangers in the first game of a double-header in Arlington. Texas won the second tilt 2–1.

JULY 8   The Red Sox explode for nine runs in the 10th inning to win 11–2 over the White Sox in the second game of a double-header at Comiskey Park. The White Sox won the opener 6–1.

JULY 10   The White Sox release Mike Andrews.

Andrews had been involved in a salary squabble with the White Sox (see February 27, 1973). The Athletics signed Andrews on August 1, where he became involved in a firestorm during the World Series against the Mets. Andrews made two critical errors at second base that led to an Oakland loss in Game Two. A's owner Charlie Finley claimed that Andrews was incapacitated by a shoulder injury and tried to replace him with another player on the roster. Commissioner Bowie Kuhn ordered that Andrews be reinstated and leveled a heavy fine on Finley for his attempts to "fire" Andrews by making false statements about the infielder's health. Andrews made a pinch-hitting appearance in the fourth game and received a standing ovation from the Shea Stadium crowd when he stepped to the plate. Andrews grounded out in what proved to be his last plate appearance in the majors.

JULY 13   The White Sox score three runs in the ninth inning to beat the Orioles 3–2 at Comiskey Park. Ken Henderson doubled in the tying run and scored on a single by Del Unser.

JULY 20   Wilbur Wood starts both ends of a double-header against the Yankees in New York and is the losing pitcher in both games by scores of 12–2 and 7–0. The second tilt was stopped by rain after six innings. Oddly, Wood had the same pitching line in both starts. In each, he pitched 4⅓ innings, allowed seven runs, five earned, surrendered seven hits, walked no one and fanned two.

JULY 27   Stu Holcomb resigns from his position as executive vice president and general manager of the White Sox. Roland Hemond, who had been director of player personnel, became vice president and general manager.

Holcomb was in charge of the promotional and marketing aspects of the club as well as negotiating player contracts. He accused Chuck Tanner and Hemond of undermining his authority. The media had been criticizing Holcomb for months because of the contentious contract disputes with several players, which led to the release of Rick Reichardt and Mike Andrews (see February 27, 1973).

JULY 29   In the White Sox's 103rd game of 1973, Wilbur Wood wins his 20th game with an 8–6 win over the Twins in Minnesota. It was Wood's third consecutive season with 20 or more wins.

AUGUST 7   Down 5–0, the White Sox score three runs in the sixth inning, two in the eighth and one in the 12th to defeat the Indians 6–5 at Comiskey Park. In the 12th, Bill Melton singled, stole second and scored on a single by Jerry Hairston.

After missing most of the 1972 season with a herniated disc, Melton hit .277 with 20 homers in 1973.

AUGUST 11   Brian Downing's first major league hit is an inside-the-park homer off Mickey Lolich during a 6–3 loss to the Tigers in Detroit.

AUGUST 15   The White Sox purchase Jim Kaat from the Twins.

Kaat was 34 years old and looked to be on his way out of the majors when purchased by the Sox. Under pitching coach Johnny Sain, Kaat revived his career in Chicago, winning 21 games in 1974 and 20 in 1975.

AUGUST 21   Facing the Indians in Cleveland, Stan Bahnsen loses a one-hitter with one out in the ninth inning when Walt Williams hits a single. Bahnsen had to settle for a 4–0 win and a one-hitter.

AUGUST 22   The White Sox lose 1–0 to the Indians in 12 innings in Cleveland.

AUGUST 29   The White Sox sell Eddie Fisher to the Cardinals.

SEPTEMBER 2   Outfielder Johnny Jeter has a big day in a 13–2 win over the Angels at Comiskey Park. Jeter led off the first inning with a home run on Clyde Wright's first pitch. During the White Sox's eight-run seventh inning, Jeter hit a double and a single.

SEPTEMBER 4   The White Sox whip the Rangers 14–0 at Comiskey Park.

SEPTEMBER 11   In his major league debut, White Sox first baseman Samuel Ewing strikes out four times in four plate appearances against Nolan Ryan during a 3–1 loss in Anaheim.

SEPTEMBER 22   Stan Bahnsen loses his 20th game of the season, allowing five runs in one-third of an inning during a 9–3 loss to the Athletics at Comiskey Park.

Bahnsen had a record of 18–21 with a 3.57 ERA in 282⅓ innings in 1973.

SEPTEMBER 23   Wilbur Wood loses his 20th game of the season with a 10–5 defeat at the hands of the Athletics at Comiskey Park.

Ten different pitchers have accounted for the 12 seasons of 20 or more losses in a season during the history of the White Sox. Wood and Ted Lyons both lost 20 or more twice. Wood and Bahnsen are the only two to lose at least 20 in the same season, and were the first since Bill Wight was 9–20 in 1948. The last White Sox pitcher with 20 losses was Wood in 1975 when he posted a 16–20 record.

SEPTEMBER 26   Buddy Bradford hits a walk-off homer in the 10th inning to beat the Royals at Comiskey Park.

SEPTEMBER 30   In the final game of the season, the White Sox win 1–0 in 10 innings against the Athletics at Comiskey Park. The run scored on a bases-loaded walk to Bucky Dent. Steve Stone (9⅓ innings) and Cy Acosta (two-thirds of an inning) combined on the shutout.

> *Acosta had a 10–6 record, 18 saves and a 2.25 ERA out of the White Sox bullpen in 1973. A growth on the cornea of his right eye disabled him for much of 1974, however, and he never won another big-league game.*

DECEMBER 11   Two months after Vice President Spiro Agnew resigns due to financial improprieties, the White Sox trade Steve Stone, Ken Frailing, Steve Swisher and Jim Kremmel to the Cubs for Ron Santo.

> *Santo was 33 years old and in the decline phase of his career, but he was still one of the best third basemen in the game when acquired by the White Sox. He made his ninth career All-Star team in 1973. Acquiring him was a useless transaction, however, as the Sox already had Bill Melton at third base. With Melton playing the bulk of the time at the position, Santo moved to second base and designated hitter. With the Sox, he played only one season, the last of his career, and batted only .221 with five home runs in 375 at-bats. Stone and Frailing could have helped a pitching staff that finished 11th in a 12-team league in ERA in 1974.*

1974   Sox

Season in a Sentence

At the end of a tumultuous .500 season, Richie Allen "retires" and is dealt to the Atlanta Braves.

Finish • Won • Lost • Pct • GB

Finish	Won	Lost	Pct	GB
Fourth	80	80	.500	9.0

Manager

Chuck Tanner

Stats

Stats	WS	AL	Rank
Batting Avg:	.268	.258	3
On-Base Pct:	.333	.326	4
Slugging Pct:	.389	.371	1
Home Runs:	135		1
Stolen Bases:	64		11
ERA:	3.94	3.62	11
Fielding Avg:	.977	.977	6
Runs Scored:	684		4
Runs Allowed:	721		11

Starting Lineup

Ed Herrmann, c
Richie Allen, 1b
Jorge Orta, 2b
Bill Melton, 3b
Bucky Dent, ss
Carlos May, lf
Ken Henderson, cf
Bill Sharp, rf
Pat Kelly, dh-rf
Ron Santo, dh-2b-3b
Brian Downing, c-rf
Tony Muser, 1b

Pitchers

Wilbur Wood, sp
Jim Kaat, sp
Stan Bahnsen, sp
Bart Johnson, sp
Terry Forster, rp
Skip Pitlock, rp
Goose Gossage, rp

Attendance

1,149,596 (sixth in AL)

Club Leaders

Batting Avg:	Jorge Orta	.316
On-Base Pct:	Richie Allen	.375
Slugging Pct:	Richie Allen	.563
Home Runs:	Richie Allen	32
RBIs:	Ken Henderson	95
Runs:	Richie Allen	84
Stolen Bases:	Pat Kelly	18
Wins:	Jim Kaat	21
Strikeouts:	Wilbur Wood	169
ERA:	Jim Kaat	2.92
Saves:	Terry Forster	24

APRIL 5

Two months after the kidnapping of Patty Hearst, the White Sox open the season with an 8–2 loss to the Angels before 30,041 at Comiskey Park. Wilbur Wood was the starting and losing pitcher. California broke apart a close game with five runs in the eighth inning off Terry Forster.

> *On a day in which the game-time temperature was 37 degrees, the crowd was unruly. The streaking craze was at its height, and several took a nude romp through the stands. One streaker made a run across the outfield. Fights broke out frequently in almost every area of the stands, and at least one person was carried from the scene of a brawl on a stretcher.*

APRIL 7

The game between the White Sox and Angels at Comiskey Park is called after 10 innings by blowing snow and cold. The snow made it almost impossible for the players to see the baseball. The score was 4–4 and went into the books as a tie. The game began in 39-degree temperatures and a 22-mile-per-hour wind.

APRIL 13

After opening the season with five losses and two ties in their first seven games, the White Sox finally win with a 5–4 decision over the Angels in Anaheim.

> *The Sox fell to 1–8 before righting the ship. The club was 17–14 on May 16 and were in first place in the AL West. From there, the White Sox were consistently mediocre, never more than a few games above or below the .500 mark before finishing the season at 80–80.*

APRIL 21

Trailing 6–4, the White Sox score seven runs in the sixth inning and win 11–6 over the Royals at Comiskey Park. Jorge Orta collected five hits, including a double, in six at-bats.

APRIL 24

Terry Forster strikes out eight batters in three innings of relief to close out a 7–2 win over the Brewers at Comiskey Park.

APRIL 27

Cushion Night at Comiskey Park turns into a fiasco during an 8–3 loss to the Tigers. Spectators were given seat cushions bearing the White Sox insignia when they entered the park. Many littered the field with the cushions, causing a five-minute delay, after an error by second baseman Ron Santo in the sixth inning. Then in the home half of the sixth, another barrage followed Bill Melton's home run, creating a 10-minute halt to play and a warning from umpire Bill Haller that the game would be forfeited if there was another demonstration.

MAY 3

The White Sox score seven runs in the third inning of a 10–3 win over the Brewers in Milwaukee.

MAY 7

Wilbur Wood pitches an eleven-inning complete game, allowing only two hits to defeat the Tigers 1–0 in Detroit. Ed Herrmann accounted for the lone run with a homer off Lerrin LaGrow, who hurled a complete game for the Tigers. The only hits off Wood were singles by Mickey Stanley in the fourth inning and Willie Horton in the 10th.

MAY 10

Terry Forster pitches $8^2/_3$ innings of shutout relief during a 14-inning, 8–7 win over the Rangers in Arlington. The winning run scored on a double by Richie Allen and a single from Jorge Orta.

A 23-year-old second baseman in 1974, Orta burst into stardom with a .316 batting average, which ranked second in the AL behind Rod Carew, and 10 home runs. A native of Mexico, Orta turned down a basketball scholarship from John Wooden at UCLA to sign with the White Sox. Orta's father, Pedro, was known in his day as the Babe Ruth of the Mexican League for his slugging exploits over two decades, but like other dark-skinned players of his generation, Pedro Orta never reached the majors because of the color barrier. Like many White Sox batters of the 1960s and 1970s, Orta seemed to peak during his early 20s and was a role player by the time he was in his early 30s. Shaky defense contributed to Orta's decline, as he was tried out at shortstop before shifting to second base. Later, Orta was moved to third base and the outfield without success.

MAY 15   Stan Bahnsen retires the first 23 batters to face him before beating the Twins 1–0 at Comiskey Park with a two-hitter. Bobby Darwin collected the first Minnesota hit with a single with two out in the eighth inning. Jerry Terrell added a single in the ninth. The lone run of the contest was driven in on a single from Ron Santo off Bert Blyleven in the second inning.

MAY 24   A brawl punctuates a 4–2 loss to the Royals in Kansas City. John Mayberry homered in the second inning, then was hit in the knee by a pitch from Stan Bahnsen in the third. Dropping his bat, Mayberry walked to the mound and exchanged punches with Bahnsen. Mayberry was ejected, but Bahnsen was allowed to remain in the game.

MAY 27   The White Sox play at Shea Stadium for the first time and win 5–3 over the Yankees.

The Yankees used Shea Stadium as a home field in 1974 and 1975 while Yankee Stadium was being remodeled.

JUNE 4   Richie Allen hits a grand slam off Pat Dobson in the fifth inning of a 9–2 win over the Yankees at Comiskey Park.

JUNE 5   The White Sox outlast the Yankees in 15 innings at Comiskey Park. The Sox trailed 5–0 before scoring six runs in the third. The game remained at 6–5 until the Yanks scored in the ninth. The winning run crossed the plate on a double by Jorge Orta.

On the same day, the White Sox selected pitcher Larry Monroe from Forest View High School in the Chicago suburb of Mount Prospect, Illinois, in the first round of the amateur draft. Monroe played in only eight major league games. Other future major leaguers drafted and signed by the White Sox in June 1974 were Jack Kucek (second round), Pete Vuckovich (third round) and Dave Frost (18th round). Kevin Bell was chosen in the first round of the January draft.

JUNE 7   An 8–6 win over the Red Sox at Comiskey Park is delayed for 70 minutes by a fire in a popcorn machine in the eighth inning. Gusty winds carried clouds of smoke from the right-field concession stands onto the playing field. More than 2,000 fans fled for safety. The Chicago Fire Department had 25 pieces of equipment and 125 men on the scene. Eleven people were treated for smoke inhalation. The blaze started when a bundle of paper bags fell into a gas burner used for popping corn.

JUNE 8   The White Sox score seven runs in the sixth inning and defeat the Red Sox 13–6 at Comiskey Park. Ron Santo hit a grand slam off Diego Segui.

JUNE 18   Jim Kaat records the 200th victory of his career with a 7–3 decision over the Indians in Cleveland. The White Sox hit six home runs during the contest. Richie Allen and Jorge Orta each slugged two while Ken Henderson and Carlos May contributed one each.

               Kaat finished his career in 1983 with a record of 288–237. He was 45–28 as a member of the White Sox from 1973 through 1975.

JUNE 19   The White Sox score seven runs in the sixth inning and win 15–4 against the Indians in Cleveland.

JUNE 21   Ken Henderson drives in six runs on two homers and a sacrifice fly during an 11–7 win over the Twins in Minnesota. The Sox collected 21 hits. Carlos May picked up five of them in five at-bats on three singles and two doubles.

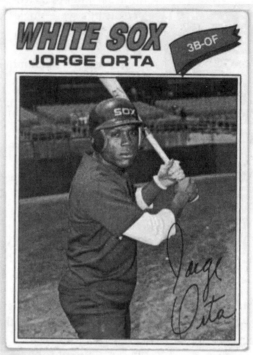

JUNE 30   Jorge Orta collects five hits, including two doubles and a triple, in five at-bats during an 8–3 win over the Twins in the first game of a double-header at Comiskey Park. Minnesota won the second tilt 6–3.

               Orta collected hits in eight consecutive at-bats over two games. During the June 29 contest, a 4–3 win over the Twins, Orta picked up a double and two singles in his last three plate appearances. The eight consecutive hits were four singles, three doubles and a triple.

Second baseman Jorge Orta hit .316 to finish second in the American League in hitting in 1974. He provided an excellent bat and superb defense during his years with the team.

JULY 1   Twenty people are taken into custody by security officers and police after a free-for-all breaks out beneath the stands at Comiskey Park late in a 9–0 loss to the Royals. Security officers and ushers brought the situation under control before the game ended. A streaker, wearing only a shirt, appeared in the seventh inning but was hauled away by security.

JULY 3   Chuck Tanner is struck in the face by umpire Joe Brinkman during a 5–3 loss to the Royals at Comiskey Park. Tanner was ejected in the eighth inning for vigorously protesting a called third strike on Carlos May, who was also ejected. Brinkman accidentally struck Tanner on the left cheek when he gave the thumb in a sweeping gesture.

JULY 7   In his first start following a recall from the White Sox's Iowa farm club in the American Association, Bart Johnson pitches a two-hitter to defeat the Tigers 3–1 in Detroit. Norm Cash homered in the second inning and Mickey Stanley singled in the ninth. In between the two Detroit hits, Johnson retired 20 batters in a row.

Johnson was demoted to the minors at the end of spring training and announced he was retiring to pursue a career in basketball. Johnson changed his mind two weeks later and reported to Iowa. Over the second half of the 1974 season, he was 10–4 with a 2.72 ERA.

JULY 14   Ken Henderson's walk-off homer in the ninth inning beats the Tigers 3–2 at Comiskey Park.

JULY 16   Jim Kaat pitches a two-hitter to defeat the Tigers 6–0 at Comiskey Park. The only Detroit hits were singles by Mickey Stanley in the third inning and Jerry Moses in the eighth.

JULY 23   At Three Rivers Stadium in Pittsburgh, Richie Allen drives in a run in the All-Star Game with a single, but the American League loses 7–2.

JULY 30   Ed Herrmann hits a home run in the 10th inning to beat the Angels 3–2 in Anaheim.

AUGUST 4   The White Sox sweep the Rangers 6–3 and 13–10 at Comiskey Park.

AUGUST 6   The White Sox score seven runs in the second inning and wallop the Angels 12–2 at Comiskey Park.

AUGUST 7   Two outs from being no-hit by Nolan Ryan, the White Sox rally to defeat the Angels 2–1 at Comiskey Park. With one out in the ninth, Richie Allen beat out an infield single. Carlos May reached on an error, and Ken Henderson and Bill Sharp each drove in runs with singles.

AUGUST 16   Eight days after the resignation of Richard Nixon as president, Richie Allen hits a home run in the top of the 13th inning to give the White Sox an 8–7 lead over the Yankees in New York. But Thurman Munson hits a two-run walk-off home run in the bottom half for a 9–8 Chicago loss. Jorge Orta collected five hits, two of them home runs, in seven at-bats. It was Orta's third five-hit game of 1974.

With 135 home runs, the White Sox led the American League for the first time in club history. The Sox didn't lead the AL in homers again until 2004.

AUGUST 31   The Yankees explode for 25 hits and hammer the White Sox 18–6.

SEPTEMBER 3   Wilbur Wood records his 20th win of the season with a complete game to defeat the Royals 6–4 in Kansas City. Jorge Orta smacked a two-run double in the 10th.

The victory gave Wood 20 or more wins four seasons in a row. He was 20–19 with a 3.60 ERA in 320⅓ innings in 1974.

SEPTEMBER 5   The White Sox edge the Angels 1–0 in Anaheim. Bart Johnson (7⅔ innings) and Terry Forster (1⅔ innings) combined on the shutout. Ken Henderson drove in the lone run with a double in the sixth inning.

SEPTEMBER 8   The White Sox collect only one hit off Andy Hassler, but they beat the Angels 1–0 in Anaheim. The lone hit and run came in the third inning. Lee Richard doubled, Bucky Dent was hit by a pitch, Richie Allen advanced both runners with an infield out, and

Richard crossed the plate on an error by third baseman Dave Chalk. Jim Kaat (6⅔ innings) and Terry Forster (2⅓ innings) combined on the shutout.

SEPTEMBER 10   The White Sox suffer an excruciating 8–7 loss to the Twins in Minnesota in 15 innings. The Sox tied the score 5–5 on a three-run homer in the ninth by Brian Downing. The club then took the lead three times in extra innings, by scoring in the 11th, 13th and 14th innings, but on all three occasions the Twins rallied with a run in their half, each of them off Terry Forster. Goose Gossage gave up the run in the 15th.

SEPTEMBER 14   Richie Allen announces his retirement from baseball and leaves the club.

Coming off a season in which he missed the second half with a broken leg (see June 28, 1973), Allen led the AL in home runs (32) and slugging percentage (.563) while playing in 128 games in 1974. His batting average was .301. While the retirement startled some teammates, there were those who accepted it with less than surprise. Despite his batting numbers, Allen didn't display the same enthusiasm he had during his first two seasons in Chicago. Ron Santo was among those who were vocal in their criticisms of the special privileges that Allen received from Chuck Tanner and the front office. The ball club was split into pro-Allen and anti-Allen factions as the slugger grew increasingly moody and self-absorbed. Despite Tanner bending over backwards to appease him, Allen ridiculed the Sox manager behind his back and expressed his dislike of three teammates in the newspaper. Later, when Allen failed to follow up with an official letter of retirement, he was switched from the voluntary retired list, which would have made him ineligible to play for 60 days, to the disqualified list, making his status more flexible and allowing him to be traded to another organization. The 60-day period of ineligibility would have left Allen unable to play for the first 41 days of the 1975 regular season, counting the 19 at the end of 1974 after he left the Sox. He was traded less than three months after his "retirement." (see December 3, 1974)

SEPTEMBER 26   Jim Kaat records his 20th win of the season with a 5–1 decision over the Rangers in the first game of a double-header in Arlington. The Sox also won the second game 7–2.

After a 3–6 start, Kaat finished the 1974 season with a record of 21–13 and a 2.92 ERA in 277⅓ innings. During the month of September, he won all seven of his starts, allowing only two earned runs in 60⅔ innings for an ERA of 0.30.

DECEMBER 3   The White Sox trade Richie Allen to the Braves for a player to be named later.

The deal included a player to be named later pending successful contract negotiations between Allen and the Braves. Speculation as to who would move from Atlanta to Chicago centered around Phil Niekro, who had a 20–13 record with a 2.38 ERA in 1974 and led the NL in wins, innings pitched and complete games. Other rumors had starting second baseman Dave Johnson coming to the Sox. Johnson hit 43 homers in 1973 before tailing off in 1974 with a .251 average and 15 homers. The rumors about Johnson were scoffed at because it was certain the Sox would get a better player in exchange for Allen, who led the AL in home runs and slugging percentage in 1974. Allen had no desire to play in the South, however, and refused to play for the Braves, who sold his contract to the Phillies. In the end, all the White Sox were able to receive as compensation for Allen was Jim Essian, who was sent to the White Sox on May 15, 1975. At the time of the deal, Essian was 24 and had a .125 career batting average in 21 games, an indication how far Allen's trade value had plummeted. Essian was on the White Sox roster for 65 days and didn't appear in a single game before being sent to the minors. He was seldom more than a backup catcher during his big-league career. Allen played three more seasons in the majors and hit .246 with 32 home runs in 885 at-bats. He finished his 15-year career with a .292 average, a .534 slugging percentage 351 homers, 1,099 runs scored and 1,119 runs batted in over 1,749 games, but he should have posted much better numbers. Emotional immaturity and instability kept him from becoming one of the best players ever.

1975   Sox

Season in a Sentence

A losing season and plummeting attendance nearly results in the White Sox moving to Seattle before Bill Veeck purchases the franchise in December.

Finish • Won • Lost • Pct • GB

Finish	Won	Lost	Pct	GB
Fifth	75	86	.466	22.5

Manager

Chuck Tanner

Stats

Stats	WS	AL	Rank
Batting Avg:	.255	.258	7
On-Base Pct:	.334	.331	5
Slugging Pct:	.358	.379	11
Home Runs:	94		11
Stolen Bases:	101		8
ERA:	3.93	3.78	8
Fielding Avg:	.978	.975	3
Runs Scored:	655		10
Runs Allowed:	703		5 (tie)

Starting Lineup

Brian Downing, c
Carlos May, 1b-lf
Jorge Orta, 2b
Bill Melton, 3b
Bucky Dent, ss
Nyls Nyman, lf
Ken Henderson, cf
Pat Kelly, rf
Deron Johnson, dh-1b
Bill Stein, 2b-3b-dh
Jerry Hairston, lf
Bob Coluccio, rf

Pitchers

Jim Kaat, sp
Wilbur Wood, sp
Claude Osteen, sp
Jesse Jefferson, sp
Goose Gossage, rp

Attendance

750,802 (11th in AL)

Club Leaders

Batting Avg:	Jorge Orta	.304
On-Base Pct:	Carlos May	.373
Slugging Pct:	Jorge Orta	.450
Home Runs:	Deron Johnson	18
RBIs:	Jorge Orta	83
Runs:	Pat Kelly	73
Stolen Bases:	Pat Kelly	18
Wins:	Jim Kaat	20
Strikeouts:	Jim Kaat	142
ERA:	Jim Kaat	3.11
Saves:	Goose Gossage	26

APRIL 1   The White Sox trade Ed Herrmann to the Yankees for Ken Bennett, Terry Quinn, Fred Anyzeski and John Narron.

Herrmann was traded to cut salary costs. In exchange, the White Sox received four players who never played a single game in the majors.

APRIL 7   The White Sox sign Claude Osteen as a free agent following his release by the Cardinals.

APRIL 8   The White Sox open the season with a 3–2 loss to the Athletics in Oakland.

On the same day, the White Sox signed Deron Johnson as a free agent following his release by the Red Sox.

APRIL 15   In the home opener, the White Sox lose 6–5 in 13 innings to the Rangers before 20,202 at Comiskey Park.

J. C. Martin joined Harry Caray in the TV booth in 1975, but he lasted only a year on the job.

APRIL 24   Trailing 3–0, the White Sox score four runs in the ninth inning to win 4–3 over the Twins in Minnesota. Carlos May homered off Bert Blyleven, followed by a triple from Ken Henderson and a single from Lee Richard. After Tom Burgmeier was sent in to relieve Blyleven, Lamar Johnson batted for Tony Muser, and Johnson clobbered Burgmeier's first pitch for a two-run homer.

MAY 7   The White Sox score three runs in the ninth inning to down the Twins 3–2 at Comiskey Park. Four singles and a walk produced the victory, and all three runs were driven in by pinch-hitters. Ken Henderson drove in the first tally before Deron Johnson singled in two with the bases loaded.

MAY 9   Jim Kaat records his 12th consecutive victory over two seasons with a 2–0 decision over the Indians in Cleveland. He needed relief help from Goose Gossage (one-third of an inning) and Terry Forster (two-thirds of an inning). Pat Kelly drove in both runs with a homer off Gaylord Perry in the eighth inning.

Kaat won his last seven games in 1974 and his first five in 1975. The winning streak was aided by the development of a quick pitch in which Kaat delivered a pitch to the plate almost immediately after receiving the ball from the catcher. He finished several complete games in under two hours. Kaat finished the 1975 season with a 20–14 record and a 3.11 ERA in 303²/₃ innings.

MAY 16   The White Sox score three runs in the ninth inning to win 3–2 over the Indians at Comiskey Park. The first run was driven in on a single by Tony Muser. Dennis Eckersley loaded the bases, then hit Buddy Bradford with a pitch and walked Jorge Orta to force in the tying and winning runs.

Orta hit .304 with 11 homers in 1975.

MAY 17   The White Sox score seven runs in the first inning and defeat the Indians 10–1 at Comiskey Park.

MAY 27   Before a game against the White Sox in Milwaukee, Brewers manager Del Crandall picks his batting order by drawing names out of a hat and beats the White Sox 9–8.

JUNE 4   In the first round of the amateur draft, the White Sox draft pitcher Chris Knapp from Central Michigan University.

Knapp made his major league debut in September 1975 and had a six-year career, three of them with the Sox, posting a 36–32 record and a 4.99 ERA. The only other future major leaguer taken in the June 1975 draft was 17th-rounder Marv Foley. During the secondary phase of the draft the previous January, the Sox chose pitcher Tim Stoddard from North Carolina State University. Stoddard was also a basketball player in college, playing as a starting forward for N. C. State's 1974 NCAA championship team. He played 14 seasons in the majors, but appeared in just one game for the Sox before he was released by the organization in 1977.

JUNE 14   Deron Johnson clubs two homers and drives in five runs during a 7–2 win over the Yankees in New York.

The White Sox retired Luke Appling's uniform number 4 in 1975. He was the first Sox player to be so honored. Appling played for the club from 1930 through 1950 and served as a coach in 1970 and 1971. The Sox issued uniform numbers for the first time in 1931, and Luke wore number 5 that season and number 8 in 1932 before settling on number 4 in 1933. Others to wear number 4 from 1951 until it was retired in 1975 included Marty Marion, Ron Jackson, Gene Freese, Ken Berry, Ron Hansen and Tim Cullen.

JUNE 15   The White Sox trade Stan Bahnsen and Skip Pitlock to the Athletics for Chet Lemon and Dave Hamilton. On the same day, the Sox dealt Tony Muser to the Orioles for Jesse Jefferson.

The White Sox traded Bahnsen to the A's to trim payroll, but came out ahead in the deal by acquiring Lemon, who was the White Sox's starting center fielder from 1976 through 1981. While with the club, he played in two All-Star Games, hit over .300 three times and led the AL in doubles in 1979.

JUNE 17   The White Sox wallop the Rangers 13–3 in Arlington.

JUNE 22   Jesse Jefferson (5⅔ innings) and Cecil Upshaw (3⅓ innings) combine on a two-hitter to defeat the Twins 9–2 in the second game of a double-header at Comiskey Park. Jefferson held the opposition hitless until Eric Soderholm singled in the sixth. The pitcher had to leave the game because his arm was beginning to feel the effects of being hit by a batted ball. Johnny Briggs homered in the seventh off Upshaw. The Sox also won the first game 6–5 in 10 innings.

JUNE 26   Bill Melton hits a grand slam off Ferguson Jenkins in the eighth inning of an 8–3 win over the Rangers at Comiskey Park.

JUNE 30   The White Sox record their ninth win in a row with a 6–1 decision over the Athletics at Comiskey Park.

JULY 13   In the last game before the All-Star break, Wilbur Wood pitches a three-hitter to defeat the Brewers 5–0 in Milwaukee.

JULY 15   Entering the All-Star Game in the fifth inning, Jim Kaat retires all six batters he faces, including Lou Brock, Joe Morgan and Johnny Bench, but the American League loses 6–3 at County Stadium in Milwaukee.

JULY 17   In the first game following the All-Star break, Wilbur Wood pitches his second
                 consecutive shutout in the White Sox's second straight game, defeating the Tigers
                 4–0 on two hits at Comiskey Park. The only Detroit base hits were singles by
                 Ron LeFlore in the third inning and Jack Pierce in the eighth.

JULY 19   Pat Kelly's grand slam off Bill Travers in the second inning accounts for all four
                 Chicago runs in a 4–2 win over the Brewers at Comiskey Park.

JULY 20   Bill Stein hits a grand slam off Pete Broberg in the fourth inning of a 10–5 win over
                 the Brewers in the second game of a double-header at Comiskey Park. The Sox also
                 won the opener 9–2.

JULY 24   The White Sox win an exciting double-header by scores of 4–3 and 1–0 over the
                 Yankees at Comiskey Park. A walk-off homer in the ninth inning by Brian Downing
                 won the opener. Jesse Jefferson (7⅔ innings) and Dave Hamilton (1⅓ innings)
                 combined on the second-game shutout.

JULY 25   The White Sox suffer a frustrating 8–6 loss in 13 innings to the Athletics in Oakland.
                 The Sox scored a run in the 11th inning and two in the 12th, but the A's came back
                 to tie the contest in the bottom half of both innings. Oakland won on a two-run,
                 walk-off homer by Reggie Jackson.

AUGUST 6   The White Sox trounce the Angels 11–1 at Comiskey Park.

AUGUST 10   The White Sox score three runs in the ninth inning to defeat the Orioles 3–2 at
                 Comiskey Park. A two-run homer by Brian Downing tied the score. After a walk to
                 Pat Kelly, Jorge Orta drove in the winning run with a double.

AUGUST 27   The White Sox win 2–0 over the Indians in the first game of a double-header in
                 Cleveland on a pair of solo homers. Jorge Orta homered in the third inning and
                 Bill Melton went deep in the seventh.

AUGUST 29   Switch-hitting Ken Henderson homers from both sides of the plate during a 4–2 win
                 over the Orioles in Baltimore. He clubbed home runs off lefty Ross Grimsley in the first
                 inning and right-hander Wayne Garland in the eighth. All four Chicago runs scored on
                 solo home runs. The other two were from Lamar Johnson and Bob Coluccio.

                 *Henderson was the first White Sox player to hit home runs from both sides
                 of the plate in the same game. It didn't happen again until Tim Raines
                 accomplished the feat in 1993.*

SEPTEMBER 1   In a statistical oddity, the 10 White Sox runs are scored by 10 different players
                 during a 10–6 win over the Royals in the first game of a double-header at Comiskey
                 Park. Kansas City won the second game 3–1.

SEPTEMBER 4   White Sox pitchers combine to walk 15 batters during a 7–0 loss to the Royals
                 at Comiskey Park. The bases on balls were issued by Ken Kravec (seven), Danny
                 Osborn (five), Rich Hinton (one) and Chris Knapp (two).

SEPTEMBER 6   Jim Kaat records his 20th win of the season with a 5–2 decision over the Twins at
                 Comiskey Park.

Without Richie Allen as a gate attraction and with a 75–86 record, the White Sox drew only 750,802 in 1975 after attracting 1,149,596 the previous season and 1,302,527 in 1973.

SEPTEMBER 22   The White Sox lose 3–0 in 16 innings to the Angels in Anaheim. The game ended on a three-run homer by Wayne Garrett off Goose Gossage. Jim Kaat (8⅓ innings) and Gossage (seven innings) had shut out the Angels up to that point.

On the same day, the White Sox traded Deron Johnson to the Red Sox for Chuck Erickson.

SEPTEMBER 27   The White Sox edge the Twins 1–0 in Minnesota. Claude Osteen (four innings) and Goose Gossage (five innings) combined on the shutout. Jerry Hairston drove in the lone run with a sacrifice fly.

Gossage pitched 141⅔ innings in 62 relief appearances in 1975. He had a 9–8 record, 26 saves and a 1.84 ERA.

OCTOBER 2   White Sox owner John Allyn fires radio and TV announcer Harry Caray.

Allyn dismissed the broadcaster because of Caray's critical comments of the White Sox's listless and lackluster play during the 1975 season. Allyn claimed that the broadcaster was "a disruptive influence." Caray's unvarnished fault-finding caused a serious rift in the clubhouse and was in direct contrast to the unbridled cheerful optimism of manager Chuck Tanner. Caray nearly came to blows with both Tanner and Bill Melton on separate occasions. Many players insisted that Harry's almost constant belittling turned fans against them and was among the reasons for their poor production. Caray took his firing lightly, believing that the majority of White Sox fans were on his side in his dispute with management and that Allyn would soon sell the club. "There's nothing to worry about," he said. "I don't think he's going to own the ball club. He's run the damn club into the ground. He's got to sell." At the time, Allyn was in the process of seeking buyers for the White Sox. Two months later, he sold the Sox to Bill Veeck (see December 9, 1976). One of Veeck's first acts was to rehire Caray.

DECEMBER 9   Bill Veeck completes negotiations to purchase the White Sox from John Allyn for $9.5 million. American League owners officially approved the sale the following day.

One of the most imaginative and controversial promoters in baseball history, Veeck returned to Chicago after a 14-year absence from the game. He previously owned the Sox from March 1959 through June 1961, leaving because of ill health. He was 61 years old when he returned. Allyn had spent months seeking a buyer for the club. A group from Seattle had been eager to purchase the White Sox and transfer the franchise to the Pacific Northwest. Seattle had a big-league club, nicknamed the Pilots, as an expansion club in 1969, but near bankruptcy, the team moved to Milwaukee in 1970 and was renamed the Brewers. The city of Seattle filed a $32.5 million lawsuit against baseball after the Pilots fled to Milwaukee, and moving the Sox to the city would settle the suit. Seattle built the Kingdome to house a major league baseball team and the Seattle Seahawks, who began play as an NFL expansion team in 1976. Oakland Athletics owner Charlie Finley had hoped that the Sox would move to Seattle. He then planned to transfer the A's to Chicago. At first, AL owners were reluctant to allow Veeck to own the Sox. He had repeatedly antagonized them in the past with his non-conformity, and many believed he was underfinanced. The owners rejected Veeck's bid to purchase the club on December 3 by a vote of 8–3 with one abstention. Nine votes were needed to approve the offer. AL President Lee MacPhail said the bid "did not meet league standards of financing" and gave him a week to raise an additional $1.2 million. Veeck met the criteria, and his purchase was approved by a vote of 10–2. Two weeks after Veeck bought the White Sox, however, arbitrator Peter Seitz ruled that Andy Messersmith and Dave McNally were free agents, which made the reserve clause invalid. No longer could a club hold onto a player in perpetuity, as had been the case for nearly 100 years. In March 1976, the players and owners negotiated an agreement that allowed a player to seek free agency after six years in the majors. Salaries escalated, and the owners harmed the most were those like Veeck who were operating on a limited budget. In his second term as owner of the White Sox, only one of Veeck's five clubs finished above the .500 mark and none of them closed a season within 12 games of first place. He sold the Sox in January 1981.

DECEMBER 10   The White Sox trade Jim Kaat and Mike Buskey to the Phillies for Dick Ruthven, Alan Bannister and Roy Thomas.

DECEMBER 11   The White Sox trade Bill Melton and Steve Dunning to the Angels for Jim Spencer and Morris Nettles.

DECEMBER 12   The White Sox trade Ken Henderson, Dick Ruthven and Danny Osborn to the Braves for Ralph Garr and Larvell Blanks, then deal Blanks to the Indians for Jack Brohamer. On the same day, Rich Hinton was dealt to the Reds for Clay Carroll.

Nicknamed the Road Runner, for his speed and high, squeaky voice, Garr hit an even .300 in each of his first two seasons with the Sox. But he negated much of that with low on-base percentages because of his reluctance to take a walk, and with atrocious defense in left field.

DECEMBER 16   Bill Veeck fires Chuck Tanner as manager.

Tanner was dismissed with three years remaining on his contract. He had a record of 430–403 with the White Sox. The following day he became manager of the Athletics, but he lasted only a year in Oakland. Tanner quickly landed a job managing the Pirates, which he held from 1977 through 1985. At Pittsburgh, he led the franchise to a world championship in 1979 with the theme "We Are Family." The Pirates never came close to the post-season again under Tanner, however, and bottomed out with a 57–104 record in 1985 and the franchise mired in a drug scandal. Tanner finished his career as manager with a rebuilding Braves team from 1986 through 1988. Overall, he was 1,352–1,381 as a big-league skipper. The Tanner family wasn't completely finished with the White Sox. Chuck's son Bruce pitched in 10 games for the club in 1985.

DECEMBER 17   The White Sox hire Paul Richards as manager.

Richards had previously managed the club from 1951 through 1954. He took *over one of the worst clubs in baseball and immediately transformed it into a pennant contender (see October 10, 1950) but couldn't lift the club into first place. Richards left Chicago to become both field manager and general manager of the Orioles. Again, he took a moribund club to contention but failed to win a pennant. Richards went searching for a new challenge and became general manager of the new Houston franchise in the National League, which began play in 1962. After four years with the Astros, which included the opening of baseball's first domed stadium, Richards was general manager of the Atlanta Braves from 1966 through 1973 before retiring. Bill Veeck talked Richards into returning to the playing field, but it wasn't a good fit. Richards was 68 years old, hadn't managed a team on the field since 1961 and could no longer relate to younger players during a period in which the generation gap was a chasm. After a horrible 64–97 record in 1976, Richards went back into retirement.*

1976   Sox

Season in a Sentence

The return of Bill Veeck and Paul Richards fails to revive the glories of the past, as the White Sox lose 97 games.

Finish • Won • Lost • Pct • GB

Sixth   64   97   .398   25.5

Manager

Paul Richards

Stats

Stats	WS	AL	Rank
Batting Avg:	.255	.256	7
On-Base Pct:	.317	.323	9
Slugging Pct:	.349	.361	9
Home Runs:	73		10
Stolen Bases:	120		7
ERA:	4.25	3.52	12
Fielding Avg:	.979	.977	4
Runs Scored:	586		10
Runs Allowed:	745		12

Starting Lineup

Brian Downing, c
Jim Spencer, 1b
Jack Brohamer, 2b
Bill Stein, 3b-2b
Bucky Dent, ss
Jorge Orta, lf-3b
Chet Lemon, cf
Ralph Garr, rf-cf-lf
Kevin Bell, 3b
Lamar Johnson, dh-1b
Jim Essian, c
Buddy Bradford, rf

Pitchers

Goose Gossage, sp
Ken Brett, sp
Bart Johnson, sp
Terry Forster, sp-rp
Dave Hamilton, rp
Francisco Barrios, rp-sp
Pete Vuckovich, rp
Clay Carroll, rp

Attendance

914,954 (tenth in AL)

Club Leaders

Batting Avg:	Ralph Garr	.300
On-Base Pct:	Ralph Garr	.322
Slugging Pct:	Jorge Orta	.410
Home Runs:	Jorge Orta	14
	Jim Spencer	14
RBIs:	Jorge Orta	72
Runs:	Jorge Orta	74
Stolen Bases:	Jorge Orta	24
Wins:	Ken Brett	10
Strikeouts:	Goose Gossage	135
ERA:	Ken Brett	3.32
Saves:	Dave Hamilton	10

APRIL 9   The White Sox win the season opener 6–0 before a crowd of 40,318 at Comiskey Park. Wilbur Wood pitched a shutout. In his debut with the Sox, Jim Spencer hit a home run in the fifth inning. He also collected a bases-loaded walk and hit two singles. With the nation celebrating its bicentennial year, returning owner Bill Veeck got into the spirit of things when he hobbled onto the field with his wooden leg as part of a fife and drum corps in pre-game ceremonies.

A Chicago tradition was born at the 1976 opener. Like many fans, Harry Caray loved to sing "Take Me Out to the Ball Game" during the seventh-inning stretch. And like many fans, Harry sang with gusto but with a decided lack of musical training. As a practical joke, without the broadcaster's knowledge, Bill Veeck had a microphone set up in the TV booth and Caray's raspy singing voice was soon bellowing throughout the stadium. The fans loved it, and from then on Caray's enthusiastic rendition of the song was an event. When Harry moved to Wrigley Field to broadcast Cubs games beginning in 1982, the tradition went with him and soon was eagerly anticipated by television viewers across the country as WGN-TV entered "superstation" status over cable outlets from coast to coast. WGN-TV did not cut away to a commercial until Caray completed the song. When Caray died in February 1998, the Cubs and the station were faced with a dilemma. How could they keep the tradition of the sing-along and still preserve Caray's memory? With a stroke of genius, it was decided that guest "conductors" would lead the fans in the baseball anthem, and it is still an important aspect of the Wrigley Field experience.

APRIL 20   The White Sox play their first game at remodeled Yankee Stadium and lose 5–4.

Bill Veeck commissioned innovative new uniforms for the White Sox for the bicentennial year of 1976. The vivid red of the previous five seasons was replaced by navy blue. But the dramatic change in color was of lesser significance than the radical tailoring of the jerseys. The new shirts were of a pullover style with a straight bottom to be worn pajama style outside the trousers. The V-neck collar included a simulated collar flap, recalling the uniforms of the 19th and early 20th centuries. The shirts and pants were made of white or navy blue and could be intermixed for home games. The road version was usually all-navy. The CHICAGO lettering was a throwback to the uniforms of the early days of the franchise. The pants had a clam-digger style leg opening. The Sox also occasionally wore shorts instead of long pants. The club became the first in major league history to wear shorts (see August 8, 1976). The cap was solid navy with SOX in horizontal lettering. The socks were basically white with navy stripes. The White Sox wore the unconventional jerseys through the 1981 season.

APRIL 28   A crowd of only 1,114 shows up for a 4–1 loss to the Brewers at Comiskey Park.

The center field wall at Comiskey Park was moved from 410 feet to 440 with the removal of the inner fence. Veeck also tore up the artificial turf in the infield and seeded it with grass.

MAY 9   Wilbur Wood suffers a fractured kneecap during a 4–2 win over the Tigers in Detroit. Wood was struck by a line drive off the bat of Ron LeFlore.

Wood missed the remainder of the season. He played two more years but was never again an effective pitcher. Wood had a combined record of 17–18 and a 5.11 ERA in 1977 and 1978.

MAY 18   The White Sox trade Carlos May to the Yankees for Ken Brett and Rich Coggins.

The older brother of George, Brett played for 10 big league clubs from 1967 through 1981, The White Sox were stop number six. After the end of his career, the much-traveled Brett made a Miller Lite beer commercial in which he couldn't remember what town he was in.

MAY 21   In his first game with the White Sox, Ken Brett hurls five shutout innings while allowing only one hit and is the winning pitcher in a 6–0 win over the Athletics at Comiskey Park. Clay Carroll pitched the final four innings.

MAY 26   In his second start with the White Sox, Ken Brett holds the Angels hitless for the first $8^2/_3$ innings and is the winning pitcher in an 11-inning, 1–0 victory at Anaheim. Brett retired the first 23 batters to face him before Lee Stanton walked with two out in the eighth. He held California without a hit until Jerry Remy reached first base on an infield single. Remy's hit was the result of a controversial scoring decision by official scorer Don Merry of the *Long Beach Independent Telegram*. Jorge Orta, playing third base, had trouble picking up Remy's slow roller as it skidded under his glove, and most observers believed the play should have gone into the books as an error. Bill Melton collected the second Angels hit with a single off Brett in the 10th. The Sox scored in the top of the 11th on successive one-base hits by Jack Brohamer, Pat Kelly and Bucky Dent. Clay Carroll earned a save by retiring the Angels in order in the bottom half. The victory ran the White Sox's winning streak to 10 games.

MAY 31   The White Sox defeat the Rangers 9–4 at Comiskey Park with the help of the fog. With the Sox trailing 2–0 in the first inning and visibility near zero, Chet Lemon hit a fly ball with the bases loaded that landed between Texas left fielder Tom Grieve and shortstop Toby Harrah as both completely lost sight of the ball until it plopped into the wet grass about 20 feet beyond the edge of the infield dirt. Lemon wound up on third base with a three-run triple.

JUNE 1   The White Sox are held to two hits by Rangers pitcher Jim Umbarger through the first 10 innings before scoring a run in the 11th to win 1–0 at Comiskey Park. Jim Essian started the rally with a double. Jorge Orta drove in the winning run with a single. Bart Johnson (nine innings) and Dave Hamilton (two innings) combined on the shutout.

JUNE 8   In the first round of the amateur draft, the White Sox select pitcher Steve Trout from Thornwood High School in South Holland, Illinois.

> *Steve was the son of Dizzy Trout, who won 170 games as a major league pitcher from 1939 through 1952, mostly with the Tigers. The Dizzy nickname could have applied to the younger Trout as well. He joined the Sox in 1978 and was soon considered the team flake. Steve was 37–40 in five seasons with the club before a trade to the Cubs. Others future major leaguers drafted and signed in June 1976 were Mike Colbern (second round) and Lorenzo Gray (eighth round), both of whom played only two years. In January, the Sox picked Fred Howard, Leo Sutherland, Rick Wortham and Harry Chappas, another group with short big-league careers.*

JUNE 13   Pat Kelly collects seven hits in nine at-bats during the double-header against the Indians in Cleveland, but the White Sox lose twice 8–5 and 9–7. Kelly had five singles, a double and a homer.

JUNE 15   The White Sox trade Pete Varney to the Braves for Blue Moon Odom.

JUNE 20   The White Sox lose their 10th game in a row by dropping a 6–3 decision to the Yankees at Comiskey Park.

The White Sox had a 27–22 record on June 10, but they were 37–75 the rest of the way.

JUNE 22   Kevin Bell hits an inside-the-park homer off Steve Busby in the third inning of a 14–8 win over the Royals in Kansas City. Left fielder Tom Poquette crashed into the left-field wall chasing Bell's drive and was knocked unconscious. Poquette suffered a triple fracture of his cheekbone.

JUNE 25   The White Sox defeat the Rangers 14–9 in the second game of a double-header in Arlington. The Sox took a 9–7 lead with five runs in the sixth inning. Texas won the opener 8–4 with five runs in the ninth inning, the last four on a walk-off grand slam by Dave Hamilton.

JUNE 26   The White Sox waste a stellar pitching performance by Ken Brett and lose 1–0 in 10 innings to the Rangers in Arlington.

JULY 3   The White Sox play a Saturday morning game at 9:30 a.m. in what Bill Veeck calls a "breakfast special." The game drew 10,099 and the Sox lost 3–0 to the Rangers.

JULY 4   With the nation celebrating the bicentennial, the White Sox split a double-header against the Rangers at Comiskey Park. The Sox won the opener 7–6 in 12 innings but lost the nightcap 3–2.

JULY 6   Pitcher Ken Brett bats ninth in the starting lineup in lieu of using a designated hitter. Brett was hitless in three at-bats during a 4–0 loss to the Red Sox in Boston.

Brett had a lifetime batting average of .262 and hit 10 homers in 347 major league at-bats.

JULY 15   Pat Kelly smashes a three-run, walk-off homer in the 10th inning to beat the Brewers 5–3 at Comiskey Park.

In July, Bill Veeck installed a shower in the center-field bleachers at Comiskey Park to allow fans to cool off on hot days.

JULY 18   The White Sox trounce the Brewers 13–3 at Comiskey Park.

JULY 24   The Twins overwhelm the White Sox 17–2 at Comiskey Park.

JULY 28   Blue Moon Odom (five innings) and Francisco Barrios (four innings) combine on a no-hitter and a 2–1 win over the Athletics in Oakland. Odom was removed from the game after issuing a walk to the first batter he faced in the sixth inning. Odom had not surrendered a hit, but he walked nine batters. The A's scored a run in the fourth inning on two walks and an error. Francisco Barrios was brought in by Paul Richards to relieve Odom. Barrios walked two more batters over the final four innings, but he completed the no-hitter. In the ninth, Sal Bando was out on a slow roller to second baseman Jack Brohamer. The ball and runner arrived at first almost simultaneously, and the A's argued vehemently with umpire George Maloney that

Bando was safe. Gene Tenace looked at strike three for the second out. Claudell Washington then reached base on a walk. Ken McMullen ended the game by grounding out to shortstop Bucky Dent. Jim Spencer had a hand in both Chicago runs. He doubled in the second inning and scored on a single by Bucky Dent. Spencer broke the 1–1 tie with a homer in the sixth.

> *Odom pitched only eight games with the White Sox, which were the last eight of his 13-year big-league career. As a member of the Sox, he had a 2–2 record and a 5.79 ERA in 28 innings. The July 28 combined no-hitter was the last of Odom's 84 lifetime victories. Barrios was a 23-year-old rookie in 1976. He had some success in 1977 with a 14–7 record, but bad-tempered, he often engaged in verbal tirades against umpires and his composure on the mound was easily rattled. Barrios once fought teammate Steve Stone in a Cleveland hotel, and on another occasion in 1979 had to be restrained from punching Ralph Garr on a flight to Seattle. Francisco's career ended in 1981 after he was arrested on a narcotics charge in a Chicago nightclub on Rush Street. He died of a drug overdose in his native Mexico in 1982 when he was only 28.*

AUGUST 8   The White Sox become the first major league team to wear shorts, donning the unusual uniforms for the first game of a double-header against the Royals at Comiskey Park. The Sox won 5–2. The club donned their conventional long pants in the second tilt, and lost 7–1.

AUGUST 14   The White Sox brawl with the Orioles during a 6–5 loss in the second game of a double-header at Memorial Stadium. Baltimore won the opener 8–6. Reggie Jackson had homered in each game, including a grand slam in the fifth inning of the second tilt off Ken Brett. Jackson had been hit by a pitch in the opener, and Brett threw close to the slugger before he delivered the grand slam. As Reggie circled the bases, he yelled and gestured at Brett with every step. On his next at-bat, Jackson was spun to the ground when Clay Carroll's first pitch was in the area of his chin. On the next serve from Carroll, Jackson let go of his bat and started for the mound. He was intercepted by catcher Jim Essian, who applied a bear hug that took Jackson to the ground. At least four separate battles broke out and the brawl raged for 10 minutes before order was restored. Jackson and Lamar Johnson were the only players ejected.

AUGUST 21   The White Sox wind up a high-scoring contest with a run in the 12th inning to beat the Orioles 11–10 at Comiskey Park. The winning run scored on a single by Bill Stein that struck third base and bounced away from Brooks Robinson.

> *Bill Veeck did his best to promote a losing club. There were Frisbee-catching dogs, belly dancers, farm animal giveaways, beer-case stacking contests, an invasion of fans with musical instruments on the field billed as the "world's largest band" and games dedicated to nearly every ethnic group in Chicago, including a Mexican Fiesta Day in which Sox players wore sombreros on the field. Attendance increased from 750,802 to 914,945, but the Sox outdrew only two other AL clubs (Oakland and Minnesota).*

AUGUST 24   The White Sox score seven runs in the ninth inning to defeat the Tigers 12–7 in Detroit.

SEPTEMBER 5   The Twins score 10 runs in the fifth inning and beat the White Sox 18–1 in Minnesota.

SEPTEMBER 8   The Athletics score five runs in the first inning, but the White Sox come back with three runs in the fifth inning and three in the eighth to win 6–5 in Oakland.

SEPTEMBER 10   Nolan Ryan strikes out 18 batters, walks nine and is the Angels winning pitcher in a 2–1 decision over the White Sox at Comiskey Park.

SEPTEMBER 11   At 53, Minnie Minoso is in the starting lineup as the designated hitter. He was hitless in three at-bats during a 7–3 loss to the Royals at Comiskey Park.

Minoso was a coach for the Sox in 1976. The September 11 contest was his first in the majors since 1964.

SEPTEMBER 12   Minnie Minoso becomes the oldest player in major league history to collect a hit with a single in three at-bats during a 10-inning, 2–1 victory over the Angels in the first game of a double-header at Comiskey Park. California won the second tilt 5–1.

Minoso played two more games in 1980 to become the second player in major league history to play in five different decades (see October 4, 1980).

SEPTEMBER 14   White Sox pitcher Larry Monroe is embarrassed by manager Paul Richards during his major league debut, a 2–1 loss to the Royals at Comiskey Park. Richards planned to use Monroe, a 20-year-old right-hander, for just two innings then switch to lefty Terry Forster against Kansas City's predominantly left-handed lineup. Richards didn't tell Monroe of the strategy, however, and the rookie was stunned when he was removed at the end of the second after allowing just one run. Monroe's big-league career lasted just eight games, two of them starts, and 21²/₃ innings.

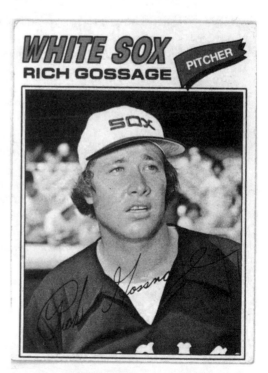

After success in the bullpen, Rich Gossage was shifted to the starting rotation in 1976 and performed poorly. After the season, the Sox dealt him, along with reliever Terry Forster, in a trade with the Pirates, letting go of two of the game's best relievers.

OCTOBER 21   The White Sox trade Phil Roof to the Blue Jays for Larry Anderson.

NOVEMBER 5   Three days after Jimmy Carter defeats Gerald Ford in the presidential election, the White Sox lose Pete Vuckovich, Jesse Jefferson and Samuel Ewing to the Blue Jays and Bill Stein and Roy Thomas to the Mariners in the expansion draft.

Vuckovich proved to be a big loss. With the Cardinals and Brewers from 1979 through 1982, he had a record of 59–29.

NOVEMBER 16   The White Sox announce the hiring of Bob Lemon as manager, replacing Paul Richards.

Lemon was elected to the Hall of Fame in 1976, based on a pitching career in which he won 207 games and lost 128. He spent his entire playing career with the Indians, breaking into the big leagues in 1941 as a third baseman. Lemon spent three years in the Navy during World War II, when he pitched in service games. The Indians converted Lemon into a pitcher in 1946, about the time that Bill Veeck purchased the club. After his playing career ended in 1958, Lemon managed in the minors and was a big-league pitching coach with the Indians, Phillies, Angels and Royals. He also managed the Royals from 1970 through 1972 to a 207–218 record. Lemon was a coach with the Yankees when hired to manage the White Sox. He patterned his reserved, thoughtful, low-key managerial style after Al Lopez, for whom Lemon played in Cleveland from 1951 through 1956. The White Sox lost 97 games in 1976, but Lemon's approach proved to be just what the club needed. The Sox were in first place in August in 1977 and finished the year with a 90–72 record. But, after a 34–40 start in 1978, Lemon was dismissed by Veeck.

NOVEMBER 18   The White Sox trade Pat Kelly to the Orioles for Dave Duncan.

NOVEMBER 24   The White Sox sign Steve Stone, most recently with the Cubs, as a free agent.

Stone was the first free agent to sign with the White Sox after the system went into effect at the end of the 1976 season. He previously played for the Sox in 1973.

NOVEMBER 26   The White Sox sign Eric Soderholm as a free agent following his release by the Twins.

Soderholm missed the entire 1976 season after falling into a storm sewer on a piece of property he had purchased in Minnesota. The mishap broke two ribs and shattered portions of his leg. Bill Veeck had lost a leg as a result of a World War II combat injury and had endured numerous health problems during his life. The Sox owner was a sucker for hard-luck stories and those who persevered through adversity and signed Soderholm at a time when almost every big-league club believed that he was finished. In a remarkable comeback, Soderholm hit .280 with 25 home runs for the White Sox in 1977.

DECEMBER 10   The White Sox trade Goose Gossage and Terry Forster to the Pirates for Richie Zisk and Silvio Martinez.

The White Sox tried to convert Gossage and Forster from relievers into starters in 1976, with poor results. They were dealt together to Pittsburgh. Zisk gave the White Sox one thrill-packed season in 1977 before departing as a free agent. He hit 30 homers with 101 runs batted in and a .290 batting average. In the long run, Zisk wasn't worth the loss of either Gossage or Forster, much less both. Gossage never started another big-league game after leaving Chicago. After one solid season in Pittsburgh, he went to the Yankees as a free agent. He pitched in the World Series for the Yanks in 1978 and 1981 and with the Padres in 1984. Gossage was named to eight All-Star teams during his career, including two with the White Sox, and finished his career with 124 wins, 310 saves and a 3.10 earned run average. Forster was an effective reliever until his career ended in 1986 while his weight steadily increased. He is perhaps best remembered for David Letterman, who during a 1985 monologue on his late-night talk show referred to Forster, then with the Braves, as a "fat tub of goo." Forster later did a video called "Fat Is In."

1977   Sox

Season in a Sentence

The White Sox are expected to lose 100 games, but fans enjoy a glorious summer and turn out in record numbers at Comiskey Park as the club holds first place from July 1 through August 12 before fading to third.

Finish • Won • Lost • Pct • GB

Finish	Won	Lost	Pct	GB
Third	90	72	.556	12.0

Manager

Bob Lemon

Stats

Stats	WS	AL	Rank
Batting Avg:	.278	.266	4
On-Base Pct:	.347	.333	3
Slugging Pct:	.444	.405	2
Home Runs:	192		2
Stolen Bases:	42		12
ERA:	4.25	4.06	8
Fielding Avg:	.974	.977	10
Runs Scored:	844		3
Runs Allowed:	771		9

Starting Lineup

Jim Essian, c
Jim Spencer, 1b
Jorge Orta, 2b
Eric Soderholm, 3b
Alan Bannister, ss
Ralph Garr, lf
Chet Lemon, cf
Richie Zisk, rf
Oscar Gamble, dh-rf
Lamar Johnson, dh-1b
Brian Downing, c
Jack Brohamer, 3b-2b

Pitchers

Francisco Barrios, sp
Steve Stone, sp
Ken Kravec, sp
Chris Knapp, sp
Wilbur Wood, sp
Ken Brett, sp
Lerrin LaGrow, rp
Dave Hamilton, rp
Bart Johnson, rp

Attendance

1,657,135 (fifth in AL)

Club Leaders

Batting Avg:	Ralph Garr	.300
On-Base Pct:	Oscar Gamble	.388
Slugging Pct:	Oscar Gamble	.588
Home Runs:	Oscar Gamble	31
RBIs:	Richie Zisk	101
Runs:	Chet Lemon	99
Stolen Bases:	Ralph Garr	12
Wins:	Steve Stone	15
Strikeouts:	Ken Kravec	125
ERA:	Ken Kravec	4.10
Saves:	Lerrin LaGrow	25

MARCH 23   The White Sox trade Clay Carroll to the Cardinals for Lerrin LaGrow.

APRIL 5   The White Sox trade Bucky Dent to the Yankees for Oscar Gamble, LaMarr Hoyt, Bob Polinsky and cash.

Dent demanded a three-year guaranteed deal from the White Sox and Veeck, unable to afford Bucky's salary request, dealt him to the Yankees. In New York, he went down in baseball history for his home run in the 1978 playoff game against the Red Sox at Fenway Park that gave the Yanks the AL East crown. Although Dent had some success with the Yanks, it was a great trade for the White Sox. Gamble gave the White Sox one great season with 31 homers and a .297 batting average in 1977 before departing to San Diego as a free agent. Hoyt didn't reach the majors until 1979, but was 19–15 for the Sox in 1982 and had a season in 1983 in which he won the Cy Young Award with a 24–10 record.

APRIL 7   The White Sox participate in the first-ever regular season game in Toronto, losing 9–5 to the Blue Jays at Exhibition Stadium. It was also the first American League game ever played outside the United States. The contest was played in near-freezing weather amid snow flurries. The Sox left an incredible 19 men on base. Toronto pitchers allowed 15 hits and seven walks and their fielders made three errors. In his White Sox debut, Richie Zisk collected four hits, including a homer and a double, in four at-bats.

APRIL 12   In the home opener, the White Sox win 5–2 over the Red Sox before 34,612 at Comiskey Park.

During Harry Caray's first five years with the White Sox, none of his broadcasting partners on radio or television lasted very long. There was Ralph Faucher (1971–72), Gene Osborn (1973), Bob Waller (1973–74), Bill Mercer (1974–75) and J. C. Martin (1975). Lorn Brown teamed with Caray in 1976, and in 1977, Jimmy Piersall and Mary Shane joined the team. Shane was the first female to broadcast games for a major league club on a regular basis. A 28-year-old former history teacher, Shane had previously worked at a radio station in Milwaukee. Like many of her predecessors, Shane lasted only a year. A combination of her inexperience and prejudice against her as a woman limited her to brief appearances on 35 games. Shane returned to sports writing and died of a heart attack in 1987. In contrast, Piersall was an immediate hit with fans. He was outspoken, critical and amusing and proved to be a perfect accomplice for Caray.

APRIL 15   The Blue Jays play at Comiskey Park for the first time and lose 7–5 to the White Sox.

APRIL 26   The White Sox come from behind to defeat the Tigers 10–7 in 14 innings in Detroit. Down 6–1, the Sox scored one run in the seventh inning and four in the eighth to deadlock the contest 6–6. Eric Soderholm gave Chicago a 7–6 lead in the top of the 13th, but the Tigers tied it in their half. The Sox put the game away with three tallies in the 14th.

APRIL 27   The White Sox hit five home runs but lose 10–9 to the Tigers in Detroit. The homers were struck by Richie Zisk, Royle Stillman, Chet Lemon, Oscar Gamble and Eric Soderholm.

MAY 1   The White Sox score eight runs in the first inning and four in the second to win 12–4 over the Rangers at Comiskey Park. The Sox collected six extra-base hits in the opening inning on home runs by Jorge Orta and Jim Essian, a triple from Oscar Gamble and doubles by Chet Lemon, Ralph Garr and Jim Spencer.

MAY 8   Chet Lemon collects five hits, including two doubles, in five at-bats during an 8–3 win over the Indians in Cleveland.

| MAY 14 | The White Sox play a "breakfast special" at 10:30 a.m., but Jim Spencer is wide awake, driving in eight runs to lead the White Sox to an 18–2 win over the Indians at Comiskey Park. The Sox scored seven runs in the second inning and Spencer batted twice, contributing a two-run homer and a two-run single. He capped the slugging spree with a grand slam off Pat Dobson in the fourth. |

MAY 22   Richie Zisk hits a home run into the center-field bleachers at Comiskey Park, but the White Sox lose 14–3 to the Tigers.

JUNE 3   The White Sox score four runs in the fourth inning and defeat the Yankees 9–5 at Comiskey Park.

JUNE 6   The White Sox score four runs in the 12th inning, three of them on a home run by Oscar Gamble, and defeat the Twins 9–5 in Minnesota.

JUNE 7   With the first overall pick in the amateur draft, the White Sox select outfielder Harold Baines from St. Michaels High School in St. Michaels, Maryland.

Bill Veeck had an estate in Easton on Maryland's eastern shore less than 10 miles from St. Michaels and had been scouting Baines since Little League. Baines signed a contract on the spot for $40,000, the smallest amount ever paid to a number-one pick. Although most major league scouts ranked Baines among the 10 best amateurs in the country, Veeck stood almost alone rating him number one. Many accused Veeck of drafting Baines simply to save money. Nearly anyone else would have commanded a six-figure bonus, and number-two choice Bill Gullickson, signed by the Expos, drew a bonus of over $100,000. It's difficult to argue with the choice of Baines today, however. Of all of the players chosen in the draft, only Paul Molitor (third overall pick in the first round by the Brewers), Ozzie Smith (fourth-round choice by the Padres) and Tim Raines (fifth-round selection by the Expos) had better careers. Baines played for the White Sox from 1980 through 1989 and again in 1996, 1997, 2000 and 2001. Quiet, unassuming, phlegmatic and rarely changing his facial expression, Baines provided the White Sox with steady play in right field while steadfastly avoiding publicity whenever possible. Among Sox players, Baines ranks sixth all-time in games played (1,670), fourth in at-bats (6,149), third in home runs (221), third in runs batted in (981), third in extra-base hits (585), fourth in total bases (2,844), fourth in doubles (320), fifth in hits (1,773), seventh in runs (786) and ninth in walks (565). At the close of his career in 2001, Baines had 2,866 hits, 488 doubles, 384 home runs and 1,628 RBIs. Because he refused to blow his own horn or call attention to himself, Baines never received the acclaim he deserved, however. Other future major leaguers drafted and signed by the Sox in June 1977 were Rich Barnes (second round), Rod Allen (sixth round), Rusty Kuntz (11th round), Dewey Robinson (19th round) and Ross Baumgartner (20th round).

JUNE 9   Alan Bannister collects five hits, including a double, in six at-bats during an 11-inning, 4–3 win over the Rangers in Arlington.

JUNE 15   The White Sox trade Ken Brett to the Angels for Don Kirkwood, John Verhoeven and John Flannery.

JUNE 19   Lamar Johnson sings the national anthem before a double-header against the Athletics at Comiskey Park, then stars in the 2–1 opening-game victory. Johnson not only collected all three of Chicago's hits, but he accounted for both runs with a pair of homers off Mike Norris. Johnson's third hit, a double, also went for extra bases. Wilbur Wood was the winning pitcher, his first victory in over a year. The Sox also won the second game 5–1.

JUNE 24   Ralph Garr loses a home run because of some inventive base running during a 7–6 loss to the Twins in Minnesota. Garr's drive cleared the fence at Metropolitan Stadium, but Jim Essian, the Chicago base runner at first, thought that right fielder Dan Ford made a tumbling catch and retreated to the bag. Garr, running full tilt, passed Essian and was called out. Garr was credited with a single on the play.

JUNE 26   The White Sox lose a 19–12 swatfest to the Twins in Minnesota.

            Jim Essian hit five homers during the three-game set in Minnesota. A devout believer in transcendental meditation, Essian psyched himself up with a series of body twists before each game.

JUNE 27   The White Sox play the Mariners for the first time and win 10–4 at Comiskey Park.

JULY 1   Richie Zisk drives in all five runs with a pair of homers to spark the White Sox to a 5–2 win over the Twins at Comiskey Park. Zisk hit a three-run homer in the first inning and a two-run blast in the third, both off Dave Goltz. The win allowed the White Sox to pass the Twins into first place.

JULY 2   Jim Spencer drives in eight runs for the second time in 1977 (see May 14, 1977) to lead the White Sox to a 13–8 victory over the Twins at Comiskey Park. Spencer hit a grand slam off Bill Butler in the fourth inning, then added an RBI-single in the sixth and a three-run homer in the eighth, an inning in which the Sox scored seven times to overcome a 7–6 deficit.

            The pair of eight-RBI games by Spencer in 1977 tied the club record. The only others to drive in eight runs in a single contest are Carl Reynolds (July 2, 1930), Tommy McCraw (May 24, 1967) and Robin Ventura (September 4, 1995).

JULY 3   The White Sox sweep the Twins 6–0 and 10–8 during a double-header at Comiskey Park.

            White Sox fans were giddy with excitement over the club's unexpected position in first place. Fans cheered with such persistence and clamor that the players had to respond to "curtain calls." It was believed to be a first in baseball and began with the July 3 sweep. Wilbur Wood stopped the Twins with a three-hit shutout in the first game. To acknowledge a three-minute ovation, Wood re-appeared from the dugout and waved his cap. Jim Spencer, Jim Essian and Alan Bannister hit home runs in the second game. So thunderous and lengthy was the applause heralding each blow that play could not resume until the sluggers took a bow. Pictures of the "curtain calls" were published in the newspapers, and almost every night on the TV news there was footage, not only of the home runs and the key plays, but of the players being urged out of the dugout by the cheering spectators. Most opposing players were less than enamored with the practice, accusing the Sox of "showboating." Hal McRae of the Royals was among the most vocal, insisting the Sox players were allowing the fans to make "fools" of them by coming out of the dugout. "This isn't a circus or a nightclub," said McRae. "It's baseball." Soon, however, the "curtain calls" spread to other cities as well, including Kansas City. In addition to the "curtain calls," the exit of an opposing pitcher after being relieved brought a chorus of "Na, Na, Hey, Hey Kiss Him Goodbye," a 1969 number-one hit by Steam. The song became a rallying cry for Sox fans. The thrill of the pennant race, which included 61 days in first place, helped the White Sox draw 1,657,135 fans in 1977, breaking the previous record of 1,644,460 in 1960. Like Steam, the 1977 White Sox proved to be one-hit wonders, however. The club didn't post another winning record until 1981 or draw over 1.6 million again until 1983.

JULY 4
The White Sox play in Seattle for the first time and win 6–2 over the Mariners at the Kingdome.

JULY 9
The White Sox extend their winning streak to nine games with a 5–2 decision over the Tigers in Detroit.

JULY 13
Oscar Gamble collects two homers and two singles during a 6–3 win over the Blue Jays in the first game of a double-header at Comiskey Park. Toronto won the opener 5–3 in 11 innings.

JULY 19
At the All-Star Game in Yankee Stadium, Richie Zisk drives in two runs with a single and double in three at-bats, but the American League loses 7–5.

JULY 25
Down 6–1, the White Sox rally to defeat the Red Sox 8–7 at Fenway Park. Four runs in the eighth inning, capped by a three-run homer from Jim Spencer, tied the score 7–7. A home run by Brian Downing in the ninth broke the deadlock.

JULY 31
The White Sox score three runs in the 10th inning to defeat the Royals 5–4 in the first game of a double-header at Comiskey Park. Kansas City scored two runs in the top of the 10th. Chet Lemon tied the game 4–4 with a two-run homer. Lemon's blast was followed by a walk to Eric Soderholm, who moved to second on a sacrifice and scored on a single by Ralph Garr. The Royals won the second tilt 8–4.

The White Sox ended July with a 62–38 record and a 5½-game lead in the AL West. The Cubs also entered August in first place. It was the first time that both Chicago teams were in first place in August since 1907. The Sox were 28–34 from August 1 through the end of the season and, like the Cubs, were out of the pennant race by Labor Day.

AUGUST 5
White Sox pitcher Bart Johnson and Royals catcher Darrell Porter exchange angry words in the fourth inning and engage in a fistfight in the seventh during a 12–2 Chicago loss in Kansas City. A fan threw a glass of beer at Johnson, who replied with an obscene gesture. Jim Essian had to be restrained from going into the stands.

AUGUST 8
A walk-off homer by Lamar Johnson in the ninth inning beats the Mariners 5–4 at Comiskey Park. It was Johnson's second homer of the game.

AUGUST 9   The White Sox club six homers during a 13–3 win over the Mariners at Comiskey Park. Eric Soderholm hit two, with Chet Lemon, Oscar Gamble, Jim Essian and Royle Stillman adding one each.

> *The Sox hit 192 home runs in 1977, shattering the old club record of 138 set in 1961 and tied in 1971. It was a dramatic increase over the 73 home runs that the club struck in 1976. The home run leaders in 1977 were Oscar Gamble (31), Richie Zisk (30), Eric Soderholm (25), Chet Lemon (19), Jim Spencer (18), Lamar Johnson (18), Jorge Orta (11), Ralph Garr (10) and Jim Essian (10). As a result of the 1977 offenseive explosion, the club became known as the "South Side Hit Men." The number of home runs would have been greater if Bill Veeck had restored the 410-foot fence in center field that had been in place before 1976 (see April 28, 1976). Veeck was ready to put the fence back in place, but Bob Lemon talked him out of it, believing the shortened distance would harm the White Sox pitchers more than it would help the hitters. The 1977 White Sox hit 107 homers on the road and 85 at home. The power-hitting fueled an overall increase in runs scored from 586 in 1976 to 844 in 1977. It proved to be a one-year aberration, however. With Zisk and Gamble gone via the free agency route, the Sox hit 106 homers and scored 634 runs in 1978.*

AUGUST 16   The White Sox suffer a tough 11–10 loss to the Yankees in New York. The Sox scored six runs in the ninth inning for a 10–9 lead, but the Yankees rallied with two in their half on a home run by Chris Chambliss off Randy Wiles.

AUGUST 18   The White Sox trade Larry Anderson to the Cubs for Steve Renko.

AUGUST 20   The White Sox are knocked out of first place with a 4–2 loss to the Brewers in Milwaukee.

> *On the same day, the White Sox traded Steve Staniland to the Cardinals for Don Kessinger. Kessinger was a member of the Cubs from 1964 through 1975 and played in six All-Star Games. He was near the end of his career by the time he donned a White Sox uniform but was the club's regular shortstop in 1978 and was a player-manager in 1979.*

AUGUST 25   Wayne Nordhagen hits the first two home runs of his career in consecutive at-bats in the sixth and eighth innings of a 6–4 win over the Orioles in Baltimore. A native of Thief River Falls, Minnesota, Nordhagen had 127 career at-bats before the home runs.

AUGUST 29   Duane Kuiper of the Indians hits the only home run of his career during a 9–2 win over the White Sox in Cleveland. The pitching victim was Steve Stone. Kuiper accumulated 3,379 at-bats during his 12-year career.

AUGUST 31   The White Sox trade Dave Hamilton, Silvio Martinez and Nyls Nyman to the Cardinals for Clay Carroll.

SEPTEMBER 10   Wilbur Wood ties a major league record by hitting three batters in a row in the first inning of a 6–1 loss to the Angels in Anaheim. Wood plunked Dave Kingman, Don Baylor and Dave Chalk.

SEPTEMBER 11   Chris Knapp strikes out 13 batters and allows only four hits during a 6–2 win over the Angels in the first game of a double-header in Anaheim. Knapp had a no-hitter until Rance Mulliniks singled with two out in the seventh. California won the second game 5–4.

SEPTEMBER 24   Jack Brohamer hits for the cycle during an 8–3 win over the Mariners in Seattle. Among his five hits were two doubles. Brohamer was the first White Sox player to hit for the cycle since Ray Schalk in 1922. Facing Greg Erardi, Brohamer struck a three-run homer in the first inning, a double in the third and another double in the fifth. Against Bob Galasso, Brohamer had a single in the sixth, then completed the cycle by belting a triple in the ninth.

The homer was one of only two hit by Brohamer in 152 at-bats in 1977.

NOVEMBER 9   Richie Zisk signs a contract as a free agent with the Rangers.

NOVEMBER 29   Oscar Gamble signs a contract as a free agent with the Padres.

DECEMBER 5   The White Sox trade Brian Downing, Chris Knapp and Dave Frost to the Angels for Bobby Bonds, Rich Dotson and Thad Bosley.

The trade proved to be one of the worst in White Sox history. Downing was 27 at the time of the trade and never developed to the satisfaction of White Sox management. He found new life in Southern California, however, and made the All-Star team with the Angels in 1979 with a .326 average and 12 homers. Downing was converted into an outfielder in 1982 and a designated hitter in 1987 and continued to give the Angels, and later the Rangers, above-average production until he passed his 40th birthday. The White Sox were Bonds's fourth team in five years. He lasted only 26 games in Chicago before a May 1977 trade to Texas. Dotson was in the Sox starting rotation from 1980 through 1987 and showed flashes of brilliance. He led the AL in shutouts in 1981 and was 22–7 in 1983.

DECEMBER 12   The White Sox trade Jim Spencer, Cirilio Cruz and Bob Polinsky to the Yankees for Stan Thomas and Ed Ricks.

1978

Season in a Sentence

In a season in which almost everything goes wrong, Bob Lemon is fired by the White Sox in June, lands a job as manager of the Yankees in July and leads the Yanks to the world championship.

Finish • Won • Lost • Pct • GB

Fifth   71   90   .441   20.5

Managers

Bob Lemon (34–40) and Larry Doby (37–50)

Stats

Stats	WS	AL	Rank
Batting Avg:	.264	.261	7
On-Base Pct:	.320	.329	11
Slugging Pct:	.379	.385	8
Home Runs:	106		9 (tie)
Stolen Bases:	83		10
ERA:	4.21	3.76	12
Fielding Avg:	.977	.978	10
Runs Scored:	634		11
Runs Allowed:	731		12

Starting Lineup

Bill Nahorodny, c
Lamar Johnson, 1b
Jorge Orta, 2b
Eric Soderholm, 3b
Don Kessinger, ss
Ralph Garr, lf
Chet Lemon, cf
Claudell Washington, rf
Bob Molinaro, dh-rf
Greg Pryor, 2b-3b-ss
Thad Bosley, cf
Wayne Nordhagen, lf-rf-dh
Ron Blomberg, dh

Pitchers

Steve Stone, sp
Ken Kravec, sp
Francisco Barrios, sp
Wilbur Wood, sp
Lerrin LaGrow, rp
Jim Willoughby, rp

Attendance

1,492,100 (eighth in AL)

Club Leaders

Batting Avg:	Lamar Johnson	.273
On-Base Pct:	Lamar Johnson	.329
Slugging Pct:	Eric Soderholm	.431
Home Runs:	Eric Soderholm	20
RBIs:	Lamar Johnson	72
Runs:	Ralph Garr	67
Stolen Bases:	Bob Molinaro	22
Wins:	Steve Stone	12
Strikeouts:	Ken Kravec	154
ERA:	Francisco Barrios	4.05
Saves:	Lerrin LaGrow	16

MARCH 30   The White Sox trade Jim Essian and Steve Renko to the Athletics for Pablo Torrealba.

APRIL 7   Before a record Opening Day crowd of 50,754 at Comiskey Park, the White Sox rally for two runs in the ninth inning to defeat the Red Sox 6–5. Ron Blomberg, in his White Sox debut, homered to tie the score 5–5. The winning run scored on a single by Chet Lemon and a double from Wayne Nordhagen.

The home run was Blomberg's first major league hit since 1975. He had only one at-bat with the Yankees in 1976 and sat out all of the 1977 season with injuries. Blomberg was acquired by the White Sox as a free agent.

APRIL 8   The White Sox rally for the second day in a row to win 6–5 over the Red Sox at Comiskey Park. Trailing 5–0, the White Sox scored twice in the fifth inning and four times in the eighth.

After a strong season in 1977, the White Sox opened the 1978 campaign with four wins in their first five games, then sank to 12–28 by May 27. A streak of 17 wins in 19 games revived the hopes of the fans, but the club was unable to get over the .500 mark before the close of the season.

MAY 16   The White Sox trade Bobby Bonds to the Rangers for Claudell Washington and Rusty Torres.

Washington didn't report to the White Sox for five days, then he arrived as damaged goods. He was hobbled by a gimpy ankle suffered in a basketball game the previous January. The ankle was injured much more seriously than the Sox were led to believe. After playing one game for the club, Washington was placed on the disabled list from May 22 through June 16.

MAY 28   Francisco Barrios pitches a two-hitter to defeat the Athletics 4–0 in the second game of a double-header at Comiskey Park. The only Oakland hits were singles by Jeff Newman in the fifth inning and Gary Thomasson in the eighth. The Sox also won the second game 3–2.

MAY 31   The White Sox score 11 runs in the fifth inning and defeat the Angels 17–2 at Comiskey Park. Twelve batters reached base during the big inning on five singles, three doubles, three errors and a walk. Jorge Orta collected two of the singles, with Greg Pryor, Ralph Garr and Thad Bosley accounting for the rest of the one-base hits. Bill Nahorodny, Chet Lemon and Pryor doubled. Nahorodny's bases-loaded two-bagger drove in three runs. The Sox collected 22 hits during the contest, five of them by Orta in six at-bats. Orta had a homer and four singles.

JUNE 5   A two-run double by Bill Nahorodny in the fourth inning accounts for the only two runs in a 2–0 victory over the Indians in Cleveland. Steve Stone pitched the shutout.

JUNE 8   In the second round of the amateur draft, the White Sox select pitcher Britt Burns from Huffman High School in Birmingham, Alabama.

Burns was the only future major leaguer drafted and signed by the White Sox in 1978. He pitched his first game with the Sox less than two months later at the age of 19. Burns was 70–60 in eight seasons in Chicago.

JUNE 12   The White Sox edge the Indians 1–0 at Comiskey Park. A sacrifice fly by Wayne Nordhagen in the first inning drove in the lone run of the contest. Ken Kravec (seven innings) and Jim Willoughby (two innings) combined on the shutout.

JUNE 13   After trailing 9–0, the White Sox complete an incredible comeback to win 10–9 over the Indians at Comiskey Park. Cleveland scored four runs in the first inning, four in the second and one in the third. The Sox countered with six in their half of the third and four in the fourth. The Chicago runs were driven in by Wayne Nordhagen (three), Cliff Johnson (two), Jorge Orta (two), Bill Nahorodny (one) and Ralph Garr (one). Another scored on an error.

JUNE 18   The White Sox rout the Royals 11–0 in the second game of a double-header at Comiskey Park. The Sox lose the opener 3–2.

JUNE 27   The White Sox clobber five homers during a 10–6 win over the Mariners in Seattle. Chet Lemon hit two of the homers, with Don Kessinger, Bob Molinaro and Jim Breazeale adding the other three.

The home run by Kessinger was the only one he struck in 1978. He hit only 14 homers in 7,651 career at-bats.

JUNE 30   Larry Doby replaces Bob Lemon as manager of the White Sox.

In his first year with the White Sox, Lemon guided an overachieving club to a 90–72 record. Bill Veeck expected another miracle and was frustrated over the slow start and dwindling attendance figures in 1978. Before Lemon was fired, there was talk of trading managers with the Yankees, with Billy Martin coming to Chicago. In a bizarre chain of events, Martin was fired by the Yankees on July 24 and replaced the following day by Lemon. Then, on July 29, George Steinbrenner announced that Martin would return as Yankees manager in 1980. With Lemon at the helm, the Yanks trailed the Red Sox by 14½ games in July, but they recovered to win the AL East and then won the World Series over the Dodgers. Just 65 games into the 1979 season, Lemon was fired by Steinbrenner and replaced by Martin. Lemon returned to the Yanks late in the 1981 season and managed the club in another World Series, this time losing to the Dodgers. Doby became the second African-American to play in the major leagues in the modern era and the first in the American League when he signed with the Indians in 1947 when Veeck owned the club. Doby also became the second African-American to manage a team in the majors, following Frank Robinson, who ran the Indians from 1975 through 1977. A center fielder, Doby played in seven consecutive All-Star Games from 1949 through 1955. He played for the White Sox in 1956 and 1957 and again in 1959. While in Cleveland, Larry was a teammate of Lemon. Doby was a coach with the White Sox when elevated to the position of manager. The Sox failed to reverse their slide under Doby, posting a 37–50 record over the remainder of 1978, and he was dismissed at the end of the season.

JULY 3   The White Sox score three runs in the ninth inning to defeat the Rangers 7–6 at Comiskey Park. Chet Lemon hit a homer to pull the Sox within one before Lamar Johnson beat out an infield hit and Jorge Orta hit a two-run walk-off homer. The game was Larry Doby's first as manager in Chicago.

Larry Doby Johnson played three games as a catcher for the White Sox in 1978. He was born in Cleveland in 1950 and was named after his parents' favorite Indians player.

SEPTEMBER 1   In his major league debut, Sammy Stewart strikes out seven White Sox batters in a row during a 9–3 Baltimore win in the second game of a double-header at Memorial Stadium. The Sox also lost the opener 3–0.

SEPTEMBER 3   In his first at-bat since July 14, Wayne Nordhagen hits a three-run pinch-hit homer in the ninth inning for a 4–2 win over the Orioles in Baltimore. Nordhagen had been on the disabled list with hepatitis.

SEPTEMBER 6   Ken Kravec pitches the White Sox to a 1–0 win over the Twins in Minnesota. The lone run scored on a double by Chet Lemon and a single by Greg Pryor.

SEPTEMBER 7   Harry Chappas makes his major league debut, going hitless in four at-bats during a 5–3 loss to the Mariners at Comiskey Park.

A shortstop, Chappas stood only five-foot-three and weighed 150 pounds. His status as the shortest player in baseball since Eddie Gaedel appeared in a game in 1951 earned Chappas a spot on the cover of Sports Illustrated *on March 19, 1979. He disliked the publicity surrounding his size, however, and turned inward, avoiding reporters at all costs. In 72 games and 184 at-bats over three seasons with the White Sox, Chappas hit .246 and compiled a slugging percentage of just .283.*

SEPTEMBER 8   Greg Pryor hits his first two major league homers in consecutive at-bats to drive in all three runs of a 3–2 win over the Mariners at Comiskey Park. Pryor homered in the first and third innings. He had accumulated 184 major league at-bats before connecting for the back-to-back blasts.

The game was played on Don Kessinger Night. Before the contest, he received a number of gifts, including two ponies and a round-trip ticket to Hawaii for his entire family.

SEPTEMBER 15   The White Sox explode for five runs in the 10th inning to defeat the Mariners 8–3 in Seattle.

SEPTEMBER 16   Francisco Barrios pitches a one-hitter and beats the Mariners 9–1 at the Kingdome. The only Seattle hit was a single by Julio Cruz in the sixth inning.

SEPTEMBER 19   Ron Blomberg hits a grand slam off Alan Wirth in the eighth inning of an 8–4 win over the Athletics in the first game of a double-header in Oakland. The White Sox completed the sweep with a 7–3 win in the second tilt.

SEPTEMBER 23   While his team is in Chicago for a series against the White Sox, Angels outfielder Lyman Bostock is shot to death in Gary, Indiana. He was in Gary to visit an uncle, who was driving a car containing Bostock and two women he'd met only a few minutes earlier. Another vehicle pulled alongside and the husband of one of the women fired shots at the car. One of the bullets struck Bostock and he died three hours later.

OCTOBER 19   Don Kessinger replaces Larry Doby as manager.

Doby was never given another chance to manage in the majors. Kessinger was a long-time favorite in Chicago because of his years with the Cubs. Bill Veeck admitted that he was in the business of selling tickets, and that Kessinger's popularity was one factor in the decision. Only 36, Kessinger served as player-manager in 1979, appearing in 58 games. He didn't last a full season as manager, resigning on August 2, 1979, with the Sox holding a record of 46–60.

NOVEMBER 29   Steve Stone signs a contract with the Orioles as a free agent.

When he signed with the Orioles, Stone was 31 and had a career record of 67–72. He had a career year with 25 wins and seven losses in 1980, but his playing career ended a year later with an elbow injury. Stone later was a television announcer for the Cubs from 1983 through 2000 and again from 2003 until 2005. He teamed with Harry Caray from 1983 until Harry's death in 1998.

1979   Sox

Season in a Sentence

Tony LaRussa takes over in August in the midst of a season in which the White Sox lose 87 games, one of them by forfeit following the destruction of disco records.

Finish • Won • Lost • Pct • GB

Fifth   73   87   .456   14.0

Managers

Don Kessinger (46–60) and Tony LaRussa (27–27)

Stats

Stats	WS	AL	Rank
Batting Avg:	.275	.270	7
On-Base Pct:	.335	.338	10
Slugging Pct:	.410	.408	7
Home Runs:	127		10
Stolen Bases:	97		9
ERA:	4.10	4.22	6
Fielding Avg:	.972	.978	13
Runs Scored:	730		11
Runs Allowed:	748		8

Starting Lineup

Milt May, c
Lance Johnson, 1b
Alan Bannister, 2b-lf
Kevin Bell, 3b
Greg Pryor, ss
Ralph Garr, lf
Chet Lemon, cf
Claudell Washington, rf
Jorge Orta, dh-2b
Mike Squires, 1b
Jim Morrison, 2b-3b
Eric Soderholm, 3b
Junior Moore, lf
Wayne Nordhagen, dh
Bill Nahorodny, c
Rusty Torres, lf-rf

Pitchers

Ken Kravec, sp
Rich Wortham, sp
Ross Baumgarten, sp
Steve Trout, sp
Francisco Barrios, sp
Ed Farmer, rp
Randy Scarberry, rp
Mike Proly, rp

Attendance

1,280,702 (tenth in AL)

Club Leaders

Batting Avg:	Chet Lemon	.318
On-Base Pct:	Chet Lemon	.391
Slugging Pct:	Chet Lemon	.496
Home Runs:	Chet Lemon	17
RBIs:	Chet Lemon	86
Runs:	Chet Lemon	79
	Claudell Washington	79
Stolen Bases:	Alan Bannister	22
Wins:	Ken Kravec	15
Strikeouts:	Ken Kravec	132
ERA:	Ross Baumgarten	3.54
Saves:	Ed Farmer	14

APRIL 6   Six days after the nuclear disaster at Three Mile Island and three days after Jane Byrne is elected mayor of Chicago, the White Sox lose the season opener 5–2 to the Orioles in Baltimore.

APRIL 10   The White Sox lose the first game of the season at Comiskey Park 10–2 to the Blue Jays before 41,043 in 40-degree weather.

               Bill Veeck was so disgusted with his team's performance that he gave fans who attended the opener free admission to the next home game two days later. All the fans had to present was a rain check to be admitted to Comiskey Park without charge. Only 2,220 fans took advantage of the offer, joining a meager 1,205 others who paid to get into the ballpark. The White Sox blew a 7–2 lead by giving up six runs in the eighth inning and lost 9–7 to the Blue Jays.

APRIL 13   The White Sox pound the Yankees 12–2 at Comiskey Park.

On the same day, the White Sox traded Jack Kucek to the Phillies for Jim Morrison.

APRIL 27   The White Sox rout the Rangers 11–0 at Comiskey Park. The game started with the temperature at 36 degrees and the wind chill at 19.

MAY 3   The White Sox score three runs in the ninth inning to defeat the Rangers 7–5 in the first game of a double-header at Arlington. A single by Chet Lemon tied the score. A two-run double by Eric Soderholm put the Sox into the lead. Chicago held a 6–0 lead in the seventh inning of the second game, but they lost 7–6.

MAY 17   Ken Kravec (seven innings) and Mike Proly (two innings) combine on a two-hitter to beat the Athletics 5–1 in Oakland. The only hits collected by the A's were a single by Jim Essian in the third inning and a homer by Jeff Newman in the seventh.

MAY 25   Ross Baumgarten (eight innings) and Randy Scarberry (one inning) combine on a one-hitter to defeat the Angels 6–1 at Comiskey Park. Bobby Grich accounted for the lone California hit with a double in the seventh inning. Baumgarten was relieved because he walked eight batters during the contest, including the first two batters of the ninth inning.

            A native of Highland Park, Illinois, Baumgarten was 13–8 as a 24-year-old in 1979. While playing for the White Sox in 1980 and 1981 and the Phillies in 1982, he posted a record of only 7–26.

MAY 27   The White Sox purchase Milt May from the Tigers.

JUNE 5   Seven days after the crash of a DC-10 kills 275 at O'Hare Airport, the highest death toll in a single aircraft crash in U.S. history, the White Sox select shortstop Steve Buechele from Servite High School in Fullerton, California, and Rick Seilheimer of Brenham, Texas in Brenham, Texas in the first round of the amateur draft. The Sox had two picks due to free agent compensation.

            Buechele elected to attend Stanford University instead of signing with the White Sox. He was drafted by the Rangers in 1982 and had an 11-year career in the majors. Seilheimer made his major league debut at the age of 19 in 1980, but his big-league career lasted only 21 games. The only other players drafted and signed by the Sox in 1979 to reach the majors were Randy Johnson (third round in January), Frank Mullins (third round in the regular phase in June) and Bob Fallon (first round of the secondary phase in June). The Randy Johnson selected by the Sox was not the famous pitcher, but a first baseman who ended up with just two seasons as a big-leaguer.

JUNE 10   The White Sox unleash a 21-hit attack and romp to a 13–3 win over the Brewers in Milwaukee.

JUNE 11   White Sox pitching coach Fred Martin dies of lung cancer at the age of 63.

JUNE 12   The White Sox score seven runs in the second inning and beat the Orioles 12–4 at Comiskey Park.

JUNE 15   The White Sox trade Eric Soderholm to the Rangers for Ed Farmer and Gary Holle.

JULY 4   The White Sox score 10 runs in the fifth inning and beat the Indians 16–4 in
                Cleveland. Wayne Nordhagen hit a grand slam off Rick Waits. Alan Bannister
                collected five hits, including a double, in six at-bats.

JULY 12   Disco Demolition Night at Comiskey Park backfires and results in a forfeit to
                the Tigers.

                *The promotion was initiated by WLUP-FM disc jockey Steve Dahl with the
                involvement of Mike Veeck, son of owner Bill Veeck Jr. Dahl and the younger
                Veeck shared a bitter distaste for the trend toward the disco beat in popular
                music. Dahl had been bashing disco music on his program for some time.
                The disco craze was already on the wane by 1979, but Veeck knew a great
                promotional idea when he heard one. Fans who brought disco records to
                Comiskey Park received tickets for a double-header with the Tigers for 98 cents.
                The 98 cents was a tie-in to the radio station's frequency of 98 on the FM dial.
                Some 50,000 turned up with records, which were to be placed in a crate and
                burned between games. But rowdiness began with the discs being thrown like
                Frisbees onto the field during the first game, won by Detroit 4–1. Between games,
                Dahl, dressed in army fatigues and riding in a jeep, drove out to center field and
                set off an explosive charge, sending thousands of vinyl disco records skyward.
                Smoke billowed about as many of the records ignited, creating a bonfire in center
                field. Moments later, a swarm of 5,000 to 8,000 fans invaded the field and refused
                to leave the field despite pleas from Veeck and radio announcer Harry Caray.
                The mob dug up home plate and pieces of turf. After a delay of one hour and
                16 minutes, umpire-in-chief Dave Phillips decided that the field was unplayable
                and called the contest. A day later, AL president Lee McPhail ruled it a forfeit.*

JULY 14   The White Sox club six home runs, three of them by Claudell Washington, to defeat
                the Tigers 12–4 at Comiskey Park. Washington hit a solo shot off Steve Baker in the
                third inning and a pair of two-run homers against Dave Tobik in the seventh and
                eighth. The other Chicago home runs were hit by Ralph Garr, Rusty Torres and
                Jim Morrison.

JULY 22   Randy Scarberry (seven innings) and Ed Farmer (one inning) combine on a two-
                hitter, but the White Sox lose 1–0 to the Tigers in Detroit. The lone run scored in the
                second inning on a walk, a stolen base and a single by Jerry Morales.

AUGUST 2   Tony LaRussa replaces Don Kessinger as manager.

                *Kessinger resigned with the White Sox holding a record of 46–60. He never
                managed another big-league club. LaRussa was only 34 years old and had been
                managing the White Sox's Class AAA farm club in Des Moines. He made his big-
                league debut as a player as an 18-year-old infielder in 1963 with the Kansas City
                Athletics. By the time he played his last game in 1973, LaRussa had logged only
                132 games in the majors, with a batting average of .199 without a single home
                run in 176 at-bats. Between baseball seasons, LaRussa attended Florida State
                University Law School and was admitted to the Florida bar during the 1979–80
                off-season. Over the balance of the 1979 season, the White Sox were 27–27
                under LaRussa and he was given a shot at managing the club again in 1980. He
                methodically built a winner, and by 1983 the Sox were 99–63 and won the AL
                West. The club was 159–165 over the next two seasons, however, and LaRussa
                was let go on June 19, 1986, with the Sox standing at 26–38.*

AUGUST 5   A crowd of about 70,000 jams Comiskey Park for nine hours of music that includes the Beach Boys, Blondie and Sha Na Na.

AUGUST 9   Rich Wortham pitches a two-hitter and beats the Yankees 5–1 in New York. The only hits off Wortham were a single by Lenny Randle in the third inning and a home run by Lou Piniella in the fourth.

The White Sox tried to convert former Chicago Bears quarterback Bobby Douglass into a pitcher in 1979. He pitched four games in Des Moines in the American Association without success.

Outfielder Chet Lemon enjoyed his best year in many offensive categories in 1979, including a league-leading 44 doubles.

AUGUST 12   Ross Baumgarten pitches a two-hitter to defeat the Blue Jays 7–0 in the first game of a double-header at Comiskey Park. The only Toronto hits were a single by Bob Bailor in the first inning and a triple by Al Woods in the seventh.

AUGUST 21   Chet Lemon walks out on the White Sox before a double-header against the Brewers in Milwaukee. Lemon was angry because he wasn't permitted to bat out of turn during practice. He returned the following day and was docked one day's pay.

Despite the unexcused absence, Lemon was the White Sox's best player in 1979, with a .318 batting average, 44 doubles and 17 homers.

AUGUST 24   The game between the White Sox and Orioles at Comiskey Park is called off because of unplayable field conditions. Due to a rock concert days earlier, loose turf was strewn all over the diamond and the outfield was a sandy quagmire.

SEPTEMBER 4   Down 7–2, the White Sox score five runs in the sixth inning, one in the eighth and two in the ninth to beat the Angels 10–7 in Anaheim.

SEPTEMBER 18   Ken Kravec pitches a 10-inning complete game, allowing only three hits, to defeat the Twins 1–0 at Comiskey Park. Kravec held Minnesota hitless until Ron Jackson doubled in the eighth.

SEPTEMBER 20   The White Sox sell Ralph Garr to the Angels.

OCTOBER 3   The White Sox purchase Bob Molinaro from the Orioles.

NOVEMBER 1   Milt May signs as a free agent with the Giants.

DECEMBER 19   Six weeks after Iranian militants seize the U.S. Embassy in Teheran, taking 52 hostages, Jorge Orta signs as a free agent with the Indians.

White Sox by the Numbers

Uniforms have long been an intregal part of the game of baseball. The following is a list of uniform numbers and the key White Sox players, managers and coaches who wore them since 1931, when the club affixed numerals on the jerseys for the first time. Retired numbers are those for Nellie Fox (2), Harold Baines (3), Luke Appling (4), Minnie Minoso (9), Luis Aparicio (11), Ted Lyons (16), Billy Pierce (19), Jackie Robinson (42) and Carlton Fisk (72). In addition, the White Sox haven't assigned number 35 since Frank Thomas left the club via free agency at the end of the 2005 season. Number 6 is also in "limbo." The last two individuals to wear the numeral were hitting coaches Charlie Lau from 1982 through 1984 and Walt Hriniak from 1989 through 1995. Both died while active coaches with the Sox.

1   Lew Fonseca (1933–34), George Kell (1954–56), Jim Landis (1957–64), Tommie Agee (1965–67), Scott Fletcher (1983–85), Lance Johnson (1988–95)

2   Jackie Hayes (1933–35), Marv Owen (1938–39), Bill Knickerbocker (1941), Thurman Tucker (1946–47), Al Zarilla (1950–51), Nellie Fox (1953–62), Mike Andrews (1971–73). Retired in honor of Fox in 1976.

3   Carl Reynolds (1931), Zeke Bonura (1933–37), Joe Kuhel (1938–43), Rudy York (1947), Tony Lupien (1948), Jim Busby (1951), Fred Hatfield (1956–57), Floyd Robinson (1960–66), Walt Williams (1967–72), Jim Spencer (1976–77), Harold Baines (1980–89, 1996–97, 2000–01). Retired in honor of Baines in 1989.

4   Luke Appling (1933–43, 1945–50), Marty Marion (1954–55), Gene Freese (1960), Ron Hansen (1963–69). Retired in honor of Baines in 1989.

5   Al Simmons (1933), Jimmy Dykes (1934–46), Pat Seerey (1948–49), Hank Majeski (1950–51), Sam Mele (1953), Johnny Groth (1954–55), Bubba Phillips (1955–59), Roy Sievers (1960–61), Joe Cunningham (1962–64), Bill Skowron (1964), Johnny Romano (1965–66), Duane Josephson (1967–70), Bob Molinaro (1978–81), Vance Law (1982–84), Ray Durham (1995–2002), Juan Uribe (2004–07)

6   Cliff Watwood (1931), Mule Haas (1933–37), Eddie Smith (1939), Taffy Wright (1940–42, 1946–48), Roy Schalk (1944–45), Gus Zernial (1949–51), Cass Michaels (1954), Billy Goodman (1958–61), Jorge Orta (1972–79)

7   Lew Fonseca (1931), Jimmie Dykes (1933), Al Simmons (1934–35), Dixie Walker (1937), Hal Trosky (1944, 1946), Cass Michaels (1947–50), Jim Rivera (1953–60), Charlie Maxwell (1962–64), Don Buford (1965–67), Chuck Tanner (1971–75), Alan Bannister (1976–80), Kenny Williams (1987–88), Scott Fletcher (1989–91), Gene Lamont (1992), Jerry Manuel (1998–2003)

8   Luke Appling (1932), Mike Kreevich (1936–41), Thurman Tucker (1943–44), Floyd Baker (1945–51), Ferris Fain (1953–54), Walt Dropo (1955–58), Pete Ward (1963–68), Tom Egan (1971–73), Mike Devereaux (1995), Tony Phillips (1996), Albert Belle (1997–98), Brook Fordyce (1999–2000), Charles Johnson (2000), Carl Everett (2004–05)

9   Evar Swanson (1933–34), Rip Radcliff (1935–39), Moose Solters (1940–41), Wally Moses (1942–46), Dave Philley (1947–51), Minnie Minoso (1951–57, 1960–61, 1964, 1976, 1980), Danny Cater (1965). Retired in honor of Minoso in 1983.

10 Sherm Lollar (1953–63), Al Lopez (1964–65, 1969), J. C. Martin (1966–67), Jay Johnstone (1971–72), Jack Brohamer (1976–77), Tony LaRussa (1979–86), Jeff Torborg (1989–91), Royce Clayton (2000–01), Shingo Takatsu (2004–05)

11 Luis Aparicio (1956–62, 1968–70), Dave Nicholson (1963–65), Jim Essian (1976–77), Don Kessinger (1979), Rudy Law (1982–84). Retired in honor of Aparicio in 1984.

12 Lew Fonseca (1932), Larry Rosenthal (1936–41), Guy Curtwright (1943–46), Harry Dorish (1951–55), J. C. Martin (1960–65), Eddie Stanky (1966–68), Ed Herrmann (1969–74), Paul Richards (1976), Eric Soderholm (1977–79), Jim Morrison (1979–82), Steve Lyons (1987–91), Chris Singleton (1999–2001), A. J. Pierzynski (2005–07)

13 Ozzie Guillen (1985–97, 2004–07)
14 Luke Sewell (1935–38), Sam Mele (1952), Larry Doby (1956–57, 1977–79), Tom McCraw (1963–64), Bill Skowron (1965–67), Bill Melton (1968–75), Tony Bernazard (1978–81), Craig Grebeck (1990–93), Julio Franco (1994), Dave Martinez (1995–97), Paul Konerko (1999–2007)
15 Tommy Thomas (1931), Mike Tresh (1938–48), Bob Keegan (1953–58), Richie Allen (1972–74), Tadahito Iguchi (2005–07)
16 Ted Lyons (1932–42, 1946–48), Mike Fornieles (1953–56), Al Smith (1958–62), Ken Berry (1965–70), Brian Downing (1973–77), Greg Pryor (1978–79), Julio Cruz (1983–84), Jim Fregosi (1986–87). Retired in honor of Lyons in 1987.
17 Sugar Cain (1936–38), Frank Papish (1945–48), Chico Carrasquel (1950–55), Earl Torgeson (1957–60), Carlos May (1969–76), Oscar Gamble (1977), Dave Gallagher (1988–90), Mike Caruso (1998–99)
18 Red Faber (1931), George Earnshaw (1934), Bill Dietrich (1938–48), Randy Gumpert (1949–51), Bob Nieman (1955–56), Gail Hopkins (1968–70), Pat Kelly (1971–76), Claudell Washington (1978–80), Jim Fregosi (1987–88), Terry Bevington (1995–97)
19 Les Tiejte (1935), Buck Ross (1941–45), Billy Pierce (1949–61), Bruce Howard (1964–67), Greg Luzinski (1981–84), Alan Bannister (1986–87). Retired in honor of Pierce in 1987.
20 Sandy Consuegra (1953–56), Joe Horlen (1961–71), Wayne Nordhagen (1978–81), Ron Karkovice (1989–97), Jon Garland (2003–07)
21 Gerry Staley (1956–61), Ray Herbert (1961–64), Bart Johnson (1971–76), Bob Lemon (1977–78), Gary Redus (1987–88), George Bell (1992–93), Esteban Loaiza (2003–04)
22 Donie Bush (1931), Paul Richards (1951–54), Dick Donovan (1955–60), Richie Zisk (1977), Ed Farmer (1979–81), Steve Kemp (1982), Ivan Calderon (1986–90), Darrin Jackson (1994), Jose Valentin (2000–04), Scott Podsednik (2005–07)
23 Eddie Smith (1940), Jack Onslow (1949–50), Virgil Trucks (1953–55), Bob Locker (1965–69), Lamar Johnson (1976–81), Rudy Law (1985), Robin Ventura (1990–98), Jermaine Dye (2005–07)
24 Vic Frasier (1931), Red Kress (1932), Vern Kennedy (1934–37), Jack Knott (1938–40), Eddie Carnett (1944), Early Wynn (1958–62), Tommy McCraw (1965–68), Tom Bradley (1971–72), Ken Henderson (1973–75), Mike Proly (1978–80), Floyd Bannister (1983–85, 1987), Mike Cameron (1995–98), Joe Crede (2000–07)
25 Joe Heving (1933–34), Monte Stratton (1936–41), Ralph Hodgin (1943–44), Oris Hockett (1945), Tommy John (1965–71), Tony Muser (1972–75), Sammy Sosa (1989–91), Jim Thome (2006–07)
26 Clint Brown (1936–40), Johnny Humphries (1941–45), Nellie Fox (1950–52), Don Johnson (1954), Jose DeLeon (1986–87), Ellis Burks (1993)
27 Lu Blue (1931), Thornton Lee (1937–47), Turk Lown (1958–62), Ken Kravec (1976–80)
28 Sad Sam Jones (1933–34), Cass Michaels (1944–47), Al Gettel (1948–49), Dixie Howell (1955–58), Eddie Fisher (1962–66), Wilbur Wood (1967–78), Joey Cora (1992–94)
29 John Kerr (1931), Johnny Rigney (1937–42, 1946–47), Bill Wight (1948–50), Joe Dobson (1951–53), Jack Harshman (1954–57), Greg Walker (1983–90), Jack McDowell (1990–94), Chris Foulke (1998–2002)
30 Jim Wilson (1956–58), John Buzhardt (1962–67), Bucky Dent (1973–76), Ross Baumgarten (1979–81), Salome Barojas (1982–84), Gene Nelson (1984–86), Tim Raines (1991–95), Magglio Ordonez (1997–2004)
31 Hoyt Wilhelm (1963–68), LaMarr Hoyt (1981–84), Scott Radinsky (1990–95), Greg Norton (1996–2000)
32 Juan Pizarro (1961–66), Steve Stone (1973, 1977–78), Tim Hulett (1983–87), Tony Fernandez (1990–96), Dustin Hermanson (2005–06)
33 Steve Trout (1979–82), Melido Perez (1988–91), Gene Lamont (1992–95), Mike Sirotka (1997–2000), Aaron Rowand (2003–05)
34 John Whitehead (1935), Ken Holcombe (1951–52), Ken Brett (1976–77), Bill Almon (1981–82), Rich Dotson (1983–87, 1989), Freddy Garcia (2004–06)

35 Joe Haynes (1941–48), Saul Rogovin (1951–52), Bob Shaw (1958–60), Frank Thomas (1990–2005)

36 Johnny Dickshot (1944–45), Hector Rodriguez (1952), Jim Kaat (1973–75), Lerrin LaGrow (1977–79), Jerry Koosman (1981–83), Ron Reed (1984), Eric King (1989–90), Kevin Tapani (1996–98)

37 Tony Piet (1935), Gordon Maltzberger (1943–44), Bobby Thigpen (1987–93), James Baldwin (1995–2001)

38 Phil Masi (1950–52), Frank Baumann (1960–64), Dave LaPoint (1987–88)

39 Don Gutteridge (1970), Roberto Hernandez (1991–97)

40 Mike Hershberger (1961–64), Britt Burns (1980–85), Joe Cowley (1986), Wilson Alvarez (1990–97), Jim Parque (1998–2002)

41 Cy Acosta (1972–74), Tom Seaver (1984–86), Jerry Reuss (1988–89), Bill Simas (1995–2001)

42 Al Lopez (1957–63, 1968), Ron Kittle (1983–86, 1989–91). Retired in honor of Jackie Robinson in 1997.

43 Gary Peters (1963–69), Bob James (1985–87), Herbert Perry (2000–01), Damaso Marte (2002–05)

44 Russ Kemmerer (1960–62), Don McMahon (1967–68), Chet Lemon (1976–81), Tom Paciorek (1982–85), John Cangelosi (1986), Dan Pasqua (1988–94)

45 Orval Grove (1940–49), Sherm Lollar (1952), Camilo Carreon (1960–64), Stan Bahnsen (1972–75), Danny Tartabull (1996), Carlos Lee (1999–2004), Bobby Jenks (2005–07)

46 Hank Steinbacher (1937–39), Eddie Smith (1940–43), Earl Caldwell (1945–48), Bob Kuzava (1949–50), Eddie Robinson (1950–52), Francisco Barrios (1976–80), Bill Long (1985, 1987), Jason Bere (1994–98), Bobby Howry (1999–2002)

47 Eric McNair (1939), Don Kolloway (1941–43, 1946–49), Tony Cuccinello (1943–45)

48 Ed Lopat (1944–47), Rick Reichardt (1971–73), Ralph Garr (1976–79)

49 Rich Dotson (1979–82), Charlie Hough (1991–92)

50 Barry Jones (1989–90), Sean Lowe (1999–2001)

51 Terry Forster (1971–76), Jason Bere (1993)

52 John Garland (2000–02), Jose Contreras (2004–07)

53 Dennis Lamp (1981–83)

54 Goose Gossage (1972–76)

56 Mark Buehrle (2000–07)

59 Luis Aloma (1950–52)

72 Carlton Fisk (1982–93). Retired in honor of Fisk in 1997.

THE STATE OF THE WHITE SOX

Four of the 10 White Sox teams during the 1980s posted winning records, including the Western Division champions of 1983. Tony LaRussa managed all four of the winning clubs, the last in 1985. Overall, the White Sox were 758–802 during the decade, a winning percentage of .486 that ranked 10th among the 14 AL clubs. AL clubs that reached the World Series were the Royals (1980 and 1985), Yankees (1981), Brewers (1982), Orioles (1983), Tigers (1984), Red Sox (1986), Twins (1987) and Athletics (1988 and 1989). AL West champs, other than the White Sox, were the Royals (1980, 1984 and 1985), Athletics (1981, 1988 and 1989), Angels (1982 and 1986) and Twins (1987).

THE BEST TEAM

The 1983 White Sox, with the slogan "Winning Ugly", were 99–63 and won the AL West before losing the American League Championship Series to the Orioles.

THE WORST TEAM

The 1989 White Sox tumbled into last place with a record of 69–92.

THE BEST MOMENT

On June 30, 1988, at a midnight session, the Illinois General Assembly approved the funds to provide the White Sox with a new stadium to replace Comiskey Park. Without the legislation, it's likely that the Sox would have moved to St. Petersburg, Florida.

THE WORST MOMENT

After winning 99 regular season games in 1983, the most in the major leagues, the White Sox seemed to be headed for their first World Series since 1959, but they lost the American League Championship Series to the Orioles.

THE ALL-DECADE TEAM • YEARS WITH WS

Carlton Fisk, c	1981–93
Greg Walker, 1b	1982–90
Tony Bernazard, 2b	1981–83
Vance Law, 3b	1982–85
Ozzie Guillen, ss	1985–97
Ron Kittle, lf	1982–86, 1989–91
Rudy Law, cf	1982–85
Harold Baines, rf	1980–89, 1996–97, 2000–01
Greg Luzinski, dh	1981–84
Rich Dotson, p	1979–87, 1989
Britt Burns, p	1978–85
Floyd Bannister, p	1983–87
Bobby Thigpen, p	1986–93

Fisk is in the Hall of Fame. Right fielder Ivan Calderon (1986–90, 1993) and pitcher LaMarr Hoyt (1979–84) were also outstanding players on the White Sox during the 1980s. Second base and third base were problem positions for most of the decade.

THE DECADE LEADERS

Batting Avg:	Harold Baines	.289
On-Base Pct:	Greg Luzinski	.361
Slugging Pct:	Harold Baines	.464
Home Runs:	Harold Baines	186
RBIs:	Harold Baines	819
Runs:	Harold Baines	661
Stolen Bases:	Rudy Law	239
Wins:	Rich Dotson	92
Strikeouts:	Rich Dotson	805
ERA:	Britt Burns	3.59
Saves:	Bobby Thigpen	91

THE HOME FIELD

One of the first priorities of Jerry Reinsdorf and Eddie Einhorn when they purchased the club in 1981 was to replace Comiskey Park. The two believed that the White Sox couldn't compete for players in the free-agent era playing at the aging ballpark. The owners explored the possibility of moving the club to the western Chicago suburbs, and when that failed, looked to shifting the franchise to St. Petersburg, Florida. Finally in 1988, the government financing needed to build a new Comiskey Park adjacent to the old one was voted upon by the Illinois General Assembly. The new stadium opened in 1991. Before building the new ballpark, Reinsdorf and Einhorn did much to rehabilitate the original Comiskey Park, extend its life and make it more of a family-oriented attraction. Under previous administrations, the ballpark had a reputation as the world's "largest outdoor saloon." Under Reinsdorf and Einhorn, sales of hard liquor were banned and security was increased. In 1982, renovations included new dugouts, box seats, and an all-electronic DiamondVision scoreboard. In 1983, home plate was moved forward eight feet to increase the number of home runs, then was shifted back to its original location in 1986.

THE GAME YOU WISHED YOU HAD SEEN

In a game that took two days to complete, the White Sox and Brewers played 25 innings, the longest in American League history, on May 8 and 9, 1984. The White Sox won 7–6 on a walk-off home run by Harold Baines.

THE WAY THE GAME WAS PLAYED

The 1980s had a little something for everybody. Trends that surfaced in the 1970s continued, with teams still emphasizing speed. In 1987, offense spiked in a year that combined the speed of the dead-ball era with the power of the 1950s. AL teams averaged 124 stolen bases and 188 home runs.

THE MANAGEMENT

Bill Veeck sold the White Sox in January 1981 to Jerry Reinsdorf and Eddie Einhorn. Reinsdorf became chairman of the board and Einhorn was installed as president. General managers were Roland Hemond (1970–85), Ken Harrelson (1985–86) and Larry Himes (1986–90). Field managers were Tony LaRussa (1979–86), Doug Rader (1986), Jim Fregosi (1986–88) and Jeff Torborg (1989–91).

THE BEST PLAYER MOVE

The best player move was the selection of Frank Thomas in the 1989 amateur draft. The signing of Carlton Fisk as a free agent in 1981 was another significant move in White Sox history.

THE WORST PLAYER MOVE

The worst move sent Bobby Bonilla to the Pirates in July 1986 for Jose DeLeon.

1980

Season in a Sentence

With one of the youngest teams in the league, the White Sox lose 90 games, largely the result of a woeful offense and severe fielding deficiencies.

Finish Won · Lost · Pct · GB

Fifth   70   90   .438   26.0

Manager

Tony LaRussa

Stats

Stats	WS	AL	Rank
Batting Avg:	.259	.269	12
On-Base Pct:	.314	.335	12
Slugging Pct:	.370	.399	13
Home Runs:	91		13
Stolen Bases:	68		12
ERA:	3.92	4.03	6
Fielding Avg:	.973	.978	14
Runs Scored:	587		14
Runs Allowed:	722		6

Starting Lineup

Bruce Kimm, c
Mike Squires, 1b
Jim Morrison, 2b
Greg Pryor, 3b-ss
Todd Cruz, ss
Wayne Nordhagen, lf-rf
Chet Lemon, cf
Harold Baines, rf
Lamar Johnson, dh-1b
Bob Molinaro, lf-dh
Kevin Bell, 3b

Pitchers

Britt Burns, sp
Rich Dotson, sp
Steve Trout, sp
LaMarr Hoyt, sp-rp
Ross Baumgarten, sp
Ken Kravec, sp
Ed Farmer, rp
Mike Proly, rp
Rick Wortham, rp

Attendance

1,200,365 (ninth in AL)

Club Leaders

Batting Avg:	Chet Lemon	.292
On-Base Pct:	Chet Lemon	.388
Slugging Pct:	Chet Lemon	.442
Home Runs:	Wayne Nordhagen	15
RBIs:	Lamar Johnson	81
Runs:	Chet Lemon	76
Stolen Bases:	Bob Molinaro	18
Wins:	Britt Burns	15
Strikeouts:	Britt Burns	133
ERA:	Britt Burns	2.84
Saves:	Ed Farmer	30

APRIL 10   The White Sox lose 5–3 to the Orioles before an Opening Day crowd of 35,539 at Comiskey Park. Starter Steve Trout gave up four runs in the first inning and one in the fifth. Alan Bannister collected three hits, including a double. In his major league debut, Harold Baines was hitless in four at-bats.

Harold Baines was assigned uniform number 3, which would be retired by the club in his honor in 1989. The last individual to wear number 3 prior to Baines was coach Joe Sparks in 1979.

APRIL 15   Chet Lemon singles to drive in the winning run in the 14th inning of a 4–3 decision over the Yankees at Comiskey Park.

The White Sox's radio and TV teams in 1980 consisted of Harry Caray, Jimmy Piersall, Joe McConnell and Rick King.

APRIL 19   Catcher Marv Foley hits a home run in the 12th inning to beat the Orioles 5–4 in Baltimore.

APRIL 20   The White Sox score three runs in the ninth inning to defeat the Orioles 9–6 at Memorial Stadium. The contest featured a bench-clearing brawl in the sixth.

Sox hurler Mike Proly hit Doug DeCinces with a pitch. DeCinces charged the mound, and Proly tackled him at the knees. The Baltimore third baseman responded by punching the pitcher several times in the back. DeCinces was ejected.

APRIL 26   In the 12th inning, Mike Squires scores Thad Bosley from third base on a suicide squeeze for the winning run in an 8–7 decision over the Yankees in New York. Kevin Bell struck out five times in five plate appearances.

The victory gave the White Sox an 11–4 record. The club was still 22–15 on May 20 and held first place in the AL West, but it went 40–73 from May 21 through September 24.

MAY 4   Mike Squires becomes the first left-handed catcher in the major leagues in 22 years during an 11–1 loss to the Brewers at Comiskey Park. Squires went into the game in the ninth inning.

The last lefty catcher prior to Squires was Dale Long of the Cubs in 1958. Squires caught one other game before the experiment ended.

MAY 5   Mike Proly is again in a fight, this time during an 11–7 win over the Brewers at Comiskey Park. In the fourth inning, Proly struck Ben Oglivie with a pitch, and the Milwaukee hitter charged the mound. Bruce Kimm tried to stop Oglivie, who reached around the Sox catcher to punch Proly, causing both benches to empty. Tony LaRussa suffered a separated shoulder in the melee.

MAY 19   The day after the volcanic eruption of Mount St. Helens, the White Sox edge the Twins 1–0 at Comiskey Park. Ken Kravec (eight innings) and Ed Farmer (one inning) combined on the shutout. The lone run scored in the third inning on a double by Alan Bannister.

JUNE 3   In the first round of the amateur draft, the White Sox select outfielder Cecil Espy from Point Loma High School in San Diego, California.

The Sox sent Espy to the Dodgers in 1982 in a deal that brought Rudy Law in Chicago. A light-hitting outfielder, Espy hit seven homers and batted .244 in 1,248 major league at-bats. The only other future major leaguers drafted and signed by the Sox in 1980 were Jim Siwy and Tim Hulett.

JUNE 7   The White Sox trade Claudell Washington to the Mets for Jesse Anderson.

JUNE 20   A vicious brawl punctuates an 11-inning, 5–3 loss to the Tigers at Comiskey Park. Al Cowens, batting in the 11th, grounded to shortstop but instead of running to first base, charged Sox pitcher Ed Farmer, who had his back turned and didn't see Cowens coming. In May 1979 while playing for the Royals, Cowens was hit in the face by a pitch from Farmer, then with the Rangers. Cowens was suspended for seven days by the American League. Farmer swore out a warrant for Cowens's arrest on assault charges. Cowens missed a series in Chicago in August to avoid arrest. Finally, on September 1, Farmer dropped the charges and the two shook hands at home plate before a game in Detroit, receiving a standing ovation from the Tiger Stadium crowd.

JULY 2   Ross Baumgarten pitches a one-hitter to defeat the Angels 1–0 at Comiskey Park. Rod Carew led off the seventh inning with a single for the only California hit. Earlier in the at-bat, left fielder Wayne Nordhagen dropped Carew's pop foul.

After the game, Jimmy Piersall attacked Rob Gallas, a writer from the Daily Herald, *a suburban newspaper. The fight resulted from Piersall's trials and tribulations throughout the season. Piersall was not only a radio and television announcer, but served as a part-time outfield and base-running coach for the Sox. Because of his controversial style in front of the mike, the* Chicago Sun-Times *conducted a fan poll in May asking fans whether not he should be fired. By an 8–1 margin, those responding wanted to keep Piersall on the air. In mid-June, he lost his job as a coach because of his barbs criticizing Tony LaRussa and Sox players. He also called Bill Veeck's wife. Mary Francis. a "colossal bore" on a daytime TV talk show. Gallas made light of Piersall's misfortunes, and Piersall responded by grabbing the writer by the neck. Fortunately, there were several people on hand who were able to pull Piersall off Gallas before he could inflict serious injury. Veeck gave Piersall a chance to remain on the broadcast team because of his popularity, but not before Piersall spent two days in the hospital for "exhaustion," rested for a week at a Wisconsin resort and sought medical help from a psychiatrist and a heart specialist.*

Rookie sensation Britt Burns was a bright spot in a weak season for the Sox in 1980. Burns won 70 games in six full seasons with the team, but a degenerative hip condition shortened his career.

JULY 6   A two-run, walk-off, pinch-hit home run by Greg Pryor in the ninth inning beats the Athletics 5–4 in the second game of a double-header at Comiskey Park. The Sox trailed 4–0 before scoring a run in the seventh and two in the eighth. The three runs scored on solo homers by Thad Bosley, Lamar Johnson (as a pinch-hitter) and Todd Cruz. The two pinch-hit home runs tied a major league record. The Sox also won the opener 2–0.

JULY 13   Steve Trout holds the Yankees hitless for seven innings, then gives up three runs and three hits in the eighth inning and the White Sox lose 3–1 at Comiskey Park. Neither team had a hit until the bottom of the seventh. Rudy May held the Sox without a hit for the first 6⅓ innings and finished with a two-hitter.

The White Sox had one of the youngest starting rotations in baseball history in 1980 with Trout (age 22), Rich Dotson (21), Britt Burns (21), Ross Baumgarten (25) and LaMarr Hoyt (25).

JULY 26

Harold Baines hits a walk-off homer in the ninth inning to defeat the Rangers 4–3 in the first game of a double-header at Comiskey Park. The second contest ended in a 1–1 tie when called by rain in the sixth inning.

AUGUST 20

White Sox rookie outfielder Leo Sutherland breaks up the no-hit bid of Indians hurler Dan Spillner with a single with one out in the ninth inning at Comiskey Park. Spillner had to settle for a one-hitter and a 3–0 win.

AUGUST 22

Bill Veeck announces that the White Sox board of directors has agreed to accept a buyout offer of $20 million made by Edward J. DeBartolo, Sr., of Youngstown, Ohio.

Veeck had been trying to sell the club for two years. He contended he could no longer afford to operate under the sport's inflating player salaries. DeBartolo was a 69-year-old shopping center magnate with an estimated worth of $500 million. His only partner in the deal was his daughter, Marie Denise York, whose husband, John, was a physician at Vanderbilt University. Edward Sr. also owned the Pittsburgh Penguins of the National Hockey League. His son, Edward, Jr., owned the San Francisco 49ers. Soon after DeBartolo's offer was accepted, several American League owners and commissioner Bowie Kuhn expressed their opposition to the sale. Among their fears was that DeBartolo might try to move the White Sox out of Chicago. Several years earlier, he had tried to purchase the Oakland Athletics with the idea of moving them to New Orleans. DeBartolo also had made inquiries into purchasing the Mariners without success. Kuhn said it would not be in baseball's best interests to have an owner based in a city other than the one in which the club was located. The commissioner's major concern was DeBartolo's ownership of three race tracks and therefore, his connection to gambling interests. This was one of many inconsistencies in Kuhn's adamant refusal to allow DeBartolo into baseball, because other owners had racing interests and were absentee owners. George Steinbrenner of the Yankees was based in Tampa and owned a race track in the city. John Galbreath of the Pirates not only owned a piece of Churchill Downs, but raised horses. There were also unfounded rumors that DeBartolo was connected to organized crime. He offered to sign a long-term lease and to sell his race tracks, but his detractors could not be swayed. AL magnates met on October 24, and although the vote was 8–6 in favor of the sale of the Sox to DeBartolo, 10 votes were needed for approval. Another vote was taken on December 11, when 11 of the 14 AL owners voted to reject the bid of DeBartolo, who leveled charges of anti-Italian bias and threatened to sue. Veeck's fellow owners urged him to sell the club to a group from Chicago (see January 8, 1981). DeBartolo tried to buy the Indians in 1982, but he ran into the same road blocks. Shortly after the DeBartolo deal to purchase the Sox was voted down, his family built the 49ers into one of the greatest dynasties in NFL history. In 2008, the DeBartolo clan still owned the San Francisco club.

AUGUST 27

The White Sox win 3–2 over the Tigers in a 14-inning battle at Comiskey Park. Lamar Johnson drove in the winning run with a single.

SEPTEMBER 5

LaMarr Hoyt pitches a two-hitter to defeat the Blue Jays 3–0 at Exhibition Stadium. The only Toronto hits were singles by Al Woods in the second inning and Garth Iorg in the sixth.

SEPTEMBER 8   Against the Mariners at Comiskey Park, Rich Dotson has a no-hitter in progress into the eighth inning before Larry Milbourne and Jerry Narron both homered to tie the score 2–2. The Sox won the game 3–2 in the 12th. The winning run scored when Chet Lemon was hit by a pitch, stole second and crossed the plate on a single from Wayne Nordhagen.

OCTOBER 4   At the age of 57, Minnie Minoso bats as a pinch-hitter during a 4–2 win over the Angels at Comiskey Park. Minoso fouled out. The appearance allowed Minoso, who made his major league debut in 1949, to become only the second individual to play in five different decades (see September 21, 1990). The first was Nick Altrock, who played his first game in 1898 and his last in 1933. Altrock was a member of the White Sox from 1903 through 1909.

OCTOBER 5   In the final game of the season, Minoso bats again as a pinch-hitter and grounds out as the White Sox win 5–3 over the Angels at Comiskey Park.

NOVEMBER 20   Two weeks after Ronald Reagan defeats Jimmy Carter in the presidential election, the White Sox sign Jim Essian, most recently with the Athletics, as a free agent.

DECEMBER 6   The White Sox sign Ron LeFlore, most recently with the Expos, as a free agent.

    LeFlore stole 97 bases for the Expos in 1980, but he proved to be a disappointment in Chicago. In 671 at-bats with the Sox over two seasons, he stole 64 bases and hit .267 with just four home runs. LeFlore first played baseball while serving a 5 to 15-year sentence for armed robbery at Jackson State Prison in Michigan. He reached the majors in 1974 with the Tigers. LeFlore's life story was published in Breakout, *later made into the movie* One in a Million.

DECEMBER 12   The White Sox trade Rich Wortham to the Expos for Tony Bernazard.

1981

Season in a Sentence

The acquisitions of Carlton Fisk and Greg Luzinski by Jerry Reinsdorf and Eddie Einhorn in their first season as owners signal a new era in White Sox baseball, as the club posts a winning record in the strike-marred campaign.

Finish • Won • Lost • Pct • GB

*   54   52   .509   *
* Because of the player's strike, the season was split in two. The White Sox finished in third place in the first half with a 31–22 record, 2½ games behind, and sixth in the second half with a record of 23–30, seven games behind.

Manager

Tony LaRussa

Stats

	WS	AL	Rank
Batting Avg:	.272	.256	2
On-Base Pct:	.338	.324	2
Slugging Pct:	.387	.373	4
Home Runs:	76		8
Stolen Bases:	86		5
ERA:	3.47	3.66	4
Fielding Avg:	.979	.980	9
Runs Scored:	476		4
Runs Allowed:	423		6

Starting Lineup

Carlton Fisk, c
Mike Squires, 1b
Tony Bernazard, 2b
Jim Morrison, 3b
Bill Almon, ss
Ron LeFlore, lf
Chet Lemon, cf
Harold Baines, rf
Greg Luzinski, dh
Wayne Nordhagen, rf-lf
Lamar Johnson, 1b

Pitchers

Britt Burns, sp
Rich Dotson, sp
Steve Trout, sp
Ross Baumgarten, sp
LaMarr Hoyt, rp
Ed Farmer, rp
Kevin Hickey, rp
Dennis Lamp, rp-sp

Attendance

946,651 (eighth in AL)

Club Leaders

Batting Avg:	Bill Almon	.301
On-Base Pct:	Tony Bernazard	.367
Slugging Pct:	Chet Lemon	.491
Home Runs:	Greg Luzinski	21
RBIs:	Greg Luzinski	62
Runs:	Greg Luzinski	55
Stolen Bases:	Ron LeFlore	36
Wins:	Britt Burns	10
Strikeouts:	Britt Burns	108
ERA:	Britt Burns	2.64
Saves:	LaMarr Hoyt	10
	Ed Farmer	10

JANUARY 8   Bill Veeck agrees to sell the White Sox to 44-year-old real estate tycoon Jerry Reinsdorf and 45-year-old television executive Eddie Einhorn for $20 million. Reinsdorf disclosed he would serve as chairman of the board and run the baseball end of the operation. Einhorn became president and took charge of business side of the franchise.

Reinsdorf and Einhorn grew up in the Northeast and were classmates at Northwestern Law School. Reinsdorf spent his youth in Brooklyn and attended Dodgers games at Ebbets Field. Einhorn hailed from New Jersey. After graduation, they settled in Chicago. At the press conference announcing the sale, Einhorn said that the White Sox would be a "class organization." Veeck took that as a slap against his administration and attended only a handful of Sox games over the remainder of his life. He became a Cubs fan and was seen often at Wrigley Field prior to his death in 1986. Reinsdorf always praised Veeck in public and was respectful in person, doing everything he could to apologize and salve the wounds. Veeck would have none of it, however. In 1983, Veeck turned down an offer by Reinsdorf to throw out the ceremonial first pitch during the

American League Championship Series, the first post-season game at Comiskey Park since 1959. The new regime did have much more money to spend than Veeck, and within a year's time it doubled the number of people employed by the club and intensified the marketing and promotional end of the business. The strategy was tied to selling the team as a more family-oriented attraction. Sales of hard liquor were immediately banned, and security was stepped up to roust the grandstand brawlers. Reinsdorf and Einhorn were still running the Sox more than a quarter-century later.

FEBRUARY 4   Two weeks after Ronald Reagan is inaugurated as president and the American hostages in Iran are released from captivity, the White Sox sign Bill Almon, most recently with the Mets, as a free agent.

Almon was chosen by the Padres as the first overall choice in the June 1974 draft. He gave the White Sox one solid season, batting .301 as a starting shortstop in 1981.

MARCH 9   The White Sox sign Carlton Fisk, most recently with the Red Sox, as a free agent.

Fisk played 11 seasons with the Red Sox, highlighted by his dramatic home run in the sixth game of the 1975 World Series, and made six All-Star Game appearances. He became a free agent because the Red Sox were late in sending him his contract for the 1981 season. New White Sox owners Jerry Reinsdorf and Eddie Einhorn were anxious to give their organization instant credibility and landed Fisk. The catcher was 33 years old at the time he was signed, and no one dreamed he would spend 13 seasons in Chicago. By the time his career was over, Fisk caught in 2,226 major league games, the most of anyone in history. Among White Sox players, he ranks ninth in games (1,421), 10th in at-bats (4,869), fourth in home runs (214), sixth in extra-base hits (442), sixth in runs batted in (762) and eighth in total bases (2,143).

MARCH 28   The White Sox trade Ken Kravec to the White Sox for Dennis Lamp.

MARCH 30   On the day that Ronald Reagan is wounded by John Hinckley in an assassination attempt, the White Sox purchase Greg Luzinski from the Phillies.

A native of the Chicago area, Luzinski was a hit with White Sox fans as a designated hitter and power source in the lineup. He struck 84 homers in 1,875 at-bats over four seasons.

APRIL 10   In the first game of the 1981 season and his first with the White Sox, Carlton Fisk stars in a 5–3 win over his former Red Sox teammates in Boston. Chicago trailed 2–0 when Fisk clobbered a three-run homer in the eighth inning for a 3–2 lead.

APRIL 14   Two days after the launch of the Columbia, the first space shuttle, Carlton Fisk continues the storybook start to his career with the White Sox by hitting a grand slam off Reggie Cleveland during a 9–3 Chicago win over the Red Sox in the home opener before 51,560 at Comiskey Park.

Fisk took the unusual uniform number 72 with the White Sox. It was the reverse of the number 27 he wore with the Red Sox. He hit .263 with seven homers in 1981.

APRIL 22   Orioles pitcher Dennis Martinez is struck above the right eye with a beer bottle thrown by a spectator at Comiskey Park before a game that is eventually rained out. Martinez was hit as he stood alongside the bat rack. He needed four stitches to close the wound. The culprit was Perry Galanos, who was nabbed by stadium security and turned over to the police. In November, Galanos was sentenced to 26 weekends in jail.

APRIL 23   The White Sox sweep the Orioles 18–5 and 5–3 in a double-header against the Orioles at Comiskey Park. The Sox collected 26 hits in the first game, including 21 singles, two doubles, two triples and a home run. Chicago collected seven runs in both the fourth and sixth innings.

The center-field fence at Comiskey Park was shortened from 445 feet to 402 in 1981.

APRIL 24   Greg Luzinski homers in the 10th inning to beat the Tigers 3–2 in Detroit.

The White Sox started the season winning 11 of their first 15 games and were 25–16 on May 30.

MAY 11   Indians players break up a mugging near Comiskey Park after beating the White Sox 3–1. On the bus back to the hotel, the players witnessed two men and a woman walking when a car pulled up alongside them. Three men leaped out of the vehicle and began beating Tim McKimson and Kathy Mancyzk, both 19, and 20-year-old Craig Denemark. One of the assailants was using a baseball bat. Indians coach Dave Duncan and several Cleveland players yelled at the bus driver to pull to the curb. The players interrupted the brawl, and the three attackers were held until police arrived. Several Indians were sued for assault by the three arrested, but the case was thrown out of court a few months later.

MAY 18   Greg Luzinski hits two homers and drives in five runs during a 7–2 win over the Blue Jays in Toronto.

MAY 19   Todd Cruz is arrested in an Edmonton, Saskatchewan, department store for pilfering $2,000 worth of watches. After playing as the Sox's starting shortstop for much of the 1980 season, Cruz was at Edmonton, the Sox Class AAA affiliate, following a spring training back injury. He was traded to the Mariners in December 1981.

MAY 23   The White Sox thrash the Angels 15–4 in Anaheim.

MAY 31   Broadcaster Jimmy Piersall nearly causes a forfeit during a double-header before a packed house at Comiskey Park. The Angels won the opener 7–4 and the White Sox came back to win 2–1 in 10 innings in game two. According to umpire Dale Ford, Piersall leaned out of the broadcast booth and made obscene gestures toward the umpiring crew during the first game. Ford said the actions were done to incite the crowd. The arbiters told Piersall that if he continued his actions during the second tilt, they would walk off the field and call a forfeit.

JUNE 8   In the first round of the amateur draft, the White Sox select outfielder Daryl Boston from Woodward High School in Cincinnati, Ohio.

Boston played 11 years in the majors, the first seven with the White Sox, mostly as a reserve outfielder. Boston was a tremendous talent who always seemed to be ready to take his place among the best players in the game, but he never panned out. During his career, he hit .249 with 63 homers in 1,058 games. Although he never held down a job as a starter and failed to live up to his reputation, Boston was easily the best player chosen by the White Sox in 1981 Other future major leaguers drafted and signed were Craig Smajstrla (fourth round), Wade Rowdon (eighth round) and Al Jones (13th round).

JUNE 11　In the last game before the strike, the White Sox defeat the Yankees 3–2 before 33,777 at Comiskey Park.

JUNE 12　Major League Baseball players begin a strike that lasts 50 days and wipes out nearly two months of the 1981 season. The strike reduced the White Sox's schedule to 106 games.

JULY 31　Two days after Prince Charles marries Lady Diana Spencer in London, the players and owners hammer out an agreement that ends the strike.

AUGUST 6　The owners vote to split the 1981 pennant race, with the winners of the two halves of the season to compete in an extra round of the playoffs for the division race.

AUGUST 10　In the first game following the strike, the White Sox defeat the Red Sox 7–1 in Boston.

The White Sox played their first 16 games of the second half on a long road trip through Boston, Baltimore, New York, Toronto and Milwaukee. The Sox were 10–6 on the trip, but were 3–11 on a 14-game homestand starting on August 27.

AUGUST 15　The White Sox trade Bob Molinaro to the Cubs for Lynn McGlothen.

AUGUST 22　Britt Burns shuts out the Blue Jays 8–0 in Toronto.

Burns put together a streak of 30 consecutive scoreless innings during the second half amid personal tragedy. He commuted from Chicago to Birmingham, Alabama, between pitching assignments to spend time at the bedside of his critically injured father, who later died from injuries suffered after being hit by a car.

AUGUST 23　The White Sox collect 21 hits and wallop the Blue Jays 13–2 in Toronto.

AUGUST 25　A bloop double by Robin Yount leading off the ninth inning deprives Dennis Lamp of a no-hitter as the White Sox down the Brewers 5–1 in Milwaukee. Yount scored on two infield outs and Lamp completed a one-hitter. After walking Cecil Cooper with two out in the first, Lamp retired 22 batters in a row.

AUGUST 27　The White Sox play at home for the first time since June 11 and win 3–1 over the Yankees in a game called in the eighth inning by rain.

AUGUST 30　The White Sox trade Ivan Mesa, Ronnie Perry and Randy Johnson to the Twins for Jerry Koosman.

SEPTEMBER 9   Jimmy Piersall is suspended by White Sox owner Jerry Reinsdorf because of comments made on television about the wives of the players. The suspension, with pay, lasted until the end of the season. Appearing on a show hosted by *Chicago Sun-Times* columnist Mike Royko, Piersall said, "I think each ball club should have a clinic once a week for the wives, because I don't think they know what the hell baseball is. First of all, they were horny broads that wanted to get married and they wanted a little money, a little security and a big, strong ballplayer." Several of the Sox players' wives complained and Reinsdorf described it as "an embarrassment to the organization."

SEPTEMBER 13   The White Sox play at Metropolitan Stadium in Bloomington, Minnesota, for the last time and lose 7–6 to the Twins.

The Twins moved into the Metrodome in downtown Minneapolis in 1982.

SEPTEMBER 27   The White Sox sweep the Athletics 9–5 and 10–3 during a double-header in Oakland. In the opener, the A's tied an American League record with eight consecutive singles at the start of the first inning to take a 5–0 lead. Ross Baumgarten allowed five of the hits and was removed from the game for LaMarr Hoyt. Hoyt allowed singles to the first three batters he faced, than surrendered only two more hits in finishing the game with a nine-inning relief performance. The Sox came back to win with three runs in the third, four in the sixth, one in the seventh and one in the eighth.

SEPTEMBER 30   The White Sox score seven runs in the second inning and win 10–3 over the Angels at Comiskey Park.

OCTOBER 4   In the final game of the season, the White Sox overcome a seven-run deficit to beat the Twins 13–12 at Comiskey Park. Trailing 12–5, the Sox scored four runs in the eighth inning and four in the ninth. Jerry Hairston hit a grand slam off Dan Cooper in the eighth. In the ninth, Chicago was still down 12–9 with two out and no one on base. Mike Squires and pinch-hitters Bob Molinaro and Jerry Turner singled. Leo Sutherland walked to load the bases. A two-run single by Tony Bernazard tied the score. Hairston then stroked a walk-off single for his sixth RBI of the game. The victory gave the Sox a winning record on the season.

NOVEMBER 16   The Cubs hire Harry Caray as play-by-play announcer.

Caray was hired away from the White Sox. The club wanted him to move from WGN-TV to a new cable venture called SportsVision, which was part of big changes planned for the 1982 season. Jerry Reinsdorf and Eddie Einhorn planned to drastically reduce the number of games offered for free over WGN-TV in favor of airing the games on a subscription basis on SportsVision. Caray bluntly told Reinsdorf and Einhorn it wouldn't work. Caray believed that Chicago area fans wouldn't pay for the privilege of watching the Sox when nearly every game was offered for free on WGN. He also believed he would be losing his connection to much of his core audience, which might not be able to fit pay television into their budget. In addition, Caray was upset at being offered only a one-year contract extension by the Sox, and that Reinsdorf and Einhorn wanted him to tone down his criticism of the club. Timing is everything, and the timing for Caray's move from the South Side to the North Side was perfect. He felt that if he continued with the Sox in the club's new TV package, it would be the end of his career. Reinsdorf and Einhorn spoke confidently of wiring 50,000 for SportsVision by the start of the 1982 season. Meanwhile, WGN was going national with its "superstation" cable and was available in eight million homes nationwide. It took a couple of years for Cubs fans to warm up to Caray, and for a time it appeared as though he made the wrong move. In 1983, the White Sox won the division title while drawing 2.1 million fans, while the Cubs lost 91 games and attracted 1.4 million to Wrigley Field. As the Sox celebrated their first post-season since 1959, Reinsdorf didn't disguise his feelings about Caray and Jimmy Piersall, Harry's former broadcast partner. "I hope people realize what scum they are," Reinsdorf said. But everything changed in 1984 when the tables turned and the Cubs won a division championship and the Sox finished in fifth place with a 74–88 record. With Cubs games carried all over the country, Harry became a national institution with his bubbling enthusiasm and love for the game while cheering the Cubs on to another win. He also helped turn Wrigley Field into a Chicago tourist attraction. The national telecasts placed Wrigley on the list of must-see attractions for visitors to the Windy City. Caray broadcast major league games for 53 years with the Cardinals, Athletics, White Sox and Cubs. Although just 16 of those years were with the Cubs, just five more than he spent with the White Sox, he will always be associated with the club and with Wrigley Field.

NOVEMBER 27   The White Sox trade Chet Lemon to the Tigers for Steve Kemp.

The White Sox came out on the wrong end of the deal. Lemon played nine more seasons in the majors and was on Detroit's world championship club in 1984. Kemp lasted one season and bolted for the Yankees as a free agent.

DECEMBER 11   The White Sox trade Todd Cruz, Jim Essian and Rod Allen to the Mariners for Tom Paciorek.

Paciorek played for the White Sox from 1982 through 1985 and was a television commentator teaming with Ken Harrelson on White Sox game from 1988 through 1999. A defensive back at the University of Houston, Paciorek was good enough to be drafted by the Miami Dolphins, but he chose baseball as a career. Tom's brothers Jim and John also played in the majors. John was the first to reach the big leagues at the age of 18 with Houston in 1963. He collected three hits in three at-bats in his debut and never played in the majors again.

1982

Season in a Sentence

The White Sox continue to build a winning club, starting the season with eight consecutive victories, before spending 43 days in first place and remaining in contention for the pennant into mid-September.

Finish • Won • Lost • Pct • GB

Third   87   75   .537   6.0

Manager

Tony LaRussa

Stats

	WS	AL	Rank
Batting Avg:	.272	.264	5
On-Base Pct:	.340	.331	5
Slugging Pct:	.413	.402	6
Home Runs:	136		8 (tie)
Stolen Bases:	136		3
ERA:	3.87	4.07	3
Fielding Avg:	.976	.980	13
Runs Scored:	786		3
Runs Allowed:	710		5

Starting Lineup

Carlton Fisk, c
Mike Squires, 1b
Tony Bernazard, 2b
Aurelio Rodriguez, 3b
Bill Almon, ss
Steve Kemp, lf
Rudy Law, cf
Harold Baines, rf
Greg Luzinski, dh
Tom Paciorek, 1b
Vance Law, ss-3b
Ron LeFlore, cf
Jim Morrison, 3b

Pitchers

LaMarr Hoyt, sp
Britt Burns, sp
Rich Dotson, sp
Dennis Lamp, sp-rp
Steve Trout, sp
Salome Barojas, rp
Kevin Hickey, rp
Jerry Koosman, rp-sp

Attendance

1,567,787 (ninth in AL)

Club Leaders

Batting Avg:	Greg Luzinski	.292
On-Base Pct:	Greg Luzinski	.386
Slugging Pct:	Harold Baines	.469
Home Runs:	Harold Baines	25
RBIs:	Harold Baines	105
Runs:	Steve Kemp	91
Stolen Bases:	Rudy Law	36
Wins:	LaMarr Hoyt	19
Strikeouts:	LaMarr Hoyt	124
ERA:	LaMarr Hoyt	3.53
Saves:	Salome Barojas	21

JANUARY 15   Lamar Johnson signs a contract with the Rangers as a free agent.

JANUARY 28   Ed Farmer signs a contract with the Phillies as a free agent.

MARCH 21   The White Sox trade Ross Baumgarten and Butch Edge to the Pirates for Vance Law and Ernie Camacho.

MARCH 30   The White Sox trade Bert Geiger and Cecil Espy to the Dodgers for Rudy Law.

In a span of a little more than a week, the White Sox acquired two players named Law for a club that had a lawyer as a manager. Rudy Law played four seasons as one of the White Sox's starting outfielders. In 1983, he stole a club-record 77 bases.

APRIL 2   The White Sox trade Wayne Nordhagen to the Blue Jays for Aurelio Rodriguez.

APRIL 6   Snow postpones the White Sox season opener against the Red Sox at Comiskey Park. The wintry weather, which spread across the Midwest and Northeast, also postponed the April 7 and 8 games against Boston in Chicago and the contests versus the Yankees in New York on April 9 and 10.

APRIL 11   The White Sox finally get the 1982 season under way five days late and sweep the Yankees 7–6 and 2–0 in a double-header in New York. The first game went 12 innings. The 6–6 tie was broken on a triple by Bill Almon and a single from Ron LeFlore. Jim Morrison hit a home run and Tom Paciorek collected three hits, including a double. In game two, Britt Burns (six innings) and Salome Barojas (three innings) combined on the shutout.

The second tilt was Barojas's major league debut. He was discovered by Tony LaRussa on a scouting trip to Mexico during the 1981 strike. Barojas began his career by pitching 14 consecutive shutout innings, allowing only four hits. He finished the year with 21 saves and saved 12 more for the 1983 division championship club before his career went south.

APRIL 17   The White Sox play their first home games and sweep the Orioles 3–1 and 10–6 in a double-header before 28,977 at Comiskey Park.

Comiskey Park was partially renovated during the 1981–82 off-season with longer and more modern dugouts, new box seats and an all-electronic scoreboard. The new board integrated the firing towers which stood on top of the old structure and shot fireworks after White Sox home runs.

APRIL 18   The White Sox run their season record to 8–0 with a 6–4 win over the Orioles at Comiskey Park.

The 8–0 start is the best in White Sox history. It was accomplished with a club that included only three players left from the 1979 team. The Sox were 28–14 on May 26, then lost seven in a row. By July 29, the Sox had a record of 49–49 amid considerable speculation that Tony LaRussa was about to be fired. LaRussa kept his job, but pitching coach Ron Schueler was dismissed. The team won 27 of the next 42 and was 3½ games out of first place on September 11. Chances of a pennant evaporated, however, with eight defeats in 11 games from September 12 through September 22.

APRIL 27   The White Sox score seven runs in the second inning and beat the Brewers 11–2 in Milwaukee. Ron LeFlore hit a grand slam off Jim Slaton.

The White Sox new announcing teams in 1982 were Ken Harrelson and Don Drysdale on television and Joe McConnell and Early Wynn on radio. Jimmy Piersall did the pre-game and post-game shows on WMAQ and frequently used his forum to heap unbridled abuse on what Piersall believed were the managerial shortcomings of Tony LaRussa.

MAY 13   The White Sox unleash a 20-hit attack and romp past the Brewers 13–2 at Comiskey Park.

The White Sox replaced the untraditional uniforms worn from 1976 through 1981 (see April 20, 1976) with another unique set in 1982. Scarlet red returned to the club's uniforms for the first time since 1975 in addition to navy blue.

The word "Sox" was splashed horizontally across the front of the shirt in white outlined in a five-inch high blue strip with borders of red on the top and bottom of the blue background. The pants had a blue waistband and the uniform number was in red on the front of the trousers. The undershirts, socks and shoes were solid red. The caps were navy, with a red bill and "Sox" written horizontally in white. The uniforms were voted upon by the fans the previous season among six combinations selected by new club owners Jerry Reinsdorf and Eddie Einhorn. The Sox wore the jerseys until 1987.

MAY 23   Rudy Law walks down 20 flights of stairs to safety during a fire at the Conrad Hilton Hotel that kills four. His room was two stories below the blaze. Later in the day, he collected two hits in a 14-inning, 6–4 loss to the Indians at Comiskey Park.

MAY 24   LaMarr Hoyt extends his record to 9–0 with a 3–1 decision over the Royals at Comiskey Park.

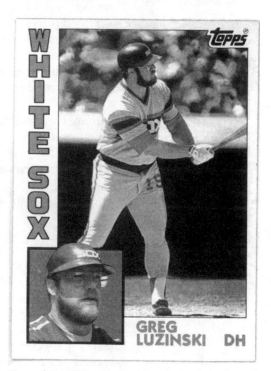

Hoyt won 14 decisions in a row, with his last five in 1981 and first nine in 1982. He finished the 1982 season with a 19–15 record and a 3.53 ERA. He later had a 15-game winning streak in 1983 and 1984. Hoyt won 63 of his first 94 decisions with the Sox.

MAY 27   Greg Luzinski hits two homers and drives in six runs during a 7–5 win over the Royals at Comiskey Park. Luzinski had a sacrifice fly in the first inning, a two-run homer in the fourth and a three-run homer in the fifth.

Luzinski hit 18 home runs, drove in 102 runs and batted .292 in 1982.

Heavy-hitting Greg Luzinski gave the Sox a feared hitter in the middle of the lineup as well as a player with a lot of post-season experience. In 1982 he knocked in 102 runs.

JUNE 3   In the first round of the amateur draft, the White Sox select catcher Ron Karkovice from Boone High School in Orlando, Florida.

Karkovice played 12 seasons in the majors, all with the White Sox, and hit 96 homers along with a .221 batting average in 939 games. Other future major leaguers drafted and signed by the White Sox in 1982 were John Cangelosi (fourth round of the January draft), Kenny Williams (third round) and Mike Trujillo (seventh round) in the regular phase in June, and Joel McKeon (first round of the secondary phase in June).

JUNE 7   Trailing 5–0, the White Sox score three runs in the seventh inning, one in the eighth, one in the ninth and one in the 11th to defeat the Athletics 6–5 at Comiskey Park.

Carlton Fisk's homer in the ninth tied the score. In the 11th, Harold Baines singled, Fisk doubled and Bill Almon singled.

Baines hit 25 homers, drove in 105 runs and hit .271 in 1982.

JUNE 14   The White Sox trade Jim Morrison to the Pirates for Eddie Solomon.

JUNE 16   After trailing 5–0, the White Sox rally to win 7–6 in 10 innings against the Athletics in Oakland. The Sox took the lead with a run in the fifth inning, three in the seventh and two in the eighth, but they allowed the A's to tie the contest in the ninth. In the 10th, Greg Luzinski drove in the winning run with a single.

JUNE 19   Steve Kemp hits a grand slam off Luis Sanchez in the fifth inning of a 7–6 victory over the Angels in Anaheim.

JUNE 26   The White Sox club five home runs during a 13–3 win over the Mariners in Seattle. The homers were struck by Tony Bernazard, Vance Law, Carlton Fisk, Steve Kemp and Jerry Hairston.

The home run was the first of Law's career. His father Vern pitched in the majors for the Pirates from 1950 through 1967. Vern and his wife VaNita had six children named Veldon, Veryl, Vaughn, Varlin, VaLynda and Vance.

JUNE 28   The White Sox break a scoreless tie with seven runs in the fourth inning and hang on to defeat the Twins 8–7 in Minneapolis. It was the first time that the White Sox played at the Metrodome and also marked the club's first game in a domed stadium.

JULY 7   Harold Baines hits three homers and drives in six runs during a 7–0 victory over the Tigers at Comiskey Park. Baines hits solo shots off Jerry Ujdur in the fifth and seventh innings and a grand slam facing Elias Sosa in the eighth.

JULY 8   Jerry Hairston hits a two-out, two-run, pinch-hit, walk-off home run to defeat the Tigers 3–2 at Comiskey Park.

Hairston is the White Sox's all-time leader in career pinch-hits with 87. Smoky Burgess is second with 50.

JULY 11   Harold Baines hits two homers, one of them a grand slam, during a 16–7 thumping of the Blue Jays at Comiskey Park. The slam was struck in the second inning off Jerry Garvin.

JULY 19   Former White Sox star Luke Appling becomes a hero to a new generation of fans during the first Cracker Jack Old-Timers Classic at RFK Stadium in Washington. Appling led off the game with a home run off Warren Spahn. At 75, Appling was the oldest player in the game and hadn't played in the majors since 1950. During his 21 years in the big leagues, he hit only 45 homers in 8,856 at-bats. The American League won the game 7–2.

JULY 21   The White Sox score six runs in the 12th inning to win 9–3 over the Mariners at Seattle. Greg Luzinski broke the 3–3 tie with a solo homer before the Sox added five insurance runs.

AUGUST 3 — The White Sox sweep the Yankees 1–0 and 14–2 over the Yankees in New York. Steve Trout (5⅓ innings), Salome Barojas (two innings) and Dennis Lamp (1⅔ innings) combined on the shutout. A single by Aurelio Rodriguez drove in the lone run with a single in the fifth inning.

AUGUST 4 — Britt Burns pitches a two-hitter to defeat the Yankees 7–0 in the second game of a double-header in New York. The only hits off Burns were singles by Graig Nettles in the second inning and Rick Cerone in the sixth. The Sox lost the opener 6–2.

AUGUST 9 — Down 5–0, the White Sox score a run in the fourth inning, two in the sixth and six in the seventh to beat the Orioles 9–5 at Comiskey Park.

AUGUST 21 — The White Sox purchase Sparky Lyle from the Phillies.

AUGUST 23 — The White Sox trade Wade Rowdon and Leo Garcia to the Reds for Jim Kern.

AUGUST 31 — The White Sox break a 5–5 tie with eight runs in the sixth inning and beat the Indians 14–6 at Comiskey Park.

SEPTEMBER 11 — A two-run homer by Carlton Fisk off Chris Codiroli are the only runs in a 2–0 victory over the Athletics in Oakland. Jerry Koosman (eight innings) and Salome Barojas (one inning) combined on the shutout.

SEPTEMBER 25 — The White Sox pummel the Twins 13–1 at Comiskey Park.

SEPTEMBER 27 — In his first major league start, Greg Walker homers during a 4–1 win over the Mariners in the second game of a double-header at Comiskey Park. As a pinch-hitter in the opener, Walker hit a three-run double in the ninth inning, but the Sox lost 8–4.

DECEMBER 9 — Steve Kemp sings a contract with the Yankees as a free agent.

DECEMBER 13 — The White Sox sign Floyd Bannister as a free agent.

Bannister was the number-one overall pick of the Astros in the 1976 draft after a stellar career at Arizona State University. He led the AL in strikeouts with the Mariners in 1982 but had a 12–13 record. Bannister seemed to have all of the tools to become one of the best pitchers in baseball and it appeared that all Bannister needed to become a 20-game winner was a solid team behind him. Bannister never reached the greatness predicted of him, however. He was 16–10 with the White Sox in 1983 and 16–11 in 1987, but he was just 34–39 in the intervening three seasons. Bannister finished his career with a 134–143 record, but he had only four winning seasons out of 15 in the majors.

1983

Sox

Season in a Sentence

Buoyed by the slogan "Winning Ugly," the White Sox win 50 of their last 66 regular-season games to capture the AL West pennant and post the best record in the major leagues before losing the ALCS to the Orioles.

Finish • Won • Lost • Pct • GB

First   99   63   .611 +20.0

American League Championship Series

The White Sox lost three games to one to the Baltimore Orioles.

Manager

Tony LaRussa

Stats

Stats	WS	AL	Rank
Batting Avg:	.262	.266	9
On-Base Pct:	.332	.331	8
Slugging Pct:	.413	.401	6
Home Runs:	157		3
Stolen Bases:	165		3
ERA:	3.67	4.06	3
Fielding Avg:	.981	.979	3
Runs Scored:	800		1
Runs Allowed:	650		2

Starting Lineup

Carlton Fisk, c
Tom Paciorek, 1b-lf-rf
Julio Cruz, 2b
Vance Law, 3b
Scott Fletcher, ss
Ron Kittle, lf
Rudy Law, cf
Harold Baines, rf
Greg Luzinski, dh
Greg Walker, 1b
Jerry Dybzinski, ss
Tony Bernazard, 2b
Mike Squires, 1b

Pitchers

LaMarr Hoyt, sp
Rich Dotson, sp
Floyd Bannister, sp
Jerry Koosman, sp-rp
Britt Burns, sp
Dennis Lamp, rp
Salome Barojas, rp
Dick Tidrow, rp

Attendance

2,132,821 (fourth in AL)

Club Leaders

Batting Avg:	Carlton Fisk	.289
On-Base Pct:	Carlton Fisk	.355
Slugging Pct:	Carlton Fisk	.518
Home Runs:	Ron Kittle	35
RBIs:	Ron Kittle	100
Runs:	Rudy Law	95
Stolen Bases:	Rudy Law	77
Wins:	LaMarr Hoyt	24
Strikeouts:	Floyd Bannister	193
ERA:	Rich Dotson	3.23
Saves:	Dennis Lamp	15

JANUARY 18   Bill Almon signs a contract with the Athletics as a free agent.

JANUARY 25   The White Sox trade Steve Trout and Warren Brusstar to the Cubs for Scott Fletcher, Pat Tabler, Dick Tidrow and Randy Martz.

FEBRUARY 7   Aurelio Rodriguez signs a contract as a free agent with the Orioles.

APRIL 1   The White Sox trade Pat Tabler to the Indians for Jerry Dybzinski.

                The Sox came out on the short end of the deal, as Tabler was a regular in the Indians' lineup for five seasons. Dybzinski spent two seasons in Chicago as a weak-hitting shortstop and made a terrible base-running gaffe in the 1983 playoff against the Orioles.

APRIL 4   In the season opener, the White Sox lose 5–3 to the Rangers in Arlington. The Sox scored three runs in the first inning but were shut out the rest of the way. LaMarr Hoyt was the losing pitcher.

Hoyt recovered from the Opening Day loss to post a record of 24–10 with an ERA of 3.66, numbers which earned him the AL Cy Young Award. Hoyt walked only 31 batters in 260²/₃ innings.

APRIL 12   On the day that Harold Washington is elected mayor of Chicago, the White Sox lose 10–8 to the Orioles before 38,306 in the first game of the season at Comiskey Park. Baltimore took an early 7–0 lead, but the Sox went ahead 8–7 with five runs in the second inning, two in the third and one in the sixth. The Orioles rallied with three in the eighth for the victory, however. Tony Bernazard, Tom Paciorek and Ron Kittle all homered.

A 25-year-old rookie in 1983 and a native of nearby Gary, Indiana, Kittle became an instant hero to White Sox fans. He had been released by the Dodgers organization after a spinal fusion operation in 1978 and was working in iron construction when he was invited to Comiskey Park for a tryout. After hitting 90 home runs in the minors in 1981 and 1982, Kittle made the White Sox's roster in 1983 as a left fielder. He made the All-Star team and won the Rookie of the Year Award by clubbing 35 homers with 100 RBIs and a .254 average. On the negative side, he struck out 150 times and walked only 39. Poor strike zone judgment and injuries kept Kittle from reaching his rookie numbers in a career that lasted until 1991. During the 1984, 1985 and 1986 seasons, he hit 75 homers in 1,141 at-bats, but he batted only .219 and was traded to the Yankees. Kittle returned to play for the Sox again from 1989 through 1991.

APRIL 14   The White Sox outlast the Orioles 12–11 at Comiskey Park. The Sox took a 9–2 lead with six runs in the fifth inning, but they allowed Baltimore to come back and tie the contest. Chicago took a 12–9 lead with three tallies in eighth, then survived a two-run Orioles rally in the ninth. Ron Kittle drove in six runs on a three-run homer, a sacrifice fly and a two-run single.

In order to increase the number of home runs at Comiskey Park, home plate was moved eight feet closer to the fences in 1983. The new dimensions were 341 feet down the foul lines, 374 feet to the power alleys and 401 feet to center field. In 1986, home plate was moved back to its original location.

APRIL 15   At Comiskey Park, Milt Wilcox of the Tigers retires the first 26 White Sox batters to face him, but his bid for a perfect game ends when pinch-hitter Jerry Hairston hits a clean single up the middle with two out in the ninth inning. Wilcox then retired Rudy Law to close out a one-hit, 6–0 victory.

APRIL 17   Dennis Lamp pitches a two-hitter to defeat the Tigers 6–1 at Comiskey Park. The only Detroit hits were a single by Lou Whitaker in the first inning and a homer from Larry Herndon in the fifth.

APRIL 19   Greg Luzinski hits two homers and drives in five runs as the White Sox shell the Yankees 13–3 at Comiskey Park.

MAY 8   The White Sox retire Minnie Minoso's number 9 in ceremonies prior to a 13–6 loss to the Indians at Comiskey Park.

Minoso wore number 9 from 1951 through 1957, 1960 and 1961, 1964, and 1976 through 1980. Others who wore number 9 before it was retired included Johnny Callison, Al Smith, Ramon Conde, Danny Cater, Wayne Causey, Woodie Held, Ossie Blanco, Lee Richard and Bob Molinaro.

MAY 18   Rich Dotson pitches a one-hitter but loses 1–0 to the Orioles in Baltimore. Dotson had a no-hitter in progress until Dan Ford homered with one out in the eighth inning for the lone run of the contest.

Dotson had a 22–7 record and a 3.23 earned run average in 1983. He was 17–2 from June 26 through the end of the season.

MAY 24   The White Sox score eight runs in the first inning and wallop the Red Sox 12–4 at Comiskey Park. There were five Chicago home runs in the game, by Greg Luzinski, Lorenzo Gray, Carlton Fisk, Ron Kittle and Jerry Hairston. It was the fifth consecutive game in which Luzinski homered.

The homer by Gray was the only one of his career in 58 games and 106 at-bats.

MAY 26   The White Sox lose 3–1 to the Rangers in Arlington.

The defeat dropped the White Sox's record on the 1983 season to 16–24 and a position in sixth place, seven games behind the first-place Angels. At the time, LaRussa's career record as a manager was 254–268. He was booed heavily every time he stepped out of the dugout at Comiskey Park. But in an amazing turnaround, the White Sox were 83–39 from May 27 through the end of the 1983 regular season, including 50 wins in their last 66 games.

JUNE 6   In the first round of the amateur draft, the White Sox select pitcher Joel Davis from Sandalwood High School in Jacksonville, Florida.

Davis was rushed through the minors and pitched for the White Sox in 1985 at the age of 20. He pitched only 49 big-league games, however, with an 8–14 record and a 4.91 ERA. Other future major leaguers drafted and signed by the White Sox in 1983 were Russ Morman (second round), Bruce Tanner (fourth round) and Doug Drabek (tenth round).

JUNE 7   The White Sox edge the Angels 12–11 in 10 innings Anaheim. Greg Luzinski drove in the winning run with a two-out double in the 10th. California tied the score 11–11 with four tallies in the ninth.

JUNE 12   The White Sox sweep the Athletics 12–10 and 8–1 in Oakland. The first game went 11 innings. The Sox scored three runs in the 10th inning, the last two on a homer by Greg Walker, to take an 8–5 lead, but the A's rallied with three tallies in their half. Chicago put the game away by scoring two times in the 11th.

JUNE 15   The White Sox trade Tony Bernazard to the Mariners for Julio Cruz.

JUNE 19   Britt Burns pitches the White Sox to a 1–0 victory over the Athletics in Oakland. The lone run scored in the fourth inning on back-to-back doubles by Harold Baines and Ron Kittle.

JULY 6   The All-Star Game is played at Comiskey Park, and the American League wins 13–3. Heading into the contest, the AL had lost the last 11 All-Star Games and 19 of the previous 20. The American League led 2–1 before exploding seven runs in the third, all off Atlee Hammaker of the Giants. Fred Lynn provided the highlight with the first grand slam in All-Star history. Jim Rice also homered, and Dave Winfield collected three hits, including a double, in three at-bats.

The game was played on the 50th anniversary of the very first All-Star Game, held at Comiskey Park on July 6, 1933. Lefty Gomez, the winning pitcher of the 1933 classic, threw out the ceremonial first pitch flanked by 11 survivors of the inaugural tilt. Future Hall of Famers on the rosters of the two clubs were Johnny Bench, George Brett, Rod Carew, Gary Carter, Reggie Jackson, Eddie Murray, Cal Ripken, Mike Schmidt, Ozzie Smith, Dave Winfield, Carl Yastrzemski and Robin Yount. Other prominent players included Rickey Henderson, Jim Rice, Andre Dawson, Tim Raines, Lee Smith, Fernando Valenzuela, Bill Madlock, Dale Murphy, Ted Simmons and Ron Guidry.

JULY 18   The White Sox take first place with a 5–3 win over the Indians in Cleveland.

AUGUST 14   The White Sox lose a controversial 2–1 decision to the Orioles at Comiskey Park. With Rudy Law the base runner on first, Carlton Fisk hit an apparent two-run homer in the fifth inning, but the umpires ruled it a ground-rule double, contending that a fan reached over the edge of the wall and deflected it into the stands. Television replays showed that the ball cleared the wall. Tony LaRussa was ejected arguing the call and heaved third base 30 feet into the dugout.

AUGUST 18   Just prior to a series against the White Sox, Rangers manager Doug Rader says the White Sox are "winning ugly." "Their bubble has got to burst," Rader said. "They're not playing that well. They're winning ugly. At least that's what our reports say." The club picked up the phrase "winning ugly" and it became a rallying cry through the final weeks of the season.

AUGUST 19   During a double-header sweep of the Rangers in Arlington, won 3–2 in 10 innings and 6–1, Rudy Law breaks the club's single-season stolen base record of 56, set by Wally Moses in 1943 and tied by Luis Aparicio in 1959. Jerry Koosman recorded his 200th career victory in the second tilt.

Law finished the season with 77 stolen bases. No one else in White Sox history has more than 60. Law broke the record wearing number 11, which adorned the uniform of Aparicio during his career with the Sox. Number 11 was retired by the franchise in 1984, and Law switched to number 23.

AUGUST 23   On the day the Soviets shoot down a South Korean passenger plane, resulting in the deaths of 269 people, left-handed throwing Mike Squires plays an inning at third base during a 10–2 loss to the Royals in Kansas City after Tony LaRussa runs short of position players.

Previously, Squires played two games as a catcher in 1980. He played in 13 more games at third base in 1984, four of them as a starter.

SEPTEMBER 1   The White Sox pummel the Royals 12–0 at Comiskey Park.

The White Sox shattered the previous Chicago attendance record in 1983 by drawing 2,132,821 into Comiskey Park. The previous mark was 1,674,993 by the Cubs in 1969. The pre-1983 White Sox standard was 1,657,135 in 1977. The Cubs drew 1,479,717 fans in 1983, some 650,000 fewer than the Sox.

SEPTEMBER 5   The White Sox wallop the Athletics 11–1 at Comiskey Park.

SEPTEMBER 9   A one-hitter by Britt Burns and three consecutive homers highlight an 11–0 triumph over the Angels at Comiskey Park. The only California hit was a two-out single to Mike Brown in the seventh inning. Carlton Fisk, Tom Paciorek and Greg Luzinski launched back-to-back-to-back homers off Tommy John in the first inning. It was the first time in club history that the White Sox hit three homers in a row.

Fisk hit .289 with 26 homers and 86 RBIs in 1983.

SEPTEMBER 11   LaMarr Hoyt records his 20th win of the season with a 10-inning, 5–4 decision over the Angels at Comiskey Park.

SEPTEMBER 13   The White Sox extend their winning streak to eight games with a 5–1 victory over the Twins in Minneapolis.

SEPTEMBER 15   The White Sox erupt for 11 runs in the sixth inning, highlighted by a grand slam by Harold Baines off Karl Best, and win 12–0 over the Mariners in a contest at Comiskey Park called after 6½ innings by rain. Greg Luzinski contributed a two-run homer during the big inning and Vance Law smacked a two-run single.

SEPTEMBER 16   Floyd Bannister pitches a two-hitter and strikes out 12 batters for a 7–0 victory over the Mariners at Comiskey Park. The only Seattle hits were singles by Spike Owen in the third inning and Pat Putnam in the eighth.

Bannister won 13 of his 14 decisions after the All-Star break to finish the year at 16–11.

SEPTEMBER 17   The White Sox clinch the AL West with a 4–3 win over the Mariners at Comiskey Park. The winning run scored in the ninth inning on a sacrifice fly by Harold Baines.

SEPTEMBER 18   The White Sox win their 17th consecutive home game with a 6–0 decision over the Mariners at Comiskey Park.

SEPTEMBER 23   Rich Dotson records his 20th win of the season with a 2–1 decision over the Angels in Anaheim.

SEPTEMBER 24   Britt Burns pitches a two-hitter to defeat the Angels 2–0 in Anaheim. The only California hits were a pair of singles in the first inning by Gary Pettis and Steve Lubratich.

SEPTEMBER 29   Mike Warren of the Athletics pitches a no-hitter to defeat the White Sox 3–0 in Oakland. It was only the ninth career start for Warren, a 22-year-old rookie, during a brief career in which he had a 9–13 record and a 5.06 ERA. The final out was recorded on a fly ball by Carlton Fisk to Rickey Henderson in left field.

SEPTEMBER 30   LaMarr Hoyt records his 13th consecutive victory and 24th of the season with a 9–4 decision over the Mariners in Seattle.

OCTOBER 2   On the final day of the regular season, Rich Dotson records his 10th victory in a row and 22nd of the season with a 3–0 decision over the Mariners in Seattle.

The White Sox played the Baltimore Orioles in the American League Championship Series. Managed by Joe Altobelli, the Orioles were 98–64 in 1983. The series was a best-of-five affair.

OCTOBER 5   In the first game of the American League Championship Series, the White Sox defeat the Orioles 2–1 in Baltimore behind the five-hit pitching of LaMarr Hoyt, who had finished the regular season with 13 consecutive wins. Singles by Rudy Law, Carlton Fisk and Tom Paciorek in the fourth inning produced the first run. Another scored in the sixth on Paciorek's single, an error that sent him to third and a double-play grounder. The lone Baltimore run crossed the plate with two out in the ninth.

On their way to the best record in the American League, the White Sox rode the arm of Cy Young Award winner LaMarr Hoyt, who posted 24 victories as well as the team's only win in the ALCS.

OCTOBER 6   Orioles pitcher Mike Boddicker strikes out 14 batters and beats the White Sox 4–0 in game two of the ALCS in Baltimore.

OCTOBER 7   In the first post-season game in Chicago in 24 years, the White Sox lose 11–1 to the Orioles before 46,635 at Comiskey Park. A brouhaha developed in the fourth inning when Baltimore hurler Mike Flanagan plunked Ron Kittle with a pitch. Both benches emptied. An inning later, Rich Dotson hit Cal Ripken in the left side. When Eddie Murray followed Ripken to the plate and a Dotson delivery buzzed the batter, Murray threatened Dotson by pointing his bat and both benches emptied again. Peace was maintained, however, and there were no ejections. The loss put the Sox down two games to one, and left them just one defeat from elimination.

OCTOBER 8   The Orioles clinch the American League pennant by beating the White Sox 3–0 in 10 innings in game four of the ALCS before 45,477 at Comiskey Park. The Sox blew an opportunity to win in the seventh when Jerry Dybzinski committed a base-running blunder. Greg Walker and Vance Law opened the inning with singles. Mike Squires pinch-ran for Walker. Dybzinski was asked to bunt the runners along. On a 3–1 count, he forced Squires at third base when catcher Rick Dempsey pounced on the bunt. Julio Cruz followed with a single to center. Third-base coach Jim Leyland held Law at third, but Dybzinski rounded second base and headed for third, was too late in realizing his mistake and became caught in a rundown. Law tried to score during the rundown and was gunned down at the plate in a jarring collision with Dempsey, snuffing out the rally. Britt Burns pitched nine innings of shutout ball for the Sox and was sent out to the mound again in the 10th. With one out, Burns gave up a home run to Tito Landrum. It was Burns's 150th pitch of the afternoon. Baltimore added two more runs off relievers Salome Barojas and Juan Agosto. Storm Davis (six innings) and Tippy Martinez (four innings) combined on the shutout for the Orioles.

Scott Fletcher started the first three games of the Series at shortstop, but he was held without a hit. LaRussa substituted Dybzynski for Fletcher in game four to "provide some spark." The White Sox scored only one run in the last 31 innings of the ALCS after leading the league in runs scored during the regular season. The Orioles played the Phillies in the World Series, and won in five games.

DECEMBER 5   Six weeks after a bomb rips through a Marine compound in Beirut, Lebanon, killing 241, the White Sox trade Jerry Koosman to the Phillies for Ron Reed.

Reed was 41 years old at the time of the trade. He had a 3.08 ERA and 12 saves in 51 appearances for the White Sox in 1984, but his won-lost record was 0–6. Reed played basketball at Notre Dame and played with the Detroit Pistons in the NBA from 1965 through 1967.

1984

Season in a Sentence

The defending AL West champions are in first place in early July, but they skid to fifth by the end of the season with 25 fewer wins than in 1983.

Finish • Won • Lost • Pct • GB

Fifth (tie) 74 88 .457 10.0

Manager

Tony LaRussa

Stats

Stats	WS	AL	Rank
Batting Avg:	.247	.264	14
On-Base Pct:	.316	.329	13
Slugging Pct:	.395	.398	7
Home Runs:	172		3
Stolen Bases:	109		5
ERA:	4.13	3.99	10
Fielding Avg:	.981	.979	2
Runs Scored:	679		10
Runs Allowed:	736		10

Starting Lineup

Carlton Fisk, c
Greg Walker, 1b
Julio Cruz, 2b
Vance Law, 3b
Scott Fletcher, ss
Ron Kittle, lf
Rudy Law, cf
Harold Baines, rf
Greg Luzinski, dh
Tom Paciorek, 1b-lf-rf
Jerry Hairston, lf-cf-dh
Marc Hill, c

Pitchers

Tom Seaver, sp
Rich Dotson, sp
Floyd Bannister, sp
LaMarr Hoyt, sp
Ron Reed, rp
Juan Agosto, rp
Britt Burns, rp-sp

Attendance

2,136,988 (third in AL)

Club Leaders

Batting Avg:	Harold Baines	.304
On-Base Pct:	Harold Baines	.361
Slugging Pct:	Harold Baines	.541
Home Runs:	Ron Kittle	32
RBIs:	Harold Baines	94
Runs:	Harold Baines	72
Stolen Bases:	Rudy Law	29
Wins:	Tom Seaver	15
Strikeouts:	Floyd Bannister	152
ERA:	Rich Dotson	3.59
Saves:	Ron Reed	12

JANUARY 10   Dennis Lamp signs a contract with the Blue Jays as a free agent.

JANUARY 20   The White Sox select Tom Seaver off the roster of the Mets as compensation for losing Dennis Lamp, who signed with the Blue Jays as a free agent on January 10.

At the time, rules called for teams who lost a Class A free agent, of which Lamp was one, to select a player from a list submitted by the other 25 big-league teams. Each team was allowed to protect 25 players. The Mets inexplicably left Seaver off the list, and the White Sox jumped at the chance to sign him. Commissioner Bowie Kuhn tried to dissuade the Sox from selecting Seaver because of what Kuhn believed would be a negative impact on baseball in general and on the Mets franchise in particular. Seaver was livid that the Mets failed to place him on their protected list, believing he would be able to end his storied career in New York. He considered retiring before the White Sox re-negotiated his contract. Seaver had a career record of 273–170 with an earned run average of 2.73 when acquired by the Sox, but he was just 14–27 while compiling an earned run average of 4.18 over the previous two seasons. Seaver gave the Sox two solid seasons. In 1984 and 1985 combined, his record was 31–22 and his ERA was 3.56. Seaver won his 300th career game in a White Sox uniform. After a slow start in 1986, his last in the majors, Seaver was dealt to the Red Sox.

JANUARY 27   Dick Tidrow signs a contract as a free agent with the Mets.

FEBRUARY 14   Former White Sox coach Loren Babe dies at the age of 56.

Babe was a coach with the Sox in 1983 when it was determined in April that he was suffering from cancer. Batting coach Charlie Lau voluntarily gave up his spot with the White Sox so that Babe could spend enough time with the club to qualify for a pension. Ironically, a month later, cancer was discovered in Lau's colon. He succumbed to the disease five weeks after Babe's death on March 18, 1984. Lau was considered to be one of the greatest hitting coaches of the era. In 1982, the Sox signed him to a six-year contract. Tony LaRussa deemed his signing "more important than if we'd signed a free agent like Reggie Jackson."

APRIL 2   In the season opener, the White Sox win 5–2 over the Orioles in Baltimore. President Ronald Reagan threw out the first pitch. Harold Baines led the offensive attack with three RBIs. LaMarr Hoyt was the winning pitcher. It was his 14th consecutive regular season victory. Hoyt won his last 13 decisions in 1983.

APRIL 6   In the home opener, the White Sox lose 3–2 to the Tigers before 42,692 at Comiskey Park.

APRIL 7   Tigers pitcher Jack Morris hurls a no-hitter against the White Sox for a 4–0 Detroit win at Comiskey Park. Morris struck out Ron Kittle for the final out.

APRIL 10   LaMarr Hoyt runs his winning streak over two seasons to 15 with a 7–3 decision over the Indians at Comiskey Park.

The 15-game winning streak included his last 13 decisions in 1983 and the first two in 1984. The streak ended with a 4–1 loss to the Tigers in Detroit on April 21. Hoyt's 15 wins in succession is still the White Sox club record. It was matched by Wilson Alvarez in 1993 and 1994.

APRIL 22   Mike Squires plays first base, third base and pitches during a 9–1 loss to the Tigers in Detroit. On the mound, Squires faced one batter in the eighth inning and recorded an out.

APRIL 28   Red Sox slugger Tony Armas homers into the center-field bleachers at Comiskey Park during an 8–7 Boston win over the White Sox.

MAY 2   LaMarr Hoyt allows only one base runner and faces the minimum 27 batters in beating the Yankees 3–0 at Comiskey Park. The only batter to reach base off Hoyt was Don Mattingly with an opposite-field bloop single with one out in the seventh inning after Hoyt retired the first 19 batters to face him. Mattingly was erased on a double play.

MAY 8   The White Sox and the Brewers play 17 innings at Comiskey Park before the contest is stopped with the score 3–3 because of the American League curfew rule, which stipulates that no inning can start after 12:59 a.m. Play was halted at 1:10 a.m. The Brewers took a 3–1 lead with two tallies in the ninth, but the Sox tied it in their half. Julio Cruz drove in the first ninth-inning run with a double and scored on Rudy Law's single. There was no scoring between the 10th and 17th innings. The game was scheduled for completion the following evening.

MAY 9

The White Sox and the Brewers complete the longest game ever played in the American League, with the Sox prevailing 7–6 in 25 innings. It was one inning shy of the longest game in major league history. The Sox-Brewers contest started the previous day when play was suspended after 17 innings with the score 3–3. Juan Agosto, who hurled the 14th, 15th, 16th and 17th innings without allowing a run the previous evening, took the mound at again on this date at the start of the 18th and pitched three more scoreless innings. Ron Reed came into the game in the 21st and allowed a three-run homer to Ben Oglivie to put the White Sox in a 6–3 hole. But Tony LaRussa's club was undaunted. In the bottom of the 21st, Rudy Law was safe on a error by third baseman Randy Ready, whose throw sailed 10 rows into the seats. Carlton Fisk, who set a major league record by catching all 25 innings, singled to drive in Law. Marc Hill followed with another single. Dave Stegman struck out, and Harold Baines walked to load the bases. Tom Paciorek drove in two runs with another base hit to tie the score at 6–6. It was one of five hits by Paciorek in nine at-bats during the long game. In the 23rd, it appeared that the Sox had won when Stegman was called safe on a play at the plate. But he had slipped rounding third, and was helped to his feet by third base coach Jim Leyland. Stegman was ruled out on coach's interference. The game continued until the 25th, when Baines finally ended the tilt with a walk-off homer off Chuck Porter. Tom Seaver, who pitched the 25th inning, was the winning pitcher. It was his first relief appearance since 1976. Seaver also tossed a complete game in the regularly scheduled contest, won by the White Sox 5–4.

The 25-inning game was the second-longest in major league history. The only longer one was played on May 2, 1920, between the Boston Braves and Brooklyn Dodgers in Boston. It lasted 26 innings and resulted in a 1–1 tie when called on account of darkness. The Cardinals and Mets also played 25 innings on September 11, 1974, with the Cards winning 4–3 in New York. The White Sox and Brewers did set a record for the longest game by time at eight hours and six minutes. Ted Simmons and Marc Hill played in both the 1974 and 1984 25-inning games. Simmons and Hill both played for the Cards in 1974. Simmons competed for the Brewers and Hill for the Sox in 1984.

MAY 10

After the Rangers score three runs in the top of the ninth inning to take a 6–5 lead, the White Sox come back with three in their half to win 8–6 at Comiskey Park. Each of the three Chicago runs in the ninth scored with two out. Harold Baines and Tom Paciorek hit back-to-back doubles to tie the contest and pinch-hitter Jerry Hairston followed with a two-run, walk-off homer.

Hairston led the American League in pinch-hits three seasons in a row with 17 in 1983, 18 in 1984 and 14 in 1985. He played 808 games for the White Sox over 14 seasons from 1973 through 1977 and again from 1981 through 1989. In between his two stints with the White Sox, Hairston played in the Mexican League.

MAY 13

In his first major league game, Daryl Boston hits a triple and two singles in leading the White Sox to an 8–1 win over the Rangers at Comiskey Park.

MAY 16

Carlton Fisk hits for the cycle in a 7–6 loss to the Royals at Comiskey Park. Fisk doubled in the first inning and singled in the second off Larry Gura, homered in the fourth against John Beckwith and completed the cycle by smacking a triple facing Dan Quisenberry in the seventh. Fisk went into the game mired in an 0-for-17 slump.

Fisk hit 21 homers in 1984 but drove in only 43 runs.

JUNE 4   In the first round of the amateur draft, the White Sox select pitcher Tony Menendez from American High School in Carol City, Florida, and outfielder Tom Hartley from Hudson Bay High School in Vancouver, Washington.

By the time Menendez reached the majors in 1992, he was out of the White Sox organization. Hartley was a complete bust, never advancing past the Class A level. The only future major leaguer drafted and signed by the Sox in 1984 was fifth-rounder Adam Peterson.

JUNE 7   Harold Baines hits a pair of three-run homers during an 11–10 comeback win over the Angels at Comiskey Park. The Sox trailed 7–0 before scoring six times in the third inning, with Baines hitting the first of his two homers. He added his second home run in the fifth, putting Chicago ahead 9–7.

Baines hit .304 with 29 homers and 94 RBIs in 1984.

JUNE 8   Greg Luzinski hits a grand slam off Frank Viola in the first inning of a 6–1 win over the Twins at Comiskey Park.

JUNE 9   Greg Luzinski hits a grand slam for the second game in a row, connecting off Mike Walters in the seventh inning of an 8–4 victory over the Twins at Comiskey Park.

Luzinski is the only player in White Sox history with grand slams in consecutive games.

JUNE 21   Two days after the Bulls draft Michael Jordan, the White Sox trade Jim Siwy to the Indians for Dan Spillner.

JUNE 22   The White Sox score three runs in the ninth inning to defeat the Twins 8–6 in Minneapolis. Scott Fletcher drove in the first run with a single, then Harold Baines smacked a two-run homer.

JUNE 24   The White Sox lose a heartbreaking 3–2 decision to the Twins in Minneapolis on a walk-off, inside-the-park homer. With one out and two on base in the ninth, the Sox led 2–0. Facing Rich Dotson, Tim Teufel hit a blooper to right field that bounced over Harold Baines's head into the corner, allowing Teufel to circle the bases.

Between the 1983 and 1984 All-Star Games, Dotson had a record of 25–6 with an ERA of 2.45. From the 1984 All-Star Game through the end of his career, Dotson had a record of 47–66 as a promising career was derailed by shoulder surgery to relieve pressure on a blood vessel.

JUNE 27   Harold Baines hits a two-run, walk-off homer in the ninth inning that defeats the Mariners 9–7 at Comiskey Park. It was Harold's fourth hit of the game.

On the same day, the White Sox traded Salome Barojas to the Mariners for Gene Nelson and Jerry Don Gleaton.

JUNE 30   A walk-off homer by Vance Law in the 11th inning beats the Orioles 5–4 at Comiskey Park.

JULY 5   A walk-off homer in the ninth inning by Greg Walker defeats the Indians 7–6 at Comiskey Park. Greg Luzinski hit his 300th career homer in the sixth inning. His milestone home run was struck off Tom Waddell.

JULY 8   The White Sox win their seventh game in a row with a 9–8 decision over the Indians at Comiskey Park.

The Sox headed into the All-Star break with a 44–40 record and a one-game lead in the AL West. The team looked for another surge, just like in 1983, when the Sox were 44–42 on July 16 and finished with a record of 99–63. It didn't happen in 1984. From the All-Star break through the end of the season, Chicago won 30 and lost 48.

JULY 18   The White Sox trade Doug Drabek and Kevin Hickey to the Yankees for Roy Smalley.

Roy Smalley III was the son of Roy Smalley Jr., who played shortstop for the Cubs from 1948 through 1953, and the nephew of Gene Mauch. The younger Smalley was in the 10th season of a productive career when he first donned a White Sox uniform, but for some reason he couldn't hit in Chicago. With the Sox, he batted .170 with four homers in 135 at-bats. It proved to be a disastrous deal. Drabek lasted only a year in New York before being traded to the Pirates, where he became the ace of a club that reached the post-season three years in a row. From 1988 through 1992, Drabek was 81–50 for Pittsburgh, including a 22–6 mark in 1990. In February 1985, Smalley was dealt to the Twins for two minor leaguers.

JULY 19   The White Sox score three runs in the ninth inning, two of them on a home run by Ron Kittle, and beat the Indians 3–0 in Cleveland. Tom Seaver (eight innings) and Jerry Don Gleaton (one inning) combined on the shutout.

AUGUST 1   Carlton Fisk and Ron Kittle both launch home runs over the left-field roof at Comiskey Park during a 5–3 win over the Red Sox.

Both Chicago teams drew two million fans in 1984. The Sox attracted 2,136,988 and the Cubs 2,104,219. It was the first time in major league history that two clubs from one city drew two million or more in the same season.

AUGUST 9   Harold Baines hits a grand slam off Dennis Rasmussen in the sixth inning of a 7–6 loss to the Yankees in New York.

SEPTEMBER 4   Greg Walker drives in six runs on a pair of three-run homers in the second and seventh innings during a 12–2 victory over the Athletics at Comiskey Park.

SEPTEMBER 10   A brawl erupts during a 1–0 loss to the Athletics in Oakland. In the third inning, Dave Kingman was hit by a pitch from Rich Dotson to load the bases. Kingman charged the mound and struck Dotson with two punches to the head while both benches emptied. After Kingman was ejected, Dotson walked Bruce Bochte on four pitches for the game's only run.

SEPTEMBER 17   Harold Baines hits three homers during a 7–3 win over the Twins in Minneapolis. Baines struck solo shots off Bert Blyleven in the first and fifth innings and a two-run homer against Ed Hodge in the seventh.

The White Sox retired Luis Aparicio's number 11 during the 1984 season. He wore the number from 1956 through 1962 and again from 1968 through 1970. Others who wore number 11 with the Sox included Dave Nicholson, Jerry Adair, Sandy Alomar, Sr., Chuck Brinkman, Gerry Moses, Jim Essian, Don Kessinger, Greg Pryor and Rudy Law.

SEPTEMBER 25   The White Sox score seven runs in the second inning of an 8–4 win over the Twins at Comiskey Park.

DECEMBER 6   The White Sox trade LaMarr Hoyt, Kevin Kristan and Todd Simmons to the Padres for Ozzie Guillen, Tim Lollar, Luis Salazar and Bill Long.

Hoyt won the Cy Young Award in 1983 with a 24–10 record but slipped to 13–18 in 1984. He started the 1985 All-Star Game for the National League and was 16–8 that season in San Diego, but he was plagued by a drug addiction and was out of baseball a year later. Hoyt served two jail terms, one of 45 days in 1987 and another of a year in 1988 and 1989, for marijuana possession. At the time of the trade, Guillen was 20 years old and had yet to make his major league debut. He won the starting shortstop job with the Sox in 1985, in addition to winning the AL Rookie of the Year Award. Ozzie was the regular at short until 1997 and played in two All-Star Games with Chicago. He was part of a tradition of White Sox shortstops from Venezuela, which started with Chico Carrasquel and continued under Luis Aparicio. In all, Guillen played in 1,743 games with the White Sox, a figure exceeded only by Luke Appling, Nellie Fox, Frank Thomas and Ray Schalk. Ozzie also ranks fifth in at-bats (6,067), fourth in singles (1,276), sixth in hits (1,608), eighth in total bases (2,056), 10th in runs (693), 10th in triples (68) and 10th in doubles (240). Of course, Guillen's greatest contribution to White Sox baseball has been as manager. In 2005, he led the club to its first world championship since 1917.

DECEMBER 7   The White Sox trade Vance Law to the Expos for Bob James.

James was six-foot-four and was generously listed at 215 pounds. He gave the White Sox one terrific season, with 32 saves and a 2.13 ERA in 69 games and 110 innings in 1985, but faded quickly afterward and was out of the majors two years later.

1985

Sox

Season in a Sentence

The White Sox win 11 more games than the disastrous season of 1984, but still disappoint their fans because of the expectations raised by the division pennant in 1983.

Finish • Won • Lost • Pct • GB

Third   85   77   .525   6.0

Manager

Tony LaRussa

Stats

	WS • AL • Rank		
Batting Avg:	.253	.261	12
On-Base Pct:	.318	.330	13
Slugging Pct:	.392	.406	10
Home Runs:	146		10
Stolen Bases:	108		7
ERA:	4.07	4.15	7
Fielding Avg:	.982	.979	2
Runs Scored:	736		6
Runs Allowed:	720		6 (tie)

Starting Lineup

Carlton Fisk, c
Greg Walker, 1b
Julio Cruz, 2b
Tim Hulett, 3b
Ozzie Guillen, ss
Rudy Law, lf
Luis Salazar, cf-3b
Harold Baines, rf
Ron Kittle, dh-lf
Scott Fletcher, 3b-ss-2b
Daryl Boston, cf
Brian Little, 2b
Oscar Gamble, dh
Jerry Hairston, dh

Pitchers

Britt Burns, sp
Tom Seaver, sp
Floyd Bannister, sp
Tim Lollar, sp
Bob James, rp
Juan Agosto, rp
Dan Spillner, rp
Gene Nelson, rp-sp

Attendance

1,669,888 (eighth in AL)

Club Leaders

Batting Avg:	Harold Baines	.309
On-Base Pct:	Harold Baines	.348
Slugging Pct:	Carlton Fisk	.488
Home Runs:	Carlton Fisk	37
RBIs:	Harold Baines	113
Runs:	Harold Baines	86
Stolen Bases:	Rudy Law	29
Wins:	Britt Burns	18
Strikeouts:	Floyd Bannister	198
ERA:	Tom Seaver	3.17
Saves:	Bob James	32

FEBRUARY 8   A group of investors headed by Jerry Reinsdorf purchases the Chicago Bulls.

Reinsdorf bought into the club during Michael Jordan's rookie year. Under Reinsdorf's leadership, and with considerable help from Jordan, the Bulls won the NBA championship in 1991, 1992, 1993, 1996, 1997 and 1998.

MARCH 23   The White Sox sign Oscar Gamble, formerly with the Yankees, as a free agent.

Gamble failed to produce in his second tour of duty with the White Sox. He hit only .203 in 70 games in 1985.

APRIL 9   The White Sox win the season opener 4–2 against the Brewers in Milwaukee. Tom Seaver was the winning pitcher.

APRIL 19   In the home opener, the White Sox win 8–1 over the Red Sox before 40,087 at Comiskey Park. Rudy Law, Carlton Fisk, Luis Salazar and Harold Baines hit home runs.

APRIL 21   Seven runs in the seventh inning gives the White Sox a 7–2 triumph over the Red Sox at Comiskey Park.

APRIL 27   The White Sox win a thrilling 5–4 decision in 11 innings over the Yankees at Comiskey Park. Two Chicago tallies in the ninth tied the score 3–3. After New York scored in the top of the 11th, the Sox plated two in their half. The game-winning rally consisted of singles by Tim Hulett, Scott Fletcher, Harold Baines, Tom Paciorek and Carlton Fisk.

MAY 29   Ron Kittle and Carlton Fisk each slam two homers during an 8–5 win over the Blue Jays at Comiskey Park.

Fisk hit only .238 in 1985, but he clubbed 37 homers and drove in 107 RBIs at the age of 37. The 37 homers were 11 more than his second-best season in the majors. Fisk clubbed 26 for the Red Sox in 1973 and 1977 and 26 again for the White Sox in 1983.

JUNE 3   In the first round of the amateur draft, the White Sox select catcher Kurt Brown from Glendora High School in Glendora, California.

Brown was the fifth overall pick in the 1985 draft, but he never appeared in a big league game. To make matters worse, Barry Bonds was selected by the Pirates with the sixth overall pick, one spot behind Brown. The club signed eight future major leaguers. Tony Scruggs was picked in the third round of the January draft. In June, the Sox chose Jose Mora (second round), Bobby Thigpen (fourth round), John Pawlowski (sixth round), Wayne Edwards (tenth round), Tom Drees (17th round), Randy Velarde (19th round) and Donn Pall (23rd round). Of those eight, only Thigpen had a significant career with the Sox, however. Velarde played 16 years in the majors, but the White Sox traded him prior to his big-league debut.

JUNE 12   Bruce Tanner, son of former manager Chuck Tanner, makes his major league debut, allowing two runs and seven hits in 6⅔ innings and is the winning pitcher in a 6–3 victory over the Mariners in Seattle.

The win proved to be the only one of Tanner's career. He pitched in 10 big-league games, four of them starts, all with the 1985 White Sox. Tanner ended up with a 1–2 lifetime record and a 5.33 earned run average.

JUNE 18   A walk-off homer in the 13th inning by Harold Baines defeats the Athletics 4–3 at Comiskey Park.

JUNE 19   The White Sox score three runs in the ninth inning and one in the 12th to beat the Athletics 8–7 at Comiskey Park. The three tallies in the ninth were achieved with a home run from Carlton Fisk, a walk to Oscar Gamble and another homer by Greg Walker. In the 12th, Ozzie Guillen reached base on a bunt single, advanced to second on a sacrifice and scored from second on a wild pitch.

The June 19 win was the high point of the 1985 season. It gave the White Sox a 34–26 record and a 1½-game lead in the AL West. The Sox lost 10 of their next 11 games, however, and failed to reach the top spot in the division again before the end of the season.

JULY 1   On the 75th anniversary of the opening of Comiskey Park, the White Sox lose 3–1 to the Mariners. Eleven people who attended the first game at the South Side ballpark on July 1, 1910, were on hand for the festivities.

JULY 2   Harold Baines hits a grand slam off Salome Barojas in the eighth inning of a 12–4 win over the Mariners at Comiskey Park.

JULY 8   Carlton Fisk hits two homers, one of them a grand slam, to lead the White Sox to a 9–4 win over the Tigers in Detroit. Fisk hit a solo home run off Dan Petry in the second inning and the slam in the fifth facing Aurelio Lopez.

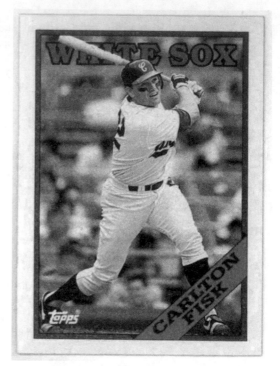

JULY 11   The White Sox suffer a galling 7–6 defeat at the hands of the Orioles in Baltimore. The Sox led 6–3 with none out in the ninth inning when Bob James twisted his ankle throwing an 0–1 pitch to Lee Lacy. Mike Stanton replaced James and allowed a single to Lacy, a walk to Cal Ripken, an RBI-single to Eddie Murray and a walk-off, three-run homer to Fred Lynn.

JULY 16   The White Sox trade Tom Paciorek to the Mets for Dave Cochrane.

JULY 18   The White Sox score six runs in the first inning and beat the Indians 10–0 at Comiskey Park. Bill Veeck sat in the bleachers with his wife

Carlton "Pudge" Fisk was already 33 years old when he joined the Sox in 1981, but he played thirteen years in Chicago, a hard-nosed team leader who inspired the players around him.

Mary Frances. It was only his second appearance at the ballpark since he sold the club in January 1981. The other time was at the 1983 All-Star Game.

JULY 19   The White Sox edge the Indians 1–0 at Comiskey Park. Tom Seaver pitched the complete-game shutout for the 298th win of his career. The lone run scored in the second inning on a home run by Carlton Fisk off Bert Blyleven.

JULY 20   A three-run, walk-off homer by Harold Baines in the ninth inning beats the Indians 8–6 at Comiskey Park.

JULY 26   A two-run, walk-off triple by Carlton Fisk in the ninth inning beats the Orioles 9–8 at Comiskey Park.

The triple was the only one that Fisk struck in 1985. He didn't hit another one until 1987.

JULY 29   Tom Seaver wins the 299th game of his career with a 10-inning, 7–5 decision over the Red Sox in Boston.

AUGUST 2   The White Sox win an eventful 6–5 decision over the Yankees in New York. Both teams scored twice in the 10th inning to knot the score at 5–5. In the 11th, Ozzie Guillen scored from second base on an infield single by Luis Salazar for the winning run. Salazar hit a slow roller up the first-base line that was fielded by Yankee pitcher Rich Bordi. Bordi had no play on Salazar, and the speedy Guillen never stopped running. The spectacular play wasn't the highlight of the game, however. That came with one out in the Yankee seventh when the White Sox retired two runners at the plate on one play with the score 3–3. With Bobby Meacham as the New York runner on first and Dale Berra at second, Rickey Henderson hit a fly ball into the gap in left-center. Meacham held up to see if center fielder Salazar would catch the ball, and once he started running, slipped rounding third base. Berra was just a few steps behind Meacham when Guillen received the relay throw. The throw by Guillen to Carlton Fisk nailed Meacham by 10 feet, and Berra was also nabbed easily.

               Guillen wore number 13 in honor of fellow Venezuelan countryman Dave Concepcion. Other White Sox players to don number 13 were Bob Fothergill (1932), Blue Moon Odom (1976), Harry Chappas (1979–80) and Jamie Quirk (1984).

AUGUST 6   The game between the White Sox and Red Sox in Chicago is canceled by a strike of the major league players. The August 7 game was also called off before the strike was settled on August 8. The two missed games were made up with double-headers.

AUGUST 17   Harold Baines collects five hits, including two doubles, in six at-bats during a 12–7 win over the Brewers in Milwaukee.

AUGUST 23   George Bell of the Blue Jays hits a home run into the center-field bleachers during a 10–3 Toronto win over the White Sox in the second game of a double-header at Comiskey Park. The Blue Jays also won the opener 6–3.

AUGUST 24   Blue Jays pitcher Dave Steib carries a 6–0 lead and a no-hitter into the ninth inning against the White Sox at Comiskey Park, then surrenders home runs to Rudy Law and Bryan Little. Gary Lavelle relieved Steib and gave up a home run to Harold Baines, the first batter Lavelle faced, giving the Sox three homers in succession. The Sox didn't score again, resulting in a 6–3 loss. George Bell hit a second mammoth long ball in consecutive days, launching a drive onto the left-field roof.

AUGUST 25   George Bell continues his long distance assault with another home run onto the roof during a 5–3 White Sox win over the Blue Jays at Comiskey Park.

AUGUST 26   A walk-off homer by Greg Walker in the 10th inning defeats the Red Sox 7–6 at Comiskey Park.

SEPTEMBER 6   Carlton Fisk drives in seven runs during a 12–1 rout of the Rangers in Arlington. Fisk hit a three-run homer in the first inning, another three-run homer in the fourth and an RBI-single in the sixth.

SEPTEMBER 13   A grand slam by pinch-hitter Joe DeSa caps a five-run ninth inning that beats the Mariners 6–1 in Seattle. DeSa homered off Dave Tobik.

DeSa was a native of Honolulu, Hawaii. The homer was the second of only two that he struck in 55 major league at-bats. DeSa died at the age of 27 in an auto accident in Puerto Rico on December 20, 1986.

SEPTEMBER 22   A two-run, walk-off homer by Luis Salazar in the 10th inning beats the Athletics 7–5 at Comiskey Park.

OCTOBER 1   The White Sox score seven runs in the fifth inning of a 12–6 win over the Twins in Minnesota.

OCTOBER 2   Ken Harrelson is hired as general manager, replacing Roland Hemond.

Hemond had been in the White Sox organization since 1970. With the hiring of Harrelson, Hemond was bumped into a meaningless front office assignment and in May 1986 joined the commissioner's office. Hemond later served as general manager of the Orioles from 1987 through 1995. The appointment of Harrelson was a complete surprise. He had no experience running a baseball team. Harrelson had been a player in the majors from 1963 through 1971, followed by a career as a television announcer with the Red Sox (1975–81) and White Sox (1982–85). Jerry Reinsdorf and Eddie Einhorn were concerned over the decline in attendance at Comiskey Park at the same time fans were flocking to Wrigley Field. The Sox attendance had dropped from 2,136,988 in 1983 to 1,424,313 in 1985. The Cubs figures rose from 575,637 in the strike-shortened season of 1981 and 1,249,278 in 1982 to 2,161,534 in 1985. If nothing else, the colorful, outspoken and flamboyant Harrelson would create newspaper headlines. During his year as general manager, Harrelson did just that, but most of them were negative. He proved to be ill-equipped for the job in nearly all aspects, as he lacked the knowledge, people skills, public relations acumen and personality that were conducive to running a team. Harrelson submitted his resignation in September 1986, near the end of a 72–90 season as attendance fell even further to 1,208,660. His short tenure as general manager would have long-lasting effects because among Harrelson's acts were the firing of Tony LaRussa and Dave Dombrowski (see June 20, 1986), both of whom would build championship clubs elsewhere.

NOVEMBER 25   The White Sox trade Scott Fletcher, Ed Correa and Jose Mota to the Rangers for Wayne Tolleson and Dave Schmidt.

The Sox made a big mistake letting Fletcher out of the organization. He was dealt to make room at shortstop for Ozzie Guillen. At the time of the trade, Fletcher was 27 years old and had a .245 batting average with eight homers in 413 big-league games. He blossomed in Texas, however, batting .300 in 1986. Fletcher played for the White Sox again from 1989 through 1991 as a starting second baseman.

DECEMBER 10   In the minor league draft, the White Sox select Bobby Bonilla from the Pirates organization (see July 23, 1986).

DECEMBER 12   The White Sox trade Britt Burns, Mike Soper and Glen Braxton to the Yankees for Ron Hassey and Joe Cowley.

> *Ken Harrelson peddled Burns to the Yankees with the knowledge that the pitcher suffered from a chronic degenerative hip condition that had plagued him since childhood. Burns compiled an 18–11 record in 1985 despite pitching in almost constant pain. He underwent surgery in the spring of 1986 and never pitched in the majors again.*

1986   Sox

Season in a Sentence

The bold experiment of hiring Ken Harrelson as general manager fails miserably, and near the end of a 90-loss season that includes the firing of Tony LaRussa, Harrelson resigns his post.

Finish • Won • Lost • Pct • GB

Fifth   72   90   .444   20.0

Managers

Tony LaRussa (28–38),
Doug Rader (1–1) and
Jim Fregosi (45–51)

Stats

Stats	WS	AL	Rank
Batting Avg:	.247	.262	14
On-Base Pct:	.310	.330	14
Slugging Pct:	.363	.408	14
Home Runs:	121		14
Stolen Bases:	115		5
ERA:	3.93		3
Fielding Avg:	.981	.979	4
Runs Scored:	644		14
Runs Allowed:	699		4

Starting Lineup

Carlton Fisk, c
Greg Walker, 1b
Julio Cruz, 2b
Tim Hulett, 3b-2b
Ozzie Guillen, ss
Bobby Bonilla, lf-1b
John Cangelsoi, cf
Harold Baines, rf
Ron Kittle, dh
Wayne Tolleson, 3b
Jerry Hairston, dh
Daryl Boston, cf

Pitchers

Rich Dotson, sp
Joe Cowley, sp
Floyd Bannister, sp
Joel Davis, sp
Neil Allen, sp
Bob James, rp
Gene Nelson, rp
Dave Schmidt, rp
Bill Dawley, rp

Attendance

1,424,313 (10th in AL)

Club Leaders

Batting Avg:	Harold Baines	.296
On-Base Pct:	Harold Baines	.349
Slugging Pct:	Harold Baines	.465
Home Runs:	Harold Baines	21
RBIs:	Harold Baines	88
Runs:	Harold Baines	72
Stolen Bases:	John Cangelosi	50
Wins:	Joe Cowley	11
Strikeouts:	Joe Cowley	132
ERA:	Floyd Bannister	3.54
Saves:	Bob James	14

FEBRUARY 13   Two weeks after the space shuttle Challenger explodes, killing six astronauts and teacher Christa McAuliffe, the White Sox trade Ron Hassey, Matt Winters, Eric Schmidt and Chris Alvarez to the Yankees for Neil Allen, Scott Bradley and Glen Braxton.

APRIL 7   The White Sox open the season with a 5–3 loss to the Brewers before 42,265 at Comiskey Park. Harold Baines collected four hits in five at-bats. Tom Seaver was the starting and losing pitcher. It was the 16th time in his career that he was the starter on Opening Day, the most of any pitcher in baseball history. Seaver started for the Mets 10 times in a row from 1968 through 1977, the Reds in 1978, 1979, 1981 and 1983, and the White Sox in 1985 and 1986.

Carlton Fisk began the year as the starting left fielder in a controversial move. He was 38 years old and had difficulty adjusting to the new position. Joel Skinner replaced Fisk as the catcher, and early in the season both were mired in a batting slump. In mid-May, Skinner was benched and Fisk was once again the White Sox's first option as a catcher. Left field was a problem all season, as nine different players started at the position. Bobby Bonilla led the club in games started in left with only 32. John Cangelosi was the Opening Day starter in center field. He was a 23-year-old non-roster player at the start of spring training, but he impressed Sox management with his hustle and determination. Cangelosi was only five-foot eight and weighed just 150 pounds and looked even smaller by hitting out of an unorthodox crouched batting stance. He also bore a striking resemblance to Bruce Springsteen. Cangelosi had 39 stolen bases by the 1986 All-Star break, but he had trouble hitting and was benched for most of the second half. He finished the season with 50 steals, a .235 batting average and just two homers. Cangelosi was traded to the Pirates in March 1987.

MAY 1   Two weeks after the U.S. bombs Libya in response to terrorist attacks, and a week after Geraldo Rivera opens Al Capone's vault on national television only to find nothing inside, White Sox co-owners Jerry Reinsdorf and Eddie Einhorn meet with Illinois Governor James Thompson to discuss Chicago Mayor Harold Washington's proposal for a $255 million South Loop stadium complex to share with the Bears.

With a retractable dome and movable seats, the stadium would hold 45,000 for baseball and 80,000 for football. If built, it would be the first new stadium or arena in the city since Chicago Stadium, home of the Blackhawks and Bulls, opened in 1929. Reinsdorf admitted that he was "close to giving up on the city" in his quest for a new stadium to replace aging Comiskey Park, which was in its 77th year of operation. "We have given them some time, but things are moving along so slowly we have to bring this to a head." In December 1984, Reinsdorf's firm, Balcor-American Express, purchased a 140-acre parcel of land at Swift Road and Lake Street in Addison, Illinois, a DuPage County suburb west of Chicago about 30 miles from the Loop. Reinsdorf and Einhorn were exploring the possibility of building a stadium on the Addison site. The two were also looking at other cities and visited Denver, Miami, Orlando, New Orleans, St. Petersburg and several locations in northwest Indiana in 1986. The Bears, who had won the Super Bowl the previous January, were looking to build their own stadium and showed little inclination toward sharing a home with the Sox. The city made it clear that it would not build a baseball-only stadium for the Sox alone. The Bears would have to be involved for the project to move forward. In December 1985, the White Sox received an engineering report stating that Comiskey Park would be impossible to maintain. The major problem was the rusting of the structural beams supporting the upper deck. At the same time, the American League office informed the White Sox that they would have to find a new home. "I don't think we can stay here for more than three years,"

Reinsdorf said of Comiskey Park. Many expressed the opinion that Reinsdorf was lying about the crumbling condition of the ballpark, however. Reinsdorf further alienated his critics by refusing to release or publish the entirety of the engineering report detailing the structural analysis of Comiskey. The ballpark had never achieved the charm of Wrigley Field, the stateliness of Yankee Stadium, the quirky characteristics of Fenway Park or the enthusiastic fan base of Ebbets Field, but many couldn't imagine the Sox playing anywhere else. Meanwhile, Addison residents were less than enthused about a stadium being built in their midst, citing traffic congestion, noise pollution and the spoilage of 22 acres of wetlands. There was also a racial undertone as many in the all-white community of Addison were afraid of the arrival of African-American fans who would follow the White Sox to Addison (see November 4, 1986).

MAY 9   The White Sox rally for three runs in the ninth inning to beat the Indians 4–3 at Municipal Stadium. The Chicago victory ended Cleveland's 10-game winning streak. The Sox scored their trio of last-at-bat runs on an RBI-single by Carlton Fisk, followed by a two-run pinch-hit single from Tim Hulett.

The White Sox headed into the contest with a 7–18 record amid rumors that Tony LaRussa's firing was imminent. A few days earlier, general manager Ken Harrelson admitted as much in a bizarre statement. "There was a feud between the cautious Ken Harrelson and the flamboyant Hawk Harrelson," he said. "The way things were going I think they were a little confused. Hawk wanted to make a change and Ken didn't." Before the May 9 contest, Harrelson called a press conference to confirm speculation that preliminary negotiations had been held to hire Billy Martin to replace LaRussa. Harrelson said that those discussions had ended and that LaRussa would remain as manager. A week later, Harrelson said, "If there's a mistake made here, it's that I've been too honest with everybody. I'm going to correct that in the future. Does that mean lying? You're danged right. You try to be honest and everybody knows what's going on and you get it shoved right up your keister."

MAY 10   The White Sox down the Indians 4–0 in 11 innings in Cleveland. A two-run homer by Carlton Fisk was the big blow of the inning. Neil Allen (seven innings), Gene Nelson (three innings) and Bob James (one inning) combined on a three-hit shutout.

MAY 14   The White Sox score three runs in the ninth inning to defeat the Yankees 3–2 in New York. The runs scored on an RBI-single by Greg Walker and a two-out, two-run triple by Ozzie Guillen.

MAY 28   Joe Cowley sets an American League record by striking out the first seven Texas batters, but the White Sox lose 6–3 in Arlington. Cowley fanned Oddibe McDowell, Scott Fletcher, Pete O'Brien, Pete Incaviglia, Gary Ward, George Wright and Steve Buechele. The streak was broken by Orlando Merced, who flied out. Cowley lasted only 4⅔ innings, however, giving up six runs, five earned, and six hits while striking out eight overall.

The game was Cowley's third as a member of the White Sox and his second start with the club. He was acquired in a trade with the Yankees in December 1985. In his debut with the White Sox on April 13, Cowley gave up five runs in 2⅓ innings against the Red Sox. Two days later, he was demoted to the minors and was recalled on May 22. Later in the year, Cowley pitched a no-hitter (see September 19, 1986).

JUNE 2   In the first round of the amateur draft, the White Sox select pitcher Grady Hall from Northwestern University.

Hall never reached the majors in what was a largely wasted draft. The only future major leaguers drafted and signed by the White Sox in 1986 were Scott Radinsky (third round), Matt Merullo (seventh round) and Mark Davis (12th round).

JUNE 11   A five-run rally in the ninth inning comes up short as the White Sox lose 12–11 to the Angels at Comiskey Park.

JUNE 12   The White Sox score five runs in the ninth inning for the second day in a row, this time winning 8–4 over the Mariners in Seattle. The Sox plated three in the eighth to cut the margin to 4–3. The big blows in the ninth were a two-run double by Carlton Fisk and a two-run homer from Harold Baines.

JUNE 13   After trailing the Mariners 6–0 in the third inning in Seattle, the White Sox take a 9–6 lead with four runs in the fourth and five in the fifth, but wind up losing 11–10.

JUNE 15   The White Sox turn an unusual triple play during a 10–5 loss to the Mariners in the Kingdome. Alvin Davis was the Seattle runner on third and Jim Presley was on first when Ken Phelps lifted a fly ball to Jerry Hairston in left field. Hairston threw out Alvin Davis at the plate and Presley, who had hesitated, was thrown out at second by Carlton Fisk.

JUNE 18   The Twins score four runs in the ninth inning and one in the 10th to defeat the White Sox 10–9 in Minnesota.

In 1986, the White Sox finished last in the American League in runs (644), batting average (.247), on-base percentage (.310), slugging percentage (.363), home runs (121) and doubles (197). Part of the problem was Ken Harrelson's decision to move the fences back at Comiskey Park. The distances were increased from 341 feet to 347 down the foul lines, 374 feet to 382 in the power alleys and 401 feet to 409 in center field.

JUNE 20   The White Sox fire Tony LaRussa as manager. Coach Doug Rader served as interim manager for two days until a replacement was hired (see June 22, 1986).

At the time LaRussa was fired, the White Sox had a record of 26–38. He was 522–510 overall as skipper of the Sox since he took over on August 2, 1979. On July 2, 1986 less than two weeks after his ouster by the Sox, LaRussa became manager of the Athletics, a position he held through the end of the 1995 season. In Oakland, Tony guided the A's to four division titles, three consecutive World Series beginning in 1988 and the world championship in 1989. In 1996, LaRussa was hired to manage the Cardinals. He was still on the job in 2008, the 30th consecutive year that he managed a big league club. At the end of that season, LaRussa was third all-time in wins by a manager, trailing only Connie Mack and John McGraw. In the more than 90 seasons since 1916, no one has more victories as a major league manager than LaRussa. In 2006, LaRussa won the world championship by leading the Cards to victory over the Detroit Tigers, a club whose general manager was Dave Dombrowski. Dombrowski was assistant general manager of the White Sox before being fired by the club on June 5, 1986, two weeks prior to LaRussa. Like the dismissal of LaRussa, Dombrowski's departure proved to be a disastrous move. He was the general manager of the Montreal Expos from 1988 through 1991, then moved to the expansion Florida Marlins, where he was the general manager until 2001. The Marlins won the World Series in 1997 and again in 2003 with a team consisting chiefly of players acquired by Dombrowski. After leaving Florida following an ownership change, Dombrowski became president and CEO of the Tigers. He helped lift the Tigers from a 43–119 season in 2003 to the World Series in 2006.

JUNE 22   Jim Fregosi is hired as manager of the White Sox and guides the club to a 10–4 win over the Mariners at Comiskey Park. When he arrived at the ballpark, he found the name of his uniform spelled "FERGOSI."

Fregosi had an 18-year big-league career from 1961 through 1978, mostly with the Angels. He was a six-time All-Star and a Gold Glove winner at shortstop. Fregosi previously managed the Angels from 1978 through 1981 and won the AL West title in 1979. He led the Sox through the close of the 1988 season and had a record of 193–226 with the club.

JUNE 23   Greg Walker hits a grand slam off Bert Blyleven in the second inning of an 11–2 win over the Twins at Comiskey Park.

JUNE 26   The White Sox trade Scott Bradley to the Mariners for Ivan Calderon.

Calderon looked like a coming star in 1987 when he hit .293 with 28 homers and 38 doubles as a 25-year-old, but injuries curtailed a promising career.

JUNE 29   The White Sox trade Tom Seaver to the Red Sox for Steve Lyons.

In the last year of his stellar career, Seaver was 2–6 with the White Sox in 1986 and desired to be dealt to a contending team on the East Coast near his Connecticut home. Nicknamed "Psycho," Lyons was a fan favorite while serving as a utility player with the White Sox from 1986 through 1990, due to his incessant hustle, sense of humor, and eccentric behavior. Lyons is best known for dropping his pants during a game in Detroit (see July 16, 1990). While with the Sox, Lyons played all nine defensive positions and also served time as a designated hitter. He appeared in 215 games at third base, 103 at first, 90 at second, 40 in left field, 27 in right, 26 in center, 11 as a DH, three as a catcher and one as a pitcher.

JULY 20   Neil Allen pitches a two-hitter and defeats the Yankees 8–0 at Yankee Stadium. The only two New York hits were a single by Dave Winfield in the fifth inning and a double by Rickey Henderson in the sixth.

JULY 23   The White Sox trade Bobby Bonilla to the Pirates for Jose DeLeon.

Bonilla was drafted from the Pirates organization the previous December, then was sent back to Pittsburgh after hitting .269 with two homers in 75 games for the White Sox. The Sox made a terrible trade. After leaving Chicago, Bonilla hit 285 home runs and played in six All-Star Games and a World Series. At the time of the trade, DeLeon had a career record of 17–38. He was 15–17 with the White Sox over two seasons.

JULY 26   Gene Nelson touches off a bench-clearing incident in the sixth inning of a 2–1 loss to the Orioles in Baltimore by drilling Rick Dempsey with a curveball.

JULY 29   Joe Cowley (8⅔ innings) and Bob James (one-third of an inning) combine on a two-hitter to beat the Red Sox 4–1 at Comiskey Park to end an eight-game losing streak. The only Boston hits were singles by Jim Rice in the second and fourth innings.

On the same day, the White Sox traded Ron Kittle, Wayne Tolleson and Joel Skinner to the Yankees for Ron Hassey, Carlos Martinez and Bill Lindsey. Hassey was on a Chicago-to-New York shuttle over a period of 19 months. He was traded by the Cubs to the Yankees in December 1984, sent by the Yankees to the White Sox in December 1985, swapped by the White Sox to the Yankees in February 1986 and dealt by the Yanks to the Sox in July 1986. Hassey reported to the Sox with an arthritic condition in his knees that prevented him from catching on a regular basis. The Sox complained that Hassey was "damaged goods" and wanted another player. When the Yankees offered to rescind the deal, the Sox kept him and put him to use as a pinch-hitter and designated hitter. Although he was limited defensively, there were few problems with Hassey's bat. Over the remainder of the 1986 season, he hit .353 in 150 at-bats.

AUGUST 3   In his major league debut, first baseman Russ Morman collects two hits during a six-run fourth inning and three overall as the White Sox defeat the Tigers 10–1 at Comiskey Park. Morman collected two singles and a home run during the contest.

AUGUST 4   The White Sox defeat Roger Clemens and the Red Sox 1–0 in Boston. Jose DeLeon (seven innings), Bob James (1⅓ innings) and Dave Schmidt (two-thirds of an inning) combined on the shutout. The lone run scored on a sacrifice fly by Julio Cruz in the eighth inning.

DeLeon was the winning pitcher. He also beat Clemens in a 7–2 decision on July 30 in Chicago. Those two games accounted for half of Clemens's losses in a 1986 season in which he posted a 24–4 record. Entering the July 30 contest, DeLeon had lost 27 of his previous 31 decisions over three seasons. The White Sox defeated Clemens five straight times between 1986 and 1988.

AUGUST 12   The White Sox sign Steve Carlton following his release from the Giants.

Carlton was 41 years old and had 319 career wins when he arrived in Chicago. Carlton started 10 games for the Sox and had a 4–3 record and a 3.69 ERA.

AUGUST 15   In his first game with the White Sox, George Foster homers during a 4–3 loss to the Brewers at Comiskey Park.

A former MVP and five-time All-Star, Foster was signed by the Sox after his release by the Mets. He lasted only 15 games in Chicago, batting .216 and hit no more homers after his debut.

SEPTEMBER 18   Harold Baines collects five hits, including a double, in five at-bats during a 6–4 victory over the Mariners in Seattle.

SEPTEMBER 19   Joe Cowley pitches a no-hitter and beats the Angels 7–1 in Anaheim. It was hardly a masterpiece, as Cowley struck out eight and walked seven batters. Of the 138 pitches he threw, 69 were balls and 69 were strikes. Cowley was nearly removed from the game by manager Jim Fregosi after walking the bases loaded with none out in the sixth inning. "He was one pitch away from being taken out," said Fregosi. "When he was 3–1 on Reggie (Jackson), if he'd thrown one more ball he would have come out." Instead, Cowley coaxed Jackson, who had hit three homers the night before in an 18–3 California rout of the Royals, to hit a sacrifice fly and got out of the inning with only one run being scored. In the ninth, Cowley walked Brian Downing, retired Jackson on a fly ball to center fielder Daryl Boston and induced Doug DeCinces to hit into a double play that went from shortstop Ozzie Guillen to second baseman Jack Perconte to first baseman Russ Morman.

Cowley made only two more starts as a member of the White Sox, and he lost them both. He finished the 1986 season with an 11–11 record and a 3.88 ERA. Cowley was traded to the Phillies in March 1987, where he was 0–4 in his last season in the majors. The no-hitter proved to be Cowley's 33rd, and last, big-league victory.

SEPTEMBER 26   Ken Harrelson resigns as general manager.

After the Sox were 85–77 in 1985, Harrelson thought the club could take the next step and reach the post-season, but he lasted only one year as general manager after a 90-loss season in 1986. Harrelson made a series of bad trades, most of them with the Yankees, and fired Tony LaRussa and Dave Dombrowski, two of the brightest minds in the game, after feuding with both. Harrelson's "blueprint for success" seemed to have little coherent direction and was ridiculed in the press. "I put mistrust in the minds of a lot of White Sox fans," said Harrelson in a statement after his resignation. "I'm not the most tactful person in the world. I know I made some P.R. gaffes." He admitted the pressures of the job got to him. "I don't go anywhere without Anacin," revealed Harrelson. "I was taking 15 a day the last couple of months." Community divisiveness over the stadium issue gave Harrelson additional headaches. He returned to his former job as a television announcer for White Sox games in 1990 and was still on the job in 2008.

SEPTEMBER 30   Only about 150 fans are in the stands in Comiskey Park at the start of a 4:00 p.m. double-header on a Tuesday afternoon against the Mariners. Official attendance was 8,528 because of season tickets sold. The White Sox won both contests by identical 5–4 scores, the first coming in 10 innings.

OCTOBER 29   The White Sox hire 46-year-old Larry Himes as general manager.

Himes had been the scouting director of the Angels, a club that won the AL West in 1986. He had earned high marks for drafting players who played key roles on the division-title team. The White Sox also drafted extremely well under Himes's leadership, selecting Jack McDowell, Robin Ventura, Frank Thomas, Ray Durham and Alex Fernandez over a four-year period. Success at the major league level wasn't forthcoming, however, and Himes was fired in September 1990.

NOVEMBER 4   A non-binding referendum to build a stadium for the White Sox in suburban Addison fails by a 43-vote margin, 3,787 to 3,744. On November 21, Illinois Governor James Thompson informed White Sox ownership that they must find a site other than Addison because of the referendum and political opposition from prominent DuPage County officials. The White Sox then turned to building on the South Side near Comiskey Park. It would take another 18 months before public funding became available for the project, however (see June 30, 1988).

1987   Sox

Season in a Sentence

The White Sox lose 46 of their first 71 games before going 52–39 the rest of the way.

Finish • Won • Lost • Pct • GB

Fifth   77   85   .475   8.0

Manager

Jim Fregosi

Stats

Stats	WS	AL	Rank
Batting Avg:	.258	.265	13
On-Base Pct:	.319	.333	14
Slugging Pct:	.415	.425	12
Home Runs:	173		10
Stolen Bases:	138		5
ERA:	4.30	4.46	4
Fielding Avg:	.981	.980	6
Runs Scored:	748		11
Runs Allowed:	691		4

Starting Lineup

Carlton Fisk, c
Greg Walker, 1b
Donnie Hill, 2b
Tim Hulett, 3b
Ozzie Guillen, ss
Gary Redus, lf
Kenny Williams, cf
Ivan Calderon, rf
Harold Baines, dh
Fred Manrique, 2b
Daryl Boston, lf-cf

Pitchers

Floyd Bannister, sp
Rich Dotson, sp
Jose DeLeon, sp
Bill Long, sp
Dave LaPoint, sp
Bobby Thigpen, rp
Bob James, rp
Ray Searage, rp
Jim Winn, rp

Attendance

1,208,060 (12th in AL)

Club Leaders

Batting Avg:	Ivan Calderon	.293
On-Base Pct:	Ivan Calderon	.362
Slugging Pct:	Ivan Calderon	.526
Home Runs:	Ivan Calderon	28
RBIs:	Greg Walker	94
Runs:	Ivan Calderon	93
Stolen Bases:	Gary Redus	52
Wins:	Floyd Bannister	16
Strikeouts:	Jose DeLeon	153
ERA:	Floyd Bannister	3.58
Saves:	Bobby Thigpen	16

JANUARY 5   The White Sox trade Pete Filson and Randy Velarde to the Yankees for Scott Nielsen and Mike Soper.

JANUARY 21   The White Sox sign Jerry Royster, most recently with the Padres, as a free agent.

MARCH 26   The White Sox trade Joe Cowley to the Phillies for Gary Redus.

APRIL 6   The White Sox win the season opener 5–4 against the Royals in Kansas City. The Sox took a 4–1 lead with four runs in the second inning. Rich Dotson was the winning pitcher.

> *The White Sox had new uniforms in 1987, going for a more traditional look, after more than a decade of designs that were unique to baseball jerseys before or since (see January 8, 1971, April 20, 1976 and May 13, 1982). The new look at home had "White Sox" displayed in slanted script in navy blue outlined in red with an underlining flourish. On the road grays, "Chicago" was in blue slanted script and outlined in red. Caps had navy blue skulls with red bills and a white script "C" outlined in red. Uniform numbers were on the top front of the left pants legs just below the belt.*

APRIL 10   In the home opener, the White Sox lose 11–4 to the Tigers before 40,025 at Comiskey Park.

> *A section of concrete overhang crashed into the lower deck seating area in right field just before the season started. The grandstand in that area was closed for several weeks until repairs were completed.*

APRIL 20   At Comiskey Park, the Brewers beat the White Sox 5–4 for their 13th straight victory to tie the major league record for the longest winning streak at the start of a season.

APRIL 21   The White Sox beat the Brewers 7–1 at Comiskey Park to end Milwaukee's season-opening 13-game winning streak.

> *Before the game, Jerry Royster broke his nose when his batted ball ricocheted off the top rail of the batting cage and went back into his face. It wasn't the most unusual injury of the year. In May, Donnie Hill had a problem with his contact lenses causing conjunctivitis. He was given a medical rehabilitation assignment in the minors to adjust to wearing glasses.*

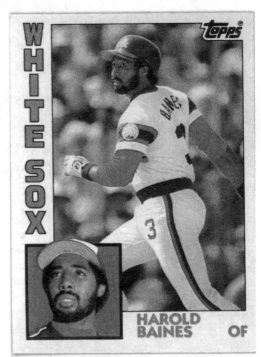

Perhaps the most consistent player for the team in the 1980s, Harold Baines produced good numbers every year during his ten seasons with the Sox.

MAY 5   White Sox pitcher Bill Long and Yankees hurler Phil Niekro both pitch two-hitters in a 2–0 Chicago victory at Comiskey Park. Both Sox runs scored in the third inning on RBI-singles by Gary Redus and Ron Hassey. The only New York hits were singles by Dan Pasqua in the second and seventh innings.

MAY 20   Less than a month after having a 13-game winning streak ended by the White Sox, the Brewers stop a 12-game losing streak by beating the Sox 5–1 at County Stadium.

MAY 23   Floyd Bannister tosses a two-hitter, leading the White Sox to a 9–1 win over the Red Sox at Fenway Park. Bannister retired the first 17 batters before center fielder Gary Redus dropped a liner struck by Rich Gedman. The play was scored a double. The second Boston hit was a homer by Ellis Burks in the ninth inning. Heading into the game, Bannister had lost 11 decisions in a row to the Red Sox dating back to 1982.

MAY 31   The White Sox lose a 10–9 heart-breaker to the Red Sox at Comiskey Park. Ivan Calderon drove in six runs on a pair of three-run homers in the first and second innings for a 9–2 Chicago lead. Boston scored eight unanswered runs, the last two on a two-run double by Mike Greenwell off Bob James in the ninth.

JUNE 1   Ivan Calderon hits a two-run homer in the top of the 12th inning for a 9–7 lead over the Rangers in Arlington, but Texas rallies to win 11–9 in the bottom half on a walk-off grand slam by Oddibe McDowell off Joel Davis. The Rangers scored five runs in the ninth inning to tie the score 7–7.

JUNE 2   Greg Walker hits a grand slam off Ron Meridith in the second inning of a 15–5 mauling of the Rangers in Arlington.

             On the same day, the White Sox selected Jack McDowell from Stanford University in the first round of the amateur draft. Other future major leaguers drafted and signed by the White Sox in 1987 were Brent Knackert (second round), Dan Rohrmeier (fifth round), Jerry Kutzier (sixth round), Rob Lukachyk (tenth round), Buddy Groom (12th round) and Dwayne Hosey (13th round). McDowell was the only one of the group to have a successful career in the majors, but he more than made up for the failure of the others. McDowell debuted with the White Sox in September 1987 and won all three of his decisions before the end of the season. Nicknamed "Black Jack," he played for the White Sox for eight seasons and posted a record of 91–58 to rank fourth all-time among franchise pitchers in winning percentage (.611). McDowell's best seasons were 1992 (20–10) and 1993 (22–10). He was a fan favorite, not only for his pitching excellence, but for his intimidating presence on the mound. McDowell wasn't often a favorite of club management, however, because of his protracted contract disputes and late-night reveling that included performing with his grunge rock band V.I.E.W. In 1993, the pitcher became involved in a bar fight in New Orleans with Pearl Jam's Eddie Vedder. A year later, after another hassle over salary that resulted in McDowell losing a bitter arbitration case, the pitcher informed the White Sox that he had no intention of returning to the club for the 1995 season and was traded to the Yankees.

JUNE 9   The only Chicago hit off Athletics pitcher Matt Young is a two-run homer by Ken Williams in the eighth inning of an 8–3 loss in Oakland.

JUNE 20   The White Sox score eight runs in the seventh inning of a 10–5 win over the Twins in Minnesota.

JUNE 23   The White Sox pound the Mariners 13–3 at Comiskey Park.

The White Sox bottomed out with a record of 25–46 on June 28. General manager Larry Himes responded by banning alcohol from the clubhouse and from team charter flights. He also fined Ivan Calderon, Scott Nielsen and Jose DeLeon for failing to wear socks with their dress clothes while in the clubhouse. In addition, Himes ordered players to display three inches of blue on their uniform socks and fined those who didn't comply with the edict. The players grumbled profusely, but play improved. The Sox had a record of 52–39 the rest of the way, including 17 wins in their last 21 games.

JULY 1   A two-out, two-run, walk-off homer in the 10th inning by Greg Walker beats the Athletics 5–3 in Oakland. A White Sox run in the ninth inning tied the score 3–3.

Catcher Ron Karkovice had a nightmare season for the White Sox in 1987. He collected only six hits and struck out 40 times in 85 at-bats for an .071 batting average. The previous off-season, the Sox sent Karkovice to Seattle for a course in positive thinking, which obviously failed to have the desired effects.

JULY 3   After the Indians score six runs in the eighth inning to take a 9–8 lead, the White Sox rebound with six in the ninth to win 14–9 at Municipal Stadium. Brook Jacoby hit three home runs for Cleveland.

JULY 5   The White Sox clobber the Indians 17–0 in Cleveland. Scott Nielsen pitched the shutout.

The pitching performance was a rarity during Nielsen's three years with the White Sox in which he was 5–7 with a 6.44 ERA in 86²/₃ innings.

JULY 9   Ozzie Guillen collects five hits, including a double, in five at-bats to lead the White Sox to a 6–3 victory over the Yankees in New York.

JULY 11   Carlton Fisk hits a two-run homer during a three-run 15th inning to defeat the Yankees 5–2 in New York.

JULY 25   The White Sox retire the uniform numbers of Ted Lyons (16) and Billy Pierce (19) in ceremonies prior to a 3–2 win over the Yankees at Comiskey Park.

Lyons made his debut with the White Sox in 1923 at a time when teams did not use uniform numbers to identify players. He wore number 16 from 1932 through 1948. Others who sported number 16 from 1949 until it was retired in 1987 included Max Surkont, Gordon Goldsberry, Bob Mahoney, Marv Grissom, Mike Fornieles, Sammy Esposito, Ted Beard, Al Smith, Brian McCall, Ken Berry, Brian Downing, Greg Pryor, Bruce Kimm, Jim Essian, Marv Foley and Julio Cruz. Pierce was number 19 during his entire White Sox career, which lasted from 1949 through 1962. Others who wore number 19 from 1963 through 1987 included Dom Zanni, Joe Shipley, Bruce Howard, Dennis Ribant, Buddy Bradford, Barry Moore, Steve Huntz, Lee Mays, Rudy Hernandez, Jim Qualls, Ken Tatum, Sam Ewing, Mike Colbern, Greg Luzinski and Floyd Bannister.

JULY 26   Rich Dotson retires the first 22 batters to face him, then gives up five runs and five hits in the eighth and ninth innings to lose 5–2 to the Yankees in New York.

JULY 27   A spectacular catch by Ivan Calderon in left field highlights an otherwise drab 4–1 loss to the Tigers in Detroit. Timing a leap, Calderon planted his right foot on the thin ledge of the auxiliary scoreboard, gripped the wire mesh with his right hand, and made the catch above the fence to rob Alan Trammell of a home run.

The White Sox finished first in the AL in doubles in 1987 with 283 after hitting 197 two-baggers in 1986 to finish last in the circuit.

JULY 30   The White Sox trade Bryce Hulstrom to the Cardinals for Dave LaPoint.

AUGUST 1   In his first game with the White Sox, Dave LaPoint holds the Brewers hitless until Steve Kiefer singles in the seventh inning. Overall, LaPoint allowed no runs and two hits in 6²/₃ innings. The Sox won 3–2 in Milwaukee.

AUGUST 3   The Blue Jays score 10 runs in the sixth inning off Floyd Bannister and Jose DeLeon and defeat the White Sox 14–5 at Comiskey Park.

AUGUST 15   Rich Dotson shuts out the Blue Jays 1–0 in Toronto.

AUGUST 26   The White Sox trade Jerry Royster and Mike Soper to the Yankees for Ken Patterson and Jeff Pries.

AUGUST 29   The White Sox release Neil Allen.

Allen was horrendous for the White Sox in 1987, with an 0–7 record and a 7.07 ERA.

AUGUST 31   Carlton Fisk drives in all five Chicago runs for a 5–3 win over the Royals at Comiskey Park. Fisk hit a three-run homer in the first inning, an RBI-single in the third and a sacrifice fly in the fifth.

SEPTEMBER 5   Carlton Fisk hits his 300th career homer during a 4–2 loss to the Royals in Kansas City. The milestone was struck off Danny Jackson.

SEPTEMBER 8   With one out in the ninth inning and the White Sox leading the Twins 4–3 in Minnesota, Ken Williams starts a game-ending double play by catching a ball in center field and throwing out the potential tying run at home plate.

SEPTEMBER 9   The White Sox allow only two hits, but both are home runs in a 2–1 loss to the Twins in Minnesota. Kirby Puckett homered off Dave LaPoint in the fourth inning and Tim Laudner connected for a walk-off blast against Jim Winn in the ninth.

SEPTEMBER 13   Floyd Bannister faces the minimum 27 batters while pitching a one-hitter as the White Sox win 2–0 over the Mariners in Seattle. The only base runner was Harold Reynolds in the third inning. Reynolds was out trying to stretch a single into a double. Mark Langston pitched a two-hitter for the Mariners. The only White Sox hits were a pair of home runs by Pat Keedy in the third inning and Donnie Hill in the seventh.

SEPTEMBER 15   Jack McDowell makes his major league debut and pitches seven shutout innings in a 6–2 win over the Twins at Comiskey Park.

McDowell started his career by pitching 13 consecutive shutout innings.

SEPTEMBER 16   The White Sox score five runs in the fifth inning and seven in the sixth to take a 13–3 lead, then hang on to beat the Twins 13–10 at Comiskey Park.

SEPTEMBER 17   Carlton Fisk leads off the 10th inning with a home run that beats the Mariners 9–8 at Comiskey Park.

SEPTEMBER 27   Dave LaPoint pitches a two-hitter and beats the Athletics 5–0 in Oakland. The only hits off LaPoint were by Terry Steinbach in the fifth inning and Mike Gallego in the eighth.

SEPTEMBER 29   The White Sox nip the Angels 1–0 at Comiskey Park. The lone run scored on an RBI-double by Steve Lyons in the fifth inning. Floyd Bannister (seven innings) and Bobby Thigpen (two innings) combined on the shutout.

Thigpen was an outfielder at Mississippi State on a team that included Rafael Palmeiro and Will Clark. Thigpen was converted into a starting pitcher in the minors in 1985, and then into a reliever. Thigpen recorded 34 saves in both 1988 and 1989, although they came with earned run averages of 3.30 and 3.76. In 1990, he put it all together. Thigpen set an all-time major league record that season with 57 saves. In 88²/₃ innings over 77 games, he compiled an ERA of 1.83. Mysteriously, Thigpen quickly declined soon afterward. By 1993, he was traded to the Phillies and a year later was out of the majors.

OCTOBER 3   The White Sox score 11 runs in the fifth inning and thrash the Athletics 17–1 at Comiskey Park. Gary Redus contributed two hits in the big inning with a two-run single and a two-run double.

Redus hit only .236 for the White Sox in 1987, but he clubbed 12 homers and stole 52 bases.

NOVEMBER 12   Three weeks after the end of the six-month Congressional hearings investigating the Iran-Contra scandal, and two weeks after the sudden death of Chicago Mayor Harold Washington, the White Sox trade Rich Dotson and Scott Nielsen to the Yankees for Dan Pasqua, Mark Salas and Steve Rosenberg.

DECEMBER 10   The White Sox trade Floyd Bannister and Dave Cochrane to the Royals for Melido Perez, Greg Hibbard, John Davis and Chuck Mount.

1988

Season in a Sentence

During another losing season, it appears as though the White Sox will leave Chicago for Florida when on June 30 the Illinois General Assembly narrowly passes a $150 million funding bill for a new stadium seconds ahead of a midnight deadline.

Finish • Won • Lost • Pct • GB

Fifth   71   90   .441   32.5

Manager

Jim Fregosi

Stats

Stats	WS	AL	Rank
Batting Avg:	.244	.259	13
On-Base Pct:	.303	.324	14
Slugging Pct:	.370	.391	12
Home Runs:	132		9
Stolen Bases:	98		8
ERA:	4.12	3.97	9
Fielding Avg:	.976	.981	14
Runs Scored:	631		13
Runs Allowed:	757		12

Starting Lineup

Carlton Fisk, c
Greg Walker, 1b
Fred Manrique, 2b
Steve Lyons, 3b
Ozzie Guillen, ss
Daryl Boston, lf-cf
Dave Gallagher, cf
Dan Pasqua, rf-lf
Harold Baines, dh
Ivan Calderon, rf
Gary Redus, lf
Donnie Hill, 2b
Kenny Williams, rf-3b

Pitchers

Jerry Reuss, sp
Melido Perez, sp
Dave LaPoint, sp
Jack McDowell, sp
Bobby Thigpen, rp
Ricky Horton, rp
Bill Long, rp-sp

Attendance

1,115,749 (13th in AL)

Club Leaders

Batting Avg:	Harold Baines	.277
On-Base Pct:	Harold Baines	.347
Slugging Pct:	Harold Baines	.411
Home Runs:	Dan Pasqua	20
RBIs:	Harold Baines	81
Runs:	Steve Lyons	59
	Dave Gallagher	59
Stolen Bases:	Gary Redus	26
Wins:	Jerry Reuss	13
Strikeouts:	Melido Perez	138
ERA:	Dave LaPoint	3.40
Saves:	Bobby Thigpen	34

FEBRUARY 9   The White Sox trade Jose DeLeon to the Cardinals for Lance Johnson and Ricky Horton.

The White Sox pulled off a tremendous deal, as Johnson was the club's starting center fielder from 1990 through 1995. He led the AL in triples four times and in hits once and twice batted over .300.

MARCH 30   The White Sox sign Jerry Reuss as a free agent following his release by the Angels.

Reuss came to the White Sox at the age of 38 with 198 lifetime wins, but over the previous two seasons he was only 6–16 with a 5.92 ERA. Reuss was invited to spring training as a non-roster player and made the club during a youth movement only because a couple of the young hurlers had to be placed on the disabled list with arm woes. Reuss gave the Sox a strong season in 1988, winning 13 and losing nine with an earned run average of 3.44. He led the team in victories, one of nine pitchers to lead in the category over an eight-year period. The nine were LaMarr Hoyt (1983), Tom Seaver (1984), Britt Burns (1985),

Joe Cowley (1986), Floyd Bannister (1987), Reuss (1988), Melido Perez (1989), and Jack McDowell and Greg Hibbard (tied in 1990).

APRIL 4   Trailing 4–3, the White Sox score five runs in the seventh inning and win 8–5 against the Angels before an Opening Day crowd of 35,899 at Comiskey Park. Ken Williams contributed a homer and a double and drove in three runs.

In a terribly ill-conceived move, the White Sox moved Williams from the outfield to third base in 1988. Williams had been one of the best defensive center fielders in the game as a rookie in 1987, but the Sox had a glut of outfielders and no third baseman, and Williams was designated to switch positions. He struggled mightily both offensively and defensively and was sent to the minors in July. Williams hit .159 in 220 at-bats and made 14 errors in 32 games at third. He was traded to the Tigers in March 1989.

APRIL 19   The White Sox smack five home runs during a 7–2 win over the Mariners in Seattle. Carlton Fisk hit two homers and Kenny Williams, Ivan Calderon and Harold Baines added one each.

APRIL 22   A two-run, walk-off homer in the 10th inning by Carlton Fisk beats the Athletics 7–5 at Comiskey Park. The Sox scored two runs in the ninth inning to tie the game.

APRIL 29   Coming into the game with an 0–21 record on the 1988 season, the Orioles beat the White Sox 9–0 at Comiskey Park. The 21 setbacks by the Baltimore club set an all-time major league record for losses at the start of a season and an American League mark for consecutive defeats at any point in a season.

MAY 9   Jerry Reuss earns his 200th career win with a 3–0 decision over the Orioles in Baltimore. He pitched 7²⁄₃ innings and was backed by 1¹⁄₃ innings of relief by Bobby Thigpen. Dan Pasqua drove in all three White Sox runs with a sacrifice fly in the second inning and a two-run homer in the fourth.

Reuss finished his career in 1990 with a record of 220–191.

MAY 15   Dave Gallagher's walk-off homer in the 11th inning beats the Blue Jays 6–5 at Comiskey Park. The White Sox led 3–1 before Toronto scored two times in the ninth and two more in the 10th. The Sox stayed alive with a pair of tallies in their half of the 10th.

Gallagher held a U.S. patent for a device called the Stride Tutor, which was an adjustable chained ankle bracelet that kept a batter from overstriding.

MAY 19   Cory Snyder of the Indians hits a walk-off homer in the ninth inning off Bobby Thigpen for the only run in a 1–0 loss in Cleveland.

MAY 31   Gary Redus hits a grand slam off Frank Tanana in the second inning of a 10–1 triumph over the Tigers in Detroit.

JUNE 1   In the first round of the amateur draft, the White Sox select third baseman Robin
              Ventura from Oklahoma State University. Other future major leaguers drafted and
              signed by the White Sox in 1988 were Stacy Jones (third round), Johnny Ruffin
              (fourth round), John Hudek (tenth round) and Derek Lee (42nd round).

              *Ventura was the only long-term success of the group, but his selection alone
              made it a successful draft. He had been named as the College Player of the
              Decade by* Baseball America *and was also the publication's third baseman on
              the All-Time College All-Star Team. Among Ventura's accomplishments at
              Oklahoma State were a 58-game hitting streak. During the summer of 1988, he
              played for the U.S. Olympic baseball team in Seoul and batted .409 in helping to
              win a gold medal. By 1990, he was the Sox starting third baseman and in 1992
              made the All-Star team. He played for the White Sox from 1989 through 1998,
              and on the all-time franchise lists he ranks fourth in walks (668), sixth in home
              runs (171), seventh in runs batted in (741), ninth in extra base hits (402) and
              10th in total bases (2,000).*

JUNE 4   Gary Redus hits his second grand slam in five days to cap a six-run ninth that lifts
              the White Sox to a 10–8 victory over the Rangers at Comiskey Park. Ivan Calderon
              led off the ninth with a home run. Greg Walker and Dave Gallagher followed with
              singles. After a walk to Donnie Hill, Mike Woodard contributed an RBI-single.
              Redus then cleared the bases with a walk-off grand slam off Dale Mohorcic.

JUNE 7   Trailing 4–3, the White Sox score seven runs in the seventh inning and hold on to
              defeat the Twins 10–8 at Comiskey Park.

JUNE 10   The White Sox register a 10-inning 1–0 decision over the Brewers at Comiskey
              Park. A walk-off single by Greg Walker sent home the lone run of the contest.
              Jack McDowell (nine innings) and Bill Long (one inning) combined on the shutout.

JUNE 20   A two-run, walk-off homer by Steve Lyons in the ninth beats the Royals 5–3 at
              Comiskey Park.

JUNE 26   Daryl Boston hits a grand slam off Jeff Russell in the sixth inning of a 7–5 win over
              the Rangers in Arlington.

JUNE 30   Just prior to a midnight deadline, Illinois legislators narrowly approve a proposal
              for a new state-financed stadium and lease deal that keeps the White Sox in Chicago.
              The measure cleared the Senate by a vote of 30–26 and the House by a 60–55
              margin. Legislators had been backed into a corner because the White Sox ownership
              had agreed three days earlier to accept a lucrative deal to move to a domed stadium
              in St. Petersburg, Florida. St. Petersburg had just begun building the stadium, which
              would later house the Devil Rays. Jerry Reinsdorf and Eddie Einhorn vowed not to
              leave the Windy City if lawmakers approved the deal. The money allowed for a new
              stadium to be built across the street from Comiskey Park.

              *The White Sox's existence on the South Side of Chicago appeared doomed when
              the day began. There was little optimism from legislators or the media who
              covered the story that the measure would pass. Some legislators were singing
              "Na-na-na-na, hey-hey-hey, goodbye," as the adjournment deadline approached.
              Opponents decried the plan to benefit the White Sox and considered funding*

The Bess Plan and the Second Comiskey Park

Once the White Sox received the state financing to build a new stadium on June 30, 1988, the next step was to decide upon the design of the club's new home. At the time, 18 of the 26 teams in Major League Baseball shared their stadium with a National Football League franchise. The Cubs, Red Sox, Tigers and White Sox played their games in ballparks built prior to World War I. Yankee Stadium originally opened in 1923 and underwent an almost complete renovation during the 1970s. The Rangers played in a former minor league park that was expanded when the club moved to Texas in 1972. The only two stadiums existing in 1988 that were built expressly for baseball in the previous 30 years and had never been converted to a multi-purpose facility were Dodger Stadium and Royals Stadium, which opened in 1962 and 1973, respectively. The White Sox decided to build a new Comiskey Park using Dodger Stadium and Royals Stadium as a model.

One of the proposals for the White Sox's new home was radically different. It was submitted by Chicago architect Philip Bess, who wanted to build a neighborhood ballpark on a smaller scale, similar to Fenway Park or Wrigley Field. Called Armour Field, Bess's design would have preserved the playing field and part of the grandstand of the old Comiskey Park as a new public park, which would include a diamond for use by high school and American Legion teams. Surrounding both the new park and the new ballpark would have been mixed-use commercial and residential loft structures. Parking garages capable of holding 6,000 cars were to be hidden behind row houses and would have provided most of the parking necessary for capacity crowds, with the rest scattered throughout the neighborhood within a five-minute walk. Bess had some support among Chicago city officials, but most rejected the notion. Armour Field remains one of the great "what-ifs" in Chicago history.

The new Comiskey Park opened on April 18, 1991. Unlike the Bess plan, it had little connection with the city or the surrounding neighborhood. The third-tier upper deck was an issue almost

immediately. It sat far from the playing field and was pitched at 35 degrees. The first row of seats was farther away than the last row at the first Comiskey. Sections had to be closed off when heavy winds whipping off Lake Michigan created potential safety problems.

No one has built another stadium like the new Comiskey. In 1992, a year after the White Sox played their first game at the stadium, Camden Yards in Baltimore opened to rave reviews and started an age in which baseball parks echoed the past. The second Comiskey Park had few such illusions, with the exception of the arched windows on the outside similar to those of the first Comiskey and the exploding scoreboard.

Nonetheless, the White Sox set attendance records when the stadium opened. With the help of a winning team, the Sox attracted 2,934,154, shattering the old mark of 2,136,988 set in 1984. The club exceeded 2.5 million in each of the first three years, for a total of 8,196,401. The best three-year total of old Comiskey was 5,939,697 from 1983 through 1985.

The Sox were on a pace to draw over 2.5 million again in 1994 when the players went on strike on August 12. When the athletes returned in 1995, club attendance dipped well below two million and plummeted to 1,338,851 in 1999. Lingering resentment over the strike, a succession of mediocre teams and concerns over the safety of the surrounding neighborhood were the major factors in the decline. The club didn't draw over two million again until the world championship year of 2005.

Efforts were made beginning in 2001 to make the new Comiskey, which became known as U.S. Cellular Field in 2003, more fan-friendly. With the changes at the stadium, another pennant-contending team and the euphoria over the city's first World Series win since 1917, the White Sox set another attendance record in 2006 with 2,957,414. It exceeded the figure of many franchises playing in the post-1991 "retro" parks, such as those of the Orioles, Indians, Rangers, Mariners, Pirates, Tigers, Rockies, Reds, Phillies and Padres.

for education and the state infrastructure to be of a greater concern. They also alleged that a new Comiskey Park would suffer from many of the same problems as the old one, since it would be built in the same neighborhood. In addition, a group was formed in Chicago to save Comiskey Park, affirming that it would be more cost-effective to rebuild the old ballpark. Others believed that the Sox would never be a success in a "Cubs town" and that it would be better just to see them leave Chicago. The uniqueness of Illinois politics came into play as well. Historically, legislators from Chicago, tucked in the northeast corner of the state, battled those from the small towns and farming communities in the rest of the state. The stadium issue was no different. "It's hard to assess the machinations of politics," said Paul Jensen, the White Sox's assistant vice president of public relations, "but I know that this vote was considered a political miracle." In the end, the 11th-hour strong-arm tactics and political maneuvering of Governor James Thompson, a native of the South Side of Chicago, swayed lawmakers, many at the last minute, to change their votes as the clock was ticking toward midnight. According to state law, that was the last moment in which a vote could be cast during that legislative session with a simple majority. Opponents claimed that the vote in the House took place some four minutes after midnight, but it stood nonetheless. A new Comiskey Park would open in 1991.

JULY 3

After the Yankees score in the top of the 10th inning, Dan Pasqua hits a two-run, walk-off homer in the bottom half to lift the White Sox to a 4–3 victory at Comiskey Park.

JULY 6

In a ceremony at home plate prior to a 4–1 win over the Orioles, Governor James Thompson signs the stadium bill into law at home plate at Comiskey Park (see June 30, 1988).

JULY 9

Dan Pasqua, Greg Walker and Daryl Boston hit consecutive homers in the fourth inning of an 8–7 win over the Red Sox in the first game of a double-header at Comiskey Park. All three homers were struck off Wes Gardner.

JULY 26

The White Sox edge the Mariners 1–0 in 11 innings at Comiskey Park. A bases-loaded walk to Ozzie Guillen by Mike Jackson scored the lone run. Jack McDowell (eight innings), Bobby Thigpen (two innings) and Ricky Horton (one inning) combined on the shutout.

JULY 30

The White Sox lose a 15–14 slugfest to the Angels at Comiskey Park. The Sox led 9–5 at the end of the third inning and fell behind 15–11 before mounting a fruitless three-run rally in the ninth.

Greg Walker was felled during batting practice by a viral infection on his brain. Trainer Herm Schneider saved Walker's life by forcing a pair of scissors into his mouth which prevented the Sox first baseman from swallowing his tongue. Walker had a second seizure in the hospital the following day. He didn't play for the remainder of the season. Walker's recovery was slow and painful, but he returned to play again in 1989.

AUGUST 8

Across town, the Cubs play their first night game at Wrigley Field, but the contest is halted by rain in the fourth inning with the Cubs leading the Phillies 3–1. The first official night game was played the following day, with the Cubs defeating the Mets 6–4.

AUGUST 13   The White Sox trade Dave LaPoint to the Pirates for Barry Jones.

AUGUST 19   In five at-bats, Carlton Fisk collects five hits, including his only triple of the 1988 season, but the White Sox lose 5–4 to the Tigers in Detroit.

On the same day, the White Sox traded Gary Redus to the Pirates for Mike Diaz.

SEPTEMBER 2   Three Venezuelans are starting infielders for the White Sox against the Indians in Cleveland. Carlos Martinez played third base, Ozzie Guillen at shortstop and Fred Manrique at second. It was Martinez's major league debut. The Sox lost 4–3.

On the same day, Eight Men Out *opened in theaters. Written and directed by John Sayles, the film was a meticulously detailed period piece about the infamous 1919 "Black Sox." Among the actors in the movie were Charlie Sheen (as Happy Felsch), John Cusack (as Buck Weaver) and David Strathairn (as Eddie Cicotte).*

SEPTEMBER 4   The White Sox score four runs in the ninth inning to win 5–2 over the Indians in the second game of a double-header in Cleveland. The big blow was a two-run double by Steve Lyons. The Sox lost the opener 3–2.

SEPTEMBER 25   The White Sox score four runs in the ninth inning to defeat the Royals 6–5 at Comiskey Park. The Chicago tallies in the ninth came on an RBI-double by Ozzie Guillen, a run-scoring ground out by Carlton Fisk and RBI-singles from Dave Gallagher and Harold Baines.

SEPTEMBER 27   Shawn Hillegas (six innings) and Tom McCarthy (three innings) combine on a two-hitter for a 3–2 win over the Rangers at Comiskey Park. The only Texas hits were a triple by Steve Buechele in the third inning and a homer by Kevin Reimer in the fourth.

OCTOBER 1   Melido Perez pitches a two-hitter to defeat the Royals 3–0 in Kansas City. The only hits off Perez were a single by Danny Tartabull in the fifth inning and a double by Kevin Seitzer in the sixth.

OCTOBER 7   The White Sox fire Jim Fregosi as manager. Larry Himes cited "philosophical differences" as reasons for the dismissal. Fregosi favored a "win now" approach to constructing the team by acquiring free agents and trading for veterans, while Himes preferred to build within the farm system.

NOVEMBER 3   The White Sox hire 46-year-old Jeff Torborg as manager.

Torborg was a catcher, mainly in a reserve role, with the Dodgers and Angels from 1964 through 1973. He previously managed the Indians from 1977 through 1979 to a 157–201 record, and then served as coach of the Yankees for 10 seasons. Torborg was 69–92 with the White Sox in 1989, but the club improved to 94–68 in 1990, earning him a clean sweep of the Manager of the Year Awards. Near the end of that season, Larry Himes was let go as general manager and was replaced by Ron Schueler. The Sox were still strong in 1991, with an 87–75 record, but Torborg and Schueler seldom saw eye to eye on issues involving the club. At the end of the season, Torborg took a job managing the New York Mets.

NOVEMBER 22   Two weeks after George Bush defeats Michael Dukakis in the presidential election, the White Sox sign Ron Kittle, most recently with the Indians, as a free agent.

Kittle returned to Chicago after playing for the White Sox from 1982 through 1986. In 1989 he was batting .302 with 11 homers in 51 games before he was shelved for the season with a back injury in June.

1989   Sox

Season in a Sentence

With a new manager, a new ballpark being constructed and a youth movement on the field, the White Sox lose 92 games and finish last in the AL in attendance.

Finish • Won • Lost • Pct • GB

Seventh   69   92   .429   29.5

Manager

Jeff Torborg

Stats

Stats	WS	AL	Rank
Batting Avg:	.271	.326	3
On-Base Pct:	.328	.326	6
Slugging Pct:	.383	.384	8
Home Runs:	94		14
Stolen Bases:	97		10
ERA:	4.23	3.88	11
Fielding Avg:	.975	.980	13
Runs Scored:	693		10
Runs Allowed:	750		12

Starting Lineup

Carlton Fisk, c
Greg Walker, 1b
Steve Lyons, 2b-1b
Carlos Martinez, 3b-1b
Ozzie Guillen, ss
Dan Pasqua, lf
Dave Gallagher, cf
Ivan Calderon, rf
Harold Baines, dh
Scott Fletcher, 2b
Daryl Boston, lf
Eddie Williams, 3b

Pitchers

Melido Perez, sp
Eric King, sp
Greg Hibbard, sp
Steve Rosenberg, sp
Jerry Reuss, sp
Rich Dotson, sp
Bobby Thigpen, rp
Donn Pall, rp
Shawn Hillegas, rp
Ken Patterson, rp
Bill Long, rp

Attendance

1,045,651 (14th in AL)

Club Leaders

Batting Avg:	Ivan Calderon	.286
On-Base Pct:	Ivan Calderon	.332
Slugging Pct:	Ivan Calderon	.437
Home Runs:	Ivan Calderon	14
RBIs:	Ivan Calderon	87
Runs:	Ivan Calderon	83
Stolen Bases:	Ozzie Guillen	36
Wins:	Melido Perez	11
Strikeouts:	Melido Perez	141
ERA:	Eric King	3.39
Saves:	Bobby Thigpen	34

MARCH 23   The White Sox trade Kenny Williams to the Tigers for Eric King.

APRIL 4   Eleven days after the Exxon Valdez spills oil into Alaska's Prince William Sound, the White Sox win 9–2 over the Angels in the season opener in Anaheim. Jerry Reuss pitched seven innings, allowing a run and two hits. He retired 17 straight batters between the first and seventh innings. Carlton Fisk and Harold Baines hit home runs and Eddie Williams contributed three hits, including a double.

APRIL 8   Ivan Calderon hits a grand slam off Rick Honeycutt in the sixth inning of a 7–4 win over the Athletics in Oakland.

APRIL 10   Facing Eric King, Ken Griffey Jr. hits his first major league homer during a 6–5 Mariners win over the White Sox in Seattle.

APRIL 11   The White Sox score three runs in the ninth inning to defeat the Mariners 8–6 in Seattle. Steve Lyons hit a two-run homer to give the Sox a 7–6 lead. An insurance run crossed the plate on a double by Eddie Williams and a single from Ron Karkovice.

APRIL 14   In the home opener, the White Sox lose 7–4 to the Athletics before 37,950 at Comiskey Park.

APRIL 22   Eric King pitches the White Sox to a 1–0 win over the Mariners at Comiskey Park. Ron Kittle drove in the lone run of the game with a single in the third inning.

APRIL 27   The White Sox edge the Red Sox 3–1 in 16 innings at Fenway Park. The contest lasted five hours and nine minutes. In the 16th, Ron Karkovice beat out a bunt, followed by a triple from Ozzie Guillen and a single by Dave Gallagher. Eric King (nine innings), Bobby Thigpen (three innings) and Donn Pall (four innings) pitched for Chicago.

MAY 6   The White Sox lose 5–2 to the Yankees in a game at Comiskey Park that was delayed for 29 minutes by snow. There were piles of snow in foul territory. The game-time temperature was 36 degrees.

MAY 7   Ground-breaking ceremonies take place for the new Comiskey Park. Mayor Richard M. Daley and Governor James Thompson were among the dignitaries taking part in the event.

MAY 10   The White Sox clobber the Brewers 12–2 in Milwaukee.

MAY 17   The White Sox score five runs in the ninth inning and beat the Tigers 10–7 in Detroit. The runs in the ninth scored on a two-run double by Carlos Martinez to tie the game 7–7 and a three-run two-bagger from Fred Manrique.

MAY 28   The White Sox participate in the last game at Exhibition Stadium in Toronto. George Bell hit a two-run, walk-off homer in the 10th inning to lift the Blue Jays to a 7–5 victory. The White Sox also played in the first game at Exhibition Stadium in 1977. The Blue Jays moved into SkyDome on June 5.

JUNE 3   The White Sox lose their 11th consecutive game at home, dropping a 5–4 decision to the Twins in the first game of a double-header at Comiskey Park. The Sox ended the skein with a 2–1 victory in the second tilt. It was the club's first win in Chicago since May 7.

JUNE 5   In the first round of the amateur draft, the White Sox select first baseman Frank Thomas from Auburn University. Three others who were drafted and signed by the White Sox in 1989 also reached the majors. They were Kevin Tolar (ninth round), Brian Keyser (19th round) and Joe Borowski (32nd round).

            It wasn't a deep draft by any means, but the selection of Thomas more than made up for it. Nicknamed "Big Hurt," he became the best offensive player to don a White Sox uniform since the days of Shoeless Joe Jackson. At Auburn, the imposing six-foot-five and 257-pound Thomas played tight end on the football team as a freshman. When the Sox chose him with the seventh overall pick in the 1989 draft, the club was widely ridiculed in the scouting community because few had him ranked that highly. Thomas made his debut with the Sox on August 2, 1990, and made an immediate impression, batting .330 with seven homers in 60 games as a rookie. He would hit over .300 in each of his first 11 big-league seasons, along with four seasons of 40 or more homers, 10 with at least 100 RBIs and nine with 100 or more runs scored. While with the White Sox, Thomas led the AL in both on-base percentage and walks four times, and in batting average, slugging percentage, doubles and runs scored once each. He won the MVP award in 1993. Playing with the Sox through 2005, Thomas shattered the club's record books. He ranks first all-time in home runs (448), first in runs batted in (1,465), first in runs scored (1,327), first in doubles (447), first in extra-base hits (906), first in slugging percentage (.568), first in on-base percentage (.427), first in walks (1,466), third in hits (2,136), third in games played (1,959), third in at-bats (6,956), sixth in singles (1,230) and ninth in batting average (.307). Thomas holds single-season records for highest slugging percentage (.729 in 1994), on-base percentage (.487 in 1994) and walks (138 in 1991).

JUNE 8   The White Sox hit four homers off Nolan Ryan but still lose 11–7 to the Rangers in Arlington. Harold Baines clubbed two of the home runs, with Ron Kittle and Ivan Calderon each hitting one.

JUNE 20   The White Sox down the Yankees 13–6 in New York. All 13 Chicago runs scored in the first five innings.

JUNE 23   Melido Perez strikes out 12 batters in 7²/₃ innings and is the winning pitcher in a 6–4 decision over the Brewers in the second game of a double-header at County Stadium. In the opener, the Sox took a 5–0 lead in the second inning before Milwaukee scored 17 unanswered runs for a 17–5 victory.

JUNE 29   The White Sox score seven runs in the sixth inning and win 12–5 over the Royals at Comiskey Park.

On the same day, the White Sox signed Rich Dotson following his release by the Yankees.

JULY 11   In the third inning of the All-Star Game, played at Anaheim Stadium, Harold Baines drives in a run with a single and later scores. The American League won 5–3.

The White Sox had a 32–56 record before the All-Star break and were 37–36 afterward.

JULY 16   Rich Dotson (7¹/₃ innings), Donn Pall (one inning) and Bobby Thigpen (two-thirds of an inning) combine on a two-hitter and a 2–0 win over the Brewers at County Stadium. The only Milwaukee hits were singles by Robin Yount in the sixth inning off Dotson and B. J. Surhoff in the ninth against Pall.

JULY 17   Carlton Fisk collects his 2,000th career hit during a 7–3 victory over the Yankees at Comiskey Park. The milestone was a single off Dave LaPoint.

JULY 21   Carlton Fisk homers off Eric Hetzel for the lone run in a 1–0 triumph over the Red Sox in Boston. Melido Perez (seven innings) and Bobby Thigpen (two innings) combined on the shutout.

JULY 22   The White Sox win their eighth straight game with a 10–6 decision over the Red Sox in Boston.

Earlier in the season, with the White Sox mired in last place, television announcer Tom Paciorek vowed to shave his head if the club won eight games in a row. Two days later, Paciorek received his buzz cut on the field at Comiskey Park during practice.

JULY 24   Both the starting pitcher and starting catcher for the White Sox against the Mariners at Comiskey Park are past their 40th birthday. Jerry Reuss, age 40, pitched six innings and was the winning pitcher. Carlton Fisk, age 41, hit a bases-loaded walk-off single in the ninth inning for a 5–4 victory.

Fisk hit .293 with 13 home runs in 1989.

JULY 29   The White Sox trade Harold Baines and Fred Manrique to the Rangers for Sammy Sosa, Scott Fletcher and Wilson Alvarez.

White Sox fans were outraged at the loss of fan-favorite Baines, but the Sox were in a youth movement and Baines was 30 years old. It would have been one of the greatest trades in White Sox history if the White Sox had hung on to Sosa instead of trading him to the Cubs (March 30, 1992).

JULY 30   The White Sox trade Jerry Reuss to the Brewers for Brian Drahman.

AUGUST 3   The White Sox trade Mark Davis to the Angels for Roberto Hernandez.

The Sox pulled off an excellent deal. Hernandez didn't play for the Sox until 1991, in part because of a life-threatening medical scare while in the minors. He began suffering from numbness in his pitching hand. Blood clots were discovered and doctors needed to transfer veins from his inner thigh to his right forearm. By 1992, Hernandez was the Sox closer and saved 161 games for the Sox before being traded in 1997. He is second all-time to Bobby Thigpen's club-record 201 saves.

AUGUST 5   The White Sox win their 13th consecutive game at home by beating the Tigers 7–6 at Comiskey Park. The streak started on July 1.

AUGUST 20   The White Sox announce the retirement of the number 3 worn by Harold Baines from the start of his career in 1980 until he was traded to the Rangers on July 29, 1989. Baines wore number 3 with the White Sox again as a player in 1996, 1997, 2000 and 2001 and as a coach since 2005.

AUGUST 27   Ron Karkovice clubs a grand slam off John Farrell in the third inning of a 9–3 win over the Indians in Cleveland.

AUGUST 29   The White Sox play at SkyDome in Toronto for the first time and lose 3–2 to the Blue Jays.

SEPTEMBER 1   Daryl Boston hits a grand slam off Bob Milacki in the first inning of a 10–1 victory over the Orioles at Comiskey Park.

SEPTEMBER 10   The White Sox score seven runs in the first inning and beat the Tigers 13–3 in Detroit. Steve Lyons hit a grand slam off Frank Williams in the eighth inning.

SEPTEMBER 12   The White Sox rout the Orioles 11–1 in Baltimore. Robin Ventura made his major league debut and collected a single in four at-bats along with a run scored and a run batted in.

SEPTEMBER 15   Melido Perez pitches a two-hitter to defeat the Angels 3–1 in the first game of a double-header at Comiskey Park. The only California hits were a single by Devon White in the sixth inning and a double by Brian Downing in the seventh. The Angels won the second contest 2–1.

               The White Sox finished last in the American League in attendance in 1989 by drawing only 1,045,651. It was the lowest by any Sox club in a non-strike season between 1976 and the present.

DECEMBER 5   Seven weeks after an earthquake strikes San Francisco during the World Series, the Royals sign Rich Dotson as a free agent.

THE STATE OF THE WHITE SOX

The White Sox began the decade with a surprising 94–68 team that finished second to the Athletics in the AL West. With a roster full of young, emerging stars, the Sox looked to a bright future that included World Series appearances. That never came to pass before the start of the new millennium, but the franchise had its moments during the 1990s.
The White Sox won a division title in 1993 and were in first place when the strike was declared in 1994. During the period from 1990 through 1997, the Sox had a better winning percentage (.538) than any other American League team, but they failed to reach the World Series or to post the best won-lost record in any single one of those years. Overall, the team was 816–735 during the '90s, a winning percentage of .526 that was the third-best in the AL behind only the Yankees and Indians. AL pennant-winners were the Athletics (1990), Twins (1991), Blue Jays (1992–93), Indians (1995 and 1997) and Yankees (1996, 1998 and 1999). During the years in which the Sox were in the AL West, they finished behind the Athletics in 1990, 1991 and 1992. Following the formation of the three-division format, the Indians won all five titles from 1995 through 1999.

THE BEST TEAM

The 1990 and 1993 clubs were both 94–68, but the 1990 outfit finished second while the 1993 team won the AL West title before losing to the Blue Jays in the ALCS.

THE WORST TEAM

The 1999 White Sox were 75–86. The team finished in second place in a weak division, 21½ games behind the Indians.

THE BEST MOMENT

Sparked by a three-run homer from Bo Jackson, the White Sox clinched the AL West title on September 27, 1993, with a 4–2 win over the Mariners at Comiskey Park.

THE WORST MOMENT

With the White Sox in first place, the 1994 season comes to an end on August 11 with a players' strike.

THE ALL-DECADE TEAM • YEARS WITH WS

Ron Karkovice, c	1986–97
Frank Thomas, 1b	1990–2005
Ray Durham, 2b	1995–2002
Robin Ventura, 3b	1989–98
Ozzie Guillen, ss	1995–97
Tim Raines, lf	1991–95
Lance Johnson, cf	1998–95
Dave Martinez, rf	1995–97
Dan Pasqua, dh	1998–94
Jack McDowell, p	1987–88, 1990–94
Alex Fernandez, p	1990–96
Wilson Alvarez, p	1991–97
Roberto Hernandez, p	1991–97

Guillen was also on the 1980s All-Decade Team. Thomas is almost a certainty to reach the Hall of Fame when he becomes eligible. Albert Belle (1997–98) was the third-best outfielder with the White Sox during the 1990s, but he played left field and ranks behind Raines. Finding a capable right fielder was a decade-long problem after the Sox traded Sammy Sosa in March 1992.

THE DECADE LEADERS

Batting Avg:	Frank Thomas	.320
On-Base Pct:	Frank Thomas	.440
Slugging Pct:	Frank Thomas	.573
Home Runs:	Frank Thomas	301
RBIs:	Frank Thomas	1,040
Runs:	Frank Thomas	968
Stolen Bases:	Lance Johnson	204
Wins:	Jack McDowell	83
Strikeouts:	Alex Fernandez	951
ERA:	Jack McDowell	3.50
Saves:	Roberto Hernandez	161

THE HOME FIELD

Old Comiskey Park celebrated its 80th anniversary on July 1, 1990. On September 30 of that year, the venerable old ballpark hosted its last game. At the time it closed, old Comiskey was the oldest major league ballpark in existence, a distinction it had held since 1971. It was also one of only four pre-1920 big-league ballparks in existence. The others were Fenway Park (1912), Tiger Stadium (1912) and Wrigley Field (1914). The new Comiskey Park opened on April 18, 1991, across 35th Street to the south of old Comiskey.

THE GAME YOU WISHED YOU HAD SEEN

The White Sox beat the Yankees 4–0 on July 1, 1990, without collecting a single hit off Andy Hawkins.

THE WAY THE GAME WAS PLAYED

Baseball experienced one of its most pivotal transitions during the 1990s, as offensive numbers soared to new heights. Fueled by expansion to 30 teams and newer ballparks with fences closer to home plate, the average number increased from 123 per team in 1989 to 188 per team in 1999, with a peak of 196 in 1996. Performance-enhancing drugs may have also been a factor in the home-run explosion. The average number of runs per game leaped from 8.6 in 1989 to 10.4 in 1999 with a high of 10.8 in 1996. The trend of the 1970s and 1980s toward artificial turf ended as every new ballpark that opened or was on the drawing board had a grass field. The "retro" look, beginning with Camden Yards in Baltimore in 1992, was the feature of most of the new facilities that tried to emulate the older, classic venues like Fenway Park. Four new teams were added in Miami, Denver, St. Petersburg and Phoenix. Beginning in 1994, there were three divisions in each league, adding a new tier of playoffs. Interleague play started in 1997, providing the White Sox with a chance to settle their intra-city rivalry with the Cubs on the field.

THE MANAGEMENT

Jerry Reinsdorf and Eddie Einhorn began their 10th year of ownership in 1990. On the organizational chart, Reinsdorf was listed as chairman and Einhorn as vice chairman. General managers were Larry Himes (1986–90) and Ron Schueler (1990–2000). Field managers were Jeff Torborg (1989–91), Gene Lamont (1992–95), Terry Bevington (1995–97) and Jerry Manuel (1998–2003).

THE BEST PLAYER MOVE

The best move was drafting Mark Buehrle in the 38th round of the 1998 amateur draft. The best trade brought Jon Garland from the Cubs for Matt Karchner in July 1998.

THE WORST PLAYER MOVE

The worst move was trading Sammy Sosa to the Cubs with Ken Patterson for George Bell in March 1992.

1990

Season in a Sentence

Expected to finish in last place again with a youthful roster in the final year at Comiskey Park, the White Sox stun everyone by winning 94 games.

Finish • Won • Lost • Pct • GB

Second   94   68   .580   9.0

Manager

Jeff Torborg

Stats

	WS	AL	Rank
Batting Avg:	.258	.259	10
On-Base Pct:	.320	.327	12
Slugging Pct:	.379	.388	10
Home Runs:	106		12 (tie)
Stolen Bases:	140		3
ERA:	3.61	3.91	2
Fielding Avg:	.980	.981	7
Runs Scored:	682		9
Runs Allowed:	633		2

Starting Lineup

Carlton Fisk, c
Carlos Martinez, 1b
Scott Fletcher, 2b
Robin Ventura, 3b
Ozzie Guillen, ss
Ivan Calderon, lf
Lance Johnson, cf
Sammy Sosa, rf
Dan Pasqua, dh-rf-lf
Ron Kittle, dh-1b
Frank Thomas, 1b

Pitchers

Greg Hibbard, sp
Jack McDowell, sp
Melido Perez, sp
Eric King, sp
Alex Fernandez, sp
Adam Peterson, sp-rp
Bobby Thigpen, rp
Barry Jones, rp
Scott Radinsky, rp
Donn Pall, rp
Ken Patterson, rp
Wayne Edwards, rp

Attendance

2,002,357 (ninth in AL)

Club Leaders

Batting Avg:	Carlton Fisk	.285
	Lance Johnson	.285
On-Base Pct:	Carlton Fisk	.378
Slugging Pct:	Carlton Fisk	.451
Home Runs:	Carlton Fisk	18
RBIs:	Ivan Calderon	74
Runs:	Ivan Calderon	85
Stolen Bases:	Lance Johnson	36
Wins:	Greg Hibbard	14
	Jack McDowell	14
Strikeouts:	Jack McDowell	165
ERA:	Greg Hibbard	3.16
Saves:	Bobby Thigpen	57

FEBRUARY 15   The owners lock the players out of spring training because of a lack of progress during negotiations for a new basic agreement.

MARCH 18   The dispute between the players and owners is resolved.

Spring training camps opened on March 20. The season, scheduled to open April 2, was delayed a week with the games to be made up on open dates, with double-headers and by extending the close of the campaign by three days. The Sox were scheduled to open against the Brewers in Chicago on April 2. The contest was moved to April 9, which was originally an open date.

APRIL 9   The White Sox open their final season at Comiskey Park with a 2–1 win over the Brewers before 40,008. A sacrifice fly by Scott Fletcher in the seventh inning broke a 1–1 tie. Barry Jones, with 1²/₃ innings of perfect relief, was the winning pitcher.

Ken Harrelson returned to the White Sox in 1990 as a television announcer, teaming with Tom Paciorek. The Sox also returned to WGN-TV in 1990.

APRIL 11   The White Sox game against the Brewers in Milwaukee is postponed by snow.

APRIL 23   Steve Lyons plays all nine positions during a 5–4 win over the Cubs during a charity exhibition game at Wrigley Field (see June 16, 1990).

APRIL 24   The Rangers score five runs in the ninth inning to stun the White Sox 5–4 in Arlington. The game ended on a one-out, two-run homer by Pete Incaviglia off Bobby Thigpen.

This was one of the rare lapses by Thigpen during the 1990 season. He established a major league record with 57 saves, shattering the previous mark of 46 set by Dave Righetti of the Yankees in 1986. Thigpen still holds the mark. The closest anyone has come to matching Thigpen is John Smoltz with the Braves in 2002 and Eric Gagne of the Dodgers in 2003. Both had 55. In addition to his 57 saves, Thigpen had a 1.83 ERA in 88²/₃ innings over 77 games. The Sox also set a still-standing club record for saves in a season with 68. The 11 saves by relievers other than Thigpen were recorded by Scott Radinsky (four), Wayne Edwards (two), Donn Pall (two), Ken Patterson (two) and Barry Jones (one).

APRIL 27   Greg Hibbard (eight innings) and Bobby Thigpen (one inning) combine on a two-hitter to defeat the Blue Jays 6–1 at Comiskey Park. The only Toronto hits were singles by Glenallen Hill and Junior Felix in the fifth inning.

APRIL 30   The White Sox trade Bill Long to the Cubs for Frank Campos.

MAY 22   Carlton Fisk squares off against Deion Sanders during a 5–2 loss to the Yankees in New York. In the fifth inning, Fisk yelled at Sanders for failing to hustle down the line on a pop-up to shortstop Ozzie Guillen. When Sanders batted in the sixth, a heated and animated discussion took place and the two were separated by umpire John Hirschbeck. Players from both benches and bullpens streamed onto the field and gathered near home plate, but no punches were thrown.

At 42, Fisk hit .285 with 18 homers in 1990.

MAY 23   Eric King (six innings), Donn Pall (two innings) and Bobby Thigpen (one inning) combine on a two-hitter to defeat the Orioles 6–3 at Memorial Stadium. The only Baltimore hits were a single by Cal Ripken Jr. and a homer from Joe Orsulak, both in the fourth inning.

Pall grew up as a White Sox fan in Chicago's south suburbs.

MAY 29   Both the White Sox and the Cubs play at home on the same night for the first time in history. The Cubs drew 28,925 for a 6–2 loss to the Giants at Wrigley Field, while the Sox attracted 15,353 for a 5–4 win over the Yankees at Comiskey Park.

JUNE 3   The White Sox play a scheduled Sunday night game at home for the first time and beat the Twins 5–2 at Comiskey Park. The game was part of ESPN's new Sunday Night Game of the Week package.

JUNE 4 | In the first round of the amateur draft, the White Sox select pitcher Alex Fernandez from Miami Dade South Community College.

Fernandez made his major league debut less than two months later, on August 2, at the age of 20. He remained a part of the starting rotation until 1996 and posted a 79–63 record for the Sox. It's possible that no club has ever made better first-round choices four years in a row than the bonanza reaped by the White Sox from 1987 through 1990, when the club selected Jack McDowell, Robin Ventura, Frank Thomas and Fernandez. The best player chosen by the White Sox in the 1990 draft was not Fernandez, however, but fifth-rounder Ray Durham, who starred for the Sox from 1995 through 2002. The 1990 draft is arguably the most productive draft in White Sox history. Other future major leaguers chosen and signed by the Sox that season included Bob Wickman (second round), Robert Ellis (third round), James Baldwin (fourth round), Jimmy Hurst (12th round), Rod Bolton (13th round) and Jason Bere (36th round).

JUNE 6 | Five runs in the first inning is enough to beat the Mariners 5–0 at Comiskey Park. Melido Perez pitched the shutout.

JUNE 13 | The White Sox score in seven of their nine turns at bat in defeating the Mariners 11–2 in Seattle. The Sox scored once in both the first and second innings, three times in the third, once each in the fourth and sixth, three more in the seventh and once in the ninth.

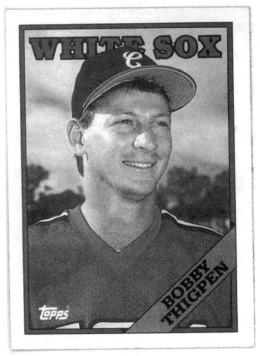

JUNE 16 | Steve Lyons pitches the eighth and ninth innings of a 12–3 loss to the Athletics at Comiskey Park. He allowed one run and two hits, walked four and struck out one. The pitching performance completed the circuit for Lyons, giving him appearances at all nine defensive positions in a regular season game during his big-league career. Counting games as a designated hitter, Lyons played 10 positions.

JUNE 23 | Jack McDowell angers the Athletics by hitting both Mark McGwire and Jose Canseco with pitches during a 5–3 White Sox win in Oakland.

One of the game's top closers in the late '80s and early '90s, Bobby Thigpen led the major leagues in 1990 with 57 saves.

JUNE 24 | Dan Pasqua hits a home run in the 10th inning off Dave Stewart to defeat the Athletics 3–2 in Oakland. Stewart and most everyone else in the ballpark thought the game was over in the ninth before Dave Henderson hit a two-out, two-run homer off Bobby Thigpen to tie the game 2–2. Stewart was in the clubhouse with his uniform shirt off and ice on his arm when Henderson homered. Stewart rushed back to the mound, only to surrender the homer to Pasqua, the first batter of the 10th.

After the game, Stewart had some pointed comments about the White Sox, who had surprised everyone with their winning ways during the early months of the 1990 season. Stewart called the Sox a "second-rate club" and suggested that Jack McDowell and Steve Lyons didn't possess enough talent to be in the majors. "Lyons is a borderline jerk," said the Oakland pitcher. "He's Mr. False Hustle." Stewart continued his tirade in the stunning postgame scene at his locker by saying "with the exception of Carlton Fisk, (Ron) Kittle and (Ivan) Calderon, maybe, nobody over there can hold my jock as far as I'm concerned. (see August 20, 1990)."

JUNE 26   The White Sox score two runs in the ninth inning to defeat the Angels 11–9 in Anaheim. The Sox took a 9–1 lead with seven runs in the sixth inning, but they allowed California to plate eight unanswered runs, including six in the seventh.

JUNE 27   The White Sox move into first place with a 5–2 win over the Angels in Anaheim.

JUNE 29   In the second inning at Comiskey Park, Ron Kittle hits a home run estimated at 454 feet off Chuck Cary for the lone run in a 1–0 win over the Yankees. Jack McDowell (seven innings), Barry Jones (one inning) and Bobby Thigpen (one inning) combined on the shutout. It was the White Sox's eighth win in a row and gave the club a 45–25 record on the 1990 season, after finishing 69–92 in 1989.

Kittle hit 176 career homers without a single grand slam.

JULY 1   In one of the most bizarre games in major league history, the White Sox fail to collect a hit off Andy Hawkins, yet defeat the Yankees 4–0 at Comiskey Park. The game was played on the 80th anniversary of the opening of the ballpark on July 1, 1910. The four White Sox runs scored in the eighth inning. Sammy Sosa hit a bouncer to third that Mike Blowers dropped, and Sosa was safe at first with a headfirst slide. The scoreboard flashed that it was a hit, causing players and coaches in the Yankees' dugout to wave wildly toward the press box. Official scorer Bob Rosenberg ruled the play an error. Hawkins then walked Ozzie Guillen and Lance Johnson to load the bases. Robin Ventura followed by hitting a fly ball to left field that should have ended the inning, but Jim Leyritz, circling near the warning track, dropped the ball after it fell into his glove and all three runners crossed the plate. Ventura wound up on second base and scored on another outfield error when right fielder Jesse Barfield dropped a fly hit by Ivan Calderon after Barfield lost the ball in the sun. Hawkins retired the first 14 White Sox batters of the game. Greg Hibbard was even better, retiring the first 16 batters to face him, and left the contest after allowing four hits in seven innings. Barry Jones and Scott Radinsky both hurled an inning to complete the shutout.

JULY 8   The White Sox drop out of first place with an 8–6 loss to the Orioles in 11 innings in Baltimore.

The Sox slowly fell farther and farther behind the Athletics, who had won the American League pennant in 1988 and 1989 and swept the Giants in the 1989 World Series. The Sox were three games behind Oakland at the end of July, 6½ out at the end of August and nine back at the close of the season.

JULY 11   The White Sox hold "Turn Back The Clock Day" at Comiskey Park. The Sox wore replica 1917 uniforms for the game against the Brewers and club management did its best to re-create that season, the most recent in which the Sox won a World Series at that time. An organ grinder and his monkey made their rounds at the ballpark and a barbershop quartet and a Dixieland band harmonized in the pathways under the stands. General admission seats sold for 50 cents. Popcorn went for a nickel a bag. Many of the men wore bow ties and straw hats, and the women donned ankle-length skirts with bonnets and parasols. Batters were announced by megaphone, even though Gene Honda's voice could not be heard into the far reaches of the crowd of 40,666. The electronic scoreboard was turned off. In its place was a hand-operated model that cost the team $12,000. The Brewers won 12–9 in 13 innings in a contest that lasted four hours and 44 minutes.

JULY 12   Melido Perez pitches a rain-shortened, six-inning no-hitter in defeating the Yankees 8–0 in New York. With one out in the top of the seventh, home plate umpire Tim Tschida ordered the field to be covered as the rainfall increased. The game was called after a 63-minute delay. Perez walked four batters and recorded eight strikeouts. The losing pitcher was Andy Hawkins, who lost a no-hitter to the White Sox 11 days earlier. Lance Johnson backed Perez by hitting his first career home run. Johnson also saved the no-hitter with a great catch against Alvaro Espinoza. Melido's brother Pascual, a pitcher for the Yankees, was in the opposition dugout. While with the Expos, Pascual pitched a rain-shortened, five-inning no-hitter on September 24, 1988.

         Johnson didn't hit another home run until 1992. Over his first 1,500 career at-bats, he hit only one home run.

JULY 14   Ron Karkovice hits a homer in the 10th inning to beat the Yankees 8–7 in New York. It was his fourth hit of the game. The White Sox led 7–0 in the second inning before allowing the Yanks back in the contest.

JULY 16   In a severe breach of decorum, Steve (Psycho) Lyons drops his pants during a 5–4 loss to the Tigers in Detroit. In the fifth inning, Lyons slid headfirst into first base for a single. Apparently forgetting where he was, Lyons unbuckled his belt, dropped his pants and bent over to brush away some dirt. Fans roared at the sight of Lyons wearing only an athletic supporter over long johns. Realizing the gaffe, an embarrassed Lyons quickly pulled his pants back up. At the end of the inning, women in the stands waved dollar bills at Lyons as he came to the dugout.

JULY 18   The White Sox score three runs in the ninth inning, capped by Sammy Sosa's two-run double, and defeat the Tigers 7–5 in Detroit.

JULY 28   Ozzie Guillen's two-run, walk-off single in the ninth inning beats the Brewers 5–4 at Comiskey Park. Ron Karkovice started the rally with a double.

JULY 29   The White Sox trade Ron Kittle to the Orioles for Phil Bradley.

AUGUST 2   On the day that Iraq invades Kuwait, and five days before Operation Desert Storm troops leave for Saudi Arabia to combat the incursion, Frank Thomas makes his major league debut during a 4–3 win over the Brewers in the first game of a double-header in Milwaukee. Batting fifth and playing first base, Thomas was hitless in four at-bats, but his slow hopper in the ninth inning scored the winning run from third base. The White Sox completed the sweep in the second tilt with a 4–2 victory.

> *Thomas was assigned number 35. It was previously worn by pitcher Jeff Bitteger in 1989.*

AUGUST 10   Ozzie Guillen and Craig Grebeck both hit their first homers of the 1990 season on consecutive pitches from Nolan Ryan in the second inning of a 5–1 win over the Rangers in the second game of a double-header at Comiskey Park. Neither Guillen nor Grebeck hit another homer for the rest of the 1990 season. Guillen had 516 at-bats in 1990, and Grebeck accumulated 119. The White Sox also won the opener 5–2.

> *The first Comiskey Park lasted for 80 years, but no one hit as many as 100 career home runs at the ballpark. The all-time leader was Carlton Fisk with 94. He hit 87 of those with the White Sox and seven as a member of the Red Sox. Second on the list of home run hitters at old Comiskey Park is Bill Melton with 91. Melton hit 90 of those 91 with the White Sox and one as an Angel.*

AUGUST 12   The White Sox finally call a game against the Rangers at Comiskey Park after a seven hour and 23-minute rain delay. The Sunday afternoon game was scheduled to start at 1:35 p.m. and was finally called at 8:58 p.m. The decision to postpone the game was in the hands of White Sox management. The home club has that power until the game starts, when the umpires take over. It was the Rangers' last scheduled game in Chicago during the 1990 season. The Sox wanted Texas to return to Comiskey on Thursday, August 16, an off day for both clubs, to make up the postponement, but the Rangers refused. This made the Sox management more determined than ever to play the game no matter how long the wait. Had the game not been played, it would have been made up in Arlington, costing the Sox a home game in a tight pennant race. More than 30,000 tickets were sold for the contest, but only about 200 remained when the rainout was announced. In the final hour before it was called, fans were invited to go to the concession stands for free sandwiches, coffee and soft drinks. The game was made up as part of a double-header in Texas on Friday, August 17.

AUGUST 17   Carlton Fisk breaks Johnny Bench's all-time record for home runs by a catcher during a 4–2 win over the Rangers in the second game of a double-header in Arlington. It was Fisk's 328th home run while playing as a catcher. The homer was also Fisk's 187th with the White Sox, breaking Harold Baines's club record. The milestone was struck off Charlie Hough. The first game resulted in a 13-inning, 1–0 loss in a contest marred by a fifth-inning brawl. Greg Hibbard hit Steve Buechele with a pitch, and Buechele responded by charging the mound and tackling Hibbard. Buechele was later suspended for three days for the incident.

> *Fisk finished his career with 376 home runs, 351 as a catcher. He held the major league record for most homers by a catcher until 2003, when he was passed by Mike Piazza. Fisk still holds the American League mark.*

AUGUST 20   The White Sox rout the Athletics 11–1 at Comiskey Park in a game of revenge following Dave Stewart's comments of June 24. Jack McDowell, who Stewart claimed didn't belong in the major leagues, hurled a three-hit complete game. Stewart was pummeled with six runs, five of them earned, in seven innings.

During the summer, the White Sox began taking down signs and photographs at Comiskey Park because fans were trying to steal them as souvenirs. By August, the upper deck of the new Comiskey Park had been built, and it dwarfed the old ballpark by comparison.

AUGUST 30   Ron Karkovice hits an inside-the-park grand slam in the fourth inning off David West for the only Chicago runs in a 4–3 victory over the Twins in Minneapolis. The drive went over the glove of shortstop Greg Gagne and rolled to the fence, where left fielder Dan Gladden had trouble fielding the ball.

SEPTEMBER 15   In a surprise move, the White Sox announce that by mutual agreement Larry Himes would not return as general manager for the 1991 season. "Himes was not fired," said Jerry Reinsdorf, "and he did not resign."

"Larry Himes took us from point A to point B," added Reinsdorf. "It's our opinion Larry Himes is not the best person to get us to point C: a world's championship." Despite building the White Sox from also-rans into a contending club, Himes was let go by the organization because of personality conflicts with White Sox officials and league executives. "There are an awful lot of general managers who wouldn't talk to Larry Himes because they didn't like him and didn't like his style," elaborated Reinsdorf. "This is a man with a severe personality problem." Reinsdorf was livid over the fact that the Athletics were able to acquire Harold Baines in a waiver deal with the Rangers on August 28 at a time when the White Sox were only six games behind the A's in the standings. The Sox had made a bid to re-acquire Baines, but Himes was unsuccessful in completing the deal. The departure of Himes took place near the end of an unexpected 94-win season with a roster of impressive young players acquired by Himes in four short years, including Lance Johnson (age 26), Greg Hibbard (25), Jack McDowell (24), Melido Perez (24), Robin Ventura (22), Frank Thomas (22), Sammy Sosa (21) and Alex Fernandez (20). Himes was later general manager with the Cubs from 1991 through 1994. Ron Schueler replaced Himes as the White Sox general manager. Schueler was a pitcher in the majors from 1972 through 1979, the last two of which were spent with the Sox. He then embarked on a front-office career, starting with the Athletics. As Oakland's vice president of baseball operations, he helped develop many of the players who played on the World Series clubs of 1988, 1989 and 1990, including Mark McGwire and Jose Canseco. Schueler was 42 when he was hired as general manager of the Sox and would remain with the organization in that capacity through the 2000 season.

SEPTEMBER 21   Commissioner Fay Vincent announces he will not allow 67-year-old Minnie Minoso to play in a major league game.

The White Sox had planned to use Minoso as a pinch-hitter or designated hitter during the final three games at Comiskey Park on September 28, 29 and 30. But Vincent squashed the idea, claiming it was "not in the best interests of baseball." Had Minoso played, he would have been the oldest player in big-league history. The oldest individual ever to play in a big-league contest is 59-year-old Satchel

Paige, who pitched in one game with the Charlie Finley-owned Kansas City Athletics in 1965, 12 years following Paige's previous appearance in the majors.

SEPTEMBER 22   The White Sox rout the Mariners 14–5 in Seattle. The Sox fell behind 5–2 in the second inning, then scored 12 unanswered runs.

SEPTEMBER 28   The White Sox display new uniforms during a 13–4 loss to the Mariners at Comiskey Park.

The Sox had designed new uniforms for the 1991 season, but rather than wait to unveil them, the club wore the duds during the final two series of the 1990 season against the Mariners in Chicago and the Red Sox in Boston. The home uniforms had black pinstripes, and a button-down front with the Old English "Sox" logo in black on the left front, outlined in silver. The uniform number was on the right front. The road jersey was gray with a script "Chicago" in black with a white outline. The cap was black with "Sox" in Old English in white. The Sox also had an alternative black shirt with "Sox" in white outlined in silver, which was worn both at home and on the road. The change led to the team slogan, "Good Guys Wear Black." The new uniforms were an homage to those worn by the club during the 1950s and 1960s. The Sox had changed uniform schemes and colors frequently during the 1970s and 1980s, but the ones worn for the first time on September 28, 1990, had staying power. They have been essentially unchanged since then.

SEPTEMBER 30   The White Sox play the final game at Comiskey Park and win 2–1 win over the Mariners in the closing act before 42,849 fans. Bobby Thigpen was on the mound at the end of the game and induced Harold Reynolds to ground to second baseman Scott Fletcher for the final out, earning Thigpen his 57th save of the 1990 season. Mayor Richard M. Daley threw out the first pitch. Among those in attendance were Goldie Hawn, Kurt Russell and Ron Howard, who were in town to film *Backdraft*. Extra security was on hand and Chicago's mounted police ringed the field when the game was over, but there was none of the vandalism the club had feared. The game pushed the White Sox's final attendance for the season to 2,002,359. It was only the third time that the Sox drew over two million in a season.

The White Sox final won-lost record at the ballpark was 3,024–2,926.

DECEMBER 4   The White Sox trade Eric King and Shawn Hillegas to the Indians for Cory Snyder and Lindsay Foster.

DECEMBER 20   The White Sox sign Charlie Hough, most recently with the Rangers, as a free agent.

Hough was 42 years old when signed by the White Sox. He pitched two seasons with the club and had a 15–22 record.

DECEMBER 23   The White Sox trade Ivan Calderon and Barry Jones to the Expos for Tim Raines, Jeff Carter and Mario Brito.

This proved to be the best deal completed by the White Sox during the 1990s, as Raines was the starting left fielder for five seasons.

1991

Season in a Sentence

The opening of a new Comiskey Park and another second-place finish helps the White Sox shatter all previous club attendance records.

Finish • Won • Lost • Pct • GB

Second   87   75   .537   8.0

Manager

Jeff Torborg

Stats

	WS	AL	Rank
Batting Avg:	.262	.260	7
On-Base Pct:	.336	.329	5
Slugging Pct:	.391	.395	9
Home Runs:	139		7
Stolen Bases:	134		3
ERA:	3.79	4.10	4
Fielding Avg:	.982	.981	7
Runs Scored:	758		6
Runs Allowed:	681		5

Starting Lineup

Carlton Fisk, c
Dan Pasqua, 1b-rf
Scott Fletcher, 2b
Robin Ventura, 3b
Ozzie Guillen, ss
Tim Raines, lf
Lance Johnson, cf
Sammy Sosa, rf
Frank Thomas, dh-1b
Joey Cora, 2b
Craig Grebeck, 3b-2b-ss

Pitchers

Jack McDowell, sp
Greg Hibbard, sp
Charlie Hough, sp
Alex Fernandez, sp
Bobby Thigpen, rp
Scott Radinsky, rp
Donn Pall, rp
Melido Perez, rp
Ken Patterson, rp

Attendance

2,934,154 (second in AL)

Club Leaders

Batting Avg:	Frank Thomas	.318
On-Base Pct:	Frank Thomas	.453
Slugging Pct:	Frank Thomas	.553
Home Runs:	Frank Thomas	32
RBIs:	Frank Thomas	109
Runs:	Frank Thomas	104
Stolen Bases:	Tim Raines	51
Wins:	Jack McDowell	17
Strikeouts:	Jack McDowell	191
ERA:	Jack McDowell	3.41
Saves:	Bobby Thigpen	30

MARCH 31   Two months after the United States and its allies attack Iraq to start the Persian Gulf War, the White Sox trade Adam Peterson and Steve Rosenberg to the Padres for Joey Cora, Warren Newson and Kevin Garner.

APRIL 3   Five weeks after President George Bush orders a cease fire to end the Persian Gulf War against Iraq, the White Sox sign Bo Jackson to a contract.

At the time, 28-year-old Vincent (Bo) Jackson was one of the most celebrated athletes in the world. He won the Heisman Trophy in 1985 in addition to starring as a baseball player at Auburn, then embarked on a career in both professional baseball and football. In baseball, Jackson reached the majors with the Royals in 1985. He played in the All-Star Game in 1989 and hit a lead-off homer. In 1990, Bo batted .272 with 28 homers for Kansas City. Jackson played for the Raiders from 1987 through 1990, gaining 2,872 yards in 515 attempts, for an average of 5.4 yards per carry, and earned a Pro Bowl berth. He is the only athlete ever to play in an All-Star Game in two sports. Even casual sports fans knew Jackson through his "Bo Knows" commercials for Nike. Unfortunately, he suffered a severe hip injury on the football field during a playoff game against the Bengals in January 1991. The Royals believed that Jackson's athletic career was over and released him on March 18. The Sox were willing to take a chance on Jackson, however. Throughout the 1991 season, there were almost daily updates of Jackson's medical condition and rehabilitation until he made his debut with the White Sox in September (see September 2, 1991).

APRIL 8   The White Sox win the season opener 9–1 over the Orioles in Baltimore. Sammy Sosa clubbed two homers and a single, drove in five runs and scored four. He was the first Sox hitter to homer twice on Opening Day since Minnie Minoso in 1960. Jack McDowell pitched a four-hit complete game.

McDowell was the White Sox's sixth different Opening Day starting pitcher in six years, following Tom Seaver (1986), Rich Dotson (1987), Ricky Horton (1988), Jerry Reuss (1989) and Melido Perez (1990).

APRIL 10   Scott Fletcher drives in both Chicago runs with a double in the sixth inning for a 2–0 win over the Orioles in Baltimore. Greg Hibbard (eight innings) and Bobby Thigpen (one inning) combined on the shutout.

APRIL 13   Jack McDowell pitches a two-hitter and defeats the Tigers 4–1 in Detroit. The only two hits off McDowell were a home run by Tony Phillips leading off the first inning and a double in the third by Dave Bergman.

The White Sox allowed only three runs in the first four games of the season.

APRIL 16   The White Sox run their 1991 season record to 6–0 with a 4–3 triumph over the Yankees in 10 innings in New York. Robin Ventura drove in the winning run with a double.

After winning their first six games, the Sox lost their next two by the combined score of 26–1.

APRIL 18   The White Sox open new Comiskey Park with a 16–0 loss to the Tigers before 42,191. The Tigers scored six runs in the third inning off Jack McDowell and 10 in the fourth against Brian Drahman and Ken Patterson. Rob Deer hit two home runs and Tony Phillips and Cecil Fielder one each. Phillips was also the first batter of the game and flied out to Cory Snyder. Fielder's homer was the first at the new ballpark. Frank Tanana pitched the complete-game shutout. The Oak Ridge Boys sang the national anthem. Among the dignitaries were Mayor Richard M. Daley, Illinois governor Jim Edgar, Vice President Dan Quayle, Defense Secretary and future Vice President Dick Cheney, and Major League Baseball Commissioner Fay Vincent. Former Illinois Governor James Thompson, whose efforts got the stadium built (see June 30, 1988), threw out the ceremonial first pitch.

The new Comiskey Park was the first new sports facility in Chicago in over 60 years. At the time, the Cubs were playing in Wrigley Field (opened in 1914), the Bears in Soldier Field (1925) and the Bulls in Chicago Stadium (1929). The field dimensions when the ballpark opened were 347 feet down the foul lines and 400 feet to center field.

APRIL 21   After two losses, the White Sox win for the first time at new Comiskey Park, beating the Tigers 5–4 with two runs in the ninth inning. Lance Johnson drove in the game-winner with a single.

APRIL 22 Frank Thomas becomes the first White Sox player to homer at new Comiskey Park during an 8–7 victory over the Orioles.

In his first full season in the majors, Thomas led the AL in on-base percentage (.453) and walks (138). The walks figure is a White Sox single-season record. Thomas also hit 32 homers, accumulated 109 RBIs, scored 104 runs and batted .318.

APRIL 27 The White Sox collect 20 hits and beat the Yankees 14–9 at Comiskey Park. The Yanks scored four runs in the first inning. The Sox broke a 7–7 tie with four tallies in the fourth.

Demolition of the original Comiskey Park took place during the season. It started in the right-field corner. The last portion to come down was the center-field bleachers and the exploding scoreboard. The site of the old park was turned into a parking lot for the new one. The location of home plate at the first Comiskey was marked by a marble plaque. The foul lines were painted on the parking lot.

MAY 1 The White Sox lose 10–9 to the Brewers in a 19-inning marathon at County Stadium. Willie Randolph drove in the winning run with a two-out single off Wayne Edwards. The Sox led 5–0 before Milwaukee scored six times in the fifth. Chicago tied the game with a tally in the seventh. The Pale Hose took a 9–6 lead in the 15th, only to have the Brewers tie the contest in their half. The game lasted six hours and five minutes.

MAY 7 Sammy Sosa hits a homer in the 12th inning to beat the Brewers 2–1 at Comiskey Park.

MAY 8 Ozzie Guillen hits a walk-off sacrifice fly in the ninth inning to beat the Brewers 2–1 at Comiskey Park. It was the second day in a row that the White Sox won 2–1 in their final turn at bat.

MAY 10 Sammy Sosa hits a 12th-inning homer for the second time in four days. The two-run blast beat the Blue Jays 5–3 at SkyDome. Toronto tied the game in the ninth and 11th innings with a pair of solo homers by Roberto Alomar.

MAY 13 The White Sox beat the Red Sox 4–3 in Boston. Matt Merullo tied the game with a pinch-hit homer off Roger Clemens with two out in the ninth inning. Ron Karkovice drove in the winning run with a single in the 10th inning.

Merullo's grandfather Lennie played for the Cubs from 1941 through 1947.

MAY 19 Mark Whiten of the Blue Jays punches Jack McDowell in the face during the fifth inning of a 5–4 White Sox win at Comiskey Park. Whiten charged the mound after McDowell zipped a pitch behind him about waist-high. Whiten struck the Sox pitcher with a roundhouse right just below the right eye. Whiten and McDowell were both ejected.

MAY 23 The White Sox rout the Athletics 11–1 in Oakland.

MAY 28
The White Sox score two runs in the ninth inning to beat the Angels 6–5 at Comiskey Park. Ozzie Guillen doubled in a run and scored on a single by Tim Raines. In the eighth, Raines hit a two-run double to pull the Sox within a run.

JUNE 2
A brawl interrupts a 4–3 win over the Athletics at Comiskey Park. The incident stemmed from a pitch from Bobby Thigpen that struck Terry Steinbach in the head. During the skirmish that followed, Oakland manager Tony LaRussa shouted at Jeff Torborg, and LaRussa was ejected for throwing a bat at the screen behind home plate.

JUNE 3
In the first round of the amateur draft, the White Sox select pitcher Scott Ruffcorn from Baylor University.

Ruffcorn looked like a great prospect after putting up sterling numbers in the minor leagues. At Class AAA Nashville in 1994, Ruffcorn was 15–3 with a 2.72 ERA and a 144–40 strikeout-to-walk ratio in 166 innings. But Ruffcorn seemed intimidated by big-league hitters and was roughed up frequently in the majors while compiling a career record of 0–8 with an ERA of 8.57 in 30 games over five seasons, four of them with the White Sox. In 70⅓ innings, Ruffcorn walked an astonishing 70 batters while striking out 46. Other future major leaguers drafted and signed by the White Sox in 1991 were Larry Thomas (second round), Mike Robertson (third round), Brian Boehringer (fourth round), Alan Levine (11th round), Doug Brady (12th round), Mike Heathcott (13th round), Mike Cameron (18th round) and Mike Bertotti (31st round). Among the draftees, only Cameron had a successful big-league career.

JUNE 6
Tim Raines collects four hits and scores the winning run in the 10th inning on a suicide squeeze by Robin Ventura to lead the White Sox to a 2–1 win over the Indians in Cleveland.

JUNE 7
Tim Raines scores the only two runs of a 2–0 win over the Royals in Kansas City. Charlie Hough (7⅔ innings) and Scott Radinsky (1⅓ innings) combined on the shutout.

Radinsky was one of two 1991 White Sox pitchers who played in rock bands. Jack McDowell was the lead singer and guitarist for "V.I.E.W." while Radinsky was the drummer for "Scared Straight."

JUNE 8
The White Sox rout the Royals 14–7 in Kansas City.

JUNE 9
Jack McDowell retires the first 18 batters to face him and finishes with a four-hitter in beating the Royals 8–2 in Kansas City. Gary Thurman broke up McDowell's no-hit bid with a single leading off the seventh.

JUNE 12
On the day the Bulls win their first NBA championship in a series with the Lakers, Charlie Hough pitches a two-hitter but loses 4–2 to the Rangers in Arlington. Ruben Sierra broke the game open with a bases-loaded triple in the third inning.

During his two years with the White Sox (1991–92), Hough pitched 58 games at the ages of 43 and 44, but he was never teamed with Carlton Fisk, who was 10 days older than Hough. If they had been the battery just once in 1992, they would have been the only pitcher-catcher combo in major league history in which each was at least 44 years old.

JUNE 18   With the White Sox trailing 4–2 in the sixth inning, Robin Ventura smacks a grand slam off Tom Candiotti, leading to a 6–5 victory over the Indians at Comiskey Park.

JUNE 23   After the Rangers score two runs in the 10th inning, the White Sox rally for three in their half to win 6–5 at Comiskey Park. Warren Newson drove in the tying run with a single and scored the game-winner on a wild pitch. Two days earlier, Newson had been sent to the minors, but he was recalled the following day after Joey Cora went on the disabled list.

JUNE 24   Frank Thomas hits a grand slam off Mike Jackson in the eighth inning of a 6–2 win over the Mariners at Comiskey Park.

JUNE 25   Jack McDowell holds the Mariners hitless for 7⅓ innings and finishes with a three-hitter and a 4–0 win at Comiskey Park. Scott Bradley collected Seattle's first hit with a single to left field.

JULY 1   Carlton Fisk hits a homer in the 10th to beat the Twins 5–4 in Minneapolis.

Fisk hit 68 career homers after his 40th birthday, which was the all-time record until Barry Bonds passed him in 2007.

JULY 12   The White Sox overcome a five-run deficit to beat the Brewers 8–6 in Milwaukee. The Sox scored four runs in the sixth inning and four in the ninth.

JULY 14   Jack McDowell pitches a one-hitter in a 15–1 thrashing of the Brewers at County Stadium. The only Milwaukee hit was a homer by Paul Molitor leading off the first inning.

On the same day, the White Sox traded Cory Snyder to the Blue Jays for Shawn Jeter.

JULY 19   Robin Ventura drives in six runs on two homers and two doubles in a 14–3 pounding of the Brewers at Comiskey Park. Ventura hit a solo homer in the first inning and a two-run blast in the second, both off Don August. Ventura added a two-run double in the fourth facing John Machado and a run-scoring double in the sixth against Darren Holmes. The four extra-base hits tied a White Sox club record.

JULY 20   Robin Ventura is the hero for the second day in a row with a walk-off homer in the 10th inning that defeats the Brewers 7–6 at Comiskey Park.

JULY 27   The White Sox win 10–8 in 14 innings over the Red Sox in the first game of a double-header in Boston. Dan Pasqua broke the tie in the 14th with a two-run single. The White Sox also won the second tilt 7–4.

JULY 31   Robin Ventura hits a two-out, walk-off grand slam off Goose Gossage in the ninth inning to down the Rangers 10–8 at Comiskey Park. It was Ventura's second homer and fourth hit of the game. The Sox loaded the bases in the ninth on a walk to Craig Grebeck, a single by Ron Karkovice and a walk to Tim Raines.

AUGUST 1   The White Sox extend their winning streak to eight games with a 13–2 rout of the Rangers at Comiskey Park.

AUGUST 4   Frank Thomas hits a homer off Mike Mussina in the sixth inning for the lone run of a 1–0 win over the Orioles at Comiskey Park. It was Mussina's major league debut. Charlie Hough pitched the shutout.

             At 43, Hough is the oldest pitcher to White Sox history to hurl a shutout.

AUGUST 6   The Yankees score five runs in the top of the first inning, but the White Sox recover and win 14–5 at Comiskey Park. The Sox tied the game 5–5 with five tallies in the fourth and, after building an 8–5 lead, broke it open with six in the eighth.

AUGUST 11   Wilson Alvarez pitches one of the most improbable no-hitters in major league history, beating the Orioles 7–0 in Baltimore. It was only his second appearance in a big-league game and his first with the White Sox. Alvarez made his big-league debut on July 24, 1989, at the age of 19 and failed to retire any of the five batters he faced. Alvarez was quickly sent back to the minors and five days later was traded to the White Sox. He spent more than two years in the Sox minor league system before being recalled from Class AA Birmingham the day before his no-hitter. Alvarez received some help from official scorer Phil Wood. In the seventh inning, Cal Ripken bounced a dribbler in front of the plate that catcher Ron Karkovice grabbed and threw wildly to first as Ripken arrived. After watching several replays, Wood ruled the play an error. Center fielder Lance Johnson helped preserve the no-hitter with a diving catch inches off the ground in the eighth. In the ninth, Alvarez retired Mike Devereaux on a routine fly and Juan Bell on a strikeout before walking Cal Ripken on four pitches and Dwight Evans on five throws. Alvarez recorded the final out by fanning Randy Milligan on an 0–2 pitch. The no-hit gem included seven strikeouts and five walks.

AUGUST 12   The White Sox play at Memorial Stadium in Baltimore for the last time and lose 5–4 in 11 innings.

             The loss began a stretch of 15 losses in 17 games that knocked the White Sox out of the pennant race. The Sox were 22–25 on June 3, then won 43 of their next 63 games to pull within one game of the division-leading Twins.

AUGUST 21   The White Sox club five home runs but lose 12–9 to the Tigers in Detroit. Frank Thomas and Robin Ventura each hit two homers, with Warren Newson adding one.

AUGUST 25   Swarms of flying insects repeatedly interrupt a 3–0 loss to the Indians in Cleveland. Batters continually stepped out of the box and pitchers walked off the mound to clear the tiny bugs from their eyes.

AUGUST 26   Bret Saberhagen of the Royals no-hits the White Sox and wins 7–0 in Kansas City.

SEPTEMBER 2 Bo Jackson plays his first game for the White Sox. In the lineup as a designated hitter, he was hitless in three at-bats, but he collected a sacrifice fly during a 5–1 win over the Royals at Comiskey Park. The Royals had released Jackson in March, believing that his injured hip would never allow him to play again.

SEPTEMBER 3   Making his major league debut, White Sox pitcher Tom Drees gives up a home run to Danny Tartabull, the first batter he faces, during an 8–0 loss to the Royals at Comiskey Park.

Drees pitched in only four major league games, compiled an ERA of 12.27 and surrendered four homers in 7⅓ innings.

SEPTEMBER 5   The White Sox erupt for 10 runs in the fourth inning and rout the Royals 11–2 at Comiskey Park. Those driving in runs in the big inning were Ozzie Guillen (four on a grand slam off Storm Davis), Bo Jackson (two), Robin Ventura (one), Warren Newson (one), Craig Grebeck (one) and Ron Karkovice (one). Scoring runs were Grebeck, with two and one each from Tim Raines, Newson, Dan Pasqua, Jackson, Lance Johnson, Karkovice, Guillen and Ventura.

SEPTEMBER 6   The White Sox defeat the Rangers 11–6 in Arlington.

SEPTEMBER 7   The White Sox score 11 runs for the third consecutive day and win 11–6 over the Rangers in Arlington for the second day in a row. The Sox scored seven runs in the second inning.

SEPTEMBER 15   Craig Grebeck hits a grand slam off Kyle Abbott in the third inning of a 9–2 win over the Angels in Anaheim.

On the way from Southern California to Chicago, the Air America West Boeing 737 carrying the White Sox lost power in one of two engines and made an unscheduled stop in Des Moines. Another plane was dispatched from Chicago to pick up the team.

SEPTEMBER 17   Bo Jackson hits a home run off Ron Darling in the seventh inning for the lone run of a 1–0 victory over the Athletics at Comiskey Park. It was one of only two Chicago hits. Greg Hibbard (7⅔ innings), Melido Perez (one-third of an inning) and Bobby Thigpen (one inning) combined on the shutout.

During the 1991 season, Jackson batted .217 with two homers in 69 at-bats. His hip condition continued to worsen, however, and Jackson had hip replacement surgery in April 1992. Despite the artificial hip, Jackson wasn't finished. He returned to baseball in 1993 (see April 9, 1993).

SEPTEMBER 24   The only hit off Scott Erickson is a homer by Dan Pasqua in a 9–2 loss to the Twins in Minneapolis.

SEPTEMBER 29   Charlie Hough (eight innings) and Scott Radinsky (one inning) combine on a two-hitter, but the White Sox lose 2–1 to the Mariners at Comiskey Park.

OCTOBER 3   The White Sox win twice in extra innings against the Twins at Comiskey Park. In the opener, the Sox scored two runs in the ninth inning and once in the 10th to win 3–2. Warren Newson drove in the winning run with a single. The second tilt was a 13–12 slugfest pulled out by the Sox in the 12th. Chicago trailed 6–1, then rallied to lead 12–8, only to have the Twins score four times in the ninth to tie the contest 12–12. Carlton Fisk drove in six runs, including a grand slam in the seventh off Steve Bedrosian. Robin Ventura drove in the winning run with a sacrifice fly.

OCTOBER 10   Jeff Torborg leaves the White Sox to become manager of the Mets.

Torborg said he left Chicago to be closer to his New Jersey home, but he had seldom been in agreement with the policies of Jerry Reinsdorf and general manager Ron Schueler. The Sox did little to keep Torborg within the organization, even though he helped lift the White Sox from one of the worst teams in the majors to consistent winners with a 94–68 record in 1990 and 87–75 in 1991. Torborg managed the Mets in 1992 and 1993, the Expos in 2001 and the Marlins in 2002 and 2003, but he never guided another club to a winning record.

NOVEMBER 26   Gene Lamont becomes manager of the White Sox.

Lamont had been the third-base coach with the Pirates the previous six seasons leading up to his appointment as manager of the Sox. Under the easy-going Lamont, the club was 86–76 in 1992, 94–68 with a division title in 1993 and 67–46 in the strike-shortened campaign of 1994. An 11–20 start in 1995 led to his dismissal, however.

DECEMBER 28   The White Sox sign Kirk McCaskill, most recently with the Angels, as a free agent.

1992   Sox

Season in a Sentence

The new management team of Ron Schueler and Gene Lamont trades promising youngsters, including Sammy Sosa, for useless veterans and the White Sox continue to tread water on the fringes of pennant contention.

Finish • Won • Lost • Pct • GB

Third   86   76   .531   10.0

Manager

Gene Lamont

Stats

	WS	AL	Rank
Batting Avg:	.261	.259	6
On-Base Pct:	.336	.328	5
Slugging Pct:	.383	.385	9
Home Runs:	110		9
Stolen Bases:	160		2 (tie)
ERA:	3.84	3.95	7
Fielding Avg:	.979	.981	9
Runs Scored:	738		6
Runs Allowed:	690		9

Starting Lineup

Ron Karkovice, c
Frank Thomas, 1b
Steve Sax, 2b
Robin Ventura, 3b
Craig Grebeck, ss
Tim Raines, lf
Lance Johnson, cf
Shawn Abner, rf
George Bell, dh
Dan Pasqua, rf

Pitchers

Jack McDowell, sp
Kirk McCaskill, sp
Greg Hibbard, sp
Alex Fernandez, sp
Charlie Hough, sp
Bobby Thigpen, rp
Scott Radinsky, rp
Roberto Hernandez, rp
Terry Leach, rp

Attendance

2,618,156 (third in AL)

Club Leaders

Batting Avg:	Frank Thomas	.323
On-Base Pct:	Frank Thomas	.439
Slugging Pct:	Frank Thomas	.536
Home Runs:	George Bell	25
RBIs:	Frank Thomas	115
Runs:	Frank Thomas	108
Stolen Bases:	Tim Raines	45
Wins:	Jack McDowell	20
Strikeouts:	Jack McDowell	178
ERA:	Jack McDowell	3.18
Saves:	Bobby Thigpen	22

JANUARY 10   The White Sox trade Melido Perez, Bob Wickman and Domingo Jean to the Yankees for Steve Sax.

This was not an inspired deal, as Sax hit just .236 and led all major league second basemen in errors in his lone season as a White Sox regular. He was so abysmal defensively that the Sox moved Sax to left field in 1993. Perez gave the Yankees a couple of good seasons and Wickman was still active in the majors in 2008.

MARCH 30   The White Sox trade Sammy Sosa and Ken Patterson to the Cubs for George Bell.

This rates as the worst trade in White Sox history. The second-worst deal ever executed by the franchise is debatable, but no matter which transaction one chooses it ranks a distant second to letting Sosa out of the organization. Sosa was just starting his fourth season in the majors and had shown flashes of the brilliance that would make him a superstar, although he was extremely erratic. He played in 327 big-league games with the Rangers in 1989 and the Sox in 1990 and 1991. In 1,031 at-bats over those three seasons, Sosa hit 29 homers and stole 52 bases, with a batting average of only .227. His strike-zone judgment was abysmal, with 295 strikeouts and only 58 walks. On defense, Sammy was the American League leader in errors by an outfielder in 1990. Sosa also seemed to be regressing in his development and had such a miserable year in 1991 that there were fears his career was in an irreversible freefall. He batted only .203 in 116 games that season with a 98–14 strikeout-to-walk ratio. In July, Sosa was sent to the Sox's Triple-A affiliate in Vancouver and didn't exactly tear up the Pacific Coast League, with a .267 average and three homers in 116 at-bats. But he was only 22 years old in 1991. The White Sox felt they were a power hitter away from winning a pennant in 1992, and they couldn't wait for Sosa to develop. White Sox outfielders hit only 27 homers combined in 1991. It was Larry Himes who had brought Sosa into the Sox organization in a trade with the Rangers in 1989. It was also Himes, who became general manager of the Cubs in November 1991, who took Sammy to the North Side of Chicago. Sosa's development continued in slow increments over the next few more years, but by 1994 he had moved into the top tier of big-league hitters. In 1998 he clubbed 66 homers during his thrilling race with Mark McGwire for the single-season record. Sammy followed that historic campaign with 63 homers in 1999, 50 in 2001, 64 in 2002 and 49 in 2003. With the Rangers in 2007, he struck his 600th career homer. Bell came to the Sox at the age of 32 after making the All-Star team in 1991 for the third time in his career. But he could no longer play in the outfield because of a knee injury that forced him to wear a brace, and he was used almost exclusively as a designated hitter with the Sox. In two seasons with the club, the last two of his big-league career, Bell hit 38 homers and drove in 182 runs in 1,037 at-bats. But he hit only .240 with an anemic on-base percentage of .274.

APRIL 7   The White Sox open the season with a 10–4 win over the Angels in Anaheim. Tim Raines drove in three runs and scored three. Frank Thomas hit a home run. Mike Huff collected three hits, including a double.

Thomas led the American League in on-base percentage (.439), doubles (46) and walks (122) in addition to batting .323 with 24 homers, 115 RBIs, 108 runs and 185 hits.

APRIL 11   Dan Pasqua hits a grand slam off Dave Stewart in the third inning to give the White Sox a 6–0 lead, but the Athletics rally to win 7–6 in Oakland.

                Ed Farmer joined John Rooney in the WMAQ radio booth in 1992. Farmer was the color commentator alongside Rooney through the 2005 season. In 2006, Farmer became the lead announcer on the White Sox radio broadcasts, with Chris Singleton handling the commentary.

APRIL 13   The White Sox win the home opener 1–0 against the Mariners before 42,290 at Comiskey Park. Greg Hibbard (eight innings) and Bobby Thigpen (one inning) combined on the shutout. A triple by Frank Thomas in the third inning drove in the lone run. Bo Jackson, standing on crutches nine days after hip replacement surgery, threw out the ceremonial first pitch.

                On the same day, a large breach in the roof of a freight tunnel beneath the Chicago River caused flooding in downtown Chicago, preventing some fans from reaching Comiskey Park for the game and making it difficult for many others. The flood paralyzed the Loop for two weeks.

APRIL 21   Ozzie Guillen suffers a season-ending knee injury during a 4–3 loss to the Yankees at Comiskey Park. Guillen tore two ligaments in a collision with left fielder Tim Raines. Guillen's knee tangled with Raines in a collision when the shortstop backed up to catch Mel Hall's fly ball in the ninth inning.

APRIL 24   Jack McDowell (seven innings), Donn Pall (one inning) and Bobby Thigpen (one inning) combine on a two-hitter to defeat the Tigers 9–1 in Detroit. The only Tiger hits were a home run by Mickey Tettleton and a single from Mark Carreon, both in the fifth inning.

                McDowell started the season 7–0 and finished 20–10 with a 3.18 ERA and 178 strikeouts in 260²/₃ innings.

APRIL 30   On the day that riots begin in the South Central section of Los Angeles, George Bell collects five hits, including two doubles and a homer, in five at-bats during a 12–1 victory over the Rangers at Comiskey Park. Bell scored four runs. Batting out of the ninth spot in the order, Craig Grebeck drove in six runs on a homer, a double and a single.

MAY 2   After a pre-game salute to some of the stars of the Negro Leagues, the White Sox take the field for a game at Comiskey Park against the Rangers wearing the caps of the Chicago American Giants. The American Giants played their home games at South Side Park from 1920 through 1940 and at the first Comiskey Park from 1941 through 1952. The Sox lost 4–1 in 11 innings.

MAY 4   Alex Fernandez pitches a one-hitter for a 7–0 win over the Brewers at Comiskey Park. The only Milwaukee hit was a double by Dante Bichette in the second inning. After Bichette's hit, Fernandez retired 22 batters in a row.

MAY 5   George Bell hits a grand slam off Chris Bosio in the first inning of a 12–2 win over the Brewers at Comiskey Park.

MAY 7	The White Sox rally from an early 6–0 deficit to defeat the Red Sox 7–6 at Comiskey Park. The Pale Hose tied the score 6–6 with three runs in the second and three more in the third, then went ahead with a tally in the sixth. Charlie Hough and Wilson Alvarez combined to walk 10 batters in the first two innings, and five Sox hurlers combined to issue 15 bases on balls and six hits during the contest.
MAY 8	Frank Thomas's homer in the 10th inning, his second of the game, beats the Orioles 4–3 in Baltimore. It was the first game that the White Sox played at Oriole Park at Camden Yards.
MAY 13	Kirk McCaskill (7⅓ innings) and Bobby Thigpen (1⅔ innings) combine on a two-hitter to defeat the Brewers 1–0 in Milwaukee. The first hit was a single by Kevin Seitzer with two out in the seventh inning. McCaskill was relieved after allowing a double to Jim Gantner in the eighth. Robin Ventura drove in the lone run of the game with a double in the first inning.
MAY 17	The White Sox outlast the Orioles 14–10 at Comiskey Park. The Sox took a 7–6 lead with three runs in the fifth inning, then added five more in the sixth.

> *At the end of the day, the White Sox had a 20–14 record and were in first place in the AL West. The club lost 21 of its next 33 games, however, to drop out of the race. At the All-Star break, the Sox were 9½ games out of first.*

JUNE 1	In the first round of the amateur draft, the White Sox select first baseman Eddie Pearson from Bishop State (Alabama) Junior College.

> *The only future major leaguers drafted and signed that season were A. J. Hinch (second round), Chris Snopek (sixth round), Craig Wilson (13th round), Brendan Donnelly (27th round), and Chris Tremie (39th round).*

JUNE 16	Two days after the Bulls win their second NBA championship in a series against the Portland Trail Blazers, Steve Sax hits a grand slam off Mike Walker in the sixth inning to give the White Sox a 5–0 lead, but the Mariners rally to win 9–6 in Seattle.
JULY 1	Craig Grebeck collects five hits, including three doubles, in five at-bats to lead the White Sox to an 8–5 win over the Indians in Cleveland.
JULY 2	Wilson Alvarez takes a no-hitter into the seventh inning of an 8–3 win over the Red Sox at Comiskey Park. The no-hit bid was broken up with a single by Wade Boggs, followed by a Tom Brunansky homer. Alvarez retired the last three hitters in the seventh, then exited for a reliever.
JULY 4	George Bell hits a sixth-inning solo home run and a walk-off single in the 10th to account for the only two runs in a 2–1 win over the Red Sox at Comiskey Park.
JULY 5	George Bell hits a grand slam off Wes Gardner in the fifth inning for the only White Sox runs in a 4–2 victory over the Red Sox at Comiskey Park. Over two consecutive games, Bell drove in the only six Chicago runs.
JULY 14	Robin Ventura and Jack McDowell contribute to a 13–6 American League win in the All-Star Game at Jack Murphy Stadium in San Diego. McDowell pitched the second

inning and retired the National League in order. In two plate appearances, Ventura hit an RBI-double in the sixth inning and a single in the eighth. It proved to be the only All-Star appearance of Ventura's career.

Ventura batted .282 with 16 homers and 93 RBIs in 1992.

JULY 16 — The White Sox win a thrilling 5–4 contest in 12 innings against the Brewers at Comiskey Park. The Sox scored twice in the ninth inning to tie the game 3–3. After Milwaukee tallied in the 10th, the Sox matched it in their half. George Bell drove in the game-winner with a walk-off single in the 12th.

JULY 21 — Trailing 8–2, the White Sox score eight runs in the eighth inning and beat the Orioles 10–7 at Comiskey Park.

AUGUST 4 — The White Sox rout the Twins 19–11 at Comiskey Park. The Sox took a 12–4 lead with nine runs in the third inning, then added four more in the sixth.

AUGUST 5 — Charlie Hough wins his 200th career game with a 9–5 decision over the Twins at Comiskey Park.

Hough finished his career with a record of 216–216 and recorded 61 saves. He won 163 games after celebrating his 34th birthday. Hough played 25 seasons in the majors from 1970 through 1994.

AUGUST 8 — The White Sox break a 2–2 tie with six runs in the ninth inning and defeat the Angels 8–2 in Anaheim.

AUGUST 9 — The White Sox score four runs in the 14th inning to down the Angels 12–8 in Anaheim. Ron Karkovice broke the 8–8 tie with a single. The Sox collected 20 hits during the contest.

AUGUST 11 — Lance Johnson extends his hitting streak to 25 games during a 10–6 win over the Athletics in Oakland.

AUGUST 25 — The White Sox defeat the Blue Jays 6–3 at Comiskey Park in a game delayed for 19 minutes due to an electrical failure that knocks out four sets of lights.

SEPTEMBER 8 — Jack McDowell wins his 20th game of the season with a 4–3 decision over the Tigers in the first game of a double-header at Comiskey Park. The Sox won the second tilt by the same 4–3 score. McDowell made five more starts in 1992 and failed to win another game, with three losses and two no decisions.

"Black Jack" McDowell won 20 games in 1992 and in 1993, when he was one of the most dominating pitchers in the game.

SEPTEMBER 14   A bench-clearing incident in the eighth inning mars an 8–6 win over the Yankees in New York. George Bell thought that Yankee hurler Greg Caderet was throwing at him and took a few steps toward the mound as the benches and bullpens came onto the field. Yankees batting coach Frank Howard, who stood six-foot-eight, walked to the plate and challenged Bell, but the White Sox player was held off by teammates and order was then restored by the umpires.

SEPTEMBER 16   Frank Thomas collects five hits, including two doubles, in five at-bats to lead the White Sox to a 9–6 win over the Yankees in New York.

SEPTEMBER 23   The White Sox score seven runs in the fifth inning and beat the Athletics 17–6 at Comiskey Park.

SEPTEMBER 25   Robin Ventura hits a two-run, walk-off double in the ninth inning to beat the Angels 6–5 at Comiskey Park.

NOVEMBER 17   Two weeks after Bill Clinton defeats George Bush in the presidential election, the White Sox lose Greg Hibbard and Robert Person to the Marlins in the expansion draft.

DECEMBER 8   Charlie Hough signs as a free agent with the Marlins. On the same day, the White Sox signed Dave Stieb, most recently with the Blue Jays, as a free agent.

1993

Sox

Season in a Sentence

After the clumsy "retirement" of Carlton Fisk in June, the White Sox win their first division title in 10 years before losing the American League Championship Series to the Blue Jays.

Finish • Won • Lost • Pct • GB

First   94   68   .580   +8.0

American League Championship Series

The White Sox lost four games to two to the Toronto Blue Jays.

Manager

Gene Lamont

Stats

Stats	WS	AL	Rank
Batting Avg:	.265	.267	7
On-Base Pct:	.338	.337	6
Slugging Pct:	.411	.408	7
Home Runs:	162		5
Stolen Bases:	106		7
ERA:	3.70	4.32	1
Fielding Avg:	.982	.981	8
Runs Scored:	776		7
Runs Allowed:	664		1

Starting Lineup

Ron Karkovice, c
Frank Thomas, 1b
Joey Cora, 2b
Robin Ventura, 3b
Ozzie Guillen, ss
Tim Raines, lf
Lance Johnson, cf
Ellis Burks, rf
George Bell, dh
Bo Jackson, lf-dh

Pitchers

Jack McDowell, sp
Alex Fernandez, sp
Wilson Alvarez, sp
Jason Bere, sp
Roberto Hernandez, rp
Scott Radinsky, rp
Jeff Schwarz, rp
Kirk McCaskill, rp-sp

Attendance

2,581,091 (third in AL)

Club Leaders

Batting Avg:	Frank Thomas	.317
On-Base Pct:	Frank Thomas	.426
Slugging Pct:	Frank Thomas	.607
Home Runs:	Frank Thomas	41
RBIs:	Frank Thomas	128
Runs:	Frank Thomas	106
Stolen Bases:	Lance Johnson	35
Wins:	Jack McDowell	22
Strikeouts:	Alex Fernandez	169
ERA:	Wilson Alvarez	2.95
Saves:	Roberto Hernandez	38

JANUARY 3   The White Sox sign Ellis Burks, most recently with the Red Sox, as a free agent.

APRIL 6   Five weeks after a terrorist bomb explodes in the parking garage of the World Trade Center, killing six people, the White Sox win the season opener 10–5 against the Twins in Minneapolis. It was the seventh consecutive year that the Sox won the first game of the season. Tim Raines hit a three-run homer during a six-run fourth inning that put the Sox ahead 9–4.

Raines batted .306 with 16 homers in 1993.

APRIL 9   In the home opener, Bo Jackson homers during an 11–6 loss to the Yankees before 42,775. It was Jackson's first at-bat in a major league game since undergoing hip replacement surgery on April 4, 1992. He was inserted into the lineup in the seventh inning as a pinch-hitter for Dan Pasqua.

Jackson batted .232 with 16 homers and 45 RBIs in 284 at-bats in 1993. At the end of the season, the Sox decided not to renew his contract, and he signed a free agent deal with the Angels in 1994, which proved to be Bo's last season in baseball.

APRIL 20   On the day after the raid on the Branch Davidian compound in Waco, Texas, Frank Thomas hits a sacrifice fly in the 14th inning to provide the winning run in a 2–1 win over the Orioles in Baltimore. Wilson Alvarez (eight innings), Roberto Hernandez (2⅓ innings), Scott Radinsky (1⅔ innings) and Donn Pall (two innings) combined on a seven-hitter. The Orioles collected only one hit over the last eight innings.

Frank Thomas was the AL MVP in a unanimous vote in 1993. He hit .317 with 41 homers, 128 RBIs and 112 walks. Oddly, Thomas won the MVP award in what statistically was not close to his best season. In his seasons of 100 or more games through 2007, he has had a higher batting average six times, a better on-base percentage in seven seasons and a greater slugging percentage in four years than he did in 1993. In addition, he hit more home runs than in 1993 twice and also drove in more runs twice and scored more often four times. Thomas won the award again in 1994.

APRIL 23   The White Sox sign Mike LaValliere, most recently with the Pirates, as a free agent.

APRIL 30   Frank Thomas hits a grand slam off Todd Stottlemyre in the third inning of a 10–2 victory over the Blue Jays at Comiskey Park.

MAY 10   The White Sox rout the Mariners 13–2 in Seattle.

MAY 16   Ellis Burks drives in six runs during a 15–6 win over the Rangers in Texas. Burks hit a grand slam off Kenny Rogers in the first inning, a solo homer against Brian Bohannon in the seventh and a sacrifice fly.

MAY 23   George Bell stars in a come-from-behind 5–4 win in 10 innings over the Athletics at Comiskey Park. Bell hit a two-run homer in the eighth inning to cut the A's lead to 4–3. After the Sox scored in the ninth, Bell smacked a walk-off triple in the 10th.

JUNE 2   Ron Karkovice hits two homers, including a grand slam, during a 10–1 win over the Tigers in Detroit. The slam was struck during a six-run first inning off Mike Moore.

JUNE 3   In the first round of the amateur draft, the White Sox select pitcher Scott Christman from Oregon State University.

Christman failed to reach the majors. Those who were drafted and signed by the White Sox in 1993 who did play in the big leagues in a largely unproductive draft included Greg Norton (second round), Tom Fordham (11th), Mike Sirotka (15th), Mario Valdez (28th) and Frank Menechino (45th).

JUNE 12   Ron Karkovice hits a home run in the 15th inning to defeat the Royals 2–1 in Kansas City. The White Sox scored their first run on a homer by Tim Raines leading off the first inning, then were shut out for 13 consecutive innings. Alex Fernandez (10 innings), Scott Radinsky (one inning), Jeff Schwarz (three innings) and Roberto Hernandez (one inning) pitched for the Sox.

Fernandez was 18–9 with a 3.13 ERA in 247⅓ innings in 1993. Hernandez collected 38 saves and compiled a 2.29 ERA in 78⅔ innings over 70 games.

JUNE 20   On the day the Bulls win their third consecutive NBA championship in a series against the Suns, George Bell hits a grand slam and a solo homer to pace the White Sox to an 11–6 win over the Angels in Anaheim. The slam was struck in the first inning off Russ Springer.

JUNE 21   The White Sox move into a three-way tie for first place in the AL West with a 7–2 win over the Rangers at Comiskey Park.

            The win gave the White Sox a 35–32 record. Two days later, the club took sole possession of the top spot in the division and held it for the rest of the year. From July 11 through the end of the season, the Sox had a record of 50–27.

JUNE 22   Carlton Fisk breaks the record for most games played by a catcher in a 3–2 win over the Rangers at Comiskey Park. It was his 2,226th game behind the plate, breaking the mark set by Bob Boone between 1972 and 1990.

            Fisk was honored before the game by teammates and fans. It proved to be his last big-league game. Fisk was released by the White Sox six days later. He was seven months past his 45th birthday. The club would have preferred that Fisk retire at the end of the 1992 season, but he needed 25 games to break Boone's record and wanted to stay in the game long enough to set the mark. The Sox relented and reluctantly placed Fisk on the roster and the awkward situation between the player and club management led to a bitter feud. Jerry Reinsdorf, Ron Schueler and other top White Sox brass were noticeably absent from the pre-game ceremonies before the June 22 contest that honored Fisk for his historic achievement. On the day Fisk was released, Reinsdorf said: "It is not fair to Gene Lamont and to our fans to carry somebody who can't possibly help the ballclub." Fisk hit .189 in 53 at-bats during the 1993 season before his release. In 2000, he was elected to the Hall of Fame. Later, Fisk and White Sox management had a reconciliation. The club retired his uniform number in 1997. A life-sized statue of Fisk was erected outside U.S. Cellular Field in 2005.

JUNE 26   Ellis Burks hits a grand slam off Erik Hanson in the third inning of a 7–4 win over the Mariners at Comiskey Park.

JULY 2   The White Sox score seven runs in the fourth inning of a 12–1 triumph over the Orioles at Comiskey Park. Robin Ventura hit a grand slam off Mike Mussina.

JULY 4   Rod Bolton (seven innings), Donn Pall (one inning) and Roberto Hernandez (one inning) combine on a three-hitter and retire the last 20 batters in a row to defeat the Orioles 3–1 at Comiskey Park.

            The win was Bolton's first in the major leagues. He finished his two-year big league career with a 2–8 record and a 7.69 ERA.

JULY 13   Jack McDowell pitches a perfect fifth inning during a 9–3 American League win in the All-Star Game played at Oriole Park in Camden Yards in Baltimore.

In three career All-Star Games, McDowell pitched four scoreless innings.

JULY 24   Bo Jackson's fourth hit of the game is a walk-off single in the ninth inning to beat the Brewers 6–5 at Comiskey Park.

JULY 28   Robin Ventura hits a grand slam off Albie Lopez in the first inning of a 9–4 win over the Indians at Comiskey Park.

JULY 30   The White Sox score two runs in the ninth inning and two in the 10th to defeat the Mariners 6–4 in Seattle. In the 10th, Lance Johnson drove in a run with a triple, then scored on a suicide squeeze by Craig Grebeck.

               Johnson led the American League in triples four seasons in a row from 1991 through 1994. During that period, he hit 58 doubles, 53 triples and six home runs. Johnson is the only player to lead his league in triples for four consecutive seasons.

JULY 31   The White Sox defeat the Mariners 13–10 in Seattle. The Sox trailed 4–0 before scoring four runs in the third inning, three in the fourth and four in the fifth.

               On the same day, the White Sox traded Johnny Ruffin and Jeff Pierce to the Reds for Tim Belcher. The Sox hoped that Belcher would be the solution to their problems in finding a capable fifth starter, but he was only 3–5 in the Chicago uniform. Starting pitchers Jack McDowell, Alex Fernandez, Wilson Alvarez and Jason Bere combined for a 67–32 record and a 3.21 earned run average in 1993. The rest of the starters were 8–23 with a 5.75 ERA. That season, McDowell was 27 years old, Fernandez and Alvarez were both 23 and Bere was 22. It appeared that the top four spots in the Sox starting rotation were set for several years, but in 1995 McDowell joined the Yankees after being dealt for two minor leaguers, while Fernandez, Alvarez and Bere combined for a 28–34 record and an earned run average of 4.88.

AUGUST 1   Jack McDowell pitches a two-hitter and defeats the Mariners 4–0 at the Kingdome. The only Seattle hits were a triple by Bret Boone in the second inning and a single by Ken Griffey Jr. in the third.

               McDowell won the Cy Young Award in 1993. He was the American League's only 20-game winner by compiling a 22–10 record with a 3.37 ERA in $256^2/_3$ innings and a league-leading four shutouts.

AUGUST 4   Robin Ventura battles with Nolan Ryan during a 5–2 loss to the Rangers in Arlington. Believing that the legendary strikeout pitcher was throwing at him, the 26-year-old Ventura charged the mound in the third inning, which fired up Ryan, then 46 and baseball's oldest player. Ryan put Ventura in a headlock and reeled off six quick punches, two of which landed in his protagonist's face and four on the top of his head before players from both teams joined the fracas. After the fight with Ventura, Ryan didn't allow another hit, setting down 12 of the 13 batters he faced before being relieved in the seventh inning. Ventura received a two-game suspension.

AUGUST 5   The White Sox play at Arlington Stadium for the last time and lose 7–1 to the Rangers.

AUGUST 10   In just his second start with the White Sox, Tim Belcher pitches a two-hitter for a 4–0 win over the Athletics at Comiskey Park. Brent Gates collected both of the Oakland hits with singles in the fourth and ninth innings.

On the same day, the White Sox traded Bobby Thigpen to the Phillies for Jose DeLeon.

AUGUST 12   Tim Raines collects his 2,000th career hit during a 4–2 loss to the Royals at Comiskey Park. The milestone hit was a home run off Kevin Appier.

AUGUST 14   Alex Fernandez (8²/₃ innings) and Scott Radinsky (one-third of an inning) combine on a two-hitter to defeat the Royals 4–1 at Comiskey Park. The only Kansas City hits were a single by Brian McRae in the first inning and a homer from Brent Mayne in the second. After the Mayne hit, Fernandez retired 22 batters in a row.

AUGUST 22   Jack McDowell pitches a complete-game shutout for a 1–0 win over the Twins in Minneapolis for his 20th win of the year. The lone run was a homer by Frank Thomas off Jim Deshaies in the first inning.

AUGUST 29   The White Sox rout the Twins 13–5 at Comiskey Park.

AUGUST 31   Tom Raines homers from both sides of the plate during an 11–3 win over the Yankees in New York. Raines homered off lefty Sterling Hitchcock and right-hander Rich Monteleone.

On the same day, the White Sox signed Ivan Calderon, most recently with the Red Sox, as a free agent.

SEPTEMBER 5   Frank Thomas becomes the first player in White Sox history to hit 40 homers in a season during a 5–3 win over the Tigers in Detroit. The previous single season club home run record was 37 by Richie Allen in 1972 and Carlton Fisk in 1985. The victory gave the White Sox a 6½-game lead in the AL West.

SEPTEMBER 6   The White Sox lose 3–1 to the Red Sox in a brawl-marred game at Comiskey Park. In the second inning, George Bell was ejected for charging Boston hurler Aaron Sele after being hit by a pitch and both dugouts and bullpens emptied. During the ensuing altercation, Bell was flipped by Red Sox infielder John Valentin, who suffered a pulled muscle. Order was restored after 10 minutes of pushing and shoving. After Boston's Rob Deer hit his second homer of the game in the ninth, Jack McDowell was ejected for arguing a previous pitch.

SEPTEMBER 8   Jason Bere strikes out 13 batters and allows only two hits over eight shutout innings in leading the White Sox to an 8–1 win over the Red Sox at Comiskey Park.

SEPTEMBER 13   The White Sox's lead over the second-place Rangers falls to 2½ games after a 9–0 loss to the Royals in Kansas City.

The Sox salted away the pennant by winning 14 of their last 19 games.

SEPTEMBER 14   Major League Baseball announces its three-division alignment, plus an extra round of playoffs, to be put into effect in the 1994 season. The White Sox were placed in the Central Division with the Indians, Royals, Brewers and Twins. In 1998, the Brewers moved to the National League and were replaced in the AL Central by the Tigers, who moved from the AL East.

SEPTEMBER 19   Robin Ventura hits a two-run homer off Dennis Eckersley in the ninth inning to lift the White Sox to a 3–1 victory over the Athletics in Oakland. The win gave the Sox a 4½-game lead in the AL West with 14 contests left on the schedule.

SEPTEMBER 22   Wilson Alvarez (eight innings) and Roberto Hernandez (one inning) combine to shut out the Angels 1–0 in Anaheim. Robin Ventura drove in the lone run of the game with a double in the fourth inning.

Alvarez won his last seven decisions and put together a scoreless streak of 30 innings.

SEPTEMBER 27   The White Sox clinch the pennant with a 4–2 win over the Mariners before 42,116 sock-waving fans at Comiskey Park. Bo Jackson broke a 0–0 tie with a three-run homer in the sixth inning on a 3–0 pitch. Wilson Alvarez (7²/₃ innings) and Kirk McCaskill (1²/₃ innings) combined on the shutout.

OCTOBER 3   The White Sox participate in the final baseball game ever played at Municipal Stadium in Cleveland. The Sox won 4–0 before a crowd of 72,390. Jose DeLeon fanned Mark Lewis for the final out.

The White Sox played the Toronto Blue Jays in the American League Championship Series. The Blue Jays won the World Series in 1992. Managed by Cito Gaston, they compiled a record of 95–67 in 1993.

OCTOBER 5   In the first game of the American League Championship Series, the White Sox lose 7–3 to the Blue Jays before 46,246 at Comiskey Park. Jack McDowell gave up all seven Toronto runs in 6²/₃ innings.

Michael Jordan threw out the ceremonial first ball, then stunned the sports world the next day by announcing his retirement from basketball after 10 seasons, the last three of which resulted in championships for the Bulls. Rumors of Jordan's retirement had spread among the media and the Comiskey Park throng throughout the game. Jordan said his loss of passion for the game, particularly after the murder of his father the previous June, was the primary reason for his exit from basketball. Within a few months, Jordan would become a baseball player in the Sox organization (see February 7, 1994).

OCTOBER 6   The White Sox start the 1993 ALCS by losing the first two games at home with a 3–1 defeat at the hands of the Blue Jays before 46,101 at Comiskey Park.

OCTOBER 8   The White Sox win game three by a 6–1 score at SkyDome in Toronto. The Sox broke open a scoreless tie with five runs in the third inning. Wilson Alvarez pitched a complete-game seven-hitter. Tim Raines collected four hits, including two doubles, in four at-bats.

OCTOBER 9   The White Sox even the ALCS with a 7–4 win over the Blue Jays in Toronto in game four. Lance Johnson put the Sox into the lead with a two-run homer in the second inning off Todd Stottlemyre. The Sox fell behind 3–2, but they pulled ahead to stay with three in the sixth. Johnson was the hero again by breaking the 3–3 tie with a two-out, two-run triple. Tim Raines collected three hits in five at-bats, giving him seven hits in consecutive games. Frank Thomas homered in the seventh.

Johnson failed to homer in 540 regular-season at-bats in 1993. He came into the post-season with four home runs in 2,599 at-bats.

OCTOBER 10   The White Sox are one game from elimination after a 5–3 loss to the Blue Jays in Toronto. Jack McDowell had his second bad outing in the series by allowing three runs in 2⅓ innings. Ellis Burks homered in the fifth inning and Robin Ventura smacked a two-run homer in the ninth.

Following a season in which he won the Cy Young Award, McDowell allowed 10 runs and 18 hits in nine innings in two starts in the 1993 ALCS.

OCTOBER 12   The Blue Jays win the 1993 American League pennant by defeating the White Sox 6–3 before 45,527 at Comiskey Park. Warren Newson hit a ninth-inning homer, but it was too little, too late.

The Sox won two of three in Toronto, but they were 0–3 at Comiskey Park.

NOVEMBER 18   Jack McDowell is knocked unconscious following a scuffle involving Pearl Jam singer Eddie Vedder in a nightclub in the French Quarter in New Orleans. The fight started about 4:15 a.m. when Vedder spat in the face of another man. The two went tumbling into the street. McDowell came charging into the fray, but he was stopped short by the club bouncer. McDowell was knocked out when he hit his head on the wheel of a Jeep. The Sox pitcher was treated for a cut lip and scalp lacerations.

NOVEMBER 30   Ellis Burks signs a contract as a free agent with the Rockies.

DECEMBER 17   The White Sox sign Julio Franco, most recently with the Rangers, as a free agent.

Despite the fact that the 1994 season was shortened to 113 games by the strike, Franco hit 20 homers and drove in 98 runs, both career highs in his 23-year big league career. He also batted .319.

DECEMBER 28   The White Sox sign Darrin Jackson, most recently with the Yankees, as a free agent.

Jackson hit .312 for the White Sox in 1994, then spent the 1995 and 1996 seasons in Japan with the Seibu Lions. Jackson ended his playing career with the Sox in 1999, and in 2000 he moved alongside Ken Harrelson in the television booth for WGN-TV, WCIU-TV and FOX Sports Net.

1994

Season in a Sentence

The defending AL West champs are in first place in the newly formed AL Central when the players call a strike on August 12, ending the season.

Finish • Won • Lost • Pct • GB

First   67   46   .593   +1.0

Manager

Gene Lamont

Stats

	WS	AL	Rank
Batting Avg:	.287	.273	3
On-Base Pct:	.366	.345	2
Slugging Pct:	.444	.434	5
Home Runs:	121		7
Stolen Bases:	77		8
ERA:	3.96	4.80	1
Fielding Avg:	.981	.981	10
Runs Scored:	633		4
Runs Allowed:	498		2

Starting Lineup

Ron Karkovice, c
Frank Thomas, 1b
Joey Cora, 2b
Robin Ventura, 3b
Ozzie Guillen, ss
Tim Raines, lf
Lance Johnson, cf
Darrin Jackson, rf
Julio Franco, dh
Mike LaValliere, c

Pitchers

Wilson Alvarez, sp
Alex Fernandez, sp
Jack McDowell, sp
Jason Bere, sp
Scott Sanderson, sp
Roberto Hernandez, rp
Paul Assenmacher, rp
Jose DeLeon, rp
Kirk McCaskill, rp

Attendance

1,697,398 (sixth in AL)

Club Leaders

Batting Avg:	Frank Thomas	.353
On-Base Pct:	Frank Thomas	.487
Slugging Pct:	Frank Thomas	.729
Home Runs:	Frank Thomas	38
RBIs:	Frank Thomas	101
Runs:	Frank Thomas	106
Stolen Bases:	Lance Johnson	26
Wins:	Wilson Alvarez	12
	Jason Bere	12
Strikeouts:	Jack McDowell	127
	Jason Bere	127
ERA:	Wilson Alvarez	3.45
Saves:	Roberto Hernandez	14

JANUARY 31   Three weeks after Nancy Kerrigan is attacked by assailants connected to rival skater Tonya Harding, Bo Jackson signs a contract as a free agent with the Angels.

FEBRUARY 6   Tim Belcher signs a contract as a free agent with the Tigers.

FEBRUARY 7   Michael Jordan sign a minor league contract with the White Sox.

Jordan retired from basketball on October 6, 1993, after 10 seasons. He decided to embark on a baseball career at the age of 31, despite the fact that he hadn't played the sport since he was 16, when he batted .257 in Babe Ruth ball. But Jordan had often taken batting practice with the Sox during his years with the Bulls and had impressed players with his power. More than once, Jordan launched a ball onto to the roof at old Comiskey Park. Although general manager Ron Schueler called Jordan's chances of reaching the majors "a million to one," Jerry Reinsdorf, who also owned the Bulls, believed that Jordan had a shot at succeeding in baseball. If nothing else, his celebrity would draw people to the ballpark. Part of Jordan's reasons for leaving basketball was the media circus surrounding his celebrity, but ironically, his every move on the baseball field was *scrutinized. Even his workouts were carried live on cable TV outlets. During the 1994 training camp in Sarasota, more attention was given to Jordan than to anyone on the major league roster. He hit just .152 in spring training games and was assigned to the Sox's Class AA farm club in Birmingham on March 21. Not wishing to ride on an old bus on 12-hour trips, Jordan purchased a new one for the Birmingham club for $350,000. The luxury bus, similar to those used by touring rock stars, had 35 reclining passenger seats, six TVs, a VCR and a lounge area with a wet bar. Again, Jordan was followed nearly everywhere by minicams, and the Birmingham Barons received more national media attention than many major league clubs. At Birmingham, Jordan batted .202 with three homers, 51 RBIs, 30 stolen bases and a league-leading 11 errors as an outfielder in 127 games. He returned to the Sox's training camp in 1995, during the strike, but quit after two weeks and returned to basketball near the end of the 1994–95 season. Jordan played on three more NBA champions before calling it a career.*

MARCH 1   The White Sox sign Scott Sanderson, most recently with the Giants, as a free agent.

MARCH 24   The White Sox trade Brian Boehringer to the Yankees for Paul Assenmacher.

APRIL 4   In a re-match of the 1993 ALCS, the White Sox open the 1994 season against the Blue Jays and lose 7–3 in Toronto. Ron Karkovice homered for the Sox.

APRIL 6   Robin Ventura hits two homers, including a grand slam in the seventh inning off Paul Spoljaric, during a 9–2 win over the Blue Jays in Toronto. Ventura struck two of Chicago's five homers. Dan Pasqua homered in the fourth. Darrin Jackson, batting for Pasqua in the seventh, hit a pinch-hit homer. Jackson stayed in the game as a right fielder and homered again in the ninth.

APRIL 7   Michael Jordan plays right field for the White Sox in the Windy City Classic charity exhibition game at Wrigley Field. Wearing uniform number 45, Jordan collected two hits and drove in two runs in five at-bats in addition to making an error and committing a base-running miscue. The game ended in a 4–4 tie after 10 innings.

APRIL 8   In the home opener, the White Sox lose 8–6 to the Red Sox before 42,990 at Comiskey Park. Tim Raines hit two homers, and Julio Franco and Robin Ventura added one each. It was Franco's first game in Chicago as a member of the White Sox.

APRIL 18   Tim Raines hits three homers during a 12–1 thrashing of the Red Sox in Boston. The contest was played on Patriots Day and started at 11:05 a.m. Raines's homers were helped by a 12 m.p.h. wind blowing out to right field. He smacked solo blasts in the first and second innings off Danny Darwin and a two-run shot against Ricky Trlicek in the eighth. Raines also singled and reached on an error, and tied a White Sox club record by scoring five runs.

APRIL 20   Tim Raines stars again by reaching base seven times in seven plate appearances during a 12-inning, 8–6 win over the Brewers in Milwaukee. Raines had three singles and four walks. Julio Franco singled home the go-ahead run in the 12th.

             Pitcher Scott Radinsky missed the 1994 season with Hodgkin's disease, a form of lymphatic cancer.

APRIL 21	The White Sox release Steve Sax.
APRIL 27	The White Sox play at Jacobs Field for the first time and lose 8–7 to the Indians in 12 innings. The Sox scored twice in the top of the 12th, only to have Cleveland rally for three in their half.
MAY 3	The White Sox rout the Indians 12–1 at Comiskey Park. In five plate appearances, Frank Thomas hit a home run and drew four walks.
MAY 10	The White Sox clobber the Mariners 16–2 at Comiskey Park.
MAY 11	The White Sox score seven runs with two out in the third inning of a 14–6 victory over the Mariners at Comiskey Park. The seven runs scored on a grand slam by Ron Karkovice and a three-run homer by Julio Franco, both off Chris Bosio. Combined with the 16-run outburst the previous day, the Sox scored 30 runs in consecutive games.

Frank Thomas won the MVP Award in 1993 and 1994. A feared hitter throughout the league, he knocked in over 100 runs 10 times for the Sox.

MAY 13	The White Sox play at The Ballpark in Arlington (now known as Ameriquest Field) for the first time and lose 11–7 to the Rangers.
MAY 20	The White Sox score eight runs in the second inning and beat the Athletics 13–6 in Oakland. Darrin Jackson collected four hits, including a homer, in five at-bats and drove in five runs.
MAY 25	The White Sox pound the Twins 12–1 at Comiskey Park. Frank Thomas collected two homers and two singles and drove in five runs.
MAY 27	Wilson Alvarez runs his record on the 1994 season to 8–0 and wins his 15th consecutive decision over two seasons with a 3–0 victory over the Orioles at Comiskey Park.

> *Alvarez won his last seven decisions in 1993 en route to a 15–8 record. His 15 wins in a row tied the club record for consecutive wins, set by LaMarr Hoyt in 1983 and 1984. It was broken by Jose Contreras, who won 17 in succession in 2005 and 2006. The single-season record for consecutive wins is 13 by Hoyt in 1983. After starting the 1994 campaign with eight wins in succession, Alvarez lost eight of 12 decisions to finish at 12–8 and was 71–78 over the remainder of his career, which ended in 2005.*

MAY 29   Frank Thomas homers in his fifth consecutive game, but the White Sox lose 8–4 to
                the Orioles at Comiskey Park.

                *In five games from May 24 through May 29, Thomas hit six home runs in 18
                at-bats. In the first 46 games of 1994, he clubbed 20 home runs. It would have
                been interesting to see what Thomas could have accomplished in 1994 had all
                162 games been played. The season was limited to 113 contests due to the strike.
                Thomas led the AL in runs scored (106), walks (109), slugging percentage (.729)
                and on-base percentage (.487). He also batted .353, hit 38 homers, drove in 101
                runs, collected 34 doubles and won his second straight MVP award.*

JUNE 1   The White Sox score three runs in the ninth inning to defeat the Yankees 5–4 in
                New York.

JUNE 2   With two choices in the first round of the amateur draft, the White Sox select catcher
                Mark Johnson from Warner Robins High School in Warner Robins, Georgia, and
                pitcher Chris Clemons from Texas A&M University. Other future major leaguers
                drafted and signed by the White Sox in 1994 were Carlos Castillo (third round), Jeff
                Abbott (fourth), Luis Garcia (19th) and Adam Bernero (21st). The Sox also drafted
                Eric Gagne in the 30th round, but he didn't sign a contract. Gagne was picked up by
                the Dodgers as an undrafted free agent in 1995. None of the group signed by the Sox
                was able to hold down a job as a regular in the majors. First-rounder Johnson hit
                only .217 in 322 games over seven seasons in the big leagues. Clemons pitched just
                five games with an 0–2 record and an 8.53 ERA.

JUNE 4   Norberto Martin hits a grand slam off Jim Poole in the ninth inning of a 7–1 win
                over the Orioles in Baltimore. It was the first career homer for Martin and the only
                one he would hit in 131 at-bats in 1994.

JUNE 7   Darrin Jackson drives in all five White Sox runs on a grand slam off Pat Hentgen in
                the first inning and an RBI-single in the ninth, but the Sox lose 9–5 to the Blue Jays
                at Comiskey Park. The defeat ended the 15-game, two-season winning streak of
                Wilson Alvarez (see May 27, 1994).

                *The White Sox had a 33–21 record on June 8 and a two-game lead in the AL
                Central. Ten losses in the next 12 games sent the Sox reeling to third place, six
                games behind. With a sudden reversal, Gene Lamont's club was 23–5 from June 21
                through July 21 to take first again with a three-game advantage. When the strike
                was called on August 12, the Sox were 67–46 and led the Indians by one game.*

JUNE 13   Jason Bere strikes out 14 batters in eight innings while allowing only two hits in a
                1–0 triumph over the Athletics at Comiskey Park. The lone run scored on a single by
                Tim Raines in the fifth inning.

                *Bere looked like a future Cy Young Award winner in 1994. As a rookie in
                1993, he won his last seven games in finishing 12–5. In 1994, his record was
                12–2, giving him 19 wins in 21 decisions over two seasons and a career mark
                of 24–7 at the age of 23. Bere was only 8–15 in 1995, however, while his ERA
                skyrocketed to 7.19. He walked 106 batters in 137²/₃ innings. Bere was never
                again able to consistently regain his effectiveness, or his control, in a career that
                ended in 2003 with a lifetime record of 71–65 and a 5.14 ERA.*

JUNE 19 — Scott Sanderson pitches no-hit ball for the first 6⅔ innings and finishes with a three-hitter and a 7–1 win over the Angels at Comiskey Park. The first California hit was a double by Chili Davis with two out in the seventh.

JUNE 22 — Wilson Alvarez (eight innings) and Paul Assenmacher (one inning) combine on a two-hitter to defeat the Rangers 4–0 at Comiskey Park. Assenmacher struck out all three batters he faced. The only Texas hits were singles by Dean Palmer in the fifth inning and Junior Ortiz in the sixth.

JUNE 23 — The White Sox sink the Mariners 13–2 in Seattle.

JULY 12 — In three plate appearances in the All-Star Game at Three Rivers Stadium in Pittsburgh, Frank Thomas collects two singles and a walk. He also scored a run and drove in one, but the American League lost 8–7. Pitching in the eighth inning, Wilson Alvarez retired Barry Bonds, Mike Piazza and Ken Caminiti in order.

In three career All-Star Games, Thomas collected four hits in five-bats, for a batting average of .800. One of his hits was a home run in 1995, and he drove in a total of seven runs.

JULY 15 — Albert Belle of the Indians has his bat confiscated during a 3–2 Cleveland win at Comiskey Park. White Sox manager Gene Lamont alleged that Belle's bat was corked, leading to a caper with all of the intrigue of a mystery novel. The incident became known in the media as "Batgate."

The bat in question was removed to the umpires' locker room, but before the game was over, someone broke into the area and replaced Belle's bat with one belonging to Paul Sorrento, another Cleveland player. Apparently, someone entered the locker room through ceiling tiles. A bat thought to be the original was returned to the umpires on July 17 and sent to the league office in New York. There it was X-rayed and sawed in half and found to be corked. AL President Bobby Brown suspended Belle for 10 games. The Indians admitted that someone connected with the club had switched the bats, but they wouldn't identify the individual. Five years later, Jason Grimsley, who pitched for the Indians in 1994, admitted that he was the bandit.

JULY 18 — Down 9–3, the White Sox score two runs in the sixth inning, four in the seventh on a Frank Thomas grand slam off Joe Boever and one in the 13th to win 10–9 over the Tigers at Comiskey Park. The winning run crossed the plate on a throwing error by Alan Trammell.

JULY 22 — Jim Thome hits three homers for the Indians during a 9–8 win over the White Sox in Cleveland.

JULY 30 — The White Sox take over sole possession of first place with a 4–2 win over the Mariners at Comiskey Park.

JULY 31 — Lance Johnson hits a grand slam off Jim Converse in the sixth inning of an 8–1 victory over the Mariners at Comiskey Park.

The contest was the last one at Comiskey Park before the strike. In the three games against Seattle on July 29, 30 and 31, the White Sox drew 126,025 fans. The final season attendance figure in 1994 was 1,697,398 in 53 home games, which projects to 2,594,136 over a full 81-game home slate. The Sox failed to draw over 2,000,000 again until the world championship year of 2005.

AUGUST 6

The White Sox explode for six runs in the 10th inning and beat the Angels 16–10 in Anaheim.

AUGUST 7

The White Sox put together a big extra inning for the second day in a row by scoring five times in the 12th to win 10–5 over the Angels in Anaheim. Mike LaValliere tied the contest 5–5 with a two-run homer in the ninth. It was his first home run since August 22, 1992.

AUGUST 10

In the final game before the strike, the White Sox beat the Athletics 2–1 in Oakland.

AUGUST 12

With about 70 percent of the season completed, the major league players go on strike.

The strike, baseball's eighth interruption since 1972, had been anticipated all season. The owners wanted to put a lid on escalating payrolls by capping salaries and revising, if not eliminating, salary arbitration procedures. The players, who were obviously not interested in these reforms, had only one weapon once talks broke down: a strike.

SEPTEMBER 14

The owners of the 28 major league clubs vote 26–2 to cancel the remainder of the season, including the playoffs and the World Series.

DECEMBER 14

The White Sox trade Jack McDowell to the Yankees for Keith Heberling and Lyle Mouton.

After winning the 1993 Cy Young Award, McDowell lost a bitter arbitration case to the Sox before the start of the 1994 season and announced he would not be returning in 1995. He started the 1994 campaign badly, with a 2–7 record and a 6.24 ERA after 11 starts. From June 1 to the end of the season, McDowell compiled an 8–2 mark and an earned run average of 2.28. The White Sox unloaded McDowell eight days before he was to become an unrestricted free agent. He was 15–10 with the Yankees in 1995 and 13–9 as an Indian in 1996 before his career went south and ended in 1999. The Sox received next to nothing in exchange for McDowell.

DECEMBER 21

Julio Franco signs a contract with the Chiba Lotte Marines of the Japanese Pacific League.

Franco played in Japan for one season, and later in Korea and Mexico. He was still active in the majors with the Mets in 2007 at the age of 48.

1995   Sox

Season in a Sentence

After finishing first in 1993 and 1994, the White Sox are expected to contend again, but the pitching staff collapses, Gene Lamont is fired after an 11–20 start and the club posts its first losing season since 1989.

Finish • Won • Lost • Pct • GB

Third   68   76   .472   32.0
In the wild-card race, the White Sox finished in sixth place, 10 games behind.

Managers

Gene Lamont (11–20) and Terry Bevington (57–56)

Stats

Stats	WS	AL	Rank
Batting Avg:	.280	.270	2
On-Base Pct:	.354	.344	4
Slugging Pct:	.431	.427	5
Home Runs:	146		8
Stolen Bases:	110		4 (tie)
ERA:	4.85	4.71	10
Fielding Avg:	.980	.982	13
Runs Scored:	755		5
Runs Allowed:	758		10

Starting Lineup

Ron Karkovice, c
Frank Thomas, 1b
Ray Durham, 2b
Robin Ventura, 3b
Ozzie Guillen, ss
Tim Raines, lf
Lance Johnson, cf
Mike Devereaux, rf
John Kruk, dh
Dave Martinez, rf-lf
Lyle Mouton, rf-lf

Pitchers

Alex Fernandez, sp
Wilson Alvarez, sp
Jason Bere, sp
Jim Abbott, sp
Roberto Hernandez, rp
Kirk McCaskill, rp
Scott Radinsky, rp
Jose DeLeon, rp
Tim Fortugno, rp

Attendance

1,609,773 (ninth in AL)

Club Leaders

Batting Avg:	Frank Thomas	.308
On-Base Pct:	Frank Thomas	.454
Slugging Pct:	Frank Thomas	.606
Home Runs:	Frank Thomas	40
RBIs:	Frank Thomas	111
Runs:	Frank Thomas	102
Stolen Bases:	Lance Johnson	40
Wins:	Alex Fernandez	12
Strikeouts:	Alex Fernandez	159
ERA:	Alex Fernandez	3.80
Saves:	Roberto Hernandez	32

JANUARY 13   Major league owners vote to use replacement players during the 1995 season if the players' strike, begun on August 12, 1994, is not settled.

Among the White Sox replacement players was Pete Rose Jr., then a minor leaguer in the White Sox system, and former Red Sox pitcher Dennis (Oil Can) Boyd.

APRIL 2   The 234-day strike of major league baseball players comes to an end.

The opening of the season, originally scheduled to begin on April 3, was pushed back to April 26 with each team playing 144 games. The replacement players were either released or sent to the minors.

APRIL 4   The White Sox sign Dave Righetti, most recently with the Blue Jays, as a free agent.

APRIL 8   The White Sox sign Mike Devereaux, most recently with the Orioles, and Jim
           Abbott, most recently with the Yankees, as free agents.

           *Abbott was born without a right hand and overcame the obstacle to fashion a
           10-year big-league career. While delivering a pitch, he tucked his glove under
           his right arm, then quickly placed his left hand into the mitt to field a batted ball
           if necessary. Abbott pitched 17 games with the White Sox in 1995 and was 6–4.
           He played for the club again in 1998, winning all five of his starts.*

APRIL 10   The White Sox sign Chris Sabo, most recently with the Orioles, as a free agent.
           On the same day, Paul Assenmacher signed a contract as a free agent with the Indians.

APRIL 11   Scott Sanderson signs a contract with the Angels as a free agent.

APRIL 26   In the season opener, the White Sox lose 12–3 to the Brewers.

APRIL 27   In the home opener, the White Sox lose 9–4 to the Brewers at Comiskey Park before
           31,073, the smallest Opening Day crowd for the club since 1982.

APRIL 30   The White Sox outlast the Red Sox 17–11 in Boston. Ron Karkovice hit a grand slam
           off Alejandro Pena in the eighth inning. It was the White Sox's first win after starting
           the 1995 season with four losses.

MAY 7   Jim Abbott (seven innings), Jose DeLeon (one inning) and Kirk McCaskill (one
           inning) combine on a two-hitter and a 6–1 win over the Twins at Comiskey Park.
           The only Minnesota hits were a single by Chuck Knoblauch in the fourth inning and
           a homer by Pedro Munoz in the seventh.

MAY 14   The White Sox sign John Kruk as a free agent.

           *Prior to the 1994 season, Kruk underwent surgery for testicular cancer. He made
           a full recovery, but aching knees forced him to retire. The Sox convinced him to
           come out of retirement to play again, but Kruk left the game as a player for good
           after just 10 weeks (see July 30, 1995).*

MAY 27   Ron Karkovice accounts for the lone run of a 1–0 win over the Tigers in Detroit with
           a homer in the fifth inning off Felipe Lira. Jason Bere (eight innings) and Roberto
           Hernandez (one inning) combined on the shutout.

MAY 28   The day after the White Sox and Tigers score only one run, the two clubs combine
           for a major league-record 12 home runs. The White Sox won 14–12 at Tiger Stadium
           in Detroit. The Sox overcame a second-inning 7–1 deficit for the win and broke an
           11–11 tie with three runs in the eighth. Cecil Fielder, Chad Curtis and Kirk Gibson
           each homered twice for the Tigers, while Ron Karkovice hit two for the Sox.
           The others were struck by Chicago's Ray Durham, Craig Grebeck and Frank Thomas
           and Detroit's Lou Whitaker. The home runs by Durham, Karkovice and Grebeck
           in the fourth were back-to-back-to-back. All three were struck against David Wells.
           James Baldwin gave up four of Detroit's homers in the first four innings.

           *This was the first of two occasions in which 12 home runs would be struck in a
           major league game. The second happened in another White Sox-Tigers contest
           on July 2, 2002, in Chicago.*

Home Run Derby in the Motor City

There have been only two games in major league history in which two teams combined for 12 home runs, and both involved the White Sox and Tigers. The first one happened on May 28, 1995, at Tiger Stadium in Detroit. Four players hit two home runs to tie a major league mark set in 1947 by the Cardinals and Pirates. Ten solo homers set another record. The Sox won the slugfest 14–12.

Before the game, a show from the 1959 television series *Home Run Derby* was played on Tiger Stadium's closed-circuit TV system. Later, the Sox and Tigers staged their own version.

The 12 home runs:

1. Detroit first inning. Chad Curtis with none on base off James Baldwin. Detroit 1, Chicago 0.
2. Detroit first inning. Cecil Fielder with one on off Baldwin. Detroit 3, Chicago 0.
3. Detroit second inning. Curtis with none on off Baldwin. Detroit 4, Chicago 1.
4. Detroit second inning. Fielder with two on off Baldwin. Detroit 7, Chicago 1.
5. Chicago fourth inning. Ray Durham with none on off David Wells. Detroit 7, Chicago 5.
6. Chicago fourth inning. Ron Karkovice with none on off Wells. Detroit 7, Chicago 6.
7. Chicago fourth inning. Craig Grebeck with none on off Wells. Chicago 7, Detroit 7.
8. Detroit fourth inning. Kirk Gibson with none on of Kirk McCaskill. Detroit 8, Chicago 7.
9. Chicago sixth inning. Frank Thomas with none on off John Doherty. Chicago 10, Detroit 10.
10. Detroit sixth inning. Gibson with none on off Rob Dibble. Detroit 11, Chicago 10.
11. Chicago seventh inning. Karkovice with none on off Doherty. Chicago 11, Detroit 11.
12. Detroit eighth inning. Lou Whitaker with none on off Scott Radinsky. Chicago 14, Chicago 12.

JUNE 1   In the first round of the amateur draft, the White Sox select third baseman Jeff Liefer from Long Beach State University.

Liefer looked as though he might deliver on his promise in 2001 with 18 homers in 256 at-bats for the Sox, but he never developed into a regular. He played on five big-league clubs from 2002 through 2005. Other future major leaguers drafted by the White Sox in 1995 included Brian Simmons (second round), J. J. Putz (third round) and Kevin Beirne (11th round). Putz opted to attend the University of Michigan instead of signing with the Sox, however. He was drafted by the Mariners in the sixth round in 1999. It took Putz a while to become a successful big league pitcher, but by 2007 he was an All-Star.

JUNE 2   In Terry Bevington's debut as a major league manager, the White Sox defeat the Tigers 5–4 in 15 innings at Comiskey Park. Detroit scored in the top of the 15th before the Sox rallied for two in their half. Mike LaValliere drove in the tying run with a single and scored on Ozzie Guillen's double.

Earlier in the day, Gene Lamont was fired as the White Sox manager and was replaced by Bevington. The Sox had a record of 11–20 at the time of the switch. Lamont was considered by the White Sox brass to be too easy-going to manage the club, even when the team was leading their division. Under Lamont's leadership, the Sox were 247–190 from 1992 through 1994, a three-year winning percentage of .565 that was the best by the franchise since 1963–65 and hasn't been exceeded since. A Tom Selleck look-alike, Bevington was a 38-year-old third base coach with the Sox. His communication skills came under fire, both in the way he dealt with the media and in his relationships with his own players. Bevington needlessly alienated reporters with curt and sarcastic answers to questions. He also had fights in separate incidents with Brewers manager Phil Garner and umpire Rich Garcia. By 1997, Bevington was replaced by Jerry Manuel.

JUNE 3

Dave Martinez hits a walk-off grand slam off Joe Boever in the ninth inning to beat the Tigers 10–6 at Comiskey Park. Detroit led 6–1 before the Sox scored a run in the fourth, three in the fifth, one in the sixth and one in the seventh.

JUNE 23

The White Sox score five runs in the fifth inning and seven in the sixth in beating the Indians 12–5 at Comiskey Park. The Sox collected 20 hits in the contest.

JUNE 28

Jason Bere strikes out 14 batters in 8²/₃ innings during a 4–3 win over the Twins at Comiskey Park.

JUNE 29

Robin Ventura collects five of the White Sox's 22 hits during a 17–13 win over the Brewers at County Stadium. Ventura hit a homer and four singles in six at-bats, scored four runs and drove in three. The Sox took an 8–4 lead with five runs in the third inning and extended the advantage to 16–6 in the eighth. The contest was marred by a couple of altercations. Milwaukee's Bill Wegman was ejected after hitting Ron Karkovice in the ribs with a pitch in the sixth inning. Karkovice, who was brushed back on the previous two pitches, threw his bat and started jawing at Wegman. Brewers manager Phil Garner was tossed by the umps for arguing about Wegman's ejection. In the ninth, White Sox pitcher Rob Dibble retaliated when he threw his first pitch near Pat Listach's head. Listach charged the mound and exchanged punches with Dibble. Karkovice ran out from behind the plate and tackled Listach while several other players traded blows. "This is not over," said Milwaukee's Jose Valentin. "We will not forget." For the next few years, there was bad blood between the Sox and Brewers (see July 22, 1995).

JULY 5

John Kruk hits a grand slam off Brian Boehringer in the first inning of an 11–5 win over the Yankees at Comiskey Park. Kruk's slam came after Boehringer walked the first four batters of the game.

JULY 11

Frank Thomas hits a two-run homer off John Smiley in the All-Star Game at The Ballpark at Arlington, but the American League loses 3–2.

Thomas's home run was the first ever by a White Sox player in an All-Star Game. There were 16 big-league clubs when the mid-summer classic started in 1933. By 1967, every one of those franchises had accounted for a home run in the contest except the Sox. In addition, a player from eight of the 10 1961–77 expansion clubs hit an All-Star home run before Thomas's 1995 blast. Since then, the only White Sox player with a homer is Magglio Ordonez in 2001.

JULY 13

With game-time temperatures at County Stadium in Milwaukee at 104 degrees, the White Sox lose 8–7 to the Brewers in 10 innings.

JULY 18

Frank Thomas collects seven hits in nine at-bats during a 9–4 and 11–4 sweep of the Yankees in a double-header in New York. Thomas had five singles, a double and a homer. Jack McDowell started the second game. It was the first time he had faced his former White Sox teammates. McDowell was removed in the fifth inning to a chorus of boos from the Yankee Stadium crowd and flashed an obscene gesture.

JULY 22	A fight interrupts a 4–2 win over the Brewers at Comiskey Park. In the seventh inning, Ozzie Guillen and Milwaukee third baseman Jeff Cirillo became tangled on the base paths. Cirillo fell backwards into Guillen, who pushed him off, and the two exchanged words. Both clubs left the dugouts and Terry Bevington and Brewers manager Phil Garner had heated words and had to be separated. Bevington was suspended for four games by the American League.
JULY 27	The White Sox trade Jim Abbott and Tim Fortugno to the Angels for Bill Simas, Andrew Lorraine, John Snyder and McKay Christensen.
JULY 30	John Kruk plays his last major league game, with a single in his only at-bat of an 8–3 loss to the Orioles in Baltimore. He started the game as a designated hitter, then was replaced by Frank Thomas. Kruk wanted to go out with a hit in front of his family members, many of whom traveled to the game from West Virginia.
AUGUST 4	Dave Martinez pitches the eighth inning of a 13–3 loss to the Indians in Cleveland. Martinez walked two batters but didn't give up a hit or a run.
AUGUST 11	The White Sox rout the Athletics 13–5 at Comiskey Park.
AUGUST 22	The White Sox collect five homers during a 15–7 victory over the Tigers in Detroit. Robin Ventura struck two of the homers, with Dave Martinez, Norberto Martin and Ron Karkovice adding one each.

Ventura hit .295 with 26 homers in 1995.

AUGUST 25	The White Sox score seven runs in the sixth inning to take an 8–0 lead and hang on to win 8–7 over the Blue Jays in Toronto. Ray Durham hit a grand slam off Pat Hentgen.
AUGUST 26	The White Sox trade Mike Devereaux to the Braves for Andre King.
AUGUST 27	The White Sox trade Jose DeLeon to the Expos for Jeff Shaw.
SEPTEMBER 2	Tim Raines's American League-record streak of 40 consecutive stolen base attempts is stopped during a 10–4 win over the Blue Jays at Comiskey Park. He was thrown out by Randy Knorr. The streak started on July 23, 1993.
SEPTEMBER 4	Robin Ventura hits two grand slams during a 14–3 win over the Rangers in Arlington. Ventura cleared the bases with a homer off Dennis Cook in the fourth and another against Danny Darwin in the fifth. Ventura's eight RBIs tied a White Sox record set by Carl Reynolds in 1930 and tied by Tommy McCraw in 1967 and twice by Jim Spencer in 1977.

Ventura is one of only 12 batters in big-league history with two grand slams in a game. He hit 10 career grand slams with the White Sox, a club record. Ventura smacked 18 grand slams during his career, which was tied with Willie McCovey for fourth all-time at the end of the 2008 season. With the Mets in 1999, Ventura became the only player in history to hit grand slams in both games of a double-header. (Update at the end of the 2008 season).

SEPTEMBER 5 — Mike LaValliere hits a homer in the 11th inning to beat the Rangers 2–1 in Arlington. It was LaValliere's first homer since August 7, 1994, and the last of 18 he hit during his 12-year big-league career.

SEPTEMBER 6 — The White Sox extend their winning streak to eight games with a 7–5 decision over the Rangers in Arlington.

SEPTEMBER 19 — Albert Belle hits three home runs for the Indians in an 8–2 win over the White Sox at Comiskey Park.

SEPTEMBER 23 — Lance Johnson collects six hits in six at-bats during a 14–4 victory over the Twins in Minneapolis. Johnson had three triples and three singles. He also scored four runs and drove in four. The six hits tied a White Sox club record set by Rip Radcliff in 1936 and tied by Hank Steinbacher in 1938 and Floyd Robinson in 1962. Johnson is the only player in Sox history with three triples in a game. The three triples also tied an American League record. In addition, Johnson is one of only two batters in big-league history with three triples in a game of six or more hits. The other was Jack Glasscock of the New York Giants in 1890.

Johnson collected nine hits in nine consecutive at-bats in three games played on September 22, 23 and 24. He led the league in triples each year from 1991 through 1994 and fell one triple shy of a fifth straight triples title in 1995. He did lead the AL in hits in 1995 with 186 in addition to his 12 three-baggers. Johnson led the NL in triples in 1996 with the Mets, which means that one more triple in 1995 would have given him six league triples championships in a row. No one else in major league history has more than three.

OCTOBER 1 — The White Sox close the 1995 season with an 11-inning, 2–1 win over the Twins at Comiskey Park. Frank Thomas hit a home run in the ninth to tie the contest. Robin Ventura drove in the winning run with a single.

Although he failed to win the MVP award for the third consecutive season, Thomas had a tremendous year in 1995. He batted .308 with 40 homers and 111 RBIs and led the league in walks with 136.

DECEMBER 12 — Two months after O. J. Simpson is found innocent of the double murder of his ex-wife and her companion, the White Sox sign Darren Lewis, most recently with the Reds, as a free agent.

DECEMBER 14 — Lance Johnson signs a contract with the Mets as a free agent.

Johnson gave the Mets the best season of his career in 1996, with a .333 batting average and league-leading totals in hits (227) and triples (21). He returned to the Sox in a trade in 1997.

DECEMBER 22 — Craig Grebeck signs a contract as a free agent with the Marlins.

DECEMBER 28 — The White Sox trade Tim Raines to the Yankees for Blaise Kozeniewski.

1996

Season in a Sentence

Expected to contend with one of the highest payrolls in baseball, the White Sox win 40 of their first 61 games, but they fail to reach the post-season and suffer an alarming drop in attendance.

Finish • Won • Lost • Pct • GB

Second   85   77   .525   14.5
In the wild-card race, the White Sox finished tied for third place, three games behind.

Manager

Terry Bevington

Stats	WS	AL	Rank
Batting Avg:	.281	.277	7
On-Base Pct:	.360	.350	4
Slugging Pct:	.447	.445	7
Home Runs:	195		8
Stolen Bases:	105		5
ERA:	4.52	4.99	2
Fielding Avg:	.982	.982	6
Runs Scored:	898		6
Runs Allowed:	794		4

Starting Lineup

Ron Karkovice, c
Frank Thomas, 1b
Ray Durham, 2b
Robin Ventura, 3b
Ozzie Guillen, ss
Tony Phillips, lf
Dave Martinez, cf-rf
Danny Tartabull, rf
Harold Baines, dh
Darren Lewis, cf
Lyle Mouton, lf-rf

Pitchers

Alex Fernandez, sp
Wilson Alvarez, sp
Kevin Tapani, sp
James Baldwin, sp
Roberto Hernandez, rp
Bill Simas, rp
Larry Thomas, rp
Matt Karchner, rp

Attendance

1,676,403 (ninth in AL)

Club Leaders

Batting Avg:	Frank Thomas	.349
On-Base Pct:	Frank Thomas	.459
Slugging Pct:	Frank Thomas	.626
Home Runs:	Frank Thomas	40
RBIs:	Frank Thomas	134
Runs:	Tony Phillips	119
Stolen Bases:	Ray Durham	30
Wins:	Alex Fernandez	16
Strikeouts:	Alex Fernandez	200
ERA:	Alex Fernandez	3.45
Saves:	Roberto Hernandez	38

JANUARY 2   Jeff Shaw signs a contract as a free agent with the Reds.

Shaw was nearly 30 when he left the Sox organization and had a less-than-impressive career at that point with an 11–25 record and a 4.50 ERA. He soon found his groove, however, and saved 194 games for the Reds and Dodgers from 1997 through 2001 in addition to playing in two All-Star Games.

JANUARY 5   The White Sox sign Harold Baines, most recently with the Orioles, as a free agent.

White Sox fans were thrilled with the return of the popular Baines to Chicago. He played two seasons in his return engagement with the Sox as a starting designated hitter.

JANUARY 20   The White Sox sign Tony Phillips, most recently with the Angels, as a free agent.

As the White Sox's leadoff hitter and left fielder in 1996, Phillips led the AL in walks with 125 and scored 119 runs, but he became embroiled in plenty of controversy. He left spring training camp in Sarasota for 48 hours after announcing his "retirement" and went back to his home in Scottsdale, Arizona. In May, Phillips fought a fan in Milwaukee (see May 15, 1996).

JANUARY 22   The White Sox trade Andrew Lorraine and Charles Poe to the Athletics for Danny Tartabull.

FEBRUARY 3   The White Sox sign Kevin Tapani, most recently with the Dodgers, as a free agent.

MARCH 31   At the Kingdome in Seattle, the White Sox and Mariners participate in the first-ever regular season game played in the month of March. The contest was played on a Sunday night on national television over ESPN. The Mariners won 3–2 in 12 innings, with Alex Rodriguez driving in the winning run with a single. White Sox batters struck out 21 times, including 14 in the first seven innings facing Randy Johnson. Frank Thomas hit a two-run homer in the first inning to account for the only two Chicago runs.

Thomas had another outstanding season in 1996 with a .349 average, 40 homers, 134 RBIs and 110 runs scored.

APRIL 9   Six days after "Unabomber" Theodore Kaczynski is arrested in Montana, the White Sox lose the home opener 3–2 to the Rangers before 34,750 at Comiskey Park.

The Sox started the season 2–5 with five one-run losses.

APRIL 11   Lyle Mouton hits a three-run walk-off homer in the 11th to beat the Rangers 8–5 at Comiskey Park. Will Clark put Texas ahead 5–4 with a home run in the top of the 10th, but the Sox tied it in their half on a sacrifice fly by Ozzie Guillen.

APRIL 13   The White Sox scored three runs in the ninth and one in the 12th to beat the Athletics 6–5 at Comiskey Park. Tony Phillips drove in the winning run with a single.

APRIL 15   The White Sox blow a 10–0 lead, but escape with an 11–10 victory over the Royals in Kansas City. The Sox scored five runs in the first inning and five more in the second, but the Royals came back with six in their half of the second and eventually tied the score 10–10 with two tallies in the eighth. Ozzie Guillen's double drove in the winning run.

APRIL 26   The White Sox-Angels game at Comiskey Park is postponed because of cold weather.

APRIL 30   A blackout in Cleveland caused by a computer glitch causes a 14-minute delay during the fourth inning of a 5–3 loss to the Indians at Jacobs Field.

MAY 4   Harold Baines hits a grand slam off Steve Howe in the ninth inning of an 11–5 victory over the Yankees in New York. Baines entered the game as a pinch-hitter in the eighth inning.

MAY 11   A two-run, walk-off homer by Harold Baines off John Wetteland in the ninth inning beats the Yankees 7–4 at Comiskey Park.

MAY 15   In a game halted early by fog, the White Sox clobber the Brewers 20–8 in Milwaukee. The contest was stopped in the first inning when Sox right fielder

Danny Tartabull barely reacted to a fly ball because he couldn't see it coming toward him in the thick haze. Play was held up for one hour and 50 minutes because of the fog. The contest resumed when Brewers outfielder Chuck Carr and Dave Martinez of the Sox fielded several fungo flies without difficulty. The Pale Hose scored two runs in the first inning, six in the second, three in the third, six in the sixth and three in the eighth. Frank Thomas drove in six runs on a homer and a double. Others driving in runs were Robin Ventura (three), Harold Baines (three), Tony Phillips (two), Ozzie Guillen (two), Martinez (two), Tartabull (one) and Ron Karkovice (one). Scoring were Guillen (four), Martinez (three), Thomas (three), Phillips (two), Robin Ventura (two), Karkovice (two), Tartabull (one), Baines (one), Ray Durham (one) and Jose Munoz (one).

Tony Phillips punched a heckling fan in the ninth inning. For striking 23-year-old Chris Hovorka of Racine, Wisconsin, the Milwaukee County Sheriff's office recommended that Phillips be charged with misdemeanor battery, which carried penalties of up to nine months in jail. A week later, the criminal charges were dropped and both Phillips and Hovorka were fined $287 for disorderly conduct.

MAY 17   Harold Baines hits a three-run homer during a five-run 10th inning to beat the Tigers 11–6 in Detroit.

MAY 18   Ray Durham hits a grand slam off Greg Keagle in the ninth inning of a 16–4 win over the Tigers in Detroit.

MAY 19   Robin Ventura and Darren Lewis both hit grand slams during a 14–3 victory over the Tigers in Detroit. Ventura hit his slam in the third inning off Gregg Olson, while Lewis connected against Greg Gohr in the ninth. It was the third straight game that the White Sox reached double digits in runs, all against the Tigers at Tiger Stadium. The Sox scored 63 runs in five games between May 15 and May 19.

MAY 21   The White Sox collect only two hits, but defeat the Blue Jays 2–1 at Comiskey Park. Both hits were run-scoring doubles off Jeff Ware by Frank Thomas in the first inning and Darren Lewis in the third.

MAY 22   With the White Sox trailing 1–0, a two-run, walk-off triple by Lyle Mouton in the 11th inning beats the Blue Jays 2–1 at Comiskey Park.

Third baseman Robin Ventura was a mainstay of the Chicago lineup through most of the 1990s, a consistent hitter and fielder.

MAY 26   The White Sox connect for four homers in a seven-run eighth inning, including three in a row, to cap a 12–1 win over the Brewers at Comiskey Park. It was the Sox's eighth win in a row. Frank Thomas, Harold Baines and Robin Ventura hit back-to-back-to-back home runs off Mike Potts. After Lyle Mouton was retired, Chad Kreuter hit Chicago's fourth homer of the inning. They were the only four homers that were struck by the White Sox during the game.

Terry Bevington got himself in hot water for his comments to the media about the heated rivalry between the White Sox and Brewers, which the Sox manager called "women's stuff, gossip." Bevington made things worse by trying to explain himself. "What I said had nothing to do with women. It's just that a woman takes an eight-minute call and turns it into 30 minutes talking about soap operas and stuff," Bevington said. "A man gets on the phone and gets right to the point."

MAY 28   Robin Ventura leads the White Sox to a 9–5 win over the Blue Jays in Toronto. Pinch-hitting for Chris Snopek, Ventura hit a long homer in the sixth inning that struck the glass of the Windows Restaurant in center field. He stayed in the game at third base and hit another home run in the eighth.

Ventura hit .287 with 34 homers and 105 RBIs in 1996 along with winning his fourth career Gold Glove.

JUNE 2   The White Sox sweep the Tigers 4–2 and 13–5 at Comiskey Park.

JUNE 4   In the first round of the amateur draft, the White Sox select pitcher Bobby Seay from Sarasota High School in Sarasota, Florida.

Seay didn't reach the majors until 2001, when he was with the Devil Rays. As of 2008, he was a journeyman relief pitcher. Other future major leaguers drafted and signed by the White Sox in 1996 were Josh Paul (second round), Joe Crede (fifth), Marcus Jones (eighth), Chad Bradford (13th) and Chris Heintz (19th).

JUNE 9   Down 6–2, the White Sox score eight runs in the fourth inning and win 12–9 against the Orioles in Baltimore.

JUNE 10   The White Sox tie the Indians for first with an 8–2 win over the Red Sox at Comiskey Park.

The Sox had a record of 40–21 on June 10. An eight-game losing streak from June 15 through June 22 knocked the club five games behind, but by July 7 the Sox clawed their way to only one game back of Cleveland. Terry Bevington's team couldn't keep pace, however, and finished 14½ games out in the AL Central. The Sox were in the wild-card chase well into September, however.

JUNE 12   Alex Fernandez strikes out 13 batters in nine innings, but the White Sox lose 3–2 in 12 innings to the Red Sox at Comiskey Park.

Fernandez was 16–10 with a 3.45 ERA and fanned 200 batters in 258 innings in 1996. A Miami native, Fernandez signed a free-agent deal with the Marlins at the end of the season.

JUNE 27   Eleven days after the Bulls win the NBA championship in a series against the Sonics following a 72–10 record in the regular season, the White Sox take a 14–3 lead after five innings and beat the Indians 15–10 at Comiskey Park.

JULY 16	Wilson Alvarez strikes out 12 batters in seven innings during an 11–2 win over the Twins in Minneapolis.
JULY 27	The White Sox trade Robert Ellis to the Angels for Pat Borders.
JULY 30	James Baldwin allows only one hit in eight shutout innings during a 2–1 victory over the Athletics in Oakland. The only hit off Baldwin was a bloop single in the fourth inning by Damon Mashore.
AUGUST 3	The White Sox outlast the Rangers 11–9 in Arlington. The Sox led 8–2 before Texas tied the score. Ray Durham broke the 8–8 deadlock with an eighth-inning homer.
AUGUST 4	Harold Baines hits a grand slam off Ed Vosberg in the eighth inning, but the White Sox lose 9–5 to the Rangers in Arlington.
AUGUST 5	The White Sox clobber the Rangers 15–5 in Arlington.
AUGUST 6	Darryl Strawberry hits three homers for the Yankees in a 9–2 win over the White Sox in New York. All three were struck off Kevin Tapani.
AUGUST 7	The White Sox score five runs in the 10th inning and beat the Yankees 8–4 in New York.
AUGUST 9	Robin Ventura hits a walk-off homer in the ninth inning to lift the White Sox to a 4–3 win over the Orioles at Comiskey Park.
AUGUST 12	Harold Baines hits a walk-off homer in the ninth inning off John Wetteland for a 3–2 win over the Yankees at Comiskey Park. It was Harold's second walk-off homer against Wetteland in 1996. The first was on May 11.
AUGUST 13	With the White Sox trailing 4–2 in the fifth inning, Robin Ventura hits a 3–0 pitch off David Weathers for a grand slam, leading to an 8–4 victory over the Yankees at Comiskey Park.

The win gave the White Sox a 67–53 record. The Sox were five games behind the Indians in the AL Central, but they seemed headed for the post-season by virtue of a 4½-game advantage over the Orioles in the wild-card race.

AUGUST 19	Trailing 7–5, the White Sox erupt for seven runs in the ninth inning to win 12–7 over the Tigers in Detroit. Ozzie Guillen and Danny Tartabull both hit three-run homers during the outburst.
AUGUST 31	The White Sox trade Scott Vollmer to the Angels for Don Slaught.
SEPTEMBER 10	The White Sox fall out of first place in the wild card race with a 5–1 loss to the Orioles in Baltimore.
SEPTEMBER 14	Danny Tartabull drives in six runs during a 13–5 win over the Red Sox in Boston. Tartabull hit a sacrifice fly in the first inning, an RBI-single in the fifth and a grand slam in the eighth. The slam was struck off Mark Brandenburg.

SEPTEMBER 15   Frank Thomas homers in his first three at-bats, but the White Sox lose 9–8 to the Red Sox in Boston. All three were struck off Tim Wakefield. In all, Chicago batters hit five home runs off Wakefield, but each came with no one on base. Robin Ventura and Danny Tartabull hit the others.

Thomas came into the game tied with Carlton Fisk as the all-time White Sox home run leader. Fisk hit 214 homers with the White Sox.

SEPTEMBER 20   Frank Thomas hits a grand slam off Rich Robertson in the second inning of a 7–3 win over the Twins at Comiskey Park.

The win gave the White Sox an 82–73 record and a spot in third place in the wild-card race, two games back of the Orioles. The Mariners were second, one-half game behind Baltimore. The Sox lost four of their last seven games to wreck any chances for post-season play.

SEPTEMBER 24   The White Sox score three runs in the ninth inning to defeat the Royals 3–2 at Comiskey Park. The runs were driven home on a Frank Thomas single, a Robin Ventura double and a walk-off single from Ray Durham.

OCTOBER 5   Jim Leyland takes a job managing the Marlins.

The White Sox had offered Leyland a lucrative contract to manage the club. After Leyland accepted the position in Florida, the Sox signed Terry Bevington to a new two-year deal.

NOVEMBER 19   Two weeks after Bill Clinton wins a second term as president by defeating Bob Dole, the White Sox sign Albert Belle, most recently with the Indians, as a free agent.

The signing of the controversial Belle showed fans that the White Sox meant business in trying to reach the post-season. His $11 million-per-year salary over five years made him the highest-paid player in baseball history at the time, both as annual compensation and as a total package. White Sox owner Jerry Reinsdorf had been a vocal proponent of fiscal restraint and made his beliefs known publicly on several occasions. The deal with Belle shocked and angered the other owners in baseball, many of whom labeled Reinsdorf a hypocrite. Notoriously antisocial, Belle certainly came with considerable baggage, despite his lofty batting numbers while playing eight seasons with Cleveland. Battling constantly with both the media and the fans, Belle was saddled with a well-earned and unsavory reputation as a malcontent. Once, he threw a baseball at a photographer. On another occasion, he purposely hit a heckling fan with a ball at a distance of less than 20 feet. There was also the infamous "Batgate" incident among Belle's transgressions (see July 15, 1994). Overall, he drew five suspensions either from the league or his team in his first eight years in the majors. Although Belle hit 30 homers and drove in 116 runs for the White Sox in 1997, it was considered a down year for him in comparison to previous seasons. In 1998, he had one of the best seasons of anyone in White Sox history, with 49 homers, 152 RBIs, 113 runs scored, a .328 batting average and a league-leading .655 slugging percentage. When Belle fell out of the top three in major league salaries following the season, he invoked a free agent clause in his contract and signed a five-year deal with the Orioles. Belle seemed headed for the Hall of

Fame in spite of his personal problems, but his power and ability to run soon deteriorated due to a serious hip condition. Belle's last big-league season was in 2001, at the age of 34.

DECEMBER 8   Alex Fernandez signs a contract as a free agent with the Marlins.

DECEMBER 11   The White Sox sign Jaime Navarro, most recently with the Cubs, as a free agent.

After signing a four-year contract, Navarro was expected to become the club's number-one starter, but he proved to be a huge flop. He spent three seasons with the White Sox and had a record of 25–43 with an earned run average of 6.06.

DECEMBER 13   Kevin Tapani signs a contract as a free agent with the Cubs, and Pat Borders signs as a free agent with the Indians.

DECEMBER 23   The White Sox sign Don Slaught, most recently with the Padres, as a free agent.

1997   Sox

Season in a Sentence

In the infamous "white flag" trade, the White Sox deal three of their top pitchers to the Giants at the July 31 trading deadline with the club only three games out of first place.

Finish • Won • Lost • Pct • GB

Second   80   81   .497   6.0
In the wild-card race, the White Sox finished in third place, 15½ games behind.

Manager

Terry Bevington

Stats

Stats	WS	AL	Rank
Batting Avg:	.273	.271	6
On-Base Pct:	.341	.340	7
Slugging Pct:	.417	.428	10
Home Runs:	158		10 (tie)
Stolen Bases:	106		7
ERA:	4.74	4.57	10
Fielding Avg:	.978	.982	13
Runs Scored:	779		9
Runs Allowed:	833		10 (tie)

Starting Lineup

Jorge Fabregas, c
Frank Thomas, 1b-dh
Ray Durham, 2b
Chris Snopek, 3b
Ozzie Guillen, ss
Albert Belle, lf
Mike Cameron, cf
Dave Martinez, rf-cf
Harold Baines, dh
Lyle Mouton, rf

Pitchers

James Baldwin, sp
Doug Drabek, sp
Jaime Navarro, sp
Wilson Alvarez, sp
Danny Darwin, sp
Roberto Hernandez, rp
Tony Castillo, rp
Matt Karchner, rp
Chuck McElroy, rp

Attendance

1,864,782 (eighth in AL)

Club Leaders

Batting Avg:	Frank Thomas	.347
On-Base Pct:	Frank Thomas	.456
Slugging Pct:	Frank Thomas	.611
Home Runs:	Frank Thomas	35
RBIs:	Frank Thomas	125
Runs:	Frank Thomas	110
Stolen Bases:	Ray Durham	33
Wins:	Doug Drabek	12
	James Baldwin	12
Strikeouts:	Jaime Navarro	142
ERA:	Wilson Alvarez	3.03
Saves:	Roberto Hernandez	28

JANUARY 11   The White Sox sign Tony Pena, most recently with the Indians, as a free agent.

JANUARY 14   The White Sox sign Doug Drabek, most recently with the Astros, as a free agent.

FEBRUARY 26   A man is jailed for trying to attack Albert Belle at the White Sox's training complex in Sarasota. David Henry, age 38, from North Ridgeville, Ohio, told police he was "on a mission from God." Henry, who was angry that Belle left the Indians to sign with the Sox, scaled an eight-foot fence to confront Belle.

MARCH 21   Robin Ventura breaks his right leg and tears ligaments in his ankle sliding into home plate during an exhibition game against the Red Sox in Sarasota. Ventura didn't play again until July 24.

APRIL 1   The White Sox open with a 6–5 win over the Blue Jays in 10 innings in Toronto. The Sox scored three runs in the eighth inning, the first two on a home run by Albert Belle, who was making his regular-season debut with the Sox. Belle had gone 67 at-bats during spring training without a homer. Chicago tied the game 5–5 on a pinch-hit homer from Norberto Martin. In the 10th, Ray Durham reached on a two-out walk, then scored all the way from first base when a grounder rolled under the glove of shortstop Alex Gonzalez. Durham just beat the throw to the plate. Tony Phillips collected three hits, including a double.

APRIL 4   The White Sox lose the home opener 8–7 in 10 innings against the Tigers before 38,560 at Comiskey Park. The Sox came back from a 7–1 deficit to tie the game with six runs in the eighth. Ron Karkovice homered in the losing cause.

APRIL 5   The White Sox lose a 15–12 slugfest to the Tigers at Comiskey Park. The Sox scored seven runs in the fourth inning to move ahead 10–8, but they couldn't hold the lead.

APRIL 6   Wind causes a seven-minute delay during the third inning of a 5–3 loss to the Tigers at Comiskey Park. Gusts were clocked at 43 miles per hour. One of them ripped a giant banner off the center-field scoreboard, stopping play.

APRIL 8   The game against the Blue Jays at Comiskey Park is postponed by cold weather. The contest on April 9 was moved from a 7:05 p.m. start to 1:05 p.m. because of a forecast of continuing cold.

APRIL 9   The attendance at Comiskey Park is only 746 with a game-time temperature of 34 degrees. The White Sox lost 5–0 to the Blue Jays.

APRIL 13   After trailing 7–0 after five innings, the White Sox rally to beat the Tigers 11–8 in 12 innings in the first game of a double-header in Detroit. The Sox tied the score 7–7 with three runs in the ninth. Both teams scored in the 11th before Chicago added three tallies in the 12th. Roberto Hernandez was the winning pitcher despite blowing a save opportunity in the 11th. In the nightcap, Hernandez was the losing pitcher in a 4–2 decision, the result of surrendering a three-run, walk-off homer to Travis Fryman.

Jackie Robinson's number 42 was retired throughout baseball in 1997. The last White Sox player to wear the number was Scott Ruffcorn in 1996.

APRIL 20   Tony Phillips walks with the bases loaded during a wacky at-bat in the 11th inning to provide the winning run in an 8–7 win over the Yankees in New York. With Brian Boehringer on the mound and the count 3–1, Phillips stepped out of the box and would not return until Boehringer moved into the stretch position. Phillips pointed at the Yankee pitcher and took umbrage when first-base umpire John Shulock snapped at him to resume hitting. Phillips walked toward Shulock shouting and waving, and had to be restrained by first-base coach Ron Jackson. After a three-minute delay, Phillips went back to the plate and drew the walk.

APRIL 21   In his first at-bat of the game against the Yankees in New York, Tony Phillips is ejected by umpire John Shulock after continuing the argument over the incident of the previous evening. The White Sox lost 5–4. Phillips was suspended for two days by the American League.

APRIL 23   The White Sox blow a seven-run lead, but they recover to beat the Orioles 11–9 in 10 innings at Camden Yards. The Sox were ahead 9–2 in the sixth, but Baltimore scored two in the sixth and five in the seventh. Lyle Mouton broke the 9–9 tie with a sacrifice fly.

APRIL 30   The White Sox lose 6–2 to the Rangers at Comiskey Park in a contest stopped in the top of the seventh inning by rain driven by winds clocked at 60 miles per hour.

On May 3, the White Sox had a record of 8–18. By June 25, the club fought its way back to the .500 mark with a record of 37–37.

MAY 11   Albert Belle hits a grand slam off Willie Adams in the third inning of an 8–6 win over the Athletics at Comiskey Park. The slam followed an intentional walk to Frank Thomas. Wilson Alvarez struck out 12 batters in seven innings.

MAY 12   Leading 6–2 against the Angels in Anaheim, the White Sox allow 13 runs in the seventh inning and lose 16–8. The 13 runs scored on 11 hits, two walks and an error with Danny Darwin, Larry Thomas, Al Levine and Tony Castillo on the mound.

MAY 15   Chris Snopek hits a two-out, two-run double in the ninth inning to beat the Mariners 4–3 in Seattle.

MAY 18   The White Sox defeat the Athletics 10–4 in Oakland.

On the same day, the White Sox traded Tony Phillips and Chad Kreuter to the Angels for Chuck McElroy and Jorge Fabregas. In August, Phillips was arrested on a charge of cocaine possession. He pled guilty and entered a court-ordered drug diversion program.

MAY 20   The White Sox hammer the Red Sox 10–1 at Comiskey Park. Frank Thomas reached base in his first three plate appearances on a double and two walks to extend his streak of reaching base in consecutive plate appearances to 15. Thomas flied out in the fifth inning to attempt to tie the major league record of 16, set by Ted Williams in 1957. In the 15 plate appearances, which took place over four games, Thomas reached on 10 hits (six singles, three doubles and a homer) and five walks. The 10 hits in consecutive official at-bats tied a White Sox record set by Harry McCurdy in 1926 and tied by Rip Radcliff in 1938.

Thomas became the first White Sox batter since Luke Appling in 1943 to lead the AL in batting average. Thomas hit .347 in 1997 and also led the league in on-base percentage (.456), in addition to 35 homers, 125 RBIs and 109 runs scored.

MAY 21   The White Sox score exactly 10 runs for the third game in a row and defeat the Red Sox 10–5 at Comiskey Park.

MAY 25   The White Sox lose 11–7 to the Brewers at Comiskey Park in a game highlighted by a bizarre bench-clearing incident. In the Milwaukee fourth, both benches and bullpens emptied when Gerald Williams of the Brewers, who was on second base, and Chicago pitcher James Baldwin started yelling at each other behind the mound. Baldwin accused Williams of trying to steal the signs of the catcher. No punches were thrown.

MAY 27   Albert Belle haunts his former teammates by hitting a grand slam off Albie Lopez in the fourth inning of an 8–2 win over the Indians at Comiskey Park. The slam followed an intentional walk to Frank Thomas. It was the second time in less than three weeks that Belle homered after an intentional pass to Thomas loaded the bases.

MAY 29   Jorge Fabregas hits a two-run homer during a four-run 11th inning to lead the White Sox to a 5–2 win over the Red Sox in Boston.

JUNE 1   Albert Belle extends his hitting streak to 27 games during a 7–4 loss to the Brewers in Milwaukee.

JUNE 3   Dave Martinez hits two homers and two singles during a 9–5 win over the Indians at Jacobs Field, but Albert Belle is the focal point in his first game in Cleveland since signing his lucrative contract with the White Sox the previous off-season. Belle was booed incessantly. A plane circled overhead pulling a banner reading: "Will Rogers never met Albert Belle." Fans in left field threw fake money, ice, cups and other debris, including a pair of binoculars, in his direction. The game was briefly delayed twice to pick up the objects. Belle kicked away the debris and motioned to fans to bring it on. Belle's three-run homer intensified the problem. When Belle fouled off a pitch behind the plate in the ninth, a fan threw it back, missing the White Sox slugger by about 30 feet. At the end of the contest, Belle flipped an obscene gesture toward the stands. He was fined $5,000 by the American League for the act.

On the same day, the White Sox selected shortstop Jason Dellaero from the University of South Florida with the first pick of the amateur draft. The White Sox had six first-round choices due to free agent compensation. Later in the opening round, the Sox chose Aaron Myette and Jim Parque. Other future major leaguers drafted and signed by the Sox in 1997 included Pat Daneker (fifth round) and Matt Smith (44th round).

JUNE 4   Tensions between the White Sox and Indians continue during a 9–4 win in Cleveland. Albert Belle was hit by a pitch from Jose Mesa in the eighth inning, setting off a series of hit batsmen and close calls. White Sox reliever Bill Simas threw inside to Marquis Grissom in the ninth, prompting Grissom to walk toward the mound, pointing his bat. Both benches and bullpens emptied, but no punches were thrown.

JUNE 7	The White Sox edge the Orioles in an 11-inning, 1–0 battle in Baltimore. Harold Baines ended the game with a bases-loaded single. Wilson Alvarez (eight innings), Matt Karchner (one-third of an inning), Tony Castillo (one inning) and Roberto Hernandez ($1^2/_3$ innings) combined on the shutout. Hernandez pitched out of bases-loaded jams in both the 10th and 11th innings.
JUNE 13	On the day the Bulls complete a six-game victory over the Utah Jazz in the NBA finals, the White Sox play a National League team during the regular season for the first time and beat the Reds 3–1 at Cinergy Field in Cincinnati. The Sox and the Reds hadn't played a meaningful game since the 1919 World Series.
	Albert Belle sneered at Reds owner Marge Schott when she tried to say hello during batting practice. Schott, who had previously been suspended by Major League Baseball for racist comments, tried to introduce herself and her dog to Belle. Instead, Belle waved her off and walked away muttering, "The hell with her."
JUNE 15	The White Sox pummel the Reds 14–6 in Cincinnati. Jorge Fabregas collected four hits, including a homer, in four at-bats and drove in five runs.
JUNE 16	The White Sox play the Cubs for the first time during the regular season and lose 8–3 at Comiskey Park. With the exception of the post-season City Series played between the White Sox and the Cubs from 1903 through 1942, it was the first meaningful game between Chicago's two teams since the 1906 World Series.
	The Sox won the last two games of the three-game series by scores of 5–3 and 3–0. The series drew 124,666 into Comiskey Park on a Monday, Tuesday and Wednesday.
JUNE 25	Trailing 7–2, the White Sox score five runs in the eighth inning and one in the 10th for an 8–7 win over the Royals at Comiskey Park. Harold Baines hit a three-run homer in the eighth. The winning run scored on a pinch-single by Mario Valdez with the bases loaded.
	The White Sox were 11–1 against the Royals in 1997.
JUNE 26	The White Sox rout the Twins 11–1 in Minneapolis.
JUNE 27	Albert Belle collects five hits, including a homer, in five at-bats during a 10–6 win over the Twins in Minneapolis.
JUNE 30	The White Sox play the Pirates for the first time during the regular season and lose 3–1 at Three Rivers Stadium.
JULY 8	Albert Belle fails to play in the American League's 3–1 win in the All-Star Game at Jacobs Field in Cleveland. Belle asked AL manager Joe Torre not to play him unless he was needed due to the rough treatment he received five weeks earlier in the city (see June 3, 1997) and because of the cascade of boos showered upon him during pre-game introductions. Belle was the only position player not to play.
JULY 21	During a 3–0 win over the Tigers in Detroit, Wilson Alvarez becomes the first White Sox pitcher to strike out four batters in an inning. In the seventh, Alvarez fanned Tony Clark, then Phil Nevin reached first base by swinging at and missing a wild

pitch with two strikes. Alvarez struck out Melvin Nieves and Orlando Miller to end the inning.

JULY 24   Robin Ventura plays for the first time since breaking his leg on March 21 and drives in the winning run with a double in the eighth inning to beat the Rangers 2–1 at Comiskey Park.

JULY 29   The White Sox trade Harold Baines to the Orioles for Juan Bautista.

Baines was the White Sox's starting designated hitter and one of the club's most popular players. The deal was made to reduce payroll. After signing Albert Belle to a record-breaking contract the previous November, the Sox were averaging only 23,596 fans per game at Comiskey Park and the club faced heavy financial losses.

JULY 31   The White Sox blow a nine-run lead, but still manage to defeat the Angels 14–12 in Anaheim. The Sox scored three runs in the first inning and six in the second for a 9–0 lead, but starting pitcher Jaime Navarro allowed 11 runs in $4^2/_3$ innings. At the end of the fifth, the score was 11–11. It was 12–12 heading into the ninth, when Chicago added two runs for the victory.

Earlier on the same day, the White Sox traded Roberto Hernandez, Wilson Alvarez and Danny Darwin to the Giants for Keith Foulke, Bob Howry, Mike Caruso, Ken Vining, Brian Manning and Lorenzo Barcello. This deal has become known in White Sox lore as the "white flag trade" because club management conceded the 1997 division title. At the time, the White Sox were 52–53, but despite the losing record were in third place, just 3½ games behind the Indians. By signing off on the deal, Jerry Reinsdorf became less popular in Chicago than Mrs. O'Leary's cow. He further outraged Sox fans with his justification of the trade of two starting pitchers and the team's closer. "Anyone who thinks this White Sox team will catch Cleveland is crazy," said Reinsdorf. "We're not even in second place, so we have to prepare for next year and the future." General manager Ron Schueler defended the deal on the grounds that all three pitchers would be free agents after the 1997 season. The Giants won the NL West with the help of Alvarez, Darwin and Hernandez. Sox fans felt betrayed by the trade as management seemed more interested in the bottom line than in winning a pennant. The resentment lingered for several years, seriously injuring the club's ability to sell tickets. Attendance dropped dramatically in both 1998 and 1999, as the Sox ranked 12th and 13th in the AL those two seasons. But in 2000, the White Sox won the AL Central with significant help out of the bullpen from both Foulke and Howry, who were acquired in the July 31, 1997 "white flag" trade. That season, neither Alvarez nor Darwin were pitching in the major leagues.

AUGUST 8   Randy Johnson strikes out 19 White Sox batters, one shy of the record for a nine-inning game, in a 5–0 Mariners win in Seattle.

AUGUST 14   The White Sox trade Tony Pena to the Astros for Julien Tucker.

AUGUST 16   Nellie Fox Day is held at Comiskey Park to honor the former second baseman who played for the White Sox from 1950 through 1963. Fox died in 1975. He was elected to the Hall of Fame earlier in 1997. The first ceremonial pitch was thrown by Nellie's widow, Joanne.

AUGUST 22   Albert Belle hits two homers off Darren Oliver, one of them a grand slam in the
                 sixth inning, and drives in six runs, but the White Sox lose 17–8 to the Rangers in
                 Arlington.

                 *It wasn't easy living with Albert Belle and his idiosyncrasies. The following
                 incidents occurred during the 1997 season, in addition to his obscene gesture (see
                 June 3, 1997) and refusal to play in the All-Star Game (see July 8, 1997). The
                 Sox held a Kid's Day autograph session for the players, but Belle decided not to
                 attend and spent the time reading a newspaper in the clubhouse. He didn't like
                 the color of the hitting background, so the club accommodated him and pained
                 it black. Belle was allowed his own flavor of Gatorade in the dugout. The club
                 hired his best friend to be a security guard. Batting practice was re-scheduled so
                 that a specific coach could soft-toss to Belle while music he selected blasted in
                 everyone's ears. He also insisted on keeping the temperature in the clubhouse so
                 low that his teammates resorted to dressing in the dugout.*

AUGUST 29   The White Sox play the Astros for the first time during the regular season and win
                 5–4 at Comiskey Park.

SEPTEMBER 1   The day after Princess Diana dies following a car accident in Paris, the White Sox
                 play the Cardinals for the first time during the regular season and win 5–4 in
                 St. Louis. Magglio Ordonez broke the 4–4 tie with a homer in the ninth inning.

                 *The win gave the White Sox a 69–68 record and a position in third place in
                 the AL Central, four games behind the Indians and one-half game back of the
                 Brewers. Beginning on September 2, the Sox lost six games in a row, including
                 three to Cleveland, to put an end to post-season dreams.*

SEPTEMBER 2   The White Sox trade Darren Lewis to the Dodgers for Chad Fonville.

SEPTEMBER 14   The White Sox retire Carlton Fisk's number 72 prior to an 8–3 loss to the Indians at
                 Comiskey Park. The Sox led 2–0 heading into the eighth before the Indians scored
                 seven runs. Terry Bevington used nine pitchers, five of them in the eighth, in an effort
                 to stem the tide. Keith Foulke entered the game without warming up in the bullpen.

SEPTEMBER 15   The White Sox play the Brewers for the last time as American League rivals and lose
                 11–10 in Milwaukee. The Brewers moved to the National League in 1998.

SEPTEMBER 19   The White Sox sneak past the Red Sox 5–4 in 10 innings at Fenway Park. Albert Belle's
                 grand slam off Tom Gordon in the ninth gave Chicago a 4–1 lead, but Boston retaliated
                 with three in their half. Frank Thomas drove in the game-winner with a single.

                 *The White Sox hit four grand slams in 1997, and Belle accounted for all four of
                 them. The four slams is also an individual club record.*

SEPTEMBER 30   The White Sox fire Terry Bevington as manager. He compiled a record of 222–214
                 with the Sox since being hired in June 1995. Bevington had considerable trouble
                 communicating with his players, had strained relations with some of his coaches and
                 alienated the media and the fans. He has yet to manage another big-league team (see
                 December 4, 1997).

NOVEMBER 18   In the expansion draft, the White Sox lose Jorge Fabregas, Chris Clemons and Chuck McElroy to the Diamondbacks.

DECEMBER 3   Dave Martinez signs with the Devil Rays as a free agent.

DECEMBER 4   The White Sox hire 41-year-old Jerry Manuel as manager. Manuel's only prior experience as a manager was in the Expos' minor league system in 1990. He was a second baseman in the majors with three clubs from 1975 through 1982 and hit only .150 in 96 games and 127 at-bats. Manuel was a coach with the Expos from 1991 through 1996 and was Jim Leyland's bench coach on the 1997 world champion Marlins. Manuel was the White Sox's second African-American manager, following Larry Doby in 1978.

DECEMBER 10   The White Sox sign two catchers as free agents on the same day in Charlie O'Brien, most recently with the Blue Jays, and Chad Kreuter, most recently with the Angels.

DECEMBER 11   Doug Drabek signs with the Orioles as a free agent.

1998   Sox

Season in a Sentence

With the youngest team in the American League, the White Sox overcome a slow start under new manager Jerry Manuel to win 45 of their last 75 games.

Finish •Won • Lost • Pct • GB

Second   80   82   .494   9.0
In the wild-card race, the White Sox finish in fourth place, 12 games behind.

Manager

Jerry Manuel

Stats

Stats	WS	AL	Rank
Batting Avg:	.271	.271	8
On-Base Pct:	.339	.340	8
Slugging Pct:	.444	.432	6
Home Runs:	198		7
Stolen Bases:	127		6
ERA:	5.22	4.65	14
Fielding Avg:	.977	.981	13
Runs Scored:	861		4
Runs Allowed:	931		14

Starting Lineup

Chad Kreuter, c
Wil Cordero, 1b
Ray Durham, 2b
Robin Ventura, 3b
Mike Caruso, ss
Albert Belle, lf
Mike Cameron, cf
Magglio Ordonez, rf
Frank Thomas, dh
Greg Norton, 1b
Jeff Abbott, cf-rf-lf

Pitchers

Mike Sirotka, sp
James Baldwin, sp
Jaime Navarro, sp
Jim Parque, sp
John Snyder, sp
Jason Bere, sp
Scott Eyre, sp-rp
Bill Simas, rp
Keith Foulke, rp
Bob Howry, rp

Attendance

1,391,146 (12th in AL)

Club Leaders

Batting Avg:	Albert Belle	.328
On-Base Pct:	Albert Belle	.399
Slugging Pct:	Albert Belle	.655
Home Runs:	Albert Belle	49
RBIs:	Albert Belle	152
Runs:	Albert Belle	113
Stolen Bases:	Ray Durham	36
Wins:	Mike Sirotka	14
Strikeouts:	Mike Sirotka	128
ERA:	Mike Sirotka	5.06
Saves:	Bill Simas	18

JANUARY 8   The White Sox sign Ruben Sierra, most recently with the Blue Jays, as a free agent.

JANUARY 29   Eight days after the sexual relationship between Bill Clinton and Monica Lewinsky is exposed, Ozzie Guillen signs with the Orioles as a free agent. Guillen had played for the White Sox since 1985.

FEBRUARY 18 Broadcasting legend Harry Caray dies at the age of 83 from the after-effects of a heart attack four days after collapsing at a nightclub in Rancho Mirage, California, while having a Valentine's Day dinner with his wife.

             The White Sox began training in Tucson, Arizona, in 1998. The club had been training in Sarasota, Florida, from 1960 through 1997.

MARCH 23   The White Sox sign Wil Cordero, most recently with the Red Sox, as a free agent.

             The acquisition of Cordero was controversial. He was arrested twice in 1997 on domestic violence charges while with the Red Sox. In November 1997, Cordero received a 90-day sentence, suspended for two years. He played one season with the White Sox and hit .267 with 13 home runs in 96 games as a first baseman.

MARCH 31   The White Sox win Jerry Manuel's debut as manager with a 9–2 Opening Day decision over the Rangers in Arlington. The Sox broke a scoreless tie with seven runs in the fifth inning. Robin Ventura homered and Magglio Ordonez and Charlie O'Brien each had three hits. The contest was O'Brien's first with the White Sox.

             Ordonez played for the White Sox from 1997 through 2004 and played in four All-Star Games while with the club. For four seasons in a row beginning in 1999, Ordonez topped the 30-home run and 100-RBI marks. On the all-time White Sox career lists, Ordonez ranks second in slugging percentage (.525), fifth in home runs (187) and tied for seventh in extra-base hits (442).

APRIL 2   In the second game of the 1998 season, the Rangers clobber the White Sox 20–4 in Arlington. Texas scored 10 runs in the seventh inning. White Sox reliever Todd Rizzo had a disastrous major league debut, allowing six earned runs without retiring a batter.

             Rizzo lasted 12 games in the majors over two seasons and had a 12.38 ERA in eight innings.

APRIL 3   The White Sox play the Devil Rays for the first time and win 10–4 in St. Petersburg.

APRIL 4   Frank Thomas hits a disputed home run during an 8–2 loss to the Devil Rays at the Tropicana Dome in St. Petersburg. The fourth-inning drive struck a catwalk in left field and landed in foul territory. The umpires discussed the play for nearly five minutes before ruling it was a home run.

APRIL 6   In the home opener, the White Sox defeat the Rangers 5–4 before 25,358 at Comiskey Park. It was the smallest crowd for a Sox opener since 1975. Magglio Ordonez homered and broke a 4–4 tie with an RBI-single in the eighth.

APRIL 10   The White Sox play the Devil Rays for the first time at Comiskey Park and win 3–0. Robin Ventura collected four hits, including a triple and two doubles, in four at-bats.

APRIL 19   Center fielder Lou Frazier steals four bases during a 12-inning, 5–4 loss to the Blue Jays in Toronto. Frazier stole the bases without collecting a hit. He reached base on two walks and a force out.

The four bases stolen by Frazier on April 19, 1998, constituted one of the strangest statistical oddities in franchise history. The four he swiped on that date were the only four he collected while playing for the White Sox and were the last four of his major league career. He played in only seven games with the Sox and was hitless in seven at-bats with six strikeouts.

APRIL 22   The White Sox score nine runs in the fifth inning and win 14–7 over the Indians in Cleveland. Ray Durham reached base on an error in three consecutive plate appearances to tie a major league record.

Durham hit .285 with 19 home runs and 126 runs scored in 1998.

APRIL 23   Wil Cordero hits the first pitch thrown to him as a member of the White Sox for a home run, but the Sox lose 5–4 to the Indians in Cleveland.

APRIL 29   The White Sox hit six home runs and rout the Orioles 16–7 at Comiskey Park. Wil Cordero smacked a solo homer in the third inning and broke a 4–4 tie with a grand slam off Terry Mathews in the fifth. The Sox twice had consecutive home runs. Frank Thomas and Albert Belle hit back-to-back homers in the third inning, and Belle and Robin Ventura accomplished the feat in the seventh.

MAY 3   Albert Belle drives in six runs with a single, double and homer during a 12–1 win over the Angels in Anaheim.

MAY 12   The White Sox hit into six double plays in eight turns at bat, but they defeat the Angels 5–2 at Comiskey Park.

MAY 27   The White Sox outlast the Yankees 12–9 at Comiskey Park. The Sox broke a 3–3 tie with three runs in the seventh inning. Mike Caruso collected four hits on his 21st birthday, but he also dropped a fly ball with the bases loaded and two out in the third inning, allowing three runs to score.

Caruso was acquired by the White Sox in the "white flag" trade with the Giants in 1997. He made the jump from Class-A ball in 1997 to the starting shortstop job with the Sox in 1998 and hit .306 as a rookie. Caruso declined considerably during his sophomore season in 1999, however, as his inexperience showed in a flurry of mental mistakes at bat, on defense and on the base paths. By 2000, he was back in the minors. Caruso played in only 12 big-league games after his 23rd birthday.

MAY 28   The White Sox win a weird 11–7 decision over the Tigers in 10 innings in Detroit. The Sox scored five runs in the eighth inning for a 7–2 lead, but the Tigers responded with five tallies in the bottom of the ninth to tie the score 7–7. Chicago scored four times in the 10th without a hit on five walks, a wild pitch and a sacrifice fly.

JUNE 2   With two picks in the first round of the amateur draft, the White Sox select pitcher Kip Wells from Baylor University and outfielder Aaron Rowand from Cal State

Fullerton. Other future major leaguers drafted and signed by the White Sox in 1998 included Gary Majewski (second round), Josh Fogg (third round), Edwin Almonte (26th round) and Mark Buehrle (38th round). Buehrle is the best player ever drafted by the White Sox in the 20th round or later.

JUNE 5

The White Sox play at Wrigley Field in a regular season game for the first time and lose 6–5 to the Cubs on Brant Brown's walk-off homer in the 12th inning. Ray Durham struck out five times during the contest.

The Sox lost all three games of the series at Wrigley.

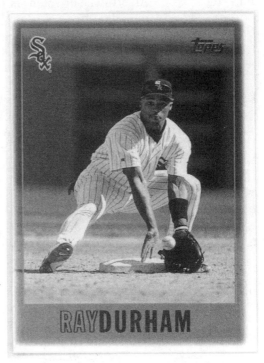

JUNE 8

The White Sox play the Cardinals at Comiskey Park for the first time and win 8–6.

JUNE 10

The White Sox overcome a seven-run deficit to defeat the Cardinals 10–8 in 11 innings at Comiskey Park. The Sox trailed 7–0 after five innings and were still down 8–4 heading into the ninth when a four-run rally sent the game into extra innings. Robin Ventura tied the score 8–8 with a two-out homer. In the 11th, Ventura came to the rescue again with a two-run walk-off home run. Albert Belle was also a hero with six runs batted in on a pair of three homers, the second of which brought Chicago within a run in the ninth.

Often overshadowed by the team's bigger stars, Ray Durham provided a blend of speed and power unique for a second baseman.

JUNE 20

Six days after the Bulls win the NBA finals against the Utah Jazz for their sixth championship just prior to the second of Michael Jordan's three retirements, run-scoring singles from Wil Cordero and Greg Norton in the 11th inning beat the Twins 8–7 at Comiskey Park. The Sox survived four Minnesota runs in the ninth that tied the score 5–5, then came back after the opposition scored in both the top of the 10th and 11th innings.

JUNE 24

The White Sox play the Reds at Comiskey Park for the first time and win 4–2.

JUNE 30

The White Sox play in Houston for the first time and lose 17–2 to the Astros at the Astrodome.

The Sox's ERA of 5.22 in 1998 ranked last in the American League.

JULY 5

Trailing 11–3, the White Sox explode for eight runs in the sixth inning to tie the score 11–11, but they wind up losing 15–14 to the Red Sox in Boston.

JULY 9   The White Sox reach the low point of the 1998 season with a 6–4 loss to the Royals at Comiskey Park to drop the club's record to 35–52. The Sox were 45–20 the rest of the way.

JULY 10   Albert Belle drives in six runs with two homers and two singles during a 10–3 win over the Royals at Comiskey Park.

JULY 14   The White Sox score four runs in the ninth inning, the last three on a walk-off homer by Frank Thomas, to defeat the Twins 8–5 at Comiskey Park.

JULY 15   Albert Belle homers in both games of a double-header as the White Sox sweep the Blue Jays 9–3 and 5–2 at Comiskey Park. Belle hit nine homers in a span of eight games in seven days from July 9 through July 15. In the seventh inning of the second game, Bob Howry and Keith Foulke hit three batters in an inning to tie a major league record. Howry struck Jose Canseco and Foulke plunked Shannon Stewart and Craig Grebeck.

JULY 16   The White Sox release Jason Bere.

JULY 17   Albert Belle hits his 300th career homer during a 4–3 win over the Indians at Comiskey Park.

JULY 21   On the day he appears in court to face charges of domestic violence against a 25-year-old woman, Albert Belle collects four hits in five at-bats to lead the White Sox to a 6–3 win over the Blue Jays in Toronto.

              Indians manager Mike Hargrove was the American League All-Star manager in 1998 and failed to select Belle for the team. Using the snub as motivation, Belle hit 12 homers in the first 14 games after the All-Star break. In those 14 games, he had 27 hits in 55 at-bats, for a batting average of .491, along with 17 runs and 24 RBIs.

JULY 29   The White Sox trade Matt Karchner to the Cubs for Jon Garland.

              The trade proved to be one of the best in White Sox history. At the time of the transaction, Garland was a 19-year-old minor league pitcher. He played for the Sox from 2000 through 2007 and compiled a 92–81 record. Garland won 18 games in both 2005 and 2006.

JULY 30   The White Sox trade Charlie O'Brien to the Angels for Jason Stockstill and Brian Tokarse.

JULY 31   Albert Belle sets an American League record for most home runs in the month of July with his 16th during a 16–2 rout of the Rangers in Arlington. Frank Thomas hit a grand slam off John Burkett in the fifth inning.

              In the 76 games after the All-Star break, Belle batted .387 with 31 homers and 86 RBIs. He finished the season with league-leading figures in slugging percentage (.655), total bases (399) and extra-base hits (100). Belle also hit .328 with 200 hits, 48 doubles, 49 homers and 152 runs batted in. He set single-season club records for homers, doubles, total bases, RBIs and extra-base hits.

AUGUST 6   Jack Brickhouse dies at the age of 82. Brickhouse announced the White Sox games on radio and television in 1945 and from 1948 through 1967. He also did the Cubs contests from 1948 through 1982 and had stints in the broadcast booths of both the Bears and the Bulls.

AUGUST 8   Mike Cameron hits a walk-off homer in the ninth inning to beat the Angels 4–3 in the second game of a double-header at Comiskey Park. The Sox also won the opener 7–5.

AUGUST 12   On the day before the birth of his first child, Scott Eyre makes a rare start and pitches five no-hit innings in a 2–0 win over the Athletics at Comiskey Park. It was his first start since June 17. Eyre was moved from the bullpen because the August 8 double-header left the Sox without a starter on fewer than four days of rest. Eyre was taken out after 67 pitches despite having a no-hitter in progress. Keith Foulke followed Eyre to the mound and pitched two no-hit innings in the sixth and seventh. The first of two Oakland hits was a single leading off the eighth inning by Jason Giambi against Bob Howry.

AUGUST 14   The White Sox score nine runs in the sixth inning and rout the Mariners 14–2 at Comiskey Park.

AUGUST 24   Robin Ventura hits a grand slam off Mike Timlin in the eighth inning, but it's too late to prevent an 11–10 loss to the Mariners in Seattle.

AUGUST 28   The White Sox and Rangers tie an American League record by combining for 14 homers during a double-header at Comiskey Park. In the first game, Texas hit four home runs and Chicago three in a 6–5 Rangers victory in 10 innings. In the fourth inning, John Snyder gave up consecutive homers to Juan Gonzalez, Will Clark and Ivan Rodriguez. During the second tilt, the Sox smacked four homers to the Rangers' three for an 8–7 Chicago win. Ray Durham hit two homers for the Sox during the twin bill, with Albert Belle, Jeff Abbott, Mike Caruso, Mike Cameron and Robin Ventura adding the rest. Clark hit a pair for Texas, with Rodriguez, Gonzalez, Rusty Greer, Royce Clayton and Roberto Kelly connecting for one each.

Snyder had a strange three-year career in the majors, the first two of which were spent with the White Sox. He had a record of 13–3 in his first 22 games, 21 of them starts, but was 6–21 with a 7.37 earned run average thereafter.

SEPTEMBER 5   Jim Abbott is the winning pitcher in a 9–5 decision over the Yankees at Comiskey Park.

It was Abbott's first big-league win since 1996, when he was 2–18 with an earned run average of 7.48 with the Angels. He fought his way back to the majors in the Sox's farm system. Abbott previously played for the club in 1995. He was the feel-good story of the final month of the 1998 campaign by winning all five of his starts, although Abbott's ERA was 4.55. He went to the Brewers as a free agent in 1999 and was 2–8 with a 6.91 earned run average in his last big-league season.

SEPTEMBER 12   Four days after Mark McGwire hits his 62nd home run to break Roger Maris's single-season record, the White Sox defeat the Indians 6–4 in a tension-filled game at Jacobs Field. There was a fiery confrontation between Belle and Cleveland starter Dave Burba in the sixth inning. Belle was restrained by home plate umpire Ted Hendry from going after Burba after an exchange of words. Extra security and police on hand for Belle's visit raced down the aisles toward the field, but no one left the dugouts.

SEPTEMBER 13   The Indians beat the White Sox 6–3 at Jacobs Field in a second day of brushback wars resulting in a bench-clearing brawl. Cleveland's Omar Vizquel and manager Mike Hargrove were ejected in the third inning after Sox pitcher Jim Parque threw a pitch over Vizquel's head, resulting in a 10-minute fracas.

Standing only five-foot-eleven and weighing 165 pounds, Parque was drafted out of UCLA as the 46th overall selection of the 1997 draft. He was the first player from that draft to reach the majors. Parque grew up in Los Angeles with a father who was an ex-Marine and a mother who was from Vietnam. His given name is Jim Vo Parque.

SEPTEMBER 14   The White Sox outslug the Tigers 17–16 in 12 innings in Detroit. There were 18 pitchers in the game, 10 of them for Detroit. Albert Belle collected five hits, including three doubles, in eight at-bats. Shortstop Craig Wilson, playing in only his sixth big-league game, had four hits, including two homers, in seven at-bats and drove in five runs. The Sox scored six runs in the sixth inning for a 12–8 lead, but the Tigers countered with two tallies in the seventh and added two more in the ninth. Chicago scored three in the 10th for a 15–12 advantage, but Detroit tied the contest 15–15 with three in their half. The Sox plated two in the top of the 12th and the Tigers scored one in their half.

SEPTEMBER 18   The White Sox sell Chad Kreuter to the Angels.

SEPTEMBER 26   Switch-hitting Brian Simmons hits his first two major league homers during a 13–5 triumph over the Royals in Kansas City. Simmons homered from each side of the plate against right-hander Brian Barber and lefty Allen McDill.

Simmons finished his big-league career in 2001 with eight homers and a .218 batting average in 119 games and 252 at-bats.

OCTOBER 23   Albert Belle becomes a free agent. Belle signed a five-year deal with the White Sox in November 1996, but the contract contained a unique clause that stated within three days following the World Series he could demand the Sox keep him among the top three highest-paid players in the game. Jerry Reinsdorf had a choice between raising Belle's salary over each of the three remaining years from $11 million to $12,416,667 or allow him to become a free agent. Despite putting together one of the greatest seasons in club history in 1998, Reinsdorf chose to let Belle walk (see December 1, 1998).

NOVEMBER 11   The White Sox trade Mike Cameron to the Reds for Paul Konerko.

At the time of the trade, Cameron was 25 and Paul Konerko was 22, and both had stellar careers ahead of them. Konerko became one of the most popular players in club history and was still the club's starting first baseman in 2008.

DECEMBER 1   Albert Belle signs as a free agent with the Orioles. On the same day, Robin Ventura signed with the Mets as a free agent.

Belle signed a five-year deal with the Orioles for $65 million. The White Sox dodged a bullet by declining to retain Belle, however. He played only three more big-league seasons because of a degenerative hip condition. Ventura had been the White Sox's starting third baseman since 1990. He had a great year with the Mets in 1999 with 32 homers and 120 RBIs, then started two more seasons with the Mets and one with the Yankees.

1999   Sox

Season in a Sentence

The White Sox win six fewer games than the previous season, but a young lineup shows considerable potential.

Finish • Won • Lost • Pct • GB

Second   75   86   .466   21.5
In the wild-card race, the White Sox finished in sixth place, 18½ games behind.

Manager

Jerry Manuel

Stats	WS	• AL •	Rank
Batting Avg:	.277	.275	8
On-Base Pct:	.337	.347	11
Slugging Pct:	.429	.439	11
Home Runs:	162		11
Stolen Bases:	73		11
ERA:	4.92	4.86	7
Fielding Avg:	.977	.981	14
Runs Scored:	777		10
Runs Allowed:	870		10

Starting Lineup

Brook Fordyce, c
Paul Konerko, 1b
Ray Durham, 2b
Greg Norton, 3b
Mike Caruso, ss
Carlos Lee, lf
Chris Singleton, cf
Magglio Ordonez, rf
Frank Thomas, dh
Craig Wilson, 3b
Mark Johnson, c

Pitchers

James Baldwin, sp
Mike Sirotka, sp
Jim Parque, sp
Jaime Navarro, sp
John Snyder, sp
Bob Howry, rp
Bill Simas, rp
Sean Lowe, rp
Keith Foulke, rp

Attendance

1,338,851 (13th in AL)

Club Leaders

Batting Avg:	Frank Thomas	.305
On-Base Pct:	Frank Thomas	.414
Slugging Pct:	Paul Konerko	.511
Home Runs:	Magglio Ordonez	30
RBIs:	Magglio Ordonez	117
Runs:	Ray Durham	109
Stolen Bases:	Ray Durham	34
Wins:	James Baldwin	12
Strikeouts:	Mike Sirotka	125
ERA:	Mike Sirotka	4.00
Saves:	Bob Howry	28

JANUARY 10   The White Sox trade Rich Pratt to the Yankees for Chris Singleton.

JANUARY 18   Wil Cordero signs with the Blue Jays as a free agent.

JANUARY 27   Jim Abbott signs with the Brewers as a free agent.

MARCH 25   Six weeks after Bill Clinton is acquitted in his impeachment trial in the Senate, the White Sox trade Jake Meyer to the Reds for Brook Fordyce.

APRIL 5   In the season opener, the White Sox defeat the Mariners 8–2 in Seattle. Darrin Jackson and Paul Konerko both hit two-run homers. Frank Thomas and Ray Durham each collected three hits.

APRIL 7   The White Sox play at the Kingdome in Seattle for the last time and lose 7–3 to the Mariners.

APRIL 9   In the home opener, Mike Sirotka ties a major league record for pitchers with three errors in the fifth inning, leading to five unearned runs and a 10–5 loss to the Royals before 26,243 at Comiskey Park. The temperature was in the 40s with wind whipping up to 33 miles per hour. The cold may have contributed to Sirotka's misadventures. Two of his errors came on one play when he dropped Johnny Damon's one-hopper and threw wildly to first. Three batters later, Sirotka pulled Paul Konerko off the first-base bag on another throw.

The White Sox drew 1,338,851 fans in 1999, the lowest in the history of the second Comiskey Park. It was less the than half of the figure of 2,914,154 the club attracted in 1991, the year the stadium opened, and about 45 percent of the record total of 2,957,414 drawn in 2006.

APRIL 17   Trailing 5–3 and down to their last out, the White Sox score three runs on one play and defeat the Royals 6–5 in Kansas City. With two out and a runner on first base, pinch-hitter Mike Caruso singled and Frank Thomas drew a walk to load the bases. Magglio Ordonez then singled to center and the ball got past Carlos Beltran, scoring all three runners.

APRIL 21   The day after 14 students are killed at a shooting at Columbine High School in Littleton, Colorado, the White Sox score twice on a fielder's choice in the eighth inning for the only runs of a 2–1 win over the Mariners at Comiskey Park. With the bases loaded, Frank Thomas hit a grounder to shortstop Domingo Cedeno, forcing Mike Caruso at second. But McKay Christensen and Ray Durham both scored on the play, with Durham coming home after second baseman David Bell paused before throwing late to the plate.

The White Sox added an alternative sleeveless home jersey to the club's wardrobe in 1999.

APRIL 28   Magglio Ordonez hits a grand slam off Tony Saunders in the third inning, then adds another homer in his next at-bat, to lead the White Sox to a 9–1 win over the Devil Rays in the second game of a double-header at Comiskey Park. Ordonez also homered in the opener, a 10–7 Chicago victory.

MAY 4   Harold Baines hits a walk-off grand slam off David Lundquist in the 10th inning to lift the Orioles to a 9–5 win over the White Sox in Baltimore.

MAY 7   Facing Tom Candiotti, Carlos Lee homers in his first major league at-bat during the second inning of a 7–1 win over the Athletics at Comiskey Park. Lee was called up from Triple-A Charlotte earlier in the day.

A native of Panama, Lee played for the White Sox through the 2004 season and hit 152 home runs with the club to rank eighth all-time. His slugging percentage of .488 with the Sox ranks seventh.

MAY 17	Carlos Lee hits a grand slam off Bartolo Colon in the first inning, but the White Sox lose 13–9 to the Indians at Comiskey Park. Cleveland scored five runs in the first and the Sox countered with six in their half. At the end of the third inning, the Indians led 12–9.
MAY 18	The Indians pummel the White Sox 13–0 at Comiskey Park.
MAY 19	The White Sox allow exactly 13 runs to the Indians for the third game in a row, dropping a 13–7 decision at Comiskey Park.
MAY 22	Mike Sirotka (eight innings), Bob Howry (two-thirds of an inning) and Bill Simas (one-third of an inning) combine on a two-hitter to beat the Yankees 2–1 in the second game of a double-header at Comiskey Park. Chad Curtis collected both New York hits with singles in the first and fourth innings. In the first game, the Yanks won 10–2 behind Roger Clemens, who won his 18th consecutive decision over two seasons.
MAY 23	A balk leads to a bench-clearing incident during an 8–7 loss to the Yankees at Comiskey Park. Bill Simas came apart at the seams as Derek Jeter trotted home from third on the balk, capping New York's four-run ninth, which tied the score 7–7. Simas angrily went to the plate and began pointing and screaming at Jeter. Both dugouts emptied before order was quickly restored. Simas claimed either Jeter or third base coach Willie Randolph yelled "balk," causing the pitcher to flinch and prompting the real balk. The Yanks won on a homer by Chad Curtis in the 10th.
MAY 27	Greg Norton hits two homers, but the White Sox lose 10–5 to the Tigers in Detroit.
MAY 28	The White Sox collect six home runs during a 9–1 victory over the Tigers in Detroit. Greg Norton hit two homers for the second game in a row. The others were struck by Brook Fordyce, Ray Durham, Frank Thomas and Paul Konerko.

> *Thomas endured a disappointing season in 1999, with only 15 home runs in 135 games. Personal problems were a contributing factor. Thomas got divorced, his agent died in a plane crash, both of his business ventures flopped and his father underwent dialysis while struggling with heart failure.*

MAY 29	Greg Norton hits his fifth homer in a span of three games during a 7–1 triumph over the Tigers in Detroit.
JUNE 2	In the first round of the amateur draft, the White Sox select pitcher Jason Stumm from Centralia High School in Centralia, Washington.

> *Stumm never reached the majors. Those drafted and signed by the White Sox in 1999 who did become big leaguers include Matt Ginter (supplemental choice in the first round), Dan Wright (second round), Jon Rauch (third round), Josh Stewart (fifth round), Dave Sanders (sixth round), Matt Guerrier (tenth round), Joe Valentine (26th round) and Jeff Bajenara (36th round).*

JUNE 4	The White Sox play the Pirates for the first time at Comiskey Park and lose 6–3.

JUNE 9 — Jeff Bagwell hits three home runs for the Astros during a 13–4 win over the White Sox at Comiskey Park. It was the second time in 1999 that Bagwell hit three homers in a game in Chicago. He also accomplished the feat against the Cubs at Wrigley Field on April 12.

JUNE 13 — The White Sox complete a three-game sweep of the Cubs at Wrigley Field with a 6–4 victory. Ray Durham collected nine hits in 14 games during the series.

JUNE 15 — Frank Thomas extends his hitting streak to 21 games during a 3–2 loss to the Devil Rays at Comiskey Park.

JUNE 17 — Paul Konerko hits a grand slam off Jesse Orosco in the seventh inning of a 9–3 win over the Orioles at Comiskey Park.

JUNE 26 — The Red Sox score 11 runs in the first inning off James Baldwin and Scott Eyre and go on to demolish the White Sox 17–1 in Boston.

JUNE 27 — The White Sox rally from a 5–0 second-inning deficit and beat the Red Sox 7–6 in Boston. Chicago capped the comeback by scoring three runs in the ninth inning, the last two on a homer by Craig Wilson, to defeat the Red Sox 7–6 in Boston. Wilson also homered in the fourth. They were his first two homers of the 1998 season.

JUNE 30 — Mike Caruso triples in the 10th inning and scores on Ray Durham's sacrifice fly to beat the Royals 10–9 at Comiskey Park.

JULY 6 — Chris Singleton hits for the cycle during an 8–7 White Sox loss in 10 innings to the Royals at Comiskey Park. Singleton singled in the first inning, tripled in the fourth, doubled in the fifth and homered in the seventh, all off Jeff Suppan. Singleton added a single in the ninth facing Jeff Montgomery for his fifth hit. Trying for a club record-tying sixth hit, Singleton flied out to end the game.

> *A 26-year-old rookie, Singleton was the last player to make the Opening Day roster in 1999 after being acquired in an off-season trade with the Yankees, but he soon established himself as the starting center fielder. He hit .300 with 17 home runs, but never came close to reaching those numbers again. In 2006, Singleton became the White Sox's color commentator on the club's radio broadcasts, teaming with Ed Farmer.*

JULY 8 — Magglio Ordonez hits a two-run, walk-off double in the ninth inning to lift the White Sox to a 6–5 win over the Royals at Comiskey Park. Carlos Beltran gave Kansas City a 5–4 lead with a two-run homer in the top of the ninth.

JULY 17 — The day after John F. Kennedy Jr. dies in a plane crash along with his wife and sister-in-law, Magglio Ordonez hits a grand slam off Kent Bottenfield during a six-run fifth inning, but the White Sox lose 8–6 to the Cardinals in St. Louis.

JULY 19 — Chris Singleton and Ray Durham hit back-to-back homers in the 12th inning to beat the Brewers 10–8 in Milwaukee. Singleton finished the game with five hits in six at-bats. It was his second five-hit game in less than two weeks.

JULY 21 — A three-run homer by Paul Konerko in the 10th inning gives the White Sox a 6–3 win over the Twins in Minneapolis.

AUGUST 3   The White Sox play at Tiger Stadium in Detroit for the last time and beat the Tigers 9–6.

AUGUST 9   The White Sox play at Safeco Field in Seattle for the first time and lose 6–4 to the Mariners.

AUGUST 21   Brady Anderson leads off the Orioles' first inning with homers in both ends of a double-header, but the White Sox rally to win 8–5 and 4–3 in Baltimore. Allowing the homers to Anderson were John Snyder (first game) and Mike Sirotka (second).

SEPTEMBER 4   Trailing 3–2, the White Sox score seven runs in the seventh inning and win 12–3 over the Rangers in Arlington.

SEPTEMBER 6   On the bench because of an injured ankle, Frank Thomas refuses to pinch-hit during an 8–6 and 6–3 double-header loss to the Rangers in Arlington. An angry Jerry Manuel sent Thomas back to Chicago in the middle of the road trip. Many in the organization accused Thomas of quitting on the team. He didn't play for the remainder of the season and underwent surgery to remove a bone spur from his right ankle.

SEPTEMBER 10   The Indians score 12 runs in the fourth inning off Kip Wells and Sean Lowe and beat the White Sox 14–6 at Comiskey Park. As part of "Turn Ahead the Clock Night," both clubs wore "futuristic" uniforms with digitized numbers and names running sideways down the backs of the shirts.

SEPTEMBER 18   Carlos Lee hits a tie-breaking three-run homer in the ninth inning to defeat the Blue Jays 7–4 in Toronto.

SEPTEMBER 25   Magglio Ordonez collects four hits, including a double and a homer, and drives in five runs to lead the White Sox to a 13–4 win over the Twins in Minneapolis. The Sox led 13–0 at the end of the sixth inning.

OCTOBER 1   Carlos Lee hits a grand slam off Jay Ryan in the first inning to spark the White Sox to a 9–8 win over the Twins at Comiskey Park.

THE STATE OF THE WHITE SOX

The 2000 White Sox had the best record in the American League, with a young roster, before folding in the first round of the playoffs. The future looked bright, but in the next four years the Sox stagnated, never winning more than 86 games or fewer than 81. Then came the season White Sox fans had waited for all their lives. In 2005, the team was in first place all season, and then won its first world championship since 1917. All told, the team has an overall record of ... since 2000.

THE BEST TEAM

Is there any doubt? The 2005 White Sox spent the entire season in first place to finish the regular season with a 99–63 record, then they went 11–1 in the post-season, including a sweep of the Astros in the World Series, to win the team's first world championship since 1917.

THE WORST TEAM

The 2007 edition had a record of 72–90 and finished in fourth place in the AL Central.

THE BEST MOMENT

The best moment was the final out of the 2005 World Series against the Astros in Houston. On a Bobby Jenks pitch, Orlando Palmeiro grounded to shortstop Juan Uribe, who threw to first baseman Paul Konerko for the out to close the 1–0 victory and a four-game sweep.

THE WORST MOMENT

A father and son jumped out of the Comiskey Park stands on September 19, 2002, to attack Royals first-base coach Tom Gamboa. A similar incident occurred on April 15, 2003, when an umpire was assaulted.

THE ALL-DECADE TEAM • YEARS WITH WS

A. J. Pierzynski, c	2005–08
Paul Konerko, 1b	1999–2008
Ray Durham, 2b	1995–2002
Joe Crede, 3b	2000–08
Jose Valentin, ss	2000–04
Carlos Lee, lf	1999–04
Aaron Rowand, cf	2001–05
Magglio Ordonez, rf	1997–2004
Frank Thomas, dh	1991–2005
Mark Buehrle, p	2000–08
Jon Garland, p	2000–08
Jose Contreras, p	2004–08
Bobby Jenks, p	2005–08

Durham and Thomas were also on the 1990s All-Decade Team. Jermaine Dye (2005–08) has been the third-best outfielder during the 2000s, but he ranks behind Ordonez in right field. Other prominent White Sox players have included shortstop Juan Uribe (2004–08) and designated hitter Jim Thome (2006–08).

THE DECADE LEADERS

Batting Avg:	Magglio Ordonez	.313	
On-Base Pct:	Frank Thomas	.395	
Slugging Pct:	Frank Thomas	.555	
Home Runs:	Paul Konerko	?	Set after 2008 season
RBIs:	Paul Konerko	?	" " "
Runs:	Paul Konerko	?	" " "
Stolen Bases:	Scott Podsednik	111	
Wins:	Mark Buehrle	?	Set after 2008 season
Strikeouts:	Mark Buehrle	?	" " "
ERA:	Mark Buehrle	?	" " "
Saves:	Bobby Jenks	?	" " "

THE HOME FIELD

The name of the White Sox's home field changed from Comiskey Park to U.S. Cellular Field in 2003. It was one of many changes since 2000, as the club has attempted to transform what had been perceived as a sterile edifice into a more fan-friendly environment. The most significant was the elimination of eight rows and 6,600 seats from the top of the upper deck. The sloped canopy-style roof was replaced by a flat roof. Other changes included the addition of nearly 2,000 seats along the foul lines in front of the existing seating. Outfield seating was extended to the fence and a two-tiered seating area was constructed outside the Bullpen Sports Bar. The bullpens were relocated to allow fans to see the pitchers warming up, and the former bullpens were filled with seats. A full-color, high-resolution 28-by-53-foot video screen was added to the center-field scoreboard and ribbon boards were placed along the upper-deck facade. The Fan Deck, featuring tiered seating and food and beverage service in a patio-like atmosphere, was built on the center-field concourse. Concourses throughout the ballpark were upgraded. New green seats were installed to replace the existing blue ones. In 2008, the White Sox finished in the top half of the American League in attendance for the fourth year in a row, marking the first time they accomplished that since 1991 through 1994. The club hasn't been in the top half in attendance five or more season in succession since 1959 through 1965.

THE GAME YOU WISHED YOU HAD SEEN

The White Sox began their sweep of the 2005 World Series with a Game One 5–3 win over the Astros on October 22. It was the first time the Fall Classic was played in Chicago since 1959.

THE WAY THE GAME WAS PLAYED

An offensive explosion took place during the last half of the 2000s, as did the trend toward new baseball-only ballparks with grass fields. About mid-decade, allegations of the use of performance-enhancing drugs became a hot topic, and Major League Baseball instituted much harsher penalties for players caught using the substances. The disparity in payrolls and success on the field between the large and small-market clubs continued to increase.

THE MANAGEMENT

Chairman Jerry Reinsdorf and vice chairman Eddie Einhorn have run the White Sox since 1981. General managers have been Ron Schueler (1990–2000) and Kenny Williams (2000-present). Field managers have been Jerry Manuel (1998–2003) and Ozzie Guillen (2004-present).

THE BEST PLAYER MOVE

The jury is still out on the best move of the 2000s, but thus far it appears to be the signing of Jermaine Dye as a free agent in December 2004. The best trade sent Jaime Navarro and John Snyder to the Brewers for Jose Valentin and Cal Eldred in January 2000.

THE WORST PLAYER MOVE

Time will determine the worst player move of the 2000s, but so far it's the trade of Carlos Lee to the Brewers for Scott Podsednik, Luis Vizcaino and Travis Hinton in December 2004. During the same off-season, the Sox let Magglio Ordonez go to the Tigers via free agency.

2000

Sox

Season in a Sentence

After three straight losing seasons, the White Sox are the surprise team of the year, posting the best record in the American League before being swept by the Mariners in the first round of the playoffs.

Finish • Won • Lost • Pct • GB

First   95   67   .586   +5.0

Manager

Jerry Manuel

American League Division Series

The White Sox lost three games to none to the Seattle Mariners.

Stats

Stats	WS	AL	Rank
Batting Avg:	.286	.276	3
On-Base Pct:	.356	.349	4
Slugging Pct:	.470	.443	2
Home Runs:	216		5
Stolen Bases:	119		4
ERA:	4.66	4.91	4
Fielding Avg:	.978	.982	12
Runs Scored:	978		1
Runs Allowed:	839		7

Starting Lineup

Brook Fordyce, c
Paul Konerko, 1b
Ray Durham, 2b
Herbert Perry, 3b
Jose Valentin, ss
Carlos Lee, lf
Chris Singleton, cf
Magglio Ordonez, rf
Frank Thomas, 1b
Jeff Abbott, cf-lf-rf
Mark Johnson, c

Pitchers

Mike Sirotka, sp
James Baldwin, sp
Jim Parque, sp
Cal Eldred, sp
Kip Wells, sp
Keith Foulke, rp
Kelly Wunsch, rp
Bob Howry, rp
Bill Simas, rp
Sean Lowe, rp

Attendance

1,947,799 (ninth in AL)

Club Leaders

Batting Avg:	Frank Thomas	.328
On-Base Pct:	Frank Thomas	.436
Slugging Pct:	Frank Thomas	.625
Home Runs:	Frank Thomas	43
RBIs:	Frank Thomas	143
Runs:	Ray Durham	121
Stolen Bases:	Ray Durham	25
Wins:	Mike Sirotka	15
Strikeouts:	Mike Sirotka	128
Saves:	Keith Foulke	34

JANUARY 12   Eleven days after the start of the new millennium and worries over the Y2K computer problem, the White Sox trade Jaime Navarro and John Snyder to the Brewers for Jose Valentin and Cal Eldred.

The White Sox pulled off a brilliant deal. Navarro never won another big-league game, and Snyder pitched only one more year with a 3–10 record. After batting .224 in 1998 and .227 in 1999, Valentin revived his career and was a starter at shortstop and third base for the next five seasons in Chicago, a span in which he hit 136 home runs. Over the previous two seasons in Milwaukee, Eldred was 6–16 while battling elbow problems. Making a remarkable recovery, he had an 8–0 record on June 28 in 2000, but the elbow miseries returned and Eldred finished the season with a 10–2 record.

FEBRUARY 26   Frank Thomas and Jerry Manuel become involved in a heated clash during a spring training workout in Tucson. The argument stemmed from Thomas's refusal to participate in Manuel's "shuttle run" drill. Thomas, whose salary made up one-third of the team's 2000 payroll, wanted to sit out because of a sore heel following off-season surgery.

APRIL 3   In the season opener, the White Sox lose 10–4 to the Rangers in Arlington. Carlos Lee collected three hits in a losing cause.

Darrin Jackson, who retired as a player after the 1999 season, joined Ken Harrelson in the White Sox TV booth in 2000. Jackson replaced Tom Paciorek.

APRIL 5   The White Sox outlast the Rangers 12–8 in Arlington. The Sox broke a 7–7 tie with five runs in the ninth inning.

APRIL 6   Ray Durham hits a home run on the first pitch of the game off Rangers starter Esteban Loaiza, sparking the White Sox to a 6–2 win at Arlington.

APRIL 8   Jose Valentin commits four errors at shortstop, but the White Sox win 7–3 over the Athletics in Oakland.

Valentin made six errors in his first six games with the White Sox on the way to a league-leading total of 36. Few were complaining about his abilities with the bat, however. Valentin hit .273 with 25 home runs in 2000.

APRIL 11   The White Sox outlast the Devil Rays 13–6 at St. Petersburg. Paul Konerko collected four hits, including a double and a homer, in five at-bats, along with four runs and four RBIs.

The Sox started the season with a grueling 10-game road trip that sent the club from Texas to California to Florida. Chicago won six of the 10 games.

APRIL 14   The White Sox play their first game of the season at Comiskey Park and win 9–4 over the Angels before a crowd of 38,912.

APRIL 18   In a slugfest at Comiskey Park, the White Sox prevail 18–11 over the Mariners. The Sox broke the game open in the fourth inning by scoring 11 runs to take a 13–6 lead. Those driving in runs in the 11-run inning were Mark Johnson (three on a home run), Greg Norton (two on a home run), Chris Singleton (two), Carlos Lee (two), Frank Thomas (one) and Paul Konerko (one).

Ray Durham used his speed to score 121 runs and hit nine triples in 2000.

APRIL 19   The White Sox take first place with a 5–2 win over the Mariners at Comiskey Park.

The Sox remained in first for the rest of the year.

APRIL 22   Chris Singleton collects five hits, including a homer and a double, and drives in five runs during a fight-filled 14–6 win over the Tigers at Comiskey Park. Eleven individuals were ejected in one of the most vicious brawls in club history. The bad blood started when Jeff Weaver hit Paul Konerko with a pitch in the fourth inning and then plunked Carlos Lee in the sixth. The fighting began in the seventh inning when Dean Palmer of Detroit charged Sox pitcher Jim Parque after Parque's throw to the plate struck Palmer in the arm. During the ensuing brawl, Magglio Ordonez was ejected for kicking. The scrum turned into a mosh pit that started near the mound and eventually moved into the outfield. There were breaks, but then a punch would be thrown and the fighting would begin again. The most vicious blow was struck by Detroit coach Juan Samuel, who sucker-punched Bill Simas. Parque was not ejected because he stayed on the mound, but Palmer was tossed by the umpires. Rob Fick of the Tigers was seen taunting the fans in the visitor's bullpen and fans doused him with beer. In the ninth, Chicago pitcher Tanyon Sturtze was ejected after he hit Deivi Cruz with a pitch. Later in the inning, Bob Howry hit Shane Halter. Detroit hurler Doug Brocail led the charge from the dugout,

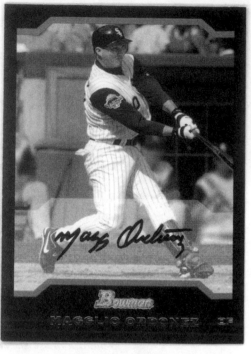

A key part of Chicago's power-packed lineup in 2000, Magglio Ordonez put up big numbers throughout his years with the Sox.

prompting a second brawl that lasted about five minutes. Keith Foulke suffered a bloody cut that required five stitches after he was attacked from behind. Palmer, who was ejected in the first altercation, left the clubhouse to participate in the second. Weaver, who had started the beanball war, joined in the fight in street clothes. In addition to Brocail, Palmer and Fick, Jeff Weaver and Danny Patterson of the Tigers were given the heave-ho by the arbiters. In addition to Ordonez and Sturtze, those from the White Sox who were ejected were Howry, Bill Simas, manager Jerry Manuel and coach Joe Nossek.

Five days later, Major League Baseball suspended 16 members of the White Sox and Tigers, eight from each team, a total of 82 games and fined 24 players, managers and coaches. The longest suspensions were given to Samuel (15 games), Palmer (eight), Manuel (eight), Tigers skipper Phil Garner (eight), Fick (five), Detroit outfielder Bobby Higginson (five) and Ordonez (five).

APRIL 24   Cal Eldred pitches a two-hitter and retires 26 of the last 27 batters to face him for an 8–2 win over the Orioles at Comiskey Park. The only Baltimore hits were a double by Delino DeShields in the first inning and a homer from Charles Johnson in the sixth.

APRIL 26   Frank Thomas hits a grand slam off Sidney Ponson in the fourth inning of an 11–6 win over the Orioles at Comiskey Park.

APRIL 27   Jose Valentin hits for the cycle and drives in five runs during a 13–4 win over the Orioles at Comiskey Park. Valentin singled in the first inning and doubled in the second off Jose Mercedes, then added a three-run triple against Calvin Maduro in the third and a home run facing Mike Trombley in the seventh.

White Sox players who have hit for the cycle are Ray Schalk (1922), Jack Brohamer (1977), Carlton Fisk (1984), Chris Singleton (1999) and Valentin.

APRIL 28   The White Sox play at Comerica Park in Detroit for the first time and beat the Tigers 3–2.

MAY 3   The White Sox hit four homers in the sixth inning, including three in a row, and five in the game to defeat the Blue Jays 7–3 at Comiskey Park. Mark Johnson led off the sixth with a homer. After Ray Durham was retired, Jose Valentin, Frank Thomas and Paul Konerko hit consecutive home runs in a span of eight pitches. Valentin hit another homer earlier in the contest.

Thomas batted .328 along with 44 doubles, 43 home runs, 143 RBIs and 115 runs in 2000.

MAY 13   Pinch-hitter Jeff Abbott hits a two-out, two-run, walk-off homer in the ninth inning to give the White Sox a 4–3 win over the Twins at Comiskey Park.

MAY 23   The White Sox hit five homers during an 8–2 win over the Yankees at Comiskey Park. The home run hitters were Magglio Ordonez, Paul Konerko, Ray Durham, Brook Fordyce and Jose Valentin.

Ordonez hit .315 with 32 homers and 126 RBIs in 2000.

MAY 27   Jose Valentin drives in six runs during a 14–3 win over the Indians at Comiskey Park. Valentin smacked a two-run homer in the first inning, a bases-loaded triple in the second and a run-scoring double in the third. Valentin finished the game just a single shy of becoming the second player in major league history to hit for the cycle twice in a season.

The White Sox scored a club-record 978 runs in 2000. The figure also led the American League.

MAY 30   Ray Durham and Carlos Lee hit solo homers for the only two runs of a 2–1 win over the Mariners in Seattle.

JUNE 2   The White Sox play at Enron Field (now Minute Maid Park) in Houston for the first time and beat the Astros 7–4.

JUNE 4   Ray Durham hits a home run on the first pitch of the game from Octavio Dotel, sparking the White Sox to a 7–3 win over the Astros in Houston.

JUNE 5   In the first round of the amateur draft, the White Sox select outfielder Joe Borchard from Stanford University.

Borchard was a backup quarterback with Stanford University in both 1998 and 1999 and was slated to become a starter in 2000 and projected to be a first-round NFL draft choice. He was the 12th overall pick in the 2000 baseball *draft, but in order to persuade him to give up football, Borchard received a signing bonus of $5.3 million, the highest ever for an amateur in major league history up to that time. It remained the record until Justin Upton signed with the Diamondbacks for $6.1 million in 2005. Borchard was extremely unimpressive with the Sox, however. He played for the club from 2002 through 2005 and hit only .191 with 12 home runs in 298 at-bats. Other future big-leaguers drafted and signed by the White Sox in 2000 include Tim Hummel (second round), Mike Morse (third round) and Heath Phillips (tenth round).*

JUNE 6   The White Sox outlast the Reds 17–12 in Cincinnati. The Sox had leads of 7–0 in the second inning, 13–1 in the seventh and 17–6 heading into the bottom of the ninth before the Reds scored six times in a futile rally.

JUNE 9   Ray Durham's single in the 14th inning provides the winning run in a 6–5 decision over the Cubs at Comiskey Park.

JUNE 11   The White Sox collect five homers, but all are struck with no one on base, resulting in a 6–5 loss to the Cubs at Comiskey Park. Jose Valentin hit two of the solo shots, with the others coming from Ray Durham, Frank Thomas and Magglio Ordonez.

JUNE 13   Ray Durham homers in the 10th inning to beat the Indians 4–3 in Cleveland.

JUNE 18   A nine-run first inning is highlighted by Jose Valentin's grand slam off Orlando Hernandez, and the White Sox rout the Yankees 17–4 in New York.

JUNE 19   The White Sox win their eighth game in a row with a 6–1 decision over the Indians at Comiskey Park. The Monday night sellout crowd gave the Sox a standing ovation as they took the field.

          The victory gave the White Sox a 45–24 record and an 8½-game lead in the AL Central.

JUNE 25   Taking the mound with an 8–1 lead, Keith Foulke gives up six runs in the ninth, but the White Sox escape with an 8–7 win over the Yankees at Comiskey Park.

JUNE 30   Two days after six-year-old Elian Gonzalez returns to Cuba following a bitter legal battle, the White Sox hit five home runs during a 10–4 win over the Red Sox at Comiskey Park. Frank Thomas and Brook Fordyce each hit two homers, with Carlos Lee adding one more.

JULY 1   Magglio Ordonez hits two homers and drives in five runs during an 8–2 victory over the Red Sox at Comiskey Park.

JULY 3   Trailing 9–3, the White Sox erupt for eight runs in the fifth inning and defeat the Royals 14–10 in Kansas City. The Sox collected 22 hits in the contest.

          The White Sox won 12 road games in a row from June 4 through July 3. The Sox were 49–32 away from home in 2000.

JULY 4   Ray Durham and Jose Valentin lead off the first inning with back-to-back homers off Chad Durbin, but the White Sox lose 10–7 to the Royals in Kansas City.

JULY 5

Herbert Perry hits a two-run homer in the 13th inning and Mark Johnson follows with a solo shot, leading the White Sox to a 6–3 win over the Royals at Kauffman Stadium. In the bottom of the 11th, Kansas City loaded the bases with one out. Left fielder Carlos Lee was brought in as a fifth infielder, and Mike Sweeney hit a bouncer up the middle to second baseman Ray Durham, who stepped on second and threw to first for a double play.

As a collegian, Perry played quarterback at the University of Florida. Pitcher Kevin Beirne also played college football as a wide receiver with Texas A&M. Beirne's father, Jim, played in the NFL from 1968 through 1976 as a wide receiver and tight end, mostly with the Houston Oilers.

JULY 11

In the All-Star Game, played at Turner Field in Atlanta, Magglio Ordonez drives in a run in the ninth inning with a sacrifice fly. The American League won 6–3.

JULY 15

Frank Thomas drives in six runs during a 15–7 triumph over the Cardinals at Comiskey Park. Thomas hit a three-run homer in the first inning and a three-run double in the seventh.

JULY 16

For the second game in a row, a White Sox batter drives in six runs against a National League club as the White Sox trounce the Brewers 10–5 at Comiskey Park. Magglio Ordonez accounted for an even half-dozen RBIs with a grand slam off Juan Acevedo in the sixth inning and a two-run homer against David Weathers in the eighth.

JULY 17

The White Sox reach double-figures in runs for the third game in a row with an 11–2 victory over the Brewers at Comiskey Park.

JULY 19

The White Sox take an 11½-game lead in the AL Central pennant race with a 3–2 decision over the Twins in Minneapolis.

The Sox had a record of 60–34 on July 19, their best after 94 games since 1917. From July 20 through the end of the 2002 regular season, the White Sox were 35–33.

JULY 29

The White Sox trade Brook Fordyce, Miguel Felix, Juan Figueroa and Jason Lakman to the Orioles for Charles Johnson and Harold Baines.

One of the most popular players in franchise history, Baines joined the White Sox for the third time. He previously played for the White Sox from 1980 through 1989 and again in 1996 and 1997. Baines's return was a nice nostalgic gesture, but on his third tour with the Sox, Harold hit only .166 with just one homer in 145 at-bats before retiring at the end of the 2001 season.

JULY 30

A late-inning rally beats the Angels 11–7 in 10 innings at Edison International Field. The White Sox trailed 6–2 before scoring two runs in the eighth inning and three in the ninth for a 7–6 lead, only to have Anaheim tie the score in the bottom of the ninth. The Sox broke the game open with four runs in the 10th.

AUGUST 1

In his first game with the White Sox, Charles Johnson hits a homer in the ninth inning to beat the Rangers 4–3 in Arlington.

AUGUST 6 — The White Sox clobber the Athletics 13–0 at Comiskey Park. James Baldwin pitched the shutout.

> *Baldwin won his first seven decisions in 2000 and had records of 10–1 on June 16 and 13–4 with the August 6 shutout. He won only one more game the rest of the season, however, and finished at 14–7 with a 4.65 earned run average. Baldwin underwent shoulder surgery during the following off-season.*

AUGUST 8 — The Mariners hit two grand slams during a 12–4 win over the White Sox in the first game of a double-header at Comiskey Park. Jay Buhner hit the first Seattle slam off Jon Garland in the first inning, and Edgar Martinez added another in the eighth off Bill Simas. The Mariners also won the second tilt 7–5.

AUGUST 9 — The White Sox win a 19–3 laugher over the Mariners at Comiskey Park. Tony Graffanino hit a grand slam off Rob Ramsay in a seven-run sixth inning. The Sox scored all 19 runs in the first six innings. Frank Thomas hit two homers and a double, scored four runs and drove in five.

AUGUST 11 — Down 5–0, the White Sox score two runs in the third inning, one in the fourth, two in the fifth and one in the seventh for a 6–5 win over the Devil Rays in St. Petersburg.

AUGUST 14 — The White Sox rout the Orioles 14–4 in Baltimore.

AUGUST 18 — The White Sox sign Ken Hill following his release by the Angels.

AUGUST 29 — Paul Konerko hits a three-run homer in the second inning off Barry Zito to account for all of the runs of a 3–0 win over the Athletics in Oakland. James Baldwin (five innings), Mark Buehrle (three innings) and Keith Foulke (one inning) combined on the shutout.

SEPTEMBER 1 — Trailing 8–2, the White Sox score a run in the seventh inning and six in the eighth to defeat the Angels 9–8 at Comiskey Park. A two-run homer by Magglio Ordonez made the score 8–5. The Sox were still down by three runs with two out and two runners on base when Charles Johnson hit an RBI-single, Ray Durham doubled in a run and Jose Valentin contributed a two-run pinch single.

SEPTEMBER 2 — Charles Johnson drives in seven runs during a 13–6 win over the Angels at Comiskey Park. Johnson hit a three-run double in the first inning, a run-scoring single in the fourth and a three-run homer in the seventh.

SEPTEMBER 3 — The White Sox outlast the Angels 13–12 at Comiskey Park. Anaheim scored four runs in the first, but the White Sox responded with a nine-run outburst in their half of the inning. The Angels went back on top 12–10 before the Sox scored a run in the seventh and two in the eighth.

SEPTEMBER 8 — The White Sox hammer the Rangers 13–1 in Arlington. As a sidelight, Scott Sheldon of Texas became the third player in major league history to play all nine positions in a regular season game. The first two were Bert Campaneris with the Athletics in 1965 and Cesar Tovar with the Twins in 1968.

SEPTEMBER 11 — Frank Thomas hits a grand slam off Nelson Cruz in the eighth inning of a 10–3 win over the Tigers at Comiskey Park.

SEPTEMBER 13   The White Sox edge the Tigers 1–0 at Comiskey Park. The lone run scored on back-to-back doubles by Frank Thomas and Harold Baines in the first inning. Jim Parque (seven innings), Bob Howry (one inning) and Keith Foulke (one inning) combined on the shutout.

> *Parque moonlighted as a sportswriter for the* Chicago Sun-Times *during the 2000 season. He was a candid columnist who criticized the official scoring and the size of the bonuses paid to high school and college players. Parque quit his weekly gig after an unproductive stretch of pitching in midseason. He was 13–6 with the Sox in 2000, but then encountered arm trouble. From 2001 through 2003 in Chicago and Tampa Bay, Parque had a 2–8 record with a stratospheric 9.68 earned run average in 70²/₃ innings.*

SEPTEMBER 20   Ray Durham hits a grand slam off Matt Anderson in the eighth inning of a 13–6 win over the Tigers in Detroit.

SEPTEMBER 22   Ray Durham passes out and collapses first face into the Metrodome artificial turf during the third inning of a 5–4 win over the Twins. Durham was carted off the field and taken to a hospital, but a CT was normal. The diagnosis was bruised ribs from a head-first slide and collision with Minnesota catcher A. J. Pierzynski minutes before his collapse. Durham was playing again in less than a week.

SEPTEMBER 24   The White Sox lose 6–5 to the Twins in 10 innings in Minneapolis on a two-run, walk-off homer by Matt Lawton, but they clinch the AL Central crown and their first post-season berth since 1993 when the Indians lose 9–0 to the Royals in Kansas City. The clinching caused a strange scene at the Metrodome, with both teams celebrating on the field at the end of the game.

SEPTEMBER 25   The White Sox participate in a three-team double-header involving the Twins and Indians at Jacobs Field in Cleveland. It was only the second three-team double-header in the majors since 1900. The other one happened on September 13, 1951, when the Cardinals played both the Boston Braves and New York Giants in St. Louis. The unique double-header in Cleveland came about when the AL re-scheduled a September 10 rainout between the Sox and the Indians. With the Indians involved in the wild-card race, the White Sox were forced to go to Cleveland for a one-game series. The Sox played a day game before the regularly scheduled night game between the Indians and Twins. The logistical nightmare came off smoothly with four team buses, two equipment trucks, three TV crews, nearly 100 players, 80,000 fans and eight umpires. There was little goodwill between the Sox and Indians in the opener. Tribe second baseman Roberto Alomar took exception to a hard slide from Tony Graffanino on a forceout in the top of the sixth, and by the bottom of the inning the lingering animosity sent both teams onto the field, although no punches were thrown. The Indians beat the White Sox 9–2 and then lost 4–3 to Minnesota.

SEPTEMBER 26   The White Sox lose 4–3 to the Red Sox at Comiskey Park, but they clinch home field advantage throughout the playoffs.

SEPTEMBER 30   Jose Valentin hits two home runs, one from each side of the plate, during a 9–1 win over the Royals at Comiskey Park. Valentin's homers were off right-hander Blake Stein and lefty Scott Mullen.

OCTOBER 1   On the last day of the season, Jerry Manuel pulls his starters one by one beginning in the sixth inning, letting them come off the field so they could be cheered by the Comiskey Park crowd. The Sox lost 6–2 to the Royals.

The White Sox met the Mariners in the first round of the playoffs. Managed by Lou Piniella, the Mariners won the wild-card race with a 91–71 record.

OCTOBER 3   The White Sox open the American League Division Series with a 7–4 loss to the Mariners in 10 innings before 45,290 at Comiskey Park. Seattle struck first with two runs in the first inning and one in the second before the Sox took a 4–3 advantage with two tallies in the bottom of the second and two more in the third. Ray Durham hit a home run and Chris Singleton and Magglio Ordonez both contributed RBI-triples. The Mariners tied the contest with a run in the seventh and won with three in the 10th. Keith Foulke surrendered a single to Mike Cameron, who stole second after several pick-off attempts. Apparently rattled, Foulke gave up a homer to Edgar Martinez that broke the 4–4 tie. John Olerud followed with another home run. Mark Johnson hit three singles in a losing cause.

After leading the AL in runs scored in 2000, the Sox would score only seven times in the three-game sweep at the hands of the Mariners. Frank Thomas, Magglio Ordonez, Paul Konerko and Carlos Lee combined for only three hits in 40 at-bats.

OCTOBER 4   The White Sox lose again 5–2 in game two before 45,383 at Comiskey Park. The Mariners broke a 2–2 tie with a run in the fourth inning and added two more runs in the fifth and ninth. Mike Sirotka gamely pitched $5^2/_3$ innings after injuring his elbow in his last regular-season appearance. The October 4 game proved to be Sirotka's last in the majors (see January 14, 2001).

OCTOBER 6   The Mariners complete the sweep of the White Sox with a 2–1 win at Safeco Field in Seattle. The game and the series ended in an unlikely manner when Carlos Guillen successfully squeezed home Rickey Henderson from third base with the winning run.

Despite the post-season disappointment, the White Sox's future looked bright because of the relative youth of the roster. Jon Garland was 20 years old; Mark Buehrle, 21; Joe Crede, 22; Kip Wells, 23; Paul Konerko and Carlos Lee, 24; Jim Parque, 25; Magglio Ordonez, 26; Keith Foulke, Kelly Wunsch and Chris Singleton, 27; and James Baldwin and Ray Durham, 28. Frank Thomas was 32, but he was coming off one of the best seasons of his career. The team slogan that season was "The Kids Can Play." The Sox looked like a power for years to come, but they sank back near the .500 mark in both 2001 and 2002. Much of the problem stemmed from injuries to Thomas and pitchers such as Cal Eldred, Bill Simas, Baldwin, Wunsch and Parque.

OCTOBER 24   Ron Schueler resigns as general manager and is replaced by 36-year-old Ken Williams.

Schueler had been general manager since 1990. He resigned to spend more time with his family. Schueler had hoped to make the move before the 2000 season, but Jerry Reinsdorf convinced him to stay one more year. Williams had been the team's Vice president of player development for five years. With his promotion,

Williams became the first African-American general manager in Chicago sports history and just the third in baseball. He attended Stanford University, where he played both baseball and football. Williams was on the field during the infamous final play of the Cal-Stanford football game in 1982 in which Cal's Kevin Moen collided with a Stanford trombone player in the end zone after a series of laterals. Williams played outfield and third base with the White Sox from 1986 through 1988 at the start of a six-year big league career. In his fifth season as the club's general manager, the Sox won their first world championship since 1917.

DECEMBER 14   Two days after the Supreme Court declares George Bush the winner in the disputed presidential election with Al Gore, the White Sox trade Aaron Myette and Brian Schmack to the Rangers for Royce Clayton.

DECEMBER 18   The White Sox lose and gain a catcher through free agency on the same day. Charles Johnson left Chicago to sign with the Marlins and the Sox added Sandy Alomar Jr., most recently with the Indians.

Alomar appeared in six All-Star Games as an Indian from 1990 through 1998, but chronic knee trouble prevented him from coming close to that level of play with the White Sox.

2001   Sox

Season in a Sentence

A year after winning the AL Central, the White Sox lose Frank Thomas to a season-ending injury in April and fall 15 games under .500 in May before a late rally results in a winning season.

Finish • Won • Lost • Pct • GB

Third   83   79   .512   8.0
In the wild-card race, the White Sox finished in third place, 19 games behind.

Manager

Jerry Manuel

Stats

Stats	WS	AL	Rank
Batting Avg:	.268	.267	5
On-Base Pct:	.334	.334	6
Slugging Pct:	.451	.428	3
Home Runs:	214		2
Stolen Bases:	123		7
ERA:	4.55	4.47	8
Fielding Avg:	.981	.981	8
Runs Scored:	798		6
Runs Allowed:	795		8

Starting Lineup

Sandy Alomar Jr., c
Paul Konerko, 1b
Ray Durham, 2b
Jose Valentin, 3b-ss
Royce Clayton, ss
Carlos Lee, lf
Chris Singleton, cf
Magglio Ordonez, rf
Jose Canseco, dh
Herbert Perry, 3b
Jeff Liefer, lf

Pitchers

Mark Buehrle, sp
Kip Wells, sp-rp
Rocky Biddle, sp
David Wells, sp
Keith Foulke, rp
Bob Howry, rp
Gary Glover, rp
Sean Lowe, rp
Jon Garland, rp-sp

Attendance

1,766,172 (12th in AL)

Club Leaders

Batting Avg:	Magglio Ordonez	.301
On-Base Pct:	Magglio Ordonez	.382
Slugging Pct:	Magglio Ordonez	.533
Home Runs:	Paul Konerko	32
RBIs:	Magglio Ordonez	113
Runs:	Ray Durham	104
Stolen Bases:	Magglio Ordonez	25
Wins:	Mark Buehrle	16
Strikeouts:	Mark Buehrle	126
ERA:	Mark Buehrle	3.29
Saves:	Keith Foulke	42

JANUARY 14   The White Sox trade Mike Sirotka, Kevin Beirne, Matt DeWitt and Mike Williams to the Blue Jays for David Wells.

Sirotka led the White Sox in wins in 2000 with 15, but during his last regular-season start, he tore a labrum in his left (pitching) shoulder. Sox general manager Ken Williams was aware of the injury, but he failed to inform Toronto G.M. Gord Ash. Sirotka never pitched another big-league game. The Blue Jays appealed to Bud Selig to overturn the deal, but the commissioner refused.
The Sox didn't benefit from the transaction, however, because Wells had a rare bad year in Chicago. He was 5–7 in 2001 at the age of 38, his only year with the club, and spent the last three months on the disabled list with back problems that eventually required surgery. Wells had a record of 20–8 with the Blue Jays in 2000 and was 19–7 as a Yankee in 2002. In addition, he was 71–32 in the four seasons before playing for the Sox and 61–29 in the four years afterward.

FEBRUARY 28 Frank Thomas reports to Tucson and apologizes to the fans and club management for his boycott of the White Sox's training camp. Thomas missed the first six days of full-squad workouts after claiming his $9.9 million a year salary was too low. Two days later, Thomas's agents severed ties with the ball player because of the incident.

APRIL 2 The White Sox win the season opener 7–4 over the Indians in Cleveland. David Wells was the winning pitcher in his Sox debut. Magglio Ordonez contributed a three-run homer.

Ordonez hit .305 with 40 doubles, 31 homers and 113 RBIs in 2001.

APRIL 6 In the home opener, the White Sox lose 10–9 in 10 innings to the Tigers before 43.9?? ??skey Park. Frank Thomas, Jose Valentin and Ray Durham each

?? changes to Comiskey Park in 2001, the start of a multi-year ?? park more fan-friendly and less sterile. Nearly 2,000 seats ?? along the foul lines in front of existing seating. The bullpens were ?? a point just behind the outfield fences to allow fans to see pitchers ?? The former bullpens were filled with new seats. The outfield seating ?? to the fence. A two-tiered terrace seating area was added ?? Sports Bar. With the modifications, the foul lines were ?? 347 feet in both directions to 330 feet in left field and 335 feet

?? a walk-off homer in the 11th inning to down the Athletics 2–1 at

?? ??seman Eric Chavez hits a home run that clears the right-field ??iskey Park in the ninth inning of a 16–6 Oakland victory. The ?? the drive, which was estimated to have traveled 490 feet, was

?? ffers a serious injury during an 8–3 loss to the Mariners at ?? the second inning, Ichiro Suzuki hit a grounder to first base and ?? his left, landing awkwardly on his right arm. He wound up tearing ?? lay and had season-ending surgery.

?? ??rko hits a walk-off single in the 14th inning that beats the Mariners 2–1 at Comiskey Park. Mark Buehrle (eight innings), Keith Foulke (two innings), Kelly Wunsch (one inning) and Gary Glover (three innings) combined on a four-hitter.

The Mariners had a record of 116–46 in 2001.

MAY 11 Jose Valentin hits a walk-off homer in the 10th inning to beat the Rangers 6–5 at Comiskey Park. It was Valentin's second home run of the game.

The White Sox wore 1917 replica uniforms on Sundays at Comiskey Park in 2001. At the time, 1917 represented the last year the franchise won the World Series.

MAY 23   The White Sox reach the low point of the 2001 season with a 9–6 loss to the Blue Jays in Toronto. Wells, who pitched for the Jays for eight seasons, lost track of the outs in the first inning and tossed the ball to an umpire, allowing a run to score.

With the defeat, the White Sox had a record of 14–29. The club won 16 of the next 19 games, but they couldn't get back into the pennant race.

MAY 25   The White Sox score six runs in the ninth inning to stun the Tigers 8–4 in Detroit. Ray Durham put the Sox into the lead with a three-run double.

JUNE 3   A two-out, three-run, walk-off homer by Paul Konerko in the 10th inning beats the Tigers 9–6 at Comiskey Park. The blast capped a tremendous comeback. The Sox were held hitless until the sixth inning and trailed 6–0 with six outs to go, before scoring four times in the eighth inning and twice in the ninth.

JUNE 5   In the first round of the amateur draft, the White Sox select pitcher Kris Honel from Providence Catholic High School in New Lenox, Illinois. Those drafted and signed by the Sox in 2002 who had reached the majors by the end of the 2007 season were Andy Gonzalez (fifth round), Chris Stewart (12th round), Chris Young (16th round) and Charlie Haeger (25th round).

JUNE 8   Carlos Lee hits a walk-off grand slam off Courtney Duncan in the 10th inning to beat the Cubs 7–3 at Comiskey Park.

JUNE 9   A defensive lapse by Tony Graffanino at third base leads to a 4–3 loss to the Cubs in 10 innings at Comiskey Park. With Eric Young sliding into third base, Graffanino thought it was a force play and stepped on the bag instead of tagging the runner. Young scored on a game-winning sacrifice fly by Matt Stairs.

JUNE 14   Paul Konerko hits a grand slam off Osvaldo Fernandez in the first inning of a 7–5 win over the Reds at Comiskey Park.

JUNE 18   Magglio Ordonez hits his sixth home run in a span of seven games during a 6–4 win over the Royals at Comiskey Park.

JUNE 20   The White Sox sign Jose Canseco as a free agent following his release by the Angels.

At the time he was signed by the Sox, Canseco was playing for the Newark Bears in the independent Atlantic League. He was a week shy of his 37th birthday and had 446 career homers. Canseco desperately wanted to end his career with at least 500 home runs, which he believed would be a ticket to the Hall of Fame. Canseco had been a star of the first order earlier in his career, when he became the first player in major league history to hit at least 40 homers and steal 40 bases in a season in 1988 while with the Athletics. Jose played in three consecutive World Series in Oakland, teaming with fellow home run hitter Mark McGwire to form the "Bash Brothers." Canseco's career was slowed by injuries and immature behavior, however. The Sox were his seventh big-league club. Canseco hit .258 with 16 homers in 76 games with the White Sox in 2001, his last season in the majors. Canseco played 18 games with the Sox's Triple-A farm club at Charlotte in 2002 before announcing his retirement in May. In 2005, he admitted to using anabolic steroids in a tell-all book titled Juiced: Wild Times,

Rampant 'Roids, Smash Hits and How Baseball Got Big. In it, Canseco claimed up to 85 percent of major league players took steroids.

JULY 5   The White Sox score two runs in the ninth inning to defeat the Twins 4–3 at Comiskey Park. Herb Perry hit a run-scoring single to tie the score, and then crossed the plate on a double by Sandy Alomar Jr.

JULY 7   Four solo homers account for all four runs of a 4–1 win over the Pirates at Comiskey Park. The home runs were struck by Paul Konerko, Aaron Rowand, Mark Johnson and Chris Singleton.

          Rowand captured the hearts of White Sox fans during his five seasons with the club with his all-out hustle. He was the starting center fielder on the 2005 world championship team.

JULY 10   In the All-Star Game at Safeco Field in Seattle, Derek Jeter and Magglio Ordonez hit back-to-back homers in the sixth inning off Jon Lieber of the Cubs, helping the American League to a 4–1 victory.

JULY 15   The White Sox play at Miller Park in Milwaukee for the first time and defeat the Brewers 3–2.

JULY 21   Paul Konerko keys a seven-run third inning with a grand slam off Tomo Ohka, leading to a 10–3 triumph over the Red Sox at Comiskey Park.

JULY 22   The White Sox score in seven of eight turns at bat and defeat the Red Sox 13–8 at Comiskey Park.

JULY 26   The White Sox trade James Baldwin to the Dodgers for Gary Majewski, Oman Masaoka and Jeff Barry.

AUGUST 1 Jose Canseco lives up to a pre-game promise he made to four young cancer patients by homering in his first two at-bats in the White Sox's 7–6 victory over the Royals at Comiskey Park. On Cancer Survivors Night, 450 patients and their families turned out for the game. Four children, two male and two female, were on the field for batting practice when Canseco promised them he would hit home runs for them.

AUGUST 3 Mark Buehrle pitches a one-hitter to defeat the Devil Rays 4–0 at Comiskey Park. Buehrle held Tampa Bay hitless until Damion Rolls led off the seventh with a single. The only other base runner was Steve Cox, who was hit in the helmet with a pitch in the sixth.

AUGUST 4 Down 5–0, the White Sox score six runs in the fourth inning and beat the Devil Rays 8–6 at Comiskey Park.

AUGUST 6 Dan Wright takes a no-hitter into the seventh inning of his second major league start, leading the White Sox to a 5–2 win over the Devil Rays at Comiskey Park. The no-hit bid was stopped by Chris Gomez, who doubled with one out. Wright who had walked seven and made 115 pitches, was taken out of the game immediately after the two-base hit.

AUGUST 8   The White Sox pummel the Angels 15–1 in Anaheim.

AUGUST 10   The White Sox score five runs in the ninth inning to defeat the Mariners 8–6 in
              Seattle. Herbert Perry drew a bases-loaded walk to score the first run. Jose Valentin
              tied the score with a two-run double and Magglio Ordonez broke the deadlock with
              another two-run double.

AUGUST 22   Big innings by both clubs highlight a 13–12 win over the Royals at Kauffman
              Stadium. Kansas City scored seven runs in the first inning for a 7–2 lead. The White
              Sox trailed 8–5 before exploding for eight runs in the sixth, then survived a four-run
              Royals rally in the seventh to nail down the victory. Ray Durham hit two homers
              and a double.

AUGUST 25   An 8–4 loss in St. Petersburg is delayed for 24 minutes in the bottom of the first
              inning when lightning strikes near Tropicana Field, knocking out a bank of lights.

AUGUST 28   Down 6–1 after two innings, the White Sox chip away at the deficit by scoring in five
              different innings and win 8–6 over the Tigers in Detroit. The Sox broke the 6–6 tie
              with a two-run homer from Jose Valentin in the eighth.

AUGUST 31   Jose Valentin hits two homers and drives in five runs during an 11–8 win over the
              Indians at Comiskey Park. Royce Clayton broke the 8–8 tie with a three-run homer
              in the eighth.

SEPTEMBER 2   The White Sox rally from six down to beat the Indians 19–10 at Comiskey Park.
              All of the Pale Hose scoring occurred in three different innings. Cleveland scored six
              times in the top of the second, but the Sox rallied with eight runs in their half, then
              scored five more in the third for a 13–6 lead. Chicago put the game away with a
              six-run rally in the seventh.

SEPTEMBER 11 Two hijacked commercial airliners strike and destroy the twin towers of the World
              Trade Center in New York in the worst terrorist attack ever on American soil. A
              third hijacked plane destroyed a portion of the Pentagon, and a fourth crashed in
              rural Pennsylvania. Some 3,000 were killed, including 2,800 at the World Trade
              Center. Almost immediately, commissioner Bud Selig canceled the slate of games that
              day, including the White Sox-Yankees match-up in New York. As the tragic events
              were unfolding at the World Trade Center, most of the White Sox players and staff
              were asleep in their Manhattan hotel a few miles north. The club's team charter
              arrived at Newark Airport early that morning after a flight from Cleveland. They got
              to their rooms about 2:00 a.m. The smoke from the twin towers was visible from the
              team hotel. Coach Art Kusyner witnessed the fall of the towers while walking down
              Fifth Avenue.

              *Later in the week, Selig announced that all games through Sunday, September
              16, would be postponed. The contests were made up by extending the regular
              season a week. When play resumed, an air of heightened security and patriotism
              imbued every game. Fans endured close scrutiny by stadium personnel. "God
              Bless America" replaced "Take Me Out to the Ball Game" as the song of choice
              during the seventh-inning stretch.*

SEPTEMBER 18   After eight days of unimaginable horror in the city where they live and play, the Yankees play their first game following the September 11 attacks with the White Sox as their opponent at Comiskey Park. The Yanks won 11–3 in a contest filled with displays of patriotism and solidarity. All through the night, the United States and New York City were saluted, from the small flags handed out to fans to signs like "Chicago Luvs NY."

SEPTEMBER 19   Roger Clemens becomes the first pitcher in major league history to start a season with a 20–1 record by leading the Yankees to a 6–3 win over the White Sox at Comiskey Park. It was Clemens's 16th consecutive win. He ended the season with a record of 20–3.

SEPTEMBER 23   Magglio Ordonez hits a grand slam off Chad Durbin in the fifth inning of a 10–2 win over the Royals at Comiskey Park. The Sox scored their runs with a pair of five-run innings in the third and the fifth.

SEPTEMBER 27   Harold Baines makes the last appearance of his 22-year playing career during a 9–3 win over the Twins at Comiskey Park. Baines had been on the disabled list since June. He was given a standing ovation as he stepped to the plate, but he then struck out.

                  Baines had hoped to finish his career with at least 3,000 hits, but he finished with 2,866 after collecting only 11 hits in 84 at-bats in 2001 for an average of .131.

SEPTEMBER 30   Carlos Lee's leaping catch above the fence in left field robs Raul Ibanez of a grand slam in the third inning of a 5–2 win in Kansas City.

OCTOBER 1   Six days before the United States launches a sustained air campaign in Afghanistan against al-Qaeda, the White Sox beat the Yankees 8–1 in New York in a contest originally scheduled for September 11. The crowd at Yankee Stadium was only 8,112.

DECEMBER 13   The White Sox trade Josh Fogg, Kip Wells and Sean Lowe to the Pirates for Todd Ritchie and Lee Evans.

                  The White Sox showed poor judgment in giving up useful pitchers in Fogg and Wells for Ritchie, who was 5–15 with a 6.06 ERA in 2002, his only year in Chicago.

2002

Sox

Season in a Sentence

The White Sox continue their failure to build on the success of the young club that won the 2000 division title, as a mid-season slump leads management to trade veterans for prospects.

Finish • Won • Lost • Pct • GB

Second   81   81   .500   13.5
In the wild-card race, the White Sox finished in fourth place, 18 games behind.

Manager

Jerry Manuel

Stats

Stats	WS	AL	Rank
Batting Avg:	.268	.264	7
On-Base Pct:	.338	.331	6
Slugging Pct:	.449	.424	3
Home Runs:	217		3
Stolen Bases:	75		9
ERA:	4.53	4.46	8
Fielding Avg:	.984	.983	6
Runs Scored:	856		3
Runs Allowed:	798		8

Starting Lineup

Mark Johnson, c
Paul Konerko, 1b
Ray Durham, 2b
Jose Valentin, 3b-ss
Royce Clayton, ss
Carlos Lee, lf
Kenny Lofton, cf
Magglio Ordonez, rf
Frank Thomas, dh
Aaron Rowand, cf-lf
Tony Graffanino, 3b-2b

Pitchers

Mark Buehrle, sp
Dan Wright, sp
Jon Garland, sp
Gary Glover, sp-rp
Todd Ritchie, sp
Keith Foulke, rp
Antonio Osuna, rp
Damaso Marte, rp
Bob Howry, rp
Rocky Biddle, rp

Attendance

1,676,804 (10th in AL)

Club Leaders

Batting Avg:	Magglio Ordonez	.320
On-Base Pct:	Magglio Ordonez	.381
Slugging Pct:	Magglio Ordonez	.597
Home Runs:	Magglio Ordonez	38
RBIs:	Magglio Ordonez	135
Runs:	Magglio Ordonez	116
Stolen Bases:	Kenny Lofton	22
Wins:	Mark Buehrle	19
Strikeouts:	Dan Wright	136
ERA:	Mark Buehrle	3.58
Saves:	Antonio Osuna	11
	Keith Foulke	11

JANUARY 10   David Wells signs with the Yankees as a free agent.

The White Sox had a $10 million option on Wells for the 2002 season, but they declined to exercise it after he won only five games for the club in 2001. The Sox should have held on to him. Wells was 19–7 in New York in 2002 and had a 61–29 record with the Yankees, Padres and Red Sox from 2002 through 2005.

JANUARY 29   The White Sox trade Chris Singleton to the Orioles for Willie Harris.

FEBRUARY 1   The White Sox sign Kenny Lofton, most recently with the Indians, as a free agent.

A native of East Chicago, Indiana, Lofton was 34 years old and on the downside of a career in which he was named to six All-Star teams. He was the Sox's starting center fielder until being traded to the Giants in July 2002.

APRIL 1   The White Sox win the season opener 6–5 over the Mariners at Safeco Field. The Sox scored four runs in the seventh inning for a 6–1 lead, then survived a four-run

Seattle rally in the eighth. Mark Buehrle allowed a run and two hits in six innings for the win. Carlos Lee contributed a homer, double and single. Paul Konerko collected three hits, including a double.

APRIL 2   Six-foot-11-inch White Sox pitcher Jon Rauch becomes the tallest player in major league history with his debut during a 7–4 loss to the Mariners in Seattle.

APRIL 6   The White Sox mash the Royals 14–0 in Kansas City.

APRIL 12   In the home opener, the White Sox win 5–2 over the Orioles before 41,128 at Comiskey Park. Sandy Alomar Jr. and Ray Durham each homered.

             The White Sox added a multi-tiered batter's eye, with the upper levels covered with ivy, to the center field area at Comiskey Park in 2002.

APRIL 15   The White Sox rout the Orioles 13–4 at Comiskey Park. The Sox led 13–0 after five innings.

APRIL 16   The White Sox score nine runs in the second inning and beat the Indians 10–5 at Comiskey Park. Magglio Ordonez hit a grand slam off Chuck Finley.

             Ordonez had another terrific season in 2002. He collected 47 doubles and 38 homers, drove in 135 runs, scored 116 and batted .320.

APRIL 20   Paul Konerko hits a grand slam off Nate Cornejo in the third inning of a 12–5 win over the Tigers at Comiskey Park. Frank Thomas reached base five times in five plate appearances on a homer, double, single and two walks.

APRIL 21   The White Sox score eight runs in the first inning and beat the Tigers 11–8 at Comiskey Park.

APRIL 24   Frank Thomas hits his first triple since 1998 during a 9–2 win over the Indians in Cleveland.

             Thomas didn't hit another triple until 2008, when he was playing for the Athletics.

APRIL 27   The White Sox give up four homers to the Athletics in the seventh inning of a 16–1 loss at Network Associates Coliseum. The Oakland homers were struck by Scott Hatteberg, Terrence Long, Carlos Pena and Frank Menechino in a span of six batters. Mark Buehrle gave up three of the homers, and Mike Porzio one.

             The White Sox had a record of 4–23 in Oakland from 2001 through 2006.

MAY 2   Mike Cameron hits a major league record-tying four homers for the Mariners during a 15–4 win over the White Sox at Comiskey Park. Cameron, who played for the White Sox from 1995 through 1998, homered in his first four plate appearances. He started the night with two home runs in the first inning. The first was struck off Jon Rauch and followed a homer by Bret Boone. Later in the 10-run Seattle inning, Boone and Cameron hit back-to-back homers again, this time facing Jim Parque. It is the only time in major league history that teammates hit back-to-back homers in the same inning. Cameron followed with solo homers in the third and fifth, both against Parque. In the seventh, Cameron was hit by a pitch from Mike Porzio in the back of the left thigh, drawing boos from the crowd of 12,891. With another chance to hit a record-breaking fifth home run in the ninth, Cameron hit a long opposite-field drive, but right fielder Jeff Liefer made a running, back-handed catch at the front of the warning track.

Through 2008, there have been 15 players who have homered four times in a game. Cameron is the only one to accomplish the feat against the White Sox. Pat Seerey hit four homers for the Sox on July 16, 1948.

MAY 7   Trailing 4–3, the White Sox score eight runs in the sixth inning and win 11–8 over the Rangers in Arlington.

MAY 10   The Angels unleash a 24-hit attack and demolish the White Sox 19–0 in Anaheim. The 19-run loss is the worst in White Sox history. The 19 runs scored in five consecutive innings from the third through the seventh off Dan Wright, Matt Ginter and Mike Porzio. The Sox collected only three hits.

MAY 14   Tony Graffanino hits two homers and two singles and drives in six runs during a 15–4 win over the Rangers at Comiskey Park.

Graffanino was born Anthony Graffagnino, but dropped the "g" after several mispronunciations by minor-league announcers.

MAY 24   The White Sox use three-run homers from Frank Thomas, Magglio Ordonez and Paul Konerko to account for nine runs in a 12–1 win over the Tigers at Comiskey Park.

MAY 25   The White Sox take a one-game lead in the AL Central with a 6–4 win over the Tigers at Comiskey Park.

The White Sox dropped out of first place two days later in the midst of a seven-game losing streak that dropped the club's record to 28–28. The Sox bottomed out at 59–69 on August 23 and Jerry Manuel's job appeared to be in jeopardy before the club rallied to finish the season with 81 wins and 81 losses.

JUNE 4   In the first round of the amateur draft, the White Sox select pitcher Royce Ring from San Diego State University.

Ring was traded to the Mets in July 2003 in a deal that brought Roberto Alomar to Chicago. Ring reached the majors in 2005, but thus far has had an unproductive career. Other future big-leaguers drafted and signed by the White Sox in 2002 include Jeremy Reed (second round), Josh Rupe (third round), Sean Tracy (eighth round), Brandon McCarthy (17th round), Boone Logan (20th round) and Jay Marshall (25th round).

JUNE 7   The White Sox play the Expos during the regular season for the first time and win 4–3 at Comiskey Park. In the sixth inning, Kenny Lofton stole his 500th career base.

Lofton is one of only two athletes to play in both a Final Four and a World Series. He played in the Final Four with the University of Arizona in 1988 and in the Fall Classic with the Indians in 1995. The other individual to accomplish the feat was Tim Stoddard, who played for the 1974 NCAA champions at North Carolina State and pitched in the World Series for the Orioles in 1979. Oddly, Stoddard and Lofton both attended Washington High School in East Chicago, Indiana.

JUNE 9 — Magglio Ordonez drives in six runs with two doubles and a single during a 13–2 rout of the Expos at Comiskey Park.

JUNE 10 — The White Sox play the Mets for the first time during the regular season and lose 3–1 at Comiskey Park.

JUNE 16 — Carlos Lee drives in seven runs during a 10–7 win over the Cubs at Wrigley Field. Lee smacked a grand slam off Kerry Wood in the third inning and a three-run homer in the fifth against Carlos Zambrano.

JUNE 18 — The White Sox play the Phillies for the first time during the regular season and win 6–3 in 12 innings at Veterans Stadium. In the 12th, Kenny Lofton hit a two-run triple and then scored on an error. It was the Sox's first appearance in Philadelphia since playing the Athletics in 1954.

JUNE 21 — The White Sox play in Atlanta for the first time and lose 3–2 to the Braves at Turner Field.

JUNE 25 — The White Sox collect 23 hits and defeat the Twins 15–7 in Minneapolis. Magglio Ordonez led the way with four hits, including a double, and five runs batted in.

JUNE 27 — Paul Konerko collects four hits, including a home run, in five at-bats during a 7–4 victory over the Twins in Minneapolis.

JUNE 28 — Paul Konerko homers twice after being beaned, leading the White Sox from an eight-run deficit to beat the Cubs 13–9 before 46,027 at Comiskey Park, the largest regular-season crowd in the history of the ballpark. Konerko was plunked in the head by a pitch from Kerry Wood in the fourth inning after singling in the second. Konerko retaliated by collecting three more hits, including the two homers. It was his second consecutive four-hit game. The Cubs led 8–0 after three innings, but the Sox rallied with a run in the fourth, three in the fifth and six in the sixth. In the sixth, Magglio Ordonez's two-run single tied the score 8–8, then Konerko hit his second homer for a 10–8 lead. After the Cubs narrowed the gap to a run, the White Sox added three insurance runs in the eighth.

In 17 games from June 10 through June 28, Konerko hit .439 with 12 homers and 21 RBIs.

JULY 2 — The White Sox and Tigers tie a major league record by combining for 12 homers during a 17–9 Chicago win at Comiskey Park. The same two clubs set the record on May 28, 1995, in Detroit. A 93-degree night and a 14 mile-per-hour wind blowing out contributed to the home run output. Each team hit six. Homering for the Sox were Sandy Alomar (two), Magglio Ordonez (two), Jose Valentin (one) and Kenny Lofton (one) off Detroit hurlers Adam Bernero (four), Jose Lima (one) and Jose Paniagua (one). The Tiger homers came from Dmitri Young (two),

Damion Easley (one), Wendell Magee (one), George Lombard (one) and Rob Fick (one) off Chicago pitchers Todd Ritchie (three) and Bob Howry (three). The second home run by Ordonez was a grand slam off Paniagua during the White Sox's seven-run eighth inning.

Ray Durham played in both of the 12-home run games in 1995 and 2002. He homered in the 1995 contest.

JULY 9   In the All-Star Game at Miller Park in Milwaukee, Paul Konerko collects two doubles in two at-bats and drives in two runs. The game ended in a 7–7 tie after 11 innings because the two teams ran out of pitchers.

JULY 14   Carlos Lee collects four hits, two of them homers, to lead the White Sox to a 6–4 win over the Tigers in Detroit.

JULY 18   Kenny Lofton leads off the first inning with a home run off Paul Byrd, but the White Sox lose 5–3 to the Royals in Kansas City.

JULY 19   For the second straight game, Kenny Lofton leads off the first inning with a home run, this time facing Rodrigo Lopez of the Orioles in Baltimore, but the White Sox lose again 10–4.

Lofton is the only batter in White Sox history to lead off two consecutive games with home runs.

JULY 23   Frank Thomas clears the left-field bleachers at Comiskey Park with a homer estimated to have traveled 495 feet during an 8–7 win over the Twins.

Home Run Derby in the Windy City

There have been only two instances in major league history in which two teams combined for 12 home runs in a game. Both involved the White Sox and Tigers. The first happened on May 28, 1995, at Tiger Stadium. The second occurred on July 2, 2002, at Comiskey Park. The White Sox won the second tilt 17–9.

The 12 home runs:
1. Detroit first inning. Dmitri Young with none on base off Todd Ritchie. Detroit 1, Chicago 0.
2. Detroit first inning. Rob Fick with one on base off Ritchie. Detroit 3, Chicago 0.
3. Chicago first inning. Leadoff batter Kenny Lofton with none on base off Adam Bernero. Detroit 3, Chicago 1.
4. Chicago first inning. Magglio Ordonez with none on base off Bernero. Detroit 3, Chicago 2.
5. Chicago second inning. Jose Valentin with none on base off Bernero. Detroit 3, Chicago 3.
6. Chicago fourth inning. Sandy Alomar Jr. with none on base off Bernero. Detroit 4, Chicago 4.
7. Chicago sixth inning. Alomar with none on base off Jose Lima. Chicago 8, Detroit 4.
8. Detroit seventh inning. George Lombard with none on base off Ritchie. The blow was Lombard's first home run in the majors since 1998. Chicago 8, Detroit 5.
9. Chicago eighth inning. Ordonez with three on base off Jose Paniagua. Chicago 15, Detroit 5.
10. Detroit ninth inning. Wendell Magee with none on base off Bob Howry. Chicago 17, Detroit 6.
11. Detroit ninth inning. Damion Easley with one on base off Howry. Chicago 17, Detroit 8.
12. Detroit ninth inning. Young with none on base off Howry. Chicago 17, Detroit 9.

JULY 25   The White Sox trade Ray Durham to the Athletics for Jon Adkins.

Durham excelled in relative obscurity during his eight seasons in Chicago and never received the recognition he deserved. Durham was eligible for free agency at the end of the 2002 season, and the White Sox jettisoned his salary for a minor-league pitcher. He signed with the Giants and was a starter for the club at second base for five seasons. Adkins had an ineffective three seasons with the Sox.

JULY 28   The White Sox trade Kenny Lofton to the Giants for Felix Diaz and Ryan Meaux.

JULY 29   The White Sox trade Sandy Alomar Jr. to the Rockies for Enemencio Pacheco.

Alomar returned to the White Sox as a free agent in December 2002.

JULY 30   A three-run homer by Magglio Ordonez off Kyle Lohse in the sixth inning provides all of the runs in a 3–0 victory over the Twins in Minneapolis. Mark Buehrle pitched the shutout.

JULY 31   The White Sox trade Bob Howry to the Red Sox for Franklin Francisco and Byeong An.

In yet another mid-season transaction to reduce the payroll, Howry was swapped for two minor leaguers who never panned out. After spending most of the 2003 season on the disabled list, Howry gave the Indians and Cubs several solid seasons out of the bullpen. The trades of Durham, Alomar, Lofton and Howry during the last week of July yielded next to nothing in return.

Though only 23 years old, lefty Mark Buehrle won 19 games in 2002, and he has won 122 games in nine years with the Sox.

AUGUST 13   Jose Valentin hits home runs from both sides of the plate and drives in six runs during a 12–3 win over the Rangers in Arlington. Valentin homered off lefty Dennys Reyes in the fourth inning and right-hander Todd Van Poppel in the sixth. The drive off Reyes was a grand slam.

AUGUST 21   Jose Valentin hits home runs in his first two at-bats and drives in five runs during a 10–1 win over the Twins at Comiskey Park.

AUGUST 27   Joe Crede contributes seven RBIs, six of them in the ninth and 10th innings, to lead the White Sox to an 8–4 victory over the Blue Jays at Comiskey Park. Crede tied the score 4–4 with a two-run homer in the ninth, then clubbed a walk-off grand slam against Felix Heredia in the 10th.

SEPTEMBER 2   In the second at-bat of his first major league game, Joe Borchard homers for his first hit to help the White Sox to a 5–3 win over the Blue Jays in Toronto.

SEPTEMBER 7   The White Sox release Royce Clayton.

SEPTEMBER 8   The White Sox score four runs in the ninth inning to stun the Indians 7–6 at Comiskey Park. Frank Thomas hit a game-tying three-run homer and Joe Crede drove in the winning run with a walk-off single.

SEPTEMBER 10   Jeff Liefer hits a grand slam in the ninth inning off Jeremy Affeldt to cap a 12–4 triumph over the Royals in Kansas City.

SEPTEMBER 13   The White Sox erupt for eight runs in the ninth inning to close out a 13–2 win over the Yankees in New York.

SEPTEMBER 15   In his first major league at-bat, White Sox catcher Miguel Olivo homers off Andy Pettitte for a 3–0 lead before the Yankees rally to win 8–4 in a contest in New York called in the bottom of the sixth by rain.

SEPTEMBER 19   An ugly incident occurs in the ninth inning of a 2–1 loss to the Royals at Comiskey Park when a father and son attack Kansas City's first-base coach, 54-year-old Tom Gamboa. The two attackers were 34-year-old William Ligue Jr., who was bare-chested, and his 15-year-old son Michael. The pair ran out of the first-base stands and landed several blows on Gamboa and a member of the Comiskey Park security team, who attempted to protect the Royals coach. With his back to the stands, Gamboa never saw his attackers coming. The two assailants were charged with two counts of felony assault. Gamboa suffered a small cut above one eye and bruises. Later, it was determined that he also sustained partial hearing loss in his right ear as a result of the blows. The White Sox beefed up security at the ballpark, but a similar incident would occur about seven months later (see April 15, 2003).

               The elder Ligue claimed that Gamboa flashed his son an obscene gesture after an exchange, but Gamboa denied the accusation. With his arms and torso covered in tattoos, Ligue was photographed being led into a police car with a defiant look on his face. He told officers that Gamboa "got what he deserved." In court, however, Ligue was repentant and in August 2003 received a sentence of only 30 months' probation, which a vast majority of people believed was shockingly lenient. Ligue violated his probation in April 2004 by breaking into a car in suburban Harvey, Illinois, and stealing a stereo. He was sentenced to five years in prison for the crime in 2006.

SEPTEMBER 21   Carlos Lee hits a grand slam off Bob Wells in the seventh inning of a 14–4 win over the Twins at Comiskey Park.

SEPTEMBER 28   In an attempt to win his 20th game of the season, Mark Buehrle carries a 2–1 lead into the eighth inning, but he allows a two-run homer to Bobby Kielty, resulting in a 3–2 defeat at the hands of the Twins in Minneapolis.

               Buehrle finished the season with a 19–12 record and a 3.58 ERA in 239 innings.

NOVEMBER 1   Aaron Rowand breaks his left shoulder blade and two ribs in a dirt bike accident near his home near Las Vegas. Rowand was traveling at 25 miles per hour when he tumbled down a 25-foot embankment. He was ready to play by Opening Day in 2003.

DECEMBER 3   The White Sox trade Keith Foulke, Mark Johnson and Joe Valentine to the Athletics for Billy Koch.

Koch was one of the top closers in the game when acquired by the White Sox. He saved 144 games for the Blue Jays and Athletics over the previous four seasons, with a high of 44 at the age of 27 in 2002. Koch was a flop in Chicago, however, with a 5.66 ERA in 76⅓ innings in 79 games over two seasons. Foulke, on the other hand, saved 43 games for the A's in 2003 and was the Red Sox's closer on the 2004 world championship club

DECEMBER 11   Royce Clayton signs with the Brewers as a free agent.

DECEMBER 20   The White Sox sign Sandy Alomar Jr., most recently with the Rockies, as a free agent.

2003   Sox

Season in a Sentence

After falling five games under .500 in July, the White Sox spend 25 days in August and September in first place, but a second-place finish costs Jerry Manuel his job.

Finish • Won • Lost • Pct • GB

Second 86 76 .531 4.0
In the wild-card race, the White Sox finished tied for third place, nine games behind.

Manager

Jerry Manuel

Stats

Stats	WS	AL	Rank
Batting Avg:	.263	.267	11
On-Base Pct:	.331	.333	7
Slugging Pct:	.446	.428	5
Home Runs:	220		4
Stolen Bases:	77		11
ERA:	4.17	4.52	4
Fielding Avg:	.984	.983	4
Runs Scored:	791		7
Runs Allowed:	715		3

Starting Lineup

Miguel Olivo, c
Paul Konerko, 1b
D'Angelo Jimenez, 2b
Joe Crede, 3b
Jose Valentin, ss
Carlos Lee, lf
Carl Everett, cf
Magglio Ordonez, rf
Frank Thomas, 1b
Tony Graffanino, ss-3b-2b
Roberto Alomar, 2b
Brian Daubach, 1b
Aaron Rowand, cf

Pitchers

Esteban Loaiza, sp
Bartolo Colon, sp
Mark Buehrle, sp
Jon Garland, sp
Dan Wright, sp
Tom Gordon, rp
Billy Koch, rp
Damaso Marte, rp
Kelly Wunsch, rp

Attendance

1,939,611 (ninth in AL)

Club Leaders

Batting Avg: Magglio Ordonez .317
On-Base Pct: Frank Thomas .390
Slugging Pct: Frank Thomas .562
Home Runs: Frank Thomas 42
RBIs: Carlos Lee 113
Runs: Carlos Lee 100
Stolen Bases: Carlos Lee 18
Wins: Esteban Loaiza 21
Strikeouts: Esteban Loaiza 207
ERA: Esteban Loaiza 2.90
Saves: Tom Gordon 12

JANUARY 15   The White Sox trade Antonio Osuna and Deivi Lantigua to the Yankees for Orlando Hernandez, then swap Hernandez, Rocky Biddle and Jeff Liefer to the Expos for Bartolo Colon and Jorge Nunez.

Colon was being shopped by Montreal because he was eligible to become a free agent after the 2003 season. With a combined record of 20–8 with the Indians and Expos in 2002, he was desired by nearly every club in the majors. In his only season in Chicago, Colon was 15–13. In a strange twist, the White Sox lost Colon to the Angels via free agency in December 2003 and then signed Hernandez.

JANUARY 20   The White Sox sign Tom Gordon, most recently with the Astros, as a free agent. On the same day, Jim Parque signed with the Devil Rays as a free agent.

JANUARY 27   The White Sox sign Esteban Loaiza, most recently with the Blue Jays, as a free agent.

Loaiza gave the White Sox one great, and totally unexpected, season. There was no rush to the box office when he was signed. After all, Loaiza was 31 years old and had a lifetime record of 69–73, a career ERA of 4.88 and had never won more than 11 games in a season. His stock had fallen so low that Loaiza was signed to a minor-league deal and wasn't even on the 40-man roster during spring training. But in 2003, Loaiza was the starting American League pitcher in the All-Star Game and finished the season second in the Cy Young Award voting with a 21–9 record, a 2.90 earned run average and a league-leading 207 strikeouts in 226⅓ innings. Loaiza's success was fleeting, however. After winning his first four starts in 2004, he reverted back to his previous state of mediocrity.

JANUARY 31   The wireless phone company U.S. Cellular purchases the naming rights to Comiskey Park for 20 years at a price of $68 million. In the process, the ballpark became known as U.S. Cellular Field. It was a radical break with tradition. Charles Comiskey founded the franchise in 1900 and opened the original Comiskey Park in 1910. His son, daughter-in-law and grandson were club executives after Charles's death in 1931. The Comiskey family sold the club in 1959 to Bill Veeck, but the ballpark at 35th and Shields continued to be known as Comiskey Park. When the new stadium across the street opened in 1991, it, too, took the name Comiskey Park. Jerry Reinsdorf said that the money the club received for the naming rights would be used to upgrade the stadium, including a remodeling of the much-criticized upper deck. In 2003, a full-color, high-resolution, 28-foot-by-53-foot video screen was added to the center-field scoreboard. In addition, two 300-foot long, five-foot high "ribbon" boards were added along the upper-deck facade. A life-sized statue of franchise founder Charles Comiskey was unveiled. And a Fan Deck was built on the center-field concourse, featuring food and beverage service in a patio-like setting.

MARCH 31   Twelve days after U.S. forces invade Iraq, the White Sox lose the season opener 3–0 to the Royals at Kauffman Stadium. The Sox collected only three hits off three Kansas City pitchers. Mark Buehrle was the losing pitcher.

Buehrle won his next two decisions, then lost nine in a row to drop his record to 2–10 on June 11. He turned things around quickly and won seven in succession from June 16 through July 29 before ending the season at 14–14.

| APRIL 4 | The White Sox win the season opener 5–2 against the Tigers before 40,395 at U.S. Cellular Field. The game-time temperature was 37 degrees and the contest was interrupted by a two-hour rain delay. |

Despite the change in the name of the White Sox's home to U.S. Cellular Field, many fans and sportscasters continued to refer to the ballpark by the old name of Comiskey Park. Veteran radio host Steve Dahl, best known for his role in "Disco Demolition Night" (see July 12, 1979), referred to U.S. Cellular Field as "The Joan" in honor of actress and Chicago native Joan Cusack for her television commercials for the U.S. Cellular company.

| APRIL 5 | With a game-time temperature of only 32 degrees at U.S. Cellular Field, the White Sox beat the Tigers 7–0. |

| APRIL 6 | Trailing 2–1, the White Sox erupt for nine runs in the eighth inning and defeat the Tigers 10–2 at U.S. Cellular Field. |

The White Sox had a 14–5 record against a Tiger club that finished the 2003 season with a record of 43–119.

| APRIL 11 | Esteban Loaiza (eight innings) and Billy Koch (one inning) combine on a two-hitter to defeat the Tigers 5–0 at Comerica Park. The only Detroit hits were singles by Shane Halter in the fourth inning and Ramon Santiago in the sixth. |

| APRIL 15 | An umpire is attacked by a fan during an 8–5 win over the Royals at U.S. Cellular Field. The situation was eerily similar to that of September 19, 2002, when Royals first-base coach Tom Gamboa was assaulted by a father and son. Oddly, Gamboa was also in attendance for the April 15, 2003, attack, this time as Kansas City's bullpen coach. The umpire was 30-year-old Laz Diaz, who was stationed near first base. The fan was 24-year-old Eric Dybas of Bolingbrook, Illinois, who ran onto the field and tried to tackle Diaz, wrapping his arms around the umpire's legs. Diaz was standing about 100 feet from where Gamboa was knocked down. The game had been delayed three times before Dybas ran onto the field, because other fans had invaded the diamond before being escorted from the premises by security guards. |

Dybas was charged with aggravated battery and criminal trespassing. He was later sentenced to six months in jail.

| APRIL 17 | Carlos Lee hits a grand slam off Chris George in the fifth inning of an 8–2 win over the Royals at U.S. Cellular Field. |

Lee tied the White Sox record by homering in five straight games from April 17–21.

| APRIL 26 | The White Sox defeat the Twins 7–4 in a tension-filled matchup at U.S. Cellular Field. The benches emptied in the sixth inning after Chicago starter Jon Garland was tossed for hitting Doug Mientkiewicz with a pitch, one inning after Magglio Ordonez was plunked for the second straight night. Sox center fielder Armando Rios was also ejected along with Minnesota reliever LaTroy Hawkins, who was not in the game. |

| APRIL 30 | A 4–1 loss to the Athletics at U.S. Cellular Field is delayed twice by fog for a total of 45 minutes. |

MAY 7 — The White Sox defeat the Athletics 8–4 on a weird night in Oakland. First, Magglio Ordonez hit a peculiar triple in the third inning. Eric Byrnes robbed Ordonez of a home run when he reached over the fence in left and had the ball in his glove before it got loose. The ball rolled along the top of the fence and eventually fell onto the warning track. A few minutes later, part of the left field wall fell to the field just below the left-field scoreboard. Byrnes and center fielder Chris Singleton attempted to punch it back in place but were unsuccessful until receiving help from the grounds crew. It caused a delay of about 10 minutes.

MAY 13 — Esteban Loaiza (seven innings), Tom Gordon (one inning) and Billy Koch (one inning) combine on a shutout to defeat the Orioles 1–0 at U.S. Cellular Field.

MAY 16 — The Twins rout the White Sox 18–3 in Minneapolis.

MAY 25 — A three-run, walk-off homer by Joe Crede in the 12th inning beats the Tigers 8–5 at U.S. Cellular Field. Carlos Lee hit a grand slam off Adam Bernero in the fifth inning.

JUNE 3 — The White Sox play the Diamondbacks for the first time during the regular season and lose 2–1 in Phoenix.

> *On the same day, the White Sox selected outfielder Brian Anderson from the University of Arizona in the first round of the amateur draft. Anderson made the White Sox roster in 2005, but thus far has been a bust in the majors. Other future major leaguers drafted and signed by the White Sox in 2003 include second-rounder Ryan Sweeney.*

JUNE 6 — The White Sox play the Dodgers for the first time during the regular season and lose 2–1 in Los Angeles.

JUNE 10 — The White Sox play the Giants for the first time during the regular season and win 5–3 at U.S. Cellular Field.

JUNE 13 — The White Sox play the Padres for the first time during the regular season and win 5–3 at U.S. Cellular Field.

JUNE 20 — Miguel Olivo hits a grand slam off Shawn Estes during a six-run first inning, sparking a 12–3 triumph over the Cubs at Wrigley Field.

JUNE 30 — Magglio Ordonez hits two of the White Sox's five homers during a 10–3 win over the Twins at U.S. Cellular Field. The others were struck by Carlos Lee, Joe Crede and Jose Valentin.

JULY 1 — The White Sox trade Royce Ring, Edwin Almonte and Andrew Salvo to the Mets for Roberto Alomar. On the same day, the Sox also traded Frankie Francisco, Josh Rupe and Anthony Webster to the Rangers for Carl Everett.

> *Alomar joined his brother Sandy Jr. on the White Sox roster. Roberto played in 12 consecutive All-Star Games from 1990 through 2001, but by the time he arrived in Chicago, his skills were in a rapid decline. Alomar batted only .253 with three homers in 67 games with the Sox. Everett came to the White Sox with considerable baggage. In 1997, he and his wife were charged with abusing*

their children with "excessive corporal punishment." Everett had also made disparaging remarks about gays and claimed dinosaurs didn't exist because they weren't mentioned in the Bible. He was a starting outfielder for the remainder of the 2003 season before going to the Expos as a free agent. The Sox re-acquired Everett in a trade with Montreal in July 2004 and he remained in Chicago through the end of the 2005 season.

JULY 2   Frank Thomas hits a two-run walk-off homer in the 12th inning to defeat the Twins 8–6 at U.S. Cellular Field. Making his White Sox debut, Roberto Alomar trotted home ahead of Thomas. After Minnesota scored in the top of the 11th, Paul Konerko responded with a solo home run in the bottom half to tie the contest 6–6.

                Remaining healthy for the bulk of the season, Thomas hit 42 homers and drove in 105 runs in 2003 along with a .267 batting average.

JULY 12   Paul Konerko hits a three-run homer in the 10th inning to beat the Indians 7–4 in the first game of a double-header at Jacobs Field. The Sox scored twice in the ninth to tie the game. Cleveland won the second tilt 4–2.

JULY 15   The All-Star Game is played at U.S. Cellular Field and results in a 7–6 American League victory. White Sox hurler Esteban Loaiza was the starting pitcher for the AL and pitched two scoreless innings. The American League struck first with a run in the third inning, but the Nationals responded with five in the fifth, including a home run by Todd Helton. Brady Anderson belted a two-run homer in the sixth for the AL and Andruw Jones put the NL ahead 6–3 with a solo shot in the seventh. Jason Giambi brought the AL back to 6–4 with a home run in the seventh. The American League scored three in the eighth for the victory on an RBI-double by Vernon Wells and a two-run homer from Hank Blalock.

                The 2003 All-Star Game was the first in which the league champion of the winning team gained home field advantage in the World Series. It was the fourth time that the White Sox hosted an All-Star Game. The others were all staged at the original Comiskey Park in 1933, the first ever in the series, and in 1950 and 1983.

JULY 17   The White Sox hit the low point of the 2003 season with a 10–9 loss to the Tigers at U.S. Cellular Field.

                The Sox's record dipped to 45–50 with the defeat. The club won 13 of 14 between July 18 and August 1 to vault back into the AL Central pennant race.

JULY 20   Frank Thomas hits two of the White Sox's five homers during a 10–1 win over the Tigers at U.S. Cellular Field. The others were struck by Jose Valentin, Paul Konerko and Magglio Ordonez.

JULY 23   The White Sox score three runs in the ninth inning to defeat the Blue Jays 7–6 at SkyDome. Magglio Ordonez hit a game-tying two-run double. Toronto pitcher Dan Reichert struck Paul Konerko with a pitch with the bases loaded to score the winning run.

JULY 24   Rain causes a 26-minute delay during a 4–3 win over the Blue Jays in Toronto. A sudden shower caused the stoppage at SkyDome, where the retractable roof was open when the shower moved in during the top of the sixth inning.

JULY 25   Frank Thomas hits his 400th career homer during a 7–2 win over the Devil Rays at Comiskey Park. It was the White Sox's eighth win in a row.

JULY 30   Jose Valentin hits three homers in his first three at-bats during a 15–4 win over the Royals in Kansas City. Valentin hit a solo homer in the second inning and a three-run shot in the third batting left-handed against Runelvys Hernandez. Switching to the right side against lefty Jeremy Affeldt, Valentin hit another solo homer in the fifth. Paul Konerko also starred with six runs batted in, including a grand slam off Sean Lowe in the seventh. The Sox hit six homers in all, with Magglio Ordonez and Carlos Lee adding the others.

AUGUST 1   The White Sox rout the Mariners 12–1 in Seattle.

AUGUST 18   A two-run walk-off homer by Frank Thomas beats the Angels 4–2 at U.S. Cellular Field.

AUGUST 20   Roberto Alomar collects four infield singles, two of them on bunts, in five at-bats during a 5–3 win over the Angels at U.S. Cellular Field.

AUGUST 21   The White Sox move into first place with a 7–3 win over the Rangers at U.S. Cellular Field.

The White Sox spent 23 of the next 25 days in first place.

AUGUST 23   Frank Thomas hits two homers and drives in five runs during a 13–2 rout of the Rangers at U.S. Cellular Field. Carlos Lee, Jose Valentin and Joe Crede also homered.

AUGUST 26   The White Sox win 13–2 for the second time in a span of four days, this time over the Yankees in New York. Frank Thomas hit a grand slam off Roger Clemens in the fifth inning on a drive that clanged high off the foul pole near the upper deck. It was one of six Chicago homers in the contest. Magglio Ordonez and Paul Konerko each homered twice and Joe Crede hit one. Clemens gave up four of the homers.

AUGUST 27   The White Sox score seven runs in the fourth inning and thrash the Yankees for the second night in a row with an 11–2 decision in New York.

SEPTEMBER 2   Bartolo Colon pitches a two-hitter, but both are home runs and the White Sox lose 2–1 to the Red Sox at U.S. Cellular Field. The homers were by Trot Nixon in the second inning and Gabe Kapler in the sixth.

SEPTEMBER 9   The White Sox take a two-game lead in the AL Central with an 8–6 win over the Twins at U.S. Cellular Field. The Sox had to squirm through a four-run Minnesota ninth inning off reliever Jose Paniagua before sealing the victory. Paniagua entered the contest at the start of the ninth. It was his first big-league appearance since September 2002 and his first with the Sox. After being removed from the game by Jerry Manuel with one out, Paniagua flashed an obscene gesture toward home-plate umpire Mark Carlson. Before the game ended, Jerry Reinsdorf personally removed Paniagua's photo from the team display on the first floor of U.S. Cellular Field. Paniagua was released the next day and never pitched another game in the majors, ending his eight-year career.

The win was the White Sox's 33rd in their last 49 games since July 17. The club lost nine of their next 13, however, to blow a chance at the post-season.

SEPTEMBER 15   The idle White Sox are knocked out of a first-place tie when the Twins beat the Indians 13–6 in Cleveland.

SEPTEMBER 18   The Twins complete a three-game sweep of the White Sox in Minneapolis with a 5–3 win. The debacle at the Metrodome left the Sox 3½ games out of first with 10 contests left on the schedule.

SEPTEMBER 22   Magglio Ordonez hits a three-run, walk-off homer in the 10th inning that beats the Yankees 6–3 at U.S. Cellular Field.

Ordonez hits .317 with 26 doubles, and 29 homers in 2003.

SEPTEMBER 24   Esteban Loaiza wins his 20th game of the season with a 9–4 decision over the Yankees at U.S. Cellular Field.

SEPTEMBER 26   Jose Valentin hits a grand slam off D. J. Carrasco in the eighth inning of an 11–2 triumph over the Royals in Kansas City.

SEPTEMBER 27   The White Sox score seven runs in the third inning and clobber the Royals 19–3 in Kansas City.

SEPTEMBER 28   On the last day of the season, Esteban Loaiza takes a no-hitter into the seventh inning and finishes by allowing a run and three hits in 7²/₃ innings in a 5–1 victory over the Royals in Kansas City.

SEPTEMBER 29   The White Sox fire Jerry Manuel as manager.

Manuel took the fall after the White Sox fell apart down the stretch after holding first place during the first half of September. "This wasn't a case of not having enough talent," said general manager Ken Williams, who added that the club needed to change its "voice and direction."

NOVEMBER 3   The White Sox hire 39-year-old Ozzie Guillen as manager.

A native of Venezuela, Guillen played as a shortstop for the White Sox from 1985 through 1997. He was a three-time All-Star and won over fans with his desire and determination. Gregarious, enthusiastic, candid and quotable, Guillen wore his heart on his sleeve and was the opposite of predecessor Jerry Manuel, who was introverted, solemn and aloof. Guillen had no managerial experience when hired by the Sox. He had been a coach with the Expos in 2002 and on the world champion Marlins in 2003. In his second year at the helm of the Sox, he rewarded the fans and the organization by leading the franchise to its first World Series win since 1917. In 2007, Guillen was given a contract extension through 2012. During his tenure, Guillen gained a reputation as an eccentric manager who was not afraid to speak his mind. He has often come under fire in the media for controversial, and sometimes incendiary, comments made about managers, players and journalists. Ozzie's television and radio interviews often had to be "bleeped" to delete profanity.

DECEMBER 2   The White Sox trade Aaron Miles to the Rockies for Juan Uribe.

DECEMBER 10   Bartolo Colon signs with the Angels as a free agent.

                  *Colon was one of the biggest names on the free agent market and the White
                  Sox tried hard to sign him, but they were outbid by the Angels. In his first two
                  seasons in Anaheim, Colon had records of 18–12 in 2004 and 21–8 in 2005
                  before he was sidetracked by shoulder trouble.*

DECEMBER 16   Tom Gordon signs with the Yankees as a free agent.

DECEMBER 19   Carl Everett signs with the Expos as a free agent.

DECEMBER 22   The White Sox sign Mike Jackson, most recently with the Twins, as a free agent.

2004   Sox

Season in a Sentence

After holding first place as late as July 25, the White Sox sink out of the race and finish four games above .500, marking the fourth straight year the club wins between 81 and 86 games.

Finish • Won • Lost • Pct • GB

Second   83   79   .512   9.0
In the wild-card race, the White Sox finished in fourth place, 15 games behind.

Manager

Ozzie Guillen

Stats

Stats	WS	AL	Rank
Batting Avg:	.268	.270	9
On-Base Pct:	.333	.338	8
Slugging Pct:	.457	.433	4
Home Runs:	242		1 (tie)
Stolen Bases:	78		9
ERA:	4.91	4.63	12
Fielding Avg:	.984	.982	5
Runs Scored:	865		3
Runs Allowed:	831		11

Starting Lineup

Ben Davis, c
Paul Konerko, 1b
Juan Uribe, 2b-ss
Joe Crede, 3b
Jose Valentin, ss
Carlos Lee, lf
Aaron Rowand, cf
Magglio Ordonez, rf
Frank Thomas, dh
Willie Harris, 2b
Timo Perez, rf-cf
Ross Gload, 1b-lf-rf

Pitchers

Mark Buehrle, sp
Jon Garland, sp
Esteban Loaiza, sp
Freddy Garcia, sp
Scott Schoeneweis, sp
Shingo Takatsu, rp
Damaso Marte, rp
Neal Cotts, rp
Cliff Politte, rp
Jon Adkins, rp
Mike Jackson, rp

Attendance

1,930,537 (eighth in AL)

Club Leaders

Batting Avg:	Aaron Rowand	.310
On-Base Pct:	Carlos Lee	.366
Slugging Pct:	Aaron Rowand	.544
Home Runs:	Paul Konerko	41
RBIs:	Paul Konerko	117
Runs:	Carlos Lee	103
Stolen Bases:	Willie Harris	19
Wins:	Mark Buehrle	16
Strikeouts:	Mark Buehrle	165
ERA:	Mark Buehrle	3.89
Saves:	Shingo Takatsu	19

JANUARY 6   Roberto Alomar signs with the Diamondbacks as a free agent.

                   Alomar returned to the White Sox in a trade with Arizona on August 5, 2004.

JANUARY 22   The White Sox sign Shingo Takatsu, most recently with the Yakult Swallows in the
                   Japanese Central League, as a free agent.

                   *Takatsu gave the White Sox one great season with 19 saves and a 2.31 ERA in
                   62$\frac{1}{3}$ innings over 59 games and in the process became a cult hero in Chicago.
                   He was known as "Mr. Zero" in Japan because he had not given up a single
                   run in 11 Japan Series championship games and was his country's all-time saves
                   leader. During the 2004 season, Takatsu's entrance into games at U.S. Cellular
                   Field was accompanied by a video montage that informed the crowd "It's Shingo
                   Time" along with a loud gong. He threw pitches with an unorthodox submarine
                   delivery that included 90-mile-per-hour fastballs followed by 60-mile-per-hour
                   change-ups that froze hitters in their tracks. Takatsu struggled in 2005, however,
                   and was sent to the minors. He returned to Japan in 2006.*

APRIL 5   In Ozzie Guillen's debut as manager, the White Sox give up six runs in the ninth
                   inning and lose 9–7 to the Royals in Kansas City. Damaso Marte surrendered a
                   three-run homer to Mendy Lopez that tied the score 7–7, and then allowed a two-
                   run, walk-off blast to Carlos Beltran. Carlos Lee and Sandy Alomar Jr. homered for
                   Chicago in the loss. Paul Konerko contributed three hits, including a double.

APRIL 13   In the home opener, the White Sox win 12–5 over the Royals before 37,706 at U.S.
                   Cellular Field. Paul Konerko put the Sox into the lead with a three-run homer in the
                   fifth. Juan Uribe homered in his first game as a member of the White Sox in Chicago.

                   *The White Sox tied for the American League lead in home runs in 2004 with
                   242. It was only the second time in club history that the Sox led the AL in
                   homers. The other was in 1974. The 242 homers were also a team record. The
                   major contributors to the mark were Paul Konerko (42), Carlos Lee (31), Jose
                   Valentin (30), Aaron Rowand (24), Juan Uribe (23), Joe Crede (21) and Frank
                   Thomas (18).*

APRIL 14   After the Royals score four runs in the ninth inning for a 9–8 lead, the White Sox
                   respond with two in their half for a 10–9 victory at U.S. Cellular Field. Joe Crede's
                   single drove in the winning run.

                   *U.S. Cellular Field had a different look in 2004. Eight rows and 6,600 seats were
                   removed from the controversial upper deck. A sloped canopy-style roof was
                   replaced by a flat roof that covered all but the first six rows of the upper deck.
                   To give the park a more "retro" look, the roof was constructed with black steel
                   truss supports. The upper concourse was enclosed by a translucent wall. Tiiered
                   seating was also added to the Fan Deck.*

APRIL 15   A walk-off homer by Magglio Ordonez in the 10th inning defeats the Royals 6–5 at
                   U.S. Cellular Field.

APRIL 18   Esteban Loaiza pitches a two-hitter for a 5–0 win over the Devil Rays in
                   St. Petersburg. The only Tampa Bay hits were singles by Tino Martinez in the
                   fifth inning and Aubrey Huff in the seventh.

APRIL 25   The White Sox score three runs in the ninth inning to beat the Devil Rays 6–5 at U.S. Cellular Field. Pinch-hitter Kelly Dransfeldt tied the score with a two-out single. The winning run crossed the plate on a bases-loaded walk from Lance Carter to Juan Uribe.

APRIL 28   The White Sox stage another incredible ninth-inning rally with five runs to defeat the Indians 9–8 at U.S. Cellular Field. The Sox were down 8–2 before scoring a run in the seventh and another in the eighth. A two-run homer by Magglio Ordonez made the score 8–6. Carlos Lee doubled and scored on an error to bring Chicago within a run. Joe Crede and Timo Perez followed with run-scoring, two-out singles.

MAY 1   Frank Catalanotto collects six hits in six at-bats for the Blue Jays during a 10–6 win over the White Sox in the second game of a double-header at U.S. Cellular Field. Catalanotto had five singles and a double. The Sox won the first game 4–3 in 10 innings.

MAY 8   At SkyDome, Josh Phelps of the Blue Jays hits a tie-breaking, two-run homer against the White Sox in the eighth inning, four pitches after having one overturned by the umpires. Phelps hit the first pitch of the at-bat from Neal Cotts down the right-field line for what first-base umpire Larry Vanover ruled a home run. Ozzie Guillen argued the call, the umpires huddled and overturned the decision, ruling it foul. Four pitches later, Phelps homered over the left-field wall and the Toronto won the game 4–2.

MAY 11   Magglio Ordonez collects four hits, including two doubles, and drives in five runs during a 15–0 rout of the Orioles at U.S. Cellular Field.

MAY 19   The White Sox rout the Indians 15–3 in Cleveland. The victory was costly, however, as Magglio Ordonez and Willie Harris collided while trying to run down a fly ball in the seventh inning. Ordonez suffered a knee injury and played in only 14 more games over the remainder of the season.

MAY 29   After being roughed up for five runs in 3$\frac{1}{3}$ innings in a 5–1 loss to the Angels at U.S. Cellular Field, Jon Rauch showers and leaves the stadium without permission from the club. Furious at the pitcher's behavior, the White Sox fined Rauch and demoted him to the minors. He was traded to the Expos in July.

JUNE 7   In the first round of the amateur draft, the White Sox select third baseman Josh Fields from Oklahoma State University.

            Fields won a job as the White Sox's starting third baseman in 2007. Other future big-leaguers drafted and signed by the Sox in 2004 include second-rounder Donny Lucy.

JUNE 8   The White Sox play the Phillies for the first time at U.S. Cellular Field and win 14–11. The Sox hit six homers. Paul Konerko and Juan Uribe each hit two home runs, with one apiece from Frank Thomas and Carlos Lee.

JUNE 9   The White Sox hit five more home runs, but lose 13–10 to the Phillies at U.S. Cellular Field. Going deep for the Sox were Joe Crede, Miguel Olivo, Aaron Rowand, Jose Valentin and Paul Konerko.

Valentin hit 30 home runs in 2004, but they came with a batting average of only .216.

JUNE 11   The White Sox play the Braves for the first time at U.S. Cellular Field and lose 6–1.

JUNE 14   During a 7–5, 10-inning win over the Marlins in Miami, Carlos Lee breaks the club hitting streak record with a base hit in his 28th consecutive game. Lee broke the record with a double in the 10th. Timo Perez tied the game with a two-run homer in the ninth. It was also the first ever regular-season meeting between the White Sox and the Marlins.

Lee broke the hitting streak record of 27 set by Luke Appling in 1936 and tied by Albert Belle in 1997. Lee's streak was stopped when he went hitless in four at-bats during a 4–0 loss to the Marlins in Miami on June 15.

JUNE 18   The White Sox play in Montreal for the first time and win 11–7 over the Expos at Olympic Stadium.

JUNE 19   Juan Uribe drives in seven runs, but the White Sox lose 17–14 to the Expos in Montreal. Uribe hit a homer, double and single. The Sox trailed 11–1 in the third inning and battled back to within a run at 15–14 before the Expos scored twice in the eighth.

JUNE 22   Jose Valentin caps a five-RBI night with a two-run, walk-off homer in the 10th inning to beat the Indians 11–9 in Cleveland. The White Sox led 8–0 after three innings but fell behind 9–8 in the eighth before rallying to win. Shingo Takatsu gave up a single to Ron Belliard to end a streak in which he retired 29 consecutive batters, dating back to May 26.

In addition to retiring 29 batters in a row, Takatsu had a streak of 26²/₃ consecutive scoreless innings during the 2004 season.

JUNE 27   In his last game with the White Sox, Miguel Olivo hits a home run during a 9–4 win over the Cubs at U.S. Cellular Field.

After the game, the White Sox traded Olivo, Jeremy Reed and Michael Morse to the Mariners for Freddy Garcia and Ben Davis. Ken Williams was able to obtain two-fifths of the 2005 world championship starting rotation with brilliant trades during the summer of 2004. The acquisition of Garcia was the first. Garcia was 9–4 over the remainder of the 2004 season, 14–8 in 2005 and 17–9 in 2006 before being traded to the Phillies.

JULY 1   The White Sox open a two-game lead in the AL Central with a 2–1 win over the Twins in Minneapolis. Carlos Lee accounted for both Chicago runs with a homer in the first. The Sox's record was 42–33.

JULY 2   White Sox right fielder Ross Gload has a grand slam reversed during a 6–2 loss to the Cubs in Wrigley Field. In the first inning, Gload fouled off three, 3–2 pitches from Carlos Zambrano and then sent a drive that cleared the wall close to the foul pole in right field. First-base umpire Charlie Reliford signaled fair, but the Cubs argued the call. Reliford then huddled with his fellow officials and the call was changed.

Replays showed the ball was foul. Gload returned to the plate and smacked a two-run double to left, but the Sox failed to score again.

JULY 9   Carlos Lee hits two homers and drives in five runs during a 6–2 win over the Mariners in Seattle.

JULY 18   The White Sox trade Jon Rauch and Gary Majewski to the Expos for Carl Everett.

Everett played previously for the White Sox in 2003.

JULY 19   In his first game back with the White Sox, Carl Everett hits a home run, helping the club to a 12–6 win over the Rangers in Arlington.

JULY 21   Mark Buehrle pitches a two-hitter after retiring the first 19 batters to face him during a 14–0 drubbing of the Indians at Jacobs Field. He also faced the minimum 27 hitters. The first Cleveland base runner was Omar Vizquel, who singled in the seventh inning. Tim Laker added another single in the eighth. Both were erased on double plays.

Buehrle had a 16–10 record and a 3.89 ERA in 2004.

JULY 22   The White Sox defeat the Indians 3–0 in Cleveland despite some confusion during a pitching change in the eighth inning. Ozzie Guillen came out to bring in left-hander Damaso Marte to face Travis Hafner. First-base umpire Joe West thought Guillen was signaling with his right hand, and West walked to the bullpen to escort right-hander Cliff Politte to the mound instead. Politte induced Hafner to pop out.

JULY 24   Joe Crede's walk-off homer in the ninth inning beats the Tigers 7–6 at U.S. Cellular Field and puts the White Sox into first place.

The Sox remained atop the AL Central for only one day. The club started a seven-game losing streak on July 25 and was out of the pennant race by the end of August.

JULY 28   Justin Morneau of the Twins has a strange day during a 10-inning 5–4 Minnesota win over the White Sox at U.S. Cellular Field by having two home runs reversed. In the second, Morneau hit a fly ball to left that third-base umpire Ed Montague ruled a home run. But after an argument by Ozzie Guillen and left fielder Carlos Lee, the arbiters huddled and ruled the play a double because it was determined that the ball hit the top of the wall and bounced back onto the field of play. In the fifth, a drive by Morneau down the right-field line was initially signaled a home run by first-base umpire Matt Hollowell. It was changed to a foul ball after Guillen and right fielder Timo Perez objected and the umps conferred. Replays were inconclusive. Morneau returned to the plate and flied out.

JULY 31   The White Sox trade Esteban Loaiza to the Yankees for Jose Contreras.

Contreras was a Cuban defector who began pitching in the majors with the Yankees in 2003 at the age of 31. He defected in October 2002 while pitching for the Cuban national team during the Americas Series in Mexico. Contreras helped the White Sox win a world championship in 2005 with a mark of 15–7 and followed that with a 13–9 ledger in 2006. He won a club-record 17 straight regular-season decisions by winning his last eight games in 2005 and the first nine in 2006.

AUGUST 3   Paul Konerko hits a grand slam off Mike Wood in the fifth inning of a 12–4 win over the Royals in Kansas City.

AUGUST 4   Aaron Rowand is the only Chicago batter to reach base as Brian Anderson of the Royals pitches a two-hitter and beats the White Sox 11–0 in Kansas City. Rowand doubled leading off the first inning, walked in the third and doubled again in the ninth.

AUGUST 5   A 6–4 loss to the Royals in Kansas City is delayed for 24 minutes in the ninth inning by a power outage.

On the same day, the White Sox re-acquired Roberto Alomar from the Diamondbacks for Brad Murray. Alomar previously played for the Sox in 2003 before leaving for Arizona as a free agent.

Paul Konerko led the Sox in home runs and RBIs in 2004 and has been one of the team's most productive hitters throughout the decade.

AUGUST 8   Timo Perez scores from first base on a ninth-inning single to account for the deciding run in a 3–2 victory over the Indians at U.S. Cellular Field. With the score 2–2 and two out in the ninth, Ben Davis lined a hit to right-center after Perez singled. Cleveland center fielder Grady Sizemore cut off Davis's drive before it could reach the wall, but Perez never stopped running and slid safely under catcher Victor Martinez's tag.

AUGUST 9   Trailing 8–0 to the Indians, the White Sox score seven runs in the sixth inning, but they can't take the lead and lose 13–11 at U.S. Cellular Field.

AUGUST 10   Willie Harris collects five hits, including three doubles, in five at-bats during a 9–3 victory over the Royals at U.S. Cellular Field.

AUGUST 18   Aaron Rowand homers twice, including a grand slam off Jeremy Bonderman in the first inning, in leading the White Sox to a 9–2 triumph over the Tigers at U.S. Cellular Field.

AUGUST 26   The White Sox score six runs in the top of the first inning and outlast the Indians 14–9 in Cleveland.

AUGUST 30   Joe Borchard hits a home run estimated at 504 feet, the longest ever at U.S. Cellular Field, during a 9–8 win over the Phillies at U.S. Cellular Field. The drive cleared the bleachers and landed in the middle of the right-field concourse. The game was a makeup of a June 10 rainout between the two clubs.

SEPTEMBER 11   The White Sox score eight runs in the second inning and rout the Angels 13–6 in Anaheim.

SEPTEMBER 13   The Florida Marlins are the home team at U.S. Cellular Field and beat the Montreal Expos 6–3 before a crowd of 4,003. The game was moved to Chicago because Hurricane Ivan struck South Florida. The Marlins were already in the Windy City, having played the Cubs on September 10, 11 and 12. The price of a ticket for the September 13 game was $15, with $5 going to hurricane relief.

SEPTEMBER 14   In the second of two games in which the Marlins host the Expos at U.S. Cellular Field, Florida wins 8–6 before 5,457.

SEPTEMBER 18   The White Sox edge the Tigers 9–8 in 12 innings at U.S. Cellular Field after the two clubs combine for four home runs in the 10th. In the top half of the 10th, Dmitri Young and Carlos Pena each hit two-run homers to give Detroit an 8–4 lead. In the bottom half, Joe Borchard and Aaron Rowand both responded with two-run shots of their own. In the 12th, Rowand's walk-off single scored Borchard from second base.

SEPTEMBER 21   With the White Sox trailing 6–4 in the seventh inning, Juan Uribe hits a pinch-hit grand slam off Jesse Crain to lift Chicago to an 8–6 win over the Twins at U.S. Cellular Field.

SEPTEMBER 23   Down 6–1, the White Sox rally with three runs in the eighth inning and three in the ninth to defeat the Royals 7–6 at U.S. Cellular Field. All three ninth-inning runs scored on a walk-off homer by Joe Crede.

SEPTEMBER 29   Carlos Lee drives in six runs with a two-run homer and a grand slam during an 11–2 win over the Tigers in Detroit. The slam was struck in the ninth inning off John Ennis.

OCTOBER 3   In the last game of the season, Jose Contreras takes a no-hit bid into the seventh inning of a 5–0 win over the Royals at Kauffman Stadium. The first Kansas City hit was a single by Ruben Gotay leading off the seventh inning. Contreras finished his stint on the mound by allowing two hits in eight innings.

DECEMBER 6   A month after George Bush wins a second term by defeating John Kerry in the presidential election, the White Sox sign Dustin Hermanson, most recently with the Giants, as a free agent.

Hermanson was another great short-term acquisition by Ken Williams that helped lead to the White Sox's first World Series win since 1917. During the 2005 season, Hermanson was a pleasant surprise by compiling the best season of his career at the age of 32 with 34 saves and a 2.05 earned run average in $57^1/3$ innings over 57 games. Back trouble ended his career in 2006, however.

DECEMBER 8   Sandy Alomar Jr. signs with the Rangers as a free agent.

DECEMBER 9   The White Sox sign Jermaine Dye, most recently with the Athletics, as a free agent.

Dye has proven to be one of the best free agent pickups in club history. In 2008, he was in his fourth season as the club's starting right fielder.

DECEMBER 13   The White Sox trade Carlos Lee to the Brewers for Scott Podsednik, Luis Vizcaino and Travis Hinton.

The trade was part of the White Sox's efforts to move from a power-laden offense to one that was more diverse and speed-oriented. It worked in 2005, when Podsednik made the All-Star team and the Sox won a world championship, but the long-term consequences of the deal with the Brewers appear to be overwhelmingly negative. By 2007, Podsednik was a part-time outfielder, while Lee was starring for the Astros.

DECEMBER 17   The White Sox purchase Bobby Jenks from the Angels.

Jenks was another great acquisition by the Sox. Standing six-foot-three and weighing in the neighborhood of 275 pounds, he regularly threw fastballs close to 100 miles per hour. Jenks became the club's closer in 2006 and tied a major league record in 2007 by retiring 41 batters in a row in addition to making the All-Star team in 2006 and 2007.

DECEMBER 21   Jose Valentin signs with the Dodgers as a free agent.

DECEMBER 22   The White Sox sign Orlando Hernandez, most recently with the Yankees, as a free agent.

Hernandez was one of two Cuban defectors in the White Sox's starting rotation in 2005. The other was Jose Contreras. Hernandez left Cuba on Christmas Day in 1997 in a boat that departed from the small city of Caibarien. There were seven others in the craft, which was intercepted by the U.S. Coast Guard. Attorney General Janet Reno granted Hernandez "humanitarian parole," allowing him to enter the United States. He signed with the Yankees in 1998 and earned the nickname "El Duque" while pitching in four World Series in New York. Hernanadez would pitch in his fifth Fall Classic with the Sox in 2005. Orlando's half-brother Livan Hernandez defected from Cuba in 1995 and also has had a successful major league career.

2005

Sox

Season in a Sentence

The White Sox stun the baseball world by leading the AL Central the entire season, posting the best record in the American League and claiming the franchise's first World Series appearance since 1959 and the first world championship since 1917.

Finish • Won • Lost • Pct • GB

First   99   63   .611   +6.0

Manager

Jerry Manuel

American League Division Series

The White Sox defeated the Boston Red Sox three games to none.

American League Championship Series

The White Sox defeated the Los Angeles Angels four games to one.

World Series

The White Sox defeated the Houston Astros four games to none.

Stats

Stats	WS	AL	Rank
Batting Avg:	.262	.268	12
On-Base Pct:	.322	.330	11
Slugging Pct:	.425	.424	8
Home Runs:	200		4
Stolen Bases:	137		3
ERA:	3.61	4.35	2
Fielding Avg:	.985	.983	4
Runs Scored:	741		9
Runs Allowed:	645		3

Starting Lineup

A. J. Pierzynski, c
Paul Konerko, 1b
Tadahito Iguchi, 2b
Joe Crede, 3b
Juan Uribe, ss
Scott Podsednik, lf
Aaron Rowand, cf
Jermaine Dye, rf
Carl Everett, dh

Pitchers

Jon Garland, sp
Mark Buehrle, sp
Freddy Garcia, sp
Jose Contreras, sp
Orlando Hernandez, sp
Dustin Hermanson, rp
Neal Cotts, rp
Luis Vizcaino, rp
Damaso Marte, rp

Attendance

2,342,833 (seventh in AL)

Club Leaders

Batting Avg:	Scott Podsednik	.290
On-Base Pct:	Paul Konerko	.375
Slugging Pct:	Paul Konerko	.534
Home Runs:	Paul Konerko	40
RBIs:	Paul Konerko	100
Runs:	Paul Konerko	98
Stolen Bases:	Scott Podsednik	59
Wins:	Jon Garland	18
Strikeouts:	Jose Contreras	154
ERA:	Mark Buehrle	3.12
Saves:	Dustin Hermanson	34

JANUARY 6   The White Sox sign A. J. Pierzynski, most recently with the Giants, as a free agent.

Pierzynski has given the White Sox their best seasons by a catcher since the heyday of Carlton Fisk. A. J. rubbed many people the wrong way, however. In 2006, Sports Illustrated asked 470 baseball players which player they would most like to see beaned. Pierzynski, received 18 percent of the vote, higher than anyone else.

JANUARY 17   Roberto Alomar signs with the Devil Rays as a free agent.

JANUARY 24   The White Sox sign Tadahito Iguchi, most recently with the Fukuoka Daiei Hawks in the Japanese Pacific League, as a free agent.

Iguchi immediately stepped in as the starting second baseman.

FEBRUARY 7   Magglio Ordonez signs with the
                  Tigers as a free agent.

                  The White Sox were fearful of
                  signing Ordonez to a long-term
                  contract because of his knee
                  injury suffered in 2004 and his
                  strained relationship with fellow
                  Venezuelan Ozzie Guillen. The
                  injury continued to adversely
                  affect Ordonez in 2005, but he
                  was back to playing as a regular
                  in 2006 and had the best season
                  of his career in 2007 by winning
                  the AL batting title with an
                  average of .363 along with 28
                  homers and 139 RBIs.

APRIL 4   The White Sox win the season opener
                  1–0 before 38,141 at U.S. Cellular
                  Field. Mark Buehrle pitched eight
                  innings and allowed only two hits.
                  Buehrle retired the first 12 batters he
                  faced. The only two Cleveland hits
                  were singles by Victor Martinez in
                  the fifth inning and Coco Crisp in the
                  seventh. Shingo Takatsu pitched a

Many players contributed to Chicago's World
Championship in 2005, but fiery manager Ozzie
Guillen played perhaps the most important role
of all. Outspoken and unpredictable, Guillen brings
a competitive spirit to every game.

perfect ninth. The lone run scored in the seventh inning. Paul Konerko doubled,
went to third on a fly ball and crossed the plate on a ground out.

                  The 2005 season was the first time the White Sox opened the season at home
                  since 1990. The Sox would also end the season with a 1–0 victory that had far
                  greater meaning (see October 26, 2005).

APRIL 6   The White Sox score four runs in the ninth inning to stun the Indians 4–3 at U.S.
                  Cellular Field. Paul Konerko hit a two-run homer to bring the Sox within a run, and
                  Jermaine Dye tied the contest with a solo blast. The winning run crossed the plate on
                  a sacrifice fly from Juan Uribe.

                  Konerko hit .283 with 40 homers and 100 RBIs in 2005.

APRIL 7   The Indians score three runs in the ninth inning and six in the 11th to defeat the
                  White Sox 11–5 at U.S. Cellular Field.

APRIL 15   Jon Garland retires the first 19 batters to face him before giving up two runs and two
                  hits in seven innings to lead the White Sox past the Mariners 6–4 at U.S. Cellular
                  Field. Garland lost his bid for a perfect game when he walked Jeremy Reed with one
                  out in the seventh. Then, in rapid succession, he surrendered a single, another walk
                  and a two-run single.

Garland had a 15–4 record on July 22 and finished the season at 18–10 with a 3.50 ERA in 228 innings.

APRIL 16   Mark Buehrle strikes out 12 batters and pitches a three-hitter to defeat the Mariners 2–1 at U.S. Cellular Field. Paul Konerko drove in both Chicago runs with homers in the second and seventh innings off Ryan Franklin. The game lasted only one hour and 39 minutes, the shortest nine-inning contest in the major leagues since 1984.

Buehrle was 16–8 with a 3.12 ERA in a league-leading 236⅔ innings in 2005.

APRIL 25   The White Sox win their eighth game in a row with a 6–0 decision over the Athletics in Oakland. The victory gave the Sox a 16–4 record in the 2005 season.

After scoring 865 runs in 2004, the offensive output declined to 741 runs in 2005. But the improvement in the pitching staff more than made up for the difference. The Sox gave up 831 runs in 2004, but only 645 in 2005.

MAY 7   Paul Konerko hits two homers and drives in five runs during a 10–7 win over the Blue Jays in Toronto. Aaron Rowand, Tadahito Iguchi and Juan Uribe also homered for the White Sox. Scott Podsednik stole four bases.

MAY 8   The White Sox win their eighth game in a row with a 5–4 decision over the Blue Jays in Toronto. It was the club's second eight-game winning streak in 2005. The victory ran the club's record to 24–7. There was a scary moment in the ninth inning when Toronto's Gregg Zaun was knocked unconscious after being kneed in the head by White Sox second baseman Pedro Lopez while trying to break up a double play. Zaun was down on the field for nearly 15 minutes and was fitted with an oxygen mask and a head and neck brace. Fortunately, Zaun wasn't seriously injured and was playing again by the end of May.

The White Sox had a lead in each of the first 37 games of the season while compiling a record of 27–10. It is the longest streak in major league history at the start of a season, and the third-longest at any point. The all-time record is 48 by the 1998 Yankees.

MAY 14   Scott Podsednik steals four bases, but the White Sox lose 9–6 to the Orioles in Baltimore.

MAY 16   A. J. Pierzynski hits a grand slam off Chan Ho Park in the first inning, but the White Sox lose 7–6 to the Rangers at U.S. Cellular Field.

MAY 17   Jon Garland becomes the first White Sox pitcher since John Whitehead in 1935 to win his first eight starts of a season with a 5–2 decision over the Rangers at U.S. Cellular Field.

MAY 24   The White Sox edge the Los Angeles Angels 2–1 in 11 innings in Anaheim. The winning run scored on a double by Tadahito Iguchi. Mark Buehrle (nine innings) and Damaso Marte (two innings) combined on a four-hitter.

MAY 30   A two-out, two-run, walk-off single by Timo Perez beats the Angels 5–4 at U.S. Cellular Field. Perez entered the game in the seventh inning as a pinch-hitter for Frank Thomas.

MAY 31	A walk-off home run by Jermaine Dye in the ninth inning beats the Angels 5–4 at U.S. Cellular Field. It was the second consecutive 5–4 victory over the Angels with a walk-off base hit.
JUNE 6	The White Sox play the Rockies for the first time and win 9–3 at Coors Field in Denver. Freddy Garcia gave up three runs in the first inning on a single, a walk and a three-run homer by Brad Hawpe. After the home run, Garcia retired 22 batters in a row before being relieved at the end of the eighth. Shingo Takatsu pitched a hitless ninth.
JUNE 7	In the first round of the amateur draft, the White Sox select pitcher Lance Broadway from Texas Christian University. Broadway reached the majors with the Sox in 2007.
JUNE 8	The White Sox collect 22 hits during a 15–3 rout of the Rockies in Denver. The Sox scored 10 runs in the last two innings, including six in the eighth. Thirteen different players collected hits, including pitchers Orlando Hernandez and Cliff Politte.
JUNE 10	The White Sox play in San Diego for the first time and beat the Padres 4–2 at Petco Park.
JUNE 12	A three-run homer by Aaron Rowand off Trevor Hoffman in the 10th inning beats the Padres 8–5 in San Diego.
JUNE 13	The White Sox play the Diamondbacks at U.S. Cellular Field for the first time and lose 8–1.
JUNE 15	Trailing 6–2, the White Sox explode for 10 runs in the sixth inning to beat the Diamondbacks 12–6 at U.S. Cellular Field. The 10 runs scored on six hits, including homers from Frank Thomas, Paul Konerko and Juan Uribe, along with two walks and two errors. Driving in runs in the big inning were Konerko (three), Uribe (three), Thomas (one), Jermaine Dye (one) and Joe Crede (one).
JUNE 17	The White Sox play the Dodgers in Chicago for the first time during the regular season and win 6–0 at U.S. Cellular Field.
JUNE 18	The White Sox stage a dramatic four-run rally in the ninth inning rally to beat the Dodgers 5–3 at U.S. Cellular Field. The Sox were down to their last strike six times. With two out, a runner on second, and the score 3–1, Carl Everett hit a two-strike RBI-single. Willie Harris ran for Everett and stole second. Aaron Rowand fouled off a 3–2 pitch before scoring Harris with a single to tie the contest 3–3. A. J. Pierzynski fouled off three pitches on a full count before delivering a two-run, walk-off homer.
	Harris is one of only two major league players born in Cairo, Georgia. The other was Jackie Robinson. Both Harris and Robinson have streets named after them in the town.
JUNE 24	The White Sox win their eighth game in a row with a 12–2 decision over the Cubs at U.S. Cellular Field. It was the Sox's third eight-game winning streak of the season. The club's record after the June 24 win was 56–22.
JUNE 29	Frank Thomas homers leading off the 13th inning to beat the Tigers 4–3 in Detroit.

JULY 4   Jermaine Dye drives in six runs on a grand slam and a two-run single during a 10–8 victory over the Devil Rays in St. Petersburg. The slam was struck off Hideo Nomo in the first inning.

JULY 10   Paul Konerko collects five hits, including a homer, in six at-bats, but the White Sox lose 9–8 in 11 innings against the Athletics at U.S. Cellular Field.

JULY 12   Mark Buehrle is the American League starter in the All-Star Game and allows no runs and three hits in two innings. The American League won 7–5 at Comerica Park in Detroit.

JULY 14   The White Sox edge the Indians 1–0 at U.S. Cellular Field. The lone run scored on a double by Frank Thomas in the first inning. Jose Contreras (seven innings), Cliff Politte (one-third of an inning), Damaso Marte (one inning) and Dustin Hermanson (two-thirds of an inning) combined on the shutout.

              The White Sox were 35–19 in one-run games in 2005.

JULY 18   A 7–5 win over the Tigers at U.S. Cellular Field lifts the White Sox's record to 62–29.

              The White Sox found it impossible to sustain that kind of momentum. From July 19 through September 27, the club was 32–34.

JULY 24   Playing on a Sunday afternoon in which the high temperature in Chicago is 102 degrees, the White Sox defeat the Red Sox 6–4 at U.S. Cellular Field.

JULY 25   The White Sox collect 22 hits and pummel the Royals 14–6 in Kansas City. Six Sox batters (Scott Podsednik, Aaron Rowand, A. J. Pierzynski, Jermaine Dye, Willie Harris and Juan Uribe) each had three hits.

AUGUST 1   The White Sox take a 15-game lead over the second-place Indians in the AL Central with a 6–3 victory over the Orioles in Baltimore. Paul Konerko homered in his fourth consecutive game.

              The August 1 win gave the White Sox a 69–35 record. By September 22, the Sox lead in the division dwindled to 1$\frac{1}{2}$ games.

AUGUST 7   The White Sox unveil a life-sized statue of Carlton Fisk outside U.S. Cellular Field prior to a 3–1 win over the Mariners. The statue depicted Fisk standing in his catcher's gear.

AUGUST 9   Solo homers from Tadahito Iguchi in the fourth inning and Paul Konerko in the ninth provide the only two runs of a 2–1 win over the Yankees in New York.

              The game was delayed for four minutes in the eighth inning when 18-year-old Scott Harper jumped from the Yankee Stadium upper deck onto the netting behind home plate. Harper said he took the leap after he and three friends discussed how much weight the net could hold.

AUGUST 21   The White Sox tie a club record with four homers in the fourth inning of a 6–2 win over the Yankees in New York. The homers accounted for all six Chicago runs in the contest, and each was struck off Randy Johnson during a 16-pitch sequence. With one out, Tadahito Iguchi, Aaron Rowand and Paul Konerko hit back-to-back-to-back homers. After singles to Jermaine Dye and Juan Uribe, Chris Widger smacked a three-run blast.

AUGUST 23   Freddy Garcia pitches a one-hitter, but he loses 1–0 to the Twins in Minneapolis. Jacque Jones ended Garcia's no-hit bid with a homer to lead off the eighth. Johan Santana and Joe Nathan combined to hold the White Sox to three hits.

AUGUST 26   Tadahito Iguchi hits a two-run homer in the 12th inning to beat the Mariners 5–3 in Seattle. Playing in his fifth major league game, Brian Anderson hit his first two major league homers to drive in the first three Chicago runs.

AUGUST 29   On the day Hurricane Katrina strikes the Gulf Coast, Tadahito Iguchi commits three errors at second base during a 7–5 loss to the Rangers in Arlington.

AUGUST 30   On the day Hurricane Katrina causes massive flooding in New Orleans, Jermaine Dye drives in six runs on two homers and a single during an 8–0 triumph in the second game of a double-header against the Rangers at Ameriquest Field. Texas won the opener 8–6.

SEPTEMBER 7   Paul Konerko homers off Mike Wood in the third inning for the lone run of a 1–0 win over the Royals at U.S. Cellular Field. It was the fourth consecutive game in which Konerko homered. Jose Contreras (7²/₃ innings), Bobby Jenks (two-thirds of an inning) and Dustin Hermanson (two-thirds of an inning) combined on the shutout.

SEPTEMBER 17   The White Sox's once-commanding lead over the second-place Indians, which reached 15 games on August 1, shrinks to 3¹/₂ games with a 5–0 loss to the Twins in Minneapolis. Johan Santana and Joe Nathan combined to strike out 16 Chicago batters.

SEPTEMBER 19   The struggling White Sox lose again 7–5 to the Indians at U.S. Cellular Field. The lead over Cleveland shriveled to 2¹/₂ games.

SEPTEMBER 20   Joe Crede's walk-off homer in the 10th inning beats the Indians 7–6 at U.S. Cellular Field. It was Crede's second home run of the game.

SEPTEMBER 22   The White Sox's lead over the Indians falls to 1¹/₂ games after losing 4–1 in 11 innings against the Twins at U.S. Cellular Field.

                 From July 28 through September 24, the Indians had a 40–13 record, while the Sox were 28–26.

SEPTEMBER 27   The White Sox suffer another crucial loss, dropping a 3–2 decision to the Tigers in Detroit.

                 With five games left, the White Sox had a 94–63 record and led the Indians by two games in the AL Central. The Sox, Indians, Red Sox and Yankees were battling for three of the four AL berths in the post-season. The Indians, Red Sox and Yankees all had records of 92–65 with the Red Sox and Yankees playing each other three times during the final weekend.

SEPTEMBER 28   The White Sox clinch a spot in the playoffs for at least a wild-card berth with a 6–2 win over the Tigers in Detroit. Jose Contreras won his eighth consecutive start.

SEPTEMBER 29   The White Sox clinch the division title with a 4–2 win over the Tigers in Detroit.

The Sox closed the season with three games against the Indians at Jacobs Field and won all three to finish with a 99–63 record, the best in the American League. The defeats knocked the Cleveland club out of the playoffs. Chicago met the Red Sox in the playoffs. Boston broke the "Curse of the Bambino" the previous season by winning their first World Series title since 1918. Managed by Terry Francona, the Red Sox were 96–66 in 2005.

OCTOBER 4   The White Sox open the American League Division Series with a 14–2 win over the Red Sox before 40,717 at U.S. Cellular Field. The White Sox opened the scoring with five runs in the first inning, the final two coming on a home run by A. J. Pierzynski. It was the first of five Chicago homers. Paul Konerko went deep in the third, Juan Uribe in the fourth, Scott Podsednik in the sixth and Pierzynski again in the eighth. Pierzynski also doubled and scored four runs in addition to driving in four. Clutch hitting aided the victory as the Pale Hose left only two runners on base. Jose Contreras was the winning pitcher, allowing two runs in 7²/₃ innings. Out with injuries, Frank Thomas threw out the ceremonial first pitch.

Podsednik didn't hit a single home run in 507 regular season at-bats. He homered again in Game Two of the World Series.

OCTOBER 5   The White Sox win game two with a 5–4 decision over the Red Sox before 40,799 at U.S. Cellular Field. The Red Sox took a 4–0 lead with two runs in the first inning and two more in the third. The White Sox won the contest by exploding for five tallies in the fifth. With Chicago trailing 3–2 and two out, Tadahito Iguchi hit a three-run homer off David Wells.

OCTOBER 7   The White Sox complete a three-game sweep of the Red Sox with a 5–3 victory at Fenway Park. Paul Konerko broke a 2–2 tie with a two-run homer in the sixth inning. Chicago added an insurance run in the ninth on a suicide squeeze by Juan Uribe, which scored A. J. Pierzynski from third base.

Counting the final five games of the regular season, the October 7 victory was the White Sox's eighth in a row. After losing the opening game of the ALCS to the Los Angeles Angels, the Sox would win eight more in succession for 16 wins in 17 games, including 11–1 in the post-season. Managed by Mike Scioscia, the Angels were 95–67 during the regular season in 2005 and beat the Yankees in five games in the Division Series.

OCTOBER 11   The White Sox lose the first game of the ALCS 3–2 to the Angels before 40,659 at U.S. Cellular Field. The Angels led 3–0 when Joe Crede hit a third-inning home run. The Sox added a run in the third, but they couldn't close the gap.

Billy Pierce, who pitched on the 1959 pennant-winning White Sox, threw out the ceremonial first pitch.

OCTOBER 12   The White Sox win game two 2–1 following a controversial play before 41,013 at U.S. Cellular Field. The score was 1–1 in the Chicago half of the ninth with two out and no one on base. A. J. Pierzynski struck out swinging at a low pitch. Catcher Josh Paul thought he caught the ball cleanly and rolled it back to the mound. Pitcher Kelvim Escobar headed toward the dugout. After taking a few steps in the direction of the third-base dugout, Pierzynski ran toward first base and arrived safely. Home-plate umpire Doug Eddings ruled that the ball had hit the dirt before Paul grabbed it, and his partners agreed. Pablo Ozuna ran for Pierzynski, stole second and scored the winning run on Joe Crede's walk-off double. Mark Buehrle pitched a five-hit complete game.

OCTOBER 14   The White Sox take a two-games-to-one lead in the ALCS with a 5–2 victory over the Angels in Anaheim. Paul Konerko got things rolling with a three-run homer in the first inning on a full count. Jon Garland pitched a four-hit complete game.

OCTOBER 15   The White Sox move within one game of the American League pennant with an 8–2 win over the Angels in Anaheim. For the second straight game, Paul Konerko hit a three-run homer in the first inning. The Angels had a rally snuffed out in the second by another controversial call. They scored a run and had two men on when Steve Finley argued that A. J. Pierzynski's mitt had tipped his bat, which should have resulted in a call of catcher's interference. The umpires disagreed. Pierzynski hit a solo homer in the fourth inning. Freddy Garcia pitched a six-hitter for the White Sox's third consecutive complete game.

OCTOBER 16   The White Sox reach the World Series for the first time since 1959 with a game five, 6–3 victory over the Angels in Anaheim. Joe Crede tied the score 3–3 with a solo home run in the seventh and broke the deadlock with an RBI-single in the eighth. The Sox added two insurance runs in the ninth. Jose Contreras pitched a five-hitter for the White Sox's fourth consecutive complete game. The Sox were the first team since the 1928 Yankees with four straight complete games in the post-season. Starting pitchers hurled 44⅓ of the 45 innings in the series against the Angels and went at least seven innings in 11 of the 12 post-season games.

> *The White Sox met the Houston Astros in the World Series. It was the first time that Houston hosted a Fall Classic. In was also the first time the Fall Classic was played in the state of Texas. Managed by Phil Garner, the Astros reached the post-season as a wild card with an 89–73 record. They proceeded to upset the Braves in four games and the Cardinals in six contests in the playoffs. Media attention had focused for decades on the "Curse of the Bambino," which allegedly kept the Red Sox from winning the World Series from 1918 until 2004, and the "Curse of the Billy Goat," which helped explain the Cubs' failure to play in a World Series since 1945 or win one since 1908. The White Sox's failure to win the Series since 1917 had grieved the club's followers just as deeply as those of the Red Sox or Cubs, but that had grabbed far fewer national headlines and didn't have a catchphrase attached to the "curse."*

OCTOBER 22   The White Sox win Game One of the World Series with a 5–3 win over the Astros before 41,206 at U.S. Cellular Field. Jermaine Dye started the scoring with a solo homer in the first inning. Joe Crede broke a 3–3 tie with a solo home run in the fourth. Jose Contreras pitched seven innings for the victory and tied a World Series record by hitting three batters.

OCTOBER 23   The White Sox win an exciting 7–6 decision over the Astros in Game Two before 41,432 at U.S. Cellular Field. The Astros led 4–2 when the Sox took a two-run lead in the seventh. With two out and two runners on base, home-plate umpire Jeff Nelson ruled that Jermaine Dye was hit by a pitch. Replays suggested that the play could have been a foul ball. Paul Konerko followed with a grand slam on the first pitch from Chad Qualls. Houston tied the score with two runs in the ninth. In the bottom half, Scott Podsednik homered to center field with one out against Brad Lidge.

OCTOBER 25   The White Sox move within one game of the world championship with a 7–5 win in 14 innings at Minute Maid Park in Houston. Among those in attendance was former President George H. W. Bush. The Astros led 4–0 when the Sox scored five times in the fifth inning. Joe Crede homered, Tadahito Iguchi and Jermaine Dye each singled in runs and A. J. Pierzynski hit a two-run double. Houston tied the contest in the eighth. Geoff Blum, who entered the game for the Sox as a second baseman in a double switch in the 13th, broke the 5–5 tie with a home run. The Sox added another run later in the inning. Mark Buehrle, who was the winning pitcher in Game Two, came out of the bullpen to record the final out for the save. In the process, he became the first pitcher in World Series history to start and earn a save in consecutive games. The game tied a record for the longest by innings with Game Two between the Red Sox and Dodgers in 1916, which featured Babe Ruth posting a complete-game win. At five hours and 41 minutes, the White Sox-Astros clash is the longest by time in the Series. The two clubs set more records by using 43 players and 17 pitchers, as well by totaling 30 men left on base and 21 walks. Six double plays tied another mark. The Sox used a record nine pitchers, who combined to post an unusual stat line by holding the Astros to one run and just one hit over the last nine innings while walking 10 batters. Sox pitchers walked a record 12 in all.

Blum's homer came in his first career World Series at-bat and his only plate appearance of the 2005 Fall Classic. His White Sox career included only 31 regular-season games, in which he batted .200 with one home run, and two at-bats in two post-season contests. Blum was acquired from the Padres on July 31, 2005 and signed with the same club as a free agent on November 16.

OCTOBER 26   The White Sox win their first world championship since 1917 and complete their sweep of the Astros with a 1–0 victory in Houston. The lone run scored in the eighth on a pinch-hit single by Willie Harris, a sacrifice, and a two-out single by Jermaine Dye. Freddy Garcia (seven innings), Cliff Politte (two-thirds of an inning), Neal Cotts (one-third of an inning) and Bobby Jenks (one inning) combined on the shutout. The final out came on a grounder by Orlando Palmeiro, who was thrown out by shortstop Juan Uribe to first baseman Paul Konerko and stranded the potential tying run on second base.

OCTOBER 28   The White Sox ride triumphantly through the streets of downtown Chicago lined with thousands of cheering fans during a World Series victory parade. Earlier in the day, the players appeared on the "Oprah Winfrey Show."

OCTOBER 29   Scott Podsednik appears on "Saturday Night Live," acting as himself on Weekend Update.

Podsednik married former Playboy Playmate Lisa Dergan in February 2006. Dergan appeared in the July 1998 issue.

OCTOBER 30   Al Lopez dies at the age of 97 in Tampa, Florida. Lopez lived just long enough to see the White Sox win the World Series. He managed the club from 1957 through 1966 and again in 1968 and 1969. Under Lopez, the Sox won the American League pennant in 1959, the only one for the franchise between 1919 and 2005.

NOVEMBER 25   The White Sox trade Aaron Rowand, Dan Haigwood and Gio Gonzalez to the Phillies for Jim Thome.

A native of Peoria, Thome found himself at home in Chicago. He hit 42 homers for the club in 2006, and in 2008 he was in his third season as the club's starting designated hitter.

DECEMBER 14   Carl Everett signs with the Mariners as a free agent.

DECEMBER 20   The White Sox trade Orlando Hernandez, Chris Young and Luis Vizcaino to the Diamondbacks for Javier Vazquez.

Vazquez was in his third season in the White Sox's starting rotation in 2008, but it may be years before this trade can be properly evaluated, depending upon the development of Young.

2006

Sox

Season in a Sentence

Playing as defending world champions for the first time in 88 years, the White Sox win 56 of their first 85 games, but they fade in the second half and finish third in the AL Central.

Finish • Won • Lost • Pct • GB

Third   90   72   .556   6.0
In the wild-card race, the White Sox finished in second place, five games behind.

Manager

Ozzie Guillen

Stats

Stats	WS	AL	Rank
Batting Avg:	.280	.275	4
On-Base Pct:	.342	.339	6
Slugging Pct:	.464	.437	1
Home Runs:	236		1
Stolen Bases:	93		7
ERA:	4.61	4.56	10
Fielding Avg:	.985	.984	5
Runs Scored:	868		3
Runs Allowed:	794		10

Starting Lineup

A. J. Pierzynski, c
Paul Konerko, 1b
Tadahito Iguchi, 2b
Joe Crede, 3b
Juan Uribe, ss
Scott Podsednik, lf
Brian Anderson, cf
Jermaine Dye, rf
Jim Thome, dh
Rob Mackowiak, cf-lf
Alex Cintron, ss

Pitchers

Jon Garland, sp
Freddy Garcia, sp
Jose Contreras, sp
Mark Buehrle, sp
Javier Vazquez, sp
Bobby Jenks, rp
Neal Cotts, rp
Matt Thornton, rp
Brandon McCarthy, rp

Attendance

2,957,414 (third in AL)

Club Leaders

Batting Avg:	Jermaine Dye	.315
On-Base Pct:	Jim Thome	.416
Slugging Pct:	Jermaine Dye	.622
Home Runs:	Jermaine Dye	44
RBIs:	Jermaine Dye	120
Runs:	Jim Thome	108
Stolen Bases:	Scott Podsednik	40
Wins:	Jon Garland	18
Strikeouts:	Freddy Garcia	135
ERA:	Jose Contreras	4.27
Saves:	Bobby Jenks	41

JANUARY 20   Ozzie Guillen becomes a U.S. citizen on his 42nd birthday along with his wife Ibis and son Oney during ceremonies in Chicago.

JANUARY 24   Frank Thomas signs a contract as a free agent with the Athletics.

Once the cornerstone of the franchise, Thomas had often angered fans and management alike during his last few years with the White Sox by acting like a prima donna and distancing himself from his teammates. From 2001 through 2005, Thomas played 429 games, an average of 86 per year. Although he could still hit for power, with 104 homers in 1,482 at-bats over those five seasons, Thomas's batting average was only .257. During the 2005 season, Thomas played in only 34 games and hit .219 with 12 homers. He revived his career with the A's in 2006 with 39 homers and collected his 500th career home run with the Blue Jays in 2007.

FEBRUARY 13   President George Bush honors the world champion White Sox in ceremonies at the White House.

FEBRUARY 27   General manager Ken Williams lashes out at Frank Thomas, calling the former White Sox star "selfish" and an "idiot" during a spring training interview. "If you go out there and ask any one of my players or staff members," added Williams, "we don't miss him. We don't miss his attitude. We don't miss his whining. We don't miss it. Good riddance."

APRIL 2   The White Sox open the season before 38,802 at U.S. Cellular Field and a Sunday night national television audience on ESPN2 and defeat the Indians 10–4. The game was tied 3–3 in the fourth inning when rain delayed play for two hours and 57 minutes. After play resumed, Jim Thome hit a home run in his White Sox debut. The contest ended at 1:10 a.m. Chicago time.

After winning the opener, the White Sox lost four games in a row, then won 12 of their next 13.

APRIL 4   The White Sox receive their World Series rings prior to an 8–2 loss to the Indians at U.S. Cellular Field. The rings were made of 14-karat yellow gold with a 14-karat white gold insert and contained 95 diamonds of varying sizes. In all, 432 rings were made for the team's players, staff and employees. Also getting rings were Luis Aparicio, Carlton Fisk and families of past team owners, including Charles Comiskey, Mary Frances Veeck and John Allyn. The rings were designed by Jerry Reinsdorf's wife Martyl, who also designed five of the six championship rings for the Chicago Bulls.

Installation of new green seats to replace the original blue ones at U.S. Cellular Field began in 2006. Two blue ones remained, locating the spots where key home runs landed during the 2005 World Series. One was the grand slam by Paul Konerko, the other was the walk-off blast by Scott Podsednik.

APRIL 13   The White Sox take a 9–1 lead in the fourth inning and outlast the Tigers 13–9 at Detroit. Jim Thome homered in his fourth consecutive game.

Thome collected six home runs in his first nine games with the White Sox and scored in his first 17 games with the club. The 17-game run-scoring streak was one short of the major league record. Thome finished the season with 42 homers, 109 runs batted in and hit .283.

APRIL 17   Jose Contreras (seven innings), Boone Logan (one inning) and Cliff Politte (one inning) combine on a one-hitter to defeat the Royals 9–0 in Kansas City. The only Royals hit was a double by Mark Grudzielanek in the fourth inning.

APRIL 19   Javier Vazquez pitches eight innings of two-hit, shutout ball during a 4–0 victory over the Royals in Kansas City. Vazquez held the Royals hitless until Doug Mientkiewicz singled on a checked-swing roller down the third-base line with one out in the seventh inning.

APRIL 23   The White Sox extend their winning streak to eight games with a 7–3 decision over the Twins at U.S. Cellular Field.

APRIL 25   The White Sox club five homers during a 13–3 win over the Mariners in Seattle. Jermaine Dye accounted for two of the home runs, with Tadahito Iguchi, Paul Konerko and Joe Crede adding one each.

Dye had the best season of his career in 2006 with 44 home runs, 120 RBIs, 103 runs and a .315 batting average.

MAY 9
The White Sox take a 3½-game lead with a 9–1 victory over the Angels at U.S. Cellular Field. The Sox had a record of 23–9.

MAY 14
Mark Buehrle allows seven runs in the first inning to fall behind 7–3, but he emerges as the winning pitcher in a 9–7 decision over the Royals in Kansas City. Buehrle became only the second pitcher in major league history to allow seven runs in the first and win the game. The other was Jack Powell of the Cardinals in 1900. The Sox pulled off a triple play in the sixth. Luis Castillo popped a bunt in the air with runners on first and second. Paul Konerko charged in from first and made a shoestring catch. He then threw to Tadahito Iguchi covering first to retire Shannon Stewart. Iguchi fired to Juan Uribe to get Nick Punto at second.

MAY 19
Mark Buehrle pitches a two-hitter to defeat the Cubs 6–1 at U.S. Cellular Field. The only hits off Buehrle were singles by Juan Pierre leading off the first inning and Ronny Cedeno in the seventh.

MAY 20
The White Sox-Cubs rivalry becomes more heated when a fight breaks out between the opposing catchers during a 7–0 Sox victory at U.S. Cellular Field. In the second inning, Pierzynski knocked over Michael Barrett just before the throw arrived and slapped the plate emphatically after the collision as the ball got away. Barrett got up and grabbed Pierzynski before landing a right to the left side of his face. The punch caused a benches-clearing melee. Scott Podsednik wrestled Barrett to the ground. White Sox center fielder Brian Anderson got into a fight with John Mabry of the Cubs. Mabry injured his ribs during the commotion and was taken to a hospital for X-rays. As Pierzynski went back to the dugout, he raised his hands in the air as the sellout crowd cheered and he then began slapping hands with teammates. Pierzynski, Barrett, Anderson and Mabry were all ejected. Minutes after the game resumed, Tadahito Iguchi hit a grand slam off Rich Hill.

Barrett was suspended for 10 days for the incident. Anderson was suspended for five days. Pierzynski escaped a suspension but received a fine.

MAY 21
The White Sox are knocked out of first place with a 7–4 loss to the Cubs at U.S. Cellular Field.

The Sox failed to regain the top spot in the AL Central for the remainder of the season, but they stayed on the heels of the surprising Tigers into late August and led the wild-card race in early September.

MAY 29
The White Sox rout the Indians 11–0 at Jacobs Field. Javier Vazquez (six innings), Neal Cotts (two innings) and Jeff Nelson (one inning) combined on a two-hitter. The only Cleveland hits were singles by Grady Sizemore and Jason Michaels with two out in the third inning.

JUNE 1
Jermaine Dye hits two homers and drives in five runs, but the White Sox lose 12–8 to the Indians in Cleveland.

JUNE 3   The White Sox score seven runs in the fourth inning and defeat the Rangers 8–6 in Arlington.

JUNE 6   In the first round of the amateur draft, the White Sox select University of Texas pitcher Kyle McCullough.

JUNE 16   Joe Crede hits a grand slam off Brandon Claussen in the first inning to spark a 12–4 win over the Reds in Cincinnati. It was the Sox's first game at Great American Ball Park.

JUNE 17   Jose Contreras strikes out 13 batters in six innings, but he allows five runs and leaves the game trailing 5–3. Still, the White Sox rally to win 8–6 in Cincinnati.

JUNE 18   Jon Garland becomes the first White Sox pitcher to hit a home run since the designated hitter rule was passed in 1973 with a shot during an 8–1 victory over the Reds in Cincinnati. The last Sox pitcher to homer was Steve Kealey on September 6, 1971.

Garland was 18–7 with a 4.51 ERA in 2006.

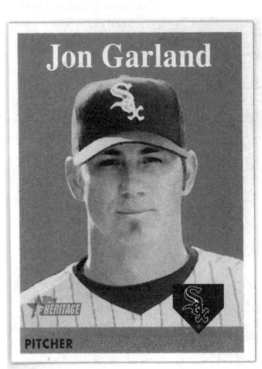

JUNE 20   The White Sox score 11 runs in the third inning and shell the Cardinals 20–6 at U.S. Cellular Field. The Sox collected 24 hits during the game, 12 of them in the big inning including two doubles and two homers. Joe Crede led the attack with two homers, a double and a single. Ozzie Guillen and reliever David Riske were ejected in the seventh after Chris Duncan was hit by a pitch. The benches had been warned in the sixth after Sidney Ponson hit two Chicago batters with the bases loaded.

Though the Sox were unable to repeat in 2006, Jon Garland won 18 games that year, matching his total from the previous year.

Tony LaRussa was forced to watch the Sox score 20 runs against his club. The game was played on the 20th anniversary of the day the Sox fired LaRussa.

JUNE 21   The White Sox pummel the Cardinals for the second night in a row at U.S. Cellular Field, winning 13–5.

JUNE 22   The only hit by the White Sox off Cardinals pitcher Anthony Reyes is a seventh-inning home run by Jim Thome that lifts Chicago to a 1–0 victory at U.S. Cellular Field. Thome's drive landed deep into the right-field bleachers. Reyes was recalled from Triple-A Memphis just before the game to face a Sox team that scored 33 runs in the first two games of the series. Freddy Garcia (eight innings) and Bobby Jenks (one inning) combined on the shutout.

On the same day, Ozzie Guillen was fined an unspecified amount and ordered to undergo sensitivity training by commissioner Bud Selig for using a slur during a tirade against sports columnist Jay Mariotti of the Chicago Sun-Times. *In a separate penalty, Guillen was suspended for one game as a result of reliever David Riske hitting Chris Duncan of the Cardinals with a pitch on June 20. Guillen went into a profanity-laced diatribe against Mariotti and called him a number of names, including a derogatory term that is often used to describe someone's sexual orientation. Guillen admitted that he was wrong to make use of the slur but refused to back down from his criticism of Mariotti. "One thing I want to make clear," said Guillen, "is that I apologize to the community, but to Jay, no chance. This thing is on and on for good." Mariotti had recently been critical of Guillen's handling of rookie pitcher Sean Tracey, who could be seen distraught in the dugout after Guillen berated Tracey when he failed to throw at Rangers hitters on June 14 in Arlington in retaliation for A. J. Pierzynski twice being hit by pitches earlier in the contest. A few days later, Tracey was demoted to the minors.*

JUNE 23   In a match-up of the 2005 World Series participants, Scott Podsednik hits a grand slam off Andy Pettitte in the fourth inning of a 7–4 win over the Astros at U.S. Cellular Field. It was the White Sox's eighth win in a row. Also, Jose Contreras extended his regular season winning streak to 16 games over two seasons.

JUNE 24   A grand slam by Joe Crede off Chad Qualls in the seventh inning ties the score 5–5, and the White Sox go on to win 6–5 in 10 innings over the Astros at U.S. Cellular Field. Alex Cintron singled home the winning run with a bases-loaded single. It was the White Sox's ninth victory in succession.

JUNE 25   The heroics of Tadahito Iguchi, who drives in seven runs, aren't enough to prevent a 13-inning, 10–9 loss to the Astros at U.S. Cellular Field. The Sox trailed 9–1 early and were still down 9–2 when Iguchi blasted a three-run home run in the eighth inning to make the score 9–5. With two out in the ninth, Iguchi struck a dramatic grand slam off Brad Lidge to tie the game 9–9. The blast was the Sox's third grand slam in three games against Houston. The Astros prevailed with a tally in the 13th, however.

JUNE 30   In response to their May 20 fight, A. J. Pierzynski and Michael Barrett shake hands on the field before a 6–2 White Sox win over the Cubs at Wrigley Field.

JULY 1   A. J. Pierzynski gains a measure of revenge for the May 20 fight with Michael Barrett by clubbing a three-run homer with two out in the ninth inning to give the White Sox an 8–6 win over the Cubs at Wrigley Field. After Pierzynski's homer, the game was delayed for about five minutes as fans pelted the field with debris.

JULY 4   The White Sox pummel the Orioles 13–0 at U.S. Cellular Field. Jose Contreras was the winning pitcher, earning his 17th consecutive victory over two seasons.

JULY 6   Jim Thome hits two homers and drives in six runs during an 11–8 victory over the Orioles at U.S. Cellular Field. Thome hit a grand slam in the third inning and a two-run shot in the fifth. Both were struck off Russ Ortiz.

The Sox had a record of 56–29 and were one game out of first place with the July 6 victory. The club was 34–43 the rest of the way.

JULY 9   The White Sox outlast the Red Sox 6–5 in a 19-inning, six hour and 19 minute marathon at U.S. Cellular Field. In the 19th, Chicago loaded the bases with consecutive singles from Alex Cintron, Rob Mackowiak and Scott Podsednik before Tadahito Iguchi drove in the winning tally with another single. Jermaine Dye homered in the ninth to tie the score 3–3. Boston scored twice in the top of the 11th, but the White Sox tied it in their half. Both teams used eight pitchers.

JULY 11   Ozzie Guillen manages the American League to a 3–2 win in the All-Star Game, played at PNC Park in Pittsburgh. Paul Konerko delivered a key hit. With the AL trailing 2–1 in the ninth with two out and no one on base, Konerko singled off Trevor Hoffman. Jose Lopez ran for Konerko and went to third on a double by Troy Glaus. Both Lopez and Glaus scored on Michael Young's triple. The hit by Konerko was his second of the game in two at-bats.

          There were seven members of the White Sox on the AL All-Star team, although none was in the starting lineup. The others besides Konerko were A. J. Pierzynski, Jim Thome, Jermaine Dye, Mark Buehrle, Jose Contreras and Bobby Jenks.

JULY 14   The 17-game winning streak of Jose Contreras over two seasons comes to an end with a 6–5 loss to the Yankees in New York. Contreras won his last eight regular season decisions in 2005 and his first nine in 2006.

JULY 23   Prior to a 5–0 win over the Rangers, the White Sox honor double-play combination Nellie Fox and Luis Aparicio with life-sized bronze sculptures on the center-field concourse at U.S. Cellular Field. The statues show second baseman Fox flipping the ball toward Aparicio, who is waiting with outstretched arms and his right foot touching the base a few feet away. They joined club founder Charles Comiskey, Minnie Minoso and Carlton Fisk with sculptures at the stadium. Another honoring Billy Pierce was added in 2007. A statue of Harold Baines was unveiled in 2008.

          On the same day, the White Sox traded B. J. LaMura to the Dodgers for Sandy Alomar Jr. It was Alomar's third tour of duty with the Sox.

JULY 28   With the White Sox trailing 4–2 in the ninth, Ross Gload smacks a grand slam off Chris Ray to defeat the Orioles 6–4 in Baltimore. Gload entered the game in the sixth inning as a replacement for Paul Konerko at first base.

          Konerko hit 35 homers and drove in 113 runs with a .313 batting average in 2006.

JULY 29   The White Sox score seven runs in the third inning to spark a 13–11 win over the Orioles in Baltimore. A. J. Pierzynski collected five hits, including a home run, in five at-bats. Jim Thome was hitless in two at-bats, but he scored four times after drawing four walks.

AUGUST 5 Javier Vazquez strikes out 13 batters in eight innings during a 7–1 win over the Blue Jays in Toronto.

AUGUST 14   The White Sox score eight runs in the fourth inning of a 12–2 rout of the Royals at U.S. Cellular Field.

AUGUST 17   All four lead-off hitters homer in the first two innings of the White Sox's 5–4 win over the Royals at U.S. Cellular Field. It was the first such occurrence in major league history. Kansas City's David DeJesus and Emil Brown homered to lead off the first and second innings, respectively, while Pablo Ozuna and Jermaine Dye of the Sox did the same. The pitchers were Chicago's Mark Buehrle and the Royals' Oliver Perez.

AUGUST 24   The White Sox wallop the Tigers 10–0 in Detroit.

AUGUST 29   The White Sox build a 7–0 lead after two innings and hold on to defeat the Devil Rays 12–9 at U.S. Cellular Field.

> *The White Sox drew 2,957,414 fans in 2006, breaking the single-season record of 2,934,154 set in 1991, the first year of Comiskey Park II/U.S. Cellular Field. There were 22 consecutive sellouts from July 5 through August 17.*

SEPTEMBER 4   The White Sox drop out of the lead in the wild-card race with a 3–2 loss to the Red Sox in Boston.

> *The White Sox blew a chance at the post-season by losing 16 of their last 27 games.*

SEPTEMBER 8   A. J. Pierzynski hits a two-run, walk-off homer in the bottom of the ninth inning to beat the Indians 7–6 at U.S. Cellular Field. Bobby Jenks blew a save opportunity in the top of the ninth by giving up four straight doubles that produced three Cleveland runs.

> *The White Sox wore uniforms with green pinstripes and green trim along with green caps and socks, and they sold green beer as part of a "Halfway to St. Patrick's Day" celebration.*

SEPTEMBER 13   Freddy Garcia makes a bid for a perfect game by retiring the first 23 batters to face him in a 9–0 win over the Angels in Anaheim. The only Los Angeles base runner during the entire game was Adam Kennedy, who singled on a 3–2 pitch with two out in the eighth. Garcia retired Kendry Morales to end the eighth before being relieved by Neal Cotts, who pitched a 1–2–3 ninth.

SEPTEMBER 18   Josh Fields homers in his first big league at-bat during an 8–2 loss to the Tigers at U.S. Cellular Field. He homered as a pinch-hitter for A. J. Pierzynski in the ninth inning. Fields was the third member of the White Sox to homer in his first plate appearance in the majors. The first two were Carlos Lee in 1999 and Miguel Olivo in 2002.

> *The defeat dropped the White Sox six games behind the Tigers in the AL Central and 4¹/₂ games back of the Twins in the wild-card race. The Sox had 12 games left to play.*

SEPTEMBER 19   Freddy Garcia pitches eight shutout innings and allows just one hit during a 7–0 win over the Tigers at U.S. Cellular Field. The only base hit off Garcia was a single by Ivan Rodriguez in the first inning. Garcia retired 23 straight batters after the Rodriguez single. It was the second start in a row in which Garcia allow just one hit and retired 23 in succession (see September 13, 2006). Over those two starts, he retired 48 of the 52 batters to face him.

Garcia was 17–9 with a 4.53 earned run average in 2006.

SEPTEMBER 23   Down 7–2, the White Sox score four runs in the sixth inning and five in the eighth to defeat the Mariners 11–7 at U.S. Cellular Field. The rally came after a rain delay of one hour and 57 minutes in the top of the sixth.

SEPTEMBER 24   The White Sox utilize five home runs to defeat the Mariners 12–7 at U.S. Cellular Field. Paul Konerko hit two homers and Joe Crede, Juan Uribe and Brian Anderson added one each.

The White Sox won at least 90 games for the second consecutive season. It was the first time the franchise accomplished the feat since Al Lopez's teams of 1963 (94–68), 1964 (98–64) and 1965 (95–67).

OCTOBER 11   The White Sox announce they will start weeknight home games at 7:11 p.m. as part of a three-year sponsorship deal with the 7-Eleven convenience store chain. Previously, games had begun at 7:07 p.m.

DECEMBER 6   The White Sox trade Freddy Garcia to the Phillies for Gavin Floyd and Gio Gonzalez.

2007

Season in a Sentence

With the league's worst offense, the White Sox lose 90 games just two years after winning the World Series.

Finish • Won • Lost • Pct • GB

Fourth   72   90   .444   24.0
In the wild-card race, the White Sox finished in eighth place, 22 games behind.

Manager

Ozzie Guillen

Stats

Stats	WS	AL	Rank
Batting Avg:	.246	.271	14
On-Base Pct:	.318	.338	14
Slugging Pct:	.404	.423	12
Home Runs:	190		2
Stolen Bases:	78		10 (tie)
ERA:	4.77	4.50	12
Fielding Avg:	.982	.984	12
Runs Scored:	693		14
Runs Allowed:	839		11

Starting Lineup

A. J. Pierzynski, c
Paul Konerko, 1b
Tadahito Iguchi, 2b
Josh Fields, 3b
Juan Uribe, ss
Rob Mackowiak, lf
Jerry Owens, cf
Jermaine Dye, rf
Jim Thome, dh
Darrin Erstad, cf
Scott Podsednik, lf

Pitchers

Javier Vazquez, sp
Jon Garland, sp
Mark Buehrle, sp
Jose Contreras, sp
John Danks, sp
Bobby Jenks, rp
Mike Myers, rp
Boone Logan, rp
Matt Thornton, rp
Mike McDougal, rp
Ryan Bukvich, rp

Attendance

2,684,395 (fifth in AL)

Club Leaders

Batting Avg:	Jim Thome	.275
On-Base Pct:	Jim Thome	.410
Slugging Pct:	Jim Thome	.563
Home Runs:	Jim Thome	35
RBIs:	Jim Thome	96
Runs:	Jim Thome	79
Stolen Bases:	Jerry Owens	32
Wins:	Javier Vazquez	15
Strikeouts:	Javier Vazquez	213
ERA:	Mark Buehrle	3.63
Saves:	Bobby Jenks	40

JANUARY 25   The White Sox sign Darrin Erstad, most recently with the Angels, as a free agent.

Erstad is the only athlete to play on a collegiate football champion and a World Series winner. He was a punter on Nebraska's 1994 NCAA championship squad and played center field for the 2002 world champion Anaheim Angels.

APRIL 2   The White Sox lose the opener 12–5 to the Indians before 38,088 at U.S. Cellular Field. Grady Sizemore struck the second pitch of the game from Jose Contreras for a home run. Contreras allowed eight runs, seven of them earned, before being relieved with none out in the second inning. Cleveland led 11–2 in the third inning. Darrin Erstad hit a home run in his first at-bat with the Sox. Paul Konerko also homered.

Among the changes at U.S. Cellular Field in 2007 were the addition of a new press box on the first-base side of the upper seating level and the beginnings of a brick plaza in front of the stadium.

APRIL 5   Indians reliever Roberto Hernandez hits Paul Konerko with a bases-loaded pitch to force in the winning run in a 4–3 White Sox win at U.S. Cellular Field.

APRIL 7   With a game-time temperature of 31 degrees and a wind chill of 20 because of a 19-mile-per-hour wind, the White Sox beat the Twins 3–0 at U.S. Cellular Field.

APRIL 15   Jose Contreras (five innings), Nick Masset (two-thirds of an inning), Andy Sisco (one-third of an inning), and Dave Aardsma (two innings) combine on a one-hitter, but the White Sox lose 2–1 to the Indians at Jacobs Field. The only hit was a double by Grady Sizemore leading off the first inning. Sizemore scored on a passed ball and a ground out. Another Cleveland run was added in the fourth on three walks and an error.

           Aardsma is listed first among all major leaguers alphabetically. Hank Aaron is second.

APRIL 18   Two days after 32 die in a shooting on the campus of Virginia Tech University, Mark Buehrle pitches a no-hitter to defeat the Rangers 6–0 at U.S. Cellular Field. The only Texas batter to reach base was Sammy Sosa with a fifth-inning walk. Sosa was picked off first base before the inning ended. Buehrle faced the minimum 27 batters and threw 94 pitches. The game-time temperature was 40 degrees with an 11-mile-per-hour wind. In the ninth inning, Buehrle struck out Matt Kata and Nelson Cruz and induced Gerald Laird to hit a ground ball to third baseman Joe Crede, who threw across the diamond to Paul Konerko at first. On offense, Jermaine Dye hit a grand slam off Kevin Millwood in the fifth inning. The other two Chicago runs scored on solo homers from Jim Thome.

           Buehrle's gem was the first no-hitter by a White Sox pitcher since Wilson Alvarez on August 11, 1991, and the first in Chicago since Joel Horlen on September 10, 1967.

APRIL 19   Jim Thome walks five times in five plate appearances during a 6–4 win over the Rangers in Arlington.

APRIL 23   Paul Konerko hits two homers and drives in five runs during a 7–4 victory over the Royals in Kansas City.

MAY 6   A. J. Pierzynski ties the score with a two-run, pinch-hit homer in the eighth inning and singles in the go-ahead tally in the 10th to lead the White Sox to a 6–3 triumph over the Angels in Anaheim.

MAY 20   The White Sox score seven runs in the seventh inning during a 10–6 victory over the Cubs at Wrigley Field. A. J. Pierzynski hit a grand slam off Neal Cotts.

MAY 25   The White Sox defeat the Devil Rays 5–4 at U.S. Cellular Field. Joe Crede drove in the winning run with a sacrifice fly in the ninth inning.

           The win gave the White Sox a 24–20 record, but the club lost 22 of its next 27 games through June 24. There was another horrible stretch of baseball that included 18 defeats in 21 games from August 11 through September 1.

JUNE 7   In the first round of the amateur draft, the White Sox select pitcher Aaron Poreda from the University of San Francisco.

JUNE 11   The White Sox play at Citizens Bank Park in Philadelphia for the first time and lose 3–0 to the Phillies.

JUNE 18   The White Sox play the Florida Marlins in Chicago for the first time and win 10–6 at U.S. Cellular Field. The Marlins had played at U.S. Cellular previously, however, against the Montreal Expos on September 13 and 14, 2004. The games were transferred from Miami to Chicago because of Hurricane Ivan.

JULY 5   Tadahito Iguchi hits a homer, triple and double during an 11–6 victory over the Orioles at U.S. Cellular Field.

JULY 6   The White Sox surrender 32 runs during a day-night double-header at U.S. Cellular Field. It was the most runs given up by any major league club in a double-header since 1939, and the most by the White Sox in consecutive games since 1930. The opener, played in the afternoon, was a 20–14 slugfest won by Minnesota. Starting pitcher Jon Garland gave up 12 runs, 11 of them earned, in 3$^{1}/_{3}$ innings. The Sox trailed 14–4 in the fourth inning and 18–8 in the seventh. In the night game, the Twins thrashed the Pale Hose 12–0. Justin Morneau clubbed three home runs for the visitors. The 34 runs scored in the opener was one shy of the most ever by two teams in a game involving the White Sox. The record of 35 was set on May 31, 1970, in a 22–13 win over the Red Sox in Boston.

JULY 16   The White Sox edge the Indians 11–10 at Jacobs Field. The Sox broke a 2–2 tie by exploding for nine runs in the top of the sixth inning. They then survived three Cleveland tallies in the bottom half of the inning and five more in the eighth.

JULY 23   The White Sox unveil a statue of Billy Pierce prior to a 9–6 loss to the Tigers at U.S. Cellular Field.

JULY 27   The White Sox trade Tadahito Iguchi to the Phillies for Michael Dubee.

JULY 28   Jerry Owens hits a two-run homer off Roy Halladay in the seventh inning to provide the only two runs of a 2–0 win over the Blue Jays at U.S. Cellular Field. It was the first homer of Owens's career. Mike Buehrle (eight innings) and Bobby Jenks (one inning) combined on the shutout.

JULY 31   The White Sox surrender eight home runs during a 16–3 loss to the Yankees in New York. It was the first time that the Sox ever allowed eight homers in a game. Starter Jose Contreras gave up home runs to Miguel Cairo, Hideki Matsui and Bobby Abreu in 2$^{2}/_{3}$ innings. In an inning-and-a-third, Charlie Haeger allowed round-trippers

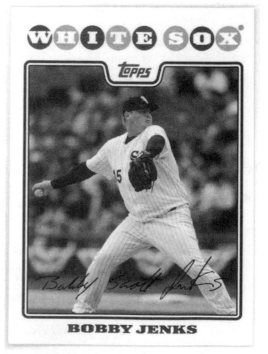

Intimidating hitters with his size as well as his fastball, closer Bobby Jenks racked up 111 saves from 2006 through 2008.

to Melky Cabrera and Jorge Posada. During a three-inning stint, Gavin Floyd yielded home runs to Shelley Duncan, Johnny Damon and Matsui.

AUGUST 2   The White Sox outlast the Yankees 13–9 at Yankee Stadium. The Sox broke a scoreless tie with eight runs in the top of the second inning, only to have the Yanks retaliate with eight tallies in their half. It was only the second time in major league history that both clubs scored at least eight runs in an inning. The 16 runs were the most ever in the second inning of a game. Jermaine Dye tied a White Sox record with four extra-base hits. He collected two homers and two doubles in four at-bats. The pair of doubles came in the big second inning, both off Roger Clemens. Dye's first homer broke the 8–8 tie in the fourth inning.

AUGUST 3   Juan Uribe hits a grand slam off Andrew Miller in the fourth inning of a 7–4 win over the Tigers in Detroit.

AUGUST 8   A. J. Pierzynski and Juan Uribe redeem themselves with extra-inning homers as the White Sox beat the Indians 6–4 in 13 innings at U.S. Cellular Field. Acting as a pinch-hitter in the ninth, Pierzynski ended a rally by grounding into a double play. In the top of the 12th, Uribe made an error that gave Cleveland a 4–3 lead. In the bottom of the 12th, Pierzynski homered to tie the score and Uribe smacked a two-run walk-off home run in the 13th.

AUGUST 11   Josh Fields hits a grand slam off J. J. Putz in the ninth inning, but it comes too late to prevent a 7–6 loss to the Mariners at U.S. Cellular Field.

AUGUST 12   Bobby Jenks ties the all-time major league record for most consecutive batters retired with 41 over 14 relief appearances dating back to July 17. Jenks tied the record set by Jim Barr of the Giants set in 1972 by retiring all three batters he faced in the ninth inning of a 6–0 loss to the Mariners at U.S. Cellular Field. Jenks did break the American League record of 38, established by David Wells with the Yankees in 1998 (see August 20, 2007).

AUGUST 17   Danny Richar hits a grand slam off George Sherrill in the seventh inning, but it comes too late to prevent a 5–4 loss to the Mariners in Seattle. It was Richar's first big-league homer.

AUGUST 20   Pitching for the first time in eight days, Bobby Jenks fails to break the record for most consecutive batters retired. Jenks entered the game against the Royals at U.S. Cellular Field with the White Sox holding a 4–3 lead in the ninth inning and his streak of 41 consecutive batters retired still intact. Jenks gave up a lead-off single to Joey Gathright, but he then retired three batters in a row for the save.

Following the single to Gathright, Jenks retired 14 of the next 15 batters to face him over six relief appearances through September 4. The only one to reach base was on an error. Therefore, from July 17 through September 4, Jenks retired 55 of 57 batters he faced, with the two reaching base on a single and an error.

AUGUST 26   The White Sox lose 11–1 to the Red Sox on a Sunday afternoon at U.S. Cellular Field to cap a nightmare weekend. The White Sox lost 11–3 and 10–1 to Boston in a Friday night double-header and 14–2 in a single game on Saturday night.

41 in a Row

Bobby Jenks tied a major league record by retiring 41 batters in a row from July 17 through August 12, 2007, over 14 relief appearances. The record was set by Jim Barr of the Giants in 1972. Jenks did established records for most consecutive batters retired in the American League and the most ever retired in succession by a reliever. Jenks retired 41 in a row by throwing 153 pitches, 101 of them for strikes. He recorded 42 outs during the streak including a double-play ball erasing a runner he inherited. The streak ended when Jenks gave up a single to Joey Gathright of the Royals on August 20.

Date	Opponent	Batters	Pitches	Strikes
July 17	at Cleveland	3	14	9
July 19	at Boston	3	13	7
July 24	Detroit (game one)	3	9	5
July 24	Detroit (game two)	2	12	8
July 26	Detroit	3	15	13
July 27	Toronto	3	10	6
July 28	Toronto	3	11	9
August 1	at NY Yankees	3	8	4
August 2	at NY Yankees	3	12	8
August 4	at Detroit	3	12	8
August 5	at Detroit	3	11	8
August 8	Cleveland	3	9	5
August 10	Seattle	3	10	6
August 12	Seattle	3	7	5

AUGUST 27 Trailing 4–0, the White Sox hit four homers in the seventh inning to account for five runs and defeat the Devil Rays 5–4 at U.S. Cellular Field. With none out, A. J. Pierzynski, Jermaine Dye and Juan Uribe hit consecutive homers off Edwin Jackson in a span of nine pitches. After Danny Richar doubled, Dan Wheeler relieved Jackson. Following two strikeouts, Wheeler surrendered a homer to Josh Fields.

AUGUST 30 The White Sox make four errors, three by third baseman Andy Gonzalez, during the third inning of a 5–1 loss to the Rangers in Arlington. The other error was made by pitcher John Danks.

SEPTEMBER 7 The White Sox take a thrilling 13-inning, 11–10 decision from the Twins at U.S. Cellular Field. The score was 4–4 after eight innings. Minnesota scored six times in the top of the ninth for a 10–4 lead and it looked like another frustrating loss in an extremely disappointing season. But the Sox came off the mat and scored six runs in their half of the ninth. Following a two-run double from Josh Fields, Jim Thome hit a three-run homer to make the score 10–9. Darrin Erstad drove in the tying run with a double. The winning run came across the plate on A. J. Pierzynski's walk-off single.

SEPTEMBER 12 Jim Thome hits his 499th career homer during a 7–4 win over the Indians at U.S. Cellular Field.

SEPTEMBER 16 Jim Thome hits his 500th career homer in dramatic fashion with a two-run walk-off blast off Dustin Moseley to defeat the Angels 9–7 at U.S. Cellular Field. The homer broke Thome's 0-for-11 slump. The White Sox rallied from a 7–1 deficit. After the Angels scored four times in the top of the seventh, the Sox responded with four in their half, three of them on a home run by Josh Fields. Danny Richar's two-run homer in the eighth tied the contest 7–7.

Thome was the 23rd player to reach the 500-home run plateau. He was the only one of the 23 to hit number 500 with a walk-off homer.

SEPTEMBER 17   The White Sox pack all of their runs into one inning, scoring 11 times in the fifth inning for an 11–3 victory over the Royals in Kansas City. There were nine hits in the inning. Danny Richar led off the 11-run explosion with a home run and later added a run-scoring triple. Jermaine Dye and Josh Fields also homered. Those driving in runs were Fields (four), Dye (three), Richar (two), Juan Uribe (one) and Alex Cintron (one).

SEPTEMBER 27   The White Sox hammer the Royals 10–0 at U.S. Cellular Field. Lance Broadway pitched six innings for his first major league win.

NOVEMBER 19   The White Sox trade Jon Garland to the Angels for Orlando Cabrera.

NOVEMBER 20   The White Sox release Scott Podsednik.

DECEMBER 3   The White Sox trade Chris Carter to the Diamondbacks for Carlos Quentin.

2008

Season in a Sentence

Few expected the White Sox to contend for a pennant, but helped by an offensive resurgence, the club wins the AL Central before losing in the first round of the playoffs.

Finish • Won • Lost • Pct • GB

Finish	Won	Lost	Pct	GB
First	89	74	.546	+1.0

Manager

Ozzie Guillen

American League Division Series

The White Sox lost to the Tampa Bay Rays three games to one.

Stats

Stats	WS	AL	Rank
Batting Avg:	.263	.268	10
On-Base Pct:	.332	.336	9
Slugging Pct:	.448	.420	2
Home Runs:	235		1
Stolen Bases:	67		13
ERA:	4.11	4.36	6
Fielding Avg:	.983	.984	12
Runs Scored:	811		5
Runs Allowed:	729		7

Starting Lineup

A. J. Pierzynski, c
Paul Konerko, 1b
Alexei Ramirez, 2b
Joe Crede, 3b
Orlando Cabrera, ss
Carlos Quentin, lf
Nick Swisher, cf-1b
Jermaine Dye, rf
Jim Thome, dh
Juan Uribe, 3b-2b

Pitchers

Gavin Floyd, sp
Mark Buehrle, sp
Javier Vazquez, sp
John Danks, sp
Jose Contreras, sp
Bobby Jenks, rp
Matt Thornton, rp
Octavio Dotel, rp
Boone Logan, rp
Scott Linebrink, rp

Attendance

2,500,648 (fifth in AL)

Club Leaders

Batting Avg:	Jermaine Dye	.292
On-Base Pct:	Carlos Quentin	.394
Slugging Pct:	Carlos Quentin	.571
Home Runs:	Carlos Quentin	36
RBIs:	Carlos Quentin	100
Runs:	Carlos Quentin	96
	Jermaine Dye	96
Stolen Bases:	Orlando Cabrera	19
Wins:	Gavin Floyd	17
Strikeouts:	Javier Vasquez	200
ERA:	John Danks	3.32
Saves:	Bobby Jenks	30

JANUARY 3　　The White Sox trade Fautino De Los Santos, Gio Gonzalez and Ryan Sweeney to the Athletics for Nick Swisher.

JANUARY 22　　The White Sox sign Octavio Dotel, most recently with the Braves, as a free agent.

MARCH 31　　The White Sox open the season with a 10–8 loss to the Indians in Cleveland. Mark Buehrle gave up seven runs in the second inning to put the Sox in a 7–2 hole. Chicago rallied to deadlock the contest 7–7 before Cleveland scored three in the eighth on Casey Blake's bases-loaded double against Octavio Dotel, who was making his White Sox debut. Jim Thome hit two home runs and drove in four runs. Jermaine Dye hit a homer, a double and a single.

Thome became the second White Sox player to homer twice on Opening Day. The first was Minnie Minoso in 1960.

APRIL 3   John Danks (6²/₃ innings), Octavio Dotel (one-third of an inning), Scott Linebrink (one inning) and Bobby Jenks (one inning) combine on a two-hitter to defeat the Indians at Progressive Field. The only Cleveland hits were a single by Casey Blake in the sixth inning and a double from Ryan Garko in the seventh, both off Danks. The two White Sox runs scored on solo homers by Juan Uribe in the sixth inning and Joe Crede in the eighth.

APRIL 6   The White Sox rout the Tigers 13–2 in Detroit. Nick Swisher hit the second pitch of the game for a home run. The Sox snapped a 1–1 tie with two runs in the fifth, then added six more in the fifth.

APRIL 7   Joe Crede breaks a 3–3 tie with a grand slam off Pat Neshek in the seventh inning and the White Sox take a 7–4 decision over the Twins in the home opener at U.S. Cellular Field before a crowd of 38,082.

APRIL 11   Prior to a 5–2 loss against the Tigers, the White Sox pay tribute to the 2005 world championship team by unveiling a new plaza and monument at U.S. Cellular Field. It is called the Champions Monument in Champions Plaza, located outside of Gate 4. The diamond-shaped plaza contains legacy bricks, which are inscribed with fan messages. The plaza also commemorates key moments in franchise history. Large bronze images of Joe Crede, Paul Konerko, Juan Uribe, Geoff Blum and Orlando Hernandez stand out prominently on the monument. Among those in attendance were Illinois governor Rod Blagojevich. A Cubs fans, the governor was booed when introduced.

APRIL 12   Gavin Floyd holds the Tigers hitless until Edgar Renteria singles with one out in the eighth inning of a 7–0 win over the Tigers at U.S. Cellular Field. Floyd, threw 107 pitches and had never before pitched more than seven innings in a game, was immediately relieved. Scott Linebrink (two-thirds of an inning) and Bobby Jenks (one inning) completed the shutout.

APRIL 13   The White Sox use two grand slams to defeat the Tigers 11–0 at U.S. Cellular Field. Paul Konerko hit the first one off Kenny Rogers in the third inning. Joe Crede clubbed his second grand slam in seven days with a blast off Zach Miner in the fifth.

           The game marked the fourth time that the Sox hit two grand slams in a game. Dummy Hoy and Herm McFarland accomplished the feat on May 1, 1901. Robin Ventura hit two slams on September 4, 1995, and Ventura and Darren Lewis both hit bases-loaded homers on May 19, 1996.

APRIL 28   On a cold and rainy day at U.S. Cellular Field, a game between the White Sox and Orioles is suspended after 11 innings with the score 3–3. In the 11th, Ramon Hernandez homered in the top half and Juan Uribe in the bottom half. At the conclusion of the inning, the umpires called for the tarp as conditions became unplayable and an announcement was made a few minutes later that the contest was suspended. It was completed on August 24 in Baltimore. The Orioles scored a run in the 14th to win 4–3.

MAY 4   The White Sox cause controversy by trying to break out of a batting slump in a creative manner when an unidentified player arranges the team's bats around two nude blow-up dolls before a game against the Blue Jays in Toronto. Many found the display offensive, but Ozzie Guillen refused to apologize, stating it was done in the privacy of the clubhouse where everyone was "over 18" and dismissed it as a "joke blown out of proportion." "I don't think we did anything illegal," said the Sox manager. "It was just a funny doll." Guillen made matters worse during a tirade laced with profanity and vulgarities while complaining about the White Sox's second-class status in Chicago. During his rant, Guillen said the Sox were not sufficiently appreciated in the Windy City despite winning the World Series in 2005. "That's what ticks me off about Chicago fans and Chicago media, they forget pretty quickly," Guillen said. He bemoaned the fact that the Cubs were considered the "best" in Chicago even though they hadn't won a World Series since 1908. Guillen feared his club would never get respect "no matter how many World Series we win."

MAY 6   Gavin Floyd carries a no-hitter into the ninth inning during a 7–1 victory over the Twins at U.S. Cellular Field. Minnesota scored a run in the fourth on a walk, an error and a sacrifice fly. With one out in the ninth, Joe Mauer hit a double that broke up Floyd's second no-hit bid of the young 2008 season (see April 12, 2008). Floyd was taken out of the game immediately and replaced by Bobby Jenks, who retired the only two batters he faced.

MAY 7   Four days before Mother's Day, Bobby Jenks, Nick Swisher, John Danks and Toby Hall die their facial hair pink in support of breast cancer awareness before a 13–1 loss to the Twins at U.S. Cellular Field. Each player made a donation on behalf of the Lynn Sage Cancer Research Foundation.

MAY 14   Carlos Quentin hits a grand slam off Scot Shields in the eighth inning to break a 1–1 tie to lead the White Sox to a 6–1 victory over the Angels in Anaheim.

MAY 16   Alexei Ramirez hits a two-run homer off Jonathan Sanchez for the only two runs of a 2–0 win over the Giants in San Francisco. It was the first major league home run for Ramirez, who was a Cuban defector. The contest was also the first ever game for the White Sox in San Francisco. Gavin Floyd (six innings), Ehren Wasserman (one-third of an inning), Boone Logan (two-thirds of an inning), Scott Linebrink (one inning) and Bobby Jenks (one inning) combined on the shutout.

             Ramirez led the Cuban pro league in home runs in 2007.

MAY 18   The White Sox outlast the Giants 13–8 in San Francisco. Nick Swisher broke a 6–6 tie in the eighth inning with a three-run double.

MAY 22   The White Sox extend their winning streak to eight games with a 3–1 win over the Indians at U.S. Cellular Field. The victory gave the Sox a 26–20 record and a 3$\frac{1}{2}$-game lead in the AL Central.

             Carlton Fisk, who had recently been named team ambassador, was honored in ceremonies prior to the game.

JUNE 4   Paul Konerko hits a two-run walk-off homer in the 15th inning to defeat the Royals 6–4 at U.S. Cellular Field. Kansas City scored twice in the ninth to tie the score 4–4.

             Among players in franchise history at the end of the 2008 season, Konerko ranked ninth in games played (1,467), eighth in at-bats (5,324), second in home runs (291), fourth in RBIs (928), fifth in doubles (275), fifth in total bases (2,651), sixth in slugging percentage (.498), seventh in runs (786) and eighth in walks (586).

JUNE 5   In the first round of the amateur draft, the White Sox select shortstop Gordon Beckham from the University of Georgia.

JUNE 6   Joe Crede collects four hits, two of them homers, in four at-bats during a 10–6 triumph over the Twins at U.S. Cellular Field. Carlos Quentin hit a three-run homer in the fifth inning which deflected off the glove of Minnesota right fielder Michael Cuddyer.

JUNE 7   Joe Crede hits two homers for the second game in a row, leading the White Sox to an 11–2 win over the Twins at U.S. Cellular Field. Paul Konerko hit his first triple since 2000.

          In four games from June 5 through June 8, Crede collected 10 in 15 at-bats, struck four homers and drove in 12 runs.

JUNE 8   The White Sox rout the Twins 12–2 at U.S. Cellular Field. It was the third consecutive game in which the Sox scored at least 10 runs, all against Minnesota.

          Ozzie Guillen publicly criticized his club's lack of offensive production in his usual colorful manner on June 1. "If anyone thinks we can win with the offense we have," said Guillen, "they're full of (expletive deleted). I'm just being honest." Over the next seven games, all wins, the White Sox scored 61 runs and hit 19 homers. Before Guillen's harangue, the Sox averaged 4.2 runs per game in 58 games. Afterward, the club averaged 5.4 runs per game over the remaining 105 regular-season contests.

JUNE 9   Nick Swisher homers from both sides of the plate during a 7–5 win over the Twins at U.S. Cellular Field. Swisher homered off lefty Glen Perkins in the fourth inning and right-hander Jesse Crain in the sixth.

JUNE 13   The White Sox play the Rockies for the first time at U.S. Cellular Field and win 5–4.

JUNE 17   The White Sox pummel the Pirates 16–5 at U.S. Cellular Field. The score was tied 5–5 after four innings before the Sox scored 11 unanswered runs.

JUNE 19   After the Pirates score six runs in the top of the second, the White Sox score six in their half and go on to win 13–8 at U.S. Cellular Field. Jermaine Dye led the way with six RBIs. He hit a two-run homer off Phil Dumatrait in the second inning and a grand slam against John Grabow in the seventh.

          At the end of the 2008 season, Jermaine Dye's slugging percentage of .541 as a member of the White Sox ranked second among White Sox players in franchise history with at least 2,000 plate appearances.

JUNE 21   The Cubs hit four homers during a nine-run fourth inning and beat the White Sox 11–7 at Wrigley Field. Jim Edmonds homered twice in the big inning off Jose Contreras and Boone Logan.

JUNE 27   The White Sox score seven runs in the third inning and beat the Cubs 10–3 at U.S.
           Cellular Field. Steve Swisher hit a grand slam off Ryan Dempster.

           *Derrick Rose threw out the ceremonial first pitch the day after being selected as
           the number one pick in the NBA draft by the Bulls.*

JUNE 30   Nick Swisher homers from both sides of the plate, including a grand slam off lefty
           Jeremy Sowers in the third inning of a 9–7 win over the Indians at U.S. Cellular
           Field. It was Swisher's second grand slam in a span of four days. In the sixth inning,
           Swisher hit a solo homer against right-hander Tom Mastny.

JULY 1   After the Indians score in the top of the 10th inning, the White Sox rally for two
           in their half after the first two batters are retired to win 3–2 at U.S. Cellular Field.
           Alexei Ramirez tied the score with a home run. Dewayne Wise then singled, stole
           second, and scored the winning run on a one-base hit by Alexei Ramirez.

JULY 2   With rain pouring down, A. J. Pierzynski hits a walk-off homer in the 10th inning to
           defeat the Indians 7–6 at U.S. Cellular Field. It was his second homer of the game.
           It was also the second game in a row won by the Sox with a walk-off hit in the 10th
           inning.

JULY 8   A two-run sacrifice fly helps the White Sox defeat the Royals 8–7 in 13 innings in
           Kansas City. In the 11th inning, A. J. Pierzynski hit a deep fly to right-center in which
           outfielders Joey Gathright and Mark Teahen collided. Gathright caught the ball, but
           fell to the turf allowing Joe Crede to score from third base and Alexei Ramirez from
           second. The Royals scored twice in their half of the 11th to tie the contest, but the
           White Sox won on an RBI-double from Orlando Cabrera in the 13th.

JULY 9   Trailing 5–0, the White Sox score two runs in the fourth inning, two in the sixth,
           one in the seventh and two in the eighth, and defeat the Royals 7–6 in Kansas City.
           Carlos Quentin hit a pair of two-run homers during the comeback and scored the
           winning run from third base on a balk.

           *Quentin was a huge surprise. He was acquired in an off-season trade with the
           Diamondbacks and came to Chicago with a .230 batting average and 14 homers
           in 395 at-bats over the seasons. All the Sox had to give up to obtain Quentin
           was first baseman Chris Carter, who played at the Class A level in 2007.
           For the Sox in 2008, Quentin batted .288 with 36 home runs and 100 RBIs in
           130 games before a broken hand ended his season on September 1. Quentin
           headed a batting attack which clubbed a league-leading 235 home runs, 35 more
           than any other AL club. Others who hit double digits in homers for the White
           Sox were Jermaine Dye (34), Jim Thome (34), Nick Swisher (24), Paul Konerko
           (22), Alexei Ramirez (21), Joe Crede (17) and A. J. Pierzynski (13).*

JULY 13   The White Sox collect 22 hits, but lose 12–11 to the Rangers in Arlington.

JULY 20   The White Sox unveil a statue of Harold Baines prior to an 8–7 loss to the Royals at
           U.S. Cellular Field. Jim Thome collected his 2,000th career hit with a double in the
           seventh inning.

JULY 21   Alexei Ramirez hits a grand slam off Dustin Nippert in the seventh inning of a 10–2
           win over the Rangers at U.S. Cellular Field.

| JULY 25 | Jermaine Dye clubs a two-out, two-run, walk-off homer in the ninth inning to defeat the Tigers 6–5 at U.S. Cellular Field. |

JULY 31   Ozzie Guillen pulls his team off the field in the seventh inning of a 10–6 loss to the Twins in Minneapolis. Guillen's action was in response to fans throwing hats and baseballs onto the field following an umpiring call adverse to the home team.

On the same day, the White Sox traded Nick Masset and Danny Richar to the Reds for Ken Griffey, Jr. At the time of the trade, Griffey was 38 years old and had 608 career homers. He was acquired to fill a need for a center fielder. Over the remainder of the season, Griffey hit .260 with three homers in 131 at-bats.

A team leader since joining the Sox in 2005, Jermaine Dye was many people's choice for the MVP Award in 2008.

AUGUST 1   Ken Griffey, Jr. plays in his first game with the White Sox. Batting seventh and playing center field, Griffey singled and drove in two runs in three at-bats during a 4–2 win over the Royals in Kansas City.

Griffey took number 17. He previously wore number 24 with the Mariners and numbers 30 and 3 with the Reds.

AUGUST 3   A brawl erupts during a 14–3 loss to the Royals in Kansas City. In the fifth inning, Miguel Olivo of the Royals had to duck out of the way of a high-and-tight pitch from D. J. Carrasco. On Carrasco's next pitch, Olivo was struck on the wrist and charged the mound, causing both benches to empty. Olivo was grabbed from behind by A. J. Pierzynski, then turned and punched the White Sox catcher. Olivo, Carrasco and Ozzie Guillen were all ejected. In the seventh inning, Kansas City pitcher Zack Greinke was also ejected for hitting Nick Swisher with a pitch.

AUGUST 5   After the Tigers score twice in the top of the 14th inning, the White Sox come back with four in their half, the last three on a two-out, three-run walk-off homer by Steve Swisher, to win 10–8 at U.S. Cellular Field. Swisher entered the game in the 11th inning as a first baseman after Paul Konerko was lifted for a pinch-runner. It was also Ken Griffey Jr.'s first game as a member of the White Sox in Chicago. He collected a single in six at-bats.

AUGUST 14   The White Sox hit four home runs in a row during the sixth inning of a 9–2 win over the Royals at U.S. Cellular Field. With the Sox leading 3–2 and Joel Peralta on the mound, Jim Thome hit the first homer in the sequence deep to right field. On the next pitch, Paul Konerko homered to deep left near the foul line. Six pitches later,

Alexei Ramirez homered to left-center. Robinson Tejada relieved Peralta, and on Tejada's fourth pitch, Juan Uribe homered to left. They were the only four homers by the Sox in the game. The club hadn't hit a home run in the previous 15 innings over three games. In addition, Carlos Quentin was hit by a pitch for the sixth consecutive game. It was the longest streak in the majors since at least 1920.

The White Sox were the sixth team in baseball history to hit four home runs in a row. The others were the 1961 Milwaukee Braves, the 1963 Indians, the 1964 Twins, the 2006 Dodgers and the 2007 Red Sox.

AUGUST 17   Alexei Ramirez hits a grand slam off Dan Meyer in the seventh inning of a 13–1 trouncing of the Athletics in Oakland. With the game well in hand, two players with 500 or more career homers were lifted for pinch-hitters. Toby Hall batted for Jim Thomas and Dewayne Wise for Ken Griffey, Jr.

AUGUST 18   The White Sox score 13 runs for the second game in a row, and clobber the Mariners 13–5 at U.S. Cellular Field.

AUGUST 20   The White Sox offense continues to roll with a 15–3 hammering of the Mariners at U.S. Cellular Field. Ken Griffey Jr. hit his 609th career homer to tie Sammy Sosa for fifth all-time. It was Griffey's first home run with the White Sox.

The Sox scored 46 runs in four games from August 17 through August 20.

AUGUST 24   A. J. Pierzynski is again in the eye of a storm during a ten-inning, 6–5 win over the Rays at U.S. Cellular Field. With the score 5–5 in the tenth, Pierzynski was caught in a rundown between second and third and fell as he was being tagged out. Umpire Doug Eddings ruled that Pierzynski was safe because of interference from third baseman Willy Aybar. Replays indicated that Pierzynski initiated the contact. He scored the winning run on a walk-off single by Alexei Ramirez.

Coincidentally, Eddings and Pierzynski were at the center of another disputed call during the 2005 ALCS (see October 12, 2005).

AUGUST 26   Ken Griffey, Jr. plays in his 2,500th career game and collects two hits and an RBI in four at-bats during an 8–3 win over the Orioles in Baltimore.

SEPTEMBER 6   Jim Thome hits a walk-off homer in the 15th inning to defeat the Angels 7–6 at U.S. Cellular Field.

SEPTEMBER 14   Dewayne Wise hits a pinch-hit grand slam in the eighth inning off Kyle Farnsworth to break a 7–7 tie for an 11–7 triumph over the Tigers in the second game of a double-header at U.S. Cellular Field. The White Sox also won the first game 4–2.

SEPTEMBER 18   The White Sox play at the original Yankee Stadium for the last time, and lose 9–2.

The White Sox were 54–28 at home in 2008, and 35–46 on the road.

SEPTEMBER 19   Alexei Ramirez hits a grand slam off Brian Bannister in the fourth inning of a 9–4 victory over the Royals in Kansas City.

SEPTEMBER 23   Ken Griffey, Jr. hits his 610th career homer during a 9–3 loss to the Twins in Minneapolis. The home run put Griffey past Sammy Sosa into fifth place on the all-time list.

SEPTEMBER 24   The White Sox lose 3–2 to the Twins in Minneapolis to cut their lead to one-half game.

SEPTEMBER 25   With first place on the line, the White Sox take a 6–1 lead in the fourth inning, but wind up losing 7–6 in 10 innings to the Twins in Minneapolis. The defeat sent the Sox into second place—one-half game behind the Twins. The White Sox had four games remaining, and the Twins had three left.

The White Sox lost their next two games to the Indians at U.S. Cellular Field. Fortunately, the Twins also lost twice to the Royals in Kansas City.

SEPTEMBER 28   Needing a win on the last scheduled day of the regular season to stay alive for a postseason berth, the White Sox defeat the Indians 5–1 at U.S. Cellular Field. Pitching on three days' rest, Mark Buehrle went seven innings. The Twins beat the Royals 6–0 in Kansas City to remain one-half game ahead of the Sox.

The White Sox needed to play a make-up of a postponed game against the Tigers at U.S. Cellular Field the following day to settle the AL Central championship.

SEPTEMBER 29   The White Sox down the Tigers 8–2 at U.S. Cellular Field to move into a tie for first place with the Twins. Alexei Ramirez broke a 2–2 tie with a grand slam off Gary Glover in the sixth inning. It was the fourth slam of the year for Ramirez. Pitching on three days' rest, Gavin Floyd went six innings.

After 162 games, both Chicago and Minnesota had records of 88–74. To determine the AL Central champ, a tiebreaking playoff game was set for U.S. Cellular Field on September 30.

SEPTEMBER 30   The White Sox win the AL Central crown with a tension-filled 1–0 victory over the Twins at U.S. Cellular Field. Jim Thome provided the lone run with a homer in the seventh inning off Nick Blackburn which traveled an estimated 461 feet. John Danks pitched eight innings on three days' rest and allowed only two hits. He had a no-hitter in progress until Michael Cuddyer doubled in the fifth. The other Minnesota hit was a single by Brandan Harris in the eighth. Jenks retired the Twins in order in the ninth, with the last out recorded on a diving catch by Brian Anderson in center field.

The White Sox played the Tampa Bay Rays in the first round of the playoffs. Managed by Joe Maddon, the Rays were 97–65 as the surprise team of 2008. In the first 10 seasons of its existence, from 1998 through 2007, the franchise never won more than 70 games. In 2007, the club was 66–96, the worst record in the major leagues.

OCTOBER 2   The White Sox open the Division Series with a 6–4 loss to the Rays in St. Petersburg. The Sox took a 3–1 lead in the second inning on a home run by Dewayne Wise, but couldn't hold the advantage. Evan Longoria led the Tampa Bay comeback with two homers in his first two at-bats off Javier Vasquez. Paul Konerko homered for Chicago in the ninth.

OCTOBER 3   The White Sox lose game two 6–2 to the Devil Rays in St. Petersburg. The Sox
                 scored twice in the first inning, but were shut down the rest of the way.

OCTOBER 5   The White Sox stay alive in the Division Series by beating the Rays 5–3 before
                 40,142 at U.S. Cellular Field. The Sox broke a 1–1 tie with three runs in the fourth
                 inning.

OCTOBER 6   The White Sox are eliminated from the playoffs with a 6–2 loss to the Rays before
                 40,454 at U.S. Cellular Field. B. J. Upton hit two home runs off Gavin Floyd to lead
                 Tampa Bay.

White Sox Uniform Numbers

Uniform numbers have long been part of the fabric of baseball. The following is a list of uniform numbers and the key players, managers and coaches who have worn them since the White Sox introduced numbers in 1931. In parentheses are the years that the individuals wore those particular numbers. Numbers that are retired include those for Nellie Fox (2), Harold Baines (3), Luke Appling (4), Minnie Minoso (9), Luis Aparicio (11), Ted Lyons (16), Billy Pierce (19), Jackie Robinson (42) and Carlton Fisk (72).

1   Lew Fonseca (1933–34), George Kell (1954–56), Jim Landis (1957–64), Tommie Agee (1965–67), Scott Fletcher (1983–85), Kenny Williams (1986–87), Lance Johnson (1988–95, 1997–98), Willie Harris (2004–05)

2   Jackie Hayes (1933–35), Tony Piet (1936–37), Marv Owen (1938–39), Bill Knickerbocker (1941), Thurman Tucker (1946–47), Al Zarilla (1951–52), Nellie Fox (1953–63), Mike Andrews (1971–73). Retired in honor of Fox in 1976.

3   Carl Reynolds (1931), Zeke Bonura (1933–37), Joe Kuhel (1938–43), Rudy York (1947), Tony Lupien (1948), Jim Busby (1951), Fred Hatfield (1956–57), Floyd Robinson (1960–66), Walt Williams (1967–72), Jim Spencer (1976–77), Harold Baines (1980–89, 1996–97, 2000–01, 2004–08). Retired in honor of Baines in 1989.

4–   Luke Appling (1933–43, 1945–50, 1970–71), Marty Marion (1954–56), Gene Freese (1960), Ron Hansen (1963–69). Retired in honor of Appling in 1975.

5   Al Simmons (1933), Jimmy Dykes (1934–46), Pat Seerey (1948–49), Hank Majeski (1950–51), Sam Mele (1953), Johnny Groth (1954–55), Bubba Phillips (1956–59), Roy Sievers (1960–61), Joe Cunningham (1962–64), Bill Skowron (1964), Johnny Romano (1965–66), Duane Josephson (1967–70), Bob Molinaro (1978–81), Vance Law (1982–84), Ray Durham (1995–2002), Juan Uribe (2005–07)

6   Cliff Watwood (1931), Mule Haas (1933–37), Eddie Smith (1939), Taffy Wright (1940–42, 1946–48), Roy Schalk (1944–45), Gus Zernial (1949–51), Cass Michaels (1954), Billy Goodman (1958–61), Jorge Orta (1972–79)

7   Lew Fonseca (1931), Jimmy Dykes (1933), Al Simmons (1934–35), Dixie Walker (1937), Gee Walker (1938–39), Hal Trosky (1944, 1946), Cass Michaels (1947–50), Jim Rivera (1953–60), Charlie Maxwell (1962–64), Don Buford (1965–67), Chuck Tanner (1971–75), Alan Bannister (1976–80), Jerry Manuel (1998–2003)

8   Luke Appling (1932), Mike Kreevich (1936–41), Thurman Tucker (1943–44), Floyd Baker (1945–51), Ferris Fain (1953–54), Walt Dropo (1955–58), Pete Ward (1963–69), Tom Egan (1971–73), Mike Devereaux (1995), Tony Phillips (1996), Albert Belle (1997–98), Brook Fordyce (1999–2000), Charles Johnson (2000), Carl Everett (2004–05)

9   Evar Swanson (1933–34), Rip Radcliff (1935–39), Moose Solters (1940–41), Wally Moses (1942–46), Dave Philley (1947–51), Minnie Minoso (1951–57, 1960–61, 1964, 1976–79), Danny Cater (1965). Retired in honor of Minoso in 1983.

10 Sherm Lollar (1953–63), Al Lopez (1964–65, 1969), J. C. Martin (1966–67), Jay Johnstone (1971–72), Jack Brohamer (1976–77), Tony LaRussa (1979–86), Jeff Torborg (1989–91), Royce Clayton (2000–01), Shingo Takatsu (2004–05)

11 Luis Aparicio (1956–62, 1968–70), Dave Nicholson (1963–65), Jim Essian (1976–77), Don Kessinger (1978–79). Retired in honor of Aparicio in 1984.

12 Lew Fonseca (1932), Larry Rosenthal (1936–41), Guy Curtwright (1943–46), Harry Dorish (1951–55), J. C. Martin (1960–65), Eddie Stanky (1966–68), Ed Herrmann (1969–74), Paul Richards (1976), Eric Soderholm (1977–79), Jim Morrison (1979–82), Steve Lyons (1987–90), Chris Singleton (1999–2001), A. J. Pierzynski (2005–08)

13 Ozzie Guillen (1985–97, 2004–08)

14 Luke Sewell (1935–38), Sam Mele (1952), Larry Doby (1956–57, 1977–79), Tom McCraw (1963–64), Bill Skowron (1965–67), Bill Melton (1968–75), Tony Bernazard (1981–83), Craig Grebeck (1990–93), Julio Franco (1994), Dave Martinez (1995–97), Paul Konerko (1999–2008)

15 Tommy Thomas (1931), Mike Tresh (1938–48), Bob Keegan (1953–58), Richie Allen (1972–74), Tadahito Iguchi (2005–07)

16 Ted Lyons (1932–42, 1946–48), Mike Fornieles (1953–56), Al Smith (1958–62), Ken Berry (1965–70), Brian Downing (1973–77), Greg Pryor (1978–79), Julio Cruz (1983–84), Jim Fregosi (1986–87). Retired in honor of Lyons in 1987.

17 Sugar Cain (1936–38), Frank Papish (1945–48), Chico Carrasquel (1950–55), Earl Torgeson (1957–60), Carlos May (1969–76), Oscar Gamble (1977), Dave Gallagher (1988–90), Mike Caruso (1998–99)

18 Red Faber (1931), George Earnshaw (1934), Bill Dietrich (1937–46), Randy Gumpert (1949–51), Bob Nieman (1955–56), Gail Hopkins (1968–70), Pat Kelly (1971–76), Claudell Washington (1978–80), Jim Fregosi (1987–88), Terry Bevington (1995–97)

19 Les Tietje (1935), Buck Ross (1941–45), Billy Pierce (1949–61), Bruce Howard (1964–67), Greg Luzinski (1981–84). Retired in honor of Pierce in 1987.

20 Sandy Consuegra (1953–56), Joe Horlen (1961–71), Wayne Nordhagen (1978–81), Ron Karkovice (1989–97), Jon Garland (2003–07)

21 Gerry Staley (1956–61), Ray Herbert (1961–64), Bart Johnson (1971–76), Bob Lemon (1977–78), Gary Redus (1987–88), George Bell (1992–93), Esteban Loaiza (2003–04)

22 Donie Bush (1931), Paul Richards (1951–54), Dick Donovan (1955–60), Richie Zisk (1977), Ed Farmer (1979–81), Steve Kemp (1982), Ivan Calderon (1986–90), Darrin Jackson (1994), Jose Valentin (2000–04), Scott Podsednik (2005–07)

23 Jack Onslow (1949–50), Virgil Trucks (1953–55), Bob Locker (1965–69), Lamar Johnson (1976–81), Robin Ventura (1989–98), Jermaine Dye (2005–08)

24 Vic Frasier (1931), Red Kress (1932), Vern Kennedy (1934–37), Eddie Carnett (1944), Early Wynn (1958–62), Don Buford (1964), Tom McCraw (1965–68), Tom Bradley (1971–72), Ken Henderson (1973–75), Mike Proly (1978–80), Floyd Bannister (1983–85, 1987), Mike Cameron (1995–98), Joe Crede (2000–08)

25 Joe Heving (1933–34). Monty Stratton (1936–41), Ralph Hodgin (1943–44), Oris Hockett (1945), Tommy John (1965–71), Tony Muser (1972–75), Sammy Sosa (1989–91), Jim Thome (2006–08)

26 Clint Brown (1936–40), Bill Humphries (1941–45), Nellie Fox (1950–52), Don Johnson (1954), Jose DeLeon (1986–87), Ellis Burks (1993)

27 Lu Blue (1931), Thornton Lee (1937–47), Turk Lown (1958–62), Ken Kravec (1976–80), Greg Hibbard (1989–92)

28 Sad Sam Jones (1933–34), Cass Michaels (1944–47), Al Gettel (1948–49), Dixie Howell (1955–58), Eddie Fisher (1962–66), Wilbur Wood (1967–78), Joey Cora (1992–94)

29 John Kerr (1931), Johnny Rigney (1937–42, 1946–47), Bill Wight (1948–50), Joe Dobson (1951–53), Jack Harshman (1954–57), Greg Walker (1982–90, 2003–08), Jack McDowell (1990–94), Keith Foulke (1998–2002)

30 Jim Wilson (1956–58), John Buzhardt (1962–66), Bucky Dent (1973–76), Ross Baumgarten (1979–81), Salome Barojas (1982–84), Gene Nelson (1984–86), Tim Raines (1991–95, 2005–06), Magglio Ordonez (1997–2004)

31 Hoyt Wilhelm (1963–68), Lamarr Hoyt (1980–84), Scott Radinsky (1990–93, 1995), Greg Norton (1996–2000)

32 Juan Pizarro (1962–66), Steve Stone (1973, 1977–78), Tim Hulett (1983–87), Alex Fernandez (1990–96), Dustin Hermanson (2005–06)

33 Steve Trout (1979–82), Melido Perez (1988–91), Gene Lamont (1992–95), Mike Sirotka (1997–2000), Aaron Rowand (2003–05), Javier Vazquez (2006–08)

34 John Whitehead (1935–39), Ken Holcombe (1950–52), Ken Brett (1976–77), Bill Almon (1981–82), Rich Dotson (1983–87, 1989), Freddy Garcia (2004–06)

35 Joe Haynes (1941–48), Saul Rogovin (1951–53), Bob Shaw (1958–60), Frank Thomas (1990–2005)

36 Johnny Dickshot (1944–45), Hector Rodriguez (1952), Jim Kaat (1973–75), Lerrin LaGrow (1976–79), Jerry Koosman (1981–83), Ron Reed (1984), Eric King (1989–90), Kevin Tapani (1996–98), Dan Wright (2002, 2004), Tom Gordon (2003)

37 Tony Piet (1935), Gordon Maltzberger (1943–44, 1947), Bobby Thigpen (1987–93), James Baldwin (1995–2001)

38 Phil Masi (1950–51), Frank Baumann (1960–63), Dave LaPoint (1988)

39 Don Gutteridge (1970), Roberto Hernandez (1991–97)

40 Mike Hershberger (1960–64), Britt Burns (1980–85), Joe Cowley (1986), Wilson Alvarez (1992–97), Jim Parque (1998–2002), Bartolo Colon (2003)

41 Cy Acosta (1972–74), Tom Seaver (1984–86), Jerry Reuss (1988–89), Bill Simas (1995–2000)

42 Al Lopez (1957–63, 1968), Ron Kittle (1982–86, 1989–91). Retired in honor of Jackie Robinson in 1997.

43 Gary Peters (1963–69), Bob James (1985–87), Herbert Perry (2000–01), Damaso Marte (2002–05)

44 Russ Kemmerer (1960–62), Don McMahon (1967–68), Chet Lemon (1976–81), Tom Paciorek (1982–85), John Cangelosi (1986), Dan Pasqua (1988–94)

45 Orval Grove (1940, 1942–49), Sherm Lollar (1952), Cam Carreon (1960–64), Stan Bahnsen (1972–75), Danny Tartabull (1996), Carlos Lee (1999–2004), Bobby Jenks (2005–08)

46 Hank Steinbacher (1937–39), Eddie Smith (1940–43), Earl Caldwell (1945–48), Eddie Robinson (1950–52), Francisco Barrios (1976–81), Bill Long (1986–87), Jason Bere (1994–97), Bob Howry (1999–2002)

47 Eric McNair (1939), Don Kolloway (1941–43, 1946–49), Tony Cuccinello (1943–45)

48 Ed Lopat (1944–47), Rick Reichardt (1971–73), Ralph Garr (1976–79)

49 Bob Kuzava (1949–50), Rich Dotson (1979–82), Charlie Hough (1991–92)

50 Barry Jones (1989–90), Sean Lowe (1999–01)

51 Terry Forster (1971–76), Jason Bere (1993)

52 Jon Garland (2000–02), Jose Contreras (2004–08)

53 Dennis Lamp (1981–83)

54 Goose Gossage (1972–76)

56 Mark Buehrle (2000–08)

59 Luis Aloma (1950–52)

72 Carlton Fisk (1981–93). Retired in honor of Fisk in 1997.

CHICAGO WS ALL-TIME BATTING LEADERS 1901–2008

Batting Average

(minimum 2,000 plate appearances)

1	Joe Jackson	.339
2	Eddie Collins	.331
3	Carl Reynolds	.322
4	Zeke Bonura	.317
5	Bibb Falk	.315
6	Taffy Wright	.312
7	Luke Appling	.310
8	Rip Radcliff	.310
9	Magglio Ordonez	.307
10	Frank Thomas	.307
11	Earl Sheely	.305
12	Minnie Minoso	.304
13	Harry Hooper	.302
14	Johnny Mostil	.301
15	Bill Barrett	.294
16	Happy Felsch	.293
17	Nellie Fox	.291
18	Lamar Johnson	.291
19	Mike Kreevich	.290
20	Harold Baines	.288

Home Runs

1	Frank Thomas	448
2	Paul Konerko	291
3	Harold Baines	221
4	Carlton Fisk	214
5	Magglio Ordonez	187
6	Robin Ventura	171
7	Bill Melton	154
8	Carlos Lee	152
9	Ron Kittle1	140
10	Jermaine Dye	137
11	Jose Valentin	136
12	Minnie Minoso	135
13	Joe Crede	125
14	Sherm Lollar	124
15	Greg Walker	113
16	Jim Thome	111
17	Ray Durham	106
18	Pete Ward	97
19	Ron Karkovice	96
20	Juan Uribe	87

Runs Batted In

1	Frank Thomas	1,465
2	Luke Appling	1,116
3	Harold Baines	981
4	Paul Konerko	928
5	Minnie Minoso	808
6	Eddie Collins	806
7	Carlton Fisk	762
8	Robin Ventura	741
9	Nellie Fox	740
10	Magglio Ordonez	703
11	Sherm Lollar	631
12	Bibb Falk	627
13	Ray Schalk	594
14	Willie Kamm	587
15	Earl Sheely	582
16	Ozzie Guillen	565
17	Carlos Lee	552
18	Shano Collins	541
19	Bill Melton	535
20	Ray Durham	484

Runs

1	Frank Thomas	1,327
2	Luke Appling	1,319
3	Nellie Fox	1,187
4	Eddie Collins	1,065
5	Minnie Minoso	893
6	Luis Aparicio	791
7	Harold Baines	786
8	Paul Konerko	786
9	Ray Durham	784
10	Fielder Jones	693
11	Ozzie Guillen	693
12	Robin Ventura	658
13	Carlton Fisk	649
14	Magglio Ordonez	624
15	Buck Weaver	623
16	Johnny Mostil	618
17	Ray Schalk	579
18	Shano Collins	572
19	Willie Kamm	545
20	Carlos Lee	533

Doubles

1	Frank Thomas	447
2	Luke Appling	440
3	Nellie Fox	335
4	Harold Baines	320
5	Paul Konerko	275
6	Eddie Collins	266
7	Minnie Minoso	260
8	Ray Durham	249
9	Bibb Falk	245
10	Willie Kamm	243
11	Ozzie Guillen	240
12	Magglio Ordonez	240
13	Shano Collins	230
14	Luis Aparicio	223
15	Robin Ventura	219
16	Carlton Fisk	214
17	Johnny Mostil	209
18	Earl Sheely	207
19	Ray Schalk	199
20	Buck Weaver	198

Triples

1	Shano Collins	104
2	Nellie Fox	104
3	Eddie Collins	102
4	Luke Appling	102
5	Johnny Mostil	82
6	Joe Jackson	79
7	Minnie Minoso	79
8	Lance Johnson	77
9	Buck Weaver	69
10	Ozzie Guillen	68
11	Willie Kamm	67
12	Mike Kreevich	65
13	Happy Felsch	64
14	Frank Isbell	62
15	Carl Reynolds	55
16	Luis Aparicio	54
17	Ray Durham	53
18	Bibb Falk	50
19	Jim Rivera	50
20	Ray Schalk	49

Games

1	Luke Appling	2,422
2	Nellie Fox	2,115
3	Frank Thomas	1,959
4	Ray Schalk	1,755
5	Ozzie Guillen	1,743
6	Harold Baines	1,670
7	Eddie Collins	1,670
8	Luis Aparicio	1,511
9	Paul Konerko	1,467
10	Carlton Fisk	1,421
11	Minnie Minoso	1,373
12	Sherm Lollar	1,358
13	Shano Collins	1,335
14	Robin Ventura	1,254
15	Buck Weaver	1,254
16	Willie Kamm	1,170
17	Fielder Jones	1,153
18	Ray Durham	1,146
19	Lee Tannehill	1,090
20	Frank Isbell	1,074

At-Bats

1	Luke Appling	8,857
2	Nellie Fox	8,486
3	Frank Thomas	6,956
4	Harold Baines	6,149
5	Ozzie Guillen	6,067
6	Eddie Collins	6,065
7	Luis Aparicio	5,856
8	Paul Konerko	5,324
9	Ray Schalk	5,304
10	Minnie Minoso	5,011
11	Carlton Fisk	4,896
12	Buck Weaver	4,809
13	Shano Collins	4,791
14	Robin Ventura	4,542
15	Ray Durham	4,479
16	Fielder Jones	4,282
17	Sherm Lollar	4,229
18	Willie Kamm	4,066
19	Frank Isbell	4,060
20	Bibb Falk	3,874

Walks

1	Frank Thomas	1,466
2	Luke Appling	1,302
3	Eddie Collins	965
4	Robin Ventura	668
5	Nellie Fox	658
6	Minnie Minoso	658
7	Ray Schalk	638
8	Paul Konerko	586
9	Willie Kamm	569
10	Harold Baines	565
11	Fielder Jones	550
12	Sherm Lollar	525
13	Ray Durham	484
14	Jim Landis	483
15	Carlton Fisk	460
16	Carlos May	456
17	Earl Sheely	454
18	Joe Kuhel	450
19	Luis Aparicio	439
20	Bill Melton	418

Stolen Bases

1	Eddie Collins	368
2	Luis Aparicio	318
3	Frank Isbell	250
4	Lance Johnson	226
5	Ray Durham	219
6	Fielder Jones	206
7	Shano Collins	192
8	Luke Appling	179
9	Ray Schalk	176
10	Johnny Mostil	176
11	Buck Weaver	172
12	Minnie Minoso	171
13	Rudy Law	171
14	Patsy Dougherty	168
15	Ozzie Guillen	163
16	George Davis	162
17	Nixey Callahan	157
18	Jim Rivera	146
19	Tim Raines	143
20	Three tied at	127

Slugging Percentage

(minimum 2,000 plate appearances)

1	Frank Thomas	.568
2	Jermaine Dye	.541
3	Magglio Ordonez	.525
4	Zeke Bonura	.518
5	Carl Reynolds	.499
6	Joe Jackson	.498
7	Paul Konerko	.496
8	Carlos Lee	.488
9	Jose Valentin	.483
10	Ron Kittle	.470
11	Minnie Minoso	.468
12	Harold Baines	.463
13	Greg Walker	.453
14	Ivan Calderon	.451
15	Chet Lemon	.451
16	Greg Luzinski	.451
17	Joe Crede	.447
18	Al Smith	.444
19	Bibb Falk	.442
20	Robin Ventura	.440

CHICAGO WS ALL-TIME PITCHING LEADERS 1901–2008

Wins

1	Ted Lyons	260
2	Red Faber	230
3	Ed Walsh	195
4	Billy Pierce	186
5	Wilbur Wood	163
6	Doc White	159
7	Eddie Cicotte	156
8	Mark Buehrle	122
9	Joe Horlen	113
10	Frank Smith	107
11	Jim Scott	107
12	Thornton Lee	104
13	Rich Dotson	97
14	Jon Garland	92
15	Gary Peters	91
16	Jack McDowell	91
17	Tommy Thomas	83
18	Tommy John	82
19	Roy Patterson	81
20	Frank Owen	81
	Lefty Williams	81

Losses

1	Ted Lyons	230
2	Red Faber	213
3	Billy Pierce	152
4	Wilbur Wood	148
5	Ed Walsh	125
6	Doc White	123
7	Jim Scott	113
8	Joe Horlen	113
9	Thornton Lee	104
10	Eddie Cicotte	102
11	Rich Dotson	95
12	Tommy Thomas	92
13	Bill Dietrich	91
14	Mark Buehrle	87
15	Eddie Smith	82
16	Jon Garland	81
17	Frank Smith	80
18	Tommy John	80
19	Ted Blankenship	79
20	Gary Peters	78

Winning Percentage
(minimum 100 decisions)

1	Lefty Williams	.648
2	Juan Pizarro	.615
3	Jack McDowell	.611
4	Ed Walsh	.609
5	Eddie Cicotte	.605
6	LaMarr Hoyt	.602
7	Dick Donovan	.593
8	Mark Buehrle	.584
9	Reb Russell	.579
10	Wilson Alvarez	.573
11	Frank Smith	.569
12	Doc White	.564
13	Nick Altrock	.560
14	Frank Owen	.559
15	Alex Fernandez	.556
16	Billy Pierce	.550
17	Red Faber	.544
18	Gary Peters	.538
19	Britt Burns	.538
20	Early Wynn	.538

Strikeouts

1	Billy Pierce	1,796
2	Ed Walsh	1,732
3	Red Faber	1,471
4	Wilbur Wood	1,332
5	Gary Peters	1,098
6	Mark Buehrle	1,083
7	Ted Lyons	1,073
8	Doc White	1,067
9	Joe Horlen	1,007
10	Eddie Cicotte	961
11	Alex Fernandez	951
12	Jim Scott	945
13	Jack McDowell	918
14	Tommy John	888
15	Rich Dotson	873
16	Frank Smith	826
17	Juan Pizarro	793
18	Wilson Alvarez	770
19	Jon Garland	761
20	Floyd Bannister	759

ERA

1	Ed Walsh	1.80
2	Frank Smith	2.18
3	Eddie Cicotte	2.24
4	Jim Scott	2.30
5	Doc White	2.30
6	Red Russell	2.33
7	Nick Altrock	2.40
8	Joe Benz	2.42
9	Frank Owen	2.48
10	Roy Patterson	2.75
11	Gary Peters	2.92
12	Tommy John	2.95
13	Juan Pizarro	3.05
14	Lefty Williams	3.09
15	Joe Horlen	3.11
16	Joe Haynes	3.14
17	Red Faber	3.15
18	Wilbur Wood	3.18
19	Billy Pierce	3.19
20	Thornton Lee	3.33

Games

1	Red Faber	669
2	Ted Lyons	594
3	Wilbur Wood	578
4	Billy Pierce	456
5	Ed Walsh	427
6	Bobby Thigpen	424
7	Hoyt Wilhelm	361
8	Doc White	360
9	Eddie Cicotte	353
10	Keith Foulke	346
11	Roberto Hernandez	345
12	Joe Horlen	329
13	Jim Scott	317
14	Scott Radinsky	316
15	Bill Simas	308
16	Bobby Howry	294
17	Mark Buehrle	293
18	Eddie Fisher	286
19	Damaso Marte	279
20	Bob Locker	271

Games Started

1	Ted Lyons	484
2	Red Faber	483
3	Billy Pierce	390
4	Ed Walsh	312
5	Doc White	301
6	Wilbur Wood	286
7	Joe Horlen	284
8	Mark Buehrle	268
9	Eddie Cicotte	258
10	Rich Dotson	250
11	Thornton Lee	232
12	Jim Scott	225
13	Jon Garland	223
14	Tommy John	219
15	Gary Peters	216
16	Bill Dietrich	199
17	Tommy Thomas	197
18	Alex Fernandez	197
19	Frank Smith	195
20	Jack McDowell	191

Innings Pitched

1	Ted Lyons	4,161.0
2	Red Faber	4,087.2
3	Ed Walsh	2,947.1
4	Billy Pierce	2,931.0
5	Wilbur Wood	2,524.1
6	Doc White	2,498.1
7	Eddie Cicotte	2,321.2
8	Joe Horlen	1,918.0
9	Jim Scott	1,892.0
10	Thornton Lee	1,888.0
11	Mark Buehrle	1,847.2
12	Frank Smith	1,717.1
13	Rich Dotson	1,606.0
14	Gary Peters	1,560.0
15	Tommy Thomas	1,557.1
16	Tommy John	1,493.1
17	Bill Dietrich	1,437.2
18	Jon Garland	1,428.2
19	Roy Patterson	1,365.0
20	Joe Benz	1,359.1

Complete Games

1	Ted Lyons	356
2	Red Faber	274
3	Ed Walsh	249
4	Doc White	206
5	Eddie Cicotte	183
6	Billy Pierce	183
7	Frank Smith	156
8	Thornton Lee	142
9	Jim Scott	125
10	Roy Patterson	119
11	Nick Altrock	117
12	Frank Owen	116
13	Wilbur Wood	113
14	Tommy Thomas	104
15	Reb Russell	81
16	Lefty Williams	78
17	Joe Benz	76
18	Eddie Smith	75
19	Ted Blankenship	73
20	Ed Lopat	72

Shutouts

1	Ed Walsh	57
2	Doc White	43
3	Billy Pierce	35
4	Red Faber	30
5	Eddie Cicotte	28
6	Ted Lyons	27
7	Jim Scott	26
8	Frank Smith	25
9	Wilbur Wood	24
10	Reb Russell	24
11	Tommy John	21
12	Gary Peters	18
13	Joe Horlen	18
14	Joe Benz	17
15	Roy Patterson	16
16	Frank Owen	16
17	Nick Altrock	16
18	Early Wynn	16
19	Dick Donovan	15
20	John Buzhardt	13
	Thornton Lee	13

Walks

1	Red Faber	1,213
2	Ted Lyons	1,121
3	Billy Pierce	1,052
4	Wilbur Wood	671
5	Rich Dotson	637
6	Thornton Lee	633
7	Jim Scott	609
8	Ed Walsh	608
9	Bill Dietrich	561
10	Eddie Smith	545
11	Doc White	542
12	Joe Horlen	534
13	Eddie Cicotte	533
14	Wilson Alvarez	523
15	Gary Peters	515
16	Frank Smith	496
17	Ted Blankenship	489
18	Jon Garland	473
19	Tommy Thomas	468
20	Tommy John	460

Saves

1	Bobby Thigpen	201
2	Roberto Hernandez	161
3	Bobby Jenks	117
4	Keith Foulke	100
5	Hoyt Wilhelm	98
6	Terry Forster	75
7	Wilbur Wood	57
8	Bob James	56
9	Ed Farmer	54
10	Clint Brown	53
11	Bobby Howry	49
12	Bob Locker	48
13	Turk Lown	45
14	Eddie Fisher	42
15	Lerrin LaGrow	42
16	Gerry Staley	39
17	Harry Dorish	36
18	Ed Walsh	34
19	Salome Barojas	34
20	Gordon Maltzberger	33

Books of Interest

Rollie's Follies:
A Hall of Fame Revue of
Baseball Stories and Stats, Lists and Lore
By Rollie Fingers and Yellowstone Ritter

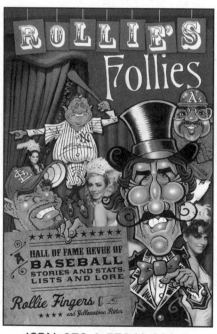

ISBN: 978-1-57860-233-9
$14.95 Paperback

Rollie's Follies is, like the pitcher it celebrates, a singular creation. Before Fingers, the role of closer didn't exist: starting pitchers threw far more innings, and the bullpen was an ever-changing group of pitchers working their way into, or out of, the rotation. Fingers' dominance in relief, coupled with the advent of the designated hitter, changed all that. Today he's considered baseball's first true closer and a pioneer of modern relief pitching. *Rollie's Follies* transcends the typical baseball book — not a dull litany of stats, this book is akin to *Schott's Miscellany* or the *Uncle John* series. Its engaging format features fun, fact-filled lists and sidebars, and colorful stories from Fingers' career. A must-read for all lovers of the game, this breakthrough book is as fascinating as baseball's mustachioed, groundbreaking first closer.

Rollie Fingers is one of the most recognizable players in major league history, due to his playful charisma and handlebar moustache as much as to his 17-year career with the Oakland A's, San Diego Padres, and Milwaukee Brewers. He is one of only two relief pitchers in history to have won a Cy Young Award, a league Most Valuable Player Award, and to be enshrined in the Baseball Hall of Fame.